Fundamentals of Taxation

2018

Fundamentals of Taxation

2018

Ana Cruz
Miami Dade College

Michael Deschamps
MiraCosta College

Frederick Niswander
East Carolina University

Debra Prendergast
Prairie State College

Dan Schisler
East Carolina University

Mc Graw Hill Education

FUNDAMENTALS OF TAXATION 2018 EDITION, ELEVENTH EDITION

This book is printed on acid-free paper.

1 2 3 4 5 6 7 8 9 LMN 21 20 19 18

ISBN 978-1-259-71373-6
MHID 1-259-71373-3
ISSN 1993-8066

Portfolio Manager: *Kathleen Klehr*
Product Developers: *Jaroslaw Szymanski / Danielle Andries*
Marketing Manager: *Zachary Rudin*
Content Project Managers: *Dana M. Pauley / Angela Norris*
Buyer: *Susan K. Culbertson*
Design: *Matt Backhaus*
Content Licensing Specialist: *Shannon Manderscheid*
Cover Image: ©*Caiaimage/Glow Images (People working at table in office);* ©*Blend Images - JGI/Jamie Grill/ Getty Images (Woman paying bills);* ©*Blend Images - Mike Kemp/Brand X/Getty Images (Family);* ©*John Fedele/ Blend Images LLC (Business people using digital tablet);* ©*mmgunn/Getty Images (Tax form)*
Compositor: *SPi Global*

mheducation.com/highered

I dedicate this work to my parents.

– Ana Cruz

To my lovely wife Shannon for all of her support and encouragement and to my students whose curiosity and enthusiasm greatly enrich this experience.

– Michael Deschamps

To my wife Debi, who keeps me grounded.

– Rick Niswander

To my family: You are the parts that make me whole. I dedicate this work to you.

– Debra Prendergast

I would like to dedicate this text to my wife Debra, and my daughters Jessica and Samantha.

– Dan Schisler

Updates to the 2018 Edition

For the 2018 edition of *Fundamentals of Taxation*, the Cruz author team has spent considerable time making careful revisions to the textbook and its supplements. **All chapters and tax forms have been updated for new tax law, making them current through September 2017.** Other updates beyond September can be found in *Connect*.

Additional chapter-by-chapter enhancements that have been made in the 2018 edition include the following:

Chapter 1

- Updated text for new tax rate schedules and tax tables as well as permitted deductions from income.
- Updated text for new social security limit.

Chapter 2

- Revised the exemption amounts for the dependency deduction and the standard deduction to reflect applicable inflation-adjustments.

Chapter 3

- Changed the maximum deduction and phase out ranges for employer-provided adoption assistance.
- Included updated inflation-adjusted phase out amounts for interest income exclusion for savings bonds.

Chapter 4

- Revised the limits for Health Savings Accounts (HSAs)
- The phase out limits for student loan interest were updated.
- Moving expense mileage rates were revised.
- Expanded coverage of the educator expense deduction.

Chapter 5

- Modified coverage of deductible medical expenses to reflect that the 10% AGI threshold now applies to all taxpayers.
- Medical-related mileage rates were revised.
- The maximum deductible premiums for medical insurance and long-term care were revised.
- Revised the phase-out amounts for the limitation of total itemized deductions for high income taxpayers.

Chapter 6

- The rules and limits for section 179 expense were revised and updated.
- Mileage rates for travel expense were revised.

Chapter 9

- Revised phase out amounts for limitation of education credits.
- Revised modified adjusted gross income thresholds for the retirement savings contribution credit.
- Revised credit amount and income phase out limitations for the adoption credit.
- Revised income and phase out limitations for the Earned Income Tax Credit.
- Adjusted poverty level amounts used to calculate the premium tax credit.

Chapter 10

- Modified and clarified text related to reporting payroll taxes and Form 941.
- Revised penalty amounts for incorrect or late filing of W-2s.

Chapter 11

- Revised contribution limits for defined contribution plans.
- Revised phase out thresholds for traditional IRA and Roth IRA plans.

Chapter 15

- Updated text for changes to filing due dates for corporations.

Four Primary Teaching Advantages of *Fundamentals of Taxation*

1

First, we organize the content of *Fundamentals of Taxation* to **closely follow IRS tax forms.** We introduce students to standard IRS forms early and reinforce their use throughout the text. **Actual tax forms are incorporated throughout** giving students the opportunity to understand the principles behind tax law while they learn how to work with clients to obtain the information they will need to complete tax forms.

2

Second, we **illustrate the proper reporting of tax issues.** We present a tax issue, discuss the legal requirements, illustrate the proper tax form placement, and show the completed form in the text. By effectively leading the student through each issue, we demonstrate how tax form preparation is the result of a careful process that balances legal knowledge with practical experience using tax forms.

3

Third, we **integrate an individual income tax software package** into the content and refer to its examples. We instruct students how to use the software to complete returns using sample "taxpayers" who appear from chapter to chapter. An important consideration in writing *Fundamentals of Taxation* was to allow instructor flexibility. You can choose to rely heavily on the software, you can incorporate the software only after you cover the law and the reporting, or you can deemphasize the software component. This flexible approach allows you to structure your taxation course the way you want to.

4

Fourth, we supplement the content with **citations of relevant tax authorities** such as the Internal Revenue Code, Treasury Regulations, Revenue Rulings, Revenue Procedures, and court cases. These citations are almost always provided in **footnotes.** Thus, you and your students can easily use, or not use, the footnote material.

Ana Cruz

Dr. Ana Cruz is Chair of the Business Department at Miami Dade College, Wolfson Campus, where she utilizes her extensive experience in the areas of general business, management, accounting, and taxes. She has worked in the service, retailing, and manufacturing industries, as well as in the federal government sector, where she served as a field examiner for the Internal Revenue Service. Dr. Cruz, a certified public accountant, has published several articles in business journals, has participated in several SACS On-Site Committiees, and has received the Southeast Banking Corporation Foundation Endowed Teaching Chair (1998) and the Wolfson Senior Foundation Endowed Teaching Chair (2002). She was also named the Professor of the Year for the State of Florida by the Council for Advancement and Support of Education and the Carnegie Foundation (2005).

How Does *Fundamentals of Taxation* Help Students Better Understand Tax?

Forms-Based Approach

Examples of completed tax forms demonstrate how tax theory covered in the text translates to real returns.

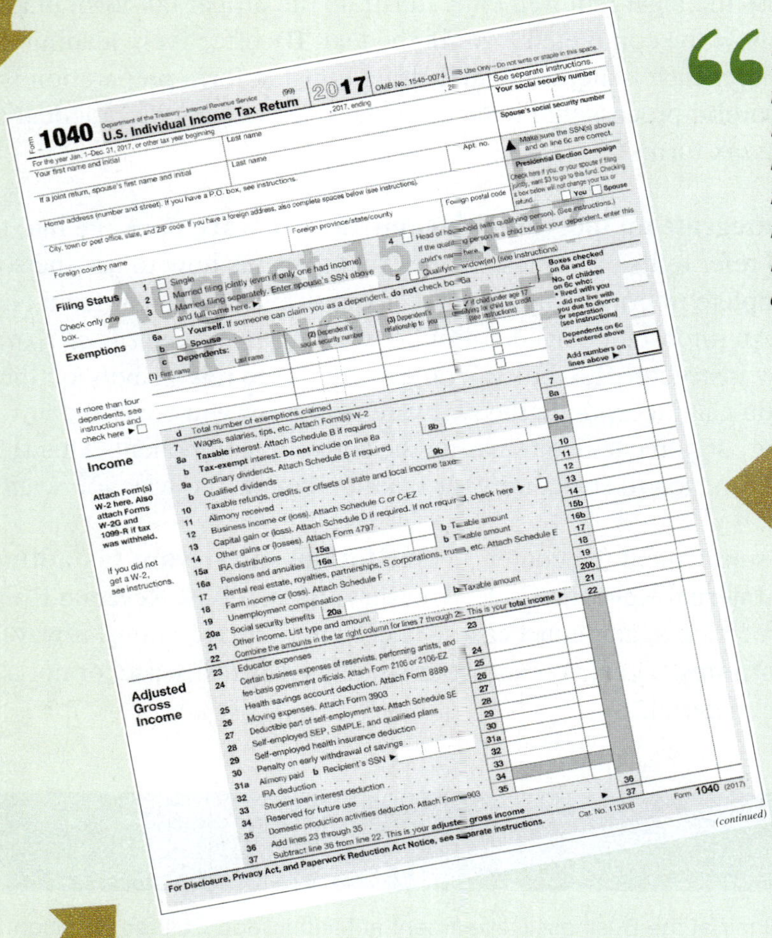

Form 1040 — Department of the Treasury—Internal Revenue Service — U.S. Individual Income Tax Return 2017

Filing Status

Exemptions

Income

Adjusted Gross Income

For Disclosure, Privacy Act, and Paperwork Reduction Act Notice, see separate instructions. Cat. No. 11320B Form 1040 (2017)

(continued)

> ***The forms-based approach*** *to tax concepts in this text gives students the opportunity to apply concepts by completing actual tax forms both manually and through tax software—not only giving them a valuable skill but* ***ultimately making them more employable in today's workplace.***
>
> —Angela Deaton Mott, Northeast Mississippi Community College

Appendix B includes comprehensive problems for 1040 Schedules A, C, D, and E. These longer problems include both easy and difficult schedules to test students'' comprehension of a range of topics covered across multiple chapters.

Incorporation of real-world tax returns into the text for electronic as well as manual preparation forces students to learn hands-on skills.

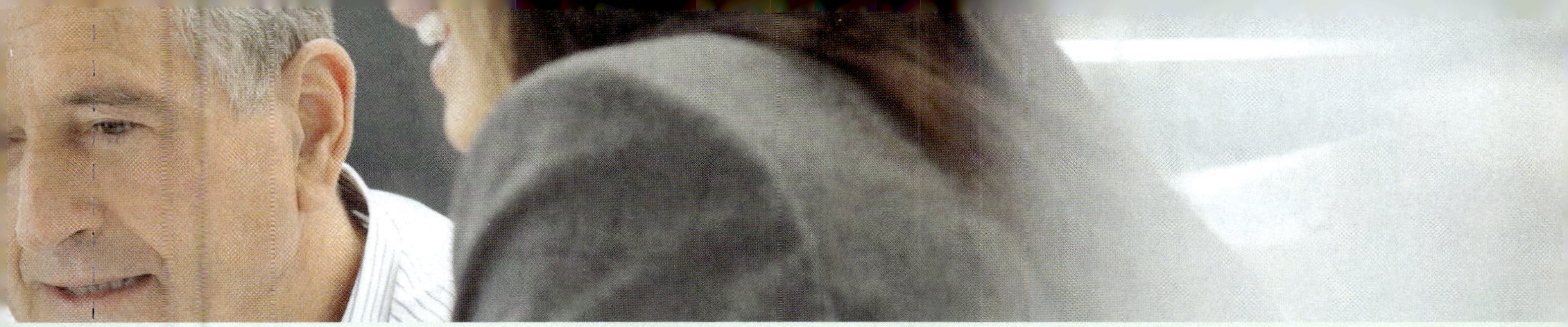

Connect Tax Form Simulations

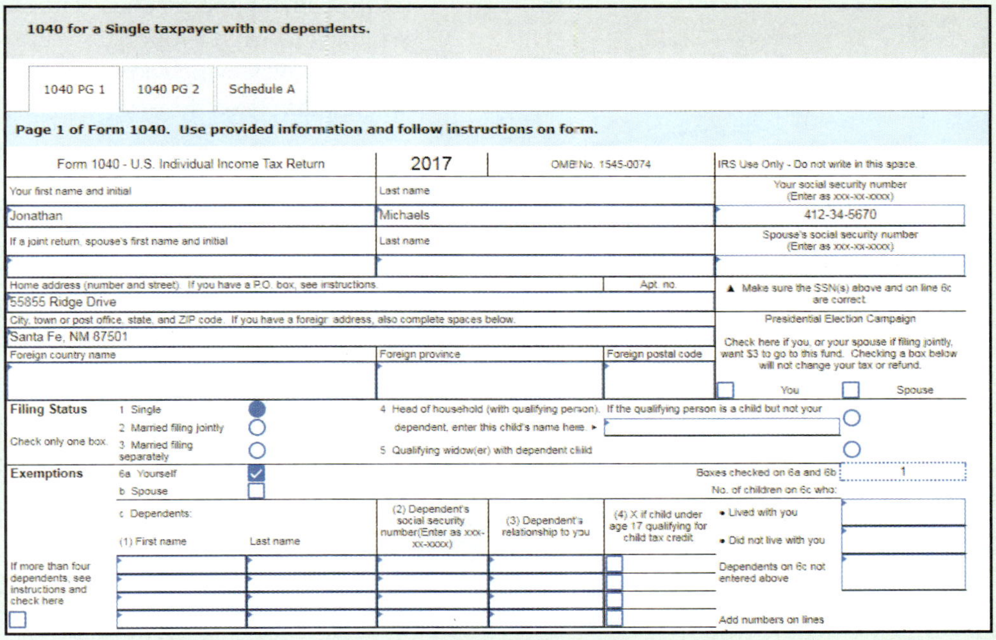

1040 for a Single taxpayer with no dependents.

1040 PG 1 | 1040 PG 2 | Schedule A

Page 1 of Form 1040. Use provided information and follow instructions on form.

Form 1040 - U.S. Individual Income Tax Return 2017 OMB No. 1545-0074 IRS Use Only - Do not write in this space.

Your first name and initial: Jonathan
Last name: Michaels
Your social security number (Enter as xxx-xx-xxxx): 412-34-5670

If a joint return, spouse's first name and initial
Last name
Spouse's social security number (Enter as xxx-xx-xxxx)

Home address (number and street). If you have a P.O. box, see instructions. Apt. no.
55855 Ridge Drive
▲ Make sure the SSN(s) above and on line 6c are correct.

City, town or post office, state, and ZIP code. If you have a foreign address, also complete spaces below.
Santa Fe, NM 87501

Presidential Election Campaign
Check here if you, or your spouse if filing jointly, want $3 to go to this fund. Checking a box below will not change your tax or refund. You / Spouse

Foreign country name | Foreign province | Foreign postal code

Filing Status — Check only one box.
1 Single
2 Married filing jointly
3 Married filing separately
4 Head of household (with qualifying person). If the qualifying person is a child but not your dependent, enter this child's name here. ▸
5 Qualifying widow(er) with dependent child

Exemptions
6a Yourself
b Spouse
Boxes checked on 6a and 6b: 1
No. of children on 6c who:
• Lived with you
• Did not live with you
Dependents on 6c not entered above
Add numbers on lines

c Dependents:

(1) First name	Last name	(2) Dependent's social security number (Enter as xxx-xx-xxxx)	(3) Dependent's relationship to you	(4) X if child under age 17 qualifying for child tax credit

If more than four dependents, see instructions and check here

The **Auto-graded Tax Form Simulation,** assignable within *Connect,* provides a much-improved student experience when solving the tax-form based problems. The **Auto-graded Tax Form Simulation** allows students to apply tax concepts by completing the actual tax forms online with automatic feedback and grading for both students and professors.

Michael P. Deschamps

Michael P. Deschamps received a bachelor of science degree in accounting, graduating magna cum laude from the University of San Diego, where he served as the chapter president for Beta Alpha Psi, the accounting honor society. After working in public accounting and obtaining his CPA license, he returned to San Diego State University, where he earned a master's degree in taxation and a certificate in financial planning. In addition, he earned his Enrolled Agent Certificate in 2004. He is currently the lead accounting instructor at MiraCosta College in Oceanside, CA, where he has developed a highly regarded tax program certified by the State of California. He is an active member of Teachers of Accounting at Two Year Colleges (TACTYC) and has been a frequent presenter on tax topics at the organization's national conventions. He has also given presentations on tax issues to a variety of organizations.

How Does *Fundamentals of Taxation* Provide a Clear Path to Student Success?

Clear Objectives for Your Students

or without the footnotes. If you would like to become familiar with ... and other tax authority, the footnotes are a good place to start exploring.

Learning Objectives

When you have completed this chapter, you should understand the following learning objectives (LO):

- LO 1-1 Understand progressive, proportional, and regressive tax structures.
- LO 1-2 Understand the concepts of marginal and average tax rates as well as a simple income tax formula.
- LO 1-3 Understand the components of a Form 1040EZ income tax return.
- LO 1-4 Determine tax liability in instances when a Form 1040EZ return is appropriate.
- LO 1-5 Understand the types of tax authority and how they interrelate (Appendix A).
- LO 1-6 Understand the provisions of IRS Circular 230 for paid tax preparers (Appendix B).

Learning income tax return preparation requires constant reinforcement and practice. The authors have set up *the text* to provide an easy-to-follow format starting with a list of learning objectives, which are then repeated throughout the text where the related material appears.

Concept Checks are mini-quizzes that test students' understanding of each objective.

CONCEPT CHECK 2-2— LO 2-2

1. Even though you are in the process of getting a divorce, you can file as married filing jointly. True or false?
2. The social security number of the taxpayer's spouse must be shown on the taxpayer's tax return when filing as married filing separately. True or false?
3. A surviving spouse who qualified as married filing jointly when the spouse died can file as a qualifying widow(er) for the next two years as long as the surviving spouse pays for more than half the cost of keeping up a household and does not remarry. True or false?

LO 12-3: Apply the tax rules to report an installment sale.	• The taxpayer calculates a gross profit percentage based on the basis of the property sold divided by the selling price. • As the taxpayer receives cash in installments, the gain is recognized based on the gross profit percentage. • The interest income on any note receivable is a separate calculation.
LO 12-4: Explain how to exclude a gain on the sale of a personal residence.	• A taxpayer can exclude up to $500,000 ($250,000 if single) of gain on the sale of a personal residence. • The residence exclusion applies only to the taxpayer's principal residence. • The taxpayer must live there two of the last five years. • Reduced exclusions are available if a move is the result of employment transfers or health issues.

A summary of the learning objectives appears at the end of each chapter, providing a quick reference chart for students as they prepare for exams.

The same learning objectives are also referenced in the end-of-chapter material next to each discussion question, multiple-choice question, and problem. Additionally, **marginal EA tags** in the end-of-chapter material help instructors and students identify specific questions that will help prepare students for the Enrolled Agent Exam.

Problems connect

All applicable problems are available with *Connect*®

EA LO 4-1 46. What are some of the limitations concerning deductibility of student loan interest? Be specific and comprehensive.

Debra Prendergast

Dr. Debra Prendergast has a doctor of philosophy degree in public policy from the University of Illinois at Chicago, a master's of business administration degree from Governors State University, and a bachelor of arts degree in business administration with a concentration in accounting from Saint Xavier University in Chicago. She is a licensed and practicing certified public accountant in Illinois and a certified management accountant. She began her professional accounting career as a management advisory services consultant with Grant Thornton before taking a position as the controller for a corporation in Chicago. To spend more time with her family, she left her controller position in 1988 and began a 21-year career with Northwestern College. In 2010, Dr. Prendergast became the dean of Business, Mathematics, and Science at Prairie State College. She served as an officer on the board of Teachers of Accounting at Two Year Colleges (TACTYC) and on the Precertification Education Executive committee of the AICPA.

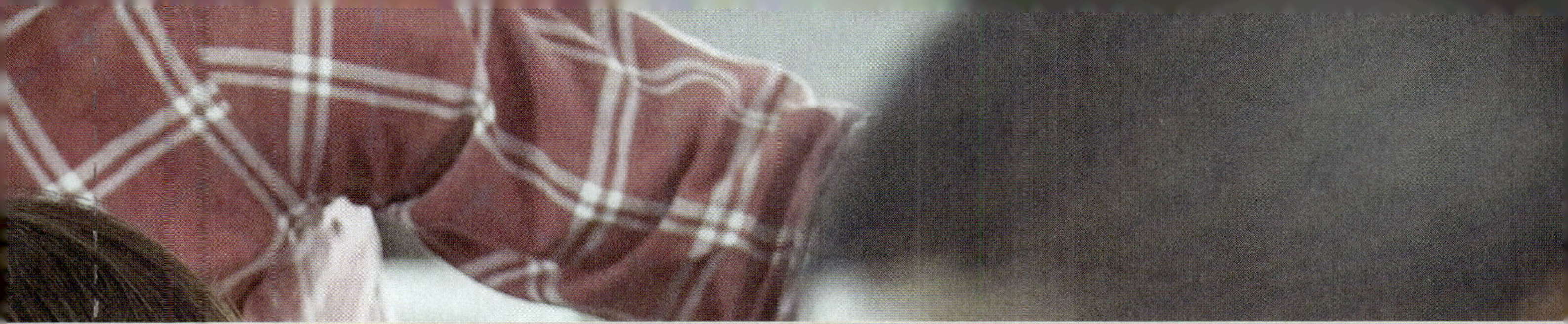

Surgent Enrolled Agent Exam Review Course!

Surgent EAreview

Surgent has partnered with McGraw Hill Education and is making the Enrolled Agent Exam Review Course available to you. The Enrolled Agent credential is awarded by the Internal Revenue Service to tax preparers who pass the three-part IRS Special Enrollment Examination. By earning the Enrolled Agent credential, tax preparers are awarded the same client representation rights as CPAs and attorneys. In addition, Enrolled Agents historically have a higher lifetime earning potential than tax preparers who do not earn the Enrolled Agent credential.

As a student using Cruz, *Fundamentals of Taxation 2018* edition, you are eligible to receive six months of free access to Part One (Individual Taxation) of the Surgent Enrolled Agent Exam Review. To start your free access, please visit **https://www.Surgent.com/McGrawHill/EA** and complete the registration form. In addition, you are entitled to a discount on the remaining exam sections of our Enrolled Agent Exam Review course. Please see the website above for additional information or to enroll.

McGraw-Hill Customer Experience Group Contact Information

At McGraw-Hill, we understand that getting the most from new technology can be challenging. That's why our services don't stop after you purchase our products. You can contact our Product Specialists 24 hours a day to get product training online. Or you can search the knowledge bank of Frequently Asked Questions on our support Web site. For Customer Support, call **800-331-5094,** or visit **www.mhhe.com/support.** One of our Technical Support Analysts will be able to assist you in a timely fashion.

Dan Schisler

Dr. Dan Schisler is a Professor and Research Fellow in the Accounting Department at East Carolina University. He holds a doctor of philosophy degree from Memphis State University, a master's degree in accounting—tax concentration from Auburn University, and a bachelor of science degree in accounting from Southeastern Louisiana University. In addition to public accounting experience with Peat Marwick Main & Co, Dr. Schisler has published numerous articles in national academic and practitioner journals such as *Journal of the American Taxation Association, Advances in Taxation,* and *Accounting Horizons.* He teaches tax and accounting at the graduate and undergraduate levels at East Carolina, where he has been recognized for teaching excellence by numerous teaching awards at the department, school, and university levels. Dr. Schisler holds CPA certificates in North Carolina and Louisiana.

TaxAct Professional

Fundamentals of Taxation features an integrated tax software package from TaxAct, one of the leading tax preparation software companies in the market today. Students are instructed in the practical applications of tax software with exercises that teach how software can be used to prepare all types of tax returns.

Sample "taxpayers" are used throughout the book, in varying situations, to give students full exposure to the many types of tax preparation challenges they will face. This exposure allows students to **make the connection** between the **tax law,** the **software inputs,** and the **tax output** on the appropriate tax forms

> ***I currently use TaxAct** for my tax practice, and I like your choice.*
>
> —Natasha Librizzi, Milwaukee Area Technical College

Fundamentals of Taxation also provides the instructor with the flexibility needed in an individual income tax course. Each chapter can be used **with or without the tax software,** depending on the objectives of an individual instructor's course.

TaxAct features **in-depth form instructions** that supplement the *Fundamentals of Taxation,* making it easier than ever to integrate software into the classroom. Students are provided with the latest tax forms via the **Check for Updates from the Online tab in the program,** so that at the start of the semester, each student will be prepared to work with the most up-to-date information available. With over **120 tax forms, schedules, and worksheets**, TaxAct is sure to have the course materials you will need throughout the semester.

For instructions on how to install the software, please refer to Chapter 1, Appendix C of this text. You can also visit **www.TaxAct.com** today for more information. Please note, at the time of printing, TaxAct is accessible by PC computers only. To ensure all students are able to access TaxAct, a free-of-charge site license is available to schools permitting downloading of the TaxAct software to school lab computers. Please see the online Instructor Resource site for the site license agreement and instructions for submittal.

How Does *Fundamentals of Taxation* Better Prepare My Students?

From Shoebox to Software

TaxAct Professional

The From Shoebox to Software examples in each chapter help students understand how they start with a mass of paper provided by a client and proceed to a completed tax return using tax software. The student can actually see the jump from the theoretical tax world to practical application.

> "*Most importantly,* ***students learn how to apply*** *what they learned by preparing tax returns at the end of the chapter, and the bonus is they learn how to use tax software. In 16 weeks,* ***students would have prepared over 30 tax returns.*** *This is what attracts students to enroll in the course. It not only meets their requirement for their course of study—they walk away with a life skill.*"
>
> —Lolita M. Lockett, Florida Community College at Jacksonville

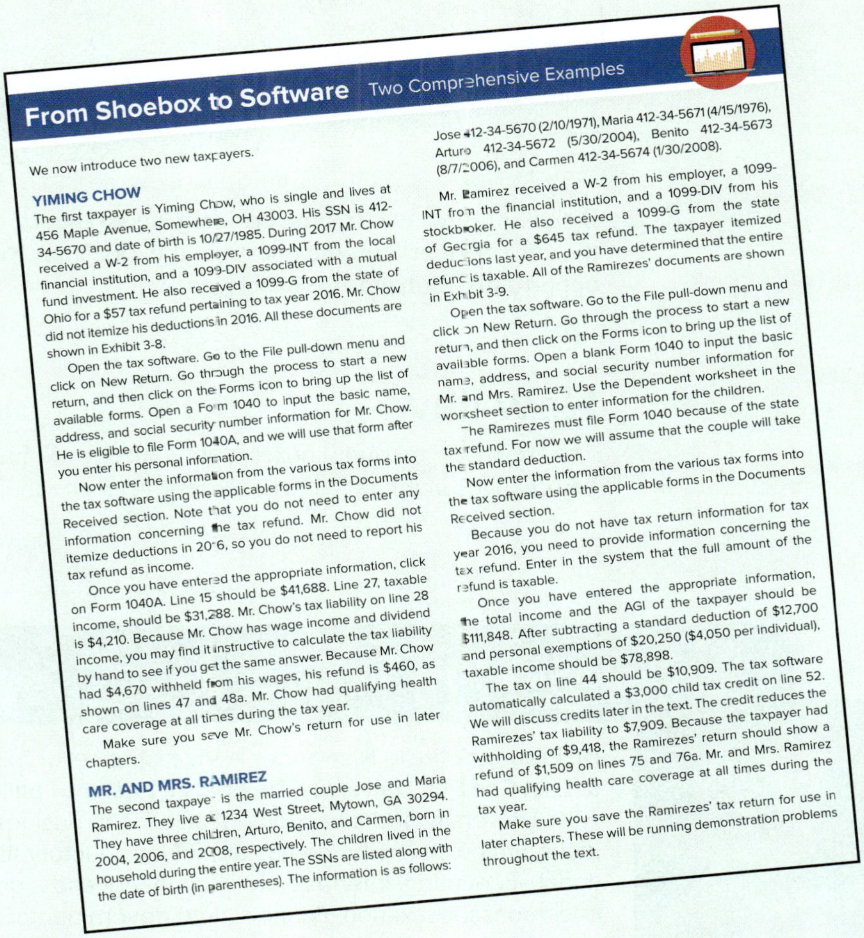

From Shoebox to Software Two Comprehensive Examples

We now introduce two new taxpayers.

YIMING CHOW

The first taxpayer is Yiming Chow, who is single and lives at 456 Maple Avenue, Somewhere, OH 43003. His SSN is 412-34-5670 and date of birth is 10/27/1985. During 2017 Mr. Chow received a W-2 from his employer, a 1099-INT from the local financial institution, and a 1099-DIV associated with a mutual fund investment. He also received a 1099-G from the state of Ohio for a $57 tax refund pertaining to tax year 2016. Mr. Chow did not itemize his deductions in 2016. All these documents are shown in Exhibit 3-8.

Open the tax software. Go to the File pull-down menu and click on New Return. Go through the process to start a new return, and then click on the Forms icon to bring up the list of available forms. Open a Form 1040 to input the basic name, address, and social security number information for Mr. Chow. He is eligible to file Form 1040A, and we will use that form after you enter his personal information.

Now enter the information from the various tax forms into the tax software using the applicable forms in the Documents Received section. Note that you do not need to enter any information concerning the tax refund. Mr. Chow did not itemize deductions in 2016, so you do not need to report his tax refund as income.

Once you have entered the appropriate information, click on Form 1040A. Line 15 should be $41,688. Line 27, taxable income, should be $31,288. Mr. Chow's tax liability on line 28 is $4,210. Because Mr. Chow has wage income and dividend income, you may find it instructive to calculate the tax liability by hand to see if you get the same answer. Because Mr. Chow had $4,670 withheld from his wages, his refund is $460, as shown on lines 47 and 48a. Mr. Chow had qualifying health care coverage at all times during the tax year.

Make sure you save Mr. Chow's return for use in later chapters.

MR. AND MRS. RAMIREZ

The second taxpayer is the married couple Jose and Maria Ramirez. They live at 1234 West Street, Mytown, GA 30294. They have three children, Arturo, Benito, and Carmen, born in 2004, 2006, and 2008, respectively. The children lived in the household during the entire year. The SSNs are listed along with the date of birth (in parentheses). The information is as follows: Jose 412-34-5670 (2/10/1971), Maria 412-34-5671 (4/15/1976), Arturo 412-34-5672 (5/30/2004), Benito 412-34-5673 (8/7/2006), and Carmen 412-34-5674 (1/30/2008).

Mr. Ramirez received a W-2 from his employer, a 1099-INT from the financial institution, and a 1099-DIV from his stockbroker. He also received a 1099-G from the state of Georgia for a $645 tax refund. The taxpayer itemized deductions last year, and you have determined that the entire refund is taxable. All of the Ramirezes' documents are shown in Exhibit 3-9.

Open the tax software. Go to the File pull-down menu and click on New Return. Go through the process to start a new return, and then click on the Forms icon to bring up the list of available forms. Open a blank Form 1040 to input the basic name, address, and social security number information for Mr. and Mrs. Ramirez. Use the Dependent worksheet in the worksheet section to enter information for the children.

The Ramirezes must file Form 1040 because of the state tax refund. For now we will assume that the couple will take the standard deduction.

Now enter the information from the various tax forms into the tax software using the applicable forms in the Documents Received section.

Because you do not have tax return information for tax year 2016, you need to provide information concerning the tax refund. Enter in the system that the full amount of the refund is taxable.

Once you have entered the appropriate information, the total income and the AGI of the taxpayer should be $111,848. After subtracting a standard deduction of $12,700 and personal exemptions of $20,250 ($4,050 per individual), taxable income should be $78,898.

The tax on line 44 should be $10,909. The tax software automatically calculated a $3,000 child tax credit on line 52. We will discuss credits later in the text. The credit reduces the Ramirezes' tax liability to $7,909. Because the taxpayer had withholding of $9,418, the Ramirezes' return should show a refund of $1,509 on lines 75 and 76a. Mr. and Mrs. Ramirez had qualifying health care coverage at all times during the tax year.

Make sure you save the Ramirezes' tax return for use in later chapters. These will be running demonstration problems throughout the text.

The simulation of real-world situations in each Shoebox example helps students become professional tax preparers. Their first day of work is far less stressful because it is not the first time they have seen a Form 1040 or a Schedule D. They are far more productive because they know where to start and how to complete the work.

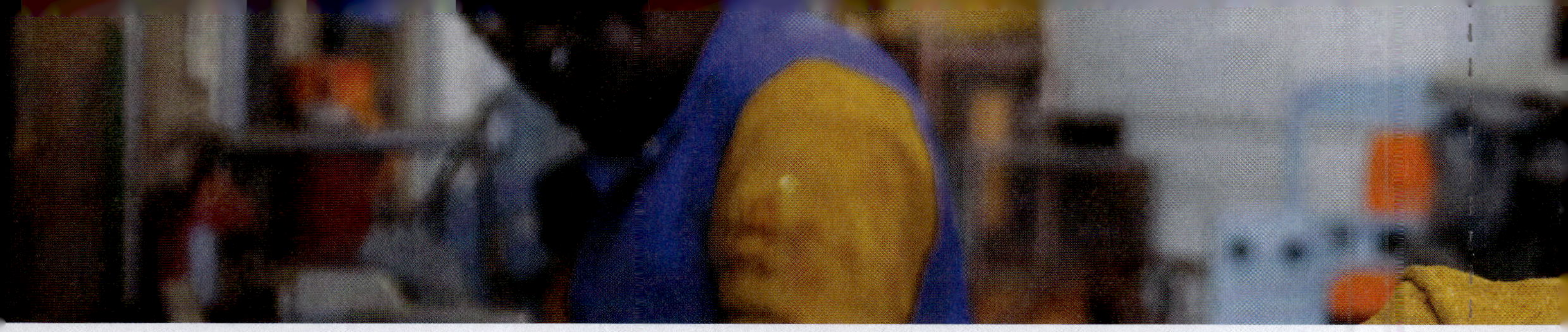

Tax Your Brain

The Tax Your Brain feature is designed to work with the examples in the text to reinforce the understanding of key concepts. Students are given information in an example and then asked to apply what they have learned to a different situation.

TAX YOUR BRAIN

Assume that Janice's year 2018 wage income will be $50,000 (she worked full-time) and she will have $8,300 withheld from her wages. Also assume that she expects to sell a large number of paintings and that she estimates her total 2018 tax liability will be $18,000. To avoid an underpayment penalty, does Janice need to pay estimated payments during 2018 and, if so, how much must she pay?

ANSWER

Janice does not need to make any estimated payments. Her required annual payment is $6,995, which is the lower of (a) 90% of $18,000 (the estimate of her 2018 tax liability) or (b) $6,995 (her tax liability for 2017). Because her estimated tax withholdings are $8,300, she is not obligated to make estimated payments. She will need to pay the remaining $9,700 ($18,000 – $8,300) no later than April 15, 2019.

By asking students to think critically about theories and concepts while supplying the answer right after the question, the Tax Your Brain examples provide another opportunity for hands-on experience.

New Law

The New Law marginal boxes alert students and instructors to key changes in tax law for the current year's textbook.

NEW LAW

Personal and dependency exemptions is $4,050, phasing out at different adjusted gross income amounts.

Frederick Niswander

Dr. Frederick (Rick) Niswander is Vice Chancellor for Administration and Finance at East Carolina University. He holds a doctor of philosophy degree from Texas A&M University and a bachelor of science in business administration degree from Idaho State University. He has taught introductory financial accounting, international accounting, intermediate accounting, and a graduate accounting course that encompasses taxation, financial, and governmental accounting. Prior to obtaining his doctorate and joining the ECU faculty in 1993, he was the chief financial officer of a privately held real estate company in Phoenix, Arizona, for eight years. Dr. Niswander first became a CPA in 1981 and has been a North Carolina CPA since 1994. He is a member of the North Carolina Association of CPAs, the American Institute of Certified Public Accountants, and the American Accounting Association. He has held leadership roles in the American Institute of CPAs including chair of the Board of Examiners and as a member of the AIPCA Board of Directors.

Robust and Relevant End-of-Chapter Material

Fundamentals of Taxation offers a robust selection of end-of-chapter material.

EA LO 3-3 9. Sam owns all of the stock in a newly formed corporation. During 2017, the first year of operation, the corporation realized current earnings and profits of $10,000. Sam received a $12,000 distribution from the corporation. How much, if any, of the distribution is taxable to Sam? Why?

Discussion questions test the basic concepts of each chapter. Students supply short answers to a variety of questions covering each of the major concepts in the chapter.

Multiple-Choice Questions connect

All applicable multiple-choice questions are available with *Connect*©

EA 26. (Introduction) *For* AGI, or above-the-line, deductions
a. Are determined by the taxpayer.
b. Are set by statute.
c. Increase tax liability.
d. Are reported in Schedule A.

EA 27. (Introduction) *For* AGI, or above-the-line, deductions
a. Increase AGI.
b. Reduce tax credits.
c. Are available only for married filing jointly.
d. Can reduce overall tax liability.

Multiple-choice questions complement the discussion questions as an alternative way to quickly test a variety of learning objectives. They range from easy to more complex computational multiple choices.

d. Provide records requested by the IRS in all circumstances.

Tax Return Problems connect

All applicable tax return problems are available with *Connect*©

Use your tax software to complete the following problems. If you are manually preparing the tax returns, you will need a Form 1040EZ for each problem.

Tax Return Problem 1 Alex Montgomery is single and lives at 3344 Bayview Drive, Richmond Hill, GA 31324. His SSN is 412-34-5670. He recently graduated from the Savannah College of Art and Design and works as a video game developer. His Form W-2 contained the following information.

Wages (box 1) = $61,011.30
Federal W/H (box 2) = $ 8,528.10
Social security wages (box 3) = $61,011.30
Social security W/H (box 4) = $ 3,782.70

Now available in Connect, **Tax Return Problems** incorporate the TaxAct software and encourage students to apply a range of concepts they have learned throughout the chapter. All Tax Return Problems can also be done by hand. The authors indicate which forms are needed for each problem.

McGraw-Hill Education connect®

McGraw-Hill Connect® is a highly reliable, easy-to-use homework and learning management solution that utilizes learning science and award-winning adaptive tools to improve student results.

Homework and Adaptive Learning

- Connect's assignments help students contextualize what they've learned through application, so they can better understand the material and think critically.
- Connect will create a personalized study path customized to individual student needs through SmartBook®.
- SmartBook helps students study more efficiently by delivering an interactive reading experience through adaptive highlighting and review.

Connect's Impact on Retention Rates, Pass Rates, and Average Exam Scores

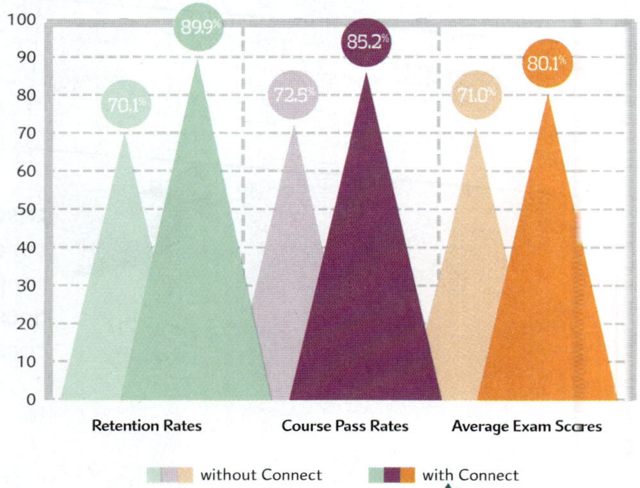

Using **Connect** improves retention rates by **19.8%**, passing rates by **12.7%**, and exam scores by **9.1%**.

Over **7 billion questions** have been answered, making McGraw-Hill Education products more intelligent, reliable, and precise.

73% of instructors who use **Connect** require it; instructor satisfaction **increases** by 28% when **Connect** is required.

Quality Content and Learning Resources

- Connect content is authored by the world's best subject matter experts, and is available to your class through a simple and intuitive interface.
- The Connect eBook makes it easy for students to access their reading material on smartphones and tablets. They can study on the go and don't need internet access to use the eBook as a reference, with full functionality.
- Multimedia content such as videos, simulations, and games drive student engagement and critical thinking skills.

Robust Analytics and Reporting

©Hero Images/Getty Images

- Connect Insight® generates easy-to-read reports on individual students, the class as a whole, and on specific assignments.
- The Connect Insight dashboard delivers data on performance, study behavior, and effort. Instructors can quickly identify students who struggle and focus on material that the class has yet to master.
- Connect automatically grades assignments and quizzes, providing easy-to-read reports on individual and class performance.

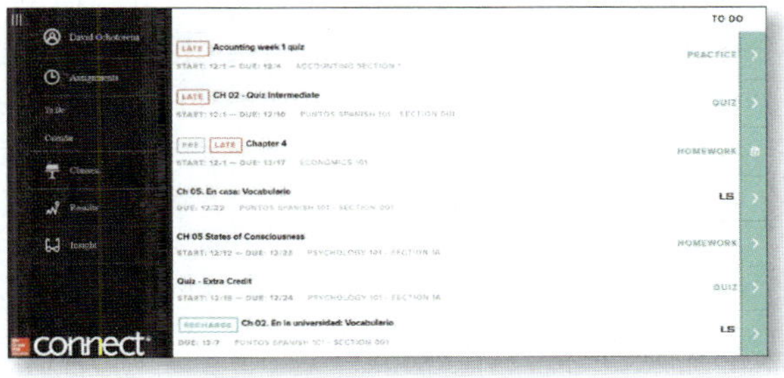

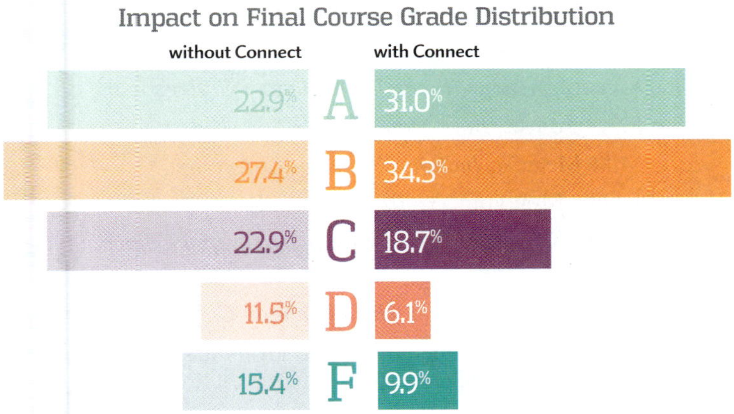

More students earn **As** and **Bs** when they use **Connect.**

Trusted Service and Support

- Connect integrates with your LMS to provide single sign-on and automatic syncing of grades. Integration with Blackboard®, D2L®, and Canvas also provides automatic syncing of the course calendar and assignment-level linking.
- Connect offers comprehensive service, support, and training throughout every phase of your implementation.
- If you're looking for some guidance on how to use Connect, or want to learn tips and tricks from super users, you can find tutorials as you work. Our Digital Faculty Consultants and Student Ambassadors offer insight into how to achieve the results you want with Connect.

www.mheducation.com/connect

A Monumental Development Effort

Acknowledgments

Writing a textbook is always a collaborative effort among authors, the publisher, authors' families, and instructors. The professors listed here contributed their time and insight to help this new edition launch successfully. By attending focus groups, reviewing selected chapters, reading through the whole manuscript, and reviewing page proofs, they contributed careful observations that enabled us to make significant improvements. Each person contributed something different—either a well-deserved criticism or a helpful word of encouragement. We sincerely appreciate their help and professionalism:

Nancy Batch, *Mountain View College*
Margaret Black, *San Jacinto College–North*
Joy Bruce, *Gaston College*
Bernard Bugg, *Shaw University*
Marian Canada, *Ivy Tech Community College*
Amy Chataginer, *Mississippi Gulf Coast Community College–Jefferson Davis*
Amy Conley, *Genesee Community College*
Curtis Crocker, *Central Georgia Technical College*
Geoffrey Danzig, *Miami Dade College–North*
John Daugherty, *Pitt Community College*
Patricia Davis, *Keystone College*
Susan Davis, *Green River Community College*
Peggy DeJong, *Kirkwood Community College*
George DeOrio, *Kaplan Career Institute–ICM Campus Technical College*
Scott Edelman, *Dominican College*
Don Furman, *State University of New York–New Paltz*
Kim W. Gatzke, *Delgado Community College*
Michelle Hayes, *Kalamazoo Valley Community College*
Margaret (Peggy) Helms, *Wayne Community College*
Gary Hollingsworth, *Antonelli College*
Carol Hughes, *Asheville Buncombe Tech Community College*
Norma Hunting, *Chabot College*
Kimberly Hurt, *Central Community College–Grand Island*
Karen Kettelson, *Western Technical College*
Mary Lou Kline, *Reading Area Community College*
Becky Knickel, *Brookhaven College*
Natasha Librizzi, *Milwaukee Area Technical College*
William Lloyd, *Lock Haven University of Pennsylvania*
Susan Logorda, *Lehigh Carbon Community College*
Ivan Lowe, *York Technical College*
Ming Lu, *West LA College*
William Lyle, *Georgia Piedmont Technical College*
Ted Lynch, *Hocking College*
Richard Mandau, *Piedmont Technical College*
Stacie Mayes, *Rose State College*
Mike Metzcar, *Indiana Wesleyan University*
Janelle Montgomery, *Rose State College*
Angela Deaton Mott, *Northeast Mississippi Community College*
Michelle Nickla, *Ivy Tech Community College*
Patricia Diane Nipper, *Southside Virginia Community College–Keysville*
Irene Novikov, *Foothill College*
Chris O'Byrne, *Cuyamaca College*
Cynthia Phipps, *Lake Land College*
Betty Pilchard, *Heartland Community College*
Jennifer Robinson, *Trident Technical College*
Patrick Rogan, *Cosumnes River College*
Dennis Sheridan, *Fayetteville Technical Community College*
Amy Shigley, *Edmonds Community College*
Mark Siegel, *South Texas College of Law*
Bonnie Silbernagel, *Lakeshore Technical College*
Barb Squires, *Corning Community College*
Carolyn Strauch, *Crowder College*
Denise Teixeira, *Chemeketa Community College*
Jerri Tittle, *Rose State College*
Alan Viersen, *MiraCosta College*
Shunda Ware, *Atlanta Technical College*
Kenneth Wise, *Wilkes Community College*
Edwin J. Wu, *Norfolk State University*

We greatly appreciate the accuracy-checking work completed by Matt Lowenkron (Glendale Community College). His attention to detail has helped us achieve the accuracy of the 2018 edition.

We also appreciate the expert attention given to this project by the staff at McGraw-Hill Education, especially Tim Vertovec, managing director; Kathleen Klehr, executive portfolio manager; Zach Rudin, marketing manager; Danielle Andries, senior product developer; Jaroslaw Szymanski, product developer; Dana Pauley, Angela Norris, and Erika Jordan, content project managers; Matt Backhaus, designer; and Susan Culbertson, buyer.

Ana Cruz

Michael Deschamps

Rick Niswander

Debra Prendergast

Dan Schisler

Assurance of Accuracy

Dear Colleague,

As textbook authors, and more importantly, as instructors of taxation, we recognize the great importance placed on accuracy—not only in the book you are now holding but also in the supplements. With this in mind, we have taken the following steps to ensure that *Fundamentals of Taxation* is error-free:

1. We received detailed feedback from dozens of instructor reviews. Each review contributed in significant ways to the accuracy of the content.
2. Each of us wrote, reviewed, and carefully checked the end-of-chapter material.
3. Multiple accuracy checkers reviewed each chapter and its accompanying end-of-chapter material.
4. A copy editor checked the grammar of the final manuscript.
5. A proofreader reviewed each page to ensure that no errors remained.
6. Our Solutions Manual and Testbank were created by the authors and reviewed by independent accuracy checkers.
7. *Connect* content was verified first by independent accuracy checkers and again by the author team.

Given these steps taken, we have the utmost confidence that you and your students will have a great experience using *Fundamentals of Taxation.*

As We Go To Press

This book is completed in mid-October and printed in early December. We picked that publication date to provide you a book that is as up-to-date as possible. A consequence of using that time frame is that Congress or the IRS may change some aspect of the tax law (especially around year-end or election time) that will affect the material in this book. Thus, it is important that students and instructors utilize *Connect* for information on how tax law changes have affected material in this book.

This book makes liberal use of IRS tax forms to illustrate how the tax law is implemented in practice. In fact, that notion—applying the tax law to practice—is one of the key features of the text.

As noted, we send the book to the printer in late October so we can provide the most up-to-date book as possible to be used for the 2017 tax filing season, which begins in January 2018. When we couple these two notions—using IRS tax forms and an October printing deadline—we must rely on draft tax forms that the IRS releases starting in June and running through the end of the year (see the note about draft tax forms on page 1-8 for more information). Go to the IRS website at www.irs.gov to obtain the final forms.

Sincerely,

Ana Cruz
Mike Deschamps
Rick Niswander
Debra Prendergast
Dan Schisler

Contents

Chapter 13
At-Risk/Passive Activity Loss Rules and the Individual Alternative Minimum Tax 13-1

Chapter 14
Partnership Taxation 14-1

Chapter 15
Corporate Taxation 15-1

Fundamentals of Taxation

2018

Chapter One

Introduction to Taxation, the Income Tax Formula, and Form 1040EZ

This chapter introduces the federal tax system and presents a broad overview of the tax formula. We begin with a wide-angle look at the U.S. tax system and the three types of tax rate structures. We introduce a simplified income tax formula using Form 1040EZ as a guide.

Throughout the entire text, the footnotes generally provide citations to the Internal Revenue Code (IRC) and other tax law or regulations. You can read this text either with or without the footnotes. If you would like to become familiar with the IRC and other tax authority, the footnotes are a good place to start exploring.

Learning Objectives

When you have completed this chapter, you should understand the following learning objectives (LO):

LO 1-1 Understand progressive, proportional, and regressive tax structures.

LO 1-2 Understand the concepts of marginal and average tax rates as well as a simple income tax formula.

LO 1-3 Understand the components of a Form 1040EZ income tax return.

LO 1-4 Determine tax liability in instances when a Form 1040EZ return is appropriate.

LO 1-5 Understand the types of tax authority and how they interrelate (Appendix A).

LO 1-6 Understand the provisions of IRS Circular 230 for paid tax preparers (Appendix B).

INTRODUCTION

The federal government enacted the first federal income tax in 1861 as a method to finance the Civil War. Prior to that time, federal tax revenues came primarily from excise taxes and duties on imported goods. Once the war was over, Congress repealed the income tax. Congress again passed a federal income tax in 1894 to broaden the types of taxes and to increase federal revenues. However, in 1895 the Supreme Court held that the federal income tax was unconstitutional. That ruling resulted in the Sixteenth Amendment to the Constitution in 1913:

Sixteenth Amendment to the Constitution of the United States of America

> The Congress shall have power to lay and collect taxes on incomes, from whatever source derived, without apportionment among the several States, and without regard to any census or enumeration.

TABLE 1-1
Type and Number of Individual Tax Returns

Source: *IRS Statistics of Income Bulletin,* Spring 2017, 2016, and 2015, Table A.

Type of Tax Return	2015	2014	2013	2012
Form 1040 returns	85,421,307	84,573,730	84,484,712	83,225,812
Form 1040A returns	41,133,634	40,853,006	39,788,033	38,607,172
Form 1040EZ returns	24,010,976	23,259,850	23,463,055	23,115,401
Total returns	150,565,918	148,686,586	147,735,801	144,948,385
Returns electronically filed (included in figures above)	132,251,035	129,076,138	126,531,029	122,266,344

The Sixteenth Amendment provides the underlying legal and statutory authority for the administration and enforcement of individual income taxes. Congress has promulgated tax law that is the primary source of information for what is, and is not, permitted. That tax law is the Internal Revenue Code (IRC). The IRC covers taxation of individuals, corporations, and partnerships, as well as other tax rules. Appendix A in this chapter discusses the types of tax laws, regulations, and court cases that compose what we refer to as *tax authority.* The material in Appendix A is of particular importance to students who want to be involved in tax planning, tax research, and other tax-related activities that require an understanding of taxes beyond a fill-in-the-forms level.

Currently the federal government collects revenue from various types of taxes. The largest revenue generators are the individual income tax, social security tax, corporate income tax, federal gift and estate tax, and various excise taxes. This text focuses on the largest revenue generator for the federal government: the individual income tax.[1] In tax year 2015, the federal government collected $1.45 trillion in income tax on almost $10.2 trillion of gross income ($7.3 trillion of taxable income) as reported on 150.6 million individual tax returns.[2] Table 1-1 presents a breakdown of the number and type of individual tax returns filed for 2012 through 2015.

One major criticism of the current tax system is the complexity of the law and the length of the forms. However, taxpayers filed over 65 million returns using the two easiest forms—Forms 1040A and 1040EZ. We will introduce you to Form 1040EZ in this chapter. Complexity in the tax system is not necessarily bad. Taxpayers often do not realize that many provisions that require use of the more complex tax forms are deduction or credit provisions that actually *benefit* the taxpayer. This text will help you understand the tax system's complexity, the rationale behind some of the complexity, and how to complete a tax return effectively.

TAX RATE STRUCTURES
LO 1-1

The study of taxation must begin with a basic understanding of rate structures and the tax system. We will discuss three different types of tax rate structures:

- Progressive rate structure.
- Proportional rate structure.
- Regressive rate structure.

Each of these rate structures is present in the tax collection system at the local, state, or federal level. Taxing authorities use one or more of these structures to assess most taxes.

Progressive Rate Structure

With a *progressive structure,* the tax rate increases as the tax base increases. The tax rate is applied to the tax base to determine the amount of tax. The most obvious progressive tax in

[1] The last two chapters are an overview of partnership and corporate taxation.

[2] IRS Statistics of Income Bulletin (Spring 2017), Table A.

TABLE 1-2
Individual Income Tax Rate Brackets for Married Taxpayers for Tax Year 2017

Taxable Income	Tax Rate
Up to $18,650	10.0%
$18,651–$75,900	15.0%
$75,901–$153,100	25.0%
$153,101–$233,350	28.0%
$233,351–$416,700	33.0%
$416,701–$470,700	35.0%
Over $470,700	39.6%

the United States, and the focus of this text, is the federal income tax. Table 1-2 illustrates the progressive rate structure of the individual income tax for married taxpayers who file joint returns.

The federal income tax is progressive because the tax rate gets larger as the taxable income (tax base) increases. For very low taxable income, the tax rate is 10% per additional dollar of income, and for very high taxable income, the tax rate is 39.6% per additional dollar.

EXAMPLE 1-1

Mary and George are married, file a joint federal tax return, and have taxable income of $240,000. Their tax liability is

$18,650 × 10% =	$ 1,865.00
($75,900 – $18,650) × 15% =	8,587.50
($153,100 – $75,900) × 25% =	19,300.00
($233,350 – $153,100) × 28% =	22,470.00
($240,000 – $233,350) × 33% =	2,194.50
Total tax liability	$54,417.00

Note from Example 1-1 that as the tax base (taxable income) increases, the tax rate per dollar of income gets progressively larger, rising from 10% to 33%.

TAX YOUR BRAIN

On average, how much income tax did Mary and George pay on their taxable income, and how do you interpret your answer?

ANSWER

Mary and George had an average tax rate of 22.67% calculated as their tax liability of $54,417 divided by their taxable income of $240,000. This means that, on average, for each dollar of taxable income, Mary and George paid 22.67 cents to the federal government for income tax.

Table 1-3 provides some additional evidence of the progressivity of the U.S. tax system. The average tax rates in Table 1-3 confirm that the individual income tax is indeed a progressive tax.

TAX YOUR BRAIN

In Table 1-3, compare those taxpayers with incomes less than $100,000 to those taxpayers with incomes greater than $100,000. What does your comparison suggest about income progressivity?

ANSWER

Over 125 million taxpayers had adjusted gross income of less than $100,000 and this group paid over $284 billion of individual income tax. There were about 25 million taxpayers with income over $100,000 and they paid tax of almost $1.2 trillion. This is further support for the notion that the U.S. individual income tax system is a progressive system.

TABLE 1-3 Individual Income Tax Returns from 2015, Number of Tax Returns, Taxable Income (in thousands), Total Tax Liability (in thousands), and Average Tax Rate by Ranges of Adjusted Gross Income

Source: *IRS Statistics of Income Bulletin,* Spring 2017, Table 1.

	Ranges of Adjusted Gross Income					
Item	**Under $15,000**	**$15,000 to under $30,000**	**$30,000 to under $50,000**	**$50,000 to under $100,000**	**$100,000 to under $200,000**	**$200,000 or more**
Number of returns	35,584,745	30,103,270	26,564,740	32,892,457	18,634,133	6,786,573
Taxable income	$21,528,894	$212,137,755	$562,835,017	$1,584,027,809	$1,907,435,602	$3,044,839,049
Total tax liability	$1,891,308	$18,379,300	$57,708,083	$206,278,362	$318,137,530	$851,380,935
Average tax rate*	8.78%	8.66%	10.25%	13.02%	16.68%	27.96%

*The average tax rate is total tax liability divided by taxable income.

Proportional Rate Structure

With a proportional tax structure, the tax *rate* remains the same regardless of the tax base. The popular name for a proportional tax is a *flat tax.* The most common flat or proportional taxes in existence in the United States are state and local taxes levied on either property or sales. For example, a local sales tax could be 6% on the purchase of a new car. Regardless of whether the price of the car (the tax base) was $15,000 or $80,000, the tax rate would still be 6% and the taxpayer would pay either $900 or $4,800 in sales tax, depending on the car purchased.

Another proportional tax is the Medicare tax. This tax pays for medical expenses for individuals over age 65. The rate is 2.9% of every dollar of wage income or self-employment income (there is an additional 0.9% tax on income over $250,000 for married taxpayers and $200,000 for most others. We discuss this in Chapter 10. We also discuss an additional 3.8% Medicare tax for high income taxpayers in Chapter 7.). Thus a doctor will pay Medicare tax of $4,350 on the $150,000 of net income from her medical practice (2.9% × $150,000), and a golf professional will pay $2,900 from his $100,000 tournament winnings (2.9% × $100,000). Although the doctor pays more total tax, the *rate* of tax is the same for both the doctor and the golf professional.

In recent years, there have been numerous political movements to replace the current progressive tax system with a flat tax. One plan called for a 17% flat tax on income. Compared to the current system, the 17% flat tax would result in an increase in tax liability for taxpayers with income of less than $200,000 and a decrease in tax liability for taxpayers with income of more than $200,000 (see Table 1-3).

Regressive Rate Structure

With a regressive tax, the rate decreases as the tax base increases. The social security tax is the most common regressive tax. The rate for social security taxes is 6.2% (12.4% for self-employed taxpayers) on the first $127,200 of wages in tax year 2017. Once wages exceed the $127,200 ceiling, social security taxes cease. Thus the rate drops (from 6.2% to 0%) as the tax base increases.

CONCEPT CHECK 1-1— LO 1-1

1. The three types of tax rate structures are __________, __________, and __________.
2. The tax rate structure for which the tax rate remains the same for all levels of the tax base is the __________ rate structure.
3. The federal income tax system is an example of a __________ tax structure.

MARGINAL TAX RATES AND AVERAGE TAX RATES
LO 1-2

Newspaper and magazine articles often discuss taxes and use the terms *average tax rate* and *marginal tax rate*. These two terms are not interchangeable; they mean very different things.

The average tax rate is the percentage that a taxpayer pays in tax given a certain amount of taxable income. The marginal tax rate represents the proportion of tax that he or she pays on the last dollar (or more accurately, the *next* dollar) of taxable income.

Let us assume that Ben and Martha have taxable income of $38,450 and file an income tax return as a married couple. Using the tax rates in Table 1-2, they determine that their tax liability is

$18,650 × 10% =	$1,865.00
($38,450 − $18,650) × 15% =	2,970.00
Total tax liability	$4,835.00

If you refer to Table 1-2, you will see that, for a married couple, each dollar of taxable income between $18,650 and $75,900 is taxed at a rate of 15%. In other words, if Ben and Martha earned an additional $100 of taxable income, they would owe the federal government an additional $15. Thus their marginal tax rate (the rate they would pay for an additional dollar of income) is 15%.

Conversely, the average rate is the percentage of total tax paid on the entire amount of taxable income. Ben and Martha have taxable income of $38,450 on which they had a tax liability of $4,835. Their average rate is 12.57% ($4,835.00/$38,450). The average rate is, in effect, a blended rate. Ben and Martha paid tax at a 10% rate on some of their taxable income and at a 15% rate on the rest of their income. Their average rate is a mixture of 10% and 15% that, in their case, averages out to 12.57%.

TAX YOUR BRAIN

For Ben and Martha, the marginal rate was larger than the average rate. Is that always the case?

ANSWER

No. When taxable income is zero or is within the lowest tax bracket (from $0 to $18,650 for married couples), the marginal rate will be equal to the average rate. When taxable income is more than the lowest tax bracket, the marginal rate will always be larger than the average rate.

A SIMPLE INCOME TAX FORMULA
LO 1-2

Taxpayers must annually report their taxable income, deductions, and other items to the Internal Revenue Service (IRS). Taxpayers do so by filing an income tax return. In its most simplified form, an individual income tax return has the following components:

Income
− Permitted deductions from income

= Taxable income
× Appropriate tax rates

= Tax liability
− Tax payments and tax credits

= Tax refund or tax due with return

Although many income tax returns are complex, the basic structure of every tax return follows this simplified formula. For many taxpayers, this simplified formula is sufficient.

For example, most individuals who receive all their income from an hourly or salaried job have a tax return that conforms to this basic structure. In later chapters we will expand on this tax formula, and we will provide more information about complexities in our tax laws. However, for this chapter the simplified version is appropriate.

CONCEPT CHECK 1-2— LO 1-2

1. The marginal tax rate is the rate of tax imposed on the next dollar of taxable income. True or false?
2. What is the marginal tax rate for a married couple with taxable income of $85,350?
3. Average tax rate and marginal tax rate mean the same thing. True or false?
4. Complex tax returns do not follow the basic (or simplified) income tax formula. True or false?

THE COMPONENTS OF FORM 1040EZ
LO 1-3

Taxpayers must annually report their income, deductions, tax liability, and other items to the federal government. They do so by filing a tax return. Taxpayers may file Form 1040, Form 1040A, or Form 1040EZ (listed in order from complex to simple). The return selected and filed generally depends on the complexity of the tax situation of the individual taxpayer.

A taxpayer who has a simple tax structure may be eligible to file the least complex individual income tax return—the 14-line Form 1040EZ, shown in Exhibit 1-1.

To use Form 1040EZ, a taxpayer must meet all of the following criteria:

- File the return as either single or married filing jointly.
- Be under age 65 and not blind.
- Have no dependents.
- Have total taxable income under $100,000.
- Have income only from wages, salary, tips, unemployment compensation, or taxable interest income of $1,500 or less.
- Claim no tax credits except for the Earned Income Credit.

Let us review the components of the simplified tax formula and the restrictions for filing Form 1040EZ. We will refer to the line numbers from the form in much of the discussion.

CONCEPT CHECK 1-3— LO 1-3

1. Almost all taxpayers can file Form 1040EZ. True or false?
2. Max, who is 74 years old and single, is eligible to file Form 1040EZ if his taxable income is under $100,000. True or false?
3. Erma, a 28-year-old single taxpayer with no dependents, has wage income of $40,000. She is eligible to file Form 1040EZ. True or false?

Filing Status

To use Form 1040EZ, a taxpayer must be either single or married and file a joint return with his or her spouse. Other filing categories that may apply to taxpayers include married filing separately, head of household, or qualifying widow(er). We explain these additional categories and expand our discussion of filing status in Chapter 2.

For purposes of this chapter, we will assume the taxpayer is either single or married filing a joint return.

Income

To use Form 1040EZ, taxpayers can have income only from wages, salary, tips, interest of $1,500 or less, and unemployment compensation.

EXHIBIT 1-1

Form **1040EZ**

Department of the Treasury—Internal Revenue Service

Income Tax Return for Single and Joint Filers With No Dependents (99) **2017** OMB No. 1545-0074

Your first name and initial	Last name		**Your social security number**
If a joint return, spouse's first name and initial	Last name		**Spouse's social security number**
Home address (number and street). If you have a P.O. box, see instructions.		Apt. no.	▲ Make sure the SSN(s) above are correct.
City, town or post office, state, and ZIP code. If you have a foreign address, also complete spaces below (see instructions).			**Presidential Election Campaign** Check here if you, or your spouse if filing jointly, want $3 to go to this fund. Checking a box below will not change your tax or refund. ☐ You ☐ Spouse
Foreign country name	Foreign province/state/county	Foreign postal code	

Income

Attach Form(s) W-2 here.

Enclose, but do not attach, any payment.

1	Wages, salaries, and tips. This should be shown in box 1 of your Form(s) W-2. Attach your Form(s) W-2.	1
2	Taxable interest. If the total is over $1,500, you cannot use Form 1040EZ.	2
3	Unemployment compensation and Alaska Permanent Fund dividends (see instructions).	3
4	Add lines 1, 2, and 3. This is your **adjusted gross income.**	4
5	If someone can claim you (or your spouse if a joint return) as a dependent, check the applicable box(es) below and enter the amount from the worksheet on back. ☐ **You** ☐ **Spouse** If no one can claim you (or your spouse if a joint return), enter $10,400 if **single;** $20,800 if **married filing jointly.** See back for explanation.	5
6	Subtract line 5 from line 4. If line 5 is larger than line 4, enter -0-. This is your **taxable income.** ▶	6

Payments, Credits, and Tax

7	Federal income tax withheld from Form(s) W-2 and 1099.	7
8a	**Earned income credit (EIC)** (see instructions)	8a
b	Nontaxable combat pay election. 8b	
9	Add lines 7 and 8a. These are your **total payments and credits.** ▶	9
10	**Tax.** Use the amount on **line 6 above** to find your tax in the tax table in the instructions. Then, enter the tax from the table on this line.	10
11	Health care: individual responsibility (see instructions) Full-year coverage ☐	11
12	Add lines 10 and 11. This is your **total tax.**	12

Refund

Have it directly deposited! See instructions and fill in 13b, 13c, and 13d, or Form 8888.

13a	If line 9 is larger than line 12, subtract line 12 from line 9. This is your **refund.** If Form 8888 is attached, check here ▶ ☐	13a
▶ b	Routing number ▶ **c** Type: ☐ Checking ☐ Savings	
▶ d	Account number	

Amount You Owe

14	If line 12 is larger than line 9, subtract line 9 from line 12. This is the **amount you owe.** For details on how to pay, see instructions. ▶	14

Third Party Designee

Do you want to allow another person to discuss this return with the IRS (see instructions)? ☐ **Yes.** Complete below. ☐ **No**

Designee's name ▶ Phone no. ▶ Personal identification number (PIN) ▶

Sign Here

Joint return? See instructions.

Keep a copy for your records.

Under penalties of perjury, I declare that I have examined this return and, to the best of my knowledge and belief, it is true, correct, and accurately lists all amounts and sources of income I received during the tax year. Declaration of preparer (other than the taxpayer) is based on all information of which the preparer has any knowledge.

Your signature	Date	Your occupation	Daytime phone number
Spouse's signature. If a joint return, **both** must sign.	Date	Spouse's occupation	If the IRS sent you an Identity Protection PIN, enter it here (see inst.)

Paid Preparer Use Only

Print/Type preparer's name	Preparer's signature	Date	Check ☐ if self-employed	PTIN
Firm's name ▶		Firm's EIN ▶		
Firm's address ▶		Phone no.		

For Disclosure, Privacy Act, and Paperwork Reduction Act Notice, see separate instructions. Cat. No. 11329W Form **1040EZ** (2017)

Source: U.S. Department of the Treasury, Internal Revenue Service, Form 1040EZ. Washington, DC: 2017.

A Note about Draft Tax Forms

Many of the IRS tax forms used throughout the text have the word "Draft" and a date printed across the form (see Exhibit 1-1). The IRS creates and modifies tax forms during the tax year. These forms are in draft form until they have obtained final approval within the IRS and by the federal Office of Management and Budget. The IRS distributes the draft forms internally, to tax professionals, and to tax software companies. By doing so, the IRS seeks comments to catch errors or to improve the forms. Final approval usually occurs on a rolling basis between mid-October and mid-December. Once the form has received final approval, the "Draft" label is removed and taxpayers can use the final form as they prepare their tax returns.

This text went to press in late October, when most IRS forms were available only in draft form. By the time you read this, final forms will be available on the IRS Web site (www.irs.gov) and in your tax software after you have updated it.

Wages, Salaries, and Tips (1040EZ, line 1)

Wages, salaries, and tips are the major sources of gross income for most taxpayers. In fact, for millions of Americans, these items are their only source of income. Individuals receive wages, salaries, and tips as "compensation for services."[3] This category is quite broad and encompasses commissions, bonuses, severance pay, sick pay, meals and lodging,[4] vacation trips or prizes given in lieu of cash, fringe benefits, and similar items.[5]

Employees receive wages and related income from their employers. Income received as a self-employed individual (independent contractor) does not meet the definition of wages and is reported on Schedule C. We discuss Schedule C in Chapter 6.

Wages include tips.[6] Employees receiving tip income must report the amount of tips to their employers.[7] They use IRS Form 4070 for that purpose. Large food and beverage establishments (those at which tipping is customary and that employ more than 10 employees on a typical business day) must report certain information to the IRS and to employees.[8] These employers must also allocate tip income to employees who normally receive tips. You can find more information about reporting tip income in IRS Publication 531, available on the IRS Web site at www.irs.gov.

Taxpayers classified as employees who receive compensation will receive a Form W-2 from their employer indicating the amount of wage income in box 1, "Wages, tips, and other compensation." This amount is reported on line 1 of Form 1040EZ.

An example of a Form W-2 is shown in Exhibit 1-2.

Taxable Interest (1040EZ, line 2)

Interest is compensation for the use of money with respect to a bona fide debt or obligation imposed by law (such as loans, judgments, or installment sales). Interest received by or credited to a taxpayer is taxable unless specifically exempt.[9] Interest paid is often deductible.[10] This section covers interest received.

For individuals, interest income is most often earned in conjunction with savings accounts, certificates of deposit, U.S. savings bonds, corporate bonds owned, seller-financed mortgages, loans made to others, and similar activities.

Generally, interest income is determined based on the interest rate stated in the documents associated with the transaction. Some exceptions exist, and some interest income is nontaxable. These items are discussed in the Appendix to Chapter 3.

Normally, taxpayers will receive a Form 1099-INT that will report the amount of interest earned (see Exhibit 1-3). The amount in box 1 is reported on Form 1040EZ, line 2.

[3] IRC § 61(a)(1).
[4] Unless excluded under IRC § 119.
[5] Reg. § 1.61-2 and Reg. § 1.61-21.
[6] IRC § 3401(f).
[7] IRC § 6053(a).
[8] IRC § 6053(c).
[9] IRC § 61(a)(4).
[10] Interest paid in conjunction with a trade or business is covered in Chapter 6. Personal interest paid is in Chapters 4 and 5.

EXHIBIT 1-2

	a Employee's social security number	OMB No. 1545-0008	Safe, accurate, FAST! Use IRS e-file	Visit the IRS website at *www.irs.gov/efile*
b Employer identification number (EIN)			1 Wages, tips, other compensation	2 Federal income tax withheld
c Employer's name, address, and ZIP code			3 Social security wages	4 Social security tax withheld
			5 Medicare wages and tips	6 Medicare tax withheld
			7 Social security tips	8 Allocated tips
d Control number			9 Verification code	10 Dependent care benefits
e Employee's first name and initial	Last name	Suff.	11 Nonqualified plans	12a See instructions for box 12 Code
			13 Statutory employee ☐ Retirement plan ☐ Third-party sick pay ☐	12b Code
			14 Other	12c Code
				12d Code
f Employee's address and ZIP code				

15 State	Employer's state ID number	16 State wages, tips, etc.	17 State income tax	18 Local wages, tips, etc.	19 Local income tax	20 Locality name

Form **W-2** **Wage and Tax Statement** **2017** Department of the Treasury—Internal Revenue Service

Copy B—To Be Filed With Employee's FEDERAL Tax Return.
This information is being furnished to the Internal Revenue Service.

Source: U.S. Department of the Treasury, Internal Revenue Service, Form W-2 Wage and Tax Statement. Washington, DC: 2017.

EXHIBIT 1-3

☐ CORRECTED (if checked)

PAYER'S name, street address, city or town, state or province, country, ZIP or foreign postal code, and telephone no.		Payer's RTN (optional)		OMB No. 1545-0112 **2017** Form **1099-INT**	**Interest Income**
		1 Interest income $			
		2 Early withdrawal penalty $			**Copy B**
PAYER'S federal identification number	RECIPIENT'S identification number	3 Interest on U.S. Savings Bonds and Treas. obligations $			**For Recipient**
RECIPIENT'S name		4 Federal income tax withheld $	5 Investment expenses $		This is important tax information and is being furnished to the Internal Revenue Service. If you are required to file a return, a negligence penalty or other sanction may be imposed on you if this income is taxable and the IRS determines that it has not been reported.
Street address (including apt. no.)		6 Foreign tax paid $	7 Foreign country or U.S. possession		
City or town, state or province, country, and ZIP or foreign postal code		8 Tax-exempt interest $	9 Specified private activity bond interest $		
		10 Market discount $	11 Bond premium $		
	FATCA filing requirement ☐	12 Bond premium on Treasury obligations $	13 Bond premium on tax-exempt bond $		
Account number (see instructions)		14 Tax-exempt and tax credit bond CUSIP no.	15 State	16 State identification no.	17 State tax withheld $ $

Form **1099-INT** (keep for your records) www.irs.gov/form1099int Department of the Treasury - Internal Revenue Service

Source: U.S. Department of the Treasury, Internal Revenue Service, Form 1099-INT. Washington, DC: 2017.

EXHIBIT 1-4

☐ CORRECTED (if checked)

PAYER'S name, street address, city or town, state or province, country, ZIP or foreign postal code, and telephone no.		1 Unemployment compensation $ 2 State or local income tax refunds, credits, or offsets $	OMB No. 1545-0120 **2017** Form **1099-G**	**Certain Government Payments**
PAYER'S federal identification number	RECIPIENT'S identification number	3 Box 2 amount is for tax year	4 Federal income tax withheld $	**Copy B For Recipient**
RECIPIENT'S name Street address (including apt. no.) City or town, state or province, country, and ZIP or foreign postal code		5 RTAA payments $ 7 Agriculture payments $ 9 Market gain $	6 Taxable grants $ 8 If checked, box 2 is trade or business income ► ☐	This is important tax information and is being furnished to the Internal Revenue Service. If you are required to file a return, a negligence penalty or other sanction may be imposed on you if this income is taxable and the IRS determines that it has not been reported.
Account number (see instructions)		**10a** State / **10b** State identification no.	**11** State income tax withheld $ $	

Form **1099-G** (keep for your records) www.irs.gov/form1099g Department of the Treasury - Internal Revenue Service

Source: U.S. Department of the Treasury, Internal Revenue Service, 1099-G. Washington, DC: 2017.

Unemployment Compensation (1040EZ, line 3)

Federal and state unemployment compensation benefits are taxable.[11] The rationale behind taxing these payments is that they are a substitute for taxable wages. Unemployment benefits are reported to recipients on Form 1099-G in box 1 (see Exhibit 1-4). The amount in box 1 is reported on line 3 of Form 1040EZ.

Citizens of Alaska also report any Alaska Permanent Fund dividends they receive on line 3 of Form 1040EZ.

Permitted Deductions from Income (1040EZ, line 5)

On Form 1040EZ, the only permitted deduction from income is on line 5. Although not labeled as such, this deduction is actually a combination of a standard deduction and a personal exemption. We will explain these two items in more detail in Chapter 2. For purposes of this chapter, the line 5 deduction is either $10,400 if the taxpayer is single or $20,800 if the taxpayer is filing a return as married. These dollar amounts represent the amount of income that is not taxed.

Taxable Income (1040EZ, line 6)

Taxable income refers to the wages, interest, and unemployment income on lines 1 through 3 minus the permitted deduction on line 5. Taxable income is the tax base used to determine the amount of tax.

CONCEPT CHECK 1-4—
LO 1-3

1. Only certain types of income can be reported on Form 1040EZ. They are ______________________________.
2. Unemployment compensation is reported to the taxpayer on a Form __________.
3. To be able to use Form 1040EZ, a taxpayer must be either filing status __________ or filing status __________.

[11] IRC § 85(a).

CALCULATION OF INCOME TAX AND HEALTH CARE TAX (FORM 1040EZ, LINES 10 AND 11)

LO 1-4

Income Tax (1040EZ, line 10)

We will now skip ahead to line 10, total tax, and line 11, health care. (Later we will come back to lines 7 through 9.)

The total amount of tax liability on line 10 of Form 1040EZ is determined based on the amount of taxable income (line 6). Taxpayers could calculate their tax using the tax rate schedule shown in Table 1-2 (or a similar one if the taxpayer were single). However, that method can be a bit complicated and can result in calculation errors. To make things easier, the IRS has prepared tax tables that predetermine the amount of tax liability for taxable incomes of up to $100,000. Remember that taxpayers must have total taxable income of less than $100,000 to use Form 1040EZ; otherwise they must use Form 1040A or 1040.

The tax tables applicable for tax year 2017 are printed in Appendix D of this text. Please refer to the 2017 tax tables when reviewing the examples and when working the problems at the end of this chapter unless you are told otherwise.

EXAMPLE 1-2

Art is a single taxpayer and has taxable income of $42,787. Referring to the tax table, his income is between $42,750 and $42,800. Reading across the table to the Single column gives a tax (for Form 1040EZ, line 10) of $6,433.

EXAMPLE 1-3

Joe and Marsha are married and are filing a joint tax return. They have taxable income of $45,059. In the tax table, their income is between $45,050 and $45,100. Their corresponding tax liability is $5,829.

Notice the effect of a differing filing status. Art had lower taxable income than did Joe and Marsha, but Art's tax liability was higher. All other things being equal, for equivalent amounts of taxable income, the highest tax will be paid by married persons filing separately, followed by single persons, then heads of household, and finally by married persons filing jointly. There are two exceptions to this general observation. The first is that, at low levels of taxable income, tax liability will be the same for all groups. The second is that married persons filing separately and single persons will have equal tax liability at taxable income levels up to $76,550.

In the preceding examples, we used the tax tables in Appendix D of this text to determine the amount of tax liability. If we calculated the amount of tax using the tax rate schedules provided in Appendix F of this text (or in Table 1-2 for married taxpayers), we would have computed a slightly different number.

EXAMPLE 1-4

Bill and Andrea Chappell, a married couple, have taxable income of $48,305. Using the tax tables in Appendix D, their tax liability is $6,316. Using the tax rate schedule in Table 1-2 (and printed in Appendix F of this text), their tax liability is

Tax on $18,650 × 10%	$1,865.00
Tax on ($48,305 − $18,650) × 15%	$4,448.25
Total tax	$6,313.25

Here the difference between the two tax numbers is $2.75. There will usually be a slight difference between the amount of tax calculated using the tax tables and the amount calculated using the tax rate schedules. The reason is that the tax rate schedules are precise, whereas the tax tables in Appendix D determine tax liability in $50 increments. In fact, the amount of tax liability shown in the tax tables represents the tax due on taxable income exactly in the middle of the $50 increment (as an exercise, check this out for yourself). Thus a taxpayer with taxable income in the lower half of the increment (like Bill and Andrea in the example) will pay a little extra in tax while someone in the upper half of the increment will pay a little less.

Again, unless instructed otherwise, for taxable income under $100,000 use the tax tables in Appendix D when you calculate tax liability.

TAX YOUR BRAIN

Determine the precise tax liability using the tax rate schedules in Appendix F for Art in Example 1-2 and for Joe and Marsha in Example 1-3.

ANSWER

Using the tax rate schedules, Art's tax liability is $6,435.50. The tax liability of Joe and Marsha is $5,826.35.

Health Care Tax (1040EZ, line 11)

The Affordable Care Act requires all individuals to either have health care coverage, or qualify for a health coverage exemption, or make a shared responsibility payment with their tax return. The shared responsibility payment is reported on Form 1040EZ, line 11.

Most health care coverage that people have is qualifying health care coverage (also called *minimum essential coverage*). Common examples of qualifying coverage are:

- Health coverage provided by the taxpayer's employer,
- Health coverage obtained through the Health Insurance Marketplace (also known as an "Exchange"), and
- Most government-sponsored coverage including Medicare, most Medicaid, and coverage for veterans and active duty service members.

If a taxpayer or a taxpayer and spouse (if filing jointly) had qualifying health care coverage for every month of 2017, then no additional tax due. In this case, the taxpayer checks the box on line 11 and leaves the line blank. Most taxpayers will have qualifying coverage.

If a taxpayer did not have qualifying coverage, the taxpayer may be eligible for an exemption from health care coverage. Some of the exemptions include:

- Cost of the lowest-cost qualifying coverage exceeds 8% of household income.
- Taxpayer income is below the minimum level required to file a return. Generally, for single taxpayers this amount is gross income less than $10,400 and for married taxpayers it is gross income less than $20,800. These amounts are increased if the taxpayer or spouse is over age 65.
- If a taxpayer went without coverage for less than three consecutive months during the year.

For a complete list of exemptions, refer to the instructions for Form 8965, available on the IRS Web site.

Taxpayers who qualify for an exemption must file a Form 8965 and no additional tax is due on Form 1040EZ, line 11.

If a taxpayer does not have qualifying coverage and is not eligible for an exemption, the taxpayer will be required to report a shared responsibility payment on line 11.

In general, the annual shared responsibility payment is the greater of:

- 2.5% of household income that is greater than the tax return filing threshold (see on the following page), or
- A flat dollar amount, which is $695 per adult and $347.50 per child under age 18, limited to a family maximum of $2,085.

Taxpayers owe 1/12 of the calculated annual shared responsibility payment for each month they do not have coverage and do not qualify for an exemption.

The annual shared responsibility payment cannot exceed the national average premium for a bronze-level qualified health plan available through the Marketplace. Practically, this limitation is unlikely to apply.

The tax return filing threshold amounts are shown in the following chart.

Filing Status	Household Income Threshold
Single, under age 65	$10,400
Single, age 65 or older	$11,950
Married, filing jointly, both spouses under age 65	$20,800
Married, filing jointly, one spouse age 65 or older	$22,050
Married, filing jointly, both spouses age 65 or older	$23,300
Married filing separately	$4,050
Head of household, under age 65	$13,400
Head of household, age 65 or older	$14,950

We discuss married filing separately and head of household filing statuses in Chapter 2.

EXAMPLE 1-5

Debra is age 37 and single. During all of 2017, she did not have qualifying health care coverage, nor was she eligible for an exemption. The national average premium limitation does not apply. Her household income was $50,000. Her annual shared responsibility payment is the greater of:

- 2.5% of household income that is greater than the threshold. This is ($50,000 – $10,400) × 2.5% = $990.
- $695.

Thus, her annual shared responsibility payment, shown on Form 1040EZ, line 11, is $990.

EXAMPLE 1-6

George and Deloris are both under age 65 and file as married, filing jointly. During all of 2017, they did not have qualifying health care coverage, nor were they eligible for an exemption. The national average premium limitation does not apply. Their household income was $30,000. Their annual shared responsibility payment is the greater of:

- 2.5% of household income that is greater than the threshold. This is ($30,000 – $20,800) × 2.5% = $230.
- $695 × 2 = $1,390.

Thus, their annual shared responsibility payment, shown on Form 1040EZ, line 11, is $1,390.

Certain taxpayers are eligible for a premium tax credit. In general, eligible taxpayers have income that is 400% or less than the federal poverty line for the taxpayer's family size. Those eligible for the premium tax credit cannot file a Form 1040EZ but must file a Form 1040 or Form 1040A. We discuss the premium tax credit in Chapter 9, Tax Credits.

The IRS issues publications which provide additional details related to application of the Affordable Care Act. These include Publication 5187, Publication 5201, and the instructions to Form 8965. All are available on the IRS Web site at www.irs.gov.

Total Tax (1040EZ, line 12)

Line 12 is the total of income tax plus any health care individual responsibility payment. It represents the total amount the taxpayer must pay to the government for the tax year. As we will see when we discuss lines 7 through 9, the taxpayer has likely already paid all or most of this liability.

CONCEPT CHECK 1-5— LO 1-4

1. Taxpayers eligible to use Form 1040EZ *must* calculate their tax liability using the tax tables. True or false?
2. Refer to the tax tables. What is the tax liability of a married couple with taxable income of $93,262? ____________
3. Using the tax rate schedule in Table 1-2 (or Appendix F), determine the tax liability (to the nearest penny) for a married couple with taxable income of $93,262. ____________
4. Taxpayers who do *not* have qualifying health care coverage must pay a shared responsibility payment of 2.5% of household income. True or False?

TAX PAYMENTS (FORM 1040EZ, LINE 9)

LO 1-3

Usually, taxpayers pay most of their tax liability prior to the due date of the tax return. Commonly, taxpayers pay through income tax withholding or quarterly estimated tax payments.

When certain taxable payments are made to individuals, the law requires the payer to retain (withhold) a portion of the payment otherwise due and to remit the amount withheld to the Treasury.[12] The withheld amount represents an approximation of the amount of income tax that would be due for the year on the taxable payment. Withholding, credited to the account of the taxpayer, reduces the amount of tax otherwise due to the government on the due date of the return.

Taxpayers have taxes withheld from their wages. When an employer pays a salary or wages to an employee, the employer is required to retain part of the amount otherwise due the employee. The amount retained is payroll tax withholding and is a part of virtually every pay stub in the country. The total amount of individual income tax withheld from the earnings of an employee is shown in box 2 of the Form W-2 given to each employee shortly after the end of the calendar year. The amount in box 2 is transferred to line 7 of Form 1040EZ.

Earned Income Credit (1040EZ, line 8a)

An Earned Income Credit (EIC) is available for certain low-income taxpayers. The EIC is a percentage of earned income with a phaseout of the credit at higher earned income amounts. For purposes of this chapter, we will assume the EIC is zero. We discuss the EIC in more detail in Chapter 9.

Members of the U.S. armed forces who serve in a combat zone can exclude certain combat zone pay from their income. However, because the exclusion reduces the amount of earned income, the exclusion may reduce the amount of EIC. Armed forces personnel can elect to include the combat zone pay in earned income (on line 8b) for purposes of determining their EIC, thus receiving a larger tax credit (and paying less tax).

Total Payments (1040EZ, line 9)

Line 9 is the sum of the tax withholding from line 7 and the credits on lines 8a and 8b.

Tax Refund (line 13a) or Tax Due with Return (line 14)

Compare the amount owed (line 12) with the total amount already paid (line 9). Excess payment results in a refund; remaining tax liability means the taxpayer must pay the remaining amount owed when filing the return.

(text continues on page 1-19)

[12] See Chapter 10 for discussion of the rules associated with withholding and remitting payroll taxes.

From Shoebox to Software An Introduction

Throughout this text, we provide a series of features called From Shoebox to Software. These sections explain how a tax preparer goes about putting together all or part of a tax return. Because this is the first time we have presented a From Shoebox to Software feature, let's explain what it is and how it works.

The majority of the information that appears on a tax return comes from some sort of source document. The most common document is an IRS form. Almost all taxpayers receive source documents provided on standardized IRS forms. These documents include a W-2 for wages, a 1099-INT for interest payments, a 1099-B for stock brokerage transactions, and many others. These documents serve a dual purpose. First, they provide taxpayers information necessary to prepare a portion of their tax returns in a standardized and easy-to-use format. Second, the IRS receives a copy of each document and uses the information to check whether individual taxpayers have properly reported items on their tax returns.

The second type of document used for tax return preparation is a nonstandardized, free-form document. It could be a charge card receipt from a restaurant meal with a business customer, a bill from a hospital for medical care, or a written record (such as a journal) of business car expenses.

Taxpayers accumulate documents during the tax year and then use them when the tax return is prepared. Tax return preparers have a standard joke about clients coming to their office with a pile of documents—some useful, some not. This pile of documents is often called a "shoebox" because many times that's what the documents are kept in during the year. Virtually every tax preparer has a story (often many) about a client who drops a shoebox full of documents on the preparer's desk—often on April 14, the day before the individual income tax return filing deadline.

The tax return preparer must then make sense of the shoebox full of documents. One challenge is to separate the documents useful in the preparation of the return (W-2s, medical receipts, etc.) from documents that do not matter (the receipt for a new gas grill used by the taxpayer at home). The series of From Shoebox to Software explanations (and your future understanding of tax rules and regulations) will help you extract the valuable documents from the rest of the papers.

From Shoebox to Software explanations will also help you determine how the information from the document is "put into" tax software so the completed return is accurate. It is one thing to have the correct data and quite another to be able to efficiently, effectively, and correctly use them in the software. Many tax software products are available for use. Some are very simple, and others are extremely complex. In this book we use TaxAct software produced by 2nd Story Software. However, it doesn't matter what software product you use because almost all tax software has a similar structure: Source document information is entered into a series of input forms that then feed into a tax return form that is then assembled with other tax return forms into a final completed tax return. The drawing below illustrates the process.

When you use the tax software, you initially record the information from the source document on a source document input form. For example, you record information from a W-2 source document on a W-2 input form in the tax software. You record most tax information in a similar manner.

Sometimes you record source document data directly on a tax return form. This occurs if the item is unusual or does not "flow" to another form.

The From Shoebox to Software text boxes will show you how to take raw data and enter them correctly on the tax forms. Before you start to use the software, you should take a few minutes to read Appendix C of this chapter, where we provide some basic information and guidelines concerning the TaxAct software that is included with this text.

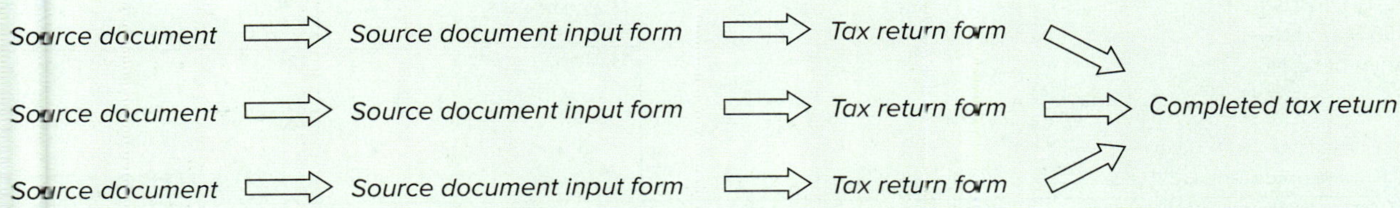

From Shoebox to Software A Comprehensive Example

This comprehensive example allows you to use what you have learned. Use your tax software and follow along as we explain the procedure. When you have finished, you will have prepared a 1040EZ using the information in the example.

Your clients are Ed and Betty Davidson, a married couple. They live at 456 Main Street, Anywhere, NC 27890. Ed's social security number is 412-34-5670 and Betty's is 412-34-5671.[13] You have determined that they qualify to file Form 1040EZ.

Betty worked at Brenden Manufacturing and received a W-2 from the company. Ed performed volunteer work during the year and received no compensation. They received $372.33 in interest income from First Savings Bank during the year.

You received the following documents (see below and the next page) from the Davidsons.

Open TaxAct. Click on Forms on the toolbar at the top of the page. This will open the Forms Explorer and allow you to select the form you wish to work on. You will use the Forms method to input information into the TaxAct software. We realize that the software has a mode, called Q&A, that will ask the user a series of questions and will create a tax return based on the answers. Tax practitioners seldom use this mode. If you plan to become a tax practitioner (or even if you just want to do your own return yourself), you will need to get in the habit of using the Forms mode to become more familiar with the various IRS forms used when filing a return.

The Forms Explorer has three primary categories of forms from which to choose:

Forms and schedules: This section includes all of the IRS forms that you need to complete a tax return. At this point, we care about only one form—the 1040EZ.

Documents received: Earlier we mentioned that the Shoebox contains two types of source documents. One type of source document is an IRS form. In the Documents Received section, you will find input screens for many IRS forms received by taxpayers. When you properly input the IRS form information on the appropriate screen, the data will automatically flow to all other applicable forms. For the Davidsons, we are interested in the input forms for their W-2 and the 1099-INT.

Worksheets: This section contains worksheets for you to input information that the software will summarize and then show on the appropriate tax form. These worksheets are helpful to collect supporting information in one place. The software worksheets also help the tax practitioner have consistent work paper files and procedures. For this example, we will not use any of the worksheets.

a Employee's social security number: 412-34-5671 | OMB No. 1545-0008 | Safe, accurate, FAST! Use e-file | Visit the IRS website at www.irs.gov/efile

b Employer identification number (EIN)		1 Wages, tips, other compensation	53,766.00
		2 Federal income tax withheld	4,279.00
c Employer's name, address, and ZIP code	Brendon Manufacturing 6789 Main Street Anywhere, NC 27890	3 Social security wages	53,766.00
		4 Social security tax withheld	3,333.49
		5 Medicare wages and tips	53,766.00
		6 Medicare tax withheld	779.61
		7 Social security tips	
		8 Allocated tips	
d Control number		9 Verification code	
		10 Dependent care benefits	
e Employee's first name and initial / Last name / Suff.	Betty Davidson 456 Main Street Anywhere, NC 27890	11 Nonqualified plans	
		12a See instructions for box 12	
		13 Statutory employee / Retirement plan / Third-party sick pay	☐ ☐ ☐
		12b	
		14 Other	
		12c	
f Employee's address and ZIP code		12d	

15 State	Employer's state ID number	16 State wages, tips, etc.	17 State income tax	18 Local wages, tips, etc.	19 Local income tax	20 Locality name
NC		53,766.00	1,201.22			

Form **W-2** Wage and Tax Statement **2017**

Department of the Treasury—Internal Revenue Service

Copy B—To Be Filed With Employee's FEDERAL Tax Return.
This information is being furnished to the Internal Revenue Service.

Source: U.S. Department of the Treasury, Internal Revenue Service, Form W-2 Wage and Tax Statement. Washington, DC: 2017.

[13] Throughout the text we use common fictional social security numbers for all our fictional taxpayers.

☐ CORRECTED (if checked)

PAYER'S name, street address, city or town, state or province, country, ZIP or foreign postal code, and telephone no.	Payer's RTN (optional)	OMB No. 1545-0112	
First Savings Bank 123 Main Street Anywhere NC 27890	1 Interest income $ 372.33	**2017** Form **1099-INT**	**Interest Income**
	2 Early withdrawal penalty $		**Copy B** **For Recipient**
PAYER'S federal identification number: 33-1234500	RECIPIENT'S identification number: 412-34-5670	3 Interest on U.S. Savings Bonds and Treas. obligations $	
RECIPIENT'S name Ed Davidson	4 Federal income tax withheld $	5 Investment expenses $	This is important tax information and is being furnished to the Internal Revenue Service. If you are required to file a return, a negligence penalty or other sanction may be imposed on you if this income is taxable and the IRS determines that it has not been reported.
Street address (including apt. no.) 456 Main Street	6 Foreign tax paid $	7 Foreign country or U.S. possession	
City or town, state or province, country, and ZIP or foreign postal code Anywhere NC 27890	8 Tax-exempt interest $	9 Specified private activity bond interest $	
FATCA filing requirement ☐	10 Market discount $	11 Bond premium $	
	12 Bond premium on Treasury obligations $	13 Bond premium on tax-exempt bond $	
Account number (see instructions)	14 Tax-exempt and tax credit bond CUSIP no.	15 State | 16 State identification no.	17 State tax withheld $ $

Form **1099-INT** (keep for your records) www.irs.gov/form1099int Department of the Treasury - Internal Revenue Service

Source: U.S. Department of the Treasury, Internal Revenue Service, Form 1099-INT. Washington, DC: 2017.

To start, you must input the basic information about the Davidsons. Go to the File menu (upper left) and click on New Return. The system will then give you the opportunity to import data from a prior year's tax return. For all examples in this text, there is no prior year information.

You will now be at the main TaxAct screen in the Q&A mode. Click on the Forms icon on the taskbar. This will take you to the Forms Explorer. Click on Forms and Schedules and then double-click on Federal Form 1040. TaxAct will print out the appropriate return depending on the data provided. Information related to the taxpayer is recorded on Form 1040.

You now need to input the basic name and address information for the Davidsons. Click on the appropriate boxes in the white area on the upper portion of the 1040 form. You also need to input their social security numbers in the appropriate boxes. When you have entered the information, click the Forms icon and then double-click on Federal Form 1040EZ. You should now be looking at Form 1040EZ with the Davidsons' information at the top of the form. Check to see that the information is correct. If not, go back to Form 1040 and correct it.

We now need to input the W-2 and 1099-INT information. Click on the Forms icon and then click on Documents Received. Input the W-2 first. Double-click on Federal Form W-2. This will bring up a W-2 input form. You now need to input the information from Betty's W-2 from Brenden Manufacturing. Fill in all appropriate boxes, including the employer name and address. Make sure you input the correct social security number and name for Betty. When you have completed the W-2 for Brenden Manufacturing, click the Back button at the bottom. You will be back at the Forms Explorer.

Now input the information from the 1099-INT.

You have now input the tax information for the Davidsons. Let's look at the result. Go to the Forms Explorer, click on Forms and Schedules, and double-click on Federal Form 1040EZ. This will bring up the completed 1040EZ of the Davidsons.

Your completed 1040EZ should look like the form shown on the next page.

Line 1, wages, salaries, and tips, is $53,766. This is the wage information from the W-2 of Betty.

Line 2, taxable interest, shows the $372 of interest income from First Savings Bank. When you typed in the information, you put in $372.33, yet line 2 only shows $372. What happened to the 33 cents? When you input information, you use dollars and cents. When the software completes the forms, it will round all numbers to the nearest dollar (the IRS says we need to round down amounts below 50 cents and round up amounts of 50 cents or more).

Line 4, Adjusted Gross Income, is the summation of lines 1 and 2. Line 5 is the $20,800 deduction for a married couple. Taxable income, line 6, is $33,338 and represents line 4 minus line 5.

Line 7, federal income tax withheld, is the amount from box 2 from Betty's W-2.

Line 10 is the total tax liability of $4,066. You can check this figure with reference to the 2017 tax tables.

When you compare the Davidsons' total liability of $4,066 to the $4,279 they have already paid in withholding and credits, you see that the Davidsons will receive a refund of $213. This amount is on line 13a.

Form **1040EZ** Department of the Treasury—Internal Revenue Service
Income Tax Return for Single and Joint Filers With No Dependents (99) **2017** OMB No. 1545-0074

Your first name and initial	Last name	Your social security number
Ed	Davidson	4 1 2 3 4 5 6 7 0
If a joint return, spouse's first name and initial	Last name	Spouse's social security number
Betty	Davidson	4 1 2 3 4 5 6 7 1
Home address (number and street). If you have a P.O. box, see instructions. 456 Main Street	Apt. no.	▲ Make sure the SSN(s) above are correct.
City, town or post office, state, and ZIP code. If you have a foreign address, also complete spaces below (see instructions). Anywhere, NC 27890		**Presidential Election Campaign** Check here if you, or your spouse if filing jointly, want $3 to go to this fund. Checking a box below will not change your tax or refund. ☐ You ☐ Spouse
Foreign country name	Foreign province/state/county	Foreign postal code

Section	Line	Description	Line	Amount
Income Attach Form(s) W-2 here. Enclose, but do not attach, any payment.	1	Wages, salaries, and tips. This should be shown in box 1 of your Form(s) W-2. Attach your Form(s) W-2.	1	53,766
	2	Taxable interest. If the total is over $1,500, you cannot use Form 1040EZ.	2	372
	3	Unemployment compensation and Alaska Permanent Fund dividends (see instructions).	3	
	4	Add lines 1, 2, and 3. This is your **adjusted gross income.**	4	54,138
	5	If someone can claim you (or your spouse if a joint return) as a dependent, check the applicable box(es) below and enter the amount from the worksheet on back. ☐ **You** ☐ **Spouse** If no one can claim you (or your spouse if a joint return), enter $10,400 if **single;** $20,800 if **married filing jointly.** See back for explanation.	5	20,800
	6	Subtract line 5 from line 4. If line 5 is larger than line 4, enter -0-. This is your **taxable income.** ▶	6	33,338
Payments, Credits, and Tax	7	Federal income tax withheld from Form(s) W-2 and 1099.	7	4,279
	8a	**Earned income credit (EIC)** (see instructions)	8a	
	b	Nontaxable combat pay election. 8b		
	9	Add lines 7 and 8a. These are your **total payments and credits.** ▶	9	4,279
	10	**Tax.** Use the amount on **line 6 above** to find your tax in the tax table in the instructions. Then, enter the tax from the table on this line.	10	4,066
	11	Health care: individual responsibility (see instructions) Full-year coverage ☑	11	
	12	Add lines 10 and 11. This is your **total tax.**	12	4,066
Refund Have it directly deposited! See instructions and fill in 13b, 13c, and 13d, or Form 8888.	13a	If line 9 is larger than line 12, subtract line 12 from line 9. This is your **refund.** If Form 8888 is attached, check here ▶ ☐	13a	213
	▶ b	Routing number ▶ c Type: ☐ Checking ☐ Savings		
	▶ d	Account number		
Amount You Owe	14	If line 12 is larger than line 9, subtract line 9 from line 12. This is the **amount you owe.** For details on how to pay, see instructions. ▶	14	

Third Party Designee Do you want to allow another person to discuss this return with the IRS (see instructions)? ☐ **Yes.** Complete below. ☐ **No**
Designee's name ▶ Phone no. ▶ Personal identification number (PIN) ▶

Sign Here Under penalties of perjury, I declare that I have examined this return and, to the best of my knowledge and belief, it is true, correct, and accurately lists all amounts and sources of income I received during the tax year. Declaration of preparer (other than the taxpayer) is based on all information of which the preparer has any knowledge.

Joint return? See instructions. Keep a copy for your records.

Your signature	Date	Your occupation	Daytime phone number
Spouse's signature. If a joint return, **both** must sign.	Date	Spouse's occupation	If the IRS sent you an Identity Protection PIN, enter it here (see inst.)

Paid Preparer Use Only

Print/Type preparer's name	Preparer's signature	Date	Check ☐ if self-employed	PTIN
Firm's name ▶		Firm's EIN ▶		
Firm's address ▶		Phone no.		

For Disclosure, Privacy Act, and Paperwork Reduction Act Notice, see separate instructions. Cat. No. 11329W Form **1040EZ** (2017)

Source: U.S. Department of the Treasury, Internal Revenue Service, Form 1040EZ. Washington, DC: 2017.

A taxpayer who is entitled to a refund can elect to (a) receive a check or (b) have the refund deposited directly in the taxpayer's bank account by supplying account information on lines 13b, c, and d.

In many ways, a tax return is the document a taxpayer uses to "settle up" with the IRS after a tax year is over. On it, the taxpayer reports income and deductions, the amount of tax, and the tax already paid. The refund (line 13a) or tax due (line 14) is simply the balancing figure required to make total net payments equal to the amount of total tax liability.

Individual income tax returns must be filed with the IRS no later than April 15 of the following year. Thus tax returns for calendar year 2017 must be filed (postmarked) no later than April 15, 2018. If April 15 falls on a weekend, taxpayers must file by the following Monday. Taxpayers can receive a six-month extension to file their returns if they file Form 4868 no later than April 15. Any remaining tax liability is still due by April 15—the extension of time pertains only to the tax return, not the tax due.

EXAMPLE 1-7

Nora, who is single, has determined that her total tax liability for 2017 is $4,486. In 2017 her employer withheld $4,392 from Nora's paychecks. When Nora files her return, she will need to enclose a check for $94. Thus Nora's total payment for tax year 2017 is $4,486 ($4,392 withholdings plus $94 paid with her return), which is equal to her total liability for 2017.

EXAMPLE 1-8

Todd and Ellen, a married couple, determined that their total tax liability for 2017 is $8,859. In 2017 Ellen's employer withheld $5,278 from her paycheck and Todd's employer withheld $3,691. Todd and Ellen will receive a refund of $110 ($5,278 + $3,691 – $8,859). Thus Ellen and Todd's total payment for tax year 2017 is $8,859 ($5,278 and $3,691 of withholdings minus the $110 refund), which is equal to their total liability for 2017.

CONCEPT CHECK 1-6—
LO 1-3

1. Taxpayers pay all of their tax liability when they file their tax returns. True or false?
2. Bret's tax liability is $15,759. His employer withheld $15,367 from his wages. When Bret files his tax return, will he be required to pay or will he get a refund? ____________ What will be the amount of payment or refund? ____________
3. An Earned Income Credit will increase the amount of tax liability. True or false?

Appendix A

TAX AUTHORITY
LO 1-5

Throughout this text, there are many references to "tax authority." As a beginning tax student, you need to understand what tax authority is. The best definition of *tax authority* is that the term refers to the guidelines that give the taxpayer not only guidance to report taxable income correctly but also guidelines and precedent for judicial decisions concerning conflicts between the IRS and the taxpayer. There are three types of primary tax authority:

Statutory sources
Administrative sources
Judicial sources

TABLE 1-4
Legislative Process of U.S. Tax Laws

- U.S. House of Representatives Ways and Means Committee.
- Voted on by the House of Representatives.
- U.S. Senate Finance Committee.
- Voted on by the Senate.
- Joint Conference Committee (if differences between the House and Senate versions).
- Joint Conference bill voted on by the House of Representatives and the Senate.
- If the bill passes the House and Senate—signed or vetoed by the president of the United States.
- If signed—incorporated into the Internal Revenue Code.

Statutory Sources of Tax Authority

The ultimate statutory tax authority is the Sixteenth Amendment to the U.S. Constitution. By far the most commonly relied-upon statutory authority is the IRC. Congress writes the IRC. Changes to it must pass through the entire legislative process to become law. Table 1-4 shows the legislative process for tax laws.

Typically federal tax legislation begins in the Ways and Means Committee of the House of Representatives (although bills can start in the Senate Finance Committee). A tax bill passed by the House is sent to the Senate for consideration. If the Senate agrees to the bill with no changes, it sends the bill to the president for a signature or veto. If, as is more likely, the Senate passes a bill different from the House version, both houses of Congress select some of their members to be on a Joint Conference Committee. The committee's goal is to resolve the conflict(s) between the House and Senate versions of the bill. Once conflicts are resolved in the Conference Committee, both the House and the Senate vote on the common bill. If passed by both bodies, the bill goes to the president and, if signed, becomes law and part of the IRC.

Each enacted law receives a public law number. For example, Public Law 99-272 means the enacted legislation was the 272nd bill of the 99th Congress (the January 2017 to January 2019 legislative years of the Congress will be the 115th Congress).

Throughout the legislative process, each taxation committee (Ways and Means, Senate Finance, and the Joint Conference Committee) generates one or more committee reports that note the "intent of Congress" in developing legislation. These committee reports can provide courts, the IRS, and tax professionals guidance as to the proper application of enacted tax law. The public law number of the bill is used to reference committee reports. Public Law 99-272 would have a House Ways and Means Committee report, a Senate Finance Committee report and possibly a Joint Conference Committee report.[14]

The IRS publishes the congressional reports in the *IRS Cumulative Bulletin. Cumulative Bulletins* are in most libraries in the government documents section. The reports are also on various governmental Internet sites. Use an Internet search engine to help you find these sites. *Cumulative Bulletins* for the last five years are available on the IRS Web site (www.irs.gov).

The IRC is organized by subtitle, as shown in Table 1-5.

TABLE 1-5
Subtitles of the Internal Revenue Code

Subtitle	Subject
A	Income taxes
B	Estate and gift taxes
C	Employment taxes
D	Excise taxes
E	Alcohol and tobacco taxes
F	Procedure and administration
G	Joint Committee on Taxation
H	Presidential election campaign financing
I	Trust funds

[14] Not all bills have committee reports from each house of Congress. If there are no conflicts between the House and Senate, additional committee reports are not necessary. Such an outcome is unusual.

Most of this text pertains to subtitle A of the IRC (income taxes). The IRC is hundreds of pages in length. An excerpt from the IRC follows:

> IRC § 61. Gross Income Defined
> General Definition—Except as otherwise provided in this subtitle, gross income means all income from whatever source derived, including (but not limited to) the following items:
> Compensation for services, including fees, commissions, fringe benefits, and similar items;
> Gross income derived from business;
> Gains derived from dealings in property;
> Interest;
> Rents;
> Royalties;
> Dividends;
> Alimony and separate maintenance payments;
> Annuities;
> Income from life insurance and endowment contracts;
> Pensions;
> Income from discharge of indebtedness;
> Distributive share of partnership gross income;
> Income in respect of a decedent; and
> Income from an interest in an estate or trust.

The major national tax publishers such as Research Institute of America (RIA) and Commerce Clearing House (CCH) publish the IRC in bound versions and on their respective Web sites. The IRC can also be located on numerous tax Internet sites, although students are cautioned that the content of most generic Web sites is often not up to date (RIA and CCH are current).

CONCEPT CHECK 1-7— LO 1-5

1. The committee charged with considering tax legislation in the House of Representatives is called the ________________ Committee.
2. The most commonly relied-on statutory authority is ________________.
3. All tax legislation must pass both the House of Representatives and the Senate and be signed by the president of the United States in order to become law. True or false?

As authorized by Congress, the president of the United States enters into tax treaties. Thus treaties between the United States and other countries are also statutory tax authority.

A problem with the IRC is that it is usually extremely broad and sometimes difficult to apply to specific tax situations. Because of this limitation, administrative and judicial tax authorities have evolved.

Administrative Tax Authority

The IRS, a division of the U.S. Treasury Department, develops administrative tax authority. The tax authority created by the IRS is, in effect, the IRS's interpretation of the IRC. Table 1-6 presents a list of the major IRS administrative authorities. These are the rulings or interpretations of the IRS at the national level. Each region of the IRS also publishes several authoritative guidelines.

TABLE 1-6
Examples of Administrative Authority (in order of strength of authority, from highest to lowest)

Type of Administrative Authority	Example of Typical Research Citation
IRS Regulations (Treasury Regulations)	Reg. § 1.351-1
Revenue Rulings	Rev. Rul. 80-198, 1980-2 CB 113
Revenue Procedures	Rev. Proc. 87-32, 1987-2 CB 396
Private Letter Rulings	PLR 8922063
IRS Notices	Notice 97-69, 1997-2 CB 331

Treasury Regulations

IRS Regulations are by far the strongest administrative authority. Regulations are the IRS's direct interpretation of the IRC. There are four types of IRS Regulations (listed in order of strength of authority, high to low):

Legislative Regulations: The IRS writes these regulations under a direct mandate by Congress. Legislative Regulations actually take the place of the IRC and have the full effect of law.

General or Final Regulations: The IRS writes these regulations under its general legislative authority to interpret the IRC. Most sections of the IRC have General Regulations to help interpret the law.

Temporary Regulations: These regulations have the same authority as General Regulations until they expire three years after issuance. The IRS issues Temporary Regulations to give taxpayers immediate guidance related to a new law. Temporary Regulations are noted with a "T" in the citation (for example, Reg. § 1.671-2T).

Proposed Regulations: These regulations do not have the effect of law. The IRS writes Proposed Regulations during the hearing process leading up to the promulgation of General Regulations. The purpose of the Proposed Regulations is to generate discussion and critical evaluation of the IRS's interpretation of the IRC.

Regulations are referred to (or cited) by using an IRC subtitle prefix, the referring code section, and the regulation number. For example, Reg. § 1.162-5 refers to the prefix (1) denoting the income tax subtitle, IRC section 162, and regulation number 5. Here are some examples of regulation subtitle prefixes:

1. Income Taxes (Reg. § 1.162-5).
20. Estate Tax (Reg. § 20.2032-1).
25. Gift Tax (Reg. § 25.2503-4).
31. Employment Taxes (Reg. § 31.3301-1).
301. Procedural Matters (Reg. § 301.7701-1).[15]

Like the IRS, the national publishers (RIA and CCH) publish and sell paperback and hardbound versions of IRS Regulations. You can also find regulations on a number of tax Internet sites including the IRS Web site (www.irs.gov).

Revenue Rulings and Revenue Procedures

Revenue Rulings (Rev. Rul.) and Revenue Procedures (Rev. Proc.) are excellent sources of information for taxpayers and tax preparers. When issuing a Revenue Ruling, the IRS is reacting to an area of the tax law that is confusing to many taxpayers or that has substantive tax implications for numerous taxpayers. After many taxpayers have requested additional guidance on a given situation, the IRS may issue a Rev. Rul. The Rev. Rul. lists a factual situation, the relevant tax authority, and the IRS's conclusion as to the manner in which taxpayers should treat the issue.

Revenue Procedures (Rev. Proc.), on the other hand, are primarily proactive. Through a Rev. Proc., the IRS illustrates how it wants something reported. Often the IRS provides guidelines or safe harbors to help taxpayers follow the law as interpreted by the IRS. For example, after the Tax Reform Act of 1986, the allowable depreciation methods were drastically changed. The IRS issued Rev. Proc. 87-56 and 87-57 to help taxpayers and preparers properly calculate and report depreciation expense under the new rules.

[15] Various other prefixes are used in specific situations. When dealing with income taxes, however, the first (1) is used most often.

The citations for Revenue Rulings and Revenue Procedures indicate the year of the ruling or procedure and a consecutive number (reset to 1 each year). For example, Rev. Proc. 87-56 was the 56th Revenue Procedure issued in 1987. Revenue Rulings and Procedures are in the *Cumulative Bulletins* published by the IRS and available on its Web site.

Other IRS Pronouncements

Other pronouncements issued by the IRS include Private Letter Rulings (PLRs) and IRS Notices. Each of these has limited authority. The IRS issues PLRs when a taxpayer requests a ruling on a certain tax situation. The PLR is tax authority only to the taxpayer to whom it is issued, although it does indicate the thinking of the IRS.

When there is a change in a rate or allowance, the IRS issues an IRS Notice. For example, if there is a change to the standard mileage rate for business travel from 55 cents a mile to 50 cents a mile, the IRS will issue an IRS Notice to publicize the change.

In addition to the administrative authority discussed in this section, the IRS also publishes various other sources of information that can benefit taxpayers, such as Technical Advice Memorandums and Determination Letters.

CONCEPT CHECK 1-8— LO 1-5

1. Administrative tax authority takes precedence over statutory tax authority. True or false?
2. IRS Revenue Procedures are applicable only to the taxpayer to whom issued. True or false?
3. The administrative tax authority with the most strength of authority is ________________.

Judicial Tax Authority

The tax laws and regulations are complex. There can be differences of opinion as to how a taxpayer should report certain income or whether an item is a permitted deduction on a tax return. When conflict occurs between the IRS and taxpayers, it is the job of the court system to settle the dispute. The rulings of the various courts that hear tax cases are the third primary tax authority.

Figure 1-1 depicts the court system with regard to tax disputes. Three different trial courts hear tax cases: (1) the U.S. Tax Court, (2) the U.S. District Court, and (3) the U.S. Court of Federal Claims. Decisions by the Tax Court and the district courts may be appealed to the U.S. Court of Appeals and then to the Supreme Court. U.S. Court of Federal Claims cases are appealed to the U.S. Court of Appeals—Federal Claims, and then to the Supreme Court.

The Tax Court hears most litigated tax disputes between the IRS and taxpayers. The Tax Court is a national court with judges who travel throughout the nation to hear cases. Judges are tax law specialists and hear tax cases in major cities several times a year.

FIGURE 1-1
Court System for Tax Disputes

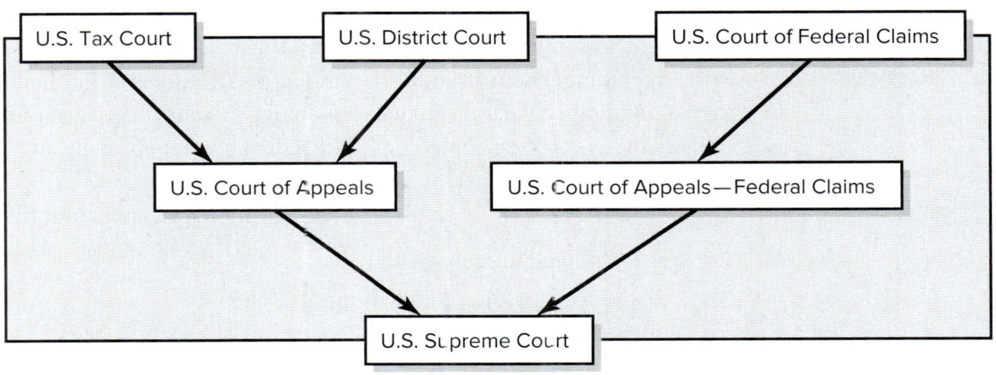

The court system becomes involved when a taxpayer and the IRS do not agree. Typically the IRS assesses the taxpayer for the tax the IRS believes is due. The taxpayer then needs to decide whether to go to court to contest the IRS's position and, if so, determine a court venue. One major advantage the taxpayer has when filing a petition with the Tax Court is that the taxpayer does not need to pay the IRS's proposed tax assessment prior to trial. With the other two judicial outlets (the district court and the Court of Federal Claims), the taxpayer must pay the government and then sue for a refund.

CONCEPT CHECK 1-9—
LO 1-5

1. The U.S. Supreme Court does not accept appeals of tax cases. True or false?
2. A taxpayer who does not agree with an assessment of tax by the IRS has no recourse. True or false?
3. A taxpayer who does not want to pay the tax assessed by the IRS prior to filing a legal proceeding must use the ____________ Court.

Appendix B

IRS RULES FOR PAID TAX PREPARERS

LO 1-6

Anyone can prepare a tax return; in fact each year, millions of Americans do so. It is also the case that millions benefit from the services of a paid tax preparer. The IRS has established rules that must be followed by any person who receives compensation to prepare a tax return or provide tax advice. These rules are found in Circular 230. You can download Circular 230 from the IRS Web site at www.irs.gov.

The provisions of Circular 230 apply to Certified Public Accountants (CPAs), attorneys, enrolled agents, registered tax return preparers, or any other person who, for compensation, prepares a tax return, provides tax advice, or practices before the IRS. Practicing before the IRS includes all communications with the IRS with respect to a client. If a practitioner fails to comply with the provisions, he or she can be suspended or disbarred from practice before the IRS, receive a public censure, be fined, or be subject to civil or criminal penalties.

The rules are far reaching and complex. They affect not only tax return preparation but also tax opinions, marketing and advertising, client records, fees, tax preparer registration, and other matters.

A paid preparer is someone who, for compensation, prepares all or substantially all of a tax return or tax form submitted to the IRS or a claim for refund. There is an exemption for individuals who do not sign the tax return and who are supervised by a CPA, attorney, or enrolled agent.

Paid preparers must register with the IRS and obtain a preparer tax identification number (PTIN). Preparers who are not CPAs, attorneys, or enrolled agents must also pass a competency examination and fulfill continuing education requirements of at least 15 hours annually (including 2 hours of ethics or professional conduct). Enrolled agents must obtain 72 hours of continuing education annually (including 2 hours of ethics or professional conduct). CPAs and attorneys are subject to continuing education requirements under the rules of each state. Paid preparers must renew their PTIN annually.

Under the provisions of Circular 230, paid preparers or individuals giving tax advice must:

- Sign all tax returns they prepare.
- Provide a copy of the returns to clients.
- Return records to clients.
- Exercise due diligence.

- Exercise best practices in preparing submissions to the IRS.
- Disclose all nonfrivolous tax positions when such disclosure is required to avoid penalties.
- Promptly notify clients of any error or omission on a client tax return.
- Provide records and information requested by the IRS unless the records or information are privileged.
- Inform a client if the client has made an error or omission in a document submitted to the IRS.

Paid preparers or individuals giving tax advice must *not:*

- Take a tax position on a return unless there is a "realistic possibility" of the position being sustained.
- Charge a fee contingent on the outcome of the return or any position, except in certain limited situations.
- Charge an "unconscionable fee."
- Unreasonably delay the prompt disposition of any matter before the IRS.
- Cash an IRS check for a client for whom the return was prepared.
- Represent a client before the IRS if the representation involves a conflict of interest.
- Make false, fraudulent, or coercive statements or claims or make misleading or deceptive statements or claims. In part, this item pertains to claims made with respect to advertising or marketing.

Circular 230 contains detailed requirements associated with providing clients with a tax opinion that the client can rely upon to avoid a potential penalty related to a tax position. These opinions are called "covered opinions."

Paid preparers who are in willful violation of the provisions of Circular 230 may be censured, suspended, or disbarred. They may also be subject to monetary penalty or to civil or criminal penalties.

Appendix C

GETTING STARTED WITH TAXACT

This text includes an online version of the TaxAct tax preparation software for individual income tax returns. Throughout this text, we provide examples and end-of-chapter questions and problems that you can solve using tax software.

The tax return problems can be completed either by hand using the tax forms available in this text and on the IRS Web site or by using the TaxAct software. Your instructor will tell you how to prepare the problems. If you are using the tax software, this section will help you get started.

Many tax software products are on the market. They are all similar. Because of that, except for this chapter, we have purposefully written the text in a "software-neutral" manner. What we discuss for TaxAct will generally apply to any individual income tax product you would be likely to use.

The following information will help you get started using the TaxAct software:

- Visit the *Connect* Library and select TaxAct Program under Course-wide content.
- Select each TaxAct program you wish to download and follow the prompts to complete installation.
- Once download is complete, TaxAct will automatically open. The program may ask you a number of questions that you will skip or respond with "Cancel." Subsequent times you start the software, it may ask about state tax software. Respond with "Cancel."
- You will eventually arrive at the Home screen.

The TaxAct software allows the user to input tax information in two formats. One is the Interview Method (called Q&A). With this method, the computer asks a series of questions that guides the user through the issues pertaining to his or her tax return. This method is active when the program starts and is sometimes helpful for individuals preparing a tax return who know very little about taxes.

The second method is the Forms Method. With it, the user selects the appropriate tax form or input form and types the correct information onto the appropriate line or lines. This method is suited to those who have some familiarity with the tax forms and how they interact. Using this text, you will quickly reach the necessary level of familiarity.

We will exclusively use the Forms Method throughout the text. We do this for three reasons. First, we strongly believe that when preparing taxes, the user needs to understand the forms that are needed, how they interact, and where the numbers come from and go to. Otherwise it is like memorizing only one way to get to work—if something changes, the individual is totally lost. Second, in the text, we often focus on one or two forms at a time, not an entire tax return (except for the comprehensive examples). The Q&A method is not designed to zero in on a form or two—instead it guides a user through an entire return. Third, the Q&A method makes assumptions that are sometimes difficult to change.

Other tax software uses similar Q&A (interview) or Forms approaches. No matter what software you end up using after you graduate from school, the basic approach and input methodology found in TaxAct will be the same from program to program.

To get the program into the proper input method and to get it ready to accept data, you need to click on the Forms icon on the toolbar, toward the top of the page in the middle.

When you want to start a new "client," perform the following steps:

1. Click on the File pull-down menu at the upper left.
2. Click on New Return.
3. The system may ask you whether you want to order a state tax product. Click Continue.

Now click on the Forms icon to get to the Forms Method.

The TaxAct program is a highly complex computer program. The software recognizes that information "starts" on a certain form or schedule and then is carried forward to other forms or schedules. For example, the name and address of the taxpayer are initially entered on Form 1040. TaxAct automatically transfers these data to other forms that require that information.

As you use the TaxAct software, you will notice that most numerical information is in either a green or blue color. Green numbers are numbers that you can enter directly on the form you are working on. Blue numbers are calculated on (or derived from) another form or worksheet. If you click on a blue number, you can then click on the Folder icon and go to the supporting form or worksheet.

If you click on a blue number and try to enter a figure, the software will warn you that you are trying to alter a calculated value. You can then choose to go to the supporting schedule, or you can choose to override the value. The software strongly advises you *not* to enter information directly but to go to the appropriate supporting form. We concur. Until you have a much better understanding of how tax software works (or unless we specifically tell you otherwise), you should use the supporting schedules. If you fail to do so, you can get unanticipated results that may create an erroneous return. This can occur, for example, when the software transfers a number to two or more follow-up forms. If you change the number on one of the follow-up forms but not on the other(s), you will have an erroneous return.

Important note: Preliminary versions of tax software are generally issued in October with final versions coming out around January. Software vendors want to make sure you are using the most up-to-date versions of their software and tax forms. This text comes with a preliminary version of the software, and the vendors require you to get an updated version before you can print any tax forms. **Before TaxAct will allow you to print out a tax return, you need to**

update your software. To confirm you have the latest version go to your TaxAct home screen and complete the following:

1. Click on Online in the upper menu of TaxAct program.
2. Click on Check for Updates.
3. Click the program you wish to update.
4. Follow the instructions to choose the federal or state update required to complete the update.

Finally, we use a number of example "taxpayers" who will reappear off and on throughout the text (the Davidsons introduced in this chapter are an example). Note two important things about these taxpayers. First, they are entirely fictional. They are constructed for illustrative purposes only and do not represent any existing taxpayers. Second, because we will also use the example taxpayers in later chapters (some more often than others), it is important that you save the tax return information in the TaxAct software. That way, you do not have to rekey the data later.

Summary

LO 1-1: Understand progressive, proportional, and regressive tax structures.

- Taxes are levied by multiplying a tax rate (the rate of tax) by a tax base (the amount taxed).
- Progressive: The tax rate increases as the tax base increases.
- Proportional: The tax rate remains the same regardless of the tax base.
- Regressive: The tax rate decreases as the tax base increases.

LO 1-2: Understand the concepts of marginal and average tax rates as well as a simple income tax formula.

- The marginal tax rate is the proportion of tax paid on the next dollar of income.
- The average tax rate is the percentage of total tax paid on the amount of taxable income.
- The simple tax formula is

  Income
  − Permitted deductions from income
  = Taxable income
  × Appropriate tax rates
  = Tax liability
  − Tax payments and tax credits
  = Tax refund or tax due with return

LO 1-3: Understand the components of a Form 1040EZ income tax return.

- Must meet six criteria to be eligible to file Form 1040EZ.
- Major components of Form 1040EZ return are filing status, wage income, taxable interest income, unemployment compensation, permitted deductions, taxable income, tax liability, tax payments, earned income credit, and amount owed or refund.

LO 1-4: Determine tax liability in instances when a Form 1040EZ return is appropriate.

- Tax liability is determined with reference to the tax tables issued by the IRS (and printed in Appendix D of this text).
- Tax liability can also be determined by using the tax rate schedules printed in Appendix F.
- Tax liability includes any shared responsibility payment related to health insurance as required under the Affordable Care Act.

LO 1-5: Understand the types of tax authority and how they interrelate (Appendix A).	• Statutory tax authority is the Internal Revenue Code and committee reports from appropriate congressional committees.
	• Administrative tax authority is issued by the IRS. It includes
	  • IRS Regulations.
	  • Revenue Rulings.
	  • Revenue Procedures.
	  • Private Letter Rulings.
	  • IRS Notices.
	• Judicial tax authority is developed by the courts as a result of court cases between taxpayers and the IRS.

LO 1-6: Understand the provisions of IRS Circular 230 for paid tax preparers (Appendix B).	• Circular 230 covers individuals who are compensated for preparing a tax return, providing tax advice, or practicing before the IRS. • Includes CPAs, attorneys, enrolled agents, registered tax preparers, and others. • Paid tax preparers must register with the IRS and receive a preparer tax identification number (PTIN). • Circular 230 sets forth actions paid preparers must do and must not do.

Discussion Questions connect

All applicable discussion questions are available with ***Connect***®

LO 1-1 1. (Introduction) Give a brief history of the income tax in the United States.

LO 1-1 2. (Introduction) For tax year 2015, what proportion of individual income tax returns was filed on a Form 1040EZ, Form 1040A, and Form 1040? What proportion was electronically filed?

LO 1-1 3. Name the three types of tax rate structures and give an example of each.

LO 1-1 4. What is a *progressive tax*? Why do you think the government believes it is a more equitable tax than, say, a regressive tax or proportional tax?

LO 1-1 5. What type of tax is a sales tax? Explain your answer.

LO 1-1 6. What is the definition of *tax base,* and how does it affect the amount of tax levied?

LO 1-1 7. What type of tax rate structure is the U.S. federal income tax? Explain your answer.

LO 1-1 8. A change to a 17% flat tax could cause a considerable increase in many taxpayers' taxes and a considerable decrease in the case of others. Explain this statement in light of the statistics in Table 1-3.

LO 1-1 9. Explain what is meant by *regressive tax.* Why is the social security tax considered a regressive tax?

LO 1-2 10. Define and compare these terms: *average tax rate* and *marginal tax rate.*

EA LO 1-3 11. What is meant by *compensation for services*? Give some examples.

EA LO 1-3 12. What is the definition of *interest*?

EA LO 1-3 13. What federal tax forms do taxpayers normally receive to inform them of the amount of wages and interest they earned during the year?

EA LO 1-3 14. Explain why unemployment compensation is taxable.

EA LO 1-3 15. What is the amount of the permitted deduction for single and married taxpayers who use Form 1040EZ?

LO 1-3, 1-4 16. What is the most common way taxpayers pay their income tax liability during the year?

EA LO 1-4 17. Explain how to calculate the shared responsibility payment under the Affordable Care Act.

Multiple-Choice Questions

All applicable multiple-choice questions are available with ***Connect***©

LO 1-1 18. A tax rate that decreases as the tax base increases is an example of what kind of tax rate structure?

a. Progressive.
b. Proportional.
c. Regressive.
d. Recessive.

LO 1-1 19. A tax rate that decreases as the tax base decreases is an example of what kind of tax rate structure?

a. Progressive.
b. Proportional.
c. Regressive.
d. Recessive.

LO 1-1 20. Jake earned $15,000 and paid $1,500 of income tax; Jill earned $40,000 and paid $3,500 of income tax. The tax rate structure they are subject to is

a. Progressive.
b. Proportional.
c. Regressive.
d. Recessive.

LO 1-1 21. Margaret earned $15,000 and paid $1,500 of income tax; Mike earned $50,000 and paid $5,000 of income tax. The tax rate structure they are subject to is

a. Progressive.
b. Proportional.
c. Regressive.
d. Recessive.

LO 1-1 22. Which of the following is an example of a regressive tax?

a. Federal income tax.

b. State and local taxes levied on property.

c. Sales tax.

d. Social security tax.

LO 1-1 23. Which of the following is an example of a progressive tax?

a. Federal income tax.

b. State and local taxes levied on property.

c. Sales tax.

d. Social security tax.

LO 1-2 24. Jennifer and Paul, who file a joint return, have taxable income of $94,625 and the following tax liability:

$18,650 × 10% =	$ 1,865.00
($75,900 − $18,650) × 15% =	8,587.50
($94,625 − $75,900) × 25% =	4,681.25
Total tax liability	$15,133.75

Their marginal tax rate is

a. 10%.

b. 15%.

c. 16%.

d. 25%.

LO 1-2 25. Jennifer and Paul, who file a joint return, have taxable income of $94,625 and the following tax liability:

$18,650 × 10% =	$ 1,865.00
($75,900 − $18,650) × 15% =	8,587.50
($94,625 − $75,900) × 25% =	4,681.25
Total tax liability	$15,133.75

Their average tax rate is

a. 10%.

b. 15%.

c. 16%.

d. 25%.

EA LO 1-3 26. Which of the following would disqualify a taxpayer from filing Form 1040EZ?

a. The taxpayer is married.

b. The taxpayer is age 66.

c. The taxpayer received unemployment compensation.

d. The taxpayer had adjusted gross income (line 4 of Form 1040EZ) of $101,000.

EA LO 1-3 27. The most complex individual income tax return is a Form

a. 1040.

b. 1040A.

c. 1040C.

d. 1040EZ.

EA LO 1-3 28. Wage income is reported to a taxpayer on a Form

a. W-2.

b. 1099-G.

c. 1099-W.

d. 1099-INT.

EA LO 1-3 29. Interest income is reported to a taxpayer on a Form

a. W-2.

b. W-2-INT.

c. 1099-G.

d. 1099-INT.

EA LO 1-3 30. On Form 1040EZ, the amount of the permitted deduction from income for taxpayers filing a joint return is

a. $1,500.

b. $10,400.

c. $20,800.

d. $31,200.

EA LO 1-3 31. Elizabeth determined that her tax liability was $3,492. Her employer withheld $3,942 from her paychecks during the year. Elizabeth's tax return would show

a. A refund of $450.

b. A refund of $3,492.

c. Tax due of $450.

d. Tax due of $3,942.

EA LO 1-4 32. Sandra, a single taxpayer, has taxable income of $79,238. Using the tax tables, she has determined that her tax liability is

a. $11,284.

b. $14,059.

c. $15,545.

d. $15,625.

LO 1-4 33. A married taxpayer has taxable income of $47,861. You have calculated tax liability using the tax tables and using the tax rate schedules. What can you say about the two figures?

a. Tax liability determined using the tax tables will be more than tax liability determined using the tax rate schedules.

b. Tax liability determined using the tax tables will be less than tax liability determined using the tax rate schedules.

c. Tax liability determined using the tax tables will be the same as tax liability determined using the tax rate schedules.

d. The answer cannot be determined with the information provided.

EA LO 1-3, 1-4 34. Eddie, a single taxpayer, has W-2 income of $38,189. Using the tax tables, he has determined that his tax liability is

a. $5,283.

b. $3,909.

c. $3,700.

d. $3,234.

EA LO 1-3, 1-4 35. Arno and Bridgette are married and have combined W-2 income of $75,612. They paid $344 when they filed their taxes. How much income tax did their employers withhold during the year?

a. $7,635.

b. $7,291.

c. $6,947.

d. The answer cannot be determined with the information provided.

EA LO 1-4 36. Benito is age 29 and single. During all of 2017, he did not have qualifying health coverage, nor was he eligible for an exemption. His household income was $47,650. What is the amount of shared responsibility payment he must report on his 2017 income tax return?

a. $0.

b. $695.00.

c. $931.25.

d. $1,191.25.

EA LO 1-4 37. Wanda and Austin are under the age of 65 and file their tax return as married filing jointly. They had qualifying health coverage for three months during 2017. They were not eligible for an exemption. Their household income was $77,760. What is the amount of shared responsibility payment they must report on their 2017 income tax return?

a. $1,944

b. $1,424.

c. $1,390.

d. $1,068.

Problems connect

All applicable problems are available with ***Connect***©

LO 1-1 38. Using the information in Table 1-3, determine the average amount of taxable income per tax return, rounded to the nearest dollar, for each of the ranges of taxable income provided.

LO 1-1 39. Using the information in Table 1-3, determine the amount of average income tax liability per tax return, rounded to the nearest dollar, for each income range provided.

LO 1-1 40. Use the information in Table 1-3. If the federal tax system was changed to a proportional tax rate structure with a tax rate of 17%, calculate the amount of tax liability for 2015 for all taxpayers. How does this amount differ from the actual liability?

EA LO 1-2 41. What is the income tax formula in simplified form?

____

____

____

EA LO 1-3 42. What six criteria must a taxpayer meet in order to file Form 1040EZ?

______________________ ______________________

______________________ ______________________

______________________ ______________________

EA LO 1-3 43. When taxpayers file a tax return, they will either pay an additional amount or receive a refund of excess taxes paid. Briefly explain how this "settling up" process works. Why might a taxpayer pay too much during the year?

____

____

____

EA LO 1-4 44. Cameron is single and has taxable income of $84,192. Determine his tax liability using the tax tables and using the tax rate schedule. Why is there a difference between the two amounts?

____

____

____

EA LO 1-4 45. Havel and Petra are married, will file a joint tax return, and meet the requirements to file Form 1040EZ. Havel has W-2 income of $46,152, and Petra has W-2 income of $47,289. What is their tax liability? Determine their tax liability using both the tax tables and the tax rate schedule.

____

____

____

EA LO 1-2, 1-4 46. Determine the tax liability, marginal tax rate, and average tax rate (rounded to two decimal places) in each of the following cases. Use the Form 1040EZ tax tables to determine tax liability.

a. Single taxpayer, taxable income of $33,862:
Liability = __________ Marginal = __________ Average = __________

b. Single taxpayer, taxable income of $83,877:
Liability = __________ Marginal = __________ Average = __________

EA LO 1-2, 1-4 47. Determine the tax liability, marginal tax rate, and average tax rate (rounded to two decimal places) in each of the following cases. Use the Form 1040EZ tax tables to determine tax liability.

a. Married taxpayers, taxable income of $83,877:
Liability = __________ Marginal = __________ Average = __________

b. Married taxpayers, taxable income of $91,229:
Liability = __________ Marginal = __________ Average = __________

EA LO 1-2, 1-4 48. Determine the tax liability, marginal tax rate, and average tax rate (rounded to two decimal places) in each of the following cases. Use the Form 1040EZ tax tables to determine tax liability.

a. Married taxpayers, taxable income of $33,862:
Liability = __________ Marginal = __________ Average = __________

b. Single taxpayer, taxable income of $91,229:
Liability = __________ Marginal = __________ Average = __________

EA LO 1-4 49. Use the tax rate schedules to determine the tax liability for each of the cases in Problems 46, 47, and 48.

a. Liability for 46*a* = ____________ 46*b* = ____________

b. Liability for 47*a* = ____________ 47*b* = ____________

c. Liability for 48*a* = ____________ 48*b* = ____________

EA LO 1-3, 1-4 50. The W-2 income of Sandra, a single taxpayer, was $98,793. Using the tax tables, determine Sandra's tax liability.

____

____

EA LO 1-3, 1-4 51. The W-2 incomes of Betty and her husband Ronald were $48,466 and $45,128, respectively. If Betty and Ronald use a filing status of married filing jointly, determine their tax liability using the tax tables.

____

____

EA LO 1-3, 1-4 52. Sheniqua, a single taxpayer, had taxable income of $93,678. Her employer withheld $19,003 in federal income tax from her paychecks throughout the year. Using the tax tables, would Sheniqua receive a refund or would she be required to pay additional tax? What is the amount?

____

____

EA LO 1-3, 1-4 53. Xavier and his wife Maria have total W-2 income of $91,932. They will file their tax return as married filing jointly. They had a total of $10,149 withheld from their paychecks for federal income tax. Using the tax tables, determine the amount of refund or additional tax due upon filing their tax return. Indicate whether the amount is a refund or additional tax.

____

____

Discussion Questions Pertaining to Appendix A (LO 1-5)

54. Discuss the concept of *tax authority*. How does tax authority help taxpayers and tax preparers report tax items properly?

____

____

____

55. What are the three types of tax authority? Who issues each type?

____

____

____

56. Discuss the concept of *statutory tax authority*. Why is there a need for additional types of authority when statutory authority is the law?

____

____

____

57. What is the legislative process concerning tax laws? Where does tax legislation often begin?

58. What are committee reports, and how can they help the taxpayer or tax preparer?

59. What is the purpose of a Joint Conference Committee? Its reports are considered more important or are more authoritative. Why?

60. Explain what is meant by *Public Law 100-14.*

61. What is administrative authority, and who publishes it?

62. What is a Proposed Regulation? Can a taxpayer rely on a Proposed Regulation as authority on how to treat a certain tax item?

63. Can a taxpayer rely on a Temporary Regulation as authority on how to treat a certain tax item? If so, how long is a Temporary Regulation valid?

64. Differentiate between a General Regulation and a Legislative Regulation. Which one is the stronger tax authority?

65. Where are Revenue Rulings and Revenue Procedures found? When might a Revenue Ruling be useful to a taxpayer? When might a Revenue Procedure be useful to a taxpayer?

66. In what courts are disputes between the IRS and a taxpayer heard?

67. What are the advantages of petitioning the Tax Court versus other trial courts?

68. When would a taxpayer want to sue the government in a district court versus the Tax Court?

69. If a taxpayer loses a case against the IRS in one of the three trial courts, does the taxpayer have any avenue for appeals?

70. After the Court of Appeals, does a taxpayer have any additional avenue for appeals? If so, what are the taxpayer's probabilities of receiving an appeal after the Court of Appeals? Why?

71. Why might a district court's opinion regarding a tax decision be more likely to be reversed on appeal?

72. (Longer answer) What is a Treasury Regulation? What are the four types of regulations and how do they differ?

73. (Longer answer) What is the difference between a Revenue Ruling and a Revenue Procedure? How does the level of authority of a ruling or procedure compare with regulations and statutory authority?

Multiple-Choice Questions Pertaining to Appendix A (LO 1-5)

All applicable multiple-choice questions are available with ***Connect***©

74. Which of the following is (are) primary sources of tax authority?
    a. Statutory sources.
    b. Administrative sources.
    c. Judicial sources.
    d. All of the above.

75. Which of the following is a statutory source of tax authority?
    a. Internal Revenue Code.
    b. Regulations.
    c. Revenue Rulings.
    d. Tax Court decision.

76. Which of the following types of IRS Regulations have the greatest strength of authority?
    a. General or Final Regulations.
    b. Legislative Regulations.
    c. Proposed Regulations.
    d. Temporary Regulations.

77. Which of the following refers to an income tax regulation?
    a. Reg. § 1.162-5.
    b. Reg. § 20.2032-1.
    c. Reg. § 25.2503-4.
    d. Reg. § 31.3301-1.

78. Which of the following trial court(s) hear tax cases?
    a. U.S. Tax Court.
    b. U.S. district courts.
    c. U.S. Court of Federal Claims.
    d. All of the above.

Discussion Questions Pertaining to Appendix B (LO 1-6)

EA 79. IRS rules for paid tax preparers apply to what types of tax professionals?

EA 80. Who must obtain a preparer tax identification number?

EA 81. List at least five items that paid preparers must do to comply with Circular 230.

EA 82. List at least five items that paid preparers must *not* do to comply with Circular 230.

____

____

Multiple-Choice Questions Pertaining to Appendix B (LO 1-6)

All applicable multiple-choice questions are available with ***Connect***©

EA 83. A preparer tax identification number must be obtained by

a. Only CPAs, attorneys, and enrolled agents.
b. Only individuals who are not CPAs, attorneys, or enrolled agents.
c. Any individual who is paid to prepare a tax return.
d. Only individuals who prepare a Form 1040EZ

EA 84. A paid preparer must *not*

a. Cash a client's IRS check.
b. Charge a reasonable fee.
c. Inform a client if the preparer makes a mistake on the client's tax return.
d. Provide a client with a copy of his or her return.

EA 85. A paid preparer must

a. Ignore a conflict of interest when representing a client before the IRS.
b. Charge a contingent fee.
c. Sign all tax returns she or he prepares.
d. Provide records requested by the IRS in all circumstances.

Tax Return Problems

All applicable tax return problems are available with ***Connect***©

Use your tax software to complete the following problems. If you are manually preparing the tax returns, you will need a Form 1040EZ for each problem.

Tax Return Problem 1 Alex Montgomery is single and lives at 3344 Bayview Drive, Richmond Hill, GA 31324. His SSN is 412-34-5670. He recently graduated from the Savannah College of Art and Design and works as a video game developer. His Form W-2 contained the following information.

Wages (box 1) =	$61,011.30
Federal W/H (box 2) =	$ 8,528.10
Social security wages (box 3) =	$61,011.30
Social security W/H (box 4) =	$ 3,782.70
Medicare wages (box 5) =	$61,011.30
Medicare W/H (box 6) =	$ 884.66

Alex had qualifying health care coverage at all times during the year. Prepare a Form 1040EZ for Alex.

Tax Return Problem 2 Brenda Peterson is single and lives at 567 East Street, Beantown, MA 02043. Her SSN is 412-34-5670. She worked the entire year for Applebee Consulting in Beantown. Her Form W-2 contained information in the following boxes:

Wages (box 1) = $65,155.65
Federal W/H (box 2) = $ 9,771.12
Social security wages (box 3) = $65,155.65
Social security W/H (box 4) = $ 4,039.65
Medicare wages (box 5) = $65,155.65
Medicare W/H (box 6) = $ 944.76

She also received two Forms 1099-INT. One was from First National Bank of Beantown and showed interest income of $537.39 in box 1. The other Form 1099-INT was from Eaystate Savings and Loan and showed interest income of $281.70 in box 1.

Brenda had qualifying health care coverage at all times during the tax year.

Prepare a Form 1040EZ for Brenda.

Tax Return Problem 3 Jin Xiang is single and lives at 2468 North Lake Road in Lakeland, MN 56444. Her SSN is 412-34-5670. She worked the entire year for Lakeland Automotive. The Form W-2 from Lakeland contained information in the following boxes:

Wages (box 1) = $37,811.89
Federal W/H (box 2) = $ 4,833.91
Social security wages (box 3) = $37,811.89
Social security W/H (box 4) = $ 2,344.34
Medicare wages (box 5) = $37,811.89
Medicare W/H (box 6) = $ 548.27

On the weekends, Jin worked at Parts-Galore, a local auto parts store. The Form W-2 from Parts-Galore contained information in the following boxes:

Wages (box 1) = $9,167.02
Federal W/H (box 2) = $ 348.39
Social security wages (box 3) = $9,167.02
Social security W/H (box 4) = $ 568.36
Medicare wages (box 5) = $9,167.02
Medicare W/H (box 6) = $ 132.92

Jin also received a Form 1099-INT from Minnesota Savings and Loan. The amount of interest income in box 1 of the Form 1099-INT was $51.92.

Jin had qualifying health care coverage at all times during the tax year.

Prepare a Form 1040EZ for Jin.

Tax Return Problem 4 Jose and Maria Suarez are married and live at 9876 Main Street, Denver, CO 80205. Jose's SSN is 412-34-5670 and Maria's SSN is 412-34-5671.

For the first five months of the year, Jose was employed by Mountain Mortgage Company. The Form W-2 from Mountain Mortgage contained information in the following boxes

Wages (box 1) = $35,028.52
Federal W/H (box 2) = $ 4,923.89
Social security wages (box 3) = $35,028.52
Social security W/H (box 4) = $ 2,171.77

Medicare wages (box 5) = $35,028.52
Medicare W/H (box 6) = $ 507.91

Jose was laid off from his job at Mountain Mortgage and was unemployed for three months. He received $1,000 of unemployment insurance payments. The Form 1099-G Jose received from the state of Colorado contained $1,000 of unemployment compensation in box 1 and $100 of federal income tax withholding in box 4.

During the last four months of the year, Jose was employed by First Mountain Bank in Denver. The Form W-2 Jose received from the bank contained information in the following boxes:

Wages (box 1) = $19,820.20
Federal W/H (box 2) = $ 2,667.74
Social security wages (box 3) = $19,820.20
Social security W/H (box 4) = $ 1,228.85
Medicare wages (box 5) = $19,820.20
Medicare W/H (box 6) = $ 287.39

Maria was employed the entire year by Blue Sky Properties in Denver. The Form W-2 Maria received from Blue Sky contained information in the following boxes:

Wages (box 1) = $52,455.05
Federal W/H (box 2) = $ 6,408.82
Social security wages (box 3) = $52,455.05
Social security W/H (box 4) = $ 3,207.14
Medicare wages (box 5) = $52,455.05
Medicare W/H (box 6) = $ 750.06

The Suarezes also received two Forms 1099-INT showing interest they received on two savings accounts. One Form 1099-INT from the First National Bank of Northeastern Denver showed interest income of $59.36 in box 1. The other Form 1099-INT from Second National Bank of Northwestern Denver showed interest income of $82.45 in box 1.

Jose and Maria had qualifying health care coverage at all times during the tax year.

Prepare a Form 1040EZ for Mr. and Mrs. Suarez.

We have provided selected filled-in source documents that are available in the *Connect Library*.

Chapter Two

Expanded Tax Formula, Forms 1040A and 1040, and Basic Concepts

This chapter expands the basic tax formula introduced in the previous chapter. We also introduce you to two additional tax forms, Form 1040A and Form 1040, and to tax situations common to most taxpayers including determination of filing status, personal exemptions, dependents, and the standard deduction.

Learning Objectives

When you have completed this chapter, you should understand the following learning objectives (LO):

- **LO 2-1** Describe the expanded tax formula and the components of the major sections of Form 1040A and Form 1040.
- **LO 2-2** Determine the proper filing status.
- **LO 2-3** Calculate personal exemptions.
- **LO 2-4** Calculate dependency exemptions.
- **LO 2-5** Determine the standard deduction.
- **LO 2-6** Compute the amount of tax due to the Internal Revenue Service (IRS).
- **LO 2-7** Determine what interest and penalties the IRS can assess and in what instances certain penalties are applicable.

INTRODUCTION

This chapter introduces two complex tax forms, the 1040A and 1040. It is important to familiarize yourself with the concept and calculation of personal and dependency exemptions and the difference between the standard deduction and itemized deductions. This will enable you to determine which form is the most appropriate for a taxpayer to use.

Furthermore, our discussion takes you through the body of the forms to arrive at the amount due to the IRS or the refund due. The last section of the chapter presents some of the possible penalties the IRS can assess a taxpayer for failure to file and pay, failure to pay estimated tax, accuracy-related errors, and fraud.

THE INCOME TAX FORMULA AND FORMS 1040A AND 1040

LO 2-1

In Chapter 1 we introduced a very simple tax formula:

Income
– Permitted deductions from income

= Taxable income
× Appropriate tax rates

= Tax liability
– Tax payments and tax credits

= Tax refund or tax due with return

This simple formula is the basis of Form 1040EZ. Most taxpayers, however, have a more complex tax situation. In this chapter, we begin to explore the intricacies of a tax return.

Of the two new forms introduced in this chapter, the 1040A is more complex than a 1040EZ, and the 1040 is more complex than a 1040A. Both forms follow the basic tax formula noted previously, but each has more detail to accommodate the complexity of the tax code and regulations.

An expanded tax formula, using the more complex return (Form 1040), is as follows:

Gross income (GI)
– Permitted deductions from gross income

= Adjusted Gross Income (AGI)
– Standard deduction or itemized deductions
– Personal and dependency exemptions

= Taxable income (TI)
× Appropriate tax rates

= Tax liability
– Tax credits
+ Other taxes
– Tax payments and refundable credits

= Tax refund or tax due with return

We provide copies of Forms 1040 and 1040A in Exhibits 2-1 and 2-2, respectively. At first glance the forms look complicated, and in some ways they are. Form 1040 is the most complex and will accommodate the tax situation of any taxpayer. Form 1040A has about half the lines of Form 1040. To aid you in understanding the differences between Form 1040A and Form 1040, Table 2-1 lists all items on the forms, indicating the line numbers that are applicable on each of the forms. This table also indicates the chapter in which we discuss each of the tax form lines.

Note that both forms have sections pertaining to income, deductions from income (split into two sections), credits, and payments. The 1040 is more detailed than the 1040A in each case.

With more than 70 lines of information, it is clear that Form 1040 is more complex than Form 1040A and that both are more complex than Form 1040EZ.

Because Form 1040 is the most complex, it can accommodate any taxpayer situation. However, to save taxpayers and the IRS some time, taxpayers can choose from three levels of complexity when they file their taxes. Less complexity is beneficial to taxpayers and the IRS alike.

EXHIBIT 2-1

Form **1040** Department of the Treasury—Internal Revenue Service (99) **U.S. Individual Income Tax Return** **2017** OMB No. 1545-0074 IRS Use Only—Do not write or staple in this space.

For the year Jan. 1–Dec. 31, 2017, or other tax year beginning , 2017, ending , 20 | See separate instructions.

Your first name and initial	Last name	Your social security number
If a joint return, spouse's first name and initial	Last name	Spouse's social security number
Home address (number and street). If you have a P.O. box, see instructions.	Apt. no.	▲ Make sure the SSN(s) above and on line 6c are correct.
City, town or post office, state, and ZIP code. If you have a foreign address, also complete spaces below (see instructions).		**Presidential Election Campaign** Check here if you, or your spouse if filing jointly, want $3 to go to this fund. Checking a box below will not change your tax or refund. ☐ You ☐ Spouse
Foreign country name	Foreign province/state/county	Foreign postal code

Filing Status

Check only one box.

1 ☐ Single
2 ☐ Married filing jointly (even if only one had income)
3 ☐ Married filing separately. Enter spouse's SSN above and full name here. ▶
4 ☐ Head of household (with qualifying person). (See instructions.) If the qualifying person is a child but not your dependent, enter this child's name here. ▶
5 ☐ Qualifying widow(er) (see instructions)

Exemptions

6a ☐ **Yourself.** If someone can claim you as a dependent, **do not** check box 6a . . . . .
b ☐ **Spouse** . . . .

c **Dependents:**

(1) First name Last name	(2) Dependent's social security number	(3) Dependent's relationship to you	(4) ✓ if child under age 17 qualifying for child tax credit (see instructions)
			☐
			☐
			☐
			☐

If more than four dependents, see instructions and check here ▶ ☐

d Total number of exemptions claimed . . . .

Boxes checked on 6a and 6b ____
No. of children on 6c who:
• lived with you ____
• did not live with you due to divorce or separation (see instructions) ____
Dependents on 6c not entered above ____
Add numbers on lines above ▶ ☐

Income

Attach Form(s) W-2 here. Also attach Forms W-2G and 1099-R if tax was withheld.

If you did not get a W-2, see instructions.

7	Wages, salaries, tips, etc. Attach Form(s) W-2		7
8a	**Taxable** interest. Attach Schedule B if required		8a
b	**Tax-exempt** interest. **Do not** include on line 8a	8b	
9a	Ordinary dividends. Attach Schedule B if required		9a
b	Qualified dividends	9b	
10	Taxable refunds, credits, or offsets of state and local income taxes		10
11	Alimony received		11
12	Business income or (loss). Attach Schedule C or C-EZ		12
13	Capital gain or (loss). Attach Schedule D if required. If not required, check here ▶ ☐		13
14	Other gains or (losses). Attach Form 4797		14
15a	IRA distributions	15a	b Taxable amount 15b
16a	Pensions and annuities	16a	b Taxable amount 16b
17	Rental real estate, royalties, partnerships, S corporations, trusts, etc. Attach Schedule E		17
18	Farm income or (loss). Attach Schedule F		18
19	Unemployment compensation		19
20a	Social security benefits	20a	b Taxable amount 20b
21	Other income. List type and amount		21
22	Combine the amounts in the far right column for lines 7 through 21. This is your **total income** ▶		22

Adjusted Gross Income

23	Educator expenses	23	
24	Certain business expenses of reservists, performing artists, and fee-basis government officials. Attach Form 2106 or 2106-EZ	24	
25	Health savings account deduction. Attach Form 8889	25	
26	Moving expenses. Attach Form 3903	26	
27	Deductible part of self-employment tax. Attach Schedule SE	27	
28	Self-employed SEP, SIMPLE, and qualified plans	28	
29	Self-employed health insurance deduction	29	
30	Penalty on early withdrawal of savings	30	
31a	Alimony paid **b** Recipient's SSN ▶	31a	
32	IRA deduction	32	
33	Student loan interest deduction	33	
34	Reserved for future use	34	
35	Domestic production activities deduction. Attach Form 8903	35	
36	Add lines 23 through 35		36
37	Subtract line 36 from line 22. This is your **adjusted gross income** ▶		37

For Disclosure, Privacy Act, and Paperwork Reduction Act Notice, see separate instructions. Cat. No. 11320B Form **1040** (2017)

Source: U.S. Department of the Treasury, Internal Revenue Service, Form 1040. Washington, DC: 2017

(continued)

EXHIBIT 2-1 *(concluded)*

Form 1040 (2017) Page **2**

Tax and Credits	38	Amount from line 37 (adjusted gross income)		38
	39a	Check if: ☐ **You** were born before January 2, 1953, ☐ Blind. ☐ **Spouse** was born before January 2, 1953, ☐ Blind. **Total boxes checked** ▶ **39a** ☐		
	b	If your spouse itemizes on a separate return or you were a dual-status alien, check here ▶ 39b☐		
Standard Deduction for— • People who check any box on line 39a or 39b **or** who can be claimed as a dependent, see instructions. • All others: Single or Married filing separately, $6,350 Married filing jointly or Qualifying widow(er), $12,700 Head of household, $9,350	40	**Itemized deductions** (from Schedule A) **or** your **standard deduction** (see left margin)		40
	41	Subtract line 40 from line 38		41
	42	**Exemptions.** If line 38 is $156,900 or less, multiply $4,050 by the number on line 6d. Otherwise, see instructions		42
	43	**Taxable income.** Subtract line 42 from line 41. If line 42 is more than line 41, enter -0-		43
	44	**Tax** (see instructions). Check if any from: **a** ☐ Form(s) 8814 **b** ☐ Form 4972 **c** ☐		44
	45	**Alternative minimum tax** (see instructions). Attach Form 6251		45
	46	Excess advance premium tax credit repayment. Attach Form 8962		46
	47	Add lines 44, 45, and 46 ▶		47
	48	Foreign tax credit. Attach Form 1116 if required	48	
	49	Credit for child and dependent care expenses. Attach Form 2441	49	
	50	Education credits from Form 8863, line 19	50	
	51	Retirement savings contributions credit. Attach Form 8880	51	
	52	Child tax credit. Attach Schedule 8812, if required	52	
	53	Residential energy credit. Attach Form 5695	53	
	54	Other credits from Form: **a** ☐ 3800 **b** ☐ 8801 **c** ☐	54	
	55	Add lines 48 through 54. These are your **total credits**		55
	56	Subtract line 55 from line 47. If line 55 is more than line 47, enter -0- ▶		56
Other Taxes	57	Self-employment tax. Attach Schedule SE		57
	58	Unreported social security and Medicare tax from Form: **a** ☐ 4137 **b** ☐ 8919		58
	59	Additional tax on IRAs, other qualified retirement plans, etc. Attach Form 5329 if required		59
	60a	Household employment taxes from Schedule H		60a
	b	First-time homebuyer credit repayment. Attach Form 5405 if required		60b
	61	Health care: individual responsibility (see instructions) Full-year coverage ☐		61
	62	Taxes from: **a** ☐ Form 8959 **b** ☐ Form 8960 **c** ☐ Instructions; enter code(s)		62
	63	Add lines 56 through 62. This is your **total tax** ▶		63
Payments	64	Federal income tax withheld from Forms W-2 and 1099	64	
If you have a qualifying child, attach Schedule EIC.	65	2017 estimated tax payments and amount applied from 2016 return	65	
	66a	**Earned income credit (EIC)**	66a	
	b	Nontaxable combat pay election 66b		
	67	Additional child tax credit. Attach Schedule 8812	67	
	68	American opportunity credit from Form 8863, line 8	68	
	69	Net premium tax credit. Attach Form 8962	69	
	70	Amount paid with request for extension to file	70	
	71	Excess social security and tier 1 RRTA tax withheld	71	
	72	Credit for federal tax on fuels. Attach Form 4136	72	
	73	Credits from Form: **a** ☐ 2439 **b** ☐ Reserved **c** ☐ 8885 **d** ☐	73	
	74	Add lines 64, 65, 66a, and 67 through 73. These are your **total payments** ▶		74
Refund	75	If line 74 is more than line 63, subtract line 63 from line 74. This is the amount you **overpaid**		75
	76a	Amount of line 75 you want **refunded to you.** If Form 8888 is attached, check here ▶ ☐		76a
Direct deposit? See instructions.	▶ b	Routing number ▶ c Type: ☐ Checking ☐ Savings		
	▶ d	Account number		
	77	Amount of line 75 you want **applied to your 2018 estimated tax** ▶	77	
Amount You Owe	78	**Amount you owe.** Subtract line 74 from line 63. For details on how to pay, see instructions ▶		78
	79	Estimated tax penalty (see instructions)	79	

Third Party Designee Do you want to allow another person to discuss this return with the IRS (see instructions)? ☐ **Yes.** Complete below. ☐ **No**

Designee's name ▶ Phone no. ▶ Personal identification number (PIN) ▶

Sign Here

Under penalties of perjury, I declare that I have examined this return and accompanying schedules and statements, and to the best of my knowledge and belief, they are true, correct, and accurately list all amounts and sources of income I received during the tax year. Declaration of preparer (other than taxpayer) is based on all information of which preparer has any knowledge.

Joint return? See instructions. Keep a copy for your records.

Your signature	Date	Your occupation	Daytime phone number
Spouse's signature. If a joint return, **both** must sign.	Date	Spouse's occupation	If the IRS sent you an Identity Protection PIN, enter it here (see inst.)

Paid Preparer Use Only

Print/Type preparer's name	Preparer's signature	Date	Check ☐ if self-employed	PTIN
Firm's name ▶			Firm's EIN ▶	
Firm's address ▶			Phone no.	

Go to *www.irs.gov/Form1040* for instructions and the latest information. Form **1040** (2017)

EXHIBIT 2-2

Form **1040A** Department of the Treasury—Internal Revenue Service
U.S. Individual Income Tax Return (99) **2017** IRS Use Only—Do not write or staple in this space.

August 11, 2017
DO NOT FILE

Your first name and initial	Last name	OMB No. 1545-0074 **Your social security number**
If a joint return, spouse's first name and initial	Last name	**Spouse's social security number**
Home address (number and street). If you have a P.O. box, see instructions.	Apt. no.	▲ Make sure the SSN(s) above and on line 6c are correct.
City, town or post office, state, and ZIP code. If you have a foreign address, also complete spaces below (see instructions).		**Presidential Election Campaign** Check here if you, or your spouse if filing jointly, want $3 to go to this fund. Checking a box below will not change your tax or refund. ☐ **You** ☐ **Spouse**
Foreign country name	Foreign province/state/county / Foreign postal code	

Filing status
Check only one box.

1 ☐ Single
2 ☐ Married filing jointly (even if only one had income)
3 ☐ Married filing separately. Enter spouse's SSN above and full name here. ▶
4 ☐ Head of household (with qualifying person). (See instructions.) If the qualifying person is a child but not your dependent, enter this child's name here. ▶
5 ☐ Qualifying widow(er) (see instructions)

Exemptions

6a ☐ **Yourself.** If someone can claim you as a dependent, **do not** check box 6a.
b ☐ **Spouse**

Boxes checked on 6a and 6b

c **Dependents:**

If more than six dependents, see instructions.

(1) First name Last name	(2) Dependent's social security number	(3) Dependent's relationship to you	(4) ✓ if child under age 17 qualifying for child tax credit (see instructions)
			☐
			☐
			☐
			☐
			☐
			☐

No. of children on 6c who:
• lived with you
• did not live with you due to divorce or separation (see instructions)
Dependents on 6c not entered above

d Total number of exemptions claimed. **Add numbers on lines above ▶**

Income

Attach Form(s) W-2 here. Also attach Form(s) 1099-R if tax was withheld.

If you did not get a W-2, see instructions.

7	Wages, salaries, tips, etc. Attach Form(s) W-2.		7
8a	**Taxable** interest. Attach Schedule B if required.		8a
b	**Tax-exempt** interest. **Do not** include on line 8a.	8b	
9a	Ordinary dividends. Attach Schedule B if required.		9a
b	Qualified dividends (see instructions).	9b	
10	Capital gain distributions (see instructions).		10
11a	IRA distributions. 11a	**11b** Taxable amount (see instructions).	11b
12a	Pensions and annuities. 12a	**12b** Taxable amount (see instructions).	12b
13	Unemployment compensation and Alaska Permanent Fund dividends.		13
14a	Social security benefits. 14a	**14b** Taxable amount (see instructions).	14b
15	Add lines 7 through 14b (far right column). This is your **total income.** ▶		15

Adjusted gross income

16	Educator expenses (see instructions).	16	
17	IRA deduction (see instructions).	17	
18	Student loan interest deduction (see instructions).	18	
19	Reserved for future use.	19	
20	Add lines 16 through 19. These are your **total adjustments.**		20
21	Subtract line 20 from line 15. This is your **adjusted gross income.** ▶		21

For Disclosure, Privacy Act, and Paperwork Reduction Act Notice, see separate instructions. Cat. No. 11327A Form **1040A** (2017)

Source: U.S. Department of the Treasury, Internal Revenue Service, Form 1040A. Washington, DC: 2017.

(continued)

EXHIBIT 2-2 *(concluded)*

Form 1040A (2017) Page **2**

Tax, credits, and payments

22	Enter the amount from line 21 (adjusted gross income).			22
23a	Check if: { ☐ **You** were born before January 2, 1953, ☐ Blind / ☐ **Spouse** was born before January 2, 1953, ☐ Blind } **Total boxes checked** ▶ 23a ☐			
b	If you are married filing separately and your spouse itemizes deductions, check here ▶ 23b ☐			
24	Enter your **standard deduction**.			24
25	Subtract line 24 from line 22. If line 24 is more than line 22, enter -0-.			25
26	**Exemptions.** Multiply $4,050 by the number on line 6d.			26
27	Subtract line 26 from line 25. If line 26 is more than line 25, enter -0-. This is your **taxable income.** ▶			27
28	**Tax,** including any alternative minimum tax (see instructions).	28		
29	Excess advance premium tax credit repayment. Attach Form 8962.	29		
30	Add lines 28 and 29.			30
31	Credit for child and dependent care expenses. Attach Form 2441.	31		
32	Credit for the elderly or the disabled. Attach Schedule R.	32		
33	Education credits from Form 8863, line 19.	33		
34	Retirement savings contributions credit. Attach Form 8880.	34		
35	Child tax credit. Attach Schedule 8812, if required.	35		
36	Add lines 31 through 35. These are your **total credits.**			36
37	Subtract line 36 from line 30. If line 36 is more than line 30, enter -0-.			37
38	Health care: individual responsibility (see instructions). Full-year coverage ☐			38
39	Add line 37 and line 38. This is your **total tax.**			39
40	Federal income tax withheld from Forms W-2 and 1099.	40		
41	2017 estimated tax payments and amount applied from 2016 return.	41		
42a	**Earned income credit (EIC).**	42a		
b	Nontaxable combat pay election. 42b			
43	Additional child tax credit. Attach Schedule 8812.	43		
44	American opportunity credit from Form 8863, line 8.	44		
45	Net premium tax credit. Attach Form 8962.	45		
46	Add lines 40, 41, 42a, 43, 44, and 45. These are your **total payments.** ▶			46

Standard Deduction for—
- People who check any box on line 23a or 23b **or** who can be claimed as a dependent, see instructions.
- All others:

Single or Married filing separately, $6,350

Married filing jointly or Qualifying widow(er), $12,700

Head of household, $9,350

If you have a qualifying child, attach Schedule EIC.

Refund

47	If line 46 is more than line 39, subtract line 39 from line 46. This is the amount you **overpaid.**		47
48a	Amount of line 47 you want **refunded to you.** If Form 8888 is attached, check here ▶ ☐		48a
▶ b	Routing number	▶ c Type: ☐ Checking ☐ Savings	
▶ d	Account number		
49	Amount of line 47 you want **applied to your 2018 estimated tax.**	49	

Direct deposit? See instructions and fill in 48b, 48c, and 48d or Form 8888.

Amount you owe

50	**Amount you owe.** Subtract line 46 from line 39. For details on how to pay, see instructions. ▶		50
51	Estimated tax penalty (see instructions).	51	

Third party designee

Do you want to allow another person to discuss this return with the IRS (see instructions)? ☐ **Yes.** Complete the following. ☐ **No**

Designee's name ▶ | Phone no. ▶ | Personal identification number (PIN) ▶

Sign here

Joint return? See instructions. Keep a copy for your records.

Under penalties of perjury, I declare that I have examined this return and accompanying schedules and statements, and to the best of my knowledge and belief, they are true, correct, and accurately list all amounts and sources of income I received during the tax year. Declaration of preparer (other than the taxpayer) is based on all information of which the preparer has any knowledge.

Your signature	Date	Your occupation	Daytime phone number
Spouse's signature. If a joint return, **both** must sign.	Date	Spouse's occupation	If the IRS sent you an Identity Protection PIN, enter it here (see inst.)

Paid preparer use only

Print/Type preparer's name	Preparer's signature	Date	Check ▶ ☐ if self-employed	PTIN
Firm's name ▶			Firm's EIN ▶	
Firm's address ▶			Phone no.	

Go to *www.irs.gov/Form1040A* for instructions and the latest information. Form **1040A** (2017)

TABLE 2-1
Line-by-Line Comparison of Form 1040 and Form 1040A

Description	Form 1040 Line Location	Form 1040A Line Location	Chapter Where Discussed
Filing Status	1–5	1–5	1, 2
Exemptions	6a–d	6a–d	1, 2
Gross Income			
Wages, salaries, and tips	7	7	1, 3
Taxable and nontaxable interest	8a/b	8a/b	1, 3
Ordinary and qualified dividends	9a/b	9a/b	3
Taxable refunds of state/local taxes	10	—	3
Alimony received	11	—	3
Business income/loss (Schedule C)	12	—	6
Capital gain/loss (Schedule D)	13	10	7
Other gains/losses (Form 4797)	14	—	7
IRA distributions	15a/b	11a/b	11
Pension distributions	16a/b	12a/b	11
Rentals, partnerships, etc. (Schedule E)	17	—	8, 13
Farm income/loss (Schedule F)	18	—	—
Unemployment compensation	19	13	1, 3
Social security benefits	20a/b	14a/b	3
Other income	21	—	3
Total Income	22	15	
Deductions for Adjusted Gross Income			
Educator expenses	23	16	4
Certain business expenses	24	—	—
Health savings account deduction	25	—	4
Moving expenses	26	—	4
Half of self-employment tax	27	—	4
SEP, SIMPLE, and other retirement plans	28	—	11
Self-employed health insurance	29	—	4
Penalty on early withdrawal of savings	30	—	4
Alimony paid	31a	—	4
IRA deduction	32	17	11
Student loan interest deduction	33	18	4
Tuition and fees	34	19	4
Domestic production activities	35	—	—
Total *for* AGI deductions	36	20	
Adjusted Gross Income (AGI)	37	21	
Itemized or Standard Deduction*	40*	24	2, 5
Personal Exemptions	42	26	2
Taxable Income	43	27	
Regular Income Tax	44	28	1, 2
Alternative Minimum Tax (AMT)	45	(in line 28)	13
Excess advance premium tax credit repayment	46	29	9
Tax Credits			
Foreign tax credit	48	—	9
Child and dependent care	49	31	9
Elderly and disabled	—	32	9
Education credits	50	33	9
Retirement savings contributions credit	51	34	9
Child tax credit	52	35	9
Residential energy credits	53	—	—
Miscellaneous other credits	54	—	—
Total Credits	55	36	—
Income Tax Subtotal	56	37	
Other Taxes			
Self-employment tax	57	—	6
Unreported social security tax	58	—	—
Tax on retirement plans	59	—	11
Household employment taxes	60a	—	10
First time homebuyer credit repayment	60b	—	
Health care: individual responsibility	61	38	—
Other taxes	62	—	10
Total Tax before Payments (tax liability)	63	39	

(continued)

TABLE 2-1
(concluded)

Description	Form 1040 Line Location	Form 1040A Line Location	Chapter Where Discussed
Payments			
Withholding	64	40	1, 2, 10
Estimated tax payments	65	41	2
Earned income credit	66a	42a	2, 9
Nontaxable combat pay election	66b	42b	
Additional child tax credit	67	43	2, 9
American opportunity credit	68	44	9
Net premium tax credit	69	45	9
Amount paid with extension	70	—	2
Excess social security tax withheld	71	—	2
Credit for federal tax on fuels	72	—	—
Other miscellaneous payments	73	—	—
Total payments	74	46	—
Overpayment	75	47	—
Amount of refund	76a	48a	1, 2
Amount owed	78	50	1, 2
Estimated tax penalty	79	51	2

*Itemized deductions are permitted only on Form 1040.

A taxpayer should use the form that is right for him or her. For example, a taxpayer who is single or married and has only wage income can use any of the three forms (although Form 1040EZ is the most logical). However, a taxpayer who has dividend income cannot use Form 1040EZ—because taxpayers cannot report dividend income on that form—but could use either Form 1040A or Form 1040. Similarly, if a taxpayer needs to itemize deductions or has self-employed business income, Form 1040 is the only appropriate form.

In the remainder of the chapter, we will discuss some basic topics that pertain to both Form 1040A and Form 1040.

Adjusted Gross Income (Form 1040A, line 21, or Form 1040, line 37)

Before we begin to discuss some of the items introduced on Form 1040A or 1040, we need to introduce the concept of *Adjusted Gross Income* (AGI). The tax code defines AGI as gross income minus a list of permitted deductions.[1] In practice, calculation of AGI is simple: Just subtract all of the *for* AGI deductions (summarized on Form 1040A line 20 or Form 1040 line 36) from total income (shown on Form 1040A line 15 or Form 1040 line 22). *For* AGI deductions are deductions that a taxpayer can take prior to calculating AGI.

AGI is an extremely important concept. Many deductions and credits are determined with reference to it. Furthermore, when a taxpayer's AGI exceeds certain levels, certain tax benefits are reduced or eliminated. We will refer to AGI throughout this text.

CONCEPT CHECK 2-1— LO 2-1

1. When preparing a tax return, you should always use Form 1040. True or false?
2. The concept of Adjusted Gross Income (AGI) is important because many deductions and credits reported on the tax return are computed based on the amount shown as AGI. True or false?

[1] The permitted deductions are given in IRC § 62(a).

FILING STATUS (FORMS 1040A AND 1040, LINES 1–5)

LO 2-2

The amount of tax liability depends on many factors, including the filing status of the taxpayer(s). Because of individual circumstances, taxpayers file their returns as one of the following: (1) single, (2) married filing jointly, (3) married filing separately, (4) head of household, or (5) qualifying widow(er) with dependent child. Taxpayers must choose the filing status that is appropriate for them. We discuss each of these filing statuses next.

Single

Individuals use a filing status of single if they are not married and if they do not qualify as either head of household or qualifying widow(er). Marital status is determined on the last day of the tax year.

For purposes of this section, individuals also are single if a divorce or separate maintenance decree was legally executed on or before December 31 of the tax year.

Married Filing Jointly

A couple that is legally married on the last day of the tax year can file one joint tax return that combines all income, deductions, and credits of both spouses.[2] It does not matter if only one spouse earns all of the income. The marital status of a couple is determined under the laws of the state in which they reside. If a spouse dies during the year, the surviving taxpayer can file a joint return if the couple was married on the date of death and the surviving spouse has not remarried as of December 31 of the tax year.

As stated in the section for single status, a person who is legally separated from his or her spouse under a decree of divorce or separate maintenance is not considered married.[3] However, couples in the process of obtaining a divorce (that is not yet final) can file a joint return.

If either spouse is a nonresident alien at any time during the year, generally that person cannot file a joint return. This is because the non-U.S. income of a nonresident spouse is not taxable in the United States. However, if both spouses agree to subject their worldwide income to U.S. taxation, they can file a joint return.

Married Filing Separately

A married couple can elect to file two separate returns rather than one joint return.[4] Only in unusual circumstances is it advantageous for a married couple to file separate returns rather than a joint return.

A taxpayer who files as married filing separately must show the name and social security number of his or her spouse on Form 1040 or Form 1040A. (See Exhibits 2-1 and 2-2.) Additionally, if one taxpayer itemizes deductions, the other spouse must also itemize even if his or her itemized deductions are less than the standard deduction. The standard deduction can be taken only if both of them choose the standard deduction. For a more detailed discussion of this topic, see the sections about standard deductions later in this chapter and about itemized deductions in Chapter 5.

Head of Household

To qualify as head of household, a taxpayer must be unmarried at the end of the tax year, be a U.S. citizen or resident throughout the year, not be a qualifying widow(er), and maintain a household that is the principal place of abode of a *qualifying person* for more than half of the year. Temporary absences, such as attending school, do not disqualify the person under this section.

[2] IRC § 7703(a)(1) and IRC § 6013(a).

[3] IRC § 7703(a)(2).

[4] IRC § 1(d).

EXHIBIT 2-3 Who Is a Qualifying Person for Filing as Head of Household?[1]

Caution: See the text of this chapter for the other requirements you must meet to claim head of household filing status.

Note: The references to "chapter 3" noted below are to Chapter 3 in Publication 17, not Chapter 3 in this book.

Source: IRS *Publication 17.*

IF the person is your . . .	AND . . .	THEN that person is . . .
qualifying child (such as a son, daughter, or grandchild who lived with you more than half the year and meets certain other tests)[2]	he or she is single	a qualifying person, whether or not you can claim an exemption for the person.
	he or she is married <u>and</u> you can claim an exemption for him or her	a qualifying person.
	he or she is married <u>and</u> you cannot claim an exemption for him or her	not a qualifying person. [3]
qualifying relative [4] who is your father or mother	you can claim an exemption for him or her[5]	a qualifying person.[6]
	you cannot claim an exemption for him or her	not a qualifying person.
qualifying relative [4] other than your father or mother (such as a grandparent, brother, or sister who meets certain tests)	he or she lived with you more than half the year, <u>and</u> he or she is related to you in one of the ways listed under *Relatives who do not have to live with you* in chapter 3 <u>and</u> you can claim an exemption for him or her [5]	a qualifying person.
	he or she did not live with you more than half the year	not a qualifying person.
	he or she is not related to you in one of the ways listed under *Relatives who do not have to live with you* in chapter 3 and is your qualifying relative only because he or she lived with you all year as a member of your household	not a qualifying person.
	you cannot claim an exemption for him or her	not a qualifying person.

[1]A person cannot qualify more than one taxpayer to use the head of household filing status for the year.
[2]The term "qualifying child" is defined in chapter 3. **Note.** If you are a noncustodial parent, the term "qualifying child" for head of household filing status does not include a child who is your qualifying child for exemption purposes only because of the rules described under *Children of divorced or separated parents* under *Qualifying Child* in chapter 3. If you are the custodial parent and those rules apply, the child generally is your qualifying child for head of household filing status even though the child is not a qualifying child for whom you can claim an exemption.
[3] This person is a qualifying person if the only reason you cannot claim the exemption is that you can be claimed as a dependent on someone else's return.
[4]The term "qualifying relative" is defined in chapter 3.
[5]If you can claim an exemption for a person only because of a multiple support agreement, that person is not a qualifying person. See *Multiple Support Agreement* in chapter 3.
[6]See *Special rule for parent* for an additional requirement.

Also to qualify as maintaining a household, a taxpayer must pay for more than half the cost of keeping up a home for the year. These costs include rent or mortgage payments, real estate taxes, home insurance, utilities, maintenance and repair, and food eaten in the home. Nonqualifying costs are personal expenditures such as clothing, medical costs, transportation costs, and the like.[5]

A special rule allows a taxpayer's parents to live in a household separate from that of the taxpayer and still permits the taxpayer to qualify for head of household status. However, the taxpayer must pay for more than half of the cost of the household where the parents live.

To understand the definition of a qualifying person for head of household filing status, refer to Exhibit 2-3, from IRS Publication 17. Notice that a *qualifying relative* who is a dependent only because this person lived with the taxpayer for the entire year is not a qualifying person for head of household. In addition, a married individual who lives apart from his or her spouse for at least the last six months of the year can qualify as head of household.

[5] Reg. § 1.2-2(d).

Qualifying Widow(er) with Dependent Child

If a spouse dies during the tax year, the surviving spouse usually can file a joint return. For the two tax years following the death of a spouse, the surviving spouse may be eligible to file as a qualifying widow(er) if all the following conditions are satisfied:

- The taxpayer was eligible to file a joint return in the year the spouse died.
- The taxpayer did not remarry before the end of the tax year in question.
- The taxpayer paid more than half the cost of keeping up a household (see the "Head of Household" section for costs that qualify).
- The household was the principal place of abode for the entire year (except for temporary absences) of both the taxpayer and a child, stepchild, or adopted child who can be claimed as a dependent by the taxpayer (see the rules concerning dependents given later).

This filing status is also called *surviving spouse*.[6]

CONCEPT CHECK 2-2—
LO 2-2

1. Even though you are in the process of getting a divorce, you can file as married filing jointly. True or false?
2. The social security number of the taxpayer's spouse must be shown on the taxpayer's tax return when filing as married filing separately. True or false?
3. A surviving spouse who qualified as married filing jointly when the spouse died can file as a qualifying widow(er) for the next two years as long as the surviving spouse pays for more than half the cost of keeping up a household and does not remarry. True or false?

PERSONAL EXEMPTIONS (FORMS 1040A AND 1040, LINES 6A–B)

LO 2-3

In computing taxable income, taxpayers can deduct an exemption amount from AGI for each personal and dependency exemption.[7] The taxpayer receives an exemption for himself or herself, his or her spouse, and each dependent.[8] Dependency exemptions are explained in the next section.

NEW LAW

Personal and dependency exemptions is $4,050, phasing out at different adjusted gross income amounts.

The exemption amount is subject to annual adjustment for inflation. For 2017 the exemption amount is $4,050 per individual.

For taxable years beginning in 2017, the exemption phases out for taxpayers with the following adjusted gross income amounts:

	AGI—Phaseout Starts	AGI—Exemption Is Eliminated
Single	$261,500	$384,000
Married filing jointly	$313,800	$436,300
Married filing separately	$156,900	$218,150
Head of household	$287,650	$410,150
Qualifying widow(er)	$313,800	$436,300

Someone can be claimed as an exemption only once. If a taxpayer is claimed as a dependent on another return, no personal exemption is allowed on the taxpayer's return. This may occur, for example, when a dependent child must file his or her own return because of earnings from a part-time job. The child cannot claim a personal exemption on his or her own return because the parents can claim him or her as a dependent on their return.

[6] IRC § 2(a).
[7] IRC § 151.
[8] IRC § 151(b) and IRC §151(c).

CONCEPT CHECK 2-3—
LO 2-3

1. If you file a tax return with your spouse, you can claim a total of $8,100 for personal exemptions. True or false?

DEPENDENCY EXEMPTIONS (FORMS 1040A AND 1040, LINE 6C)

LO 2-4

Dependents are listed on line 6c of Forms 1040A and 1040, and line 6d shows the total number of personal and dependency exemptions claimed by the taxpayer. The existence and number of dependents affect the determination of total tax liability in areas such as personal and dependency exemptions, child credits, and filing status.

The amount on line 26 (Form 1040A) or line 42 (Form 1040) represents the number of exemptions (from the box on line 6d) multiplied by the exemption amount ($4,050 in 2017).

Since 2005, a taxpayer can claim a dependency exemption if the person is *a qualifying child or a qualifying relative* and the person meets all of the following tests:

1. Dependent taxpayer test.
2. Joint return test.
3. Citizen or resident test.

The dependent taxpayer test means that if an individual can be claimed as a dependent by someone else, then the taxpayer cannot claim a dependency exemption for that person. This is the case even if the person is a qualifying child or qualifying relative of the taxpayer.

For the joint return test, the taxpayer cannot claim a dependency exemption for someone who files a joint return with his or her spouse.[9] However, if the dependent files a joint return simply to claim a refund (that is, if there is no tax liability on the joint return and there would be no tax liability on separate returns), then a dependency exemption is allowed.[10]

EXAMPLE 2-1

Mary is the daughter of Joseph and Iris Jefferson. Mary married Peter Young in January 2017. The Youngs are both 18 years old, are full-time students at State University, and have lived, for the entire year, with the Jeffersons, who paid for all the living expenses of both Mary and Peter. Mary and Peter both work part-time at the university, and each earned $1,000 during the year, from which their employer withheld income taxes. The Youngs had no other sources of income, and they filed a joint tax return for 2017. Assume that, in all respects other than the joint return test, the Jeffersons can claim Mary and Peter as dependents. In this case, the Jeffersons will receive the dependency exemptions for Mary and Peter. Even though Mary and Peter filed a joint return, it was solely to claim a refund. The tax liability on a joint return would be zero, and if they filed separate returns, there would still be no liability.

TAX YOUR BRAIN

Use the information in Example 2-1, but assume that Mary and Peter each earned $20,000 from their university employment. Who is entitled to the dependency exemptions?

ANSWER

No one. The joint tax return of Mary and Peter would show a tax liability. Thus the Jeffersons cannot claim the dependency exemptions because Mary and Peter do not meet the joint return test. Mary and Peter would not receive the dependency exemptions either. The IRS deems that the person or persons filing a tax return are not dependents. Mary and Peter would, however, each be entitled to a personal exemption on their joint tax return. Note that the answer would be the same even if Mary and Peter filed separate returns.

[9] IRC § 152(b)(2).

[10] Rev. Rul. 54-567, Rev. Rul. 65-34.

An individual meets the citizen or resident test if the person is (a) a U.S. citizen, resident, or national, (b) a resident of Canada or Mexico, or (c) an adopted child of the taxpayer if the child is a member of the taxpayer's household all year and the taxpayer is a U.S. citizen or national.[11]

Recall that to claim someone as a dependent, the individual must meet the three tests just noted, *and* the individual must be either a qualifying child or a qualifying relative. We will define those terms next.

Qualifying Child

A person is a qualifying child if he or she meets *all five* of the following tests:

1. Relationship test.
2. Age test.
3. Residency test.
4. Support test.
5. Special test for qualifying child of more than one taxpayer.

Relationship Test

The relationship test is met if the dependent is *one* of the following:

- Child or descendant of child (grandchild or great-grandchild).
- Stepchild.
- Eligible foster child.
- Brother, sister, half-brother, half-sister, stepbrother, or stepsister, or a descendant of them.[12]

A child includes an adopted child and includes a child placed for adoption in the taxpayer's household by an authorized adoption agency even if the adoption is not finalized.[13] Cousins are not included in the definition of qualifying child.

Age Test

At the end of the tax year, the child must be *one* of the following:

- Under the age of 19.
- Under the age of 24 and a full-time student. A full-time student is a person who was in school full-time during any part of each of five calendar months during the calendar year.
- Totally and permanently disabled regardless of age.

For years after 2008, the child must be younger than the person claiming the dependency.

Residency Test

The child must live with the taxpayer for more than half of the year to meet this requirement. Temporary absences are exceptions to this rule if the absences are due to education, vacation, illness, or military service.

Support Test

The child must not provide more than half of his or her support. The definition of *support* is broad. It "includes food, shelter, clothing, medical and dental care, education, and the like."[14] Items such as medical insurance premiums, child care, toys, gifts, and vacations have been found to be includable in support, whereas life insurance premiums have been excluded. A scholarship is not counted as support if it is received by, and used in support of, a child (including stepchild, foster child, adopted child, or child placed for adoption) who is a full-time student at an educational institution.[15]

[11] IRC § 152(b)(3).

[12] IRC § 152(c)(2).

[13] Reg. § 1.152-2(c)(2).

[14] Reg. § 1.152-1(a)(2)(i).

[15] IRC § 152(F)(5).

EXHIBIT 2-4
When More Than One Person Files a Return Claiming the Same Qualifying Child (Tie-Breaker Rule)

Source: IRS *Publication 17.*

IF more than one person files a return claiming the same qualifying child and . . .	THEN the child will be treated as the qualifying child of the. .
only one of the persons is the child's parent,	parent.
two of the persons are parents of the child and they do not file a joint return together,	parent with whom the child lived for the longer period of time during the year.
two of the persons are parents of the child, they do not file a joint return together, and the child lived with each parent the same amount of time during the year,	parent with the highest adjusted gross income (AGI).
none of the persons are the child's parent,	person with the highest AGI.

For items paid for in cash, support is the amount paid. For noncash items such as lodging, use the fair market value of the item to determine the amount of support.

Special Test for Qualifying Child of More Than One Taxpayer

If a child meets the other four tests and can be a qualifying child for more than one taxpayer, only one individual can claim the exemption. The IRS lets you decide who the taxpayer claiming the exemption should be. However, if you cannot make a decision, the IRS will use the tie-breaker rule as shown in Exhibit 2-4 (from IRS Publication 17).

Child of Divorced or Separated Parents

In most cases, a child of divorced or separated parents will be the qualifying child of the parent with custody. However, the child will be deemed to be the qualifying child of the noncustodial parent if *all* the following tests are met:

- The child has been in the custody of either or both parents for more than half of the year.
- Either or both parents provided more than half the child's support.
- The parents are (a) divorced or legally separated, (b) separated under a written separation agreement, or (c) living apart at all times during the last six months of the year.
- The decree or separation agreement for 2017 states that the noncustodial parent can claim the child as a dependent, or the custodial parent signs a written document specifying that the child will not be claimed as a dependent.

Beginning after July 2, 2008, Form 8332 or a similar form must be used to revoke a release of claim to exemption that was previously released to the noncustodial parent. Additionally, if the custodial parent gives notice of revocation in 2017, the revocation takes effect in tax year 2018.

CONCEPT CHECK 2-4— LO 2-4

1. What are the five specific tests you need to meet to claim someone as a qualifying child? ______________________________

2. To meet the age test, a child who is not disabled must be __________ or __________ if a full-time student.

Qualifying Relative

A person is a qualifying relative if he or she meets *all four* of the following tests:

1. Not a qualifying child test.
2. Relationship or member of household test.
3. Gross income test.
4. Support test.

The four tests are discussed in the next paragraphs.

Not a Qualifying Child Test

If a child is your qualifying child or the qualifying child of another taxpayer, he or she cannot be your qualifying relative.

Relationship or Member of Household Test

The person either must be a member of the taxpayer's household for the entire year *or* must be related to the taxpayer in *one* of the following ways:

- Child or descendant of child (grandchild or great-grandchild).
- Stepchild.
- Eligible foster child.
- Brother, sister, half-brother, half-sister, or a descendant of them.
- Stepbrother or stepsister.
- Father or mother.
- Brother or sister of parents.
- Son-in-law, daughter-in-law, father-in-law, mother-in-law, brother-in-law, or sister-in-law.

Note that if someone is related to the taxpayer (as indicated in the preceding list), it is not necessary that the person live with the taxpayer for the entire year or, actually, any part of the year. But it may be difficult to meet the support test if the individual does not live in the household.

Gross Income Test

The dependent must *not* have gross income equal to or greater than the amount of the exemption. The amount of the exemption is subject to annual adjustment for inflation. For tax years 2016 and 2017, the exemption amount is $4,050.

For purposes of this test, gross income does not include certain items such as tax-exempt interest, the nontaxable portion of social security benefits, and the nontaxable portion of a scholarship or fellowship.

Support Test

The taxpayer must provide over 50% of the dependent's support.[16] Recall that the definition of support was explained in the "Qualifying Child" section.

In practice, a taxpayer must determine how much was paid for the support of the dependent (regardless of who paid it) and then determine whether the taxpayer provided over half of that support.

If several dependents receive the benefits of an item of support, allocate the cost of the item to the dependents on a pro rata basis unless the taxpayer can show that a different allocation is appropriate.[17] Money received by a dependent and spent by him or her counts as support. Examples include wages from a part-time job or social security benefits paid to a dependent.

Do not confuse the issue of what expenditures qualify for support with the issue of who paid for the expenditures. These are different but related concepts. Confusion can arise because sometimes it is easier to determine the total amount of support by reference to where the money came from rather than by creating an itemized list of support paid on behalf of an individual.

The support test has two exceptions. The first occurs when several persons provide for more than half the support of someone, but no one person meets the 50% threshold.[18] If each person in the group would be able to claim the individual as a dependent (absent the support test) and no one person in the group furnished more than half of the individual's support, then one of the persons in the group who provided more than 10% of the support can claim the dependent with the agreement of the other persons in the group. Such a multiple support agreement must

[16] IRC § 152(a).

[17] Rev. Rul. 64-222, 1964-2 CB 47

[18] IRC § 152(d)(3).

be in writing; taxpayers use Form 2120 for this purpose. Each person who meets the 10% test but who will not be claiming the dependency exemption must fill out Form 2120. The taxpayer who will receive the exemption must file all the Forms 2120 with his or her return.

If someone is the subject of a multiple support agreement over a number of years, it is not necessary that the same individual claim the dependency exemption each year.

EXAMPLE 2-2

Lisa, Monique, Terry, Robert, and Angie provided all the support for Donald in the following percentages:

Lisa (friend)	30%
Monique (neighbor)	5%
Terry (son)	40%
Robert (son)	10%
Angie (daughter)	15%

Initially you need to determine the members of the group who could claim Donald as a dependent, absent the support test. These are Terry, Robert, and Angie, who are Donald's children (Lisa and Monique cannot claim Donald because he does not meet the relationship test). Next determine whether Terry, Robert, and Angie (as a group) contributed more than 50% of Donald's support. In this case, they contributed 65%. If a multiple support agreement is prepared, either Terry or Angie would be entitled to claim Donald as a dependent. Robert is not entitled to the exemption because he did not contribute *more* than 10% of Donald's support.

TAX YOUR BRAIN

Using Example 2-2, assume that Donald had a part-time job that provided 25% of his support. The other five people provided the remaining 75% of Donald's support in the same proportions given. Which person(s) would be entitled to the dependency exemption for purposes of a multiple support agreement?

ANSWER

No one would be entitled to the dependency exemption. We previously determined that only Terry, Robert, and Angie would have been entitled to claim Donald as a dependent, absent the support test. These three people must supply over half of Donald's support. Here the three individuals contributed only 48.75% of Donald's support (65% of the 75% not paid by Donald). Thus no one can claim Donald as a dependent.

The second exception to the 50% support test is the case of a child of divorced or separated parents. If the child is not a qualifying child, he or she can be treated as a qualifying relative of the noncustodial parent if the following are true:

- The child has been in the custody of either or both parents for more than half the year.
- Either or both parents provided more than half the child's support.
- The parents are (1) divorced or legally separated, (2) separated under a written separation agreement, or (3) living apart at all times during the last six months of the year.
- The decree or separation agreement for 2017 states that the noncustodial parent can claim the child as a dependent, or the custodial parent relinquishes the dependency exemption to the noncustodial parent by signing a written agreement to that effect.[19] However, the agreement is not binding on future tax years.

The preceding tests do not apply if the support of the child is determined based on a multiple support agreement.

[19] IRC § 152(e)(2).

CONCEPT CHECK 2-5— LO 2-4

1. You must meet one of these four tests to be a qualifying relative: not a qualifying child test, relationship or member of household test, gross income test, and support test. True or false?
2. A qualifying relative can earn up to $6,350 for the year 2017. True or false?

STANDARD DEDUCTION (FORM 1040A, LINE 24, OR FORM 1040, LINE 40)

LO 2-5

Taxpayers can subtract a standard deduction from AGI.[20] Taxpayers may alternatively elect to subtract itemized deductions and should do so if their itemized deductions are larger than the standard deduction amount.[21] Note that taxpayers who elect to itemize their deductions cannot use Form 1040A—that form permits taxpayers to use only standard deductions.

The standard deduction is the sum of the basic standard deduction and the additional standard deduction.[22] Both components depend on filing status and are subject to annual adjustment for inflation. The basic standard deduction for tax year 2017 is as follows:

NEW LAW

For 2017 the standard deduction for each filing status has increased.

Filing Status	Basic Standard Deduction
Single	$ 6,350
Married filing jointly	$12,700
Married filing separately	$ 6,350
Head of household	$ 9,350
Qualifying widow(er)	$12,700

Taxpayers who either are 65 or older or are blind can claim an additional standard deduction. Taxpayers who are both 65 or older and blind get two additional standard deductions. Note that blind taxpayers are entitled to the additional standard deduction regardless of their age. The additional standard deductions for taxpayers who are 65 or older or blind are:

Filing Status	Tax Year 2017
Single	$1,550
Married filing jointly	$1,250
Married filing separately	$1,250
Head of household	$1,550
Qualifying widow(er)	$1,250

EXAMPLE 2-3

Flora is 56 years old, single and blind. She is entitled to a standard deduction of $7,900 ($6,350 + $1,550). If she were 70 instead of 56, she would have a standard deduction of $9,450 ($6,350 + $1,550 + $1,550).

EXAMPLE 2-4

Victor and Marvel are married and have an 8-year-old dependent child who is blind. Victor and Marvel are entitled to a standard deduction of $12,700. This example illustrates that the additional standard deduction applies only to the taxpayer and the spouse, if any. Dependents do not affect the standard deduction computation.

[20] IRC § 63(c).

[21] We discuss itemized deductions in Chapter 5.

[22] IRC § 63(c)(1).

The standard deduction is zero in any of the following instances:

- A married couple files separate returns and one spouse itemizes deductions. In this case, the other spouse must also itemize.
- A taxpayer is a nonresident alien.
- A taxpayer files a return for a period of less than 12 months because of a change in accounting period.

When a taxpayer can be claimed as a dependent on the tax return of another individual, the basic standard deduction for the taxpayer is limited to the greater of (1) $1,050 or (2) the taxpayer's earned income plus $350, but not more than the amount of the basic standard deduction.[23] Earned income is generally income from work or the efforts of the taxpayer. Salaries and wages are the most common type of earned income.

Congress enacted the preceding rule to prevent taxpayers from shifting income to their children or other dependents. For example, a couple could give a child a bond that pays interest of $3,500 per year. Without the rule, the entire $3,500 interest income would be tax-free because the basic standard deduction for any filing status exceeds the amount of income. With the rule in place, the standard deduction for the child would be $1,050.

The standard deduction increases, in effect, for the wages of the dependent person. This permits children, for example, to work a part-time summer job for some extra spending money but not have to pay income taxes.

EXAMPLE 2-5

Sherry's parents can claim her as a dependent on their tax return. In 2017 her only source of income was a part-time job in a local store where she earned $2,500 during the year. Sherry's standard deduction is $2,850, which is the greater of (a) $1,050 or (b) $2,500 + $350. As a result, Sherry would owe no income tax on her wages.

EXAMPLE 2-6

In 2017 Joe received $1,350 of interest income from a local bank. The interest was his only source of income for the year. His standard deduction is $1,050, which is the greater of (a) $1,050 or (b) $0 + $350.

CONCEPT CHECK 2-6—
LO 2-5

1. What is the amount of the standard deduction in each of the following cases?
   a. The taxpayer is single, 42 years of age, and blind. ____________
   b. The taxpayer is head of household, 37 years of age, and not blind. ____________
   c. The taxpayers are married filing jointly, the husband is 67 and the wife is 61 years of age, and neither is blind. ____________

TAX DUE TO IRS
LO 2-6

It is important to learn how to compute the amount of tax and arrive at the total liability amount. We illustrate some steps to help you determine these two items before we discuss tax payments.

[23] IRC § 63(c)(5). The dollar value given in (1) is for tax year 2017 and is adjusted annually for inflation.

Amount of Tax (Form 1040A, line 28, or Form 1040, line 44)

Most taxpayers determine the amount of tax by looking up the applicable tax due in a tax table.

The tax tables used in the preparation of Form 1040A or 1040 are in Appendix D of this text. As you can see, there are columns for (1) single, (2) married filing jointly, (3) married filing separately, and (4) head of household. The qualifying widow(er) filing status uses the same column as married filing jointly.

EXAMPLE 2-7

A taxpayer has taxable income of $71,330. Referring to the tax tables, we can see that the amount of tax for line 28 (Form 1040A) or line 44 (Form 1040) would be $13,570 for a single person, $9,766 for a married couple filing jointly or a qualifying widow(er), $12,084 for a head of household, or $13,570 for a married couple filing separately.

The tax tables stop at taxable income of less than $100,000. Taxpayers with taxable income of $100,000 or more must use the tax rate schedules provided on the inside front cover of this text. Recall that the IRS uses tax rate schedules to create the tax tables according to the midpoint of each $50 range.

Total Tax Liability (Form 1040A, line 39, or Form 1040, line 63)

This line represents the total amount the taxpayer must pay to the government for the tax year.

Tax Payments (Form 1040A, lines 40–45, or Form 1040, lines 64–73)

Taxpayers must pay the amount of tax indicated on the total tax line (line 39 on Form 1040A or line 63 on Form 1040). Normally taxpayers pay some or all of their tax liability prior to the due date of the tax return. Most commonly, taxpayers make payment through income tax withholding and quarterly estimated tax payments, although other payment methods are also possible.

Income Tax Withholding (Form 1040A, line 40, or Form 1040, line 64)

When certain taxable payments are made to individuals, the payer must retain (withhold) a proportion of the payment otherwise due and remit the amount withheld to the U.S. Treasury. The withheld amount represents an estimate of the amount of income tax that would be due for the year on the taxable payment. The IRS credits withholding to the account of the appropriate taxpayer. Withholding reduces the amount otherwise due the IRS on the due date of the return.

For most taxpayers, withholding comes from two sources. First, when an employer pays a salary or wages to an employee, the employer is required to retain part of the amount otherwise due the employee and to pay the retained amount, for the benefit of the employee, to the federal government. The amount retained is the payroll tax withholding, which is a part of virtually every pay stub in the country.[24] Employers report the total amount withheld from the earnings of an employee on a Form W-2 given to each employee shortly after the end of the calendar year.

Second, income tax withholding can also occur when a taxpayer receives interest, dividends, rents, royalties, pension plan distributions, and similar payments. In certain circumstances, payers are required to withhold a portion of the payment and remit it to the government. The concept is similar to that used for wage payments. Payers report the amount of the total payment and the amount withheld on a Form 1099 provided to the taxpayer. Pension plan distributions are the most common payments requiring or permitting withholding.

[24] Chapter 10 discusses payer rules associated with determining and remitting withholding taxes, social security tax, and Medicare tax.

Estimated Tax Payments (Form 1040A, line 41, or Form 1040, line 65)

Taxpayers must pay their tax liability throughout the tax year, not at the time they file their tax return. If taxes withheld approximate the total tax liability for the year (the situation for most taxpayers), no estimated payments are due. However, a taxpayer who has income that is not subject to withholding may be required to make estimated payments during the year.[25] Failure to do so may subject the taxpayer to an underpayment penalty.[26]

Taxpayers must make periodic payments based on the *required annual payment,* which is defined as the lesser of 90% of the tax shown on the return or 100% of the tax shown on the return for the preceding year.[27] Payments are equal to 25% of the required annual payment and are due on April 15, June 15, September 15 in the current year, and January 15 of the next calendar year. For taxpayers with prior year AGI over $150,000, the 100% figure increases to 110%.

As noted previously, failure to make required estimated payments will subject the taxpayer to a potential underpayment penalty plus interest. However, taxpayers are not assessed a penalty if the difference between the tax shown on the return and the amount of tax withheld for wages is less than $1,000.[28]

Exhibit 2-5 is a flowchart from IRS Publication 17 that illustrates the decision process associated with determining whether estimated payments are required.

EXHIBIT 2-5 Do You Have to Pay Estimated Tax?

Source: IRS *Publication 17.*

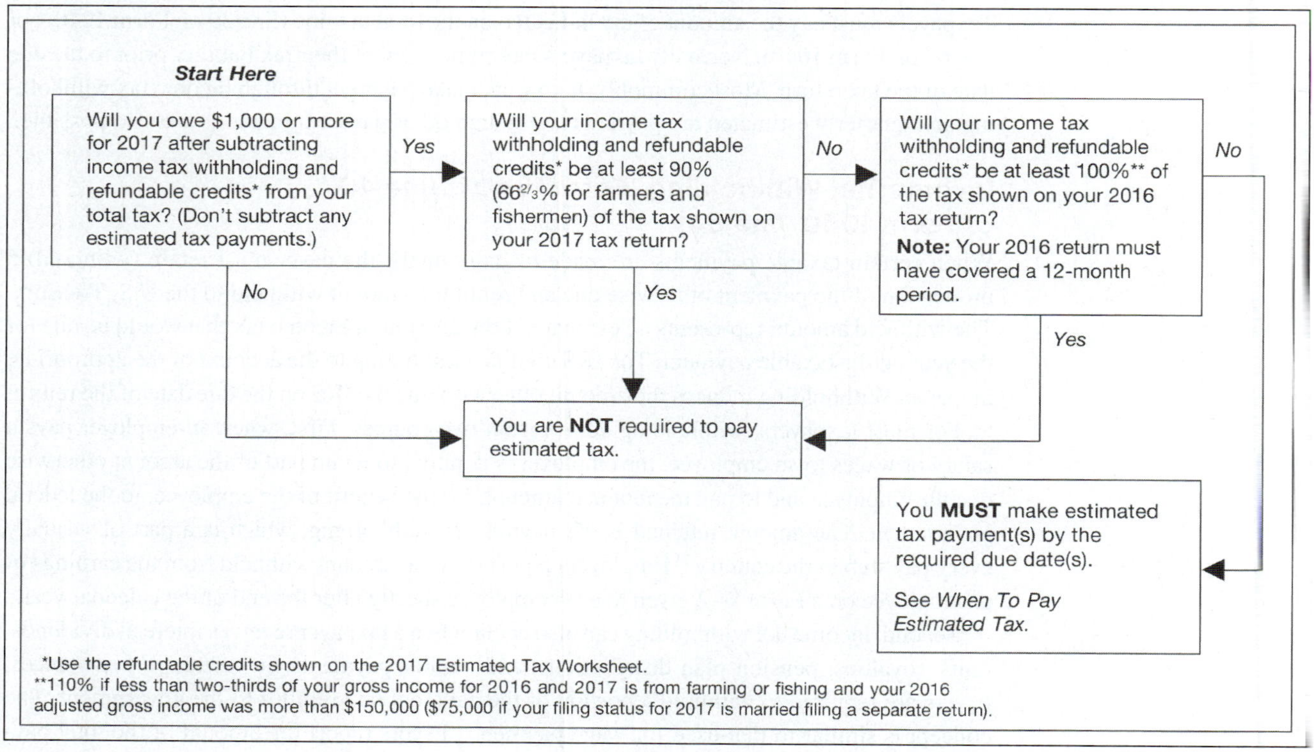

[25] IRC § 6654(d).

[26] IRC § 6654(a).

[27] IRC § 6654(d)(1)(B).

[28] IRC § 6654(e)(1).

EXAMPLE 2-8

Janice, who is single, had taxable income of $45,000 in 2017 and had a total tax liability for the year of $6,995. During 2018 she will work only part-time, earn $25,000, and have income tax withholding of $4,100. She receives additional income from selling paintings. Based on her expected painting sales and wage earnings, she expects her tax liability for 2018 will be $6,350. To avoid an underpayment penalty, Janice must make estimated tax payments during 2018. Janice's required annual payment is $5,715, which is the lower of (a) 90% of $6,350 (the tax expected to show on her 2018 return) or (b) $6,995 (the amount of her 2017 liability). Because she expects to have taxes of $4,100 withheld from her paycheck, she must pay the remaining $1,615 ($5,715 – $4,100) in estimated payments during 2018. She must pay the amount in four equal installments of $403.75 on the dates indicated previously. Note that if Janice's 2018 tax liability actually turns out to be exactly $6,350, she will still owe $635 ($6,350 liability minus withholding of $4,100 minus estimated payments of $1 615) when she files her 2018 tax return.

TAX YOUR BRAIN

Assume that Janice's year 2018 wage income will be $50,000 (she worked full-time) and she will have $8,300 withheld from her wages. Also assume that she expects to sell a large number of paintings and that she estimates her total 2018 tax liability will be $18,000. To avoid an underpayment penalty, does Janice need to pay estimated payments during 2018 and, if so, how much must she pay?

ANSWER

Janice does not need to make any estimated payments. Her required annual payment is $6,995, which is the lower of (a) 90% of $18,000 (the estimate of her 2018 tax liability) or (b) $6,995 (her tax liability for 2017). Because her estimated tax withholdings are $8,300, she is not obligated to make estimated payments. She will need to pay the remaining $9,700 ($18,000 – $8,300) no later than April 15, 2019.

Other Payments (Form 1040A, lines 42a–45, or Form 1040, lines 66a–73)

NEW LAW

The social security wage limitation increased to $127,200.

Taxpayers with earned income (wages, salaries, tips, or earnings from self-employment) below certain limits are entitled to a tax credit.[29] Usually credits are shown on lines 31–35 (1040A) or 48–54 (Form 1040), but the earned income credit is reported in the payments section. The amount of this credit is calculated on Schedule EIC and is reported on line 42a (Form 1040A) or 66(a) (Form 1040). We cover the EIC in Chapter 9.

Employers are required to withhold FICA (social security and Medicare) taxes from wages paid to employees. However, once wages paid to an individual employee exceed a certain limit ($127,200 in 2017), social security withholding ceases.[30] Each employer calculates the FICA withholding without regard to other employers. However, the employee simply needs to reach the limit during the calendar year. Thus an employee who works for more than one employer can have excess social security taxes withheld from his or her paychecks. Excess social security taxes are a payment toward income taxes due and are reported on Form 1040, line 71. Note that the $127,200 wage limitation is determined per taxpayer, not per tax return. Someone who has excess social security taxes withheld cannot use Form 1040A.

Qualifying taxpayers can receive a child tax credit. This credit is reported in the credits section on line 35 (Form 1040A) or line 52 (Form 1040). In certain circumstances, taxpayers can receive an additional child tax credit beyond the amount reported in the credits section. This additional credit is on line 43 or 67 on Form 1040A or 1040, respectively. We discuss the child tax credit in Chapter 9.

[29] IRC § 32.

[30] The limitation amount is adjusted annually based on the national average wage index. Go to www.ssa.gov for future limitation amounts. This applies only to social security, not to Medicare, which has no limit on the amount of earnings.

A taxpayer may request an automatic 6-month extension of time to file his or her tax return.[31] Extending the time to file the return does not extend the time to pay the applicable tax. As a result, if a taxpayer filing an extension determines that he or she owes additional tax, the payment must accompany the extension request (Form 4868). The additional payment is on Form 1040, line 70. Taxpayers paying additional tax with an extension request cannot use Form 1040A.

Taxpayers can use Form 1040, lines 72 and 73, to claim certain other payments (Form 1040A cannot be used). Farmers and fishermen may be entitled to a refund of federal fuel taxes paid on fuel that was not used in a motor vehicle on the highway (such as fuel used in a farm tractor or a commercial fishing boat). The total from Form 4136 is on line 72. Certain undistributed long-term capital gains (Form 2439), and other credits are reported on line 73.

Tax Refund (Form 1040A, line 48a, or Form 1040, line 76a) or Tax Due with Return (Form 1040A, line 50, or Form 1040, line 78)

Compare the amount owed with the total amount paid (line 39 versus line 46 on Form 1040A or line 63 versus line 74 on Form 1040). Excess payment results in a refund; excess remaining tax liability means the taxpayer must pay the remaining amount owed when filing the return.

A taxpayer who is entitled to a refund can elect to (1) receive a check, (2) have the refund deposited directly in his or her bank account, or (3) apply the excess to next year's tax return. The taxpayer who selects the direct deposit option must supply account information on lines 48b through d on Form 1040A or lines 76b through d on Form 1040.

The estimated tax penalty shown on line 51 (1040A) or 79 (1040) comes from Form 2210 and is a result of paying insufficient tax amounts throughout the year. We discuss the penalty in the following section.

CONCEPT CHECK 2-7— LO 2-6

1. Use the tables in Appendix D of the text to determine the tax amounts for the following situations:
   a. Single taxpayer with taxable income of $34,640. ____________
   b. Married taxpayers filing jointly with taxable income of $67,706. ____________
2. What is the limit on the FICA (social security) amount for 2017? ____________

INTEREST AND TAX PENALTIES

LO 2-7

Failure to adhere to the tax law can subject a taxpayer to IRS assessments for penalties and interest. Although the IRS can assess a number of different penalties, it assesses only a few to individual taxpayers. In this section, we discuss the most common civil and criminal penalties applicable to individuals. We provide details on the following penalties:

- Interest charged on assessments.
- Failure to file a tax return.
- Failure to pay tax.
- Failure to pay estimated taxes.
- Substantial understatement of tax liability (accuracy-related penalties).
- Fraud penalties.
- Erroneous claim for refund or credit penalty.

[31] IRC § 6081.

From Shoebox to Software

The amount of federal tax withholding is the amount in box 2 of Form W-2 plus the amount in box 4 of all Forms 1099 received (1099-MISC, 1099-B, 1099-INT, etc.). Taxpayers may have multiple W-2 and 1099 forms. Information from W-2s and 1099s is entered into the appropriate forms in the Documents Received section of the tax return software. The software will automatically sum the various documents and will place the total on line 63. The tax preparer should check the amount on line 63 to ensure that all appropriate documentation was correctly entered.

Amounts for estimated payments will come from canceled checks or worksheets prepared when determining the appropriate payment amounts. You enter appropriate amounts in the tax software on a supporting schedule. The software utilizes this supporting schedule to record amounts paid during the year for federal and state estimated tax payments.

The Earned Income Credit and the additional child tax credit are from Schedule EIC and Form 8812, respectively.

A taxpayer who files Form 4868, Application for Automatic Extension of Time to File U.S. Individual Income Tax Return, must pay any additional tax owed with that form. The amount paid should be included on line 70 (Form 1040 only). If the tax software is used to prepare Form 4868, the amount on line 10 (amount paid) will normally be transferred to line 70. Otherwise you must directly enter any additional payment onto line 70. Retain the canceled check or other evidence of payment.

Tax preparers should determine whether excess social security taxes have been withheld when total wages (Form 1040 or 1040A, line 7) exceed the social security limit ($127,200 in 2017) and the taxpayer has received multiple Forms W-2. The tax software will automatically calculate this amount from W-2s entered into the W-2 worksheets.

Entries on lines 72 and 73 (Form 1040 only) are relatively unusual.

Interest Charged on All Assessments

Many taxpayers are under the false impression that filing a tax return extension also delays the payment of any remaining tax liability. An extension is an extension of time to file, *not* an extension of time to pay. The amount of unpaid tax liability is still due on April 15 for individual taxpayers. If the taxpayer still owes tax after April 15, the IRS assesses interest based on the remaining amount owed. The IRS charges interest on all nonpayments, underpayments, and late payments of tax. The rate charged is the federal short-term rate plus 3 percentage points.[32] Rates are set quarterly. Here are the annualized rates of interest on assessments for the past several years:

Time Period	Percentage Rate
Jan. 1, 2017, to June 30, 2017	4%
Apr. 1, 2016, to Dec. 31, 2016	4
July 1, 2015, to Mar. 31, 2016	3
Oct. 1, 2011, to June 30, 2015	3
Apr. 1, 2011, to Sept. 30, 2011	4
Jan. 1, 2011, to Mar. 31, 2011	3
Apr. 1, 2009, to Dec. 31, 2010	4
Jan. 1, 2009, to Mar. 31, 2009	5
Oct. 1, 2008, to Dec. 31, 2008	6
July 1, 2008, to Sept. 30, 2008	5
Apr. 1, 2008, to June 30, 2008	6
Jan. 1, 2008, to Mar. 31, 2008	7
July 1, 2007, to Dec. 31, 2007	8
July 1, 2006, to June 30, 2007	8
Oct. 1, 2005, to June 30, 2006	7
Apr. 1, 2005, to Sept. 30, 2005	6
Oct. 1, 2004, to Mar. 31, 2005	5

[32] IRC § 6621(a)(2).

Failure to File a Tax Return

A taxpayer who does not file a tax return by the due date of the return, plus extensions, must pay a failure to file penalty. The penalty for failure to file is 5% of the amount of tax due on the return if the failure is less than one month. For each additional month or fraction of a month, the IRS adds an additional 5% penalty, up to a maximum of 25%. Any income tax return not filed within 60 days of its due date is subject to a minimum penalty of the lesser of $210 or the amount of tax required on the return. If failure to file is due to fraud, the penalty is 15% per month, up to a maximum of 75%.[33] The IRS calculates the penalty on the tax liability shown on the return reduced by any payments made by withholding, estimated payments, or credits.

EXAMPLE 2-9

Ernest was extremely busy during April and forgot to file his tax return by April 15. He did not file an extension. Ernest finally filed his tax return on June 1 and had a remaining tax liability of $2,000. Ernest has a $200 failure to file penalty, calculated as follows:

Underpayment	$2,000
Penalty per month or fraction thereof (2 months × 5%)	10%
Failure to file penalty	$ 200

If a taxpayer can show the delay in filing was due to a reasonable cause, the IRS could agree to abate (forgive) the penalty. Reasonable cause occurs when the taxpayer shows that he or she exercised ordinary business care and prudence in providing for payment of his or her liability but, nevertheless, either was unable to pay the tax or would suffer an undue hardship if he or she paid on the due date.[34]

The IRS makes the abatement determination case by case based on the facts and circumstances of the particular situation.

Failure to Pay Tax

The failure to pay and the failure to file penalties are interrelated. The failure to pay penalty is 0.5% of the tax shown on the return for each month (or fraction of a month) the tax is unpaid, up to a maximum of 25%.[35]

However, the failure to file penalty (discussed earlier) is reduced by the failure to pay penalty when both apply. This means that the maximum monthly penalty is 5% when both penalties apply. The IRS will also abate the failure to pay penalty if the taxpayer can show a reasonable cause for not paying. If the taxpayer filed a proper extension to file his or her tax return, the IRS will presume a reasonable cause exists when both of the following conditions apply:

- The amount due with the tax return is less than 10% of the amount of tax shown on the tax return.
- Any balance due shown on the tax return is paid with the return.

EXAMPLE 2-10

Assume the same facts as in Example 2-9. However, Ernest filed a proper automatic six-month extension to file his return. Thus his new due date is October 15. If the $2,000 owed by Ernest is less than 10% of the amount of tax on the return, then there is no failure to pay penalty. There is also not a failure to file penalty because Ernest obtained an extension of time to file.

[33] IRC § 6651(f).

[34] Reg. § 301.6651-1(c).

[35] IRC § 6651(a)(2).

EXAMPLE 2-11

Assume the same facts as in Example 2-10 except that Ernest does not file his tax return until December 1 and the $2,000 tax due is more than 10% of his total tax shown on the return. In this case, Ernest would be subject to both the failure to file penalty and the failure to pay penalty. Because the return was due on October 15, the failure to *file* penalty runs from October 15 to December 1 (two months of penalty). Because the $2,000 is more than 10% of the total tax, the failure to pay penalty runs from April 15 to December 1 (eight months of penalty).

The calculations are as follows:

Failure to pay	Underpayment	$2,000
	0.5% for 8 months	4%
	Failure to pay penalty	$ 80
Failure to file	Underpayment	$2,000
	5% for 2 months	10%
	Failure to file penalty	$ 200
Less failure to pay penalty for the months when both apply (2 months × 0.5% × $2,000)		($20)
	Adjusted failure to file	$ 180

Ernest must pay $2,260 ($2,000 + $80 + $180) in taxes and penalties (plus interest) when the return is filed.

Penalty for Failure to Pay Estimated Income Tax

Normally individuals pay income taxes throughout the tax year, not just in April when they file their returns. Taxpayers whose primary income is wages or salary make tax payments through employer withholding. However, taxpayers who earn a large portion of their income from sources other than wages may have little or no income tax withheld.[36]

These taxpayers must pay estimated tax payments throughout the year on a quarterly basis. The quarterly payments are due on April 15, June 15, September 15 in the current year, and January 15 of the next calendar year. The IRS will impose an estimated tax penalty on taxpayers who do not pay enough estimated tax.[37]

To avoid this penalty, the taxpayer must pay during the year, either through withholding or estimated payments, a minimum of the following:

- 90% of the current year's tax liability.
- 100% of the prior year's tax liability if the taxpayer's AGI in the prior year is less than $150,000.

If the taxpayer's prior year AGI is more than $150,000, the percentage for the prior year rule increases to 110%.[38]

No estimated tax penalty applies if the tax due after withholding or estimated payments is less than $1,000. The IRS calculates the penalty on a per quarter basis using the same rate at which it charges interest (the short-term federal rate plus 3 percentage points).

Taxpayers use Form 2210 to calculate the failure to pay estimated tax penalty. The tax software automatically calculates the amount of underpayment penalty, if any.

Accuracy-Related Penalties

On a return when negligence or any substantial understatement of income occurs, the IRS will assess a penalty equal to 20% of the tax due.[39]

36 Self-employment and investment income are discussed in Chapters 6 and 3, respectively.

37 Even taxpayers subject to withholding may be required to make estimated payments if nonwage income is sufficiently large.

38 IRC § 6654(d)(1)(C).

39 IRC § 6662(a).

Negligence includes any failure to make a reasonable attempt to comply with the provisions of the IRC. Negligence also includes any careless, reckless, or intentional disregard for tax authority. The IRS may waive the negligence penalty if the taxpayer makes a good-faith effort to comply with the IRC. If the taxpayer were to take a position contrary to established law, the filing of Form 8275R (the form used to disclose a contrary position) can help avoid the negligence penalty. The 20% penalty also applies when the taxpayer has substantially understated his or her income tax. *Substantial understatement* occurs when the understatement is either

- More than 10% of the tax required to be shown on the return.
- $5,000 or more.[40]

The IRS may reduce the amount of the understatement subject to the 20% penalty if the taxpayer has substantial tax authority for his or her tax treatment.[41] Substantial authority exists only if the weight of tax authority supporting the taxpayer's treatment is substantial in relation to the tax authority supporting the IRS's position.

Fraud Penalties

The IRS can impose a 75% penalty on any portion of understatement of tax that is attributable to fraud.[42] Although the IRC does not define *fraud,* the courts provide a comprehensive definition. One court defined it as intentional wrongdoing with the purpose of evading tax.[43] Another court said it is the intent to conceal, mislead, or otherwise prevent the collection of tax.[44] If any underpayment is due to fraud, the IRS assesses the 75% penalty.[45]

Fraud on a tax return can also lead to criminal charges. Criminal penalties apply only to tax evasion (attempt to evade or defeat tax), willful failure to collect or pay tax, and willful failure to file a return. The IRS can assess criminal penalties in addition to civil penalties. Possible criminal penalties include the following:

- **Any person who willfully attempts to evade or defeat any tax:** The charge is a felony punishable by fines of not more than $100,000 or imprisonment of not more than five years or both.[46]
- **Any person who fails to collect, account for, and pay over any tax:** The charge is a felony punishable by fines of not more than $10,000 or imprisonment of not more than five years or both.[47]
- **Any person who willfully fails to pay estimated tax or other tax and file a return:** The charge is a misdemeanor punishable by fines of not more than $25,000 or imprisonment of not more than one year or both.[48]

Penalty for Erroneous Claim for Refund or Credit

A 20% penalty could be assessed by the IRS on the disallowed amount of the claim if the claim for refund or credit of income filed is found to be excessive. An amount for a claim is classified as "excessive" if the claim amount exceeds the amount of the allowable claim. This penalty does not apply if the fraud or the accuracy-related penalty has been assessed.

[40] IRC § 6662(d)(1)(A).

[41] IRC § 6662(d)(2)(B).

[42] IRC § 6663.

[43] *Mitchell v. Comm.*, 118 F2d 308 (5th-CA 1941).

[44] *Stoltzfus v. U.S.*, 398 F2d 1002 (3rd-CA 1968).

[45] IRC § 6663(b).

[46] IRC § 7201.

[47] IRC § 7202.

[48] IRC § 7203.

CONCEPT CHECK 2-8— LO 2-7

1. A taxpayer filed an automatic extension before April 15 but sent no money to the IRS. He then filed his return by June 2 and paid the amount due of $3,000. What are the amounts for the failure to file a tax return penalty and the failure to pay penalty? ____________
2. Fraud on a tax return can also lead to criminal charges. True or false?

Summary

LO 2-1: Describe the expanded tax formula and the components of the major sections of Form 1040A and Form 1040.	• Forms 1040A and 1040 are more complex than Form 1040EZ. • The taxpayer must use the form that is right for him or her. • Adjusted Gross Income (AGI) is gross income minus a list of permitted deductions. • Many deductions and credits are determined with reference to AGI.

LO 2-2: Determine the proper filing status.	• There are five filing statuses.
	  • Single: not married as of the last day of the year.
	  • Married filing jointly: legally married on the last day of the year; the marital status is determined by state law.
	  • Married filing separately: married but elect to file separately. The standard deduction can be taken only if both take it.
	  • Head of household: unmarried at the end of the year and must maintain a household for a qualifying person for more than half the year.
	  • Qualifying widow(er) with dependent child: eligible to file a joint return the year the spouse died, unmarried, and paying more than half the cost of a household that was the principal place of residence of the taxpayer and child for the year.

LO 2-3: Calculate personal exemptions.	• Personal exemptions are for the taxpayer and spouse. • The amount of the personal exemption for 2017 is $4,050 (subject to annual inflation adjustment). • No personal exemption is allowed on a taxpayer's return if he or she can be claimed as a dependent on another return.
LO 2-4: Calculate dependency exemptions.	• Must meet the following: dependent taxpayer test, joint return test, and citizen or resident test. • Must be a qualifying child or a qualifying relative. • A qualifying child must meet five tests: relationship test, age test, residency test, support test, and special test for qualifying child of more than one taxpayer. • A qualifying relative must meet four tests: not a qualifying child test, relationship or member of household test, gross income test, and support test.
LO 2-5: Determine the standard deduction.	• Standard deduction for each filing status: single—$6,350; married filing jointly—$12,700; married filing separately—$6,350; head of household—$9,350; and qualifying widow(er)—$12,700. • The amount of the standard deduction increases for people who are age 65 and/or blind. • Dependent taxpayers are limited to the higher of $1,050 or the taxpayer's earned income plus $350. Limited to the basic standard deduction.

LO 2-6: Compute the amount of tax due to the Internal Revenue Service (IRS).	• The tax liability is computed by using the tables or the tax rate schedule. • Tax payments (withholding by the employer and estimated payments sent to IRS) and tax credits reduce the tax due to IRS. • Excess payment results in a refund; excess remaining tax liability means an amount is owed to IRS.
LO 2-7: Determine what interest and penalties the IRS can assess and in what instances certain penalties are applicable.	• Interest on assessments: The rate charged is the federal short-term rate plus 3 percentage points. • The failure to file a tax return penalty is 5% per month or fraction of a month, not to exceed 25%. • The failure to pay tax penalty is 0.5% per month or fraction of a month, not to exceed 25%. If an income tax return is filed more than 60 days after its due date, the minimum penalty is $135 or 100% of the unpaid tax. • The maximum amount is 5% per month or fraction of a month, not to exceed 25% when both penalties, failure to file a tax return and failure to pay tax, apply. • The failure to pay estimated income tax penalty applies if a taxpayer fails to pay during the year a minimum of 90% of the current year's tax liability or 100% of the prior year's tax liability. If AGI is more than $150,000, the percentage increases to 110%. • The accuracy-related penalty applies when negligence or any substantial understatement occurs. The rate is 20% of the tax due. • Fraud penalties are 75% on any portion of the understatement of tax that is attributable to fraud. • A 20% penalty for erroneous claim for refund or credit could be assessed by the IRS if the amount is found to be excessive.

Discussion Questions connect

All applicable discussion questions are available with ***Connect***©

EA LO 2-1 1. What is a *for* AGI deduction? Give three examples.

EA LO 2-2 2. What are the five types of filing status?

EA LO 2-2 3. What qualifications are necessary to file as head of household?

EA LO 2-2 4. George and Debbie were legally married on December 31, 2017. Can they file their 2017 income tax return using the status of married filing jointly? Why or why not? What other filing status choices do they have, if any?

EA LO 2-3, 2-4 5. What is the amount of the personal and dependency exemptions for 2017?

EA LO 2-4 6. What are the three general tests that a qualifying person must meet to be a dependent of the taxpayer?

EA LO 2-4 7. What are the five specific tests necessary to be a qualifying child of the taxpayer?

EA LO 2-4 8. What age must a child be at the end of the year to meet the age test under the qualifying child rules?

EA LO 2-4 9. What are the four specific tests necessary to be a qualifying relative of the taxpayer?

EA LO 2-4 10. What is a multiple support agreement, and what is its purpose?

EA LO 2-4 11. Mimi is 22 years old and is a full-time student at Ocean County Community College. She lives with her parents, who provide all of her support. During the summer, she put her Web design skills to work and earned $4,150. Can Mimi's parents claim her as a dependent on their joint tax return? Why or why not? Assume that all five tests under qualifying child are met.

EA LO 2-5 12. What is the standard deduction for each filing status?

EA LO 2-6 13. Under what circumstances must a taxpayer use a tax rate schedule rather than using a tax table?

EA LO 2-7 14. When and at what rate is interest calculated on amounts owed to the IRS?

____

____

____

EA LO 2-7 15. Prepare a table of the possible IRS penalties listed in the text and give a brief summary of the purpose of each penalty.

IRS Penalties	Purpose of Penalty

Multiple-Choice Questions connect

All applicable multiple-choice questions are available with ***Connect***©

EA LO 2-1 16. A single taxpayer is 26 years old and has wages of $18,000 and interest income of $450. Which is the simplest tax form this person can file?

a. 1040.
b. 1040EZ.
c. 1040A.
d. 1040Z.

EA LO 2-1 17. Payment of alimony by the taxpayer is a *for* AGI deduction. Which form can the taxpayer use to claim this benefit?

a. Either 1040 or 1040A.
b. 1040.
c. 1040A.
d. None of the above.

EA LO 2-2 18. A taxpayer is married with a qualifying child (dependent), but she has been living separately from her spouse for the last eight months of the year. However, she paid for more than half of the cost of keeping up the household. Her spouse does not want to file jointly. What filing status must she use when filing her tax return? She wants to obtain the maximum legal benefit.

a. Married filing separately.
b. Single.
c. Qualifying widow(er).
d. Head of household.

EA LO 2-2 19. A taxpayer's spouse died on December 31, 2016. He has no qualifying child. Which status should the taxpayer select when filing his 2017 tax return?

a. Qualifying widow(er).
b. Married filing jointly.
c. Single.
d. Married filing separately.

EA LO 2-3 20. Esmeralda is 20 years of age and a full-time student living with her parents. She had wages of $500 ($50 of income tax withholding) for 2017. Can Esmeralda claim her own exemption on her return even though her parents will claim her as a dependent?

a. Yes, Esmeralda can claim the exemption.

b. No, Esmeralda cannot claim the exemption.

c. Esmeralda and her parents can both claim the exemption.

d. No one can claim the exemption for Esmeralda.

EA LO 2-3, 2-4 21. What is the amount of the personal and dependency exemptions for 2017?

a. $3,950.

b. $4,100.

c. $4,000.

d. $4,050.

EA LO 2-4 22. To be a qualifying child, the taxpayer must meet three general tests and five specific tests. Which of the following is *not* part of the five specific tests?

a. Support test.

b. Age test.

c. Gross income test.

d. Relationship test.

EA LO 2-4 23. To be a qualifying relative, who has to live in the home of the taxpayer for the entire year?

a. Cousin.

b. Child.

c. Stepchild.

d. Father.

EA LO 2-5 24. Which amount represents the standard deduction for a taxpayer who is 44 years old and claiming head of household status?

a. $9,250.

b. $9,300.

c. $9,350.

d. $6,350.

EA LO 2-5 25. A married couple, both of whom are under 65 years old, decided to file as married filing separately. One of the spouses is going to itemize deductions instead of taking the standard deduction. What is the standard deduction permitted to the other spouse when she files her tax return?

a. $12,700.

b. $9,350.

c. $6,350.

d. $0.

EA LO 2-6 26. Employers are required to withhold social security taxes from wages paid to employees. What is the amount of the social security wage limitation for 2017?

a. $127,200.

b. $118,500.

c. $113,700.

d. $106,800.

EA **LO 2-6** 27. What is the amount of the tax liability for a married couple filing jointly with taxable income of $135,500?

a. $33,875.
b. $28,333.
c. $20,325.
d. $25,353.

EA **LO 2-7** 28. What is the percentage of interest the IRS was charging on assessment (amount of unpaid tax liability) during March 2017? You might want to do this research by going to the IRS Web site (www.irs.gov).

a. 6%.
b. 5%.
c. 3%.
d. 4%.

EA **LO 2-7** 29. When there is negligence on a return, the IRS charges a penalty of ______ of the tax due.

a. 25%.
b. 20%.
c. 18%.
d. 10%.

EA **LO 2-7** 30. When there is fraud on a return, the IRS charges a penalty of ______ on any portion of understatement of tax that is attributable to the fraud.

a. 20%.
b. 25%.
c. 75%.
d. 100%.

Problems connect

All applicable problems are available with ***Connect***©

EA **LO 2-1** 31. The benefits of many deductions, credits, or other benefits are limited to taxpayers with Adjusted Gross Income below certain limits.

a. Explain how the limitation (phaseout) process works.

____
____
____

b. Give two examples of deductions, credits, or other benefits that are limited.

____
____

c. Why would Congress wish to limit the benefits of these items?

____
____

EA **LO 2-2** 32. List the five types of filing status and briefly explain the requirements for the use of each one.

____
____
____
____
____

EA LO 2-2 33. In which of the following cases may the taxpayer claim head of household filing status?

a. The taxpayer is single and maintains a household that is the principal place of abode of her infant son.

____

b. The taxpayer is single, maintains a household for herself, and maintains a separate household that is the principal place of abode of her dependent widowed mother.

____

c. The taxpayer was married from January to October and lived with his spouse from January to May. From June 1 to December 31, the taxpayer maintained a household that was the principal place of abode of his married son and daughter-in-law, whom the taxpayer can claim as dependents.

____

d. Same as (c) except the taxpayer lived with his ex-spouse until August and maintained the household from September 1 to the end of the year.

____

EA LO 2-3 34. How many personal exemptions can a taxpayer claim on his or her tax return? Explain your answer.

____

____

____

____

EA LO 2-4 35. Roberta is widowed and lives in an apartment complex. She receives $8,000 of social security income that she uses to pay for rent and other household expenses. The remainder of her living expenses is paid by relatives and neighbors. The total amount of support paid by Roberta and the others totals $22,000. Amounts paid for support during the year are as follows:

Roberta	$8,000
Ed (neighbor)	4,000
Bill (son)	5,000
Jose (neighbor)	2,000
Alicia (niece)	3,000

a. Which of these persons is entitled to claim Roberta as a dependent absent a multiple support agreement?

____

b. Under a multiple support agreement, which of these persons is entitled to claim Roberta as a dependent? Explain your answer.

____

c. If Roberta saved all of her social security income and the other persons paid for the shortfall in the same proportions as shown, which of these persons would be entitled to claim Roberta as a dependent under a multiple support agreement? Explain your answer.

____

____

EA LO 2-4 36. Shandra is a U.S. citizen and is the 68-year-old widowed mother of Janet. After retirement, Shandra decided to fulfill a lifelong dream and move to Paris. Shandra receives $1,000 of interest income, but all of her other living expenses (including rent on her Paris apartment with spectacular views of the Eiffel Tower) are paid by Janet. Janet resides in Chicago. Is Janet entitled to a dependency exemption for Shandra? Explain your answer.

EA LO 2-5 37. Donald is a 21-year-old full-time college student. During 2017 he earned $2,550 from a part-time job and $1,150 in interest income. If Donald is a dependent of his parents, what is his standard deduction amount? If Donald supports himself and is not a dependent of someone else, what is his standard deduction amount?

EA LO 2-5 38. Raphael and Martina are engaged and are planning to travel to Las Vegas during the 2017 Christmas season and get married around the end of the year. In 2017 Raphael expects to earn $45,000 and Martina expects to earn $15,000. Their employers have deducted the appropriate amount of withholding from their paychecks throughout the year. Neither Raphael nor Martina has any itemized deductions. They are trying to decide whether they should get married on December 31, 2017, or on January 1, 2018. What do you recommend? Explain your answer.

EA LO 2-5 39. Determine the amount of the standard deduction for each of the following taxpayers for tax year 2017:

a. Christina, who is single.

b. Adrian and Carol, who are filing a joint return. Their son is blind.

c. Peter and Elizabeth, who are married and file separate tax returns. Elizabeth will itemize her deductions.

d. Karen, who earned $1,100 working a part-time job. She can be claimed as a dependent by her parents.

e. Rodolfo, who is over 65 and is single.

f. Bernard, who is a nonresident alien with U.S. income.

g. Manuel, who is 70, and Esther, who is 63 and blind, will file a joint return.

h. Herman, who is 75 and a qualifying widower with a dependent child.

EA LO 2-6 40. Using the appropriate tax tables or tax rate schedules, determine the amount of tax liability in each of the following instances:

a. A married couple filing jointly with taxable income of $32,991.

____

b. A married couple filing jointly with taxable income of $192,257.

____

c. A married couple filing separately, one spouse with taxable income of $43,885 and the other with $56,218.

____

d. A single person with taxable income of $79,436.

____

e. A single person with taxable income of $297,784.

____

f. A head of household with taxable income of $96,592.

____

g. A qualifying widow with taxable income of $14,019.

____

h. A married couple filing jointly with taxable income of $11,216.

____

EA LO 2-6 41. Determine the average tax rate and the marginal tax rate for each instance in question 40.

a. Average = ______________________ Marginal = ______________________
b. Average = ______________________ Marginal = ______________________
c. Average = ______________________ Marginal = ______________________
d. Average = ______________________ Marginal = ______________________
e. Average = ______________________ Marginal = ______________________
f. Average = ______________________ Marginal = ______________________
g. Average = ______________________ Marginal = ______________________
h. Average = ______________________ Marginal = ______________________

EA LO 2-6 42. Using the appropriate tax tables or tax rate schedules, determine the tax liability for tax year 2017 in each of the following instances. In each case, assume the taxpayer can take only the standard deduction.

a. A single taxpayer, not head of household, with AGI of $23,493 and one dependent.

____

b. A single taxpayer, not head of household, with AGI of $169,783 and no dependents.

____

c. A married couple filing jointly with AGI of $39,945 and two dependents.

____

d. A married couple filing jointly with AGI of $162,288 and three dependents.

____

e. A married couple filing jointly with AGI of $301,947 and one dependent.

____

f. A taxpayer filing married filing separately with AGI of $68,996 and one dependent.

____

g. A qualifying widow, age 66, with AGI of $49,240 and one dependent.

____

h. A head of household with AGI of $14,392 and two dependents.

____

i. A head of household with AGI of $59,226 and one dependent.

____

EA LO 2-7 43. Victoria's 2017 tax return was due on April 15, 2018, but she did not file it until June 12, 2018. Victoria did not file an extension. The tax due on the tax return when filed was $8,500. In 2017, Victoria paid in $12,000 through withholding. Her 2016 tax liability was $11,500. Victoria's AGI for 2017 is less than $150,000. How much penalty will Victoria have to pay (disregard interest)?

____

____

____

____

____

EA LO 2-7 44. Paul has the following information:

AGI for 2017	$155,000
Withholding for 2017	24,000
Total tax for 2016	29,000
Total tax for 2017	33,470

a. How much must Paul pay in estimated taxes to avoid a penalty?

____

____

____

b. If Paul had paid $1,000 per quarter, would he have avoided the estimated tax penalty?

____

____

EA LO 2-7 45. Charles and Joan Thompson file a joint return. In 2016 they had taxable income of $92,370 and paid tax of $14,636. Charles is an advertising executive, and Joan is a college professor. During the fall 2017 semester, Joan is planning to take a leave of absence without pay. The Thompsons expect their taxable income to drop to $70,000 in 2017. They expect their 2017 tax liability will be $9,571, which will be the approximate amount of their withholding. Joan anticipates that she will work on academic research during the fall semester.

During September, Joan decides to perform consulting services for some local businesses. Charles and Joan had not anticipated this development. Joan is paid a total of $35,000 during October, November, and December for her work.

What estimated tax payments are Charles and Joan required to make, if any, for tax year 2017? Do you anticipate that the Thompsons will be required to pay an underpayment penalty when they file their 2017 tax return? Explain your answer.

____

____

____

____

____

Tax Return Problems

All applicable tax return problems are available with ***Connect***©

Use your tax software to complete the following problems. If you are manually preparing the tax returns, you will need to use a Form 1040 or Form 1040A, depending on the complexity of the problem. *Note to instructors and students:* When using software, certain tax credits, such as the Child Tax Credit, may appear on the tax return even though we have not yet discussed those tax credits. This occurs because the taxpayer may be entitled to the credits and the software will automatically include the credit on the final tax return.

Tax Return Problem 1

Jose and Dora Hernandez are married filing jointly. They are 50 and 45 years old, respectively. Their address is 32010 Lake Street, Atlanta, GA 30294. Additional information about Mr. and Mrs. Hernandez is as follows:

Social security numbers:

Jose: 412-34-5670	Dora: 412-34-5671
Date of birth: 4/23/1967	Date of birth: 7/12/1972
W-2 for Jose shows these amounts:	W-2 for Dora shows these amounts:
Wages (box 1) = $45,800.00	Wages (box 1) = $31,000.00
Federal W/H (box 2) = $ 6,160.00	Federal W/H (box 2) = $ 3,650.00
Social security wages (box 3) = $45,800.00	Social security wages (box 3) = $31,000.00
Social security W/H (box 4) = $ 2,839.60	Social security W/H (box 4) = $ 1,922.00
Medicare wages (box 5) = $45,800.00	Medicare wages (box 5) = $31,000.00
Medicare W/H (box 6) = $ 664.10	Medicare W/H (box 6) = $ 449.50

Form 1099-INT for Jose and Dora shows this amount:

Box 1 = $300.00 from City Bank.

Dependent: Daughter Adela is 5 years old. Her date of birth is 3/15/2012. Her social security number is 412-34-5672.

Jose is a store manager, and Dora is a receptionist.

Prepare the tax return for Mr. and Mrs. Hernandez using the appropriate form. They are entitled to a $1,000 child tax credit (this credit is discussed in Chapter 9). For now, enter the credit on the appropriate line of the form. They want to contribute to the presidential election campaign. Mr. and Mrs. Hernandez had qualifying health care coverage at all times during the tax year.

Tax Return Problem 2

Marie Lincoln is a head of household. She is 37 years old and her address is 4110 N.E. 13th Street, Miami, FL 33127. Additional information about Ms. Lincoln is as follows:

Social security number: 412-34-5670

Date of birth: 1/14/1980

W-2 for Marie shows these amounts:

Wages (box 1) = $43,600.00
Federal W/H (box 2) = $ 4,540.00
Social security wages (box 3) = $43,600.00
Social security W/H (box 4) = $ 2,703.20
Medicare wages (box 5) = $43,600.00
Medicare W/H (box 6) = $ 632.20

Form 1099-INT for Marie shows this amount:

Box 1 = $500.00 from A & D Bank.

Dependent: Son Steven is 10 years old. His date of birth is 5/11/2007. His social security number is 412-34-5672.

Marie is an administrative assistant.

Prepare the tax return for Ms. Lincoln using the appropriate form. She is entitled to a $1,000 child tax credit (this credit is discussed in Chapter 9). For now, enter the credit on the appropriate line of the form. She wants to contribute to the presidential election campaign. Ms. Lincoln had qualifying health care coverage at all times during the tax year.

Tax Return Problem 3 Margaret O'Hara has been divorced for about two years. She is 28 years old, and her address is 979 Adams Street, Jacksonville, FL 32202. Additional information about Ms. O'Hara is as follows:

Social security number: 412-34-5670

Date of birth: 6/17/1989

Alimony received = $24,000.00

W-2 for Margaret shows these amounts:

Wages (box 1) =	$38,000.00
Federal W/H (box 2) =	$ 9,500.00
Social security wages (box 3) =	$38,000.00
Social security W/H (box 4) =	$ 2,356.00
Medicare wages (box 5) =	$38,000.00
Medicare W/H (box 6) =	$ 551.00

Margaret is a research assistant.

Prepare the tax return for Ms. O'Hara using the appropriate form. She does not want to contribute to the presidential election campaign. Ms. O'Hara had qualifying health care coverage at all times during the tax year.

We have provided selected filled-in source documents that are available in the *Connect Library*.

Chapter Three

Gross Income: Inclusions and Exclusions

We now explore the details associated with a tax return. This chapter covers many of the items that compose *gross income*. These items are reported on lines 7 to 14 on Form 1040A or lines 7 to 21 on Form 1040.

Learning Objectives

When you have completed this chapter, you should understand the following learning objectives (LO):

LO 3-1 Describe when and how to record income for tax purposes.

LO 3-2 Apply the cash method of accounting to income taxes.

LO 3-3 Explain the taxability of components of gross income, including interest, dividends, tax refunds, and social security benefits.

LO 3-4 Apply the rules concerning items excluded from gross income.

LO 3-5 Apply the rules associated with tax accounting for savings bond interest used for education expenses, below-market interest loans, gift loans, and original issue discount debt (Appendix).

INTRODUCTION

This chapter encompasses major components of total income (line 15 on Form 1040A or line 22 on Form 1040) and many types of nontaxable income. Total income is composed of gross income (excluding nontaxable income) minus permitted deductions.

You will recall that gross income is ". . . all income from whatever source derived . . ."[1] Obviously, gross income is an extremely broad, all-encompassing concept. Much of this book is devoted to the discussion of various components of gross income and taxable income.

Not all income is subject to tax. In practice, all income is gross income unless the Internal Revenue Code (IRC) specifically excludes it from taxation. In this chapter, you will learn about many gross income exclusions.

WHEN AND HOW TO RECORD INCOME

LO 3-1

Accountants record (recognize) income for financial statement purposes when it is both realized and earned (the *accrual method of accounting*). *Realization* is the process of converting a noncash resource into cash or a right to cash. Conversion occurs when a company or person

[1] IRC § 61(a).

exchanges a noncash asset or resource for cash or a receivable in a transaction with a third party. Although the most commonly used example is selling inventory for cash or an account receivable, the realization concept applies to professional services (exchanging knowledge for cash), asset sales (exchanging a building for cash or a right to cash), licensing a patent (exchanging an idea for cash or a right to cash), or wages (exchanging time, knowledge, and effort for cash).

Income has been earned when companies or persons have performed all actions necessary to complete the transaction. When a grocery store sells you a can of beans, it has earned the income because it has done everything it needs to do to complete the transaction. The store does not need to open the can, heat the contents, and serve you at the dinner table.

For tax purposes, income recognition follows similar rules with a few twists. In general, an individual must recognize income on his or her tax return if a transaction meets *all* of the following three conditions:

- There must be an economic benefit. If a person is economically better off because of a transaction, the person must normally record income. If someone works for an employer and receives cash for that work, the person has income. If a person sells his or her car to a friend for a note receivable, the person has income.[2] It is important to note that the benefit may be indirect. If an accountant performs some tax work for a client and the client agrees to pay a $500 debt the accountant owes to a local bank, the accountant has $500 of income because he or she has received an economic benefit (less debt) even if the $500 cash was never in the possession of the accountant.
- A transaction must actually have reached a conclusion. Two factors are at work here. First, a transaction must occur. Simply owning an asset that has increased in value does not create income (even though there may be an economic benefit). If an individual owns 100 shares of IBM common stock and the stock increases in price by $1 per share, no income will result because no transaction has occurred. The second factor is that the transaction process must be complete. Often a time gap occurs between the agreement to enter into a transaction and the completion of the transaction. In general, the completion date is the date when income is recognized.
- Finally, the income cannot be tax-exempt. Certain income is statutorily excluded from taxation and will not be included in gross income even if the preceding two conditions are met.

EXAMPLE 3-1

On December 29, 2016, Raul agreed to repair a damaged roof and started to work on that date. On January 6, 2017, he completed the job and received payment. Raul would record income in 2017, not 2016.

CONCEPT CHECK 3-1— LO 3-1

1. An individual must recognize income on his or her tax return if the transaction meets three conditions. Name the three conditions: ______________________________, ______________________________, ______________________________.
2. An individual can exclude certain income from taxation even though a transaction that has economic benefits has occurred. True or false?

[2] Taxpayers likely have a "cost" or "basis" that can be subtracted from the proceeds to arrive at the net amount of income that must be reported.

CASH METHOD OF ACCOUNTING

LO 3-2

Almost all individuals use the cash receipts and disbursements method of accounting.[3] Unincorporated businesses without inventories often use the cash method as well. Under the *cash method,* a taxpayer reports income in the year he or she receives or constructively receives the income rather than the year in which the taxpayer earns the income. *Constructive receipt* means that the income is available to or in the control of the taxpayer regardless of whether the taxpayer chooses to utilize the income. Thus interest credited to a taxpayer's savings account on December 31 is income in the year credited, not the year withdrawn.

Income can be "realized in any form, whether in money, property, or services."[4] Note that even cash basis taxpayers do not actually have to receive cash before they record income (although that is quite often the case). Receipt of property or services triggers income recognition. Furthermore, taxpayers recognize income even if they receive it indirectly.

EXAMPLE 3-2

If a lawyer agrees to give legal advice to a neighbor in exchange for the neighbor agreeing to paint the lawyer's house, both parties will have income equal to the fair market value of the services received by them.

EXAMPLE 3-3

Heather owns an unincorporated cash basis architectural firm. She performs architectural services for a client during December 2016. She completed the work in 2016 (so the income was earned), but she did not receive payment by the end of the year. Heather received payment for her services on January 23, 2017, and recognizes income in 2017.

EXAMPLE 3-4

Antonio provided golf lessons worth $300 to Arturo in December 2016. Antonio owed Millie $300, and he asked Arturo to pay the $300 to Millie. In January 2017 Arturo paid Millie $300. Antonio recognizes income of $300 in 2017.

In some instances, a cash basis taxpayer can report income as though he or she were an accrual basis taxpayer. For instance, in the case of interest income on Series EE and Series I U.S. savings bonds, taxpayers can defer the income until the maturity of the bond or can elect to report the interest annually.[5] Special rules also apply to farmers and ranchers, who can elect to average their income over a three-year period and can elect to defer certain insurance proceeds and federal disaster payments.[6]

CONCEPT CHECK 3-2— LO 3-2

1. Income may be realized in any form, whether in money, property, or services. True or false?
2. If you provide consulting services to your friend and, in exchange, he fixes your car, you and your friend must report on both tax returns the fair market value of the services provided. True or false?

[3] The method of accounting (cash or accrual) used for an individual taxpayer's first tax return effectively establishes that person's accounting method. See Reg. § 1.446-1(c)(1)(i). Thus, although it is possible that an individual can use the accrual method of accounting, it is unlikely that he or she uses the accrual method for the first return.

[4] Reg. § 1.61-1(a).

[5] IRC § 454.

[6] IRC § 1301 and IRC § 451(d).

TAXABILITY OF COMPONENTS OF GROSS INCOME

LO 3-3

This section discusses the taxability of various types of gross income, including interest, dividends, tax refunds, and social security benefits.

Interest Income (Forms 1040A and 1040, line 8)

Recall that interest is compensation for the use of money with respect to a bona fide debt or obligation imposed by law. For most individuals, interest income comes from interest-earning deposits at financial institutions—banks, savings and loans, or credit unions. These institutions report interest income to taxpayers on Form 1099-INT. Taxpayers can also earn interest income in other ways not reported on an IRS form. An example is a creditor–debtor arrangement between two individuals in which taxpayer A lends some money to taxpayer B and taxpayer A receives $50 in interest. In this instance, taxpayer A would earn interest income, but no IRS document would be required to record the interest income.

Some tax issues pertaining to interest income are complex and less common. These include below-market interest rate loans, gifts, shareholder and similar loans, and interest from original issue discount (OID). The Appendix of this chapter provides further details about these subjects. Next we discuss common types of interest income.

Interest on U.S. Savings Bonds

Individuals purchased Series EE and Series E (before July 1980) U.S. savings bonds at a discount from face value. The owners of the bonds do not receive a periodic cash interest payment. Instead the face value of the bond increases over the period to maturity, and that increase represents the amount of interest earned. The owner of such bonds can defer reporting any interest (that is, the increase in bond value) until the bonds mature, are redeemed, or are otherwise disposed of, whichever comes first. Alternatively, the owner can elect to report the annual increase in face value as interest income on each year's income tax return (on an accrual basis).[7] Such election applies to all bonds owned at the time of the election and to any bonds subsequently acquired.

EXAMPLE 3-5

Donna purchased a $1,000 face value Series EE U.S. savings bond for $500 on January 1, 2017. The bond earned interest at a rate of 6% throughout 2017 so that at year-end, the bond had a face value of $530. If Donna does nothing, she does not need to report the $30 interest income for 2017 until she cashes the bond upon maturity. Alternatively, Donna can elect to report the $30 as interest income in 2017. If she does, she must report all future interest income on the bond in the same manner.

Until August 2004, the U.S. Treasury sold Series HH bonds at face value. Interest on these bonds is paid by check semiannually and is included in income in the year received.

Tax-Exempt Interest

Certain interest income is exempt from taxation. Taxpayers can exclude from gross income any interest earned on bonds issued by any state, any possession of the United States, any political subdivision of either of the foregoing, or the District of Columbia (such as municipal bonds).[8] However, interest is taxable if received from state or local bonds issued for private activities such as convention centers, industrial parks, or stadiums.[9]

[7] IRC § 454(a).

[8] IRC § 103(a), IRC § 103(c).

[9] IRC § 103(b)(1).

From Shoebox to Software Interest Income

Taxable interest income is on line 8a of Form 1040A and Form 1040. Tax-exempt interest is on line 8b. If any of the following is true, the taxpayer must complete and file Schedule B (Forms 1040A and 1040):

- Had more than $1,500 of interest income.
- Received seller-financed mortgage interest.
- Received tax-exempt interest in any amount.
- Received interest as a nominee.
- Claimed an exclusion for interest on Series EE U.S. savings bonds issued after 1989 or Series I bonds.
- Reported any adjustments for accrued interest, amortizable bond premium, or original issue discount (see the Appendix at the end of this chapter).
- Had a foreign account; received a distribution from or was the grantor of or a transferor to a foreign trust.

Schedule B is shown in Exhibit 3-1. The total from line 4 of the applicable schedule is reported on line 8a of Form 1040A or Form 1040, as appropriate.

Information concerning interest income comes from a number of sources:

- If interest is received from a financial institution, corporation, or branch of government, the taxpayer will receive Form 1099-INT that will indicate, in box 1, the amount of interest received or credited to the taxpayer's account during the year. Form 1099-INT is shown in Exhibit 3-2.
- Taxpayers who are partners of a partnership or who are shareholders of a Subchapter S corporation will receive Schedule K-1 that will reflect the taxpayer's proportionate share of interest income. We discuss partnerships and Subchapter S corporations in Chapters 14 and 15, respectively.
- If the taxpayer owns bonds that were purchased at a discount (see the chapter Appendix), the taxpayer should receive Form 1099-OID showing, in box 1, the amount of original issue discount that must be reported as income in the current year. A Form 1099-OID is shown in Exhibit 3-3.
- Taxpayers who receive interest from other sources will need to calculate the appropriate amount of interest to include on Schedule B. Other sources of interest income include
  - Payments received from seller-financed mortgages.
  - Receipts from installment sale receivables or other receivables received over time.
  - Imputed interest on loans made at a below-market interest rate (see the chapter Appendix).
  - Interest on bonds sold between interest dates.

When using the tax software, you record the information from all Forms 1099 received onto the appropriate input form in the Documents Received section.

Taxpayers who are eligible to exclude U.S. savings bond interest because they paid qualified higher education expenses (see the chapter Appendix) must complete Form 8815 and attach it to their tax return. With the tax software, you enter the required information directly on Form 8815.

Self-employed individuals who receive interest income as a part of their business report the amounts on Schedule C (see Chapter 6).

CONCEPT CHECK 3-3— LO 3-3

1. All interest received from state or local bonds is not taxable. True or false?
2. Schedule B (Forms 1040A and 1040) is required if an individual receives $1,500 of interest for the tax year. True or false?

Dividends (Form 1040 and Form 1040A, line 9)

Dividends are distributions of property by a corporation to its shareholders. Dividends are generally taxed at capital gains rates to the extent they are made from either a corporation's current earnings and profits or its accumulated earnings and profits.[10] Distributions in excess of earnings and profits represent a nontaxable return of capital that reduces the taxpayer's cost basis in the stock. If the distribution is greater than the basis of the stock, the excess is a capital gain.[11]

[10] IRC § 316(a). Earnings and profits are similar, but not identical, to retained earnings for financial statement purposes. Earnings and profits are beyond the scope of this book.

[11] IRC § 301(c).

EXHIBIT 3-1

SCHEDULE B (Form 1040A or 1040)
Department of the Treasury Internal Revenue Service (99)

Interest and Ordinary Dividends

▶ Attach to Form 1040A or 1040.
▶ Go to *www.irs.gov/ScheduleB* for instructions and the latest information.

OMB No. 1545-0074
2017
Attachment Sequence No. 08

Name(s) shown on return | **Your social security number**

Part I Interest

(See instructions and the instructions for Form 1040A, or Form 1040, line 8a.)

Note: If you received a Form 1099-INT, Form 1099-OID, or substitute statement from a brokerage firm, list the firm's name as the payer and enter the total interest shown on that form.

			Amount
1	List name of payer. If any interest is from a seller-financed mortgage and the buyer used the property as a personal residence, see the instructions and list this interest first. Also, show that buyer's social security number and address ▶	1	
2	Add the amounts on line 1	2	
3	Excludable interest on series EE and I U.S. savings bonds issued after 1989. Attach Form 8815	3	
4	Subtract line 3 from line 2. Enter the result here and on Form 1040A, or Form 1040, line 8a ▶	4	

Note: If line 4 is over $1,500, you must complete Part III.

Part II Ordinary Dividends

(See instructions and the instructions for Form 1040A, or Form 1040, line 9a.)

Note: If you received a Form 1099-DIV or substitute statement from a brokerage firm, list the firm's name as the payer and enter the ordinary dividends shown on that form.

			Amount
5	List name of payer ▶	5	
6	Add the amounts on line 5. Enter the total here and on Form 1040A, or Form 1040, line 9a ▶	6	

Note: If line 6 is over $1,500, you must complete Part III.

Part III Foreign Accounts and Trusts

(See instructions.)

You must complete this part if you **(a)** had over $1,500 of taxable interest or ordinary dividends; **(b)** had a foreign account; or **(c)** received a distribution from, or were a grantor of, or a transferor to, a foreign trust.

		Yes	**No**
7a	At any time during 2017, did you have a financial interest in or signature authority over a financial account (such as a bank account, securities account, or brokerage account) located in a foreign country? See instructions		
	If "Yes," are you required to file FinCEN Form 114, Report of Foreign Bank and Financial Accounts (FBAR), to report that financial interest or signature authority? See FinCEN Form 114 and its instructions for filing requirements and exceptions to those requirements		
b	If you are required to file FinCEN Form 114, enter the name of the foreign country where the financial account is located ▶		
8	During 2017, did you receive a distribution from, or were you the grantor of, or transferor to, a foreign trust? If "Yes," you may have to file Form 3520. See instructions		

For Paperwork Reduction Act Notice, see your tax return instructions. Cat. No. 17146N **Schedule B (Form 1040A or 1040) 2017**

Source: U.S. Department of the Treasury, Internal Revenue Service, SCHEDULE B Form 1040A or 1040. Washington, DC: 2017.

EXHIBIT 3-2

☐ CORRECTED (if checked)

PAYER'S name, street address, city or town, state or province, country, ZIP or foreign postal code, and telephone no.

Payer's RTN (optional)

OMB No. 1545-0112

2017

Form 1099-INT

Interest Income

1 Interest income
$

2 Early withdrawal penalty
$

Copy B

For Recipient

PAYER'S federal identification number | RECIPIENT'S identification number

3 Interest on U.S. Savings Bonds and Treas. obligations
$

RECIPIENT'S name

4 Federal income tax withheld
$

5 Investment expenses
$

Street address (including apt. no.)

6 Foreign tax paid
$

7 Foreign country or U.S. possession

8 Tax-exempt interest
$

9 Specified private activity bond interest
$

City or town, state or province, country, and ZIP or foreign postal code

10 Market discount
$

11 Bond premium
$

FATCA filing requirement ☐

12 Bond premium on Treasury obligations
$

13 Bond premium on tax-exempt bond
$

This is important tax information and is being furnished to the Internal Revenue Service. If you are required to file a return, a negligence penalty or other sanction may be imposed on you if this income is taxable and the IRS determines that it has not been reported.

Account number (see instructions)

14 Tax-exempt and tax credit bond CUSIP no.

15 State | 16 State identification no. | 17 State tax withheld
$
$

Form **1099-INT** (keep for your records) www.irs.gov/form1099int Department of the Treasury - Internal Revenue Service

Source: U.S. Department of the Treasury, Internal Revenue Service, Form 1099-INT. Washington, DC: 2017.

EXHIBIT 3-3

☐ CORRECTED (if checked)

PAYER'S name, street address, city or town, state or province, country, ZIP or foreign postal code, and telephone no.

1 Original issue discount for 2017*
$

* This may not be the correct figure to report on your income tax return. See instructions on the back.

OMB No. 1545-0117

2017

Form 1099-OID

Original Issue Discount

2 Other periodic interest
$

PAYER'S federal identification number | RECIPIENT'S identification number

3 Early withdrawal penalty
$

4 Federal income tax withheld
$

Copy B

For Recipient

5 Market discount
$

6 Acquisition premium
$

RECIPIENT'S name

7 Description

Street address (including apt. no.)

City or town, state or province, country, and ZIP or foreign postal code

8 Original issue discount on U.S. Treasury obligations*
$

9 Investment expenses
$

This is important tax information and is being furnished to the Internal Revenue Service. If you are required to file a return, a negligence penalty or other sanction may be imposed on you if this income is taxable and the IRS determines that it has not been reported.

FATCA filing requirement ☐

10 Bond premium
$

11 Tax-exempt OID
$

Account number (see instructions)

12 State | 13 State identification no. | 14 State tax withheld
$
$

Form **1099-OID** (keep for your records) www.irs.gov/form1099oid Department of the Treasury - Internal Revenue Service

Source: U.S. Department of the Treasury, Internal Revenue Service, Form 1099-OID. Washington, DC: 2017.

Corporations normally pay dividends in the form of cash, but they may pay them in property or anything of economic value. The basis of the property received as a dividend in the hands of the shareholder is the property's fair market value at the date of distribution.[12]

A *stock dividend* is a distribution of shares of the corporation's own stock to shareholders. Stock dividends (and stock splits) are generally not taxable to a shareholder.[13] Shareholders allocate the basis of the stock originally held between the old and the new stock in proportion to the fair market value of each on the date of the distribution. Certain stock dividends are taxable, including these:

- Stock dividends in which a shareholder has the option to receive stock or cash or other property.
- Disproportionate dividends in which some shareholders receive property and other shareholders receive an increase in their stock interest in the corporation.
- Distributions of preferred stock to some common shareholders and common stock to other common shareholders.
- Distributions made on preferred stock.[14]

Mutual funds (known as *regulated investment companies*) are entities that pool the financial resources of thousands of individuals to purchase stocks or bonds. Mutual funds are required to distribute the income they receive, whether in the form of dividends from holding stocks or capital gains and losses from sales of a portion of the portfolio. Real estate investment trusts make similar distributions.

Taxation of Dividends

To this point in the text, all income is the same for purposes of determining the amount of tax. However, certain types of income are taxed at different rates.

Prior to passage of the 2003 Jobs and Growth Act (the "2003 Act") in June 2003, dividends and ordinary income were taxed at the same rate. The 2003 Act states that qualified dividends received in 2003 or later may receive preferential treatment.[15] Specifically, when an individual's marginal ordinary income tax rate is 25% or more, the taxation rate on qualified dividends is 15% with the exception starting in 2015 that if an individual's marginal ordinary income tax rate is 39.60%, the tax rate on qualified dividends is 20%. When the marginal rate is less than 25%, the tax rate on qualified dividends is 0% for years beginning after 2007.

Qualified dividends (1) are made from the earnings and profits of the payer corporation and (2) are from domestic corporations or qualified foreign corporations.[16]

EXAMPLE 3-6

Refer to the tax rate schedules inside the front cover of the text. A single individual who has taxable income of $110,000 before dividends will be in the 28% marginal tax bracket. If that individual then receives a qualified dividend of $1,000, the tax rate applied to the dividend would be 15%. The tax liability of the individual would be determined as follows:

Taxable income (before dividend)	$110,000.00
Less lower bracket amount	91,900
Income taxed at 28%	$ 18,100
Tax rate	× 28%
Tax at highest bracket	$ 5,068
Plus tax on first $91,900	18,713.75
Tax before dividend	$ 23,781.75
Tax on dividend ($1,000 × 15%)	150.00
Total tax liability	$ 23,931.75

[12] IRC § 301(d).

[13] IRC § 305(a).

[14] IRC § 1.305-5(a).

[15] IRC § 1(h)(11)(A).

[16] IRC § 1(h)(11)(B)(i).

From Shoebox to Software Dividends

Dividends are reported on line 9 of Form 1040A or Form 1040. A taxpayer who receives more than $1,500 of dividend income must complete and file Schedule B (Forms 1040A and 1040). Refer to Exhibit 3-1 for Schedule B. Note that Schedule B contains information about both interest and dividends. The total from line 6 of Schedule B is reported on line 9 of Forms 1040A or 1040.

Corporate and mutual fund payers are required to provide shareholders a Form 1099-DIV (see Exhibit 3-4) that indicates the amount of dividends in box 1a. Note that the amount in box 1b represents how much of box 1a is *qualified* dividends. If all dividends received by an individual are qualified dividends, the amount in box 1a will be the same as the amount in box 1b. The total amount of qualified dividends is reported on line 9b of Form 1040A or 1040.

Most taxpayers will have no other sources of dividend income other than that reported on Form 1099-DIV.

As was the case with interest payments reported on Form 1099-INT, any dividend income from Form 1099-DIV should be recorded in the tax software using the appropriate supporting form located in the Documents Received section of the software.

The example also illustrates that taxpayers add the dividend income "at the end" no matter when in the tax year they earned the dividend. In other words, tax is computed first on the nondividend income and then on the dividend income.

CONCEPT CHECK 3-4— LO 3-3

1. Qualified dividends arise from the earnings and profits of the payer corporation. True or false?
2. A corporation can pay only cash dividends to its shareholders. True or false?

EXHIBIT 3-4

☐ CORRECTED (if checked)

PAYER'S name, street address, city or town, state or province, country, ZIP or foreign postal code, and telephone no.	1a Total ordinary dividends $ 1b Qualified dividends $	OMB No. 1545-0110 2017 Form 1099-DIV	**Dividends and Distributions**
	2a Total capital gain distr. $	2b Unrecap. Sec. 1250 gain $	**Copy B For Recipient**
PAYER'S federal identification number | RECIPIENT'S identification number	2c Section 1202 gain $	2d Collectibles (28%) gain $	
RECIPIENT'S name	3 Nondividend distributions $	4 Federal income tax withheld $	This is important tax information and is being furnished to the Internal Revenue Service. If you are required to file a return, a negligence penalty or other sanction may be imposed on you if this income is taxable and the IRS determines that it has not been reported.
Street address (including apt. no.)		5 Investment expenses $	
City or town, state or province, country, and ZIP or foreign postal code	6 Foreign tax paid $	7 Foreign country or U.S. possession	
	8 Cash liquidation distributions $	9 Noncash liquidation distributions $	
FATCA filing requirement ☐	10 Exempt-interest dividends $	11 Specified private activity bond interest dividends $	
Account number (see instructions)	12 State | 13 State identification no.	14 State tax withheld $ $	

Form **1099-DIV** (keep for your records) www.irs.gov/form1099div Department of the Treasury - Internal Revenue Service

Source: U.S. Department of the Treasury, Internal Revenue Service, Form 1099-DIV. Washington, DC: 2017.

State and Local Tax Refunds (Form 1040, line 10)

Taxpayers may receive a refund of state or local taxes paid in a prior year. If a taxpayer deducted state or local taxes as an itemized deduction on Schedule A (see Chapter 5) in the prior year, the taxpayer must report the refund as income in the year in which it was received. The taxable amount is the lesser of (a) the amount received, (b) the amount deducted on Schedule A, or (c) the amount by which the itemized deductions exceed the standard deduction. If the taxpayer did not itemize deductions in the prior year (that is, the taxpayer took the standard deduction), no amount of the refund is taxable.[17]

EXAMPLE 3-7

Rose, who is single, reported itemized deductions of $9,900 on her 2016 tax return. Her itemized deductions included $1,150 of state taxes paid. In 2017 she received a $120 refund of state taxes paid in 2016. She must include the entire $120 in income in 2017.

EXAMPLE 3-8

Assume that Rose reported itemized deductions of $6,340 in 2016. Only $40 of her $120 tax refund would be taxable in 2017 because her itemized deductions exceeded her standard deduction by only $40 (in 2016, the standard deduction for single individuals was $6,300)

State and local tax refunds are reported to taxpayers on Form 1099-G, box 2 (see Exhibit 3-5). The applicable amount of the refund is reported on line 10 of Form 1040.

TAX YOUR BRAIN

Steve received a state tax refund of $200 from the state of California and, at the end of the year, received a Form 1099-G showing the payment in box 2. Must Steve report the refund on his Form 1040?

ANSWER

Not necessarily. Just because Steve received a 1099-G does not mean that the amount indicated in box 2 is actually taxable to him. Steve must determine whether he itemized deductions in the prior year and, if so, how much of the $200 is taxable based on how much tax benefit he received in the prior year, if any.

Unemployment Compensation (Form 1040A, line 13, or Form 1040, line 19)

Federal and state unemployment compensation benefits are taxable.[18] The rationale behind taxing these payments is that they are a substitute for taxable wages. Unemployment benefits are reported to recipients on Form 1099-G in box 1 (see Exhibit 3-5).

A taxpayer who repays some or all of the unemployment compensation received subtracts the repayment from the amount otherwise received. The repayment is reported by indicating, on line 13 (Form 1040A) or line 19 (Form 1040), the net amount of unemployment compensation received (amount received minus amount repaid) and, on the dotted line, writing *repaid* followed by the amount repaid.

[17] IRC § 111(a).

[18] IRC § 85(a), (b).

EXHIBIT 3-5

☐ CORRECTED (if checked)

PAYER'S name, street address, city or town, state or province, country, ZIP or foreign postal code, and telephone no.		1 Unemployment compensation $	OMB No. 1545-0120	**Certain Government Payments**
		2 State or local income tax refunds, credits, or offsets $	**2017** Form **1099-G**	
PAYER'S federal identification number	RECIPIENT'S identification number	3 Box 2 amount is for tax year	4 Federal income tax withheld $	**Copy B** **For Recipient**
RECIPIENT'S name		5 RTAA payments $	6 Taxable grants $	This is important tax information and is being furnished to the Internal Revenue Service. If you are required to file a return, a negligence penalty or other sanction may be imposed on you if this income is taxable and the IRS determines that it has not been reported.
Street address (including apt. no.)		7 Agriculture payments $	8 If checked, box 2 is trade or business income ▶ ☐	
City or town, state or province, country, and ZIP or foreign postal code		9 Market gain $		
Account number (see instructions)		10a State | 10b State identification no.	11 State income tax withheld $ $	

Form **1099-G** (keep for your records) www.irs.gov/form1099g Department of the Treasury - Internal Revenue Service

Source: U.S. Department of the Treasury, Internal Revenue Service, Form 1099-G. Washington, DC: 2017.

Social Security Benefits (Form 1040, line 20, or Form 1040A, line 14)

The taxability of social security benefits depends on the provisional income and filing status of the taxpayer.[19] The effect of the rules is to exclude social security benefits from taxation for lower-income individuals but tax up to 85% of benefits for taxpayers with higher income. You can find additional information concerning the tax treatment of social security benefits in IRS Publication 915.

Provisional income (also called *modified Adjusted Gross Income*) is calculated as follows:[20]

Adjusted Gross Income (before social security benefits)
Plus: Interest on U.S. savings bonds excluded for educational purposes[21]
Most tax-exempt interest[22]
Employer-provided adoption benefits[23]
Excluded foreign income[24]
Deducted interest on educational loans[25]
Deducted tuition and fees (Tax Extenders Act of 2008)
50% of social security benefits

[19] Social security benefits refer to the monthly retirement and disability benefits payable under social security and to tier-one railroad retirement benefits. They do not include tier-two railroad benefits or supplementary Medicare benefits that cover medical expenses.

[20] IRC § 86(b)(2).

[21] Interest excluded under IRC § 135.

[22] Exclusion under IRC § 103.

[23] IRC § 137.

[24] Under IRC § 911, 931, or 933.

[25] Interest deductible under IRC § 221.

From Shoebox to Software Social Security Benefits

Taxpayers will receive Form SSA-1099 or RRB-1099 showing the amount of social security benefits or railroad retirement benefits received, respectively. See Exhibit 3-6 for Form SSA-1099.

The amount of benefits to use in taxability calculations is in box 5. As with other 1099 forms, you record the information on the appropriate form within the tax software. Specifically, you record both social security and railroad retirement benefits on the Social Security Benefits worksheet in the worksheet section of the tax software.

If provisional income exceeds certain thresholds, 50% of social security benefits are taxable. As provisional income increases, the proportion of benefits included in taxable income increases to as much as 85%. The thresholds and taxability are shown in the following chart:

	Married, Filing Jointly	**Single, Head of Household, or Qualifying Widow(er)**
Lower limit of provisional income	$32,000	$25,000
Upper limit of provisional income	$44,000	$34,000
Taxable portion of benefits if provisional income is between the two limits	Lesser of 50% of benefits or 50% of the excess of provisional income over $32,000	Lesser of 50% of benefits or 50% of the excess of provisional income over $25,000
Taxable portion of benefits if provisional income is above the upper limit	Lesser of (a) 85% of benefits or (b) 85% of the excess of provisional income over $44,000 *plus* the lesser of (1) $6,000 or (2) 50% of benefits	Lesser of (a) 85% of benefits or (b) 85% of the excess of provisional income over $34,000 *plus* the lesser of (1) $4,500 or (2) 50% of benefits

Taxpayers use the single column if they are married filing separately and have lived apart from their spouse for the entire year. If such persons lived with their spouse at any time during the year, the lower and upper limits are zero. Thus for these persons, social security benefits are taxable to the extent of the lesser of 85% of social security benefits or 85% of provisional income.

EXAMPLE 3-9

Robert and Cindy file a joint return. Their AGI before social security was $15,000, and they received $8,000 in benefits. They had no items to add back to AGI. Their provisional income is $19,000 ($15,000 + $4,000). No social security benefits are taxable.

EXAMPLE 3-10

Karen files a return as a qualifying widow. She received $7,000 of social security benefits, $19,000 of interest income, and $5,000 of nontaxable municipal bond interest. Her provisional income is $27,500 ($3,500 + $19,000 + $5,000). Karen will report taxable social security benefits equal to the lesser of 50% of social security benefits ($3,500) or 50% of the excess of provisional income over $25,000 ($1,250). Thus her taxable benefits total $1,250. (See Exhibit 3-7.)

EXHIBIT 3-6

FORM SSA-1099 – SOCIAL SECURITY BENEFIT STATEMENT

2016
- PART OF YOUR SOCIAL SECURITY BENEFITS SHOWN IN BOX 5 MAY BE TAXABLE INCOME.
- SEE THE REVERSE FOR MORE INFORMATION.

Box 1. Name		Box 2. Beneficiary's Social Security Number
Box 3. Benefits Paid in 2016	Box 4. Benefits Repaid to SSA in 2016	Box 5. Net Benefits for 2016 *(Box 3 minus Box 4)*

DESCRIPTION OF AMOUNT IN BOX 3	DESCRIPTION OF AMOUNT IN BOX 4
	Box 6. Voluntary Federal Income Tax Withheld
	Box 7. Address
	Box 8. Claim Number *(Use this number if you need to contact SSA.)*

SAMPLE

Form **SSA-1099-SM** (1-2017) **DO NOT RETURN THIS FORM TO SSA OR IRS**

Source: U.S. Department of the Treasury, Internal Revenue Service, Form SSA-1099. Washington, DC: 2016.

EXAMPLE 3-11

Carson and Maureen file a joint return showing interest and dividend income of $46,000, self-employment income for Carson of $31,000, and nontaxable municipal bond interest of $10,000. They excluded $1,000 of interest on educational loans. They received social security benefits of $9,000. Their provisional income is $92,500 ($46,000 + $31,000 + $10,000 + $1,000 + $4,500). They will report taxable social security benefits equal to the lesser of 85% of social security benefits ($7,650) or 85% of the excess of provisional income over $44,000 (which is $41,225) plus the lesser of $6,000 or $4,500 (50% of social security benefits). Thus their taxable benefits total $7,650.

CONCEPT CHECK 3-5— LO 3-3

1. Linda and Mason file a joint return. Their AGI before social security was $22,000, social security benefits received were $9,000, and tax-exempt interest was $1,250. What is the amount of their provisional income? ______________________

EXHIBIT 3-7

1.	Enter the total amount from **box 5** of **all** your **Forms SSA-1099** and **Forms RRB-1099.** Also, enter this amount on Form 1040, line 20a 1. 7,000		
2.	Multiply line 1 by 50% (0.50)	2.	3,500
3.	Combine the amounts from Form 1040, lines 7, 8a, 9a, 10 through 14, 15b, 16b, 17 through 19, and 21	3.	19,000
4.	Enter the amount, if any, from Form 1040, line 8b	4.	5,000
5.	Combine lines 2, 3, and 4	5.	27,500
6.	Enter the total of the amounts from Form 1040, lines 23 through 32, plus any write-in adjustments you entered on the dotted line next to line 36	6.	0
7.	Is the amount on line 6 less than the amount on line 5? ☐ **No.** STOP None of your social security benefits are taxable. Enter -0- on Form 1040, line 20b. ☒ **Yes.** Subtract line 6 from line 5	7.	27,500
8.	If you are: • Married filing jointly, enter $32,000 • Single, head of household, qualifying widow(er), or married filing separately and you **lived apart** from your spouse for all of 2017, enter $25,000 • Married filing separately and you lived with your spouse at any time in 2017, skip lines 8 through 15; multiply line 7 by 85% (0.85) and enter the result on line 16. Then, go to line 17	8.	25,000
9.	Is the amount on line 8 less than the amount on line 7? ☐ **No.** STOP None of your social security benefits are taxable. Enter -0- on Form 1040, line 20b. If you are married filing separately and you **lived apart** from your spouse for all of 2017, be sure you entered "D" to the right of the word "benefits" on line 20a. ☒ **Yes.** Subtract line 8 from line 7	9.	2,500
10.	Enter: $12,000 if married filing jointly; $9,000 if single, head of household, qualifying widow(er), or married filing separately and you **lived apart** from your spouse for all of 2017	10.	9,000
11.	Subtract line 10 from line 9. If zero or less, enter -0-	11.	0
12.	Enter the **smaller** of line 9 or line 10	12.	2,500
13.	Enter one-half of line 12	13.	1,250
14.	Enter the **smaller** of line 2 or line 13	14.	1,250
15.	Multiply line 11 by 85% (0.85). If line 11 is zero, enter -0-	15.	0
16.	Add lines 14 and 15	16.	1,250
17.	Multiply line 1 by 85% (0.85)	17.	5,950
18.	**Taxable social security benefits.** Enter the **smaller** of line 16 or line 17. Also enter this amount on Form 1040, line 20b	18.	1,250

Source: U.S. Department of the Treasury, Internal Revenue Service, Forms SSA-1099 and RRB-1099. Washington, DC: 2017.

Other Income (Form 1040, line 21)

Gross income includes ". . . all income from whatever source derived . . .".[26] The concept is broad, and taxpayers often receive income that does not neatly fit into lines 7 through 20 of Form 1040. Line 21 is where taxpayers report other taxable gross income. A taxpayer who has any other taxable income reportable on line 21 can use only Form 1040. Items that taxpayers must report on line 21 include these:

- **Jury duty pay:** Individuals who serve jury duty receive a small amount of pay for each day served. This pay is included in other income. If the individual is required to remit the payment to his or her employer, the payment is deductible, the net effect of which is that the taxpayer reports zero.[27]
- **Prizes and awards:** If an employee receives a prize or award from his or her employer, the award is included in W-2 income. Prizes and awards received from other sources are taxable as other income unless specifically excluded (such as a scholarship award).

[26] *IRS Publication* 17.

[27] IRC § 62(a)(13).

- **Forgiveness of debt:** If a taxpayer borrows money, it is not taxable income because the taxpayer must repay the loan (that is, the taxpayer does not have a complete, unfettered right to the money). If a lender fully or partially forgives a loan, the taxpayer has income to the extent of the forgiveness.[28] However, a borrower does not report income if payment of the debt would have given rise to a deduction.[29] For example, a lender forgives some interest otherwise due on a loan to a self-employed cash basis taxpayer. A taxpayer who had paid the interest would have recorded a business deduction for the interest paid. Thus the taxpayer reports no income. Other exceptions to the general forgiveness of debt rule (such as forgiveness during bankruptcy proceedings or when the taxpayer is insolvent) are beyond the scope of this text.[30]
- **Certain insurance proceeds:** Taxpayers receiving insurance proceeds in excess of the adjusted basis of the property insured must report taxable income equal to the excess. This category does not include life insurance or health insurance proceeds.

CONCEPT CHECK 3-6— LO 3-3

1. Name a type of income item that is listed on line 21 of Form 1040.

____

ITEMS EXCLUDED FROM GROSS INCOME
LO 3-4

Congress has exempted certain income from tax by statute. These exemptions include the following items.

Nontaxable Employee Fringe Benefits

The general rule is that employee compensation, in whatever form, is taxable to the employee. However, certain types of fringe benefits are tax-free to the employee, and the employer can deduct the cost of providing the benefits.[31] Most benefits are subject to nondiscrimination rules.[32]

The following fringe benefits provided by an employer are not taxable to the employee:

- **No-additional-cost services** provided to an employee, his or her spouse, or dependent children:[33] The employer must ordinarily offer the services for sale to outside customers, and the employer must incur no substantial additional cost (including forgone revenue) to provide the service. Examples include unsold hotel rooms or airline seats (but not if the benefit bumps a paying customer).
- **Discounts** provided employees for products or services normally sold by the business:[34] Examples are reduced priced meals in restaurants, discounts on clothing at a retail store, and reduced interest rate loans from a financial institution. In the case of products, the discount cannot exceed the gross profit percentage, and in the case of services, the maximum discount is 20% of the normal selling price.

[28] IRC § 61(a)(12).

[29] IRC § 108(e)(2).

[30] These exceptions are found in IRC § 108 and the regulations thereunder.

[31] Employer deductibility is not a focus of this text.

[32] Generally, nondiscrimination rules prohibit or limit the nontaxability of certain benefits if highly compensated employees disproportionately receive the benefits at the expense of lower-paid employees. For example, if discounts (see the text) are given only to employees with salaries over $500,000, it is likely that the nondiscrimination rules would apply and make the discount amount a taxable benefit rather than a tax-free benefit.

[33] IRC § 132(b).

[34] IRC § 132(c).

- **Working condition fringe benefits:** These are services or properties provided to an employee that would have been deductible as a trade or business expense or as depreciation expense had the employee paid for them.[35] Working condition fringes include professional organization dues paid by an employer or the use of an employer-provided vehicle for business purposes.
- **Qualified transportation fringe benefits:** These benefits include transit passes, parking near the employer's business or near a mass transit location, and use of an employer-provided vanpool that holds six or more persons and is used 80% or more for commuting.[36] In 2017 parking benefits cannot exceed $255 per month, and transit passes and vanpool benefits cannot exceed $255 per month.
- **Moving expense reimbursements:** In certain circumstances, an employee can exclude from income any moving reimbursements paid by his or her employer to the extent that the employee does not deduct moving expenses.
- ***De minimis* benefits:** (holiday turkeys, company picnics, flowers or fruit sent when an employee is sick, etc.) A *de minimis* benefit is one whose value is so small that keeping track of which employees received the benefit is administratively impractical.[37]

Employees can exclude from income additional employer-provided benefits. Commonly used benefits follow:

- Employers often provide reduced-cost or fully paid accident and health insurance to employees. The value of the premium paid by the employer is not taxable to the employee.[38] Reimbursement for medical care paid by the insurance policy (or paid directly by the employer if no policy exists or if the policy does not cover the cost) is not taxable income to the employee unless the reimbursement exceeds the cost of the care.
- Employers can pay (or reimburse employees) for up to $5,250 per year of educational assistance, whether or not it is job-related.[39] Expenses include, but are not limited to, tuition, fees, books, and supplies.
- Employer-paid premiums on group term life insurance are not taxable to employees.[40] Tax-free coverage is limited to $50,000 per person. Coverage in excess of the $50,000 limit is taxable to the employee based on the cost of the excess.[41]
- The costs of employer-paid meals and lodging are tax-exempt if the meals and lodging are furnished for the convenience of the employer and are furnished on the business premises (in the case of meals), or the employee is required to accept the lodging as a condition of employment.[42] Examples meeting these criteria would be lodging for employees on an oil rig, at a lumber camp, or on a ship at sea, or meals provided employees who work at a business location far from eating places.
- Payments under written dependent care assistance plans are tax-free.[43] The exclusion cannot exceed $5,000 ($2,500 for married filing separately) and cannot exceed earned income (earned income of the lesser earning spouse for married filing jointly). Dependent care expenses are those that are considered to be employment-related expenses for purposes of the child care credit rules.
- Flexible benefit plans (often referred to as *cafeteria plans* or *flexible spending accounts*) are written plans that permit employees to choose their own benefits (which may include

[35] IRC § 132(d).

[36] IRC § 132(f).

[37] IRC § 132(e).

[38] IRC § 106(a).

[39] IRC § 127(a).

[40] IRC § 79(a).

[41] To determine the cost of the excess, see Reg. § 1.79-3(d)(2).

[42] IRC § 119(a).

[43] IRC § 129(a).

cash payments).[44] Normally the law provides that if a person has an opportunity to receive cash but elects to defer the payment or take payment in a noncash asset, income is still recognized. In the case of cafeteria plans (which by their very nature permit employees to choose), the value of the *benefits* received is not taxed to the employee. However, if employees elect to receive cash, the cash is taxable. The menu of options from which employees can choose often includes many of the fringe benefits discussed earlier (health care insurance, group life insurance, educational expenses, transportation fringe benefits, and the like). Under a cafeteria plan, the employee gets to choose the components that he or she finds the most beneficial.

Other Nontaxable Income

Taxpayers can receive certain nontaxable income not directly related to employment. This nontaxable income includes the following items.

Scholarships and Fellowships

In general, scholarships and fellowships are tax-free.[45] The individual must be a degree-seeking student at an educational institution and must use the proceeds for qualified tuition and related expenses (tuition, fees, books, supplies, and equipment). If the scholarship or fellowship payment exceeds permitted expenses, the excess is taxable income. Benefits under tuition reduction plans provided to employees of educational institutions are not taxable. If a student must perform certain services for the educational institution (such as graduate assistantships), the amount paid for the services is not a scholarship or fellowship but is a taxable wage.

EXAMPLE 3-12

Hilda is a graduate student at State University. In 2017 she received a scholarship of $7,000 ($4,000 toward tuition and fees and $3,000 to pay for campus housing) and a graduate assistantship that paid $5,000. Tuition, fees, and books cost $6,000 during the year. Hilda can exclude $4,000 from income. She will be required to report wage income of $5,000 from the graduate assistantship and $3,000 of other income for the housing benefit.

Qualified Tuition Program Withdrawals

A *Qualified Tuition Program (QTP)* is a state program that, in effect, is a tax-free savings account when used exclusively for educational expenses. Individuals make cash contributions to the QTP, and the state invests the contributions. If the contributor makes withdrawals from the QTP and uses the money to pay for qualified higher education expenses at an eligible educational institution, the withdrawal is tax-free. For tax years 2009 through 2017, the definition of qualified higher education expenses includes the purchase of computer equipment or Internet access that will be used by the beneficiary while the beneficiary is enrolled at an eligible educational institution.[46] These programs are also called *529 plans* (from the IRC section that created them).

Life Insurance Proceeds

Life insurance proceeds, payable because of the death of the insured, are fully excludable from the gross income of the recipient.[47] If proceeds are paid over time (rather than as a lump sum), payments are tax-free except to the extent that the payments exceed the amount payable at the time of death (for example, if there are earnings on the proceeds). The proportion of each payment that is tax-free is the excludable amount divided by the expected number of payments.[48]

44 IRC § 125(a).

45 IRC § 117(a), (b).

46 IRC § 529.

47 IRC § 101(a)(1).

48 IRC § 101(d)(1). If payments are made over the life of the recipient, the denominator is determined by reference to appropriate life expectancy tables. Changes are not made to the calculations even if the recipient exceeds the life expectancy.

EXAMPLE 3-13

Bill is entitled to receive $50,000 of life insurance payable because of his wife's death. Instead of receiving a lump sum, he agreed to take five annual payments of $12,000 each. The excluded amount is $50,000/5 = $10,000 per payment. Thus the remaining $2,000 of each payment is interest income.[49]

Accelerated death benefits are amounts received under a life insurance policy on the life of an individual who is terminally ill or chronically ill. Taxpayers can exclude such payments from gross income.[50] A person is *terminally ill* if a physician certifies that he or she is likely to die within 24 months. A *chronically ill* person has a disability requiring long-term care or substantial supervision.[51]

Gifts and Inheritances

Gifts and inheritances are tax-free to the recipient.[52] *Gifts* are transfers made during the lifetime of the giver; *inheritances* are transfers of property at or after death. An individual can classify a transfer as a tax-free gift only if the giver was motivated by kindness, generosity, affection, or similar emotions.

TAX YOUR BRAIN

Norma was the 100,000th customer at her local grocery store. Because of that, the store gave Norma a free trip to Australia as a gift. Is the trip taxable or tax-free?

ANSWER

The trip to Australia is taxable. The owners did not give Norma the trip because they were motivated by kindness or generosity; they gave it to her for promotional reasons. The fair value of the trip is taxable to Norma.

Gifts may be subject to a gift tax that is the responsibility of the giver. Rules concerning gift taxes are beyond the scope of this text.

Compensation for Sickness or Injury

The following items are exempt from income under the umbrella of compensation for injuries or sickness:[53]

- Payments received under workers' compensation acts.
- Damages (other than punitive damages) received as a result of personal physical injuries or sickness.
- Pensions or annuities received for personal injuries or sickness from active service in the armed forces, Coast Guard, public health service, or foreign service.
- Disability income resulting from a terrorist attack while in the employ of the United States engaged in official duties outside the United States.

Other

Other nontaxable income includes:

- Child support (nontaxable to the recipient and not deductible by the payer).[54]
- Public assistance payments (such as welfare).
- Employer-provided adoption assistance up to $13,570 per child. In 2017, the amount excludable from an employee's gross income starts to phase out when modified Adjusted Gross Income is in excess of $203,540 and is eliminated when modified Adjusted Gross Income reaches $243,540.

NEW LAW

The amount of $13,570 excludable under employer-provided adoption assistance starts phasing out when modified Adjusted Gross Income reaches $203,540 and is eliminated at $243,540.

[49] Generally the taxpayer will receive a form 1099-INT from the insurance company disclosing the amount of interest income.

[50] IRC § 101(g)(1).

[51] IRC § 101(g)(4).

[52] IRC § 102(a).

[53] IRC § 104(a).

[54] IRC § 71(c)(1).

From Shoebox to Software Two Comprehensive Examples

We now introduce two new taxpayers.

YIMING CHOW

The first taxpayer is Yiming Chow, who is single and lives at 456 Maple Avenue, Somewhere, OH 43003. His SSN is 412-34-5670 and date of birth is 10/27/1985. During 2017 Mr. Chow received a W-2 from his employer, a 1099-INT from the local financial institution, and a 1099-DIV associated with a mutual fund investment. He also received a 1099-G from the state of Ohio for a $57 tax refund pertaining to tax year 2016. Mr. Chow did not itemize his deductions in 2016. All these documents are shown in Exhibit 3-8.

Open the tax software. Go to the File pull-down menu and click on New Return. Go through the process to start a new return, and then click on the Forms icon to bring up the list of available forms. Open a Form 1040 to input the basic name, address, and social security number information for Mr. Chow. He is eligible to file Form 1040A, and we will use that form after you enter his personal information.

Now enter the information from the various tax forms into the tax software using the applicable forms in the Documents Received section. Note that you do not need to enter any information concerning the tax refund. Mr. Chow did not itemize deductions in 2016, so you do not need to report his tax refund as income.

Once you have entered the appropriate information, click on Form 1040A. Line 15 should be $41,688. Line 27, taxable income, should be $31,288. Mr. Chow's tax liability on line 28 is $4,210. Because Mr. Chow has wage income and dividend income, you may find it instructive to calculate the tax liability by hand to see if you get the same answer. Because Mr. Chow had $4,670 withheld from his wages, his refund is $460, as shown on lines 47 and 48a. Mr. Chow had qualifying health care coverage at all times during the tax year.

Make sure you save Mr. Chow's return for use in later chapters.

MR. AND MRS. RAMIREZ

The second taxpayer is the married couple Jose and Maria Ramirez. They live at 1234 West Street, Mytown, GA 30294. They have three children, Arturo, Benito, and Carmen, born in 2004, 2006, and 2008, respectively. The children lived in the household during the entire year. The SSNs are listed along with the date of birth (in parentheses). The information is as follows: Jose 412-34-5670 (2/10/1971), Maria 412-34-5671 (4/15/1976), Arturo 412-34-5672 (5/30/2004), Benito 412-34-5673 (8/7/2006), and Carmen 412-34-5674 (1/30/2008).

Mr. Ramirez received a W-2 from his employer, a 1099-INT from the financial institution, and a 1099-DIV from his stockbroker. He also received a 1099-G from the state of Georgia for a $645 tax refund. The taxpayer itemized deductions last year, and you have determined that the entire refund is taxable. All of the Ramirezes' documents are shown in Exhibit 3-9.

Open the tax software. Go to the File pull-down menu and click on New Return. Go through the process to start a new return, and then click on the Forms icon to bring up the list of available forms. Open a blank Form 1040 to input the basic name, address, and social security number information for Mr. and Mrs. Ramirez. Use the Dependent worksheet in the worksheet section to enter information for the children.

The Ramirezes must file Form 1040 because of the state tax refund. For now we will assume that the couple will take the standard deduction.

Now enter the information from the various tax forms into the tax software using the applicable forms in the Documents Received section.

Because you do not have tax return information for tax year 2016, you need to provide information concerning the tax refund. Enter in the system that the full amount of the refund is taxable.

Once you have entered the appropriate information, the total income and the AGI of the taxpayer should be $111,848. After subtracting a standard deduction of $12,700 and personal exemptions of $20,250 ($4,050 per individual), taxable income should be $78,898.

The tax on line 44 should be $10,909. The tax software automatically calculated a $3,000 child tax credit on line 52. We will discuss credits later in the text. The credit reduces the Ramirezes' tax liability to $7,909. Because the taxpayer had withholding of $9,418, the Ramirezes' return should show a refund of $1,509 on lines 75 and 76a. Mr. and Mrs. Ramirez had qualifying health care coverage at all times during the tax year.

Make sure you save the Ramirezes' tax return for use in later chapters. These will be running demonstration problems throughout the text.

CONCEPT CHECK 3-7— LO 3-4

1. Holiday turkeys given to employees are included in gross income. True or false?
2. In general, scholarships are not taxable if the use of the money is to pay tuition, fees, books, supplies, and equipment. True or false?

EXHIBIT 3-8

☐ CORRECTED (if checked)

PAYER'S name, street address, city or town, state or province, country, ZIP or foreign postal code, and telephone no.		1a Total ordinary dividends	OMB No. 1545-0110	Dividends and Distributions
Jones Brokerage P.O. Box 500 Somewhere, OH 43003		$ 96.71	2017	
		1b Qualified dividends $ 96.71	Form **1099-DIV**	
		2a Total capital gain distr. $	2b Unrecap. Sec. 1250 gain $	**Copy B** **For Recipient**
PAYER'S federal identification number 56-4456789	RECIPIENT'S identification number 412-34-5670	2c Section 1202 gain $	2d Collectibles (28%) gain $	
RECIPIENT'S name Yiming Chow		3 Nondividend distributions $	4 Federal income tax withheld $	This is important tax information and is being furnished to the Internal Revenue Service. If you are required to file a return, a negligence penalty or other sanction may be imposed on you if this income is taxable and the IRS determines that it has not been reported.
			5 Investment expenses $	
Street address (including apt. no.) 456 Maple Ave.		6 Foreign tax paid $	7 Foreign country or U.S. possession	
City or town, state or province, country, and ZIP or foreign postal code Somewhere, OH 43003		8 Cash liquidation distributions $	9 Noncash liquidation distributions $	
	FATCA filing requirement ☐	10 Exempt-interest dividends $	11 Specified private activity bond interest dividends $	
Account number (see instructions)		12 State / 13 State identification no.	14 State tax withheld $ $	

Form **1099-DIV** (keep for your records) www.irs.gov/form1099div Department of the Treasury - Internal Revenue Service

	a Employee's social security number 412-34-5670	OMB No. 1545-0008	Safe, accurate, FAST! Use IRS e-file	Visit the IRS website at *www.irs.gov/efile*
b Employer identification number (EIN)			1 Wages, tips, other compensation 41,321.34	2 Federal income tax withheld 4,670.00
c Employer's name, address, and ZIP code Acme Company 900 Oak Street Somewhere, OH 43003			3 Social security wages 41,321.34	4 Social security tax withheld 2,561.92
			5 Medicare wages and tips 41,321.34	6 Medicare tax withheld 599.16
			7 Social security tips	8 Allocated tips
d Control number			9 Verification code	10 Dependent care benefits
e Employee's first name and initial	Last name	Suff.	11 Nonqualified plans	12a See instructions for box 12
Yiming Chow 456 Maple Street Somewhere, OH 43003			13 Statutory employee ☐ Retirement plan ☐ Third-party sick pay ☐	12b
			14 Other	12c
f Employee's address and ZIP code				12d

15 State	Employer's state ID number	16 State wages, tips, etc.	17 State income tax	18 Local wages, tips, etc.	19 Local income tax	20 Locality name
OH		41,321.34	1,039.63			

Form **W-2** **Wage and Tax Statement** 2017 Department of the Treasury—Internal Revenue Service

Copy B—To Be Filed With Employee's FEDERAL Tax Return.
This information is being furnished to the Internal Revenue Service.

Source: U.S. Department of the Treasury, Internal Revenue Service, Form 1099-DIV. Washington, DC: 2017.

EXHIBIT 3-8 *(concluded)*

☐ CORRECTED (if checked)

PAYER'S name, street address, city or town, state or province, country, ZIP or foreign postal code, and telephone no.	State of Ohio P.O. Box 500 Columbus, OH 45555
1 Unemployment compensation	$
2 State or local income tax refunds, credits, or offsets	$ 57.00
OMB No. 1545-0120	2017, Form 1099-G
PAYER'S federal identification number	47-4450000
RECIPIENT'S identification number	412-34-5670
3 Box 2 amount is for tax year	2016
4 Federal income tax withheld	$
RECIPIENT'S name	Yiming Chow
5 RTAA payments	$
6 Taxable grants	$
Street address (including apt. no.)	456 Maple Street
7 Agriculture payments	$
8 If checked, box 2 is trade or business income ►	☐
9 Market gain	$
City or town, state or province, country, and ZIP or foreign postal code	Somewhere, OH 43003
10a State	
10b State identification no.	
11 State income tax withheld	$ $
Account number (see instructions)	

Certain Government Payments

Copy B

For Recipient

This is important tax information and is being furnished to the Internal Revenue Service. If you are required to file a return, a negligence penalty or other sanction may be imposed on you if this income is taxable and the IRS determines that it has not been reported.

Form **1099-G** (keep for your records) www.irs.gov/form1099g Department of the Treasury - Internal Revenue Service

☐ CORRECTED (if checked)

PAYER'S name, street address, city or town, state or province, country, ZIP or foreign postal code, and telephone no.	First National Bank 125 Main Street Somewhere, OH 43003
Payer's RTN (optional)	
1 Interest income	$ 270.12
OMB No. 1545-0112	2017, Form 1099-INT
2 Early withdrawal penalty	$
PAYER'S federal identification number	46-6735241
RECIPIENT'S identification number	412-34-5670
3 Interest on U.S. Savings Bonds and Treas. obligations	$
RECIPIENT'S name	Yiming Chow
4 Federal income tax withheld	$
5 Investment expenses	$
Street address (including apt. no.)	456 Maple Street
6 Foreign tax paid	$
7 Foreign country or U.S. possession	
8 Tax-exempt interest	$
9 Specified private activity bond interest	$
City or town, state or province, country, and ZIP or foreign postal code	Somewhere, OH 43003
10 Market discount	$
11 Bond premium	$
FATCA filing requirement	☐
12 Bond premium on Treasury obligations	$
13 Bond premium on tax-exempt bond	$
Account number (see instructions)	
14 Tax-exempt and tax credit bond CUSIP no.	
15 State	
16 State identification no.	
17 State tax withheld	$ $

Interest Income

Copy B

For Recipient

This is important tax information and is being furnished to the Internal Revenue Service. If you are required to file a return, a negligence penalty or other sanction may be imposed on you if this income is taxable and the IRS determines that it has not been reported.

Form **1099-INT** (keep for your records) www.irs.gov/form1099int Department of the Treasury - Internal Revenue Service

EXHIBIT 3-9

☐ CORRECTED (if checked)

PAYER'S name, street address, city or town, state or province, country, ZIP or foreign postal code, and telephone no. First National Bank 1000 Main Street Mytown, GA 30294	Payer's RTN (optional) 1 Interest income $ 3,150.00	OMB No. 1545-0112 **2017** Form **1099-INT**	**Interest Income**
PAYER'S federal identification number 56-3455667 / RECIPIENT'S identification number 412-34-5670	2 Early withdrawal penalty $ 3 Interest on U.S. Savings Bonds and Treas. obligations $		**Copy B** **For Recipient**
RECIPIENT'S name Jose Ramirez	4 Federal income tax withheld $	5 Investment expenses $	This is important tax information and is being furnished to the Internal Revenue Service. If you are required to file a return, a negligence penalty or other sanction may be imposed on you if this income is taxable and the IRS determines that it has not been reported.
Street address (including apt. no.) 1234 West Street	6 Foreign tax paid $	7 Foreign country or U.S. possession	
City or town, state or province, country, and ZIP or foreign postal code Mytown, GA 30294	8 Tax-exempt interest $	9 Specified private activity bond interest $	
FATCA filing requirement ☐	10 Market discount $	11 Bond premium $	
	12 Bond premium on Treasury obligations $	13 Bond premium on tax-exempt bond $	
Account number (see instructions)	14 Tax-exempt and tax credit bond CUSIP no.	15 State / 16 State identification no.	17 State tax withheld $ $

Form **1099-INT** (keep for your records) www.irs.gov/form1099int Department of the Treasury - Internal Revenue Service

☐ CORRECTED (if checked)

PAYER'S name, street address, city or town, state or province, country, ZIP or foreign postal code, and telephone no. Smith Brokerage P.O. Box 100 Mytown, GA 30294	1a Total ordinary dividends $ 2,916.00 1b Qualified dividends $ 2,916.00	OMB No. 1545-0110 **2017** Form **1099-DIV**	**Dividends and Distributions**
	2a Total capital gain distr. $	2b Unrecap. Sec. 1250 gain $	**Copy B** **For Recipient**
PAYER'S federal identification number 56-4456789 / RECIPIENT'S identification number 412-34-5670	2c Section 1202 gain $	2d Collectibles (28%) gain $	
RECIPIENT'S name Jose Ramirez	3 Nondividend distributions $	4 Federal income tax withheld $	This is important tax information and is being furnished to the Internal Revenue Service. If you are required to file a return, a negligence penalty or other sanction may be imposed on you if this income is taxable and the IRS determines that it has not been reported.
Street address (including apt. no.) 1234 West Street		5 Investment expenses $	
	6 Foreign tax paid $	7 Foreign country or U.S. possession	
City or town, state or province, country, and ZIP or foreign postal code Mytown, GA 30294	8 Cash liquidation distributions $	9 Noncash liquidation distributions $	
FATCA filing requirement ☐	10 Exempt-interest dividends $	11 Specified private activity bond interest dividends $	
Account number (see instructions)	12 State / 13 State identification no.	14 State tax withheld $ $	

Form **1099-DIV** (keep for your records) www.irs.gov/form1099div Department of the Treasury - Internal Revenue Service

Source: U.S. Department of the Treasury, Internal Revenue Service, Form 1099-INT. Washington, DC: 2017.

EXHIBIT 3-9 *(concluded)*

	a Employee's social security number 412-34-5670	OMB No. 1545-0008	Safe, accurate, FAST! Use IRS e-file	Visit the IRS website at *www.irs.gov/efile*

b Employer identification number (EIN)	1 Wages, tips, other compensation 105,137.10	2 Federal income tax withheld 9,418.32
c Employer's name, address, and ZIP code Beta Tech 500 East Street Mytown, GA 30294	3 Social security wages 105,137.10	4 Social security tax withheld 6,518.50
	5 Medicare wages and tips 105,137.10	6 Medicare tax withheld 1,524.49
	7 Social security tips	8 Allocated tips
d Control number	9 Verification code	10 Dependent care benefits
e Employee's first name and initial Last name Suff. Jose Ramirez 1234 West Street Mytown, GA 30294	11 Nonqualified plans	12a See instructions for box 12 Code
	13 Statutory employee ☐ Retirement plan ☐ Third-party sick pay ☐	12b Code
	14 Other	12c Code
f Employee's address and ZIP code		12d Code

15 State	Employer's state ID number	16 State wages, tips, etc.	17 State income tax	18 Local wages, tips, etc.	19 Local income tax	20 Locality name
GA		105,137.10	3,469.52			

Form **W-2 Wage and Tax Statement** **2017** Department of the Treasury—Internal Revenue Service

Copy B—To Be Filed With Employee's FEDERAL Tax Return.
This information is being furnished to the Internal Revenue Service.

☐ CORRECTED (if checked)

PAYER'S name, street address, city or town, state or province, country, ZIP or foreign postal code, and telephone no. State of Georgia P.O. Box 500 Atlanta, GA 34567	1 Unemployment compensation $	OMB No. 1545-0120 **2017** Form **1099-G**	**Certain Government Payments**
	2 State or local income tax refunds, credits, or offsets $ 645.00		
PAYER'S federal identification number 41-3500000 / RECIPIENT'S identification number 412-34-5670	3 Box 2 amount is for tax year 2016	4 Federal income tax withheld $	**Copy B** **For Recipient**
RECIPIENT'S name Jose Ramirez	5 RTAA payments $	6 Taxable grants $	This is important tax information and is being furnished to the Internal Revenue Service. If you are required to file a return, a negligence penalty or other sanction may be imposed on you if this income is taxable and the IRS determines that it has not been reported.
Street address (including apt. no.) 1234 West Street	7 Agriculture payments $	8 If checked, box 2 is trade or business income ▶ ☐	
City or town, state or province, country, and ZIP or foreign postal code Mytown, GA 30294	9 Market gain $		
Account number (see instructions)	10a State / 10b State identification no.	11 State income tax withheld $ $	

Form **1099-G** (keep for your records) www.irs.gov/form1099g Department of the Treasury - Internal Revenue Service

Appendix

TAX ACCOUNTING FOR SAVINGS BOND INTEREST USED FOR EDUCATION EXPENSES, BELOW-MARKET INTEREST LOANS, GIFT LOANS, AND ORIGINAL ISSUE DISCOUNT DEBT

LO 3-5

This Appendix covers topics pertaining to interest that are important but less common.

NEW LAW

For years beginning in 2017, the savings bond interest exclusion for paying qualified higher education expenses starts to phase out for modified AGI in excess of $117,250 (joint return) and $78,150 (other returns) and is eliminated at $147,250 (joint return) and $93,150 (other returns).

Savings Bond Interest Exclusion

Interest on Series EE or Series I savings bonds is not taxable if the taxpayer uses the bond proceeds to pay qualified higher education expenses for the taxpayer, his or her spouse, or their dependent(s).[55] The bonds must have been purchased (not received by gift) after 1989 by an individual at least 24 years old at the time of purchase who is the sole owner of the bonds (or joint owner with his or her spouse). Qualified higher education expenses are tuition and fees at a qualified educational institution.[56] However, the taxpayer must reduce qualified expenses by tax-exempt scholarships, certain educational assistance allowances, certain benefits under a qualified state tuition program, and expenses used in determining Hope and lifetime learning credits or a Coverdell Education Savings Account distribution exclusion.[57] Married persons living together must file a joint return in the year of exclusion.

Taxpayers can exclude the full amount of interest subject to the phaseout amount, only if the amount of qualified higher education expense paid in a year exceeds the redemption proceeds (principal plus interest) for the year. If proceeds exceed expenses, the amount of interest that is excludable is limited to the interest multiplied by a fraction calculated as qualified expenses paid during the year divided by aggregate redemption proceeds.

EXAMPLE 3-14

In 2017, Angeline and Albert redeemed $4,000 (principal of $3,000 and interest of $1,000) of Series I savings bonds to pay qualified higher education expenses. Qualified expenses for the year totaled $3,500. Angeline and Albert may exclude interest of $875 from income in 2017 [$1,000 × ($3,500/$4,000)]. The remaining $125 is taxable interest income.

The amount of savings bond interest exempt from tax is further limited if the modified AGI of the taxpayer for tax year 2017 exceeds $117,250 on a joint return or $78,150 on other returns.[58] If modified AGI exceeds those limits, the amount of the reduction is equal to

$$\text{Amount otherwise excludable} \times \frac{\text{Modified AGI} - \text{Limitation amount}}{\$30{,}000\ (\$15{,}000 \text{ for single filers})}$$

When modified AGI reaches $147,250 for joint returns and $93,150 for other returns, the amount of exempt interest phases out. Taxpayers calculate the modified AGI limitation after all other limitations.

[55] IRC § 135(a).

[56] IRC § 529(e)(5).

[57] IRC § 135(c)(2) and IRC § 135(d).

[58] These amounts are subject to annual adjustment for inflation.

EXAMPLE 3-15

Steve, a single taxpayer, has determined that his excludable savings bond interest is $1,400 prior to any modified AGI limitation. His modified AGI is $78,900. Steve will be able to exclude $1,330 of savings bond interest on his 2017 tax return, calculated as follows: $1,400 × [($78,900 – $78,150)/$15,000] = reduction amount of $70. Thus the excludable savings bond interest will be $1,400 – $70 = $1,330. Steve must report savings bond interest of $70 on his 2017 tax return.

Modified AGI is AGI adjusted as follows:

Adjusted Gross Income

Plus: Deduction for student loan interest[59]

Deduction for tuition and fees (Tax Extenders Act of 2008)

The savings bond interest exclusion itself[60]

Excluded foreign income and allowances[61]

Excluded adoption assistance from an employer[62]

EXAMPLE 3-16

Virginia has AGI of $41,000 that includes a student loan interest deduction of $800. Her modified AGI for purposes of the savings bond interest exclusion is $41,800.

Below-Market Interest Rate Loans

Most interest-bearing instruments carry an interest rate that approximates the market rate of interest for instruments of similar maturity, credit risk, and collateral. For example, if two persons of equal loan-paying ability and credit rating obtain a loan at a financial institution to finance the purchase of a Ford F-150 on a four-year repayment schedule, the interest rates on the two loans should be approximately equal.

In some circumstances, one party in a transaction wishes to charge a low rate of interest rather than a market rate.[63] Assume that an individual is selling a parcel of land for $100,000 and will accept $10,000 down with annual interest-only payments on the balance at an interest rate of 10% with principal due at the end of five years. Total payments would be $100,000 in principal and $45,000 of interest. Because interest income is taxable at a rate up to 35% and capital gains are generally taxed at 15% unless the taxpayer's marginal ordinary income tax rate is 39.60%, it would be beneficial to the seller if the price were raised to, say, $130,000 while lowering the interest rate to 2.5%. Total payments will still be $145,000 ($130,000 principal and $15,000 interest), but the seller will have, in effect, converted $30,000 of interest income into capital gain income, thereby saving almost $6,000 in tax.[64]

The law limits the ability of taxpayers to create debt instruments with interest rates that materially vary from market rates on the date the instrument is created.[65] Taxpayers are required to "impute interest" on a deferred payment contract for which no interest, or a low rate of interest, is stated. Imputing interest reallocates payments so that more of each payment is interest and less is principal. The imputed interest rules apply to installment transactions that are due more than six months after the date of the sale or exchange of property.

[59] Under IRC § 221.

[60] Under IRC § 135.

[61] Under IRC § 911, 931, and 933.

[62] Under § 137.

[63] Charging above-market rates is also possible but less likely.

[64] The $30,000 difference is taxed at 15% rather than 35%, so the taxpayer will save 20%, or $6,000.

[65] IRC § 483 and § 1274.

An installment obligation arises when a taxpayer sells property and does not receive the entire sales price at the time of sale. The imputed interest rules apply when the gross payments due under an installment contract are greater than the present value of the payments due under the contract, discounted at the applicable federal rate (AFR).[66] In effect, installment contracts with stated interest rates below the AFR will result in the imposition of the imputed interest rules. The AFR is determined monthly, varies with the term of the loan (short-, mid-, or long-term), and is based on the rate paid by the federal government on borrowed funds.

EXAMPLE 3-17

In 2017 Lloyd sells land for $40,000, payable with $5,000 down and the balance in five equal annual installments of $7,642, which include interest at 3%. Lloyd's basis in the land is $30,000. The AFR at the time of sale is 8%. The present value (PV) of the five annual payments discounted at 8% is $30,512. Thus the sales price is $35,512 (the PV of the payments plus the down payment), and Lloyd's capital gain is $5,512.

Here is the amortization schedule:

Year	Payment	Principal	Interest	Balance
				$30,512
2017	$7,642	$5,201	$2,441	25,311
2018	7,642	5,617	2,025	19,694
2019	7,642	6,067	1,575	13,627
2020	7,642	6,552	1,090	7,075
2021	7,642	7,075	567	–0–

The preceding calculations illustrate that Lloyd will have a capital gain of $5,512 and interest income of $7,698 rather than a capital gain of $10,000 and $3,210 of interest income.

The imputed interest rules do not apply to the following:[67]

- Debt subject to the original issue discount rules (see the following).
- Sales of property for $3,000 or less.
- Certain carrying charges.[68]
- Sales in which all payments are due in six months or less.
- In the case of sales of patents, any portion of the sales price that is contingent on the productivity, use, or disposition of the patent.

Taxpayers use the accrual basis to calculate imputed interest (even if the taxpayer reports on the cash basis) except in the following instances when cash basis reporting is permitted:[69]

- Sale of a personal residence.
- Sales of farms for $1 million or less.
- Sales in which total payments are $250,000 or less.
- Certain land transfers between related parties.[70]
- Debt in which the stated principal is $2 million or less and the lender and borrower elect to use the cash method (not applicable to accrual method lenders or dealers).

[66] The imputed interest rules in question are in IRC § 483(b). The AFR is determined under IRC § 1274(d).

[67] IRC § 483(d).

[68] Covered in IRC § 163(b).

[69] IRC § 1274(c)(3) and IRC § 1274A(c).

[70] Described in IRC § 483(e).

Gift, Shareholder, and Similar Loans

The concepts associated with imputed interest rules also apply to certain low-interest or interest-free loans involving related parties.[71] Imputed interest rules apply to term loans or demand loans in which the interest rate is less than the AFR and that occur in the following situations:

- Gift loans over $14,000 in which interest forgone is in the form of a gift. An example of a gift loan is a loan from a parent to a child in which no interest rate is stated. The $14,000 limit does not apply if the loan is for acquisition of income-producing assets.[72] However, imputed interest is limited to net investment income if the loan amount is $100,000 or less. No interest imputation is necessary if net investment income is less than $1,000.
- Compensation-related loans over $10,000 between an employee and employer or between an independent contractor and the corporation for which he or she works or any shareholder thereof.
- Loans over $10,000 between a corporation and any shareholder.
- Other loans in which the principal purpose is to avoid tax.
- Other loans in which the below-market or interest-free loan would have a significant effect on the tax liability of the borrower or lender.

EXAMPLE 3-18

Marty made interest-free loans to his three brothers, Pete, Bob, and Bill, of $8,000, $30,000, and $150,000, respectively. Pete used his $8,000 to buy a boat; Bob purchased IBM bonds with his $30,000 and earned $1,500 of investment income; and Bill bought a personal residence with his $150,000. The imputed interest rules would not apply to Pete because the loan is less than $10,000. The loans to Bob and Bill fall under the imputed interest rules because Bob purchased income-producing property (the interest expense would be limited to the $1,500 of net investment income) and Bill's loan was over $100,000.

Imputed interest is determined in a manner similar to that outlined earlier. The lender is deemed to give the borrower the amount of the calculated imputed interest, which the borrower then repays to the lender. Thus the transaction results in taxable interest income to the lender and interest expense to the borrower (which may or may not be deductible). For loans between an employer and employee, the deemed payment from the lender to the borrower creates compensation income to the employee. Similarly, deemed payments on loans between a corporation and a shareholder create dividend income to the shareholder.

Original Issue Discount

If someone purchases a debt instrument (such as a bond) from an issuer for an amount less than par, the transaction creates OID. The initial OID is equal to the difference between the acquisition price and the maturity value.[73]

EXAMPLE 3-19

On January 1, 2017, Leonardo purchased $200,000 of Meno Corporation's newly issued bonds for $176,100, to yield 11%. The bonds carry an interest rate of 9% and mature in 10 years. The initial OID on these bonds is $23,900 (the $200,000 face amount less the $176,100 payment).

OID is deemed to be zero if it is less than 0.25% of the maturity value, multiplied by the number of complete years to maturity.[74] In Example 3-19, this *de minimis* threshold is $5,000

[71] IRC § 7872.

[72] In the case of gift loans between individuals that total $100,000 or less, the amount of imputed interest is limited to the borrower's net investment income.

[73] IRC § 1273(a)(1).

[74] IRC § 1273(a)(3).

(0.0025 × 10 years × $200,000). Thus if Leonardo purchased the bonds for any amount more than $195,000, no OID is recognized.

If OID exists, the holder must include part of the OID in interest income every year, regardless of the holder's method of accounting (that is, the holder accounts for the income under the accrual method).[75] The taxpayer calculates the imputed interest using the constant interest rate method (sometimes referred to as the *effective interest method* that you probably learned in your financial accounting class). In this method, total interest income is equal to the carrying amount (basis) of the bond multiplied by the effective interest rate (the yield to maturity on the date of purchase). The amount of OID is the difference between interest income as calculated using the effective interest method and the amount of cash received. The carrying amount of the bond increases by the amount of OID.

EXAMPLE 3-20

Using the information from Example 3-19, we see that the effective interest calculations for the first four bond payments are as follows (remember that bond interest is paid semiannually):

Payment Date	(1) Interest Income	(2) Cash Received	(3) OID	(4) Carrying Amount
				$176,100
June 30, 2017	$9,686	$9,000	$686	176,786
Dec. 31, 2017	9,723	9,000	723	177,509
June 30, 2018	9,763	9,000	763	178,272
Dec. 31, 2018	9,805	9,000	805	179,077

Column (1) is the prior balance in column (4) times 11% divided by 2.
Column (2) is the $200,000 face amount multiplied by the 9% face rate divided by 2.
Column (3) is column (1) minus column (2).
Column (4) is the prior balance in column (4) plus the OID amount in column (3).

In 2017 Leonardo would report interest income of $19,409 ($9,686 + $9,723). Leonardo's interest income in 2018 would be $19,568.

OID rules apply to all debt instruments with OID except for[76]

- Tax-exempt debt.
- U.S. savings bonds.
- Debt with a maturity of one year or less on the date of issue.
- Any obligation issued by a natural person before March 2, 1984.
- Nonbusiness loans of $10,000 or less between natural persons.

An individual who sells a debt instrument with OID prior to maturity calculates OID on a daily basis until the date of sale.

The OID rules stated earlier apply to the original purchaser only. The Revenue Reconciliation Act of 1993 extended many of the provisions of the OID rules to market discount bonds,[77] which are bonds purchased in the bond market at a discount. The market discount is the difference between the redemption price (normally par) and the basis (cost) of the bond immediately after purchase.[78] The *de minimis* rule for OID also applies to market discount bonds.

With OID instruments, taxpayers report a portion of the OID as interest income annually. Such is not the case with market discount bonds. Rather, the gain on disposition of the bond, if any, is ordinary income to the extent of the accrued market discount (determined ratably on

[75] IRC § 1272(a)(1).

[76] IRC § 1272(a)(2).

[77] IRC § 1278.

[78] IRC § 1278(a)(2)(A).

a straight-line method computed on a daily basis). If a person holds the bond to maturity, the entire market discount amount is ordinary income.

EXAMPLE 3-21

Yvonne purchased $100,000 of the seven-year bonds of Ruby Company on July 1, 2017, for $90,000. The bonds were originally issued on January 1, 2015 (so at the time of purchase they had a remaining maturity of 4½ years). One year later, Yvonne sold the bonds for $96,000. Without the market discount bond rules, Yvonne would recognize a capital gain of $6,000. However, her capital gain is reduced (and her ordinary income is increased) by a portion of the market discount. Yvonne spreads the $10,000 discount over the maturity period (as of the date of purchase) on a straight-line basis, resulting in an allocation of $2,222 per year ($10,000 / 4.5). Thus Yvonne will recognize a capital gain of $3,778 and ordinary income of $2,222.

CONCEPT CHECK 3-8—
LO 3-5

1. An individual is required to impute interest on a deferred payment contract where no interest, or a low rate of interest, is stated. True or false?
2. If someone purchases a debt instrument (such as a bond) from an issuer for an amount less than par value, the transaction creates OID. True or false?

Summary

LO 3-1: Describe when and how to record income for tax purposes.

- Recognition of income for accounting takes place when the income has been realized and earned.
- Recognition of income for tax purposes is similar to the recognition of income for accounting, but three additional conditions must be met: economic benefit of the transaction, conclusion of the transaction, and the income derived from the transaction must not be tax-exempt income.

LO 3-2: Apply the cash method of accounting to income taxes.

- Almost all individuals use the cash receipts and disbursements method of accounting for taxes.
- An individual reports income in the year he or she receives or constructively receives the income rather than the year in which he or she earns the income.
- Receipt of property or services will trigger income recognition.
- Special situations exist in which a cash basis taxpayer can report income as though he or she were an accrual basis taxpayer.

LO 3-3: Explain the taxability of components of gross income, including interest, dividends, tax refunds, and social security benefits.

- If the amount of interest is over $1,500, use Schedule B for Forms 1040A and 1040.
- Interest from banks, savings and loans, or credit unions is reported on Form 1099-INT and is taxable.
- Interest earned on Series E, EE, and I U.S. savings bonds can be reported gradually on an annual basis or fully at maturity.
- Some interest received is tax-exempt if the debt is issued by a U.S. state, possession, or subdivision thereof (such as municipal bonds).
- Other sources of interest that must be reported: payments received from seller-financed mortgages, receipts from installment sale receivables, imputed interest on loans made with below-market interest rates, and interest on bonds sold between interest dates.

- If the amount of dividends is over $1,500, use Schedule B for Forms 1040A and 1040.
- Dividends are distributions to shareholders.
- Dividends are taxed at capital gain rates if they are qualified dividends.
- Stock dividends and stock splits are generally not taxable.
- State and local tax refunds are taxable if, in the prior tax year, the tax was deducted as an itemized deduction.
- Unemployment compensation is taxable.
- Part of social security benefits may be taxable. Provisional income must be calculated and compared to the information on the chart (see the text) showing the thresholds and taxability.
- Other income to be reported on the tax return: jury duty pay, prizes and awards, forgiveness of debt, and insurance proceeds in excess of the adjusted basis of the property.

LO 3-4: Apply the rules concerning items excluded from gross income.

- Congress has exempted certain income from tax by statute.
- Fringe benefits must be subject to nondiscrimination rules by the employer to qualify.
- Examples of fringe benefits not taxable in most circumstances: no-additional-cost services provided to an employee, discounts provided to employees for products or services normally sold by the business, a working condition fringe benefit, qualified transportation, moving expense reimbursements, and *de minimis* benefits.
- Nontaxable fringe benefits with certain limitations: life insurance, educational assistance, dependent care assistance, and cafeteria plans offered to employees.
- Other nontaxable income includes scholarships and fellowships, qualified tuition program (QTP) withdrawals, life insurance proceeds, gifts and inheritances, compensation for sickness or injury, child support, welfare, and employer-provided adoption assistance.

LO 3-5: Apply the rules associated with tax accounting for savings bond interest used for education expenses, below-market interest loans, gift loans, and original issue discount debt (Appendix).

- Savings bond interest exclusion can be taken for the full amount if the amount of qualified higher education expense paid in a year exceeds the redemption proceeds (principal plus interest).
- Limitation applies if modified AGI exceeds $117,250 on a joint return or $78,150 on other returns.
- Taxpayers are required to impute interest on a deferred payment contract if no interest, or a low rate of interest, is stated. Certain exceptions apply.
- Original issue discount (OID) is equal to the difference between the acquisition price and the maturity value.
- If OID exists, the holder must report part of the OID as income every year.

Discussion Questions

All applicable Discussion Questions are available with ***Connect***®

EA LO 3-2 1. Explain how income is recognized under the cash method of accounting.

____

____

____

____

EA LO 3-2 2. Are there circumstances in which income is recognized even when a cash basis taxpayer does not receive cash? Explain.

EA LO 3-2 3. What is meant by the concept of *constructive receipt*?

EA LO 3-2 4. Refer to Example 3-4 in the chapter. Explain why Antonio is required to report income even though he did not receive an asset (either cash or property).

EA LO 3-3 5. Your friend John files his own tax returns. He received a computer as a dividend from a closely held corporation. He says that he does not need to report the computer as dividend income because the dividend was not paid in cash. Is he right? Why?

EA LO 3-3 6. Interest on corporate bonds is taxable to the recipient whereas interest on municipal bonds is tax-free. Would you expect that the interest rate on a corporate bond would be higher or lower than the rate on a municipal bond of comparable quality and term? Why?

EA LO 3-3 7. What is a *dividend*?

EA LO 3-3 8. How are dividends taxed?

EA LO 3-3 9. Sam owns all of the stock in a newly formed corporation. During 2017, the first year of operation, the corporation realized current earnings and profits of $10,000. Sam received a $12,000 distribution from the corporation. How much, if any, of the distribution is taxable to Sam? Why?

EA LO 3-3 10. Under what circumstances is a dividend nontaxable to a shareholder recipient?

EA LO 3-3 11. How do *dividends* and *earnings and profits* relate to each other?

EA LO 3-3 12. Under what circumstances is a state or local income tax refund included in the taxable income of a taxpayer?

EA LO 3-3 13. Under what circumstances are social security benefits taxable to a single taxpayer?

EA LO 3-3 14. When determining the taxability of social security benefits, the IRC uses the concept of *provisional income*. How is provisional income calculated?

EA LO 3-4 15. Congress has chosen to exempt certain income from taxation, such as scholarships, gifts, life insurance proceeds, municipal bond interest, and employee fringe benefits. Given that one of the primary purposes of the IRC is to raise revenue for the government, why do you think Congress would provide these and other exemptions?

EA LO 3-4 16. What is an employer-provided fringe benefit?

EA LO 3-4 17. Define and give examples of a *de minimis* employee fringe benefit.

EA LO 3-4 18. Explain the requirements necessary for a scholarship to be tax-free to the recipient.

Multiple-Choice Questions connect

All applicable multiple-choice questions are available with ***Connect***®

EA LO 3-1 19. Accountants recognize revenue when it is both realized and

a. Recorded.
b. Accumulated.
c. Collected.
d. Earned.

EA LO 3-1 20. For tax purposes, one of the requirements to recognize income is that

a. There must be an economic benefit.
b. The income must be tax-exempt.
c. The transaction must occur but completion of the transaction is not necessary.
d. There must be a cash transaction.

EA LO 3-2 21. Income may be realized in the form of

a. Money or services.
b. Only money.
c. Money, services, or property.
d. None of the above.

EA LO 3-2 22. When filing their tax returns, almost all individuals use

a. The cash receipts and disbursements method.
b. The accrual method.
c. The recognition method.
d. The hybrid method.

EA LO 3-3 23. An individual must complete Schedule B (Forms 1040A or 1040) if the following situation occurs:

a. Receives child support payments of $1,600.

b. Receives interest income over $1,500.

c. Receives qualified dividends of $1,050.

d. Receives interest income of $1,450.

EA LO 3-3 24. The basis of the property received as a dividend by a shareholder of a corporation is

a. The book value at the date of distribution.

b. The original cost at the date of purchase.

c. The accounting value at the date of distribution.

d. The fair market value at the date of distribution.

EA LO 3-3 25. When an individual's marginal ordinary income tax rate is 25%, the tax rate on qualified dividends is

a. 0%.

b. 15%.

c. 25%.

d. 5%.

EA LO 3-3 26. Graciela, who is single, reported itemized deductions of $6,400 on her 2016 tax return. Her itemized deductions included $200 of state taxes paid. In 2017, she received a $150 refund of state taxes paid in 2016. What is the amount that Graciela needs to report on her 2017 tax return? Use the Internet (www.irs.gov) to find out how much the standard deduction was for 2016.

a. $200.

b. $100.

c. $0.

d. She needs to amend her 2016 tax return.

EA LO 3-3 27. Provisional income is calculated by starting with AGI before social security benefits and adding back specific items. One of these items is

a. Employer-provided adoption benefits.

b. Taxable interest income.

c. Wages earned.

d. Qualified dividends.

EA LO 3-3 28. Frank, who is single, received $7,000 of social security benefits. His AGI before the social security benefits was $15,000. He also had $100 of tax-exempt interest. What is the amount of taxable social security benefits?

a. $18,600.

b. $7,000.

c. $0.

d. $3,500.

EA LO 3-3 29. Items that must be reported on line 21 (other income) of Form 1040 include

a. Dividend income.

b. Capital gains.

c. Interest income.

d. Jury duty pay.

EA LO 3-4 30. Which of the following fringe benefits provided by the employer is *not* taxable to the employee?

a. Sick pay.

b. Vacation pay.

c. Bonus.

d. 10% discount on products sold by the business; the gross profit percentage for the business is 20%.

EA LO 3-4 31. Payments to employees under written dependent care assistance plans are tax-free. The exclusion cannot exceed the earned income of the lesser earning spouse and cannot exceed ____________ for an individual filing as married filing jointly.

a. $2,500.

b. $5,000.

c. $5,150.

d. $5,250.

EA LO 3-4 32. Employers can pay (or reimburse) employees for up to ____________ per year of educational assistance, whether or not the education is job-related.

a. $5,250.

b. $5,150.

c. $5,000.

d. $2,500.

EA LO 3-4 33. An example of nontaxable income is

a. Wages.

b. Dividend income.

c. Alimony payment.

d. Child support payment.

Problems connect

All applicable problems are available with ***Connect***©

EA LO 3-1 34. In 2012 Marie borrowed $10,000. In 2017 the debt was forgiven. Marie does not believe she should report the forgiveness of debt as income because she received nothing at the time the debt was forgiven in 2017. Do you agree or disagree? Support your position.

____

____

____

____

EA LO 3-2 35. Determine the amount of taxable income that should be reported by a cash-basis taxpayer in 2017 in each of the following independent cases:

a. A taxpayer completes $500 of accounting services in December 2017 for a client who pays for the accounting work in January 2018.

____

b. A taxpayer is in the business of renting computers on a short-term basis. On December 1, 2017, she rents a computer for a $200 rental fee and receives a $500 deposit. The customer returns the computer and is refunded the deposit on December 20, 2017.

____

c. Same facts as (b) except that the computer is returned on January 5, 2018.

d. On December 18, 2017, a landlord rents an apartment for $700 per month and collects the first and last months' rent up front. It is customary that tenants apply the security deposit to their last month's rent upon moving out.

e. An accountant agrees to perform $500 of tax services for an auto mechanic who has agreed to perform repairs on the car of the accountant's wife. The mechanic repairs the car in December 2017 and the accountant starts and completes the tax work in March 2018.

EA LO 3-3 36. A taxpayer who purchases a Series EE U.S. savings bond must report the interest income (i.e., increase in value) on the bond on the date the bond is redeemed, or the taxpayer can elect to report the interest currently in income. Under what circumstances should a taxpayer report income at maturity? Under what circumstances is it more advantageous to report income currently?

EA LO 3-3 37. Nancy, who is 59 years old, is the beneficiary of a $200,000 life insurance policy. What amount of the insurance proceeds is taxable under each of the following scenarios?

a. She receives the $200,000 proceeds as a lump-sum payment.

b. She receives the proceeds at the rate of $4,000 a month for five years.

c. She receives the proceeds in monthly payments of $1,300 over her remaining life expectancy (assume she will live 25 years).

d. Use the information from (c). If Nancy lives beyond her 25-year life expectancy, what amount of each monthly payment will be taxable in the 26th year?

EA LO 3-3 38. Determine the amount of tax liability in the following situations. In all cases, the taxpayer is using the filing status of married filing jointly.

a. Taxable income of $62,449 that includes a qualified dividend of $560.

b. Taxable income of $12,932 that includes a qualified dividend of $322.

c. Taxable income of $144,290 that includes a qualified dividend of $4,384.

d. Taxable income of $43,297 that includes a qualified dividend of $971.

e. Taxable income of $262,403 that includes a qualified dividend of $12,396.

EA LO 3-3 39. Each of the following taxpayers received a state income tax refund in 2017. In all cases, the taxpayer has a filing status of married filing jointly. What amount of the refund is properly included in 2017 income?

a. Refund of $729; taxpayer did not itemize deductions in 2016.

b. Refund of $591; taxpayer had $13,220 of itemized deductions in 2016.

c. Refund of $927; taxpayer had itemized deductions of $13,000 in 2016.

EA LO 3-3 40. A married couple received $10,000 of social security benefits. Calculate the taxable amount of those benefits if the couple's provisional income is (a) $20,000, (b) $41,000, and (c) $63,000.

EA LO 3-3 41. Carl and Karina file a joint return. Karina earned a salary of $38,000 and received dividends of $3,000, taxable interest income of $2,000, and nontaxable interest of $1,000. Carl received $9,000 of social security benefits and a gift of $6,000 from his brother. What amount of social security benefits is taxable to Carl and Karina?

EA LO 3-3 42. Sean, who is single, received social security benefits of $8,000, dividend income of $13,000, and interest income of $2,000. Except as noted, those income items are reasonably consistent from year to year. At the end of 2017, Sean is considering selling stock that would result in an immediate gain of $10,000, a reduction in future dividends of $1,000, and an increase in future interest income of $1,500. He has asked you for advice. What course of action do you recommend?

EA LO 3-4 43. Burger Store is located near many large office buildings, so at lunch it is extremely busy. Burger Store management previously permitted lunchtime employees a half-hour off-premises lunch break. However, employees could not easily return in a timely manner. Thus a new policy was instituted to allow employees a 20-minute break for free lunch (only on the Burger Store premises). The company's accountant believes that the cost of these meals must be allocated to employees as additional compensation because the meals do not qualify as a nontaxable fringe benefit for employee discounts. In your opinion, should the cost of these meals be taxable or tax-free to employees? Support your answer.

Discussion Questions Pertaining to Appendix (LO 3-5)

EA 44. Explain the rules governing the exemption of interest on U.S. savings bonds from taxation if it is used for educational purposes.

EA 45. Define *imputed interest.*

EA 46. Why were the interest imputation rules created?

EA 47. Briefly explain the application of the imputed interest rules.

EA 48. The interest imputation rules indirectly use a market rate of interest. What is meant by a *market rate of interest*?

EA 49. Define *original issue discount* (OID). Under what circumstances are the OID rules applied?

EA 50. Concerning the exemption for U.S. savings bond interest used for education expenses, what are the lower and upper income limitations for married taxpayers, and how is the exemption determined when taxpayer income falls between the limitation amounts?

EA 51. On July 1, 2017, Rene, a cash-basis taxpayer, purchased $500,000 of the newly issued bonds of Acce Corporation for $452,260. The 10-year bonds carry an interest rate of 8% and were sold to yield 9.5%. What amount of interest income must Rene report in 2017, 2018, and 2019?

EA 52. In 2017, Joseph and Patricia Jefferson redeemed $8,000 of Series EE U.S. savings bonds (principal of $5,500 and interest of $2,500), the proceeds from which were used to pay for qualified higher education expenses of their dependent daughter who is attending a qualified educational institution. For the year, tuition and fees were $8,000 and room and board cost $7,000. The daughter received a $2,000 tax-exempt scholarship during the year that was used to pay tuition and fees. The Jeffersons' modified AGI was $96,000 in 2017. They do not participate in any other higher education–related programs. Calculate the amount of savings bond interest that the Jeffersons can exclude from gross income in 2017.

EA 53. Daniel and Alexis, both 28, are interested in saving for the college education of their twin daughters Alie and Amber. They decide to purchase some Series EE U.S. savings bonds because they know that the interest on the bonds is tax-free in certain circumstances. To easily keep track of the savings for each child, they purchase half of the bonds in the names of Daniel and Alie and the other half in the names of Daniel and Amber. Assuming that current tax law does not change, under what circumstances will Daniel and Alexis be permitted to exclude interest on redemption of these bonds?

EA 54. A person is selling some property and wishes to obtain payment partially in cash with the remainder in the form of a carryback note receivable.

a. Why might the seller wish to increase the sales price and reduce the interest rate on the carryback note? Assume that the cash down payment and the total amount of payments will not change.

b. Would the buyer likely agree to the increased price and decreased interest rate? Why or why not?

Multiple-Choice Questions Pertaining to the Appendix (LO 3-5)

All applicable multiple-choice questions are available with ***Connect***©

EA 55. The amount of savings bond interest exempt from tax is limited when an individual is single and his or her AGI reaches

a. $117,250.

b. $77,550.

c. $78,150.

d. $76,000.

EA 56. Original issue discount (OID) is deemed to be zero if it is less than ___________ of the maturity value, multiplied by the number of complete years to maturity.

a. 0.25%.

b. 5%.

c. 25%.

d. 15%.

EA 57. An individual with an OID instrument must annually report a portion of the OID as

a. Dividend income.

b. Pension income.

c. Capital gain income.

d. Interest income.

Tax Return Problems

All applicable tax return problems are available with ***Connect***©

Use your tax software to complete the following problems. If you are manually preparing the tax returns, you will need to use a Form 1040 or Form 1040A, depending on the complexity of the problem.

Tax Return Problem 1

John and Martha Holloway are married filing jointly. They are 35 and 31 years old, respectively. Their address is 10010 Dove Street, Atlanta, GA 30294. Additional information about Mr. and Mrs. Holloway is as follows:

Social security numbers:

John: 412-34-5670	Martha: 412-34-5671
Date of birth: 3/4/1982	Date of birth: 8/20/1986
W-2 for John shows these amounts:	W-2 for Martha shows these amounts:
Wages (box 1) = $22,000.00	Wages (box 1) = $35,500.00
Federal W/H (box 2) = $ 2,200.00	Federal W/H (box 2) = $ 4,100.00
Social security wages (box 3) = $22,000.00	Social security wages (box 3) = $35,500.00
Social security W/H (box 4) = $ 1,364.00	Social security W/H (box 4) = $ 2,201.00
Medicare wages (box 5) = $22,000.00	Medicare wages (box 5) = $35,500.00
Medicare W/H (box 6) = $ 319.00	Medicare W/H (box 6) = $ 514.75

Form 1099-DIV for Martha shows this amount:
Box 1a and box 1b = $345.00 from MAR Brokerage.

Form 1099-INT for Martha shows these amounts:
Box 1 = $450.00 from ABC Bank.
Box 4 = $35.00.

John is a maintenance worker, and Martha is a human resources manager.

Prepare the tax return for Mr. and Mrs. Holloway using the appropriate form. They want to contribute to the presidential election campaign. Mr. and Mrs. Holloway had qualifying health care coverage at all times during the tax year.

Tax Return Problem 2 Carl and Elizabeth Williams are married filing jointly. They are 45 and 40 years old, respectively. Their address is 19010 N.W. 135th Street, Miami, FL 33054. Additional information about Mr. and Mrs. Williams is as follows:

Social security numbers:

Carl: 412-34-5670	Elizabeth: 412-34-5671
Date of birth: 7/13/1972	Date of birth: 9/19/1977
W-2 for Carl shows these amounts:	W-2 for Elizabeth shows these amounts:
Wages (box 1) = $75,000.00	Wages (box 1) = $31,000.00
Federal W/H (box 2) = $ 8,950.00	Federal W/H (box 2) = $ 3,700.00
Social security wages (box 3) = $75,000.00	Social security wages (box 3) = $31,000.00
Social security W/H (box 4) = $ 4,650.00	Social security W/H (box 4) = $ 1,922.00
Medicare wages (box 5) = $75,000.00	Medicare wages (box 5) = $31,000.00
Medicare W/H (box 6) = $ 1,087.50	Medicare W/H (box 6) = $ 449.50

Form 1099-INT for Carl and Elizabeth shows this amount:

Box 1 = $2,450.00 from Global Bank.

They also received tax-exempt interest of $500.00, as well as $45.00 for jury duty pay when Carl went to court to serve for a few days.

Carl received two weeks of workers' compensation pay for a total of $3,100.00.

Dependent: Son, Carl Jr., who is 7 years old. His date of birth is 3/25/2010. His social security number is 412-34-5672.

Carl is a sales manager, and Elizabeth is an office clerk.

Prepare the tax return for Mr. and Mrs. Williams using the appropriate form. They are entitled to a $1,000 child tax credit (this credit is discussed in Chapter 9). For now, enter the credit on the appropriate line of the form. They do not want to contribute to the presidential election campaign. Mr. and Mrs. Williams had qualifying health care coverage at all times during the tax year.

Tax Return Problem 3 Robert and Vilma Greene are married filing jointly. They are 68 and 66 years old, respectively. Their address is 1001 N.W. 93 Street, Miami, FL 33168. Additional information about Mr. and Mrs. Greene, who are retired, is as follows:

Social security numbers:

Robert: 412-34-5670	Vilma: 412-34-5671
Date of birth: 10/9/1949	Date of birth: 11/9/1951
SSA-1099 for Robert shows this amount:	SSA-1099 for Vilma shows this amount:
Box 5 = $21,600.00	Box 5 = $15,600.00
Form 1099-INT for Robert shows this amount:	Form 1099-INT for Vilma shows this amount:
Box 1 = $9,100.00 from CD Bank.	Box 1 = $7,500.00 from CD Bank.

Prepare the tax return for Mr. and Mrs. Greene using the appropriate form. They want to contribute to the presidential election campaign. Mr. and Mrs. Greene had qualifying health care coverage at all times during the tax year.

We have provided selected filled-in source documents that are available in the *Connect Library*.

Chapter **Four**

Adjustments *for* Adjusted Gross Income

Taxpayers can deduct certain items from total income for purposes of computing Adjusted Gross Income (AGI). In this chapter, we introduce you to most of these *for* AGI deductions. This is a key step in determining the actual tax liability of the individual.

Learning Objectives

When you have completed this chapter, you should understand the following learning objectives (LO):

- **LO 4-1** Describe the tax rules for student loan interest.
- **LO 4-2** Be able to determine eligibility requirements and applicable dollar limits related to the Health Savings Account deduction.
- **LO 4-3** Determine the deduction for moving expenses.
- **LO 4-4** Explain the deduction for half of self-employment taxes.
- **LO 4-5** Discuss the self-employed health insurance deduction.
- **LO 4-6** Explain the penalty on early withdrawal of savings.
- **LO 4-7** Be able to calculate the deduction for alimony paid.
- **LO 4-8** Determine the deduction for educator expenses.
- **LO 4-9** Be able to calculate the deduction for eligible tuition and fees.

INTRODUCTION

In previous chapters, we primarily discussed tax rules and the presentation of many components of total income (line 22 on Form 1040). Taxpayers can also deduct certain items from total income to arrive at Adjusted Gross Income (AGI). These deductible items are *for* AGI deductions, commonly referred to as *above-the-line* deductions (AGI is considered to be "the line"). AGI is critically important to the calculation of other key items on the tax return. *For* AGI deductions are on Form 1040, lines 23 to 35, or Form 1040A, lines 16 to 19.[1] See Exhibit 4-1 for the AGI portion of Form 1040.

You may recall that certain deductions are also subtracted from AGI to arrive at taxable income. These *from* AGI deductions, or *below-the-line* deductions, are standard or itemized deductions and personal exemptions. In effect, gross income minus *for* AGI (above-the-line) deductions equals AGI. If you then subtract *from* AGI (below-the-line) deductions, you will get taxable income.

[1] We do not discuss all *for* AGI deductions in this chapter. Taxpayers may also take *for* AGI deductions for contributions to Individual Retirement Accounts (Form 1040, line 32) and to retirement plans for self-employed individuals (Form 1040, line 28). We discuss these deductions in Chapter 11.

EXHIBIT 4-1

Adjusted Gross Income				
23	Educator expenses	23		
24	Certain business expenses of reservists, performing artists, and fee-basis government officials. Attach Form 2106 or 2106-EZ	24		
25	Health savings account deduction. Attach Form 8889	25		
26	Moving expenses. Attach Form 3903	26		
27	Deductible part of self-employment tax. Attach Schedule SE	27		
28	Self-employed SEP, SIMPLE, and qualified plans	28		
29	Self-employed health insurance deduction	29		
30	Penalty on early withdrawal of savings	30		
31a	Alimony paid **b** Recipient's SSN ►	31a		
32	IRA deduction	32		
33	Student loan interest deduction	33		
34	Reserved for future use	34		
35	Domestic production activities deduction. Attach Form 8903	35		
36	Add lines 23 through 35		36	
37	Subtract line 36 from line 22. This is your **adjusted gross income** ►		37	

Source: U.S. Department of the Treasury, Internal Revenue Service, Form 1040. Washington, DC: 2017.

STUDENT LOAN INTEREST (FORM 1040, LINE 33, OR FORM 1040A, LINE 18) LO 4-1

Tax law provides numerous tax benefits for expenses associated with obtaining education beyond high school. These benefits are available for individuals saving for higher education (Coverdell Education Savings Accounts, state tuition programs, and qualified U.S. savings bonds), for many expenses incurred while attending a qualified educational institution (American opportunity/Hope and lifetime learning credits), and for interest paid on loans incurred for higher education expenses.[2]

Paying higher education expenses often requires students or their parents or guardians to borrow money from lending institutions such as banks or from federal or state student loan programs. An individual can take a deduction for "an amount equal to the interest paid by the taxpayer during the taxable year on any qualified education loan."[3] Only the person legally obligated to make the interest payments can take the deduction.[4] *A person who is claimed as a dependent on another person's return cannot claim the deduction,*[5] *nor can persons whose filing status is married filing separately.*[6]

EXAMPLE 4-1

In 2013 Juana borrowed $5,000 for higher education expenses on a qualified education loan. In 2017, when she began making payments on the loan, she was still living at home and her parents appropriately claimed her as a dependent. Juana cannot claim the student interest deduction. Although she was the person legally obligated to repay the loan, she was claimed on the return of another person.

The amount of this deduction is limited to $2,500 per year.[7] The deduction may be further limited based on the modified Adjusted Gross Income of the taxpayer.

[2] Coverdell Education Savings Accounts and the American opportunity (AOTC) and lifetime learning credits are discussed in Chapters 9 and 11, respectively.

[3] IRC § 221(a).

[4] Reg. § 1.221-1(b).

[5] IRC § 221(c).

[6] IRC § 221(e)(2).

[7] IRC § 221(b)(1).

Qualified Education Loan

A *qualified education loan* is one incurred by the taxpayer solely to pay qualified education expenses on behalf of the taxpayer, taxpayer's spouse, or any dependent of the taxpayer at the time the loan was incurred.[8] Note that the loan must be *solely* to pay for educational expenses. Thus home equity loans or revolving lines of credit often do not qualify. Qualified education expenses must be paid or incurred within a reasonable period before or after the loan date.[9] Expenses meet this test if the proceeds of the loan are disbursed within 90 days of the start or 90 days after the end of the academic period. Federal education loan programs meet this criterion. The expenses also must occur during the period the recipient was carrying at least half the normal full-time workload for the intended course of study.[10] The course of study can be at the undergraduate or graduate level.

Qualified Education Expenses

Qualified education expenses are the costs of attending an eligible educational institution.[11] These costs include tuition, fees, books, supplies, equipment, room, board, transportation, and other necessary expenses of attendance. However, taxpayers must reduce qualified expenses by the amount of income excluded from gross income in each of the following cases. In each instance, because the income is not included, the item does *not* create a deduction:

- An employer-paid educational assistance program.[12]
- Redemption of U.S. savings bonds used to pay higher education tuition and fees.[13]
- Funds withdrawn from a Coverdell Education Savings Account.[14]
- Qualified tax-free scholarships and fellowships.[15]
- Armed forces' or veterans' educational assistance allowances.[16]
- Any other educational assistance excludable from gross income (not including gifts, bequests, devises, or inheritances).[17] This category includes a state-qualified tuition plan.

EXAMPLE 4-2

In September Reggie spent $3,000 on qualified educational expenses. He received a loan for $2,800 in the same month as he paid the expenses. During the semester, he received a scholarship of $500 that she properly excluded from income. Reggie's qualified educational expenses are $2,500 ($3,000 − $500). As a result, interest on $2,500 of the $2,800 loan will be eligible for student loan interest treatment while interest on the remaining $300 is nondeductible personal interest.

Other Provisions and Limitations

As noted earlier, deductible education expenses must occur in conjunction with attendance at an eligible educational institution. An *eligible institution* is generally a postsecondary educational institution that meets the requirements to participate in the federal student loan program.[18] The Health Care and Reconciliation Act of 2010 made some substantial changes to the administration of the federal student loan program. This includes almost all four-year colleges and

[8] IRC § 221(d)(1)(A).

[9] IRC § 221(d)(1)(B), Reg. § 1.221-1(e)(3)(ii).

[10] IRC § 221(d)(3), IRC § 25A(b)(3).

[11] IRC § 221(d)(2).

[12] IRC § 127.

[13] IRC § 135.

[14] IRC § 530.

[15] IRC § 117.

[16] IRC § 25A(g)(2)(B).

[17] IRC § 25A(g)(2)(C).

[18] IRC § 221(d)(2), IRC § 25A(f)(2).

universities, two-year community colleges, and many trade and technical schools. The classification also incorporates institutions with an internship or residency program leading to a degree or certificate awarded by an institute of higher education, a hospital, or a health care facility that offers postgraduate training.[19] Qualified expenses must be for an academic period during which the student was enrolled at least half-time in one of these qualifying programs.

The deduction for interest on qualified education loans may be limited based on the modified Adjusted Gross Income of the taxpayer.[20] *Modified AGI* is equal to the AGI on the taxpayer's tax return plus (a) any deduction for student loan interest, (b) any foreign, U.S. possession, or Puerto Rican income excluded from taxable income, (c) any deduction taken for tuition and fees, and (d) any deduction taken with regard to domestic activities production.[21]

The deductible amount of student loan interest is reduced when modified AGI reaches \$135,000 on a joint return (\$65,000 for a single return) and is totally eliminated when modified AGI reaches \$165,000 (\$80,0000 for single returns).[22] The following formula is used:

Preliminary deduction × Fraction (see below) = Disallowed interest

For married taxpayers, the fraction is (Modified AGI – \$135,000)/\$30,000.

For single taxpayers, the fraction is (Modified AGI – \$65,000)/\$15,000.

The denominators in these fractions represent the difference between the beginning and the end of the phaseout range (that is, for married filing jointly, the \$30,000 denominator is the difference between \$135,000 and \$165,000). These fractions represent the disallowed proportion of the preliminary deduction.

Note that the preliminary deduction amount cannot exceed the \$2,500 maximum allowed deduction.

EXAMPLE 4-3

Al and Marian borrowed \$30,000 on a qualified educational loan to pay for qualified higher education expenses for their two children. During 2017 they paid \$1,800 interest on the loan. Al and Marian's modified AGI on their joint return was \$155,000. They are entitled to deduct \$600 as follows:

$$\$1{,}800 \times \frac{\$155{,}000 - \$135{,}000}{\$30{,}000} = \$1{,}200 \text{ disallowed}$$

Permitted deduction = \$1,800 – \$1,200 = \$600.

TAX YOUR BRAIN

If Al and Marian paid \$3,200 interest on the loan in 2017, what is the allowed deduction for student loan interest?

ANSWER

Because the interest deduction is limited to a total of \$2,500 before the AGI limitation, the couple would be entitled to an \$833 deduction as follows:

$$\$2{,}500 \times \frac{\$155{,}000 - \$135{,}000}{\$30{,}000} = \$1{,}667 \text{ disallowed}$$

Permitted deduction = \$2,500 – \$1,667 = \$833.

[19] IRC § 221(d)(2)(B).

[20] IRC § 221(b)(2).

[21] IRC § 221(b)(2)(C)(i).

[22] These limitation amounts are adjusted for inflation under IRC § 221(f).

From Shoebox to Software

There are generally four critical issues concerning student loan interest:

- Whether the loan was taken out solely for education expenses.
- Whether loan funds were used for education expenses.
- The amount of the interest payment for the year.
- Limitation of the deduction based on AGI phaseouts.

Identifying applicable loans and maintaining (or in some cases obtaining) proper documentation is more difficult because a number of years usually transpire between the date that the loan is created, the date that the expenses are paid, and the date the interest deduction is sought. On many student loans, the student can elect to defer payments while enrolled in college and even after that point for certain economic hardship reasons. Be careful, however; deferral does not prevent interest from accruing.

Loans made through the federal student loan program usually meet the first two critical issues because the U.S. government intends that these loans cover education expenses not paid by student earnings or parental contributions. The federal government provides an annual report to the taxpayer (often a substitute Form 1099-INT) that provides the amount of interest paid during the year.

Loans from financial institutions require a higher level of documentation. The taxpayer should review loan documents and canceled checks to determine whether the loan and the expenditures qualify for favored treatment. Lenders normally provide Form 1098-E (see Exhibit 4-2) indicating the amount of interest paid by the taxpayer in a year.

In both cases, when preparing a return using tax software, you enter applicable information on a Student Loan Interest Deduction worksheet. The Student Loan Interest Deduction worksheet can be found in IRS Publication 970, Tax Benefits for Education (Exhibit 4-3).

EXHIBIT 4-2

☐ CORRECTED (if checked)

RECIPIENT'S/LENDER'S name, street address, city or town, state or province, country, ZIP or foreign postal code, and telephone number		OMB No. 1545-1576 **2017** Form **1098-E**	**Student Loan Interest Statement**
RECIPIENT'S federal identification no.	BORROWER'S social security number	**1** Student loan interest received by lender $	**Copy B** **For Borrower**
BORROWER'S name Street address (including apt. no.) City or town, state or province, country, and ZIP or foreign postal code			This is important tax information and is being furnished to the Internal Revenue Service. If you are required to file a return, a negligence penalty or other sanction may be imposed on you if the IRS determines that an underpayment of tax results because you overstated a deduction for student loan interest.
Account number (see instructions)		**2** If checked, box 1 does **not** include loan origination fees and/or capitalized interest for loans made before September 1, 2004 . . . . ☐	

Form **1098-E** (keep for your records) www.irs.gov/form1098e Department of the Treasury - Internal Revenue Service

Source: U.S. Department of the Treasury, Internal Revenue Service, Form 1098-E. Washington, DC: 2017.

(continued)

EXHIBIT 4-3

Student Loan Interest Deduction Worksheet—Line 33

Keep for Your Records

Before you begin:
- √ Figure any write-in adjustments to be entered on the dotted line next to line 36 (see the instructions for line 36).
- √ Be sure you have read the **Exception** in the instructions for this line to see if you can use this worksheet instead of Pub. 970 to figure your deduction.

1.	Enter the total interest you paid in 2017 on qualified student loans (see the instructions for line 33). **Don't** enter more than $2,500		**1.** ______
2.	Enter the amount from Form 1040, line 22	**2.** ______	
3.	Enter the total of the amounts from Form 1040, lines 23 through 32, plus any write-in adjustments you entered on the dotted line next to line 36	**3.** ______	
4.	Subtract line 3 from line 2	**4.** ______	
5.	Enter the amount shown below for your filing status. • Single, head of household, or qualifying widow(er)—$65,000 • Married filing jointly—$135,000	**5.** ______	
6.	Is the amount on line 4 more than the amount on line 5? ☐ **No.** Skip lines 6 and 7, enter -0- on line 8, and go to line 9. ☐ **Yes.** Subtract line 5 from line 4	**6.** ______	
7.	Divide line 6 by $15,000 ($30,000 if married filing jointly). Enter the result as a decimal (rounded to at least three places). If the result is 1.000 or more, enter 1.000		**7.** ___.___
8.	Multiply line 1 by line 7		**8.** ______
9.	**Student loan interest deduction.** Subtract line 8 from line 1. Enter the result here and on Form 1040, line 33. **Don't** include this amount in figuring any other deduction on your return (such as on Schedule A, C, E, etc.)		**9.** ______

Source: IRS *Publication 970*

CONCEPT CHECK 4-1— LO 4-1

1. For the interest on a student loan to qualify for the deduction, the student must be enrolled at least ____________.
2. Under the student loan program, qualified educational expenses include ____________ and ____________.
3. The deductible amount of student loan interest is reduced when modified AGI for those filing married jointly reaches ____________.

HEALTH SAVINGS ACCOUNT DEDUCTION (FORM 1040, LINE 25)

LO 4-2

A Health Savings Account (HSA) is a tax-exempt savings account used for qualified medical expenses for the account holder, his or her spouse, and dependents. In general, qualified taxpayers can take a *for* AGI deduction for contributions to the HSA.[23] Contributions grow tax-free, and distributions are not taxable if used for qualified medical expenses.

To be eligible to fund an HSA, a taxpayer, under the age of 65, must be self-employed; an employee (or spouse) of an employer who maintains a high-deductible health plan (HDHP); or an employee of a company that has no health coverage, and the employee has purchased a high-deductible policy on his or her own. In addition, the individual cannot have other health insurance except for coverage for accidents, disability, dental care, vision care, long-term care, or workers' compensation.[24] In addition, the taxpayer cannot be enrolled in Medicare and cannot be claimed as a dependent on someone else's return. No permission or authorization from the IRS is required to establish an HSA. In order to set up an HSA, the taxpayer must work with a trustee who serves as custodian of the account.

[23] IRC § 223(a).

[24] IRC § 223(c)(1)(B).

From Shoebox to Software

Taxpayers who contribute to or withdraw from an HSA during the year must file Form 8889 and attach it to their Form 1040. Form 8889 is shown in Exhibit 4-4.

EXHIBIT 4-4

Form **8889** Department of the Treasury Internal Revenue Service

Health Savings Accounts (HSAs)

▶ Attach to Form 1040 or Form 1040NR.
▶ Go to *www.irs.gov/Form8889* for instructions and the latest information.

OMB No. 1545-0074 **2017** Attachment Sequence No. **52**

Name(s) shown on Form 1040 or Form 1040NR | Social security number of HSA beneficiary. If both spouses have HSAs, see instructions ▶

Before you begin: Complete Form 8853, Archer MSAs and Long-Term Care Insurance Contracts, if required.

DRAFT AS OF JULY 25 2017 DO NOT FILE

Part I **HSA Contributions and Deduction.** See the instructions before completing this part. If you are filing jointly and both you and your spouse each have separate HSAs, complete a separate Part I for each spouse.

1	Check the box to indicate your coverage under a high-deductible health plan (HDHP) during 2017 (see instructions) . . . ▶	☐ Self-only ☐ Family	
2	HSA contributions you made for 2017 (or those made on your behalf), including those made from January 1, 2018, through April 17, 2018, that were for 2017. **Do not** include employer contributions, contributions through a cafeteria plan, or rollovers (see instructions) . . .	2	
3	If you were under age 55 at the end of 2017, and on the first day of **every** month during 2017, you were, or were considered, an eligible individual with the **same** coverage, enter $3,400 ($6,750 for family coverage). **All others,** see the instructions for the amount to enter . . .	3	
4	Enter the amount you and your employer contributed to your Archer MSAs for 2017 from Form 8853, lines 1 and 2. If you or your spouse had family coverage under an HDHP at any time during 2017, also include any amount contributed to your spouse's Archer MSAs . . .	4	
5	Subtract line 4 from line 3. If zero or less, enter -0- . . .	5	
6	Enter the amount from line 5. But if you and your spouse each have separate HSAs and had family coverage under an HDHP at any time during 2017, see the instructions for the amount to enter . . .	6	
7	If you were age 55 or older at the end of 2017, married, and you or your spouse had family coverage under an HDHP at any time during 2017, enter your additional contribution amount (see instructions) . . .	7	
8	Add lines 6 and 7 . . .	8	
9	Employer contributions made to your HSAs for 2017 . . . **9**		
10	Qualified HSA funding distributions . . . **10**		
11	Add lines 9 and 10 . . .	11	
12	Subtract line 11 from line 8. If zero or less, enter -0- . . .	12	
13	**HSA deduction.** Enter the **smaller** of line 2 or line 12 here and on Form 1040, line 25, or Form 1040NR, line 25 . . .	13	
	Caution: *If line 2 is more than line 13, you may have to pay an additional tax (see instructions).*		

Part II **HSA Distributions.** If you are filing jointly and both you and your spouse each have separate HSAs, complete a separate Part II for each spouse.

14a	Total distributions you received in 2017 from all HSAs (see instructions) . . .	14a	
b	Distributions included on line 14a that you rolled over to another HSA. Also include any excess contributions (and the earnings on those excess contributions) included on line 14a that were withdrawn by the due date of your return (see instructions) . . .	14b	
c	Subtract line 14b from line 14a . . .	14c	
15	Qualified medical expenses paid using HSA distributions (see instructions) . . .	15	
16	**Taxable HSA distributions.** Subtract line 15 from line 14c. If zero or less, enter -0-. Also, include this amount in the total on Form 1040, line 21, or Form 1040NR, line 21. On the dotted line next to line 21, enter "HSA" and the amount . . .	16	
17a	If any of the distributions included on line 16 meet any of the **Exceptions to the Additional 20% Tax** (see instructions), check here . . . ▶ ☐		
b	**Additional 20% tax** (see instructions). Enter 20% (0.20) of the distributions included on line 16 that are subject to the additional 20% tax. Also include this amount in the total on Form 1040, line 62, or Form 1040NR, line 60. Check box c on Form 1040, line 62, or box b on Form 1040NR, line 60. Enter "HSA" and the amount on the line next to the box . . .	17b	

For Paperwork Reduction Act Notice, see your tax return instructions. Cat. No. 37621P Form **8889** (2017)

Source: U.S. Department of the Treasury, Internal Revenue Service, Form 8889. Washington, DC: 2017.

(continued)

A trustee, normally a bank or insurance company, administers the HSA. Trustees are required to provide HSA holders contribution and distribution information. Contributions are reported on Form 5498-SA (see Exhibit 4-5). Taxpayers use contribution information to prepare Part I of Form 8889.

Distributions are reported by the trustee on Form 1099-SA, shown in Exhibit 4-6. The distributions are reported on Part II of Form 8889 (see Exhibit 4-4).

EXHIBIT 4-5

☐ CORRECTED (if checked)

TRUSTEE'S name, street address, city or town, state or province, country, ZIP or foreign postal code, and telephone number		1 Employee or self-employed person's Archer MSA contributions made in 2017 and 2018 for 2017 $	OMB No. 1545-1518 **2017** Form **5498-SA**	**HSA, Archer MSA, or Medicare Advantage MSA Information**
		2 Total contributions made in 2017 $		
TRUSTEE'S federal identification number	PARTICIPANT'S social security number	3 Total HSA or Archer MSA contributions made in 2018 for 2017 $		**Copy B** **For Participant**
PARTICIPANT'S name		4 Rollover contributions $	5 Fair market value of HSA, Archer MSA, or MA MSA $	
Street address (including apt. no.) City or town, state or province, country, and ZIP or foreign postal code		6 HSA ☐ Archer MSA ☐ MA MSA ☐		This information is being furnished to the Internal Revenue Service.
Account number (see instructions)				

Form **5498-SA** (keep for your records) www.irs.gov/form5498sa Department of the Treasury - Internal Revenue Service

Source: U.S. Department of the Treasury, Internal Revenue Service, Form 5498-SA. Washington, DC: 2017.

EXHIBIT 4-6

☐ CORRECTED (if checked)

TRUSTEE'S/PAYER'S name, street address, city or town, state or province, country, ZIP or foreign postal code, and telephone number			OMB No. 1545-1517 **2017** Form **1099-SA**	**Distributions From an HSA, Archer MSA, or Medicare Advantage MSA**
PAYER'S federal identification number	RECIPIENT'S identification number	1 Gross distribution $	2 Earnings on excess cont. $	**Copy B** **For Recipient**
RECIPIENT'S name		3 Distribution code	4 FMV on date of death $	
Street address (including apt. no.) City or town, state or province, country, and ZIP or foreign postal code		5 HSA ☐ Archer MSA ☐ MA MSA ☐		This information is being furnished to the Internal Revenue Service.
Account number (see instructions)				

Form **1099-SA** (keep for your records) www.irs.gov/form1099sa Department of the Treasury - Internal Revenue Service

Source: U.S. Department of the Treasury, Internal Revenue Service, Form 1099-SA. Washington, DC: 2017.

Any insurance company or any bank (including a similar financial institution as defined in section 408(n)) can be an HSA trustee or custodian. In addition, any other person already approved by the IRS to be a trustee or custodian of IRAs or Archer MSAs is automatically approved to be an HSA trustee or custodian. Other persons may request approval to be a trustee or custodian in accordance with the procedures set forth in Treas. Reg. § 1.408-2(e) (relating to IRA nonbank trustees).

An HDHP is a health plan with specified minimum deductible amounts and a maximum annual deductible and out-of-pocket expense limitation.[25] *Out-of-pocket expense* represents the amount the health plan requires the policyholder to pay for covered benefits (other than the premium). Essentially, an HDHP is a health insurance plan with lower premiums and higher deductibles than a traditional health plan. It is a form of catastrophic coverage. For calendar year 2017, these amounts are as follows:

	Minimum Deductible	Maximum Deductible and Annual Out-of-Pocket Expenses
Individual coverage	$1,300	$ 6,550
Family coverage	$2,600	$13,100

The employee or employer contributes to the HSA. For individual coverage maximum, the aggregate contribution an individual under age 55 can make to an HSA is $3,400. For family coverage, with a contributor under age 55, the maximum aggregate annual contribution is $6,750.[26]

If the taxpayer is 55 or older, he or she may contribute an additional $1,000 in 2017. This assumes that only one spouse has an HSA. If both spouses have separate HSAs, see IRS Publication 969 for further information. Individuals are now allowed to make a one-time contribution to an HSA of an amount distributed from their IRA. The contribution must be made in a direct trustee-to-trustee transfer. Amounts distributed from the IRA are not includable in the individual's income to the extent that the distribution would otherwise be includable in income. Such distributions are not subject to the 20% additional tax on early distributions. An individual who becomes covered by a high-deductible plan during the year can make a contribution to an HSA as if he or she was eligible for the entire year. Contributions for a tax year must be made by the due date of the return.

Contributions made by a qualified individual are a *for* AGI deduction, assuming that the limitations are met. If an employer contributes, the amount is not deductible (because the employee paid nothing), but the payment is not counted as income to the employee. The funds in the account are allowed to accumulate from year to year and the interest or other earnings on the assets in the account are tax free.

Distributions from HSAs are tax-free if they are used to pay for qualified medical expenses.[27] Part I of Form 8889, Health Savings Accounts, is used to report the amount of the deduction that is reported on line 25. Form 8889 must be attached to the taxpayer's return. The form is also used to report the taxable and nontaxable amounts of a distribution from an HSA. You can find additional information about HSAs in IRS Publication 969.

Funds contained within an HSA account are exempt from tax. An employee is always 100% vested in his or her HSA. Amounts that remain in the HSA at the end of the year are carried over to the next year. Earnings on amounts in an HSA are not included in income while held in the HSA.

CONCEPT CHECK 4-2— LO 4-2

1. To be eligible to fund an HSA, a taxpayer must be __________, an employee (or spouse) of an employer who maintains a high-deductible health plan, or an uninsured employee who has purchased a high-deductible policy on his or her own.
2. If they are used to pay for qualified medical expenses, distributions from HSAs are __________.
3. If taxpayers make contributions to or withdrawals from an HSA during the year, they must file Form __________ and attach it to their Form __________.

[25] IRC § 223(c)(2).
[26] IRC § 223(b).
[27] IRC § 223(d)(2).

MOVING EXPENSES (FORM 1040, LINE 26)

LO 4-3

An employee or self-employed individual who moves his or her principal residence because of a change in employment may deduct certain moving expenses.[28] *Moving expenses* are reasonable expenses for the following:

- Moving household goods and personal effects from the old residence to the new residence.
- Traveling from the old residence to the new residence (including lodging but excluding meals).[29]

Additionally, moving expenses include temporary storage of household goods within a consecutive 30-day period after items are moved from the former home and actual expenses or mileage for driving a personal auto at a rate of 17 cents per mile for 2017. Nonqualified moving expenses generally include house-hunting costs before the move, costs incurred in buying and selling a home, and temporary living expenses and costs of meals incurred while moving.

Moving expenses of persons other than the taxpayer are permitted if the other persons are members of the taxpayer's household and both the old and new residences are the persons' principal place of abode.[30] This situation most often occurs in the case of family members or other dependents who also move with the taxpayer. Travel is limited to one trip per person.

Tests for Moving Expense Deductibility

To qualify for a moving expense deduction, taxpayers must meet three tests.

Change in Employment Test

For the first test, the move must be the result of a change in the taxpayer's principal place of work.[31] The move will be considered due to a new work location if the move is within one year of the date the taxpayer started working at the new location. If there is no change of job location, the taxpayer cannot take the moving expense deduction. However, a taxpayer starting work for the first time qualifies provided he or she meets the distance test outlined next. In addition, there is no requirement that the new job be in the same line of work as the old job.

Distance Test

The second test is the distance test. The new job location must be at least 50 miles farther from the taxpayer's old residence than was the old job location.[32] For example, if the old residence was 15 miles from the old job, the new job must be at least 65 miles away from the old residence. If the taxpayer had no old job (that is, the taxpayer was unemployed), the new job must be more than 50 miles away from his or her old residence.[33] A diagram illustrating the application of the distance test is shown in Exhibit 4-7.

EXHIBIT 4-7
Distance Test Diagram

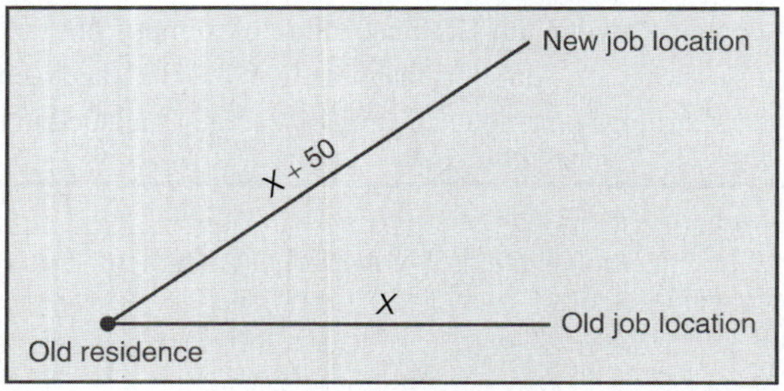

[28] IRC § 217(a).
[29] IRC § 217(b)(1).
[30] IRC § 217(b)(2).
[31] IRC § 217(a).
[32] IRC § 217(c)(1).
[33] IRC § 217(c)(1)(B).

So if the distance between the old residence and the old job is defined as X miles, the new job must be at least $X + 50$ miles from the old residence. An easy way to determine whether this test is met is to use the following table:

Worksheet 1. **Distance Test**

	Note. Members of the U.S. armed forces may not have to meet this test. See *Members of the Armed Forces.*		
1.	Enter the number of miles from your old home to your new workplace	**1.**	miles
2.	Enter the number of miles from your old home to your old workplace	**2.**	miles
3.	Subtract line 2 from line 1. If zero or less, enter -0-	**3.**	miles
4.	Is line 3 at least 50 miles? ☐ Yes. You meet this test. ☐ No. You do not meet this test. You cannot deduct your moving expenses.		

Time Test

The third test is the time test. To meet this test, a taxpayer must meet either of the following:

- Be a full-time employee for a period of 39 weeks during the 12 months immediately following arrival in the new area.
- Be self-employed for at least 78 weeks during the 24 months immediately following arrival in the new area. At least 39 of the 78 weeks must be during the first 12-month period.[34]

To meet the time test, the taxpayer need not remain employed in the new job for the entire 39- or 78-week period; but the full-time employment (or self-employment) must be in the same general location as the new job for which the taxpayer moved.[35] Therefore, a taxpayer who gets a job in a new city, moves there, works for the new employer for 2 months, and then obtains a different full-time job in the same area for the next 10 months meets the time test.

For a married couple, if both obtain new jobs in a new area, the taxpayers can deduct moving expenses if either spouse satisfies the time test.[36] However, spouses must separately account for their weeks worked (weeks worked by one spouse cannot be added to weeks worked by the other spouse).

Moving expenses are deductible only in the year incurred. Often taxpayers do not meet the time test by the due date of the tax return for the appropriate tax year. If the taxpayer expects to be able to comply with the time test, the taxpayer can choose either to deduct the moving expenses in the year incurred or to wait until he or she meets the test and then file an amended return claiming the deduction.[37] If the taxpayer elects to deduct the moving expenses prior to satisfying the time test and later does not meet the test, the moving expenses are disallowed, and the taxpayer must include the previously deducted expenses in income in the subsequent year or file an amended return for the year in which the expenses were deducted.[38]

EXAMPLE 4-4

Becca moved from Atlanta to Chicago in October 2017 because of a new job and incurred moving expenses of $4,000. She filed her 2017 return in March 2018. As of that date, the time test was not satisfied. Becca was employed full time in Chicago from October 2017 to March 2018; thus it was still possible that the time test could be satisfied. Becca elected to deduct the $4,000 moving expenses on her 2017 tax return. If, by the end of 2018, she satisfied the time test, Becca would take no further action. However, if she did not satisfy the time test by the end of 2018, she must include $4,000 in her 2018 gross income or file an amended return for 2017.

[34] IRC § 217(c)(2).
[35] Reg. § 1.217-2(c)(4)(iii).
[36] Reg. § 1.217-2(c)(4)(v).
[37] IRC § 217(d)(2) and Reg. § 1.217-2(d)(2).
[38] Reg. § 1.217-2(d)(3).

From Shoebox to Software

When using tax software to report moving expenses, there are multiple sources of tax-related information and two different forms used by taxpayers. Open the tax software using any of the clients we have used in the book so you can look at the worksheets and forms used for moving expenses.

To determine whether a taxpayer can take the moving expense deduction, the first task is to provide information concerning the time and distance tests. *This information is usually provided on the Form 3903—Distance and Time Tests worksheet section.* On this worksheet, you enter information concerning the two tests. If the taxpayer does not meet one or both of the tests, it is not necessary to continue because no moving expense deduction is permitted.

If a taxpayer meets the tests, you must then provide information concerning the amount of moving expenses and associated reimbursement, if any. Form 3903 is used for this purpose (see Exhibit 4-8).

Note that lines 1 and 2 of Form 3903 are shown in green in the tax software. This means that you input the data for these lines directly on Form 3903. The amount on line 1 pertains to the cost of moving and storing the household goods, and line 2 is for reporting the travel and lodging expenses for the individuals being moved.

Employers report reimbursements (if any) to the employee on Form W-2. The reimbursement amount is in box 12 and will have a code of P. When you enter the W-2 data, any code P amount will automatically be shown on line 4 of Form 3903. If expenses exceed reimbursements, the software will show the excess on Form 1040, line 26. Similarly, the software will report reimbursements in excess of expenses on Form 1040, line 21, as other income.

Sources of information for moving expenses include canceled checks and credit card statements (accompanied by supporting documentation) and miscellaneous cash receipts. If the taxpayer obtains reimbursement from his or her employer, the documentation provided to the employer is often an excellent source document.

EXHIBIT 4-8

Form **3903** — Department of the Treasury, Internal Revenue Service (99)

Moving Expenses

► Go to *www.irs.gov/Form3903* for the latest information.
► Attach to Form 1040 or Form 1040NR.

OMB No. 1545-0074 — **2017** — Attachment Sequence No. **170**

Name(s) shown on return | **Your social security number**

Before you begin: ✓ See the **Distance Test** and **Time Test** in the instructions to find out if you can deduct your moving expenses.
✓ See **Members of the Armed Forces** in the instructions, if applicable.

1	Transportation and storage of household goods and personal effects (see instructions)	1	
2	Travel (including lodging) from your old home to your new home (see instructions). **Do not** include the cost of meals	2	
3	Add lines 1 and 2	3	
4	Enter the total amount your employer paid you for the expenses listed on lines 1 and 2 that is **not** included in box 1 of your Form W-2 (wages). This amount should be shown in box 12 of your Form W-2 with code **P**	4	
5	Is line 3 **more than** line 4? ☐ **No.** You **cannot** deduct your moving expenses. If line 3 is less than line 4, subtract line 3 from line 4 and include the result on Form 1040, line 7, or Form 1040NR, line 8. ☐ **Yes.** Subtract line 4 from line 3. Enter the result here and on Form 1040, line 26, or Form 1040NR, line 26. This is your **moving expense deduction**	5	

For Paperwork Reduction Act Notice, see your tax return instructions. Cat. No. 12490K Form **3903** (2017)

Source: U.S. Department of the Treasury, Internal Revenue Service, Form 3903. Washington, DC: 2017.

The time test does not apply if failure to meet the test was a result of any of the following:

- Death or disability of the taxpayer.
- Involuntary separation from employment (other than for willful misconduct).
- A retransfer of the employee for the benefit of the employer (that was not initiated by the employee).[39]

In each of the last two exceptions, the taxpayer must have had a reasonable expectation to meet the time test, absent the noted cause.

Neither the distance nor the time test applies to moves made by members of the U.S. armed forces who are on active duty and who have moved pursuant to a military order including a permanent change of station.[40] There are also some separate rules that apply to the moving expenses incurred by those moving to a new work location outside of the United States. Additional information on these and other issues can be found in IRS Publication 521.

Employer Moving Expense Reimbursements

Employers may reimburse employees for some or all of their moving expenses. If the taxpayer would have been able to deduct the reimbursed expenses had the taxpayer paid them directly, the taxpayer can exclude the reimbursement from income.[41] In such a case, the taxpayer cannot deduct the reimbursed moving expenses.[42] If the employer reimburses less than the amount of deductible expenses, the taxpayer can deduct the excess expenses. If the reimbursement is more than the amount of deductible expenses (for example, if the employer reimburses the employee for meals), the excess reimbursement is gross income.

CONCEPT CHECK 4-3—
LO 4-3

1. Moving expenses can be deducted either as a *for* AGI deduction or as an itemized deduction on Schedule A. True or false?
2. A taxpayer who meets the time test does not have to be concerned about the distance test. True or false?
3. If an employer reimburses an employee for moving costs, the employee cannot deduct those expenses on the tax return. True or false?

DEDUCTION FOR HALF OF SELF-EMPLOYMENT TAX (FORM 1040, LINE 27)

LO 4-4

Self-employed individuals must normally pay self-employment tax equal to 15.3% of their net earnings from self-employment.[43] The self-employment tax is the FICA tax for social security and Medicare that W-2 employees have deducted from their paychecks at a rate of 7.65% and that employers must match at the same rate. Self-employed individuals are responsible for both halves of the tax, and the tax is calculated on the net earnings of the business. Self-employed persons are allowed a *for* AGI deduction equal to one-half of the self-employment tax imposed.[44] The tax software will automatically calculate the appropriate amount for line 27. Self-employment tax is calculated on Form SE; it is covered in more detail in Chapter 6.

One ObamaCare provision, that is now in effect, relates to the portion of FICA taxes pertaining to the Medicare tax. It requires that an additional Medicare tax of 0.9% be assessed for

[39] IRC § 217(d)(1).

[40] IRC § 217(g).

[41] IRC § 132(a)(6) and IRC § 132(g).

[42] See Reg. § 1.217-2(a)(2) for guidance when the reimbursement and moving expenses occur in different tax years.

[43] IRC § 1401.

[44] IRC § 164(f).

those individuals, according to filing status, whose income exceeds the following threshold amounts:

Filing Status	Threshold Amount
Married filing jointly	$250,000
Married filing separately	$125,000
Single	$200,000
Head of household	$200,000
Qualifying widow(er)	$200,000

An employer is required by law to withhold the additional Medicare tax from wages it pays to individuals in excess of $200,000 in a calendar year. This added tax raises the wage earner's Medicare portion of FICA compensation to 2.35 percent, above the regular 1.45 percent.

CONCEPT CHECK 4-4— LO 4-4

1. Self-employment tax is calculated on the ______________ earnings of the business.
2. For W-2 employees, for 2017 the total FICA tax is calculated at a rate of ______________ of their gross earnings.
3. An employer is required by law to withhold the additional Medicare tax from wages it pays to individuals in excess of $______________ in a calendar year.

SELF-EMPLOYED HEALTH INSURANCE DEDUCTION (FORM 1040, LINE 29) LO 4-5

Payments for health insurance for self-employed individuals, their spouse, and their dependents are not deductible as a business expense on Schedule C.[45] However, applicable taxpayers can deduct, as a *for* AGI deduction, 100% of self-employed health insurance premiums.[46]

The amount of the deduction may be limited in two respects. First, taxpayers cannot take a deduction for any amount in excess of net earnings from self-employment from the trade or business under which coverage is provided.[47] Net earnings from self-employment are determined by reducing gross income by the regular expenses of the business as well as the deduction for one-half of the self-employment tax and any deduction for contributions to qualified retirement plans.

EXAMPLE 4-5

Gia had net earnings of $2,800 from self-employment. She paid $160 per month for health insurance ($1,920 per year). Gia is entitled to a *for* AGI deduction of $1,920 for health insurance. If Gia net earnings from self-employment were $1,500, her deduction would have been limited to $1,500.

The second limitation pertains to availability of other health insurance coverage. If the taxpayer is entitled to participate in any subsidized health plan maintained by any employer of the taxpayer or of the taxpayer's spouse, a deduction is not allowed.[48] Eligibility for alternative coverage is determined on a monthly basis. A *subsidized health plan* is one in which someone other than the employee pays for part or all of the cost of the plan.

EXAMPLE 4-6

Wendy is self-employed and had net earnings from self-employment of $17,000 for the year. She has an individual-only health insurance policy through her business for which she pays $145 per month. An unrelated local business employs Taylor, her husband. Taylor's employer provides health insurance coverage for all employees and pays $100 toward the monthly premium of each employee. Taylor can cover Wendy under his policy, but the couple has chosen not to do so because the cost would be higher than Wendy's current policy. In this case, Wendy cannot deduct any of her health insurance premiums because she is entitled to participate under a subsidized plan. The fact that she chooses not to be covered does not matter.

[45] IRC § 162(l)(4). Chapter 6 covers the taxation of self-employed individuals.

[46] IRC § 162(l)(1)(B).

[47] Generally, net earnings from self-employment are defined in IRC § 1402(a). For purposes of the health insurance deduction, that definition is modified by IRC § 401(c)(2).

[48] IRC § 162(l)(2)(B).

TAX YOUR BRAIN

Using the information from Example 4-6, assume that Taylor did not begin work at the local business until April 1, 2017. Prior to that time, he was an employee of Wendy's business, and both he and Wendy were covered under a group policy that cost $300 per month. On April 1 Wendy changed to an individual policy at $145 per month. How much can Wendy deduct for self-employed health insurance in 2017?

ANSWER

$900. Wendy is entitled to deduct the health insurance costs for herself and her spouse for the first three months of the year ($300 × 3 months). After that time, she is eligible under Taylor's policy, so she cannot take any additional deductions.

The alternative coverage rule is applied separately to plans that provide long-term care services or are qualified long-term care insurance contracts and to plans that do not provide such services.[49]

EXAMPLE 4-7

Patrick is self-employed and is entitled to participate in a subsidized qualified long-term care insurance plan through his wife Jennifer's employer. The general health care plan offered by Jennifer's employer is not subsidized. Patrick is entitled to participate in both health plans. He chooses to obtain general health care and qualified long-term care insurance through his own business. Patrick will be able to deduct the cost of the general health care plan (subject to the income limitation), but he cannot deduct the cost of the long-term care insurance. The general rule is that if someone else is willing to pay for insurance coverage, fully or partially, the premiums are not deductible.

The self-employed health insurance deduction is also available to a partner in a partnership and to a shareholder in a Subchapter S corporation who owns more than 2% of the stock in the corporation.[50] In the case of a Subchapter S shareholder, wages from the corporation are included in self-employed income for purposes of determining the deduction limitation based on net earnings from self-employment.

CONCEPT CHECK 4-5—
LC 4-5

1. Self-employed individuals are allowed to take a *for* AGI deduction for up to 80% of the cost of their self-employed health insurance premiums. True or false?
2. One limitation on this deduction is that taxpayers cannot deduct the premium cost that exceeds gross earnings from self-employment. True or false?
3. Another limitation on this deduction is that eligible participation in a health plan subsidized by the employer of either the taxpayer or the taxpayer's spouse will prohibit the deduction.

PENALTY ON EARLY WITHDRAWAL OF SAVINGS (FORM 1040, LINE 30)

LO 4-6

Certificates of deposit (CDs) and time savings accounts normally require holding an investment for a fixed period ranging from three months to five years. Often the rules associated with these financial instruments state that a depositor who withdraws the funds prior to the end of the fixed term will forfeit a certain amount of interest to which he or she would otherwise be entitled. For example, a two-year CD might state that the depositor will forfeit three months of interest on the CD in the event the depositor withdraws the money before the end of the two-year period. If such a premature withdrawal occurs, the taxpayer will be credited with the entire amount of interest (and that amount must be reported as interest income), but the financial institution will deduct three months of interest as a penalty.

If a taxpayer incurs an early withdrawal of savings penalty, the taxpayer is entitled to report the penalty as a *for* AGI deduction on line 30 of Form 1040.[51]

[49] IRC § 162(l)(2)(B)(i)&(ii).

[50] IRC § 162(l)(5) and IRC § 1372(a).

[51] IRC § 62(a)(9).

From Shoebox to Software

Financial institutions report early withdrawal penalties in box 2 of Form 1099-INT (see Exhibit 4-9). When you record the Form 1099-INT, the software automatically carries forward the box 2 amount onto line 30 of Form 1040.

EXHIBIT 4-9

☐ CORRECTED (if checked)

PAYER'S name, street address, city or town, state or province, country, ZIP or foreign postal code, and telephone no.	Payer's RTN (optional) 1 Interest income $	OMB No. 1545-0112 2017 Form **1099-INT**	**Interest Income**
	2 Early withdrawal penalty $		**Copy B** **For Recipient**
PAYER'S federal identification number | RECIPIENT'S identification number	3 Interest on U.S. Savings Bonds and Treas. obligations $		
RECIPIENT'S name	4 Federal income tax withheld $	5 Investment expenses $	This is important tax information and is being furnished to the Internal Revenue Service. If you are required to file a return, a negligence penalty or other sanction may be imposed on you if this income is taxable and the IRS determines that it has not been reported.
Street address (including apt. no.)	6 Foreign tax paid $	7 Foreign country or U.S. possession	
City or town, state or province, country, and ZIP or foreign postal code	8 Tax-exempt interest $	9 Specified private activity bond interest $	
	10 Market discount $	11 Bond premium $	
FATCA filing requirement ☐	12 Bond premium on Treasury obligations $	13 Bond premium on tax-exempt bond $	
Account number (see instructions)	14 Tax-exempt and tax credit bond CUSIP no.	15 State | 16 State identification no.	17 State tax withheld $ $

Form **1099-INT** (keep for your records) www.irs.gov/form1099int Department of the Treasury - Internal Revenue Service

Source: U.S. Department of the Treasury, Internal Revenue Service, Form 1099-INT. Washington, DC: 2017.

EXAMPLE 4-8

On February 1, 2017, Ricardo and Marie deposited $10,000 into a one-year CD earning 2% interest at State Bank and Trust. If the couple withdrew their money prior to the end of the term, they would forfeit one month's interest as a penalty. On October 1, 2017, they withdrew their money. Ricardo and Marie would report $133 interest income on line 8A of the 1040 or, if required, on Schedule B ($10,000 × 2% × 8/12). They would also report a *for* AGI deduction of $17 ($10,000 × 2% × 1/12) as a penalty on early withdrawal of savings.

CONCEPT CHECK 4-6—
LO 4-6

1. The early withdrawal penalty is reported on Form 1040 as a(n) ________________ deduction.
2. The amount of the penalty is reported to the taxpayer by the financial institution on Form ________________.

ALIMONY PAID (FORM 1040, LINE 31A)

LO 4-7

In a divorce or legal separation, certain payments may flow from one party to the other. These payments are (a) alimony, (b) child support, or (c) a property settlement. Of the three, only alimony has a tax consequence, and it is important to be able to distinguish it from the other two types of payments.

Child support is a fixed payment (in terms of dollars or a proportion of the payment) that is payable for the support of children of the payer spouse.[52] A *property settlement* is a division of property of the marital community incident to a divorce.[53] For tax purposes, child support payments and property settlement payments do not result in income to either spouse; nor does either spouse receive a tax deduction.

The payment of alimony, however, has tax ramifications.[54] Alimony received is taxable to the payee (receiving) spouse in the year received.[55] It is income on line 11 of Form 1040. Alimony payments are deductible by the payer spouse in the year paid as a *for* AGI deduction.[56]

To qualify as *alimony,* a payment must be cash and must be required under the provisions of a decree of divorce or separate maintenance or the provisions of a written separation agreement or other decree requiring one spouse to make payments to support the other spouse.[57] All payments must occur after the decree or after the execution of the agreement. Any payments made prior to this time would be neither deductible by the payer spouse nor included in the income of the payee spouse.

All payments must end at the payee spouse's death. There can be no provisions to make payments to the estate of the spouse or in any other manner after the death of the spouse. If this rule is not satisfied, then none of the payments are alimony, even those made during the life of the spouse.[58]

Alimony includes payments made to third parties on behalf of the payee spouse under the terms of the divorce decree or separate maintenance agreement.[59] Such payments might include paying the spouse's rent, mortgage, car payment, or property taxes. Payments made to maintain property owned by the payer spouse but used by the payee spouse do not qualify as alimony.[60]

Payments are not alimony if the spouses file a joint return or if they live in the same household when payments occur.[61] However, if a payment is made when the spouses are living together and one spouse is preparing to leave the household and does so within one month after the payment, such payment will be considered alimony. Furthermore, if the spouses are not yet legally separated under a decree of divorce and a payment is made under a written separation agreement, such payment will count as alimony even if the spouses are members of the same household when the payment is made.[62]

Finally, if the divorce decree or separate maintenance agreement states that certain payments are not alimony, the agreement will control.[63]

[52] IRC § 71(c)(1).

[53] IRC § 1041.

[54] The IRC refers to payments for "alimony or separate maintenance." In general, *separate maintenance* refers to payments made by one spouse to another while separated but still married, whereas *alimony* payments are those made after the divorce becomes final. For purposes of this section, we will refer to these payments simply as *alimony.*

[55] IRC § 71.

[56] IRC § 62(a)(10) and IRC § 215(a).

[57] IRC § 71(b)(2).

[58] IRC § 71(b)(1)(D) and Reg. § 1.71-1T(b), Q&A-10.

[59] IRC § 71(b)(1).

[60] Reg. § 1.71-1T(b), Q&A-6.

[61] IRC § 71(e) and IRC § 71(b)(1)(C).

[62] Reg. § 1.71-T(b), Q&A-9.

[63] IRC § 71(b)(1)(B).

From Shoebox to Software

Alimony received is reported on line 11 of Form 1040. Alimony paid is reported on line 31a. Persons making alimony payments must report the taxpayer identification number of the recipient on line 31b.

In the tax software, you report information concerning alimony received or paid on a worksheet (Alimony Income or Alimony Paid Adjustment, as the case may be). The tax software carries the information forward to the appropriate line on Form 1040.

Canceled checks or other forms of payment provide information about the amount of alimony payments. Whether the payments constitute alimony is determined by reference to the divorce decree or separation agreement. In particularly complex cases, the taxpayer should obtain the advice of an attorney.

EXAMPLE 4-9

Akeem, who had previously moved out of the home, and Taylor entered into a separation agreement on July 20, 2017. The agreement required Akeem to make payments of $300 per month to Taylor beginning on July 20, 2017. Their divorce decree was final on December 12, 2017. Under terms of the divorce, Akeem transferred title on the couple's house to Taylor's name. The house was worth $100,000 at the time of the transfer. The divorce decree also mandated that, beginning in December 2017, Akeem make payments on the 12th of each month of (a) $200 to Taylor for maintenance of the couple's only child, (b) $400 per month to Taylor, and (c) mortgage payments of $800 to the bank on behalf of Taylor. Payments for the child will continue until she reaches age 18; payments to or on behalf of Taylor will cease upon her death. They will file separate returns for 2017. How much can Akeem deduct in 2017 and 2018 for alimony?

In 2017, Akeem may deduct the $300 payments required under the separate maintenance agreement for July through November, one $400 payment to Taylor, and one $800 payment to the bank. The alimony payments total $2,700 for 2017. The value of the house is a property settlement, and the monthly $200 for their child is child support. Neither of these items has any tax effect for either party. For 2018, Akeem will be able to deduct $1,200 per month ($400 + $800), or $14,400 for the year. Note also that the amount of alimony income that Taylor must report is the same as the amount of alimony deduction calculated by Akeem.

TAX YOUR BRAIN

Would the answer to Example 4-9 change if Akeem did not move out until January 30, 2018?

ANSWER

Yes. The payments Akeem made on December 12 are not alimony because both he and Taylor were members of the same household on the date of the payment, and Akeem did not move out within one month thereafter. Deductible payments for 2018 would not change.

Alimony Recapture Rules

If alimony payments decrease sharply in the second or third year of payment, the payments may be subject to a recapture provision.[64] This relates to the concept of "substance over form"; the payments may be called alimony but are, in substance, a property settlement. Note that these recapture rules do not apply after the third year of payment.

[64] IRC § 71(f).

The recapture rules effectively reclassify payments from alimony to a property settlement. If recapture is required, the recipient (who previously recorded income) treats the recapture amount as a deduction, and the payer (who previously recorded a deduction) must count the recapture as income. The recapture occurs in the third postseparation year.[65]

TAX YOUR BRAIN

Why would the IRS care about the timing and magnitude of alimony payments?

ANSWER

Alimony payments create income for one taxpayer and a deduction for another, whereas property settlements have no tax effect on either party. In practice, it is likely that the tax rates of the spouses will differ after the divorce, perhaps significantly. For example, one spouse could be in the 35% bracket while the other one is in the 15% bracket. Taxpayers may try, in effect, to shift income from the high-tax spouse to the low-tax spouse.

CONCEPT CHECK 4-7— LO 4-7

1. Alimony may be paid in either cash or property, as long as the payments are made on a regular basis to a non-live-in ex-spouse. True or false?
2. For payments to qualify as alimony, the couple must be legally divorced at the time payments are made. True or false?
3. The goal of the alimony recapture rule is to properly define the substance of payments made to a former spouse to ensure proper tax treatment. True or false?

EDUCATOR EXPENSES (FORM 1040, LINE 23)

LO 4-8

Eligible educators may deduct up to $250 of qualified education expenses as an above-the-line AGI deduction.[66] The deduction is taken on Form 1040. If the taxpayer's filing status is married filing jointly and both individuals are eligible educators, the maximum deduction is $500, but neither spouse can deduct more than $250 of his or her expenses. Taxpayers must reduce otherwise permitted qualified expenses by any reimbursements received pertaining to the expenses.

An eligible educator is a teacher, instructor, counselor, principal, or aide in a kindergarten through 12th grade school who devotes at least 900 hours in the school year to that job.[67] Qualification under the 900-hour test is measured within the academic year while the $250 deduction applies to expenses paid for during the calendar year.

Qualified education expenses are those for books, supplies, equipment (including computers and software), and other materials used in the classroom. The expense must also be ordinary (common and accepted in the educational field) and necessary (helpful and appropriate in the taxpayer's educational profession). Expenses for home schooling or for nonathletic supplies for health or physical education courses do not qualify. The Protecting Americans from Tax Hikes (PATH) Act of 2015 further enhanced this deduction by allowing "professional development expenses" to qualify.

Professional development expenses cover courses related to the curriculum in which the educator provides instruction. This enhancement applies to tax years that began after 2015.

Expenses exceeding $250 and nonclassroom supplies may be deducted as an employment-related miscellaneous deduction subject to the 2% floor by eligible taxpayers who itemize. (See Chapter 5.)

[65] IRC § 71(f)(6).

[66] IRC § 62(a)(2)(D).

[67] IRC § 62(d)(1).

EXAMPLE 4-10

William and Lakeisha are married and will file a joint tax return. Both are eligible educators. William spent $420 on eligible expenses for his 4th grade class, and he received a $190 reimbursement from his school. Lakeisha spent $360 pertaining to her 11th grade science class and received no reimbursement. In total, the couple spent $780 and received reimbursement of $190, for a net expense of $590. However, William deduction is limited to his net expenses of $230 ($420 − $190), and Lakeisha's is limited to a maximum of $250. Thus the total deduction on their joint tax return is $480.

CONCEPT CHECK 4-8—
LO 4-8

Please fill in the blanks with the best answer(s).

1. To be eligible for the deduction, an educator must work at least ____________ hours in the job.
2. The maximum deduction for a couple who are both eligible educators and married filing jointly is ____________.
3. Expenses for ____________ and ____________ do not qualify for this deduction.

TUITION AND FEES DEDUCTION (FORM 1040, LINE 34)
LO 4-9

Taxpayers may be eligible to take a deduction for qualified tuition and related expenses paid during 2017 for the taxpayer, taxpayer's spouse, or a dependent.[68] The deduction is a maximum of $4,000 but can be smaller if the modified AGI of the taxpayer exceeds certain limits.[69] The full $4,000 deduction is allowed if you have AGI less than $65,000 (single, head of household, qualifying widow) or less than $130,000 (married filing jointly). The deduction is limited to $2,000 if your AGI is between $65,000 and $80,000 (unmarried taxpayers) or is between $130,000 and $160,000 (married filing jointly). The deduction is zero above those amounts. Payments must be to a qualified educational institution (see the definition in the "Student Loan Interest" section) and must be for a student taking one or more courses at that institution. Taxpayers cannot claim a deduction for tuition paid for elementary and secondary school education. Taxpayers must attach Form 8917 when claiming this deduction.

Only tuition and related expenses qualify.[70] Related expenses are student activity fees and fees for course-related books, supplies, and equipment but only if the school requires the payment as a condition of enrollment or attendance. For instance, some schools include books as part of the tuition fees. Sal enrolls in an art class at a qualified educational institution. In addition to applicable tuition, the school charges $50 to pay for supplies used in the class. The $50 fee would qualify as a related expense.

EXAMPLE 4-11

Riki enrolls in an art class at a qualified educational institution. In addition to applicable tuition, the school charges $50 to pay for supplies used in the class. The $50 fee would qualify as a related expense.

EXAMPLE 4-12

The school in Example 4-11 requires art students either to provide their own supplies or to pay the $50 fee. Riki decides to pay the $50 fee directly to the school. The fee would not be a qualified expense because the school does not require payment of the fee as a condition of enrollment or attendance.

[68] IRC § 222(a).
[69] IRC § 222(b).
[70] IRC § 25A(f).

From Shoebox to Software Comprehensive Examples

In this section, we will add information to the tax returns of two taxpayers introduced in Chapter 3.

YIMING CHOW

Open the tax return file of Yiming Chow that you saved from Chapter 3. You are now going to add some information pertaining to the two *for* AGI deductions.

Moving Expense

Mr. Chow moved from Somewhere, Colorado, to Mytown, Georgia, on February 3, 2017, as a direct result of changing jobs. The distance between those two towns is 1,844 miles, and the distance from his old house to his old workplace was 27 miles. Beta Tech has continuously employed him in Mytown since his move. He paid the moving company $1,106 to move his belongings, including his auto, and spent another $319 in air travel and lodging expenses and $71 in meals pertaining to his move. His employer reimbursed him $842 for the move.

To properly report Mr. Chow's moving expense deduction, you need to perform the following steps:

Modify the W-2 information previously entered for Mr. Chow to reflect the newly created employer reimbursement. To do this, open his W-2. Go to box 12. Click on the code area of box 12 and highlight the P code. Then enter $842 in the amount box.

Go to the worksheets area and open the federal Form 3903 Distance and Time worksheet. You might first want to enter the information in the distance worksheet at the bottom of the form and then, if applicable, continue entering the remainder of the information.

Student Loan Interest Deduction

Mr. Chow also incurred $622 of interest expense pertaining to a federal student loan incurred while he was a student at State University in Colorado.

You must perform the following steps to report the student loan interest.

Open Mr. Chow's Form 1040.

Click on line 33. Then click on the yellow folder to open the supporting form. Alternatively, you could have opened the Student Loan Interest Deduction worksheet in the worksheet section.

On line 1 enter the $622 interest payment beside Mr. Chow's name.

Line 16 of the worksheet should now read $622. If you reopen Mr. Chow's Form 1040, the $622 deduction should be reflected on line 33.

After you have entered the moving expense and student loan interest data, Mr. Chow's AGI is $40,483 and his taxable income is $30,183. His total tax liability is $4,040. Because his total tax withholdings were $4,670, he should now receive a refund of $630 (rather than having a refund of $450 as determined in Chapter 3).

As mentioned, Mr. Chow now reports on Form 1040 rather than the 1040A that he was able to use in Chapter 3. This is so because Form 1040A does not accommodate a moving expense deduction. The tax software automatically chose the proper reporting form

When you have finished, remember to save Mr. Chow's tax return for use in later chapters.

JOSE AND MARIA RAMIREZ

Open the tax return file of Mr. and Mrs. Ramirez that you saved from Chapter 3. You will now add some information pertaining to alimony. Remember that for now we are assuming the standard deduction for the Ramirezes.

Mr. Ramirez pays alimony of $150 per month to his former wife (her SSN is 412-34-5666). He paid 12 payments during the year. To record the alimony payments in the tax software, perform the following steps:

Open the Ramirezes' tax return and then open their Form 1040.

Go to the form's worksheet tab and bring up the Alimony Paid Adjustment worksheet.

On the worksheet, enter $6,000 as the amount of alimony paid by Jose and enter his ex-wife's SSN.

Open the Ramirezes' Form 1040. The $1,800 alimony payment is on line 31a and the ex-wife's SSN is on the adjacent dotted line.

After you have entered the alimony information, the AGI of the Ramirezes is $110,048. Their taxable income is $77,098, and their total tax liability is $10,373. After the child tax credit of $3,000, and income tax withheld of $9,418, they will receive a refund of $2,045.

When you have finished, make sure you save the Ramirezes' tax return for use in later chapters.

Summary

LO 4-1: Describe the tax rules for student loan interest.	• Only interest on a *qualified* student loan is potentially deductible. • A *qualified* loan is one used solely to pay for qualified education expenses. • The deduction for student loan expense may be limited based on the modified AGI of the taxpayer.
LO 4-2: Be able to determine eligibility requirements and applicable dollar limits related to the Health Savings Account deduction.	• A Health Savings Account (HSA) is a tax-exempt savings account used to pay for qualified medical expenses. • To be eligible for an HSA, the taxpayer must be self-employed, an employee (or spouse) of an employer with a high-deductible health plan, or an uninsured employee who has purchased a high-deductible policy on his or her own. • Distributions from an HSA are tax-free as long as they are used to pay for qualified medical expenses.
LO 4-3: Determine the deduction for moving expenses.	• If a taxpayer moves due to a change in employment location, certain expenses related to moving may be deducted. • The costs of moving goods and people from the old residence to the new residence are considered suitable expenses. • The deductibility of moving expenses is subject to employment, time, and distance tests.
LO 4-4: Explain the deduction for half of self-employment taxes.	• Self-employed individuals pay both halves of the FICA tax. For 2017 self-employed individuals will pay self-employment tax of 15.3%, unless their income is above the threshold for their filing status that requires them to pay the additional 0.9% Medicare tax on their earnings, effectively raising their Medicare tax on earnings from 1.45% to 2.35%. • The amount related to the employer's portion of the self-employment tax that is a *for* AGI (above-the-line deduction) deduction remains at 7.65% of self-employment income for 2017. • The tax is based on the *net* earnings from self-employment.

LO 4-5: Discuss the self-employed health insurance deduction.	• Self-employed individuals may be able to deduct 100% of self-employed health insurance premiums.
	• The amount of the deduction may be limited by two factors:
	  • Self-employed individuals cannot take a deduction in excess of the *net* earnings from self-employment.
	  • The amount is a function of the availability of other health insurance coverage.

LO 4-6: Explain the penalty on early withdrawal of savings.	• A taxpayer who withdraws funds early from a time deposit account may be subject to an early withdrawal penalty. • The amount of the penalty is reported on a Form 1099-INT issued by the financial institution.
LO 4-7: Be able to calculate the deduction for alimony paid.	• Alimony is one of three potential payments that can exist in a divorce or legal separation. • Of the three, only alimony has a tax consequence. • If payments properly qualify as alimony, they are deductible by the payer as a *for* AGI (above-the-line) deduction. • The recipient (the payee) of the payments must include these payments as income on his or her tax return. • When dealing with the character of payments in a divorce, it is important to use the "substance over form" rule.

LO 4-8: Determine the deduction for educator expenses.	• Educators may be able to deduct up to $250 of qualified out-of-pocket expenses paid in 2017. • If both spouses are eligible educators and file a joint return, each may deduct up to $250. • Qualified educators who work at least 900 hours during the school year are eligible to take the deduction. • Qualifying expenditures include classroom supplies such as paper, pens, glue, scissors, books, and computers as well as professional development expenses cover courses related to the curriculum in which the educator provides instruction.
LO 4-9: Be able to calculate the deduction for eligible tuition and fees.	• An above-the-line education tuition deduction is available for both single and joint filers in 2017. • The deduction is two-tiered ($4,000 or $2,000) that is tied to AGI thresholds. • Only higher education tuition and qualifying fees are eligible for the deduction. • Taxpayers must attach Form 8917 when claiming this deduction. • Taxpayers taking this above-the-line deduction cannot also claim the American opportunity or lifetime learning credit for the same student for additional expenses related to his or her education.

Discussion Questions connect

All applicable Discussion Questions are available with ***Connect***©

EA LO 4-1 1. What is a qualified education loan for purposes of the student loan interest deduction?

EA LO 4-1 2. What are qualified education expenses for purposes of the student loan interest deduction?

EA LO 4-1 3. For purposes of the student loan interest deduction, what is modified AGI, and how is it determined?

EA LO 4-1 4. For purposes of the student loan interest deduction, what is an eligible educational institution?

EA LO 4-1 5. Explain the limitations associated with the deductibility of student loan interest.

EA LO 4-1 6. In 2013 Chara incurred a loan to pay for qualified higher education expenses for her 20-year-old grand daughter, who was a dependent. In 2017 her grand daughter graduated from college, moved away to start a new job, and ceased to be a dependent on Chara's tax return. Chara started making payments on the loan in 2017. Without regard to any modified AGI limitations, is Chara permitted to deduct interest on the loan?

EA LO 4-2 7. Explain the purpose of a Health Savings Account (HSA).

EA LO 4-2 8. What are the qualifications to be eligible for a Health Savings Account (HSA) deduction?

EA LO 4-2 9. What are the consequences of an *employer* contribution to an employee's HSA?

EA LO 4-3 10. Explain the three tests associated with deductibility of moving expenses.

EA LO 4-3 11. Describe the types of expenses that can be deducted for moving expenses.

EA LO 4-3 12. A taxpayer incurs moving expenses in conjunction with a job-related move that meets the distance test. At the end of the year, the taxpayer has not yet met the time test. Under what circumstances can the taxpayer deduct the moving expenses?

EA LO 4-3 13. Rica quit her job in Austin, TX, and moved to Seattle, WA, incurring $1,500 of moving expenses. Upon arriving in Seattle, she sought employment and found a position three weeks later. Without regard to the time test, what amount, if any, of her moving expenses can Rica deduct?

EA LO 4-3 14. In January 2017 Tran incurred $1,200 of moving expenses when he moved from Des Moines, IA, to Detroit, MI. When he moved, he had no job but found one a week after moving. He stayed on that job for two months, changed to another job for four months, and changed again to a long-term position that he held for the remainder of the year. What is the amount of moving expense deduction Tran can report in 2017, if any?

EA LO 4-4 15. Explain why self-employed taxpayers generally pay double the amount of FICA taxes that regular wage earners do.

EA LO 4-4 16. Refer to Question 15. How does the tax code attempt to remedy this seeming inequity?

EA LO 4-5 17. Explain the two limitations associated with the deduction for health insurance by self-employed individuals.

EA LO 4-6 18. What is meant by a *penalty on early withdrawal of savings,* and under what circumstances is it deductible?

EA LO 4-7 19. Define *alimony, child support,* and *property settlement.*

EA LO 4-7 20. Why is it important to distinguish between a property settlement and alimony?

EA LO 4-8 21. Who is eligible to take an above-the-line AGI deduction for educator expenses, and what is the maximum amount of the permitted deduction?

EA LO 4-8 22. What expenses qualify as deductible educator expenses?

EA LO 4-8 23. In the case of a joint return, what is the treatment of educator expenses?

EA LO 4-9 24. Briefly explain the tax rules associated with the tuition and fees deduction.

EA LO 4-9 25. Mr. and Mrs. Chen paid tuition of $1,400 and required fees of $650 for their 25-year-old daughter, who is attending State University, living on her own, and working 30 hours per week as a restaurant hostess. Their AGI is $50,000. The daughter paid for all her other school and living expenses, which amounted to more than 50% of her total living expenses. What is the permitted amount of tuition and fees deduction for the Chens? Why?

Multiple-Choice Questions connect

All applicable multiple-choice questions are available with ***Connect***©

EA 26. (Introduction) *For* AGI, or above-the-line, deductions

a. Are determined by the taxpayer.

b. Are set by statute.

c. Increase tax liability.

d. Are reported in Schedule A.

EA 27. (Introduction) *For* AGI, or above-the-line, deductions

a. Increase AGI.

b. Reduce tax credits.

c. Are available only for married filing jointly.

d. Can reduce overall tax liability.

EA LO 4-1 28. Student loan interest is reported on Form

a. 1098-SA.

b. 1098-E.

c. 1099-S.

d. 1098-GA.

EA LO 4-1 29. Taxpayers eligible to take the student loan interest deduction do *not* include

a. A student who is claimed as a dependent on another's return.

b. A self-supporting student.

c. The parents of a dependent student who took out the loan on their child's behalf.

d. A married student filing jointly.

EA LO 4-1 30. In 2013 through 2016, Korey, who is single, borrowed a total of $25,000 for higher education expenses on qualified education loans. In 2017, while still living at home and being claimed by his parents as a dependent, he began making payments on the loan. The first year's interest on the loan was reported as $550, and his AGI for the year was less than $65,000. The amount that Korey can claim on his tax return is

a. $0.
b. $225.
c. $340.
d. $550.

EA LO 4-2 31. For 2017 the maximum aggregate annual contribution that a taxpayer, under age 55, can make to an HSA for *family coverage* is

a. $1,300.
b. $3,350.
c. $6,750.
d. $13,100.

EA LO 4-2 32. To be eligible to fund a Health Savings Account (HSA), a taxpayer must meet which of the following criteria:

a. An employee (or spouse) who works for an employer with a high-deductible health plan.
b. An uninsured employee who has purchased a high-deductible health plan on his or her own.
c. A self-employed individual.
d. Any of the above.

EA LO 4-3 33. To be eligible to deduct moving expenses, a taxpayer

a. Must meet the time test.
b. Must meet the distance test.
c. Must meet one of the change of job location, time, or distance tests.
d. Must meet all three of the change of job location, time, and distance tests.

EA LO 4-3 34. Deductible expenses for moving do *not* include

a. The cost of transporting household goods.
b. Hotel costs while moving to the new location.
c. Meals incurred during the move.
d. Storage of household goods for a limited time upon arrival at the new location.

EA LO 4-3 35. To meet the distance test, the new job location must be

a. 100 miles from the old job location.
b. At least 50 miles farther than the old residence was from the old job location.
c. At least 50 miles farther than the new residence from the old job location.
d. 100 miles from the old residence.

EA LO 4-4 36. The deduction for half of the self-employment tax is

a. Based on a total of 7.65% of FICA taxes.
b. Based on the gross earnings of the business.
c. Based on filing status.
d. Based on the net earnings of the business.

EA LO 4-5 37. As a *for* AGI deduction, self-employed health insurance premiums are deductible at

a. 50%.
b. 70%.
c. 80%.
d. 100%.

EA LO 4-5 38. Shana is a self-employed carpenter who had net earnings from self-employment of $3,500. She paid $325 per month for health insurance over the last year. Shana is entitled to a *for* AGI deduction for health insurance of

a. $0.

b. $325.

c. $3,500.

d. $3,900.

EA LO 4-6 39. Penalties for the early withdrawal of savings are reported by the financial institution on

a. Box 2 of Form 1099-INT.

b. Form EWIP.

c. A letter of notification.

d. None of the above.

EA LO 4-7 40. Mia is required under a 2016 divorce decree to pay $600 of alimony and $300 of child support per month for 12 years. In addition, Mia makes a voluntary payment of $100 per month. How much of each total monthly payment can Mia deduct in 2017?

a. $100.

b. $300.

c. $600.

d. $700.

EA LO 4-7 41. The Renfros were granted a decree of divorce in 2016. In accordance with the decree, Josh Renfro is to pay his ex-wife $24,000 a year until their only child, Evelyn, now 10, turns 18, and then the payments will decrease to $14,000 per year. For 2017, how much can Josh deduct as alimony in total?

a. $10,000.

b. $14,000.

c. $24,000.

d. None of the above.

EA LO 4-7 42. At the beginning of June 2017, Julia left her husband and is currently living in an apartment. The couple has no children. At the end of the current year, no formal proceedings have occurred in relation to the separation or potential divorce. Julia has been making a $2,000 a month maintenance payment since moving out. How much can Julia deduct in total as alimony for 2017?

a. 0.

b. $2,000.

c. $12,000.

d. $24,000.

EA LO 4-8 43. Which of the following items does not qualify as an educator expense item deduction?

a. Books.

b. Home schooling expenses.

c. Computers and software.

d. Professional development expenses related to the curriculum.

EA LO 4-8 44. Under current tax law, the deductible amount for expenses under the educator expense deduction is limited per taxpayer to:

a. $100.

b. $150.

c. $200.

d. $250.

45. The amount of the tuition and fees deduction for married filing separate is:
    a. $4,000.
    b. $3,000.
    c. $2,000.
    d. $0.

Problems connect

All applicable problems are available with ***Connect***©

EA LO 4-1 46. What are some of the limitations concerning deductibility of student loan interest? Be specific and comprehensive.

EA LO 4-1 47. Discuss the characteristics of an *eligible educational institution* as it relates to the deductibility of student loan interest.

EA LO 4-1 48. Zach attended Champion University during 2012–2016. He lived at home and was claimed by his parents as a deduction during his entire education. He incurred education expenses of $10,000 during college of which $2,000 was paid for by scholarships. To finance his education, he borrowed $7,000 through a federal student loan program and borrowed another $3,000 from a local lending institution for educational purposes. After graduation, he married and moved with his spouse to a distant city. In 2017 he incurred $700 of interest on the federal loans and $300 on the lending institution loan. He filed a joint return with his spouse showing modified AGI of $128,000. What amount of student loan interest can Zach and his spouse deduct in 2017, if any?

EA LO 4-2 49. If an employer contributes to an HSA on behalf of an employee,
    a. Is the contribution deductible by the employee?

    b. Is the payment considered income to the employee?

EA LO 4-3 50. Fabian, a single account executive, was employed and resided in New Mexico. On July 1, 2017, his company transferred him to Florida. Fabian worked full time for the entire year. During 2017 he incurred and paid the following expenses related to the move:

Pre-move house-hunting costs	$1,500
Lodging and travel expenses (not meals) while moving	1,800
Cost of moving furniture and personal belongings	2,700

He did not receive reimbursement for any of these expenses from his employer; his AGI for the year was $85,500. What amount can Fabian deduct as moving expenses on his 2017 return?

EA LO 4-3 51. In May 2017 Regina graduated from USC with a degree in accounting and moved to Portland, OR, to look for work. Shortly after arriving in Portland, she obtained work as a staff accountant in a local CPA firm. In her move to Portland, Regina incurred the following costs:

$275 in gasoline.

$250 for renting a truck from UPAYME rentals.

$100 for a tow trailer for his car.

$85 in food.

$25 in double espressos from Starbucks.

$300 for motel lodging on the way to Portland.

$405 for a previous plane trip to Portland to look for an apartment.

$175 in temporary storage costs for her collection of crystal figurines.

How much, if any, may Regina take as a moving expense deduction on her 2017 tax return? Is that deduction subject to any conditions that could change its deductibility in the future?

EA LO 4-3 52. Are the moving expenses of other people besides the taxpayer deductible? If so, what are the requirements for deductibility?

EA LO 4-4, 4-5 53. Juan, who is single, is a self-employed carpenter as well as an employee of Frame It, Inc. His self-employment net income is $35,000, and he received a W-2 from Frame It for wages of $25,000. He is covered by his employer's pension plan, but his employer does not offer a health plan in which he could participate.

a. Up to how much of his self-employed health insurance premiums could he deduct for this year, if any? Why?

b. How much of Juan's self-employment taxes would be deductible?

EA LO 4-6 54. Chantel has received a 1099-INT from her financial institution showing $75 in box 2 of the form. How should she handle this on her 2017 tax return and why?

EA LO 4-7 55. Three types of payments are associated with a decree of separation or a divorce.

a. What are those three payments?

b. Which one has a tax consequence?

c. What is the timing rule regarding the recapture period of those payments?

EA LO 4-7 56. Under the terms of a divorce decree executed May 1, 2017, Ahmed transferred a house worth $650,000 to his ex-wife, Farah, and was to make alimony payments of $3,000 per month. The property has a tax basis to Ahmed of $300,000.

a. How much of this must be reported on Farah's tax return?

b. Of that amount, how much is taxable gain or loss that Farah must recognize related to the transfer of the house?

EA LO 4-7 57. Under the alimony recapture rules, what amounts are designated for recapture reclassification, and what are the tax consequences?

EA LO 4-1–4-7 58. Indicate whether each of the following items is considered a *for* AGI (above-the-line) deduction for the 2017 tax year:

a. Student loan interest.

b. Gambling losses.

c. Early withdrawal penalty.

d. Child support payments.

e. Charitable contributions.

f. One-half of self-employment taxes.

g. Alimony.

h. Scholarships for tuition and books.

i. Moving expenses.

j. Property taxes.

k. Self-employed health insurance premiums.

Tax Return Problems

All applicable tax return problems are available with ***Connect***©

Use your tax software to complete the following problems. If you are manually preparing the tax returns, you will need a Form 1040 and associated schedules for each problem.

Tax Return Problem 1

Jason Ready attended the University of San Diego during 2013–2017. He incurred education expenses of $10,000 in total for his education, and $1,500 of that amount was incurred in 2017 for his last semester. To finance his education, he borrowed $7,000 through a federal student loan program and borrowed another $3,000 from SoCal Credit Union for educational purposes. After graduation, he accepted a position with the Portland office of KPMG and moved there in May 2017. He lives at 4560 Ranch Drive, Portland, OR 97035. His social security number is 412-34-5670 (date of birth 7/10/1995). Jason had qualifying health care coverage at all times during the tax year.

His W-2 contained the following information:

Wages (box 1) =	$67,533.05
Federal W/H (box 2) =	$ 8,994.95
Social security wages (box 3) =	$67,533.05
Social security W/H (box 4) =	$ 4,187.05
Medicare wages (box 5) =	$67,533.05
Medicare W/H (box 6) =	$ 979.23

In moving to Portland, he incurred the following moving expenses:

$495 in gasoline.

$295 for renting a truck from IGOTYA rentals.

$125 in food.

$465 for motel lodging on the way to Portland.

He also received two Forms 1098-E. One was from the federal student loan program, which showed $450 of student loan interest; the other was from SoCal Credit Union and showed $150.75 of student loan interest.

Prepare a Form 1040, a Form 3903, and a Form 8917. If manually preparing the return, the Student Loan Interest Deduction worksheet can be found in IRS Publication 970, Tax Benefits for Education.

Tax Return Problem 2

In June 2017 Phillip and Barbara Jones and their two dependent children, who are both over 17, moved from Chicago to Albuquerque, New Mexico, a distance of 1,327 miles, which they drove in their own car. The children's names are Roger and Gwen and both will be attending the University of New Mexico in the fall, Roger as a freshman and Gwen as a junior. The move was a result of a job transfer for Phillip. The distance from their old home to Phillip's old office was 30 miles. Barbara quit her job in Chicago and decided to perform volunteer work for a year before seeking further employment. Phillip and Barbara incurred expenses of $4,550 to the moving company (which included $320 for temporary furniture storage), hotel charges of $550, and meals of $712 en route from Chicago to Albuquerque. Their new home is located at 7432 Desert Springs Way, Albuquerque, NM 87101. Phillip, but not Barbara, was employed in the new location throughout the year. Phillip's social security number is 412-34-5670 (date of birth 6/12/1975), Barbara's is 412-34-5671 (date of birth 8/12/1977), Roger's is 412-34-5672 (date of birth 2/17/2000), and Gwen's is 412-34-5673 (date of birth 9/14/1998). The Joneses had qualifying health care coverage at all times during the tax year.

Phillip is a civil engineer for a national firm; his W-2 contained the following information:

Wages (box 1) = $110,220.45
Federal W/H (box 2) = $ 11,015.42
Social security wages (box 3) = $110,220.45
Social security W/H (box 4) = $ 6,833.67
Medicare wages (box 5) = $110,220.45
Medicare W/H (box 6) = $ 1,598.20

Employer moving expense reimbursement

(box 12, Code P) = $ 5,000.00

In addition, both he and Barbara received Forms 1098-E from the federal student loan program. Phillip had student loan interest of $1,050, and Barbara had student loan interest of $750.

Prepare a Form 1040 for Phillip and Barbara as well as Form 3903. If manually preparing the return, the Student Loan Interest Deduction worksheet can be found in IRS Publication 970, Tax Benefits for Education.

Tax Return Problem 3

Kathy and Rob Wright obtained a divorce effective May 1, 2017. In accordance with the divorce decree, Rob was required to pay $2,250 per month until their only child turns 18; then the payments would be reduced to $1,500 per month. Kathy has full custody of the child and appropriately takes the dependent deduction and child credit. Furthermore, Rob was to transfer title of their house, which had a cost of $150,000 and a fair value of $200,000 on the date of transfer, to Kathy and was to continue making the monthly mortgage payments of $1,235 on behalf of Kathy. Rob works for a large oil distributor in Santa Fe, NM, and after the divorce lives at 1132 Northgate Avenue, Santa Fe, NM 87501. Rob's social security number is 412-34-5671 (date of birth 11/4/1983), and Rob's social security number is 412-34-5670 (date of birth 8/14/1980). Rob had qualifying health care coverage at all times during the tax year.

His W-2 contained the following information:

Wages (box 1) = $85,100.25
Federal W/H (box 2) = $ 7,325.24
Social security wages (box 3) = $85,100.25
Social security W/H (box 4) = $ 5,276.22
Medicare wages (box 5) = $85,100.25
Medicare W/H (box 6) = $ 1,233.95

He also received a Form 1099-INT from First New Mexico Bank with $336 of interest income in box 1. In addition, Rob made a timely $2,500 contribution to his new HSA account.

Prepare a Form 1040 and a Form 8889 for Rob.

We have provided selected filled-in source documents that are available in the *Connect Library*.

Chapter **Five**

Itemized Deductions

This chapter provides a detailed investigation of Schedule A and itemized deductions. Specifically, we present the laws, rules, and complete tax authority encompassing the six basic categories of the primarily personal expenditures allowed as tax deductions. In addition to the law and rules for deductibility, we present the practical application of the law on Schedule A and related forms.

Learning Objectives

When you have completed this chapter, you should understand the following learning objectives (LO):

LO 5-1 Describe the deductibility and reporting of medical expenses.

LO 5-2 Be able to explain the state and local tax deductions.

LO 5-3 Apply the tax rules associated with the interest deduction.

LO 5-4 Explain the deductibility and reporting of charitable contributions.

LO 5-5 Discuss the casualty loss deduction.

LO 5-6 Know how to report miscellaneous expenditures.

LO 5-7 Apply the tax rules for the Pease limitations on total itemized deductions for high-income taxpayers in 2017.

INTRODUCTION

The Internal Revenue Code allows taxpayers to deduct certain items from gross income when determining taxable income. One type of permitted deduction is a *for* (or *above-the-line*) AGI deduction such as moving expenses, student loan interest, and Health Savings Accounts. We discussed these *for* AGI deductions in Chapter 4.

The other type of permitted deduction is a *from* (*below-the-line*) AGI deduction. You are already familiar with one *from* AGI deduction—the standard deduction, discussed in Chapter 2. We now introduce you to another *from* AGI deduction—the itemized deduction.

Itemized deductions are reported on Schedule A (see Exhibit 5-1). If you review Schedule A, you will see that itemized deductions are organized into six major categories:

1. Medical.
2. State and local taxes.
3. Interest.
4. Charitable gifts.
5. Casualty losses.
6. Miscellaneous deductions, including unreimbursed employee expenses.

The first six learning objectives of this chapter are tied to these six categories of itemized deductions.

Most itemized deductions are, in effect, personal living expenses: medical expenses, interest expenses, payments for taxes, and the like. Permitted personal living expenses can be deducted only if they are expressly permitted.

EXHIBIT 5-1

SCHEDULE A (Form 1040) Department of the Treasury Internal Revenue Service (99)	**Itemized Deductions** ▶ Go to *www.irs.gov/ScheduleA* for instructions and the latest information. ▶ Attach to Form 1040.	OMB No. 1545-0074 **2017** Attachment Sequence No. **07**

Name(s) shown on Form 1040 | **Your social security number**

Section	Line	Description	Box	Total
Medical and Dental Expenses		**Caution:** Do not include expenses reimbursed or paid by others.		
	1	Medical and dental expenses (see instructions)	1	
	2	Enter amount from Form 1040, line 38 [2]		
	3	Multiply line 2 by 10% (0.10)	3	
	4	Subtract line 3 from line 1. If line 3 is more than line 1, enter -0-		4
Taxes You Paid	5	State and local **(check only one box):** a ☐ Income taxes, **or** b ☐ General sales taxes	5	
	6	Real estate taxes (see instructions)	6	
	7	Personal property taxes	7	
	8	Other taxes. List type and amount ▶	8	
	9	Add lines 5 through 8		9
Interest You Paid **Note:** Your mortgage interest deduction may be limited (see instructions).	10	Home mortgage interest and points reported to you on Form 1098	10	
	11	Home mortgage interest not reported to you on Form 1098. If paid to the person from whom you bought the home, see instructions and show that person's name, identifying no., and address ▶	11	
	12	Points not reported to you on Form 1098. See instructions for special rules	12	
	13	Reserved	13	
	14	Investment interest. Attach Form 4952 if required. See instructions.	14	
	15	Add lines 10 through 14		15
Gifts to Charity If you made a gift and got a benefit for it, see instructions.	16	Gifts by cash or check. If you made any gift of $250 or more, see instructions	16	
	17	Other than by cash or check. If any gift of $250 or more, see instructions. You **must** attach Form 8283 if over $500	17	
	18	Carryover from prior year	18	
	19	Add lines 16 through 18		19
Casualty and Theft Losses	20	Casualty or theft loss(es). Attach Form 4684. See instructions		20
Job Expenses and Certain Miscellaneous Deductions	21	Unreimbursed employee expenses—job travel, union dues, job education, etc. Attach Form 2106 or 2106-EZ if required. See instructions. ▶	21	
	22	Tax preparation fees	22	
	23	Other expenses—investment, safe deposit box, etc. List type and amount ▶	23	
	24	Add lines 21 through 23	24	
	25	Enter amount from Form 1040, line 38 [25]		
	26	Multiply line 25 by 2% (0.02)	26	
	27	Subtract line 26 from line 24. If line 26 is more than line 24, enter -0-		27
Other Miscellaneous Deductions	28	Other—from list in instructions. List type and amount ▶		28
Total Itemized Deductions	29	Is Form 1040, line 38, over $156,900? ☐ **No.** Your deduction is not limited. Add the amounts in the far right column for lines 4 through 28. Also, enter this amount on Form 1040, line 40. ☐ **Yes.** Your deduction may be limited. See the Itemized Deductions Worksheet in the instructions to figure the amount to enter.		29
	30	If you elect to itemize deductions even though they are less than your standard deduction, check here ▶ ☐		

For Paperwork Reduction Act Notice, see the Instructions for Form 1040. Cat. No. 17145C **Schedule A (Form 1040) 2017**

Source: U.S. Department of the Treasury, Internal Revenue Service, Form 1040- Schedule A. Washington, DC: 2017.

Itemized deductions also include two other types of expenses: unreimbursed employee business expenses (part of miscellaneous deductions) and investment-related expenses (part of the interest category as well as miscellaneous deductions).

In practice, taxpayers determine their (1) standard deduction and (2) total itemized deductions and use the higher number. In other words, a taxpayer cannot take *both* the standard deduction *and* the itemized deduction but only the higher of the two. Recall, for example, that the standard deduction is $12,700 for a married couple.[1] Thus a married couple who has itemized deductions of $11,000 should claim the standard deduction, but if the itemized deductions total $13,500, the couple should choose to itemize the deductions.

DEDUCTIBLE MEDICAL EXPENSES (SCHEDULE A, LINE 4)

LO 5-1

Taxpayers can deduct an itemized deduction for medical expenses (net of insurance proceeds) for themselves, their spouse, and dependent(s). The qualifying relationship must exist at the date the taxpayer incurs or pays the expenses. Only the amount in excess of 10.0% of AGI is deductible.[2] Because the threshold is so high, medical expenditures usually must be substantial for the taxpayer(s) to benefit from a medical deduction. A formula for calculating the amount of deductible medical expense is shown in Table 5-1.

Beginning in 2017, under the 2010 Health Care Reform Act, all taxpayers, regardless of age, are not able to deduct medical expenses until they exceed 10% of AGI.

TABLE 5-1
Medical Expense Deduction Formula

Calculation of Deductible Medical Expenses

Allowable medical expenses
minus (insurance reimbursements)

Allowable net paid medical expenses
minus (10.0% of Adjusted Gross Income)

Deductible medical expenses

EXAMPLE 5-1

Alice and Bob are married taxpayers, with AGI of $100,000 in tax year 2017. To benefit from an itemized deduction for medical expenses, Alice and Bob must have medical costs in excess of $10,000 ($100,000 × 10.0% floor).

Two special rules apply for determining whether an individual qualifies as a dependent for purposes of the medical expense deduction:

1. The dependent child of divorced parents is treated as a dependent of both parents. The parent who pays the child's medical expenses may deduct the expenses even if the parent is not permitted to claim the child's dependency exemption.
2. The gross income and the joint return tests for the dependency exemption are waived. A taxpayer who pays the medical expenses of an individual who satisfies the relationship, citizenship, and support tests for the dependency exemption may deduct the medical expenses paid for that person.[3]

[1] The standard deduction for a qualifying widow(er) is $12,700, for head of household is $9,350, and for a single person as well as married filing separately is $6,350.

[2] IRC § 213.

[3] Reg. § 1.213-1(a)(3)(i).

A deduction may be claimed only for medical expenses actually paid during the taxable year regardless of when the care was provided and regardless of the taxpayer's method of accounting.[4] A medical expense charged to a credit card is considered paid.

The taxpayer may deduct costs for medical care, which includes the following:

1. The diagnosis, cure, mitigation, treatment, or prevention of disease, or for the purpose of affecting any structure or function of the body.
2. Transportation primarily for and essential to medical care.
3. Qualified long-term care services.
4. Insurance for medical care or qualified long-term care services.

In most instances, medical expenses are relatively straightforward and include all costs for licensed medical treatment. Ambiguity occurs when expenditures for personal, living, and family purposes (generally not deductible) are incidental to medical care (generally deductible).

TAX YOUR BRAIN

A physician prescribes a special diet consisting of low-fat, high-fiber foods to lower cholesterol. The physician's bill is definitely deductible. However, is the cost of the food a deductible medical expense?

ANSWER

The mere fact that a physician prescribes or recommends a course of action does not automatically qualify the expenditure as a deduction.[5] If an expense item is ordinarily for personal purposes, the excess of the cost of the special items (excess over the ordinary-use goods) qualifies as a medical deduction. For example, the extra cost of a specially designed auto (above the normal cost of the auto) for a taxpayer confined to a wheelchair would qualify as a medical deduction.[6] Therefore, the special food would be deductible only to the extent the food costs exceeded normal food costs. This would be difficult to substantiate. Thus it is unlikely that the food would qualify as a deductible medical expense.

Taxpayers may *not* deduct expenditures that are merely for the benefit of the general health of an individual.[7] For example, expenditures for cosmetic surgery are normally not deductible. Clearly, any payments made for operations or treatments for any part of the body or function of the body are deductible if they serve a distinct medical need. Plastic surgery to repair a birth defect would be a deductible expense. This includes payments to virtually all health care providers, such as doctors, dentists, ophthalmologists, nurses, and physical therapists as well as many unconventional medical treatments, from acupuncture to treatments by Christian Science practitioners.[8]

TAX YOUR BRAIN

Can a capital expenditure such as an addition of a swimming pool to a house qualify as a deductible medical expense?

ANSWER

If the capital expenditure for the swimming pool is for the primary medical care of the taxpayer, his or her spouse, or his or her dependent(s), it may qualify for a deduction.[9] This area has been highly litigated by the IRS. To ensure the deduction for the pool, a physician must prescribe swimming and there can be no recreational element (such as a diving board or slide) to the pool. Other factors used in determining the deductibility of a swimming pool include the availability of other types of exercise and access to a community pool.[10]

[4] IRC § 213(a).

[5] *Atkinson, H.* (1965) 44 TC 39, acq. 1965-2 CB 4.

[6] Rev. Rul. 76-80, 1976-1 CB 71.

[7] Reg. § 1.213-1(e)(1)(ii).

[8] Rev. Rul. 72-593, 1972-2 CB 180; Rev. Rul. 55-261, 1955-1 CB 307. Payments to the following medical providers are specifically included as deductible charges: psychologists, physicians, surgeons, specialists or other medical practitioners, chiropractors, dentists, optometrists, osteopaths, psychiatrists, and Christian Science practitioners.

[9] Reg. § 1.213-1(e)(1)(iii).

[10] Rev. Rul. 83-33 (1983-1 CB 70) specially addresses the swimming pool issue.

For medical capital expenditures that improve the taxpayer's property, the deduction is available only to the extent that the medical expenditure exceeds the increase in the fair market value (FMV) of the residence. Thus if the cost of a swimming pool for medical purposes was $30,000 and the increase in FMV to the residence was $20,000, the medical deduction would be limited to $10,000 (the excess cost over the FMV increase).

EXAMPLE 5-2

Renaldo suffers from a severe knee condition and is unable to climb steps. Consequently, he installed an elevator in his home at a cost of $7,000. An appraiser indicates that the elevator increased the value of the home by $2,000. The cost of the elevator, $7,000, is a medical expense to the extent that it exceeds the increase in the value of the property, $2,000. Thus $5,000 of the cost of the elevator is included in the calculation of Renaldo's medical expense deduction.

Generally, deductible medical costs do not include cosmetic surgery unless the surgery is necessary to correct a deformity arising from a congenital abnormality, personal injury, or disfiguring disease.[11]

EXAMPLE 5-3

Tamara was riding her mountain bike on a trail and lost control. Her head and face hit a tree stump, causing damage to the right side of her face. The cost of the cosmetic surgery to repair the damage, the hospital stay, and all physician fees would qualify as a medical deduction.

Medical expenses are *not* deductible if they have been "compensated for by insurance or otherwise."[12] As a result, any insurance reimbursements or partial reimbursements reduce the deductible medical expenses subject to the 10.0% AGI limitation.

Medicine and Drugs

For the cost of a drug to be deductible, a physician must first prescribe it.[13] This would include payments for birth control pills or drugs to alleviate nicotine withdrawal as long as a prescription was required.[14]

One other limitation to the deductibility of medicine or drug costs is that the taxpayer must obtain the drug legally. Thus even if a physician prescribes an otherwise illegal drug for medicinal purposes, the cost of acquiring the illegal drug is not deductible.

Prescription drugs obtained from sources outside the United States, such as Canada, are deductible if they are prescribed by a physician for the treatment of a medical condition and the FDA has approved that they can be legally imported. Amounts paid for over-the-counter medications are not reimbursable from HSAs.

TAX YOUR BRAIN

A physician prescribes marijuana for pain control purposes for a terminally ill cancer patient. The use of marijuana for medicinal purposes is legal under state law. Can a taxpayer deduct the cost of marijuana?

ANSWER

Because marijuana cannot be legally procured under federal law, its cost is not deductible.[15]

[11] IRC § 213(d)(9).

[12] IRC § 213(a).

[13] IRC § 213(b).

[14] Rev. Rul. 73-200, 1973-1 CB 140; Rev. Rul. 99-28, 1999-25 IRB 6.

[15] Reg. § 1.213-1(e)(2); Rev. Rul. 97-9, 1997-1 CB 77.

Travel and Transportation for Medical Purposes

Transportation costs for medical purposes could include such items as cab, bus, or train fares, as well as expenses for a personal auto. The cost of the transportation must be primarily for, and essential to, deductible medical care.[16]

EXAMPLE 5-4

Jake Avery, who currently lives in New Orleans, must fly to Memphis to see a specialist concerning an inner ear condition. Mrs. Avery, a big Elvis fan, decides to go along to visit Graceland. The travel costs for Jake, but not Mrs. Avery, are deductible as a medical expense. If, on the other hand, Mrs. Avery accompanied Jake because her assistance was required because of problems stemming from the ear condition, her costs would also be deductible.[17]

There are two ways to calculate the deduction for the use of a personal auto for medical transportation: (1) the *actual cost* of operating the car for medical purposes or (2) the *standard mileage allowance*.[18]

When using the actual costs, the taxpayer must keep documentation for items such as gasoline, oil, repairs, and so on that are directly associated with transportation to and from medical care. However, the taxpayer gets no deduction for general repairs, maintenance, or insurance. The simpler approach for deducting personal auto expense is to use the standard mileage allowance, which in 2017 is 17 cents per mile. The taxpayer can deduct other supplemental costs such as parking and tolls in addition to the applicable mileage rate.

EXAMPLE 5-5

Maria has an inoperable brain tumor that requires treatment at University of Texas Medical Center in Houston twice a month. It is a 500-mile round trip. She pays a total of $10 in tolls, $20 in parking, and $80 for gasoline on each round trip. Assuming that Maria made the trip six times in the current tax year, what is the maximum transportation expense deduction for medical purposes (*disregarding* the 10% AGI floor)?

ANSWER

Actual costs follow:

Gasoline ($90 × 6)	$540
Tolls ($10 × 6)	60
Parking ($20 × 6)	120
Total deduction	$720

Use of the standard mileage rate in effect for the year gives this deduction:

Mileage (500 miles × $0.17/mile × 6)	$510
Tolls ($10 × 6)	60
Parking ($20 × 6)	120
Total deduction	$690

Maria would choose the standard mileage rate in this situation because it produces a higher deduction. This is not always the case, however. In reality, the convenience and the lack of receipt substantiation make the standard mileage rate more popular even though the deduction of actual costs could be higher.

[16] IRC § 213(d)(1)(B).

[17] *Kelly, Daniel*, TC Memo 1969-231 reversed on another issue (1971, CA-7), 440 F2d 307.

[18] Rev. Proc. 80-32, 1980-2 CB 767.

In addition to the mileage, the cost of meals and lodging at a hospital or similar institution is deductible if the principal reason for being there is to receive medical care.[19] Lodging near the related medical facility is deductible as long as no significant element of personal pleasure, recreation, or vacation is involved. The lodging expenditures are limited to $50 for each night for each individual, and meals are not deductible.[20]

Long-Term Care

As the population ages, more funds will be spent providing long-term care for senior citizens. *Qualified long-term care services* are medical, maintenance, and personal care services provided to a chronically ill individual pursuant to a plan of care prescribed by a licensed health care practitioner.

The general rule concerning the deductibility of nursing home or other long-term care institution costs provides that amounts spent are deductible if the principal reason for the individual's stay is medical care as opposed to enjoyment or convenience. The entire cost of the long-term institution is deductible as a medical expense if indeed that is the case. If full-time medical care is not required, only the fee allocable to actual medical care is deductible, and costs for food and lodging are nondeductible.[21]

Determining medical expenses is usually quite easy for the individual or client who keeps good records. Generally, medical care providers supply the necessary receipts to document the medical charges incurred in a hospital or doctor's office. Other source documents for medical charges include checkbook registers, bank records, and credit card statements. Be careful, however, in taking a medical deduction for a check made out to a local drugstore that sells items in addition to prescription drugs. The IRS may require an itemized receipt for the prescription drugs. Pharmacy departments usually provide this information. Another major item, which is easy to misclassify, is the payment of health insurance premiums. These are deductible only if the taxpayer pays the premiums with after-tax funds (not in an employer pretax plan).

Insurance for Medical Care or Long-Term Care

Premiums for medical insurance, such as major medical, hospitalization, dental, and vision insurance, are deductible. This includes Medicare B premiums for voluntary supplemental coverage, but it does not include Medicare A insurance payroll taxes withheld from the taxpayer's paycheck. Premiums for long-term care policies are deductible, subject to dollar limitations. Deductible amounts for 2017[22] follow:

Age at Close of Taxable Year	2017 Amount
40 and under	$ 410
More than 40, but not more than 50	770
More than 50, but not more than 60	1,530
More than 60, but not more than 70	4,090
Age 71 and over	5,110

In the event that the long-term insurance contract pays periodic payments to an individual who is chronically ill, any amount in excess of the per diem limit is in fact taxable. The per diem rate for 2017 is $360.

[19] *Montgomery, Morris v. Comm.* (1970, CA6), 428 F2d 243 affg (1968) 51 TC 410.

[20] IRC § 213(d)(2)(A)&(B).

[21] Reg. § 1.213-1(e)(1)(v).

[22] IRS Rev. Proc. 2014-61.

From Shoebox to Software

EXAMPLE 5-6 We will return to Maria and Jose Ramirez in terms of Example 5-5. In Chapter 4, you created and saved a tax file for Jose and Maria Ramirez. They had an AGI of $110,048. For this chapter, you will reopen their return and you will add the following medical costs:

Maria's hospital charges	$13,000
Maria's physician charges	8,000
Maria's prescription drugs	3,000
Jose's high blood pressure drugs	300
Jose's eye surgery	750
Regular dental visits (4 total)	280
Jose's regular physician charges	400
Transportation (from Example 5-5)	690
Lodging for trips to the University of Texas (for both Jose and Maria—Maria could not drive because the treatments affected her vision—6 nights at $127/night)	600
High-fiber health food recommended for Jose	450

Assuming that Jose and Maria do not have health insurance, how much is their medical deduction, and how is it presented on Form 1040, Schedule A?

Tax software: Retrieve the Ramirezes' file saved from Chapter 4. Because of the numerous types of medical expenses allowed, it is easier to go directly to Schedule A to enter the medical deductions.

To complete the form, you must understand tax law. All of the expenses qualify for a deduction with the exception of the high-fiber health food. Additionally, the lodging is limited to $50 per person per night. In this case, because Jose was required to drive Maria, expenses for both of them qualify, and lodging would be limited to $100 per night ($50 for Jose, $50 for Maria) for six nights. Thus the total medical deduction before the 10.0% AGI limitation is $27,020.

The $27,020 deduction could be placed on line 1 of Schedule A; or if you wished to list all of the deductions, you could right-click on line 1 and then list the expenses on the "add line item detail" provided. The taxpayer's AGI ($110,048) would automatically transfer to line 2, and the 10.0% limitation ($11,005) would be calculated. Any changes to other areas of the tax return would automatically update AGI and thus change the allowable medical deduction.

The medical expense presentation on Schedule A (Exhibit 5-2) is as follows:

EXHIBIT 5-2

Medical and Dental Expenses		Caution: Do not include expenses reimbursed or paid by others.				
	1	Medical and dental expenses (see instructions)	1	27,020		
	2	Enter amount from Form 1040, line 38 **2** 110,048				
	3	Multiply line 2 by 10% (0.10)	3	11,005		
	4	Subtract line 3 from line 1. If line 3 is more than line 1, enter -0-			4	16,015

Source: U.S. Department of the Treasury, Internal Revenue Service, Form 1040- Schedule A. Washington, DC: 2017.

The net medical expense deduction would be $16,015.

If Jose and Maria had health insurance and received benefits of $14,000, the amount shown on line 1 would be $13,020 ($27,020 − $14,000). You could either directly enter $13,020 on line 1 or show the insurance benefits as a negative on the line item detail. The result would be a deduction of only $2,015 (see Exhibit 5-3). Save the file showing $2,015 in net medical expenses for use later in the text.

EXHIBIT 5-3

Medical and Dental Expenses		Caution: Do not include expenses reimbursed or paid by others.				
	1	Medical and dental expenses (see instructions)	1	13,020		
	2	Enter amount from Form 1040, line 38 **2** 110,048				
	3	Multiply line 2 by 10% (0.10)	3	11,005		
	4	Subtract line 3 from line 1. If line 3 is more than line 1, enter -0-			4	2,015

Source: U.S. Department of the Treasury, Internal Revenue Service, Form 1040- Schedule A. Washington, DC: 2017.

TAX YOUR BRAIN

Sofia is an elderly woman who does not require any medical or nursing care. However, she has recently become legally blind and needs help with normal living activities such as cooking, cleaning, and bathing. Sofia enters an assisted living facility where she feels she will be happier and less of a burden to her children. Does the cost of the facility qualify as a medical deduction?

ANSWER

Because medical care is not the principal reason for the woman stay at the facility, there is no medical deduction.[23] Of course any actual medical costs, such as doctor visits, are still deductible.

Exhibit 5-3 assumes that Maria and Jose received a $14,000 insurance reimbursement in the year in which they paid the medical expenses. What happens if Maria and Jose receive the insurance benefits in the subsequent year? In this case, the insurance reimbursement would be included in income in the year received to the extent of the tax benefit received in the prior year.

EXAMPLE 5-7

Use the same facts as in Exhibit 5-3. If Jose and Maria received the $14,000 medical insurance benefits in the subsequent year they must include the benefit amount in income to the extent of the tax benefit received. Their medical expense deduction would have been $16,015, so they would have received a tax benefit equal to the entire $14,000. In this case, they would report the $14,000 in income in the tax year received on line 21, Other Income, on Form 1040.

One common misconception is that the entire amount of an insurance reimbursement will always be included in income. If the insurance reimbursement caused the itemized deductions to be lower than the standard deduction, only a limited amount of the reimbursement would be included in income. The taxpayer would have to compare the taxable income in the deduction year tax return as it was reported to the taxable income that would have been reported had the insurance reimbursement been received in that year. The difference is the amount of income reported.

CONCEPT CHECK 5-1— LO 5-1

1. Medical expenses are generally deductible only to the extent that they exceed ________ of AGI.
2. Medical expenses can be deducted only in the year the expenses are ____________.
3. The deductible amount of medical expense is reduced by ________________________ for those expenses.
4. The cost of long-term care insurance premiums is deductible, but the extent of the deduction depends on the taxpayer's ____________.

DEDUCTIBLE STATE AND LOCAL TAXES (SCHEDULE A, LINE 9)

LO 5-2

Taxes are deductible in various places on a tax return. In this section, we discuss taxes that are personal; that is, they are not paid in connection with a trade or business or any other activity relating to the production of income. For example, if an individual taxpayer owns rental property, the property taxes relating to the rental property are a *for* AGI deduction and are deducted on Schedule E (see Chapter 8). Likewise, if an individual taxpayer operates a business as a sole proprietorship, any payroll or property taxes paid relating to the business are deductible on Schedule C (see Chapter 6) and thus reduce AGI (*for* AGI deductions).

There are four major categories of deductible taxes on individual returns:

1. Personal property taxes.
2. Local real estate property taxes.
3. Other state and local taxes.
4. Foreign taxes.

[23] *Robinson, John v. Comm.* (1968) 51 TC 520, affirmed, vacated, and remanded by (1970, CA9) 422 F2d 873.

The taxes that most individual taxpayers deduct on Schedule A are state and local income taxes and property taxes on real estate and personal property.[24] For cash method taxpayers, deductible taxes are generally deductible in the year paid. For accrual method taxpayers, taxes are generally deductible in the year in which the taxes are accrued. One important note is that federal taxes generally are not deductible on the federal tax return.

Personal Property Taxes

Personal property taxes paid on personal-use assets, such as the family car, are deductible on Schedule A. Personal property taxes paid on rental property are deducted on Schedule E. Personal property taxes paid on assets used in a proprietor's business are deducted on Schedule C.

State or local property taxes must meet three tests to be deductible:

- The tax must be levied on personal property.
- The tax must be an *ad valorem tax*; that is, it must be based on the value of the property.
- The tax must be imposed, at a minimum, on an annual basis with respect to personal property.

TAX YOUR BRAIN

David lives in Johnson County and his brother Joseph lives in Lee County. Johnson County imposes a property tax of 2% of the value of personal vehicles. Lee County, on the other hand, imposes a flat fee of $250 per personal auto. Both counties impose the tax on an annual basis. How should David and Joseph treat these taxes?

ANSWER

David may deduct the tax he pays because it is an annual tax based on the value of personal property. Joseph, on the other hand, cannot deduct the property tax because it is a flat fee that is not based on value.

Many counties and states have different names for the taxes they levy. For example, some counties levy vehicle registration fees, which are deductible if they meet the preceding three tests. Usually the primary determinant is whether the fee is based on the value of the vehicle. If it is, the fee is deductible (assuming that it passes the other two tests).

Property taxes on real estate must meet the three tests as well. Taxes on real property usually are much higher than personal property taxes and may create additional controversy. Problems may develop in the following situations:

1. Jointly owned real property.
2. Sale of property during the tax year.

Property Taxes on Property Owned Jointly

In most states and counties, joint owners of property are jointly and severally liable for property taxes. In other words, if an individual is a part owner of a parcel of real estate and the other owner does not pay the real estate property taxes, that individual is liable for the full payment. In this situation, the owner who pays the tax may deduct the tax amount.[25]

EXAMPLE 5-8

Two brothers, Jake and Stan, own a parcel of real estate with ownership interests of 30% to Jake and 70% to Stan. Jake pays the entire $2,300 county real estate tax. If Jake and Stan live in a state where all joint owners are jointly and severally liable for the tax, then Jake can deduct the entire $2,300 on Schedule A.[26]

---

[24] IRC § 164.

[25] Rev. Rul. 72-79, 1972-1 CB 51.

[26] This assumes the real estate is not business or "for the production of income" property. If the property were business use property, the taxes would be *for* AGI deductions and deducted on Schedule C (business), Schedule E (rental property), or Schedule F (farming property). See Chapters 6 and 8.

If local law mandates that co-owners of property do not have joint and several liability for a tax, then only the proportionate share of the taxes can be deducted.

EXAMPLE 5-9

Assume the same facts as in Example 5-8. However, Jake and Stan live in a state that does not have joint and several liability for the tax. In this case, Jake's deduction is $690 ($2,300 × 30%) even though he paid the entire amount.[27]

Property Taxes on Property Sold during the Year

When property is sold during the year, both the buyer and the seller receive a deduction for a portion of the real estate tax paid according to the number of days each owner held the property.[28]

EXAMPLE 5-10

On March 1, David sold some land to Marsha. The real estate tax of $3,300 was not due until August, and Marsha properly paid it. How much, if anything, can David and Marsha deduct? In this case, the buyer and seller prorate the real estate tax on a daily basis. Therefore, David would deduct $533 ($3,300 × 59/365), and Marsha would deduct the remainder of $2,767 ($3,300 × 306/365). Note that the day of sale is not included in David's holding period, and we are assuming a non–leap year event.

The previous example could raise a question. If Marsha paid the tax, how can David get a deduction? At the time of transfer of ownership, a closing agent (often an attorney) prepares a *closing agreement* that prorates, or divides, the taxes (and other items) between the seller and the buyer. The taxes owed by the seller are withheld from the amount otherwise due to the seller. In effect, David paid the tax at the time of sale instead of at the due date.

Real Estate Taxes

Real estate property taxes are deductible in the calculation of federal taxable income. If the tax is paid on personal-use real estate, such as the taxpayer's principal residence, it is an itemized deduction on Schedule A. If it is paid on rental real estate, it is deducted on Schedule E in the calculation of the taxpayer's net income or loss from the rental property. If it is paid on business real estate, such as an office building that the taxpayer owned and used as a proprietor, it is deducted on Schedule C in the calculation of net profit or loss from self-employment.

Many individuals make monthly mortgage payments that include real estate property taxes as well as mortgage principal and interest. Each month, the real estate tax payment is deposited into an escrow account that the mortgage company uses to pay the property taxes when they are due. In this case, the taxpayer deducts the actual amount of property taxes ultimately paid to the local taxing authority from the escrow account, not the amount paid to the mortgage holder. The mortgage company notifies the individual of the amount of the taxes paid on a year-end statement, normally a Form 1098.

EXAMPLE 5-11

Miriam's monthly mortgage payment for her principal residence is $1,500, of which $1,250 is mortgage principal and interest and $250 is for real estate property taxes. Every month the mortgage company deposits the $250 tax payment into an escrow account. In November 2017, the mortgage company paid the actual tax bill of $2,800 from the escrow account. Miriam can deduct $2,800 of real estate property taxes on her 2017 Schedule A.

State and Local Taxes

The deduction for state income taxes is one of the largest itemized deductions for many taxpayers. Only seven states in the United States do not have some form of state income tax.[29]

[27] *James, Joseph J.* (1995) TC Memo 1995-562.

[28] IRC § 164(d)(1).

[29] Currently the only states that do *not* have some form of income tax are Alaska, Florida, Nevada, South Dakota, Texas, Washington, and Wyoming.

EXAMPLE 5-12

Elijah lives in South Carolina and has state taxable income of $120,000. His state income tax is $7,200. If he itemizes, Elijah gets a deduction on Schedule A for that amount in the year the tax is paid.

In any year, an individual taxpayer can deduct the amount of state income taxes paid, whether through withholding, estimated taxes, or filing the prior year's state tax return However, if the state tax payments that were deducted result in the taxpayer receiving a refund in the following year, the state tax refund must be included as taxable income in the year of receipt. This is the *tax benefit rule,* which states that if a taxpayer receives a federal tax benefit from an expense when the expense is paid, that taxpayer is taxed on a refund of that expense when the refund is received. If the taxpayer does not receive a tax benefit from the expense when it is paid, he or she is not taxed on a refund of that expense when it is received.

EXAMPLE 5-13

In 2016 Richard had $4,700 in state income tax withheld from his paycheck. When he filed his 2016 federal tax return in April 2017, he was eligible to itemize and thus deducted the $4,700 in state income taxes paid, thus reducing his 2016 taxable income and federal tax liability. When he filed his 2016 state tax return (also in April 2017), he found that he had overpaid his state taxes and was due a refund of $800. He received the $800 state refund in June 2017. The $800 refund must be included in federal taxable income for the tax year 2017. The reasoning behind the inclusion is that Richard received a tax benefit for the entire $4,700 even though, in the end, he paid only $3,900 ($4,700 tax paid less the $800 refund). The inclusion of the $800 in income in the subsequent year corrects the excess deduction. The $800 is included on Form 1040, line 10, Taxable refunds, credits, or offsets of state and local taxes.

Taxpayers who do not itemize deductions (but claim the standard deduction) cannot deduct state income tax. Thus, if they get a refund, it is nontaxable income on their federal return because they received no tax benefit from a nondeductible expense. A refund of that expense is therefore not subject to tax. The same rules apply to taxpayers who are required to pay city or other local income taxes.

Employers may be required to withhold *state disability insurance* (SDI) from the paychecks of their employees in the state of California. California SDI is treated as state income tax for purposes of calculating federal taxable income.

Taxpayers may be able to elect to take an itemized deduction for the amount of either (1) state and local income taxes or (2) state and local general sales taxes paid during the tax year.[30] Taxpayers generally cannot deduct both. In general, taxpayers in states with an income tax will take the income tax deduction whereas taxpayers in states with no income tax will take the sales tax deduction. In states with both a state income tax and a state sales tax, the taxpayer will take the one with the greater benefit.

The amount of the sales tax deduction is determined by calculating actual sales taxes paid during the year. From a practical perspective, most taxpayers would find it difficult to determine and document actual sales tax payments. Thus a deduction is permitted using sales tax tables provided by the IRS in the instructions for Schedule A or by using the sales tax deduction calculator the IRS provides at http://apps.irs.gov/app/stdc/. To use the calculator, you can either copy and paste into your browser the URL just provided, or go to www.irs.gov and enter "sales tax deduction calculator" in the search box. When using the sales tax tables, taxpayers determine their sales tax deduction based on their income and number of exemptions. Income is defined as AGI plus any nontaxable items such as tax-exempt interest, workers' compensation, nontaxable social security or retirement income, and similar items. The number of exemptions is equal to the exemptions claimed on Form 1040, line 6d.

[30] IRC § 164(b)(5)

EXAMPLE 5-14

Lester and Charmaine live in Clearwater, FL 33755 with their two dependent children. Florida does not have a state income tax. The couple had AGI of $79,337 and interest income from a tax-exempt municipal bond of $2,190. Using the IRS sales tax deduction calculator tool for income between $80,000 and $90,000 with four exemptions and their zip code, you can calculate the itemized general sales tax deduction available to Lester and Charmaine.

Taxpayers who purchase an aircraft, boat, or in most cases a home or addition to a home, can add the amount of sales tax paid on those items to the amount of sales tax determined with reference to the IRS tables.[31]

Taxpayers claim the general sales tax deduction on Schedule A, line 5. The Schedule A instructions contain a worksheet for calculating the state and local sales tax deduction. The state and local sales tax tables are located in the appendix of the Schedule A instructions.

Foreign Taxes

Foreign taxes paid are deductible.[32] The taxpayer has the option of taking a credit (discussed in Chapter 9) for foreign taxes paid or deducting them on Schedule A. Individual taxpayers are usually better off utilizing the credit rather than the deduction because the credit is a dollar-for-dollar reduction in taxes, but the deduction reduces only taxable income, and the net tax effect depends on the taxpayer's tax rate.

EXAMPLE 5-15

Daniel, a U.S. citizen and resident, has several investments in England. The investments produced substantial income, and he had to pay $3,500 in English income taxes. Assume that Daniel's effective U.S. federal tax rate is 35%. He has a choice: File Form 1116 and take a $3,500 credit for the English tax, assuming that the foreign tax credit limitation does not apply, or deduct the taxes on Schedule A as an itemized deduction. The credit will reduce Daniel's net U.S. tax by $3,500. If he takes the deduction option, his net tax savings is only $1,225 ($3,500 × 35%). Clearly the better tax option is to file Form 1116 and take the credit.

A taxpayer cannot take both the credit and the deduction for the same foreign taxes paid. In most instances, the credit produces the better tax effect. However, if a taxpayer pays taxes to a country with which the United States has severed diplomatic relations or to a country that supports international terrorism, the credit is not allowed.[33] In this case, the deduction of the tax on Schedule A is the only option.

Documentation for State and Local Taxes

Generally the source document for property taxes (both personal and real property) is the receipt from the county or city tax collector. Other sources for property taxes are canceled checks. Many lending institutions escrow the property taxes along with the mortgage payment. If this is the case, the amount of property taxes is listed on the year-end mortgage interest statement (Form 1098) that the lending institution supplies. When real property is sold during the year, the allocation of the property taxes is usually shown on the closing statements signed when title changes hands.

For state income taxes, there are normally three source documents. For the majority of clients, the largest portion of state income taxes paid comes from the taxpayer's W-2 wage statement as state income tax withholding. Taxpayers who are self-employed or have considerable investment income could also pay quarterly estimated payments during the year. Usually, canceled checks to the state's department of revenue or other tax authority suffice as

[31] IRC § 164(b)(5)(H)(i) and IRS Publication 600.

[32] IRC § 164(a)(3).

[33] IRC § 901(j)(2).

documentation. The third source document is the prior year's state tax return. Reviewing the prior year return is crucial because it will show any tax paid with the prior year's return. If there was a refund, the tax preparer will know to include the refund in income for the current year (assuming the taxpayer itemized his or her return and deducted state taxes in the previous year).

Foreign taxes are sometimes more difficult to locate. The traditional source documents to locate foreign taxes paid include these:

1. The prior year's tax return from the foreign country.
2. Mutual fund or stock brokerage statements.
3. Canceled checks.

Some mutual funds or brokerage offices are required to withhold or pay foreign taxes on the sale of stock within the mutual fund. These taxes, in turn, pass through to investors. In addition, if a taxpayer invests in foreign stocks, taxes are often withheld from foreign dividends received. These withholdings are reported to the taxpayer on Form 1099-B.

Summary of Deductible Taxes

Type	Potential Source Documents
Personal property	County/city tax collector receipt Checkbook register/canceled check
Real estate property taxes	County/city tax collector receipt Checkbook register/canceled check Real estate closing statements Form 1098—Bank Mortgage Interest
State/local income tax	W-2 wage statement—State withholding box W-2 wage statement—Local withholding box Quarterly estimated tax payments Prior year's state/local tax return
Foreign	Prior year's foreign tax return Mutual fund/stock statements Canceled checks

CONCEPT CHECK 5-2—
LO 5-2

1. For personal property taxes to be deductible, they must be based on the value of the property. True or false?
2. When property is sold during the year, only the seller is allowed to take a deduction for taxes paid. True or false?
3. The tax benefit rule states that if a taxpayer receives a tax benefit when an expense is paid, no further action is required on the taxpayer's part if a refund is received in the future as a result of the previous expense deduction. True or false?
4. A taxpayer generally has the option to deduct foreign taxes paid either as a credit or as a deduction on Schedule A. True or false?

DEDUCTIBLE INTEREST (SCHEDULE A, LINE 15)
LO 5-3

Most taxpayers in the United States do not itemize deductions until they purchase their first residence. The main component of the interest deduction is the home mortgage deduction. In the past, almost all types of personal interest were deductible on Schedule A. However, consumer loan interest deductions (such as auto loan interest and credit card interest) have been virtually eliminated. The only types of personal interest still available as a deduction are mortgage interest on a personal residence and investment interest. Any interest connected with

From Shoebox to Software

EXAMPLE 5-16

Locate the saved tax file for Jose and Maria Ramirez from earlier in this chapter. They had the following additional information:

Property or Activity	Tax
Jose's state income tax withheld (per W-2)	$3,470
State estimated tax payments ($250 per quarter with the last payment on 12/31/17)	1,000
State taxes paid with prior year return	300
Foreign taxes paid on foreign stock investments	400
Personal residence real estate property tax	1,300
Truck	200
Van	250
Ski boat	200

Lines 5–9 on Schedule A are the appropriate lines to record deductible personal taxes. Go to Schedule A for the Ramirezes.

1. Note that the state withholding is already on line 5 from the W-2 you entered previously.
2. To enter the state estimated tax payments, double-click on the state and local estimates line. Enter the $250 per quarter payments and the dates they were paid.
3. Enter the $300 paid with last year's return (usually filed in April) on the Other state and local income taxes line.
4. Enter the personal residence property tax ($1,300) on the real estate tax line (line 6).
5. Enter the total of the taxes on the truck, van, and boat on line 7. You can use the line item detail by right-clicking on line 7 and entering each item individually. The total from the worksheet will then be carried forward to line 7.

When you have completed Schedule A for taxes, it will look like the one in Exhibit 5-4.

The total itemized deduction for taxes equals $6,720. The foreign taxes of $400 could have been placed on line 8, but the Ramirezes would most likely receive a higher tax benefit by filing Form 1116 and taking the $400 as a foreign tax credit.

EXHIBIT 5-4

Taxes You Paid	5	State and local **(check only one box):**				
		a ☑ Income taxes, **or** / b ☐ General sales taxes	5	4,770		
	6	Real estate taxes (see instructions)	6	1,300		
	7	Personal property taxes	7	650		
	8	Other taxes. List type and amount ▶	8			
	9	Add lines 5 through 8			9	6,720

Source: U.S. Department of the Treasury, Internal Revenue Service, Form 1040- Schedule A. Washington, DC: 2017.

a trade or business or for the production of income is still deductible. However, these amounts are *for* AGI deductions and are deducted on the appropriate form (Schedule C, Schedule E, or Schedule F).

Mortgage Interest and Home Equity Loans

Interest is the fee paid by a borrower to a lender for the use or forbearance of money. Congress encourages home ownership by granting an itemized deduction for qualified residence interest, better known as *home mortgage interest.* Qualified residence interest is *interest paid on acquisition indebtedness or a home equity loan secured by a qualified residence.* If the loan is not secured by a qualified residence, the interest is not qualified residence interest. *Acquisition indebtedness* means any debt incurred to acquire, construct, or substantially improve any qualified residence.[34]

[34] IRC § 163(h)(3)(B)(i).

TAX YOUR BRAIN

Suppose the taxpayer has a large unsecured personal line of credit with the local lending institution and borrows $15,000 to add a large closet to the existing residence. Does the interest charged by the institution on the $15,000 qualify as residence interest?

ANSWER

No. Because the debt was not secured by the residence, the interest would not be deductible. Had the line of credit been a home equity line, the interest would be deductible.

Taxpayers can deduct qualified residence interest on their principal residence and or a second residence selected by the taxpayer.[35] The aggregate amount treated as acquisition indebtedness for any period cannot exceed $1,000,000 ($500,000 for married individuals filing separate returns). The $1,000,000 limitation refers to the amount of *principal* of the debt, not the interest paid. Taxpayers may have more than one acquisition loan per residence (a first mortgage and a second mortgage).

If the taxpayer refinances an acquisition loan (for example, refinances a $260,000, 6% loan with a new $260,000, 4% loan), the new loan continues to qualify as acquisition debt to the extent that the principal does not increase. If the principal does increase as a result of the refinance, the interest related to that additional principal does not qualify for the deduction. There is a worksheet on page 9 of IRS Publication 936 that can be used to calculate the allowable mortgage deduction.

EXAMPLE 5-17

Cathy and Mark, who are married, incur debt of $580,000 to build their new personal residence. In the following year, they decide to build a vacation home at the beach and borrow an additional $500,000 to build it. Cathy and Mark's acquisition indebtedness is limited to $1,000,000. In this case, the additional interest on the excess $80,000 of indebtedness is allowed. However, it must be classified as home equity indebtedness. Home equity indebtedness may not exceed $100,000.[36] Thus the true debt limit to qualified residence interest is $1,100,000 for those filing MFJ.

The 9th Circuit Court of Appeals recently ruled that the mortgage interest deduction debt limits apply to unmarried co-owners *on a per-taxpayer basis, not on a per-residence basis* and the IRS, in AOD (Action on Decision) 2016-02, acquiesced to that decision.

The implication of this ruling is very important. Whereas a married couple filing jointly is seen as effectively being one taxpayer, and thus subject to the overall mortgage interest deduction limit of up to $1 million dollars in acquisition debt, an unmarried couple that owns a property together would be subject to a mortgage interest deduction of up to $1 million dollars in acquisition debt per individual.

This would also apply to the Home Equity interest deductions limitations as well. Assume that a non-married couple acquires a new house, owning the home as joint tenants. Also assume the total acquisition mortgage debt is $2,000,000 and the total home equity loan is $200,000, making the total debt $2,200,000. Under this new ruling, each person would be able to deduct the interest on their portion of the total debt which would be $1,100,000 per individual. This becomes another example of the "Marriage Penalty" that we see elsewhere in the tax code.

In Example 5-17, we noted that home equity indebtedness can increase the effective limit of the home mortgage deduction to interest on $1,100,000. What is *home equity indebtedness,* and how does it differ from acquisition indebtedness? *Home equity loans* are loans that are secured by a qualified residence in an amount that does not exceed the FMV of the residence less the acquisition debt.

35 IRC § 163(h)(4)(A)(i)(II).

36 IRC § 163(h)(3)(C)(ii).

EXAMPLE 5-18

Bryan purchased a house several years ago for $130,000. The acquisition debt still outstanding is $115,000. The house's FMV is now $150,000. Therefore, the net equity in the house is now $35,000 ($150,000 FMV − $115,000 debt). Bryan could borrow as home equity indebtedness up to $35,000, and the interest would still be deductible (most lending institutions, however, will lend only up to 80% or 90% of the net equity in the personal residence).

The aggregate amount treated as home equity indebtedness for any period cannot exceed $100,000 for MFJ ($50,000 for married filing separately) but, as pointed out in the previous paragraph, for unmarried co-owners of a property that interest limitation would be on $100,000 of home equity debt per person.[37] Interest on home equity debt is an adjustment for the Alternative Minimum Tax (AMT).

Mortgage Points

Points are amounts that borrowers pay to obtain a mortgage. The most common names of these charges are "loan origination fees" or "loan processing fees." Each point equals 1% of the loan principal. For example, Marisa pays 2 points on a $100,000 mortgage loan. The points equal $2,000 (0.01 × 2 × $100,000). Typically taxpayers deduct points ratably over the term of the loan. However, the law allows an exception for points paid in connection with a principal residence. Points are deductible by a cash basis taxpayer as mortgage interest if they meet the following "safe harbor" criteria:

1. The Uniform Settlement Statement must clearly designate the amounts as loan origination fees, loan discount, discount points, or points payable in connection with the loan.
2. The amounts must be computed as a percentage of the stated principal amount of the indebtedness incurred by the taxpayer.
3. The amounts paid must conform to an established business practice of charging points for loans for the acquisition of principal residences in the geographical area.
4. The amounts must be paid in connection with the acquisition of the taxpayer's principal residence, and that residence must secure the loan.
5. The amounts must be paid directly by the taxpayers [38]

Generally the buyer of the home incurs points when obtaining a loan. As an inducement for the sale, the seller of the residence may actually pay the points for the buyer. If this is the case, the buyer receives the tax benefit if the point amount reduces the basis of the home when the property is sold. Taxpayers can take a deduction for the points paid only if the indebtedness is incurred in connection with the purchase or improvement of their principal residence. Points paid to refinance an existing mortgage are deducted ratably over the life of the loan. If the loan is paid off before it is due, the unamortized points are deductible in the year the debt is paid.

EXAMPLE 5-19

Jason and his wife purchased a home in 2003 for $230,000. They borrowed $184,000 with a 30-year, 6.5% note from a local lending institution. In 2017, Jason decided to make an addition to the house that would cost $75,000. He and his wife borrowed the $75,000 and paid a 1% loan origination fee. In 2017, the $750 in points could be deducted because the indebtedness was in connection with the improvement of their principal residence.

EXAMPLE 5-20

Assume the same initial facts as Example 5-19. However, instead of the $75,000 addition, Jason and his wife decided to refinance their loan (balance now at $175,000) because the interest rate was now 3.5% for a 30-year loan. The 1% origination fee of $1,750 cannot be fully deducted this year because the new loan was not for the original purchase or improvement of the residence. They can deduct the points ratably over the 30-year loan period or $58 per year ($1,750/30 years). If the refinancing had occurred on June 1, then the deduction for the current year would be $34 ($1,750/30 years × 7/12).[39]

[37] IRC § 163(h)(3)(C)(ii).

[38] Rev. Proc. 94-27, 1994-1 CB 613.

[39] Rev. Proc. 87-15, 1987-1 CB 624.

Mortgage Insurance Premium Deduction

Often individuals who purchase a home with a down payment of less than 20% are required to pay a mortgage insurance premium or, as it is sometimes referred to, *private mortgage insurance* (PMI). In effect, mortgage insurance protects the lender against a loan default. In the past, the mortgage insurance premium was not deductible. For mortgage insurance contracts issued in 2017, the taxpayer may take an itemized deduction for the amount of the premium paid in 2017 on line 13 of Schedule A.

The deductible amount is reduced by 10% for every $1,000 ($500 if married filing separately) by which AGI exceeds $100,000 ($50,000 if married filing separately). Thus the deduction is not allowed when AGI exceeds $110,000 ($55,000 if married filing separately).

Investment Interest

If a taxpayer borrows money to finance the purchase of investment assets—such as stocks, bonds, or land held strictly for investment—the interest expense is investment interest expense.

Investment interest expense is any interest that is paid or accrued on indebtedness properly allocable to property held for investment. The deduction of investment interest expense is limited to the net investment income for the year and is deductible as an itemized deduction on Schedule A.[40] Net investment income is gross investment income less deductible investment expenses. If the investment interest expense exceeds the taxpayer's net investment income, he or she can carry forward the excess expense to future tax years when net investment income is available. One common example of investment interest expense is interest from a loan whose proceeds the taxpayer uses to purchase stock.

EXAMPLE 5-21

Gayle purchased a tract of land that she felt would substantially appreciate over the next several years. She borrowed $20,000 from a local lending institution and signed a 7%, 15-year note. If Gayle's only investment income is interest of $1,000, she could deduct the interest on the lending institution loan up to a maximum of $1,000 in the current year (her net investment income). Any remaining amount of interest would be carried forward to future years and would be deducted when additional net investment income becomes available.

Typical items that qualify as investment income are interest income, ordinary dividends, and short-term capital gains. However, gains and losses from the disposition of several investment properties must first be netted to determine investment income. Income from passive activities and income from rental real estate with active participation are specifically excluded from the definition of investment income, as well as net long-term capital gains and qualified dividend income.[41] However, if a taxpayer elects to treat a portion of long-term capital gain or qualified dividend income as investment income, the long-term gain or dividend income is not eligible for the lower tax rate that would otherwise apply.[42] Generally taxpayers use Form 4952 to calculate and report the amount of deductible investment interest expense. However, Form 4952 does not have to be included with the return if all three of these circumstances apply:

1. Investment interest expense does not exceed investment income from interest and ordinary dividends minus qualified dividends.
2. The taxpayer has no other deductible investment expenses.
3. The taxpayer has no disallowed investment interest expense from 2016.

Net investment income may now be subject to a 3.8% Medicare tax for AGI over certain thresholds.

[40] IRC § 163(d)(1).

[41] IRC § 163(d)(4)(D). Passive activities and rental real estate are discussed in detail in Chapters 8 and 13, respectively.

[42] IRC § 163(d)(4)(B).

From Shoebox to Software

Determining the amount of the total interest deduction usually is not difficult. In most cases, a financial institution sends the taxpayer Form 1098 reporting the interest expense. See Exhibit 5-5 for an example of a common Form 1098 from a financial institution.[43]

EXAMPLE 5-22 Assume that the Form 1098 in Exhibit 5-5 was for Jose and Maria Ramirez and had $7,300 on line 1. To enter the $7,300 on line 10 of Schedule A, you must enter the amount on a Form 1098. Enter the $7,300 on line 1, and it will automatically be transferred to Schedule A. Save the Ramirezes' return for future use.

Difficulty can arise when a taxpayer has numerous loans outstanding. Typically the lending institution labels the interest as related to the principal residence (either acquisition indebtedness or home equity indebtedness). However, if the taxpayer has several loans, some of which are personal loans (like a car loan) and others are investment loans, the tax preparer must question the client to discover which loans are for what activities.

EXHIBIT 5-5

☐ CORRECTED (if checked)

RECIPIENT'S/LENDER'S name, street address, city or town, state or province, country, ZIP or foreign postal code, and telephone no.		*Caution: The amount shown may not be fully deductible by you. Limits based on the loan amount and the cost and value of the secured property may apply. Also, you may only deduct interest to the extent it was incurred by you, actually paid by you, and not reimbursed by another person.	OMB No. 1545-0901 **2017** Form **1098**	**Mortgage Interest Statement**
		1 Mortgage interest received from payer(s)/borrower(s)* $		**Copy B** **For Payer/ Borrower**
RECIPIENT'S/LENDER'S federal identification number	PAYER'S/BORROWER'S taxpayer identification no.	2 Outstanding mortgage principal as of 1/1/2017 $	3 Mortgage origination date	The information in boxes 1 through 10 is important tax information and is being furnished to the Internal Revenue Service. If you are required to file a return, a negligence penalty or other sanction may be imposed on you if the IRS determines that an underpayment of tax results because you overstated a deduction for this mortgage interest or for these points, reported in boxes 1 and 6; or because you didn't report the refund of interest (box 4); or because you claimed a non-deductible item.
PAYER'S/BORROWER'S name		4 Refund of overpaid interest $	5 Mortgage insurance premiums $	
		6 Points paid on purchase of principal residence $		
Street address (including apt. no.)		7 Is address of property securing mortgage same as PAYER'S/BORROWER'S address? If "Yes," box is checked . . . . ☐ If "No," see box 8 or 9, below		
City or town, state or province, country, and ZIP or foreign postal code		8 Address of property securing mortgage		
10 Number of mortgaged properties	11 Other	9 If property securing mortgage has no address, below is the description of the property		
Account number (see instructions)				

Form **1098** (Keep for your records) www.irs.gov/form1098 Department of the Treasury - Internal Revenue Service

Source: U.S. Department of the Treasury, Internal Revenue Service, Form 1098. Washington, DC: 2017.

[43] Many financial institutions develop their own Form 1098 (labeled Form 1098 Substitute). Therefore, the form may differ somewhat depending on the institution. The form, however, reports the same information.

CONCEPT CHECK 5-3— LO 5-3

1. Acquisition indebtedness means any debt incurred to ______________________, ______________, or ______________ any qualified residence.
2. The aggregate amount treated as acquisition indebtedness, not home equity indebtedness, for any period cannot exceed $ ______________ for married filing jointly.
3. The deduction of investment interest expense is limited to the ________ ________ income for the year.
4. Each point paid to acquire a home loan equals ______________ of the loan principal.

DEDUCTIBLE GIFTS TO CHARITY (SCHEDULE A, LINE 19)

LO 5-4

The government encourages the private sector to support charitable organizations by granting individual taxpayers a charitable contribution deduction, which may be claimed as an itemized deduction on Schedule A. Contributions must be to one of the following five types of organizations:[44]

1. Any governmental unit or subdivision of the United States or its possession as long as the gift is for exclusively public purposes.
2. Any nonprofit organization that is organized and operated exclusively for religious, charitable, scientific, literary, or educational purposes or to foster international amateur sports competition and is not disqualified from tax-exempt status under IRC § 501(c)(3).
3. A post or organization of war veterans for which no part of the net earnings benefits any private shareholder or individual.
4. A domestic fraternal society or association that uses the contribution only for religious, charitable, scientific, or educational purposes.
5. A cemetery company owned and operated exclusively for the benefit of its members.

If you are uncertain whether an organization is a qualified donee organization, check the IRS Exempt Organization on-line search tool at www.irs.gov/charities-non-profits/exempt-organizations-select-check.

The amount of the deduction depends on the type of donated property and is subject to AGI limitations. To be deductible, the donation must be cash or other property of value. The government imposes strict documentation requirements for both types of contributions.

A taxpayer receives no deduction for services rendered to a charitable organization.[45] The services do not give rise to taxable income to the taxpayer, so no deduction is permitted.

A taxpayer who travels away from home overnight to attend a convention as a representative of a charitable organization may deduct related transportation and travel expenses, including meals and lodging. If the taxpayer incurs travel expenses as a volunteer for a qualified charity, the expenses are deductible if he or she has significant duties throughout the course of the trip and no significant amount of personal recreation is attached to the trip.

EXAMPLE 5-23

Kathy, a local CPA, is an ardent supporter of the Boys Club in Hickory Hills, AL. Each year she compiles monthly financial statements and prepares the Form 990 tax return for the club. Kathy estimates that she spends 20 hours per year working for the Boys Club. Her normal rate is $100 per hour. Because Kathy's donation is her services and she has recorded no income for those services, she receives no charitable contribution deduction.

Kathy is able to deduct any out-of-pocket expenses she paid in connection with her service to the Boys Club. Actual expenditures are deductible for automotive travel, or the taxpayer has the option to deduct 14 cents per mile as a standard rate for charitable contributions.

Property Donations: Capital versus Ordinary Income Property

Not all donations to charity are in the form of cash. In fact, many large donations are made with capital gain property (such as stocks, bonds, land, and other investments). Still other donations

[44] IRC § 170(c).

[45] Reg. § 1.170A-1(g).

are made with ordinary income property (inventory and accounts receivable). Generally, if capital gain property is donated to a public charity, the deductible donation amount is the property's FMV.

Charitable Contribution of Personal Tangible Property Clarification

A key exception to this general rule concerns the contribution of tangible personal property. If the donated property is put to a use that is unrelated to the purpose or function of the charity's tax-exempt status, the contribution must be reduced by the amount of any long-term capital gain that would have been realized if the property had been sold at its FMV at the time of the contribution. For example, if a sculpture is donated to a museum and is put on display for the public, that would be a related purpose. If, however, the museum had simply sold the sculpture without displaying it and used the funds for museum operations, that would be an unrelated purpose and would require this exception. A second exception occurs if the investment property is short-term property (held one year or less). In this case, the deduction is limited to the tax basis of the asset (its cost). The donation of investment/capital gain property is also subject to additional limitations depending on the type of the recipient organization (see the following section on limitations).

EXAMPLE 5-24

Kimberly donated her old computer to Helping Hands Industries. She had purchased the computer for personal use several years ago at a cost of $1,500. The computer's FMV at the date of donation was $400. The computer is a capital asset held for more than one year, so Kimberly may deduct the $400 FMV as a charitable contribution, subject to the overall charitable contribution limits.

Generally, when ordinary income property (such as inventory and accounts receivable) is donated to charity, the deduction amount is limited to the tax basis of the property donated. The deduction does not depend on the type of recipient organization.

Percentage Limitations of Charitable Donations

There are three limitations concerning charitable contributions by individual taxpayers: 50%, 30%, and 20% limitations. The general limitation is the 50% limitation. All charitable contributions to public charities are limited to 50% of the individual taxpayer's AGI.[46] A contribution in excess of the limitation is carried forward for the next five tax years, subject to the overall 50% limitation in those years. For each category of contributions, the taxpayer must deduct carryover contributions only after deducting all allowable contributions in that same category for the current year. The deduction of amounts from previous years is done on a first-in, first-out, basis.

EXAMPLE 5-25

Doris is a wealthy widow and has $200,000 in AGI from various investments. If she makes a $150,000 cash donation to State University, her charitable deduction is limited to $100,000. The remaining $50,000 is carried forward for up to five years.

The 30% limitation applies to contributions of long-term tangible capital gain property. When long-term tangible capital gain property is contributed to a public charity, and the property is put to a related use by the charity, the taxpayer can take a deduction for the asset's FMV. However, the deduction is limited to 30% of the taxpayer's AGI.[47] Again, any excess is carried forward for five years.

EXAMPLE 5-26

Assume the same facts as in Example 5-25. However, instead of giving cash of $150,000, Doris contributed a vacation cottage that she has owned for many years. The cottage, which is in a marshland and could be used for research purposes, has an FMV of $150,000. The university uses the cottage as a research station for biology and zoology students, which would be a related use. In this case, Doris's deduction is limited to $60,000 for this year ($200,000 AGI × 30% limitation). The excess $90,000 of eligible deduction is carried forward for the next five years.

[46] IRC § 170(b)(1)(A).

[47] IRC § 170(b)(1)(C).

There is one exception to this rule: If the taxpayer elects to reduce the FMV of the contributed property by the amount of long-term capital gain that would have been recognized if the property had been sold at its FMV at the time of the contribution, the 50% limitation would apply to the contribution, rather than the 30% of AGI limitation.[48]

EXAMPLE 5-27

Assume the same facts as in Example 5-26. However, Doris elects to reduce the fair market value FMV of the cottage by the amount of long-term capital gain she would have recognized if she had sold the cottage. Her adjusted basis in the cottage is $70,000. Her charitable contribution would therefore be $70,000 because 50% of her AGI of $200,000 would be a $100,000 limitation on charitable contributions.

Another exception to this rule concerns the donation of long-term tangible capital gain property to a charity that the charity uses for purposes unrelated to the organization's function.

EXAMPLE 5-28

Assume the same facts as in Example 5-26, except that the university promptly sells the cottage. In this case, the deduction would be limited to Doris's adjusted basis in the cottage of $70,000 because the presumption is that the use of the property was unrelated to the university's tax-exempt purpose. In this exception the 30% limit does not apply, and the deduction would be based on 50% of AGI, as seen in Example 5-27.

The 30% limitation also applies to any contribution (cash or property) to charities that are not 50% limitation charities such as war veterans' organizations, fraternal orders, cemetery companies, and certain nonoperating private foundations.

The 20% limitation refers to the donation of capital gain property to a private foundation. The deduction for cash given to a private foundation is limited to 30% of AGI, whereas capital gain property given to the same organization is limited to 20% of AGI.[49]

One final limitation involves a charitable contribution to an educational institution that gives the taxpayer the right or benefit to preferential treatment at athletic events. The most common example is preferential seating rights at football and basketball games. If an otherwise deductible contribution to a university or college allows the taxpayer to get preferential seating, that donation is limited to 80% of the payment.[50] Any portion of the payment that is for tickets is nondeductible, and the excess is limited to 80%.

EXAMPLE 5-29

Samatha, a wealthy business owner, gave the following amounts to State College: $4,500 for 30 season tickets for woman's basketball and $10,000 to its athletic foundation for preferential seating location and parking. The $4,500 is not deductible at all because the taxpayer is buying a product; the $10,000 donation is limited to $8,000 (80% of $10,000).

Required Documentation of Charitable Gifts

Recently the substantiation requirements for charitable contributions have become more stringent. The nonprofit organizations themselves bear most of the increased requirements. They are now required to provide summary receipts to donors. From the taxpayer's perspective, when a gift to a charitable organization is less than $250 in cash, the contributor is required to keep a canceled check, a receipt from the organization, or other written records to substantiate the deduction.[51] If the donation is more than $250, the taxpayer must have written acknowledgment from the recipient organization stating (1) the date and amount of the contribution, (2) whether the taxpayer received any goods or services from the charity as a result of the

[48] IRC § 170(b)(1)(C)(iii).

[49] IRC § 170(b)(1)(D).

[50] IRC § 170(l)(2).

[51] Reg. § 1.170A-13(a)(1)(i)–(iii).

contribution, and (3) a description and good-faith estimate of the value of any goods and services that the taxpayer received. A canceled check does not meet the substantiation requirements for donations of more than $250.

EXAMPLE 5-30

John goes to a church function organized to raise funds for a new youth group building. He pays $500 for a painting that has a $100 FMV. John's charitable contribution to the church is $400. To substantiate the deduction, he must get a receipt from the church and keep his canceled check.

Taxpayers are not required to aggregate multiple contributions they make to a charity during the year for purposes of the $250 limit. The required documentation is based on the amount of each separate contribution.

EXAMPLE 5-31

Every week, Adina donates $50 to her synagogue. In October 2017, she made an additional $500 contribution to the temple building fund. Adina may document each weekly contribution with a canceled check. To take the $500 contribution as a deduction, she must receive a written acknowledgment from the synagogue. It must state the date and amount of the contribution and the fact that Adina received no goods or services from the temple as a result of her donation.

From Shoebox to Software

EXAMPLE 5-32

Jose and Maria Ramirez gave the following items to their church: (1) cash $1,000, no individual contribution greater than $250, (2) a painting with an FMV of $750, basis $500, and (3) three large bags of used clothing. The Ramirezes' charitable contribution would be calculated and placed on Schedule A and Form 8283 as follows:

Cash	$1,000
Painting	750
Clothes (thrift value)[52]	200
Total	$1,950

Open their tax return. Enter the cash contributions directly on line 16 of Schedule A. Form 8283 is required for noncash gifts in excess of $500. Double-click on line 17 or open a Form 8283. Enter the required information as shown on Form 8283 in Exhibit 5-6. Make sure you save your file when you have finished.

EXHIBIT 5-6

Gifts to Charity	16	Gifts by cash or check. If you made any gift of $250 or more, see instructions	16	1,000		
If you made a gift and got a benefit for it, see instructions.	17	Other than by cash or check. If any gift of $250 or more, see instructions. You **must** attach Form 8283 if over $500	17	950		
	18	Carryover from prior year	18			
	19	Add lines 16 through 18			19	1,950

Source: U.S. Department of the Treasury, Internal Revenue Service, Form 8283. Washington, DC: 2017.

(continued)

The substantiation requirements are the same for noncash gifts. A taxpayer who donates noncash property valued at less than $250 should obtain a receipt or letter from the charity showing the name of the charity, the date and location of the contribution, and a description of the donated property. The charity is not required to value the donated property, but the taxpayer should keep a record of the property's FMV at the date of the donation and how that FMV was determined.

However, if noncash gifts are worth more than $500, the taxpayer must file Form 8283 on which he or she must list the organization's name, a description of the property, the date acquired, the

[52] *Thrift value* is the value for which the clothes could be sold. In most cases, thrift value is a very subjective value.

EXHIBIT 5-6 *(concluded)*

Form **8283** (Rev. December 2014) Department of the Treasury Internal Revenue Service

Noncash Charitable Contributions

▶ **Attach to your tax return if you claimed a total deduction of over $500 for all contributed property.**

▶ **Information about Form 8283 and its separate instructions is at *www.irs.gov/form8283*.**

OMB No. 1545-0908

Attachment Sequence No. **155**

Name(s) shown on your income tax return | **Identifying number**

Note. Figure the amount of your contribution deduction before completing this form. See your tax return instructions.

Section A. Donated Property of $5,000 or Less and Publicly Traded Securities—List in this section **only** items (or groups of similar items) for which you claimed a deduction of $5,000 or less. Also list publicly traded securities even if the deduction is more than $5,000 (see instructions).

Part I **Information on Donated Property**—If you need more space, attach a statement.

1	**(a)** Name and address of the donee organization	**(b)** If donated property is a vehicle (see instructions), check the box. Also enter the vehicle identification number (unless Form 1098-C is attached).	**(c)** Description of donated property (For a vehicle, enter the year, make, model, and mileage. For securities, enter the company name and the number of shares.)
A		☐	
B		☐	
C		☐	
D		☐	
E		☐	

Note. If the amount you claimed as a deduction for an item is $500 or less, you do not have to complete columns (e), (f), and (g).

	(d) Date of the contribution	**(e)** Date acquired by donor (mo., yr.)	**(f)** How acquired by donor	**(g)** Donor's cost or adjusted basis	**(h)** Fair market value (see instructions)	**(i)** Method used to determine the fair market value
A						
B						
C						
D						
E						

Part II **Partial Interests and Restricted Use Property**—Complete lines 2a through 2e if you gave less than an entire interest in a property listed in Part I. Complete lines 3a through 3c if conditions were placed on a contribution listed in Part I; also attach the required statement (see instructions).

2a Enter the letter from Part I that identifies the property for which you gave less than an entire interest ▶ ______
If Part II applies to more than one property, attach a separate statement.

b Total amount claimed as a deduction for the property listed in Part I: **(1)** For this tax year ▶ ______
(2) For any prior tax years ▶ ______

c Name and address of each organization to which any such contribution was made in a prior year (complete only if different from the donee organization above):

Name of charitable organization (donee)

Address (number, street, and room or suite no.)

City or town, state, and ZIP code

d For tangible property, enter the place where the property is located or kept ▶ ______

e Name of any person, other than the donee organization, having actual possession of the property ▶ ______

		Yes	**No**
3a	Is there a restriction, either temporary or permanent, on the donee's right to use or dispose of the donated property?		
b	Did you give to anyone (other than the donee organization or another organization participating with the donee organization in cooperative fundraising) the right to the income from the donated property or to the possession of the property, including the right to vote donated securities, to acquire the property by purchase or otherwise, or to designate the person having such income, possession, or right to acquire?		
c	Is there a restriction limiting the donated property for a particular use?		

For Paperwork Reduction Act Notice, see separate instructions. Cat. No. 62299J Form **8283** (Rev. 12-2014)

Source: U.S. Department of the Treasury, Internal Revenue Service, Form 8283. Washington, DC: 2017.

acquisition method of the property, the cost or basis, and the FMV. If the value of the donated property is more than $5,000, an appraisal is required within 60 days prior to the date of contribution.

CONCEPT CHECK 5-4—
LO 5-4

1. Depending on the type and amount of a charitable donation, it can be claimed either as a *for* AGI deduction or as an itemized deduction on Schedule A. True or false?
2. The overall limitation on the deductibility of charitable contributions is 30% of AGI. True or false?
3. If noncash gifts are worth more than $500, the taxpayer must file Form 8283. True or false?

DEDUCTIBLE CASUALTY AND THEFT LOSSES (SCHEDULE A, LINE 20)

LO 5-5

The Internal Revenue Code notes three instances in which an individual taxpayer can deduct a loss of property.[53] The first two deal with business or "production of income" property. Such losses are *for* AGI deductions[54] and are treated differently than losses to personal-use property. Losses discussed in this section pertain to losses of personal-use property (such as a personal residence, personal auto, or vacation home).

What Is a Casualty?

Over the years, court cases and IRS administrative rulings have developed a generally accepted definition of *casualty:* an identifiable event of a sudden, unexpected , or unusual nature.[55] *Sudden* means the event is not gradual or progressive. If a loss is due to progressive deterioration, such as termite damage, it is not deductible as a casualty. A casualty is also an unusual event caused by external forces. Common household accidents, such as accidentally breaking furniture or damage caused by a pet, are not casualties. To claim a deduction, the taxpayer must own the damaged property.

EXAMPLE 5-33

Damage to walls and flooring from the progressive deterioration of a roof is a nondeductible casualty loss because the event was not sudden but gradual and progressive.[56] Likewise, when a patio porch collapses as a result of excessive dry rot, the casualty loss is disallowed.[57]

Unexpected refers to an event that is unanticipated and occurs without the intent of the taxpayer. An *unusual* event is one that is extraordinary and nonrecurring.[58]

TAX YOUR BRAIN

Since 1995 the North Carolina coast has been hit by a number of hurricanes, each of which caused substantial casualty losses. If a hurricane strikes the North Carolina coast in 2017, is the event still a casualty?

ANSWER

With a strict reading of the tax authority concerning casualty losses, the hurricane probably would not qualify as a casualty. The hurricane is not unexpected or unusual in recent history. However, the IRS is very unlikely to challenge a natural disaster if for no other reason than the negative public opinion that would result. A hurricane could provide a sudden loss even if it were not unusual. The Tax Court has held that even if an event is foreseeable, it does not preclude a casualty loss deduction.[59]

[53] IRC § 165(c).
[54] Casualty losses of business property are discussed in Chapter 6 and Chapter 8.
[55] Rev. Rul. 76-134,1976-1 CB 54.
[56] *Whiting, Laurin* (1975) 34 TCM 241.
[57] *Chipman* (1981) 41 TCM 1318.
[58] Rev. Rul. 72-592, 1972-2 CB 101.
[59] *Heyn, Harry* (1966) 46 TC 302, acq 1967-2 CB 2.

TABLE 5-2
Personal Casualty Expense Deduction Formula

Calculation of Deductible Casualty Loss

Determine:

FMV immediately before the casualty	
minus (FMV immediately after the casualty)	
Amount A: Decline in FMV	
Amount B: Adjusted basis of the property	
Select the smaller of Amount A or Amount B	
minus (insurance recovery)	
Allowable loss	
minus ($100 per event)	
Eligible loss	
minus (10% of AGI)	
Deductible casualty loss	

The magnitude of the casualty is not the primary factor in deciding whether the event is a casualty. Thus a minor event could qualify as a casualty. A formula that can be used to determine the amount of deductible casualty loss is shown in Table 5-2.

The Amount of a Casualty Loss and the Year Deductible

The taxpayer may deduct uninsured loss or out-of-pocket loss subject to certain limits detailed here. The taxpayer's uninsured loss is calculated as follows:

$$\text{Uninsured loss} = \text{Loss due to casualty or theft} - \text{Insurance recovery}$$

In general, the casualty loss is the lower of the following:

1. The FMV immediately before the casualty reduced by the FMV immediately after the casualty.
2. The amount of the adjusted basis for determining the loss from the sale or other disposition of the property involved.[60]

The taxpayer is required to provide proof of the adjusted basis and FMV. *Adjusted basis* is the original cost or basis of the asset minus any depreciation or amortization and plus the cost of any capital improvements. The FMV is normally determined by an appraised value before and after the casualty event. Repair costs can also play an important role in determining the casualty loss. If the property is only partially destroyed, the casualty loss is its decline in value.

EXAMPLE 5-34

Tracy and Barbara purchased their personal residence in 1996 for $95,000. In March 2017, when the appraised value of the house was $250,000, it and most of their belongings in it were destroyed by fire. The amount of the casualty loss for the house is $95,000 (the lower of the adjusted basis of $95,000 or the decrease in FMV of $250,000) because Tracy and Barbara received no insurance reimbursement for the damage. Losses for the personal belongings would be calculated on an item-by-item basis (from an inventory list of everything in the house).

EXAMPLE 5-35

In 2016, Lee purchased an automobile (used for nonbusiness purposes) for $17,000. In April 2017, he had an accident with another automobile. Lee's auto had an FMV of $14,500 when the accident occurred. The FMV after the accident is difficult to determine. However, the cost to repair the auto to its precasualty condition was $5,000. The $5,000 would be a reasonable amount to deduct as a casualty loss. If Lee receives any insurance proceeds, he would reduce his loss accordingly.

[60] Reg § 1.167-7(b)(1).

Typically a taxpayer reports a casualty loss on the tax return in the tax year it took place. However, in three instances, casualty losses may be deducted in different tax years:

1. Theft losses.
2. Reimbursement by insurance or otherwise (such as from a negligence claim against an individual or company that caused the loss).
3. Disaster area losses.

Theft losses are deducted in the tax year in which the theft was discovered rather than the year of theft, if different.

EXAMPLE 5-36

As a hobby, Stefan collects rare coins. He had his collection appraised by an expert in October 2016. In January 2017, when Stefan was reviewing his collection, he noted that two extremely rare coins had been replaced with forgeries. Stefan would deduct the loss in 2017.[61]

In all cases, taxpayers must subtract any insurance reimbursement in determining their loss. Even when the insurance reimbursement has not yet been received, if a reasonable prospect of recovery exists with respect to a claim of insurance, the casualty loss should be adjusted for the anticipated recovery.[62] Should the loss be deducted and recovery occur in the subsequent tax year, the taxpayer must include the reimbursement in income in the year of reimbursement to the extent a tax benefit was gained from the casualty loss.

Individuals are required to file an insurance claim for *insured* personal casualty and theft losses to claim a deduction. If no insurance claim is filed, and there was insurance, then no deduction is permitted.

If the casualty loss occurred as the result of a major event (usually a natural disaster), and the president of the United States declares the area a national disaster area, the taxpayer can elect to deduct the casualty loss against the preceding year's taxable income. Congress added this provision to allow taxpayers suffering major disasters to get immediate assistance from a tax refund. The taxpayer files an amended return (Form 1040X) for the previous tax year including the casualty loss in the calculation. If the preceding year's tax return had not been filed at the time of the casualty, the loss can be deducted on the original return.

Limitation on Personal Casualty Losses

The tax law places two general limitations on personal casualty deductions. Each separate casualty is reduced by $100. It is important to note that this is $100 per *casualty,* not $100 per *item of property.*[63] For example, a taxpayer may lose his home, car, and other personal belongings in a tornado. This is one casualty, and only one $100 reduction is necessary. If the events are closely related, they are considered a single casualty. If the taxpayer had a theft loss early in the year and the tornado occurred later in the year, each loss would be reduced by $100.

The second and more substantial limitation is the 10% of AGI limitation. For the taxpayer to obtain any benefit from a casualty loss, the total losses for the year after the $100 per casualty deduction must exceed 10% of AGI. Because of the 10% limitation, most taxpayers do not benefit from casualty losses unless the loss was substantial.

For more information about specific issues related to casualty and theft losses, refer to IRS Publication 547—Casualties, Disasters, and Thefts.

EXAMPLE 5-37

Debra is a single taxpayer with an AGI of $75,000. For her to receive any tax benefit, a casualty loss must exceed $7,600 ($100 per casualty plus 10% of AGI). Recall that the $7,600 is net of any insurance recovery.

[61] This loss may be difficult to prove if Stefan did not have adequate documentation noting that he owned the rare coins prior to the theft.

[62] Reg. § 1.165-1(d)(2)(i).

[63] IRC § 165(h).

From Shoebox to Software

EXAMPLE 5-38 Jose and Maria Ramirez (see the saved file) had the following casualties from a large storm during the 2017 tax year. Recall that they had AGI of $110,048 in 2017. The area has not yet been declared a federal disaster area.

Asset	Cost or Basis	Decrease in FMV	Date Destroyed or Damaged	Insurance Proceeds
Furniture	$ 3,000	$ 3,000	04/11/2017	$ –0–
Auto	15,500	9,500	04/11/2017	–0–
Personal residence damaged by storm	225,000	55,000	04/11/2017	50,000

Casualty loss	
Residence (lower of cost or decrease in value)	$ 55,000
Insurance proceeds	(50,000)
Furniture	3,000
Auto (lower of cost or decrease in value)	9,500
Casualty before limitations	$ 17,500
$100 per event	(100)
10% AGI floor	(11,005)
Net casualty loss	$ 6,395

Jose and Maria would have a $6,395 casualty loss deduction for the year. If the area of the damage were declared a national disaster area, they could elect to take the deduction against their 2016 taxable income by filing an amended return.

Open the tax return file you previously saved for the Ramirezes. Report the casualty losses on line 20 of Schedule A. The taxpayers first report the losses on Form 4684. Double-click on line 20 of Schedule A to go to Form 4684 or open Form 4684 directly. Personal casualties are reported on lines 1 through 12. Click on Open Supporting Form and enter the data here. If you open Schedule A, you will see the net casualty loss of $6,395 on line 20.

The completed Form 4684 (Exhibit 5-7) follows on page 5-29.

TAX YOUR BRAIN Binh suffered a $40,000 casualty loss in a nationally declared disaster in September 2017. Assuming that he had AGI of $110,000 in 2016 and $200,000 in 2017 (the disaster also affected business), what is the best way to treat the casualty loss?

ANSWER

Binh can elect to amend his 2016 tax return and get an immediate refund against her 2016 taxes or can wait until April 2018 and deduct the loss on his 2017 return.

An amendment to the 2016 return is as follows:

Disaster loss	$40,000
$100 per casualty	(100)
10% AGI floor	(11,000)
Casualty loss deduction	$28,900

If he files on her 2017 return, the deduction is as follows:

Disaster loss	$40,000
$100 per casualty	(100)
10% AGI floor	$20,000
Casualty loss deduction	$19,900

The advantage to filing an amended return for 2016 is that he will receive a larger refund and receive the funds more quickly.

EXHIBIT 5-7

Form **4684** — Department of the Treasury, Internal Revenue Service

Casualties and Thefts

► Go to *www.irs.gov/Form4684* for instructions and the latest information.
► Attach to your tax return.
► Use a separate Form 4684 for each casualty or theft.

OMB No. 1545-0177 — **2017** — Attachment Sequence No. **26**

Name(s) shown on tax return: **Jose and Maria Ramirez** — Identifying number: **412-34-5670**

SECTION A—Personal Use Property (Use this section to report casualties and thefts of property **not** used in a trade or business or for income-producing purposes.)

1 Description of properties (show type, location, and date acquired for each property). Use a separate line for each property lost or damaged from the same casualty or theft.

Property **A** **Furniture**
Property **B** **Automobile**
Property **C** **Personal Residence**
Property **D**

Line	Description	A	B	C	D
2	Cost or other basis of each property	3,000	15,500	225,000	
3	Insurance or other reimbursement (whether or not you filed a claim) (see instructions). **Note:** *If line 2 is **more** than line 3, skip line 4.*			50,000	
4	Gain from casualty or theft. If line 3 is **more** than line 2, enter the difference here and skip lines 5 through 9 for that column. See instructions if line 3 includes insurance or other reimbursement you did not claim, or you received payment for your loss in a later tax year				
5	Fair market value **before** casualty or theft	3,000	15,500	225,000	
6	Fair market value **after** casualty or theft	0	6,000	170,000	
7	Subtract line 6 from line 5	3,000	9,500	55,000	
8	Enter the **smaller** of line 2 or line 7	3,000	9,500	55,000	
9	Subtract line 3 from line 8. If zero or less, enter -0-	3,000	9,500	5,000	

Line	Description	Amount
10	Casualty or theft loss. Add the amounts on line 9 in columns A through D	17,500
11	Enter the **smaller** of line 10 or $100	100
12	Subtract line 11 from line 10	17,400
	Caution: *Use only one Form 4684 for lines 13 through 18.*	
13	Add the amounts on line 12 of all Forms 4684	17,400
14	Add the amounts on line 4 of all Forms 4684	0
15	• If line 14 is **more** than line 13, enter the difference here and on Schedule D. **Do not** complete the rest of this section (see instructions). • If line 14 is **less** than line 13, enter -0- here and go to line 16. • If line 14 is **equal** to line 13, enter -0- here. **Do not** complete the rest of this section.	0
16	If line 14 is **less** than line 13, enter the difference	17,400
17	Enter 10% of your adjusted gross income from Form 1040, line 38, or Form 1040NR, line 37. Estates and trusts, see instructions	11,005
18	Subtract line 17 from line 16. If zero or less, enter -0-. Also enter the result on Schedule A (Form 1040), line 20, or Form 1040NR, Schedule A, line 6. Estates and trusts, enter the result on the "Other deductions" line of your tax return	6,395

For Paperwork Reduction Act Notice, see instructions. Cat. No. 12997O Form **4684** (2017)

Source: U.S. Department of the Treasury, Internal Revenue Service, Form 4684. Washington, DC: 2017.

The taxpayer must be able to prove both the fact of the casualty or theft and the amount of the loss. Newspaper articles, photographs, and police reports are commonly used to document the fact of a casualty or theft. When a casualty results from a sudden, unexpected, or unusual event, the amount of the loss is not always easy to determine. In many instances, an appraisal of the property is required to calculate the loss. Casualty losses are first reported on Form 4684, and the net loss is carried to the appropriate form (Schedule A for personal casualties). If the insurance or other reimbursement is more than the basis in the property damaged or destroyed, the reimbursement is a gain. The gain is generally taxable if the taxpayer does not use the reimbursement proceeds to purchase replacement property that is related in service or use. However, there are several circumstances where the gain may be postponed; in the instance of gain realized on homes in declared disaster areas, the gain may escape taxation.

The IRS has previously issued guidance concerning the tax treatment of investment scam losses, similar to those in the infamous Bernie Madoff scandal, and the safe harbor options for deducting such losses.[64] In a situation where a taxpayer unknowingly invested in a brokerage activity that was in fact fraudulent, and the taxpayer experienced a loss as a result of the fraudulent activities, the loss is considered a theft loss, not a capital loss. However, the loss is not subject to the general deductibility limitations just outlined. It is entered on Form 4864 and carried to line 28 of Schedule A as a miscellaneous itemized deduction, not subject to the 2% of AGI limitation.

CONCEPT CHECK 5-5—
LO 5-5

1. A casualty is an identifiable event of a ____________, ____________, or ____________ nature.
2. Casualty losses are first reported on Form ____________.
3. Generally, the tax law places ____________ limitations on personal casualty deductions. First, each separate casualty event is reduced by ____________.
4. In general, to obtain any benefit from a casualty loss, the loss must be in excess of ____________ of AGI.

MISCELLANEOUS ITEMIZED DEDUCTIONS (SCHEDULE A, LINE 27)
LO 5-6

The final category of itemized deduction is the catch-all of miscellaneous itemized deductions. Typically miscellaneous itemized deductions are subject, in aggregate, to a 2% AGI floor. In other words, the sum of all miscellaneous deductions must exceed 2% of the taxpayer's AGI before any benefit is received. The most common miscellaneous deductions are for the following:

1. Unreimbursed employee business expenses.
2. Union or professional dues and subscriptions.
3. Expenses related to investment income or property.
4. Investment counsel and advisory fees.
5. Tax return preparation fees.
6. Safe deposit box fees.
7. Gambling losses to the extent of gambling income.[65]

Unreimbursed employee business expenses are usually the largest and are most likely to cause the total miscellaneous deduction to exceed the 2% floor. These expenses are costs

[64] Rev. Rul. 2009-9.

[65] Gambling losses are one miscellaneous deduction that is not subject to the 2% floor; instead they are limited to gambling income and are reported on line 28 of Schedule A.

incurred by the taxpayer as a part of his or her employment (as opposed to being self-employed) but not reimbursed. If any travel, transportation, meals, or entertainment expenses were incurred or some expenses were reimbursed, the taxpayer must complete Form 2106. Examples of unreimbursed employee business expenses include these:

1. Safety equipment needed on the taxpayer's job.
2. Uniforms required for employment that the taxpayer would not usually wear away from work.
3. Protective clothing such as hard hats, safety shoes or boots, and glasses.
4. Business dues and subscriptions.
5. Certain business use of the taxpayer's home.
6. Certain education expenses that do not qualify the taxpayer for a new job.[66]
7. Vehicle mileage not reimbursed by the employer.

EXAMPLE 5-39

Jane's AGI is $43,000. During the year, she had unreimbursed business expenses for supplies, a computer, and travel of $5,200. Jane's deduction would be limited to $4,340 ($5,200 – $860 [$43,000 × 0.02]).

If an employee is required as a condition of employment to wear special clothing that is not suitable for general street wear, the cost of the clothing and its upkeep (such as laundry) is generally a tax-deductible expense. The determination of whether clothing is suitable for general street wear is based on "general objective standards," not personal taste. Examples include uniforms worn by safety, transportation, and health care personnel and protective clothing such as hard hats, safety goggles, and steel-tipped shoes.

A taxpayer who is looking for a new job in the same business or profession in which he or she is already employed may deduct the costs of the job search, such as the cost of preparing and printing résumés, postage, employment agency fees, and long-distance telephone calls to prospective employers. The costs of looking for a new job are deductible whether or not the taxpayer accepts a new position. However, if the taxpayer is looking for a first job or for a job in a new field, his or her job-hunting expenses are generally nondeductible. This is so because to deduct the expense, it must be related to the current occupation. If a taxpayer has no occupation or is changing occupations, the expense is not related to current employment.

Many individuals purchase portfolio investments, such as stocks, bonds, and mutual funds. Expenses to manage, conserve, or maintain these income-producing investments are deductible on Schedule A. Examples include safety deposit box rental to store stock and bond certificates, investment advisory fees, subscriptions to investment publications, software to track investment portfolios, and depreciation on a home computer used to monitor personal investments. One element of these deductions that taxpayers often miss is investment advice. If a taxpayer has a large portfolio of stock or investments, the advisory cost can be substantial. Investment fees, however, are not deductible if they are added to the cost basis of the investment. Examples include brokerage commissions or items paid with tax-deferred funds.[67]

EXAMPLE 5-40

Jason has a $1 million investment portfolio and pays a flat fee of 2% of the FMV of the portfolio. The 2% fee would be deductible if Jason paid it directly. If the portfolio were a tax-deferred account or if the fee were paid on a commission basis that increased the basis of the investment, the investment fee would not be deductible.

[66] The deduction for education expenses is explained in detail in Chapter 6 (relating to a trade or business).

[67] For example, a 1% fee (on the outstanding value) paid to a custodian of an IRA that is paid from the IRA funds would not qualify as a miscellaneous itemized deduction.

If any of these expenses were related to a trade or business or rental property, the taxpayer would receive a higher tax benefit by taking the deduction as a *for* AGI deduction on Schedule C or Schedule E (discussed in Chapters 6 and 8, respectively).

CONCEPT CHECK 5-6— LO 5-6

1. The sum of all miscellaneous deductions must exceed 3.5% of the taxpayer's AGI before receiving any benefit. True or false?
2. If a taxpayer as part of his or her employment incurs any travel, transportation, meals, and entertainment expenses or the employer reimburses him or her for some of the expenses, the taxpayer must complete Form 2106. True or false?
3. An example of deductible unreimbursed employee business expenses would include the blue suit needed by an accountant for his job. True or false?

LIMITATION OF TOTAL ITEMIZED DEDUCTIONS (SCHEDULE A, LINE 29)

LO 5-7

Individuals who are high-income taxpayers in the past have forfeited a part of their itemized deductions. This effectively increased the tax rate of high-income individuals by denying deductions rather than increasing rates. For 2017, this reduction, often referred to as the Pease limitation, is in effect.

If a taxpayer's AGI is above a certain amount, itemized deductions allowed for the year are reduced by the lessor of:

1. 3% of the excess of AGI over the applicable amount.
2. 80% of the itemized deductions otherwise allowable for the tax year.[68]

For tax year 2017, a high-income taxpayer is a person whose AGI exceeds $313,800 for married filing jointly ($156,900 for married filing separately). These amounts are adjusted for inflation in subsequent years.

The 3%/80% rule does not apply to medical expenses, investment interest, casualty or theft losses, or gambling losses. That is because most of these exempted deductions are somewhat uncommon or have high AGI qualifying hurdles.

EXAMPLE 5-41

Assume that a couple married filing jointly has AGI of $413,800. Their applicable itemized deductions total $30,000 and are as follows:

Mortgage interest deduction	$ 8,000
Real estate taxes	4,000
State income tax deduction	6,000
Charitable deduction	12,000

With a 2017 married filing jointly AGI threshold limitation of $313,800 for itemized deductions, the calculation for the limitation is as follows:

a. 3% × $100,000 ($413,800 − $313,800) = $3,000, which would reduce the taxpayers' itemized deduction by that amount.

b. 80% × $30,000 = $24,000, which would reduce the taxpayers' itemized deduction by that amount.

Because option (a) is the lesser, or lower, of the two amounts, the taxpayers' itemized deductions of $30,000 would be reduced to $27,000 ($30,000 − $3,000), which would be their deductible amount for 2017.

CONCEPT CHECK 5-7— LO 5-7

1. For 2017, there is a ____________ on the amount of itemized deductions for high income taxpayers.
2. The applicable percentages for the limitation of itemized deductions for high-income taxpayers are the lesser of ____________ of AGI over the filing status threshold *or* ____________ of the applicable itemized deductions.

[68] IRC § 68(a).

From Shoebox to Software Comprehensive Example

In this example, you will create a new return for a high-income taxpayer. Open the tax software and create a new return.

Alan (SSN 412-34-5670) and Cherie (SSN 412-34-5671) Masters are married filing a joint return and reside at 1483 Tax Street, Highland, MO 63747. They have two children under the age of 17 who are eligible for the child tax credit on line 51 of the 1040:

Scotty (SSN 412-34-5672), born 7/12/2006.

Brittney (SSN 412-34-5673), born 9/16/2008.

The couple had the following 2017 income items that you need to enter in the tax software:

Alan's W-2	
Wages	$112,505
Federal withholding	14,056
Social security wages	112,505
Social security withholding	6,975
Medicare withholding	1,631
State withholding	5,456
Cherie's W-2	
Wages	$37,495
Federal withholding	5,499
Social security wages	37,495
Social security withholding	2,325
Medicare withholding	544
State withholding	3,123
Taxable amount on 1099-G from Missouri state tax refund ($7,560 deducted on federal 2016 return)	897
1099-INT, New Bank	2,300
1099-DIV, Shake Co, Inc. (qualified)	3,100

They also had the following additional itemized deductions:

Medical expenses	$6,400
Personal property taxes	2,000
Real estate property taxes	3,532
Mortgage interest from line 1 of Form 1098	10,052
Charitable contributions (cash) (no individual contribution was more than $250)	2,750
Unreimbursed employee business expenses (travel)	2,500
Tax preparation fee	410
Safety deposit box	75

See Exhibit 5-8 for the completed Schedule A for Alan and Cherie.

Notice the following in the tax software:

1. The medical expenses are entered directly on line 1. In Alan and Cherie's case, they get no benefit from their medical expenditures due to the 10% AGI floor.
2. Note that the state income tax paid flows through to line 5 when the amounts are entered on the W-2 input form.
3. The real estate property taxes and personal property taxes are entered directly on lines 6 and 7, respectively.
4. The mortgage interest is entered through the Documents Received section. To enter it, click on Form 1098 and enter $10,052 on line 1. The interest transfers to line 10 of Schedule A.
5. The charitable contributions are entered directly on line 16 of Schedule A.
6. The miscellaneous deductions are limited. The 2% AGI floor calculations are shown on Schedule A itself. Recall that a Form 2106 must be filed for employee business expenses if any portion of the expenses is reimbursed or if job-related vehicle, travel, transportation, meals, or entertainment expenses are involved. Because travel was involved in Alan and Cherie's case, Form 2106 is required to be filed (Form 2106 is not shown). To access Form 2106 through the tax software, double-click line 21 on Schedule A. Enter the unreimbursed business expenses on the appropriate lines of Form 2106, and the amount flows through to Schedule A. In this case, $2,500 is entered on line 3 of Form 2106.

Make sure you save the return for the Masters.

EXHIBIT 5-8

SCHEDULE A (Form 1040)
Department of the Treasury Internal Revenue Service (99)

Itemized Deductions

▶ Go to *www.irs.gov/ScheduleA* for instructions and the latest information.
▶ Attach to Form 1040.

OMB No. 1545-0074
2017
Attachment Sequence No. **07**

Name(s) shown on Form 1040	Your social security number
Alan and Cherie Masters	412-34-5670

Medical and Dental Expenses

Line	Description	Box	Amount	Box	Amount
	Caution: Do not include expenses reimbursed or paid by others.				
1	Medical and dental expenses (see instructions)	1	6,400		
2	Enter amount from Form 1040, line 38 — 2: 156,297				
3	Multiply line 2 by 10% (0.10)	3	15,630		
4	Subtract line 3 from line 1. If line 3 is more than line 1, enter -0-			4	0

Taxes You Paid

Line	Description	Box	Amount	Box	Amount
5	State and local **(check only one box):** a ☑ Income taxes, **or** b ☐ General sales taxes	5	8,579		
6	Real estate taxes (see instructions)	6	3,532		
7	Personal property taxes	7	2,000		
8	Other taxes. List type and amount ▶	8			
9	Add lines 5 through 8			9	14,111

Interest You Paid

Note: Your mortgage interest deduction may be limited (see instructions).

Line	Description	Box	Amount	Box	Amount
10	Home mortgage interest and points reported to you on Form 1098	10	10,052		
11	Home mortgage interest not reported to you on Form 1098. If paid to the person from whom you bought the home, see instructions and show that person's name, identifying no., and address ▶	11			
12	Points not reported to you on Form 1098. See instructions for special rules	12			
13	Reserved	13			
14	Investment interest. Attach Form 4952 if required. See instructions.	14			
15	Add lines 10 through 14			15	10,052

Gifts to Charity

If you made a gift and got a benefit for it, see instructions.

Line	Description	Box	Amount	Box	Amount
16	Gifts by cash or check. If you made any gift of $250 or more, see instructions	16	2,750		
17	Other than by cash or check. If any gift of $250 or more, see instructions. You **must** attach Form 8283 if over $500	17			
18	Carryover from prior year	18			
19	Add lines 16 through 18			19	2,750

Casualty and Theft Losses

Line	Description	Box	Amount	Box	Amount
20	Casualty or theft loss(es). Attach Form 4684. See instructions			20	

Job Expenses and Certain Miscellaneous Deductions

Line	Description	Box	Amount	Box	Amount
21	Unreimbursed employee expenses—job travel, union dues, job education, etc. Attach Form 2106 or 2106-EZ if required. See instructions. ▶	21	2,500		
22	Tax preparation fees	22	410		
23	Other expenses—investment, safe deposit box, etc. List type and amount ▶ safe deposit box	23	75		
24	Add lines 21 through 23	24	2,985		
25	Enter amount from Form 1040, line 38 — 25: 156,297				
26	Multiply line 25 by 2% (0.02)	26	3,126		
27	Subtract line 26 from line 24. If line 26 is more than line 24, enter -0-			27	0

Other Miscellaneous Deductions

Line	Description	Box	Amount	Box	Amount
28	Other—from list in instructions. List type and amount ▶			28	

Total Itemized Deductions

Line	Description	Box	Amount	Box	Amount
29	Is Form 1040, line 38, over $156,900? ☑ **No.** Your deduction is not limited. Add the amounts in the far right column for lines 4 through 28. Also, enter this amount on Form 1040, line 40. ☐ **Yes.** Your deduction may be limited. See the Itemized Deductions Worksheet in the instructions to figure the amount to enter.			29	26,913
30	If you elect to itemize deductions even though they are less than your standard deduction, check here ▶ ☐				

For Paperwork Reduction Act Notice, see the Instructions for Form 1040. Cat. No. 17145C **Schedule A (Form 1040) 2017**

Source: U.S. Department of the Treasury, Internal Revenue Service, Form 1040- Schedule A. Washington, DC: 2017.

Summary

LO 5-1: Describe the deductibility and reporting of medical expenses.

- Itemized, or below-the-line, deductions are taken in lieu of the standard deduction. They are reported on Schedule A.
- Medical expenses are deductible to the extent that they exceed 10% of AGI.
- Taxpayers may deduct just about all medical expenses that are doctor prescribed. Expenses related to the maintenance of general health are usually not deductible.
- Medical capital expenditures are deductible only to the extent that the expenditures exceed the increase in FMV of the property.
- Premiums for long-term care insurance are deductible, but the extent to which they are depends on the taxpayer's age.

LO 5-2: Be able to explain the state and local tax deductions.

- The four major categories of deductible taxes on individual returns are personal property taxes, local real estate taxes, other state and local taxes, and foreign taxes.
- For a property tax to be deductible, it must be based on the value of the property.
- An individual taxpayer can deduct the amount of state income taxes actually paid or has the option of deducting state and local sales taxes paid.
- Taxpayers have the option of taking a credit for foreign taxes or deducting the taxes as an itemized deduction on Schedule A.

LO 5-3: Apply the tax rules associated with the interest deduction.

- Interest paid on an acquisition loan or a home equity loan secured by a qualified residence is deductible up to certain limits.
- For acquisition indebtedness, the interest is generally deductible only on principal amounts up to $1,000,000. However, in the case of unmarried co-owners of a property, that limitation is extended to $1,000,000 per person.
- For home equity indebtedness, the interest is generally deductible only on principal amounts up to $100,000. However, in the case of unmarried co-owners of a property, that limitation is extended to $100,000 per person.
- Points are amounts paid by borrowers to obtain a mortgage. Typically taxpayers deduct points ratably over the term of the loan; however, there are some exceptions.

LO 5-4: Explain the deductibility and reporting of charitable contributions.

- All charitable contributions to public charities are limited to an overall 50% of the individual taxpayer's AGI.
- Depending on the nature of the item contributed, there are three deduction limitations for charitable contributions by individual taxpayers: 50%, 30%, and 20%.
- The substantiation requirements for charitable contributions have become more stringent, and the taxpayer is subject to more stringent reporting requirements.
- Contributions above the limitation amounts can be carried forward five years.

LO 5-5: Discuss the casualty loss deduction.

- *Casualty* is defined as an identifiable event of a sudden, unexpected, or unusual nature. *Sudden* means the event is not gradual or progressive.
- The taxpayer's uninsured loss is calculated as Uninsured loss = Loss due to casualty or theft − Insurance recovery
- Typically a taxpayer reports a casualty on the tax return in the tax year the casualty took place; however, there are exceptions.
- The deductible amount is generally limited. First, each separate casualty is reduced by $100. Second, the loss must be in excess of 10% of AGI.

LO 5-6: Know how to report miscellaneous expenditures.	• The sum of all miscellaneous deductions must exceed 2% of the taxpayer's AGI before the taxpayer receives any benefit • Unreimbursed employee business expenses are usually the largest and are most likely to cause the total miscellaneous deduction to exceed the 2% floor. • One deduction often missed by taxpayers is investment advice. If a taxpayer has a large portfolio of stock or investments, the advisory cost can be substantial.

LO 5-7: Apply the tax rules for the Pease limitations on total itemized deductions for high-income taxpayers in 2017.	• "High-income" taxpayers' total itemized deductions are limited.
	• For 2017, a high-income taxpayer is a person whose AGI exceeds \$313,800 for married filing jointly (\$156,900 for married filing separately).
	• A high-income taxpayer's itemized deductions are reduced by the lower of:
	  ◦ 3% of the excess of AGI over the applicable amount.
	  ◦ 80% of the itemized deductions otherwise allowable for the tax year.

Discussion Questions connect

All applicable Discussion Questions are available with ***Connect***©

1. (Introduction) What is the difference between deductions *from* AGI and deductions *for* AGI?

2. (Introduction) What are the six types of personal expenses that can be classified as itemized deductions on Schedule A, Form 1040?

EA LO 5-1 3. Describe the concept of a 10% floor for medical deductions.

EA LO 5-1 4. Can an individual take a medical deduction for a capital improvement to his or her personal residence? If so, how is it calculated?

EA LO 5-1 5. What are the general requirements for a medical expense to be considered deductible?

LO 5-1 6. When are travel costs deductible as medical costs? How are medical travel costs calculated?

EA LO 5-1 7. What is the proper tax treatment for prescription drugs obtained outside the United States, such as from Canada?

EA LO 5-1 8. Can a taxpayer take a deduction for premiums paid for health insurance? How do reimbursements from health insurance policies affect the amount of the medical deduction? What happens if an insurance reimbursement for medical expenses is received in a subsequent tax year?

EA LO 5-2 9. What are the four major categories of deductible taxes on individual returns?

EA LO 5-2 10. For a tax to be deductible as an itemized deduction, what three tests are required?

EA LO 5-2 11. If state or local income taxes are deducted on the current year's tax return, what is required if the taxpayer receives a refund in the next year?

EA LO 5-2 12. For 2017, how can the amount of the sales tax deduction be determined?

EA LO 5-2 13. When using the IRS sales tax deduction calculator to assist in determining a sales tax deduction, what information is needed concerning the taxpayer do you need?

EA LO 5-2 14. What options does a taxpayer who paid foreign taxes have when considering his or her tax treatment? Which option is usually more tax beneficial?

EA LO 5-3 15. What is qualified residence interest? Are there any limits to the deductibility of acquisition loan interest?

EA LO 5-3 16. What is a home equity loan? Is the interest tax deductible? Are there any limits to the deductibility of home equity loan interest?

EA LO 5-3 17. What is investment interest expense? What are the limits to the deductibility of investment interest expense?

EA LO 5-4 18. Donations to what types of organizations are tax deductible?

EA LO 5-4 19. Distinguish between the tax treatment for donations to charitable organizations of cash, ordinary income property, and capital gain property.

EA LO 5-4 20. What happens to a charitable contribution that is in excess of the AGI limits?

EA LO 5-5 21. Define *personal casualty loss.* Include in your discussion the concepts of sudden, unexpected, and unusual.

EA LO 5-5 22. How is a personal casualty loss calculated? Include in your discussion how the determination of the loss is made and limits or floors that are placed on personal casualties as well as any exceptions to those limits.

EA LO 5-6 23. Give three examples of miscellaneous itemized deductions. How are miscellaneous itemized deductions limited?

EA LO 5-6 24. What is usually the largest miscellaneous deduction for individual taxpayers? Are any special reporting issues associated with it?

EA LO 5-7 25. Explain the treatment of itemized deduction limitations for high-income taxpayers in 2017.

____

____

____

Multiple-Choice Questions connect

All applicable multiple-choice questions are available with ***Connect***©

EA 26. (Introduction) Itemized deductions are taken when

a. The taxpayer wants to.

b. They are less than the standard deduction.

c. They are higher than the standard deduction.

d. The standard deduction is limited by high AGI.

EA 27. (Introduction) The majority of itemized deductions are

a. Business expenses.

b. Tax credits.

c. Personal living expenses.

d. None of the above.

EA LO 5-1 28. Generally, a taxpayer may deduct the cost of medical expenses for which of the following?

a. Marriage counseling.

b. Health club dues.

c. Doctor-prescribed birth control pills.

d. Trips for general health improvement.

EA LO 5-1 29. The threshold amount for the deductibility of allowable medical expenses ordinarily is:

a. 7.5% of AGI.

b. 10% of AGI.

c. 10% of taxable income.

d. 15% of taxable income.

EA LO 5-1 30. During 2017, Raul incurred and paid the following expenses:

Prescription drugs	$ 470
Vitamins and over-the-counter cold remedies	130
Doctors and dentist visits	700
Health club fee	250
Hair transplant surgery	2,400

What is the total amount of medical expenses (before considering the limitation based on AGI) that would enter into the calculation of itemized deductions for Raul's 2017 income tax return?

a. $1,170.

b. $1,300.

c. $1,550.

d. $3,950.

EA LO 5-1 31. Prescription drugs obtained from sources outside the United States, such as Canada, are

a. Always deductible no matter how they were obtained.

b. Deductible only for citizens of Canada living in the United States.

c. Deductible if prescribed by a physician and approved by the FDA for legal importation.

d. Never deductible.

EA LO 5-1 32. For 2017, Perla, who is single and 55 years of age, had AGI of $60,000. During the year, she incurred and paid the following medical costs:

Doctor and dentist fees	$3,350
Prescription medicines	625
Medical care insurance premiums	380
Long-term care insurance premiums	1,600
Hearing aid	150

What amount can Perla take as a medical expense deduction (after the AGI limitation) for her 2017 tax return?

a. $6,105.

b. $6,035.

c. $105.

d. $35.

EA LO 5-2 33. For 2017, the amount of the sales tax deduction is calculated by

a. Determining the actual sales tax paid during the year.

b. Using the IRS sales tax deduction calculator.

c. Using the sales worksheet and tax tables provided by the IRS in the Schedule A instructions.

d. All of the above.

EA LO 5-2 34. Daryl, who had significant itemized deductions for 2017 and therefore was eligible to use Schedule A, purchased a new vehicle in 2017 for $40,000 with a state sales tax of 10%. The allocated deduction amount for other purchases made by Daryl throughout the year, using the IRS state and local sales tax tables, would be $750. He also paid state income taxes of $4,500 for 2017. Daryl's best option to legally maximize his tax savings in 2017 would be to:

a. Deduct the amount of state sales tax for the vehicle purchase on Schedule A.

b. Take the standard deduction.

c. Take the deduction for the state income taxes paid on Schedule A.

d. Deduct his total amount of allowable state sales tax deduction on Schedule A.

EA LO 5-2 35. During 2017, Noriko paid the following taxes related to her home:

Real estate property taxes on residence (paid from escrow account)	$1,800
State personal property tax on her automobile (based on value)	600
Property taxes on land held for long-term appreciation	400

What amount can Noriko deduct as property taxes in calculating itemized deductions for 2017?

a. $400.

b. $1,000.

c. $2,400.

d. $2,800.

EA LO 5-3 36. What is the maximum amount of personal residence *acquisition* debt on which interest is fully deductible on Schedule A?

a. $1,000,000.

b. $500,000.

c. $250,000.

d. $0.

EA LO 5-3 37. For 2017, the deduction by a taxpayer for investment interest expense is

a. Not limited.

b. Limited to the taxpayer's net investment income for 2017.

c. Limited to the investment interest paid in 2017.

d. Limited to the taxpayer's gross investment income for 2017.

EA LO 5-3 38. For 2017, Thomas, a single parent, reported the following amounts relating to his investments:

Net investment income	$7,000
Interest expense on a loan to purchase stocks	2,000
Interest expense on funds borrowed to purchase land for investment	6,000

What is the maximum amount that Thomas can deduct in 2017 as investment interest expense?

a. $1,000.

b. $2,000.

c. $6,000.

d. $7,000.

EA LO 5-3 39. Referring to the previous question, what is the treatment for the interest expense that Thomas could not deduct in 2017?

a. It is lost.

b. It cannot be used except as a carryback to previous years.

c. It can be carried forward and deducted in succeeding years.

d. None of the above.

EA LO 5-4 40. Which of the following organizations qualifies for deductible charitable contributions?

a. A nonprofit educational institution.

b. The Salvation Army.

c. Churches.

d. All of the above.

EA LO 5-4 41. Which of the following statements is *not* true regarding documentation requirements for charitable contributions?

a. If the total deduction for all noncash contributions for the year is more than $500, Section A of Form 8283, Noncash Charitable Contributions, must be completed.

b. A noncash contribution of less than $250 must be supported by a receipt or other written acknowledgment from the charitable organization.

c. A contribution charged to a credit card is a noncash contribution for purposes of documentation requirements.

d. A deduction of more than $5,000 for one property item generally requires that a written appraisal be obtained and attached to the return.

EA LO 5-5 42. In 2017, the president of the United States declared a federal disaster due to brush fires in the Southwest. Lisa lives in that area and lost her home in the fires. What choice does she have regarding when she can claim the loss on her tax return?

a. It may be claimed in 2016 or 2017.

b. It must be claimed in 2016 if the loss is greater than her modified Adjusted Gross Income.

c. It may be claimed in 2018 if an election is filed with the 2017 return.

d. It must be claimed in 2016 if the return has not been filed by the date of the loss.

EA LO 5-5 43. In 2017, the Rinaldis' vacation cottage was severely damaged by an earthquake. They had an AGI of $110,000 in 2017, and following is information related to the cottage:

Cost basis	$ 95,000
FMV before casualty	135,000
FMV after casualty	20,000

The Rinaldis had insurance and received an $80,000 insurance settlement. What is the amount of allowable casualty loss deduction for the Rinaldis in 2017 *before* the AGI and event limitation?

a. $3,900.

b. $14,900.

c. $15,000.

d. $45,000.

EA LO 5-6 44. Which expense, incurred and paid in 2017, can be claimed as miscellaneous itemized deduction subject to the 2% of AGI floor?

a. Self-employed health insurance.

b. Unreimbursed moving expenses.

c. Employee's unreimbursed business car expense.

d. Self-employment taxes.

EA LO 5-6 45. Raquel, who works in medical sales, drives her own vehicle to various locations for client sales meetings. Her employer reimburses her $400 each month for various business expenses and does not expect Raquel to provide proof of her expenses. Her employer included this $4,800 reimbursement in Raquel's 2017 W-2 as part of her wages. In 2017, Raquel incurred $3,000 in transportation expense, $1,000 in parking and tolls expense, $1,800 in car repair expense, and $600 for expenses while attending a professional association convention. Assume that Raquel uses the vehicle for business purposes only and that she maintains adequate documentation to support all of these expenditures. What amount is Raquel entitled to deduct on her Schedule A for miscellaneous itemized deductions?

a. $6,400 of expenses subject to the 2% of AGI limitation.

b. $4,800 because her employer follows a nonaccountable plan.

c. $1,600, the difference between her expenditures and her reimbursement.

d. $0 because her employer follows a nonaccountable plan.

EA LO 5-6 46. Which of the following itemized deductions is *not* subject to the 2% limit on the Schedule A?

a. Tax preparation fees.

b. Safe deposit box fee.

c. Gambling losses.

d. Union dues and fees.

EA LO 5-6 47. All of the following would qualify as a deductible work or job-related expense *except:*

a. A doctor incurring expenses related to studying to become certified as a plastic surgeon.

b. An accountant taking a CPA exam review course.

c. A teacher taking courses to qualify for an educational administration position.

d. A CPA taking continuing education courses to be eligible to practice in another state.

EA LO 5-7 48. In 2017, high-income individuals are required to forfeit part of their itemized deductions. This effectively

a. Reduces their overall tax rate.

b. Does not affect their overall tax rate.

c. Increases their overall tax rate.

d. None of the above.

EA LO 5-7 49. For 2017, the high-income taxpayer limitation percent of the excess of AGI over the applicable threshold is

a. 3%.

b. 2%.

c. 1%.

d. 0%.

Problems connect

All applicable problems are available with ***Connect***©

EA LO 5-1 50. Mickey is a 12-year-old dialysis patient. Three times a week for the entire year he and his mother, Sue, drive 20 miles one way to Mickey's dialysis clinic. On the way home, they go 10 miles out of their way to stop at Mickey's favorite restaurant. Their total round trip is 50 miles per day. How many of those miles, if any, can Sue use to calculate an itemized deduction for transportation? Use the mileage rate in effect for 2017. Explain your answer.

___

___

___

EA LO 5-1 51. Reggie, who is 55, had AGI of $32,000 in 2017. During the year, he paid the following medical expenses:

Drugs (prescribed by physicians)	$ 200
Marijuana (prescribed by physicians)	1,400
Health insurance premiums–after taxes	850
Doctors' fees	1,250
Eyeglasses	375
Over-the-counter drugs	200

Reggie received $500 in 2017 for a portion of the doctors' fees from his insurance. What is Reggie's medical expense deduction?

___

___

___

EA LO 5-1 52. Dante and Rosa, both under 65 and married, have a combined AGI of $45,000 in year 2017. Due to certain heart issues, Dante has been prescribed Lipitor by a physician. For year 2017, Dante spent a total of $3,100 on the medication and $750 on doctor's bills. Can Dante deduct the medical costs as an itemized deduction? Explain your answer.

____

____

____

EA LO 5-3 53. Leslie and Jason, who are married, paid the following expenses during 2017:

Interest on a car loan	$ 100
Interest on lending institution loan (used to purchase municipal bonds)	3,000
Interest on home mortgage (home mortgage principal is less than $1,000,000)	2,100

What is the maximum amount that they can use in calculating itemized deductions for 2017?

____

____

____

EA LO 5-2 54. On April 1, 2017, Paul sold a house to Amy. The property tax on the house, which is based on a calendar year, was due September 1, 2017. Amy paid the full amount of property tax of $2,500. Calculate both Paul and Amy's allowable deductions for the property tax. Assume a 365-day year.

____

____

____

EA LO 5-2 55. In 2016, Tomas, a single taxpayer, had $3,750 in state tax withheld from his paycheck. He properly deducted that amount on his 2016 tax return as an itemized deduction that he qualified for, thus reducing his tax liability. After filing his 2016 tax return, Tomas discovered that he had overpaid his state tax by $417. He received his refund in July 2017. What must Tomas do with the $417 refund? Explain your answer.

____

____

____

EA LO 5-3 56. Steve purchased a personal residence from Adam. To sell the residence, Adam agreed to pay $4,500 in points related to Steve's mortgage. Discuss the tax consequences from the perspectives of both Steve and Adam.

____

____

____

EA LO 5-3 57. Shelby has net investment income of $18,450 and wage income of $80,500. She paid investment interest expense of $19,000. What is Shelby's deduction for investment interest expense? Explain your answer.

____

____

____

EA LO 5-3 58. Tyrone and Akira, who are married, incurred and paid the following amounts of interest during 2017:

Home acquisition debt interest	$15,000
Credit card interest	5,000
Home equity loan interest	6,500
Investment interest expense	10,000

With 2017 net investment income of $2,000, calculate the amount of their allowable deduction for investment interest expense and their total deduction for allowable interest. Home acquisition principal is less than $1,000,000, and the home equity loan principal is less than $100,000.

EA LO 5-4 59. Jinhee purchased a ticket to a concert to raise money for the local university. The ticket cost $350, but the normal cost of a ticket to this concert is $100. How much is deductible as a charitable contribution?

EA LO 5-4 60. Jaylen made a charitable contribution to his church in the current year. He donated common stock valued at $33,000 (acquired as an investment in 1998 for $14,000). Jaylen's AGI in the current year is $75,000. What is his allowable charitable contribution deduction? How are any excess amounts treated?

EA LO 5-4 61. Adrian contributed an antique vase she had owned for 25 years to a museum. At the time of the donation, the vase had a value of $35,000. The museum displayed this vase in the art gallery.

a. Assume that Adrian's AGI is $80,000, and her basis in the vase is $15,000. How much may Adrian deduct?

b. How would your answer to Part a change if, instead of displaying the vase, the museum sold the vase to an antique dealer?

EA LO 5-5 62. In 2017, Arturo's pleasure boat that he purchased in 2012 for $48,500 was destroyed by a hurricane. His loss was not totally covered by his insurance. On what form(s) will Arturo report this loss?

EA LO 5-5 63. Reynaldo and Sonya, a married couple, had flood damage in their home due to a faulty water heater during 2017, which ruined the furniture that was stored in their garage. The following items were completely destroyed and not salvageable:

Damaged Items	FMV Just Prior to Damage	Original Item Cost
Antique poster bed	$6,000	$ 5,000
Pool table	7,000	11,000
Flat-screen TV	700	2,500

Their homeowner's insurance policy had a $10,000 deductible for the personal property, which was deducted from their insurance reimbursement of $12,700, resulting in a net payment of $2,700. Their AGI for 2017 was $50,000. What is the amount of casualty loss that Reynaldo and Sonya can claim on their joint return for 2017?

EA LO 5-6 64. During the year 2017, Ricki, who is not self-employed and does not receive employer reimbursement for business expenses, drove her car 5,000 miles to visit clients, 10,000 miles to get to her office, and 500 miles to attend business-related seminars. All of this mileage was incurred ratably throughout the year. She spent $300 for airfare to another business seminar and $200 for parking at her office. Using the automobile expense rates in effect for 2017, what is her deductible transportation expense?

EA LO 5-6 65. Hortencia is employed as an accountant for a large firm in San Diego. During 2017, she paid the following miscellaneous expenses:

Unreimbursed employee business expenses	$520
AICPA dues	400
Investment journal subscriptions	175
Student loan interest	450
Job-hunting expenses within the same profession	200

Hortencia plans to itemize her deductions in 2017 because she purchased a home this year and has mortgage interest expense; what amount could she claim as miscellaneous itemized deductions *before* the AGI limitations?

Tax Return Problems

All applicable tax return problems are available with **Connect**©

Use your tax software to complete the following problems. If you are manually preparing the tax returns, you will need to prepare Form 1040 and Schedule A for each problem and a Form 8283 for the third problem and a Form 2106 for the fourth problem.

Tax Return Problem 1

Elise Dubois is single, has no dependents, and lives at 55855 Ridge Drive in Lafayette, LA 70593. His social security number is 412-34-5670 (date of birth 3/15/1976). Elise had qualifying health care coverage at all times during the tax year.

Her W-2 contained the following information:

Wages (box 1) = $48,965.25
Federal W/H (box 2) = $ 5,043.40
Social security wages (box 3) = $48,965.25
Social security W/H (box 4) = $ 3,035.85
Medicare wages (box 5) = $48,965.25
Medicare W/H (box 6) = $ 710.00

She has gambling winnings of $550 and the following expenses:

State income taxes	$2,200
Real estate property taxes	1,150
Medical expenses	5,400
Charitable cash contributions (no single contribution was more than $250)	450
Mortgage interest expense	4,605
Personal property taxes	220
Gambling losses	660
Job-hunting expenses within the same profession (she did not get the new position)	310

Prepare a Form 1040 and Schedule A for Elise using any appropriate worksheets.

Tax Return Problem 2

In 2017, John and Shannon O'Banion, who live at 3222 Pinon Drive, Mesa, CO 81643, file as married filing jointly. John's social security number is 412-34-5670 (date of birth 5/12/1979), and Shannon's is 412-34-5671 (date of birth 11/3/1981). John and Shannon had qualifying health care coverage at all times during the tax year.

John's W-2 contained the following information:

Wages (box 1) = $66,346.74

Federal W/H (box 2) = $ 6,583.85

Social security wages (box 3) = $66,346.74

Social security W/H (box 4) = $ 4,113.50

Medicare wages (box 5) = $66,346.74

Medicare W/H (box 6) = $ 962.03

Shannon did not work for the year due to a medical condition but did receive unemployment compensation of $2,711 for the year with no federal withholding. In the same year, they had the following medical costs:

Shannon's prescribed diabetes medication	$2,150
Shannon's hospital charges	8,350
Shannon's regular physician visits	835
Shannon's eye doctor	75
Shannon's diabetes blood testing supplies	185
Insurance reimbursements	1,910

In addition, they had the following other expenses:

State income taxes	$2,950
Real estate property taxes	1,170
Car loan interest	500
Personal property taxes	265
Cash charitable contributions (made ratably throughout the year to their church)	635
Mortgage interest expense	7,970
Union dues for John	575
Tax preparation fees	175

Prepare a Form 1040 and Schedule A for the O'Banions using any appropriate worksheets.

Tax Return Problem 3

Keisha Sanders, a divorced single taxpayer and practicing attorney, lives at 9551 Oak Lane in Menifee, CA 92584. Her social security number is 412-34-5670 (date of birth 2/27/1973). Keisha had qualifying health care coverage at all times during the tax year.

Her W-2 contained the following information:

Wages (box 1) = $84,601.55
Federal W/H (box 2) = $9,898.38
Social security wages (box 3) = $84,601.55
Social security W/H (box 4) = $ 5,245.30
Medicare wages (box 5) = $84,601.55
Medicare W/H (box 6) = $ 1,226.72

In addition, Keisha made alimony payments totaling $10,800 for the year to her former husband Alex, an unemployed mine worker, whose social security number is 412-34-5671. She also received a 1099 INT from Menifee Credit Union in the amount of $204.75.

Keisha also has the following information for her Schedule A itemized deductions:

Interest expense	
Home mortgage (qualified residence interest)	$8,100
MasterCard (used exclusively for personal expenses and purchases)	425
Car loan (personal use)	600
Student loan interest	1,750
Taxes paid	
State income tax withheld	2,950
State income tax deficiency (for 2015)	350
Real estate property taxes—principal residence	1,700
Personal property taxes—car	75
Registration fee—car	135
Medical expenses	
Doctors' fees	500
Prescription drugs	200
Vitamins and over-the-counter drugs	250
Dental implant to correct a bite problem	1,600
Health club fee	400
Charitable contributions (all required documentation is maintained)	
Cash:	
Church (made ratably throughout the year)	3,100
United Way	100
PBS annual campaign	200
Property:	
Pine Cove Goodwill—used clothing and household items	
Date of donation November 15, 2017	
Thrift shop value at date of donation	350
Purchase price of the items	1,300
Other	
Investment publications	150
Tax return preparation fee	275
Business dues and subscriptions	350
Safe deposit box	75

Prepare a Form 1040, a student loan worksheet, a Schedule A, and a Form 8283 for Keisha using any other appropriate worksheets.

We have provided selected filled-in source documents that are available in *Connect.*

Chapter Six

Self-Employed Business Income (Line 12 of Form 1040 and Schedule C)

Many taxpayers in the United States attribute a large portion of their taxable income to self-employment trade or businesses. Self-employment status automatically increases the complexity of a taxpayer's tax return. It also increases the importance of understanding applicable tax law to minimize a taxpayer's tax liability. In this chapter, we present and discuss the tax rules for recognizing income and maximizing expenses on Schedule C for self-employed businesses.

Learning Objectives

When you have completed this chapter, you should understand the following learning objectives (LO):

- **LO 6-1** Describe how income and expenses for a self-employed individual are recognized and reported.
- **LO 6-2** Explain the concept of ordinary and necessary business expenses.
- **LO 6-3** Explain the calculation of depreciation for trade or business assets.
- **LO 6-4** Describe travel and entertainment expenses and discuss their deductibility.
- **LO 6-5** Apply the rules for deducting the business portion of a residence and business bad debts.
- **LO 6-6** Explain the hobby loss rules and the limits on education expense deductibility.
- **LO 6-7** Describe the calculation of self-employment taxes.

INTRODUCTION

This chapter discusses the taxation of self-employed trade or businesses (sole proprietors). In Chapter 4, the concept of a *for* Adjusted Gross Income (AGI) deduction was presented. Chapter 4 discussed several income components of AGI in detail. However, this is the first chapter in which income items and *for* AGI deductions are aggregated to determine the effect on AGI. Simply put, the income from a sole proprietorship is netted with related ordinary and necessary business expenses to determine the increase (or decrease if a net loss results) in AGI. A sole proprietor reports trade or business income or loss on Schedule C of Form 1040. Taxpayers must use Schedule C when the trade or business is neither incorporated nor conducting business as some other entity form (such as a partnership or limited liability company). Schedule C is shown in Exhibit 6-1.

EXHIBIT 6-1

SCHEDULE C (Form 1040)
Department of the Treasury Internal Revenue Service (99)

Profit or Loss From Business

(Sole Proprietorship)

▶ Go to *www.irs.gov/ScheduleC* for instructions and the latest information.
▶ Attach to Form 1040, 1040NR, or 1041; partnerships generally must file Form 1065.

OMB No. 1545-0074
2017
Attachment Sequence No. 09

Name of proprietor | **Social security number (SSN)**

A Principal business or profession, including product or service (see instructions) | **B Enter code from instructions** ▶

C Business name. If no separate business name, leave blank. | **D Employer ID number (EIN)** (see instr.)

E Business address (including suite or room no.) ▶
City, town or post office, state, and ZIP code

F Accounting method: **(1)** ☐ Cash **(2)** ☐ Accrual **(3)** ☐ Other (specify) ▶

G Did you "materially participate" in the operation of this business during 2017? If "No," see instructions for limit on losses . ☐ Yes ☐ No

H If you started or acquired this business during 2017, check here . . . ▶ ☐

I Did you make any payments in 2017 that would require you to file Form(s) 1099? (see instructions) . . . ☐ Yes ☐ No

J If "Yes," did you or will you file required Forms 1099? . . . ☐ Yes ☐ No

Part I Income

1	Gross receipts or sales. See instructions for line 1 and check the box if this income was reported to you on Form W-2 and the "Statutory employee" box on that form was checked . . . ▶ ☐	1	
2	Returns and allowances . . .	2	
3	Subtract line 2 from line 1 . . .	3	
4	Cost of goods sold (from line 42) . . .	4	
5	**Gross profit.** Subtract line 4 from line 3 . . .	5	
6	Other income, including federal and state gasoline or fuel tax credit or refund (see instructions) . . .	6	
7	**Gross income.** Add lines 5 and 6 . . . ▶	7	

Part II Expenses. Enter expenses for business use of your home **only** on line 30.

8	Advertising . . .	8		18	Office expense (see instructions)	18	
9	Car and truck expenses (see instructions) . . .	9		19	Pension and profit-sharing plans .	19	
10	Commissions and fees .	10		20	Rent or lease (see instructions):		
11	Contract labor (see instructions)	11		a	Vehicles, machinery, and equipment	20a	
12	Depletion . . .	12		b	Other business property . . .	20b	
13	Depreciation and section 179 expense deduction (not included in Part III) (see instructions) .	13		21	Repairs and maintenance . . .	21	
				22	Supplies (not included in Part III) .	22	
				23	Taxes and licenses . . .	23	
				24	Travel, meals, and entertainment:		
14	Employee benefit programs (other than on line 19) . .	14		a	Travel . . .	24a	
15	Insurance (other than health)	15		b	Deductible meals and entertainment (see instructions) .	24b	
16	Interest:			25	Utilities . . .	25	
a	Mortgage (paid to banks, etc.)	16a		26	Wages (less employment credits) .	26	
b	Other . . .	16b		27a	Other expenses (from line 48) . .	27a	
17	Legal and professional services	17		b	**Reserved for future use** . . .	27b	

28	**Total expenses** before expenses for business use of home. Add lines 8 through 27a . . . ▶	28	
29	Tentative profit or (loss). Subtract line 28 from line 7 . . .	29	
30	Expenses for business use of your home. Do not report these expenses elsewhere. Attach Form 8829 unless using the simplified method (see instructions). **Simplified method filers only:** enter the total square footage of: (a) your home: ________ and (b) the part of your home used for business: ________ . Use the Simplified Method Worksheet in the instructions to figure the amount to enter on line 30 . . .	30	
31	**Net profit or (loss).** Subtract line 30 from line 29. • If a profit, enter on both **Form 1040, line 12** (or **Form 1040NR, line 13**) and on **Schedule SE, line 2.** (If you checked the box on line 1, see instructions). Estates and trusts, enter on **Form 1041, line 3.** • If a loss, you **must** go to line 32.	31	

32 If you have a loss, check the box that describes your investment in this activity (see instructions).

• If you checked 32a, enter the loss on both **Form 1040, line 12,** (or **Form 1040NR, line 13**) and on **Schedule SE, line 2.** (If you checked the box on line 1, see the line 31 instructions). Estates and trusts, enter on **Form 1041, line 3.**

• If you checked 32b, you **must** attach **Form 6198.** Your loss may be limited.

32a ☐ All investment is at risk.
32b ☐ Some investment is not at risk.

For Paperwork Reduction Act Notice, see the separate instructions. Cat. No. 11334P **Schedule C (Form 1040) 2017**

Source: U.S. Department of the Treasury, Internal Revenue Service, SCHEDULE C (Form 1040). Washington, DC: 2017.

Schedule C (Form 1040) 2017 Page **2**

Part III Cost of Goods Sold (see instructions)

33	Method(s) used to value closing inventory: **a** ☐ Cost **b** ☐ Lower of cost or market **c** ☐ Other (attach explanation)		
34	Was there any change in determining quantities, costs, or valuations between opening and closing inventory? If "Yes," attach explanation . . . . . . ☐ **Yes** ☐ **No**		
35	Inventory at beginning of year. If different from last year's closing inventory, attach explanation . . .	35	
36	Purchases less cost of items withdrawn for personal use	36	
37	Cost of labor. Do not include any amounts paid to yourself	37	
38	Materials and supplies	38	
39	Other costs	39	
40	Add lines 35 through 39	40	
41	Inventory at end of year	41	
42	**Cost of goods sold.** Subtract line 41 from line 40. Enter the result here and on line 4	42	

Part IV Information on Your Vehicle.

Complete this part **only** if you are claiming car or truck expenses on line 9 and are not required to file Form 4562 for this business. See the instructions for line 13 to find out if you must file Form 4562.

43 When did you place your vehicle in service for business purposes? (month, day, year) ▶ ____/____/____

44 Of the total number of miles you drove your vehicle during 2017, enter the number of miles you used your vehicle for:

a Business ____________ **b** Commuting (see instructions) ____________ **c** Other ____________

45 Was your vehicle available for personal use during off-duty hours? . . . . . ☐ **Yes** ☐ **No**

46 Do you (or your spouse) have another vehicle available for personal use?. . . . . ☐ **Yes** ☐ **No**

47a Do you have evidence to support your deduction? . . . . . ☐ **Yes** ☐ **No**

b If "Yes," is the evidence written? . . . . . ☐ **Yes** ☐ **No**

Part V Other Expenses.

List below business expenses not included on lines 8–26 or line 30.

48 Total other expenses. Enter here and on line 27a	48	

Schedule C (Form 1040) 2017

Neither the tax law nor the regulations directly define the term *trade* or *business*. However, the term is used quite frequently in various code sections, particularly when addressing the deductibility of expenses. The general consensus of the relevant tax authority (mainly Tax Court cases, IRS Publication 334, and the IRS instructions accompanying Schedule C) is that a "trade or business" is any activity that is engaged in for profit.[1] The profit motive is necessary, and the activity should be engaged in with continuity and regularity. Thus sporadic activity or hobby activities are not considered trade or business activity.

If an activity produces a profit, there is usually no problem with the trade or business classification. However, when substantial losses result from an activity, a profit motive may be questioned. To combat losses from hobbylike activities, Congress developed hobby loss rules.[2] Once the taxpayer can establish that an activity is a trade or business, income and expenses from the activity are reported on Schedule C.[3]

Schedule C

A review of Schedule C shows that the form is fundamentally an income statement for the trade or business. The first section is primarily information related. The proprietor's name and social security number, business address, business code, and accounting method are required for each business. A separate business name must be listed if it exists. An employer identification number is required only if the business has a Keogh retirement plan or is required to file various other tax returns.[4]

A business code for each business is required in box B.[5] The taxpayer elects the accounting method used in the first year of business.[6] However, because nearly all individual taxpayers are cash method taxpayers, the cash receipts and disbursements method is the norm for sole proprietorships. If inventory is a material income-producing factor, the accrual method of accounting is required for reporting sales, purchases, and cost of goods sold. In practice, if inventory is material, most Schedule C businesses use a hybrid method of accounting. That is, they use the accrual method for sales, inventory, and cost of goods sold, but they use the cash method to report other income and expense items.

Question G in the top section of Schedule C refers to "material participation." If the taxpayer does not materially participate in the business, the income or loss is classified as *passive*. With passive activities, losses can be taken only to the extent of passive income. We discuss the concepts of material participation and passive activities in detail in Chapter 13.

INCOME FOR A SCHEDULE C TRADE OR BUSINESS

LO 6-1

Taxpayers report the gross receipts from the trade or business on line 1 of Schedule C. Gross receipts include direct sales to customers, work performed for other businesses as an independent contractor,[7] and amounts reported to the taxpayer on a Form W-2 as a "statutory employee."

[1] *Doggett v. Burnet* (1933, CA Dist Col) 65 F2d 191; *Coffey, R. v. Comm.* (1944, CA5) 141 F2d 204; *Black Dome Corp.*, (1946) 5 TCM 455.

[2] IRC § 183 and Chapter 1 of IRS Publication 535. The hobby loss rules are discussed in detail later in this chapter.

[3] If the business has expenses of $5,000 or less, the taxpayer may be able to file Schedule C-EZ.

[4] The ID number is required if the business must file an employment, excise, estate, trust, or alcohol, tobacco, and firearms tax return. If an ID number is required, the social security number of the owner should not be listed. An ID number can be acquired by filing Form SS-4 with the IRS.

[5] The business codes are located in the instructions for Form 1040, Schedule C. The codes are also usually included with the tax software. To review the business codes in your tax software, you generally open a Schedule C and double-click on box B.

[6] IRC § 446.

[7] *Independent contractor* is a term that is used synonymously with self-employed. An individual is an independent contractor when he or she is not considered an employee of the person or business making the payment for a service.

EXAMPLE 6-1

Jason owns a drywall business. He contracts with various general contractors to complete drywall work during the construction of numerous personal residences. He is paid directly by the contractors but is not an employee of any one contractor. Jason would report the proceeds from his work on Schedule C (assuming his business is not incorporated). If Jason worked for only one contractor, he would likely be considered an employee and a Schedule C would not be required.

Amounts received by an independent contractor are usually reported to the taxpayer on Form 1099-MISC. Businesses that pay a nonemployee for services rendered are required to send a Form 1099-MISC to the independent contractor and to the IRS. A Form 1099-MISC (see Exhibit 6-2) is typically required when more than $600 is paid to an independent contractor in a given tax year.

EXAMPLE 6-2

Jake is an accounting systems professor at State University. He also has a consulting business through which he performs accounting systems analysis for local industries. Jake consulted with five different corporations and received five Forms 1099-MISC of $2,500 each (in addition to a W-2 from State University). Jake is required to report $12,500 in income on Schedule C, line 1. He reports his wages from State University on line 7 of Form 1040. He does not combine the wages with the gross receipts of his trade or business on Schedule C.

EXHIBIT 6-2

☐ CORRECTED (if checked)

PAYER'S name, street address, city or town, state or province, country, ZIP or foreign postal code, and telephone no.	1 Rents $ 2 Royalties $	OMB No. 1545-0115 **2017** Form **1099-MISC**	**Miscellaneous Income**
	3 Other income $	4 Federal income tax withheld $	**Copy B** **For Recipient**
PAYER'S federal identification number | RECIPIENT'S identification number	5 Fishing boat proceeds $	6 Medical and health care payments $	
RECIPIENT'S name Street address (including apt. no.)	7 Nonemployee compensation $	8 Substitute payments in lieu of dividends or interest $	This is important tax information and is being furnished to the Internal Revenue Service. If you are required to file a return, a negligence penalty or other sanction may be imposed on you if this income is taxable and the IRS determines that it has not been reported.
City or town, state or province, country, and ZIP or foreign postal code	9 Payer made direct sales of $5,000 or more of consumer products to a buyer (recipient) for resale ▶ ☐	10 Crop insurance proceeds $	
	11	12	
Account number (see instructions) | FATCA filing requirement ☐	13 Excess golden parachute payments $	14 Gross proceeds paid to an attorney $	
15a Section 409A deferrals $ | 15b Section 409A income $	16 State tax withheld $ $	17 State/Payer's state no.	18 State income $ $

Form **1099-MISC** (keep for your records) www.irs.gov/form1099misc Department of the Treasury - Internal Revenue Service

Source: U.S. Department of the Treasury, Internal Revenue Service, Form 1099-MISC. Washington, DC: 2017.

TAX YOUR BRAIN

Does the amount reported on line 1 of Schedule C always match the Forms 1099-MISC received by the taxpayer?

ANSWER

No; recall that a 1099-MISC is not required if the payment is below $600 or if the payments were received from individuals (businesses are required to report payments to the IRS via the 1099-MISC). Thus if one or more of the consulting jobs in Example 6-2 was for less than $600, the company involved is not required to send a 1099-MISC to Jake. However, he must still report the income on line 1 of Schedule C. If for some reason the amount reported on line 1 is less than the total from the Forms 1099-MISC, the taxpayer is required to attach a statement explaining the difference.

The final amount reported on line 1 of Schedule C is proceeds to "statutory employees." Statutory employees receive a W-2 from their employer, but box 13 (on the W-2) is checked, indicating that the employee is to be treated as a statutory employee. Statutory employees include full-time life insurance agents, certain agents or commission drivers, traveling salespersons, and certain at-home workers. These taxpayers are employees, but their statutory status allows them to reduce their income with *for* AGI expenses.[8]

Cost of Goods Sold

Recall that if inventory is a material income-producing factor, taxpayers must use the accrual method of accounting (at least for sales, cost of goods sold, and inventory). Likewise, inventory must be accounted for at the beginning and the end of each tax year. The inventory can be valued at cost or the lower of cost or market.[9] If the taxpayer's annual gross receipts in each of the three prior tax years exceed $10 million, the taxpayer must also capitalize certain indirect costs in inventory (allocate these costs between cost of goods sold and inventory) under the Uniform Capitalization Rules.[10] These indirect costs consist of costs associated with the production or resale of inventory such as equipment repairs, utilities, rent, supervisory wages, and depreciation.[11] You report cost of goods sold for a Schedule C business on page 2 (Part III). The calculation is similar to the traditional financial accounting calculation:

Beginning inventory
+ Purchases
+ Cost of labor
− Ending inventory
= Cost of goods sold

CONCEPT CHECK 6-1—
LO 6-1

1. Schedule C is used only when an individual is an employee of a company. True or false?
2. The income reported on a Schedule C will always match the amount the individual receives on one or more Forms 1099-MISC. True or false?
3. If inventory is a material income-producing factor, the accrual method of accounting must be used to account for inventory. True or false?

[8] Employers withhold social security and Medicare tax from the earnings of statutory employees. Thus statutory employees do not owe self-employment tax on these earnings. We discuss the specifics of the self-employment tax later in the chapter.

[9] If the taxpayer uses LIFO valuation, lower of cost or market cannot be used [Reg. § 1.472-2(b)].

[10] IRC § 263A.

[11] See Reg. § 1.263A-1T for a more comprehensive list of costs to be capitalized in inventory under the Uniform Capitalization Rules.

ORDINARY AND NECESSARY TRADE OR BUSINESS EXPENSES

LO 6-2

For an expense to be deductible, it must be "ordinary" and "necessary." For an expense to be *ordinary,* it must be customary or usual in the taxpayer's particular business. The *necessary* criterion refers to an expense that is appropriate and helpful rather than one that is essential to the taxpayer's business.[12] The courts have added a third standard: "reasonableness."[13] The courts have held that a trade or business expense must not only be ordinary and necessary but also reasonable in amount and reasonable in relation to its purpose. In most situations, making payments to related parties that are larger than normally required when the payee is an unrelated third party violates the reasonableness standard.

EXAMPLE 6-3

Martin owns a successful landscaping business and is in the 35% marginal tax bracket. He employs his 17-year-old son, Brian, as a laborer. To reduce his taxable income and provide money to Brian for college in the fall, Martin pays Brian $25 per hour. An unrelated laborer for the business is normally paid $10 per hour. The extra $15 per hour would be disallowed because it is unreasonable.

TAX YOUR BRAIN

The wages will be taxable to Brian, so why would the IRS contest Martin paying his son an unreasonable wage?

ANSWER

Brian would most likely pay a lower percentage of income tax on his wages than his father (probably 15%). Assuming an excess of $10,000 was paid to Brian, the tax savings for the family would be $2,000 ($10,000 × [35% – 15%]).

In addition to the three criteria of ordinary, necessary, and reasonable, certain other expenditures are expressly forbidden as deductibles. The most common forbidden expenses are

1. Illegal bribes, kickbacks, and other payments.
2. Payments for certain lobbying and political expenses.
3. Payments for fines and penalties.[14]

A taxpayer cannot deduct these expenses even if the preceding payments are ordinary, necessary, and reasonable in the taxpayer's trade or business.

EXAMPLE 6-4

Shane owns a hazardous waste management company. To transport the waste from the refining plant to the approved disposal area, he must cross a public highway with the waste. The state permit for transporting waste on state roads is $2,500 a year. However, the fine for not having the permit is only $50 per offense. Because Shane must cross the road only once every two weeks, he decides to forgo the permit and pay the penalty if he gets a ticket. Even though he can make an argument that the fines are ordinary, necessary, and reasonable business expenses (and make economic sense), the fine charges are not tax-deductible.

[12] *Welch, T.* (1933, S. Ct., 290 US 111).

[13] *Lincoln Electric Co. v. Com.* (1949, CA6, cert den 1950, S. Ct.), 176 F2d 815; *Haskel Engineering & Supply Co. v. Com.* (1967, CA9) 380 F2d 786.

[14] IRC § 162(c)(e)(f).

On Schedule C, the IRS provides a sample of possible expenses. Many are self-explanatory, but the listed expenses are not exhaustive. If the criteria of ordinary, necessary, and reasonable are met, an expense is deductible. However, many expenses have additional conditions and limits to their deductibility. The remainder of this chapter focuses on these conditions and limits.

CONCEPT CHECK 6-2— LO 6-2

1. For an expense to be deductible on Schedule C, the expense must be ____________, ____________, and ____________.
2. Certain types of expenditures are expressly forbidden from being deductible from income on Schedule C. What are two examples of forbidden expenses? ____________ and ____________.

DEPRECIATION
LO 6-3

The depreciation allowance (commonly called *cost recovery*) is the expense allowed for the wear or loss of usefulness of a business asset. Understanding the concept of depreciation is extremely important to comprehending the overall tax system. Why? Depreciation is a material noncash expense on the tax return that provides a large cash flow savings in terms of a tax reduction. Depreciation is allowed for every tangible asset (except land) used in a trade or business or for the production of income.[15] For each activity that uses depreciable assets, a taxpayer must complete Form 4562 to report depreciation.

Components of Depreciation

For depreciation to be allowed, the property must be used in a business or held for the production of income (such as rental property) and not be inventory or investment property. For property placed in service on or after January 1, 1987, depreciation is calculated under the Modified Accelerated Cost Recovery System (MACRS). For tax purposes, the depreciation calculation has four principal factors:

1. Basis (usually the cost of the asset).
2. Depreciation periods (asset class lives).
3. Depreciation convention (half-year, mid-quarter, or mid-month).
4. Depreciation method (200% or 150% declining balance or straight-line).

Depreciable Basis

Basis is a concept similar to book value on a financial accounting balance sheet. Typically the depreciable basis of property is its initial cost. Cost is equal to the cash paid for the asset plus liabilities created or assumed plus expenses associated with the purchase.

The depreciable basis can differ depending on how the property was acquired. For example, if the property is inherited, the basis is generally fair market value (FMV) at the date of death of the decedent. If the property was converted from personal use property to business use property, the depreciable cost basis is the lower of the FMV or the cost at the date of conversion. Basis can also differ from cost if the property is acquired in a nontaxable exchange (trade-in). Typically the depreciable basis of an asset received after a trade-in is the cost of the new asset less any deferred gain on the old asset.[16] Table 6-1 summarizes how basis is

[15] Thus depreciation is calculated for Schedule C (trades or businesses—discussed in this chapter), Schedule E (rents and royalties—Chapter 8), and Form 2106 (unreimbursed employee business expenses—Chapter 5).
[16] Nontaxable exchanges are discussed in greater detail in Chapter 12. For nontaxable exchanges, the basis is determined under IRC § 1031(d).

TABLE 6-1
Depreciable Basis

How Business Asset Was Acquired	Depreciable Basis
Purchase	Cost of asset
Converted from personal to business use	Lower of cost or FMV at the conversion date
Nontaxable exchange	Typically asset's cost less the deferred gain on the old asset
Inherited	Typically the FMV at the decedent's death

determined for various acquisition methods. Often the primary tax authorities refer to adjusted basis, which is the cost basis less any accumulated depreciation.

EXAMPLE 6-5

Ashley purchased a computer for $2,500 to use in her sole proprietorship business. She also inherited land and a building from her father. The land had a basis of $10,000 and an FMV of $18,000 at the death of her father. The building had a $150,000 adjusted basis and a $300,000 FMV at his death. Ashley now uses both the land and building for her office. In this case, the computer has a $2,500 depreciable basis (cost). The building's depreciable basis is $300,000 because it was inherited and its basis is "stepped up" to its FMV. The land's basis would also be the FMV of $18,000 but is not depreciable.

EXAMPLE 6-6

Ashley also converted to business use an old van (basis $13,000; FMV $6,000 on the date of conversion) that she had held for personal use. She now plans to use the van 100% for business. The van's depreciable basis is $6,000 (the lower of the adjusted basis or the FMV at conversion). Had the van been used less than 100% for business, its $6,000 basis would be multiplied by the business use percentage to determine the depreciable basis.

TAX YOUR BRAIN

If a taxpayer buys an 8-year-old piece of equipment to use in a business for $4,000, can the taxpayer depreciate the $4,000 cost even though the equipment is used and was most likely fully depreciated by the prior owner?

ANSWER

Yes, the taxpayer depreciates the $4,000 basis as if it were new. The theory in this case is that the equipment has some useful productive life; otherwise it would not have been purchased. Depreciation is based on the taxpayer's cost; it does not matter whether the asset is new or used.

CONCEPT CHECK 6-3—
LO 6-3

1. Shelly purchased a laptop computer for her personal use last year for $2,200. This year she started her own business and transferred the computer to business use. The value of the computer at transfer was $1,300. What is Shelly's depreciable basis in her computer? ____________
2. Jackson purchased a van for $22,000 and used it 100% for business. In the current year, he deducted $4,400 in depreciation related to the van. What is Jackson's adjusted basis in the van at the end of the current year? ____________

Depreciation Periods (Class Lives of Assets)

The IRS has established class lives and MACRS recovery classes for various types of assets.[17] The MACRS system makes a distinction between personal property and real property. *Personal property* includes equipment, furniture, and fixtures or anything else that is not classified as real property. *Real property* consists of land and buildings as well as any other structural components attached to land. Personal properties usually have shorter useful lives, and thus have recovery periods of 3, 5, and 7 years. Real properties have recovery periods of 27.5 years and 39 years. The other recovery classes (10, 15, and 20 years) could apply to either real or personal property. A summary of recovery periods for various types of assets is provided in Table 6-2.

Depreciation Conventions

Depreciation expense for tax purposes differs from depreciation for financial accounting calculations. With financial accounting, the depreciation calculation depends on the number of months the property was used in a given year. For the tax calculation, certain conventions (assumptions) are established:[18]

1. **Half-year convention:** The half-year convention treats all property placed in service during any taxable year as being placed in service at the midpoint of that taxable year.[19]
2. **Mid-quarter convention:** The mid-quarter convention treats all property placed in service during any quarter of a taxable year as being placed in service at the midpoint of that quarter.[20]
3. **Mid-month convention:** The mid-month convention treats all property placed in service during any month as being placed in service at the midpoint of that month.[21]

These conventions are built into the depreciation tables issued by the IRS and are shown in the Appendix of this chapter. It is important to determine the convention to use when calculating depreciation expense.

TABLE 6-2
Summary of Recovery Period and Asset Types Placed in Service on or after January 1, 1987

Source: IRS *Publication 946.*

MACRS Recovery Period	Typical Assets Included in Recovery Period
3-year	Racehorses less than 2 years old and certain specialized industry tools
5-year	Autos and light trucks; computers and peripheral equipment
7-year	Furniture, fixtures, and equipment
10-year	Vessels, barges, tugs, and fruit- or nut-bearing plants
15-year	Wastewater treatment plants and telephone distribution plants
20-year	Farm buildings
27.5-year	Residential real property (e.g., apartments)
31.5-year	Nonresidential property acquired between January 1, 1987 and May 13, 1993
39-year	Nonresidential property acquired after May 13, 1993

[17] See IRS Publication 946, *How to Depreciate Property.* Also, Rev. Proc. 87-56, 1987-2 CB 674 contains the class lives for most assets. This Rev. Proc. is essential for tax preparers to have on hand as a quick depreciation reference source.

[18] IRC § 168(d)(4).

[19] IRC § 168(d)(4)(A).

[20] IRC § 168(d)(4)(C).

[21] IRC § 168(d)(4)(B).

CONCEPT CHECK 6-4—
LO 6-3

1. An auto used in a trade or business would be depreciated over what period of time for MACRS tax purposes?
   a. 3 years.
   b. 5 years.
   c. 7 years.
   d. 10 years.
2. An apartment complex would be depreciated over what period of time for MACRS tax purposes?
   a. 10 years.
   b. 20 years.
   c. 27.5 years.
   d. 39 years.
3. A warehouse would be depreciated over what period of time for MACRS tax purposes?
   a. 10 years.
   b. 20 years.
   c. 27.5 years.
   d. 39 years.

Half-Year Convention

The convention used most often is the half-year convention. With it, one-half year of depreciation is taken no matter when the asset is purchased during the year. A taxpayer uses the half-year convention for all personal property unless required to use the mid-quarter convention (discussed next).[22]

EXAMPLE 6-7

Cal purchased the following assets during the tax year for his sole proprietorship:

January 6	Equipment	$ 7,400
May 4	Truck	20,000
December 1	Equipment	2,000

Even though he purchased the assets at different times, he takes one-half year of depreciation on each asset. The equipment (both the January and the December purchases) would be 7-year MACRS property; the truck would be 5-year MACRS property.

Mid-Quarter Convention

Taxpayers must use the mid-quarter convention when they place more than 40% of their personal property (not real property) in service during the last three months of the tax year or if the tax year consists of three months or less.[23] The 40% threshold is measured in terms of aggregate bases of the property placed in service and does not include the basis of real property acquired.[24]

TAX YOUR BRAIN

Mid-quarter convention is mandated when more than 40% of the asset purchases are made in the fourth quarter. How are assets purchased in the first quarter treated when the mid-quarter convention is required?

ANSWER

The first quarter property is treated as being placed in service at the midpoint of the first quarter. The IRS depreciation tables published in Rev. Proc. 87-57 (and reproduced in the chapter Appendix) account for the different quarters by having separate tables for assets placed in service in the first, second, third, and fourth quarters.

[22] IRC § 168(d)(1).
[23] IRC § 168(d)(3).
[24] IRC § 168(d)(3).

EXAMPLE 6-8

Assume the same facts as in Example 6-7, but Cal purchased the truck on November 5 instead of May 4. Because he purchased 75% of the assets ($22,000/$29,400) in the fourth quarter, he must use the mid-quarter convention. The January equipment is treated as being placed in service at the midpoint of the first quarter, and the other two assets are treated as being placed in service at the midpoint of the fourth quarter.

Mid-Month Convention

The final convention is mid-month, which applies only to real property (27.5-year, 31.5-year, and 39-year property). Under the mid-month convention, the property is treated as being placed in service at the midpoint of the month acquired. Thus real property acquired on March 3 is treated as acquired halfway through the month (9.5 months of depreciation would be taken in the first year).

Convention for Year of Disposal

Regardless of the convention required for a given asset (half-year, mid-quarter, or mid-month), the property is subject to the same convention in the year of disposal. For example, if a 7-year MACRS asset is disposed of in year 3, a half-year of depreciation is taken on the asset regardless of whether the date of disposal was in January or December. Likewise, mid-quarter assets receive half a quarter of depreciation, and mid-month assets receive half a month of depreciation in the month of disposition.

TAX YOUR BRAIN

Can the IRS build the percentages for the year of disposal into the depreciation tables?

ANSWER

No, the IRS can build the first-year depreciation percentages into the tables because they are known (for example, half a year of depreciation is taken in the first year). However, the IRS does not know in which year every taxpayer will dispose of the property. Thus, in the year of disposal, taxpayers must divide the table percentage by 2 for the half-year convention and by the appropriate number of months for the mid-quarter and mid-month conventions.

EXAMPLE 6-9

Jessica purchased a business computer system on November 3, 2015, for $3,000. The computer was subject to the mid-quarter convention because more than 40% of Jessica's total asset purchases occurred in the fourth quarter. Jessica sold the computer on March 5, 2017. Thus, in the 2017 tax year, Jessica would take 1.5 months of depreciation on the computer (one-half of the first quarter, or 1.5/12). If she sold the computer in December 2017, Jessica would depreciate the computer for 10.5 months (one-half of the final quarter plus the first three quarters, or 10.5/12).

CONCEPT CHECK 6-5— LO 6-3

1. A taxpayer can choose any depreciation convention as long as she or he is consistent in doing so. True or false?
2. A taxpayer must use the mid-quarter convention for personal property if more than 40% of the property is purchased in the fourth quarter. True or false?
3. The half-year convention is the most often-used convention for personal property. True or false?
4. To depreciate an apartment complex, a taxpayer should use the half-year convention. True or false?
5. The taxpayer must use the same depreciation convention in the year of disposal as the convention used in the year of acquisition. True or false?

DEPRECIATION METHODS

Only three depreciation methods are allowed for MACRS property purchased on or after January 1, 1987:

1. 200% declining balance switching to straight-line.
2. 150% declining balance switching to straight-line.
3. Straight-line.[25]

The 200% declining balance method is required for all 3-, 5-, 7-, or 10-year MACRS property (personal property). For 15-year and 20-year property, 150% declining balance is used. In both cases, the depreciation switches to straight-line in the tax year in which straight-line yields a higher depreciation allowance. Straight-line is required for all depreciable real property. In all cases, salvage value is ignored for tax purposes. The taxpayer can make an irrevocable election to use straight-line for any of the classes.[26]

Showing the Calculation

To correctly calculate depreciation, the taxpayer or tax preparer must know only the type of property, the recovery period, and the depreciable basis.

EXAMPLE 6-10

In May 2017, Samantha purchased equipment for $8,000, a work truck for $19,000, and an office building for $120,000. The depreciation calculation for each asset follows (numbers may be rounded in the final year):

Property Type	Recovery Period	Conventions	Depreciation Expense
Equipment	7-year property	Half-year	$ 8,000 basis
2017	Table 6A-1*	($8,000 × 14.29%)	1,143
2018		($8,000 × 24.49%)	1,959
2019		($8,000 × 17.49%)	1,399
2020		($8,000 × 12.49%)	999
2021		($8,000 × 8.93%)	714
2022		($8,000 × 8.92%)	714
2023		($8,000 × 8.93%)	714
2024		($8,000 × 4.46%)	358
Truck	5-year property	Half-year	$ 19,000 basis
2017	Table 6A-1*	($19,000 × 20.00%)	3,800
2018		($19,000 × 32.00%)	6,080
2019		($19,000 × 19.20%)	3,648
2020		($19,000 × 11.52%)	2,189
2021		($19,000 × 11.52%)	2,189
2022		($19,000 × 5.76%)	1,094
Building	39-year property	Mid-month	$120,000 basis
2017 App.	Table 6A-8*	($120,000 × 1.605%)	1,926
2018–2055		($120,000 × 2.564%)	3,077
2056		($120,000 × 0.963%)	1,148

* In the Appendix to this chapter.

In Example 6-10, if both the equipment and the truck had been purchased in the fourth quarter and exceeded 40% of the aggregate basis of acquired personal property, the mid-quarter convention would be required. In this case, the appropriate table for the two personal property assets would be Table 6A-5 in the Appendix to this chapter. The first-year percentage would be 3.57% for the equipment and 5.00% for the truck.

[25] Depreciation for alternative minimum tax (AMT) purposes is calculated separately for each asset using either 150% declining balance or straight-line. We provide a detailed presentation of AMT depreciation calculations in Chapter 13.

[26] IRC § 168(b)(5).

TABLE 6-3
Summary of MACRS Depreciation

Source: IRS *Publication 946.*

Asset Type	Convention	Method	Depr. Table†
Personal property			
3 yr.—racehorses	Half-year/mid-quarter*	200% double declining balance to straight-line	6A-1†
5 yr.—cars, trucks, computers	Half-year/mid-quarter*	200% double declining balance to straight-line	6A-1
7 yr.—furniture and equipment	Half-year/mid-quarter*	200% double declining balance to straight-line	6A-1
Real property			
27.5 residential	Mid-month	Straight-line	6A-6
31.5 nonresidential: 12/31/86–5/13/93	Mid-month	Straight-line	6A-7
39 nonresidential: 5/14/93 to present	Mid-month	Straight-line	6A-8

* For mid-quarter conventions, use Table 6A-2, 6A-3, 6A-4, or 6A-5 (in the Appendix to this chapter), depending on the quarter in which the asset was placed in service.
† Refers to the tables in the Appendix to this chapter.

Table 6-3 summarizes depreciation conventions and methods for various asset types. Table 6-3 also indicates the appropriate depreciation table (located in the Appendix to this chapter) to use for calculations.

CONCEPT CHECK 6-6— LO 6-3

1. Shu purchased a piece of business equipment for $12,000 on May 3, 2017. This equipment is the only business asset Shu purchased during the year. What is Shu's depreciation expense related to the equipment? ____________
2. If Shu sold the equipment on January 5, 2019, what would the depreciation expense be for 2019? ____________
3. Davis purchased an apartment complex on March 5, 2017, for $330,000. What is Davis's depreciation expense related to the complex? ____________

IRC § 179 Expense Election

Instead of MACRS depreciation, the taxpayer can elect to expense a certain portion of personal property purchased during the year (real property is excluded). See Table 6-4 for the maximum IRC § 179 amounts. The maximum Section 179 for 2017 is $510,000.

The § 179 deduction is designed to benefit small businesses by permitting them to expense the cost of the assets in the year of purchase rather than over time. The expense is allowed in full only if the total of personal property purchases is less than $2,030,000 in 2017 in aggregate cost. The expense election is phased out dollar-for-dollar for purchases in excess of $2,030,000. Thus the expense election is completely eliminated when asset purchases reach $2,540,000 ($2,030,000 + 510,000). Several other limitations apply to the § 179 expense election:

1. The property must be used in an active trade or business. Purchased property associated with investment or rental property is not eligible for the expense election.
2. The § 179 expense cannot create a net operating loss. However, the total amount of wages, salaries, tips, or other pay earned as an employee is included as income derived from a trade or business. Thus a taxpayer who is an employee and has an active business on the side can have a loss

TABLE 6-4
Applicable Maximum § 179 Expense

Year	Amount
2014	$500,000
2015	$500,000*
2016	$500,000*
2017	$510,000*

* For tax years after 2015, both the $500,000 limit and the $2,010,000 phase-out are indexed for inflation.

in the side business caused by the § 179 expense as long as his or her salary exceeds the loss. Any § 179 expense disallowed by the lack of business income can be carried over indefinitely.

3. The property cannot be acquired from a related party or by gift or inheritance.
4. If the property is acquired with a trade-in, the § 179 expense is limited to the cash paid for the property.

EXAMPLE 6-11

ABC Co. purchased $641,000 of personal property in 2017. The company can elect to expense $510,000 under § 179. The remaining $131,000 is depreciated using regular MACRS rates.

A taxpayer who purchases several assets during the year can pick the asset(s) he or she wishes to expense under § 179 (up to the yearly limit).

CONCEPT CHECK 6-7— LO 6-3

1. Assume the same asset purchase as in Concept Check 6-6. Shu purchased a piece of business equipment for $12,000 on May 3, 2017. This equipment was the only business asset purchased during the year, and the business has substantial income. What is Shu's deduction for the equipment, assuming § 179 expense is elected? Would there be any additional MACRS regular depreciation? § 179 expense $________ Additional MACRS ________
2. What if the equipment Shu purchased had cost $535,000? What would the total expense deduction be if § 179 were elected? § 179 expense $________ Additional MACRS ________

The American Relief Act of 2012 extended a provision that allows § 179 expensing for qualified real property. Qualified real property includes leasehold improvements, qualified restaurant property, and restaurant improvements (i.e., adding cabinets in a retail store). In 2017, qualified real property Section 179 limit is $510,000—subject to the same phase-out limitations.

50% Bonus Depreciation

The accelerated depreciation deduction equal to 50% of the basis of certain property has been extended through December 31, 2019, subject to a phase-down of the percentages starting after the 2017 tax year. Eligible property includes:

1. Property with a MACRS recovery period of less than 20 years.
2. Property acquired and placed in service prior to December 31, 2020.

Regular depreciation rules apply to the additional basis. Any allowable § 179 expense reduces the basis before the new 50% allowance is taken.

EXAMPLE 6-12

Jack purchased a piece of new equipment (7-year MACRS) for $570,000 for his business on March 1, 2017. Jack is allowed the following depreciation deductions for the equipment:

$570,000 × 50%	=	$285,000 (50% bonus)
$285,000 × 14.29%	=	40,727 (remaining basis at first year % – 7 year)
Depreciation		$325,727

The remaining $285,000 in basis would be depreciated as normal 7-year MACRS property.

EXAMPLE 6-13

Use the same facts as in Example 6-12 except that Jack also is eligible for $510,000 (the maximum in 2017) in § 179 expense.

§ 179 limit	$510,000
50% allowance ($60,000 × 50%)	30,000
7-yr. MACRS (570,000 – 510,000 – 30,000) × 14.29%	4,287
Total cost recovery in 2017	$544,287

Listed Property

Because of the fear of loss of revenue from the use of accelerated depreciation methods on assets that have both business and personal use components to them, Congress established limitations and restrictions on "listed property." Listed property consists of the following:

- Any passenger automobile.
- Any other property used as a means of transportation (not included are vehicles that constitute a trade or business, such as taxis).
- Any property of a type generally used for entertainment, recreation, or amusement (such as a boat).
- Any computer or peripheral equipment.
- Any cellular telephone or other telecommunications equipment.[27]

Listed property does not include the above items that are used exclusively for business at a regular business establishment.

For the normal MACRS rules discussed earlier to apply, listed property must be used predominantly for business, which means that it is used more than 50% for business. If a taxpayer is an employee (not self-employed), the use of the asset is not business use unless it is both used for the employer's convenience and required as a condition of employment.

EXAMPLE 6-14

Linda is a public relations officer for her local city government. She purchased a computer to complete work on press releases and to return e-mail from home at night. Her computer use is 70% business related, but her employer does not require the computer as a condition of employment, nor is its use for the employer's convenience. Because Linda is an employee and the computer does not meet the business use test, no depreciation is allowed.

If the listed property does not meet the predominantly business use test, the taxpayer cannot claim an IRC § 179 expense deduction for the property and must use straight-line depreciation (usually over a 5-year recovery period).[28]

EXAMPLE 6-15

Jack purchased a computer for $2,500 for use in his home office (he is self-employed). The computer is used 70% for business and 30% by his children to play computer games. Because the computer is predominantly used for business and is 5-year property, the MACRS depreciation for the first year would be $350 ($2,500 × 70% business use × 20% [Table 6A-1]). If the business use were only 30%, straight-line depreciation would be required and the depreciation deduction in the first year would be $75 ($2,500 × 30% × 10%).[29]

If in the first year of the asset's life, the 50% test is met, but in subsequent years, the business use falls below the 50% threshold, the depreciation must be calculated using the straight-line method. Additionally, depreciation must be recalculated for all years for which MACRS depreciation was used, and the excess MACRS depreciation (or IRC § 179 expense) must be included in the taxpayer's gross income (recaptured) in the year the business use test is *not* met.[30]

[27] IRC § 280F(d)(4).

[28] Chapter 5 of IRS Publication 946 discusses the treatment of listed property.

[29] The 10% is calculated by taking the straight-line rate of 20% (1/5) and applying the half-year convention (1/2).

[30] IRC § 280F(b)(2).

EXAMPLE 6-16

Assume the same facts as in Example 6-15 but the business use was 70% in year 1 and 30% in year 2. The depreciation and recapture amounts would be calculated as follows:

	MACRS	Straight-Line	Difference
Year 1	$350	$175	$175
Year 2	—	150	

The depreciation deduction would be $150 (full-year at 1/5 straight-line) in year 2, and the excess depreciation taken in year 1 ($175) would be included (recaptured) in gross income. The straight-line method would be required for future years even if the business use percentage subsequently increased above 50%.

Luxury Automobile Limitations

In addition to the business use limitation, the amount of depreciation allowed for luxury automobiles is limited. Passenger autos are defined as four-wheeled vehicles made primarily for use on public streets, roads, and highways with a gross vehicle weight of less than 6,000 pounds.[31] Light trucks or vans that are 6,000 pounds or less have a slightly higher limit.[32] The depreciation expense limits for luxury autos and light trucks placed in service in tax year 2017 follow:

	Auto Limit	Light Truck/Van Limit
Year 1 (2015)	$11,160	$11,560
Year 2 (2016)	5,100	5,700
Year 3 (2017)	3,050	3,450
Year 4 (2018) and succeeding	1,875	2,075

These limits apply to both § 179, the 50% bonus, and regular MACRS depreciation. They are reduced further if the business use of the auto is less than 100%. If for some reason the 50% bonus was not taken, the limit for regular depreciation would revert back to $3,160 for autos and $3,560 for light trucks/vans for the first year.

EXAMPLE 6-17

In 2017, Allison purchased a Toyota Camry for $25,000 to be used exclusively for business. The § 179 expense deduction would produce a deduction equal to $25,000. Because the maximum depreciation for 2017 is $11,160, the depreciation allowance is limited to $11,160.

EXAMPLE 6-18

Jackson purchased a new car for $19,000 on July 7, 2017, and used it 75% for business. The maximum amount of expense for the car in the first year is $8,370 ($11,160 × 75%).

Prior to 2005, many taxpayers circumvented the luxury auto rules by purchasing vehicles with a gross weight of more than 6,000 lbs. Thus if a taxpayer purchased a large SUV, the taxpayer could use § 179 to expense the entire purchase amount up to the § 179 limit. For purchases after October 22, 2004, the § 179 deduction is limited to $25,000 on these large SUVs. However, the regular MACRS depreciation is still unaffected by the luxury ceiling amounts, thus keeping the purchase of these vehicles attractive in terms of depreciation. However, the bonus depreciation is not limited to $25,000.

EXAMPLE 6-19

Javier purchased a new GMC Yukon for $46,000 on May 3, 2017, to be used 100% for business. During 2017, he could deduct a maximum of $25,000 in § 179 expense and $4,200 in MACRS depreciation ([$46,000 − $25,000] × 20% − 5-year/half-year convention).

31 IRC § 280F(d)(5).

32 Other information concerning the auto limitation can be found in Rev. Proc. 2014–21.

CONCEPT CHECK 6-8— LO 6-3

1. Zachary purchased a Ford Expedition (more than 6,000 lbs.) for $39,000 in March 2017. What is the maximum depreciation expense allowed, assuming that Zachary is eligible for the IRC § 179 expense election and no bonus is elected?
   a. $7,800.
   b. $25,000.
   c. $27,800.
   d. $33,400.
2. Assume the same facts as in Question 1. However, the Expedition was used only 80% for business. What is the maximum depreciation expense allowed, assuming that Zachary is eligible for the IRC § 179 expense election?
   a. $7,800.
   b. $20,000.
   c. $22,240.
   d. $26,720.

Leased Vehicles

To circumvent the luxury auto depreciation limitations, leasing business vehicles became popular. However, the IRS limited the lease deduction for vehicles by requiring taxpayers to include a certain amount in income to offset the lease deduction. The "lease inclusion amount" is based on the vehicle's FMV and the tax year in which the lease began. The full lease payment is deducted (unless the business use is less than 100%), and the income inclusion reduces the net deduction. The IRS annually provides current lease inclusion amounts in a Revenue Procedure.[33]

Adequate Records

Taxpayers must have adequate records to document the business use and the time or mileage accumulated. IRS Publication 946 (see Chapter 5) notes that "an account book, diary, log, statement of expense, trip sheet, or similar record . . . " is sufficient to establish an expenditure or use. Adequate records for a portion of the year (which is then annualized) are acceptable if the taxpayer can show that the records represent the use throughout the year.

TRANSPORTATION AND TRAVEL
LO 6-4

Ordinary and necessary travel expenses are deductible by a trade or business.[34] A distinction is made between transportation and travel. *Transportation,* in a tax sense, traditionally means the expense of getting from one workplace to another workplace within the taxpayer's home area. *Travel,* on the other hand, generally refers to business travel away from the home area that requires an overnight stay.

Local Transportation Expenses

Taxpayers may take a deduction for business transportation expenses from one place of work to another as long as the expense is not for commuting (from home to workplace). These costs could include travel by air, rail, bus, taxi, or car. To differentiate between commuting costs and business transportation expenses, a taxpayer must first determine his or her *tax home,* which is the taxpayer's regular place of business, regardless of where the taxpayer actually lives.

[33] The 2017 inclusion amounts are published in Rev. Proc. 2017–29.

[34] IRC § 162(a)(2).

From Shoebox to Software

After completing several tax returns, depreciation calculations become routine. However, for new tax preparers, depreciation calculations and proper placement on the tax return can cause a great deal of stress. In practice, tax software performs most of the calculations. However, the old computer adage "garbage in, garbage out" also holds true for tax software. All current year software calculations should be checked because the type of property, recovery class, and § 179 expense election must be input into the software. In this section, we calculate the depreciation for a new client in the insurance business. We also show the correct presentation of the depreciation information on Form 4562.

EXAMPLE 6-20

Alan Masters, a taxpayer from Chapter 5, started his own insurance agency on July 1, 2017. Later in the chapter, we incorporate business income and other nondepreciation expenses, but now we focus on depreciation. For the tax year 2017, Alan's business acquired the following assets (assume no 50% bonus is elected):

Asset	Date Purchased	Percentage of Business Use	Cost	Class and Depreciation Method
Computer	07/12/2017	100%	$ 2,500	5-yr DDB*
Phone system	07/12/2017	100	2,300	5-yr DDB
Auto	07/15/2017	90	22,000	5-yr DDB
Furniture	07/12/2017	100	23,000	7-yr DDB
Office building	07/01/2017	100	120,000	39-yr S/L†

* DDB = double declining balance method.
† S/L = straight-line method.

Assume that Alan took no IRC § 179 or bonus depreciation deduction. Because less than 40% of the aggregate basis was purchased in the fourth quarter, the mid-quarter convention is not required. The half-year convention is used for these assets.

Current Year Depreciation	
Computer ($2,500 × 20%)	$ 500
Phone system ($2,300 × 20%)	460
Auto ($22,000 × 90% × 20%)	2,844*
Furniture ($23,000 × 14.29%)	3,288
Office building ($120,000 × 1.177%)	1,412
Total depreciation expense	$8,504

* Because the 50% bonus was not taken, the luxury limit would decrease to $3,160 (90% of $3,160 in this case).

Open the tax return file of Alan and Cherie Masters and then open Schedule C. Answer the questions at the top of Schedule C. Alan uses the cash method of accounting and does "materially participate" in the business. Most tax software programs have a Form 4562 Asset Depreciation and Vehicle Expenses worksheet. Enter the information for each asset on a separate worksheet. You need to enter the business and personal mileage for the auto to determine the business percentage. In this case, use 9,000 business miles and 1,000 personal miles.

Exhibit 6-3 shows the presentation on Form 4562. Note that the listed property is individually entered on page 2 of Form 4562. The total depreciation deduction is $8,504 under the assumption that no IRC § 179 expense election was made.

If the IRC § 179 election were made, the entire amount of personal property (everything but the building) purchased could be expensed. Because the § 179 expense limit is now $510,000, most small businesses will be able to expense all of their non–real property purchases. If § 179 expense or the 50% bonus were taken, which in all likelihood it would be, all of the assets would be listed in Part I of Form 4562 and the total expense shown.

EXHIBIT 6-3

Form **4562** — Department of the Treasury, Internal Revenue Service (99)

Depreciation and Amortization
(Including Information on Listed Property)
▶ Attach to your tax return.
▶ Go to *www.irs.gov/Form4562* for instructions and the latest information.

OMB No. 1545-0172 — 2017 — Attachment Sequence No. 179

Name(s) shown on return	Business or activity to which this form relates	Identifying number
Alan Masters	Insurance	412-34-5670

Part I Election To Expense Certain Property Under Section 179
Note: If you have any listed property, complete Part V before you complete Part I.

		Line	Amount
1	Maximum amount (see instructions)	1	
2	Total cost of section 179 property placed in service (see instructions)	2	
3	Threshold cost of section 179 property before reduction in limitation (see instructions)	3	
4	Reduction in limitation. Subtract line 3 from line 2. If zero or less, enter -0-	4	
5	Dollar limitation for tax year. Subtract line 4 from line 1. If zero or less, enter -0-. If married filing separately, see instructions	5	

6	(a) Description of property	(b) Cost (business use only)	(c) Elected cost

		Line	Amount
7	Listed property. Enter the amount from line 29	7	
8	Total elected cost of section 179 property. Add amounts in column (c), lines 6 and 7	8	
9	Tentative deduction. Enter the **smaller** of line 5 or line 8	9	
10	Carryover of disallowed deduction from line 13 of your 2016 Form 4562	10	
11	Business income limitation. Enter the smaller of business income (not less than zero) or line 5 (see instructions)	11	
12	Section 179 expense deduction. Add lines 9 and 10, but don't enter more than line 11	12	
13	Carryover of disallowed deduction to 2018. Add lines 9 and 10, less line 12 ▶	13	

Note: Don't use Part II or Part III below for listed property. Instead, use Part V.

Part II Special Depreciation Allowance and Other Depreciation (Don't include listed property.) (See instructions.)

		Line	Amount
14	Special depreciation allowance for qualified property (other than listed property) placed in service during the tax year (see instructions)	14	
15	Property subject to section 168(f)(1) election	15	
16	Other depreciation (including ACRS)	16	

Part III MACRS Depreciation (Don't include listed property.) (See instructions.)

Section A

		Line	Amount
17	MACRS deductions for assets placed in service in tax years beginning before 2017	17	
18	If you are electing to group any assets placed in service during the tax year into one or more general asset accounts, check here ▶ ☐		

Section B—Assets Placed in Service During 2017 Tax Year Using the General Depreciation System

(a) Classification of property	(b) Month and year placed in service	(c) Basis for depreciation (business/investment use only—see instructions)	(d) Recovery period	(e) Convention	(f) Method	(g) Depreciation deduction
19a 3-year property						
b 5-year property		4,800	5 yr	HY	DDB	960
c 7-year property		23,000	7 yr	HY	DDB	3,288
d 10-year property						
e 15-year property						
f 20-year property						
g 25-year property			25 yrs.		S/L	
h Residential rental property			27.5 yrs.	MM	S/L	
			27.5 yrs.	MM	S/L	
i Nonresidential real property	7/17	120,000	39 yrs.	MM	S/L	1,412
				MM	S/L	

Section C—Assets Placed in Service During 2017 Tax Year Using the Alternative Depreciation System

(a) Classification of property	(b)	(c)	(d)	(e)	(f)	(g)
20a Class life					S/L	
b 12-year			12 yrs.		S/L	
c 40-year			40 yrs.	MM	S/L	

Part IV Summary (See instructions.)

		Line	Amount
21	Listed property. Enter amount from line 28	21	2,844
22	**Total.** Add amounts from line 12, lines 14 through 17, lines 19 and 20 in column (g), and line 21. Enter here and on the appropriate lines of your return. Partnerships and S corporations—see instructions	22	8,504
23	For assets shown above and placed in service during the current year, enter the portion of the basis attributable to section 263A costs	23	

For Paperwork Reduction Act Notice, see separate instructions. Cat. No. 12906N Form **4562** (2017)

Source: U.S. Department of the Treasury, Internal Revenue Service, Form 4562. Washington, DC: 2017.

EXHIBIT 6-3 *(concluded)*

Form 4562 (2017) Page **2**

Part V **Listed Property** (Include automobiles, certain other vehicles, certain aircraft, certain computers, and property used for entertainment, recreation, or amusement.)

Note: For any vehicle for which you are using the standard mileage rate or deducting lease expense, complete **only** 24a, 24b, columns (a) through (c) of Section A, all of Section B, and Section C if applicable.

Section A—Depreciation and Other Information (Caution: See the instructions for limits for passenger automobiles.)

24a Do you have evidence to support the business/investment use claimed? ☑ **Yes** ☐ **No** **24b** If "Yes," is the evidence written? ☑ **Yes** ☐ **No**

(a) Type of property (list vehicles first)	(b) Date placed in service	(c) Business/ investment use percentage	(d) Cost or other basis	(e) Basis for depreciation (business/ investment use only)	(f) Recovery period	(g) Method/ Convention	(h) Depreciation deduction	(i) Elected section 179 cost
25 Special depreciation allowance for qualified listed property placed in service during the tax year and used more than 50% in a qualified business use (see instructions) .						25		
26 Property used more than 50% in a qualified business use:								
Auto	7/15/17	90 %	22,000	19,800	5 yr	DDB	2,844	
		%						
		%						
27 Property used 50% or less in a qualified business use:								
		%				S/L –		
		%				S/L –		
		%				S/L –		
28 Add amounts in column (h), lines 25 through 27. Enter here and on line 21, page 1 .						28	2,844	
29 Add amounts in column (i), line 26. Enter here and on line 7, page 1 . . .							29	

Section B—Information on Use of Vehicles

Complete this section for vehicles used by a sole proprietor, partner, or other "more than 5% owner," or related person. If you provided vehicles to your employees, first answer the questions in Section C to see if you meet an exception to completing this section for those vehicles.

	(a) Vehicle 1		(b) Vehicle 2		(c) Vehicle 3		(d) Vehicle 4		(e) Vehicle 5		(f) Vehicle 6	
30 Total business/investment miles driven during the year (**don't** include commuting miles) .												
31 Total commuting miles driven during the year												
32 Total other personal (noncommuting) miles driven												
33 Total miles driven during the year. Add lines 30 through 32												
	Yes	**No**	**Yes**	**No**	**Yes**	**No**	**Yes**	**No**	**Yes**	**No**	**Yes**	**No**
34 Was the vehicle available for personal use during off-duty hours?												
35 Was the vehicle used primarily by a more than 5% owner or related person? . .												
36 Is another vehicle available for personal use?												

Section C—Questions for Employers Who Provide Vehicles for Use by Their Employees

Answer these questions to determine if you meet an exception to completing Section B for vehicles used by employees who **aren't** more than 5% owners or related persons (see instructions).

	Yes	**No**
37 Do you maintain a written policy statement that prohibits all personal use of vehicles, including commuting, by your employees?		
38 Do you maintain a written policy statement that prohibits personal use of vehicles, except commuting, by your employees? See the instructions for vehicles used by corporate officers, directors, or 1% or more owners . .		
39 Do you treat all use of vehicles by employees as personal use?		
40 Do you provide more than five vehicles to your employees, obtain information from your employees about the use of the vehicles, and retain the information received?		
41 Do you meet the requirements concerning qualified automobile demonstration use? (See instructions.) . . .		

Note: If your answer to 37, 38, 39, 40, or 41 is "Yes," don't complete Section B for the covered vehicles.

Part VI **Amortization**

(a) Description of costs	(b) Date amortization begins	(c) Amortizable amount	(d) Code section	(e) Amortization period or percentage	(f) Amortization for this year
42 Amortization of costs that begins during your 2017 tax year (see instructions):					
43 Amortization of costs that began before your 2017 tax year				43	
44 **Total.** Add amounts in column (f). See the instructions for where to report				44	

Form **4562** (2017)

EXHIBIT 6-4

Source: IRS *Publication 463*, 14.

Figure B. **When Are Transportation Expenses Deductible?**
Most employees and self-employed persons can use this chart.
(Do not use this chart if your home is your principal place of business.
See *Office in the home*.)

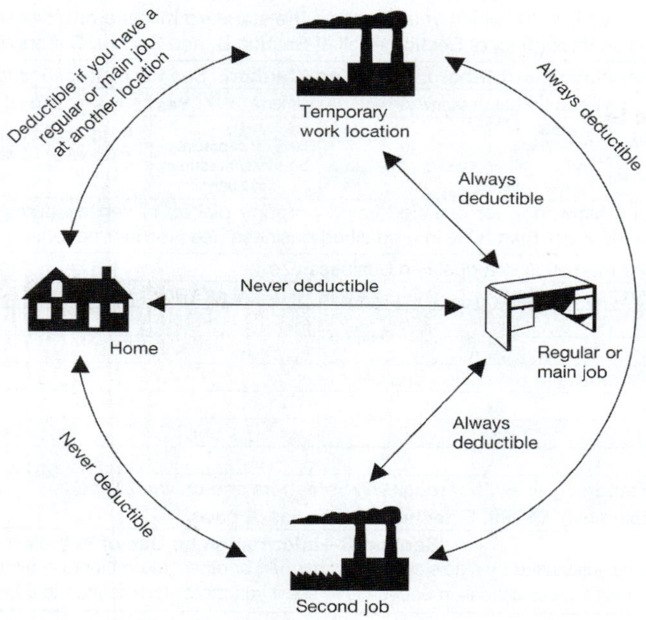

Home: The place where you reside. Transportation expenses between your home and your main or regular place of work are personal commuting expenses.

Regular or main job: Your principal place of business. If you have more than one job, you must determine which one is your regular or main job. Consider the time you spend at each, the activity you have at each, and the income you earn at each.

Temporary work location: A place where your work assignment is realistically expected to last (and does in fact last) one year or less. Unless you have a regular place of business, you can only deduct your transportation expenses to a temporary work location <u>outside</u> your metropolitan area.

Second job: If you regularly work at two or more places in one day, whether or not for the same employer, you can deduct your transportation expenses of getting from one workplace to another. If you do not go directly from your first job to your second job, you can only deduct the transportation expenses of going directly from your first job to your second job. You cannot deduct your transportation expenses between your home and a second job on a day off from your main job.

Exhibit 6-4 is an excerpt from IRS Publication 463 that summarizes when transportation costs can be deducted.

Local transportation costs are deductible in the following situations:

- Getting from one workplace to another in the course of conducting a business or profession when traveling within the city or general area of the taxpayer's tax home.
- Visiting clients or customers.
- Going to a business meeting away from the taxpayer's regular workplace.
- Getting from home to a temporary workplace when the taxpayer has one or more regular places of work. These temporary workplaces can be either inside or outside the taxpayer's tax home.[35]

[35] IRS *Publication 463*, 14.

EXAMPLE 6-21

Karen is a self-employed computer analyst in downtown Atlanta. She maintains an office at the downtown location but lives 30 miles out of town. She is currently performing a job that will last approximately a week that is 45 miles on the other side of Atlanta (75-mile one-way trip from her home). Because this is a temporary work location, Karen can deduct the cost of her transportation from her home to the temporary location.

EXAMPLE 6-22

Assume the same facts as in Example 6-21. However, every morning Karen goes to the office for two hours. In this case, only the cost of her trip from her office to the temporary workplace is deductible. The cost of the trip from home to the office is commuting.

If the taxpayer's principal residence is his or her principal place of business, the cost of transportation between the residence and either a temporary location or a client/customer is deductible.[36]

Automobile Expenses: Standard Mileage Rate

If an automobile is used as transportation in a trade or business activity, a deduction is allowed for the cost of the auto's use. Taxpayers calculate the auto deduction in one of two ways: Use either the standard mileage rate or the actual expenses of business operation.[37] A taxpayer can use the standard mileage rate if

- The taxpayer owns the vehicle and uses the standard mileage rate for the first year it was placed in service.
- The taxpayer leases the auto and uses the standard mileage rate for the entire lease period.

The standard mileage rate *cannot* be used in the following instances:

- The auto has claimed depreciation (other than straight-line), § 179, or bonus depreciation.
- The auto is for hire (taxis).
- The taxpayer operates five or more cars *simultaneously* in business operations.

For tax year 2017, the standard mileage rate is 53.5 cents per mile.[38] If the standard mileage rate is used, the taxpayer cannot deduct any actual car expenses. The mileage rate encompasses depreciation or lease payments, maintenance and repairs, gasoline, oil, insurance, and vehicle registration fees. The taxpayer simply takes the business miles driven and multiplies them by the standard rate to determine the deduction.

Certain vehicle information is required concerning the auto (date placed in service and miles driven). If Form 4562 is not required (for depreciation of other business assets), this auto information is placed in Part IV of Schedule C. Otherwise this information is shown on Form 4562.

EXAMPLE 6-23

Marta is a self-employed baker who makes wedding cakes and other pastries for parties. She owns a car for going to meetings with clients and a van that she uses for delivering cakes and pastries. Marta can use the standard mileage rate for both the car and the van.

[36] Rev. Rul. 99-7, 1999-1 CB 361; IRS Publication 463, p. 15.

[37] The standard mileage rate is available to employees (as opposed to self-employed taxpayers) for the unreimbursed portion of business miles. These costs are deducted as miscellaneous itemized deductions on Schedule A. See Chapter 5 for more information about miscellaneous itemized deductions.

[38] IRS Notice 2016–79.

A self-employed taxpayer can still deduct the business portion of any interest paid in acquiring a vehicle even if the standard mileage rate is used for the vehicle. Other permitted deductions include parking fees, tolls, and property taxes on the vehicle. If the vehicle is used less than 100% for business, the business portion of the property taxes should be reported on Schedule C, and the personal portion of the property taxes should be reported on Schedule A as an itemized deduction.

EXAMPLE 6-24

Ed purchased a vehicle for business and personal use. In 2017, he used the vehicle 60% for business (14,000 miles incurred ratably through the year) and used the standard mileage rate to calculate his vehicle expenses. He also paid $1,600 in interest and $180 in county property tax on the car. The total business deductions related to Ed's car are calculated as follows:

Standard mileage rate (14,000 × 0.535)	$7,490
Interest ($1,600 × 60%)	960
Property taxes ($180 × 60%)	108
Total auto deduction on Schedule C	$8,558

The 40% personal interest is disallowed, and the remaining $72 of personal property tax is deducted on Schedule A as an itemized deduction.

Automobile Expenses: Actual Car Expenses

The second option for deducting business auto expenses is to use actual car expenses. Actual car expenses include the following:

- Depreciation or lease payments.
- Gas, oil, tires, repairs.
- Insurance, licenses, registration fees.[39]

The expenses must be divided between business and personal use (an allocation based on mileage can be used). Once depreciation on a vehicle has been taken, the taxpayer cannot use the standard mileage rate in future years on that vehicle. A taxpayer who has used the standard mileage rate in the past and decides to switch to the actual expense method must use straight-line depreciation and must reduce the depreciable basis by 25 cents per mile in 2017.[40]

The actual expense method usually results in a larger deduction but also requires receipts for actual expenses as well as a mileage log to determine business use versus personal use. With the standard mileage rate, only mileage documentation is required. Taxpayers can use the standard mileage rate for one vehicle and actual expenses for another vehicle.

Travel Expenses

Travel expenses are different from transportation expenses because travel involves an overnight stay for business purposes. The basic travel requirement is that the trip requires sleep or rest.[41] The significance of meeting the "travel away from home" standard is that it allows the deduction of meals, lodging, and other incidental expenses such as dry cleaning. All travel expenses can be deducted if the trip was entirely business-related.

[39] IRS *Publication No. 463,* 16.

[40] The rate was 24 cents per mile in 2015 and 2016. The rate was 22 cents for 2014 and 23 cents for 2013. IRS Notice 2016–79.

[41] *U.S. v. Correll, H.* (1967, S. Ct.), 389 US 299.

EXAMPLE 6-25

Debra is self-employed and has her primary business in New York City. Debra flew to Washington, D.C., in the morning for a business meeting and then flew to Boston for an afternoon meeting with a client. She then took a late flight home that evening. The trip would not qualify as travel because Debra did not require sleep. Thus only the transportation cost is deductible.

If a temporary work assignment can be expected to last less than one year, travel from the taxpayer's tax home to the work assignment and temporary living costs at the remote location are deductible. If the work assignment is expected to last longer than one year, the position is considered permanent, and meals and lodging are considered nondeductible personal living expenses.[42] Limitations exist if the trip is partly personal or if lavish or extravagant expenditures for meals or lodging are incurred.

Limits on Travel Cost: Personal and Luxury

Tax challenges occur when a trip consists of both personal and business activity. If the trip is primarily a vacation but some business is transacted on the trip, transportation costs are not deductible. Any expenses directly related to business activities, however, are deductible. If the trip was primarily business-related even if some personal vacation was involved, the taxpayer can deduct the transportation expenses.

EXAMPLE 6-26

Timothy is currently self-employed in Raleigh, North Carolina, as a personal financial adviser. He flies to New York to visit his parents for seven days. While in New York, Timothy rents a car to meet with a business client one afternoon. The rental car and other costs associated with the business meeting are deductible, but the cost of the flight is not. The trip was primarily personal.

EXAMPLE 6-27

Assume the same facts as in Example 6-26. However, in this case, Timothy spends five days in New York conducting business and then drives to his parents' house for the weekend (two days). Because the trip is primarily business, the transportation expenses are deductible in addition to meals and lodging while on business. Expenses incurred while visiting his parents for two days are not deductible.

Additional limitations are placed on foreign business travel.[43] For foreign travel, a trip is considered entirely for business if it meets one of the following four criteria:

- The taxpayer does not have substantial control over arranging the trip.
- The taxpayer is outside the United States no more than seven consecutive days (do not count the days on which the taxpayer leaves or returns).
- The taxpayer spends less than 25% of his or her time on personal activities (the days on which the trip began and ended are counted).
- Vacation is not a major consideration for the taxpayer.

If one or more of the conditions are met and the trip to the foreign country is considered primarily business, the taxpayer still must allocate travel time between business days and nonbusiness days. To calculate the deductible amount of the round-trip travel expenses, the taxpayer multiplies total trip costs by the fraction of the number of business days to the total

[42] Rev. Rul. 93-86, 1993-2 CB 71.

[43] IRC § 274 and related regulations.

number of travel days outside of the United States. Weekends and holidays that intervene the business days are considered business days.[44] If a vacation is taken beyond the place of business activities, the travel deduction is limited to those expenses to and from the business location.[45]

Deductibility of Meals and Entertainment

In general, any business meals and entertainment expenditures are limited to 50% of the amount incurred. The 50% limit pertains to any expense for food or beverage and any expense with respect to an activity that is generally considered to constitute entertainment, amusement, or recreation. To qualify for any deduction, meals and entertainment expenses must be both ordinary and necessary business expenses as well as be either "directly related" to or "associated with 'business.'" *Directly related* or *associated with business* primarily means that the activity took place in a business setting or the entertainment directly preceded or followed business discussions. Club dues and membership fees are expressly denied as deductions.[46]

The taxpayer's meals while away from home on business may be deducted if the taxpayer either keeps track of the actual cost of meals or uses the federal per diem rates. The federal meal and incidental per diem rates vary and depend on the location of the meals and lodging.[47] For the tax year 2017, the continental standard per diem (CONUS) rate is $51 for meals and incidentals. These standard amounts are increased for business travel in IRS-designated high-cost areas. Using a per diem rate eliminates the need for detailed recordkeeping.

The 50% limit does not apply to self-employed individuals in certain circumstances.[48] Self-employed taxpayers who meet the following three requirements can deduct 100% of meals and entertainment expenses:

1. The taxpayer incurs these expenses as an independent contractor.
2. The customer or client reimburses the taxpayer or gives the taxpayer allowances for these expenses in connection with the services performed.
3. The taxpayer provides adequate records of these expenses to the customer or client.

TAX YOUR BRAIN

Why does the IRS allow self-employed taxpayers who meet the three requirements to deduct 100% of meals and entertainment expenses?

ANSWER

If the taxpayer is an independent contractor and the client reimburses him or her for meals and entertainment, the reimbursement would be included in the taxpayer's 1099-MISC from the client and thus be required to be reported in full as income. If the taxpayer is then allowed only a 50% deduction, the extra 50% would remain in taxable income (100% included in income but only 50% deductible) when, in fact, those amounts are expense reimbursements, not income.

Table 6-5 provides a summary of deductible meals and entertainment expenses.

44 Reg. § 1.274-4(d)(2)(v).

45 There are additional limitations concerning luxury water travel. See IRS Publication 463 for more information.

46 IRC § 274(a)(3).

47 These limits are subject to adjustment and depend on the location within the continental United States. Go to www.gsa.gov and click on Per Diems for the most recent figures.

48 IRS Publication 463, pp. 11–12. The 50% rule also does not apply if the expenses for meals and entertainment were for advertising or if the meals and entertainment are actually sold or provided by the business (e.g., a nightclub).

TABLE 6-5
Summary of Deductible Meals and Entertainment

Source: IRS *Publication 463*, 10.

General rule	Entertainment is deductible for clients, customers, or employees if the "directly related" business test or "associated" business test is met. Meals are deductible if the business trip is overnight or business is conducted with clients, customers, or employees.
Tests to be met	Directly related test: Activity took place in a clear business setting. Main purpose was the active conduct of business. Associated test: Activity was associated with the trade or business. Entertainment directly preceded or followed a substantial business discussion.
Limits	Expenses cannot be lavish or extravagant under the circumstances. Generally, meals and entertainment are limited to 50% of expenses.

CONCEPT CHECK 6-9— LO 6-4

1. A taxpayer can take depreciation on a business auto and use the standard mileage rate in the same year. True or false?
2. Transportation costs are allowed only when the taxpayer visits a client. True or false?
3. A deduction is allowed for meals, lodging, and incidental expenses when a taxpayer travels away from home and requires sleep. True or false?
4. A taxpayer can deduct $51/day for meals and incidentals without keeping receipts on a business trip (subject to the 50% limitation). True or false?
5. Taking five clients to a major league baseball game immediately following a substantial business discussion is deductible up to 50% of costs. True or false?

BUSINESS USE OF THE HOME AND BUSINESS BAD DEBTS
LO 6-5

Typically no deduction is allowed with respect to a taxpayer's residence (except for itemized deductions for mortgage interest, taxes, and casualty losses concerning the primary residence). Difficulties arise when a taxpayer uses the primary residence or a portion of it for business purposes.

A self-employed taxpayer can deduct expenses for the business use of the home if the business use is exclusive, regular, and for the taxpayer's trade or business.[49] The home must be the principal place of business or a place where the taxpayer meets patients, clients, or customers. The exclusive use test is satisfied if a specific area of the home is used *only* for the trade or business (such as a separate room). To meet the regular use test, a taxpayer must use the home office on a continuing basis, not just occasionally or incidentally.[50]

To determine whether the taxpayer's home is the principal place of business, several factors must be considered. First, what is the relative importance of the activities performed at each business location? Second, what amount of time is spent at each business location? Business home use also includes administration or management activities if there is no other fixed location to conduct such business.

EXAMPLE 6-28

Rob is a self-employed independent insurance agent who works exclusively from two rooms in his home. He rarely meets clients at his home because most of his client contact occurs over the phone or at the client's home or office. Even though most of Rob's client contact is not in his home, all of the administrative work is completed in the home office. The two rooms qualify as a home office if they are used exclusively for business.

[49] IRC § 280A(c)(1).

[50] *IRS Publication* No. 587, p. 3.

The preceding rules also apply both to employees and to self-employed individuals. The standards for an employee are higher because the employee must meet the exclusive use test (for business) and the home office must be *for the convenience of his or her employer.* The employee cannot rent all or part of the residence to the employer and use the rented portion to perform services as an employee. Employee home office expenses are reported on Schedule A as miscellaneous itemized deductions (see Chapter 5).

Home Office Deduction for Self-Employed Taxpayers

The home office deduction for self-employed individuals is reported on Form 8829 and transferred to Schedule C, line 30. The first objective in determining the home office deduction is to calculate the area (in square footage) used regularly and exclusively for business.

EXAMPLE 6-29

The five-room home that Rob owns (see Example 6-28) has 3,000 square feet. According to the floor plan of the house, the two rooms used exclusively for business are 750 square feet each. Thus one-half (1,500/3,000) of Rob's house is used exclusively for business.

The next objective in calculating the home office deduction for self-employed individuals is to separate the home expenses into direct and indirect expenses. *Direct expenses* are those that are only for the business part of the home. For example, repairs and painting expenses for the business portion are direct expenses. Direct expenses are deducted in full in column (a) of Form 8829. Indirect expenses are expenses of running the entire household (insurance, utilities, taxes, interest, and so on). The indirect expenses are multiplied by the business percentage calculated in Part I of Form 8829 to derive the deductible portion.

Deduction Limit

Home office expenses that are not otherwise deductible (such as insurance, utilities, and depreciation) are limited to the gross income from the business use of the home. *Gross income* is first reduced by the amount of regular trade or business expenses (non–home related) and home office expenses that would be deductible in any event (mortgage interest and property taxes). If any positive income remains, the business use portions of insurance, utilities, and depreciation (note that depreciation is last) can be deducted.

EXAMPLE 6-30

Assume the same facts as in Example 6-29. Rob had $19,000 of gross income from his home trade or business and the following expenses:

Trade or business expenses	$12,000
Mortgage interest	9,800
Real estate taxes	1,200
Utilities	1,500
Insurance	1,700
Repairs	2,000
Depreciation (for business started in January: house basis $200,000 [200,000 × 50% business × 2.461%])	2,461

Expenses allowed are calculated as follows:

Gross income	$19,000
Trade or business expenses	(12,000)
Interest ($9,800 × 50%)	(4,900)
Taxes ($1,200 × 50%)	(600)
Deduction limit	$ 1,500

Even though one-half of the utilities, insurance, repairs, and depreciation are for the exclusive use of the home office, they are limited to $1,500. The excess is indefinitely carried over (assuming continued home office use) to the following tax year and deducted, subject to the limit in that year. Exhibit 6-5 shows the presentation of the preceding example on Form 8829. Beginning for tax years 2013 and forward, taxpayers can use a simplified option for the home office deduction. With this option, taxpayers:

- use a standard of $5 per square foot for the home office to a maximum of 300 square feet,
- take mortgage interest and real estate taxes in full on Schedule A as itemized deductions, and;
- take no depreciation on the home office.

Business Bad Debts and Business Casualty Losses

Certain bad debt losses can be deducted as ordinary deductions if incurred in a trade or business.[51] Generally, the same rules for deducting trade or business expenses also apply to bad debts. In other words, if a debt is considered a bona fide business bad debt, it must have been ordinary, necessary, and reasonable in the trade or business. The distinction between a business bad debt and a nonbusiness bad debt is extremely important. A *nonbusiness bad debt* is treated as a short-term capital loss and can be deducted only when it becomes completely worthless.[52] *Business bad debts,* on the other hand, can be deducted when either partially worthless or completely worthless and are treated as an ordinary deduction.

Bona Fide Business Bad Debt

To be a business bad debt, a debt must be a *bona fide debt,* which consists of debt that arises from a debtor–creditor relationship based on a valid and enforceable obligation to pay a fixed sum of money.[53] Additionally, for a note or account receivable to be considered a debt, the receivable must have been previously included in income. Thus a cash basis taxpayer cannot write off, as a bad debt, any account receivable that is not collected. Because the receivable has not been included in income on Schedule C, it therefore has no basis, and no deduction is allowed.

EXAMPLE 6-31

Mike, a cash basis sole proprietor (consultant), gave advice to a corporate client that he billed $700. Subsequently the corporate client went out of business and filed for bankruptcy. Because the $700 receivable was never included in income, Mike cannot take a bad debt deduction.

EXAMPLE 6-32

In addition to the $700 bill for the consulting services, Mike lent the corporate client $5,000 (evidenced by a valid note) to help the client pay bills and avoid bankruptcy. The business purpose for the loan was that the corporate officers were a source of many client referrals for Mike's firm. When the corporate client later went bankrupt, Mike could take an ordinary deduction for the $5,000.

If a bad debt is deducted, any recoveries of the bad debt in subsequent years must be included in gross income.[54]

Business Casualty Losses

An individual taxpayer reports a loss from a business casualty on page 2 of Form 4684.[55] When business property is lost in a fire, storm, shipwreck, theft, or other casualty, the taxpayer normally receives an ordinary loss deduction for the basis of the property unless the

[51] IRC § 165(c).

[52] Reg. § 1.166(d).

[53] Reg. § 1.166-1(c).

[54] Reg. § 1.166-1(f).

[55] More details on casualty losses are provided in Chapter 5. The limits for casualties of personal use (nonbusiness use) property are discussed there.

EXHIBIT 6-5

Form **8829** — **Expenses for Business Use of Your Home**

► File only with Schedule C (Form 1040). Use a separate Form 8829 for each home you used for business during the year.
► Go to *www.irs.gov/Form8829* for instructions and the latest information.

Department of the Treasury Internal Revenue Service (99) | OMB No. 1545-0074 | 2017 | Attachment Sequence No. 176

Name(s) of proprietor(s): Rob Taxpayer | Your social security number: 412-34-5670

Part I — Part of Your Home Used for Business

Line	Description			Line	Amount
1	Area used regularly and exclusively for business, regularly for daycare, or for storage of inventory or product samples (see instructions)			1	1,500
2	Total area of home			2	3,000
3	Divide line 1 by line 2. Enter the result as a percentage			3	50 %
	For daycare facilities not used exclusively for business, go to line 4. All others, go to line 7.				
4	Multiply days used for daycare during year by hours used per day	4	hr.		
5	Total hours available for use during the year (365 days x 24 hours) (see instructions)	5	8,760 hr.		
6	Divide line 4 by line 5. Enter the result as a decimal amount	6	.		
7	Business percentage. For daycare facilities not used exclusively for business, multiply line 6 by line 3 (enter the result as a percentage). All others, enter the amount from line 3 ►			7	50 %

Part II — Figure Your Allowable Deduction

Line	Description	Line	(a) Direct expenses	(b) Indirect expenses	Line	Amount
8	Enter the amount from Schedule C, line 29, **plus** any gain derived from the business use of your home, **minus** any loss from the trade or business not derived from the business use of your home (see instructions)				8	7,000
	See instructions for columns (a) and (b) before completing lines 9–21.					
9	Casualty losses (see instructions)	9				
10	Deductible mortgage interest (see instructions)	10		9,800		
11	Real estate taxes (see instructions)	11		1,200		
12	Add lines 9, 10, and 11	12		11,000		
13	Multiply line 12, column (b) by line 7	13		5,500		
14	Add line 12, column (a) and line 13				14	5,500
15	Subtract line 14 from line 8. If zero or less, enter -0-				15	1,500
16	Excess mortgage interest (see instructions)	16				
17	Insurance	17		1,700		
18	Rent	18				
19	Repairs and maintenance	19		2,000		
20	Utilities	20		1,500		
21	Other expenses (see instructions)	21				
22	Add lines 16 through 21	22		5,200		
23	Multiply line 22, column (b) by line 7	23		2,600		
24	Carryover of prior year operating expenses (see instructions)	24				
25	Add line 22, column (a), line 23, and line 24				25	2,600
26	Allowable operating expenses. Enter the **smaller** of line 15 or line 25				26	1,500
27	Limit on excess casualty losses and depreciation. Subtract line 26 from line 15				27	
28	Excess casualty losses (see instructions)	28				
29	Depreciation of your home from line 41 below	29		2,461		
30	Carryover of prior year excess casualty losses and depreciation (see instructions)	30				
31	Add lines 28 through 30				31	2,461
32	Allowable excess casualty losses and depreciation. Enter the **smaller** of line 27 or line 31				32	0
33	Add lines 14, 26, and 32				33	7,000
34	Casualty loss portion, if any, from lines 14 and 32. Carry amount to **Form 4684** (see instructions)				34	
35	**Allowable expenses for business use of your home.** Subtract line 34 from line 33. Enter here and on Schedule C, line 30. If your home was used for more than one business, see instructions ►				35	7,000

Part III — Depreciation of Your Home

Line	Description	Line	Amount
36	Enter the **smaller** of your home's adjusted basis or its fair market value (see instructions)	36	200,000
37	Value of land included on line 36	37	0
38	Basis of building. Subtract line 37 from line 36	38	200,000
39	Business basis of building. Multiply line 38 by line 7	39	100,000
40	Depreciation percentage (see instructions)	40	2.461 %
41	Depreciation allowable (see instructions). Multiply line 39 by line 40. Enter here and on line 29 above	41	2,461

Part IV — Carryover of Unallowed Expenses to 2018

Line	Description	Line	Amount
42	Operating expenses. Subtract line 26 from line 25. If less than zero, enter -0-	42	1,100
43	Excess casualty losses and depreciation. Subtract line 32 from line 31. If less than zero, enter -0-	43	2,461

For Paperwork Reduction Act Notice, see your tax return instructions. Cat. No. 13232M Form **8829** (2017)

Source: U.S. Department of the Treasury, Internal Revenue Service, Form 8829. Washington, DC: 2017.

TAX YOUR BRAIN

Can a taxpayer have a casualty gain?

ANSWER

Yes. As an example, a business building purchased in 1985 for $55,000 is now worth $200,000. The building is likely to be insured for its replacement cost and to be fully depreciated ($0 adjusted basis). If the building were completely destroyed by fire and the insurance proceeds were $200,000, the taxpayer could have a gain of $200,000 ($200,000 proceeds less the $0 adjusted basis).

EXAMPLE 6-33

On September 17, 2017, Duane's office building was destroyed by a tornado. Duane had purchased the building in 1985 for $90,000 but had recently made improvements to it. The adjusted basis and FMV at the time of the tornado were $80,000 and $110,000, respectively. Duane had not updated his insurance policy in several years and thus received only $70,000 from the insurance company. Because the building was totally destroyed, the business casualty is $10,000 (the adjusted basis of $80,000 less the $70,000 insurance reimbursement). See Exhibit 6-6 for the proper reporting. The $10,000 is transferred from Form 4684, page 2, to Form 4797 and eventually to Form 1040, page 1. Note that although the loss relates to Schedule C, it does not appear on Schedule C but goes directly to Form 1040 as a *for* AGI deduction.

CONCEPT CHECK 6-10— LO 6-5

1. Jose uses 20% of his home exclusively for business. He had the entire exterior of the house painted and the interior of one room that he uses for an office painted for $3,000 and $500, respectively. What is the total deduction Jose can take as a home office expense for the painting?
   a. $500.
   b. $3,500.
   c. $700.
   d. $1,100.
2. Which of the following comments is true regarding the home office deduction?
   a. The taxpayer must see clients at home to be allowed a home office deduction.
   b. The home office deduction is limited to income from the Schedule C business.
   c. The taxpayer is allowed to take a § 179 expense election on the business portion of the home itself.
   d. Depreciation on the home is never allowed as a home office deduction.
3. When business property is partially destroyed by a casualty, the loss is calculated using which of the following?
   a. The decrease in the FMV of the property.
   b. The adjusted basis of the property.
   c. The lower of the FMV or the adjusted basis of the property.
   d. The adjusted basis of the property less 10% of AGI.

property is only partially destroyed. With partial losses, the loss is the lower of the decrease in FMV before and after the casualty or the adjusted basis. All losses are reduced by insurance proceeds.[56]

[56] The gain can be avoided by the replacement of similar property. Deferrals of gains from involuntary conversions are discussed in Chapter 12.

EXHIBIT 6-6

Form 4684 (2017) Attachment Sequence No. **26** Page **2**

Name(s) shown on tax return. Do not enter name and identifying number if shown on other side. **Duane Taxpayer**

Identifying number 412-34-5670

SECTION B—Business and Income-Producing Property

Part I **Casualty or Theft Gain or Loss** (Use a separate Part I for each casualty or theft.)

19 Description of properties (show type, location, and date acquired for each property). Use a separate line for each property lost or damaged from the same casualty or theft. **See instructions if claiming a loss due to a Ponzi-type investment scheme and Section C is not completed.**

Property **A** Office Building, 123 Ally Drive, Anywhere, USA

Property **B**

Property **C**

Property **D**

		Properties A	B	C	D
20 Cost or adjusted basis of each property	20	80,000			
21 Insurance or other reimbursement (whether or not you filed a claim). See the instructions for line 3. **Note:** *If line 20 is* ***more*** *than line 21, skip line 22.*	21	70,000			
22 Gain from casualty or theft. If line 21 is **more** than line 20, enter the difference here and on line 29 or line 34, column (c), except as provided in the instructions for line 33. Also, skip lines 23 through 27 for that column. See the instructions for line 4 if line 21 includes insurance or other reimbursement you did not claim, or you received payment for your loss in a later tax year	22				
23 Fair market value **before** casualty or theft	23	110,000			
24 Fair market value **after** casualty or theft	24	0			
25 Subtract line 24 from line 23	25	110,000			
26 Enter the **smaller** of line 20 or line 25. **Note:** *If the property was totally destroyed by casualty or lost from theft, enter on line 26 the amount from line 20.*	26	80,000			
27 Subtract line 21 from line 26. If zero or less, enter -0-	27	10,000			

28 Casualty or theft loss. Add the amounts on line 27. Enter the total here and on line 29 **or** line 34 (see instructions) . . . **28** 10,000

Part II **Summary of Gains and Losses** (from separate Parts I)

(a) Identify casualty or theft		(b) Losses from casualties or thefts: (i) Trade, business, rental or royalty property	(b)(ii) Income-producing and employee property	(c) Gains from casualties or thefts includible in income
Casualty or Theft of Property Held One Year or Less				
29		( )	( )	
		( )	( )	
30 Totals. Add the amounts on line 29	30	( )	( )	
31 Combine line 30, columns (b)(i) and (c). Enter the net gain or (loss) here and on Form 4797, line 14. If Form 4797 is not otherwise required, see instructions			31	
32 Enter the amount from line 30, column (b)(ii) here. Individuals, enter the amount from income-producing property on Schedule A (Form 1040), line 28, or Form 1040NR, Schedule A, line 14, and enter the amount from property used as an employee on Schedule A (Form 1040), line 23, or Form 1040NR, Schedule A, line 9. Estates and trusts, partnerships, and S corporations, see instructions			32	
Casualty or Theft of Property Held More Than One Year				
33 Casualty or theft gains from Form 4797, line 32			33	
34 Casualty loss from line 28		(10,000)	( )	
		( )	( )	
35 Total losses. Add amounts on line 34, columns (b)(i) and (b)(ii)	35	(10,000)	( )	
36 Total gains. Add lines 33 and 34, column (c)			36	
37 Add amounts on line 35, columns (b)(i) and (b)(ii)			37	(10,000)
38 If the loss on line 37 is **more** than the gain on line 36: **a** Combine line 35, column (b)(i) and line 36, and enter the net gain or (loss) here. Partnerships (except electing large partnerships) and S corporations, see the note below. All others, enter this amount on Form 4797, line 14. If Form 4797 is not otherwise required, see instructions			38a	(10,000)
b Enter the amount from line 35, column (b)(ii) here. Individuals, enter the amount from income-producing property on Schedule A (Form 1040), line 28, or Form 1040NR, Schedule A, line 14, and enter the amount from property used as an employee on Schedule A (Form 1040), line 23, or Form 1040NR, Schedule A, line 9. Estates and trusts, enter on the "Other deductions" line of your tax return. Partnerships (except electing large partnerships) and S corporations, see the note below. Electing large partnerships, enter on Form 1065-B, Part II, line 11			38b	
39 If the loss on line 37 is **less** than or **equal** to the gain on line 36, combine lines 36 and 37 and enter here. Partnerships (except electing large partnerships), see the note below. All others, enter this amount on Form 4797, line 3			39	

Note: *Partnerships, enter the amount from line 38a, 38b, or line 39 on Form 1065, Schedule K, line 11. S corporations, enter the amount from line 38a or 38b on Form 1120S, Schedule K, line 10.*

Form **4684** (2017)

Source: U.S. Department of the Treasury, Internal Revenue Service, Form 4684. Washington, DC: 2017.

HOBBY LOSS RULES AND EDUCATION EXPENSES

LO 6-6

To limit deductible losses from activities that are primarily for personal pleasure instead of a trade or business, Congress established the hobby loss rules.[57] If an activity is characterized as a hobby (rather than a trade or business), the tax treatment is different. Instead of reporting all income and expenses on Schedule C, the income is reported on Form 1040, line 21, as other income, and the expenses are treated as miscellaneous itemized deductions.[58] The deductible expenses are limited to the income from the activity.

EXAMPLE 6-34

Alex is a successful CPA who enjoys decorative woodworking. He makes decorative rocking chairs, tables, and other handcrafted furniture. He spends 10 to 15 hours a week (considerably less time during tax season) making the furniture and had gross sales of $3,000. His expenses for the year were $10,000. If this activity is treated as a trade or business, Alex would have a $7,000 loss to deduct against other income. If the woodworking is treated as a hobby, the deductible expenses would be limited to the $3,000 of income.

What is the deciding factor in determining whether an activity is a hobby or business? Nine factors are used in the hobby determination:

1. Manner in which the taxpayer carries on the activity.
2. Expertise of the taxpayer or his or her advisers.
3. Time and effort expended by the taxpayer in carrying on the activity.
4. Expectations that assets used in the activity can appreciate in value.
5. Success of the taxpayer in carrying on other similar or dissimilar activities.
6. Taxpayer's history of income or losses with respect to the activity.
7. Amount of occasional profits, if any, that are earned.
8. Taxpayer's financial status.
9. Elements of personal pleasure or recreation.[59]

The regulations note that taxpayers are to take *all* of the facts and circumstances into account and that no one factor is controlling in the hobby determination.[60] If the IRS asserts that an activity is a hobby, the burden to prove that the activity is a trade or business rests with the taxpayer. However, if the taxpayer has shown a profit for three out of five consecutive tax years (two out of seven for horse racing), the burden of proof shifts to the IRS.[61]

After the activity is characterized as a hobby, expenses are allowed only to the extent of income and only in the following order:

1. Expenses that would be allowed to reduce taxable income regardless of the presence of the hobby (such as mortgage interest or property taxes).
2. Expenses pertaining to the hobby that do not reduce the basis of property (utilities, supplies).
3. Expenses pertaining to the hobby that reduce the basis of property (depreciation).[62]

[57] IRC § 183.

[58] See Chapter 5 for the treatment of miscellaneous itemized deductions.

[59] Reg. § 1.183-2(b).

[60] Reg. § 1.183-2(b).

[61] IRC § 183(d).

[62] Reg. § 1.183-1(b)(1)(i)(ii)(iii).

Education Expenses

A major expense for many self-employed individuals is the cost incurred for education. However, with education expenses, it is sometimes difficult to distinguish whether the education is an ordinary and necessary business expense (deductible) or qualifies the taxpayer for a new profession (not deductible). This ambiguity has led to considerable litigation between taxpayers and the IRS. Education expenses are deductible if the education meets either of these criteria:

- Maintains or improves skills required by the individual in his or her employment or other trade or business.
- Meets the express requirements of the individual's employer or the requirements of applicable law or regulation.[63]

However, even if one of the two preceding requirements is met, the education expenses are not deductible if the education is required to meet minimum educational requirements for employment or if the education qualifies the taxpayer for a new trade or business. The definition of what constitutes a new trade or business has been the source of much confusion.

TAX YOUR BRAIN

Assume that Leon is a CPA who has been practicing for 10 years in audit. He decides that he would like to start a tax practice. He begins taking classes in a masters of taxation program. Are the expenses for the classes deductible?

ANSWER

Yes, they are because the education does not qualify Leon for a new profession. The education only improves his skills in the CPA profession for which he already qualifies.

Eligible education expenses include not only tuition but also books, supplies, fees, and travel.

CONCEPT CHECK 6-11— LO 6-6

1. If a taxpayer has shown a net profit for the last three years, the activity is not considered a hobby. True or false?
2. A taxpayer can never take a net loss on an activity considered a hobby. True or false?
3. Expenses that can be deducted elsewhere on the tax return must be the first expenses deducted from hobby income. True or false?
4. Education expenses that help qualify a taxpayer for a new trade or business (or profession) are deductible. True or false?

SELF-EMPLOYMENT TAX

LO 6-7

One of the major disadvantages to being self-employed is the requirement to pay self-employment tax. *Self-employment (SE) tax* consists of two parts: (1) the social security tax and (2) the Medicare tax.[64] Self-employed taxpayers are not discriminated against because every U.S. citizen or resident (with few exceptions) must pay these taxes. However, because most taxpayers are employees, the employer is required to pay half of these taxes,

[63] Reg. § 1.162-5.

[64] The social security tax is the old age, survivors, and disability insurance tax (OASDI), and the Medicare tax is a hospital insurance tax.

and the employee pays the other half. The employee's one-half share is commonly reported as FICA on most paychecks. Self-employed taxpayers must pay *both* the employer's and the employee's shares.[65] Any self-employed taxpayer with $400 or more in self-employment income must pay self-employment taxes. Income from Schedule C and as a partner in a partnership are sources of SE income.

The tax base for the social security tax is limited. In tax year 2017, the first $127,200 of wages and self-employment income is subject to the social security tax. The tax base for the Medicare tax, on the other hand, is not limited. Here are the social security tax and Medicare rates:

	Rate (Percent)	Income Limit
Social security	12.4%	$127,200
Medicare	2.90	Unlimited
Total SE	15.3%[66]	

An additional Medicare tax of 0.9% is imposed on self-employment income in excess of $250,000 for joint returns ($125,000 for MFS, $200,000 for all other returns). The thresholds are reduced by any wages the taxpayers have in addition to SE income.

The total SE rate is multiplied by 92.35% of SE income. The self-employed taxpayer receives a *for* AGI deduction for one-half of the SE tax paid (see Chapter 4).

EXAMPLE 6-35

In 2017, Linda is employed at a local bank and has wages of $128,000. She also has a Schedule C business of selling jewelry at night and on the weekends. Linda has net income from the Schedule C of $15,000. In this case, Linda owes zero additional social security tax because she is over the $127,200 limit for 2017. She would have to pay the Medicare tax on her Schedule C income:

$$\$15{,}000 \times 0.9235 \times 2.9\% = \$402$$

Linda paid social security tax and Medicare tax on the first $128,000 through withholding from her paycheck at the bank.

EXAMPLE 6-36

Suppose Linda's wages from the bank (see Example 6-35) were only $79,200. Linda would have to pay SE tax (both parts) on the additional $15,000 from her Schedule C business:

Social security $15,000 × 0.9235 × 12.40%	=	$1,718
Medicare $15,000 × 0.9235 × 2.90%	=	402
Total SE tax		$2,120

The SE tax is reported on Schedule SE, which must accompany any Schedule C the taxpayer files. If a taxpayer has more than one Schedule C, only one Schedule SE is required. However, if the tax return is a joint return, each spouse is individually subject to the $127,200 limit and must file his or her own Schedule SE. Exhibit 6-7 illustrates a completed Schedule SE for Linda in Example 6-36.

[65] IRC § 1401.

[66] An employee pays only 7.65% because the employer pays 7.65% (the other half).

EXHIBIT 6-8

SCHEDULE C (Form 1040)
Department of the Treasury Internal Revenue Service (99)

Profit or Loss From Business
(Sole Proprietorship)

▶ Go to *www.irs.gov/ScheduleC* for instructions and the latest information.
▶ Attach to Form 1040, 1040NR, or 1041; partnerships generally must file Form 1065.

OMB No. 1545-0074
2017
Attachment Sequence No. **09**

Name of proprietor: **Alan Masters** | Social security number (SSN): **412-34-5670**

A Principal business or profession, including product or service (see instructions): **Insurance**
B Enter code from instructions ▶ 5 2 4 2 1 0
C Business name. If no separate business name, leave blank.
D Employer ID number (EIN) (see instr.)
E Business address (including suite or room no.) ▶
City, town or post office, state, and ZIP code
F Accounting method: **(1)** ☑ Cash **(2)** ☐ Accrual **(3)** ☐ Other (specify) ▶
G Did you "materially participate" in the operation of this business during 2017? If "No," see instructions for limit on losses ☑ Yes ☐ No
H If you started or acquired this business during 2017, check here ▶ ☐
I Did you make any payments in 2017 that would require you to file Form(s) 1099? (see instructions) ☐ Yes ☑ No
J If "Yes," did you or will you file required Forms 1099? ☐ Yes ☐ No

Part I Income

		Line	Amount
1	Gross receipts or sales. See instructions for line 1 and check the box if this income was reported to you on Form W-2 and the "Statutory employee" box on that form was checked ▶ ☐	1	58,380
2	Returns and allowances	2	0
3	Subtract line 2 from line 1	3	58,380
4	Cost of goods sold (from line 42)	4	0
5	**Gross profit.** Subtract line 4 from line 3	5	58,380
6	Other income, including federal and state gasoline or fuel tax credit or refund (see instructions)	6	0
7	**Gross income.** Add lines 5 and 6 ▶	7	58,380

Part II Expenses. Enter expenses for business use of your home **only** on line 30.

		Line	Amount			Line	Amount
8	Advertising	8	1,250	18	Office expense (see instructions)	18	1,500
9	Car and truck expenses (see instructions)	9		19	Pension and profit-sharing plans	19	
				20	Rent or lease (see instructions):		
10	Commissions and fees	10		a	Vehicles, machinery, and equipment	20a	
11	Contract labor (see instructions)	11		b	Other business property	20b	
12	Depletion	12		21	Repairs and maintenance	21	
13	Depreciation and section 179 expense deduction (not included in Part III) (see instructions)	13	8,504	22	Supplies (not included in Part III)	22	2,300
				23	Taxes and licenses	23	660
				24	Travel, meals, and entertainment:		
14	Employee benefit programs (other than on line 19)	14		a	Travel	24a	588
15	Insurance (other than health)	15		b	Deductible meals and entertainment (see instructions)	24b	51
16	Interest:			25	Utilities	25	
a	Mortgage (paid to banks, etc.)	16a		26	Wages (less employment credits)	26	7,000
b	Other	16b		27a	Other expenses (from line 48)	27a	2,343
17	Legal and professional services	17		b	**Reserved for future use**	27b	

		Line	Amount
28	**Total expenses** before expenses for business use of home. Add lines 8 through 27a ▶	28	24,196
29	Tentative profit or (loss). Subtract line 28 from line 7	29	34,184
30	Expenses for business use of your home. Do not report these expenses elsewhere. Attach Form 8829 unless using the simplified method (see instructions). **Simplified method filers only:** enter the total square footage of: (a) your home: ______ and (b) the part of your home used for business: ______. Use the Simplified Method Worksheet in the instructions to figure the amount to enter on line 30	30	
31	**Net profit or (loss).** Subtract line 30 from line 29. • If a profit, enter on both **Form 1040, line 12** (or **Form 1040NR, line 13**) and on **Schedule SE, line 2.** (If you checked the box on line 1, see instructions). Estates and trusts, enter on **Form 1041, line 3.** • If a loss, you **must** go to line 32.	31	34,184

32 If you have a loss, check the box that describes your investment in this activity (see instructions).
• If you checked 32a, enter the loss on both **Form 1040, line 12,** (or **Form 1040NR, line 13**) and on **Schedule SE, line 2.** (If you checked the box on line 1, see the line 31 instructions). Estates and trusts, enter on **Form 1041, line 3.**
• If you checked 32b, you **must** attach **Form 6198.** Your loss may be limited.

32a ☐ All investment is at risk.
32b ☐ Some investment is not at risk.

For Paperwork Reduction Act Notice, see the separate instructions. Cat. No. 11334P **Schedule C (Form 1040) 2017**

Source: U.S. Department of the Treasury, Internal Revenue Service, SCHEDULE C (Form 1040). Washington, DC: 2017.

EXHIBIT 6-8 *(concluded)*

Schedule C (Form 1040) 2017 Page **2**

Part III **Cost of Goods Sold** (see instructions)

33 Method(s) used to value closing inventory: **a** ☐ Cost **b** ☐ Lower of cost or market **c** ☐ Other (attach explanation)

34 Was there any change in determining quantities, costs, or valuations between opening and closing inventory? If "Yes," attach explanation . . . ☐ Yes ☐ No

35	Inventory at beginning of year. If different from last year's closing inventory, attach explanation	35	
36	Purchases less cost of items withdrawn for personal use	36	
37	Cost of labor. Do not include any amounts paid to yourself	37	
38	Materials and supplies	38	
39	Other costs	39	
40	Add lines 35 through 39	40	
41	Inventory at end of year	41	
42	**Cost of goods sold.** Subtract line 41 from line 40. Enter the result here and on line 4	42	

Part IV **Information on Your Vehicle.** Complete this part **only** if you are claiming car or truck expenses on line 9 and are not required to file Form 4562 for this business. See the instructions for line 13 to find out if you must file Form 4562.

43 When did you place your vehicle in service for business purposes? (month, day, year) ▶ ____/____/____

44 Of the total number of miles you drove your vehicle during 2017 enter the number of miles you used your vehicle for:

a Business ________ **b** Commuting (see instructions) ________ **c** Other ________

45 Was your vehicle available for personal use during off-duty hours? . . . ☐ Yes ☐ No

46 Do you (or your spouse) have another vehicle available for personal use? . . . ☐ Yes ☐ No

47a Do you have evidence to support your deduction? . . . ☐ Yes ☐ No

b If "Yes," is the evidence written? . . . ☐ Yes ☐ No

Part V **Other Expenses.** List below business expenses not included on lines 8–26 or line 30.

Continuing Education		975
Cell Phone		588
Internet		780
48 **Total other expenses.** Enter here and on line 27a	48	2,343

Schedule C (Form 1040) 2017

EXHIBIT 6-9

Form **4562**

Department of the Treasury
Internal Revenue Service (99)

Depreciation and Amortization
(Including Information on Listed Property)

▶ Attach to your tax return.
▶ Go to *www.irs.gov/Form4562* for instructions and the latest information.

OMB No. 1545-0172
2017
Attachment Sequence No. 179

Name(s) shown on return	Business or activity to which this form relates	Identifying number
Alan Masters	Insurance	412-34-5670

Part I Election To Expense Certain Property Under Section 179
Note: If you have any listed property, complete Part V before you complete Part I.

1	Maximum amount (see instructions)	1	
2	Total cost of section 179 property placed in service (see instructions)	2	
3	Threshold cost of section 179 property before reduction in limitation (see instructions)	3	
4	Reduction in limitation. Subtract line 3 from line 2. If zero or less, enter -0-	4	
5	Dollar limitation for tax year. Subtract line 4 from line 1. If zero or less, enter -0-. If married filing separately, see instructions	5	

6	(a) Description of property	(b) Cost (business use only)	(c) Elected cost
7	Listed property. Enter the amount from line 29	7	

8	Total elected cost of section 179 property. Add amounts in column (c), lines 6 and 7	8	
9	Tentative deduction. Enter the **smaller** of line 5 or line 8	9	
10	Carryover of disallowed deduction from line 13 of your 2016 Form 4562	10	
11	Business income limitation. Enter the smaller of business income (not less than zero) or line 5 (see instructions)	11	
12	Section 179 expense deduction. Add lines 9 and 10, but don't enter more than line 11	12	
13	Carryover of disallowed deduction to 2018. Add lines 9 and 10, less line 12 ▶	13	

Note: Don't use Part II or Part III below for listed property. Instead, use Part V.

Part II Special Depreciation Allowance and Other Depreciation (Don't include listed property.**)** (See instructions.)

14	Special depreciation allowance for qualified property (other than listed property) placed in service during the tax year (see instructions)	14	
15	Property subject to section 168(f)(1) election	15	
16	Other depreciation (including ACRS)	16	

Part III MACRS Depreciation (Don't include listed property.**)** (See instructions.)

Section A

17	MACRS deductions for assets placed in service in tax years beginning before 2017	17	
18	If you are electing to group any assets placed in service during the tax year into one or more general asset accounts, check here ▶ ☐		

Section B—Assets Placed in Service During 2017 Tax Year Using the General Depreciation System

(a) Classification of property	(b) Month and year placed in service	(c) Basis for depreciation (business/investment use only—see instructions)	(d) Recovery period	(e) Convention	(f) Method	(g) Depreciation deduction
19a 3-year property						
b 5-year property		4,800	5 yr	HY	DDB	960
c 7-year property		23,000	7 yr	HY	DDB	3,288
d 10-year property						
e 15-year property						
f 20-year property						
g 25-year property			25 yrs.		S/L	
h Residential rental property			27.5 yrs.	MM	S/L	
			27.5 yrs.	MM	S/L	
i Nonresidential real property	7/17	120,000	39 yrs.	MM	S/L	1,412
				MM	S/L	

Section C—Assets Placed in Service During 2017 Tax Year Using the Alternative Depreciation System

20a Class life					S/L	
b 12-year			12 yrs.		S/L	
c 40-year			40 yrs.	MM	S/L	

Part IV Summary (See instructions.)

21	Listed property. Enter amount from line 28	21	2,844
22	**Total.** Add amounts from line 12, lines 14 through 17, lines 19 and 20 in column (g), and line 21. Enter here and on the appropriate lines of your return. Partnerships and S corporations—see instructions	22	8,504
23	For assets shown above and placed in service during the current year, enter the portion of the basis attributable to section 263A costs	23	

For Paperwork Reduction Act Notice, see separate instructions. Cat. No. 12906N Form **4562** (2017)

Source: U.S. Department of the Treasury, Internal Revenue Service, Form 4562. Washington, DC: 2017.

EXHIBIT 6-9 *(concluded)*

Form 4562 (2017) Page 2

Part V Listed Property (Include automobiles, certain other vehicles, certain aircraft, certain computers, and property used for entertainment, recreation, or amusement.)

Note: For any vehicle for which you are using the standard mileage rate or deducting lease expense, complete **only** 24a, 24b, columns (a) through (c) of Section A, all of Section B, and Section C if applicable.

Section A—Depreciation and Other Information (Caution: See the instructions for limits for passenger automobiles.)

24a Do you have evidence to support the business/investment use claimed? ☑ Yes ☐ No **24b** If "Yes," is the evidence written? ☑ Yes ☐ No

(a) Type of property (list vehicles first)	(b) Date placed in service	(c) Business/investment use percentage	(d) Cost or other basis	(e) Basis for depreciation (business/investment use only)	(f) Recovery period	(g) Method/Convention	(h) Depreciation deduction	(i) Elected section 179 cost
25 Special depreciation allowance for qualified listed property placed in service during the tax year and used more than 50% in a qualified business use (see instructions) . . **25**								
26 Property used more than 50% in a qualified business use:								
Auto	7/15/17	90 %	22,000	19,800	5 yr	DDB	2,844	
		%						
		%						
27 Property used 50% or less in a qualified business use:								
		%				S/L –		
		%				S/L –		
		%				S/L –		
28 Add amounts in column (h), lines 25 through 27. Enter here and on line 21, page 1 . **28**							2,844	
29 Add amounts in column (i), line 26. Enter here and on line 7, page 1 . . . . . **29**								

Section B—Information on Use of Vehicles

Complete this section for vehicles used by a sole proprietor, partner, or other "more than 5% owner," or related person. If you provided vehicles to your employees, first answer the questions in Section C to see if you meet an exception to completing this section for those vehicles.

	(a) Vehicle 1		(b) Vehicle 2		(c) Vehicle 3		(d) Vehicle 4		(e) Vehicle 5		(f) Vehicle 6	
30 Total business/investment miles driven during the year (**don't** include commuting miles) .												
31 Total commuting miles driven during the year												
32 Total other personal (noncommuting) miles driven												
33 Total miles driven during the year. Add lines 30 through 32												
	Yes	**No**	**Yes**	**No**	**Yes**	**No**	**Yes**	**No**	**Yes**	**No**	**Yes**	**No**
34 Was the vehicle available for personal use during off-duty hours?												
35 Was the vehicle used primarily by a more than 5% owner or related person? . .												
36 Is another vehicle available for personal use?												

Section C—Questions for Employers Who Provide Vehicles for Use by Their Employees

Answer these questions to determine if you meet an exception to completing Section B for vehicles used by employees who **aren't** more than 5% owners or related persons (see instructions).

	Yes	**No**
37 Do you maintain a written policy statement that prohibits all personal use of vehicles, including commuting, by your employees?		
38 Do you maintain a written policy statement that prohibits personal use of vehicles, except commuting, by your employees? See the instructions for vehicles used by corporate officers, directors, or 1% or more owners . .		
39 Do you treat all use of vehicles by employees as personal use?		
40 Do you provide more than five vehicles to your employees, obtain information from your employees about the use of the vehicles, and retain the information received?		
41 Do you meet the requirements concerning qualified automobile demonstration use? (See instructions.) . . .		
Note: If your answer to 37, 38, 39, 40, or 41 is "Yes," don't complete Section B for the covered vehicles.		

Part VI Amortization

(a) Description of costs	(b) Date amortization begins	(c) Amortizable amount	(d) Code section	(e) Amortization period or percentage	(f) Amortization for this year
42 Amortization of costs that begins during your 2017 tax year (see instructions):					
43 Amortization of costs that began before your 2017 tax year				**43**	
44 **Total.** Add amounts in column (f). See the instructions for where to report				**44**	

Form **4562** (2017)

EXHIBIT 6-10

Schedule SE (Form 1040) 2017 | Attachment Sequence No. **17** | Page **2**

Name of person with **self-employment** income (as shown on Form 1040 or Form 1040NR): Alan Masters | Social security number of person with **self-employment** income ▶ 412-34-5670

Section B—Long Schedule SE

Part I Self-Employment Tax

Note: If your only income subject to self-employment tax is **church employee income,** see instructions. Also see instructions for the definition of church employee income.

Line	Description	Box	Amount
A	If you are a minister, member of a religious order, or Christian Science practitioner **and** you filed Form 4361, but you had $400 or more of **other** net earnings from self-employment, check here and continue with Part I . . . . ▶ ☐		
1a	Net farm profit or (loss) from Schedule F, line 34, and farm partnerships, Schedule K-1 (Form 1065), box 14, code A. **Note:** Skip lines 1a and 1b if you use the farm optional method (see instructions)	1a	
b	If you received social security retirement or disability benefits, enter the amount of Conservation Reserve Program payments included on Schedule F, line 4b, or listed on Schedule K-1 (Form 1065), box 20, code Z	1b	( )
2	Net profit or (loss) from Schedule C, line 31; Schedule C-EZ, line 3; Schedule K-1 (Form 1065), box 14, code A (other than farming); and Schedule K-1 (Form 1065-B), box 9, code J1. Ministers and members of religious orders, see instructions for types of income to report on this line. See instructions for other income to report. **Note:** Skip this line if you use the nonfarm optional method (see instructions)	2	34,184
3	Combine lines 1a, 1b, and 2	3	34,184
4a	If line 3 is more than zero, multiply line 3 by 92.35% (0.9235). Otherwise, enter amount from line 3 **Note:** If line 4a is less than $400 due to Conservation Reserve Program payments on line 1b, see instructions.	4a	31,569
b	If you elect one or both of the optional methods, enter the total of lines 15 and 17 here . .	4b	31,569
c	Combine lines 4a and 4b. If less than $400, **stop;** you don't owe self-employment tax. **Exception:** If less than $400 and you had **church employee income,** enter -0- and continue ▶	4c	
5a	Enter your **church employee income** from Form W-2. See instructions for definition of church employee income . . . **5a**		
b	Multiply line 5a by 92.35% (0.9235). If less than $100, enter -0-	5b	
6	Add lines 4c and 5b	6	31,569
7	Maximum amount of combined wages and self-employment earnings subject to social security tax or the 6.2% portion of the 7.65% railroad retirement (tier 1) tax for 2017	7	127,200 00
8a	Total social security wages and tips (total of boxes 3 and 7 on Form(s) W-2) and railroad retirement (tier 1) compensation. If $127,200 or more, skip lines 8b through 10, and go to line 11 — **8a** 112,505		
b	Unreported tips subject to social security tax (from Form 4137, line 10) — **8b**		
c	Wages subject to social security tax (from Form 8919, line 10) — **8c**		
d	Add lines 8a, 8b, and 8c	8d	112,505
9	Subtract line 8d from line 7. If zero or less, enter -0- here and on line 10 and go to line 11 . ▶	9	14,695
10	Multiply the **smaller** of line 6 or line 9 by 12.4% (0.124)	10	1,822
11	Multiply line 6 by 2.9% (0.029)	11	916
12	**Self-employment tax.** Add lines 10 and 11. Enter here and on **Form 1040, line 57,** or **Form 1040NR, line 55**	12	2,738
13	**Deduction for one-half of self-employment tax.** Multiply line 12 by 50% (0.50). Enter the result here and on **Form 1040, line 27,** or **Form 1040NR, line 27** **13** 1,369		

Part II Optional Methods To Figure Net Earnings (see instructions)

Farm Optional Method. You may use this method **only** if **(a)** your gross farm income[1] wasn't more than $7,800, **or (b)** your net farm profits[2] were less than $5,630.

Line	Description	Box	Amount
14	Maximum income for optional methods	14	5,200 00
15	Enter the **smaller** of: two-thirds (2/3) of gross farm income[1] (not less than zero) **or** $5,200. Also include this amount on line 4b above	15	

Nonfarm Optional Method. You may use this method **only** if **(a)** your net nonfarm profits[3] were less than $5,630 and also less than 72.189% of your gross nonfarm income,[4] **and (b)** you had net earnings from self-employment of at least $400 in 2 of the prior 3 years. **Caution:** You may use this method no more than five times.

Line	Description	Box	Amount
16	Subtract line 15 from line 14	16	
17	Enter the **smaller** of: two-thirds (2/3) of gross nonfarm income[4] (not less than zero) **or** the amount on line 16. Also include this amount on line 4b above	17	

[1] From Sch. F, line 9, and Sch. K-1 (Form 1065), box 14, code B.

[2] From Sch. F, line 34, and Sch. K-1 (Form 1065), box 14, code A—minus the amount you would have entered on line 1b had you not used the optional method.

[3] From Sch. C, line 31; Sch. C-EZ, line 3; Sch. K-1 (Form 1065), box 14, code A; and Sch. K-1 (Form 1065-B), box 9, code J1.

[4] From Sch. C, line 7; Sch. C-EZ, line 1; Sch. K-1 (Form 1065), box 14, code C; and Sch. K-1 (Form 1065-B), box 9, code J2.

Schedule SE (Form 1040) 2017

Source: U.S. Department of the Treasury, Internal Revenue Service, Schedule SE (Form 1040). Washington, DC: 2017.

Summary

LO 6-1: Describe how income and expenses from a self-employed individual are recognized and reported.

- Reported on Schedule C.
- Usually reported on 1099-MISC.
- Usually reported on the cash basis except for inventory, which is reported on the accrual basis.

LO 6-2: Explain the concept of ordinary and necessary business expenses.

- Expenses must be ordinary, necessary, and reasonable.
  - Ordinary—customary or usual.
  - Necessary—appropriate and helpful.
  - Reasonable—amount and relation to business.
- Illegal payments, lobbying, or payments for fines and penalties not allowed.

LO 6-3: Explain the calculation of depreciation for trade or business assets.

- Basis—typically the cost of the asset.
- Periods—3, 5, or 7 years for personal property; 27.5 and 39 years for real property.
- Conventions—half-year, mid-quarter, and mid-month conventions.
- Methods—200% declining balance (DB), 150% DB, and straight-line.
- § 179 expense up to $510,000 in 2017.
- Luxury autos limited to $11,160 in 2017.

LO 6-4: Describe travel and entertainment expenses and discuss their deductibility.

- Transportation deductible unless for commuting.
- Standard mileage rate is 53.5 cents per mile for 2017.
- Travel—overnight stay for business purposes, meals included.
- Meals and entertainment limited to 50%.

LO 6-5: Apply the rules for deducting the business portion of a residence and business bad debts.

- Portion of the home must be used exclusively and regularly in the trade or business.
- Direct expenses 100% deductible.
- Indirect expenses deductible in relation to business ratio.
- Deductions limited to the gross income from the business.
- Business bad debts create an ordinary deduction.

LO 6-6: Explain the hobby loss rules and the limits on education expense deductibility.

- Hobby—primarily for personal pleasure.
- Not a hobby if a profit is shown for 3 of the last 5 years.
- No net loss allowed from the hobby.
- Education expenses deductible if the education maintains or improves skills.

LO 6-7: Describe the calculation of self-employment taxes.

- Reported on Schedule SE.
- Social security 12.40%.
- Medicare 2.9%.
- Social security limit $127,200 in 2017.

Appendix

General Depreciation System

TABLE 6A-1
General Depreciation System 200% or 150% Declining Balance Switching to Straight-Line*

	Half-Year Convention					
Recovery Year	3-Year	5-Year	7-Year	10-Year	15-Year	20-Year
1	33.33	20.00	14.29	10.00	5.00	3.750
2	44.45	32.00	24.49	18.00	9.50	7.219
3	14.81	19.20	17.49	14.40	8.55	6.677
4	7.41	11.52	12.49	11.52	7.70	6.177
5		11.52	8.93	9.22	6.93	5.713
6		5.76	8.92	7.37	6.23	5.285
7			8.93	6.55	5.90	4.888
8			4.46	6.55	5.90	4.522
9				6.56	5.91	4.462
10				6.55	5.90	4.461
11				3.28	5.91	4.462
12					5.90	4.461
13					5.91	4.462
14					5.90	4.461
15					5.91	4.462
16					2.95	4.461
17						4.462
18						4.461
19						4.462
20						4.461
21						2.231

* May not be used for farm business property generally placed in service after 1988. See Table 14, Rev. Proc. 87-57.

TABLE 6A-2
General Depreciation System 200% or 150% Declining Balance Switching to Straight-Line*

	Mid-Quarter Convention (Property Placed in Service in 1st Quarter)					
Recovery Year	3-Year	5-Year	7-Year	10-Year	15-Year	20-Year
1	58.33	35.00	25.00	19.50	8.75	6.563
2	27.78	26.00	21.43	16.50	9.13	7.000
3	12.35	15.60	15.31	13.20	8.21	6.482
4	1.54	11.01	10.93	10.56	7.39	5.996
5		11.01	8.75	8.45	6.65	5.546
6		1.38	8.74	6.76	5.99	5.130
7			8.75	6.55	5.90	4.746
8			1.09	6.55	5.91	4.459
9				6.56	5.90	4.459
10				6.55	5.91	4.459
11				0.82	5.90	4.459
12					5.91	4.460
13					5.90	4.459
14					5.91	4.460
15					5.90	4.459
16					0.74	4.460
17						4.459
18						4.460
19						4.459
20						4.460
21						0.557

* May not be used for farm business property generally placed in service after 1988. See Table 15, Rev. Proc. 87-57.

TABLE 6A-3
General Depreciation System 200% or 150% Declining Balance Switching to Straight-Line*

Mid-Quarter Convention (Property Placed in Service in 2nd Quarter)

Recovery Year	3-Year	5-Year	7-Year	10-Year	15-Year	20-Year
1	41.67	25.00	17.85	12.50	6.25	4.688
2	38.89	30.00	23.47	17.50	9.38	7.148
3	14.14	18.00	16.76	14.00	8.44	6.612
4	5.30	11.37	11.97	11.20	7.59	6.116
5		11.37	8.87	8.96	6.83	5.658
6		4.26	8.87	7.17	6.15	5.233
7			8.87	6.55	5.91	4.841
8			3.33	6.55	5.90	4.478
9				6.56	5.91	4.463
10				6.55	5.90	4.463
11				2.46	5.91	4.463
12					5.90	4.463
13					5.91	4.463
14					5.90	4.463
15					5.91	4.462
16					2.21	4.463
17						4.462
18						4.463
19						4.462
20						4.463
21						1.673

* May not be used for farm business property generally placed in service after 1988. See Table 16, Rev. Proc. 87-57.

TABLE 6A-4
General Depreciation System 200% or 150% Declining Balance Switching to Straight-Line*

Mid-Quarter Convention (Property Placed in Service in 3rd Quarter)

Recovery Year	3-Year	5-Year	7-Year	10-Year	15-Year	20-Year
1	25.00	15.00	10.71	7.50	3.75	2.813
2	50.00	34.00	25.51	18.50	9.63	7.289
3	16.67	20.40	18.22	14.80	8.66	6.742
4	16.67	12.24	13.02	11.84	7.80	6.237
5	8.33	11.30	9.30	9.47	7.02	5.769
6		7.06	8.85	7.58	6.31	5.336
7			8.86	6.55	5.90	4.936
8			5.53	6.55	5.90	4.566
9				6.56	5.91	4.460
10				6.55	5.90	4.460
11				4.10	5.91	4.460
12					5.90	4.460
13					5.91	4.461
14					5.90	4.460
15					5.91	4.461
16					3.69	4.460
17						4.461
18						4.460
19						4.461
20						4.460
21						2.788

* May not be used for farm business property generally placed in service after 1988. See Table 17, Rev. Proc. 87–57.

TABLE 6A-5
General Depreciation System 200% or 150% Declining Balance Switching to Straight- Line*

Mid-Quarter Convention (Property Placed in Service in 4th Quarter)

Recovery Year	3-Year	5-Year	7-Year	10-Year	15-Year	20-Year
1	8.33	5.00	3.57	2.50	1.25	0.938
2	61.11	38.00	27.55	19.50	9.88	7.430
3	20.37	22.80	19.68	15.60	8.89	6.872
4	10.19	13.68	14.06	12.48	8.00	6.357
5		10.94	10.04	9.98	7.20	5.880
6		9.58	8.73	7.99	6.48	5.439
7			8.73	6.55	5.90	5.031
8			7.64	6.55	5.90	4.654
9				6.56	5.90	4.458
10				6.55	5.91	4.458
11				5.74	5.90	4.458
12					5.91	4.458
13					5.90	4.458
14					5.91	4.458
15					5.90	4.458
16					5.17	4.458
17						4.458
18						4.459
19						4.458
20						4.459
21						3.901

* May not be used for farm business property generally placed in service after 1988. See Table 18, Rev. Proc. 87–57.

TABLE 6A-6 **General Depreciation System Straight-Line Applicable Recovery Period: 27.5 Years Mid-Month Convention**

	Month in the First Recovery Year the Property Is Placed in Service											
Recovery Year	**1**	**2**	**3**	**4**	**5**	**6**	**7**	**8**	**9**	**10**	**11**	**12**
1	3.485	3.182	2.879	2.576	2.273	1.970	1.667	1.364	1.061	0.758	0.455	0.152
2	3.636	3.636	3.636	3.636	3.636	3.636	3.636	3.636	3.636	3.636	3.636	3.636
3	3.636	3.636	3.636	3.636	3.636	3.636	3.636	3.636	3.636	3.636	3.636	3.636
4	3.636	3.636	3.636	3.636	3.636	3.636	3.636	3.636	3.636	3.636	3.636	3.636
5	3.636	3.636	3.636	3.636	3.636	3.636	3.636	3.636	3.636	3.636	3.636	3.636
6	3.636	3.636	3.636	3.636	3.636	3.636	3.636	3.636	3.636	3.636	3.636	3.636
7	3.636	3.636	3.636	3.636	3.636	3.636	3.636	3.636	3.636	3.636	3.636	3.636
8	3.636	3.636	3.636	3.636	3.636	3.636	3.636	3.636	3.636	3.636	3.636	3.636
9	3.636	3.636	3.636	3.636	3.636	3.636	3.636	3.636	3.636	3.636	3.636	3.636
10	3.637	3.637	3.637	3.637	3.637	3.637	3.636	3.636	3.636	3.636	3.636	3.636
11	3.636	3.636	3.636	3.636	3.636	3.636	3.637	3.637	3.637	3.637	3.637	3.637
12	3.637	3.637	3.637	3.637	3.637	3.637	3.636	3.636	3.636	3.636	3.636	3.636
13	3.636	3.636	3.636	3.636	3.636	3.636	3.637	3.637	3.637	3.637	3.637	3.637
14	3.637	3.637	3.637	3.637	3.637	3.637	3.636	3.636	3.636	3.636	3.636	3.636
15	3.636	3.636	3.636	3.636	3.636	3.636	3.637	3.637	3.637	3.637	3.637	3.637
16	3.637	3.637	3.637	3.637	3.637	3.637	3.636	3.636	3.636	3.636	3.636	3.636
17	3.636	3.636	3.636	3.636	3.636	3.636	3.637	3.637	3.637	3.637	3.637	3.637
18	3.637	3.637	3.637	3.637	3.637	3.637	3.636	3.636	3.636	3.636	3.636	3.636
19	3.636	3.636	3.636	3.636	3.636	3.636	3.637	3.637	3.637	3.637	3.637	3.637
20	3.637	3.637	3.637	3.637	3.637	3.637	3.636	3.636	3.636	3.636	3.636	3.636
21	3.636	3.636	3.636	3.636	3.636	3.636	3.637	3.637	3.637	3.637	3.637	3.637
22	3.637	3.637	3.637	3.637	3.637	3.637	3.636	3.636	3.636	3.636	3.636	3.636
23	3.636	3.636	3.636	3.636	3.636	3.636	3.637	3.637	3.637	3.637	3.637	3.637
24	3.637	3.637	3.637	3.637	3.637	3.637	3.636	3.636	3.636	3.636	3.636	3.636
25	3.636	3.636	3.636	3.636	3.636	3.636	3.637	3.637	3.637	3.637	3.637	3.637
26	3.637	3.637	3.637	3.637	3.637	3.637	3.636	3.636	3.636	3.636	3.636	3.636
27	3.636	3.636	3.636	3.636	3.636	3.636	3.637	3.637	3.637	3.637	3.637	3.637
28	1.970	2.273	2.576	2.879	3.182	3.485	3.636	3.636	3.636	3.636	3.636	3.636
29	0.000	0.000	0.000	0.000	0.000	0.000	0.152	0.455	0.758	1.061	1.364	1.667

TABLE 6A-7 General Depreciation System Straight-Line Applicable Recovery Period: 31.5 Years Mid-Month Convention

	Month in the First Recovery Year the Property Is Placed in Service											
Recovery Year	**1**	**2**	**3**	**4**	**5**	**6**	**7**	**8**	**9**	**10**	**11**	**12**
1	3.042	2.778	2.513	2.249	1.984	1.720	1.455	1.190	0.926	0.661	0.390	0.132
2	3.175	3.175	3.175	3.175	3.175	3.175	3.175	3.175	3.175	3.175	3.170	3.175
3	3.175	3.175	3.175	3.175	3.175	3.175	3.175	3.175	3.175	3.175	3.170	3.175
4	3.175	3.175	3.175	3.175	3.175	3.175	3.175	3.175	3.175	3.175	3.170	3.175
5	3.175	3.175	3.175	3.175	3.175	3.175	3.175	3.175	3.175	3.175	3.170	3.175
6	3.175	3.175	3.175	3.175	3.175	3.175	3.175	3.175	3.175	3.175	3.170	3.175
7	3.175	3.175	3.175	3.175	3.175	3.175	3.175	3.175	3.175	3.175	3.170	3.175
8	3.175	3.174	3.175	3.174	3.175	3.174	3.175	3.175	3.175	3.175	3.170	3.175
9	3.174	3.175	3.174	3.175	3.174	3.175	3.174	3.175	3.174	3.175	3.170	3.175
10	3.175	3.174	3.175	3.174	3.175	3.174	3.175	3.174	3.175	3.174	3.170	3.174
11	3.174	3.175	3.174	3.175	3.174	3.175	3.174	3.175	3.174	3.175	3.170	3.175
12	3.175	3.174	3.175	3.174	3.175	3.174	3.175	3.174	3.175	3.174	3.170	3.174
13	3.174	3.175	3.174	3.175	3.174	3.175	3.174	3.175	3.174	3.175	3.170	3.175
14	3.175	3.174	3.175	3.174	3.175	3.174	3.175	3.174	3.175	3.174	3.170	3.174
15	3.174	3.175	3.174	3.175	3.174	3.175	3.174	3.175	3.174	3.175	3.170	3.175
16	3.175	3.174	3.175	3.174	3.175	3.174	3.175	3.174	3.175	3.174	3.170	3.174
17	3.174	3.175	3.174	3.175	3.174	3.175	3.174	3.175	3.174	3.175	3.170	3.175
18	3.175	3.174	3.175	3.174	3.175	3.174	3.175	3.174	3.175	3.174	3.170	3.174
19	3.174	3.175	3.174	3.175	3.174	3.175	3.174	3.175	3.174	3.175	3.170	3.175
20	3.175	3.174	3.175	3.174	3.175	3.174	3.175	3.174	3.175	3.174	3.170	3.174
21	3.174	3.175	3.174	3.175	3.174	3.175	3.174	3.175	3.174	3.175	3.170	3.175
22	3.175	3.174	3.175	3.174	3.175	3.174	3.175	3.174	3.175	3.174	3.170	3.174
23	3.174	3.175	3.174	3.175	3.174	3.175	3.174	3.175	3.174	3.175	3.170	3.175
24	3.175	3.174	3.175	3.174	3.175	3.174	3.175	3.174	3.175	3.174	3.170	3.174
25	3.174	3.175	3.174	3.175	3.174	3.175	3.174	3.175	3.174	3.175	3.170	3.175
26	3.175	3.174	3.175	3.174	3.175	3.174	3.175	3.174	3.175	3.174	3.170	3.174
27	3.174	3.175	3.174	3.175	3.174	3.175	3.174	3.175	3.174	3.175	3.170	3.175
28	3.175	3.174	3.175	3.174	3.175	3.174	3.175	3.174	3.175	3.174	3.170	3.174
29	3.174	3.175	3.174	3.175	3.174	3.175	3.174	3.175	3.174	3.175	3.170	3.175
30	3.175	3.174	3.175	3.174	3.175	3.174	3.175	3.174	3.175	3.174	3.170	3.174
31	3.174	3.175	3.174	3.175	3.174	3.175	3.174	3.175	3.174	3.175	3.170	3.175
32	1.720	1.984	2.249	2.513	2.778	3.042	3.175	3.174	3.175	3.174	3.170	3.174
33	0.000	0.000	0.000	0.000	0.000	0.000	0.132	0.397	0.661	0.926	1.190	1.455

TABLE 6A-8 General Depreciation System Straight-Line Applicable Recovery Period: 39 Years Mid-Month Convention

	Month in the First Recovery Year the Property Is Placed in Service											
Recovery Year	**1**	**2**	**3**	**4**	**5**	**6**	**7**	**8**	**9**	**10**	**11**	**12**
1	2.461	2.247	2.033	1.819	1.605	1.391	1.177	.963	.749	.535	.32	.107
2–39	2.564	2.564	2.564	2.564	2.564	2.564	2.564	2.564	2.564	2.564	2.564	2.564
40	0.107	0.321	0.535	0.749	0.963	1.177	1.391	1.605	1.819	2.033	2.24	2.461

Discussion Questions connect

All applicable Discussion Questions are available with ***Connect***©

EA LO 6-1 1. Discuss the definition of *trade* or *business*. Why does it matter whether a taxpayer is classified as an employee or as self-employed?

EA LO 6-2 2. Discuss the concepts of *ordinary, necessary,* and *reasonable* in relation to trade or business expenses.

EA LO 6-3 3. On what form is depreciation reported, and how does it relate to other forms such as Schedules C, E, F, and Form 2106?

EA LO 6-3 4. On what type of property is depreciation allowed?

EA LO 6-3 5. Discuss the word *basis* in relation to the financial accounting term *book value*. What is meant by the term *adjusted basis*?

EA LO 6-3 6. Discuss the difference between personal property and real property. Give examples of each.

EA LO 6-3 7. What is a *depreciation convention*? What conventions are available under MACRS?

EA LO 6-3 8. When calculating depreciation for personal property (assuming the half-year convention) using the IRS depreciation tables, does the taxpayer need to multiply the first year table depreciation percentage by one-half? What about in the year of disposal, assuming the property is disposed of prior to the end of its recovery period?

EA LO 6-3 9. Discuss the concept of electing § 179 expense. Does the election allow a larger expense deduction in the year of asset acquisition?

EA LO 6-3 10. Discuss the concept of *listed property.*

EA LO 6-4 11. Distinguish between travel and transportation expenses.

EA LO 6-4 12. When can a taxpayer use the standard mileage rate? Is the standard mileage rate better than the actual auto costs?

EA LO 6-4 13. Discuss the limits on meals and entertainment. Are meals and entertainment expenses always limited to 50%?

EA LO 6-5 14. Discuss the limits on home office expense deductibility.

EA LO 6-6 15. Why were the hobby loss rules established? What factors determine whether an activity is a trade or business or a hobby? Is any one factor controlling?

EA LO 6-7 16. What are the two components of the self-employment tax? Is either component limited?

Multiple-Choice Questions

All applicable multiple-choice questions are available with **Connect**®

EA LO 6-1 17. Trade or business expenses are treated as

a. A deduction *for* AGI.

b. An itemized deduction if not reimbursed.

c. A deduction *from* AGI.

d. A deduction *from* AGI limited to the amount in excess of 2% of AGI.

EA LO 6-1 18. Which of the following is *not* a "trade or business" expense?

a. Interest on investment indebtedness.

b. Property taxes on business equipment.

c. Depreciation on business property.

d. Cost of goods sold.

EA LO 6-1 19. Atlas, a financial consultant, had the following income and expenses in his business:

Fee income	$235,000
Expenses:	
Rent expense	18,000
Penalties assessed by the SEC	2,500
Office expenses	6,000
Supplies	6,000
Interest paid on note used to acquire office equipment	2,700
Speeding tickets going to see clients	650

How much net income must Atlas report from this business?

a. $199,150.

b. $202,300.

c. $202,950.

d. $205,450.

EA LO 6-2 20. Mandy, a CPA, flew from Raleigh to Seattle to attend an accounting conference that lasted four days. Then she took three days of vacation to go sightseeing. Mandy's expenses for the trip are as follows:

Airfare	$ 625
Lodging (7 days × $145)	1,015
Meals (7 days × $75)	525
Taxi from airport to hotel and back	70

Mandy's travel expense deduction is

a. $1,425.

b. $1,575.

c. $1,973.

d. $2,235.

EA LO 6-3 21. On May 5, 2012, Jill purchased equipment for $40,000 to be used in her business. She did not elect to expense the equipment under § 179 or bonus depreciation. On January 1, 2017, she sells the equipment to a scrap metal dealer. What is the cost recovery deduction for 2017?

a. $892.

b. $1,784.

c. $3,568.

d. No deduction allowed.

EA LO 6-3 22. On April 15, 2015, Andy purchased some furniture and fixtures (7-year property) for $10,000 to be used in his business. He did not elect to expense the equipment under § 179 or bonus depreciation. On June 30, 2017, he sells the equipment. What is the cost recovery deduction for 2017?

a. $0.

b. $875.

c. $1,429.

d. $1,749.

EA LO 6-3 23. Lawrence purchased an apartment building on February 10, 2017, for $330,000, $30,000 of which was for the land. What is the cost recovery deduction for 2017?

a. $0.

b. $6,741.

c. $9,546.

d. $10,660.

EA LO 6-3 24. Roy purchased an office building on March 30, 2014, for $250,000, $25,000 of which was for the land. On July 30, 2017, he sold the office building. What is the cost recovery deduction for 2017?

a. $0.

b. $3,125.

c. $5,769.

d. $6,410.

EA LO 6-3 25. On June 30, 2017, Ken purchased an apartment building for $500,000. Determine the cost recovery deduction for 2017:

a. $4,925.

b. $5,335.

c. $6,955.

d. $9,850.

EA LO 6-3 26. During the year, Cory purchased a log skidder (7-year property) for $55,000 for his business. Assume that he has income from his business of $30,000, and he and his wife have combined salaries and wages income of $40,000. What is the maximum deduction he can take for his business in relation to the log skidder purchase?

a. $7,860.

b. $30,000.

c. $31,429.

d. $55,000.

EA LO 6-3 27. § 179 expense is available for all of the following business assets *except*

a. Office building.

b. Office furniture.

c. Computer.

d. Delivery truck.

EA LO 6-4 28. Jordan has two jobs. She works as a night auditor at the Moonlight Motel. When her shift at the motel is over, she works as a short-order cook at the Greasy Spoon Restaurant. On a typical day, she drives the following number of miles:

Home to Moonlight Motel	4
Moonlight Motel to Greasy Spoon Restaurant	7
Greasy Spoon Restaurant to home	12

How many miles would qualify as transportation expenses for tax purposes?

a. 4.

b. 7.

c. 11.

d. 12.

EA LO 6-4 29. Which of the following is *false* with respect to the standard mileage rate?

a. It can be used if the taxpayer owns the vehicle and uses the standard mileage rate for the first year it was placed in service.

b. It includes parking fees, tolls, and property taxes on the vehicle.

c. It encompasses depreciation or lease payments, maintenance and repairs, gasoline, oil, insurance, and vehicle registration fees.

d. It does not include interest expense on acquisition of the automobile.

EA LO 6-4 30. Frank purchased a vehicle for business and personal use. In 2017, he used the vehicle 70% for business (11,000 business miles incurred equally throughout the year) and calculated his vehicle expenses using the standard mileage rate. Frank also paid $1,800 in interest and $480 in county property tax on the car. What is the total business deduction related to business use of the car?

a. $5,885.

b. $6,365.

c. $7,481.

d. $8,165.

EA LO 6-1, 6-4 31. Jimmy took a business trip from Dallas to Brazil. He was there for a total of seven days, of which two were weekend days. Over the weekend, he spent his time sightseeing and relaxing. His expenses were as follows:

Airfare	$1,400
Lodging (7 days × $300)	2,100
Meals (7 days)	595
Taxi fares ($600 to and from business meetings)	800

How much is Jimmy allowed to deduct?

a. $3,404.

b. $3,496.

c. $4,598.

d. $4,895.

EA LO 6-5 32. Jake runs a business out of his home. He uses 600 square feet of his home exclusively for the business. His home is 2,400 square feet in total. Jake had $27,000 of business revenue and $22,000 of business expenses from his home-based business. The following expenses relate to his home:

Mortgage interest	$10,800
Real estate taxes	1,600
Utilities	2,400
Insurance	600
Repairs	2,400
Depreciation (on business use portion of home)	1,200

What is Jake's net income from his business? What amount of expenses is carried over to the following year, if any?

a. ($14,000) and $0 carryover.

b. ($650) and $0 carryover.

c. $0 and $650 carryover.

d. $550 and $0 carryover.

EA LO 6-6 33. Which of the following is *not* a relevant factor to be considered in deciding whether an activity is profit seeking or a hobby?

a. Manner in which the taxpayer carries on the activity.

b. Expertise of the taxpayer or his or her advisers.

c. Time and effort expended by the taxpayer in carrying on the activity.

d. All of the above are relevant factors.

EA LO 6-6 34. Which of the following individuals can deduct education expenses?

a. A real estate broker who attends college to get an accounting degree.

b. A CPA who attends a review course to obtain his building contractor's license.

c. A corporate executive attending an executive MBA program.

d. An accounting bookkeeper taking a CPA review course to pass the CPA exam and become a CPA.

EA LO 6-7 35. Annie is self-employed and has $58,000 in income from her business. She also has investments that generated dividends of $3,000 and interest of $2,500. What is Annie's self-employment tax for the year?

a. $8,195.

b. $8,619.

c. $8,874.

d. $8,972.

EA LO 6-7 36. The maximum tax bases and percentages for 2017 for the two portions of the self-employment tax are which of the following?

	Social Security	Medicare
a.	$127,200; 12.4%	Unlimited; 2.9%.
b.	$127,200; 12.4%	Unlimited; 15.3%.
c.	$118,500; 12.4%	Unlimited; 2.9%.
d.	$118,500; 15.3%	Unlimited; 15.3%.

Problems connect

All applicable problems are available with ***Connect***©

EA LO 6-1 37. Kelly is a self-employed tax attorney whose practice primarily involves tax planning. During the year, she attended a three-day seminar regarding new changes to the tax law. She incurred the following expenses:

Lodging	$400
Meals	95
Course registration	350
Transportation	150

a. How much can Kelly deduct? ____________

b. Kelly believes that obtaining a CPA license would improve her skills as a tax attorney. She enrolls as a part-time student at a local college to take CPA review courses. During the current year, she spends $1,500 for tuition and $300 for books. How much of these expenses can Kelly deduct? Why?

____

____

____

LO 6-1, 6-2, 6-4 EA

38. Jackie owns a temporary employment agency that hires personnel to perform accounting services for clients. During the year, her entertainment expenses for her clients include the following:

Cab fare to and from restaurants	$ 350
Gratuity at restaurants	300
Meals	4,000
Cover charges	250

Jackie also held a holiday party for her employees, which cost $1,500. All expenses are reasonable.

a. Can Jackie deduct any of these expenses? If so, how much? ________________

b. How is the deduction classified? ________________________

EA LO 6-5

39. David is a college professor who does some consulting work on the side. He uses 25% of his home exclusively for the consulting practice. He is single and 63 years old. His AGI (without consideration of consulting income) is $45,000. Other information follows:

Income from consulting business	$4,000
Consulting expenses other than home office	1,500
Total costs relating to home:	
Interest and taxes	6,500
Utilities	1,500
Maintenance and repairs	450
Depreciation (business part only)	1,500

Calculate David's AGI. ____________________________

EA LO 6-5

40. In 2015, Gerald loaned Main Street Bakery $55,000. In 2016, he learned that he would probably receive only $6,400 of the loan. In 2017, Gerald received $3,000 in final settlement of the loan. Calculate Gerald's possible deductions with respect to the loan for 2015, 2016, and 2017.

2015: ____________________________________

2016: ____________________________________

2017: ____________________________________

EA LO 6-1, 6-2

41. Charles, a self-employed real estate agent, attended a conference on the impact of some new building codes on real estate investments. His unreimbursed expenses were as follows:

Airfare	$480
Lodging	290
Meals	100
Tuition and fees	650

How much can Charles deduct on his return? ________________________

EA LO 6-3 42. Betsy acquired a new network system on June 5, 2017 (5-year class property), for $75,000. She expects taxable income from the business will always be about $175,000 without regard to the § 179 election. Betsy will elect § 179 expensing. She also acquired 7-year property in July 2017 for $350,000. Determine Betsy's maximum cost recovery deduction with respect to her purchases in 2017: ______________

EA LO 6-3 43. Janet purchased her personal residence in 2007 for $250,000. In January 2017, she converted it to rental property. The fair market value at the time of conversion was $210,000.

a. Determine the amount of cost recovery that can be taken in 2017. ______________

b. Determine the amount of cost recovery that could be taken in 2017 if the fair market value of the property were $350,000: ______________

EA LO 6-3 44. On February 4, 2017, Jackie purchased and placed in service a car she purchased for $21,500. The car was used exclusively for her business. Compute Jackie's cost recovery deduction in 2017 assuming no § 179 expense but the bonus was taken: ______________

EA LO 6-3 45. Rueben acquires a warehouse on September 1, 2017, for $3 million. On March 1, 2021, he sells the warehouse. Determine Rueben's cost recovery for 2017–2021:

____

EA LO 6-3 46. Michael is the sole proprietor of a small business. In June 2017, his business income is $12,000 before consideration of any § 179 deduction. He spends $245,000 on furniture and equipment in 2017. If Michael elects to take the § 179 deduction and no bonus on a conference table that cost $25,000 (included in the $245,000 total), determine the maximum cost recovery for 2017 with respect to the conference table: ______________

EA LO 6-3 47. On June 10, 2017, Huron purchased equipment (7-year class property) for $75,000. Determine Huron's cost recovery deduction for computing 2017 taxable income. Assume that Huron does not make the § 179 or bonus elections. ______________

EA LO 6-3 48. Brittany purchased a building for $500,000 on January 1, 2009. The purchase price does not include land. Calculate the cost recovery for 2009 and 2017 if the real property is

a. Residential real property: ______________

b. A warehouse: ______________

EA LO 6-3 49. Walt purchased a computer for $5,000. He could use the computer exclusively for his business, or he could allow his family to use the computer 60% of the time and 40% would be for business use. Determine the tax deduction for the year of acquisition under both alternatives. What is the overall tax savings between the two alternatives? Assume that Walt would not elect § 179 expensing or 50% bonus and that he is in the 25% tax bracket.

____

EA LO 6-3, 6-4 50. In 2015, Jessica bought a new heavy truck for $45,000 to use 80% for her sole proprietorship. Total miles driven include 12,000 in 2015, 14,500 in 2016, and 13,000 in 2017.

a. If Jessica uses the standard mileage method, how much may she deduct on her 2017 tax return (miles were incurred ratably throughout the year)? ______________

b. What is the deduction for 2017 assuming the actual method was used from the beginning? Calculate depreciation only; the truck is not limited by the luxury auto rules. Also assume § 179 was not elected in the year of purchase. ______________

EA LO 6-3, 6-4 51. Jose purchased a vehicle for business and personal use. In 2017, he used the vehicle 18,000 miles (80% of total) for business and calculated his vehicle expenses using the standard mileage rate (mileage was incurred ratably throughout the year). He paid $1,400 in interest and $150 in property taxes on the car. Calculate the total business deduction related to the car:

___

EA LO 6-4 52. Jordan took a business trip from New York to Denver. She spent two days in travel, conducted business for nine days, and visited friends for five days. She incurred the following expenses:

Airfare	$ 550
Lodging	3,000
Meals	900
Entertainment of clients	750

How much of these expenses can Jordan deduct?

___

EA LO 6-5 53. Derrick owns a farm in eastern North Carolina. A hurricane hit the area and destroyed a farm building and some farm equipment and damaged a barn.

Item	Adjusted Basis	FMV before Damage	FMV after Damage	Insurance Proceeds
Building	$85,000	$115,000	$ –0–	$55,000
Equipment	68,000	49,000	–0–	15,000
Barn	95,000	145,000	95,000	35,000

Due to the extensive damage throughout the area, the president of the United States declared all areas affected by the hurricane as a disaster area. Derrick, who files a joint return with his wife, had $45,000 of taxable income last year. Their taxable income for the current year is $150,000, excluding the loss from the hurricane. Calculate the amount of the loss deductible by Derrick and his wife and the years in which they should deduct the loss. (*Hint:* Chapter 5 provides information concerning nationally declared disaster areas.)

___

___

___

EA LO 6-6 54. Rebecca is a doctor with an AGI of $125,000 before consideration of income or loss from her dog breeding business. Her home is on 15 acres, 10 of which she uses to house the animals and provide them with ample space to play and exercise. Her records show the following related income and expenses for the current year:

Income from fees and sales	$2,500
Expenses:	
Dog food	$4,000
Veterinary bills	3,500
Supplies	1,200
Publications and dues	350

a. How must Rebecca treat the income and expenses of the operation if the dog breeding business is held to be a hobby? ______________________________

____

b. How would your answer differ if the operation were held to be a business?

____

EA LO 6-6 55. Eric, who is single, participates in an activity that is appropriately classified as a hobby. The activity produces the following revenue and expenses:

Revenue	$12,000
Property taxes	2,000
Materials and supplies	4,000
Utilities	1,500
Advertising	1,900
Insurance	775
Depreciation	5,000

Without regard to this activity, Eric's AGI is $55,000. Determine how much income he must report, the amount of the expenses he is permitted to deduct, and his AGI:

____

EA LO 6-7 56. In 2017, Landon has self-employment earnings of $195,000. Compute Landon's self-employment tax liability and the allowable income tax deduction of the self-employment tax paid. SE tax: ______________ SE deduction: ______________

EA LO 6-3 57. (Comprehensive) Casper used the following assets in his Schedule C trade or business in the tax year 2017.

Asset	Date Purchased	Date Sold	Business Use (percentage)	Cost
Computer 1	03/12/14		100%	$ 3,000
Computer 2	05/05/14	05/15/17	100	2,500
Printer	08/25/17		100	2,200
Computer 3	05/25/17		100	2,800
Equipment	03/20/15		100	2,700
Auto	05/01/17		90	20,000
Furniture 1	02/12/15	08/25/17	100	22,000
Furniture 2	08/15/15		100	3,600
Office building	04/01/17		100	330,000

Casper is a new client and unfortunately does not have a copy of his prior year's tax return. He recalls that all of the assets purchased in prior years used MACRS depreciation (no § 179 expense). Casper does not wish to take a § 179. Calculate the current year depreciation allowance for Casper's business. Correctly report the amounts on Form 4562.

Tax Return Problems connect

All applicable tax return problems are available with ***Connect***®

Use your tax software to complete the following problems. If you are manually preparing the tax returns, the problems indicate the forms or schedules you will need.

Tax Return Problem 1 Cassi (SSN 412-34-5670) has a home cleaning business she runs as a sole proprietorship. The following are the results from business operations for the tax year 2017:

Gross receipts		$203,000
Business mileage: 27,000 (miles incurred ratably throughout the year)		
35,000 miles total during the year 2017		
Van (over 6,000 lbs) placed in service 1/01/2017, cost 27,000		
Postage		(500)
Wages		(26,000)
Payroll taxes		(1,950)
Supplies		(12,500)
Phone		(1,250)
Internet service		(600)
Rent		(2,400)
Insurance		(2,800)
Van expenses		(4,500)
Business assets	Date Purchased	Cost
Computer 1	5/18/17	$2,200
Computer 2	6/01/17	2,700
Printer	3/01/16	900
Copier	3/02/16	2,100
Furniture	3/01/16	6,000

Determine Cassi's self-employment income and prepare Schedule C and Schedule SE. § 179 expense is elected on all eligible assets (§ 179 was not taken on assets purchased last year).

Tax Return Problem 2 During 2017, Cassandra Albright, who is single, worked part-time at a doctor's office and received a W-2. She also had a consulting practice that had the following income and expenses: Cassi had qualifying health care coverage at all times during the tax year.

Revenue	$48,000
Laptop computer purchased 4/23/17 (§ 179 elected)	2,300
Travel 2,500 miles for business, 13,000 personal	
Supplies	500
Cell phone charge	540

Cassandra (SSN 412-34-5670) resides at 1400 Medical Street, Apt. 3A, Lowland, CA 92273. Her W-2 shows the following:

Wages	$45,300
Federal withholding	4,983
Social security wages	45,300
Social security withholding	2,809
Medicare withholding	657
State withholding	2,265
Other income:	
1099-INT Old Bank	2,300
1099-DIV Bake Co., Inc.—Ordinary dividends	3,100
Qualified dividends	3,100

Cassandra had the following itemized deductions:

State income tax withholding	$ 2,265
State income tax paid with the 2016 return	350
Real estate tax	3,450
Mortgage interest	12,300

Cassandra made two federal estimated payments of $7,000 each on April 15 and June 15. Prepare Form 1040 for Cassandra for 2017. You will need Form 1040, Schedule A, Schedule B, Schedule C, Form 4562, and Schedule SE. Cassandra had qualifying health care coverage at all times during the tax year.

Tax Return Problem 3 During 2017, Jason and Vicki Hurting, who are married with two children, had the following tax information. Jason owns a landscaping business, and Vicki works as a sales executive for a manufacturing business.

Jason (SSN 412-34-5670) and Vicki (SSN 412-34-5671) reside at 123 Bate Street, Bright, AL 36116. Both children are under the age of 17:

Jason Jr. (412-34-5672) date of birth 7/20/09
Catlin (412-34-5673) date of birth 1/08/13
Vicki's W-2 information is as follows:

Wages	$94,000
Federal withholding	22,000
Social security wages	94,000
Social security withholding	5,828
Medicare withholding	1,363
State withholding	4,700
Other income:	
1099-G Alabama state tax refund is taxable because $4,700 was deducted on last year's return	$423
1099-INT First Bank of Alabama	225
1099-DIV IBM, Inc.—Ordinary dividends	125
Qualified dividends	125

The following information is for Jason's landscaping business:

Revenue	$153,000		
Wages	41,600		
Payroll tax	3,182		
Cell phone charge	425		
Assets (§ 179 elected)			
Item	**Date Purchased**	**Business Use Amount**	**Percentage**
Truck (100% business)	2/05/2017	$28,000	100%
Mower 1	3/08/2017	12,000	100
Mower 2	3/08/2017	3,400	100
Equipment	6/25/2017	1,595	100

The truck was over 6,000 lbs. The Hurtings had the following itemized deductions:

State income tax withholding (from above)	$4,700
Real estate tax	2,100
Personal property tax	425
Mortgage interest	8,300
Charitable contributions	2,400

The Hurtings made four federal estimated payments of $3,000 each on their due dates. Prepare Form 1040 for the Hurtings for 2017. You will need Form 1040, Schedule A, Schedule C, Form 4562, and Schedule SE. The Hurtings had qualifying health care coverage at all times during the tax year.

We have provided selected filled-in source documents that are available in the *Connect Library*.

Chapter Seven

Capital Gains and Other Sales of Property (Schedule D and Form 4797)

Gains and losses from the sale of assets are included in taxable income. The gain or loss can appear on a tax return in different locations, depending on the type of asset sold. Before determining the tax implications of asset sales, the property must be classified as a personal-use asset, a trade or business asset, or an investment asset. Also the length of time the taxpayer owned the property and whether the asset is subject to depreciation must be determined. Each of these items affects the taxability of asset sales. This chapter focuses on the tax treatment of asset sales with particular attention on the determination of capital gain versus ordinary gain treatment. At present, gains from the sale of capital assets receive preferential tax treatment (lower rate of tax). Thus the chapter emphasizes the proper classification and reporting of capital gain properties. IRS Publication 544 (Sales and Other Dispositions of Assets), Publication 550 (Investment Income and Expenses), and Publication 551 (Basis of Assets) can be helpful as you study this chapter.

Learning Objectives

When you have completed this chapter, you should understand the following learning objectives (LO):

- **LO 7-1** Define the terms and identify the tax forms used in sales of property transactions.
- **LO 7-2** Classify assets sold as ordinary assets, § 1221 capital assets, or § 1231 business assets.
- **LO 7-3** Explain and apply the tax rules for recognizing gains or losses on the sale of ordinary assets.
- **LO 7-4** Explain and apply the tax rules for recognizing short-term and long-term gains or losses on the sale of capital assets (§ 1221).
- **LO 7-5** Calculate the recognized gain or loss on the sale of § 1231 business assets, including gain recapture provisions of § 1245 and § 1250 property.
- **LO 7-6** Describe the tax rules for special types of sales, including block stock sales, capital gain distributions, sales of mutual funds, worthless securities, and sales of property received as a gift or through inheritance.

INTRODUCTION

Gross income includes gains derived from dealings in property.[1] The tax code also allows the deductibility of losses on the sale of property in certain situations.[2] The purpose of this chapter

[1] IRC § 61(3).

[2] IRC § 165.

is to discuss the taxability and reporting of gains and losses from the sale of various asset types. Depending on the classification of the assets sold, gains on the sale are subject to different tax rates; however, losses on the sales of assets may be limited, may be deducted in full, or may not be deductible. Form 4797 and Schedule D are the forms used to record all gains and losses from sales of property. There is a new Form 8949—Sales and Other Dispositions of Capital Assets. This form is completed first and the subtotals are then recorded on the Schedule D Part I and Part II.

TERMS AND TAX FORMS

LO 7-1

Before any gain or loss on the sale or transfer of property can be calculated, the asset's basis first must be determined. In general, the *basis* of property purchased is the cost of the asset, including cash, debt obligations, and other property or services involved in acquiring the asset. For example, if you buy stocks, the basis is the purchase price plus commission and transfer fees. If you buy a copier, additional costs could include sales tax, freight, and installation. The cost basis is adjusted for certain items such as improvements to the property, which increase basis, and depreciation deductions, which decrease basis. The result of these adjustments to the property is termed the *adjusted basis.* Using the copier as an example, assume it was purchased for use in a business at an initial cost of $10,000. Freight and installation costs added $500. The adjusted basis of the copier is $10,500. Assume depreciation allowed was $4,200; the adjusted basis of the copier is now $6,300 ($10,000 + $500 − $4,200). The concept of adjusted basis is important because this basis will be used to determine the amount of the gain or loss on the sale or disposition of the property. The lower the adjusted basis, the greater the potential gain will be when the property is sold. How these gains are taxed is explained in detail later in the chapter. Sometimes basis is other than the cost of the asset. For example, if the taxpayer receives investment property in exchange for services rendered, the basis is the fair market value (FMV) of the property. If the value of the services was known beforehand, then the asset's basis would be based on the price of the services.

The basis of assets transferred by inheritance is generally valued at the FMV of the property at the date of the individual's death or the FMV on the alternate valuation date if the personal representative for the estate chooses and qualifies to use this date. If no federal estate tax return is filed, the appraised value on the date of death for state inheritance taxes is used.[3] The basis of property transferred to a taxpayer from a spouse or former spouse incident to a divorce settlement is the same as the spouse's or former spouse's adjusted basis before the transfer.[4] The transfer must occur within one year after the date on which the marriage ends if the transfer is related to the ending of the marriage.

The rules for assets transferred by gift depend on whether the FMV is less than, equal to, or more than the donor's adjusted basis. If the FMV of the property at the time of the gift is less than the donor's adjusted basis before the gift, the donee's basis for a gain on the sale or other disposition is the donor's adjusted basis. The basis for a loss is the FMV of the property at the time the gift was given. If the FMV is equal to or greater than the donor's adjusted basis just before the gift, the donee's basis for calculating a gain or loss is the donor's adjusted basis. (Refer to the special sales section at the end of the chapter for an example.) Table 7-1 outlines some specific definitions of basis used in this chapter.[5]

Also important terms to know are *amount realized* and *amount recognized.* The *amount realized* from a sale or trade of property is everything the taxpayer receives in the transaction. This is also termed the *proceeds from the sale.* This includes cash received plus the FMV of any property or services received plus the amount of any debt assumed by the purchaser. If a taxpayer

[3] Additional rules for valuation of assets transferred by inheritance are beyond the scope of this discussion. For specific rules, refer to Publication 559—Survivors, Executors, and Administrators.

[4] Refer to Publication 504—Divorced or Separated Individuals.

[5] Publication 551—Basis of Assets.

TABLE 7-1

Basis	The amount of investment in property for tax purposes. *Basis* is the starting point in determining gain or loss on the sale or disposition of investment property.
Cost Basis	The cost of the property bought in cash, debt obligations, other property or services.
Other Cost Basis	Property acquired other than through a purchase: • Gift • Inheritance • Divorce • Exchanges
Adjusted Basis	Increases and/or decreases to the original cost basis of an asset. • Examples of increases: a room addition to a home, replacing an entire roof, the cost of defending and perfecting a title to property or a patent, commission fees for purchasing stock, and stock dividends received through dividend reinvestment plans. • Examples of decreases: § 179 deductions, deductions previously allowed such as depreciation or amortization, nontaxable stock dividends or stock splits, or postponed gain from the sale of a home (discussed in Chapter 12).
Fair Market Value	The price at which the property would change hands between a buyer and a seller, neither being forced to buy or sell and both having reasonable knowledge of all the relevant facts. Sales of similar property, around the same date, are typically used in figuring fair market value.

trades property and cash for other property, the amount realized is the FMV of the asset that the taxpayer is receiving. The difference between the amount realized and the adjusted basis determines whether there is a gain or loss on the sale. The following chart summarizes this process:

Amount realized < Adjusted basis	Loss
Amount realized > Adjusted basis	Gain

The last term to discuss is the amount of gain or loss that will be recognized for tax purposes. The *amount recognized* from a sale or trade of property is the amount that will be recorded on the tax return as a gain or loss. Gains and losses can be realized and recognized, or they can be realized and not recognized, such as in a nontaxable exchange, or a loss on the disposition of property that is held for personal use, or a gain that is excluded as with the sale of a residence (see Chapter 12)

For example, if the adjusted basis of the property sold is $8,000 and the amount realized is $10,000, there is a gain of $2,000. This $2,000 gain is recognized for tax purposes because it is not from a nontaxable exchange. If the adjusted basis of the property sold is $8,000 and the amount realized is $7,000, there is a loss of $1,000. If the loss is from the disposition of personal-use property, the $1,000 is not recognized for tax purposes. If the loss is *not* from the disposition of personal-use property, it is recognized as a loss for tax purposes.

It is possible that, when a sale occurs, the sales proceeds (amount the seller realizes) include not only cash but also the FMV of other property received as well as any assumption of liabilities by the buyer, as illustrated in Examples 7-1 and 7-2.[6]

EXAMPLE 7-1

Debra sold a parcel of land for $55,000 cash. The buyer also assumed a $15,000 note attached to the land. Debra originally purchased the land for $34,000, so she reports a gain on the land of $36,000 ($55,000 cash + $15,000 release of liability less the $34,000 basis).

EXAMPLE 7-2

Larry needed cash and sold a parcel of land for $55,000. The buyer also assumed a $15,000 note attached to the land. Larry originally purchased the land for $72,000, so he reports a loss on the land of $2,000 ($55,000 cash + $15,000 release of liability less the $72,000 basis).

[6] Reg. § 1.1001-2(a)(1).

The nature of the tax reporting for gains and losses on the sale of property depends primarily on the use of the asset rather than on its form. After the appropriate asset use has been determined, the taxpayer will possibly record the taxable event on different tax forms. Examples 7-1 and 7-2 involved the sale of land. If the land were used in a trade or business, the gain or loss would be reported on Form 4797. If the land were an investment held in a trade or business, the gain or loss would be reported on Schedule D. Exhibit 7-1 is a sample of Form 4797, and Exhibit 7-2 is a sample of Schedule D including Form 8949.

CONCEPT CHECK 7-1—
LO 7-1

1. A gain or loss on a sale is the difference between the cash received and the original cost of the asset. True or false?
2. The gain or loss on the sale of an asset used for investment or in a trade or business appears on Form 4797. True or false?
3. When the buyer assumes the seller's liability, the seller includes this amount in computing the amount realized from the sale. True or false?

CLASSIFICATION OF ASSETS
LO 7-2

All assets can be classified into one of three categories. The classification of the asset determines how gains and losses on the sale are reported for tax purposes. The three asset categories follow:

1. Ordinary income property.
2. § 1221 property (capital assets).
3. § 1231 trade or business property.

The following sections discuss the rules associated with classifying assets into each of the categories. (Refer to Table 7-2 for a summary of asset classifications.)

Ordinary Income Property

The tax code does not directly define *ordinary income property* except to state that it is any asset that is "not a capital asset." The two most common ordinary assets are inventory and accounts or notes receivable, defined in Chapter 2 of IRS Publication 544 as follows:

- Inventory: property held mainly for sale to customers or property that will physically become part of merchandise for sale to customers.
- Receivables: accounts or notes receivable acquired in the ordinary course of business or from the sale of any inventory properties.

TABLE 7-2
Asset Classification Summary

Ordinary Income Asset	§ 1221—Capital Asset	§ 1231—Trade or Business
Short-term asset used in a trade or business	Any asset held for investment	Long-term depreciable trade or business property
Inventory	Personal-use property	Long-term land used in the trade or business
Accounts receivable	Not inventory	Not short-term trade or business property
Notes receivable	Not depreciable trade or business property	Not inventory
	Not a copyright*	Not a copyright
	Not accounts receivable	
	Not notes receivable	

* Refer to new election provision for musical compositions and copyrights in musical works.

Typically the sale of inventory appears on the income statement of a business as a cost of goods sold. Gross profit (sales − cost of goods sold) is ordinary income subject to tax and is entered on Schedule C for a sole proprietorship.[7] The collection of an account or note receivable is ordinary income to a cash basis taxpayer when the cash is collected. Neither selling inventory nor collecting accounts or notes receivable requires reporting on Form 4797 or Schedule D. Other assets such as copyrights and literary, musical, and artistic compositions are also ordinary assets in the hands of the creator or artist.

§ 1221 Capital Property (Capital Assets)

In general, a *capital asset* is any asset used for personal purposes or investment.[8] A common example of a capital asset is an investment in stocks or bonds. Other capital assets include these:

- A home owned and occupied by the taxpayer and the taxpayer's family.
- Timber grown on home property or investment property, even if the taxpayer makes only casual sales of the timber.
- Household furnishings.
- A car used for pleasure or commuting.
- Coin or stamp collections, gems, and jewelry.
- Gold, silver, and other metals.[9]

The Internal Revenue Code (IRC) actually defines a capital asset not by what it *is* but by what it is *not*. Capital assets include all assets held by the taxpayer *except:*[10]

1. Those held mainly for sale to customers, including stock in trade, inventory, and other property held mainly for sale to customers in a trade or business.
2. Property used in a trade or business subject to depreciation.
3. A copyright; a literary, musical, or artistic composition; a letter or memorandum; or similar property held by a taxpayer whose personal efforts created the property or, in the case of a letter or memo, for which the letter was prepared.
4. Accounts or notes receivable acquired in the ordinary course of business.
5. Real property used in the taxpayer's trade or business.
6. Any commodities derivative financial instrument held by a dealer.
7. Certain hedging transactions entered in the normal course of a trade or business.
8. Supplies used or consumed by the taxpayer in the ordinary course of a trade or business of the taxpayer.

TAX YOUR BRAIN

Is land a capital asset?

ANSWER

The answer is the typical tax answer—it depends. Land held for investment is a capital asset. However, land used in a trade or business is not a capital asset but a § 1231 asset (discussed in the next section). Additionally, land held for resale by a real estate developer is inventory (an ordinary asset).

[7] The sale, related cost of goods sold, and gross profit are reported directly on Schedule C.

[8] *Publication 544,* Chapter 2.

[9] IRS *Publication 544,* 18.

[10] IRC § 1221.

Musical compositions and copyrights in musical works are generally not capital assets. However, there is an election available to treat these types of property as capital assets if they are sold or exchanged in the years beginning after May 17, 2006, and

- The taxpayer's personal efforts created the property, or
- The taxpayer under certain circumstances (such as by gift) is entitled to the basis of the person who created the property or for whom it was prepared or produced.

By definition, artistic works are specifically not capital assets of the taxpayer who created the property (the artist), but any artistic work purchased is a capital asset in the hands of the purchaser. In all instances of artistic works, copyrights, letters, or publications of the U.S. government, if the taxpayer's basis is determined by reference to the basis of the property in the hands of the creator of the property (such as by gift from the creator), then the property is not a capital asset.[11]

EXAMPLE 7-3

Jacque, a world-renowned artist, painted a lovely new work. He then gave the painting to his current girlfriend as a gift. Because the property is a gift, the girlfriend's basis is the same as the basis to Jacque. Consequently, the painting is not a capital asset to the girlfriend and would be treated as ordinary income property.

Trade or Business Property (§ 1231 Asset)

IRC § 1231 property is depreciable or nondepreciable property (such as land) used in a trade or business and held for more than one year.[12] Land purchased and held for investment (even if purchased through the business) is a capital asset under § 1221.

Timber, coal, domestic iron ore, and certain livestock held for breeding, dairy, or sporting purposes are also considered § 1231 property.[13] The most typical examples of § 1231 assets are machinery and equipment used in a business, business buildings, and business land. If a business asset is disposed of within one year of acquisition, it is treated as a short-term asset, and the amount received for it is considered ordinary income. Furthermore, § 1231 assets do not include property that is considered inventory or artistic works.

EXAMPLE 7-4

Jake, a sole proprietor, purchased a three-acre lot for $55,000. He constructed a building for his business on a portion of the land and used the rest of the land for customer parking. The land, building, and pavement for the parking lot are considered § 1231 property.

CONCEPT CHECK 7-2— LO 7-2

1. Inventory sold by a company is an ordinary income asset that appears on Form 4797—Sale of Business Assets. True or false?
2. A capital asset includes all of the following *except*
   a. A taxpayer's vacation home.
   b. Inherited property.
   c. Property used in a trade or business.
   d. A stock portfolio.
3. An ordinary income asset is any short-term or long-term asset used in a business. True or false?
4. A § 1221 asset is any asset held for investment. True or false?
5. A § 1231 asset is any depreciable or nondepreciable property used in a trade or business and not considered an ordinary income asset. True or false?

[11] IRC § 1221(a)(3)(A), IRC § 1221(a)(5)(B). When property is received by gift, the new basis is determined by the basis (old basis) to the person giving the gift (donor).

[12] IRC § 1231(b)(1).

[13] IRC § 1231(b)(3).

From Shoebox to Software

To report ordinary income or loss from the sale of an ordinary asset, use Form 4797, Part II. The description of the property sold, the date acquired, the date sold, the gross sales price, the depreciation allowed, the cost basis, and the gain or loss are shown on Form 4797. Exhibit 7-1 illustrates the reporting of Examples 7-5 and 7-6. Note that the gains are combined (netted if a loss had occurred) on line 18. If any ordinary gains or losses had resulted from the sale of § 1231 property (discussed later), they would also be included in the final figure on line 18. For an individual taxpayer, the $15,140 ordinary income is reported on line 14 of Form 1040.

TAX PREPARATION SOFTWARE

The sale of a receivable is a unique transaction (it does not happen often in practice). To enter this type of sale in tax preparation software, enter the information directly on Part II of Form 4797. For an asset that has already been entered on Form 4562, Asset Depreciation worksheet (see Chapter 6), simply go to the Asset Depreciation worksheet and enter the date sold. Then click the Asset Disposed Of link and enter the sales price. The depreciation should recalculate, and the gain or loss will appear in the appropriate section of Form 4797.[14]

SALES OF ORDINARY ASSETS

LO 7-3

When an asset is sold (or otherwise disposed of), the gain or loss produced is considered either "ordinary" or "capital." For example, when an ordinary asset is sold, the gain or loss is termed "an ordinary gain or loss." When a capital asset (§ 1221 asset) is sold, the gain or loss is a "capital gain or loss." When a § 1231 asset is sold, the gain can be either ordinary or capital.

Why is the distinction between ordinary and capital so important? The primary reason is that capital gains are taxed at lower capital gains tax rates compared to ordinary gains that are taxed at ordinary rates. Capital losses are also limited in their deductibility.[15] The specifics of ordinary gains and losses, capital gains and losses, and § 1231 gains and losses are described in detail in the following sections.

Recognized Gain or Loss from Ordinary Assets

Recall that the primary ordinary income assets are inventory and accounts receivable. Inventory sold in the normal course of a trade or business generates sales revenue. The cost of the inventory is a deduction (cost of goods sold). The type of transaction discussed in this chapter is the sale of an ordinary asset outside the normal course of business. Typically, ordinary gains or losses produced outside (not part of) the normal course of business relate to the sale of business property held less than one year or the sale of accounts receivable.[16]

EXAMPLE 7-5

Jason is a sole proprietor who needs cash. He decides to sell his outstanding accounts receivable. They have a $10,000 FMV and a zero basis. He is able to sell the receivables on July 1, 2017, for $8,500. Jason recognizes an $8,500 ordinary gain ($8,500 received less $0 basis).

EXAMPLE 7-6

Jason sold some equipment for $22,000 on March 7, 2017, that he had originally purchased for $24,000 on April 8, 2016. The equipment was subject to depreciation of $8,640 for 2016 and 2017. The adjusted basis is $15,360 ($24,000 cost − $8,640 depreciation). Jason recognizes a $6,640 ordinary gain ($22,000 amount realized − $15,360 adjusted basis).

[14] Remember from Chapter 6 that only a half-year of depreciation is allowed in the year of disposal for half-year convention assets. Depreciation for mid-quarter and mid-month convention assets also changes in the year of disposal.

[15] Capital gains and losses are treated differently for corporate taxpayers. The discussion in this chapter pertains exclusively to noncorporate taxpayers.

[16] The sale of § 1231 property where the gain is a result of depreciation taken also produces an ordinary gain. These gains are discussed later in the chapter.

EXHIBIT 7-1 Form 4797 for Examples 7-5 and 7-6

Form **4797**

Department of the Treasury
Internal Revenue Service

Sales of Business Property
(Also Involuntary Conversions and Recapture Amounts Under Sections 179 and 280F(b)(2))

▶ Attach to your tax return.
▶ Go to *www.irs.gov/Form4797* for instructions and the latest information.

OMB No. 1545-0184
2017
Attachment Sequence No. 27

Name(s) shown on return		Identifying number
Jason Taxpayer	For Examples 7-5 and 7-6	412-34-5670

1 Enter the gross proceeds from sales or exchanges reported to you for 2017 on Form(s) 1099-B or 1099-S (or substitute statement) that you are including on line 2, 10, or 20. See instructions . . . **1**

Part I **Sales or Exchanges of Property Used in a Trade or Business and Involuntary Conversions From Other Than Casualty or Theft—Most Property Held More Than 1 Year** (see instructions)

2 (a) Description of property	(b) Date acquired (mo., day, yr.)	(c) Date sold (mo., day, yr.)	(d) Gross sales price	(e) Depreciation allowed or allowable since acquisition	(f) Cost or other basis, plus improvements and expense of sale	(g) Gain or (loss) Subtract (f) from the sum of (d) and (e)

Line	Description	No.	Amount
3	Gain, if any, from Form 4684, line 39	3	
4	Section 1231 gain from installment sales from Form 6252, line 26 or 37	4	
5	Section 1231 gain or (loss) from like-kind exchanges from Form 8824	5	
6	Gain, if any, from line 32, from other than casualty or theft	6	
7	Combine lines 2 through 6. Enter the gain or (loss) here and on the appropriate line as follows:	7	

Partnerships (except electing large partnerships) and S corporations. Report the gain or (loss) following the instructions for Form 1065, Schedule K, line 10, or Form 1120S, Schedule K, line 9. Skip lines 8, 9, 11, and 12 below.

Individuals, partners, S corporation shareholders, and all others. If line 7 is zero or a loss, enter the amount from line 7 on line 11 below and skip lines 8 and 9. If line 7 is a gain and you didn't have any prior year section 1231 losses, or they were recaptured in an earlier year, enter the gain from line 7 as a long-term capital gain on the Schedule D filed with your return and skip lines 8, 9, 11, and 12 below.

Line	Description	No.	Amount
8	Nonrecaptured net section 1231 losses from prior years. See instructions	8	
9	Subtract line 8 from line 7. If zero or less, enter -0-. If line 9 is zero, enter the gain from line 7 on line 12 below. If line 9 is more than zero, enter the amount from line 8 on line 12 below and enter the gain from line 9 as a long-term capital gain on the Schedule D filed with your return. See instructions	9	

Part II **Ordinary Gains and Losses** (see instructions)

10 Ordinary gains and losses not included on lines 11 through 16 (include property held 1 year or less):

Description	Date acquired	Date sold	Gross sales price	Depreciation	Cost or other basis	Gain or (loss)
Accounts Receivable	various	various	8,500	0	0	8,500
Equipment	04/08/16	03/07/17	22,000	8,640	24,000	6,640

Line	Description	No.	Amount
11	Loss, if any, from line 7	11	( )
12	Gain, if any, from line 7 or amount from line 8, if applicable	12	
13	Gain, if any, from line 31	13	
14	Net gain or (loss) from Form 4684, lines 31 and 38a	14	
15	Ordinary gain from installment sales from Form 6252, line 25 or 36	15	
16	Ordinary gain or (loss) from like-kind exchanges from Form 8824	16	
17	Combine lines 10 through 16	17	15,140
18	For all except individual returns, enter the amount from line 17 on the appropriate line of your return and skip lines a and b below. For individual returns, complete lines a and b below:		
a	If the loss on line 11 includes a loss from Form 4684, line 35, column (b)(ii), enter that part of the loss here. Enter the part of the loss from income-producing property on Schedule A (Form 1040), line 28, and the part of the loss from property used as an employee on Schedule A (Form 1040), line 23. Identify as from "Form 4797, line 18a." See instructions	18a	
b	Redetermine the gain or (loss) on line 17 excluding the loss, if any, on line 18a. Enter here and on Form 1040, line 14	18b	15,140

For Paperwork Reduction Act Notice, see separate instructions. Cat. No. 13086I Form **4797** (2017)

Source: U.S. Department of the Treasury, Internal Revenue Service, Form 4797. Washington, DC: 2017.

CONCEPT CHECK 7-3—
LO 7-3

1. When an ordinary asset is sold, the gain or loss is subject to capital gain or loss tax treatment. True or false?
2. Why is the distinction between "ordinary" and "capital" so important?
3. Ordinary gains or losses produced outside the normal course of business relate to the sale of business property held for less than one year or the sale of receivables. True or false?

EXHIBIT 7-2 **Form 8949 and Schedule D for Example 7-14**

Form **8949**

Department of the Treasury
Internal Revenue Service

Sales and Other Dispositions of Capital Assets

▶ Go to *www.irs.gov/Form8949* for instructions and the latest information.

▶ File with your Schedule D to list your transactions for lines 1b, 2, 3, 8b, 9, and 10 of Schedule D.

OMB No. 1545-0074

2017

Attachment Sequence No. **12A**

Name(s) shown on return: **Alan and Cherie Masters**

Social security number or taxpayer identification number: **412-34-5670**

Before you check Box A, B, or C below, see whether you received any Form(s) 1099-B or substitute statement(s) from your broker. A substitute statement will have the same information as Form 1099-B. Either will show whether your basis (usually your cost) was reported to the IRS by your broker and may even tell you which box to check.

Part I **Short-Term.** Transactions involving capital assets you held 1 year or less are short term. For long-term transactions, see page 2.

Note: You may aggregate all short-term transactions reported on Form(s) 1099-B showing basis was reported to the IRS and for which no adjustments or codes are required. Enter the totals directly on Schedule D, line 1a; you aren't required to report these transactions on Form 8949 (see instructions).

You *must* check Box A, B, *or* C below. Check only one box. If more than one box applies for your short-term transactions, complete a separate Form 8949, page 1, for each applicable box. If you have more short-term transactions than will fit on this page for one or more of the boxes, complete as many forms with the same box checked as you need.

☑ **(A)** Short-term transactions reported on Form(s) 1099-B showing basis was reported to the IRS (see **Note** above)
☐ **(B)** Short-term transactions reported on Form(s) 1099-B showing basis **wasn't** reported to the IRS
☐ **(C)** Short-term transactions not reported to you on Form 1099-B

1 (a) Description of property (Example: 100 sh. XYZ Co.)	(b) Date acquired (Mo., day, yr.)	(c) Date sold or disposed of (Mo., day, yr.)	(d) Proceeds (sales price) (see instructions)	(e) Cost or other basis. See the **Note** below and see *Column (e)* in the separate instructions	Adjustment, if any, to gain or loss. If you enter an amount in column (g), enter a code in column (f). See the separate instructions. (f) Code(s) from instructions	(g) Amount of adjustment	(h) Gain or (loss). Subtract column (e) from column (d) and combine the result with column (g)
Stock #1	12/01/16	09/01/17	15,000	9,000			6,000
Stock #2	12/01/16	04/01/17	17,000	25,000			(8,000)
Totals to Schedule D			32,000	34,000			(2,000)

You *must* check Box D, E, *or* F below. Check only one box. If more than one box applies for your long-term transactions, complete a separate Form 8949, page 2, for each applicable box. If you have more long-term transactions than will fit on this page for one or more of the boxes, complete as many forms with the same box checked as you need.

☑ **(D)** Long-term transactions reported on Form(s) 1099-B showing basis was reported to the IRS (see **Note** above)
☐ **(E)** Long-term transactions reported on Form(s) 1099-B showing basis **wasn't** reported to the IRS
☐ **(F)** Long-term transactions not reported to you on Form 1099-B

1 (a) Description of property (Example: 100 sh. XYZ Co.)	(b) Date acquired (Mo., day, yr.)	(c) Date sold or disposed of (Mo., day, yr.)	(d) Proceeds (sales price) (see instructions)	(e) Cost or other basis. See the **Note** below and see *Column (e)* in the separate instructions	Adjustment, if any, to gain or loss. If you enter an amount in column (g), enter a code in column (f). See the separate instructions. (f) Code(s) from instructions	(g) Amount of adjustment	(h) Gain or (loss). Subtract column (e) from column (d) and combine the result with column (g)
Stock #3	06/05/15	12/05/17	38,000	20,000			18,000

You *must* check Box D, E, *or* F below. Check only one box. If more than one box applies for your long-term transactions, complete a separate Form 8949, page 2, for each applicable box. If you have more long-term transactions than will fit on this page for one or more of the boxes, complete as many forms with the same box checked as you need.

☐ **(D)** Long-term transactions reported on Form(s) 1099-B showing basis was reported to the IRS (see **Note** above)
☐ **(E)** Long-term transactions reported on Form(s) 1099-B showing basis **wasn't** reported to the IRS
☑ **(F)** Long-term transactions not reported to you on Form 1099-B

1 (a) Description of property (Example: 100 sh. XYZ Co.)	(b) Date acquired (Mo., day, yr.)	(c) Date sold or disposed of (Mo., day, yr.)	(d) Proceeds (sales price) (see instructions)	(e) Cost or other basis. See the **Note** below and see *Column (e)* in the separate instructions	Adjustment, if any, to gain or loss. If you enter an amount in column (g), enter a code in column (f). See the separate instructions. (f) Code(s) from instructions	(g) Amount of adjustment	(h) Gain or (loss). Subtract column (e) from column (d) and combine the result with column (g)
Collectibles	07/01/16	08/01/17	20,000	14,000			6,000

Source: U.S. Department of the Treasury, Internal Revenue Service, Form 8949 and Schedule D. Washington, DC: 2017.

Excess losses are carried forward to the next year and retain their original character. A short-term loss carries over as a short-term loss, and a long-term loss carries over as a long-term loss.

EXAMPLE 7-13

Mary and John Garcia sold property in 2017. The sale resulted in a long-term loss of $8,000. They had no other capital transactions and filed a joint return for 2017. They had taxable income 2017 of $50,000. The Garcias deduct $3,000 of the loss in 2017. The unused $5,000 of the loss ($8,000 – $3,000) carries over to 2018 as a long-term loss. If their loss had been less than $3,000, there would be no carryover to 2018.

EXAMPLE 7-14

Alan Masters, the taxpayer from previous chapters, had the following capital transactions:

	Purchased	Sold	Sale Price	Basis	Gain/Loss
Stock 1 (held 9 months)	12/01/2016	09/01/2017	$15,000	$ 9,000	$ 6,000
Stock 2 (held 4 months)	12/01/2016	04/01/2017	17,000	25,000	(8,000)
Stock 3 (held 30 months)	06/05/2015	12/05/2017	38,000	20,000	18,000
Collectibles	07/01/2016	08/01/2017	20,000	14,000	6,000

The results follow:

Net short-term capital loss ($8,000 – $6,000)	$ (2,000)
Net long-term capital gain	18,000
28% collectibles capital gain	6,000

The net short-term loss of $2,000 first offsets the 28% gain on the collectibles. The result is a long-term capital gain of $18,000 and a $4,000, 28% gain. The appropriate rates are applied:

$18,000 × 15% = $2,700
$ 4,000 × 28% = 1,120
$3,820 increase in tax due to capital gains

Form 8949, Schedule D, and the 28% gains worksheet are illustrated in Exhibit 7-2.

EXAMPLE 7-15

Assume similar facts from Example 7-14, except that stock 3 was sold for $20,000 with a basis of $38,000, producing a loss of $18,000.

	Purchased	Sold	Sale Price	Basis	Gain/Loss
Stock 1 (9 months)	12/01/2016	09/01/2017	$ 15,000	$ 9,000	$ 6,000
Stock 2 (4 months)	12/01/2016	04/01/2017	17,000	25,000	(8,000)
Stock 3 (30 months)	06/05/2015	12/05/2017	20,000	38,000	(18,000)
Collectibles	07/01/2016	08/01/2017	20,000	14,000	6,000

The results follow:

Net short-term capital loss ($8,000 – $6,000)	$ (2,000)
Net long-term loss against collectibles gain ($18,000) – $6,000	(12,000)

Only $3,000 of the $14,000 loss can be taken this year. The net short-term loss of $2,000 is allowed plus $1,000 of the long-term loss. The $11,000 remaining loss is carried forward indefinitely.

Form 8949 and Schedule D, created from Example 7-15, are shown in Exhibit 7-3.

From Shoebox to Software

When capital gains or losses occur, the taxpayer must file Schedule D to report the gain or loss. The following examples illustrate the preparation of Schedule D.

Taxpayers receive Form 1099-B from corporations and brokerage firms. These forms report information concerning the sale of stock by the taxpayer (see Exhibit 7-7). Often brokerage firms send a "substitute" 1099-B form to report multiple sales transactions occurring throughout the year.

Exhibit 7-2 illustrates the reporting of the gains from Example 7-14 on Form 8949 and Schedule D. A taxpayer who has 28% capital gains also uses the 28% Rate Gain worksheet shown. The taxpayer uses the rates from the tax rate schedules to calculate the tax on the ordinary income and calculates the tax on qualified dividends.

TAX PREPARATION SOFTWARE

Open the tax return for the Masters and go to the forms. Open Schedule D and double-click on the first sales price cell. This will open the Form 1099-B box. The taxpayer receives a sales confirmation after a sale throughout the year and a 1099-B (Brokerage Sales) at year-end from the brokerage company.

Open a new copy for each 1099-B received. Enter the name of the stock, the sales price, the dates purchased, and the dates sold. For the collectibles, make sure you check the box on the bottom of the input form that indicates that the asset sold is a collectible. Tax preparation software will classify the gains as short- or long-term and enter them on the correct section of Schedule D.

full NII of $80,000 because the modified AGI exceeds the threshold by $100,000. The surtax applies to the lower amount, which in this case is $80,000; the additional tax would be $3,040 ($80,000 × 3.8%). The surtax is calculated on Form 1040.

Netting Capital Gains and Capital Losses

After all long- and short-term capital gains and losses have been calculated, they need to be combined in a certain manner before applying special tax rate provisions. First, combine all short-term capital gains and short-term capital losses to obtain a *net* short-term gain or loss. Next, combine all long-term capital gains and losses to obtain a *net* long-term capital gain or loss. Finally, combine the net short-term gain or loss with the net long-term gain or loss. If netting results in a net short-term capital gain and a net long-term capital gain or a net short-term capital loss and a net long-term capital loss, the netting process ends. In this final phase, taxpayers must take care to separate the gains that are taxed at 28% (collectibles and § 1202 gains). If an overall net loss results, IRC § 1211 permits the taxpayer to deduct up to a maximum of $3,000 against other income.[23] IRC § 1212 allows any net loss exceeding $3,000 to be carried over to future years (indefinitely) to offset other capital gains.[24]

The netting process can result in the following outcomes:

- **Net short-term gain and net long-term gain:** Short-term gains are taxed at regular tax rates, and net long-term gains are taxed at the appropriate capital gain rate of 0%, 15%, 20%, 25%, or 28%.
- **Net short-term gain and net long-term loss:** A long-term loss is offset against a short-term gain. If a net short-term gain results, the short-term gain is taxed using regular tax rates. If a long-term loss results, the loss, up to $3,000, reduces other income, and any excess carries forward indefinitely.
- **Net short-term loss and net long-term gain:** In this case, separate the long-term gains into 28%, 25%, 20%, and 15% or 0% groups. Any net short-term loss is first offset against the 28% group, then the 25% group, and if any loss remains, the 20%, 15%, or 0% group.[25]
- **Net short-term loss and net long-term loss:** In this case, only $3,000 of the loss is deductible against other income in any one year. First, the short-term losses are deducted against other income, and if any of the $3,000 maximum remains, deduct the long-term loss up to the maximum $3,000 annual loss limit.

[23] IRC § 1211(b)—only a $1,500 loss is allowed for married taxpayers filing a separate return.

[24] IRC § 1212(b).

[25] IRS Notice 97-59, 1997-2 CB 309.

EXAMPLE 7-10 David purchased a business building in November 2003 for $200,000 and assumes that $69,655 of depreciation was taken on the building. The adjusted basis is $130,345 ($200,000 cost – $69,655 depreciation). If David sold the building for $190,000 in June 2017, the $59,655 gain ($190,000 amount realized – $130,345 adjusted basis) would be a long-term capital gain subject to the 25% rate because the gain is attributable to the depreciation recapture requirement.

EXAMPLE 7-11 If David sold the building for $220,000, the total gain would be $89,655 ($220,000 amount realized – $130,345 adjusted basis). Of that gain, $69,655 would be subject to the 25% rate (the unrecaptured depreciation) and $20,000 would be a § 1231 gain subject to a potential 0% or 15% rate.

The 28% capital gain rate applies to collectibles gains. A *collectibles gain or loss* is a gain or loss from the sale or exchange of a work of art, rug, antique, metal, gem, stamp, coin, or alcoholic beverage held longer than one year.[20]

The 28% rate also applies to § 1202 gains. IRC § 1202 has a provision to limit the taxation on a gain from the sale of *qualified small business (QSB) stock,* which is stock from any domestic corporation whose aggregate gross assets at all times after August 10, 1993, up to the date of issue, have been less than $50,000,000.[21] In the case of a taxpayer other than a corporation who purchased the stock after August 10, 1993, and prior to February 17, 2009, gross income excludes 50% of any gain from the sale or exchange of qualified small business stock held for more than five years.[22] Any remaining gain is taxed at a 28% rate.

EXAMPLE 7-12 Richard invested in a midsize local corporation with gross assets of $15,000,000. He purchased 500 shares for $25,000 in 1998. On April 6, 2017, he sold the stock for $45,000, realizing a gain of $20,000. One-half of the $20,000 gain is excluded from gross income under § 1202. The remaining $10,000 gain is recognized and taxed at a rate of 28%.

There is a 3.8% Medicare Surtax (IRC § 1411) on certain net investment income (NII) on individuals who have modified AGI above a threshold amount. In general, net investment income includes some of the more common types of investments such as interest, dividends, rental, and royalty income. It also includes, but is not limited to, gains from the sale of stocks, bonds, mutual funds, capital gain distributions from mutual funds, and gains from the sale of investment real estate (a second home that is not a primary residence), and sales of interests in passive investments from a partnership or S Corporation.

The 3.8% surtax is imposed on the lesser of:

- Net investment income (NII) for the year, or
- Modified Adjusted Gross Income (MAGI) over $250,000 for married filing jointly and qualifying widow(er) with dependent child; $200,000 for single and head of household (with qualified person); and $125,000 for married filing separately

For example, a single taxpayer who has NII of $40,000 and modified AGI of $180,000 will not be subject to this surtax because the modified AGI did not exceed the threshold amount of $200,000. Remember that the $40,000 is included in the modified AGI calculation. What if the same single taxpayer had NII of $40,000 and modified AGI of $210,000? The surtax would apply because modified AGI is more than the threshold of $200,000. The tax would be applied to the $10,000 amount because it is less than the NII income of $40,000. If the taxpayer had NII of $80,000 and modified AGI of $300,000, the amount of surtax would be calculated on the

[20] IRC § 408(m)(2).

[21] IRC § 1202(d)(1).

[22] IRC § 1202(a). *Note:* For stock acquired after February 17, 2009, and before September 27, 2010, this exclusion is 75%. For stock acquired after September 27, 2010, and before January 1, 2012, this exclusion is 100%. Remember that these exclusion rates are not applicable until the stock has been held for more than five years. This exclusion has been extended for stock acquired before January 1, 2014, and held for more than five years.

TABLE 7-4
Summary of Capital Gain Tax Rates

Source of Net Capital Gain	Post 2012 Sales—the Maximum Capital Gain Rate
Collectibles gain	28%
§ 1202 gain	28
Unrecaptured § 1250 gain	25
Other capital gains when in the 39.6% tax bracket	20
Other capital gains when in the 25% and up to the 39.6% tax bracket	15
Other capital gains when the tax bracket is less than 25%	–0–
Surtax on investment type and gains subject to modified AGI thresholds	3.8

EXAMPLE 7-8

Matthew gave a gift of 500 shares of GM stock to his son, Jim, on November 12, 2016, when the stock was worth $50 per share. Matthew had purchased the stock for $30 per share in 1990. Because the basis to Jim, the son, would be the same as in the hands of Matthew, the father, the holding period for Jim includes Matthew's holding period. Thus Jim's holding period is more than one year, and the stock is considered a long-term capital asset. When Jim sells the stock, any gain will be taxed using capital gain rates

Capital Gain Rates

The taxes on net long-term capital gains are calculated using 15%, 20%, 25%, and 28% rates. The 15% tax rate is for taxpayers in the 25%, 28%, 33%, or 35% regular tax brackets. The rate is 0% for taxpayers who are in the less than 15% tax rate status. In 2017 this 15% gain rate starts when taxable income is over $37,950 for single taxpayers and $75,900 for married taxpayers filing a joint return. In 2017, the rate increases to 20% for taxpayers with income over $418,400 ($470,700 for married taxpayers and $444,550 for heads of households) when the top tax rate of 39.6% applies. The lower rates of 0%, 15%, and 20% are called *maximum capital gain rates.* Table 7-4 summarizes the capital gain tax rates in effect for 2017.

EXAMPLE 7-9

Bill is a married taxpayer who files a joint return. In tax year 2017, his taxable income is $115,000. He sold stock in April 2017 that he had held for four years. The gain on the sale was $30,000. Bill is in the 25% tax bracket, so his $30,000 capital gain is taxed using a 15% tax rate.

The 25% bracket is a special rate that relates to capital gains generated from depreciable real property (buildings) used in a trade or business. The Internal Revenue Code has special tax rules for depreciable real property (buildings) used in a trade or business, called *§ 1250 property.* In general, when depreciable real property is sold for a gain, the taxpayer has to bring back (recapture) as income that part of the gain due to the difference between MACRS depreciation and straight-line depreciation. As of 1987, all § 1250 property is depreciated using the straight-line method; therefore, there is no recapture of depreciation. However, the IRS implemented a special provision for this nonrecaptured depreciation of real property; it is called *unrecaptured § 1250 gain.* Instead of the entire gain from § 1250 real property being taxed at preferential capital gain rates, the gain attributable to any depreciation allowable is taxed at a special 25% rate, and any gain in excess of this amount is given preferential capital gains tax treatment. To avoid the possibility that a taxpayer might get around this special tax provision by not claiming depreciation, the IRS included depreciation recapture in the tax law so the taxpayer must include depreciation deductions whether or not the taxpayer actually took depreciation deductions on the real property. § 1250 property is covered in more detail under LO 7-5 (Sales of Business Property) later in this chapter.

TABLE 7-3
Summary of the Different Holding Periods for Capital Assets

Source: IRS *Publication 544*.

Type of Acquisition	When the Holding Period Starts
Stock or bond purchased on a securities market	The day after the trading day the taxpayer purchased the security.
Nontaxable exchanges	The day after the taxpayer acquired the old property.
Gift	If the taxpayer's basis is the donor's basis, the holding period includes the donor's holding period. If the taxpayer's basis is the FMV, the holding period starts the day after the date of the gift.
Inherited property	The property is considered to be held longer than one year regardless of how long the property was actually held.
Real property purchase	The day after the date the taxpayer received title to the property.
Real property repossessed	The date the taxpayer originally received title to the property, but not including the time between the original sale and the date of repossession.

SALES OF CAPITAL ASSETS

LO 7-4

Recall that a capital asset is any personal-use asset or any asset held for investment that is not one of the exclusions listed earlier. The tax treatment of a capital gain or loss varies depending on several factors:

- The period of time the capital asset is held.
- Whether the sale of the asset produced a gain or loss.
- The type of capital asset sold (for example, collectibles are treated differently).
- The taxpayer's tax bracket.
- The combination (or netting) of all capital gains and losses to derive a net capital gain or a net capital loss.
- Whether a capital asset sold is stock of a qualified small business.

Holding Period of a Capital Asset

Only long-term capital gains receive preferential tax treatment. A *long-term capital asset* is any capital asset held for more than one year.[17] A *short-term capital asset* is any capital asset held for one year or less, and any gain or loss on its sale is taxed using ordinary tax rates. Typically the holding period starts the day after the taxpayer acquired the property and includes the day the property is sold. Table 7-3 summarizes the determination of holding periods for capital assets.

EXAMPLE 7-7

Jackie purchased 100 shares of IBM stock on January 6, 2016. The stock is a long-term asset on January 7, 2017. If the stock is sold prior to January 7, 2017, the gain or loss is short-term and no preferential treatment is applicable on any gain.

Capital assets are typically acquired through a purchase. However, what if an asset is received by gift, nontaxable exchange, or inheritance?[18] Generally, if the property received has the same basis as the basis in the hands of the transferor (the person giving the property), the holding period includes the transferor's holding period. The exception to this rule is for property received by inheritance. Inherited property is *always* long-term property regardless of how long the asset belonged to the decedent or beneficiary.[19]

[17] IRC § 1222(3).

[18] Often when one asset is traded for another asset, no gain or loss is recognized. These are nontaxable exchanges covered in Chapter 12.

[19] IRC § 1223(11).

EXHIBIT 7-2 *(continued)*

SCHEDULE D (Form 1040)

Department of the Treasury Internal Revenue Service (99)

Capital Gains and Losses

▶ Attach to Form 1040 or Form 1040NR.
▶ Go to *www.irs.gov/ScheduleD* for instructions and the latest information.
▶ Use Form 8949 to list your transactions for lines 1b, 2, 3, 8b, 9, and 10.

OMB No. 1545-0074

2017

Attachment Sequence No. 12

Name(s) shown on return	Your social security number
Alan and Cherie Masters	412-34-5670

Part I Short-Term Capital Gains and Losses—Assets Held One Year or Less

See instructions for how to figure the amounts to enter on the lines below. This form may be easier to complete if you round off cents to whole dollars.	(d) Proceeds (sales price)	(e) Cost (or other basis)	(g) Adjustments to gain or loss from Form(s) 8949, Part I, line 2, column (g)	(h) Gain or (loss) Subtract column (e) from column (d) and combine the result with column (g)
1a Totals for all short-term transactions reported on Form 1099-B for which basis was reported to the IRS and for which you have no adjustments (see instructions). However, if you choose to report all these transactions on Form 8949, leave this line blank and go to line 1b .				
1b Totals for all transactions reported on Form(s) 8949 with **Box A** checked	32,000	34,000		(2,000)
2 Totals for all transactions reported on Form(s) 8949 with **Box B** checked				
3 Totals for all transactions reported on Form(s) 8949 with **Box C** checked				

4 Short-term gain from Form 6252 and short-term gain or (loss) from Forms 4684, 6781, and 8824 .	4	
5 Net short-term gain or (loss) from partnerships, S corporations, estates, and trusts from Schedule(s) K-1	5	
6 Short-term capital loss carryover. Enter the amount, if any, from line 8 of your **Capital Loss Carryover Worksheet** in the instructions	6	( )
7 **Net short-term capital gain or (loss).** Combine lines 1a through 6 in column (h). If you have any long-term capital gains or losses, go to Part II below. Otherwise, go to Part III on the back	7	(2,000)

Part II Long-Term Capital Gains and Losses—Assets Held More Than One Year

See instructions for how to figure the amounts to enter on the lines below. This form may be easier to complete if you round off cents to whole dollars.	(d) Proceeds (sales price)	(e) Cost (or other basis)	(g) Adjustments to gain or loss from Form(s) 8949, Part II, line 2, column (g)	(h) Gain or (loss) Subtract column (e) from column (d) and combine the result with column (g)
8a Totals for all long-term transactions reported on Form 1099-B for which basis was reported to the IRS and for which you have no adjustments (see instructions). However, if you choose to report all these transactions on Form 8949, leave this line blank and go to line 8b .				
8b Totals for all transactions reported on Form(s) 8949 with **Box D** checked	38,000	20,000		18,000
9 Totals for all transactions reported on Form(s) 8949 with **Box E** checked				
10 Totals for all transactions reported on Form(s) 8949 with **Box F** checked.	20,000	14,000		6,000

11 Gain from Form 4797, Part I; long-term gain from Forms 2439 and 6252; and long-term gain or (loss) from Forms 4684, 6781, and 8824	11	
12 Net long-term gain or (loss) from partnerships, S corporations, estates, and trusts from Schedule(s) K-1	12	
13 Capital gain distributions. See the instructions	13	
14 Long-term capital loss carryover. Enter the amount, if any, from line 13 of your **Capital Loss Carryover Worksheet** in the instructions	14	( )
15 **Net long-term capital gain or (loss).** Combine lines 8a through 14 in column (h). Then go to Part III on the back .	15	24,000

For Paperwork Reduction Act Notice, see your tax return instructions. Cat. No. 11338H **Schedule D (Form 1040) 2017**

(continued)

EXHIBIT 7-2 *(concluded)*

Schedule D (Form 1040) 2017 Page **2**

Part III Summary

16	Combine lines 7 and 15 and enter the result	16	22,000
	• If line 16 is a **gain,** enter the amount from line 16 on Form 1040, line 13, or Form 1040NR, line 14. Then go to line 17 below. • If line 16 is a **loss,** skip lines 17 through 20 below. Then go to line 21. Also be sure to complete line 22. • If line 16 is **zero,** skip lines 17 through 21 below and enter -0- on Form 1040, line 13, or Form 1040NR, line 14. Then go to line 22.		
17	Are lines 15 and 16 **both** gains? ☑ **Yes.** Go to line 18. ☐ **No.** Skip lines 18 through 21, and go to line 22.		
18	If you are required to complete the **28% Rate Gain Worksheet** (see instructions), enter the amount, if any, from line 7 of that worksheet ▶	18	4,000
19	If you are required to complete the **Unrecaptured Section 1250 Gain Worksheet** (see instructions), enter the amount, if any, from line 18 of that worksheet ▶	19	
20	Are lines 18 and 19 **both** zero or blank? ☐ **Yes.** Complete the **Qualified Dividends and Capital Gain Tax Worksheet** in the instructions for Form 1040, line 44 (or in the instructions for Form 1040NR, line 42). **Don't** complete lines 21 and 22 below. ☑ **No.** Complete the **Schedule D Tax Worksheet** in the instructions. **Don't** complete lines 21 and 22 below.		
21	If line 16 is a loss, enter here and on Form 1040, line 13, or Form 1040NR, line 14, the **smaller** of: • The loss on line 16 or • ($3,000), or if married filing separately, ($1,500) **Note:** When figuring which amount is smaller, treat both amounts as positive numbers.	21	( )
22	Do you have qualified dividends on Form 1040, line 9b, or Form 1040NR, line 10b? ☐ **Yes.** Complete the **Qualified Dividends and Capital Gain Tax Worksheet** in the instructions for Form 1040, line 44 (or in the instructions for Form 1040NR, line 42). ☐ **No.** Complete the rest of Form 1040 or Form 1040NR.		

Schedule D (Form 1040) 2017

28% Rate Gain Worksheet—Line 18

Keep for Your Records

1.	Enter the total of all collectibles gain or (loss) from items you reported on Form 8949, Part II	1.	6,000
2.	Enter as a positive number the total of: • Any section 1202 exclusion you reported in column (g) of Form 8949, Part II, with code "Q" in column (f), that is 50% of the gain; • ⅔ of any section 1202 exclusion you reported in column (g) of Form 8949, Part II, with code "Q" in column (f), that is 60% of the gain; and • ⅓ of any section 1202 exclusion you reported in column (g) of Form 8949, Part II, with code "Q" in column (f), that is 75% of the gain. Don't make an entry for any section 1202 exclusion that is 100% of the gain.	2.	0
3.	Enter the total of all collectibles gain or (loss) from Form 4684, line 4 (but only if Form 4684, line 15, is more than zero); Form 6252; Form 6781, Part II; and Form 8824	3.	0
4.	Enter the total of any collectibles gain reported to you on: • Form 1099-DIV, box 2d; • Form 2439, box 1d; and • Schedule K-1 from a partnership, S corporation, estate, or trust.	4.	0
5.	Enter your long-term capital loss carryovers from Schedule D, line 14, and Schedule K-1 (Form 1041), box 11, code C	5.	(0)
6.	If Schedule D, line 7, is a (loss), enter that (loss) here. Otherwise, enter -0-	6.	(2,000)
7.	Combine lines 1 through 6. If zero or less, enter -0-. If more than zero, also enter this amount on Schedule D, line 18	7.	4,000

EXHIBIT 7-3 Schedule D and Capital Loss Carryover Worksheet for Example 7-15

Form **8949** Department of the Treasury Internal Revenue Service

Sales and Other Dispositions of Capital Assets

▶ Go to *www.irs.gov/Form8949* for instructions and the latest information.
▶ File with your Schedule D to list your transactions for lines 1b, 2, 3, 8b, 9, and 10 of Schedule D.

OMB No. 1545-0074 **2017** Attachment Sequence No. **12A**

Name(s) shown on return: Alan and Cherie Masters | Social security number or taxpayer identification number: 412-34-5670

Before you check Box A, B, or C below, see whether you received any Form(s) 1099-B or substitute statement(s) from your broker. A substitute statement will have the same information as Form 1099-B. Either will show whether your basis (usually your cost) was reported to the IRS by your broker and may even tell you which box to check.

Part I **Short-Term.** Transactions involving capital assets you held 1 year or less are short term. For long-term transactions, see page 2.

Note: You may aggregate all short-term transactions reported on Form(s) 1099-B showing basis was reported to the IRS and for which no adjustments or codes are required. Enter the totals directly on Schedule D, line 1a; you aren't required to report these transactions on Form 8949 (see instructions).

You *must* check Box A, B, *or* C below. Check only one box. If more than one box applies for your short-term transactions, complete a separate Form 8949, page 1, for each applicable box. If you have more short-term transactions than will fit on this page for one or more of the boxes, complete as many forms with the same box checked as you need.

☑ **(A)** Short-term transactions reported on Form(s) 1099-B showing basis was reported to the IRS (see **Note** above)
☐ **(B)** Short-term transactions reported on Form(s) 1099-B showing basis **wasn't** reported to the IRS
☐ **(C)** Short-term transactions not reported to you on Form 1099-B

1 (a) Description of property (Example: 100 sh. XYZ Co.)	(b) Date acquired (Mo., day, yr.)	(c) Date sold or disposed of (Mo., day, yr.)	(d) Proceeds (sales price) (see instructions)	(e) Cost or other basis. See the **Note** below and see *Column (e)* in the separate instructions	Adjustment, if any, to gain or loss. If you enter an amount in column (g), enter a code in column (f). See the separate instructions. (f) Code(s) from instructions	(g) Amount of adjustment	(h) Gain or (loss). Subtract column (e) from column (d) and combine the result with column (g)
Stock #1	12/01/16	09/01/17	15,000	9,000			6,000
Stock #2	12/01/16	04/01/17	17,000	25,000			(8,000)
Totals to Schedule D			32,000	34,000			(2,000)

You *must* check Box D, E, *or* F below. Check only one box. If more than one box applies for your long-term transactions, complete a separate Form 8949, page 2, for each applicable box. If you have more long-term transactions than will fit on this page for one or more of the boxes, complete as many forms with the same box checked as you need.

☑ **(D)** Long-term transactions reported on Form(s) 1099-B showing basis was reported to the IRS (see **Note** above)
☐ **(E)** Long-term transactions reported on Form(s) 1099-B showing basis **wasn't** reported to the IRS
☐ **(F)** Long-term transactions not reported to you on Form 1099-B

1 (a) Description of property (Example: 100 sh. XYZ Co.)	(b) Date acquired (Mo., day, yr.)	(c) Date sold or disposed of (Mo., day, yr.)	(d) Proceeds (sales price) (see instructions)	(e) Cost or other basis. See the **Note** below and see *Column (e)* in the separate instructions	Adjustment, if any, to gain or loss. If you enter an amount in column (g), enter a code in column (f). See the separate instructions. (f) Code(s) from instructions	(g) Amount of adjustment	(h) Gain or (loss). Subtract column (e) from column (d) and combine the result with column (g)
Stock #3	06/05/15	12/05/17	20,000	38,000			(18,000)

You *must* check Box D, E, *or* F below. Check only one box. If more than one box applies for your long-term transactions, complete a separate Form 8949, page 2, for each applicable box. If you have more long-term transactions than will fit on this page for one or more of the boxes, complete as many forms with the same box checked as you need.

☐ **(D)** Long-term transactions reported on Form(s) 1099-B showing basis was reported to the IRS (see **Note** above)
☐ **(E)** Long-term transactions reported on Form(s) 1099-B showing basis **wasn't** reported to the IRS
☑ **(F)** Long-term transactions not reported to you on Form 1099-B

1 (a) Description of property (Example: 100 sh. XYZ Co.)	(b) Date acquired (Mo., day, yr.)	(c) Date sold or disposed of (Mo., day, yr.)	(d) Proceeds (sales price) (see instructions)	(e) Cost or other basis. See the **Note** below and see *Column (e)* in the separate instructions	Adjustment, if any, to gain or loss. If you enter an amount in column (g), enter a code in column (f). See the separate instructions. (f) Code(s) from instructions	(g) Amount of adjustment	(h) Gain or (loss). Subtract column (e) from column (d) and combine the result with column (g)
Collectibles	07/01/16	08/01/17	20,000	14,000			6,000

Source: U.S. Department of the Treasury, Internal Revenue Service, Form 8949. Washington, DC: 2017.

(continued)

EXHIBIT 7-3 *(continued)*

SCHEDULE D (Form 1040)

Department of the Treasury
Internal Revenue Service (99)

Capital Gains and Losses

► Attach to Form 1040 or Form 1040NR.
► Go to *www.irs.gov/ScheduleD* for instructions and the latest information.
► Use Form 8949 to list your transactions for lines 1b, 2, 3, 8b, 9, and 10.

OMB No. 1545-0074
2017
Attachment Sequence No. 12

Name(s) shown on return: Alan and Cherie Masters
Your social security number: 412-34-5670

Part I Short-Term Capital Gains and Losses—Assets Held One Year or Less

See instructions for how to figure the amounts to enter on the lines below. This form may be easier to complete if you round off cents to whole dollars.	(d) Proceeds (sales price)	(e) Cost (or other basis)	(g) Adjustments to gain or loss from Form(s) 8949, Part I, line 2, column (g)	(h) Gain or (loss) Subtract column (e) from column (d) and combine the result with column (g)
1a Totals for all short-term transactions reported on Form 1099-B for which basis was reported to the IRS and for which you have no adjustments (see instructions). However, if you choose to report all these transactions on Form 8949, leave this line blank and go to line 1b				
1b Totals for all transactions reported on Form(s) 8949 with **Box A** checked	32,000	34,000		(2,000)
2 Totals for all transactions reported on Form(s) 8949 with **Box B** checked				
3 Totals for all transactions reported on Form(s) 8949 with **Box C** checked				

4 Short-term gain from Form 6252 and short-term gain or (loss) from Forms 4684, 6781, and 8824	4	
5 Net short-term gain or (loss) from partnerships, S corporations, estates, and trusts from Schedule(s) K-1	5	
6 Short-term capital loss carryover. Enter the amount, if any, from line 8 of your **Capital Loss Carryover Worksheet** in the instructions	6	( )
7 **Net short-term capital gain or (loss).** Combine lines 1a through 6 in column (h). If you have any long-term capital gains or losses, go to Part II below. Otherwise, go to Part III on the back	7	(2,000)

Part II Long-Term Capital Gains and Losses—Assets Held More Than One Year

See instructions for how to figure the amounts to enter on the lines below. This form may be easier to complete if you round off cents to whole dollars.	(d) Proceeds (sales price)	(e) Cost (or other basis)	(g) Adjustments to gain or loss from Form(s) 8949, Part II, line 2, column (g)	(h) Gain or (loss) Subtract column (e) from column (d) and combine the result with column (g)
8a Totals for all long-term transactions reported on Form 1099-B for which basis was reported to the IRS and for which you have no adjustments (see instructions). However, if you choose to report all these transactions on Form 8949, leave this line blank and go to line 8b				
8b Totals for all transactions reported on Form(s) 8949 with **Box D** checked	20,000	38,000		(18,000)
9 Totals for all transactions reported on Form(s) 8949 with **Box E** checked				
10 Totals for all transactions reported on Form(s) 8949 with **Box F** checked	20,000	14,000		6,000

11 Gain from Form 4797, Part I; long-term gain from Forms 2439 and 6252; and long-term gain or (loss) from Forms 4684, 6781, and 8824	11	
12 Net long-term gain or (loss) from partnerships, S corporations, estates, and trusts from Schedule(s) K-1	12	
13 Capital gain distributions. See the instructions	13	
14 Long-term capital loss carryover. Enter the amount, if any, from line 13 of your **Capital Loss Carryover Worksheet** in the instructions	14	( )
15 **Net long-term capital gain or (loss).** Combine lines 8a through 14 in column (h). Then go to Part III on the back	15	(12,000)

For Paperwork Reduction Act Notice, see your tax return instructions. Cat. No. 11338H **Schedule D (Form 1040) 2017**

EXHIBIT 7-3 *(concluded)*

Schedule D (Form 1040) 2017 — Page **2**

Part III Summary

16 Combine lines 7 and 15 and enter the result **16** (14,000)

- If line 16 is a **gain,** enter the amount from line 16 on Form 1040, line 13, or Form 1040NR, line 14. Then go to line 17 below.
- If line 16 is a **loss,** skip lines 17 through 20 below. Then go to line 21. Also be sure to complete line 22.
- If line 16 is **zero,** skip lines 17 through 21 below and enter -0- on Form 1040, line 13, or Form 1040NR, line 14. Then go to line 22.

17 Are lines 15 and 16 **both** gains?

☐ **Yes.** Go to line 18.

☐ **No.** Skip lines 18 through 21, and go to line 22.

18 If you are required to complete the **28% Rate Gain Worksheet** (see instructions), enter the amount, if any, from line 7 of that worksheet . . . . . ▶ **18**

19 If you are required to complete the **Unrecaptured Section 1250 Gain Worksheet** (see instructions), enter the amount, if any, from line 18 of that worksheet . . . . . ▶ **19**

20 Are lines 18 and 19 **both** zero or blank?

☐ **Yes.** Complete the **Qualified Dividends and Capital Gain Tax Worksheet** in the instructions for Form 1040, line 44 (or in the instructions for Form 1040NR, line 42). **Don't** complete lines 21 and 22 below.

☐ **No.** Complete the **Schedule D Tax Worksheet** in the instructions. **Don't** complete lines 21 and 22 below.

21 If line 16 is a loss, enter here and on Form 1040, line 13, or Form 1040NR, line 14, the **smaller** of:

- The loss on line 16 or
- ($3,000), or if married filing separately, ($1,500)

. . . . . **21** (3,000)

Note: When figuring which amount is smaller, treat both amounts as positive numbers.

22 Do you have qualified dividends on Form 1040, line 9b, or Form 1040NR, line 10b?

☐ **Yes.** Complete the **Qualified Dividends and Capital Gain Tax Worksheet** in the instructions for Form 1040, line 44 (or in the instructions for Form 1040NR, line 42).

☐ **No.** Complete the rest of Form 1040 or Form 1040NR.

Schedule D (Form 1040) 2017

CONCEPT CHECK 7-4— LO 7-4

1. The tax treatment of a capital gain or loss varies, depending on all of the following *except*
   a. The holding period.
   b. The basis of the asset sold.
   c. The taxpayer's tax bracket.
   d. The netting of all gains and losses.
2. If property received has the same basis as the basis in the hands of the transferor, the holding period includes the holding period of the transferor. True or false?
3. The holding period of inherited property can be either short-term or long-term to the beneficiary. True or false?
4. The 3.8% surtax is charged on long-term capital gains only if a taxpayer is in the top tax bracket. True or false?
5. For sales after 2012, what are the maximum capital gain rates on the following?
   a. Collectibles gains.
   b. § 1202 gains.
   c. Unrecaptured § 1250 gains.
   d. Taxpayer's regular tax rate is ≥ 25% and < 39.6%.
   e. Taxpayer's regular tax rate is < 25%.
   f. Taxpayer's regular tax rate is < 35%.

SALES OF BUSINESS PROPERTY
LO 7-5

§ 1231 assets are assets used in a trade or business that are held longer than one year. The sales treatment of a § 1231 asset varies depending on three factors:

1. Whether the asset was sold at a gain or loss.
2. If a gain, whether the asset had been depreciated.
3. Whether the asset was depreciable real property (such as a building) or depreciable personal property (such as equipment).

As with capital assets, gains and losses from the sale of § 1231 assets must be netted. If a net § 1231 gain results, the net gain is taxed as a long-term capital gain subject to the depreciation recapture provisions discussed in the next section.[26] Thus net § 1231 gains receive preferential tax rate treatment. If a net § 1231 loss results, the loss is treated as an ordinary loss. Ordinary loss treatment allows an unlimited loss deduction rather than the $3,000 limit placed on capital losses. The sale of § 1231 assets (both gains and losses) is initially reported on Form 4797.

EXAMPLE 7-16

Josh sold land used in his trade or business for $15,000 in 2017. He had purchased the land in 1990 for $7,000. The $8,000 gain is a § 1231 gain and goes on Form 4797, Part I. The $8,000 gain would be netted with other § 1231 transactions, and if a net § 1231 gain results, the gain is transferred to Schedule D as a long-term capital gain. If the netted transactions result in a net § 1231 loss, the loss from Form 4797 is transferred to Form 1040, page 1, as an ordinary loss.

[26] IRC § 1231(a)(1).

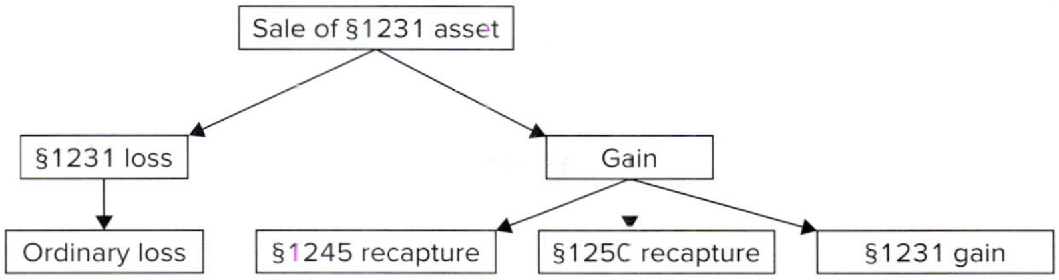

Recapture Provisions

The term *depreciation recapture* can be a difficult concept to understand. Recall from Chapter 6 that depreciation is an income tax deduction that permits the taxpayer to recover the cost or other basis of an asset used in a trade or business. The longer the taxpayer owns and uses the property, the more cost is "recovered"; therefore, the adjusted basis is reduced. The lower the adjusted basis, the greater the gain to be included in the taxpayer's taxable income. When the taxpayer sells § 1231 property for a gain, this gain can qualify for capital gain tax preference. The position of the IRS is that if a taxpayer was allowed to reduce taxable income by taking a depreciation deduction and paid less in taxes, when the property is sold, some of that gain attributable to depreciation deductions should be taxed at regular rates; this is depreciation recapture. The theory is to transform (recapture), as ordinary income, the portion of a gain that was created by taking a deduction for depreciation. For personal property (§ 1245 property) used in a business, this gain attributable to depreciation is taxed as ordinary income, whereas the gain attributable to depreciation for real property (§ 1250 property) is taxed at a special rate of 25%. Note that when a § 1231 asset is sold at a loss, the loss is always treated as an ordinary loss provided there are no § 1231 gains to offset the loss. The chart above illustrates the treatment of gains or losses on depreciable § 1231 assets. Recall that the only § 1231 asset that is not depreciated is land.

§ 1245 Recapture

§ 1245 property is personal trade or business property subject to depreciation. This definition encompasses most assets used in a trade or business with the exception of real property. Land, buildings, and building structural components (with the exception to be noted) are *not* included as § 1245 property. Although the most common example of § 1245 property is machinery and equipment used in a business, the § 1245 definition also includes such assets as autos, livestock, and certain buildings placed in service between 1981 and 1986.[27] The general rule concerning § 1245 recapture is that any gain recognized on the sale of § 1245 property is "ordinary" to the extent of depreciation taken.

For example, in May 2015, a taxpayer purchased a truck to be used 100% in a trade or business (5-year property) for $10,000. Using MACRS and the half-year convention, $6,160 of depreciation was taken. In May 2017, the truck was sold for $7,000. Here is how the gain on the sale is calculated and taxed:

Truck cost basis	$10,000
Less depreciation	6,160
Adjusted basis	$ 3,840
Selling price	$ 7,000
Less adjusted basis	3,840
Realized gain	$ 3,160

[27] IRC § 1245(a)(3). The only buildings considered § 1245 property are buildings placed in service from 1981 through 1986 and depreciated under the 15-, 18-, or 19-year ACRS rules.

From Shoebox to Software

Tax preparation software makes most of the calculations for you. When a § 1245 asset is sold, simply go to the asset's Form 4562—Asset Depreciation worksheet and double-click on the Asset Disposed of icon. Enter the date sold and the proceeds from the sale. The gain and recapture amounts will automatically be calculated and placed in the appropriate section of Form 4797. This transaction cannot be done for existing clients Alan and Cherie Masters because none of Alan's business assets have been held longer than one year. Thus do not enter this transaction on the Masters' tax return file.

The gain treated as ordinary income is the lesser of the depreciation taken ($6,160) or the realized gain ($3,160); in this example, that would be $3,160. In practice, however, a § 1231 gain (in excess of depreciation) on § 1245 property is unusual because equipment rarely appreciates, and any gain is usually caused by the depreciation taken.

EXAMPLE 7-17

On May 1, 2015, Jason purchased equipment costing $12,000 for his business. Depreciation deducted on the equipment from 2015 to 2017 was $7,392; the adjusted basis of the equipment is $4,608. Using the following independent situations, calculate the amount of any gain or loss assuming the equipment was sold on July 8, 2017, for the following amounts:

Situation	Amount Realized	Adjusted Basis ($12,000 – $7,392) (Cost – Depreciation)	Gain (Loss)	§ 1245 Recapture*	§ 1231 Gain/Loss
1	$13,000	$4,608	$8,392	$7,392	$1,000
2	$ 9,000	$4,608	$4,392	$4,392	–0–
3	$ 4,000	$4,608	$ (608)	–0–	$ (608) Ordinary loss/ no recapture

* Amount up to depreciation taken or allowed.

Exhibit 7-4 shows the reporting of the first sale situation in Example 7-17 on Form 4797. The sale and total gain appear on Part III, lines 19–24. Lines 25a and 25b separate the recapture amount. The ordinary income of $7,392 is transferred to Part II on page 1 of Form 4797, and the § 1231 gain of $1,000 is transferred to Part I on page 1 of Form 4797. Business property sales that occur during the year are netted, and these netted gains and losses are reported on page 1 of Form 4797.

§ 1250 Recapture

The phrase "§ 1250 recapture" refers to the portion of the capital gain from § 1250 property representing the tax benefit of a depreciation deduction previously taken. § 1250 property includes depreciable real property used in a trade or business that has never been considered § 1245 property. Thus § 1250 property includes all buildings, residential and nonresidential, used in a business or for the production of income.[28] The general rule for § 1250 recapture is that any gain on § 1250 property is considered ordinary to the extent the depreciation taken exceeds straight-line depreciation. Any other gain is considered § 1231 gain.

[28] One exception is for buildings placed in service from 1981 through 1986, as noted in footnote 27.

EXHIBIT 7-4 Example of § 1245 Recapture on Form 4797 from Example 7-17, Situation

Form **4797** — **Sales of Business Property** (Also Involuntary Conversions and Recapture Amounts Under Sections 179 and 280F(b)(2))

Department of the Treasury Internal Revenue Service

▶ Attach to your tax return.
▶ Go to *www.irs.gov/Form4797* for instructions and the latest information.

OMB No. 1545-0184 — **2017** — Attachment Sequence No. **27**

Name(s) shown on return		Identifying number
Jason Taxpayer	Information from Example 7-17, Situation 1	412-34-5670

1	Enter the gross proceeds from sales or exchanges reported to you for 2017 on Form(s) 1099-B or 1099-S (or substitute statement) that you are including on line 2, 10, or 20. See instructions	1	

Part I Sales or Exchanges of Property Used in a Trade or Business and Involuntary Conversions From Other Than Casualty or Theft—Most Property Held More Than 1 Year (see instructions)

2	(a) Description of property	(b) Date acquired (mo., day, yr.)	(c) Date sold (mo., day, yr.)	(d) Gross sales price	(e) Depreciation allowed or allowable since acquisition	(f) Cost or other basis, plus improvements and expense of sale	(g) Gain or (loss) Subtract (f) from the sum of (d) and (e)

3	Gain, if any, from Form 4684, line 39	3	
4	Section 1231 gain from installment sales from Form 6252, line 26 or 37	4	
5	Section 1231 gain or (loss) from like-kind exchanges from Form 8824	5	
6	Gain, if any, from line 32, from other than casualty or theft	6	1,000
7	Combine lines 2 through 6. Enter the gain or (loss) here and on the appropriate line as follows:	7	1,000
	Partnerships (except electing large partnerships) and S corporations. Report the gain or (loss) following the instructions for Form 1065, Schedule K, line 10, or Form 1120S, Schedule K, line 9. Skip lines 8, 9, 11, and 12 below.		
	Individuals, partners, S corporation shareholders, and all others. If line 7 is zero or a loss, enter the amount from line 7 on line 11 below and skip lines 8 and 9. If line 7 is a gain and you didn't have any prior year section 1231 losses, or they were recaptured in an earlier year, enter the gain from line 7 as a long-term capital gain on the Schedule D filed with your return and skip lines 8, 9, 11, and 12 below.		
8	Nonrecaptured net section 1231 losses from prior years. See instructions	8	
9	Subtract line 8 from line 7. If zero or less, enter -0-. If line 9 is zero, enter the gain from line 7 on line 12 below. If line 9 is more than zero, enter the amount from line 8 on line 12 below and enter the gain from line 9 as a long-term capital gain on the Schedule D filed with your return. See instructions	9	

Part II Ordinary Gains and Losses (see instructions)

10 Ordinary gains and losses not included on lines 11 through 16 (include property held 1 year or less):

11	Loss, if any, from line 7	11	( )
12	Gain, if any, from line 7 or amount from line 8, if applicable	12	
13	Gain, if any, from line 31	13	7,392
14	Net gain or (loss) from Form 4684, lines 31 and 38a	14	
15	Ordinary gain from installment sales from Form 6252, line 25 or 36	15	
16	Ordinary gain or (loss) from like-kind exchanges from Form 8824	16	
17	Combine lines 10 through 16	17	7,392
18	For all except individual returns, enter the amount from line 17 on the appropriate line of your return and skip lines a and b below. For individual returns, complete lines a and b below:		
a	If the loss on line 11 includes a loss from Form 4684, line 35, column (b)(ii), enter that part of the loss here. Enter the part of the loss from income-producing property on Schedule A (Form 1040), line 28, and the part of the loss from property used as an employee on Schedule A (Form 1040), line 23. Identify as from "Form 4797, line 18a." See instructions	18a	
b	Redetermine the gain or (loss) on line 17 excluding the loss, if any, on line 18a. Enter here and on Form 1040, line 14	18b	7,392

For Paperwork Reduction Act Notice, see separate instructions. Cat. No. 13086I Form **4797** (2017)

Source: U.S. Department of the Treasury, Internal Revenue Service, Form 4797. Washington, DC: 2017.

(continued)

EXHIBIT 7-4 *(continued)*

Form 4797 (2017) Page **2**

Part III Gain From Disposition of Property Under Sections 1245, 1250, 1252, 1254, and 1255 (see instructions)

19	(a) Description of section 1245, 1250, 1252, 1254, or 1255 property:	(b) Date acquired (mo., day, yr.)	(c) Date sold (mo., day, yr.)
A	Equipment	05/01/15	07/08/17
B			
C			
D			

	These columns relate to the properties on lines 19A through 19D. ▶		Property A	Property B	Property C	Property D
20	Gross sales price (**Note:** *See line 1 before completing.*)	20	13,000			
21	Cost or other basis plus expense of sale	21	13,000			
22	Depreciation (or depletion) allowed or allowable	22	7,392			
23	Adjusted basis. Subtract line 22 from line 21	23	4,608			
24	Total gain. Subtract line 23 from line 20	24	8,392			
25	**If section 1245 property:**					
a	Depreciation allowed or allowable from line 22	25a	7,392			
b	Enter the **smaller** of line 24 or 25a	25b	7,392			
26	**If section 1250 property:** If straight line depreciation was used, enter -0- on line 26g, except for a corporation subject to section 291.					
a	Additional depreciation after 1975. See instructions	26a				
b	Applicable percentage multiplied by the **smaller** of line 24 or line 26a. See instructions	26b				
c	Subtract line 26a from line 24. If residential rental property **or** line 24 isn't more than line 26a, skip lines 26d and 26e	26c				
d	Additional depreciation after 1969 and before 1976	26d				
e	Enter the **smaller** of line 26c or 26d	26e				
f	Section 291 amount (corporations only)	26f				
g	Add lines 26b, 26e, and 26f	26g				
27	**If section 1252 property:** Skip this section if you didn't dispose of farmland or if this form is being completed for a partnership (other than an electing large partnership).					
a	Soil, water, and land clearing expenses	27a				
b	Line 27a multiplied by applicable percentage. See instructions	27b				
c	Enter the **smaller** of line 24 or 27b	27c				
28	**If section 1254 property:**					
a	Intangible drilling and development costs, expenditures for development of mines and other natural deposits, mining exploration costs, and depletion. See instructions	28a				
b	Enter the **smaller** of line 24 or 28a	28b				
29	**If section 1255 property:**					
a	Applicable percentage of payments excluded from income under section 126. See instructions	29a				
b	Enter the **smaller** of line 24 or 29a. See instructions	29b				

Summary of Part III Gains. Complete property columns A through D through line 29b before going to line 30.

30	Total gains for all properties. Add property columns A through D, line 24	30	8,392
31	Add property columns A through D, lines 25b, 26g, 27c, 28b, and 29b. Enter here and on line 13	31	7,392
32	Subtract line 31 from line 30. Enter the portion from casualty or theft on Form 4684, line 33. Enter the portion from other than casualty or theft on Form 4797, line 6	32	1,000

Part IV Recapture Amounts Under Sections 179 and 280F(b)(2) When Business Use Drops to 50% or Less (see instructions)

			(a) Section 179	(b) Section 280F(b)(2)
33	Section 179 expense deduction or depreciation allowable in prior years	33		
34	Recomputed depreciation. See instructions	34		
35	Recapture amount. Subtract line 34 from line 33. See the instructions for where to report	35		

Form **4797** (2017)

TAX YOUR BRAIN

Why are fewer building sales resulting in ordinary gains for taxpayers?

ANSWER

The main reason is that any depreciable real property purchased after 1986 must be depreciated using the straight-line method.[29] If the required depreciation is straight-line, there cannot be any depreciation in *excess* of straight-line.

In recent years, few § 1250 sales have been subject to the § 1250 recapture provisions. Most real property placed in service from 1981 through 1986 used accelerated depreciation methods over periods of 15, 18, or 19 years. Although it is likely that the same taxpayers still own many of these buildings, recall that these properties are considered § 1245 property. Most other buildings placed in service prior to 1981 are likely to be fully depreciated under either straight-line or some other method.[30] Thus the depreciation taken would be the same under all methods.

The more important aspect of § 1250 property in recent years is the capital gain rate applied to the gain. The term *unrecaptured* refers to the amount of capital gain attributable to depreciation previously taken and is taxed at a 25% capital gain rate rather than the 0%, 15%, or 20% rate. For example, in February 2008, a taxpayer purchased for $200,000 a building to be used 100% in a trade or business (39-year property) and took $48,296 in total depreciation deductions. In July 2017, the taxpayer sold the building for $275,000. Assume the taxpayer is in the 33% tax bracket and is not subject to the surtax. Here is how the gain on the sale is calculated and taxed:

Building cost basis	$200,000
Less depreciation	48,296
Adjusted basis	$151,704
Selling price	$275,000
Less adjusted basis	151,704
Realized gain	$123,296
Realized gain	$123,296
Less § 1250 provision	48,296
Gain on § 1231 asset	$ 75,000

The gain treated as income subject to the 25% tax is the lesser of the depreciation taken ($48,296) or the realized gain ($123,296); in this example, that would be $48,296 taxed at a rate of 25%, resulting in $12,074 tax. If this was the only sale of a § 1231 asset, the remaining $75,000 gain due to the appreciation in value (selling price $275,000 – cost basis $200,000) would qualify for the 15% rate, resulting in $11,250 additional tax. Given this example, the total tax liability on the sale of the building would be $23,324. If there were no recapture provisions, the entire $123,296 gain would have been taxed at the 15% rate, generating only $18,494 in tax liability.

The portion of the gain that is attributable to depreciation is taxed at 25%; any gain in excess of the depreciation taken is considered a normal § 1231 gain and is potentially taxed at the preferential rate of 0%, 15%, or 20%.

[29] Recall from Chapter 6 that the required MACRS depreciation for nonresidential real property is 39-year straight-line for property acquired after May 13, 1993, and the required method for residential real property is 27.5-year straight-line.

[30] If the § 1250 property purchased before 1981 is not fully depreciated, it will be late in its depreciation life. Because most accelerated methods for tax purposes switch to straight-line late in the asset's life or the depreciation allowed goes below straight-line, any possible recapture would be limited.

EXAMPLE 7-18

Joe used a building in his trade or business that he purchased in June 2013 for $165,000. He sold the building in June 2017. Assume straight-line depreciation was taken in the amount of $16,927. The adjusted basis is $148,073 ($165,000 – $16,927). Using the following independent situations, calculate the amount of any gain or loss, assuming the building sells in 2017 for the following amounts. Assume the maximum gain rate of 15%.

Situation	Amount Realized	Adjusted Basis	Gain/ (Loss)	§ 1250 Amount	§ 1231 Gain/Loss
1	$172,000	$148,073	$23,927	$16,927 × 25% $ 4,232	$7,000 × 15% $1,050
2	160,000	$148,073	$11,927	$11,927 × 25% $ 2,982	–0–
3	140,000	$148,073	(8,073)	–0–	(8,073) ordinary loss

From Shoebox to Software

Any sale of § 1250 property is originally reported on page 2 of Form 4797, and the gain is transferred to Schedule D. Exhibit 7-5 illustrates the reporting on Form 4797 for situation 1 in Example 7-18. Note that the entire gain appears on page 1 of Form 4797. Because the gain is all capital, the gain transfers to Schedule D. On page 2 of Schedule D, separate the 25% gain and the 15% gain, and then calculate the tax. The tax preparation software will calculate the § 1250 gain. The unrecaptured § 1250 Gain worksheet shows the effect of this transaction.

CONCEPT CHECK 7-5—
LO 7-5

1. Under § 1231, gains receive preferential tax rate treatment but losses are limited to $3,000 per year. True or false?
2. The only pure § 1231 asset is land used in a trade or business. True or false?
3. What is meant by the term *depreciation recapture*?
4. What is the difference between a § 1245 asset and a § 1250 asset?
5. What is the difference between recaptured and unrecaptured gain provisions?

TAX ISSUES FOR SPECIAL TYPES OF SALES
LO 7-6

Sales of Block Stock, Mutual Fund Capital Gain Distributions, and Sales of Shares from Mutual Funds

When shares of stock are purchased on different dates or for different prices, the shares are termed purchases of *blocks* of stock. Each block of stock may differ in basis and holding period (short-term or long-term). The taxpayer can specify which block is being sold (specific identification), or if the blocks are not specified, they are treated as coming from the earliest purchases (first-in, first-out).

A *mutual fund* is an investment vehicle that pools the resources of numerous taxpayers and purchases shares of stock in a portfolio. Tax treatment of a mutual fund investment can be difficult. For example, a mutual fund buys and sells individual stocks throughout the year, generating capital gains and losses from these sales. At year-end, the individual

EXHIBIT 7-5 Sale of § 1250 Property on Form 4797 and Schedule D from Example 7-18, Situation 1

Form **4797** — **Sales of Business Property**

(Also Involuntary Conversions and Recapture Amounts Under Sections 179 and 280F(b)(2))

Department of the Treasury, Internal Revenue Service

▶ Attach to your tax return.
▶ Go to *www.irs.gov/Form4797* for instructions and the latest information.

OMB No. 1545-0184 — **2017** — Attachment Sequence No. **27**

Name(s) shown on return		Identifying number
Joe Taxpayer	Information from Example 7-18, Situation 1	412-34-5670

1	Enter the gross proceeds from sales or exchanges reported to you for 2017 on Form(s) 1099-B or 1099-S (or substitute statement) that you are including on line 2, 10, or 20. See instructions	1	

Part I — Sales or Exchanges of Property Used in a Trade or Business and Involuntary Conversions From Other Than Casualty or Theft—Most Property Held More Than 1 Year (see instructions)

2	(a) Description of property	(b) Date acquired (mo., day, yr.)	(c) Date sold (mo., day, yr.)	(d) Gross sales price	(e) Depreciation allowed or allowable since acquisition	(f) Cost or other basis, plus improvements and expense of sale	(g) Gain or (loss) Subtract (f) from the sum of (d) and (e)

3	Gain, if any, from Form 4684, line 39	3	
4	Section 1231 gain from installment sales from Form 6252, line 26 or 37	4	
5	Section 1231 gain or (loss) from like-kind exchanges from Form 8824	5	
6	Gain, if any, from line 32, from other than casualty or theft	6	23,927
7	Combine lines 2 through 6. Enter the gain or (loss) here and on the appropriate line as follows:	7	23,927
	Partnerships (except electing large partnerships) and S corporations. Report the gain or (loss) following the instructions for Form 1065, Schedule K, line 10, or Form 1120S, Schedule K, line 9. Skip lines 8, 9, 11, and 12 below.		
	Individuals, partners, S corporation shareholders, and all others. If line 7 is zero or a loss, enter the amount from line 7 on line 11 below and skip lines 8 and 9. If line 7 is a gain and you didn't have any prior year section 1231 losses, or they were recaptured in an earlier year, enter the gain from line 7 as a long-term capital gain on the Schedule D filed with your return and skip lines 8, 9, 11, and 12 below.		
8	Nonrecaptured net section 1231 losses from prior years. See instructions	8	
9	Subtract line 8 from line 7. If zero or less, enter -0-. If line 9 is zero, enter the gain from line 7 on line 12 below. If line 9 is more than zero, enter the amount from line 8 on line 12 below and enter the gain from line 9 as a long-term capital gain on the Schedule D filed with your return. See instructions	9	

Part II — Ordinary Gains and Losses (see instructions)

10 Ordinary gains and losses not included on lines 11 through 16 (include property held 1 year or less):

11	Loss, if any, from line 7	11	( )
12	Gain, if any, from line 7 or amount from line 8, if applicable	12	
13	Gain, if any, from line 31	13	
14	Net gain or (loss) from Form 4684, lines 31 and 38a	14	
15	Ordinary gain from installment sales from Form 6252, line 25 or 36	15	
16	Ordinary gain or (loss) from like-kind exchanges from Form 8824	16	
17	Combine lines 10 through 16	17	
18	For all except individual returns, enter the amount from line 17 on the appropriate line of your return and skip lines a and b below. For individual returns, complete lines a and b below:		
a	If the loss on line 11 includes a loss from Form 4684, line 35, column (b)(ii), enter that part of the loss here. Enter the part of the loss from income-producing property on Schedule A (Form 1040), line 28, and the part of the loss from property used as an employee on Schedule A (Form 1040), line 23. Identify as from "Form 4797, line 18a." See instructions	18a	
b	Redetermine the gain or (loss) on line 17 excluding the loss, if any, on line 18a. Enter here and on Form 1040, line 14	18b	

For Paperwork Reduction Act Notice, see separate instructions. Cat. No. 13086I Form **4797** (2017)

Source: U.S. Department of the Treasury, Internal Revenue Service, Form 4797. Washington, DC: 2017.

(continued)

EXHIBIT 7-5 *(continued)*

Form 4797 (2017) Page **2**

Part III Gain From Disposition of Property Under Sections 1245, 1250, 1252, 1254, and 1255 (see instructions)

19 (a) Description of section 1245, 1250, 1252, 1254, or 1255 property:	(b) Date acquired (mo., day, yr.)	(c) Date sold (mo. day, yr.)
A Building	06/01/13	06/01/17
B		
C		
D		

These columns relate to the properties on lines 19A through 19D. ▶		Property A	Property B	Property C	Property D
20 Gross sales price (**Note:** *See line 1 before completing.*)	20	172,000			
21 Cost or other basis plus expense of sale	21	165,000			
22 Depreciation (or depletion) allowed or allowable	22	16,927			
23 Adjusted basis. Subtract line 22 from line 21	23	148,073			
24 Total gain. Subtract line 23 from line 20	24	23,927			
25 **If section 1245 property:**					
a Depreciation allowed or allowable from line 22	25a				
b Enter the **smaller** of line 24 or 25a	25b				
26 **If section 1250 property:** If straight line depreciation was used, enter -0- on line 26g, except for a corporation subject to section 291.					
a Additional depreciation after 1975. See instructions	26a				
b Applicable percentage multiplied by the **smaller** of line 24 or line 26a. See instructions	26b				
c Subtract line 26a from line 24. If residential rental property **or** line 24 isn't more than line 26a, skip lines 26d and 26e	26c				
d Additional depreciation after 1969 and before 1976	26d				
e Enter the **smaller** of line 26c or 26d	26e				
f Section 291 amount (corporations only)	26f				
g Add lines 26b, 26e, and 26f	26g				
27 **If section 1252 property:** Skip this section if you didn't dispose of farmland or if this form is being completed for a partnership (other than an electing large partnership).					
a Soil, water, and land clearing expenses	27a				
b Line 27a multiplied by applicable percentage. See instructions	27b				
c Enter the **smaller** of line 24 or 27b	27c				
28 **If section 1254 property:**					
a Intangible drilling and development costs, expenditures for development of mines and other natural deposits, mining exploration costs, and depletion. See instructions	28a				
b Enter the **smaller** of line 24 or 28a	28b				
29 **If section 1255 property:**					
a Applicable percentage of payments excluded from income under section 126. See instructions	29a				
b Enter the **smaller** of line 24 or 29a. See instructions	29b				

Summary of Part III Gains. Complete property columns A through D through line 29b before going to line 30.

30 Total gains for all properties. Add property columns A through D, line 24	30	23,927
31 Add property columns A through D, lines 25b, 26g, 27c, 28b, and 29b. Enter here and on line 13	31	0
32 Subtract line 31 from line 30. Enter the portion from casualty or theft on Form 4684, line 33. Enter the portion from other than casualty or theft on Form 4797, line 6	32	23,927

Part IV Recapture Amounts Under Sections 179 and 280F(b)(2) When Business Use Drops to 50% or Less (see instructions)

		(a) Section 179	(b) Section 280F(b)(2)
33 Section 179 expense deduction or depreciation allowable in prior years	33		
34 Recomputed depreciation. See instructions	34		
35 Recapture amount. Subtract line 34 from line 33. See the instructions for where to report	35		

Form **4797** (2017)

EXHIBIT 7-5 *(continued)*

SCHEDULE D (Form 1040)

Department of the Treasury
Internal Revenue Service (99)

Capital Gains and Losses

► Attach to Form 1040 or Form 1040NR.
► Go to *www.irs.gov/ScheduleD* for instructions and the latest information.
► Use Form 8949 to list your transactions for lines 1b, 2, 3, 8b, 9, and 10.

OMB No. 1545-0074
2017
Attachment Sequence No. **12**

Name(s) shown on return: Joe Taxpayer | **Your social security number**: 412-34-5670

Part I Short-Term Capital Gains and Losses—Assets Held One Year or Less

See instructions for how to figure the amounts to enter on the lines below. This form may be easier to complete if you round off cents to whole dollars.	(d) Proceeds (sales price)	(e) Cost (or other basis)	(g) Adjustments to gain or loss from Form(s) 8949, Part I, line 2, column (g)	(h) Gain or (loss) Subtract column (e) from column (d) and combine the result with column (g)
1a Totals for all short-term transactions reported on Form 1099-B for which basis was reported to the IRS and for which you have no adjustments (see instructions). However, if you choose to report all these transactions on Form 8949, leave this line blank and go to line 1b .				
1b Totals for all transactions reported on Form(s) 8949 with **Box A** checked				
2 Totals for all transactions reported on Form(s) 8949 with **Box B** checked				
3 Totals for all transactions reported on Form(s) 8949 with **Box C** checked				

4 Short-term gain from Form 6252 and short-term gain or (loss) from Forms 4684, 6781, and 8824 .	4	
5 Net short-term gain or (loss) from partnerships, S corporations, estates, and trusts from Schedule(s) K-1	5	
6 Short-term capital loss carryover. Enter the amount, if any, from line 8 of your **Capital Loss Carryover Worksheet** in the instructions	6	( )
7 **Net short-term capital gain or (loss).** Combine lines 1a through 6 in column (h). If you have any long-term capital gains or losses, go to Part II below. Otherwise, go to Part III on the back	7	

Part II Long-Term Capital Gains and Losses—Assets Held More Than One Year

See instructions for how to figure the amounts to enter on the lines below. This form may be easier to complete if you round off cents to whole dollars.	(d) Proceeds (sales price)	(e) Cost (or other basis)	(g) Adjustments to gain or loss from Form(s) 8949, Part II, line 2, column (g)	(h) Gain or (loss) Subtract column (e) from column (d) and combine the result with column (g)
8a Totals for all long-term transactions reported on Form 1099-B for which basis was reported to the IRS and for which you have no adjustments (see instructions). However, if you choose to report all these transactions on Form 8949, leave this line blank and go to line 8b .				
8b Totals for all transactions reported on Form(s) 8949 with **Box D** checked				
9 Totals for all transactions reported on Form(s) 8949 with **Box E** checked				
10 Totals for all transactions reported on Form(s) 8949 with **Box F** checked.				

11 Gain from Form 4797, Part I; long-term gain from Forms 2439 and 6252; and long-term gain or (loss) from Forms 4684, 6781, and 8824	11	23,927
12 Net long-term gain or (loss) from partnerships, S corporations, estates, and trusts from Schedule(s) K-1	12	
13 Capital gain distributions. See the instructions	13	
14 Long-term capital loss carryover. Enter the amount, if any, from line 13 of your **Capital Loss Carryover Worksheet** in the instructions	14	( )
15 **Net long-term capital gain or (loss).** Combine lines 8a through 14 in column (h). Then go to Part III on the back	15	23,927

For Paperwork Reduction Act Notice, see your tax return instructions. Cat. No. 11338H **Schedule D (Form 1040) 2017**

(continued)

EXHIBIT 7-5
(concluded)

Schedule D (Form 1040) 2017 Page **2**

Part III **Summary**

16 Combine lines 7 and 15 and enter the result **16** 23,927

- If line 16 is a **gain,** enter the amount from line 16 on Form 1040, line 13, or Form 1040NR, line 14. Then go to line 17 below.
- If line 16 is a **loss,** skip lines 17 through 20 below. Then go to line 21. Also be sure to complete line 22.
- If line 16 is **zero,** skip lines 17 through 21 below and enter -0- on Form 1040, line 13, or Form 1040NR, line 14. Then go to line 22.

17 Are lines 15 and 16 **both** gains?
☑ **Yes.** Go to line 18.
☐ **No.** Skip lines 18 through 21, and go to line 22.

18 If you are required to complete the **28% Rate Gain Worksheet** (see instructions), enter the amount, if any, from line 7 of that worksheet . . . . ▶ **18**

19 If you are required to complete the **Unrecaptured Section 1250 Gain Worksheet** (see instructions), enter the amount, if any, from line 18 of that worksheet . . . . ▶ **19** 16,927

20 Are lines 18 and 19 **both** zero or blank?
☐ **Yes.** Complete the **Qualified Dividends and Capital Gain Tax Worksheet** in the instructions for Form 1040, line 44 (or in the instructions for Form 1040NR, line 42). **Don't** complete lines 21 and 22 below.

☑ **No.** Complete the **Schedule D Tax Worksheet** in the instructions. **Don't** complete lines 21 and 22 below.

21 If line 16 is a loss, enter here and on Form 1040, line 13, or Form 1040NR, line 14, the **smaller** of:

- The loss on line 16 or
- ($3,000), or if married filing separately, ($1,500) } . . . . **21** (   )

Note: When figuring which amount is smaller, treat both amounts as positive numbers.

22 Do you have qualified dividends on Form 1040, line 9b, or Form 1040NR, line 10b?

☐ **Yes.** Complete the **Qualified Dividends and Capital Gain Tax Worksheet** in the instructions for Form 1040, line 44 (or in the instructions for Form 1040NR, line 42).

☐ **No.** Complete the rest of Form 1040 or Form 1040NR.

Schedule D (Form 1040) 2017

Unrecaptured Section 1250 Gain Worksheet—Line 19

Keep for Your Records

If you are not reporting a gain on Form 4797, line 7, skip lines 1 through 9 and go to line 10.

Line	Description	Inner line	Inner amount	Line	Amount
1.	If you have a section 1250 property in Part III of Form 4797 for which you made an entry in Part I of Form 4797 (but not on Form 6252), enter the **smaller** of line 22 or line 24 of Form 4797 for that property. If you did not have any such property, go to line 4. If you had more than one such property, see instructions			1.	16,927
2.	Enter the amount from Form 4797, line 26g, for the property for which you made an entry on line 1			2.	0
3.	Subtract line 2 from line 1			3.	16,927
4.	Enter the total unrecaptured section 1250 gain included on line 26 or line 37 of Form(s) 6252 from installment sales of trade or business property held more than 1 year (see instructions)			4.	0
5.	Enter the total of any amounts reported to you on a Schedule K-1 from a partnership or an S corporation as "unrecaptured section 1250 gain"			5.	0
6.	Add lines 3 through 5			6.	16,927
7.	Enter the **smaller** of line 6 or the gain from Form 4797, line 7	7.	16,927		
8.	Enter the amount, if any, from Form 4797, line 8	8.	0		
9.	Subtract line 8 from line 7. If zero or less, enter -0-			9.	16,927
10.	Enter the amount of any gain from the sale or exchange of an interest in a partnership attributable to unrecaptured section 1250 gain (see instructions)			10.	0
11.	Enter the total of any amounts reported to you as "unrecaptured section 1250 gain" on a Schedule K-1, Form 1099-DIV, or Form 2439 from an estate, trust, real estate investment trust, or mutual fund (or other regulated investment company) or in connection with a Form 1099-R			11.	0
12.	Enter the total of any unrecaptured section 1250 gain from sales (including installment sales) or other dispositions of section 1250 property held more than 1 year for which you did not make an entry in Part I of Form 4797 for the year of sale (see instructions)			12.	0
13.	Add lines 9 through 12			13.	16,927
14.	If you had any section 1202 gain or collectibles gain or (loss), enter the total of lines 1 through 4 of the **28% Rate Gain Worksheet**. Otherwise, enter -0-	14.	0		
15.	Enter the (loss), if any, from Schedule D, line 7. If Schedule D, line 7, is zero or a gain, enter -0-	15.	(0)		
16.	Enter your long-term capital loss carryovers from Schedule D, line 14, and Schedule K-1 (Form 1041), box 11, code C*	16.	(0)		
17.	Combine lines 14 through 16. If the result is a (loss), enter it as a positive amount. If the result is zero or a gain, enter -0-			17.	0
18.	**Unrecaptured section 1250 gain.** Subtract line 17 from line 13. If zero or less, enter -0-. If more than zero, enter the result here and on Schedule D, line 19			18.	16,927

EXAMPLE 7-19

Mashun purchased the following blocks of stock:

Date	Shares	Price
February 5, 2015	100	$10
August 15, 2015	50	9
December 9, 2016	150	8

Mashun sold 200 shares of stock on July 26, 2017, for $8.50 per share for a total of $1,700.

Using the specific identification method:

The shares sold were identified as being 100 shares from the February 5, 2015, and 100 shares from the December 9, 2016, purchases. The basis for each block is calculated as follows:

February 5, 2015, purchase	100 shares × $10	= $1,000
July 26, 2017, sale	100 shares × $8.50	= 850
Loss on sale		$ (150) long-term
December 9, 2016, purchase	100 shares × $8	= $800
July 26, 2017, sale	100 shares × $8.50	= 850
Gain on sale		$ 50 short-term

Using the first-in, first-out method:

February 5, 2015, purchase	100 shares × $10	= $1,000
August 15, 2015, purchase	50 shares × $9	= 450
Basis		$1,450
July 26, 2017, sale	150 shares × $8.50	= $1,275
Loss on the sale		$ (175) long-term
December 9, 2016, purchase	50 shares × $8	= $400
July 26, 2017, sale	50 shares × $8.50	= 425
Gain on sale		$ 25 short-term

investors are responsible for paying taxes on their share of these gains and losses, which are considered to be long-term regardless of how long they are held by shareholders. These capital gains, known as *capital gain distributions,* are reported to the taxpayer (investor) on Form 1099-DIV.[31] The taxpayer reports the capital gain distribution on line 13 of Schedule D (any gains subject to a rate of 28% appear on the annual mutual fund statement and are reported by the taxpayer on Schedule D). If there are no other capital gains or losses, the amounts on Form 1099-DIV, line 2a, can go directly on Form 1040, line 13, or Form 1040A, line 10 (see Exhibit 7-6).

Remember that ordinary dividends are a distribution from the earnings and profits of the corporation, are ordinary income, and include short-term capital gains.[32] Ordinary dividends are reported to taxpayers on Form 1099-DIV, and sales of stock are reported on Form 1099-B. Many mutual funds and stock brokerages use a substitute Form 1099-DIV or 1099-B to record multiple events under the taxpayer's account.

Many brokerage firms provide the taxpayer with an annual statement on which all activity for the year is reported. Many firms, but not all, automatically calculate the average cost of the shares for the taxpayer's convenience. Form 1099-B—Proceeds from Broker and Barter

[31] The mutual fund may also pass through dividends to the investors.

[32] Publication 550, Chapter 1—Dividends and Other Corporate Distributions.

EXHIBIT 7-6

was withheld.				
	12	Business income or (loss). Attach Schedule C or C-EZ	12	
	13	Capital gain or (loss). Attach Schedule D if required. If not required, check here ▶ ☐	13	
If you did not	14	Other gains or (losses). Attach Form 4797	14	

12	Net long-term gain or (loss) from partnerships, S corporations, estates, and trusts from Schedule(s) K-1	12	
13	Capital gain distributions. See the instructions	13	
14	Long-term capital loss carryover. Enter the amount, if any, from line 13 of your **Capital Loss Carryover Worksheet** in the instructions	14	( )
15	**Net long-term capital gain or (loss).** Combine lines 8a through 14 in column (h). Then go to Part III on the back	15	

Source: U.S. Department of the Treasury, Internal Revenue Service, Form 1040. Washington, DC: 2016.

Exchange Transactions—has been redesigned to accommodate changes to Form 8949. One of the important changes to Form 1099-B is to box 3—if checked, basis reported to IRS. Refer to Exhibit 7-7 for a completed Form 1099-B.

A tax challenge occurs in determining the basis of units or shares of the mutual funds sold. Often mutual fund stock purchases can occur at different times with regular purchases, dividend reinvestment programs, or automatic monthly investments. The simplest case is the sale of *all* shares. The gain or loss is the difference between the sales price and the total cost basis of the shares. However, if a taxpayer who has invested in a mutual fund for 10 years at $200 per month with all of the capital gains and dividends reinvested sells *some* (not all) of those shares, the taxpayer will have a challenge in establishing a cost basis from which to calculate gain or loss. For example, suppose the taxpayer has 1,000 mutual fund shares acquired at many different times over decades. This taxpayer then sells 56.125 units of the mutual fund for $5,000. The challenge is in establishing a cost of these shares that had different purchase prices to calculate the gain or loss on the sale. To simplify this challenge, the taxpayer can use one of three methods in determining the basis of the units in the mutual fund:[33]

- **First-in, first-out:** The first shares purchased are assumed to be the first shares sold. This usually results in the largest gain when the value of the mutual fund units appreciates.
- **Specific identification:** The taxpayer specifies exactly which units are sold from the fund.
- **Average basis:** The taxpayer takes the total cost basis and divides by the total number of units to get an average cost per unit (single-category method).

After the basis has been determined, with an entry in box 3 of Form 1099-B or by separate calculations, any gain or loss is reported on Form 8949 and the totals transferred to Schedule D. Using the information in Example 7-20, the gain on the sale of the stock held in this mutual fund will be $3,500 using the first-in, first-out method; $1,500 using the specific identification method; and $2,000 using the single-category average basis method. Using the information from Example 7-20, Exhibits 7-7 and 7-8 illustrate the recording of mutual fund dividends and sales on Form 8949, Schedule D, and the Qualified Dividends and Capital Gain Tax worksheet.

[33] Reg. § 1.1012-1(e).

EXAMPLE 7-20

Jane purchased the following shares in the Get Rich Quick Mutual Fund:

Date	Shares	Price per Share	Total Cost
2014	1,000	$5	$ 5,000
2015	1,500	7	10,500
2016	500	9	4,500

The basis of the block stock purchases can be calculated as follows:

First-In, First-Out

Shares	Price per Share	Total Cost	Sale Price	Gain/Loss
1,000	$5	$5,000		
500	7	3,500		
		$8,500	**$12,000**	**$3,500**

Specific Identification

Shares	Price per Share	Total Cost	Sale Price	Gain/Loss
2014: 500	$5	$ 2,500		
2015: 500	7	3,500		
2016: 500	9	4,500		
		$10,500	$12,000	$1,500

Average Basis—Single Category

Shares	Price per Share	Total Cost	Sale Price	Gain/Loss
1,000	$5	$ 5,000		
1,500	7	10,500		
500	9	4,500		
		$20,000/3,000 shares = $6.667/share: 1,500 × $6.667 = **$10,000**	**$12,000**	**$2,000**

Assume that on May 15, 2017, Jane sold 1,500 shares at a unit price of $8 for a total sale of $12,000. Jane also received Form 1099-DIV (see Exhibit 7-7) from Get Rich Quick Mutual Fund showing $500 in ordinary dividends, $300 in qualified dividends, and $1,000 in capital gain distributions. Assume she has gross wages of $42,000, is filing as a single taxpayer, takes the standard deduction, and has taxable income (line 43) of $38,600. She is using the single-category average cost method to value her shares. See Exhibit 7-8 for a completed Schedule D and Qualified Dividends and Capital Gains worksheet.

Worthless Securities

A taxpayer cannot deduct a loss on a security until the security is sold or it becomes worthless. At issue is the definition of *worthless*. Treasury Reg. § 1.165-5 states that the act of abandonment establishes worthlessness. Therefore, worthless securities follow the capital loss limitation rules for deductibility. If a security becomes worthless during the year, the taxpayer reports a loss from a sale or exchange of a capital asset on the last day of the taxable year.[34]

EXHIBIT 7-7 **Form 1099-B and 1099-DIV from Example 7-20**

☐ CORRECTED (if checked)

PAYER'S name, street address, city or town, state or province, country, ZIP or foreign postal code, and telephone no. Get Rich Quick Mutual Fund	Applicable check box on Form 8949	OMB No. 1545-0715 2017 Form 1099-B	**Proceeds From Broker and Barter Exchange Transactions**
	1a Description of property (Example 100 sh. XYZ Co.) 1,500 shares of mutual fund		
	1b Date acquired	1c Date sold or disposed 05/15/17	
PAYER'S federal identification number: 36-8156713 RECIPIENT'S identification number: 412-34-5670	1d Proceeds $ 12,000	1e Cost or other basis $	**Copy B** **For Recipient**
	1f Accrued market discount $	1g Wash sale loss disallowed $	
RECIPIENT'S name Jane Taxpayer	2 Short-term gain or loss ☐ Long-term gain or loss ☒ Ordinary ☐	3 If checked, basis reported to IRS ☐	This is important tax information and is being furnished to the Internal Revenue Service. If you are required to file a return, a negligence penalty or other sanction may be imposed on you if this income is taxable and the IRS determines that it has not been reported.
Street address (including apt. no.)	4 Federal income tax withheld $	5 If checked, noncovered security ☐	
City or town, state or province, country, and ZIP or foreign postal code	6 Reported to IRS: Gross proceeds ☐ Net proceeds ☐	7 If checked, loss is not allowed based on amount in 1d ☐	
Account number (see instructions)	8 Profit or (loss) realized in 2017 on closed contracts $	9 Unrealized profit or (loss) on open contracts—12/31/2016 $	
CUSIP number FATCA filing requirement ☐	10 Unrealized profit or (loss) on open contracts—12/31/2017 $	11 Aggregate profit or (loss) on contracts $	
14 State name | 15 State identification no | 16 State tax withheld $ $	12 Check if proceeds from collectibles ☐	13 Bartering $	

Form **1099-B** (Keep for your records) www.irs.gov/form1099b Department of the Treasury - Internal Revenue Service

☐ CORRECTED (if checked)

PAYER'S name, street address, city or town, state or province, country, ZIP or foreign postal code, and telephone no. Get Rich Quick Mutual Fund	1a Total ordinary dividends $ 500.00	OMB No. 1545-0110 2017 Form 1099-DIV	**Dividends and Distributions**
	1b Qualified dividends $ 300.00		
	2a Total capital gain distr. $ 1,000.00	2b Unrecap. Sec. 1250 gain $	**Copy B** **For Recipient**
PAYER'S federal identification number: 36-8156713 RECIPIENT'S identification number: 412-34-5670	2c Section 1202 gain $	2d Collectibles (28%) gain $	
RECIPIENT'S name Jane Taxpayer	3 Nondividend distributions $	4 Federal income tax withheld $	This is important tax information and is being furnished to the Internal Revenue Service. If you are required to file a return, a negligence penalty or other sanction may be imposed on you if this income is taxable and the IRS determines that it has not been reported.
Street address (including apt. no.)		5 Investment expenses $	
City or town, state or province, country, and ZIP or foreign postal code	6 Foreign tax paid $	7 Foreign country or U.S. possession	
	8 Cash liquidation distributions $	9 Noncash liquidation distributions $	
FATCA filing requirement ☐	10 Exempt-interest dividends $	11 Specified private activity bond interest dividends $	
Account number (see instructions)	12 State | 13 State identification no	14 State tax withheld $ $	

Form **1099-DIV** (keep for your records) www.irs.gov/form1099div Department of the Treasury - Internal Revenue Service

Source: U.S. Department of the Treasury, Internal Revenue Service, Form 1099-B and 1099-DIV. Washington, DC: 2017.

EXHIBIT 7-8 **Form 8949 and Schedule D from Example 7-20**

SCHEDULE D (Form 1040)

Department of the Treasury Internal Revenue Service (99)

Capital Gains and Losses

► Attach to Form 1040 or Form 1040NR.
► Go to *www.irs.gov/ScheduleD* for instructions and the latest information.
► Use Form 8949 to list your transactions for lines 1b, 2, 3, 8b, 9, and 10.

OMB No. 1545-0074
2017
Attachment Sequence No. **12**

Name(s) shown on return: Jane Taxpayer
Your social security number: 412-34-5670

Part I **Short-Term Capital Gains and Losses—Assets Held One Year or Less**

See instructions for how to figure the amounts to enter on the lines below. This form may be easier to complete if you round off cents to whole dollars.	(d) Proceeds (sales price)	(e) Cost (or other basis)	(g) Adjustments to gain or loss from Form(s) 8949, Part I, line 2, column (g)	(h) Gain or (loss) Subtract column (e) from column (d) and combine the result with column (g)
1a Totals for all short-term transactions reported on Form 1099-B for which basis was reported to the IRS and for which you have no adjustments (see instructions). However, if you choose to report all these transactions on Form 8949, leave this line blank and go to line 1b				
1b Totals for all transactions reported on Form(s) 8949 with **Box A** checked				
2 Totals for all transactions reported on Form(s) 8949 with **Box B** checked				
3 Totals for all transactions reported on Form(s) 8949 with **Box C** checked				

4 Short-term gain from Form 6252 and short-term gain or (loss) from Forms 4684, 6781, and 8824	4	
5 Net short-term gain or (loss) from partnerships, S corporations, estates, and trusts from Schedule(s) K-1	5	
6 Short-term capital loss carryover. Enter the amount, if any, from line 8 of your **Capital Loss Carryover Worksheet** in the instructions	6	( )
7 **Net short-term capital gain or (loss).** Combine lines 1a through 6 in column (h). If you have any long-term capital gains or losses, go to Part II below. Otherwise, go to Part III on the back	7	

Part II **Long-Term Capital Gains and Losses—Assets Held More Than One Year**

See instructions for how to figure the amounts to enter on the lines below. This form may be easier to complete if you round off cents to whole dollars.	(d) Proceeds (sales price)	(e) Cost (or other basis)	(g) Adjustments to gain or loss from Form(s) 8949, Part II, line 2, column (g)	(h) Gain or (loss) Subtract column (e) from column (d) and combine the result with column (g)
8a Totals for all long-term transactions reported on Form 1099-B for which basis was reported to the IRS and for which you have no adjustments (see instructions). However, if you choose to report all these transactions on Form 8949, leave this line blank and go to line 8b				
8b Totals for all transactions reported on Form(s) 8949 with **Box D** checked				
9 Totals for all transactions reported on Form(s) 8949 with **Box E** checked	12,000	10,000		2,000
10 Totals for all transactions reported on Form(s) 8949 with **Box F** checked				

11 Gain from Form 4797, Part I; long-term gain from Forms 2439 and 6252; and long-term gain or (loss) from Forms 4684, 6781, and 8824	11	
12 Net long-term gain or (loss) from partnerships, S corporations, estates, and trusts from Schedule(s) K-1	12	
13 Capital gain distributions. See the instructions	13	1,000
14 Long-term capital loss carryover. Enter the amount, if any, from line 13 of your **Capital Loss Carryover Worksheet** in the instructions	14	( )
15 **Net long-term capital gain or (loss).** Combine lines 8a through 14 in column (h). Then go to Part III on the back	15	3,000

For Paperwork Reduction Act Notice, see your tax return instructions. Cat. No. 11338H **Schedule D (Form 1040) 2017**

Source: U.S. Department of the Treasury, Internal Revenue Service, Form 8949 and Schedule D (Form 1040). Washington, DC: 2017.

(continued)

EXHIBIT 7-8 *(continued)*

Schedule D (Form 1040) 2017 — Page **2**

Part III Summary

16 Combine lines 7 and 15 and enter the result **16** 3,000

- If line 16 is a **gain,** enter the amount from line 16 on Form 1040, line 13, or Form 1040NR, line 14. Then go to line 17 below.
- If line 16 is a **loss,** skip lines 17 through 20 below. Then go to line 21. Also be sure to complete line 22.
- If line 16 is **zero,** skip lines 17 through 21 below and enter -0- on Form 1040, line 13, or Form 1040NR, line 14. Then go to line 22.

17 Are lines 15 and 16 **both** gains?

☑ **Yes.** Go to line 18.

☐ **No.** Skip lines 18 through 21, and go to line 22.

18 If you are required to complete the **28% Rate Gain Worksheet** (see instructions), enter the amount, if any, from line 7 of that worksheet . . . . ▶ **18**

19 If you are required to complete the **Unrecaptured Section 1250 Gain Worksheet** (see instructions), enter the amount, if any, from line 18 of that worksheet . . . . ▶ **19**

20 Are lines 18 and 19 **both** zero or blank?

☑ **Yes.** Complete the **Qualified Dividends and Capital Gain Tax Worksheet** in the instructions for Form 1040, line 44 (or in the instructions for Form 1040NR, line 42). **Don't** complete lines 21 and 22 below.

☐ **No.** Complete the **Schedule D Tax Worksheet** in the instructions. **Don't** complete lines 21 and 22 below.

21 If line 16 is a loss, enter here and on Form 1040, line 13, or Form 1040NR, line 14, the **smaller** of:

- The loss on line 16 or
- ($3,000), or if married filing separately, ($1,500) . . . . . . **21** (   )

Note: When figuring which amount is smaller, treat both amounts as positive numbers.

22 Do you have qualified dividends on Form 1040, line 9b, or Form 1040NR, line 10b?

☐ **Yes.** Complete the **Qualified Dividends and Capital Gain Tax Worksheet** in the instructions for Form 1040, line 44 (or in the instructions for Form 1040NR, line 42).

☐ **No.** Complete the rest of Form 1040 or Form 1040NR.

Schedule D (Form 1040) 2017

Part II **Long-Term.** Transactions involving capital assets you held more than 1 year are long term. For short-term transactions, see page 1.

Note: You may aggregate all long-term transactions reported on Form(s) 1099-B showing basis was reported to the IRS and for which no adjustments or codes are required. Enter the totals directly on Schedule D, line 8a; you aren't required to report these transactions on Form 8949 (see instructions).

You *must* check Box D, E, *or* F below. Check only one box. If more than one box applies for your long-term transactions, complete a separate Form 8949, page 2, for each applicable box. If you have more long-term transactions than will fit on this page for one or more of the boxes, complete as many forms with the same box checked as you need.

☐ **(D)** Long-term transactions reported on Form(s) 1099-B showing basis was reported to the IRS (see **Note** above)

☑ **(E)** Long-term transactions reported on Form(s) 1099-B showing basis **wasn't** reported to the IRS

☐ **(F)** Long-term transactions not reported to you on Form 1099-B

1 (a) Description of property (Example: 100 sh. XYZ Co.)	(b) Date acquired (Mo., day, yr.)	(c) Date sold or disposed of (Mo., day, yr.)	(d) Proceeds (sales price) (see instructions)	(e) Cost or other basis. See the **Note** below and see *Column (e)* in the separate instructions	Adjustment, if any, to gain or loss. If you enter an amount in column (g), enter a code in column (f). **See the separate instructions.** (f) Code(s) from instructions	(g) Amount of adjustment	(h) **Gain or (loss).** Subtract column (e) from column (d) and combine the result with column (g)
1,500 shares GRQ Mutuial Fund	**various**	**05/15/17**	**12,000**	**10,000**			**2,000**

EXHIBIT 7-8 *(concluded)*

Qualified Dividends and Capital Gain Tax Worksheet—Line 44

Keep for Your Records

Before you begin:
- √ See the earlier instructions for line 44 to see if you can use this worksheet to figure your tax.
- √ Before completing this worksheet, complete Form 1040 through line 43.
- √ If you don't have to file Schedule D and you received capital gain distributions, be sure you checked the box on line 13 of Form 1040.

1.	Enter the amount from Form 1040, line 43. However, if you are filing Form 2555 or 2555-EZ (relating to foreign earned income), enter the amount from line 3 of the Foreign Earned Income Tax Worksheet . . . . . 1.		38,600		
2.	Enter the amount from Form 1040, line 9b* . . . . . 2.	300			
3.	Are you filing Schedule D?* ☒ **Yes.** Enter the **smaller** of line 15 or 16 of Schedule D. If either line 15 or 16 is blank or a loss, enter -0-. ☐ **No.** Enter the amount from Form 1040, line 13. 3.	3,000			
4.	Add lines 2 and 3 . . . . . 4.	3,300			
5.	If filing Form 4952 (used to figure investment interest expense deduction), enter any amount from line 4g of that form. Otherwise, enter -0- . . . . . 5.	0			
6.	Subtract line 5 from line 4. If zero or less, enter -0- . . . . . 6.		3,300		
7.	Subtract line 6 from line 1. If zero or less, enter -0- . . . . . 7.		35,300		
8.	Enter: $37,950 if single or married filing separately, $75,900 if married filing jointly or qualifying widow(er), $50,800 if head of household. . . . . 8.		37,950		
9.	Enter the smaller of line 1 or line 8 . . . . . 9.		37,950		
10.	Enter the smaller of line 7 or line 9 . . . . . 10.		35,300		
11.	Subtract line 10 from line 9. This amount is taxed at 0% . . . . . 11.		2,650		
12.	Enter the smaller of line 1 or line 6 . . . . . 12.		3,300		
13.	Enter the amount from line 11 . . . . . 13.		2,650		
14.	Subtract line 13 from line 12 . . . . . 14.		650		
15.	Enter: $418,400 if single, $235,350 if married filing separately, $470,700 if married filing jointly or qualifying widow(er), $444,550 if head of household. . . . . 15.		418,400		
16.	Enter the smaller of line 1 or line 15 . . . . . 16.		38,600		
17.	Add lines 7 and 11 . . . . . 17.		37,950		
18.	Subtract line 17 from line 16. If zero or less, enter -0- . . . . . 18.		650		
19.	Enter the smaller of line 14 or line 18 . . . . . 19.		650		
20.	Multiply line 19 by 15% (0.15)			20.	98
21.	Add lines 11 and 19 . . . . . 21.		3,300		
22.	Subtract line 21 from line 12 . . . . . 22.		0		
23.	Multiply line 22 by 20% (0.20)			23.	0
24.	Figure the tax on the amount on line 7. If the amount on line 7 is less than $100,000, use the Tax Table to figure the tax. If the amount on line 7 is $100,000 or more, use the Tax Computation Worksheet			24.	4,833
25.	Add lines 20, 23, and 24			25.	4,931
26.	Figure the tax on the amount on line 1. If the amount on line 1 is less than $100,000, use the Tax Table to figure the tax. If the amount on line 1 is $100,000 or more, use the Tax Computation Worksheet			26.	5,395
27.	**Tax on all taxable income.** Enter the **smaller** of line 25 or 26. Also include this amount on Form 1040, line 44. If you are filing Form 2555 or 2555-EZ, don't enter this amount on Form 1040, line 44. Instead, enter it on line 4 of the Foreign Earned Income Tax Worksheet			27.	4,931

**If you are filing Form 2555 or 2555-EZ, see the footnote in the Foreign Earned Income Tax Worksheet before completing this line.*

The mere fact that a company declares bankruptcy is not sufficient to indicate worthlessness. It is often difficult to pinpoint exactly when a security became worthless and hence determine a sale date for long-term versus short-term treatment. Thus, for these purposes, a loss on a worthless security is assumed to occur on the last day of the taxable year.[35]

[34] IRC § 165(g).

[35] IRC § 165(g).

EXAMPLE 7-21

Diane purchased 500 shares in Bad News, Inc., for $10,000 on December 12, 2016. The company promptly went bankrupt in February 2017 with no hope of recovery for the shareholders. Accordingly, the date the stock is deemed to be worthless occurs on December 31, 2017; Diane would have a long-term capital loss of $10,000 in tax year 2017.

Sales of Inherited Property

Remember that in this situation the basis to the beneficiaries is the FMV at the date of death or alternate valuation date (if the estate qualifies for and elects to use the alternate date) and that the holding period is always considered long-term. If no federal estate tax return is filed, use the FMV at the date of death. For example, Taylor inherits property from a relative with an FMV of $5,000 on June 13, 2017. On November 21, 2017, Taylor sells the property for $7,000 for a $2,000 gain. Even though Taylor held the property for less than one year, the gain is taxed as a long-term capital gain.

Sales of Property Received as a Gift

To figure the gain or loss from the sale of property received as a gift, the person who received the gift must know the adjusted basis of the property to the donor and the FMV when the gift was given. If the FMV is less than the donor's adjusted basis at the time of the gift, the basis for figuring the gain is the donor's basis and the FMV is the basis for figuring a loss. If the FMV is equal to or more than the donor's adjusted basis, the basis for any gain or loss on a sale is the donor's adjusted basis.[36]

EXAMPLE 7-22

Juan receives property as a gift. At the time of the gift, the property had an FMV of $7,000. The donor's basis was $9,000. Using the following situations, calculate Juan's gain or loss on the sale of the gifted property:

Situation	Sale Price	Donor Basis	FMV at Date of Gift	Gain/Loss
1	$11,000	$9,000	$7,000	$2,000 gain (use donor basis)
2	6,000	9,000	7,000	$(1,000) loss (use FMV at date of gift)
3	8,000	9,000	7,000	No gain or loss; sale price in between basis and FMV

Note: If the FMV of the gift was $10,000 at the date of the gift, the donor's basis of $9,000 would be used to calculate any gains or losses on a subsequent sale.

CONCEPT CHECK 7-6—
LO 7-6

1. Explain the three types of methods used to determine the basis of the units in a mutual fund.
2. It is often difficult to pinpoint exactly when a security becomes worthless, so the loss on a worthless security is treated as occurring on the last day of the taxable year. True or false?
3. The basis for property given as a gift is always the FMV of the property at the time of the gift. True or false?
4. The tax treatment of a gain on the sale of inherited property depends on the holding period of the deceased taxpayer. True or false?

Table 7-5 is a summary table for the sale of all assets. These assets include ordinary assets, § 1221 capital assets, § 1231 assets, § 1245 assets, and § 1250 assets.

[36] See Chapter 4 in Publication 550 for more detailed information about sales of property received as a gift subject to gift tax.

TABLE 7-5 Summary of Asset Sales

	Asset Type				
	Ordinary Asset	**§ 1221 Capital Asset**	**§ 1231 Asset**	**§ 1245 Asset**	**§ 1250 Asset**
	1.Short-term business assets 2. Short-term gains or losses 3. Inventory 4. Accounts receivable or notes receivable	1. Not inventory 2. Not depreciable business assets 3. Not copyrights* 4. Not accounts receivable or notes receivable	1. Depreciable or nondepreciable business assets held ≥ 1 year 2. Long-term depreciable or nondepreciable real property 3. Not inventory 4. Not copyrights 5. Not short-term business assets	1. Subset of § 1231 2. Depreciable personal property	1. Subset of § 1231 2. Depreciable real property
	Gain (Loss)				
Gain (Loss) treatment	Ordinary income/loss	**Gains** Net short-term capital gains held ≤ 1 year Net long-term capital gains held > 1 year 0%, 15%, or 20% rate† Collectibles 28% § 1202 investments **Losses** Net short-term capital losses held ≤ 1 year Net long-term capital losses held > 1 year	**Gains** Net long-term taxed at long-term capital gains preferential rates **Losses** Net capital losses deducted as an ordinary loss	**Gains** Ordinary to the extent of depreciation taken; excess is true § 1231 capital gain **Losses** § 1231 loss—ordinary loss	**Gains** Ordinary to the extent that depreciation taken exceeds straight-line; subject to 25% rate to the extent of depreciation taken; excess is true § 1231 capital gain **Losses** § 1231 loss—ordinary loss
	Form Reported				
	Form 4797 Part II	Schedule D	Form 4797 Part I	Form 4797 Part III	Form 4797 Part III
	Asset Example				
	Inventory or account receivable	Stocks and securities	Business land	Business equipment	Business building

* Refer to new election provisions for musical works.
† Sales after 2012.

Summary

LO 7-1: Define the terms and identify the tax forms used in sales of property transactions.

- The amount realized (or sales proceeds) and the adjusted basis of the asset must be determined before a gain or loss on the sale of the asset can be determined.
- *A gain or loss on the sale of property* is the difference between the amount realized from the sale and the asset's adjusted basis.
- The nature of tax reporting for gains and losses on the sale of property depends primarily on the use of the asset.
- Form 8949, Schedule D, and Form 4797 are used to record sales of property.

LO 7-2: Classify assets sold as ordinary assets, § 1221 capital assets, or § 1231 business assets.

- Ordinary income property is any asset that is "not a capital asset."
- In general, any asset used for personal purposes or investment is a *capital asset,* but there are eight basic exceptions to this definition.
- § 1231 property is property used in a trade or business that is depreciable or real and held for more than one year.
- Any business asset that is disposed of within one year of acquisition is an ordinary income asset.

LO 7-3: Explain and apply the tax rules for recognizing gains or losses on the sale of ordinary assets.

- Inventory and accounts receivable are not ordinary income assets unless they are outside (not part of) the normal course of business.
- Inventory sold is a part of the cost of goods sold, whereas accounts receivable are generated from sales of the inventory.
- Gains are taxed at the taxpayer's regular tax rate; there is no preferential tax treatment.

LO 7-4: Explain and apply the tax rules for recognizing short-term and long-term gains or losses on the sale of capital assets (§ 1221).

- Tax treatment for a capital gain or loss depends on the holding period of the asset. Assets must be held for more than one year for preferential treatment.
- Generally, the property received through a gift or nontaxable exchange has the same basis as the basis in the hands of the transferor.
- The exception to this rule is property received through inheritance, in which case the asset is always long-term property.
- Tax rates differ, depending on the holding period; short-term assets are taxed at regular taxpayer rates, whereas long-term assets are taxed at preferential rates.
- The 0%, 15%, and 20% rates are for long-term gains on capital assets.
- The 25% rate is applied to that portion of the gain attributable to the depreciation on real property used in a trade or business.
- The 28% rate applies to "collectibles" gains and gains on § 1202 property (qualified small business stock).
- There is a 3.8% surtax applied to the lesser of net investment income (NII) or when modified AGI exceeds $250,000 for MFJ and $200,000 for single taxpayers, and $125,000 for MFS.
- All short-term gains and losses are netted, as are all long-term gains and losses. The resultant gain or loss determines the deductibility of a loss and the tax rate used for gains.

LO 7-5: Calculate the recognized gain or loss on the sale of § 1231 business assets, including gain recapture provisions of § 1245 and § 1250 property.

- Gains and losses from the sale of § 1231 assets must be netted before tax rates are applied.
- A net § 1231 gain is taxed as a long-term capital gain subject to recapture provisions.
- Net § 1231 gains receive preferential tax rate treatment.
- Net § 1231 losses are treated as ordinary losses and are fully deductible.
- Losses disallowed in the current year can be carried over to future years.
- Depreciation recapture rules are designed to transform some or all of a § 1231 gain into an ordinary gain.
- § 1245 (personal trade or business property) and § 1250 (buildings, residential and nonresidential) are subsets of § 1231 property and apply only when there is a gain on the sale of a property that has been depreciated.
- The tax rate for unrecaptured depreciation on § 1250 property is 25%.

LO 7-6: Describe the tax rules for special types of sales, including block stock sales, capital gain distributions, sales of mutual funds, worthless securities, and sales of property received as a gift or through inheritance.

- Block stock sales are shares that are sold at one time but were purchased at different times or prices. Use either specific identification or the first-in, first-out method to calculate share basis.
- A mutual fund pools resources from various sources and purchases shares of stock in a portfolio.
- Capital gain distributions from mutual funds can be reported either on Schedule D or directly on Form 1040 if Schedule D is not being prepared.
- Determining the basis of mutual fund shares can be challenging. Three methods are available for calculating the basis of the shares: first-in, first-out; specific identification; and single-category average basis. Form 1099-B has been redesigned to show cost basis if known.
- Worthless securities are treated as losses from a sale or exchange of a capital asset on the last day of the taxable year.
- Property received through an inheritance is always considered to be long-term regardless of the holding period by the beneficiary. The basis to the beneficiary is valued at the FMV at the date of death or alternate valuation date chosen by the personal representative if qualified under estate tax rules.
- The FMV and adjusted basis of the property at the date given by the donor must be known for the donee to properly calculate a gain or loss on the sale of gifted property in the future.

Discussion Questions connect

All applicable discussion questions are available with ***Connect***©

EA LO 7-1 1. How are the terms *basis, adjusted basis,* and *fair market value* defined as they apply to the calculation of gains and losses?

EA LO 7-1 2. What is meant by the terms *realized gain (loss)* and *recognized gain (loss)* as they apply to the sale of assets by a taxpayer?

EA LO 7-2 3. How can the gain from the sale of property be characterized? Why is it important to correctly characterize the gain on the sale of property?

EA LO 7-2 4. What is a *capital asset*? What factors affect the determination of whether an asset is classified as a capital asset?

EA LO 7-2 5. What determines whether land is a capital asset? How else can land be classified?

EA LO 7-2 6. What is a § 1231 asset? How are gains and losses from the sale of § 1231 assets treated? On what tax form are gains and losses from the sale of § 1231 assets reported?

EA LO 7-2 7. When we determine whether an asset is a § 1231 asset, does the length of time the asset is held affect the classification? Explain.

EA LO 7-2, 7-4 8. What are the different classifications of capital assets? List each classification and the rate at which the gains are taxed.

EA LO 7-3 9. Discuss the concept of ordinary income property and give some examples.

EA LO 7-4 10. What factors affect the taxability of capital gains and losses?

EA LO 7-4 11. Does the length of time a capital asset is held affect the gain or loss on the sale of the asset? Explain.

EA LO 7-4 12. How is a net capital loss treated? Include in your answer a discussion of how a net capital loss is treated in relation to other income.

EA LO 7-4 13. In what ways can a capital asset be acquired, and how is the holding period determined for each method of acquisition?

EA LO 7-4 14. Capital gains can be taxed at several different rates. What determines the rate?

EA LO 7-4 15. What is a § 1202 gain, and how is it taxed?

EA LO 7-4 16. Discuss the netting process of capital gains and losses. What are the possible outcomes of the netting process, and how would each situation be taxed?

EA LO 7-5 17. What is a § 1245 asset? How is it related to a § 1231 asset?

EA LO 7-5 18. What is a § 1250 asset? How is it related to a § 1231 asset?

EA LO 7-5 19. Explain the terms *recapture* and *unrecaptured provisions* as they apply to § 1250 assets.

EA LO 7-6 20. What is a capital gain distribution, and how is it taxed?

EA LO 7-6 21. How can a taxpayer determine the basis of units from a mutual fund?

EA LO 7-6 22. How are gains (losses) from the sale of property acquired from a decedent taxed?

EA LO 7-6 23. Explain how gains (losses) from the sale of property acquired as a gift are taxed.

Multiple-Choice Questions connect

All applicable multiple-choice questions are available with ***Connect***©

EA LO 7-1 24. Jim sells a parcel of land for $75,000 cash, and the buyer assumes Jim's liability of $10,000 on the land. Jim's basis is $64,000. What is the gain or loss on the sale?

a. $1,000 loss.

b. $1,000 gain.

c. $11,000 gain.

d. $21,000 gain.

EA LO 7-1 25. All of the following statements regarding the definition of basis other than cost are true *except*

a. The basis for assets received as a gift depends on whether the FMV is greater than, equal to, or less than the donor's basis at the time of the gift.

b. The basis of property transferred to a taxpayer from a former spouse pursuant to a divorce decree is valued at the FMV at the date of the decree.

c. The basis of inherited property is the FMV at the date of death or alternate valuation date that the personal representative is allowed by law to choose.

d. The basis for property received in exchange for services rendered is the FMV of the property if the FMV of the services is not known beforehand.

EA LO 7-1 26. All of the following increase the basis of stock held for investment *except*

a. Commission fees on the purchase of the stock.

b. Stock splits.

c. Stock dividends from a dividend reinvestment plan.

d. All of the above increase the basis of stock held for investment.

EA LO 7-2 27. In 2014 Grant purchased land for $103,000 for use in his business. He sold it in 2017 for $114,000. What is the amount and type of gain on this sale before netting any other gains and/or losses?

a. $11,000 § 1231 gain.

b. $11,000 ordinary gain.

c. $11,000 short-term capital gain

d. $11,000 long-term capital gain.

EA LO 7-3 28. On May 20, 2016, Jessica purchased land for $105,647 to use in her business. She sold it on May 21, 2017, for $102,595. What is the amount and type of loss on this sale if Jessica does not have any other sales from a trade or business?

a. $3,052 deferred loss.

b. $3,052 long-term capital loss.

c. $3,052 ordinary loss.

d. $3,052 § 1231 loss.

EA LO 7-4 29. Medhat and Neveen, married filing jointly, have $390,000 in modified AGI and $86,000 of NII. They will pay a surtax of:

a. $0.

b. $2,052.

c. $2,580.

d. $3,268.

EA LO 7-4 30. In 2005, Duncan purchased 2,000 shares of stock for $50,000 in a midsize local company with gross assets of $15,000,000. In 2017, Duncan sold the stock for $68,000. How is the gain treated for tax purposes?

a. $18,000 capital gain and taxed at preferential rates.

b. $9,000 excluded from gross income under § 1202 and $9,000 taxed at regular rates.

c. $9,000 excluded from gross income under § 1202 and $9,000 taxed at 28%.

d. $13,500 excluded from gross income under § 1202 and $4,500 taxed at preferential rates.

EA LO 7-4 31. Blair sold the following stocks in 2017: 200 shares of Dearborn Investments, purchased May 15, 2016, for $3,050 and sold January 9, 2017, for $4,135; and 40 shares of State Street Investments, purchased November 7, 2014, for $11,875 and sold March 29, 2017, for $8,675. What is the pre-net amount and nature of the gain (loss) on the sale of these transactions on Blair's 1040 return for 2017?

a. $1,085 short-term gain and $3,000 long-term loss.

b. $1,085 short-term gain and $3,200 long-term loss.

c. $1,915 net long-term loss.

d. $2,115 net long-term loss.

EA LO 7-4 32. Which statement is true regarding short-term capital gains?

a. If there are a net short-term gain and a net long-term gain, both gains are taxed at regular rates.

b. A long-term loss offsets a short-term gain, and if a gain results, the gain is taxed at regular rates.

c. A long-term loss offsets a short-term gain, and if a gain results, the gain is taxed at preferential rates.

d. If there are a net short-term gain and a net long-term gain, both gains are taxed at preferential rates.

EA LO 7-4 33. Which is true regarding long-term capital gains?

a. A net long-term gain can be taxed at 28%, 25%, 20%, 15%, or 0%, depending on the type of gain generated.

b. A net long-term loss can be offset against a long-term gain, and if there is a resulting long-term gain, it is taxed at regular rates.

c. A long-term loss can offset a long-term gain only if the netting result produces a loss of more than $3,000.

d. A net long-term gain can offset a short-term gain but not a short-term loss.

EA LO 7-4 34. When there are a net short-term loss and a net long-term loss, which of the following is true?

a. The entire short-term loss is used to reduce other income before the long-term loss can be used to offset other income.

b. A long-term loss is used to reduce other income before the short-term loss.

c. Regardless of the amount of a short-term or long-term loss, the maximum amount of loss that can be taken in any one year is $3,000. Any remaining loss amounts can be carried forward for three years for individual taxpayers.

d. Regardless of the amount of a short-term or long-term loss, the maximum amount of loss that can be taken in any one year is $3,000. Any remaining loss amounts can be carried forward indefinitely for individual taxpayers.

EA LO 7-4 35. Alton received a Form 1099-B that shows a net sales price of $3,500 on the sale of 600 shares of FNP Company. He bought the stock on October 21, 2016, and sold it on October 22, 2017. His basis in the stock is $2,025, of which $25 is a commission fee. What is the amount and nature of Alton's gain?

a. $1,475 short-term gain.

b. $1,475 long-term gain.

c. $1,500 short-term gain.

d. $1,500 long-term gain.

EA LO 7-4, 7-6 36. Amal received a Form 1099-DIV with a capital gain distribution of $210. She also received a Form 1099-B from the sale of 240 shares of AMS stock she purchased for $2,900 plus a $28 commission fee on February 22, 2016. The net proceeds of the stock sale were $2,700 (the commission fee was $14) and the trade date was February 22, 2017. What is the amount and nature of Amal's gain (loss) on these transactions?

a. $214 short-term loss and $210 long-term gain.

b. $214 long-term loss and $210 short-term gain.

c. $228 long-term loss and $210 short-term gain.

d. $228 short-term loss and $210 long-term gain.

EA LO 7-5 37. Shannon bought an apartment building in July 2011 for $360,000 and sold it for $480,000 in 2017. There was $77,994 of accumulated depreciation allowed on the apartment building. Assuming that Shannon is in the 33% tax bracket, how much of her gain is taxed at 25%?

a. $0.

b. $42,006.

c. $77,994.

d. $120,000.

EA LO 7-4 38. Francisco, a single taxpayer, has income from his W-2 of $93,250. He also has a short-term capital loss of $7,311, a short-term capital gain of $2,100, and a long-term capital gain of $4,680. What is Francisco's AGI for 2017?

a. $92,719.

b. $93,250.

c. $95,350.

d. $100,030.

EA LO 7-6 39. In 2017 Ann received 1,000 shares of stock as a gift from her husband, Tim, who purchased them in 2008. At the time of the gift, the FMV of the stock was $29,300 and Tim's basis was $31,000. If Ann sells the stock for $32,834 in 2017, what is the nature and amount of the gain from the sale?

a. $1,834 long-term gain.

b. $3,534 long-term gain.

c. $1,834 short-term gain and $1,700 long-term gain.

d. $1,834 long-term gain and $1,700 short-term gain.

EA LO 7-6 40. In 2017 Ann received 1,000 shares of stock as a gift from her husband, Tim, who purchased them in 2008. At the time of the gift, the FMV of the stock was $29,300 and Tim's basis was $31,000. If Ann sells the stock for $26,834 in 2017, what is the nature and amount of the loss from the sale?

a. $2,466 short-term loss.

b. $1,700 long-term loss.

c. $4,166 long-term loss.

d. $2,466 short-term loss and $1,700 long-term loss.

Problems connect

All applicable problems are available with **Connect**©

EA LO 7-3 41. Umair sold some equipment he used in his business on August 29, 2017, that was originally purchased for $70,000 on November 21, 2016. The equipment was depreciated using the 7-year MACRS method for a total of $18,574. Assume there is no additional netting of gains and losses for this taxpayer.

a. Assume Umair sold the equipment for $50,000:

(1) What is the amount of realized gain or loss on the sale of the equipment?

(2) Is the nature of the gain or loss considered ordinary or long-term?

____

____

____

b. Assume Umair sold the equipment for $60,000:

(1) What is the amount of realized gain or loss on the sale of the equipment?

(2) Is the nature of the gain or loss considered ordinary or long-term?

LO 7-1, 7-2, 7-4 EA

42. Alice owns undeveloped land with an adjusted basis of $160,000. She sells the property to George for $205,000.

a. What is Alice's realized and recognized gain?

b. To what IRC section does the gain on the property apply?

c. If the land is used in a trade or business, to what IRC section does the gain on the property apply?

EA LO 7-4

43. Haneen has taxable income of $115,000 without consideration of capital gain or loss transactions. She has a short-term capital gain of $15,000, a long-term capital loss of $7,000, and a short-term capital gain of $4,000. Assume no gains or losses are from collectibles or unrecaptured § 1250 property and Haneen is in the 25% tax bracket.

a. What is the total short-term gain or loss?

b. What is the total long-term gain or loss?

c. What is the carryover amount?

d. Is the gain or loss after netting taxed at the ordinary or capital rate?

EA LO 7-4

44. Respond to the following independent situations:

a. Jacob is a single taxpayer who has net investment income consisting of $10,000 interest on a certificate of deposit, $5,000 from dividends from a mutual fund, $5,000 from capital gain distributions from mutual funds, and $40,000 in long-term capital gains from selling some stocks, and his modified AGI is $190,000.

(1) How much in surtax will Jacob be assessed on his Form 1040 for 2017?

b. Jacob is a single taxpayer who has net investment income consisting of $10,000 interest on a certificate of deposit, $5,000 from dividends from a mutual fund, $5,000 from capital gain distributions from mutual funds, and $40,000 in long-term capital gains from selling some stocks, and his modified AGI is $250,000.

(1) How much in surtax will Jacob be assessed on his Form 1040 for 2017?

____

____

c. Jacob is a single taxpayer who has net investment income consisting of $30,000 interest on a certificate of deposit, $15,000 from dividends from a mutual fund, $15,000 from capital gain distributions from mutual funds, and $40,000 in long-term capital gains from selling some stocks, and his modified AGI is $300,000.

(1) How much in surtax will Jacob be assessed on his Form 1040 for 2017?

____

____

EA LO 7-4 45. Respond to the following independent situations:

a. Masa and Haiming, husband and wife, filing jointly, earn $275,000 in salaries and do not have any net investment income.

(1) How much in surtax will Masa and Haiming be assessed on their Form 1040 for 2017? ______________________

b. Masa and Haiming, husband and wife, filing jointly, earn $200,000 in salaries and $50,000 in capital gains, $50,000 in dividends, and $25,000 in savings interest for a total modified AGI of $325,000.

(1) How much in surtax will Masa and Haiming be assessed on their Form 1040 for 2017? ______________________

c. Masa and Haiming, husband and wife, filing jointly, earn $320,000 in salaries and $50,000 in capital gains for a total modified AGI of $370,000.

(1) How much in surtax will Masa and Haiming be assessed on their Form 1040 for 2017? ______________________

EA LO 7-5 46. Jake purchased a $235,000 crane for his construction business. He sold the crane for $175,000 after taking $115,000 of depreciation. Assume Jake is in the 33% tax rate bracket.

a. On what form would the gain or loss originally be reported?

____

____

b. What is the amount of gain or loss on the sale?

____

____

c. What amount of the gain or loss is subject to ordinary tax rates?

____

____

EA LO 7-4 47. Brantley owns an automobile for personal use. The adjusted basis is $19,500, and the FMV is $16,000. Assume Brantley has owned the automobile for two years.

a. Respond to the following if Brantley sells the vehicle for $16,000.

(1) What is the amount of realized gain or loss on the sale? ______________

(2) What is the amount Brantley will recognize on his Form 1040? ______________

b. Respond to the following if Brantley sells the vehicle for $20,000.

(1) What is the amount of realized gain or loss on the sale? ______________

(2) What is the amount Brantley will recognize on his Form 1040? ______________

EA LO 7-4 48. Antoine sold the following stock in 2017. ABC, Inc., is a § 1202 qualified small business (QSB).

Asset	Cost	Acquired	Sale Price	Sale Date
ABC, Inc. 200 shares	$148,000	01/10/09	$200,000	04/30/17
DEF, Inc. 100 shares	21,000	11/15/13	14,000	02/28/17
GHI, Inc. 50 shares	18,000	03/31/16	17,000	08/30/17

a. Complete this chart.

Asset	Amount of Realized Gain (Loss)	Amount of Recognized Gain (Loss)	IRC Section
ABC	______	______	______
DEF	______	______	______
GHI	______	______	______

b. After netting, what is the total gain or loss?

____

c. If Antoine is in the 33% tax rate bracket, at what rate is the net gain or loss taxed?

____

EA LO 7-5 49. Ricardo acquired a warehouse for business purposes on August 30, 1998. The building cost $420,000. He took $227,600 of depreciation on the building and then sold it for $500,000 on July 1, 2017. What is the amount and nature of Ricardo's gain or loss on the sale of the warehouse?

a. What is the adjusted basis for the warehouse?

____

b. What amount of the gain or loss is realized on the sale of the warehouse?

____

c. What amount of the gain or loss is unrecaptured?

____

d. At what rate is the unrecaptured gain or loss taxed?

____

e. What amount of gain or loss qualifies as a § 1231 gain or loss ?

LO 7-1, 7-2, 7-3, 7-4, 7-5

EA

50. Davidson Industries, a sole proprietorship, sold the following assets in 2017:

Asset	Cost	Acquired	Depreciation	Sale Price	Sale Date
Warehouse	$150,000	10/10/10	$25,301	$175,000	03/15/17
Truck	18,000	01/15/16	6,480	16,000	01/14/17
Computer	25,000	07/31/16	6,534	17,000	08/31/17

a. The following questions relate to the sale of the warehouse:

(1) What is the adjusted basis of the warehouse?

(2) What is the realized gain on the warehouse?

(3) What amount of the gain is taxed according to § 1250 rules?

(4) What amount is considered a § 1231 gain before netting?

b. The following questions relate to the sale of the truck:

(1) What is the adjusted basis of the truck?

(2) What is the realized gain on the truck?

(3) What amount of the gain is taxed according to § 1245 rules?

(4) What amount of the gain is taxed as ordinary income?

c. The following questions relate to the sale of the computer:

(1) What is the adjusted basis of the computer?

(2) What is the realized gain or loss on the sale?

(3) Which IRC section code applies to this asset?

____

____

LO 7-3, 7-4, 7-5 EA

51. In 2017 Rosalva sold stock considered short-term for a gain of $925 and stock considered long-term for a loss of $2,165. She also had a $3,000 short-term loss carryover from 2016 and a $1,240 long-term loss carryover from 2015.

a. What amount will be shown as a short-term gain (loss) for 2017? ____________

b. What amount will be shown as a long-term gain (loss) for 2017? ____________

c. How much of the loss is deductible in 2017? ____________

d. What is the amount of long-term carryover to 2018? ____________

EA LO 7-6

52. Lois purchased the following blocks of Westgate stock:

Date	Shares	Price
June 12, 2014	1,000	$4.225
October 21, 2014	2,000	4.775
December 18, 2016	1,500	5.500

Lois sold 1,600 shares of the stock on November 20, 2017, for $5.00 per share for a total of $8,000. Using the first-in, first-out method, determine the gain or loss on the sale of the Westgate stock.

____

____

What if 750 of the shares sold were identified as being from the October 21, 2014, purchase and the remaining 850 shares from the December 18, 2016, purchase? Using the specific identification method, determine the gain or loss on the sale of the Westgate stock.

____

____

EA LO 7-6

53. During 2017 Roberto sold 830 shares of Casual Investor Mutual Fund for $8.875 per share. The shares were purchased on the following dates:

Date	Shares	Price
May 31, 2013	400	$ 9.375
September 18, 2014	225	8.500
October 21, 2014	425	10.000
January 12, 2016	276	7.125

Calculate the gain (loss) on the sale under the following assumptions (carry your calculations to three places):

a. Basis is calculated using the first-in, first-out method.

____

b. Basis is calculated using the average cost method (assume all shares are long-term).

____

LO 7-3, 7-4, 7-5, 7-6 EA

54. Suzette inherited property from her father on April 19, 2017. The FMV at the date of death was $40,000. The property was worth $35,000 six months later and had a basis to her father of $25,000.
   a. What is the basis of the inherited property to Suzette
      (1) If the alternate valuation date was not elected? ______
      (2) If this property qualifies for using the alternate valuation date? ______
   b. Assuming that Suzette sold the property on November 1, 2017, for $47,500, what is the amount and nature of the gain
      (1) If the alternate valuation date was not elected? ______
      (2) If this property qualifies for using the alternate valuation date? ______

EA LO 7-6

55. Using the following independent situations, answer the following questions:

Situation 1

Clara received from her Aunt Sona property with an FMV at the date of the gift of $40,000. Aunt Sona purchased the property five years ago for $35,000. Clara sold the property for $43,000. Assume Aunt Sona does not have modified AGI of over $200,000.

a. What is the basis to Clara? ______

b. What is Clara's gain on the sale? ______

c. If Clara is in the 33% tax bracket, what is the tax on the gain (assuming she has no other gains/losses to be netted)? ______

d. If Clara is in the 15% tax bracket, what is the tax on the gain (assuming she has no other gains/losses to be netted)? ______

Situation 2

Clara received from her Aunt Sona property with a FMV at the date of the gift of $30,000. Aunt Sona purchased the property five years ago for $35,000.

a. If Clara sold the property for $43,000, what is her gain or loss on the sale?

______

b. If Clara sold the property for $33,000, what is her gain or loss on the sale?

______

c. If Clara sold the property for $28,000, what is her gain or loss on the sale?

______

EA LO 7-6

56. Ramon received a gift of stock from his uncle. The basis of the stock to his uncle was $25,000, and it had a FMV of $18,000 at the date of the gift. The donor held the property for more than one year. Complete the following chart under the independent situations shown:

	Situation 1	Situation 2	Situation 3
Donor's basis	$25,000	$25,000	$25,000
FMV at gift date	18,000	18,000	18,000
Ramon's selling price	30,000	15,000	20,000
Basis to Ramon	____	____	____
Taxable gain (if any)	____	____	____
Deductible loss (if any)	____	____	____

Tax Return Problems

All applicable tax return problems are available with ***Connect***©

Use your tax software to complete the following problems. If you are manually preparing the tax returns, you will need Form 1040, Schedule A, Schedule B, Schedule D, Schedule D worksheets, and Form 4797, Form 8949, or other forms, depending on the problems.

Tax Return Problem 1 Jorge Gomez is a single taxpayer. His SSN is 412-34-5670, and he lives at 5037 Circle Court, Crestview, IL 60543. He is a supervisor and his 2017 W2 shows gross wages of $94,850 with $5,881 of social security and $1,375 of Medicare taxes withheld. He has $17,147 of federal withholding and $2,595 in state withholding. Jorge does not itemize. He had the following stock transactions for the year:

Stock Shares	Date Purchased	Date Sold	Sale Price	Cost Basis
5,500	7/8/16	9/12/17	$15,000	$18,000
800	3/12/17	10/21/17	43,000	47,000
2,800	2/13/10	10/21/17	30,000	22,000

He also has interest from a savings account with Local Neighborhood Bank of $250 and a dividend from a Form 1099-DIV of $1,600 in ordinary dividends, of which $1,350 are considered qualified dividends.

Prepare a 2017 Form 1040 for Jorge and all related schedules and forms. Assume that each box 3 of the 1099-Bs was not checked for all sales transactions. Jorge had qualifying health care coverage at all times during the tax year.

Tax Return Problem 2 Danae Coleman is single and lives at 5411 Melbourne Avenue, Chicago, IL 60455. She is a supervisor and her SSN is 412-34-5670. Using the following information, complete her tax return for 2017:

Kimber Company W-2:	
Gross	$90,000
Social security tax	5,580
Medicare tax	1,305
Federal withholding tax	17,300
State withholding tax	2,700
Lee Company W-2:	
Gross	$22,500
Social security tax	1,395
Medicare tax	326
Federal withholding tax	2,300
State withholding tax	600
Danae has the following itemized deductions:	
Real estate tax	$7,633
Mortgage interest	8,445
Charitable contributions	3,000
Danae has the following investments:	
1099-INT	$2,510
1099-DIV	
Ordinary dividends	2,389
Qualified dividends	1,963
Capital gain distribution	4,711
2016 short-term loss carryover	(1,000)

Danae received a gift of 2,000 shares of FNP Inc. stock from her Aunt Jane on January 19, 2017. The basis of the shares to Aunt Jane was $4,300, and they had an FMV of $4,600 on the date of the gift. Aunt Jane purchased the stock on December 30, 2015. On June 30, 2017, Danae sold all the shares for $6,000.

Danae is an avid stamp collector and purchased a rare stamp on March 20, 2007, for $4,000. She sold the stamp for $6,000 on April 8, 2017.

Prepare Form 1040 and all related schedules, forms, and worksheets for 2017. Danae does not donate to the presidential election campaign. Danae is a manager at Kimber Company and had qualifying health care coverage at all times during the tax year.

Tax Return Problem 3

Norman and Leslie Beber are married and file a joint return in 2017. They live at 12345 Hemenway Avenue, Marlborough, MA 01752. Norman is a self-employed tax preparer and his SSN is 412-34-5670. Leslie is a software programmer and her SSN is 412-34-5671. She had the following income and expenses for the year:

Leslie's W-2:	
Gross wages	$100,776
Social security tax	6,248
Medicare tax	1,461
Federal withholding tax	20,035
State withholding tax	4,800

Norman was the sole proprietor of NAMA Tax Service. His business is located at 123 Main Street, Marlborough, MA, 01752 and his business code is 541213. He had the following revenue and expenses:

Revenue	$80,000
Expenses:	
Advertising	1,200
Insurance	3,200
Telephone	2,400
Office rent	18,000
Utilities	4,800
Office supplies	5,000
Depreciation	6,041 (must be allocated to the § 1231 assets listed next)

Norman had the following business assets:

- Office furniture: Purchased for $4,950 on May 20, 2015. The equipment is being depreciated over seven-year MACRS 200% declining balance. Norman sold it on May 15, 2017, for $4,000.
- Office equipment: Purchased a copier for $13,800 on January 10, 2017. The copier is being depreciated over five-year MACRS 200% declining balance. Norman makes no elections for § 179 or bonus depreciation.
- Computer and equipment: Purchased a computer system for $8,900 on January 2, 2016. The computer is being depreciated over five-year MACRS 200% declining balance. Norman makes no elections for § 179 or bonus depreciation.

Norman and Leslie had the following other sources of income and deductions:

- Interest from a CD in the amount of $1,410.
- Long-term loss carryover from 2016 of $5,000.
- Real estate taxes of $8,459.
- Home mortgage interest of $14,041.
- Charitable contributions in cash over the year of $1,800; all receipts and acknowledgments were received from the charitable organizations.

Norman has made four (4) quarterly installments of $625 each as estimated taxes for 2017. All estimated tax payments were paid by the due date using the 1040-ES coupons.

Prepare Form 1040 and all related schedules, forms, and worksheets for Norman and Leslie Beber for 2017. The Bebers do not donate to the presidential election campaign. Norman and Leslie had qualifying health care coverage at all times during the tax year.

We have provided selected filled-in source documents that are available in the *Connect Library*.

BUS
LANE
TOW &
FINE

Chapter Eight

Rental Property, Royalties, and Income from Flow-Through Entities (Line 17, Form 1040, and Schedule E)

The Internal Revenue Code often uses the term *for the production of income.* This term relates to activities that are not trade or businesses but are activities with a profit motive. Rental property is the most common example. Because these activities have a profit motive, taxpayers can deduct most ordinary and necessary expenses to offset income. In this chapter, we discuss the most common types of activities for the production of income. Rental properties, royalty-producing property or investments, and flow-through entities such as partnerships, S corporations, LLCs, trusts, and estates are covered.

Learning Objectives

When you have completed this chapter, you should understand the following learning objectives (LO):

LO 8-1 Explain how income and expenses are recognized and reported for rental property.

LO 8-2 Understand how to report personal use of a rental property (vacation home).

LO 8-3 Know how to report royalty income on Schedule E.

LO 8-4 Discuss the different types of flow-through entities reported on Schedule E, such as partnerships, S corporations, LLCs, trusts, and estates.

INTRODUCTION

This chapter focuses on property described as *for the production of income.* These activities produce income and expenses that are *for* AGI, similar to a trade or business. Income and expenses associated with rental, royalty, and flow-through entities[1] are for the production of income property. Generally taxpayers report these items on Schedule E of Form 1040. The income and expense items are netted on Schedule E and are accumulated on line 17 of Form 1040. Examples of Schedule E can be found throughout this chapter.

[1] Common flow-through entities are partnerships, S corporations, LLCs, trusts, and estates. They are referred to in this way because, in most instances, they do not pay income taxes. Instead the net share of income or loss from the entity flows through to the tax returns of its individual partners/shareholders/owners. The partners and others then pay tax on their share of the flow-through income.

On Schedule E, income and expenses from rental properties and royalties are reported on Part I, page 1 (Exhibit 8-1); and certain items from flow-through entities such as partnerships, S corporations, LLCs, trusts, and estates are reported on Part II and Part III, page 2 (Exhibit 8-7).

RENTAL PROPERTY
LO 8-1

Taxable income includes rental income.[2] This includes any rental income received or accrued for the occupancy of real estate or for the use of personal property.[3] The taxpayer must differentiate between rental property and a trade or business involving rental property. Generally, if the taxpayer is a real estate professional and materially participates in a real property trade or business, then the business side of the rental activity should be reported on Schedule C. The business side, such as real property development, construction, acquisition, conversion, rental operation, management, leasing, or brokerage all should be reported on Schedule C. Items related to the real estate rental activity such as rental income and related expenses should be reported on Schedule E. Rental income is not subject to self-employment tax.[4]

EXAMPLE 8-1

Jack is a real estate professional who owns and operates a bed and breakfast in the North Carolina mountains. Jack provides significant services to the renters and has no other trade or business. As such, the activity is treated as a trade or business, not as rental property. Consequently, Jack reports the rental (lodging) income and expenses of this property on Schedule C.

Farm Rental Income

Any rental income from farming activities is reported on Form 4835 rather than on Schedule E. However, the provisions concerning the reporting of farm rental income are similar to the rules for reporting regular rental income. Net farm rental income or loss from Form 4835 is transferred to line 40 of Schedule E.

Rental Income

The rental activities reported on Schedule E are proceeds from the rental of real estate such as office buildings, rental houses, condominiums or town houses, and vacation homes. Taxpayers report gross rents on line 3 of Schedule E. Ordinary and necessary expenses are deducted on lines 5 through 20 to arrive at net rental income or loss on line 26. The net amount from line 26 of Schedule E is reported on line 17 of Form 1040.

Gross rent is the total rent collected from each individual property. Gross rental income includes advance rentals in the year of receipt regardless of the rental period covered or the method of accounting employed.[5] Advance rental does *not* include security deposits. Generally, if the payment is subject to an obligation to repay, it is not included in taxable income.[6]

EXAMPLE 8-2

On December 12, 2017, Della receives $7,000 from Philip to cover six months of rent from December 15, 2017, to June 15, 2018. The payment includes a $1,000 security deposit. Della must include $6,000 as rental income in the tax year 2017. The $1,000 security deposit is not reported as income.

[2] IRC § 61(a)(5).

[3] Reg. § 1.61-8(a).

[4] Additional information concerning rental activities treated as trades or businesses, and *who* qualifies as a real estate professional, is given in Chapter 13 under passive activity losses. As discussed later in this chapter, rental activities are, by definition, considered passive activities.

[5] Reg. § 1.61-8(b).

[6] The Supreme Court in *Comm. v. Indianapolis Power & Light Co.* [(1990) 493 US 203, 65 AFTR 2d 90-394, 90-1 USTC 50,007] ruled that if the taxpayer had no guarantee to keep the advance payment (contingent on events outside his or her control), the payment was not includable in taxable income.

Expenses paid by the tenant or services provided by the tenant in lieu of rent payments are also components of rental income. If the tenant pays an expense normally paid by the taxpayer, the taxpayer must include that payment in rental income. Likewise, if the tenant performs services in exchange for free rent or reduced rent, the fair market value of those services is included in rental income.[7]

EXAMPLE 8-3

Bill is the owner of a house that rents for $900 per month. During the winter while Bill was on vacation, the furnace failed. The tenants of the house had the furnace repaired and paid $300 in repair costs. On the first of the following month, the tenants reduced the rent payment by $300, paying just $600. Bill is required to include $900 as rental income: the net rental payment plus the repair cost paid by the tenants. Bill can then deduct a repair expense of $300.

EXAMPLE 8-4

Bill owns a second rental house in need of repairs. He allows a new tenant (a carpenter) to live rent-free for three months ($1,800 value); in exchange, the tenant will complete the necessary repairs. Bill must include $1,800 in rental income. He can then take a corresponding deduction for the repairs, assuming that they are not capital improvements.

Rental Expenses

Recall that an ordinary expense is customary or usual for the taxpayer's business or activity (in this case, rental property). The "necessary" criterion refers to an expense that is appropriate and helpful rather than one that is essential to the taxpayer's activity. Table 8-1 summarizes expenses that are common to most rental activities.

The information in Table 8-1 is not comprehensive because any expense that meets the ordinary and necessary criteria is deductible. We discussed the rules concerning the deductibility of many of these expenses in Chapter 6. For example, we distinguished between travel and transportation. The same rules apply to rental property. Consequently, travel costs from the taxpayer's home to a rental property are deductible if the travel is for business purposes (such as to conduct repairs or attend a condominium association meeting). Likewise, if a taxpayer stays overnight, meals are also deductible. Use caution when deducting meals, however, especially if elements of personal vacation are involved.[8] Typically the standard mileage rate is used to calculate any travel expenses concerning rental property because the rental activity (on Schedule E) is not the taxpayer's trade or business, and thus the taxpayer likely does not drive enough to merit using actual auto costs.

TABLE 8-1
Common Rental Activity Expenses

Expense	Purpose
Advertising	Payments to advertise property for rent.
Travel	Travel to and from property for rental business such as repairs or maintenance.
Repair and maintenance costs	Normal repair and maintenance costs that are not capital improvements.
Insurance	Policy to guard the property against casualty and liability.
Management fees	Fees paid to have someone manage the property and provide services such as security, rental agency, repairs, and maintenance.
Interest	Payments on mortgage to purchase or improve rental property.
Taxes	Payments for property taxes (e.g., county property taxes).
Depreciation	Residential: 27.5-year MACRS straight-line. Nonresidential: 39-year MACRS straight-line.

[7] IRS Publication 527, p. 3.

[8] The rules concerning the deduction of expenses on vacation homes that are also rented are presented in the next section.

TABLE 8-2
Examples of Capital Improvements

Source: IRS *Publication 527.*

Additions	Heating and air conditioning	Lawn and grounds landscaping	Plumbing
Bedroom	Heating system	Driveway	Septic system
Bathroom	Central air conditioning	Walkway	Water heater
Deck	Furnace	Fence	Soft water system
Garage	Ductwork	Retaining wall	Filtration system
Porch	Central humidifier	Sprinkler system	**Miscellaneous**
Patio	Filtration system	Swimming pool	Storm windows, doors
Interior improvements		**Insulation**	New roof
Built-in appliances		Attic	Central vacuum
Kitchen modernization		Walls, floor	Wiring upgrades
Flooring		Pipes, ductwork	Satellite dish
Wall-to-wall carpeting			Security system

EXAMPLE 8-5

Bryan lives in Birmingham, Alabama, and owns a rental condominium on the beach in Destin, Florida. Twice a year (in March and June) he drives to Destin to perform general maintenance on the condominium. The round-trip mileage from Birmingham to Destin is 602 miles. In tax year 2017, Bryan could deduct $644 in travel costs (602 miles × 2 trips × 53.5 cents per mile).

General repairs and maintenance are also deductible from gross rental income. However, the taxpayer cannot deduct amounts that are "capital improvements"; allowable repairs are expenditures that neither materially add to the value of the property nor appreciably prolong the property's life.[9] Any repairs as part of an extensive remodeling or restoration of the property are considered *capital improvements* and are, consequently, capitalized and depreciated over the appropriate depreciable life.[10] The distinction is important because a taxpayer receives an immediate expense deduction for repairs, whereas capital improvements require depreciation over 27.5 years (residential) or 39 years (nonresidential). Table 8-2 shows examples of expenditures that are considered capital improvements.[11] Starting in 2014, certain small rentals can elect to deduct certain improvements as expenses up to a maximum of:

1. 2% of the building's unadjusted basis; or
2. $10,000.

Taxpayers with average rental receipts over $10 million and properties with basis greater then $1 million are not eligible.[12]

Rental property is also depreciated. We provided a complete review of depreciation in Chapter 6. However, some aspects specifically relating to rental property merit additional discussion. For the rental structure, the depreciable life is 27.5 years for residential structures and 39 years for nonresidential structures. The applicable depreciation method is straight-line. The IRC § 179 deduction is not allowed for rental property.

When a furnished rental property is purchased for a lump sum, depreciation may be calculated over 27.5 (or 39) years on the total purchase price of the rental property. However, to accelerate the tax deduction, the taxpayer should allocate the purchase price to the structure separately from the furniture, appliances, carpet, and even shrubbery or fences (because depreciating over 5 or 7 years allows a much faster deduction than over 27.5 or 39 years). The depreciable lives and methods for these asset types are as follows:

[9] Reg. § 1.162–4.
[10] Reg. § 1.162–4.
[11] IRS Publication 527, p. 5.
[12] Reg. Section 1.263(a)-3(h)

Asset	**MACRS Life**	**MACRS Method**
Furniture used in rental*	5 years	200% declining balance
Appliances	5 years	200% declining balance
Carpets	5 years	200% declining balance
Office furniture	7 years	200% declining balance
Shrubbery	15 years	150% declining balance
Fences	15 years	150% declining balance

* In Chapter 6, we depreciated furniture and fixtures for a trade or business over a seven-year period. Furniture used in a rental activity has a five-year depreciation period. IRS Publication 527 makes a distinction between furniture used in a rental (five years) and office furniture and equipment (seven years).

EXAMPLE 8-6

Alan and Cherie Masters purchased a furnished beach house in San Clemente, California, for $1,364,000 on June 1, 2017. The land was valued at $700,000; furniture, $15,000; appliances, $3,000; carpet, $4,000; and landscaping, $8,000. The Masters rent the house full-time (no personal use). If the Masters depreciate the house as a single lump sum (as 27.5-year property), their first-year depreciation would be as follows (see Table 6A-6 in Chapter 6):

$$\$664,000 \times 1.970\% = \$13,081$$

On the other hand, if the Masters divided the assets into depreciable components, their first-year depreciation would be as calculated here:

House	$634,000 (27.5 years, straight-line) × 1.970% =	$12,490
Furniture	$15,000 (5 years, 200% declining balance [DB]) × 20.00% =	3,000
Appliances	$3,000 (5 years, 200% DB) × 20.00% =	600
Carpet	$4,000 (5 years, 200% DB) × 20.00% =	800
Landscaping	$8,000 (15 years, 200% DB) × 5.00% =	400
Total depreciation		$17,290

By allocating the purchase price to the structure and to the other assets, the Masters would benefit from an additional depreciation deduction of $4,209 ($17,290 − $13,081) in the first year.

From Shoebox to Software

In this section, we present a comprehensive example of rental income and expenses. The Masters, from Example 8-6, have the following income and expenses in addition to the depreciation deduction calculated earlier. During the tax year, neither the Masters nor their family used the house at any time for personal reasons.

Rental income (12 wks @ $3,500 per week)	$42,000
Rental management company (10% of gross)	4,200
Travel (1 round-trip [in April] for maintenance at 893 miles 893 miles × 53.5 cents per mile)	478
Repairs (leaking roof & plumbing repairs)	2,500
Mortgage interest	1,300
Property taxes	3,800
Insurance	1,800
Utilities	2,000
Depreciation (see Example 8-6)	17,290

Open the Masters' tax return file. Then open Schedule E and enter the type and location of the property (123 Beach Rd., San Clemente CA 92672). Next, enter the income and the expenses. Enter the auto (2016 Yukon, placed in service on June 1, 2017), and enter the Business Use worksheet to fill in the mileage. Then check the box to use the standard mileage rate and answer the questions in step 3 (all "yes" in this case).

Click on line 20 on Schedule E and add each individual asset on the asset entry worksheet (as in Chapter 6 and Schedule C). Some tax software programs do not provide an "asset type" for rental furniture, appliances, or carpet.[13] If this is the case, use the Other asset type and enter the five-year life and MACRS method on the life and method input lines. Exhibit 8-1 shows the presentation of the preceding information on Schedule E, and Exhibit 8-2 shows the depreciation reported on Form 4562.

[13] If you choose "office furniture and fixtures" on some programs, seven-year MACRS is used for the depreciation life when a five-year life is allowed.

EXHIBIT 8-1

SCHEDULE E (Form 1040)
Department of the Treasury Internal Revenue Service (99)

Supplemental Income and Loss

(From rental real estate, royalties, partnerships, S corporations, estates, trusts, REMICs, etc.)
▶ Attach to Form 1040, 1040NR, or Form 1041.
▶ Go to *www.irs.gov/ScheduleE* for instructions and the latest information.

OMB No. 1545-0074
2017
Attachment Sequence No. **13**

Name(s) shown on return: **Alan and Cherie Masters** | Your social security number: **412-34-5670**

Part I **Income or Loss From Rental Real Estate and Royalties** **Note:** If you are in the business of renting personal property, use **Schedule C** or **C-EZ** (see instructions). If you are an individual, report farm rental income or loss from **Form 4835** on page 2, line 40.

A Did you make any payments in 2017 that would require you to file Form(s) 1099? (see instructions) ☐ Yes ☑ No
B If "Yes," did you or will you file required Forms 1099? ☐ Yes ☐ No

1a	Physical address of each property (street, city, state, ZIP code)
A	123 Beach Road, San Clemente, CA 92672
B	
C	

1b	Type of Property (from list below)	2 For each rental real estate property listed above, report the number of fair rental and personal use days. Check the **QJV** box only if you meet the requirements to file as a qualified joint venture. See instructions.	Fair Rental Days	Personal Use Days	QJV
A		A	365	0	☐
B		B			☐
C		C			☐

Type of Property:
1 Single Family Residence 3 Vacation/Short-Term Rental 5 Land 7 Self-Rental
2 Multi-Family Residence 4 Commercial 6 Royalties 8 Other (describe)

Income:	**Properties:**		A	B	C
3	Rents received	3	42,000		
4	Royalties received	4			
Expenses:					
5	Advertising	5			
6	Auto and travel (see instructions)	6	478		
7	Cleaning and maintenance	7			
8	Commissions	8			
9	Insurance	9	1,800		
10	Legal and other professional fees	10			
11	Management fees	11	4,200		
12	Mortgage interest paid to banks, etc. (see instructions)	12	1,300		
13	Other interest	13			
14	Repairs	14	2,500		
15	Supplies	15			
16	Taxes	16	3,800		
17	Utilities	17	2,000		
18	Depreciation expense or depletion	18	17,290		
19	Other (list) ▶	19			
20	Total expenses. Add lines 5 through 19	20	33,368		
21	Subtract line 20 from line 3 (rents) and/or 4 (royalties). If result is a (loss), see instructions to find out if you must file **Form 6198**	21	8,632		
22	Deductible rental real estate loss after limitation, if any, on **Form 8582** (see instructions)	22	( )	( )	( )

23a	Total of all amounts reported on line 3 for all rental properties	23a	42,000
b	Total of all amounts reported on line 4 for all royalty properties	23b	0
c	Total of all amounts reported on line 12 for all properties	23c	1,300
d	Total of all amounts reported on line 18 for all properties	23d	17,290
e	Total of all amounts reported on line 20 for all properties	23e	33,368
24	**Income.** Add positive amounts shown on line 21. **Do not** include any losses	24	8,632
25	**Losses.** Add royalty losses from line 21 and rental real estate losses from line 22. Enter total losses here	25	( )
26	**Total rental real estate and royalty income or (loss).** Combine lines 24 and 25. Enter the result here. If Parts II, III, IV, and line 40 on page 2 do not apply to you, also enter this amount on Form 1040, line 17, or Form 1040NR, line 18. Otherwise, include this amount in the total on line 41 on page 2	26	8,632

For Paperwork Reduction Act Notice, see the separate instructions. Cat. No. 11344L **Schedule E (Form 1040) 2017**

Source: U.S. Department of the Treasury, Internal Revenue Service, Schedule E (Form 1040). Washington, DC: 2017.

EXHIBIT 8-2

Form **4562** Department of the Treasury Internal Revenue Service (99)

Depreciation and Amortization
(Including Information on Listed Property)
▶ Attach to your tax return.
▶ Go to *www.irs.gov/Form4562* for instructions and the latest information.

OMB No. 1545-0172 **2017** Attachment Sequence No. **179**

Name(s) shown on return	Business or activity to which this form relates	Identifying number
Alan and Cherie Masters	Rental	412-34-5670

Part I Election To Expense Certain Property Under Section 179
Note: If you have any listed property, complete Part V before you complete Part I.

1	Maximum amount (see instructions)	1	
2	Total cost of section 179 property placed in service (see instructions)	2	
3	Threshold cost of section 179 property before reduction in limitation (see instructions)	3	
4	Reduction in limitation. Subtract line 3 from line 2. If zero or less, enter -0-	4	
5	Dollar limitation for tax year. Subtract line 4 from line 1. If zero or less, enter -0-. If married filing separately, see instructions	5	

6	(a) Description of property	(b) Cost (business use only)	(c) Elected cost

7	Listed property. Enter the amount from line 29	7	
8	Total elected cost of section 179 property. Add amounts in column (c), lines 6 and 7	8	
9	Tentative deduction. Enter the **smaller** of line 5 or line 8	9	
10	Carryover of disallowed deduction from line 13 of your 2016 Form 4562	10	
11	Business income limitation. Enter the smaller of business income (not less than zero) or line 5 (see instructions)	11	
12	Section 179 expense deduction. Add lines 9 and 10, but don't enter more than line 11	12	
13	Carryover of disallowed deduction to 2018. Add lines 9 and 10, less line 12 ▶	13	

Note: Don't use Part II or Part III below for listed property. Instead, use Part V.

Part II Special Depreciation Allowance and Other Depreciation (Don't include listed property.) (See instructions.)

14	Special depreciation allowance for qualified property (other than listed property) placed in service during the tax year (see instructions)	14	
15	Property subject to section 168(f)(1) election	15	
16	Other depreciation (including ACRS)	16	

Part III MACRS Depreciation (Don't include listed property.) (See instructions.)

Section A

17	MACRS deductions for assets placed in service in tax years beginning before 2017	17	
18	If you are electing to group any assets placed in service during the tax year into one or more general asset accounts, check here ▶ ☐		

Section B—Assets Placed in Service During 2017 Tax Year Using the General Depreciation System

(a) Classification of property	(b) Month and year placed in service	(c) Basis for depreciation (business/investment use only—see instructions)	(d) Recovery period	(e) Convention	(f) Method	(g) Depreciation deduction
19a 3-year property						
b 5-year property		22,000	5 yr	HY	200 DB	4,400
c 7-year property						
d 10-year property						
e 15-year property		8,000	15 yr	HY	150 DB	400
f 20-year property						
g 25-year property			25 yrs.		S/L	
h Residential rental property	06/01/17	634,000	27.5 yrs.	MM	S/L	12,490
			27.5 yrs.	MM	S/L	
i Nonresidential real property			39 yrs.	MM	S/L	
				MM	S/L	

Section C—Assets Placed in Service During 2017 Tax Year Using the Alternative Depreciation System

20a Class life					S/L	
b 12-year			12 yrs.		S/L	
c 40-year			40 yrs.	MM	S/L	

Part IV Summary (See instructions.)

21	Listed property. Enter amount from line 28	21	
22	**Total.** Add amounts from line 12, lines 14 through 17, lines 19 and 20 in column (g), and line 21. Enter here and on the appropriate lines of your return. Partnerships and S corporations—see instructions	22	17,920
23	For assets shown above and placed in service during the current year, enter the portion of the basis attributable to section 263A costs	23	

For Paperwork Reduction Act Notice, see separate instructions. Cat. No. 12906N Form **4562** (2017)

Source: U.S. Department of the Treasury, Internal Revenue Service, Form 4562. Washington, DC: 2017.

(continued)

EXHIBIT 8-2 *(concluded)*

Form 4562 (2017) Page 2

Part V Listed Property (Include automobiles, certain other vehicles, certain aircraft, certain computers, and property used for entertainment, recreation, or amusement.)

Note: For any vehicle for which you are using the standard mileage rate or deducting lease expense, complete **only** 24a, 24b, columns (a) through (c) of Section A, all of Section B, and Section C if applicable.

Section A—Depreciation and Other Information (Caution: See the instructions for limits for passenger automobiles.)

24a Do you have evidence to support the business/investment use claimed? ☑ Yes ☐ No **24b** If "Yes," is the evidence written? ☑ Yes ☐ No

(a) Type of property (list vehicles first)	(b) Date placed in service	(c) Business/ investment use percentage	(d) Cost or other basis	(e) Basis for depreciation (business/investment use only)	(f) Recovery period	(g) Method/ Convention	(h) Depreciation deduction	(i) Elected section 179 cost
25 Special depreciation allowance for qualified listed property placed in service during the tax year and used more than 50% in a qualified business use (see instructions) . **25**								
26 Property used more than 50% in a qualified business use:								
		%						
		%						
		%						
27 Property used 50% or less in a qualified business use:								
2016 Yukon	06/01/17	5.625 %				S/L –		
		%				S/L –		
		%				S/L –		
28 Add amounts in column (h), lines 25 through 27. Enter here and on line 21, page 1 . **28**								
29 Add amounts in column (i), line 26. Enter here and on line 7, page 1 . . . **29**								

Section B—Information on Use of Vehicles

Complete this section for vehicles used by a sole proprietor, partner, or other "more than 5% owner," or related person. If you provided vehicles to your employees, first answer the questions in Section C to see if you meet an exception to completing this section for those vehicles.

	(a) Vehicle 1		(b) Vehicle 2		(c) Vehicle 3		(d) Vehicle 4		(e) Vehicle 5		(f) Vehicle 6	
30 Total business/investment miles driven during the year (**don't** include commuting miles) .												
31 Total commuting miles driven during the year												
32 Total other personal (noncommuting) miles driven . . .												
33 Total miles driven during the year. Add lines 30 through 32 . . .												
	Yes	No	Yes	No	Yes	No	Yes	No	Yes	No	Yes	No
34 Was the vehicle available for personal use during off-duty hours? . . .												
35 Was the vehicle used primarily by a more than 5% owner or related person? . .												
36 Is another vehicle available for personal use?												

Section C—Questions for Employers Who Provide Vehicles for Use by Their Employees

Answer these questions to determine if you meet an exception to completing Section B for vehicles used by employees who **aren't** more than 5% owners or related persons (see instructions).

	Yes	No
37 Do you maintain a written policy statement that prohibits all personal use of vehicles, including commuting, by your employees? . . .	✓	
38 Do you maintain a written policy statement that prohibits personal use of vehicles, except commuting, by your employees? See the instructions for vehicles used by corporate officers, directors, or 1% or more owners . .	✓	
39 Do you treat all use of vehicles by employees as personal use? . . .		✓
40 Do you provide more than five vehicles to your employees, obtain information from your employees about the use of the vehicles, and retain the information received? . . .		✓
41 Do you meet the requirements concerning qualified automobile demonstration use? (See instructions.) . . .		✓

Note: If your answer to 37, 38, 39, 40, or 41 is "Yes," don't complete Section B for the covered vehicles.

Part VI Amortization

(a) Description of costs	(b) Date amortization begins	(c) Amortizable amount	(d) Code section	(e) Amortization period or percentage	(f) Amortization for this year
42 Amortization of costs that begins during your 2017 tax year (see instructions):					
43 Amortization of costs that began before your 2017 tax year . . .				**43**	
44 Total. Add amounts in column (f). See the instructions for where to report . . .				**44**	

Form **4562** (2017)

One important exception to trade or business depreciation rules is that the IRC § 179 deduction *cannot* be claimed for property held to produce rental income. Any 50% bonus is allowed, however.

If a rental property incurs a loss, there are potential limitations on the deductibility of the losses. By definition, rental property is a *passive activity*. The rules concerning passive activity losses are complex and are discussed briefly at the end of this chapter and more fully in Chapter 13.[14]

CONCEPT CHECK 8-1— LO 8-1

1. Rental income is generally reported on Schedule E. True or false?
2. All expenses related to rental property are deductible in the current year, including capital improvements. True or false?
3. Rental property structures must be depreciated using the straight-line method. True or false?
4. If a taxpayer's rental property is considered a trade or business, he or she reports the income on Schedule E. True or false?
5. If a tenant provides a service in lieu of rent, the taxpayer is not required to report the value of that amount as rental income. True or false?

RENTAL OF VACATION HOMES
LO 8-2

When a taxpayer uses a property both for personal use (vacation home) and as rental property, tax complexities arise. Vacation home rental property falls into one of the following three possible categories: (1) primarily rental use, (2) primarily personal use, and (3) personal/rental use.

The appropriate category is determined by comparing the number of rental use days to the number of personal use days. The category determines how much of the rental income and expenses for the property may be reported. If the property

1. Is not used for more than 14 days (or 10% of the total rental days, if more) for personal use, and it is rented for 15 days or more, it is categorized as primarily rental.
2. Is rented for less than 15 days, it is categorized as primarily personal.
3. Is rented for 15 days or more and the personal use of the property is more than the greater of[15]
   a. 14 days or
   b. 10% of the total rental days at the fair rental value

it is categorized as personal/rental property.

EXAMPLE 8-7

John owns a cabin in the mountains. If he rents the cabin for the ski season (four months) and uses the property for personal use for 13 days, the cabin would be categorized as primarily rental property. If John used the property for personal use for 21 days, the property would be categorized as personal/rental. If John rented the cabin for less than 15 days, the cabin would be categorized as primarily personal.

Personal use of a dwelling is any use by

1. The taxpayer, any member of the taxpayer's family, or any other person with an interest in the unit.
2. Any individual who uses the unit under an arrangement that enables the taxpayer to use some other dwelling unit (reciprocal-use arrangement).
3. Any individual unless for such day the dwelling unit is rented for its fair rental value.[16]

[14] For a detailed discussion of the passive activity loss rules, and the loss rules of rental property in particular, see Chapter 13.

[15] IRC § 280A(d)(1).

[16] IRC § 280A(d)(2).

If a taxpayer lets anyone, family or nonfamily, use the rental property free of a rental charge, those days are considered personal-use days by the taxpayer. If any family member uses the rental property (even if the family member pays the full rental value), the days are considered personal-use days.[17] *Family* is defined as the taxpayer's brothers and sisters (whether whole or half blood), spouse, ancestors, and lineal descendants.[18] Any day spent working substantially full-time repairing and maintaining the property does not count as a personal-use day. This is true even if other family members use the property for recreational purposes on the same day.[19]

EXAMPLE 8-8

Nick owns a rental beach house. He and his two daughters spend two days at the beach house, where Nick repairs the deck and the screened porch while his daughters relax on the beach. The two days are not considered personal-use days.

Primarily Rental Use

If rental property is not used for more than 14 days for personal purposes (or 10% of the total rental days if more) and is rented for 15 days or more, it is primarily rental property. As such, the taxpayer must report all of the income and ordinary and necessary expenses (rental portion). The portion of expenses that are allocated to the personal use are not deductible unless they are normally allowed as itemized deductions (such as mortgage interest and property taxes). If a net loss results, it is deductible to the extent allowed by the passive activity loss rules (see the end of this chapter and Chapter 13).

Primarily Personal Use

A property rented for less than 15 days but otherwise used as a personal residence is considered primarily personal property. When property is rented for less than 15 days, *none* of the rental income derived from the short rental period is included in gross income. Likewise, no deduction is allowed for rental expenses (other than those normally allowed as itemized deductions).

EXAMPLE 8-9

Kirk and his family live in Augusta, Georgia. Each year during the Masters golf tournament, they rent their house to a major corporation for $10,000 for the entire week. Because Kirk rents his house for only seven days, the property is considered primarily personal, and Kirk reports none of the rental income or expenses.

Personal/Rental Property

When a rental property is used for personal use for more than 14 days, or 10% of the total rental days, and is rented for 15 days or more, the property is considered personal/rental property. In the case of personal/rental property, a taxpayer can deduct expenses only to the extent that there is rental income (that is, no net loss is allowed). A summary of vacation home rental rules is presented in Table 8-3.

EXAMPLE 8-10

Case 1: Primarily Rental Property: Frank owns a condominium at the beach that he rents for 90 days during the summer and uses the property for personal use for 13 days.

Case 2: Personal/Rental Property: Frank rents the condominium for 90 days and uses it for personal use for 16 days.

Case 3: Primarily Personal Property: Frank rents the property for 10 days, and he uses the condominium for the remainder of the year for personal use.

[17] Prop. Reg. § 1.280A-1(e)(7), ex. (1).

[18] IRC § 267(c)(4).

[19] IRS Publication 527, p. 21.

TABLE 8-3 Summary of Vacation Home Rental Rules

	Primarily Personal	**Primarily Rental**	**Personal/Rental**
Rental days	Rented less than 15 days.		Rented 15 days or more.
Personal days	No limit.	Personal use no more than the greater of (a) 14 days or (b) 10% of the total rental days.	More than the greater of (a) 14 days or (b) 10% of the total rental days.
Income and expense reporting	The income does not have to be reported. (It is not taxable!) Mortgage interest and property taxes are allowed as itemized deductions, as with any personal residence.	All rental income must be reported on Schedule E. The expenses must be allocated between personal and rental days and reported on Schedule E.	All rental income must be reported on Schedule E. The expenses must be allocated between personal and rental days and reported on Schedule E.
Net loss treatment	Not allowed; none of the net income or net loss is reported.	Losses are allowed (limited by passive activity loss rules). Usually limited to losses up to \$25,000 by passive loss rules discussed in Chapter 13.	Not allowed; expenses deducted only to the extent there is rental income (i.e., breakeven).

EXAMPLE 8-11

Susan owns a beach house in Seal Beach, California. Each year she uses her beach house for four months and rents it for three months in the summer. The property is considered personal/rental, and the expenses related to the beach house must be allocated between personal and rental use. Remember that if the rental portion of her expenses is higher than her rental income, the resulting net loss is not allowed.

CONCEPT CHECK 8-2— LO 8-2

Indicate the correct letter that identifies whether the rental property in the following situations would be categorized as (a) primarily rental, (b) primarily personal, or (c) personal/rental:

1. Jamie rented her lake home for \$2,000 for 12 days, and she and her family used it for the rest of the year, usually on weekends and holidays.
2. Julie rented her home in Solano Beach for 180 days for \$12,000; she used it for 17 days.
3. Darren rented his beach house for 45 days for \$9,000 and stayed there on weekends with his family for a total of 16 days. During his stay, he spent 7 of the days rebuilding the deck while his family enjoyed the beach.
4. Alex rented her mountain cabin for 90 days for \$13,500, and she and her family used it for 50 days.

Allocation of Rental Expenses

For both primarily rental and personal/rental properties, the expenses related to those properties must be allocated between personal and rental use. The following are the two methods used to allocate expenses between the personal and rental use of a rental property:

1. **The IRS method:** The expenses should be allocated between personal and rental days based on the ratio of the number of rental days to the total number of days used.
2. **The Tax Court method:** The interest and taxes on the rental property should be allocated based on the ratio of the number of rental days to the total number of days in the year (365),[20]

[20] The denominator in the allocation is the number of days owned during the year if the property was purchased or sold during the year.

and the remaining rental expenses should be allocated using the IRS method.[21] The court's rationale is that interest and taxes occur ratably over the entire year whereas other expenses occur only when the property is used.

Regardless of the allocation method used, certain expenses are not allocated but are deducted in full, subject to sufficient rental income. These are expenses that have no personal element to them such as travel costs and management fees. The Tax Court method nearly always results in a larger deduction for the taxpayer.

In addition, expenses must be deducted in a certain order. First, mortgage interest and property taxes and those expenses that are directly related to the rental activity (such as management fees) are deducted. Next to be deducted are indirect expenses such as utilities, insurance, and repairs. Lastly, depreciation expense is deducted and for personal/rental properties, deducted only to the extent that there is income still remaining.

EXAMPLE 8-12

Assume the same rental property example as illustrated in the "From Shoebox to Software" box for the Masters (following Example 8-6) except that rental income was $21,600 and the taxpayer used the property for 22 days for personal use and rented it for 84 days (therefore, the property would be categorized as personal/rental property). Also assume that the property was held the entire year when using the Tax Court method.

Rent income (12 weeks at $1,800 per week)	$21,600
Mortgage interest	1,300
Property taxes	3,800
Management fees (10% of gross rent)	2,160
Travel (1 round-trip [in April] for maintenance at 893 miles: 893 miles × 53.5 cents per mile)	478
Repairs (leaking roof and plumbing repairs)	2,500
Insurance	1,800
Utilities	2,000
Depreciation	17,290

IRS Method

The rental expenses are allocated based on the ratio of the number of rental days (84) to the total days used (106). The remaining expenses are allocated to personal use.

Expense	Total	Rental Ratio	Allocated to Personal	Deductible on Schedule E
Mortgage interest	$ 1,300	84/106	$270*	$1,030
Property taxes	3,800	84/106	789*	3,011
Management fees	2,160	100%	–0–	2,160
Travel	478	100%	–0–	478
Repairs	2,500	84/106	519	1,981
Insurance	1,800	84/106	374	1,426
Utilities	2,000	84/106	415	1,585
Depreciation	17,290	84/106	–0–	9,929†

* These amounts are deducted on Schedule A.
† The depreciation is $13,702. However, the deduction is limited to the remaining rental income of $9,929.
Note: Remember that the taxpayer cannot have a net loss on a personal/rental property.

Tax Court Method

Using the Tax Court allocation method, taxpayers allocate mortgage interest and property taxes by the ratio of rental days (84) to the entire year (365).[22] This yields a smaller percentage

[21] *Bolton, Dorance* (1981) 77 TC 104, affd (1982, CA9) 694 F2d 556; *McKinney, Edith* (1983, CA10) 732 F2d 414.

[22] If the property was held for less than the entire year (i.e., purchased or sold during the year), the number of days owned during the year is substituted for 365 days.

of the interest and taxes being allocated to rental income on Schedule E and more allocated to personal use as itemized deductions on Schedule A. The remaining expenses are allocated using the IRS method (84/106).

Expense	Total	Rental Ratio	Allocated to Personal	Deductible on Schedule E
Mortgage interest	$ 1,300	84/365	$1,001*	$ 299
Property taxes	3,800	84/365	2,925*	875
Management fees	2,160	100%	–0–	2,160
Travel	478	100%	–0–	478
Repairs	2,500	84/106	519	1,981
Insurance	1,800	84/106	374	1,426
Utilities	2,000	84/106	415	1,585
Depreciation	17,290	84/106	–0–	12,796†

* These amounts are deducted on Schedule A.
† The depreciation is $13,702. However, the deduction is limited to the remaining rental income of $12,796.
Note: Remember that the taxpayer cannot have a net loss on a personal/rental property.

Multifamily Residential Homes

If a taxpayer owns a multifamily home (such as a duplex or a triplex) and lives in one of the units and rents the other unit(s), the units are treated as independent units and the expenses are allocated accordingly. The expenses are allocated based on the proportion of the property that is used for rental purposes versus the portion that is used for personal purposes and deducted from the rental income.

EXAMPLE 8-13

Guadalupe owns and lives in a fourplex of identical two-bedroom units in Anaheim, California. During the year, the entire fourplex had $100,000 in expenses. She would allocate three-fourths of the expenses and deduct $75,000 in rental expenses against rental income for the year. The remaining $25,000 would be considered personal and deducted to the extent that Guadalupe can if she itemizes.

From Shoebox to Software

Tax software allocates rental expenses for you. Check whether your software calculates the expense allocation using the IRS method or the Tax Court method. Usually, if you enter the number of personal days on Schedule E (line 2), a note appears stating that the "vacation home limits will be applied." If you double-click on this note, the Vacation Home worksheet appears showing the allocation. If you wish to use a method different than your software normally does, you must make the calculations yourself and enter the expense items directly on Schedule E. Exhibits 8-3 and 8-4 illustrate the IRS method and the Tax Court method, respectively, on Schedule E, for the Masters using Example 8-12.

Note that the Tax Court method allocates more interest and taxes to personal use and deducts them on Schedule A as itemized deductions.[23] By allocating a higher percentage of interest and taxes to Schedule A, the taxpayer is able to deduct an additional $2,867 of depreciation expense ($12,796 versus $9,929) and increase the overall deductible expenses. Also note that the travel costs and management fees are 100% deductible. As discussed earlier, these expenses are 100% deductible because if this property was not rented, these expenses would not have occurred.

[23] Mortgage interest is deductible on Schedule A for interest on a personal residence and one vacation home; but if the taxpayer has more than one vacation home, the interest may not be deductible on Schedule A (for details on mortgage interest, see Chapter 5).

EXHIBIT 8-3 Schedule E Using the IRS Method

SCHEDULE E (Form 1040)
Department of the Treasury Internal Revenue Service (99)

Supplemental Income and Loss
(From rental real estate, royalties, partnerships, S corporations, estates, trusts, REMICs, etc.)
▶ Attach to Form 1040, 1040NR, or Form 1041.
▶ Go to *www.irs.gov/ScheduleE* for instructions and the latest information.

OMB No. 1545-0074
2017
Attachment Sequence No. 13

Name(s) shown on return: Alan and Cherie Masters IRS METHOD
Your social security number: 412-34-5670

Part I **Income or Loss From Rental Real Estate and Royalties** **Note:** If you are in the business of renting personal property, use **Schedule C** or **C-EZ** (see instructions). If you are an individual, report farm rental income or loss from **Form 4835** on page 2, line 40.

A Did you make any payments in 2017 that would require you to file Form(s) 1099? (see instructions) . . . ☐ Yes ☑ No
B If "Yes," did you or will you file required Forms 1099? . . . ☐ Yes ☐ No

1a	Physical address of each property (street, city, state, ZIP code)
A	123 Beach Road, San Clemente, CA 92672
B	
C	

1b	Type of Property (from list below)	2 For each rental real estate property listed above, report the number of fair rental and personal use days. Check the QJV box only if you meet the requirements to file as a qualified joint venture. See instructions.		Fair Rental Days	Personal Use Days	QJV
A	1		A	84	22	☐
B			B			☐
C			C			☐

Type of Property:
1 Single Family Residence 3 Vacation/Short-Term Rental 5 Land 7 Self-Rental
2 Multi-Family Residence 4 Commercial 6 Royalties 8 Other (describe)

Income:	**Properties:**		A	B	C
3	Rents received . . .	3	21,600		
4	Royalties received . . .	4			
Expenses:					
5	Advertising . . .	5			
6	Auto and travel (see instructions) . . .	6	478		
7	Cleaning and maintenance . . .	7			
8	Commissions. . . .	8			
9	Insurance . . .	9	1,426		
10	Legal and other professional fees . . .	10			
11	Management fees . . .	11	2,160		
12	Mortgage interest paid to banks, etc. (see instructions)	12	1,030		
13	Other interest. . . .	13			
14	Repairs. . . .	14	1,981		
15	Supplies . . .	15			
16	Taxes . . .	16	3,011		
17	Utilities. . . .	17	1,585		
18	Depreciation expense or depletion . . .	18	9,929		
19	Other (list) ▶	19			
20	Total expenses. Add lines 5 through 19 . . .	20	21,600		
21	Subtract line 20 from line 3 (rents) and/or 4 (royalties). If result is a (loss), see instructions to find out if you must file **Form 6198** . . .	21	0		
22	Deductible rental real estate loss after limitation, if any, on **Form 8582** (see instructions) . . .	22	( )	( )	( )

23a	Total of all amounts reported on line 3 for all rental properties . . .	23a	21,600
b	Total of all amounts reported on line 4 for all royalty properties . . .	23b	0
c	Total of all amounts reported on line 12 for all properties . . .	23c	1,060
d	Total of all amounts reported on line 18 for all properties . . .	23d	9,929
e	Total of all amounts reported on line 20 for all properties . . .	23e	21,600
24	**Income.** Add positive amounts shown on line 21. **Do not** include any losses . . .	24	0
25	**Losses.** Add royalty losses from line 21 and rental real estate losses from line 22. Enter total losses here .	25	(0)
26	**Total rental real estate and royalty income or (loss).** Combine lines 24 and 25. Enter the result here. If Parts II, III, IV, and line 40 on page 2 do not apply to you, also enter this amount on Form 1040, line 17, or Form 1040NR, line 18. Otherwise, include this amount in the total on line 41 on page 2 . . .	26	0

For Paperwork Reduction Act Notice, see the separate instructions. Cat. No. 11344L **Schedule E (Form 1040) 2017**

Source: U.S. Department of the Treasury, Internal Revenue Service, Schedule E (Form 1040). Washington, DC: 2017.

EXHIBIT 8-4 Schedule E Using the Tax Court Method

SCHEDULE E (Form 1040)
Department of the Treasury Internal Revenue Service (99)

Supplemental Income and Loss
(From rental real estate, royalties, partnerships, S corporations, estates, trusts, REMICs, etc.)
▶ Attach to Form 1040, 1040NR, or Form 1041.
▶ Go to *www.irs.gov/ScheduleE* for instructions and the latest information.

OMB No. 1545-0074
2017
Attachment Sequence No. 13

Name(s) shown on return: Alan and Cherie Masters TAX COURT METHOD
Your social security number: 412-34-5670

Part I Income or Loss From Rental Real Estate and Royalties **Note:** If you are in the business of renting personal property, use **Schedule C** or **C-EZ** (see instructions). If you are an individual, report farm rental income or loss from **Form 4835** on page 2, line 40.

A Did you make any payments in 2017 that would require you to file Form(s) 1099? (see instructions) ☐ Yes ☑ No
B If "Yes," did you or will you file required Forms 1099? ☐ Yes ☐ No

1a	Physical address of each property (street, city, state, ZIP code)
A	123 Beach Road, San Clemente, CA 92672
B	
C	

1b	Type of Property (from list below)	2 For each rental real estate property listed above, report the number of fair rental and personal use days. Check the QJV box only if you meet the requirements to file as a qualified joint venture. See instructions.	Fair Rental Days	Personal Use Days	QJV
A	1	A	84	22	☐
B		B			☐
C		C			☐

Type of Property:
1 Single Family Residence 3 Vacation/Short-Term Rental 5 Land 7 Self-Rental
2 Multi-Family Residence 4 Commercial 6 Royalties 8 Other (describe)

Income: Properties:		A	B	C
3 Rents received	3	21,600		
4 Royalties received	4			
Expenses:				
5 Advertising	5			
6 Auto and travel (see instructions)	6	478		
7 Cleaning and maintenance	7			
8 Commissions	8			
9 Insurance	9	1,426		
10 Legal and other professional fees	10			
11 Management fees	11	2,160		
12 Mortgage interest paid to banks, etc. (see instructions)	12	299		
13 Other interest	13			
14 Repairs	14	1,981		
15 Supplies	15			
16 Taxes	16	875		
17 Utilities	17	1,585		
18 Depreciation expense or depletion	18	12,796		
19 Other (list) ▶	19			
20 Total expenses. Add lines 5 through 19	20	21,600		
21 Subtract line 20 from line 3 (rents) and/or 4 (royalties). If result is a (loss), see instructions to find out if you must file **Form 6198**	21	0		
22 Deductible rental real estate loss after limitation, if any, on **Form 8582** (see instructions)	22	( )	( )	( )

23a Total of all amounts reported on line 3 for all rental properties	23a	21,600
b Total of all amounts reported on line 4 for all royalty properties	23b	0
c Total of all amounts reported on line 12 for all properties	23c	299
d Total of all amounts reported on line 18 for all properties	23d	12,796
e Total of all amounts reported on line 20 for all properties	23e	21,600
24 **Income.** Add positive amounts shown on line 21. **Do not** include any losses	24	0
25 **Losses.** Add royalty losses from line 21 and rental real estate losses from line 22. Enter total losses here	25	(0)
26 **Total rental real estate and royalty income or (loss).** Combine lines 24 and 25. Enter the result here. If Parts II, III, IV, and line 40 on page 2 do not apply to you, also enter this amount on Form 1040, line 17, or Form 1040NR, line 18. Otherwise, include this amount in the total on line 41 on page 2	26	0

For Paperwork Reduction Act Notice, see the separate instructions. Cat. No. 11344L **Schedule E (Form 1040) 2017**

Source: U.S. Department of the Treasury, Internal Revenue Service, Schedule E (Form 1040). Washington, DC: 2017.

From the partner's point of view, the details of the self-employment calculation are unimportant because the number on line 14 (less § 179 expense) is the amount of self-employment earnings that must be reported on Schedule SE.

The income from all other flow-through entities is not considered self-employment income (as is in a partnership). For example, an employee/shareholder in an S corporation receives a salary like any other employee, and the S corporation and employee each pays its share of social security tax. Ordinary income from an S corporation is not self-employment income.

Partnership Income or Loss—Passive Activities

We discuss passive activities in detail in Chapter 13. However, some explanation is needed at this point. A *passive activity* is an activity in which the taxpayer does not materially participate in the operations. An investment often is a passive activity, whereas an actual trade or business is considered active. After all, a trade or business such as a bakery or a retail store does not operate by itself; some person(s) must actively run the business. Rental activity and limited partnership interests are, by definition, passive activities (even if the taxpayer actively participated in that activity).[31]

Thus, if the limited partner box on a K-1 (Part II) is checked or income from rental activities is shown on line 2 or 3, the activity is likely a passive activity. The passive rules require that the taxpayer categorize income and losses into three types: active, passive, and portfolio. In general, taxpayers can deduct passive losses to the extent that there is passive income (that is, no loss is allowed). Any excess losses cannot be used to offset active or portfolio income but are carried forward instead to offset passive income in future years. In cases of rental activity, however, a taxpayer is allowed up to $25,000 of rental losses against other nonpassive income, subject to phaseout above certain AGI amounts (see Chapter 13 for details and limitations). Income or losses from passive activities are reported on line 28, column (f) or (g), of page 2, Schedule E. Form 8582 may also be required.

CONCEPT CHECK 8-5— LO 8-4

1. Flow-through entities allocate an appropriate share of the entity's income, expenses, or loss to their partners, shareholders, or owners on a Schedule K-1. True or false?
2. Ordinary income from all flow-through entities is considered self-employment income. True or false?
3. The partners (shareholders and owners) must report the income and loss from the K-1s they received on a Schedule E of their individual tax returns. True or false?
4. By definition, rental properties are passive activities. However, in certain cases, a taxpayer may deduct rental losses, subject to limitations and phaseouts. True or false?

Summary

LO 8-1: Explain how income and expenses are recognized and reported for rental property.

- Income and expenses from rental property are generally reported on Schedule E.
- Gross rent is total rent collected regardless of the period covered and includes expenses paid by the tenant or services provided by the tenant in lieu of rent payments.
- All ordinary and necessary expenses related to a rental property are deductible.
- Rental property is depreciated using straight-line depreciation over 27.5 or 39 years.
- If a taxpayer's rental property is considered a trade or business, the related income and expenses are reported on Schedule C.

[31] IRC § 469.

LO 8-2: Understand how to report personal use of a rental property (vacation home).	• A property that is used for both personal and rental activity falls into one of three categories for tax purposes: (a) primarily rental, (b) primarily personal, and (c) personal/rental. • The three categories are determined by comparing the number of rental use days versus the number of personal-use days. • If a rental property is primarily personal, no income is taxable and no expenses are deductible other than deductions usually allowed as itemized deductions. • If a rental property is primarily rental or personal/rental, the expenses must be allocated between personal and rental use. • Two methods available to allocate expenses between personal and rental uses are the IRS and the Tax Court methods. • No net loss is allowed if a rental property is considered personal/rental (i.e., expenses are deducted only to the extent that there is rental income). • In the case of multifamily homes when the taxpayer owns the home, lives in one of the units, and rents the remaining units, the units are treated as independent units and expenses allocated accordingly.
LO 8-3: Know how to report royalty income on Schedule E.	• A *royalty* is a payment for the right to use intangible property. • Royalty income is generally reported on Schedule E. • If a payment is received while performing a service related to the royalty-producing asset or the royalty is a result of a trade or business, the royalty income is reported on Schedule C.
LO 8-4: Discuss the different types of flow-through entities reported on Schedule E, such as partnerships, S corporations, LLCs, trusts, and estates.	• Partnerships, LLCs, S corporations, trusts, and estates are known as *flow-through entities.* • Flow-through entities file "informational returns" and provide their partners (shareholder or owner) with Schedule K-1s. • The income and expenses from K-1s are reported on the individual partner's (shareholder or owner) Schedule E. • Certain limited partnerships and rental activity are considered passive activities; as such, the amounts of net loss that are deductible against nonpassive income are limited by the passive activity rules (discussed in detail in Chapter 13).

Discussion Questions connect

All applicable discussion questions are available with ***Connect***©

LO 8-1 1. Can an owner of a rental property be treated as conducting a trade or business with respect to the rental property? If so, what must the owner do for it to be considered a trade or business?

EA LO 8-1 2. For rental expenses to be deductible, what criteria must be met? For this question, assume no personal use of the rental property.

EA LO 8-1 3. What is the difference between a deductible repair expense and capital improvement of rental property?

EA LO 8-1 4. When depreciation is deducted on a rental property, why is it beneficial for the taxpayer to allocate the cost of the property to other assets (furniture, appliances, etc.) connected with the property rather than allocating the entire lump sum to the building itself?

EA LO 8-2 5. Can travel expenses to and from rental property be deducted? If so, what are the rules concerning the deductibility of travel, and how is the deduction calculated? (*Hint:* You may need to review Chapter 6 to help with this answer.)

EA LO 8-2 6. Les's personal residence is in uptown New Orleans. Every year during Mardi Gras, Les rents his house for 10 days to a large corporation that uses it to entertain clients. How does Les treat the rental income? Explain.

EA LO 8-2 7. Two methods are used to allocate expenses between personal and rental uses of property. Explain the Tax Court method and the IRS method. Which method is more beneficial to the taxpayer?

LO 8-2 8. Discuss the three categories of vacation home rentals. Include in your discussion how personal use of the property affects the reporting of income and losses of vacation homes.

LO 8-2 9. What is considered personal use of a vacation rental property?

LO 8-2 10. Jake has a vacation rental house at the beach. During the tax year, he and his immediate family used the house for 12 days for personal vacation. Jake and his son spent two more weekends (4 days) repairing the steps from the property to the beach. The beach house was rented for 100 days. How is the beach house categorized this year? Explain your answer.

LO 8-2 11. Would your answer to Question 10 change if Jake also rented his house (at fair value) to his brother and his family for 7 days?

EA LO 8-3 12. What is royalty income, and which forms are used to report it? What factors determine which forms should be used?

LO 8-1, 8-2, 8-3, 8-4 EA 13. Briefly describe the types of income that are reported on Schedule E.

LO 8-4 14. What is meant by the term *flow-through entity*? Give some examples.

EA LO 8-4 15. How are the income and losses from a flow-through entity reported to the taxpayer (partner, shareholder, or owner)? Are all of the items from the flow-through entity reported on the same form? Explain.

LO 8-4 16. Why are the income and losses (or expenses) separately stated to the partner, shareholder, or owner, and on what form are they reported?

LO 8-4 17. Why are charitable contributions stated separately on the K-1 but not deducted on a partnership return?

Multiple-Choice Questions connect

All applicable multiple-choice questions are available with ***Connect***©

EA LO 8-1 18. On August 1 of the current year, Jennifer and Tyler purchased a cabin for $950,000. Of that amount, $500,000 was for the land. How much depreciation deduction can Jennifer and Tyler take in the current year assuming that the cabin was rented starting on the purchase date? (You may need to refer to the depreciation tables in Chapter 6.)

a. 0.

b. $6,138.

c. $8,865.

d. $16,364.

EA LO 8-1 19. Jermaine owns a rental home in Lake Tahoe and traveled there from his home in San Francisco for maintenance and repairs three times this year. The round trip from San Francisco to Lake Tahoe is approximately 167 miles. How much travel cost can Jermaine deduct for the current year related to the rental home in Lake Tahoe?

a. 0.

b. $89.

c. $266.

d. $271.

EA LO 8-1 20. Dennis receives $11,100 during the current tax year from Blanca for some office space in Anaheim, California. The rent covers eight months, from August 1 of the current year to March 31 of the following year. The amount also includes a security deposit of $1,500. How much should Dennis report as rental income in the current tax year?

a. $1,200.

b. $6,000.

c. $9,600.

d. $11,100.

EA LO 8-1 21. Ginny owns a house in northern Wisconsin that she rents for $1,600 per month. Ginny does not use the property personally. While she was in Europe for Christmas, the water heater on the property failed, and her tenants repaired it for $1,200. For the following month's rent (January), her tenants paid her $400 for rent ($1,600 – $1,200). What amounts should Ginny include for rental income and repair expense, respectively, for January?

a. $400; $0.

b. $1,200; $400.

c. $1,600; $400.

d. $1,600; $1,200.

EA LO 8-2 22. James owns a home in Lake Tahoe, Nevada, that he rented for $1,600 for two weeks during the summer. He lived there for a total of 120 days, and the rest of the year the house was vacant. The expenses for the home included $6,000 in mortgage interest, $900 in property taxes, $1,300 in maintenance and utilities, and $2,500 in depreciation.

How much rental income from the Lake Tahoe home would James report for the current year?

a. $0.

b. $567.

c. $1,600.

d. $9,100.

EA LO 8-2 23. Assume the same facts as Question 22 except that James rented the Lake Tahoe home for 40 days for $4,600. What is his net income or loss from the rental of his home (without considering the passive loss limitation)? Use the IRS method for allocation of expenses.

a. $0.

b. $1,925 net income.

c. $4,600 net income.

d. $6,100 net loss.

EA LO 8-2 24. Which of the following items is *not* deductible as rental expense?

a. Advertising.

b. Repairs and maintenance.

c. New bathroom addition.

d. Insurance.

EA LO 8-2 25. Darren and Nikki own a cabin in Mammoth, California. During the year, they rented it for 45 days for $9,000 and used it for 12 days for personal use. The house remained vacant for the remainder of the year. The expenses for the house included $8,000 in mortgage interest, $2,000 in property taxes, $1,200 in utilities, $750 in maintenance, and $4,000 in depreciation. What is their net income or loss from their cabin rental (without considering the passive loss limitation)? Use the IRS method for allocation of expenses.

a. $0.

b. $3,592 net loss.

c. $6,950 net loss.

d. $9,000 net income.

EA LO 8-2 26. Sean and Jenny own a home in Boulder City, Nevada, near Lake Mead. During the year, they rented the house for 40 days for $3,000 and used it for personal use for 18 days. The house remained vacant for the remainder of the year. The expenses for the house included $14,000 in mortgage interest, $3,500 in property taxes, $1,100 in utilities, $1,300 in maintenance, and $10,900 in depreciation. What is the deductible net loss for the rental of their home (without considering the passive loss limitation)? Use the Tax Court method for allocation of expenses.

a. $0.

b. $388.

c. $8,090.

d. $27,800.

EA LO 8-2 27. Nicolette and Brady own a cabin in Lake Arrowhead, California, that they rent out during the winter and use the rest of the year. The rental property is categorized as personal/rental property, and their personal use is determined to be 68% (based on the IRS method). They had the following income and expenses for the year (after allocation):

Gross rental income	$9,500
Interest and taxes	6,000
Utilities and maintenance	2,500
Depreciation	4,300

How much can Nicolette and Brady deduct for depreciation expense related to this property for the year on their tax return?

a. $0.

b. $1,000.

c. $4,300.

d. The answer cannot be determined.

EA LO 8-3 28. Colin is a high school chemistry teacher who owns some land in Oklahoma that produces oil from its small oil reserve. On what schedule should Colin report the royalty income he receives?

a. Schedule A.

b. Schedule C.

c. Schedule E.

d. Schedule SE.

EA LO 8-3 29. Sally is a full-time author and recently published her third mystery novel. The royalty income she receives from the publisher this year should be reported on what schedule?

a. Schedule E.

b. Schedule D.

c. Schedule A.

d. Schedule C.

LO 8-4 30. What is the maximum amount of passive losses from a rental activity that a taxpayer can deduct against active and portfolio income per year (assuming no passive loss limitation due to AGI or personal use of the property)?

a. $0.

b. $15,000.

c. $25,000.

d. $50,000.

LO 8-4 31. Which of the following entity(ies) is (are) considered flow-through?

a. Partnership.

b. S corporation.

c. LLC.

d. All are considered flow-through entities.

LO 8-4 32. From which of the following flow-through entities is ordinary income (K-1) considered self-employment income?

a. Partnership.

b. S corporation.

c. Trusts.

d. Estates.

Problems connect

All applicable problems are available with ***Connect***©

LO 8-1

33. Ramone is a tax attorney and he owns an office building that he rents for $8,500/month. He is responsible for paying all taxes and expenses relating to the building's operation and maintenance. Is Ramone engaged in the trade or business of renting real estate?

EA LO 8-1, 8-2

34. Kelvin owns and lives in a duplex. He rents the other unit for $750 per month. He incurs the following expenses during the current year for the entire property:

Mortgage interest	$7,500
Property taxes	2,000
Utilities	1,500
Fixed light fixture in rental unit	100
Fixed dishwasher in personal unit	250
Painted entire exterior	1,300
Insurance	1,800
Depreciation (entire structure)	7,000

How are these income and expenses reported on Kelvin's tax return? On what tax form(s) are these amounts reported?

EA LO 8-2

35. In the current year, Sandra rented her vacation home for 75 days, used it for personal use for 22 days, and left it vacant for the remainder of the year. Her income and expenses before allocation are as follows:

Rental income	$15,000
Real estate taxes	2,000
Utilities	1,500
Mortgage interest	3,800
Depreciation	7,200
Repairs and maintenance	1,300

What is Sandra's net income or loss from the rental of her vacation home? Use the Tax Court method.

EA LO 8-2 36. Alice rented her personal residence for 13 days to summer vacationers for $4,500. She has AGI of $105,000 before the rental income. Related expenses for the year include the following:

Real property taxes	$ 4,500
Utilities	5,000
Insurance	900
Mortgage interest	7,000
Repairs	800
Depreciation	15,000

Calculate the effect of the rental on Alice's AGI. Explain your rationale, citing tax authority.

EA LO 8-2 37. Matt and Marie own a vacation home at the beach. During the year, they rented the house for 42 days (6 weeks) at $890 per week and used it for personal use for 58 days. The total costs of maintaining the home are as follows:

Mortgage interest	$4,200
Property taxes	700
Insurance	1,200
Utilities	3,200
Repairs	1,900
Depreciation	5,500

a. What is the proper tax treatment of this information on their tax return using the Tax Court method?

b. Are there options available for how to allocate the expenses between personal and rental use? Explain.

c. What is the proper tax treatment of the rental income and expenses if Matt and Marie rented the house for only 14 days?

EA LO 8-2 38. Janet owns a home at the lake. She incurs the following expenses:

Mortgage interest	$1,300
Property taxes	800
Insurance	1,500
Utilities	1,800
Repairs	300
Depreciation	4,000

What is the proper treatment of the rental income and expenses in each of the following cases? Use the Tax Court allocation method, if applicable.

Case	Rental Income	Days Rented	Personal-Use Days
A	$ 9,000	45	10
B	12,000	55	25
C	6,000	10	30
D	22,000	365	–0–

EA LO 8-2 39. Randolph and Tammy own a second home. They spent 45 days there and rented it for 88 days at $150 per day during the year. The total costs relating to the home include the following:

Mortgage interest	$4,500
Property taxes	1,200
Insurance	1,800
Utilities	2,300
Repairs	1,500
Depreciation	6,500

What is the proper treatment of these items relating to the second home? Would you use the Tax Court allocation or the IRS allocation? Explain.

EA LO 8-4 40. Mabel, Loretta, and Margaret are equal partners in a local restaurant. The restaurant reports the following items for the current year:

Revenue	$ 600,000
Business expenses	310,000
Investment expenses	150,000
Short-term capital gains	157,000
Short-term capital losses	(213,000)

Each partner receives a Schedule K-1 with one-third of the preceding items reported to her. How must each individual report these results on her Form 1040?

EA LO 8-4 41. Nicole and Mohammad (married taxpayers filing jointly) are equal owners in an S corporation. The company reported sales revenue of $450,000 and expenses of $310,000. The corporation also earned $20,000 in taxable interest and dividend income and had $15,000 investment interest expense. How are these amounts treated for tax purposes?

EA LO 8-4 42. Dominique and Terrell are joint owners of a bookstore. The business operates as an S corporation. Dominique owns 65%, and Terrell owns 35%. The business has the following results in the current year:

Revenue	$1,500,000
Business expenses	750,000
Charitable contributions	50,000
Short-term capital losses	4,500
Long-term capital gains	6,000

How do Dominique and Terrell report these items for tax purposes?

EA LO 8-4 43. Shirelle and Newman are each 50% partners of a business that operates as a partnership. The business reports the following results:

Revenue	$95,000
Business expenses	48,000
Investment expenses	8,000
Short-term capital gains	15,000
Short-term capital losses	(22,000)

How do Shirelle and Newman report these items for tax purposes?

Tax Return Problems connect

All applicable tax return problems are available with ***Connect***©

Use your tax software to complete the following problems. If you are manually preparing the tax returns, see each problem for the forms you may need.

Tax Return Problem 1

Derrick and Ani Jones are married taxpayers, filing jointly and have a son named Jackson. They live at 474 Rustic Drive, Spokane, WA 99201. Ani works as the director of information systems at Washington Community College District (WCCD). Derrick is a stay-at-home dad. Their SSNs are Derrick, 412-34-5670; Ani, 412-34-5671; and Jackson, 412-34-5672. Their birth dates are as follows: Derrick, June 7, 1977; Ani, March 20, 1978; and Jackson, October 10, 2010. The Joneses own their home and paid $15,000 in mortgage interest during the year to Chase Bank and property taxes of $3,200. Assume they have no other deductible expenses.

The Form W-2 Ani received from WCCD contained the following information:

Wages (box 1) = $79,002.50
Federal W/H (box 2) = $ 8,000.14
Social security wages (box 3) = $79,002.50
Social security W/H (box 4) = $ 4,898.16
Medicare wages (box 5) = $79,002.50
Medicare W/H (box 6) = $ 1,145.54

In addition, the Joneses own a small four-unit rental at 12345 Rainbow Way, Sultan, WA 98294. The rental was purchased and placed in service on July 1, 2005, and was rented for the entire year. The following income and expense information relates to the rental activity. For the purpose of this return problem, do not consider passive activity rules or limitations.

Rental income	$24,000
Real estate taxes	2,000
State sales taxes	$1,349
Utilities	1,500
Mortgage interest	3,800
Depreciation	7,200
Repairs and maintenance	1,300

Prepare the Joneses' federal tax return for 2017. Use Form 1040, Schedule A, Schedule E, and any other appropriate schedules. Assume they do not qualify for any credits other than the child care credit. If using tax software, the software will calculate Child Tax Credit automatically. The taxpayers had qualifying health care coverage at all times during the tax year. For any missing information, make reasonable assumptions.

We have provided selected filled-in source documents available in the *Connect Library*.

Tax Return Problem 2

Warren and Young Kim are married taxpayers, filing jointly. They live at 777 Kingston Place, Anaheim, CA 92805. They are both retired. Their SSNs are Warren, 412-34-5670; and Young, 412-34-5671. Their birth dates are as follows: Warren, January 8, 1947; and Young, August 21, 1947.

They own their home, which they paid off in 2008, and another home that they paid for in cash as an investment (Warren considers it his pension). Their investment home was rented for the entire year and is located just one block over at 9021 Jasmine Way. The following income and expense information relates to the rental activity. For the purpose of this return problem, do not consider passive activity rules or limitations.

Rental income	$27,600
Real estate taxes	7,952
Utilities	1,603
Mortgage interest	–0–
Repairs and maintenance	3,616
Depreciation	See following information

They placed the rental home into service on March 1, 2011, and of the $515,000 purchase price, $426,000 was allocated to the land.

In addition to the rental, they received interest of $1,086 from American Credit Union and $2,200 from Bank of California. Social security benefits were $13,910 for Warren and $3,822 for Young, respectively.

Prepare the Kims' federal tax return for 2017. Use Form 1040, Schedule B, Schedule E, and Form 4562. Assume they do not qualify for any credits (although they may). The taxpayers had qualifying health care coverage at all times during the tax year. For any missing information, make reasonable assumptions.

We have provided selected filled-in source documents available in the *Connect Library.*

Tax Return Problem 3

Lou and Joann Girardi are married and file a joint return. They recently bought a new home on 21680 Skyline Drive, Henderson, NV, 89077. Their son, Stuart, attends the University of Pennsylvania full-time on a full scholarship. Stuart is claimed as a dependent on the Girardis' tax return. Their SSNs are Lou, 412-34-5670; Joann, 412-34-5671; and Stuart, 412-34-5672. Their birth dates are as follows: Lou, May 18, 1964; Joann, December 24, 1964; and Stuart, May 9, 1997. Their relevant tax information follows:

Joann is an attorney and owns her law firm, which is operating as an S corporation. Her W-2 information and Schedule K-1 from her law firm are as follows:

Wages (box 1) = $114,800.50
Federal W/H (box 2) = $ 15,000.14
Social security wages (box 3) = $114,800.50
Social security W/H (box 4) = $ 7,117.63
Medicare wages (box 5) = $114,800.50
Medicare W/H (box 6) = $ 1,664.61

Schedule K-1 from the law offices of Joann Girardi: Girardi - Attorney at Law
ID # 12-3456789
100% Owner
Material participation – yes

Line 1 = $22,582.00 (ordinary business income)
Line 11 = $22,582.00 (§ 179 deduction)

Lou is a full-time lecturer at Arizona State University. His W-2 information from ASU is as follows:

Wages (box 1) = $65,000.00
Federal W/H (box 2) = $ 9,950.25
Social security wages (box 3) = $65,000.00
Social security W/H (box 4) = $ 4,030.00
Medicare wages (box 5) = $65,000.00
Medicare W/H (box 6) = $ 942.50

The following are other income and expenses they received and incurred during the year:

Income	
Dividends (qualified)	$ 666
Interest	765
Expenses	
Real estate taxes	7,836
State sales tax	1,629
Mortgage interest	32,562
Charitable contribution	2,598

Prepare the Girardis' federal tax return for 2017. Use Form 1040, Schedules A, B, and E, and a Qualified Dividends worksheet. Assume that the Girardis do not qualify for any credits (although they may). For any missing information, make reasonable assumptions. The taxpayers had qualifying health care coverage at all times during the tax year. (Assume no AMT although it may apply; Form 6251 or the AMT calculation is not required.)

We have provided selected filled-in source documents that are available in the *Connect Library*.

Chapter Nine

Tax Credits (Form 1040, Lines 48 through 54 and Lines 66a through 73)

Congress has provided a variety of tax credits designed to reduce the tax liability of specific groups of taxpayers. The intended purpose of these tax credits is to accomplish certain social or economic goals or to encourage participation in certain activities deemed desirable by policymakers. Tax credits are different from tax deductions. A tax credit is subtracted directly from the total amount of tax liability, thus reducing or even eliminating the taxpayer's tax obligation. Tax deductions decrease the taxable income used to calculate tax liability. Thus tax credits provide equal relief to all taxpayers regardless of their marginal tax rate and are more beneficial to the taxpayer than a deduction.

Learning Objectives

When you have completed this chapter, you should understand the following learning objectives (LO):

LO 9-1 Apply the tax rules and calculate the credit for child and dependent care expenses.
LO 9-2 Apply the tax rules and calculate the credit for the elderly or the disabled.
LO 9-3 Apply the tax rules and calculate the education credits.
LO 9-4 Apply the tax rules and calculate the foreign tax credit (FTC).
LO 9-5 Apply the tax rules and calculate the child tax credit.
LO 9-6 Apply the tax rules and calculate the retirement savings contributions credit.
LO 9-7 Apply the tax rules and calculate the adoption credit.
LO 9-8 Apply the tax rules and calculate the Earned Income Credit (EIC).
LO 9-9 Apply the tax rules for the premium tax credit under the Affordable Care Act.

INTRODUCTION

Congress has elected to offer a number of tax credits, generally enacted to encourage certain outcomes or to accomplish specified societal goals. Some of these goals include assisting families with children, ensuring additional tax relief for low-income taxpayers, encouraging taxpayers to enhance their education, encouraging adoptions, and providing incentives for taxpayers to work.

Most individual income tax credits are *nonrefundable*. This means that a taxpayer whose credits exceed his or her tax liability will reduce tax owed to zero but will *not* receive a refund for the excess amount. There are some tax credits that are *refundable,* such as the Earned

Income Credit (EIC) and others. In these cases, a taxpayer with credits in excess of the tax liability will receive the excess amount as a refund.

Most tax credits are reported on lines 48 through 54 and lines 66a through 73 of Form 1040, and some may require additional forms or schedules. This chapter also discusses the premium tax credit, which can create additional tax on line 46 or an additional credit on line 69. The more commonly used tax credits are discussed under the appropriate learning objectives of this chapter.

CREDIT FOR CHILD AND DEPENDENT CARE EXPENSES (FORM 1040, LINE 49 [FORM 2441], OR FORM 1040A, LINE 31)

LO 9-1

Many taxpayers with dependents incur expenses to care for those dependents while they work. The credit for child and dependent care expenses provides some relief for working taxpayers by providing a credit for a portion of the expenses incurred to care for a qualified dependent.[1] To qualify for the credit, the taxpayer must incur employment-related expenses to care for one or more qualifying individuals.

Qualifying Expenses

All necessary expenses, including those paid for household services and expenses for the care of qualified individuals so that the taxpayer can be gainfully employed,[2] are eligible. Appropriate expenses include those incurred in the home for a babysitter, housekeeper, cook, or nanny. Expenses paid to a family member (such as a grandmother) are eligible as long as the relative is not a child of the taxpayer under the age of 19 nor can be claimed as a dependent by the taxpayer.[3]

If the expenses are incurred outside the home at a dependent care facility (such as a day care center) that provides care for a fee for six or more individuals, the expenses qualify only if the facility complies with all of the applicable state and local laws related to licensing.[4] In addition, out-of-the-home expenses incurred while caring for an older dependent or spouse (who is incapacitated) qualify. However, the qualifying individual(s) must live in the household of the taxpayer for at least eight hours a day. These rules allow credit for expenses incurred for an incapacitated dependent who otherwise would be institutionalized.

Qualifying Individual

A qualifying individual includes (1) a person under age 13 for whom the taxpayer is entitled to a dependency deduction or (2) a dependent or spouse of the taxpayer who is incapable of caring for himself or herself and who lived with the taxpayer for at least half of the year.[5] A child under age 13 meeting the special dependency test of divorced parents is deemed to be a qualifying individual for the custodial parent even if that parent cannot claim the child as a dependent.[6]

Generally, married taxpayers must file a joint return to claim the credit (legally separated taxpayers are not considered to be married). A married taxpayer filing a separate return is entitled to claim the credit only if he or she meets *all* the following conditions:

- Lived apart from his or her spouse.
- Furnished more than half of the cost of maintaining a household that a qualified individual lived in for more than half the year.
- Has a spouse who was not a member of the household for the last six months of the year.[7]

[1] IRC § 21.

[2] IRC § 21(b)(2)(A).

[3] *Family member* is defined in IRC § 151(c)(3).

[4] IRC § 21(b)(2)(C) and IRC § 21(b)(2)(D).

[5] IRC § 21(b)(1).

[6] IRC § 21(e)(5) and IRC § 152(e).

[7] IRC § 21(e)(4).

Credit Calculation

The credit is calculated as a percentage of employment-related expenses paid during the year. The percentage varies between 20% and 35%, depending on the taxpayer's AGI. The maximum amount of qualifying expenses for any year is limited to $3,000 if there is one qualifying individual and to $6,000 for two or more qualifying individuals.[8] These amounts are further limited to the amount of earned income of the taxpayer (or the earned income of the taxpayer's spouse, if smaller).[9] Earned income includes wages, salaries, tips, other taxable employee compensation, and net earnings from self-employment. Generally, only taxable compensation is included. Therefore, earned income does not include noncompensation income such as interest and dividends, unemployment compensation, or child support payments, among others. If a taxpayer receives dependent care assistance from an employer that is excluded from gross income, the expense limit is reduced by the amount excluded from income.[10] The amount of the credit is limited to the taxpayer's tax liability.

If the taxpayer's spouse is unable to care for himself or herself or is a full-time student, the spouse is deemed to have earned income for the purpose of the credit calculation. That amount of earned income is $250 per month if the taxpayer cares for one qualifying person and $500 per month if caring for two or more persons. In case of a full-time student, the amount is further limited by the number of months the taxpayer (or the spouse) attended school.

EXAMPLE 9-1

Bill and Suzie paid $6,400 in qualified employment-related expenses for their three children. Suzie received $2,500 of dependent care assistance that her employer properly excluded from Suzie's gross income. The amount of employment-related expenses Bill and Suzie can use to determine their credit is $3,500 (the maximum amount allowed of $6,000 reduced by $2,500 of excluded dependent care assistance). Note that the taxpayer must apply the dependent care assistance exclusion against the $6,000 limitation, not against the total amount paid of $6,400 (unless the amount paid is less than the limitation amount).

EXAMPLE 9-2

Rick and Vanessa paid $3,800 in qualified employment-related expenses for their dependent daughter. Their AGI was $42,000, which included $40,500 from Vanessa's job and $1,500 of net self-employment income from Rick's business (as reported on Schedule C). Qualified employment-related expenses would be limited to $1,500.

EXAMPLE 9-3

Ethan and Jenny paid $4,200 in qualified employment-related expenses for their dependent son. Ethan's AGI was $42,000; Jenny was a full-time student for nine months of the year. Ethan and Jenny's qualified employment-related expenses would be limited to $2,250 ($250 × 9 months).

The percentage used to determine the credit, which ranges from 20% to 35%, depends on the taxpayer's AGI. The percentage is 35% for taxpayers with AGI of $15,000 or less and is reduced by 1% for each additional $2,000 of AGI (or fraction thereof) with a minimum percentage of 20%. The following chart provides applicable percentages:

[8] IRC § 21(c).

[9] IRC § 21(d).

[10] IRC § 21(c). The income exclusion would be made in accordance with IRC § 129.

Adjusted Gross Income	Applicable Percentage
$15,000 or less	35%
15,001–17,000	34
17,001–19,000	33
19,001–21,000	32
21,001–23,000	31
23,001–25,000	30
25,001–27,000	29
27,001–29,000	28
29,001–31,000	27
31,001–33,000	26
33,001–35,000	25
35,001–37,000	24
37,001–39,000	23
39,001–41,000	22
41,001–43,000	21
43,001 or more	20

From Shoebox to Software

Taxpayers use Form 2441 to calculate and report the child and dependent care credit (Exhibit 9-1).

Complete identification of the qualifying child is required. Taxpayers must also provide information for the person or entity that provided the care, including taxpayer ID numbers. Most established day care programs provide taxpayers with end-of-year statements listing the amounts paid for day care and the taxpayer ID of the day care establishment.

Within the tax software, you enter most required information directly on Form 2441. Part I is used to report information about the child care provider, including the amount paid. Part II shows data on the qualifying individual(s) and the expenses paid for each one. The tax software automatically determines lines 3 through 11. If the taxpayer received any nontaxable dependent care benefits from his or her employer, the software will then complete Part III (not shown). The amount of tax-free benefit is in box 10 of Form W-2.

The tax software reports the final credit amount (line 11) on line 49 on Form 1040 or line 31 on Form 1040A.

EXAMPLE 9-4 Walt has AGI of $18,744 from his employment, and he spent $1,240 on qualified expenses for his child during the year. He is entitled to a tax credit of $409 ($1,240 × 33%). If Walt's AGI were $15,200, his credit would be $422 ($1,240 × 34%). If Walt's AGI were $25,500, his credit would be $360 ($1,240 × 29%).

EXAMPLE 9-5 Rachel, a single mother, maintains a household for her 4-year-old son, Eric. Rachel had AGI of $34,500 and incurred $3,800 in child care expenses for Eric during the year. Her child and dependent care tax credit will be $750 ($3,000 × 25%). Rachel is entitled to 25% of qualifying expenses, which are limited to $3,000.

TAX YOUR BRAIN

Why would Congress want to provide a credit for child and dependent care expenses?

ANSWER

Remember that the credit pertains to qualifying expenses paid to enable the taxpayer to be gainfully employed. It is reasonable to expect that the credit will allow more individuals to be employed (or be employed more hours), resulting in higher payroll and other taxes to offset at least some of the cost of providing the credit. In addition, overall employment levels should increase, which is beneficial to the economy in general.

EXHIBIT 9-1

Form **2441**

Department of the Treasury
Internal Revenue Service (99)

Child and Dependent Care Expenses

► Attach to Form 1040, Form 1040A, or Form 1040NR.

► Go to *www.irs.gov/Form2441* for instructions and the latest information.

1040 / 1040A / 1040NR / 2441

OMB No. 1545-0074

2017

Attachment Sequence No. **21**

Name(s) shown on return | **Your social security number**

Part I **Persons or Organizations Who Provided the Care**—You **must** complete this part. (If you have more than two care providers, see the instructions.)

1 (a) Care provider's name	(b) Address (number, street, apt. no., city, state, and ZIP code)	(c) Identifying number (SSN or EIN)	(d) Amount paid (see instructions)

Did you receive dependent care benefits? — **No** ► Complete only Part II below. — **Yes** ► Complete Part III on the back next.

Caution: If the care was provided in your home, you may owe employment taxes. If you do, you can't file Form 1040A. For details, see the instructions for Form 1040, line 60a, or Form 1040NR, line 59a.

Part II **Credit for Child and Dependent Care Expenses**

2 Information about your **qualifying person(s).** If you have more than two qualifying persons, see the instructions.

(a) Qualifying person's name — First	Last	(b) Qualifying person's social security number	(c) **Qualified expenses** you incurred and paid in 2017 for the person listed in column (a)

3 Add the amounts in column (c) of line 2. **Don't** enter more than $3,000 for one qualifying person or $6,000 for two or more persons. If you completed Part III, enter the amount from line 31 . . . . . . **3**

4 Enter your **earned income.** See instructions **4**

5 If married filing jointly, enter your spouse's earned income (if you or your spouse was a student or was disabled, see the instructions); **all others**, enter the amount from line 4 . **5**

6 Enter the **smallest** of line 3, 4, or 5 . . . . . . **6**

7 Enter the amount from Form 1040, line 38; Form 1040A, line 22; or Form 1040NR, line 37 . . . . . . **7**

8 Enter on line 8 the decimal amount shown below that applies to the amount on line 7

If line 7 is: Over	But not over	Decimal amount is	If line 7 is: Over	But not over	Decimal amount is
$0	15,000	.35	$29,000	31,000	.27
15,000	17,000	.34	31,000	33,000	.26
17,000	19,000	.33	33,000	35,000	.25
19,000	21,000	.32	35,000	37,000	.24
21,000	23,000	.31	37,000	39,000	.23
23,000	25,000	.30	39,000	41,000	.22
25,000	27,000	.29	41,000	43,000	.21
27,000	29,000	.28	43,000	No limit	.20

8 X.

9 Multiply line 6 by the decimal amount on line 8. If you paid 2016 expenses in 2017, see the instructions **9**

10 Tax liability limit. Enter the amount from the Credit Limit Worksheet in the instructions. **10**

11 **Credit for child and dependent care expenses.** Enter the **smaller** of line 9 or line 10 here and on Form 1040, line 49; Form 1040A, line 31; or Form 1040NR, line 47 . . . . **11**

For Paperwork Reduction Act Notice, see your tax return instructions. Cat. No. 11862M Form **2441** (2017)

Source: U.S. Department of the Treasury, Internal Revenue Service, Form 2441. Washington, DC: 2017.

CONCEPT CHECK 9-1—
LO 9-1

1. Jamie is a single mother with one dependent child, Joey, age 7. She has AGI of $75,000, and she paid $4,500 to a qualified day care center for after-school care for Joey. Calculate Jamie's child and dependent care credit.
2. Tom and Katie are married, file a joint return, and have two dependent children: Jack, age 11, and Jill, age 5. Tom has earned income of $41,000; Katie was a full-time student (for nine months) with no income. They paid a qualified day care/after-school care center $6,000. What is the maximum amount of qualified employment-related expenses that would be allowed for the child and dependent care credit calculation for Tom and Katie?
3. Antonio is a widower and cares for his son Elio, age 4. Antonio has AGI of $24,000 and paid qualified child care expenses for Elio of $2,900. In addition, Antonio received $1,000 of dependent care assistance that his employer properly excluded from Antonio's gross income. Calculate Antonio's child and dependent care credit.

CREDIT FOR THE ELDERLY OR THE DISABLED (FORM 1040, LINE 54 [SCHEDULE R], OR FORM 1040A, LINE 32)

LO 9-2

The credit for the elderly or the disabled was originally enacted to provide some tax relief to low-income elderly or disabled individuals.[11] To be eligible, the taxpayer must be age 65 or older or have retired on permanent and total disability and be receiving taxable disability income. In addition, certain AGI and nontaxable social security income limits apply.

Credit Calculation

The maximum allowable credit is equal to 15% of the taxpayer's base amount (depending on the filing status) as follows:

- $5,000 for single individuals or joint returns when only one spouse qualifies.
- $7,500 for joint returns when both spouses qualify.
- $3,750 for a married person filing a separate return.[12]

This base amount must first be reduced by (1) the amount of nontaxable social security (or similar) payments received and (2) one-half of the amount of AGI that exceeds $7,500 for single returns, $10,000 for joint returns, or $5,000 for married filing separately.[13]

EXAMPLE 9-6

Lou and Greta file a joint return. Lou is age 66, and Greta is 63. Note that only Lou is eligible for this credit. They have AGI of $11,500 and received $1,000 of nontaxable social security benefits. They would be entitled to a credit for the elderly or the disabled of $488 calculated as follows:

Base amount	$5,000
Less: Nontaxable social security	(1,000)
One-half of AGI over $10,000	(750)
Allowable base amount	$3,250
Applicable percentage	× 15%
Tax credit allowed	$ 488*

* Lou and Greta would have had a maximum credit for the elderly or disabled of $750 ($5,000 × 15%). However, the base amount must be reduced by social security and one-half of the amount of AGI over $10,000 ($750).

In practice, few elderly or disabled taxpayers are eligible for the credit because they generally receive nontaxable social security benefits in excess of the income limitations. In fact, if some social security benefits are taxable, the taxpayer will have exceeded the AGI limits. Furthermore, because the credit is not a refundable credit, the allowed credit is often zero because low-income elderly taxpayers often have no tax liability.

[11] IRC § 22.

[12] IRC § 22(c)(2).

[13] IRC § 22(c)(3) and IRC § 22(d).

From Shoebox to Software

Taxpayers use Schedule R to report the credit for the elderly or disabled. (For page 2 of Schedule R, see Exhibit 9-2.)

With the exception of checking an appropriate box in Part I denoting the taxpayer's age and filing status, the tax software automatically determines the credit for the person who is elderly or disabled. The amount on line 22 of Schedule R is included on Form 1040, line 54 (other credits), or Form 1040A, line 32.

TAX YOUR BRAIN

If a single taxpayer receives no social security benefits, what is the maximum AGI amount he or she would have to earn to become ineligible for the elderly or disabled credit?

ANSWER

The base amount for a single taxpayer is $5,000, reduced by one-half of the amount in excess of AGI of $7,500. Once excess AGI is more than $10,000, the base amount is reduced to zero. Thus, if total AGI exceeds $17,500 ($7,500 + $10,000), a single taxpayer would not be eligible for the credit.

CONCEPT CHECK 9-2— LO 9-2

1. Vincent and Maria are ages 70 and 67, respectively, and file a joint return. They have AGI of $21,000 and received $1,000 in nontaxable social security benefits. Calculate Vincent and Maria's credit for the elderly or the disabled.

EDUCATION CREDITS (FORM 1040, LINES 50 AND 68 [FORM 8863], OR FORM 1040A, LINES 33 AND 44)

LO 9-3

There are two education credits available: the American opportunity tax credit (AOTC), also known as the Hope scholarship credit, and the lifetime learning credit. Both credits are available to taxpayers for qualified higher education expenses paid for themselves, their spouses, or a dependent.[14] Qualifying expenses are amounts paid for tuition, fees, and other related expenses paid to an eligible educational institution while taxpayers (or their spouses and dependents) are pursuing undergraduate, graduate, or vocational degrees.[15] Qualified tuition and related expenses include amounts paid for course materials such as books and supplies. The qualifying expenses do not include room and board or student activity fees. The expenses must be for an academic period that begins in the same tax year as the year of the payment or that begins in the first three months of the following year. See Table 9-1 for a comparison of the two education credits.

An eligible educational institution is a postsecondary educational institution (college, university, vocational school, or the like) that is eligible to participate in a student aid program administered by the U.S. Department of Education. Almost all postsecondary institutions qualify.

EXAMPLE 9-7

In December 2017, Fred pays his son's college tuition for spring semester 2018. The semester starts in February 2018. Fred can deduct the expenses in tax year 2017.

Payments made using borrowed funds (such as student loans) are qualifying expenses. If a student receives a scholarship or other income that is excludable from gross income (such as Pell grants or employer-provided educational assistance), the excludable income reduces

[14] IRC § 25A.

[15] IRC § 25A(f)(1).

EXHIBIT 9-2

Schedule R (Form 1040A or 1040) 2017 Page **2**

Part III Figure Your Credit

10	**If you checked (in Part I):** **Enter:** Box 1, 2, 4, or 7 . . . . . $5,000 Box 3, 5, or 6 . . . . . $7,500 Box 8 or 9 . . . . . $3,750	10	
	Did you check box 2, 4, 5, 6, or 9 in Part I? **Yes** → You **must** complete line 11. **No** → Enter the amount from line 10 on line 12 and go to line 13.		
11	**If you checked (in Part I):** • Box 6, add $5,000 to the taxable disability income of the spouse who was under age 65. Enter the total. • Box 2, 4, or 9, enter your taxable disability income. • Box 5, add your taxable disability income to your spouse's taxable disability income. Enter the total.	11	
	TIP For more details on what to include on line 11, see *Figure Your Credit* in the instructions.		
12	If you completed line 11, enter the **smaller** of line 10 or line 11. **All others,** enter the amount from line 10	12	
13	Enter the following pensions, annuities, or disability income that you (and your spouse if filing jointly) received in 2017.		
a	Nontaxable part of social security benefits and nontaxable part of railroad retirement benefits treated as social security (see instructions). **13a**		
b	Nontaxable veterans' pensions and any other pension, annuity, or disability benefit that is excluded from income under any other provision of law (see instructions). **13b**		
c	Add lines 13a and 13b. (Even though these income items aren't taxable, they **must** be included here to figure your credit.) If you didn't receive any of the types of nontaxable income listed on line 13a or 13b, enter -0- on line 13c **13c**		
14	Enter the amount from Form 1040A, line 22, or Form 1040, line 38 . . . **14**		
15	**If you checked (in Part I):** **Enter:** Box 1 or 2 . . . $7,500 Box 3, 4, 5, 6, or 7 . . . $10,000 Box 8 or 9 . . . $5,000 **15**		
16	Subtract line 15 from line 14. If zero or less, enter -0- **16**		
17	Enter one-half of line 16 . . . . . **17**		
18	Add lines 13c and 17	18	
19	Subtract line 18 from line 12. If zero or less, **stop;** you **can't** take the credit. Otherwise, go to line 20	19	
20	Multiply line 19 by 15% (0.15)	20	
21	Tax liability limit. Enter the amount from the Credit Limit Worksheet in the instructions .	21	
22	**Credit for the elderly or the disabled.** Enter the **smaller** of line 20 or line 21. Also enter this amount on Form 1040A, line 32, or include on Form 1040, line 54 (check box **c** and enter "Sch R" on the line next to that box)	22	

Schedule R (Form 1040A or 1040) 2017

Source: U.S. Department of the Treasury, Internal Revenue Service, Schedule R (Form 1040A or 1040). Washington, DC: 2017.

qualifying expenses.[16] If a dependent pays for qualified expenses, the expenses are deemed paid by the taxpayer. Similarly, if someone other than the taxpayer, spouse, or dependent pays the expenses directly to the educational institution on behalf of the student, the expenses are deemed paid by the student.

[16] IRC § 25A(g)(2). Gifts, bequests, or inheritances are not excluded.

TABLE 9-1
Comparison of American Opportunity Tax and Lifetime Learning Credits

Source: IRS *Publication 17*, Chapter 35.

American Opportunity Tax (or Hope) Credit	Lifetime Learning Credit
Up to $2,500 credit per **eligible student.**	Up to $2,000 credit per **taxpayer.**
Available for the first four years of postsecondary education.	Available for all years of postsecondary education and for courses to acquire or improve job skills.
Up to 40% of credit may be refundable.	Credit is nonrefundable.
Student must be pursuing an undergraduate degree or other recognized education credential.	Student does not need to be pursuing a degree or other recognized education credential.
Student must be enrolled at least half-time for at least one academic period beginning during the year.	Available for one or more courses.
Qualified tuition and related expenses include books and supplies whether or not the materials are bought at the educational institution as a condition of enrollment or attendance.	Qualified tuition and related expenses include course-related books and supplies if the amount was required to be paid to the institution as part of the enrollment and attendance.
No felony drug conviction on student's record.	Felony drug conviction rule does not apply.

EXAMPLE 9-8

Uncle George pays the college tuition for his nephew Franklin. For purposes of the education credits, the expenses are deemed paid by Franklin. If Franklin is a dependent of his parents, his parents can take the credit.

American Opportunity Tax Credit

Also known as the *Hope credit,* the American opportunity tax credit (AOTC) is equal to 100% of the first $2,000 and 25% of the next $2,000 paid for qualified tuition and related expenses,[17] for a maximum of $2,500 per student per year.

To be eligible, a student must be carrying at least *half* of the normal full-time course load applicable to his or her course of study for at least one academic period (semester or quarter) during the year.[18] The student must be enrolled in a program leading to a degree or other educational credential. The AOTC is available for a student's first four years of postsecondary education, measured as of the beginning of the year.

Generally, up to 40% of the AOTC (that is, $1,000) may be a refundable credit. This means that a taxpayer may receive a refund even if he or she owes no taxes. However, none of the credit is refundable if the taxpayer claiming the credit is (a) a child under age 18 (or a student who is at least 18 and under 24) whose earned income is less than one-half of his or her own support, (b) who has at least one living parent, and (c) who does not file a joint return.

EXAMPLE 9-9

Ed and Lauren paid $3,600 of qualified tuition and related expenses for their son who is in his fourth year of college. These expenses included $450 for books and supplies. Without regard to AGI limitations or other credits, they can take an American opportunity tax credit of $2,400 ([$2,000 × 100%] + [$1,600 × 25%]).

Lifetime Learning Credit

The lifetime learning credit is equal to 20% of up to $10,000 of qualified tuition and related expenses paid during the year.[19] The credit is determined per taxpayer, not per student. Thus the maximum credit allowed for a taxpayer is $2,000 per year.

[17] These amounts are indexed for inflation.

[18] IRC § 25A(b)(2) and (3).

[19] IRC § 25A(c).

EXAMPLE 9-10 During the year, Emmit and Francine paid qualified higher education expenses of $3,000 for their daughter and $4,000 for their son. Without regard to AGI limitations or other credits, they can claim a lifetime learning credit of $1,400 ($7,000 × 20%).

A student can qualify for the lifetime learning credit regardless of whether he or she enrolls in a degree program or the number of courses taken in a semester. Qualified expenses for courses taken to acquire or improve job skills are eligible as well as expenses for any post-secondary education, including graduate school.

Phaseout of the Education Credits

The AOTC and the lifetime learning credit are intended to defray the cost of higher education for low- to middle-income taxpayers. As such, the credit is phased out when modified AGI (MAGI) exceeds certain limits. MAGI is equal to AGI plus income earned abroad or in certain U.S. territories or possessions.[20]

The AOTC begins to phase out at $80,000 of MAGI for single taxpayers and $160,000 for joint filers. The lifetime learning credit phases out when MAGI exceeds $56,000 and $112,000 for single and joint taxpayers, respectively.[21] You cannot claim the AOTC if your MAGI is $90,000 or more ($180,000 or more if you are filing jointly). Similarly, you cannot claim a lifetime learning credit if your MAGI exceeds $66,000 ($132,000 if you are filing jointly).

When MAGI is within the phaseout range, the amount of the credit is reduced by multiplying the amount by a fraction, calculated as follows:

American Opportunity Tax Credit

For Married Taxpayers	For Single Taxpayers
$\frac{\$180{,}000 - \text{MAGI}}{\$20{,}000}$	$\frac{\$90{,}000 - \text{MAGI}}{\$10{,}000}$

Lifetime Learning Credit

For Married Taxpayers	For Single Taxpayers
$\frac{\$132{,}000 - \text{MAGI}}{\$20{,}000}$	$\frac{\$66{,}000 - \text{MAGI}}{\$10{,}000}$

EXAMPLE 9-11 Chuck and Becky are married filing jointly and have modified AGI of $114,000 and a pre-limitation lifetime learning credit of $1,200. Because of their MAGI, their lifetime learning credit is limited to $1,080 ([$132,000 − $114,000]/$20,000 × $1,200). If they had MAGI of $112,000 or less, they would have received the entire $1,200 as credit. If they had MAGI of $132,000 or more, they would be entitled to no credit.

Coordination with Other Education-Related Benefits

Taxpayers can use qualifying expenses for the American opportunity tax credit or lifetime learning credit but not both. Similarly, if a tuition and fees deduction is taken (as discussed in Chapter 4), the taxpayer cannot claim the education credits for the same student. A taxpayer who is an eligible student, or has dependents that are eligible students, should take the credit or deduction (or a combination thereof) that yields the greatest tax savings for his or her individual tax situation.

[20] IRC § 25A(d).

[21] These income limitation amounts are indexed for inflation.

From Shoebox to Software

Taxpayers report education credits on Form 8863 (Exhibit 9-3). AOTC are in Part I, lifetime learning credits in Part II, and limitations are determined in Part III. With the tax software, you initially enter information concerning qualified expenses on a Federal Information for Higher Education worksheet located in the worksheet section. The software will automatically take the credit or deduction that is most advantageous. Alternatively, you can force the software to take the deduction or credit of your choice by placing an x in the appropriate box on the worksheet.

The data for the worksheet generally come from Form 1098-T (Exhibit 9-4). Schools and universities provide this form to report the amount of qualifying tuition and related expenses paid. You must reduce the amount in box 1 by any amount shown in box 4 prior to entering the information on the tax worksheet.

The information on the worksheet carries forward to Form 8863, and the credit is automatically calculated. Note that on line 18 of Form 8863, allowed credits may be limited to tax liability minus various other credits.

EXAMPLE 9-12

Art and Arlene paid $3,200 of qualified expenses for their dependent son, Albert, who is a freshman at State University. Their MAGI is $73,000, and they are married filing jointly. The couple could choose to take either an AOTC of $2,300 ($2,000 plus 25% of the next $1,200) or a lifetime learning credit of $640 ($3,200 × 20%) but not both.

TAX YOUR BRAIN

Using the information from Example 9-12, assume that Art and Arlene also have a dependent daughter, Chris, who is a sophomore at the same university, and they paid $6,000 of qualified expenses for her. What are the credit options for Art and Arlene? Which option should they choose?

ANSWER

Art and Arlene could take (1) two AOTCs of $2,300 and $2,500 (for a total of $4,800) or (2) an AOTC of $2,300 for Albert and a lifetime learning credit of $1,200 for Chris or (3) a lifetime learning credit of $640 for Albert and an AOTC of $2,500 for Chris or (4) a single lifetime learning credit of $1,840. In this case, they should obviously choose option 1.

A taxpayer can claim an AOTC or a lifetime learning credit in the same year he or she takes a tax-free distribution from a Coverdell Education Savings Account, as long as the taxpayer does not use the same expenses for both benefits.

CONCEPT CHECK 9-3— LO 9-3

1. Jewels is a single taxpayer and paid $2,900 in qualifying expenses for her dependent daughter, who attended the University of Arizona full-time as a freshman. How much is Jewels's lifetime learning credit without regard to modified AGI limitations or other credits?
2. Assume the same facts as in Question 1. Jewels has modified AGI of $85,000 and wants to claim the AOTC. What is her allowable credit after the credit phaseout based on AGI is taken into account?
3. Assume the same facts as in Question 1. Jewels has modified AGI of $98,000 and wants to claim the AOTC. What is her allowable credit after the credit phaseout based on AGI is taken into account?
4. Vern and Whitney paid $1,600 and $2,100 in qualifying expenses for their twin daughters Kimberly and Janet, respectively, to attend the nursing program at the community college. Without regard to modified AGI limitations or other credits, how much is their lifetime learning credit?

EXHIBIT 9-3

Form **8863**

Department of the Treasury
Internal Revenue Service (99)

Education Credits
(American Opportunity and Lifetime Learning Credits)

▶ Attach to Form 1040 or Form 1040A.
▶ Go to *www.irs.gov/Form8863* for instructions and the latest information.

OMB No. 1545-0074
2017
Attachment Sequence No. **50**

Name(s) shown on return | **Your social security number**

CAUTION: *Complete a separate Part III on page 2 for each student for whom you're claiming either credit before you complete Parts I and II.*

Part I Refundable American Opportunity Credit

Line	Description	Box	Amount
1	After completing Part III for each student, enter the total of all amounts from all Parts III, line 30	1	
2	Enter: $180,000 if married filing jointly; $90,000 if single, head of household, or qualifying widow(er)	2	
3	Enter the amount from Form 1040, line 38, or Form 1040A, line 22. If you're filing Form 2555, 2555-EZ, or 4563, or you're excluding income from Puerto Rico, see Pub. 970 for the amount to enter	3	
4	Subtract line 3 from line 2. If zero or less, **stop**; you can't take any education credit	4	
5	Enter: $20,000 if married filing jointly; $10,000 if single, head of household, or qualifying widow(er)	5	
6	If line 4 is: • Equal to or more than line 5, enter 1.000 on line 6 • Less than line 5, divide line 4 by line 5. Enter the result as a decimal (rounded to at least three places)	6	.
7	Multiply line 1 by line 6. **Caution:** If you were under age 24 at the end of the year **and** meet the conditions described in the instructions, you **can't** take the refundable American opportunity credit; skip line 8, enter the amount from line 7 on line 9, and check this box ▶ ☐	7	
8	**Refundable American opportunity credit.** Multiply line 7 by 40% (0.40). Enter the amount here and on Form 1040, line 68, or Form 1040A, line 44. Then go to line 9 below.	8	

Part II Nonrefundable Education Credits

Line	Description	Box	Amount
9	Subtract line 8 from line 7. Enter here and on line 2 of the Credit Limit Worksheet (see instructions)	9	
10	After completing Part III for each student, enter the total of all amounts from all Parts III, line 31. If zero, skip lines 11 through 17, enter -0- on line 18, and go to line 19	10	
11	Enter the smaller of line 10 or $10,000	11	
12	Multiply line 11 by 20% (0.20)	12	
13	Enter: $132,000 if married filing jointly; $66,000 if single, head of household, or qualifying widow(er)	13	
14	Enter the amount from Form 1040, line 38, or Form 1040A, line 22. If you're filing Form 2555, 2555-EZ, or 4563, or you're excluding income from Puerto Rico, see Pub. 970 for the amount to enter	14	
15	Subtract line 14 from line 13. If zero or less, skip lines 16 and 17, enter -0- on line 18, and go to line 19	15	
16	Enter: $20,000 if married filing jointly; $10,000 if single, head of household, or qualifying widow(er)	16	
17	If line 15 is: • Equal to or more than line 16, enter 1.000 on line 17 and go to line 18 • Less than line 16, divide line 15 by line 16. Enter the result as a decimal (rounded to at least three places)	17	.
18	Multiply line 12 by line 17. Enter here and on line 1 of the Credit Limit Worksheet (see instructions) ▶	18	
19	**Nonrefundable education credits.** Enter the amount from line 7 of the Credit Limit Worksheet (see instructions) here and on Form 1040, line 50, or Form 1040A, line 33	19	

For Paperwork Reduction Act Notice, see your tax return instructions. Cat. No. 25379M Form **8863** (2017)

Source: U.S. Department of the Treasury, Internal Revenue Service, Form 8863. Washington, DC: 2017.

EXHIBIT 9-3 *(concluded)*

Form 8863 (2017) Page **2**

Name(s) shown on return | **Your social security number**

CAUTION ***Complete Part III for each student for whom you're claiming either the American opportunity credit or lifetime learning credit. Use additional copies of page 2 as needed for each student.***

Part III Student and Educational Institution Information. See instructions.

20 Student name (as shown on page 1 of your tax return)

21 Student social security number (as shown on page 1 of your tax return)

22 Educational institution information (see instructions)

a. Name of first educational institution	**b.** Name of second educational institution (if any)
(1) Address. Number and street (or P.O. box). City, town or post office, state, and ZIP code. If a foreign address, see instructions.	**(1)** Address. Number and street (or P.O. box). City, town or post office, state, and ZIP code. If a foreign address, see instructions.
(2) Did the student receive Form 1098-T from this institution for 2017? ☐ Yes ☐ No	**(2)** Did the student receive Form 1098-T from this institution for 2017? ☐ Yes ☐ No
(3) Did the student receive Form 1098-T from this institution for 2016 with box 2 filled in and box 7 checked? ☐ Yes ☐ No	**(3)** Did the student receive Form 1098-T from this institution for 2016 with box 2 filled in and box 7 checked? ☐ Yes ☐ No
If you checked "No" in **both (2) and (3)**, skip **(4)**. However, you must complete **(4)** if you're claiming the American opportunity credit.	If you checked "No" in **both (2) and (3)**, skip **(4)**. However, you must complete **(4)** if you're claiming the American opportunity credit.
(4) If you checked "Yes" in **(2) or (3)**, enter the institution's employer identification number (from Form 1098-T). __ __ – __ __ __ __ __ __ __	**(4)** If you checked "Yes" in **(2) or (3)**, enter the institution's employer identification number (from Form 1098-T). __ __ – __ __ __ __ __ __ __

23	Has the Hope Scholarship Credit or American opportunity credit been claimed for this student for any 4 tax years before 2017?	☐ Yes — **Stop!** Go to line 31 for this student.	☐ No — Go to line 24.
24	Was the student enrolled at least half-time for at least one academic period that began or is treated as having begun in 2017 at an eligible educational institution in a program leading towards a postsecondary degree, certificate, or other recognized postsecondary educational credential? See instructions.	☐ Yes — Go to line 25.	☐ No — **Stop!** Go to line 31 for this student.
25	Did the student complete the first 4 years of postsecondary education before 2017? See instructions.	☐ Yes — **Stop!** Go to line 31 for this student.	☐ No — Go to line 26.
26	Was the student convicted, before the end of 2017, of a felony for possession or distribution of a controlled substance?	☐ Yes — **Stop!** Go to line 31 for this student.	☐ No — Complete lines 27 through 30 for this student.

CAUTION *You **can't** take the American opportunity credit and the lifetime learning credit for the **same student** in the same year. If you complete lines 27 through 30 for this student, don't complete line 31.*

American Opportunity Credit

27	Adjusted qualified education expenses (see instructions). **Don't enter more than $4,000**	27	
28	Subtract $2,000 from line 27. If zero or less, enter -0-	28	
29	Multiply line 28 by 25% (0.25)	29	
30	If line 28 is zero, enter the amount from line 27. Otherwise, add $2,000 to the amount on line 29 and enter the result. Skip line 31. Include the total of all amounts from all Parts III, line 30, on Part I, line 1	30	

Lifetime Learning Credit

31	Adjusted qualified education expenses (see instructions). Include the total of all amounts from all Parts III, line 31, on Part II, line 10	31	

Form **8863** (2017)

Source: U.S. Department of the Treasury, Internal Revenue Service, Form 1098-T. Washington, DC: 2017.

EXHIBIT 9-4

☐ CORRECTED

FILER'S name, street address, city or town, state or province, country, ZIP or foreign postal code, and telephone number		1 Payments received for qualified tuition and related expenses $ 2 Amounts billed for qualified tuition and related expenses $	OMB No. 1545-1574 **2017** Form **1098-T**	**Tuition Statement**
FILER'S federal identification no.	STUDENT'S taxpayer identification no.	3 If this box is checked, your educational institution changed its reporting method for 2017 ☐		**Copy B For Student** This is important tax information and is being furnished to the Internal Revenue Service. This form must be used to complete Form 8863 to claim education credits. Give it to the tax preparer or use it to prepare the tax return.
STUDENT'S name		4 Adjustments made for a prior year $	5 Scholarships or grants $	
Street address (including apt. no.) City or town, state or province, country, and ZIP or foreign postal code		6 Adjustments to scholarships or grants for a prior year $	7 Checked if the amount in box 1 or 2 includes amounts for an academic period beginning January–March 2018 ▶ ☐	
Service Provider/Acct. No. (see instr.)	8 Check if at least half-time student ☐	9 Checked if a graduate student . . . . ☐	10 Ins. contract reimb./refund $	

Form **1098-T** (keep for your records) www.irs.gov/form1098t Department of the Treasury - Internal Revenue Service

Source: U.S. Department of the Treasury, Internal Revenue Service, Form 1098-T. Washington, DC: 2017.

FOREIGN TAX CREDIT (FTC) (FORM 1040, LINE 48 [FORM 1116]) LO 9-4

U.S. citizens and residents are subject to taxation on income earned worldwide. Although most U.S. taxpayers earn income solely from U.S. sources, taxpayers with income from foreign sources may be subject to double taxation (the same income is taxed both in the United States and in the foreign country). Most often this foreign-source income is investment income such as interest or dividends, although other types are possible.[22] To mitigate double taxation, the Internal Revenue Code (IRC) provides a foreign tax credit for income taxes paid or accrued to a foreign country or U.S. possession.[23]

The foreign tax credit is available for taxes levied on income such as wages, interest, dividends, and royalties. The amount of the credit is equal to the foreign tax paid or accrued. However, the credit cannot exceed that portion of U.S. income tax attributable to the foreign income.[24] The limitation is determined as follows:[25]

$$\frac{\text{Foreign-source taxable income}}{\text{Worldwide taxable income}} \times \begin{array}{c}\text{U.S. income}\\ \text{tax liability}\\ \text{before FTC}\end{array} = \begin{array}{c}\text{Foreign tax}\\ \text{credit}\\ \text{limitation}\end{array}$$

EXAMPLE 9-13

Kim reported worldwide taxable income of $84,010 that included $1,000 of foreign-source interest income. Her U.S. tax liability was $18,273. She paid foreign taxes of $250 on the foreign income. Kim is entitled to a foreign tax credit of $218. Although she paid $250 in foreign tax, her credit is limited to $218 calculated as follows: ($1,000/$84,010) × $18,273 = $218. If Kim's foreign tax paid were $218 or less, the limitation would not apply and her credit would be equal to the amount of foreign tax paid.

[22] This section does not discuss foreign-source income earned by U.S. citizens living abroad. Law concerning the taxation and credits associated with such income is found in IRC § 911. Taxation of foreign-source wages is complex and is not discussed in this text.

[23] IRC § 901.

[24] IRC § 904(a).

[25] In practice, the limitation is calculated separately for certain categories of income as indicated in IRC § 904 (d) and as shown on the top of Form 1116. This text focuses only on the passive income category because the other categories seldom apply to individual taxpayers.

From Shoebox to Software

The majority of taxpayers who earn foreign-source income do so through mutual funds that invest in foreign stocks or bonds. These taxpayers will receive a Form 1099-INT or 1099-DIV from their mutual fund company. The statements report the amount of income and the corresponding foreign tax paid. Some taxpayers may own foreign stocks or bonds directly. If the investment is through a brokerage firm, the taxpayer will receive an appropriate Form 1099. If the taxpayer owns foreign investments outside of a brokerage account, the taxpayer often needs to gather the income and tax information separately.

Taxpayers report the foreign tax credit on Form 1116 (Exhibit 9-5). A taxpayer may elect to claim the credit without filing Form 1116 if he or she meets *all* of the following:[26]

- All of the foreign-source income is passive income.
- All of the income and foreign taxes paid are reported to the taxpayer on the appropriate Form 1099.
- Total foreign taxes paid were less than $300 ($600 if married filing a joint return).
- The taxpayer is not subject to the foreign tax limitation rules.

A taxpayer who meets all of these rules reports the foreign tax credit directly on Form 1040, line 48. No Form 1116 is required.

You enter the appropriate information directly onto Form 1116 when using the tax software. Most taxpayers enter information concerning the gross income that was taxed by the foreign country on line 1, columns (a) through (c), and enter the appropriate amount of foreign taxes paid in Part II, columns (k) through (s). In most situations, the tax software completes the remainder of the form and shows the total credit on line 30.

A taxpayer who earns passive income through investment in a mutual fund often provides the foreign country name in Parts I and II as "various" because there is seldom one country from which the income is earned. If the passive income were from a direct investment in one country, the taxpayer would enter that country's name.

Cash basis taxpayers take the foreign tax credit in the year paid. However, cash basis taxpayers can make a binding election to take the credit for all foreign taxes in the year they accrue.[27]

Taxpayers may also choose to deduct foreign taxes as an itemized deduction rather than as a credit. From a practical standpoint, it is seldom advantageous to use a deduction instead of a credit. However, there are at least two instances for which a deduction is preferred. One is when a taxpayer has income from one country (on which tax was paid) and an equal loss from another country. The net foreign taxable income would be zero, and the taxpayer would receive no credit. In such a case, the benefit for the taxes paid in the positive income country would be lost unless the taxpayer took the foreign taxes as an itemized deduction. Another instance relates to foreign taxes not based on income (e.g., property taxes). Taxpayers can take these foreign taxes as a deduction because the foreign tax credit is available only for foreign taxes paid based on income.[28]

CONCEPT CHECK 9-4— LO 9-4

1. Joy has $63,000 worldwide taxable income, which includes $8,000 of taxable income from New Zealand. She paid $2,500 in foreign income taxes, and her U.S. tax liability is $17,640. Calculate Joy's foreign tax credit.

[26] U.S. Department of the Treasury, Internal Revenue Service, IRS instructions for Form 1116. Washington, DC: 2016.

[27] IRC § 905(a).

[28] Reg. § 1.901-2(a)(1).

EXHIBIT 9-5

Form **1116**

Department of the Treasury
Internal Revenue Service (99)

Foreign Tax Credit

(Individual, Estate, or Trust)

▶ Attach to Form 1040, 1040NR, 1041, or 990-T.

▶ Go to *www.irs.gov/Form1116* for instructions and the latest information.

OMB No. 1545-0121

2017

Attachment Sequence No. **19**

Name | **Identifying number** as shown on page 1 of your tax return

Use a separate Form 1116 for each category of income listed below. See *Categories of Income* in the instructions. Check only one box on each Form 1116. Report all amounts in U.S. dollars except where specified in Part II below.

a ☐ Passive category income
b ☐ General category income
c ☐ Section 901(j) income
d ☐ Certain income re-sourced by treaty
e ☐ Lump-sum distributions

f Resident of (name of country) ▶

Note: If you paid taxes to only one foreign country or U.S. possession, use column A in Part I and line A in Part II. If you paid taxes to **more than one** foreign country or U.S. possession, use a separate column and line for each country or possession.

Part I Taxable Income or Loss From Sources Outside the United States (for Category Checked Above)

		Foreign Country or U.S. Possession A	B	C	Total (Add cols. A, B, and C.)
g	**Enter the name of the foreign country or U.S. possession** ▶				
1a	Gross income from sources within country shown above and of the type checked above (see instructions):				**1a**
b	Check if line 1a is compensation for personal services as an employee, your total compensation from all sources is $250,000 or more, and you used an alternative basis to determine its source (see instructions) ▶ ☐				
	Deductions and losses (**Caution:** See instructions.):				
2	Expenses **definitely related** to the income on line 1a (attach statement)				
3	Pro rata share of other deductions **not definitely related:**				
a	Certain itemized deductions or standard deduction (see instructions)				
b	Other deductions (attach statement)				
c	Add lines 3a and 3b				
d	Gross foreign source income (see instructions)				
e	Gross income from all sources (see instructions)				
f	Divide line 3d by line 3e (see instructions)				
g	Multiply line 3c by line 3f				
4	Pro rata share of interest expense (see instructions):				
a	Home mortgage interest (use the Worksheet for Home Mortgage Interest in the instructions)				
b	Other interest expense				
5	Losses from foreign sources				
6	Add lines 2, 3g, 4a, 4b, and 5				**6**
7	Subtract line 6 from line 1a. Enter the result here and on line 15, page 2 ▶				**7**

Part II Foreign Taxes Paid or Accrued (see instructions)

Country	Credit is claimed for taxes (you must check one) (h) ☐ Paid (i) ☐ Accrued	Foreign taxes paid or accrued								
		In foreign currency				In U.S. dollars				
		Taxes withheld at source on:				Taxes withheld at source on:				
	(j) Date paid or accrued	**(k)** Dividends	**(l)** Rents and royalties	**(m)** Interest	**(n)** Other foreign taxes paid or accrued	**(o)** Dividends	**(p)** Rents and royalties	**(q)** Interest	**(r)** Other foreign taxes paid or accrued	**(s)** Total foreign taxes paid or accrued (add cols. (o) through (r))
A										
B										
C										

8 **Add lines A through C, column (s). Enter the total here and on line 9, page 2** ▶ **8**

For Paperwork Reduction Act Notice, see instructions. Cat. No. 11440U Form **1116** (2017)

Source: U.S. Department of the Treasury, Internal Revenue Service, Form 1116. Washington, DC: 2017.

EXHIBIT 9-5 *(concluded)*

Form 1116 (2017) Page **2**

Part III Figuring the Credit

Line	Description	Line no.	Amount	Line no.	Amount
9	Enter the amount from line 8. These are your total foreign taxes paid or accrued for the category of income checked above Part I	9			
10	Carryback or carryover (attach detailed computation)	10			
11	Add lines 9 and 10	11			
12	Reduction in foreign taxes (see instructions)	12	( )		
13	Taxes reclassified under high tax kickout (see instructions)	13			
14	Combine lines 11, 12, and 13. This is the total amount of foreign taxes available for credit			14	
15	Enter the amount from line 7. This is your taxable income or (loss) from sources outside the United States (before adjustments) for the category of income checked above Part I (see instructions)	15			
16	Adjustments to line 15 (see instructions)	16			
17	Combine the amounts on lines 15 and 16. This is your net foreign source taxable income. (If the result is zero or less, you have no foreign tax credit for the category of income you checked above Part I. Skip lines 18 through 22. However, if you are filing more than one Form 1116, you must complete line 20.)	17			
18	**Individuals:** Enter the amount from Form 1040, line 41; or Form 1040NR, line 39. **Estates and trusts:** Enter your taxable income without the deduction for your exemption	18			
	Caution: If you figured your tax using the lower rates on qualified dividends or capital gains, see instructions.				
19	Divide line 17 by line 18. If line 17 is more than line 18, enter "1"			19	
20	**Individuals:** Enter the total of Form 1040, lines 44 and 46. If you are a nonresident alien, enter the total of Form 1040NR, lines 42 and 44. **Estates and trusts:** Enter the amount from Form 1041, Schedule G, line 1a; or the total of Form 990-T, lines 36, 37, and 39. Foreign estates and trusts should enter the amount from Form 1040NR, line 42			20	
	Caution: If you are completing line 20 for separate category **e** (lump-sum distributions), see instructions.				
21	Multiply line 20 by line 19 (maximum amount of credit)			21	
22	Enter the **smaller** of line 14 or line 21. If this is the only Form 1116 you are filing, skip lines 23 through 27 and enter this amount on line 28. Otherwise, complete the appropriate line in Part IV (see instructions) ▶			22	

Part IV Summary of Credits From Separate Parts III (see instructions)

Line	Description	Line no.	Amount	Line no.	Amount
23	Credit for taxes on passive category income	23			
24	Credit for taxes on general category income	24			
25	Credit for taxes on certain income re-sourced by treaty	25			
26	Credit for taxes on lump-sum distributions	26			
27	Add lines 23 through 26			27	
28	Enter the **smaller** of line 20 or line 27			28	
29	Reduction of credit for international boycott operations. See instructions for line 12			29	
30	Subtract line 29 from line 28. This is your **foreign tax credit.** Enter here and on Form 1040, line 48; Form 1040NR, line 46; Form 1041, Schedule G, line 2a; or Form 990-T, line 41a ▶			30	

Form **1116** (2017)

CHILD TAX CREDIT (FORM 1040, LINE 52, OR FORM 1040A, LINE 35)

LO 9-5

Taxpayers are allowed a $1,000 tax credit for each qualifying child.[29] The definition of a qualifying child is the same as a qualifying child for exemption purposes (see Chapter 2). The qualifying child must also be under age 17 as of the end of the tax year, be a U.S. citizen or resident,[30] be younger than the person claiming the credit for the child, and be unmarried.

The credit is reduced by $50 for each $1,000, or fraction thereof, of modified AGI in excess of $110,000 for taxpayers who are married filing jointly, $75,000 for single filers, and $55,000 for married filing separately.[31] *Modified AGI* is AGI plus income earned abroad or in certain U.S. territories or possessions.

EXAMPLE 9-14

Fred and Paula have two qualifying children and file jointly. Their modified AGI was $116,322. Their child tax credit will be $1,650; calculated as [($116,322 − $110,000) = $6,322/$1,000 = 7 (6.3 rounds up to 7) and, therefore, $2,000 − (7 × $50)].

Additional Child Tax Credit

In most cases, the child tax credit is nonrefundable (that is, any credit that exceeds the tax liability will not be refunded). In certain cases, however, if a taxpayer qualifies, a taxpayer may receive a child tax credit refund in excess of the tax liability. The additional child tax credit allows the taxpayer to receive up to 15% of the taxpayer's earned income that is above $3,000. To claim this as a refundable credit, the taxpayer must report the amount on Form 8812 and on line 67 of Form 1040 (or line 43 on Form 1040A).

CONCEPT CHECK 9-5—
LO 9-5

1. Pat and Lisa have two qualifying children, ages 11 and 8, and file jointly. Their AGI is $112,000. What amount of child tax credit can they claim after their AGI limitation is considered?

From Shoebox to Software

Taxpayers calculate the child tax credit using a worksheet found in the instructions to Form 1040. In the tax software, this document is in the worksheet section. When you examine the worksheet, you will see that the software automatically creates virtually all of it.

When we entered the tax information for Jose and Maria Ramirez in Chapter 3, we noted that they had a $3,000 child tax credit shown on line 52. This amount is $1,000 for each child. If you open the Ramirezes' tax return, click on line 52, and then click on the yellow folder, you will see the Child Tax Credit worksheet. You will note that the amount of the preliminary credit on line 1 is not limited.

If you open the tax return of Alan and Cherie Masters, you will see that there is no child tax credit listed on line 52 even though they have two children under the age of 17. If you click on line 52 and then click on the yellow folder to get to the worksheet, you will see that the preliminary credit of $2,000 is zero on line 8 of the worksheet because of the AGI limitation. Recall that the credit is limited once modified AGI reaches $110,000 for a married couple and that the credit is zero when modified AGI exceeds $150,000 (for two children). The Masters have modified AGI far in excess of $150,000, so they receive no child tax credit.

The credit is reported on Form 1040, line 52, or Form 1040A, line 35.

[29] IRC § 24(a).
[30] IRC § 24(c).
[31] IRC § 24(b).

RETIREMENT SAVINGS CONTRIBUTIONS CREDIT (SAVER'S CREDIT) (FORM 1040, LINE 51 [FORM 8880], OR FORM 1040A, LINE 34)

LO 9-6

Eligible individuals can take a tax credit based on contributions toward a retirement savings account, multiplied by an applicable percentage ranging from 0% to 50%.[32] The percentage is based on the taxpayer's modified AGI and filing status. Subject to the maximum, the credit is determined using Table 9-2.

Contributions can be made to Individual Retirement Accounts (traditional or Roth), 401(k), 403(b), or 457 plans, a SIMPLE or SEP plan, or other qualified retirement plans.[33] Distributions from the noted retirement accounts will reduce the allowed contribution. Modified AGI is equal to AGI plus income earned abroad or in certain U.S. territories or possessions. The maximum contribution amount for the credit is $2,000 per person, and on a joint return, $2,000 for each spouse.

TABLE 9-2
Rates for Retirement Savings Contributions Credit

Modified Adjusted Gross Income						
Joint Return		Head of Household		All Other Filing Status		Applicable Percentage
Over	Not Over	Over	Not Over	Over	Not Over	
$ 0	$37,000	$ 0	$27,750	$ 0	$18,500	50%
37,000	40,000	27,750	30,000	18,500	20,000	20%
40,000	62,000	30,000	46,500	20,000	31,000	10%
62,000		46,500		31,000		0%

EXAMPLE 9-15

Hector is a single filer with modified AGI of $25,000. He makes a $1,000 contribution to an IRA. His retirement savings contributions credit is $100 ($1,000 × 10%). If Hector's modified AGI was $18,500 or less, his credit would be $500 ($1,000 × 50%).

EXAMPLE 9-16

Bo and Rachelle are married filing jointly with modified AGI of $39,000. Bo makes a $2,000 contribution to a qualified retirement plan. Their credit is $400 ($2,000 × 20%).

CONCEPT CHECK 9-6— LO 9-6

1. Enrique and Lupe have AGI of $41,000, are married filing jointly, and contributed $1,500 during the year to a qualified retirement plan for Enrique. How much is their retirement savings contributions credit?
2. Roger is a head of household taxpayer with AGI of $26,000. He made a $2,200 contribution to a qualified retirement plan. How much is his retirement savings contributions credit?

[32] IRC § 25B(a).

[33] These plans are discussed in more detail in Chapter 11.

From Shoebox to Software

Taxpayers claim the retirement savings contributions credit on Form 8880 (Exhibit 9-6).

The information shown on line 1 comes from an IRA Contribution Summary in the worksheet section. You must enter any retirement account distributions on line 4. The software will calculate the remainder of the form and will report the appropriate credit on Form 1040, line 51. Distributions are generally reported to taxpayers on Form 1099-R.

ADOPTION CREDIT (FORM 1040, LINE 54 [FORM 8839])

LO 9-7

Taxpayers can claim an adoption credit of 100% of qualified adoption expenses paid, up to a maximum of $13,570 per eligible child adopted.[34] Married taxpayers generally must file jointly to take the credit.

Qualified adoption expenses include reasonable and necessary expenses such as adoption fees, court costs, attorney fees, and similar expenses directly related to the legal adoption of an eligible child.[35] Qualified expenses do not include reimbursements under an employer program. An eligible child is one who is under age 18 or is incapable of caring for himself or herself but does not include a child of an individual's spouse.

Adoption proceedings are often protracted. Taxpayers often pay expenses in a tax year other than the year in which the adoption becomes final. In the case of expenses paid in the years before the adoption becomes final, taxpayers take the credit in the year immediately after it is paid. For expenses paid in the year the adoption is finalized or after, taxpayers take the credit in the year paid.[36] The total amount of qualified adoption expenses over all years cannot exceed $13,570 per child.

EXAMPLE 9-17

Warren and Lois legally adopted a child in 2017. They incurred and paid qualified adoption expenses of $6,000 in 2016, $4,000 in 2017, and $5,000 in 2018 ($15,000 in total). Without any AGI limitations, Warren and Lois would be entitled to an adoption credit of $10,000 ($6,000 + $4,000) in 2017 and an additional $3,570 credit in 2018. Expenses over $13,570 are disallowed.

If a taxpayer adopts a child who is not a citizen or resident of the United States (a foreign adoption), the credit is allowed only in the year in which the adoption becomes final or in a later year if the expenses were paid or incurred in a later year.

Additional rules apply to a special-needs child. This is a child who has a special factor or condition that a state agency determines prevents the child from being placed with adoptive parents without providing adoption assistance. Such a child must also be a U.S. citizen or resident.[37] In the case of adoption of a special-needs child, taxpayers can take a $13,570 credit regardless of whether the taxpayer incurred any qualifying expenses.[38] Taxpayers take the credit in the year the adoption becomes final.

Phaseout of Adoption Credit

The adoption credit is subject to phaseout when modified AGI exceeds certain limits. Modified AGI is equal to AGI plus income earned abroad or in certain U.S. territories or possessions.

[34] IRC § 23(a) and (b).

[35] IRC § 23(d)(1).

[36] IRC § 23(a)(2).

[37] IRC § 23(d)(3).

[38] IRC § 23(a)(3).

EXHIBIT 9-6

Form **8880**

Department of the Treasury
Internal Revenue Service

Credit for Qualified Retirement Savings Contributions

▶ Attach to Form 1040, Form 1040A, or Form 1040NR.
▶ Go to *www.irs.gov/Form8880* for instructions and the latest information.

OMB No. 1545-0074
2017
Attachment Sequence No. **54**

Name(s) shown on return | **Your social security number**

CAUTION

You **cannot** take this credit if **either** of the following applies.

- The amount on Form 1040, line 38; Form 1040A, line 22; or Form 1040NR, line 37 is more than $31,000 ($46,500 if head of household; $62,000 if married filing jointly).
- The person(s) who made the qualified contribution or elective deferral **(a)** was born after January 1, 2000, **(b)** is claimed as a dependent on someone else's 2017 tax return, or **(c)** was a **student** (see instructions).

			(a) You		**(b) Your spouse**
1	Traditional and Roth IRA (including *my*RA) contributions for 2017. **Do not** include rollover contributions	1			
2	Elective deferrals to a 401(k) or other qualified employer plan, voluntary employee contributions, and 501(c)(18)(D) plan contributions for 2017 (see instructions)	2			
3	Add lines 1 and 2	3			
4	Certain distributions received **after** 2014 and **before** the due date (including extensions) of your 2017 tax return (see instructions). If married filing jointly, include **both** spouses' amounts in **both** columns. See instructions for an exception	4			
5	Subtract line 4 from line 3. If zero or less, enter -0-	5			
6	In each column, enter the **smaller** of line 5 or $2,000	6			
7	Add the amounts on line 6. If zero, **stop;** you cannot take this credit			7	
8	Enter the amount from Form 1040, line 38*; Form 1040A, line 22; or Form 1040NR, line 37	8			
9	Enter the applicable decimal amount shown below.			9	X.

If line 8 is—		And your filing status is—		
Over—	But not over—	Married filing jointly	Head of household	Single, Married filing separately, or Qualifying widow(er)
		Enter on line 9—		
---	$18,500	.5	.5	.5
$18,500	$20,000	.5	.5	.2
$20,000	$27,750	.5	.5	.1
$27,750	$30,000	.5	.2	.1
$30,000	$31,000	.5	.1	.1
$31,000	$37,000	.5	.1	.0
$37,000	$40,000	.2	.1	.0
$40,000	$46,500	.1	.1	.0
$46,500	$62,000	.1	.0	.0
$62,000	---	.0	.0	.0

Note: If line 9 is zero, **stop;** you cannot take this credit.

10	Multiply line 7 by line 9	10	
11	Limitation based on tax liability. Enter the amount from the Credit Limit Worksheet in the instructions	11	
12	**Credit for qualified retirement savings contributions.** Enter the **smaller** of line 10 or line 11 here and on Form 1040, line 51; Form 1040A, line 34; or Form 1040NR, line 48	12	

*See Pub. 590-A for the amount to enter if you are filing Form 2555, 2555-EZ, or 4563 or you are excluding income from Puerto Rico.

For Paperwork Reduction Act Notice, see your tax return instructions. Cat. No. 33394D Form **8880** (2017)

Source: U.S. Department of the Treasury, Internal Revenue Service, Form 8880. Washington, DC: 2017.

From Shoebox to Software

Taxpayers report the adoption credit on Form 8839 (see Exhibit 9-7).

You enter most of the required information directly onto Form 8839. In Part I, you provide information concerning the adopted child. On line 3, you enter the amount of any adoption credit taken in a prior year for the child. The tax software completes the remainder of the form. It also transfers the total adoption credit shown on line 12 onto Form 1040, line 54, and checks the box c for Form 8839.

Part III of Form 8839 (not shown) is used to report and account for employer-provided adoption benefits. Employers report any such benefits on Form W-2, box 12, with a code of T. The tax software will automatically record the box 12 amount on the proper lines on Part III of Form 8839.

The phaseout begins when modified AGI exceeds $203,540 and the credit is completely phased out when modified AGI reaches $243,540.

For taxpayers with modified AGI that is within the phaseout range (between $203,540 and $243,540), the allowable credit is equal to the tentative credit multiplied by the following fraction:

$$\frac{\$243{,}540 - \text{Modified AGI}}{\$40{,}000}$$

EXAMPLE 9-18

Nicholas and Elaine spent $18,000 in qualified adoption expenses. Their modified AGI is $210,000. Their adoption credit would be $11,378 ([($243,540 – $210,000)/$40,000] × $13,570). Note that the fraction is multiplied by the $13,570 maximum amount allowed, not the total spent of $18,000.

If a taxpayer receives employer-provided adoption benefits, the amount of qualified adoption expenses for purposes of the adoption credit is limited to the amount paid or incurred in excess of the employer-provided assistance, if any. If the assistance exceeds the expenses, the excess is taxable income. In order to claim the credit, Form 8839 must be filed along with documents supporting the adoption such as final adoption decree, court documents, and so on.

CONCEPT CHECK 9-7— LO 9-7

1. Adam and Michelle incurred the following expenses in the adoption of their infant daughter, which was finalized in 2017:

2016	$10,500
2017	3,950

   If their 2017 modified AGI is $120,000, how much can they claim in 2016? How about in 2017?
2. Zhang and Umiko spent $16,000 in qualified adoption expenses in the adoption of their son. The adoption was finalized and all of the expenses were incurred in the current year. Zhang and Umiko's modified AGI for the current year is $205,000. How much is their adoption credit?

EARNED INCOME CREDIT (EIC) (FORM 1040, LINE 66A, OR FORM 1040A, LINE 42A)

LO 9-8

The Earned Income Credit (EIC) is designed to help working taxpayers who are economically disadvantaged and to alleviate the burden of certain additional taxes such as gasoline and social security taxes.[39] Unlike most of the other personal credits, the EIC is a refundable tax credit. As discussed earlier, this means that the EIC amount is treated like payments made and may result

[39] IRC § 32.

EXHIBIT 9-7

Form **8839**

Department of the Treasury
Internal Revenue Service (99)

Qualified Adoption Expenses

▶ Attach to Form 1040 or 1040NR.
▶ Go to *www.irs.gov/Form8839* for instructions and the latest information.

OMB No. 1545-0074
2017
Attachment Sequence No. **38**

Name(s) shown on return | **Your social security number**

Part I **Information About Your Eligible Child or Children**—You **must** complete this part. See instructions for details, including what to do if you need more space.

1	(a) Child's name — First	(a) Child's name — Last	(b) Child's year of birth	Check if child was— (c) born **before** 2000 and disabled	(d) a child with special needs	(e) a foreign child	(f) Child's identifying number	(g) Check if adoption became final in 2017 or earlier
Child 1				☐	☐	☐		☐
Child 2				☐	☐	☐		☐
Child 3				☐	☐	☐		☐

Caution: If the child was a foreign child, see **Special rules** in the instructions for line 1, column (e), before you complete Part II or Part III. If you received **employer-provided adoption benefits,** complete Part III on the back next.

Part II **Adoption Credit**

			Child 1	Child 2	Child 3		
2	Maximum adoption credit per child	2	$13,570 00	$13,570 00	$13,570 00		
3	Did you file Form 8839 for a prior year for the same child? ☐ **No.** Enter -0-. ☐ **Yes.** See instructions for the amount to enter.	3					
4	Subtract line 3 from line 2	4					
5	**Qualified adoption expenses** (see instructions)	5					
	Caution: Your qualified adoption expenses may not be equal to the adoption expenses you paid in 2017.						
6	Enter the **smaller** of line 4 or line 5	6					
7	Enter modified adjusted gross income (see instructions)				7		
8	Is line 7 more than $203,540? ☐ **No.** Skip lines 8 and 9, and enter -0- on line 10. ☐ **Yes.** Subtract $203,540 from line 7				8		
9	Divide line 8 by $40,000. Enter the result as a decimal (rounded to at least three places). Do not enter more than 1.000					9	× .
10	Multiply each amount on line 6 by line 9	10					
11	Subtract line 10 from line 6	11					
12	Add the amounts on line 11					12	
13	Credit carryforward, if any, from prior years. See your Adoption Credit Carryforward Worksheet in the 2016 Form 8839 instructions					13	
14	Add lines 12 and 13					14	
15	Enter the amount from line 5 of the Credit Limit Worksheet in the instructions					15	
16	**Adoption Credit.** Enter the smaller of line 14 or line 15 here and on Form 1040, line 54, or Form 1040NR, line 51. Check box **c** on that line and enter **"8839"** in the space next to box **c.** If line 15 is smaller than line 14, you may have a credit carryforward (see instructions)					16	

For Paperwork Reduction Act Notice, see your tax return instructions. Cat. No. 22843L Form **8839** (2017)

Source: U.S. Department of the Treasury, Internal Revenue Service, Form 8839. Washington, DC: 2017.

in a tax refund even if a taxpayer has no tax liability. To claim the credit, the taxpayer must meet certain requirements and file a tax return. Taxpayers may claim the EIC with or without a qualifying child, but the amount of the credit will vary, depending on their earned income and whether the taxpayer has no qualifying children, or one, two, or three or more qualifying children.

Earned Income

The EIC is determined by multiplying the taxpayer's earned income (up to a certain maximum amount) by the appropriate EIC percentage. *Earned income* includes wages, salaries, tips, and earnings from self-employment (minus one-half of the self-employment taxes).[40] A taxpayer who has a net loss from self-employment must reduce earned income by the amount of the loss.[41]

Qualifying Child

To be eligible for the credit, a taxpayer must either have a qualifying child or meet certain criteria. A qualifying child is one of the following:

- The taxpayer's son or daughter, grandchildren, or descendants.
- A stepson or stepdaughter, or descendants of either.
- An eligible foster child, defined as someone the taxpayer cares for as his or her own child and who is (1) a brother, sister, stepbrother, or stepsister, or (2) a descendant of a person in (1), or (3) a child placed with the taxpayer by an authorized placement agency.
- An adopted child.[42]

In addition, the child must:

- Live with the taxpayer in the United States for more than half the year and be the age of 19 (or be a full-time student under the age of 24).
- Be younger than the person claiming the child.
- Not have filed a joint return other than to claim a refund.
- Have a valid social security number.

No Qualifying Child

If a taxpayer has no qualifying child, to be eligible for the credit, *all* of the following criteria must be met:

- Have a principal place of abode in the United States for more than half the tax year.
- Be older than 24 but younger than 65 before the end of the tax year. In the case of married individuals, at least one spouse must satisfy this requirement.
- Not be claimed as a dependent of another taxpayer.
- Not be a nonresident alien for any part of the tax year.

Calculating the Earned Income Credit

To calculate the EIC, multiply earned income up to a certain amount by a percentage; when earned income exceeds certain levels, the credit begins to phase out. The percentages for the credit and phaseout amounts vary depending on filing status and the number of qualifying children claimed by the taxpayer. The appropriate percentages and earned income amounts are shown in Table 9-3.[43]

At first glance, the table may appear intimidating, but its application is straightforward. For example, married taxpayers with two eligible children use the column "Two" (the second column from the right). For earned income up to $14,040, the taxpayer is entitled to a credit of

[40] IRC § 32(c)(2).

[41] Reg. § 1.32-2(c)(2).

[42] IRC § 32(c)(3).

[43] Derived from IRC § 32(b).

TABLE 9-3*
Earned Income Credit Tax Year 2017

	Number of Eligible Children			
	None	**One**	**Two**	**Three or More**
EIC percentage	7.65%	34.0%	40.0%	45.0%
For earned income up to	$6,670	$10,000	$14,040	$14,040
Maximum EIC	$510	$3,400	$5,616	$6,318
Phaseout percentage	7.65%	15.98%	21.06%	21.06%
For joint filers:				
Phaseout starts at earned income of	$13,930	$23,930	$23,930	$23,930
Phaseout ends at earned income of	$20,600	$45,207	$50,597	$53,930
For all other filers:				
Phaseout starts at earned income of	$8,340	$18,340	$18,340	$18,340
Phaseout ends at earned income of	$15,010	$39,617	$45,007	$48,340

* The dollar amounts in the table are subject to annual adjustments for inflation.

40% of earned income. For tax year 2017, $5,616 ($14,040 × 40%) is the maximum EIC for a joint filer with two qualifying children.

Married joint return filers (with two qualifying children) with earned income between $14,040 and the phaseout starting point of $23,930 are also entitled to the maximum credit. However, once earned income rises above $23,930, the EIC is reduced by 21.06% of the excess (that is, amounts over $23,930) until earned income reaches $50,597. Once earned income reaches $50,597, the EIC is eliminated.

In practice, the EIC is determined by referencing the EIC table provided by the IRS and completing a Schedule EIC (if there is a qualifying child) and a Worksheet A (Exhibits 9-8 and 9-9). A copy of the EIC table can be found at the end of this chapter in the appendix.

EXAMPLE 9-19

Danny and Wanda have two eligible children and file a joint return. They have earned income of $38,025. Their EIC is $2,648, calculated as follows:

Maximum credit	$5,616
Less: ($38,025 − $23,930) × 21.06%	2,968
Earned Income Credit	$2,648

EXAMPLE 9-20

Using the same information as in Example 9-19, look up the amount of EIC for Danny and Wanda using the EIC table in the appendix at the end of this chapter. They have earned income of $38,025, which falls between $38,000 and $38,050. Be sure to use the column for married filing jointly and "two children." The EIC amount should be $2,648, same as the amount calculated in Example 9-19.

EXAMPLE 9-21

Saul and Tammy have a 4-year-old daughter, Brenda, who is a dependent. Their combined earned income was $25,500. The couple had no other income. In this case, the couple qualifies for the EIC with one qualifying child. Their EIC is $3,149, calculated as follows:

Maximum credit	$3,400
Less: ($25,500 − $23,930) × 15.98%	$ 251
Earned Income Credit	$3,149

From Shoebox to Software

Taxpayers use Schedule EIC and Worksheet A to claim the EIC credit (Exhibits 9-8 and 9-9). The tax software will automatically calculate the amount of the credit based on the information provided elsewhere in the tax return. Taxpayers claim the credit directly on Form 1040, line 66a, or Form 1040A, line 42a.

To obtain the credit, the taxpayer must provide ID numbers of the taxpayer, the taxpayer's spouse (if applicable), and the name, age, and taxpayer ID of any qualifying child (if applicable).

A taxpayer is ineligible to take the EIC if he or she has disqualified income in excess of $3,450.[44] *Disqualified income* includes dividends, interest (taxable and nontaxable), net rental income, net royalty income, net capital gains, and net passive income.[45] If certain required forms are filed, a taxpayer with a qualifying child may receive advance payments of the EIC through his or her employer, not to exceed 60% of the total available credit.

CONCEPT CHECK 9-8— LO 9-8

1. Josh and Danielle both work and have one qualifying child. They had earned income of $20,000. Using the EIC table at the end of the chapter, look up the amount of their EIC.
2. Assume the same facts as above for Josh and Danielle except their earned income is $32,000. Calculate their EIC using the formula as shown in Example 9-21 of this chapter.
3. Tiffany is a head of household taxpayer with two qualifying children. She had earned income of $15,000. (*a*) If she qualifies for the EIC, how much is her credit (either the EIC table or the EIC formula may be used)? (*b*) If her tax liability is $800 for the tax year (before the EIC), what is the amount of her tax refund or tax owed after the EIC is taken into account?

From Shoebox to Software Comprehensive Example

Using the tax software, open the tax return for Mr. and Mrs. Ramirez.

The Ramirezes already have a $3,000 child tax credit—$1,000 for each of their three children. We will now add some education credits.

Maria Ramirez attended State University, where she is working on an undergraduate degree in accounting. She is taking three classes a semester (a full load is four classes). During the current year (while Maria was a sophomore), she paid the university $9,000 for tuition and fees, the local bookstore $700 for books, and $235 for food at the student union between classes.

Jose is taking a few graduate classes at State University to help him with certain aspects of his job. He paid the university $1,300 for tuition. He was not enrolled in a degree program.

Go to Form 1040 for the Ramirezes. Click on line 50, education credits. Click on the yellow file folder, and then click on the information sheet. Alternatively, you could go to the Documents Received section and click on the Federal Information for Higher Education sheet.

Jose and Maria's allowable expenses are tuition, fees, and books. The expenses for food are not qualified expenses for purposes of the credits. Enter the $9,700 of expenses for Maria and the $1,300 for Jose. Then click the Qualifies for the American opportunity tax credit box beside Maria's name because she is in her first four years of higher education.

Now open the Ramirezes' Form 8863. Part I should show a $2,500 credit for Maria, and Part II should show a $260 credit for Jose. If the Ramirezes have modified AGI in excess of $107,000, their credit of $2,760 will be limited in Part III, Line 19 of Form 8863 and line 50 of Form 1040 should both reflect this limited credit.

Save the Ramirezes' return for future chapters.

[44] This amount is adjusted annually for inflation.

[45] IRC § 32(i).

EXHIBIT 9-8

SCHEDULE EIC
(Form 1040A or 1040)

Department of the Treasury
Internal Revenue Service (99)

Earned Income Credit

Qualifying Child Information

▶ **Complete and attach to Form 1040A or 1040 only if you have a qualifying child.**

▶ Go to *www.irs.gov/ScheduleEIC* for the latest information.

OMB No. 1545-0074

2017

Attachment Sequence No. **43**

Name(s) shown on return

Your social security number

Before you begin:

- See the instructions for Form 1040A, lines 42a and 42b, or Form 1040, lines 66a and 66b, to make sure that **(a)** you can take the EIC, and **(b)** you have a qualifying child.
- Be sure the child's name on line 1 and social security number (SSN) on line 2 agree with the child's social security card. Otherwise, at the time we process your return, we may reduce or disallow your EIC. If the name or SSN on the child's social security card is not correct, call the Social Security Administration at 1-800-772-1213.

CAUTION

- *You can't claim the EIC for a child who didn't live with you for more than half of the year.*
- *If you take the EIC even though you are not eligible, you may not be allowed to take the credit for up to 10 years. See the instructions for details.*
- *It will take us longer to process your return and issue your refund if you do not fill in all lines that apply for each qualifying child.*

Qualifying Child Information	Child 1	Child 2	Child 3
1 Child's name If you have more than three qualifying children, you have to list only three to get the maximum credit.	First name Last name	First name Last name	First name Last name
2 Child's SSN The child must have an SSN as defined in the instructions for Form 1040A, lines 42a and 42b, or Form 1040, lines 66a and 66b, unless the child was born and died in 2017. If your child was born and died in 2017 and did not have an SSN, enter "Died" on this line and attach a copy of the child's birth certificate, death certificate, or hospital medical records showing a live birth.			
3 Child's year of birth	Year ___ ___ ___ ___ *If born after 1998* ***and*** *the child is younger than you (or your spouse, if filing jointly), skip lines 4a and 4b; go to line 5.*	Year ___ ___ ___ ___ *If born after 1998* ***and*** *the child is younger than you (or your spouse, if filing jointly), skip lines 4a and 4b; go to line 5.*	Year ___ ___ ___ ___ *If born after 1998* ***and*** *the child is younger than you (or your spouse, if filing jointly), skip lines 4a and 4b; go to line 5.*
4 a Was the child under age 24 at the end of 2017, a student, and younger than you (or your spouse, if filing jointly)?	☐ **Yes.** *Go to line 5.* ☐ **No.** *Go to line 4b.*	☐ **Yes.** *Go to line 5.* ☐ **No.** *Go to line 4b.*	☐ **Yes.** *Go to line 5.* ☐ **No.** *Go to line 4b.*
b Was the child permanently and totally disabled during any part of 2017?	☐ **Yes.** *Go to line 5.* ☐ **No.** The child is not a qualifying child.	☐ **Yes.** *Go to line 5.* ☐ **No.** The child is not a qualifying child.	☐ **Yes.** *Go to line 5.* ☐ **No.** The child is not a qualifying child.
5 Child's relationship to you (for example, son, daughter, grandchild, niece, nephew, eligible foster child, etc.)			
6 Number of months child lived with you in the United States during 2017 • If the child lived with you for more than half of 2017 but less than 7 months, enter "7." • If the child was born or died in 2017 and your home was the child's home for more than half the time he or she was alive during 2017, enter "12."	_______ months *Do not enter more than 12 months.*	_______ months *Do not enter more than 12 months.*	_______ months *Do not enter more than 12 months.*

For Paperwork Reduction Act Notice, see your tax return instructions. Cat. No. 13339M **Schedule EIC (Form 1040A or 1040) 2017**

Source: U.S. Department of the Treasury, Internal Revenue Service, SCHEDULE EIC (Form 1040A or 1040). Washington, DC: 2017.

EXHIBIT 9-9

Worksheet A—2017 EIC—Lines 66a and 66b

Keep for Your Records

Before you begin: √ Be sure you are using the correct worksheet. Use this worksheet only if you answered "No" to Step 5, question 2. Otherwise, use Worksheet B.

Part 1

All Filers Using Worksheet A

1. Enter your earned income from Step 5. **1** ______

2. Look up the amount on line 1 above in the EIC Table (right after Worksheet B) to find the credit. Be sure you use the correct column for your filing status and the number of children you have. Enter the credit here. **2** ______

If line 2 is zero, STOP You can't take the credit. Enter "No" on the dotted line next to line 66a.

3. Enter the amount from Form 1040, line 38. **3** ______

4. Are the amounts on lines 3 and 1 the same?

☐ **Yes.** Skip line 5; enter the amount from line 2 on line 6.

☐ **No.** Go to line 5.

Part 2

Filers Who Answered "No" on Line 4

5. If you have:

- No qualifying children, is the amount on line 3 less than $8,350 ($13,950 if married filing jointly)?
- 1 or more qualifying children, is the amount on line 3 less than $18,350 ($23,950 if married filing jointly)?

☐ **Yes.** Leave line 5 blank; enter the amount from line 2 on line 6.

☐ **No.** Look up the amount on line 3 in the EIC Table to find the credit. Be sure you use the correct column for your filing status and the number of children you have. Enter the credit here. **5** ______

Look at the amounts on lines 5 and 2.
Then, enter the **smaller** amount on line 6.

Part 3

Your Earned Income Credit

6. This is your earned income credit. **6** ______

Enter this amount on Form 1040, line 66a.

Reminder—

√ If you have a qualifying child, complete and attach Schedule EIC.

CAUTION *If your EIC for a year after 1996 was reduced or disallowed, see* Form 8862, who must file, *earlier, to find out if you must file Form 8862 to take the credit for 2017.*

Source: U.S. Department of the Treasury, Internal Revenue Service, Worksheet A-2017 EIC. Washington, DC: 2017.

PREMIUM TAX CREDIT (FORM 1040, LINE 69 OR LINE 46, OR FORM 1040A, LINE 45 OR 29)

LO 9-9

The Affordable Care Act (ACA) requires all individuals to either have health care coverage or qualify for a health coverage exemption or make a shared responsibility payment with their tax return. We first discussed the tax provisions related to the ACA in Chapter 1.

Taxpayers can obtain health insurance from an employer or from Medicare, or they can purchase an individual plan.

Individuals without insurance can obtain health insurance through a Health Insurance Marketplace ("Marketplace" or "Exchange"). Millions of Americans have purchased their health insurance in this manner.

Taxpayers who purchased qualified health insurance through the Marketplace may be eligible for a premium tax credit. This credit can be claimed in full on the taxpayer's Form 1040 or 1040A. Most often, the credit is used during the year to reduce the out-of-pocket cost of the insurance premiums—in effect, the taxpayer will pay for part of the premium and the credit will pay for the remainder.

In general, to receive the credit, eligible taxpayers must have household income between 100% and 400% of the federal poverty level for the taxpayer's family size. The taxpayer must also be ineligible for coverage through an employer or government plan.

Taxpayers eligible for the credit can choose to apply the credit toward their insurance premium or to receive the entire credit when they file their tax return. This determination is made at the time a taxpayer obtains insurance through the Marketplace.

At the end of the year, taxpayers who receive the credit must file a tax return and complete Form 8962. This form claims the premium tax credit and reconciles any advanced tax credits received with the tax credit for which the taxpayer is eligible. The credit is a refundable credit. Taxpayers receiving a credit will receive a Form 1095-A from the Marketplace, and the information on this form is used to complete Form 8962.

The amount of the credit is the lesser of:

- The premium for the insurance obtained from the Marketplace.
- The premium for the applicable second lowest cost silver plan (SLCSP) minus the taxpayer's contribution amount.

To calculate the monthly contribution amount the taxpayer uses an "applicable figure" determined with reference to Table 2 in the instructions to Form 8962. The table is shown in Appendix B of this chapter.

The applicable figure is based on the taxpayer's household income as a percentage of the federal poverty level for the applicable family size. The applicable poverty guidelines are those from the preceding calendar year. So, the 2016 guidelines are used to determine the 2017 premium tax credit. The 2016 federal poverty levels are as follows:

2016 Poverty Guidelines for the 48 Contiguous States and the District of Columbia

Persons in Family/Household	Poverty Guideline
1	$11,880
2	16,020
3	20,160
4	24,300
5	28,440
6	32,580
7	36,730
8	40,890

EXAMPLE 9-22

Shantae is married with one dependent and a household size of three. Her household income is $42,134. This household income is 209% of the federal poverty level for a household size of three ($42,134/$20,160 = 209%). The applicable figure from Table 2 is 0.0675.

The contribution amount is equal to the household income multiplied by the applicable figure from Table 2. This calculated contribution amount is subtracted from the taxpayer's SLCSP cost.

Let's put it all together with the following example.

EXAMPLE 9-23

Gordon is single with no dependents. He enrolled in a qualified health care plan with an annual premium of $5,000 through the Marketplace. His SLCSP premium (shown on his Form 1095-A) is $5,200. His household income in 2017 was $29,700, which is 250% of the federal poverty level for a family size of one ($29,700/$11,880 = 250%). His applicable figure using Table 2 in the instructions to Form 8962 or in Appendix B in this chapter is 0.0821. His contribution amount is equal to $2,438 (household income of $29,700 multiplied by the Table 2 factor of 0.0821).

Gordon's premium is the lesser of:

- His health plan premium of $5,000.
- His SLCSP cost of $5,200 minus his contribution amount of $2,438, which is $2,762.

Thus, his premium tax credit is $2,762.

In practice, the premium credit is calculated based on expected household income and expected family size. To the extent that actual household income varies from expected, the taxpayer may receive an additional credit (on Form 1040, line 69) or may have additional tax (Form 1040, line 46). In general, if actual income is greater than expected income, the taxpayer will owe additional tax because the credit decreases as income increases. If actual income is less than expected, the taxpayer will receive an additional credit on Form 1040. Similarly, if actual family size is larger than expected, the taxpayer will receive an additional credit, and if actual size is smaller, the taxpayer will owe additional tax.

The rules associated with the credit can be complex. In fact, the IRS suggests taxpayers use tax software to file a return. Refer to IRS Publications 974, 5187, and 5201 for additional information.

CONCEPT CHECK 9-9— LO 9-9

1. All taxpayers who have health insurance are eligible to receive a premium tax credit. True or false?
2. What is the applicable figure from the table in Appendix B for married taxpayers with no dependents and $60,534 of household income?

Other Personal Credits

The IRC provides for various other credits that are not discussed in detail here. As with the credit for the elderly or the disabled, some of these credits are reported on line 54 of Form 1040 (most require additional forms to be attached). Recall that tax credits are often used by Congress to encourage certain societal and economic outcomes and in some cases are available for only a short term.

Generally, the preceding personal credits are nonrefundable credits. The exceptions are, among others, the EIC, a portion of the American opportunity tax credit, and, for certain taxpayers with earned income in excess of $3,000, the child tax credit (discussed earlier).

Summary

LO 9-1: Apply the tax rules and calculate the credit for child and dependent care expenses.

- The credit is available to working taxpayers with dependent care expenses (of qualifying individuals).
- The credit is calculated as a percentage of the qualified expenses incurred to care for dependents.
- The maximum amount of qualifying expenses is limited to $3,000 for one and $6,000 for two or more qualifying individuals.
- For qualifying expenses and qualifying individuals, certain criteria must be met.
- The percentage (20%–35%) used in the calculation is dependent on AGI.
- Certain expense limitations exist.

LO 9-2: Apply the tax rules and calculate the credit for the elderly or the disabled.

- The credit is available to taxpayers over 65 years of age or permanently and totally disabled.
- The credit is equal to 15% of allowable base amounts.
- The base amount is reduced by certain amounts of social security benefits and excess AGI.
- The base amounts vary depending on the filing status and age of the taxpayer.

LO 9-3: Apply the tax rules and calculate the education credits.

- Two credits available are the American opportunity tax credit (AOTC) and the lifetime learning credit.
- Both allow credit for higher education expenses for the taxpayer, spouse, or dependent.
- The AOTC has a maximum of $2,500 per student.
- The lifetime learning credit has a maximum of $2,000 per taxpayer.
- Both credits are phased out at certain amounts of AGI.
- For the lifetime learning credit, married filing jointly and single filers phase out completely at MAGI amounts of $132,000 and $66,000, respectively.
- For the AOTC, married filing jointly and single filers phase out completely at MAGI amounts of $180,000 and $90,000, respectively.

LO 9-4: Apply the tax rules and calculate the foreign tax credit (FTC).

- The credit is available to taxpayers who paid foreign income taxes.
- The credit is equal to the amount of foreign taxes paid.
- The FTC, however, is limited to the portion of the U.S. income tax liability that is attributable to foreign income.

LO 9-5: Apply the tax rules and calculate the child tax credit.

- The credit is provided to taxpayers with children under age 17.
- The credit for each child is $1,000.
- The credit is phased out for AGI over certain amounts.
- Phaseout begins at AGI of $110,000 and $75,000 for married filing jointly and single, respectively.
- Although generally nonrefundable, this credit could provide a refund at certain earned income levels.

LO 9-6: Apply the tax rules and calculate the retirement savings contributions credit.

- The credit is available to taxpayers who made contributions to certain qualified retirement accounts.
- The credit is based on a percentage of the contributions made.
- The maximum amount of contributions for credit purposes is $2,000 per individual (or per spouse if filed jointly).
- The percentage used depends on filing status and AGI.
- Over certain amounts of AGI, no credit is available.

LO 9-7: Apply the tax rules and calculate the adoption credit.

- The credit is available up to $13,570 per child adopted.
- The credit is phased out for AGI above $203,540.
- No credit is available for AGI above $243,540.
- If married, the credit is generally allowed only for taxpayers filing jointly.
- To claim the credit, Form 8839 must be filed.

LO 9-8: Apply the tax rules and calculate the Earned Income Credit (EIC).

- The credit is allowed for working taxpayers who are economically disadvantaged.
- It is a refundable tax credit.
- The credit is based on filing status, number of qualifying children (including none), and AGI.
- The credit can completely phase out at certain AGI levels.
- Certain types of income (mostly unearned) in excess of $3,450 make taxpayers ineligible for the credit.

LO 9-9: Apply the tax rules for the premium tax credit under the Affordable Care Act.

- Taxpayers with health insurance purchased through the Marketplace may be eligible.
- Household income must be between 100% and 400% of the federal poverty level for the family size.
- The credit can be used to pay a portion of the insurance premium.
- To claim the credit or to reconcile advanced payments, taxpayers must file Form 8962.

Appendix A

2017 Earned Income Credit (EIC) Table
Caution. This is **not** a tax table.

1. To find your credit, read down the "At least - But less than" columns and find the line that includes the amount you were told to look up from your EIC Worksheet.

2. Then, go to the column that includes your filing status and the number of qualifying children you have. Enter the credit from that column on your EIC Worksheet.

Example. If your filing status is single, you have one qualifying child, and the amount you are looking up from your EIC Worksheet is $2,455, you would enter $842.

If the amount you are looking up from the worksheet is–		And your filing status is– Single, head of household, or qualifying widow(er) and the number of children you have is–			
		0	1	2	3
At least	But less than	Your credit is–			
2,400	2,450	186	825	970	1,091
2,450	2,500	189	842	990	1,114

If the amount you are looking up from the worksheet is–		And your filing status is– Single, head of household, or qualifying widow(er) and the number of children you have is–				Married filing jointly and the number of children you have is–			
		0	1	2	3	0	1	2	3
At least	But less than	Your credit is–				Your credit is–			
$1	$50	$2	$9	$10	$11	$2	$9	$10	$11
50	100	6	26	30	34	6	26	30	34
100	150	10	43	50	56	10	43	50	56
150	200	13	60	70	79	13	60	70	79
200	250	17	77	90	101	17	77	90	101
250	300	21	94	110	124	21	94	110	124
300	350	25	111	130	146	25	111	130	146
350	400	29	128	150	169	29	128	150	169
400	450	33	145	170	191	33	145	170	191
450	500	36	162	190	214	36	162	190	214
500	550	40	179	210	236	40	179	210	236
550	600	44	196	230	259	44	196	230	259
600	650	48	213	250	281	48	213	250	281
650	700	52	230	270	304	52	230	270	304
700	750	55	247	290	326	55	247	290	326
750	800	59	264	310	349	59	264	310	349
800	850	63	281	330	371	63	281	330	371
850	900	67	298	350	394	67	298	350	394
900	950	71	315	370	416	71	315	370	416
950	1,000	75	332	390	439	75	332	390	439
1,000	1,050	78	349	410	461	78	349	410	461
1,050	1,100	82	366	430	484	82	366	430	484
1,100	1,150	86	383	450	506	86	383	450	506
1,150	1,200	90	400	470	529	90	400	470	529
1,200	1,250	94	417	490	551	94	417	490	551
1,250	1,300	98	434	510	574	98	434	510	574
1,300	1,350	101	451	530	596	101	451	530	596
1,350	1,400	105	468	550	619	105	468	550	619
1,400	1,450	109	485	570	641	109	485	570	641
1,450	1,500	113	502	590	664	113	502	590	664
1,500	1,550	117	519	610	686	117	519	610	686
1,550	1,600	120	536	630	709	120	536	630	709
1,600	1,650	124	553	650	731	124	553	650	731
1,650	1,700	128	570	670	754	128	570	670	754
1,700	1,750	132	587	690	776	132	587	690	776
1,750	1,800	136	604	710	799	136	604	710	799
1,800	1,850	140	621	730	821	140	621	730	821
1,850	1,900	143	638	750	844	143	638	750	844
1,900	1,950	147	655	770	866	147	655	770	866
1,950	2,000	151	672	790	889	151	672	790	889
2,000	2,050	155	689	810	911	155	689	810	911
2,050	2,100	159	706	830	934	159	706	830	934
2,100	2,150	163	723	850	956	163	723	850	956
2,150	2,200	166	740	870	979	166	740	870	979
2,200	2,250	170	757	890	1,001	170	757	890	1,001
2,250	2,300	174	774	910	1,024	174	774	910	1,024
2,300	2,350	178	791	930	1,046	178	791	930	1,046
2,350	2,400	182	808	950	1,069	182	808	950	1,069
2,400	2,450	186	825	970	1,091	186	825	970	1,091
2,450	2,500	189	842	990	1,114	189	842	990	1,114
2,500	2,550	193	859	1,010	1,136	193	859	1,010	1,136
2,550	2,600	197	876	1,030	1,159	197	876	1,030	1,159
2,600	2,650	201	893	1,050	1,181	201	893	1,050	1,181
2,650	2,700	205	910	1,070	1,204	205	910	1,070	1,204
2,700	2,750	208	927	1,090	1,226	208	927	1,090	1,226
2,750	2,800	212	944	1,110	1,249	212	944	1,110	1,249
2,800	2,850	216	961	1,130	1,271	216	961	1,130	1,271
2,850	2,900	220	978	1,150	1,294	220	978	1,150	1,294
2,900	2,950	224	995	1,170	1,316	224	995	1,170	1,316
2,950	3,000	228	1,012	1,190	1,339	228	1,012	1,190	1,339
3,000	3,050	231	1,029	1,210	1,361	231	1,029	1,210	1,361
3,050	3,100	235	1,046	1,230	1,384	235	1,046	1,230	1,384
3,100	3,150	239	1,063	1,250	1,406	239	1,063	1,250	1,406
3,150	3,200	243	1,080	1,270	1,429	243	1,080	1,270	1,429
3,200	3,250	247	1,097	1,290	1,451	247	1,097	1,290	1,451
3,250	3,300	251	1,114	1,310	1,474	251	1,114	1,310	1,474
3,300	3,350	254	1,131	1,330	1,496	254	1,131	1,330	1,496
3,350	3,400	258	1,148	1,350	1,519	258	1,148	1,350	1,519
3,400	3,450	262	1,165	1,370	1,541	262	1,165	1,370	1,541
3,450	3,500	266	1,182	1,390	1,564	266	1,182	1,390	1,564
3,500	3,550	270	1,199	1,410	1,586	270	1,199	1,410	1,586
3,550	3,600	273	1,216	1,430	1,609	273	1,216	1,430	1,609
3,600	3,650	277	1,233	1,450	1,631	277	1,233	1,450	1,631
3,650	3,700	281	1,250	1,470	1,654	281	1,250	1,470	1,654
3,700	3,750	285	1,267	1,490	1,676	285	1,267	1,490	1,676
3,750	3,800	289	1,284	1,510	1,699	289	1,284	1,510	1,699
3,800	3,850	293	1,301	1,530	1,721	293	1,301	1,530	1,721
3,850	3,900	296	1,318	1,550	1,744	296	1,318	1,550	1,744
3,900	3,950	300	1,335	1,570	1,766	300	1,335	1,570	1,766
3,950	4,000	304	1,352	1,590	1,789	304	1,352	1,590	1,789
4,000	4,050	308	1,369	1,610	1,811	308	1,369	1,610	1,811
4,050	4,100	312	1,386	1,630	1,834	312	1,386	1,630	1,834
4,100	4,150	316	1,403	1,650	1,856	316	1,403	1,650	1,856
4,150	4,200	319	1,420	1,670	1,879	319	1,420	1,670	1,879
4,200	4,250	323	1,437	1,690	1,901	323	1,437	1,690	1,901
4,250	4,300	327	1,454	1,710	1,924	327	1,454	1,710	1,924
4,300	4,350	331	1,471	1,730	1,946	331	1,471	1,730	1,946
4,350	4,400	335	1,488	1,750	1,969	335	1,488	1,750	1,969
4,400	4,450	339	1,505	1,770	1,991	339	1,505	1,770	1,991
4,450	4,500	342	1,522	1,790	2,014	342	1,522	1,790	2,014
4,500	4,550	346	1,539	1,810	2,036	346	1,539	1,810	2,036
4,550	4,600	350	1,556	1,830	2,059	350	1,556	1,830	2,059
4,600	4,650	354	1,573	1,850	2,081	354	1,573	1,850	2,081
4,650	4,700	358	1,590	1,870	2,104	358	1,590	1,870	2,104
4,700	4,750	361	1,607	1,890	2,126	361	1,607	1,890	2,126
4,750	4,800	365	1,624	1,910	2,149	365	1,624	1,910	2,149
4,800	4,850	369	1,641	1,930	2,171	369	1,641	1,930	2,171
4,850	4,900	373	1,658	1,950	2,194	373	1,658	1,950	2,194
4,900	4,950	377	1,675	1,970	2,216	377	1,675	1,970	2,216
4,950	5,000	381	1,692	1,990	2,239	381	1,692	1,990	2,239
5,000	5,050	384	1,709	2,010	2,261	384	1,709	2,010	2,261
5,050	5,100	388	1,726	2,030	2,284	388	1,726	2,030	2,284
5,100	5,150	392	1,743	2,050	2,306	392	1,743	2,050	2,306
5,150	5,200	396	1,760	2,070	2,329	396	1,760	2,070	2,329
5,200	5,250	400	1,777	2,090	2,351	400	1,777	2,090	2,351
5,250	5,300	404	1,794	2,110	2,374	404	1,794	2,110	2,374
5,300	5,350	407	1,811	2,130	2,396	407	1,811	2,130	2,396
5,350	5,400	411	1,828	2,150	2,419	411	1,828	2,150	2,419
5,400	5,450	415	1,845	2,170	2,441	415	1,845	2,170	2,441
5,450	5,500	419	1,862	2,190	2,464	419	1,862	2,190	2,464
5,500	5,550	423	1,879	2,210	2,486	423	1,879	2,210	2,486
5,550	5,600	426	1,896	2,230	2,509	426	1,896	2,230	2,509

(Continued)

Source: U.S. Department of the Treasury, Internal Revenue Service, 2017 Earned Income Credit (EIC) Table Caution. Washington, DC: 2017.

Earned Income Credit (EIC) Table - *Continued*

(**Caution.** This is **not** a tax table)

If the amount you are looking up from the worksheet is–		And your filing status is–							
		Single, head of household, or **qualifying widow(er)** and the number of children you have is–				**Married filing jointly** and the number of children you have is–			
		0	1	2	3	0	1	2	3
At least	But less than	Your credit is–				Your credit is–			
5,600	**5,650**	430	1,913	2,250	2,531	430	1,913	2,250	2,531
5,650	**5,700**	434	1,930	2,270	2,554	434	1,930	2,270	2,554
5,700	**5,750**	438	1,947	2,290	2,576	438	1,947	2,290	2,576
5,750	**5,800**	442	1,964	2,310	2,599	442	1,964	2,310	2,599
5,800	**5,850**	446	1,981	2,330	2,621	446	1,981	2,330	2,621
5,850	**5,900**	449	1,998	2,350	2,644	449	1,998	2,350	2,644
5,900	**5,950**	453	2,015	2,370	2,666	453	2,015	2,370	2,666
5,950	**6,000**	457	2,032	2,390	2,689	457	2,032	2,390	2,689
6,000	**6,050**	461	2,049	2,410	2,711	461	2,049	2,410	2,711
6,050	**6,100**	465	2,066	2,430	2,734	465	2,066	2,430	2,734
6,100	**6,150**	469	2,083	2,450	2,756	469	2,083	2,450	2,756
6,150	**6,200**	472	2,100	2,470	2,779	472	2,100	2,470	2,779
6,200	**6,250**	476	2,117	2,490	2,801	476	2,117	2,490	2,801
6,250	**6,300**	480	2,134	2,510	2,824	480	2,134	2,510	2,824
6,300	**6,350**	484	2,151	2,530	2,846	484	2,151	2,530	2,846
6,350	**6,400**	488	2,168	2,550	2,869	488	2,168	2,550	2,869
6,400	**6,450**	492	2,185	2,570	2,891	492	2,185	2,570	2,891
6,450	**6,500**	495	2,202	2,590	2,914	495	2,202	2,590	2,914
6,500	**6,550**	499	2,219	2,610	2,936	499	2,219	2,610	2,936
6,550	**6,600**	503	2,236	2,630	2,959	503	2,236	2,630	2,959
6,600	**6,650**	507	2,253	2,650	2,981	507	2,253	2,650	2,981
6,650	**6,700**	510	2,270	2,670	3,004	510	2,270	2,670	3,004
6,700	**6,750**	510	2,287	2,690	3,026	510	2,287	2,690	3,026
6,750	**6,800**	510	2,304	2,710	3,049	510	2,304	2,710	3,049
6,800	**6,850**	510	2,321	2,730	3,071	510	2,321	2,730	3,071
6,850	**6,900**	510	2,338	2,750	3,094	510	2,338	2,750	3,094
6,900	**6,950**	510	2,355	2,770	3,116	510	2,355	2,770	3,116
6,950	**7,000**	510	2,372	2,790	3,139	510	2,372	2,790	3,139
7,000	**7,050**	510	2,389	2,810	3,161	510	2,389	2,810	3,161
7,050	**7,100**	510	2,406	2,830	3,184	510	2,406	2,830	3,184
7,100	**7,150**	510	2,423	2,850	3,206	510	2,423	2,850	3,206
7,150	**7,200**	510	2,440	2,870	3,229	510	2,440	2,870	3,229
7,200	**7,250**	510	2,457	2,890	3,251	510	2,457	2,890	3,251
7,250	**7,300**	510	2,474	2,910	3,274	510	2,474	2,910	3,274
7,300	**7,350**	510	2,491	2,930	3,296	510	2,491	2,930	3,296
7,350	**7,400**	510	2,508	2,950	3,319	510	2,508	2,950	3,319
7,400	**7,450**	510	2,525	2,970	3,341	510	2,525	2,970	3,341
7,450	**7,500**	510	2,542	2,990	3,364	510	2,542	2,990	3,364
7,500	**7,550**	510	2,559	3,010	3,386	510	2,559	3,010	3,386
7,550	**7,600**	510	2,576	3,030	3,409	510	2,576	3,030	3,409
7,600	**7,650**	510	2,593	3,050	3,431	510	2,593	3,050	3,431
7,650	**7,700**	510	2,610	3,070	3,454	510	2,610	3,070	3,454
7,700	**7,750**	510	2,627	3,090	3,476	510	2,627	3,090	3,476
7,750	**7,800**	510	2,644	3,110	3,499	510	2,644	3,110	3,499
7,800	**7,850**	510	2,661	3,130	3,521	510	2,661	3,130	3,521
7,850	**7,900**	510	2,678	3,150	3,544	510	2,678	3,150	3,544
7,900	**7,950**	510	2,695	3,170	3,566	510	2,695	3,170	3,566
7,950	**8,000**	510	2,712	3,190	3,589	510	2,712	3,190	3,589
8,000	**8,050**	510	2,729	3,210	3,611	510	2,729	3,210	3,611
8,050	**8,100**	510	2,746	3,230	3,634	510	2,746	3,230	3,634
8,100	**8,150**	510	2,763	3,250	3,656	510	2,763	3,250	3,656
8,150	**8,200**	510	2,780	3,270	3,679	510	2,780	3,270	3,679
8,200	**8,250**	510	2,797	3,290	3,701	510	2,797	3,290	3,701
8,250	**8,300**	510	2,814	3,310	3,724	510	2,814	3,310	3,724
8,300	**8,350**	510	2,831	3,330	3,746	510	2,831	3,330	3,746
8,350	**8,400**	508	2,848	3,350	3,769	510	2,848	3,350	3,769
8,400	**8,450**	504	2,865	3,370	3,791	510	2,865	3,370	3,791
8,450	**8,500**	500	2,882	3,390	3,814	510	2,882	3,390	3,814
8,500	**8,550**	496	2,899	3,410	3,836	510	2,899	3,410	3,836
8,550	**8,600**	492	2,916	3,430	3,859	510	2,916	3,430	3,859
8,600	**8,650**	488	2,933	3,450	3,881	510	2,933	3,450	3,881
8,650	**8,700**	485	2,950	3,470	3,904	510	2,950	3,470	3,904
8,700	**8,750**	481	2,967	3,490	3,926	510	2,967	3,490	3,926
8,750	**8,800**	477	2,984	3,510	3,949	510	2,984	3,510	3,949
8,800	**8,850**	473	3,001	3,530	3,971	510	3,001	3,530	3,971
8,850	**8,900**	469	3,018	3,550	3,994	510	3,018	3,550	3,994
8,900	**8,950**	466	3,035	3,570	4,016	510	3,035	3,570	4,016
8,950	**9,000**	462	3,052	3,590	4,039	510	3,052	3,590	4,039
9,000	**9,050**	458	3,069	3,610	4,061	510	3,069	3,610	4,061
9,050	**9,100**	454	3,086	3,630	4,084	510	3,086	3,630	4,084
9,100	**9,150**	450	3,103	3,650	4,106	510	3,103	3,650	4,106
9,150	**9,200**	446	3,120	3,670	4,129	510	3,120	3,670	4,129
9,200	**9,250**	443	3,137	3,690	4,151	510	3,137	3,690	4,151
9,250	**9,300**	439	3,154	3,710	4,174	510	3,154	3,710	4,174
9,300	**9,350**	435	3,171	3,730	4,196	510	3,171	3,730	4,196
9,350	**9,400**	431	3,188	3,750	4,219	510	3,188	3,750	4,219
9,400	**9,450**	427	3,205	3,770	4,241	510	3,205	3,770	4,241
9,450	**9,500**	423	3,222	3,790	4,264	510	3,222	3,790	4,264
9,500	**9,550**	420	3,239	3,810	4,286	510	3,239	3,810	4,286
9,550	**9,600**	416	3,256	3,830	4,309	510	3,256	3,830	4,309
9,600	**9,650**	412	3,273	3,850	4,331	510	3,273	3,850	4,331
9,650	**9,700**	408	3,290	3,870	4,354	510	3,290	3,870	4,354
9,700	**9,750**	404	3,307	3,890	4,376	510	3,307	3,890	4,376
9,750	**9,800**	400	3,324	3,910	4,399	510	3,324	3,910	4,399
9,800	**9,850**	397	3,341	3,930	4,421	510	3,341	3,930	4,421
9,850	**9,900**	393	3,358	3,950	4,444	510	3,358	3,950	4,444
9,900	**9,950**	389	3,375	3,970	4,466	510	3,375	3,970	4,466
9,950	**10,000**	385	3,392	3,990	4,489	510	3,392	3,990	4,489
10,000	**10,050**	381	3,400	4,010	4,511	510	3,400	4,010	4,511
10,050	**10,100**	378	3,400	4,030	4,534	510	3,400	4,030	4,534
10,100	**10,150**	374	3,400	4,050	4,556	510	3,400	4,050	4,556
10,150	**10,200**	370	3,400	4,070	4,579	510	3,400	4,070	4,579
10,200	**10,250**	366	3,400	4,090	4,601	510	3,400	4,090	4,601
10,250	**10,300**	362	3,400	4,110	4,624	510	3,400	4,110	4,624
10,300	**10,350**	358	3,400	4,130	4,646	510	3,400	4,130	4,646
10,350	**10,400**	355	3,400	4,150	4,669	510	3,400	4,150	4,669
10,400	**10,450**	351	3,400	4,170	4,691	510	3,400	4,170	4,691
10,450	**10,500**	347	3,400	4,190	4,714	510	3,400	4,190	4,714
10,500	**10,550**	343	3,400	4,210	4,736	510	3,400	4,210	4,736
10,550	**10,600**	339	3,400	4,230	4,759	510	3,400	4,230	4,759
10,600	**10,650**	335	3,400	4,250	4,781	510	3,400	4,250	4,781
10,650	**10,700**	332	3,400	4,270	4,804	510	3,400	4,270	4,804
10,700	**10,750**	328	3,400	4,290	4,826	510	3,400	4,290	4,826
10,750	**10,800**	324	3,400	4,310	4,849	510	3,400	4,310	4,849
10,800	**10,850**	320	3,400	4,330	4,871	510	3,400	4,330	4,871
10,850	**10,900**	316	3,400	4,350	4,894	510	3,400	4,350	4,894
10,900	**10,950**	313	3,400	4,370	4,916	510	3,400	4,370	4,916
10,950	**11,000**	309	3,400	4,390	4,939	510	3,400	4,390	4,939
11,000	**11,050**	305	3,400	4,410	4,961	510	3,400	4,410	4,961
11,050	**11,100**	301	3,400	4,430	4,984	510	3,400	4,430	4,984
11,100	**11,150**	297	3,400	4,450	5,006	510	3,400	4,450	5,006
11,150	**11,200**	293	3,400	4,470	5,029	510	3,400	4,470	5,029
11,200	**11,250**	290	3,400	4,490	5,051	510	3,400	4,490	5,051
11,250	**11,300**	286	3,400	4,510	5,074	510	3,400	4,510	5,074
11,300	**11,350**	282	3,400	4,530	5,096	510	3,400	4,530	5,096
11,350	**11,400**	278	3,400	4,550	5,119	510	3,400	4,550	5,119
11,400	**11,450**	274	3,400	4,570	5,141	510	3,400	4,570	5,141
11,450	**11,500**	270	3,400	4,590	5,164	510	3,400	4,590	5,164
11,500	**11,550**	267	3,400	4,610	5,186	510	3,400	4,610	5,186
11,550	**11,600**	263	3,400	4,630	5,209	510	3,400	4,630	5,209
11,600	**11,650**	259	3,400	4,650	5,231	510	3,400	4,650	5,231
11,650	**11,700**	255	3,400	4,670	5,254	510	3,400	4,670	5,254
11,700	**11,750**	251	3,400	4,690	5,276	510	3,400	4,690	5,276
11,750	**11,800**	247	3,400	4,710	5,299	510	3,400	4,710	5,299
11,800	**11,850**	244	3,400	4,730	5,321	510	3,400	4,730	5,321
11,850	**11,900**	240	3,400	4,750	5,344	510	3,400	4,750	5,344
11,900	**11,950**	236	3,400	4,770	5,366	510	3,400	4,770	5,366
11,950	**12,000**	232	3,400	4,790	5,389	510	3,400	4,790	5,389

(Continued)

Earned Income Credit (EIC) Table - *Continued* (**Caution.** This is **not** a tax table.)

If the amount you are looking up from the worksheet is–		And your filing status is– Single, head of household, or qualifying widow(er) and the number of children you have is–				Married filing jointly and the number of children you have is–			
		0	1	2	3	0	1	2	3
At least	But less than	Your credit is–				Your credit is–			
12,000	12,050	228	3,400	4,810	5,411	510	3,400	4,810	5,411
12,050	12,100	225	3,400	4,830	5,434	510	3,400	4,830	5,434
12,100	12,150	221	3,400	4,850	5,456	510	3,400	4,850	5,456
12,150	12,200	217	3,400	4,870	5,479	510	3,400	4,870	5,479
12,200	12,250	213	3,400	4,890	5,501	510	3,400	4,890	5,501
12,250	12,300	209	3,400	4,910	5,524	510	3,400	4,910	5,524
12,300	12,350	205	3,400	4,930	5,546	510	3,400	4,930	5,546
12,350	12,400	202	3,400	4,950	5,569	510	3,400	4,950	5,569
12,400	12,450	198	3,400	4,970	5,591	510	3,400	4,970	5,591
12,450	12,500	194	3,400	4,990	5,614	510	3,400	4,990	5,614
12,500	12,550	190	3,400	5,010	5,636	510	3,400	5,010	5,636
12,550	12,600	186	3,400	5,030	5,659	510	3,400	5,030	5,659
12,600	12,650	182	3,400	5,050	5,681	510	3,400	5,050	5,681
12,650	12,700	179	3,400	5,070	5,704	510	3,400	5,070	5,704
12,700	12,750	175	3,400	5,090	5,726	510	3,400	5,090	5,726
12,750	12,800	171	3,400	5,110	5,749	510	3,400	5,110	5,749
12,800	12,850	167	3,400	5,130	5,771	510	3,400	5,130	5,771
12,850	12,900	163	3,400	5,150	5,794	510	3,400	5,150	5,794
12,900	12,950	160	3,400	5,170	5,816	510	3,400	5,170	5,816
12,950	13,000	156	3,400	5,190	5,839	510	3,400	5,190	5,839
13,000	13,050	152	3,400	5,210	5,861	510	3,400	5,210	5,861
13,050	13,100	148	3,400	5,230	5,884	510	3,400	5,230	5,884
13,100	13,150	144	3,400	5,250	5,906	510	3,400	5,250	5,906
13,150	13,200	140	3,400	5,270	5,929	510	3,400	5,270	5,929
13,200	13,250	137	3,400	5,290	5,951	510	3,400	5,290	5,951
13,250	13,300	133	3,400	5,310	5,974	510	3,400	5,310	5,974
13,300	13,350	129	3,400	5,330	5,996	510	3,400	5,330	5,996
13,350	13,400	125	3,400	5,350	6,019	510	3,400	5,350	6,019
13,400	13,450	121	3,400	5,370	6,041	510	3,400	5,370	6,041
13,450	13,500	117	3,400	5,390	6,064	510	3,400	5,390	6,064
13,500	13,550	114	3,400	5,410	6,086	510	3,400	5,410	6,086
13,550	13,600	110	3,400	5,430	6,109	510	3,400	5,430	6,109
13,600	13,650	106	3,400	5,450	6,131	510	3,400	5,450	6,131
13,650	13,700	102	3,400	5,470	6,154	510	3,400	5,470	6,154
13,700	13,750	98	3,400	5,490	6,176	510	3,400	5,490	6,176
13,750	13,800	94	3,400	5,510	6,199	510	3,400	5,510	6,199
13,800	13,850	91	3,400	5,530	6,221	510	3,400	5,530	6,221
13,850	13,900	87	3,400	5,550	6,244	510	3,400	5,550	6,244
13,900	13,950	83	3,400	5,570	6,266	510	3,400	5,570	6,266
13,950	14,000	79	3,400	5,590	6,289	507	3,400	5,590	6,289
14,000	14,050	75	3,400	5,616	6,318	503	3,400	5,616	6,318
14,050	14,100	72	3,400	5,616	6,318	499	3,400	5,616	6,318
14,100	14,150	68	3,400	5,616	6,318	495	3,400	5,616	6,318
14,150	14,200	64	3,400	5,616	6,318	492	3,400	5,616	6,318
14,200	14,250	60	3,400	5,616	6,318	488	3,400	5,616	6,318
14,250	14,300	56	3,400	5,616	6,318	484	3,400	5,616	6,318
14,300	14,350	52	3,400	5,616	6,318	480	3,400	5,616	6,318
14,350	14,400	49	3,400	5,616	6,318	476	3,400	5,616	6,318
14,400	14,450	45	3,400	5,616	6,318	472	3,400	5,616	6,318
14,450	14,500	41	3,400	5,616	6,318	469	3,400	5,616	6,318
14,500	14,550	37	3,400	5,616	6,318	465	3,400	5,616	6,318
14,550	14,600	33	3,400	5,616	6,318	461	3,400	5,616	6,318
14,600	14,650	29	3,400	5,616	6,318	457	3,400	5,616	6,318
14,650	14,700	26	3,400	5,616	6,318	453	3,400	5,616	6,318
14,700	14,750	22	3,400	5,616	6,318	449	3,400	5,616	6,318
14,750	14,800	18	3,400	5,616	6,318	446	3,400	5,616	6,318
14,800	14,850	14	3,400	5,616	6,318	442	3,400	5,616	6,318
14,850	14,900	10	3,400	5,616	6,318	438	3,400	5,616	6,318
14,900	14,950	7	3,400	5,616	6,318	434	3,400	5,616	6,318
14,950	15,000	3	3,400	5,616	6,318	430	3,400	5,616	6,318
15,000	15,050	0	3,400	5,616	6,318	426	3,400	5,616	6,318
15,050	15,100	0	3,400	5,616	6,318	423	3,400	5,616	6,318
15,100	15,150	0	3,400	5,616	6,318	419	3,400	5,616	6,318
15,150	15,200	0	3,400	5,616	6,318	415	3,400	5,616	6,318
15,200	15,250	0	3,400	5,616	6,318	411	3,400	5,616	6,318
15,250	15,300	0	3,400	5,616	6,318	407	3,400	5,616	6,318
15,300	15,350	0	3,400	5,616	6,318	404	3,400	5,616	6,318
15,350	15,400	0	3,400	5,616	6,318	400	3,400	5,616	6,318
15,400	15,450	0	3,400	5,616	6,318	396	3,400	5,616	6,318
15,450	15,500	0	3,400	5,616	6,318	392	3,400	5,616	6,318
15,500	15,550	0	3,400	5,616	6,318	388	3,400	5,616	6,318
15,550	15,600	0	3,400	5,616	6,318	384	3,400	5,616	6,318
15,600	15,650	0	3,400	5,616	6,318	381	3,400	5,616	6,318
15,650	15,700	0	3,400	5,616	6,318	377	3,400	5,616	6,318
15,700	15,750	0	3,400	5,616	6,318	373	3,400	5,616	6,318
15,750	15,800	0	3,400	5,616	6,318	369	3,400	5,616	6,318
15,800	15,850	0	3,400	5,616	6,318	365	3,400	5,616	6,318
15,850	15,900	0	3,400	5,616	6,318	361	3,400	5,616	6,318
15,900	15,950	0	3,400	5,616	6,318	358	3,400	5,616	6,318
15,950	16,000	0	3,400	5,616	6,318	354	3,400	5,616	6,318
16,000	16,050	0	3,400	5,616	6,318	350	3,400	5,616	6,318
16,050	16,100	0	3,400	5,616	6,318	346	3,400	5,616	6,318
16,100	16,150	0	3,400	5,616	6,318	342	3,400	5,616	6,318
16,150	16,200	0	3,400	5,616	6,318	339	3,400	5,616	6,318
16,200	16,250	0	3,400	5,616	6,318	335	3,400	5,616	6,318
16,250	16,300	0	3,400	5,616	6,318	331	3,400	5,616	6,318
16,300	16,350	0	3,400	5,616	6,318	327	3,400	5,616	6,318
16,350	16,400	0	3,400	5,616	6,318	323	3,400	5,616	6,318
16,400	16,450	0	3,400	5,616	6,318	319	3,400	5,616	6,318
16,450	16,500	0	3,400	5,616	6,318	316	3,400	5,616	6,318
16,500	16,550	0	3,400	5,616	6,318	312	3,400	5,616	6,318
16,550	16,600	0	3,400	5,616	6,318	308	3,400	5,616	6,318
16,600	16,650	0	3,400	5,616	6,318	304	3,400	5,616	6,318
16,650	16,700	0	3,400	5,616	6,318	300	3,400	5,616	6,318
16,700	16,750	0	3,400	5,616	6,318	296	3,400	5,616	6,318
16,750	16,800	0	3,400	5,616	6,318	293	3,400	5,616	6,318
16,800	16,850	0	3,400	5,616	6,318	289	3,400	5,616	6,318
16,850	16,900	0	3,400	5,616	6,318	285	3,400	5,616	6,318
16,900	16,950	0	3,400	5,616	6,318	281	3,400	5,616	6,318
16,950	17,000	0	3,400	5,616	6,318	277	3,400	5,616	6,318
17,000	17,050	0	3,400	5,616	6,318	273	3,400	5,616	6,318
17,050	17,100	0	3,400	5,616	6,318	270	3,400	5,616	6,318
17,100	17,150	0	3,400	5,616	6,318	266	3,400	5,616	6,318
17,150	17,200	0	3,400	5,616	6,318	262	3,400	5,616	6,318
17,200	17,250	0	3,400	5,616	6,318	258	3,400	5,616	6,318
17,250	17,300	0	3,400	5,616	6,318	254	3,400	5,616	6,318
17,300	17,350	0	3,400	5,616	6,318	251	3,400	5,616	6,318
17,350	17,400	0	3,400	5,616	6,318	247	3,400	5,616	6,318
17,400	17,450	0	3,400	5,616	6,318	243	3,400	5,616	6,318
17,450	17,500	0	3,400	5,616	6,318	239	3,400	5,616	6,318
17,500	17,550	0	3,400	5,616	6,318	235	3,400	5,616	6,318
17,550	17,600	0	3,400	5,616	6,318	231	3,400	5,616	6,318
17,600	17,650	0	3,400	5,616	6,318	228	3,400	5,616	6,318
17,650	17,700	0	3,400	5,616	6,318	224	3,400	5,616	6,318
17,700	17,750	0	3,400	5,616	6,318	220	3,400	5,616	6,318
17,750	17,800	0	3,400	5,616	6,318	216	3,400	5,616	6,318
17,800	17,850	0	3,400	5,616	6,318	212	3,400	5,616	6,318
17,850	17,900	0	3,400	5,616	6,318	208	3,400	5,616	6,318
17,900	17,950	0	3,400	5,616	6,318	205	3,400	5,616	6,318
17,950	18,000	0	3,400	5,616	6,318	201	3,400	5,616	6,318
18,000	18,050	0	3,400	5,616	6,318	197	3,400	5,616	6,318
18,050	18,100	0	3,400	5,616	6,318	193	3,400	5,616	6,318
18,100	18,150	0	3,400	5,616	6,318	189	3,400	5,616	6,318
18,150	18,200	0	3,400	5,616	6,318	186	3,400	5,616	6,318
18,200	18,250	0	3,400	5,616	6,318	182	3,400	5,616	6,318
18,250	18,300	0	3,400	5,616	6,318	178	3,400	5,616	6,318
18,300	18,350	0	3,400	5,616	6,318	174	3,400	5,616	6,318
18,350	18,400	0	3,394	5,609	6,311	170	3,400	5,616	6,318

(Continued)

Earned Income Credit (EIC) Table - *Continued*

(Caution. This is **not** a tax table.)

If the amount you are looking up from the worksheet is–		And your filing status is– Single, head of household, or qualifying widow(er) and the number of children you have is–				Married filing jointly and the number of children you have is–			
		0	1	2	3	0	1	2	3
At least	But less than	Your credit is–				Your credit is–			
18,400	18,450	0	3,386	5,598	6,300	166	3,400	5,616	6,318
18,450	18,500	0	3,378	5,588	6,290	163	3,400	5,616	6,318
18,500	18,550	0	3,370	5,577	6,279	159	3,400	5,616	6,318
18,550	18,600	0	3,362	5,567	6,269	155	3,400	5,616	6,318
18,600	18,650	0	3,354	5,556	6,258	151	3,400	5,616	6,318
18,650	18,700	0	3,346	5,545	6,247	147	3,400	5,616	6,318
18,700	18,750	0	3,338	5,535	6,237	143	3,400	5,616	6,318
18,750	18,800	0	3,330	5,524	6,226	140	3,400	5,616	6,318
18,800	18,850	0	3,322	5,514	6,216	136	3,400	5,616	6,318
18,850	18,900	0	3,315	5,503	6,205	132	3,400	5,616	6,318
18,900	18,950	0	3,307	5,493	6,195	128	3,400	5,616	6,318
18,950	19,000	0	3,299	5,482	6,184	124	3,400	5,616	6,318
19,000	19,050	0	3,291	5,472	6,174	120	3,400	5,616	6,318
19,050	19,100	0	3,283	5,461	6,163	117	3,400	5,616	6,318
19,100	19,150	0	3,275	5,451	6,153	113	3,400	5,616	6,318
19,150	19,200	0	3,267	5,440	6,142	109	3,400	5,616	6,318
19,200	19,250	0	3,259	5,430	6,132	105	3,400	5,616	6,318
19,250	19,300	0	3,251	5,419	6,121	101	3,400	5,616	6,318
19,300	19,350	0	3,243	5,409	6,111	98	3,400	5,616	6,318
19,350	19,400	0	3,235	5,398	6,100	94	3,400	5,616	6,318
19,400	19,450	0	3,227	5,387	6,089	90	3,400	5,616	6,318
19,450	19,500	0	3,219	5,377	6,079	86	3,400	5,616	6,318
19,500	19,550	0	3,211	5,366	6,068	82	3,400	5,616	6,318
19,550	19,600	0	3,203	5,356	6,058	78	3,400	5,616	6,318
19,600	19,650	0	3,195	5,345	6,047	75	3,400	5,616	6,318
19,650	19,700	0	3,187	5,335	6,037	71	3,400	5,616	6,318
19,700	19,750	0	3,179	5,324	6,026	67	3,400	5,616	6,318
19,750	19,800	0	3,171	5,314	6,016	63	3,400	5,616	6,318
19,800	19,850	0	3,163	5,303	6,005	59	3,400	5,616	6,318
19,850	19,900	0	3,155	5,293	5,995	55	3,400	5,616	6,318
19,900	19,950	0	3,147	5,282	5,984	52	3,400	5,616	6,318
19,950	20,000	0	3,139	5,272	5,974	48	3,400	5,616	6,318
20,000	20,050	0	3,131	5,261	5,963	44	3,400	5,616	6,318
20,050	20,100	0	3,123	5,251	5,953	40	3,400	5,616	6,318
20,100	20,150	0	3,115	5,240	5,942	36	3,400	5,616	6,318
20,150	20,200	0	3,107	5,230	5,932	33	3,400	5,616	6,318
20,200	20,250	0	3,099	5,219	5,921	29	3,400	5,616	6,318
20,250	20,300	0	3,091	5,208	5,910	25	3,400	5,616	6,318
20,300	20,350	0	3,083	5,198	5,900	21	3,400	5,616	6,318
20,350	20,400	0	3,075	5,187	5,889	17	3,400	5,616	6,318
20,400	20,450	0	3,067	5,177	5,879	13	3,400	5,616	6,318
20,450	20,500	0	3,059	5,166	5,868	10	3,400	5,616	6,318
20,500	20,550	0	3,051	5,156	5,858	6	3,400	5,616	6,318
20,550	20,600	0	3,043	5,145	5,847	*	3,400	5,616	6,318
20,600	20,650	0	3,035	5,135	5,837	0	3,400	5,616	6,318
20,650	20,700	0	3,027	5,124	5,826	0	3,400	5,616	6,318
20,700	20,750	0	3,019	5,114	5,816	0	3,400	5,616	6,318
20,750	20,800	0	3,011	5,103	5,805	0	3,400	5,616	6,318
20,800	20,850	0	3,003	5,093	5,795	0	3,400	5,616	6,318
20,850	20,900	0	2,995	5,082	5,784	0	3,400	5,616	6,318
20,900	20,950	0	2,987	5,072	5,774	0	3,400	5,616	6,318
20,950	21,000	0	2,979	5,061	5,763	0	3,400	5,616	6,318
21,000	21,050	0	2,971	5,051	5,753	0	3,400	5,616	6,318
21,050	21,100	0	2,963	5,040	5,742	0	3,400	5,616	6,318
21,100	21,150	0	2,955	5,029	5,731	0	3,400	5,616	6,318
21,150	21,200	0	2,947	5,019	5,721	0	3,400	5,616	6,318
21,200	21,250	0	2,939	5,008	5,710	0	3,400	5,616	6,318
21,250	21,300	0	2,931	4,998	5,700	0	3,400	5,616	6,318
21,300	21,350	0	2,923	4,987	5,689	0	3,400	5,616	6,318
21,350	21,400	0	2,915	4,977	5,679	0	3,400	5,616	6,318
21,400	21,450	0	2,907	4,966	5,668	0	3,400	5,616	6,318
21,450	21,500	0	2,899	4,956	5,658	0	3,400	5,616	6,318
21,500	21,550	0	2,891	4,945	5,647	0	3,400	5,616	6,318
21,550	21,600	0	2,883	4,935	5,637	0	3,400	5,616	6,318
21,600	21,650	0	2,875	4,924	5,626	0	3,400	5,616	6,318
21,650	21,700	0	2,867	4,914	5,616	0	3,400	5,616	6,318
21,700	21,750	0	2,859	4,903	5,605	0	3,400	5,616	6,318
21,750	21,800	0	2,851	4,893	5,595	0	3,400	5,616	6,318
21,800	21,850	0	2,843	4,882	5,584	0	3,400	5,616	6,318
21,850	21,900	0	2,835	4,872	5,574	0	3,400	5,616	6,318
21,900	21,950	0	2,827	4,861	5,563	0	3,400	5,616	6,318
21,950	22,000	0	2,819	4,850	5,552	0	3,400	5,616	6,318
22,000	22,050	0	2,811	4,840	5,542	0	3,400	5,616	6,318
22,050	22,100	0	2,803	4,829	5,531	0	3,400	5,616	6,318
22,100	22,150	0	2,795	4,819	5,521	0	3,400	5,616	6,318
22,150	22,200	0	2,787	4,808	5,510	0	3,400	5,616	6,318
22,200	22,250	0	2,779	4,798	5,500	0	3,400	5,616	6,318
22,250	22,300	0	2,771	4,787	5,489	0	3,400	5,616	6,318
22,300	22,350	0	2,763	4,777	5,479	0	3,400	5,616	6,318
22,350	22,400	0	2,755	4,766	5,468	0	3,400	5,616	6,318
22,400	22,450	0	2,747	4,756	5,458	0	3,400	5,616	6,318
22,450	22,500	0	2,739	4,745	5,447	0	3,400	5,616	6,318
22,500	22,550	0	2,731	4,735	5,437	0	3,400	5,616	6,318
22,550	22,600	0	2,723	4,724	5,426	0	3,400	5,616	6,318
22,600	22,650	0	2,715	4,714	5,416	0	3,400	5,616	6,318
22,650	22,700	0	2,707	4,703	5,405	0	3,400	5,616	6,318
22,700	22,750	0	2,699	4,693	5,395	0	3,400	5,616	6,318
22,750	22,800	0	2,691	4,682	5,384	0	3,400	5,616	6,318
22,800	22,850	0	2,683	4,671	5,373	0	3,400	5,616	6,318
22,850	22,900	0	2,675	4,661	5,363	0	3,400	5,616	6,318
22,900	22,950	0	2,667	4,650	5,352	0	3,400	5,616	6,318
22,950	23,000	0	2,659	4,640	5,342	0	3,400	5,616	6,318
23,000	23,050	0	2,651	4,629	5,331	0	3,400	5,616	6,318
23,050	23,100	0	2,643	4,619	5,321	0	3,400	5,616	6,318
23,100	23,150	0	2,635	4,608	5,310	0	3,400	5,616	6,318
23,150	23,200	0	2,627	4,598	5,300	0	3,400	5,616	6,318
23,200	23,250	0	2,619	4,587	5,289	0	3,400	5,616	6,318
23,250	23,300	0	2,611	4,577	5,279	0	3,400	5,616	6,318
23,300	23,350	0	2,603	4,566	5,268	0	3,400	5,616	6,318
23,350	23,400	0	2,595	4,556	5,258	0	3,400	5,616	6,318
23,400	23,450	0	2,587	4,545	5,247	0	3,400	5,616	6,318
23,450	23,500	0	2,579	4,535	5,237	0	3,400	5,616	6,318
23,500	23,550	0	2,571	4,524	5,226	0	3,400	5,616	6,318
23,550	23,600	0	2,563	4,514	5,216	0	3,400	5,616	6,318
23,600	23,650	0	2,555	4,503	5,205	0	3,400	5,616	6,318
23,650	23,700	0	2,547	4,492	5,194	0	3,400	5,616	6,318
23,700	23,750	0	2,539	4,482	5,184	0	3,400	5,616	6,318
23,750	23,800	0	2,531	4,471	5,173	0	3,400	5,616	6,318
23,800	23,850	0	2,523	4,461	5,163	0	3,400	5,616	6,318
23,850	23,900	0	2,516	4,450	5,152	0	3,400	5,616	6,318
23,900	23,950	0	2,508	4,440	5,142	0	3,400	5,616	6,318
23,950	24,000	0	2,500	4,429	5,131	0	3,393	5,607	6,30[illegible]
24,000	24,050	0	2,492	4,419	5,121	0	3,385	5,596	6,29[illegible]
24,050	24,100	0	2,484	4,408	5,110	0	3,377	5,585	6,28[illegible]
24,100	24,150	0	2,476	4,398	5,100	0	3,369	5,575	6,27[illegible]
24,150	24,200	0	2,468	4,387	5,089	0	3,361	5,564	6,26[illegible]
24,200	24,250	0	2,460	4,377	5,079	0	3,353	5,554	6,25[illegible]
24,250	24,300	0	2,452	4,366	5,068	0	3,345	5,543	6,24[illegible]
24,300	24,350	0	2,444	4,356	5,058	0	3,337	5,533	6,23[illegible]
24,350	24,400	0	2,436	4,345	5,047	0	3,329	5,522	6,22[illegible]
24,400	24,450	0	2,428	4,334	5,036	0	3,321	5,512	6,21[illegible]
24,450	24,500	0	2,420	4,324	5,026	0	3,313	5,501	6,20[illegible]
24,500	24,550	0	2,412	4,313	5,015	0	3,305	5,491	6,19[illegible]
24,550	24,600	0	2,404	4,303	5,005	0	3,297	5,480	6,18[illegible]
24,600	24,650	0	2,396	4,292	4,994	0	3,289	5,470	6,17[illegible]
24,650	24,700	0	2,388	4,282	4,984	0	3,281	5,459	6,16[illegible]
24,700	24,750	0	2,380	4,271	4,973	0	3,273	5,449	6,15[illegible]
24,750	24,800	0	2,372	4,261	4,963	0	3,265	5,438	6,14[illegible]

* If the amount you're looking up from the worksheet is at least $20,550 but less than $20,600, and you have no qualifying children, your credit is $2. If the amount you're looking up from the worksheet is $20,600 or more, and you have no qualifying children, you can't take the credit.

(Continued)

Earned Income Credit (EIC) Table - *Continued*　　　　(**Caution.** This is **not** a tax table.)

If the amount you are looking up from the worksheet is–		And your filing status is– Single, head of household, or qualifying widow(er) and the number of children you have is–				Married filing jointly and the number of children you have is–			
		0	1	2	3	0	1	2	3
At least	But less than	Your credit is–				Your credit is–			
24,800	24,850	0	2,364	4,250	4,952	0	3,257	5,428	6,130
24,850	24,900	0	2,356	4,240	4,942	0	3,249	5,417	6,119
24,900	24,950	0	2,348	4,229	4,931	0	3,241	5,406	6,108
24,950	25,000	0	2,340	4,219	4,921	0	3,233	5,396	6,098
25,000	25,050	0	2,332	4,208	4,910	0	3,225	5,385	6,087
25,050	25,100	0	2,324	4,198	4,900	0	3,217	5,375	6,077
25,100	25,150	0	2,316	4,187	4,889	0	3,209	5,364	6,066
25,150	25,200	0	2,308	4,177	4,879	0	3,201	5,354	6,056
25,200	25,250	0	2,300	4,166	4,868	0	3,193	5,343	6,045
25,250	25,300	0	2,292	4,155	4,857	0	3,185	5,333	6,035
25,300	25,350	0	2,284	4,145	4,847	0	3,177	5,322	6,024
25,350	25,400	0	2,276	4,134	4,836	0	3,169	5,312	6,014
25,400	25,450	0	2,268	4,124	4,826	0	3,161	5,301	6,003
25,450	25,500	0	2,260	4,113	4,815	0	3,153	5,291	5,993
25,500	25,550	0	2,252	4,103	4,805	0	3,145	5,280	5,982
25,550	25,600	0	2,244	4,092	4,794	0	3,137	5,270	5,972
25,600	25,650	0	2,236	4,082	4,784	0	3,129	5,259	5,961
25,650	25,700	0	2,228	4,071	4,773	0	3,121	5,249	5,951
25,700	25,750	0	2,220	4,061	4,763	0	3,113	5,238	5,940
25,750	25,800	0	2,212	4,050	4,752	0	3,105	5,227	5,929
25,800	25,850	0	2,204	4,040	4,742	0	3,097	5,217	5,919
25,850	25,900	0	2,196	4,029	4,731	0	3,089	5,206	5,908
25,900	25,950	0	2,188	4,019	4,721	0	3,081	5,196	5,898
25,950	26,000	0	2,180	4,008	4,710	0	3,073	5,185	5,887
26,000	26,050	0	2,172	3,998	4,700	0	3,065	5,175	5,877
26,050	26,100	0	2,164	3,987	4,689	0	3,057	5,164	5,866
26,100	26,150	0	2,156	3,976	4,678	0	3,049	5,154	5,856
26,150	26,200	0	2,148	3,966	4,668	0	3,041	5,143	5,845
26,200	26,250	0	2,140	3,955	4,657	0	3,033	5,133	5,835
26,250	26,300	0	2,132	3,945	4,647	0	3,025	5,122	5,824
26,300	26,350	0	2,124	3,934	4,636	0	3,017	5,112	5,814
26,350	26,400	0	2,116	3,924	4,626	0	3,009	5,101	5,803
26,400	26,450	0	2,108	3,913	4,615	0	3,001	5,091	5,793
26,450	26,500	0	2,100	3,903	4,605	0	2,993	5,080	5,782
26,500	26,550	0	2,092	3,892	4,594	0	2,985	5,069	5,771
26,550	26,600	0	2,084	3,882	4,584	0	2,977	5,059	5,761
26,600	26,650	0	2,076	3,871	4,573	0	2,969	5,048	5,750
26,650	26,700	0	2,068	3,861	4,563	0	2,961	5,038	5,740
26,700	26,750	0	2,060	3,850	4,552	0	2,953	5,027	5,729
26,750	26,800	0	2,052	3,840	4,542	0	2,945	5,017	5,719
26,800	26,850	0	2,044	3,829	4,531	0	2,937	5,006	5,708
26,850	26,900	0	2,036	3,819	4,521	0	2,929	4,996	5,698
26,900	26,950	0	2,028	3,808	4,510	0	2,921	4,985	5,687
26,950	27,000	0	2,020	3,797	4,499	0	2,913	4,975	5,677
27,000	27,050	0	2,012	3,787	4,489	0	2,905	4,964	5,666
27,050	27,100	0	2,004	3,776	4,478	0	2,897	4,954	5,656
27,100	27,150	0	1,996	3,766	4,468	0	2,889	4,943	5,645
27,150	27,200	0	1,988	3,755	4,457	0	2,881	4,933	5,635
27,200	27,250	0	1,980	3,745	4,447	0	2,873	4,922	5,624
27,250	27,300	0	1,972	3,734	4,436	0	2,865	4,912	5,614
27,300	27,350	0	1,964	3,724	4,426	0	2,857	4,901	5,603
27,350	27,400	0	1,956	3,713	4,415	0	2,849	4,890	5,592
27,400	27,450	0	1,948	3,703	4,405	0	2,841	4,880	5,582
27,450	27,500	0	1,940	3,692	4,394	0	2,834	4,869	5,571
27,500	27,550	0	1,932	3,682	4,384	0	2,826	4,859	5,561
27,550	27,600	0	1,924	3,671	4,373	0	2,818	4,848	5,550
27,600	27,650	0	1,916	3,661	4,363	0	2,810	4,838	5,540
27,650	27,700	0	1,908	3,650	4,352	0	2,802	4,827	5,529
27,700	27,750	0	1,900	3,640	4,342	0	2,794	4,817	5,519
27,750	27,800	0	1,892	3,629	4,331	0	2,786	4,806	5,508
27,800	27,850	0	1,884	3,618	4,320	0	2,778	4,796	5,498
27,850	27,900	0	1,876	3,608	4,310	0	2,770	4,785	5,487
27,900	27,950	0	1,868	3,597	4,299	0	2,762	4,775	5,477
27,950	28,000	0	1,860	3,587	4,289	0	2,754	4,764	5,466

If the amount you are looking up from the worksheet is–		And your filing status is– Single, head of household, or qualifying widow(er) and the number of children you have is–				Married filing jointly and the number of children you have is–			
		0	1	2	3	0	1	2	3
At least	But less than	Your credit is–				Your credit is–			
28,000	28,050	0	,852	3,576	4,278	0	2,746	4,754	5,456
28,050	28,100	0	,844	3,566	4,268	0	2,738	4,743	5,445
28,100	28,150	0	,836	3,555	4,257	0	2,730	4,733	5,435
28,150	28,200	0	,828	3,545	4,247	0	2,722	4,722	5,424
28,200	28,250	0	1,820	3,534	4,236	0	2,714	4,711	5,413
28,250	28,300	0	1,812	3,524	4,226	0	2,706	4,701	5,403
28,300	28,350	0	1,804	3,513	4,215	0	2,698	4,690	5,392
28,350	28,400	0	1,796	3,503	4,205	0	2,690	4,680	5,382
28,400	28,450	0	1,788	3,492	4,194	0	2,682	4,669	5,371
28,450	28,500	0	1,780	3,482	4,184	0	2,674	4,659	5,361
28,500	28,550	0	1,772	3,471	4,173	0	2,666	4,648	5,350
28,550	28,600	0	1,764	3,461	4,163	0	2,658	4,638	5,340
28,600	28,650	0	1,756	3,450	4,152	0	2,650	4,627	5,329
28,650	28,700	0	1,748	3,439	4,141	0	2,642	4,617	5,319
28,700	28,750	0	1,740	3,429	4,131	0	2,634	4,606	5,308
28,750	28,800	0	1,732	3,418	4,120	0	2,626	4,596	5,298
28,800	28,850	0	1,724	3,408	4,110	0	2,618	4,585	5,287
28,850	28,900	0	1,717	3,397	4,099	0	2,610	4,575	5,277
28,900	28,950	0	1,709	3,387	4,089	0	2,602	4,564	5,266
28,950	29,000	0	1,701	3,376	4,078	0	2,594	4,554	5,256
29,000	29,050	0	1,693	3,366	4,068	0	2,586	4,543	5,245
29,050	29,100	0	1,685	3,355	4,057	0	2,578	4,532	5,234
29,100	29,150	0	1,677	3,345	4,047	0	2,570	4,522	5,224
29,150	29,200	0	1,669	3,334	4,036	0	2,562	4,511	5,213
29,200	29,250	0	1,661	3,324	4,026	0	2,554	4,501	5,203
29,250	29,300	0	1,653	3,313	4,015	0	2,546	4,490	5,192
29,300	29,350	0	1,645	3,303	4,005	0	2,538	4,480	5,182
29,350	29,400	0	1,637	3,292	3,994	0	2,530	4,469	5,171
29,400	29,450	0	1,629	3,281	3,983	0	2,522	4,459	5,161
29,450	29,500	0	1,621	3,271	3,973	0	2,514	4,448	5,150
29,500	29,550	0	1,613	3,260	3,962	0	2,506	4,438	5,140
29,550	29,600	0	1,605	3,250	3,952	0	2,498	4,427	5,129
29,600	29,650	0	1,597	3,239	3,941	0	2,490	4,417	5,119
29,650	29,700	0	1,589	3,229	3,931	0	2,482	4,406	5,108
29,700	29,750	0	1,581	3,218	3,920	0	2,474	4,396	5,098
29,750	29,800	0	1,573	3,208	3,910	0	2,466	4,385	5,087
29,800	29,850	0	1,565	3,197	3,899	0	2,458	4,375	5,077
29,850	29,900	0	1,557	3,187	3,889	0	2,450	4,364	5,066
29,900	29,950	0	1,549	3,176	3,878	0	2,442	4,353	5,055
29,950	30,000	0	1,541	3,166	3,868	0	2,434	4,343	5,045
30,000	30,050	0	1,533	3,155	3,857	0	2,426	4,332	5,034
30,050	30,100	0	1,525	3,145	3,847	0	2,418	4,322	5,024
30,100	30,150	0	1,517	3,134	3,836	0	2,410	4,311	5,013
30,150	30,200	0	1,509	3,124	3,826	0	2,402	4,301	5,003
30,200	30,250	0	1,501	3,113	3,815	0	2,394	4,290	4,992
30,250	30,300	0	1,493	3,102	3,804	0	2,386	4,280	4,982
30,300	30,350	0	1,485	3,092	3,794	0	2,378	4,269	4,971
30,350	30,400	0	1,477	3,081	3,783	0	2,370	4,259	4,961
30,400	30,450	0	1,469	3,071	3,773	0	2,362	4,248	4,950
30,450	30,500	0	1,461	3,060	3,762	0	2,354	4,238	4,940
30,500	30,550	0	1,453	3,050	3,752	0	2,346	4,227	4,929
30,550	30,600	0	1,445	3,039	3,741	0	2,338	4,217	4,919
30,600	30,650	0	1,437	3,029	3,731	0	2,330	4,206	4,908
30,650	30,700	0	1,429	3,018	3,720	0	2,322	4,196	4,898
30,700	30,750	0	1,421	3,008	3,710	0	2,314	4,185	4,887
30,750	30,800	0	1,413	2,997	3,699	0	2,306	4,174	4,876
30,800	30,850	0	1,405	2,987	3,689	0	2,298	4,164	4,866
30,850	30,900	0	1,397	2,976	3,678	0	2,290	4,153	4,855
30,900	30,950	0	1,389	2,966	3,668	0	2,282	4,143	4,845
30,950	31,000	0	1,381	2,955	3,657	0	2,274	4,132	4,834
31,000	31,050	0	1,373	2,945	3,647	0	2,266	4,122	4,824
31,050	31,100	0	1,365	2,934	3,636	0	2,258	4,111	4,813
31,100	31,150	0	1,357	2,923	3,625	0	2,250	4,101	4,803
31,150	31,200	0	1,349	2,913	3,615	0	2,242	4,090	4,792

(Continued)

Earned Income Credit (EIC) Table - *Continued*

(**Caution.** This is **not** a tax table.)

If the amount you are looking up from the worksheet is–		And your filing status is–							
		Single, head of household, or qualifying widow(er) and the number of children you have is–				Married filing jointly and the number of children you have is–			
		0	1	2	3	0	1	2	3
At least	But less than	Your credit is–				Your credit is–			
31,200	31,250	0	1,341	2,902	3,604	0	2,234	4,080	4,782
31,250	31,300	0	1,333	2,892	3,594	0	2,226	4,069	4,771
31,300	31,350	0	1,325	2,881	3,583	0	2,218	4,059	4,761
31,350	31,400	0	1,317	2,871	3,573	0	2,210	4,048	4,750
31,400	31,450	0	1,309	2,860	3,562	0	2,202	4,038	4,740
31,450	31,500	0	1,301	2,850	3,552	0	2,194	4,027	4,729
31,500	31,550	0	1,293	2,839	3,541	0	2,186	4,016	4,718
31,550	31,600	0	1,285	2,829	3,531	0	2,178	4,006	4,708
31,600	31,650	0	1,277	2,818	3,520	0	2,170	3,995	4,697
31,650	31,700	0	1,269	2,808	3,510	0	2,162	3,985	4,687
31,700	31,750	0	1,261	2,797	3,499	0	2,154	3,974	4,676
31,750	31,800	0	1,253	2,787	3,489	0	2,146	3,964	4,666
31,800	31,850	0	1,245	2,776	3,478	0	2,138	3,953	4,655
31,850	31,900	0	1,237	2,766	3,468	0	2,130	3,943	4,645
31,900	31,950	0	1,229	2,755	3,457	0	2,122	3,932	4,634
31,950	32,000	0	1,221	2,744	3,446	0	2,114	3,922	4,624
32,000	32,050	0	1,213	2,734	3,436	0	2,106	3,911	4,613
32,050	32,100	0	1,205	2,723	3,425	0	2,098	3,901	4,603
32,100	32,150	0	1,197	2,713	3,415	0	2,090	3,890	4,592
32,150	32,200	0	1,189	2,702	3,404	0	2,082	3,880	4,582
32,200	32,250	0	1,181	2,692	3,394	0	2,074	3,869	4,571
32,250	32,300	0	1,173	2,681	3,383	0	2,066	3,859	4,561
32,300	32,350	0	1,165	2,671	3,373	0	2,058	3,848	4,550
32,350	32,400	0	1,157	2,660	3,362	0	2,050	3,837	4,539
32,400	32,450	0	1,149	2,650	3,352	0	2,042	3,827	4,529
32,450	32,500	0	1,141	2,639	3,341	0	2,035	3,816	4,518
32,500	32,550	0	1,133	2,629	3,331	0	2,027	3,806	4,508
32,550	32,600	0	1,125	2,618	3,320	0	2,019	3,795	4,497
32,600	32,650	0	1,117	2,608	3,310	0	2,011	3,785	4,487
32,650	32,700	0	1,109	2,597	3,299	0	2,003	3,774	4,476
32,700	32,750	0	1,101	2,587	3,289	0	1,995	3,764	4,466
32,750	32,800	0	1,093	2,576	3,278	0	1,987	3,753	4,455
32,800	32,850	0	1,085	2,565	3,267	0	1,979	3,743	4,445
32,850	32,900	0	1,077	2,555	3,257	0	1,971	3,732	4,434
32,900	32,950	0	1,069	2,544	3,246	0	1,963	3,722	4,424
32,950	33,000	0	1,061	2,534	3,236	0	1,955	3,711	4,413
33,000	33,050	0	1,053	2,523	3,225	0	1,947	3,701	4,403
33,050	33,100	0	1,045	2,513	3,215	0	1,939	3,690	4,392
33,100	33,150	0	1,037	2,502	3,204	0	1,931	3,680	4,382
33,150	33,200	0	1,029	2,492	3,194	0	1,923	3,669	4,371
33,200	33,250	0	1,021	2,481	3,183	0	1,915	3,658	4,360
33,250	33,300	0	1,013	2,471	3,173	0	1,907	3,648	4,350
33,300	33,350	0	1,005	2,460	3,162	0	1,899	3,637	4,339
33,350	33,400	0	997	2,450	3,152	0	1,891	3,627	4,329
33,400	33,450	0	989	2,439	3,141	0	1,883	3,616	4,318
33,450	33,500	0	981	2,429	3,131	0	1,875	3,606	4,308
33,500	33,550	0	973	2,418	3,120	0	1,867	3,595	4,297
33,550	33,600	0	965	2,408	3,110	0	1,859	3,585	4,287
33,600	33,650	0	957	2,397	3,099	0	1,851	3,574	4,276
33,650	33,700	0	949	2,386	3,088	0	1,843	3,564	4,266
33,700	33,750	0	941	2,376	3,078	0	1,835	3,553	4,255
33,750	33,800	0	933	2,365	3,067	0	1,827	3,543	4,245
33,800	33,850	0	925	2,355	3,057	0	1,819	3,532	4,234
33,850	33,900	0	918	2,344	3,046	0	1,811	3,522	4,224
33,900	33,950	0	910	2,334	3,036	0	1,803	3,511	4,213
33,950	34,000	0	902	2,323	3,025	0	1,795	3,501	4,203
34,000	34,050	0	894	2,313	3,015	0	1,787	3,490	4,192
34,050	34,100	0	886	2,302	3,004	0	1,779	3,479	4,181
34,100	34,150	0	878	2,292	2,994	0	1,771	3,469	4,171
34,150	34,200	0	870	2,281	2,983	0	1,763	3,458	4,160
34,200	34,250	0	862	2,271	2,973	0	1,755	3,448	4,150
34,250	34,300	0	854	2,260	2,962	0	1,747	3,437	4,139
34,300	34,350	0	846	2,250	2,952	0	1,739	3,427	4,129
34,350	34,400	0	838	2,239	2,941	0	1,731	3,416	4,118

If the amount you are looking up from the worksheet is–		And your filing status is–							
		Single, head of household, or qualifying widow(er) and the number of children you have is–				Married filing jointly and the number of children you have is–			
		0	1	2	3	0	1	2	3
At least	But less than	Your credit is–				Your credit is–			
34,400	34,450	0	830	2,228	2,930	0	1,723	3,406	4,108
34,450	34,500	0	822	2,218	2,920	0	1,715	3,395	4,097
34,500	34,550	0	814	2,207	2,909	0	1,707	3,385	4,087
34,550	34,600	0	806	2,197	2,899	0	1,699	3,374	4,076
34,600	34,650	0	798	2,186	2,888	0	1,691	3,364	4,066
34,650	34,700	0	790	2,176	2,878	0	1,683	3,353	4,055
34,700	34,750	0	782	2,165	2,867	0	1,675	3,343	4,045
34,750	34,800	0	774	2,155	2,857	0	1,667	3,332	4,034
34,800	34,850	0	766	2,144	2,846	0	1,659	3,322	4,024
34,850	34,900	0	758	2,134	2,836	0	1,651	3,311	4,013
34,900	34,950	0	750	2,123	2,825	0	1,643	3,300	4,002
34,950	35,000	0	742	2,113	2,815	0	1,635	3,290	3,992
35,000	35,050	0	734	2,102	2,804	0	1,627	3,279	3,981
35,050	35,100	0	726	2,092	2,794	0	1,619	3,269	3,971
35,100	35,150	0	718	2,081	2,783	0	1,611	3,258	3,960
35,150	35,200	0	710	2,071	2,773	0	1,603	3,248	3,950
35,200	35,250	0	702	2,060	2,762	0	1,595	3,237	3,939
35,250	35,300	0	694	2,049	2,751	0	1,587	3,227	3,929
35,300	35,350	0	686	2,039	2,741	0	1,579	3,216	3,918
35,350	35,400	0	678	2,028	2,730	0	1,571	3,206	3,908
35,400	35,450	0	670	2,018	2,720	0	1,563	3,195	3,897
35,450	35,500	0	662	2,007	2,709	0	1,555	3,185	3,887
35,500	35,550	0	654	1,997	2,699	0	1,547	3,174	3,876
35,550	35,600	0	646	1,986	2,688	0	1,539	3,164	3,866
35,600	35,650	0	638	1,976	2,678	0	1,531	3,153	3,855
35,650	35,700	0	630	1,965	2,667	0	1,523	3,143	3,845
35,700	35,750	0	622	1,955	2,657	0	1,515	3,132	3,834
35,750	35,800	0	614	1,944	2,646	0	1,507	3,121	3,823
35,800	35,850	0	606	1,934	2,636	0	1,499	3,111	3,813
35,850	35,900	0	598	1,923	2,625	0	1,491	3,100	3,802
35,900	35,950	0	590	1,913	2,615	0	1,483	3,090	3,792
35,950	36,000	0	582	1,902	2,604	0	1,475	3,079	3,781
36,000	36,050	0	574	1,892	2,594	0	1,467	3,069	3,771
36,050	36,100	0	566	1,881	2,583	0	1,459	3,058	3,760
36,100	36,150	0	558	1,870	2,572	0	1,451	3,048	3,750
36,150	36,200	0	550	1,860	2,562	0	1,443	3,037	3,739
36,200	36,250	0	542	1,849	2,551	0	1,435	3,027	3,729
36,250	36,300	0	534	1,839	2,541	0	1,427	3,016	3,718
36,300	36,350	0	526	1,828	2,530	0	1,419	3,006	3,708
36,350	36,400	0	518	1,818	2,520	0	1,411	2,995	3,697
36,400	36,450	0	510	1,807	2,509	0	1,403	2,985	3,687
36,450	36,500	0	502	1,797	2,499	0	1,395	2,974	3,676
36,500	36,550	0	494	1,786	2,488	0	1,387	2,963	3,665
36,550	36,600	0	486	1,776	2,478	0	1,379	2,953	3,655
36,600	36,650	0	478	1,765	2,467	0	1,371	2,942	3,644
36,650	36,700	0	470	1,755	2,457	0	1,363	2,932	3,634
36,700	36,750	0	462	1,744	2,446	0	1,355	2,921	3,623
36,750	36,800	0	454	1,734	2,436	0	1,347	2,911	3,613
36,800	36,850	0	446	1,723	2,425	0	1,339	2,900	3,602
36,850	36,900	0	438	1,713	2,415	0	1,331	2,890	3,592
36,900	36,950	0	430	1,702	2,404	0	1,323	2,879	3,581
36,950	37,000	0	422	1,691	2,393	0	1,315	2,869	3,571
37,000	37,050	0	414	1,681	2,383	0	1,307	2,858	3,560
37,050	37,100	0	406	1,670	2,372	0	1,299	2,848	3,550
37,100	37,150	0	398	1,660	2,362	0	1,291	2,837	3,539
37,150	37,200	0	390	1,649	2,351	0	1,283	2,827	3,529
37,200	37,250	0	382	1,639	2,341	0	1,275	2,816	3,518
37,250	37,300	0	374	1,628	2,330	0	1,267	2,806	3,508
37,300	37,350	0	366	1,618	2,320	0	1,259	2,795	3,497
37,350	37,400	0	358	1,607	2,309	0	1,251	2,784	3,486
37,400	37,450	0	350	1,597	2,299	0	1,243	2,774	3,476
37,450	37,500	0	342	1,586	2,288	0	1,236	2,763	3,465
37,500	37,550	0	334	1,576	2,278	0	1,228	2,753	3,455
37,550	37,600	0	326	1,565	2,267	0	1,220	2,742	3,444

(Continued)

Earned Income Credit (EIC) Table - *Continued* (**Caution.** This is **not** a tax table.)

If the amount you are looking up from the worksheet is–		And your filing status is– **Single, head of household,** or **qualifying widow(er)** and the number of children you have is–				**Married filing jointly** and the number of children you have is–			
		0	1	2	3	0	1	2	3
At least	But less than	Your credit is–				Your credit is–			
37,600	37,650	0	318	1,555	2,257	0	1,212	2,732	3,434
37,650	37,700	0	310	1,544	2,246	0	1,204	2,721	3,423
37,700	37,750	0	302	1,534	2,236	0	1,196	2,711	3,413
37,750	37,800	0	294	1,523	2,225	0	1,188	2,700	3,402
37,800	37,850	0	286	1,512	2,214	0	1,180	2,690	3,392
37,850	37,900	0	278	1,502	2,204	0	1,172	2,679	3,381
37,900	37,950	0	270	1,491	2,193	0	1,164	2,669	3,371
37,950	38,000	0	262	1,481	2,183	0	1,156	2,658	3,360
38,000	38,050	0	254	1,470	2,172	0	1,148	2,648	3,350
38,050	38,100	0	246	1,460	2,162	0	1,140	2,637	3,339
38,100	38,150	0	238	1,449	2,151	0	1,132	2,627	3,329
38,150	38,200	0	230	1,439	2,141	0	1,124	2,616	3,318
38,200	38,250	0	222	1,428	2,130	0	1,116	2,605	3,307
38,250	38,300	0	214	1,418	2,120	0	1,108	2,595	3,297
38,300	38,350	0	206	1,407	2,109	0	1,100	2,584	3,286
38,350	38,400	0	198	1,397	2,099	0	1,092	2,574	3,276
38,400	38,450	0	190	1,386	2,088	0	1,084	2,563	3,265
38,450	38,500	0	182	1,376	2,078	0	1,076	2,553	3,255
38,500	38,550	0	174	1,365	2,067	0	1,068	2,542	3,244
38,550	38,600	0	166	1,355	2,057	0	1,060	2,532	3,234
38,600	38,650	0	158	1,344	2,046	0	1,052	2,521	3,223
38,650	38,700	0	150	1,333	2,035	0	1,044	2,511	3,213
38,700	38,750	0	142	1,323	2,025	0	1,036	2,500	3,202
38,750	38,800	0	134	1,312	2,014	0	1,028	2,490	3,192
38,800	38,850	0	126	1,302	2,004	0	1,020	2,479	3,181
38,850	38,900	0	119	1,291	1,993	0	1,012	2,469	3,171
38,900	38,950	0	111	1,281	1,983	0	1,004	2,458	3,160
38,950	39,000	0	103	1,270	1,972	0	996	2,448	3,150
39,000	39,050	0	95	1,260	1,962	0	988	2,437	3,139
39,050	39,100	0	87	1,249	1,951	0	980	2,426	3,128
39,100	39,150	0	79	1,239	1,941	0	972	2,416	3,118
39,150	39,200	0	71	1,228	1,930	0	964	2,405	3,107
39,200	39,250	0	63	1,218	1,920	0	956	2,395	3,097
39,250	39,300	0	55	1,207	1,909	0	948	2,384	3,086
39,300	39,350	0	47	1,197	1,899	0	940	2,374	3,076
39,350	39,400	0	39	1,186	1,888	0	932	2,363	3,065
39,400	39,450	0	31	1,175	1,877	0	924	2,353	3,055
39,450	39,500	0	23	1,165	1,867	0	916	2,342	3,044
39,500	39,550	0	15	1,154	1,856	0	908	2,332	3,034
39,550	39,600	0	7	1,144	1,846	0	900	2,321	3,023
39,600	39,650	0	*	1,133	1,835	0	892	2,311	3,013
39,650	39,700	0	0	1,123	1,825	0	884	2,300	3,002
39,700	39,750	0	0	1,112	1,814	0	876	2,290	2,992
39,750	39,800	0	0	1,102	1,804	0	868	2,279	2,981
39,800	39,850	0	0	1,091	1,793	0	860	2,269	2,971
39,850	39,900	0	0	1,081	1,783	0	852	2,258	2,960
39,900	39,950	0	0	1,070	1,772	0	844	2,247	2,949
39,950	40,000	0	0	1,060	1,762	0	836	2,237	2,939
40,000	40,050	0	0	1,049	1,751	0	828	2,226	2,928
40,050	40,100	0	0	1,039	1,741	0	820	2,216	2,918
40,100	40,150	0	0	1,028	1,730	0	812	2,205	2,907
40,150	40,200	0	0	1,018	1,720	0	804	2,195	2,897
40,200	40,250	0	0	1,007	1,709	0	796	2,184	2,886
40,250	40,300	0	0	996	1,698	0	788	2,174	2,876
40,300	40,350	0	0	986	1,688	0	780	2,163	2,865
40,350	40,400	0	0	975	1,677	0	772	2,153	2,855
40,400	40,450	0	0	965	1,667	0	764	2,142	2,844
40,450	40,500	0	0	954	1,656	0	756	2,132	2,834
40,500	40,550	0	0	944	1,646	0	748	2,121	2,823
40,550	40,600	0	0	933	1,635	0	740	2,111	2,813
40,600	40,650	0	0	923	1,625	0	732	2,100	2,802
40,650	40,700	0	0	912	1,614	0	724	2,090	2,792
40,700	40,750	0	0	902	1,604	0	716	2,079	2,781
40,750	40,800	0	0	891	1,593	0	708	2,068	2,770

If the amount you are looking up from the worksheet is–		And your filing status is– **Single, head of household,** or **qualifying widow(er)** and the number of children you have is–				**Married filing jointly** and the number of children you have is–			
		0	1	2	3	0	1	2	3
At least	But less than	Your credit is–				Your credit is–			
40,800	40,850	0	0	881	1,583	0	700	2,058	2,760
40,850	40,900	0	0	870	1,572	0	692	2,047	2,749
40,900	40,950	0	0	860	1,562	0	684	2,037	2,739
40,950	41,000	0	0	849	1,551	0	676	2,026	2,728
41,000	41,050	0	0	839	1,541	0	668	2,016	2,718
41,050	41,100	0	0	828	1,530	0	660	2,005	2,707
41,100	41,150	0	0	817	1,519	0	652	1,995	2,697
41,150	41,200	0	0	807	1,509	0	644	1,984	2,686
41,200	41,250	0	0	796	1,498	0	636	1,974	2,676
41,250	41,300	0	0	786	1,488	0	628	1,963	2,665
41,300	41,350	0	0	775	1,477	0	620	1,953	2,655
41,350	41,400	0	0	765	1,467	0	612	1,942	2,644
41,400	41,450	0	0	754	1,456	0	604	1,932	2,634
41,450	41,500	0	0	744	1,446	0	596	1,921	2,623
41,500	41,550	0	0	733	1,435	0	588	1,910	2,612
41,550	41,600	0	0	723	1,425	0	580	1,900	2,602
41,600	41,650	0	0	712	1,414	0	572	1,889	2,591
41,650	41,700	0	0	702	1,404	0	564	1,879	2,581
41,700	41,750	0	0	691	1,393	0	556	1,868	2,570
41,750	41,800	0	0	681	1,383	0	548	1,858	2,560
41,800	41,850	0	0	670	1,372	0	540	1,847	2,549
41,850	41,900	0	0	660	1,362	0	532	1,837	2,539
41,900	41,950	0	0	649	1,351	0	524	1,826	2,528
41,950	42,000	0	0	638	1,340	0	516	1,816	2,518
42,000	42,050	0	0	628	1,330	0	508	1,805	2,507
42,050	42,100	0	0	617	1,319	0	500	1,795	2,497
42,100	42,150	0	0	607	1,309	0	492	1,784	2,486
42,150	42,200	0	0	596	1,298	0	484	1,774	2,476
42,200	42,250	0	0	586	1,288	0	476	1,763	2,465
42,250	42,300	0	0	575	1,277	0	468	1,753	2,455
42,300	42,350	0	0	565	1,267	0	460	1,742	2,444
42,350	42,400	0	0	554	1,256	0	452	1,731	2,433
42,400	42,450	0	0	544	1,246	0	444	1,721	2,423
42,450	42,500	0	0	533	1,235	0	437	1,710	2,412
42,500	42,550	0	0	523	1,225	0	429	1,700	2,402
42,550	42,600	0	0	512	1,214	0	421	1,689	2,391
42,600	42,650	0	0	502	1,204	0	413	1,679	2,381
42,650	42,700	0	0	491	1,193	0	405	1,668	2,370
42,700	42,750	0	0	481	1,183	0	397	1,658	2,360
42,750	42,800	0	0	470	1,172	0	389	1,647	2,349
42,800	42,850	0	0	459	1,161	0	381	1,637	2,339
42,850	42,900	0	0	449	1,151	0	373	1,626	2,328
42,900	42,950	0	0	438	1,140	0	365	1,616	2,318
42,950	43,000	0	0	428	1,130	0	357	1,605	2,307
43,000	43,050	0	0	417	1,119	0	349	1,595	2,297
43,050	43,100	0	0	407	1,109	0	341	1,584	2,286
43,100	43,150	0	0	396	1,098	0	333	1,574	2,276
43,150	43,200	0	0	386	1,088	0	325	1,563	2,265
43,200	43,250	0	0	375	1,077	0	317	1,552	2,254
43,250	43,300	0	0	365	1,067	0	309	1,542	2,244
43,300	43,350	0	0	354	1,056	0	301	1,531	2,233
43,350	43,400	0	0	344	1,046	0	293	1,521	2,223
43,400	43,450	0	0	333	1,035	0	285	1,510	2,212
43,450	43,500	0	0	323	1,025	0	277	1,500	2,202
43,500	43,550	0	0	312	1,014	0	269	1,489	2,191
43,550	43,600	0	0	302	1,004	0	261	1,479	2,181
43,600	43,650	0	0	291	993	0	253	1,468	2,170
43,650	43,700	0	0	280	982	0	245	1,458	2,160
43,700	43,750	0	0	270	972	0	237	1,447	2,149
43,750	43,800	0	0	259	961	0	229	1,437	2,139
43,800	43,850	0	0	249	951	0	221	1,426	2,128
43,850	43,900	0	0	238	940	0	213	1,416	2,118
43,900	43,950	0	0	228	930	0	205	1,405	2,107
43,950	44,000	0	0	217	919	0	197	1,395	2,097

* If the amount you're looking up from the worksheet is at least $39,600 but less than $39,617, and you have one qualifying child, your credit is $1. If the amount you're looking up from the worksheet is $39,617 or more, and you have one qualifying child, you can't take the credit.

(Continued)

Earned Income Credit (EIC) Table - *Continued*

(**Caution.** This is **not** a tax table.)

If the amount you are looking up from the worksheet is–		And your filing status is–							
		Single, head of household, or qualifying widow(er) and the number of children you have is–				Married filing jointly and the number of children you have is–			
		0	1	2	3	0	1	2	3
At least	But less than	Your credit is–				Your credit is–			
44,000	44,050	0	0	207	909	0	189	1,384	2,086
44,050	44,100	0	0	196	898	0	181	1,373	2,075
44,100	44,150	0	0	186	888	0	173	1,363	2,065
44,150	44,200	0	0	175	877	0	165	1,352	2,054
44,200	44,250	0	0	165	867	0	157	1,342	2,044
44,250	44,300	0	0	154	856	0	149	1,331	2,033
44,300	44,350	0	0	144	846	0	141	1,321	2,023
44,350	44,400	0	0	133	835	0	133	1,310	2,012
44,400	44,450	0	0	122	824	0	125	1,300	2,002
44,450	44,500	0	0	112	814	0	117	1,289	1,991
44,500	44,550	0	0	101	803	0	109	1,279	1,981
44,550	44,600	0	0	91	793	0	101	1,268	1,970
44,600	44,650	0	0	80	782	0	93	1,258	1,960
44,650	44,700	0	0	70	772	0	85	1,247	1,949
44,700	44,750	0	0	59	761	0	77	1,237	1,939
44,750	44,800	0	0	49	751	0	69	1,226	1,928
44,800	44,850	0	0	38	740	0	61	1,216	1,918
44,850	44,900	0	0	28	730	0	53	1,205	1,907
44,900	44,950	0	0	17	719	0	45	1,194	1,896
44,950	45,000	0	0	7	709	0	37	1,184	1,886
45,000	45,050	0	0	*	698	0	29	1,173	1,875
45,050	45,100	0	0	0	688	0	21	1,163	1,865
45,100	45,150	0	0	0	677	0	13	1,152	1,854
45,150	45,200	0	0	0	667	0	5	1,142	1,844
45,200	45,250	0	0	0	656	0	*	1,131	1,833
45,250	45,300	0	0	0	645	0	0	1,121	1,823
45,300	45,350	0	0	0	635	0	0	1,110	1,812
45,350	45,400	0	0	0	624	0	0	1,100	1,802
45,400	45,450	0	0	0	614	0	0	1,089	1,791
45,450	45,500	0	0	0	603	0	0	1,079	1,781
45,500	45,550	0	0	0	593	0	0	1,068	1,770
45,550	45,600	0	0	0	582	0	0	1,058	1,760
45,600	45,650	0	0	0	572	0	0	1,047	1,749
45,650	45,700	0	0	0	561	0	0	1,037	1,739
45,700	45,750	0	0	0	551	0	0	1,026	1,728
45,750	45,800	0	0	0	540	0	0	1,015	1,717
45,800	45,850	0	0	0	530	0	0	1,005	1,707
45,850	45,900	0	0	0	519	0	0	994	1,696
45,900	45,950	0	0	0	509	0	0	984	1,686
45,950	46,000	0	0	0	498	0	0	973	1,675
46,000	46,050	0	0	0	488	0	0	963	1,665
46,050	46,100	0	0	0	477	0	0	952	1,654
46,100	46,150	0	0	0	466	0	0	942	1,644
46,150	46,200	0	0	0	456	0	0	931	1,633
46,200	46,250	0	0	0	445	0	0	921	1,623
46,250	46,300	0	0	0	435	0	0	910	1,612
46,300	46,350	0	0	0	424	0	0	900	1,602
46,350	46,400	0	0	0	414	0	0	889	1,591
46,400	46,450	0	0	0	403	0	0	879	1,581
46,450	46,500	0	0	0	393	0	0	868	1,570
46,500	46,550	0	0	0	382	0	0	857	1,559
46,550	46,600	0	0	0	372	0	0	847	1,549
46,600	46,650	0	0	0	361	0	0	836	1,538
46,650	46,700	0	0	0	351	0	0	826	1,528
46,700	46,750	0	0	0	340	0	0	815	1,517
46,750	46,800	0	0	0	330	0	0	805	1,507

If the amount you are looking up from the worksheet is–		And your filing status is–							
		Single, head of household, or qualifying widow(er) and the number of children you have is–				Married filing jointly and the number of children you have is–			
		0	1	2	3	0	1	2	3
At least	But less than	Your credit is–				Your credit is–			
46,800	46,850	0	0	0	319	0	0	794	1,496
46,850	46,900	0	0	0	309	0	0	784	1,486
46,900	46,950	0	0	0	298	0	0	773	1,475
46,950	47,000	0	0	0	287	0	0	763	1,465
47,000	47,050	0	0	0	277	0	0	752	1,454
47,050	47,100	0	0	0	266	0	0	742	1,444
47,100	47,150	0	0	0	256	0	0	731	1,433
47,150	47,200	0	0	0	245	0	0	721	1,423
47,200	47,250	0	0	0	235	0	0	710	1,412
47,250	47,300	0	0	0	224	0	0	700	1,402
47,300	47,350	0	0	0	214	0	0	689	1,391
47,350	47,400	0	0	0	203	0	0	678	1,380
47,400	47,450	0	0	0	193	0	0	668	1,370
47,450	47,500	0	0	0	182	0	0	657	1,359
47,500	47,550	0	0	0	172	0	0	647	1,349
47,550	47,600	0	0	0	161	0	0	636	1,338
47,600	47,650	0	0	0	151	0	0	626	1,328
47,650	47,700	0	0	0	140	0	0	615	1,317
47,700	47,750	0	0	0	130	0	0	605	1,307
47,750	47,800	0	0	0	119	0	0	594	1,296
47,800	47,850	0	0	0	108	0	0	584	1,286
47,850	47,900	0	0	0	98	0	0	573	1,275
47,900	47,950	0	0	0	87	0	0	563	1,265
47,950	48,000	0	0	0	77	0	0	552	1,254
48,000	48,050	0	0	0	66	0	0	542	1,244
48,050	48,100	0	0	0	56	0	0	531	1,233
48,100	48,150	0	0	0	45	0	0	521	1,223
48,150	48,200	0	0	0	35	0	0	510	1,212
48,200	48,250	0	0	0	24	0	0	499	1,201
48,250	48,300	0	0	0	14	0	0	489	1,191
48,300	48,350	0	0	0	**	0	0	478	1,180
48,350	48,400	0	0	0	0	0	0	468	1,170
48,400	48,450	0	0	0	0	0	0	457	1,159
48,450	48,500	0	0	0	0	0	0	447	1,149
48,500	48,550	0	0	0	0	0	0	436	1,138
48,550	48,600	0	0	0	0	0	0	426	1,128
48,600	48,650	0	0	0	0	0	0	415	1,117
48,650	48,700	0	0	0	0	0	0	405	1,107
48,700	48,750	0	0	0	0	0	0	394	1,096
48,750	48,800	0	0	0	0	0	0	384	1,086
48,800	48,850	0	0	0	0	0	0	373	1,075
48,850	48,900	0	0	0	0	0	0	363	1,065
48,900	48,950	0	0	0	0	0	0	352	1,054
48,950	49,000	0	0	0	0	0	0	342	1,044
49,000	49,050	0	0	0	0	0	0	331	1,033
49,050	49,100	0	0	0	0	0	0	320	1,023
49,100	49,150	0	0	0	0	0	0	310	1,012
49,150	49,200	0	0	0	0	0	0	299	1,002
49,200	49,250	0	0	0	0	0	0	289	991
49,250	49,300	0	0	0	0	0	0	278	980
49,300	49,350	0	0	0	0	0	0	268	970
49,350	49,400	0	0	0	0	0	0	257	959
49,400	49,450	0	0	0	0	0	0	247	949
49,450	49,500	0	0	0	0	0	0	236	938
49,500	49,550	0	0	0	0	0	0	226	928
49,550	49,600	0	0	0	0	0	0	215	917

* If the amount you're looking up from the worksheet is at least $45,000 but less than $45,007, and you have two qualifying children, your credit is $1. If the amount you're looking up from the worksheet is $45,007 or more, and you have two qualifying children, you can't take the credit.

** If the amount you're looking up from the worksheet is at least $48,300 but less than $48,340, and you have three or more qualifying children, your credit is $4. If the amount you're looking up from the worksheet is $48,340 or more, and you have three or more qualifying children, you can't take the credit.

(Continued)

Earned Income Credit (EIC) Table - *Continued* **(Caution.** This is **not** a tax table.)

If the amount you are looking up from the worksheet is–		And your filing status is– Single, head of household, or qualifying widow(er) and the number of children you have is–				Married filing jointly and the number of children you have is–			
		0	1	2	3	0	1	2	3
At least	But less than	Your credit is–				Your credit is–			
49,600	49,650	0	0	0	0	0	0	205	907
49,650	49,700	0	0	0	0	0	0	194	896
49,700	49,750	0	0	0	0	0	0	184	886
49,750	49,800	0	0	0	0	0	0	173	875
49,800	49,850	0	0	0	0	0	0	163	865
49,850	49,900	0	0	0	0	0	0	152	854
49,900	49,950	0	0	0	0	0	0	141	843
49,950	50,000	0	0	0	0	0	0	131	833
50,000	50,050	0	0	0	0	0	0	120	822
50,050	50,100	0	0	0	0	0	0	110	812
50,100	50,150	0	0	0	0	0	0	99	801
50,150	50,200	0	0	0	0	0	0	89	791
50,200	50,250	0	0	0	0	0	0	78	780
50,250	50,300	0	0	0	0	0	0	68	770
50,300	50,350	0	0	0	0	0	0	57	759
50,350	50,400	0	0	0	0	0	0	47	749
50,400	50,450	0	0	0	0	0	0	36	738
50,450	50,500	0	0	0	0	0	0	26	728
50,500	50,550	0	0	0	0	0	0	15	717
50,550	50,600	0	0	0	0	0	0	*	707
50,600	50,650	0	0	0	0	0	0	0	696
50,650	50,700	0	0	0	0	0	0	0	686
50,700	50,750	0	0	0	0	0	0	0	675
50,750	50,800	0	0	0	0	0	0	0	664
50,800	50,850	0	0	0	0	0	0	0	654
50,850	50,900	0	0	0	0	0	0	0	643
50,900	50,950	0	0	0	0	0	0	0	633
50,950	51,000	0	0	0	0	0	0	0	622
51,000	51,050	0	0	0	0	0	0	0	612
51,050	51,100	0	0	0	0	0	0	0	601
51,100	51,150	0	0	0	0	0	0	0	591
51,150	51,200	0	0	0	0	0	0	0	580
51,200	51,250	0	0	0	0	0	0	0	570
51,250	51,300	0	0	0	0	0	0	0	559
51,300	51,350	0	0	0	0	0	0	0	549
51,350	51,400	0	0	0	0	0	0	0	538
51,400	51,450	0	0	0	0	0	0	0	528
51,450	51,500	0	0	0	0	0	0	0	517
51,500	51,550	0	0	0	0	0	0	0	506
51,550	51,600	0	0	0	0	0	0	0	496
51,600	51,650	0	0	0	0	0	0	0	485
51,650	51,700	0	0	0	0	0	0	0	475
51,700	51,750	0	0	0	0	0	0	0	464
51,750	51,800	0	0	0	0	0	0	0	454
51,800	51,850	0	0	0	0	0	0	0	443
51,850	51,900	0	0	0	0	0	0	0	433
51,900	51,950	0	0	0	0	0	0	0	422
51,950	52,000	0	0	0	0	0	0	0	412

If the amount you are looking up from the worksheet is–		And your filing status is– Single, head of household, or qualifying widow(er) and the number of children you have is–				Married filing jointly and the number of children you have is–			
		0	1	2	3	0	1	2	3
At least	But less than	Your credit is–				Your credit is–			
52,000	52,050	0	0	0	0	0	0	0	401
52,050	52,100	0	0	0	0	0	0	0	391
52,100	52,150	0	0	0	0	0	0	0	380
52,150	52,200	0	0	0	0	0	0	0	370
52,200	52,250	0	0	0	0	0	0	0	359
52,250	52,300	0	0	0	0	0	0	0	349
52,300	52,350	0	0	0	0	0	0	0	338
52,350	52,400	0	0	0	0	0	0	0	327
52,400	52,450	0	0	0	0	0	0	0	317
52,450	52,500	0	0	0	0	0	0	0	306
52,500	52,550	0	0	0	0	0	0	0	296
52,550	52,600	0	0	0	0	0	0	0	285
52,600	52,650	0	0	0	0	0	0	0	275
52,650	52,700	0	0	0	0	0	0	0	264
52,700	52,750	0	0	0	0	0	0	0	254
52,750	52,800	0	0	0	0	0	0	0	243
52,800	52,850	0	0	0	0	0	0	0	233
52,850	52,900	0	0	0	0	0	0	0	222
52,900	52,950	0	0	0	0	0	0	0	212
52,950	53,000	0	0	0	0	0	0	0	201
53,000	53,050	0	0	0	0	0	0	0	191
53,050	53,100	0	0	0	0	0	0	0	180
53,100	53,150	0	0	0	0	0	0	0	170
53,150	53,200	0	0	0	0	0	0	0	159
53,200	53,250	0	0	0	0	0	0	0	148
53,250	53,300	0	0	0	0	0	0	0	138
53,300	53,350	0	0	0	0	0	0	0	127
53,350	53,400	0	0	0	0	0	0	0	117
53,400	53,450	0	0	0	0	0	0	0	106
53,450	53,500	0	0	0	0	0	0	0	96
53,500	53,550	0	0	0	0	0	0	0	85
53,550	53,600	0	0	0	0	0	0	0	75
53,600	53,650	0	0	0	0	0	0	0	64
53,650	53,700	0	0	0	0	0	0	0	54
53,700	53,750	0	0	0	0	0	0	0	43
53,750	53,800	0	0	0	0	0	0	0	33
53,800	53,850	0	0	0	0	0	0	0	22
53,850	53,900	0	0	0	0	0	0	0	12
53,900	53,930	0	0	0	0	0	0	0	3

* If the amount you're looking up from the worksheet is at least $50,550 but less than $50,597, and you have two qualifying children, your credit is $5. If the amount you're looking up from the worksheet is $50,597 or more, and you have two qualifying children, you can't take the credit.

Appendix **B**

TIP *If the amount on line 5 is less than 133, your applicable figure is 0.0204. If the amount on line 5 is between 300 through 400, your applicable figure is 0.0969.*

IF Form 8962, line 5 is . . .	**ENTER** on Form 8962, line 7 . . .	**IF** Form 8962, line 5 is . . .	**ENTER** on Form 8962, line 7 . . .	**IF** Form 8962, line 5 is . . .	**ENTER** on Form 8962, line 7 . . .	**IF** Form 8962, line 5 is . . .	**ENTER** on Form 8962, line 7 . . .
less than 133	0.0204	175	0.0526	218	0.0707	261	0.0854
133	0.0306	176	0.0530	219	0.0711	262	0.0857
134	0.0312	177	0.0535	220	0.0714	263	0.0859
135	0.0318	178	0.0540	221	0.0718	264	0.0862
136	0.0324	179	0.0544	222	0.0721	265	0.0865
137	0.0330	180	0.0549	223	0.0725	266	0.0868
138	0.0336	181	0.0554	224	0.0728	267	0.0871
139	0.0342	182	0.0558	225	0.0732	268	0.0874
140	0.0348	183	0.0563	226	0.0736	269	0.0877
141	0.0354	184	0.0568	227	0.0739	270	0.0880
142	0.0360	185	0.0573	228	0.0743	271	0.0883
143	0.0366	186	0.0577	229	0.0746	272	0.0886
144	0.0372	187	0.0582	230	0.0750	273	0.0889
145	0.0378	188	0.0587	231	0.0753	274	0.0892
146	0.0384	189	0.0591	232	0.0757	275	0.0895
147	0.0390	190	0.0596	233	0.0760	276	0.0898
148	0.0396	191	0.0601	234	0.0764	277	0.0901
149	0.0402	192	0.0605	235	0.0768	278	0.0904
150	0.0408	193	0.0610	236	0.0771	279	0.0907
151	0.0413	194	0.0615	237	0.0775	280	0.0910
152	0.0417	195	0.0620	238	0.0778	281	0.0913
153	0.0422	196	0.0624	239	0.0782	282	0.0916
154	0.0427	197	0.0629	240	0.0785	283	0.0919
155	0.0432	198	0.0634	241	0.0789	284	0.0922
156	0.0436	199	0.0638	242	0.0793	285	0.0925
157	0.0441	200	0.0643	243	0.0796	286	0.0928
158	0.0446	201	0.0647	244	0.0800	287	0.0931
159	0.0450	202	0.0650	245	0.0803	288	0.0933
160	0.0455	203	0.0654	246	0.0807	289	0.0936
161	0.0460	204	0.0657	247	0.0810	290	0.0939
162	0.0464	205	0.0661	248	0.0814	291	0.0942
163	0.0469	206	0.0664	249	0.0817	292	0.0945
164	0.0474	207	0.0668	250	0.0821	293	0.0948
165	0.0479	208	0.0671	251	0.0824	294	0.0951
166	0.0483	209	0.0675	252	0.0827	295	0.0954
167	0.0488	210	0.0679	253	0.0830	296	0.0957
168	0.0493	211	0.0682	254	0.0833	297	0.0960
169	0.0497	212	0.0686	255	0.0836	298	0.0963
170	0.0502	213	0.0689	256	0.0839	299	0.0966
171	0.0507	214	0.0693	257	0.0842	300 thru 400	0.0969
172	0.0511	215	0.0696	258	0.0845		
173	0.0516	216	0.0700	259	0.0848		
174	0.0521	217	0.0704	260	0.0851		

Source: U.S. Department of the Treasury, Internal Revenue Service. Washington, DC: 2017.

Discussion Questions connect

All applicable discussion questions are available with ***Connect***©

EA LO 9-1 1. A taxpayer has $2,000 of qualified employment-related expenses paid on behalf of one qualifying child. Determine the maximum and minimum amounts of the child and dependent care tax credit available to the taxpayer, and explain the circumstances in which the maximum and minimum credits would be permitted.

____

____

____

EA LO 9-1 2. Briefly explain the requirements that must be met to receive a tax credit for child and dependent care expenses.

____

____

____

EA LO 9-1 3. For purposes of the tax credit for child and dependent care expenses, explain the limitations concerning the amount of qualified expenses that can be used to calculate the credit.

____

____

____

EA LO 9-1 4. A taxpayer maintains a household and is entitled to a dependency exemption for an incapacitated adult child. The child lives during the week at an adult day care center and on the weekends at home with the taxpayer. The taxpayer pays a fee to the center so the taxpayer can be gainfully employed. Does the fee qualify for treatment as a qualifying expense for purposes of the child and dependent care tax credit? Why or why not?

____

____

____

LO 9-2 5. To determine the amount of the credit for the elderly or the disabled, the appropriate base amount must be adjusted by the effect of two items. What are those two items, and in what way is the base amount adjusted?

____

____

____

EA LO 9-3 6. Two kinds of educational tax credits are available. Name them and briefly discuss the criteria necessary to claim each of the credits.

____

____

____

EA LO 9-3 7. Explain what qualifies as educational expenses for the purposes of educational tax credits.

____

____

____

EA LO 9-3 8. Jerome is single and cannot be claimed by anyone as a dependent. He is a student at a local university enrolled full-time in an MBA program. His tuition bill was $5,000. He paid the bill by withdrawing $2,000 from his savings account and borrowing the remainder from a local bank. For purposes of the educational tax credits, what is the amount of Jerome's qualifying expenses?

EA LO 9-3 9. Briefly explain when and how each of the two education credits is phased out.

LO 9-4 10. Explain the two instances in which taxpayers may choose to deduct foreign taxes as an itemized deduction rather than as a credit.

LO 9-4 11. Explain how the foreign tax credit limitation works.

EA LO 9-5 12. Taxpayers can claim a child tax credit for a qualifying child. Define *qualifying child*.

EA LO 9-5 13. Paul and Olivia filed a joint tax return and reported modified AGI of $92,000. They have two qualifying children for the purposes of the child tax credit. What is the amount of their child tax credit? What is the amount of their credit if their modified AGI is $112,000?

EA LO 9-6 14. Explain the limitations pertaining to the retirement savings contributions credit.

EA LO 9-6 15. Leonardo's filing status is head of household. He has modified AGI of $28,000, and he made a $3,000 contribution to his IRA. What is the amount of his retirement savings contributions credit? What would the credit be if he had a filing status of single?

LO 9-7 16. What limitations are associated with the adoption credit in terms of both dollar amounts and eligibility?

LO 9-7 17. In the case of the adoption credit, what special rules apply when adopting a child who is a *child with special needs*?

LO 9-7 18. In the case of the adoption credit, what special rules apply when adopting a child who is a citizen of another country?

EA LO 9-8 19. What is the definition of *qualifying child* for purposes of the Earned Income Credit?

EA LO 9-8 20. Briefly explain the difference between a refundable and a nonrefundable tax credit and give three examples of tax credits that may be refundable (or partly refundable) discussed in this chapter.

EA LO 9-9 21. Briefly explain the purpose of the premium tax credit.

EA LO 9-9 22. The amount of the premium tax credit is the lesser of what two factors?

Multiple-Choice Questions

All applicable multiple-choice questions are available with ***Connect***©

EA LO 9-1 23. Jamison is a single dad with two dependent children: Zoey, age 7, and Conner, age 3. He has an AGI of $69,000 and paid $4,300 to a qualified day care center for the two children. What amount can Jamison receive for the child and dependent care credit?

a. $4,300.

b. $1,505.

c. $860.

d. $430.

EA LO 9-1 24. Allie and Buddy are married, file a joint return, and have one son, Zack, age 5. Buddy has earned income of $42,000, and Allie was a full-time student for eight months (with no income). They paid a qualified child care center $3,450. How much is Allie and Buddy's child and dependent care credit for the year?

a. $0.
b. $420.
c. $630.
d. $725.

LO 9-2 25. Avril and John are ages 70 and 72, respectively, and file a joint return. They have an AGI of $18,000 and received $1,000 in nontaxable social security benefits. How much can Avril and John take as a credit for the elderly or the disabled?
a. $2,700.
b. $1,000.
c. $525.
d. $375.

LO 9-2 26. Dennis and Vera are ages 69 and 59, respectively, and file a joint return. They have an AGI of $28,000 and received $2,000 in nontaxable social security benefits. How much can Dennis and Vera take as a credit for the elderly or the disabled?
a. $0.
b. $1,125.
c. $2,000.
d. $7,500.

EA LO 9-3 27. Nathan paid $2,750 in qualifying expenses for his daughter who attended a community college. How much is Nathan's lifetime learning credit *without* regard to AGI limitations or other credits?
a. $250.
b. $550.
c. $825.
d. $1,375.

EA LO 9-3 28. DJ and Gwen paid $3,200 in qualifying expenses for their son, Nikko, who is a freshman attending the University of Colorado. DJ and Gwen have AGI of $170,000 and file a joint return. What is their allowable American opportunity tax credit (AOTC) after the credit phaseout based on AGI is taken into account?
a. $0.
b. $1,150.
c. $2,300.
d. $3,200.

EA LO 9-3 29. Darren paid the following expenses during November 2017 for his son Sean's college expenses for the spring 2018 semester, which begins in January 2018:

Tuition	$12,000
Housing	8,000
Books	1,500

In addition, Sean's uncle paid $500 in fees on behalf of Sean directly to the college. Sean is claimed as Darren's dependent on his tax return. How much of the expenses qualify for the purpose of the AOTC deduction for Darren in 2017?
a. $12,000.
b. $13,500.
c. $14,000.
d. $22,000.

EA LO 9-3 30. Which of the following expenses are qualifying expenses for the purposes of the education credits?

a. Books (purchased at the institution as a condition of enrollment).
b. Tuition.
c. Room and board.
d. Both *(a)* and *(b)*.

LO 9-4 31. Which of the following conditions must be met for a taxpayer to be able to claim the foreign tax credit (FTC) *without* filing Form 1116?

a. All of the foreign-source income is passive income.
b. All of the foreign-source income was reported on Form 1099.
c. Total foreign taxes paid were less than $300 (or $600 if married filing jointly).
d. All of the above must be met to claim the FTC without Form 1116.

LO 9-4 32. Joyce has $82,000 worldwide taxable income, which includes $11,000 of taxable income from China. She paid $2,200 in foreign income taxes to China, and her U.S. tax liability is $21,610. Joyce's foreign tax credit is

a. $0.
b. $2,200.
c. $2,899.
d. $11,000.

LO 9-4 33. Michael paid $3,350 in foreign income taxes to Argentina. His total worldwide taxable income was $75,000, which included $9,800 of income from Argentina. His U.S. tax liability is $18,750. How much can Michael claim as foreign tax credit?

a. $2,450.
b. $2,800.
c. $3,350.
d. $15,400.

LO 9-4 34. Under which of the following situations would a taxpayer most likely take the foreign taxes paid as an itemized deduction rather than as a foreign tax credit?

a. The foreign tax paid was less than 15%.
b. The foreign tax was paid to a European country.
c. The foreign tax paid was a property tax.
d. The foreign tax paid was a tax on dividend income.

EA LO 9-5 35. Justin and Janet, whose AGI is $156,000, have twin boys, Jake and Jaime, age 5. How much child tax credit can they take?

a. $0.
b. $1,000.
c. $2,000.
d. $2,300.

EA LO 9-5 36. Julian is a single father with a son, Alex, who is 8 years old. If Julian's AGI is $87,000, what is his child tax credit for Alex?

a. $0.
b. $400.
c. $600.
d. $1,000.

EA LO 9-6 37. Jerry and Ellen are married filing jointly with AGI of $45,000. They made a $1,500 contribution to a qualified retirement plan. How much is their retirement savings contributions credit?

a. $0.

b. $150.

c. $300.

d. $750.

EA LO 9-6 38. Marcia is a single filer and has AGI of $26,000. During the year, she contributed $800 to a Roth IRA. What amount of retirement savings contributions credit can Marcia take?

a. $0.

b. $80.

c. $160.

d. $800.

LO 9-7 39. After two and one-half years of working with the orphanage and the government, Jake and Nikki adopted a two-year-old girl from Korea. The adoption process, which became final in January 2017, incurred the following qualified adoption expenses. For how much and in which year can Jake and Nikki take the adoption credit? (Assume no limitation of the credit due to AGI.)

Year 2016	$6,000
Year 2017	1,000

a. $6,000 in 2016.

b. $1,000 in 2017.

c. $7,000 in 2016.

d. $7,000 in 2017.

LO 9-7 40. Abel and Loni adopted a boy (a U.S. citizen) during the current tax year and incurred a total of $14,675 in qualified adoption expenses. Abel and Loni have modified AGI of $225,000. What is the amount of adoption credit they can take?

a. $6,290.

b. $7,280.

c. $13,570.

d. $14,675.

EA LO 9-8 41. Juan and Lydia both work, file a joint return, and have one qualifying child. They have AGI of $19,000. What is their EIC?

a. $510.

b. $3,400.

c. $5,616.

d. $10,000.

EA LO 9-8 42. Thomas and Stephani are married with four qualifying children. Their AGI is $26,500. Calculate their EIC using the EIC formula.

a. $6,318.

b. $5,777.

c. $5,616.

d. $4,600.

LO 9-8 43. Which of the following credits is *never* a refundable credit?

a. Earned Income Credit.

b. Foreign tax credit.

c. Child tax credit.

d. American opportunity tax credit

EA LO 9-9 44. Which of the following statements is *incorrect*?

a. Taxpayers who purchased qualified health insurance through the Marketplace may be eligible for a premium tax credit.

b. Taxpayers must apply the credit toward their health insurance premium.

c. The premium tax credit is designed to help eligible taxpayers pay some of their health insurance premium.

d. Taxpayers who receive a credit must file a federal tax return and attach Form 8962.

EA LO 9-9 45. Dwayne is single with one dependent. He enrolled in a qualified health care plan through the Marketplace at a cost of $4,200 per year. His household income was $39,890. The SLCSP premium is $4,700. What is Dwayne's premium tax credit?

a. $1,441.

b. $3,259.

c. $4,200.

d. $4,700.

Problems connect

All applicable problems are available with ***Connect***©

EA LO 9-1 46. Tim and Martha paid $7,900 in qualified employment-related expenses for their three young children who live with them in their household. Martha received $1,800 of dependent care assistance from her employer, which was properly excluded from gross income. The couple had $57,000 of AGI earned equally. What amount of child and dependent care credit can they claim on their Form 1040? How would your answer differ (if at all) if the couple had AGI of $36,000 that was earned entirely by Tim?

EA LO 9-1 47. Adrienne is a single mother with a 6-year-old daughter who lived with her during the entire year. Adrienne paid $2,900 in child care expenses so that she would be able to work. Of this amount, $500 was paid to Adrienne's mother, whom Adrienne cannot claim as a dependent. Adrienne had net earnings of $1,900 from her jewelry business. In addition, she received child support payments of $21,000 from her ex-husband. What amount, if any, of child and dependent care credit can Adrienne claim?

LO 9-2 48. What is the AGI limit above which each of the following taxpayers would *not* be eligible to receive a credit for the elderly or the disabled?

a. A single taxpayer eligible for the credit who receives $1,000 of nontaxable social security benefits.

b. Taxpayers filing a joint return for which one taxpayer is eligible for the credit and the taxpayers have received no social security benefits.

c. Taxpayers filing a joint return, and both are eligible for the credit and received $3,000 of nontaxable social security benefits.

LO 9-2 49. Assuming that an AGI limitation does not apply, what amounts of credit for the elderly or the disabled would be permitted in each of the instances in Problem 48?

EA LO 9-3 50. In each of the following cases, certain qualifying education expenses were paid during the tax year for individuals who were the taxpayer, spouse, or dependent. The taxpayer has a tax liability and no other credits. Determine the amount of the American opportunity tax credit (AOTC) and/or the lifetime learning credit that should be taken in each instance:

a. A single individual with modified AGI of $32,900 and expenses of $3,400 for a child who is a full-time college freshman.

b. A single individual with modified AGI of $44,500 and expenses of $3,800 for a child who is a full-time college junior.

c. A couple, married filing jointly, with modified AGI of $79,300 and expenses of $8,000 for a child who is a full-time graduate student.

EA LO 9-3 51. Walt and Deloris have two dependent children, Bill and Tiffany. Bill is a freshman at State University, and Tiffany is working on her graduate degree. The couple paid qualified expenses of $3,900 for Bill (who is a half-time student) and $7,800 for Tiffany. What are the amount and type of education tax credits that Walt and Deloris can take, assuming they have no modified AGI limitation?

EA LO 9-3 52. Use the information in Problem 51. What education tax credits are available if Walt and Deloris report modified AGI of $115,300? Does your answer change if Tiffany is taking one class a semester (is less than a half-time student) and not taking classes in a degree program? Why or why not?

EA LO 9-3 53. In 2017, Jeremy and Celeste, who file a joint return, paid the following amounts for their daughter, Alyssa, to attend the University of Colorado during academic year 2017–2018. Alyssa was in her first year of college and attended full-time.

Tuition and fees (for fall semester 2017)	$1,950
Tuition and fees (for spring semester 2018)	1,000
Books	600
Room and board	1,200

The spring semester at the University of Colorado begins in January. In addition to the above, Alyssa's Uncle Devin sent $800 for her tuition directly to the university. Jeremy and Celeste have modified AGI of $165,000. What is the amount of qualifying expenses for the purposes of the American opportunity tax credit (AOTC) in tax year 2017? What is the amount of the AOTC that Jeremy and Celeste can claim based on their AGI?

LO 9-4 54. Jenna paid foreign income tax of $1,326 on foreign income of $8,112. Her worldwide taxable income was $91,400, and her U.S. tax liability was $23,000. What is the amount of the foreign tax credit (FTC) allowed? What would be the allowed FTC if Jenna had paid foreign income tax of $2,400 instead?

EA LO 9-5 55. Determine the amount of the child tax credit in each of the following cases:

a. A single parent with modified AGI of $43,400 and two children.

b. A single parent with modified AGI of $77,058 and three children.

c. A married couple with modified AGI of $107,933 and one child.

EA LO 9-6 56. Determine the retirement savings contributions credit in each of the following cases:

a. A married couple filing jointly with modified AGI of $37,500 and an IRA contribution of $1,600.

b. A married couple filing jointly with modified AGI of $58,000 and an IRA contribution of $1,500.

c. A head of household taxpayer with modified AGI of $33,000 and Roth IRA contribution of $2,000.

d. A single taxpayer with modified AGI of $12,000 and an IRA contribution of $2,300.

LO 9-7 57. Niles and Marsha adopted an infant boy (a U.S. citizen). They paid $14,500 in 2016 for adoption-related expenses. The adoption was finalized in early 2017. Marsha received $3,000 of employer-provided adoption benefits. For question *(a),* assume that any adoption credit is not limited by modified AGI or by the amount of tax liability.

a. What amount of adoption credit, if any, can Niles and Marsha take in 2017?

b. Using the information in question *(a),* assume that their modified AGI was $210,000 in 2017. What amount of adoption credit is allowed in 2017?

EA LO 9-8 58. Determine the amount of the Earned Income Credit in each of the following cases. Assume that the person or persons are eligible to take the credit. Calculate the credit using the formulas.

a. A single person with earned income of $7,554 and no qualifying children.

b. A single person with earned income of $22,500 and two qualifying children.

c. A married couple filing jointly with earned income of $34,190 and one qualifying child.

Tax Return Problems connect

All applicable tax return problems are available with ***Connect***©

Use your tax software to complete the following problems. If you are manually preparing the tax returns, see each problem for the forms you may need.

Tax Return Problem 1

Juliette White is a head of household taxpayer with a daughter named Sabrina. They live at 1009 Olinda Terrace Apt. 5B, Reno, NV 78887. Juliette works at a local law firm, Law Offices of Dane Gray, and attends school in the evenings at Reno Community College (RCC). She is taking some general classes and is not sure what degree she wants to pursue yet. She is taking three units this semester. Full-time status at RCC is nine units. Juliette's mother watches Sabrina after school and in the evenings (no charge) so that Juliette can work and take classes at RCC. Social security numbers are 412-34-5670 for Juliette and 412-34-5672 for Sabrina. Their birth dates are as follows: Juliette, 10/31/1988; and Sabrina, 3/1/2013.

The Form W-2 Juliette received from the Law Offices of Dane Gray contained the following information:

Wages (box 1) = $19,502.50
Federal W/H (box 2) = $ 2,000.14
Social security wages (box 3) = $19,502.50
Social security W/H (box 4) = $ 1,209.16
Medicare wages (box 5) = $19,502.50
Medicare W/H (box 6) = $ 282.79

Juliette also had the following expenses:

Education expenses:	
Tuition for Reno Community College	$775

Juliette had qualifying health care coverage at all times during the tax year.

Prepare Juliette's federal tax return. Use Form 1040 and any additional appropriate schedules or forms she may need for credits. For any missing information, make reasonable assumptions.

Tax Return Problem 2

Married taxpayers David and Lillian Perdue file jointly and have a daughter, Erin. They live at 9510 Bluebird Canyon Drive, Seattle, WA 99201. The Perdues own their home, which was paid off last year. David works as a salesman for the Canyon Honda car dealer and Lillian works at the same dealer as the manager of the service department. The social security number for David is 412-34-5670; for Lillian, 412-34-5671; and for Erin, 412-34-5672. Their birth dates are as follows: David, 1/18/1970; Lillian, 3/14/1970; and Erin, 11/21/2008.

Erin attends school during the day and in the afternoon attends child care at the school. The Perdues paid $2,800 during the year to the school for the after-school care.

The Forms W-2 from Canyon Honda contained the following information:

Lillian Perdue:

Wages (box 1) = $72,000.00
Federal W/H (box 2) = $ 8,565.00
Social security wages (box 3) = $72,000.00
Social security W/H (box 4) = $ 4,464.00
Medicare wages (box 5) = $72,000.00
Medicare W/H (box 6) = $ 1,044.00

Chapter Ten

Payroll Taxes

The majority of taxpayers receive wages or other compensation from an employer. This employer–employee relationship has tax implications and responsibilities for both parties. In this chapter, we focus on the withholding tax collection and payment responsibilities of employers. We also discuss employment tax issues associated with household employees, such as nannies and similar individuals. IRS Publication 15, Circular E—Employer's Tax Guide and Publication 15-A—Employer's Supplemental Tax Guide are sources of additional information for taxpayers. State withholding and reporting requirements often differ. Thus the discussion in this chapter focuses mainly on federal payroll tax requirements.

Learning Objectives

When you have completed this chapter, you should understand the following learning objectives (LO):

LO 10-1 Explain the tax issues associated with payroll and Form 1040.

LO 10-2 Calculate federal income tax withholding, social security, and Medicare taxes on wages and tips.

LO 10-3 Describe the rules for reporting and paying payroll taxes, including deposit penalties and Form 941.

LO 10-4 Calculate self-employment taxes, unemployment taxes, Form 940, taxes for household employees, and Schedule H.

LO 10-5 Determine employer payroll reporting requirements, including Forms W-2 and W-3.

LO 10-6 Explain supplemental wage payments, backup withholding, Form W-9, estimated tax payments, and Form 1040-ES.

TAX ISSUES ASSOCIATED WITH PAYROLL AND FORM 1040

LO 10-1

Everyone who is an employee of a business receives a paycheck. Employees typically receive checks on a weekly, biweekly, semimonthly, or monthly basis. Some employees may receive daily or miscellaneous wages. Many employees look only at their net check amount with little understanding of how that net amount was determined. Often employees are not sure how their paychecks relate to the Form 1040 they file on or before April 15 of the next year.

Briefly, the federal government (as well as state and local governments) expects taxpayers to help fund programs and keep the government operational. Even though income tax returns are filed once a year, the government operates 365 days of the year and requires a steady flow of money to operate. To provide part of that flow of money, a payroll tax withholding system was established, sometimes referred to as a *pay-as-you-go* system. Employees pay into the system as they earn their wages rather than waiting until the end of the year.

At the end of the year, the employer is required to summarize all of an employee's earnings and taxes withheld on a Form W-2, which is the starting point for completing Form 1040.

Federal withholding taxes are the payments made by the employer on behalf of the employee. Form 1040 compares tax liability with tax payments to determine whether a taxpayer will receive a refund or will owe more money.

The payroll system also covers special tax situations for a person who is a tipped employee, a self-employed person, or a domestic worker within a home. The remaining sections of this chapter discuss general federal payroll, withholding, and reporting requirements as well as these special situations.

CONCEPT CHECK 10-1—
LO 10-1

1. The payroll tax withholding system was established to produce a stream of revenue for governmental operations. True or false?
2. Forms W-2 and 1040 are used to match tax liability with tax payments. True or false?

FEDERAL INCOME TAX WITHHOLDING, SOCIAL SECURITY, AND MEDICARE TAXES ON WAGES AND TIPS

LO 10-2

Income Tax Withholding from Wages

Wages and other compensation earned by employees are taxable. Rather than have taxpayers pay their entire tax liability when they file their tax returns, the IRC has established a payroll tax withholding system.[1] These rules require employers to retain (withhold) a portion of each paycheck based on the gross wages paid to the employee. This withholding represents an approximation of the proportionate share of total tax liability the employee will owe to the federal government. Employers must then remit (deposit) those withholdings to the U.S. Treasury on behalf of their employees. This system of withholding taxes has some advantages. First, employees pay their tax liability in small amounts throughout the year rather than in a large sum on April 15. Second, the federal government receives the tax revenue throughout the year, thus reducing the need to borrow money to fund operations.

Wages subject to withholding and other employment taxes include all pay given to employees for services performed. The payment may be in cash or other forms of compensation and includes, for example, salaries, vacation allowances, bonuses, commissions, and taxable fringe benefits. Employers withhold federal taxes on this compensation using withholding tax tables based on the number of withholding allowances selected by employees.[2]

Employees provide their employers a Form W-4 indicating their filing status and number of withholding allowances (see Exhibit 10-1). There is also a withholding calculator on the IRS Web site at www.irs.gov/individuals for help in determining the number of allowances to claim on Form W-4. The only portion of the form an employee gives the employer is the part at the bottom of the first page (just below the "cut here" line). Employees use the remainder of the form to determine the appropriate number of withholding allowances to claim. The larger the number of allowances, the smaller the amount of tax withheld from each paycheck.

To aid in making a reasonable estimate, employees generally fill out the Personal Allowances worksheet on page 1 of Form W-4. For example, Jose Mendoza is married and cannot be claimed as a dependent by someone else. He has one job and makes $96,000 annually. Using the Personal Allowance worksheet, Jose would enter 1 on lines A and B. Lines C–G do not apply, so line H will be 2. Jose wants an additional $50 to be withheld from each paycheck. See Exhibit 10-1 for a completed Form W-4 for Jose.

[1] IRC § 3402.

[2] IRC § 3402(f).

EXHIBIT 10-1

Form W-4 (2017)

Purpose. Complete Form W-4 so that your employer can withhold the correct federal income tax from your pay. Consider completing a new Form W-4 each year and when your personal or financial situation changes.

Exemption from withholding. If you are exempt, complete **only** lines 1, 2, 3, 4, and 7 and sign the form to validate it. Your exemption for 2017 expires February 15, 2018. See Pub. 505, Tax Withholding and Estimated Tax.

Note: If another person can claim you as a dependent on his or her tax return, you can't claim exemption from withholding if your total income exceeds $1,050 and includes more than $350 of unearned income (for example, interest and dividends).

Exceptions. An employee may be able to claim exemption from withholding even if the employee is a dependent, if the employee:

- Is age 65 or older,
- Is blind, or
- Will claim adjustments to income; tax credits; or itemized deductions, on his or her tax return.

The exceptions don't apply to supplemental wages greater than $1,000,000.

Basic instructions. If you aren't exempt, complete the **Personal Allowances Worksheet** below. The worksheets on page 2 further adjust your withholding allowances based on itemized deductions, certain credits, adjustments to income, or two-earners/multiple jobs situations.

Complete all worksheets that apply. However, you may claim fewer (or zero) allowances. For regular wages, withholding must be based on allowances you claimed and may not be a flat amount or percentage of wages.

Head of household. Generally, you can claim head of household filing status on your tax return only if you are unmarried and pay more than 50% of the costs of keeping up a home for yourself and your dependent(s) or other qualifying individuals. See Pub. 501, Exemptions, Standard Deduction, and Filing Information, for information.

Tax credits. You can take projected tax credits into account in figuring your allowable number of withholding allowances. Credits for child or dependent care expenses and the child tax credit may be claimed using the **Personal Allowances Worksheet** below. See Pub. 505 for information on converting your other credits into withholding allowances.

Nonwage income. If you have a large amount of nonwage income, such as interest or dividends, consider making estimated tax payments using Form 1040-ES, Estimated Tax for Individuals. Otherwise, you may owe additional tax. If you have pension or annuity income, see Pub. 505 to find out if you should adjust your withholding on Form W-4 or W-4P.

Two earners or multiple jobs. If you have a working spouse or more than one job, figure the total number of allowances you are entitled to claim on all jobs using worksheets from only one Form W-4. Your withholding usually will be most accurate when all allowances are claimed on the Form W-4 for the highest paying job and zero allowances are claimed on the others. See Pub. 505 for details.

Nonresident alien. If you are a nonresident alien, see Notice 1392, Supplemental Form W-4 Instructions for Nonresident Aliens, before completing this form.

Check your withholding. After your Form W-4 takes effect, use Pub. 505 to see how the amount you are having withheld compares to your projected total tax for 2017. See Pub. 505, especially if your earnings exceed $130,000 (Single) or $180,000 (Married).

Future developments. Information about any future developments affecting Form W-4 (such as legislation enacted after we release it) will be posted at *www.irs.gov/w4*.

Personal Allowances Worksheet (Keep for your records.)

A Enter "1" for **yourself** if no one else can claim you as a dependent . . . **A** 1

B Enter "1" if:
- You're single and have only one job; or
- You're married, have only one job, and your spouse doesn't work; or
- Your wages from a second job or your spouse's wages (or the total of both) are $1,500 or less.

. . . **B** 1

C Enter "1" for your **spouse.** But, you may choose to enter "-0-" if you are married and have either a working spouse or more than one job. (Entering "-0-" may help you avoid having too little tax withheld.) . . . **C** ____

D Enter number of **dependents** (other than your spouse or yourself) you will claim on your tax return . . . **D** ____

E Enter "1" if you will file as **head of household** on your tax return (see conditions under **Head of household** above) . . **E** ____

F Enter "1" if you have at least $2,000 of **child or dependent care expenses** for which you plan to claim a credit . . . **F** ____
(**Note:** Do **not** include child support payments. See Pub. 503, Child and Dependent Care Expenses, for details.)

G **Child Tax Credit** (including additional child tax credit). See Pub. 972, Child Tax Credit, for more information.
- If your total income will be less than $70,000 ($100,000 if married), enter "2" for each eligible child; then **less** "1" if you have two to four eligible children or **less** "2" if you have five or more eligible children.
- If your total income will be between $70,000 and $84,000 ($100,000 and $119,000 if married), enter "1" for each eligible child. **G** ____

H Add lines A through G and enter total here. (**Note:** This may be different from the number of exemptions you claim on your tax return.) ▶ **H** 2

For accuracy, **complete all worksheets that apply.**
- If you plan to **itemize** or **claim adjustments to income** and want to reduce your withholding, see the **Deductions and Adjustments Worksheet** on page 2.
- If you are **single and have more than one job** or are **married and you and your spouse both work** and the combined earnings from all jobs exceed $50,000 ($20,000 if married), see the **Two-Earners/Multiple Jobs Worksheet** on page 2 to avoid having too little tax withheld.
- If **neither** of the above situations applies, **stop here** and enter the number from line H on line 5 of Form W-4 below.

Separate here and give Form W-4 to your employer. Keep the top part for your records.

Form **W-4** — Department of the Treasury, Internal Revenue Service

Employee's Withholding Allowance Certificate

▶ **Whether you are entitled to claim a certain number of allowances or exemption from withholding is subject to review by the IRS. Your employer may be required to send a copy of this form to the IRS.**

OMB No. 1545-0074 **2017**

1 Your first name and middle initial	Last name	2 **Your social security number**
Jose	Mendoza	412-34-5670

Home address (number and street or rural route): 123 Main Street

3 ☐ Single ☑ Married ☐ Married, but withhold at higher Single rate.
Note: If married, but legally separated, or spouse is a nonresident alien, check the "Single" box.

City or town, state, and ZIP code: Savoy, IL 61874

4 **If your last name differs from that shown on your social security card, check here. You must call 1-800-772-1213 for a replacement card.** ▶ ☐

5	Total number of allowances you are claiming (from line **H** above **or** from the applicable worksheet on page 2)	5	
6	Additional amount, if any, you want withheld from each paycheck . . .	6	$ 50.00

7 I claim exemption from withholding for 2017, and I certify that I meet **both** of the following conditions for exemption.
- Last year I had a right to a refund of **all** federal income tax withheld because I had **no** tax liability, **and**
- This year I expect a refund of **all** federal income tax withheld because I expect to have **no** tax liability.

If you meet both conditions, write "Exempt" here . . . ▶ 7 ____

Under penalties of perjury, I declare that I have examined this certificate and, to the best of my knowledge and belief, it is true, correct, and complete.

Employee's signature
(This form is not valid unless you sign it.) ▶ **Date** ▶

8 Employer's name and address (Employer: Complete lines 8 and 10 only if sending to the IRS.)	9 Office code (optional)	10 Employer identification number (EIN)

For Privacy Act and Paperwork Reduction Act Notice, see page 2. Cat. No. 10220Q Form **W-4** (2017)

Source: U.S. Department of the Treasury, Internal Revenue Service, Form W-4. Washington, DC: 2017.

(continued)

EXHIBIT 10-1 *(concluded)*

Form W-4 (2017) Page 2

Deductions and Adjustments Worksheet

Note: Use this worksheet *only* if you plan to itemize deductions or claim certain credits or adjustments to income.

1 Enter an estimate of your 2017 itemized deductions. These include qualifying home mortgage interest, charitable contributions, state and local taxes, medical expenses in excess of 10% of your income, and miscellaneous deductions. For 2017, you may have to reduce your itemized deductions if your income is over $313,800 and you're married filing jointly or you're a qualifying widow(er); $287,650 if you're head of household; $261,500 if you're single, not head of household and not a qualifying widow(er); or $156,900 if you're married filing separately. See Pub. 505 for details . . . . 1 $ ______

2 Enter: { $12,700 if married filing jointly or qualifying widow(er) / $9,350 if head of household / $6,350 if single or married filing separately } . . . . 2 $ ______

3 **Subtract** line 2 from line 1. If zero or less, enter "-0-" . . . . 3 $ ______

4 Enter an estimate of your 2017 adjustments to income and any additional standard deduction (see Pub. 505) 4 $ ______

5 **Add** lines 3 and 4 and enter the total. (Include any amount for credits from the *Converting Credits to Withholding Allowances for 2017 Form W-4* worksheet in Pub. 505.) . . . . 5 $ ______

6 Enter an estimate of your 2017 nonwage income (such as dividends or interest) . . . . 6 $ ______

7 **Subtract** line 6 from line 5. If zero or less, enter "-0-" . . . . 7 $ ______

8 **Divide** the amount on line 7 by $4,050 and enter the result here. Drop any fraction . . . . . . 8 ______

9 Enter the number from the **Personal Allowances Worksheet,** line H, page 1 . . . . 9 ______

10 **Add** lines 8 and 9 and enter the total here. If you plan to use the **Two-Earners/Multiple Jobs Worksheet,** also enter this total on line 1 below. Otherwise, **stop here** and enter this total on Form W-4, line 5, page 1 10 ______

Two-Earners/Multiple Jobs Worksheet (See *Two earners or multiple jobs* on page 1.)

Note: Use this worksheet *only* if the instructions under line H on page 1 direct you here.

1 Enter the number from line H, page 1 (or from line 10 above if you used the **Deductions and Adjustments Worksheet**) 1 ______

2 Find the number in **Table 1** below that applies to the **LOWEST** paying job and enter it here. **However,** if you are married filing jointly and wages from the highest paying job are $65,000 or less, do not enter more than "3" . . . . 2 ______

3 If line 1 is **more than or equal to** line 2, subtract line 2 from line 1. Enter the result here (if zero, enter "-0-") and on Form W-4, line 5, page 1. **Do not** use the rest of this worksheet . . . . 3 ______

Note: If line 1 is **less than** line 2, enter "-0-" on Form W-4, line 5, page 1. Complete lines 4 through 9 below to figure the additional withholding amount necessary to avoid a year-end tax bill.

4 Enter the number from line 2 of this worksheet . . . . 4 ______

5 Enter the number from line 1 of this worksheet . . . . 5 ______

6 **Subtract** line 5 from line 4 . . . . 6 ______

7 Find the amount in **Table 2** below that applies to the **HIGHEST** paying job and enter it here . . . . 7 $ ______

8 **Multiply** line 7 by line 6 and enter the result here. This is the additional annual withholding needed . . 8 $ ______

9 Divide line 8 by the number of pay periods remaining in 2017. For example, divide by 25 if you are paid every two weeks and you complete this form on a date in January when there are 25 pay periods remaining in 2017. Enter the result here and on Form W-4, line 6, page 1. This is the additional amount to be withheld from each paycheck 9 $ ______

Table 1

Married Filing Jointly		All Others	
If wages from **LOWEST** paying job are—	Enter on line 2 above	If wages from **LOWEST** paying job are—	Enter on line 2 above
$0 - $7,000	0	$0 - $8,000	0
7,001 - 14,000	1	8,001 - 16,000	1
14,001 - 22,000	2	16,001 - 26,000	2
22,001 - 27,000	3	26,001 - 34,000	3
27,001 - 35,000	4	34,001 - 44,000	4
35,001 - 44,000	5	44,001 - 70,000	5
44,001 - 55,000	6	70,001 - 85,000	6
55,001 - 65,000	7	85,001 - 110,000	7
65,001 - 75,000	8	110,001 - 125,000	8
75,001 - 80,000	9	125,001 - 140,000	9
80,001 - 95,000	10	140,001 and over	10
95,001 - 115,000	11		
115,001 - 130,000	12		
130,001 - 140,000	13		
140,001 - 150,000	14		
150,001 and over	15		

Table 2

Married Filing Jointly		All Others	
If wages from **HIGHEST** paying job are—	Enter on line 7 above	If wages from **HIGHEST** paying job are—	Enter on line 7 above
$0 - $75,000	$610	$0 - $38,000	$610
75,001 - 135,000	1,010	38,001 - 85,000	1,010
135,001 - 205,000	1,130	85,001 - 185,000	1,130
205,001 - 360,000	1,340	185,001 - 400,000	1,340
360,001 - 405,000	1,420	400,001 and over	1,600
405,001 and over	1,600		

Privacy Act and Paperwork Reduction Act Notice. We ask for the information on this form to carry out the Internal Revenue laws of the United States. Internal Revenue Code sections 3402(f)(2) and 6109 and their regulations require you to provide this information; your employer uses it to determine your federal income tax withholding. Failure to provide a properly completed form will result in your being treated as a single person who claims no withholding allowances; providing fraudulent information may subject you to penalties. Routine uses of this information include giving it to the Department of Justice for civil and criminal litigation; to cities, states, the District of Columbia, and U.S. commonwealths and possessions for use in administering their tax laws; and to the Department of Health and Human Services for use in the National Directory of New Hires. We may also disclose this information to other countries under a tax treaty, to federal and state agencies to enforce federal nontax criminal laws, or to federal law enforcement and intelligence agencies to combat terrorism.

You are not required to provide the information requested on a form that is subject to the Paperwork Reduction Act unless the form displays a valid OMB control number. Books or records relating to a form or its instructions must be retained as long as their contents may become material in the administration of any Internal Revenue law. Generally, tax returns and return information are confidential, as required by Code section 6103.

The average time and expenses required to complete and file this form will vary depending on individual circumstances. For estimated averages, see the instructions for your income tax return.

If you have suggestions for making this form simpler, we would be happy to hear from you. See the instructions for your income tax return.

In concept, employees report the necessary number of allowances so the amount of tax paid during the year closely approximates the amount of expected tax liability. This worksheet is appropriate in most situations and takes into account the tax effect of a working or nonworking spouse and the child tax credit. Taxpayers who work more than one job or who anticipate itemizing their deductions should complete the appropriate worksheets on page 2 of Form W-4 to more precisely match withholdings with expected tax liability.

Employees can also claim exemption from withholding on line 7 of Form W-4. An individual can do so only if he or she did not have a federal tax liability in the prior tax year and expects to have no federal tax liability in the current year.[3] Such individuals expect either to have low Adjusted Gross Income (AGI) or to have unusually high deductions and/or credits.

Employers determine the amount of tax to withhold using either a percentage method or a wage bracket method with a withholding table.[4] Both methods require the employer to know the marital status of the employee, the number of exemptions claimed on Form W-4, and the pay period of the company (weekly, monthly, or the like). Because most payroll systems are computerized, the method most commonly used is the percentage method; see Examples 10-1 and 10-2.

To compute the amount of withholding with the percentage method, the employer first performs the following steps to determine the amount of wages subject to withholding:

1. Multiplies the number of allowances claimed by the employee (see Form W-4 in Exhibit 10-1) by the allowance amount shown in the following table.
2. Subtracts the amount calculated in step 1 from the employee's gross wages for the period.
3. Determines the amount of withholding using the tables provided by the IRS to this chapter.

The 2017 Amount for One Withholding Allowance (Used in Step 1)

Pay Period	Allowance Amount
Daily	$ 15.60
Weekly	77.90
Biweekly	155.80
Semimonthly	168.80
Monthly	337.50
Quarterly	1,012.50
Semiannually	2,025.00
Annually	4,050.00

EXAMPLE 10-1

Audrey is single and earns $500 per week. She claimed two allowances on the W-4 she provided her employer. The amount of federal income tax withheld from Audrey's paycheck is as follows:

Gross pay	$500.00
Less allowances (2 × $77.90)	(155.80)
Wages subject to withholding	$344.20

Using the percentage method table from the Appendix in this chapter, Audrey can calculate that the federal income tax withholding each pay period is

$$\$18.00 + [15\% \times (\$344.20 - 224.00)] = \$36.03$$

[3] IRC § 3402(n).

[4] IRC § 3402(b) and IRC § 3402(c).

EXAMPLE 10-2

Mauro is married and claimed five exemptions on his W-4. He is paid twice a month (semimonthly) and has gross wages of $3,900 each pay period. The proper amount of federal withholding is as follows:

Gross pay	$3,900.00
Less allowances (5 × $168.80)	(844.00)
Wages subject to withholding	$3,056.00

Using the percentage method table from the Appendix in this chapter, the taxpayer can calculate that the federal income tax withholding each pay period is

$$\$77.80 + [15\% \times (\$3,056.00 - \$1,138.00)] = \$365.50$$

Note that the withholding tables are structured so that employers withhold approximately the same amount for a given annual income regardless of how often the employee is paid. See Example 10-3.

EXAMPLE 10-3

Louisa is married, earns $66,300 per year, and claims two withholding allowances.

- If Louisa's pay period is on a weekly basis, her gross wages are $1,275 ($66,300/52) and her wages in excess of the allowance would be $1,119.20. Using the percentage method of withholding, her withholdings on a weekly basis would be $125.03. Over the period of a year, her withholdings total is $6,501.56.
- If Louisa is paid on a monthly basis, her gross wages would be $5,525.00 per month and her wages in excess of the allowance would be $4,850.00. Louisa's monthly check has tax withholdings of $541.65. For the year, her withholdings total $6,499.80.

When the wage bracket method is used, withholding allowances are *not* deducted before figuring the federal withholding amount. See Example 10-4 for an illustration of a wage bracket table. Notice that the amount of federal withholding is a whole amount based on a range of wages. This "averaging" accounts for differences in withholding using the percentage method.

EXAMPLE 10-4

Using the same information as in Example 10-1, Audrey's federal withholding will be $37 calculated as follows:

1. Find the wage bracket table for "Single persons—Weekly payroll period."
2. Go down the left side of the table and find the range of at least $500 but less than $510 in wages. Do not deduct any withholding allowances.
3. Go across this row until you find the withholding allowances column for two allowances.
4. The intersection is $37.

Note that when the percentage method is used, the amount of federal withholding is $36.03, and when the wage bracket method is used, the amount of federal withholding is $37. This is due to averaging between the range of gross wages ($500–$510).

Generally, the largest amount of federal income tax withholding occurs when an employee is single and claims no exemption allowances. The more exemptions claimed, the less tax is withheld and the higher the net paycheck. In such cases, that may not provide for sufficient withholding during the year if, for example, an individual works multiple jobs. The withholding tables are constructed under the assumption that an individual works only one job. Remember that the U.S. tax system is a *progressive tax system* in which individuals with higher levels of income are taxed at higher rates. If a single employee works one job and earns $25,000 per year, the marginal withholding rate is 15%. If that same person works two jobs paying $25,000 each, the second job is added to the first job for purposes of taxation. The second job causes the marginal withholding rate to be 25% (when both jobs are added together), yet each employer will withhold at a marginal 15% rate as though the individual works only one job.

Unless the employee requests one or both employers to withhold an amount in excess of the statutory requirement, the employee will likely be underwithheld and will be required to pay additional taxes when filing his or her return and could incur an underpayment penalty. On line 6 of Form W-4, an employee can ask the employer to withhold an additional amount from each paycheck to cover this potential shortfall.

FICA Taxes—Social Security Tax and Medicare Tax Withholding

Employers must also withhold Federal Insurance Contributions Act (FICA) taxes from the paychecks of employees. There are two parts to FICA taxes. One is the old age, survivors, and disability insurance (OASDI), commonly referred to as *social security*.[5] The other is hospital insurance for the elderly and other specified individuals, called *Medicare*.[6]

Unlike income tax withholding, which is deducted entirely from the paycheck of the employee, social security and Medicare taxes are collected equally from the employee and the employer. The employer withholds the appropriate amount from the employee (as with income tax withholding), and that amount is added to the amount from the pocket of the employer. Thus the employer pays a portion of the total FICA liability and the employee pays his or her portion.

If a taxpayer works two jobs, both employers are required to withhold FICA and match the amounts withheld. A taxpayer who has overpaid the social security portion of the tax because his or her combined taxable income from both jobs exceeds the annual wage base is entitled to receive the excess amount back when he or she files Form 1040. The excess social security tax withheld is recorded on the second page of Form 1040 under the Payments section.

In 2017 the social security tax rate is 6.2% of taxable wages for the employee and 6.2% of taxable wages for the employer, up to an annual wage base of $127,200.[7] For Medicare taxes, the rate is 1.45% for each party on an unlimited wage base. Thus the total amount collected by the federal government is 15.3%, 12.4% on the social security wages of an individual up to $127,200 and 2.9% on individual wages above that threshold. A 0.9% Additional Medicare Tax applies to combined Medicare wages and self-employment income over the threshold amount based on the taxpayer's filing status. The threshold is $250,000 for married filing jointly, $200,000 for single, head of household, and qualifying widow(er), and $125,000 for married filing separately. Self-employment losses are not considered for purposes of these threshold amounts. It also requires the employer to withhold the 0.9% on Medicare wages that it pays to the employee in excess of $200,000 in 2017. The employer is not required to match this additional medicare tax, it is an employee-only tax.

EXAMPLE 10-5

Henrietta earned $72,000 during 2017. Without regard to federal income taxes, her employer will withhold $4,464.00 ($72,000 × 0.062) from her paycheck for social security taxes and $1,044.00 ($72,000 × 0.0145) for Medicare taxes, for a total of $5,508.00. Henrietta's employer pays its share and will deposit a total of $11,016.00 with the federal government during the year.

EXAMPLE 10-6

Haito earned $132,800 during 2017. Her employer will withhold social security taxes of $7,886.40 (maximum wage base of $127,200 × 0.062) and Medicare taxes of $1,925.60 ($132,800 × 0.0145) for a total of $9,812.00. The employer pays its share and sends the federal government $19,624.00 during the year for social security and Medicare taxes.

[5] IRC § 3101(a).

[6] IRC § 3101(b).

[7] This annual wage base is subject to annual inflation adjustment.

EXHIBIT 10-2

Form **4070** (Rev. August 2005) Department of the Treasury Internal Revenue Service	**Employee's Report of Tips to Employer**	OMB No. 1545-0074
Employee's name and address		**Social security number**
Employer's name and address (include establishment name, if different)		**1** Cash tips received
		2 Credit and debit card tips received
		3 Tips paid out
Month or shorter period in which tips were received from , , to ,		**4** Net tips (lines **1 + 2 - 3**)
Signature		Date
For Paperwork Reduction Act Notice, see the instructions on the back of this form.	Cat. No. 41320P	Form **4070** (Rev. 8-2005)

Source: U.S. Department of the Treasury, Internal Revenue Service, Form 4070. Washington, DC: 2016.

Tips

Employees at restaurants or other establishments may receive tips from customers for services performed. Employees are required to report cash tips to their employer by the 10th of the month after the month in which the employee receives the tips. Employees can use Form 4070 to report tips (see Exhibit 10-2). The report must include the employee's name, address, and social security number, the period the report covers, and the total amount of tips received during the period. The report includes tips known to the employer (from credit card charges, for example) and cash tips, and the employee must sign the report. If the tips in any one month from any one job are less than $20, no reporting is required. Employers must withhold income tax, social security, and Medicare taxes on the amount of employee tips.[8]

Large food and beverage establishments may be required to "allocate" tips to employees. A large establishment is one with more than 10 employees on a typical business day during the preceding year that provides food or beverages for consumption on the premises and where tipping is customary.[9] In effect, if employees do not report tips in an amount of at least 8% of gross receipts, the employer must allocate the difference to the employees. Employers are required to report allocated tips to the IRS on Form 8027 (Exhibit 10-3).

CONCEPT CHECK 10-2—
LO 10-2

1. Withholding and other employment taxes are levied only on cash wages and salaries paid to the employee. True or false?
2. The employer fills out Form W-4 to determine how many withholding allowances the employee is entitled to take. True or false?
3. Jim is single and earns $600 per week. He claimed two allowances on his Form W-4 provided to the employer. What amount of federal withholding tax will be deducted from his gross compensation?
4. Jenny earns $130,500 in 2017. How much social security tax will be withheld from her compensation? How much Medicare tax will be withheld from her compensation?
5. Form 4070 is completed by tipped employees for any and all tips earned for the period. True or false?

[8] IRC § 3121(q) and IRC § 3402(k).

[9] IRC § 6053(c).

EXHIBIT 10-3

Form **8027**

Department of the Treasury
Internal Revenue Service

Employer's Annual Information Return of Tip Income and Allocated Tips

▶ See the separate instructions.
▶ Go to *www.irs.gov/Form8027* for instructions and the latest information.

OMB No. 1545-0714

2017

Check if:
Amended Return ☐
Final Return ☐

Name of establishment

Number and street (see instructions)

City or town, state, and ZIP code

Employer identification number

Type of establishment **(check only one box)**
☐ **1** Evening meals only
☐ **2** Evening and other meals
☐ **3** Meals other than evening meals
☐ **4** Alcoholic beverages

Employer's name (name as shown on Form 941)

Establishment number (see instructions)

Number and street (P.O. box, if applicable) | Apt. or suite no.

City, state, and ZIP code (if a foreign address, see instructions)

Does this establishment accept credit cards, debit cards, or other charges? ☐ Yes (lines 1 and 2 **must** be completed) ☐ No

1	Total charged tips for calendar year 2017	**1**	
2	Total charge receipts showing charged tips (see instructions)	**2**	
3	Total amount of service charges of less than 10% paid as wages to employees	**3**	
4a	Total tips reported by indirectly tipped employees	**4a**	
b	Total tips reported by directly tipped employees	**4b**	
	Note: Complete the **Employer's Optional Worksheet for Tipped Employees** in the instructions to determine potential unreported tips of your employees.		
c	Total tips reported (add lines 4a and 4b)	**4c**	
5	Gross receipts from food and beverages (not less than line 2—see instructions)	**5**	
6	Multiply line 5 by 8% (0.08) or the lower rate shown here ▶ ________ granted by the IRS. If you use a lower rate, attach a copy of the IRS determination letter to this return	**6**	
	Note: If you have allocated tips using other than the calendar year (semimonthly, biweekly, quarterly, etc.), mark an **"X"** on line 6 and enter the amount of allocated tips from your records on line 7.		
7	Allocation of tips. If line 6 is more than line 4c, enter the excess here	**7**	
	▶ This amount must be allocated as tips to tipped employees working in this establishment. Check the box below that shows the method used for the allocation. Show the portion, if any, allocated to each employee in box 8 of the employee's Form W-2.		
a	Allocation based on hours-worked method (see instructions for restriction) ☐		
	Note: If you marked the checkbox on line 7a, enter the average number of employee hours worked per business day during the payroll period. (see instructions) ________		
b	Allocation based on gross receipts method ☐		
c	Allocation based on good-faith agreement ☐		
8	Enter the total number of directly tipped employees at this establishment during 2017 ▶		

Under penalties of perjury, I declare that I have examined this return, including accompanying documents, and to the best of my knowledge and belief, it is true, correct, and complete.

Signature ▶ **Title ▶** **Date ▶**

For Privacy Act and Paperwork Reduction Act Notice, see the separate instructions. Cat. No. 49989U Form **8027** (2017)

Source: U.S. Department of the Treasury, Internal Revenue Service, Form 8027. Washington, DC: 2017.

Employers must use one of the following methods to allocate tips:

1. Gross receipts per employee.
2. Hours worked per employee.
3. Good-faith agreement between the employee and employer.

Employers are *not* required to withhold income, social security, or Medicare taxes on allocated tips. Allocated tips appear in box 8 on Form W-2.

REPORTING AND PAYING PAYROLL TAXES

LO 10-3

Payment of Payroll Taxes

Employers are required to pay withheld taxes (income tax, social security, Medicare) to the federal government on a timely basis.[10] These payments are called *payroll tax deposits*. The frequency of the deposits depends, in large part, on the dollar amounts withheld or otherwise owed to the government. The employer must use the electronic funds transfer to make all federal tax deposits[11]; the Electronic Federal Tax Payment System (EFTPS) is a free service provided by the Department of Treasury. This service is available for all employers. When the employer identification number (EIN) is requested from the IRS, the employer is pre-enrolled with instructions on how to activate the EFTPS account. For more information, go to www.eftps.gov.

Employers typically deposit taxes either monthly or semiweekly. New employers are deemed monthly schedule depositors except in unusual circumstances. The deposit schedule is based on the total tax liability that the employer reported on Form 941 during a four-quarter lookback period. For 2017, the lookback period runs from the quarters starting July 1, 2015, through June 30, 2016. If the employer reported total payroll taxes of $50,000 or less during the lookback period, the employer is a monthly schedule depositor. If total taxes exceed $50,000, the employer is a semiweekly schedule depositor.[12]

EXAMPLE 10-7

Smith Company is determining how often it needs to deposit payroll taxes for calendar year 2017. The company made quarterly payroll tax deposits during the lookback period as follows:

Quarter July 1–September 30, 2015	$ 8,000
Quarter October 1–December 31, 2015	9,000
Quarter January 1–March 31, 2016	10,000
Quarter April 1–June 30, 2016	10,000
Total payroll taxes paid in lookback period	$37,000

Because the total payroll taxes deposited in the lookback period were less than $50,000, Smith Company will be a monthly payroll tax depositor during 2017.

Monthly depositors are required to deposit payroll taxes through EFTPS on or before the 15th day of the following month. The taxes that must be deposited are the sum of (a) withheld income taxes, (b) social security and Medicare taxes withheld from the employee, and (c) the employer's share for social security and Medicare taxes.

EXAMPLE 10-8

XYZ Company is a monthly depositor. For payroll paid during the month of April, the company withheld $4,000 in income taxes and $2,500 in social security and $863 in Medicare taxes. The company is required to pay [$4,000 + ($2,500 + $863) + ($2,500 + $863)] and to deposit $10,726 through EFTPS no later than May 15.

[10] IRC § 6302(a) and Reg. § 31.6302-1(a).

[11] Refer to Publication 15 under "How to Deposit."

[12] Reg. §31.6302-1(b).

Semiweekly schedule depositors must remit payroll taxes more often. Payroll taxes associated with payrolls paid on a Wednesday, Thursday, or Friday must be deposited by the following Wednesday. For payrolls paid on Saturday, Sunday, Monday, or Tuesday, the semiweekly schedule depositor must deposit the taxes no later than the following Friday.

EXAMPLE 10-9

LMNO Company, which pays its employees every Friday, is a semiweekly schedule depositor. When the company paid its employees on Friday, it incurred a payroll tax liability of $19,000 on that date. LMNO must deposit applicable payroll taxes no later than Wednesday of the next week.

It is important to note that the applicable payroll date is the date the payroll is *paid,* not the end of the payroll period.

EXAMPLE 10-10

Nichols Company is a monthly schedule depositor that pays its employees on the first day of the month for the payroll period ending on the last day of the prior month. Payroll taxes withheld on June 1 are due no later than July 15 even though the payroll is for work performed by employees through May 31.

If the day on which taxes are due is a weekend or holiday, taxes are payable on the next banking day. Semiweekly schedule depositors have at least three banking days to make a deposit. Thus if a banking holiday means that an employer does not get three banking days, the payment date is extended.

EXAMPLE 10-11

LMNO Company (from Example 10-9) pays employees on Friday. The following Monday is a banking holiday. Because LMNO is a semiweekly schedule depositor, it must normally deposit applicable payroll taxes on the following Wednesday. Because Monday is a banking holiday, the company does not have at least three banking days to make its deposit. Thus the company has until Thursday to make its deposit.

Employers with a payroll tax liability of less than $2,500 at the end of any quarter can pay the payroll tax liability using 941-V form when they file their quarterly payroll tax reports rather than with the EFTPS.

If an employer accumulates $100,000 or more in taxes on any day during a deposit period, it must deposit the tax by the next banking day, whether it is a monthly or semiweekly schedule depositor. This rule applies to a single day, and the taxes do not accumulate during the period. For example, if $100,000 of taxes are accumulated on a Monday, they must be deposited by Tuesday. If on that Tuesday, additional accumulated taxes are $90,000, the taxes are deposited by Friday. An employer who is a monthly schedule depositor and accumulates a $100,000 tax liability on any day becomes a semiweekly schedule depositor on the next day and remains so for at least the rest of the calendar year and for the following year.

EXAMPLE 10-12

Price and Company started its business on August 28, 2017. On September 1 it paid wages for the first time and accumulated a tax liability of $30,000. On Friday, September 15, Price paid wages and incurred a tax liability of $70,000, which brings the accumulated tax liability to $100,000. Because this is the first year of its business, the tax liability for its lookback period is zero, so the company would be a monthly schedule depositor. However, because Price accumulated $100,000 tax liability, it became a semiweekly schedule depositor. It will be a semiweekly schedule depositor for the remainder of 2017 and 2018. In this example, Price and Company is required to deposit the $100,000 by Monday, September 18, the next banking day.

Deposit Penalties

If payroll taxes are not paid on a timely basis, the employer is subject to penalty. The penalty is based on the amount not properly or timely deposited. The penalties are as follows:

- 2% for deposits made 1 to 5 days late.
- 5% for deposits made 6 to 15 days late.
- 10% for deposits made 16 or more days late, but before 10 days from due date of the first notice the IRS sent asking for the tax due.
- 10% if electronic deposit is required but not used.
- 10% if deposits are paid directly to the IRS, paid with the return, or paid to an unauthorized financial institution.
- 15% for amounts unpaid more than 10 days after the date of the first notice the IRS sent asking for the tax due.

Employers who withhold taxes from employee paychecks are holding the withheld taxes in trust for the employee. As such, employers have a high level of responsibility. Individuals may be personally responsible for unpaid payroll taxes. If the IRS determines that an individual is responsible for collecting, accounting for, and paying payroll taxes and that the person acted willfully in not paying the taxes, the IRS can assess a penalty on the individual equal to the amount of tax due. Refer to Publication 15 under "Deposit Penalties" for additional rules.

Reporting Payroll Taxes and Form 941

Each quarter, if a company pays wages subject to income tax withholding or social security and Medicare taxes, a Form 941 must be completed. Refer to Exhibit 10-4 and Example 10-13 for a filled-in Form 941 and Schedule B. There is a requirement that any return prepared by a paid preparer be signed by the preparer.

EXAMPLE 10-13

Watson Company (EIN: 36-1234567), located at 123 Main Street, Mason City, IA, had the following payroll data for the second quarter, ended June 30, 2017:

Number of employees	6
Gross wages	$300,000
Total income tax withheld from wages	$ 24,000*
Social security wages	$300,000
Medicare wages	$300,000

* Assume $4,000 per pay period.

Assume that Watson Company pays wages on a semimonthly basis ($50,000 per pay period). Deposits for the quarter were $69,800. Exhibit 10-4 is the filled-in 941 (including Schedule B) for Watson Company for the second quarter of 2017. Exhibit 10-5 is a filled-in voucher coupon for the amount of additional tax due for the quarter. Greg Oliver is the paid preparer of Form 941.

The payroll tax liability per pay period is calculated as follows:

Social security tax	$50,000 × 12.4% =	$ 6,200
Medicare tax	$50,000 × 2.9% =	1,450
Federal income tax		4,000
Total tax liability per period		$11,650
Total tax liability for the quarter		$69,900
Deposits made for the quarter		69,800
Deposit due with 941 return		$ 100

EXHIBIT 10-4

Form **941 for 2017: Employer's QUARTERLY Federal Tax Return** 950117
(Rev. January 2017) Department of the Treasury — Internal Revenue Service OMB No. 1545-0029

Employer identification number (EIN) 3 6 – 1 2 3 4 5 6 7

Name (not your trade name) Watson Company

Trade name (if any)

Address 123 Main Street
Number Street Suite or room number

Mason City IA
City State ZIP code

Foreign country name Foreign province/county Foreign postal code

Report for this Quarter of 2017 (Check one.)

☐ **1:** January, February, March
☒ **2:** April, May, June
☐ **3:** July, August, September
☐ **4:** October, November, December

Instructions and prior year forms are available at *www.irs.gov/form941*.

Read the separate instructions before you complete Form 941. Type or print within the boxes.

Part 1: Answer these questions for this quarter.

1	**Number of employees who received wages, tips, or other compensation for the pay period including: *Mar. 12* (Quarter 1), *June 12* (Quarter 2), *Sept. 12* (Quarter 3), or *Dec. 12* (Quarter 4)**			1	6
2	**Wages, tips, and other compensation**			2	300,000 .
3	**Federal income tax withheld from wages, tips, and other compensation**			3	24,000 .
4	**If no wages, tips, and other compensation are subject to social security or Medicare tax**				☐ **Check and go to line 6.**
		Column 1	**Column 2**		
5a	**Taxable social security wages**	300,000 .	× 0.124 = 37,200 .		
5b	**Taxable social security tips**	0 .	× 0.124 = .		
5c	**Taxable Medicare wages & tips**	300,000 .	× 0.029 = 8,700 .		
5d	**Taxable wages & tips subject to Additional Medicare Tax withholding**	0 .	× 0.009 = .		
5e	**Add Column 2 from lines 5a, 5b, 5c, and 5d**			5e	45,900 .
5f	**Section 3121(q) Notice and Demand—Tax due on unreported tips** (see instructions)			5f	.
6	**Total taxes before adjustments.** Add lines 3, 5e, and 5f			6	69,900 .
7	**Current quarter's adjustment for fractions of cents**			7	.
8	**Current quarter's adjustment for sick pay**			8	.
9	**Current quarter's adjustments for tips and group-term life insurance**			9	.
10	**Total taxes after adjustments.** Combine lines 6 through 9			10	69,900 .
11	**Qualified small business payroll tax credit for increasing research activities.** Attach Form 8974			11	.
12	**Total taxes after adjustments and credits.** Subtract line 11 from line 10			12	69,900 .
13	**Total deposits for this quarter, including overpayment applied from a prior quarter and overpayments applied from Form 941-X, 941-X (PR), 944-X, or 944-X (SP) filed in the current quarter**			13	69,800 .
14	**Balance due.** If line 12 is more than line 13, enter the difference and see instructions			14	100 .
15	**Overpayment.** If line 13 is more than line 12, enter the difference .		Check one: ☐ Apply to next return. ☐ Send a refund.		

► **You MUST complete both pages of Form 941 and SIGN it.** Next ►

For Privacy Act and Paperwork Reduction Act Notice, see the back of the Payment Voucher. Cat. No. 17001Z Form **941** (Rev. 1-2017)

Source: U.S. Department of the Treasury, Internal Revenue Service, Form 941. Washington, DC: 2017.

(continued)

EXHIBIT 10-4 *(continued)*

950217

Name *(not your trade name)*	**Employer identification number (EIN)**

Part 2: Tell us about your deposit schedule and tax liability for this quarter.

If you are unsure about whether you are a monthly schedule depositor or a semiweekly schedule depositor, see section 11 of Pub. 15.

16 Check one: ☐ **Line 12 on this return is less than $2,500 or line 12 (line 10 if the prior quarter was the fourth quarter of 2016) on the return for the prior quarter was less than $2,500, and you didn't incur a $100,000 next-day deposit obligation during the current quarter.** If line 12 (line 10 if the prior quarter was the fourth quarter of 2016) for the prior quarter was less than $2,500 but line 12 on this return is $100,000 or more, you must provide a record of your federal tax liability. If you are a monthly schedule depositor, complete the deposit schedule below; if you are a semiweekly schedule depositor, attach Schedule B (Form 941). Go to Part 3.

☐ **You were a monthly schedule depositor for the entire quarter.** Enter your tax liability for each month and total liability for the quarter, then go to Part 3.

Tax liability: Month 1 ________ .

Month 2 ________ .

Month 3 ________ .

Total liability for quarter ________ . **Total must equal line 12.**

☒ **You were a semiweekly schedule depositor for any part of this quarter.** Complete Schedule B (Form 941), Report of Tax Liability for Semiweekly Schedule Depositors, and attach it to Form 941.

Part 3: Tell us about your business. If a question does NOT apply to your business, leave it blank.

17 If your business has closed or you stopped paying wages . . . . ☐ Check here, and

enter the final date you paid wages ___/___/___ .

18 If you are a seasonal employer and you don't have to file a return for every quarter of the year . . ☐ Check here.

Part 4: May we speak with your third-party designee?

Do you want to allow an employee, a paid tax preparer, or another person to discuss this return with the IRS? See the instructions for details.

☐ Yes. Designee's name and phone number ________ ________

Select a 5-digit Personal Identification Number (PIN) to use when talking to the IRS. ☐☐☐☐☐

☐ No.

Part 5: Sign here. You MUST complete both pages of Form 941 and SIGN it.

Under penalties of perjury, I declare that I have examined this return, including accompanying schedules and statements, and to the best of my knowledge and belief, it is true, correct, and complete. Declaration of preparer (other than taxpayer) is based on all information of which preparer has any knowledge.

✗ **Sign your name here** ________

Print your name here ________

Print your title here ________

Date ___/___/___

Best daytime phone ________

Paid Preparer Use Only Check if you are self-employed . . . ☐

Preparer's name		PTIN	
Preparer's signature		Date	/ /
Firm's name (or yours if self-employed)		EIN	
Address		Phone	
City	State	ZIP code	

EXHIBIT 10-4 *(concluded)*

Schedule B (Form 941):

960311

Report of Tax Liability for Semiweekly Schedule Depositors

OMB No. 1545-0029

(Rev. January 2017) Department of the Treasury — Internal Revenue Service

Employer identification number (EIN) 3 6 – 1 2 3 4 5 6 7

Name *(not your trade name)* Watson Company

Calendar year 2 0 1 7 (Also check quarter)

Report for this Quarter... (Check one.)

- [ ] **1:** January, February, March
- [x] **2:** April, May, June
- [ ] **3:** July, August, September
- [ ] **4:** October, November, December

Use this schedule to show your TAX LIABILITY for the quarter; don't use it to show your deposits. When you file this form with Form 941 or Form 941-SS, don't change your tax liability by adjustments reported on any Forms 941-X or 944-X. You must fill out this form and attach it to Form 941 or Form 941-SS if you're a semiweekly schedule depositor or became one because your accumulated tax liability on any day was $100,000 or more. Write your daily tax liability on the numbered space that corresponds to the date wages were paid. See Section 11 in Pub. 15 for details.

Month 1

Day	Amount	Day	Amount	Day	Amount	Day	Amount
1		9		17		25	
2		10		18		26	
3		11		19		27	
4		12		20		28	
5		13		21		29	
6		14		22		30	11,650
7		15	11,650	23		31	
8		16		24			

Tax liability for Month 1 23,300

Month 2

Day	Amount	Day	Amount	Day	Amount	Day	Amount
1		9		17		25	
2		10		18		26	
3		11		19		27	
4		12		20		28	
5		13		21		29	
6		14		22		30	
7		15	11,650	23		31	11,650
8		16		24			

Tax liability for Month 2 23,300

Month 3

Day	Amount	Day	Amount	Day	Amount	Day	Amount
1		9		17		25	
2		10		18		26	
3		11		19		27	
4		12		20		28	
5		13		21		29	
6		14		22		30	11,650
7		15	11,650	23		31	
8		16		24			

Tax liability for Month 3 23,300

Fill in your total liability for the quarter (Month 1 + Month 2 + Month 3) ▶
Total must equal line 12 on Form 941 or Form 941-SS.

Total liability for the quarter 69,900

For Paperwork Reduction Act Notice, see separate instructions. IRS.gov/form941 Cat. No. 11967Q **Schedule B (Form 941)** (Rev. 1-2017)

Source: U.S. Department of the Treasury, Internal Revenue Service, Form 941. Washington, DC: 2017.

EXHIBIT 10-5

Form **941-V** Department of the Treasury Internal Revenue Service	**Payment Voucher** ▶ **Don't staple this voucher or your payment to Form 941.**		OMB No. 1545-0029 **2017**
1 Enter your employer identification number (EIN). 36-1234567	2 **Enter the amount of your payment.** ▶ Make your check or money order payable to **"United States Treasury"**	Dollars 100	Cents 00
3 Tax Period	4 Enter your business name (individual name if sole proprietor). Watson Company		
○ 1st Quarter ○ 3rd Quarter	Enter your address. 123 Main Street		
◉ 2nd Quarter ○ 4th Quarter	Enter your city, state, and ZIP code or your city, foreign country name, foreign province/county, and foreign postal code. Mason City, IA		

Source: U.S. Department of the Treasury, Internal Revenue Service, Form 941-V. Washington, DC: 2017.

Schedule B is used to report an employer's payroll tax liability for each period, not for the amount of payroll tax deposits. Therefore, the amounts entered on Schedule B relate to the payroll tax liability for each month in the quarter. Using the previous example, the amount of payroll tax liability is $69,900; this amount will be allocated according to the employer payroll periods on the schedule.

There may be situations in which the total liability from Schedule B will not agree with the calculated amounts on line 6 of Form 941 by "fractions of cents" due to rounding. The difference is recorded on line 7 and totaled on line 10 and line 12. For 2017, a line 11 has been added to reflect any qualified small business payroll tax credits for increasing research activities. Line 12 is the total of subtracting line 11 from line 10. Schedule B totals will then be equal to line 12 on Form 941.

Small business employers may have the option of filing these taxes on an annual basis. Form 944—Employer's Annual Federal Tax Return is for employers who have received written notification from the IRS that they qualify for the Form 944 program. Refer to Publication 15, Chapter 12—Filing Form 941, or Form 944 for a detailed explanation of qualification requirements. Employers who are required to file Form 944 can notify the IRS if they want to file quarterly Form 941 instead of the annual form.

CONCEPT CHECK 10-3—
LO 10-3

1. All new employers must use the semiweekly deposit system. True or false?
2. The deposit schedule for an employer is based on the total tax liability that the employer reported on Form 941 during the prior four quarters starting on July 1 and ending on March 31 of the next year. The lookback period runs from the quarters starting July 1 of the current year through June 30 of the next year. True or false?
3. Semiweekly schedule depositors remit taxes on the following Wednesday if the payroll is paid on a Wednesday, Thursday, or Friday. True or false?
4. The penalty for not paying the appropriate federal taxes on time is based on the total amount of the tax liability whether or not a partial payment was made on time. True or false?
5. Form 941 is prepared by the employer to record all federal taxes withheld, including federal withholding, social security, and Medicare taxes and amounts paid for these taxes. True or false?

SELF-EMPLOYMENT TAXES, UNEMPLOYMENT TAXES, FORM 940, TAXES FOR HOUSEHOLD EMPLOYEES, AND SCHEDULE H
LO 10-4

Self-Employment Tax

To this point, this chapter has covered the rules associated with payroll taxes derived from an employee–employer relationship. Self-employed individuals (those filing Schedule C or Schedule F) pay similar taxes, called *self-employment taxes.*

Self-employment taxes are based on net earnings (profit) generated by the business. Because the self-employed taxpayer acts, in effect, as an employee and an employer, the self-employed taxpayer pays both parts of social security and Medicare taxes. For 2017, these individuals pay 12.4% social security tax on net earnings from self-employment of up to $127,200 and a 2.9% Medicare tax on all net earnings without limit.[13] If net earnings from self-employment are less than $400, no self-employment tax is payable.[14] Self-employment tax is reported on Schedule SE.

Remember that self-employed taxpayers are allowed a deduction for self-employment tax in determining AGI (line 27 on Form 1040). This deduction gives the sole proprietor a share of the employer tax expense that would be allowed for corporate businesses. The amount of net self-employment earnings subject to FICA taxes is first reduced by 7.65% before calculating the taxes. Remember from Chapter 6 that sole proprietors are not considered employees; therefore, there is no employer match of FICA taxes and no business expense allowed in reducing taxable income. To compensate self-employed individuals for this inability to take the employer share as a business deduction, they are permitted to reduce net self-employment earnings by 7.65% so that only 92.35% (100% – 7.65%) of net self-employment earnings are subject to FICA taxes.

In some situations, a taxpayer is an employee of a company as well as a sole proprietor. For example, a taxpayer can work as a teacher and sell real estate as a part-time business. The school district withholds the teacher's FICA taxes while the teacher must pay FICA taxes on the net earnings generated by the real estate business. If the earnings from the teacher's Form W-2 and the net earnings from the real estate business are less than the ceiling for social security ($127,200 in 2017), there is no problem. What if both activities combined generate more than $127,200 in earnings? In this type of situation, wages subject to social security are deducted from the ceiling amount of $127,200. The balance is then compared with the earnings from self-employment. If the taxpayer in this situation earned $100,000 as a teacher and $36,000 from the real estate business, the calculation for FICA tax is as follows:

Earnings (profit) from business (Schedule C)		$36,000
Net earnings from self-employment ($36,000 × 92.35%)		$33,246
Social security ceiling	$ 127,200	
– W2 wages	100,000	
Base for social security self-employment tax	$ 27,200	
Self-employment rate	Social security	Medicare
	$ 27,200	$33,246
	× 12.4%	× 2.9%
Self-employment tax	$3,372.80	$ 964.13
	(rounded to $3,373)	(rounded to $964)

The total self-employment tax is $4,337 ($3,373 + $964). The taxpayer's 2017 return will show net earnings from the business of $36,000 (on Schedule C), a deduction for Adjusted Gross Income of $1,687 (calculated from Schedule SE and transferred to line 27 of Form 1040), and self-employment tax of $4,337 (on Schedule SE, shown in Exhibit 10-6, and Form 1040, line 57). Note that amounts are rounded on the appropriate forms.

Unemployment Taxes

The Social Security Act of 1935 required every state to institute an unemployment compensation program to provide payments to people during temporary periods of unemployment.

[13] IRC § 1401(a) and IRC § 1401(b).

[14] IRC § 1402(b).

EXHIBIT 10-6

Schedule SE (Form 1040) 2017 — Attachment Sequence No. **17** — Page **2**

Name of person with **self-employment** income (as shown on Form 1040 or Form 1040NR) | Social security number of person with **self-employment** income ▶

Section B—Long Schedule SE

Part I Self-Employment Tax

Note: If your only income subject to self-employment tax is **church employee income,** see instructions. Also see instructions for the definition of church employee income.

A	If you are a minister, member of a religious order, or Christian Science practitioner **and** you filed Form 4361, but you had $400 or more of **other** net earnings from self-employment, check here and continue with Part I ▶ ☐		
1a	Net farm profit or (loss) from Schedule F, line 34, and farm partnerships, Schedule K-1 (Form 1065), box 14, code A. **Note:** Skip lines 1a and 1b if you use the farm optional method (see instructions)	1a	
b	If you received social security retirement or disability benefits, enter the amount of Conservation Reserve Program payments included on Schedule F, line 4b, or listed on Schedule K-1 (Form 1065), box 20, code Z	1b	( )
2	Net profit or (loss) from Schedule C, line 31; Schedule C-EZ, line 3; Schedule K-1 (Form 1065), box 14, code A (other than farming); and Schedule K-1 (Form 1065-B), box 9, code J1. Ministers and members of religious orders, see instructions for types of income to report on this line. See instructions for other income to report. **Note:** Skip this line if you use the nonfarm optional method (see instructions)	2	36,000
3	Combine lines 1a, 1b, and 2	3	36,000
4a	If line 3 is more than zero, multiply line 3 by 92.35% (0.9235). Otherwise, enter amount from line 3 **Note:** If line 4a is less than $400 due to Conservation Reserve Program payments on line 1b, see instructions.	4a	33,246
b	If you elect one or both of the optional methods, enter the total of lines 15 and 17 here	4b	0
c	Combine lines 4a and 4b. If less than $400, **stop;** you don't owe self-employment tax. **Exception:** If less than $400 and you had **church employee income,** enter -0- and continue ▶	4c	33,246
5a	Enter your **church employee income** from Form W-2. See instructions for definition of church employee income — 5a		
b	Multiply line 5a by 92.35% (0.9235). If less than $100, enter -0-	5b	
6	Add lines 4c and 5b	6	33,246
7	Maximum amount of combined wages and self-employment earnings subject to social security tax or the 6.2% portion of the 7.65% railroad retirement (tier 1) tax for 2017	7	127,200 00
8a	Total social security wages and tips (total of boxes 3 and 7 on Form(s) W-2) and railroad retirement (tier 1) compensation. If $127,200 or more, skip lines 8b through 10, and go to line 11 — 8a 100,000		
b	Unreported tips subject to social security tax (from Form 4137, line 10) — 8b		
c	Wages subject to social security tax (from Form 8919, line 10) — 8c		
d	Add lines 8a, 8b, and 8c	8d	100,000
9	Subtract line 8d from line 7. If zero or less, enter -0- here and on line 10 and go to line 11 ▶	9	27,200
10	Multiply the **smaller** of line 6 or line 9 by 12.4% (0.124)	10	3,373
11	Multiply line 6 by 2.9% (0.029)	11	964
12	**Self-employment tax.** Add lines 10 and 11. Enter here and on **Form 1040, line 57,** or **Form 1040NR, line 55**	12	4,337
13	**Deduction for one-half of self-employment tax.** Multiply line 12 by 50% (0.50). Enter the result here and on **Form 1040, line 27,** or **Form 1040NR, line 27** — 13 2,169		

Part II Optional Methods To Figure Net Earnings (see instructions)

Farm Optional Method. You may use this method **only** if **(a)** your gross farm income[1] wasn't more than $7,800, **or (b)** your net farm profits[2] were less than $5,631.

14	Maximum income for optional methods	14	5,200 00
15	Enter the **smaller** of: two-thirds (2/3) of gross farm income[1] (not less than zero) **or** $5,200. Also include this amount on line 4b above	15	

Nonfarm Optional Method. You may use this method **only** if **(a)** your net nonfarm profits[3] were less than $5,631 and also less than 72.189% of your gross nonfarm income,[4] **and (b)** you had net earnings from self-employment of at least $400 in 2 of the prior 3 years. **Caution:** You may use this method no more than five times.

16	Subtract line 15 from line 14	16	
17	Enter the **smaller** of: two-thirds (2/3) of gross nonfarm income[4] (not less than zero) **or** the amount on line 16. Also include this amount on line 4b above	17	

[1] From Sch. F, line 9, and Sch. K-1 (Form 1065), box 14, code B.

[2] From Sch. F, line 34, and Sch. K-1 (Form 1065), box 14, code A—minus the amount you would have entered on line 1b had you not used the optional method.

[3] From Sch. C, line 31; Sch. C-EZ, line 3; Sch. K-1 (Form 1065), box 14, code A; and Sch. K-1 (Form 1065-B), box 9, code J1.

[4] From Sch. C, line 7; Sch. C-EZ, line 1; Sch. K-1 (Form 1065), box 14, code C; and Sch. K-1 (Form 1065-B), box 9, code J2.

Schedule SE (Form 1040) 2017

Source: U.S. Department of the Treasury, Internal Revenue Service, Schedule SE (Form 1040). Washington, DC: 2017.

The Federal Unemployment Tax Act (FUTA) and the State Unemployment Tax Act (SUTA) provide for payments of unemployment compensation to workers who have lost their jobs. The federal and state governments fund these unemployment compensation payments in part through an unemployment tax assessed on employers.[15]

The actual benefits paid to taxpayers are from the taxpayer's SUTA program. The federal government has the responsibility of administering the state programs to ensure that each state pays into its state trust fund. Employers who pay employees who are not farmworkers or household workers are subject to the FUTA tax if *either* of these criteria applies to them:

1. Paid wages of $1,500 or more in any calendar quarter in the current or preceding calendar year.
2. Had one or more employees in any 20 different weeks in the current or preceding calendar year.

The tax rate is 6.0% of employee wages up to $7,000.[16] Employers get a credit for state unemployment taxes paid up to 5.4%. Thus the effective federal tax rate is 0.6% if employers pay the maximum amount of state tax on time. To receive the maximum credit, the employer's state agency must make the state's contributions on or before the due date for filing the annual return (Form 940) for FUTA. If the employer is late in depositing its funds, the credit is limited to 10% of the amount of deposit that would have been allowed as a credit.

EXAMPLE 10-14

Boone Company, located at 567 End Ave, Mason City, IA, has three employees who were paid the following amounts during 2017. Assume that Boone pays state unemployment taxes and is entitled to the maximum credit of 5.4% subject to a federal unemployment tax rate of 0.6%.

	Wages	FUTA Tax
Theodore	$3,000 × 0.006	= $18
Ursula	$28,000 limited to $7,000 × 0.006 =	$42
Vanessa	$51,000 limited to $7,000 × 0.006 =	$42

Boone will owe FUTA tax of $102.

EXAMPLE 10-15

Everhart Company had state wages of $100,000 subject to SUTA but did not make timely deposits for SUTA. Therefore, the credit for FUTA is limited to 90% of $5,400, or $4,860. If its payroll subject to FUTA tax is $100,000, the following amount is due on Form 940:

$100,000 × 0.060	= $6,000
Less 90% credit	= 4,860
Amount of net FUTA	= $1,140

If Everhart had made timely deposits to its state fund, the amount of FUTA tax would have been $100,000 × 0.6% = $600.

Those who employ household workers (see the next section) are subject to FUTA tax *only* if they pay cash wages of $1,000 or more in any calendar quarter in 2016 or 2017. Employers

[15] IRC § 3301.

[16] IRC § 3301.

must also pay FUTA tax for farmworkers if they paid cash wages of $20,000 or more to farmworkers during any calendar quarter in 2016 or 2017 or if the employer employed 10 or more farmworkers during at least some part of a day during any 20 or more different weeks in 2016 or 2017.

FUTA taxes are deposited quarterly with an authorized depository if the taxes for a quarter (plus undeposited taxes from prior quarters) exceed $500. The tax is deposited using EFTPS. The employer must record that the tax paid is for FUTA tax and indicate the quarter to which the payment applies. The deposit is due no later than the last day of the month following the end of the quarter. If the employer does not specify to which tax the payment is to be applied, the default is for the 941 tax payment (withholding and FICA taxes).

To report FUTA taxes, employers must file Form 940 on an annual basis. (See Exhibit 10-7 for a filled-in Form 940 using data from Example 10-14.) Form 940 is due no later than January 31 of the following year or the next business day if January 31 falls on a holiday or weekend. Deposits must be accompanied by a Form 940-V payment voucher.

Household Employees

A household worker is an employee who performs household work in a private home, local college club, or local fraternity or sorority chapter. These individuals may be nannies, gardeners, maintenance workers, cooks, maids, or the like. These workers are generally classified as employees, and the employer must pay payroll taxes.[17]

Individuals employing household workers are subject to tax rules if any of the following are true:

- They paid any one household employee wages of $2,000 or more in 2017; pay Social Security and Medicare Tax.
- Federal income taxes were withheld from employee wages.
- Household wages of at least $1,000 were paid to all household workers combined in any calendar quarter in 2016 or 2017; pay FUTA Tax.

Household workers do not include the taxpayer's spouse, father or mother, children under age 21, or anyone under age 18 unless providing household services is his or her primary occupation. An example of someone falling into the last category is a high school student who occasionally babysits for neighbors.

Household workers may be classified as employees or as independent contractors. This section deals with workers who are employees. These individuals generally work for one person and are under the direction of the employer. Independent contractors are likely to work for many individuals. For example, you may have someone clean your house every two weeks. That person may clean houses for 40 other people. It is likely that your household worker is an independent contractor, not an employee. Thus you would not need to withhold taxes from the individual.

Instead of filing Form 941 and Form 940, individuals who employ household workers report employment taxes on Schedule H (see Exhibit 10-8 for a filled-in illustration of Example 10-16). The form is not filed separately but is attached to Form 1040. The amount of tax due on line 27 of Schedule H is carried forward to line 60a of Form 1040. Thus the employment taxes due for household employees are paid when Form 1040 is filed or extended.

A taxpayer who has nonhousehold workers (that is, a taxpayer with a business) and household workers can elect to account for and report the latter according to the rules pertaining to his or her regular employees.

[17] IRC § 3510.

EXHIBIT 10-7

Form **940 for 2017: Employer's Annual Federal Unemployment (FUTA) Tax Return** 850113

Department of the Treasury — Internal Revenue Service OMB No. 1545-0028

Employer identification number (EIN) 3 6 – 5 6 7 8 9 0 1

Name *(not your trade name)* Boone Company

Trade name *(if any)*

Address 567 End Avenue

Number Street Suite or room number

Mason City IA

City State ZIP code

Foreign country name Foreign province/county Foreign postal code

Type of Return (Check all that apply.)

- ☐ **a.** Amended
- ☐ **b.** Successor employer
- ☐ **c.** No payments to employees in 2017
- ☐ **d.** Final: Business closed or stopped paying wages

Go to *www.irs.gov/Form940* for instructions and the latest information.

Read the separate instructions before you complete this form. Please type or print within the boxes.

Part 1: Tell us about your return. If any line does NOT apply, leave it blank. See instructions before completing Part 1.

1a	**If you had to pay state unemployment tax in one state only, enter the state abbreviation**	1a	I A
1b	**If you had to pay state unemployment tax in more than one state, you are a multi-state employer**	1b	☐ Check here. Complete Schedule A (Form 940).
2	**If you paid wages in a state that is subject to CREDIT REDUCTION**	2	☐ Check here. Complete Schedule A (Form 940).

Part 2: Determine your FUTA tax before adjustments. If any line does NOT apply, leave it blank.

3	**Total payments to all employees**	3	82,000 .
4	**Payments exempt from FUTA tax** (4) 0 .		
	Check all that apply: 4a ☐ Fringe benefits; 4b ☐ Group-term life insurance; 4c ☐ Retirement/Pension; 4d ☐ Dependent care; 4e ☐ Other		
5	**Total of payments made to each employee in excess of $7,000** (5) 65,000 .		
6	**Subtotal** (line 4 + line 5 = line 6)	6	65,000 .
7	**Total taxable FUTA wages** (line 3 – line 6 = line 7). See instructions	7	17,000 .
8	**FUTA tax before adjustments** (line 7 x 0.006 = line 8)	8	102 .

Part 3: Determine your adjustments. If any line does NOT apply, leave it blank.

9	**If ALL of the taxable FUTA wages you paid were excluded from state unemployment tax, multiply line 7 by 0.054** (line 7 × 0.054 = line 9). Go to line 12	9	.
10	**If SOME of the taxable FUTA wages you paid were excluded from state unemployment tax, OR you paid ANY state unemployment tax late** (after the due date for filing Form 940), complete the worksheet in the instructions. Enter the amount from line 7 of the worksheet	10	.
11	**If credit reduction applies,** enter the total from Schedule A (Form 940)	11	.

Part 4: Determine your FUTA tax and balance due or overpayment. If any line does NOT apply, leave it blank.

12	**Total FUTA tax after adjustments** (lines 8 + 9 + 10 + 11 = line 12)	12	102 .
13	**FUTA tax deposited for the year, including any overpayment applied from a prior year**	13	.
14	**Balance due.** If line 12 is more than line 13, enter the excess on line 14. • If line 14 is more than $500, you must deposit your tax. • If line 14 is $500 or less, you may pay with this return. See instructions	14	102 .
15	**Overpayment.** If line 13 is more than line 12, enter the excess on line 15 and check a box below	15	.

► You **MUST** complete both pages of this form and **SIGN** it. Check one: ☐ Apply to next return. ☐ Send a refund.

Next ►

For Privacy Act and Paperwork Reduction Act Notice, see the back of the Payment Voucher. Cat. No. 11234O Form **940** (2017)

Source: U.S. Department of the Treasury, Internal Revenue Service, Form 940. Washington, DC: 2017.

(continued)

EXHIBIT 10-7 *(concluded)*

850212

Name *(not your trade name)*	**Employer identification number (EIN)**

Part 5: Report your FUTA tax liability by quarter only if line 12 is more than $500. If not, go to Part 6.

16 **Report the amount of your FUTA tax liability for each quarter; do NOT enter the amount you deposited. If you had no liability for a quarter, leave the line blank.**

16a **1st quarter** (January 1 – March 31) . . . . **16a** ______ .

16b **2nd quarter** (April 1 – June 30) . . . . **16b** ______ .

16c **3rd quarter** (July 1 – September 30) . . . . **16c** ______ .

16d **4th quarter** (October 1 – December 31) . . . . **16d** ______ .

17 **Total tax liability for the year** (lines 16a + 16b + 16c + 16d = line 17) **17** ______ . **Total must equal line 12.**

Part 6: May we speak with your third-party designee?

Do you want to allow an employee, a paid tax preparer, or another person to discuss this return with the IRS? See the instructions for details.

☐ **Yes.** Designee's name and phone number

Select a 5-digit Personal Identification Number (PIN) to use when talking to IRS

☒ **No.**

Part 7: Sign here. You MUST complete both pages of this form and SIGN it.

Under penalties of perjury, I declare that I have examined this return, including accompanying schedules and statements, and to the best of my knowledge and belief, it is true, correct, and complete, and that no part of any payment made to a state unemployment fund claimed as a credit was, or is to be, deducted from the payments made to employees. Declaration of preparer (other than taxpayer) is based on all information of which preparer has any knowledge.

✗ Sign your name here

Print your name here

Print your title here

Date / /

Best daytime phone

Paid Preparer Use Only

Check if you are self-employed ☐

Preparer's name		PTIN	
Preparer's signature		Date	/ /
Firm's name (or yours if self-employed)		EIN	
Address		Phone	
City	State	ZIP code	

EXHIBIT 10-8

SCHEDULE H (Form 1040) Department of the Treasury Internal Revenue Service (99)	**Household Employment Taxes** (For Social Security, Medicare, Withheld Income, and Federal Unemployment (FUTA) Taxes) ▶ **Attach to Form 1040, 1040NR, 1040-SS, or 1041.** ▶ **Go to *www.irs.gov/ScheduleH* for instructions and the latest information.**	OMB No. 1545-1971 **2017** Attachment Sequence No. **44**

Name of employer	Social security number
Max and Abagail Jones	**412-34-5670**
	Employer identification number

Calendar year taxpayers having no household employees in 2017 don't have to complete this form for 2017.

A Did you pay **any one** household employee cash wages of $2,000 or more in 2017? (If any household employee was your spouse, your child under age 21, your parent, or anyone under age 18, see the line A instructions before you answer this question.)

☑ **Yes.** Skip lines B and C and go to line 1.
☐ **No.** Go to line B.

B Did you withhold federal income tax during 2017 for any household employee?

☐ **Yes.** Skip line C and go to line 7.
☐ **No.** Go to line C.

C Did you pay **total** cash wages of $1,000 or more in **any** calendar **quarter** of 2016 or 2017 to **all** household employees? (**Don't** count cash wages paid in 2016 or 2017 to your spouse, your child under age 21, or your parent.)

☐ **No. Stop.** Don't file this schedule.
☐ **Yes.** Skip lines 1–9 and go to line 10.

Part I **Social Security, Medicare, and Federal Income Taxes**

1	Total cash wages subject to social security tax	1	4,800		
2	Social security tax. Multiply line 1 by 12.4% (0.124)			2	595
3	Total cash wages subject to Medicare tax	3	4,800		
4	Medicare tax. Multiply line 3 by 2.9% (0.029)			4	139
5	Total cash wages subject to Additional Medicare Tax withholding	5	0		
6	Additional Medicare Tax withholding. Multiply line 5 by 0.9% (0.009)			6	0
7	Federal income tax withheld, if any			7	0
8	**Total social security, Medicare, and federal income taxes.** Add lines 2, 4, 6, and 7			8	734

9 Did you pay **total** cash wages of $1,000 or more in **any** calendar **quarter** of 2016 or 2017 to **all** household employees? (**Don't** count cash wages paid in 2016 or 2017 to your spouse, your child under age 21, or your parent.)

☐ **No. Stop.** Include the amount from line 8 above on Form 1040, line 60a. If you're not required to file Form 1040, see the line 9 instructions.

☑ **Yes.** Go to line 10.

For Privacy Act and Paperwork Reduction Act Notice, see the instructions. Cat. No. 12187K **Schedule H (Form 1040) 2017**

Source: U.S. Department of the Treasury, Internal Revenue Service, Schedule H (Form 1040). Washington, DC: 2017.

(continued)

EXHIBIT 10-8 *(concluded)*

Schedule H (Form 1040) 2017 Page **2**

Part II Federal Unemployment (FUTA) Tax

			Yes	No
10	Did you pay unemployment contributions to only one state? If you paid contributions to a credit reduction state, see instructions and check **"No."**	10	✓	
11	Did you pay all state unemployment contributions for 2017 by April 17, 2018? Fiscal year filers, see instructions	11	✓	
12	Were all wages that are taxable for FUTA tax also taxable for your state's unemployment tax?	12	✓	

Next: If you checked the **"Yes"** box on **all** the lines above, complete Section A.
If you checked the **"No"** box on **any** of the lines above, skip Section A and complete Section B.

Section A

13 Name of the state where you paid unemployment contributions ▶ **New Mexico**

14	Contributions paid to your state unemployment fund	14	480		
15	Total cash wages subject to FUTA tax			15	4,800
16	**FUTA tax.** Multiply line 15 by 0.6% (0.006). Enter the result here, skip Section B, and go to line 25			16	29

Section B

17 Complete all columns below that apply (if you need more space, see instructions):

(a) Name of state	(b) Taxable wages (as defined in state act)	(c) State experience rate period From	To	(d) State experience rate	(e) Multiply col. (b) by 0.054	(f) Multiply col. (b) by col. (d)	(g) Subtract col. (f) from col. (e). If zero or less, enter -0-.	(h) Contributions paid to state unemployment fund

18	Totals			18	
19	Add columns (g) and (h) of line 18	19			
20	Total cash wages subject to FUTA tax (see the line 15 instructions)			20	
21	Multiply line 20 by 6.0% (0.060)			21	
22	Multiply line 20 by 5.4% (0.054)	22			
23	Enter the **smaller** of line 19 or line 22 (If you paid state unemployment contributions late or you're in a credit reduction state, see instructions and check here) ☐			23	
24	**FUTA tax.** Subtract line 23 from line 21. Enter the result here and go to line 25			24	

Part III Total Household Employment Taxes

25	Enter the amount from line 8. If you checked the **"Yes"** box on line C of page 1, enter -0-	25	734
26	Add line 16 (or line 24) and line 25	26	763

27 Are you required to file Form 1040?

☑ **Yes. Stop.** Include the amount from line 26 above on Form 1040, line 60a. **Don't** complete Part IV below.

☐ **No.** You may have to complete Part IV. See instructions for details.

Part IV Address and Signature — Complete this part **only** if required. See the line 27 instructions.

Address (number and street) or P.O. box if mail isn't delivered to street address | Apt., room, or suite no.

City, town or post office, state, and ZIP code

Under penalties of perjury, I declare that I have examined this schedule, including accompanying statements, and to the best of my knowledge and belief, it is true, correct, and complete. No part of any payment made to a state unemployment fund claimed as a credit was, or is to be, deducted from the payments to employees. Declaration of preparer (other than taxpayer) is based on all information of which preparer has any knowledge.

▶ Employer's signature ▶ Date

Paid Preparer Use Only	Print/Type preparer's name	Preparer's signature	Date	Check ☐ if self-employed	PTIN
	Firm's name ▶			Firm's EIN ▶	
	Firm's address ▶			Phone no.	

Schedule H (Form 1040) 2017

EXAMPLE 10-16

Max and Abigail Jones employed a household worker for the entire year. They paid the household worker $400 per month for a total of $4,800 for the year. For purposes of this example, assume they live in New Mexico, have a state reporting number of J1234, and have paid $480 of state unemployment taxes for this worker.

Max and Abigail paid cash wages of $4,800 for the year and answered yes to Question A on Schedule H.

Part I Calculations

Social security tax	$4,800 × 12.4% =	$595
Medicare tax	$4,800 × 2.9% =	139
Total taxes		$734

Part II Calculations

Answer yes to Questions 9, 10, 11, and 12 and enter NM on line 13. On line 14, enter $480. All wages were subject to FUTA tax, so line 13 is $4,800. Calculate the amount for line 16.

Part III Calculations

Add the FUTA tax and the FICA taxes for a total amount due and reportable on Form 1040, line 60a.

CONCEPT CHECK 10-4— LO 10-4

1. A self-employed taxpayer is treated both as an employee and an employer and thus pays a combined total of 15.3% for FICA taxes. True or false?
2. What is the effective tax rate for FUTA, provided that employers pay into their state SUTA programs on a timely basis?
   a. 0.6%.
   b. 6.2%.
   c. 5.4%.
   d. 10%.
3. Who can use Schedule H? ____________________
4. Taxpayers who employ household workers are subject to payroll taxes under what conditions?
   ____
   ____

EMPLOYER PAYROLL REPORTING REQUIREMENTS INCLUDING FORMS W-2 AND W-3

LO 10-5

Employer Payroll Reporting to Employees

Employers must annually report payroll-related information to employees and to the IRS.[18] The information is reported to both parties on Form W-2, Wage and Tax Statement.

The W-2 is a multipart form labeled Copy A, B, C, D, 1, and 2. Each labeled part is used for a different purpose. The employer sends the employee Copies 1 and 2 (filed with the employee's state and local tax returns), Copy B (filed with the employee's federal tax return—see Exhibit 10-9), and Copy C (retained by the employee). The employer retains Copy D. The employee uses the information from the W-2 to prepare his or her federal and state income tax returns. The employer must mail each employee his or her W-2 copies no later than January 31.

Both paper and electronically filed W-2 and W-3 must be filed with the Social Security Administration (SSA) no later than January 31, 2018. Also, both paper and electronically filed 1099-MISC must be filed with the IRS no later than January 31, 2018. The SSA uses Copy A to track wages for social security purposes. The SSA also transmits the W-2 information to the IRS. Employers with 250 or more employees are required to file their W-2s electronically. The employer completes Form 4419, Application for Filing Information Returns Electronically (not shown here), and files it with the IRS.

[18] IRC § 6051.

EXHIBIT 10-9

a Employee's social security number 412-34-5670	OMB No. 1545-0008	Safe, accurate, FAST! Use IRS e-file	Visit the IRS website at www.irs.gov/efile
b Employer identification number (EIN) 36-3456789		1 Wages, tips, other compensation 130,000.00	2 Federal income tax withheld 27,603.75
c Employer's name, address, and ZIP code Flawless Company 125 Main Street Mason City, IA		3 Social security wages 127,200.00	4 Social security tax withheld 7,886.40
		5 Medicare wages and tips 130,000.00	6 Medicare tax withheld 1,885.00
		7 Social security tips	8 Allocated tips
d Control number		9 Verification code	10 Dependent care benefits
e Employee's first name and initial Last name Suff. Nichole Luketic 8965 West 178th Place Mason City, IA		11 Nonqualified plans	12a See instructions for box 12
		13 Statutory employee ☐ Retirement plan ☐ Third-party sick pay ☐	12b
		14 Other	12c
f Employee's address and ZIP code			12d

15 State	Employer's state ID number	16 State wages, tips, etc.	17 State income tax	18 Local wages, tips, etc.	19 Local income tax	20 Locality name

Form **W-2 Wage and Tax Statement** 2017 — Department of the Treasury—Internal Revenue Service

Copy B—To Be Filed With Employee's FEDERAL Tax Return.
This information is being furnished to the Internal Revenue Service.

Source: U.S. Department of the Treasury, Internal Revenue Service, Form W-2 Wages and Tax Statement. Washington, DC: 2017.

Form W-3 (Transmittal of Wage and Tax Statements) accompanies the W-2s sent by the employer (see Exhibit 10-10). The W-3 summarizes the information contained on the attached W-2s. The totals on the W-3 must equal the accumulated amounts on the W-2s. Recording payroll and preparing the governmental forms is time-consuming, so many employers use accountants or payroll services to provide these services and to prepare year-end W-2 and W-3 information in a timely manner.

EXAMPLE 10-17

Flawless Company had four employees. Selected 2017 information for the company is as follows:

Total wages, tips, and other compensation	=$480,000.00
Total social security wages	=$427,200.00
Total Medicare wages	=$480,000.00
Total federal income tax withheld	=$102,631.80
Total social security tax withheld	=$ 26,486.40
Total Medicare Xtax withheld	=$ 6,960.00

One of the employees is Nichole Luketic, who has the following payroll information for 2017:

Wages, tips, and other compensation	=$130,000.00
Federal income tax withheld	=$ 27,603.75
Social security tax withheld	=$ 7,886.40
Medicare tax withheld	=$ 1,885.00

Exhibit 10-9 is the completed 2017 Form W-2 for Nichole Luketic, and Exhibit 10-10 is the completed 2017 Form W-3 for Flawless Company.

EXHIBIT 10-10

33333	a Control number	For Official Use Only ▶ OMB No. 1545-0008	
b Kind of Payer (Check one): 941 [X] Military [ ] 943 [ ] 944 [ ] CT-1 [ ] Hshld. emp. [ ] Medicare govt. emp. [ ]		Kind of Employer (Check one): None apply [X] 501c non-govt. [ ] State/local non-501c [ ] State/local 501c [ ] Federal govt. [ ]	Third-party sick pay (Check if applicable) [ ]
c Total number of Forms W-2: 4	d Establishment number	1 Wages, tips, other compensation: 480,000.00	2 Federal income tax withheld: 102,631.80
e Employer identification number (EIN): 36-3456789		3 Social security wages: 427,200.00	4 Social security tax withheld: 26,486.40
f Employer's name: Flawless Company		5 Medicare wages and tips: 480,000.00	6 Medicare tax withheld: 6,960.00
125 Main Street Mason City, IA		7 Social security tips	8 Allocated tips
		9	10 Dependent care benefits
g Employer's address and ZIP code		11 Nonqualified plans	12a Deferred compensation
h Other EIN used this year		13 For third-party sick pay use only	12b
15 State / Employer's state ID number		14 Income tax withheld by payer of third-party sick pay	
16 State wages, tips, etc.	17 State income tax	18 Local wages, tips, etc.	19 Local income tax
Employer's contact person		Employer's telephone number	For Official Use Only
Employer's fax number		Employer's email address	

Under penalties of perjury, I declare that I have examined this return and accompanying documents and, to the best of my knowledge and belief, they are true, correct, and complete.

Signature ▶ Title ▶ Date ▶

Form **W-3** **Transmittal of Wage and Tax Statements** 2017 Department of the Treasury Internal Revenue Service

Source: U.S. Department of the Treasury, Internal Revenue Service, Form W-3 Transmittal of Wage and Tax Statements. Washington, DC: 2017.

An employer prepares a Form W-2C (Statement of Corrected Income and Tax Amounts) to correct a W-2 and provides appropriate copies to the employee. The employer files Copy A with the Social Security Administration, and a Form W-3C (Transmittal of Corrected Income and Tax Statements) accompanies Copy A to the Social Security Administration. These forms can be accessed through the IRS Web site.

The following penalties are imposed on employers for incorrect or late filing of W-2s:

- A W-2 filed within 30 days of the due date: $50 per return ($536,000 maximum penalty/$187,500 for small businesses).
- A W-2 filed between 30 days late and August 1: $100 per return ($1,609,000 maximum penalty/$536,000 for small businesses).
- A W-2 filed after August 1: $260 per return ($3,218,500 maximum penalty/$1,072,500 for small businesses).
- Penalty of $530 per return for intentional disregard of filing requirements, providing payees with incorrect statements, or reporting incorrect information (no maximum penalty).

CONCEPT CHECK 10-5— LO 10-5

1. The employee uses the information from a W-2 to prepare his or her federal, state, and local (if applicable) tax returns. True or false?
2. Where and when must the employer send Copy A of the W-2 form?
3. Explain the process by which an employer corrects an employee's W-2.
4. What are the maximum penalty amounts per return imposed on a company that prepares incorrect W-2s?

SUPPLEMENTAL WAGE PAYMENTS, BACKUP WITHHOLDING, FORM W-9, ESTIMATED TAX PAYMENTS, AND FORM 1040-ES

LO 10-6

Supplemental Wage Payments

Supplemental wages are compensation paid in addition to an employee's regular wages and include vacation pay, commissions, bonuses, accumulated sick pay, severance pay, taxable fringe benefits, and expense allowances paid under a nonaccountable plan. The amount withheld from these supplemental payments depends on whether the employer accounts for the payment separately from regular wages.

Supplemental wages can be combined with regular wages, and the total amount will be taxed as if it were a single payment for a regular payroll period. If the supplemental payments are identified separately from regular wages, the federal income tax withholding method depends on whether the employer withholds income tax from the employee's regular wages.

1. Method 1: If taxes are withheld from the employee's wages:
   a. Withhold a flat 25% (no other percentage is allowed), or
   b. Add the supplemental and regular wages for the period and figure the income tax withholding as if the total were a single payment. Subtract the tax already withheld from regular wages. Withhold the remaining tax from the supplemental wages.
2. Method 2: If taxes are not withheld from the employee's wages:
   a. Add the supplemental and regular wages and calculate the withholding tax as in part *b* of method 1. (This could occur when the value of the employee's withholding allowances claimed on the W-4 is more than the wages.)

Regardless of the method used to withhold income tax on supplemental wages, the wages are subject to social security, Medicare, and FUTA taxes as well as state withholding (if applicable) and SUTA.

EXAMPLE 10-18

Monique's base salary is $2,000, and she is paid on the first of the month. She is single and claims one withholding allowance. On June 1, 2017, she is paid $2,000, and $181.73 (using the percentage method) is withheld from her earnings. In July 2017, she receives a commission of $1,000, which is included in her regular wages. The amount of withholding is based on a total of $3,000. The amount withheld from her wages is $331.73 (using the percentage method).

EXAMPLE 10-19

Riva is paid a base salary of $2,000 on the first of each month. She is single and claims one withholding allowance. For the pay period of August 1, 2017, the amount of tax withheld (using the percentage method) is $181.73. On August 19, 2017, she receives a bonus of $1,000. Using method 1*b,* the amount subject to withholding is $3,000. The amount of withholding on the combined $3,000 is $331.73. Subtract the amount already withheld for the month. The difference of $150.00 is the amount to be withheld from the bonus payment.

EXAMPLE 10-20

Using the information from Example 10-19, the employer elects to use a flat rate of 25% of withholding on the bonus. In this situation, the amount of withholding on the bonus is $1,000 × 25% = $250.00.

Backup Withholding

Generally an employer must withhold 28% of certain taxable payments if the payee fails to furnish the employer with a correct taxpayer identification number (TIN). Payments subject to backup withholding include interest, dividends, rents, royalties, commissions, nonemployee compensation, and certain other payments made in the course of a trade or business. In addition, certain payments made by brokers and barter exchanges and certain payments made by fishing boat operators are subject to backup withholding.[19]

Payments a taxpayer receives are subject to backup withholding under these circumstances:

- The taxpayer does not furnish a TIN to the requester.
- The IRS tells the requester that a taxpayer has furnished an incorrect TIN.
- The IRS informs the payee that he or she is subject to backup withholding due to nonreporting of any interest and dividends on a tax return.
- The payee did not certify to the requester that he or she was not subject to backup withholding.

Backup withholding does not apply to wages, pensions, annuities, IRAs, Section 404(k) distributions from an employee stock ownership plan (ESOP), Health Savings Accounts, long-term care benefits, and real estate transactions. The IRS lists specific payees exempt from backup withholding as well as specific types of payments that are exempt from backup withholding. To avoid this backup withholding, payees must furnish a correct TIN to the payer via Form W-9.

Form W-9

Anyone who is required to file an information return with the IRS must supply the payer a correct TIN to report transactions such as income paid to the taxpayer, a real estate transaction, any mortgage interest the taxpayer paid, and contributions to an IRA. The form used to report this information to the payer is a Form W-9.

A U.S. person (or resident alien) uses Form W-9 to

- Certify that the TIN the taxpayer is giving is correct.
- Certify that the taxpayer is not subject to backup withholding.
- Claim exemption from backup withholding if the taxpayer is a U.S. exempt payee.

For federal purposes, a U.S. person includes but is not limited to

- An individual who is a citizen or resident of the United States.
- A partnership, corporation, company, or association created or organized in the United States or under the laws of the United States.
- Any estate (other than a foreign estate) or trust.

Special rules apply to partnerships, corporations, associations, and estates. There are 15 provisions for exemption from backup withholding; refer to the W-9 instructions located at the IRS Web site (www.irs.gov) for a complete list. Failure to furnish a correct TIN to a requester can result in a penalty of $50 for each failure unless the failure is due to reasonable cause, not willful neglect. If a taxpayer makes a false statement with no reasonable basis that results in no backup withholding, the taxpayer is subject to a $500 penalty. Willfully falsifying certifications may subject the taxpayer to criminal penalties including fines and imprisonment.[20] For example, Joe Zonca has a landscaping and snow removal service. One of his clients, Village Apartments, requires that all vendors complete Form W-9. Joe is a sole proprietor, social security number 412-34-5670, and he resides at 632 Main Street, Savoy, IL 61874. See Exhibit 10-11 for a completed Form W-9.

[19] Publication 15, page 5.

[20] IRS instructions for Requester of Form W-9 and Form W-9.

EXHIBIT 10-11

Form **W-9**
(Rev. December 2014)
Department of the Treasury
Internal Revenue Service

Request for Taxpayer Identification Number and Certification

Give Form to the requester. Do not send to the IRS.

Print or type
See Specific Instructions on page 2.

1 Name (as shown on your income tax return). Name is required on this line; do not leave this line blank.
Joe Zonca

2 Business name/disregarded entity name, if different from above

3 Check appropriate box for federal tax classification; check only **one** of the following seven boxes:
☑ Individual/sole proprietor or single-member LLC ☐ C Corporation ☐ S Corporation ☐ Partnership ☐ Trust/estate
☐ Limited liability company. Enter the tax classification (C=C corporation, S=S corporation, P=partnership) ▶
Note. For a single-member LLC that is disregarded, do not check LLC; check the appropriate box in the line above for the tax classification of the single-member owner.
☐ Other (see instructions) ▶

4 Exemptions (codes apply only to certain entities, not individuals; see instructions on page 3):
Exempt payee code (if any)
Exemption from FATCA reporting code (if any)
(Applies to accounts maintained outside the U.S.)

5 Address (number, street, and apt. or suite no.)
632 Main Street

Requester's name and address (optional)

6 City, state, and ZIP code
Savoy, IL 61874

7 List account number(s) here (optional)

Part I Taxpayer Identification Number (TIN)

Enter your TIN in the appropriate box. The TIN provided must match the name given on line 1 to avoid backup withholding. For individuals, this is generally your social security number (SSN). However, for a resident alien, sole proprietor, or disregarded entity, see the Part I instructions on page 3. For other entities, it is your employer identification number (EIN). If you do not have a number, see *How to get a TIN* on page 3.

Note. If the account is in more than one name, see the instructions for line 1 and the chart on page 4 for guidelines on whose number to enter.

Social security number
4 1 2 – 3 4 – 5 6 7 0

or

Employer identification number
–

Part II Certification

Under penalties of perjury, I certify that:

1. The number shown on this form is my correct taxpayer identification number (or I am waiting for a number to be issued to me); and
2. I am not subject to backup withholding because: (a) I am exempt from backup withholding, or (b) I have not been notified by the Internal Revenue Service (IRS) that I am subject to backup withholding as a result of a failure to report all interest or dividends, or (c) the IRS has notified me that I am no longer subject to backup withholding; and
3. I am a U.S. citizen or other U.S. person (defined below); and
4. The FATCA code(s) entered on this form (if any) indicating that I am exempt from FATCA reporting is correct.

Certification instructions. You must cross out item 2 above if you have been notified by the IRS that you are currently subject to backup withholding because you have failed to report all interest and dividends on your tax return. For real estate transactions, item 2 does not apply. For mortgage interest paid, acquisition or abandonment of secured property, cancellation of debt, contributions to an individual retirement arrangement (IRA), and generally, payments other than interest and dividends, you are not required to sign the certification, but you must provide your correct TIN. See the instructions on page 3.

Sign Here **Signature of U.S. person ▶** **Date ▶**

Source: U.S. Department of the Treasury, Internal Revenue Service, Form W-9. Washington, DC: 2014.

Estimated Tax Payments and Form 1040-ES

Estimated tax is the method individuals use to pay tax on income that is taxable but not subject to payroll withholding such as earnings from self-employment, interest, dividends, rents, and alimony. In most cases, a taxpayer must make estimated tax payments if he or she expects to owe at least $1,000 in tax and the taxpayer expects his or her withholding and credits to be less than the smaller of

- 90% of the tax shown on the taxpayer's current return.
- 100% of the tax shown on the taxpayer's prior year tax return if the AGI shown on that return is less than or equal to $150,000 or, if married filing separately, is less than or equal to $75,000.
- 110% of the tax shown on the taxpayer's prior year tax return if the AGI shown on that return is more than $150,000 or, if married filing separately, is more than $75,000.

If a taxpayer meets one of the percentage criteria just noted, it is said that he or she has met the "safe harbor" rule. *Safe harbor* is a term used to describe a provision of the IRC that protects a taxpayer from penalty.

EXHIBIT 10-12

Form **1040-ES** Department of the Treasury Internal Revenue Service	**2017 Estimated Tax**	**Payment Voucher 1**	OMB No. 1545-0074
File only if you are making a payment of estimated tax by check or money order. Mail this voucher with your check or money order payable to **"United States Treasury."** Write your social security number and "2017 Form 1040-ES" on your check or money order. Do not send cash. Enclose, but do not staple or attach, your payment with this voucher.		**Calendar year—Due April 18, 2017** Amount of estimated tax you are paying by check or money order.	Dollars 441 Cents 25

Print or type

Your first name and initial	Your last name	Your social security number
Ramon	Juarez	412-34-5670
If joint payment, complete for spouse		
Spouse's first name and initial	Spouse's last name	Spouse's social security number
Address (number, street, and apt. no.) 1234 Main Street		
City, state, and ZIP code. (If a foreign address, enter city, also complete spaces below.) Savoy, IL 61874		
Foreign country name	Foreign province/county	Foreign postal code

For Privacy Act and Paperwork Reduction Act Notice, see instructions. **Form 1040-ES (2017)**

Source: U.S. Department of the Treasury, Internal Revenue Service, Form 1040-ES. Washington, DC: 2017.

The estimated tax payments can be paid in total by April 15 (provided this date is a business day—otherwise the next business day) or in four equal amounts by the following dates:

- 1st payment—April 18, 2017.
- 2nd payment—June 15, 2017.
- 3rd payment—September 15, 2017.
- 4th payment—January 16, 2018.

Taxpayers make estimated payments using Form 1040-ES (see Exhibit 10-12). The taxpayer submits the coupon for the appropriate period. It is important to remember to include the correct taxpayer identification number (social security number) and remit the payment to the address given in the instructions. This form is also accessible on the IRS Web site. Using information from Example 10-21, Form 1040-ES is completed in Exhibit 10-12. It shows the first-quarter estimated payment due from Ramon. The total amount of all the estimated payments appears on line 65 of Form 1040 in the Payments section.

EXAMPLE 10-21

Ramon Juarez works as a professor at a local college. He also sells real estate as a part-time business. During 2017 Ramon earned $87,500 from the college. He also earned $15,000 in commissions for selling real estate. He operates his real estate business as a sole proprietorship. Ramon estimates that he will owe $1,765 more in taxes for 2017. He will make an estimated tax payment of $1,765 using Form 1040-ES. Assuming his self-employment earnings are consistent throughout the year, he would make estimated tax payments based on the commissions he earned each period. In this case, if he earned $3,750 in commissions each period, he could remit $441.25 ($1,765/4) to the IRS on each of the due dates.

CONCEPT CHECK 10-6—LO 10-6

1. Describe the two methods that are available to calculate the withholding from supplemental payments.
2. Payments subject to backup withholding are withheld at a flat tax rate of 28% if the payee fails to furnish the payer with a correct TIN. True or false?
3. What is a Form W-9?
4. What is the penalty for failing to furnish a correct TIN to a requester?
5. Taxpayers use Form 1040-ES to remit additional amounts to the IRS so that they receive a refund when they file Form 1040. True or false?

Summary

LO 10-1: Explain the tax issues associated with payroll and Form 1040.

- Withholding taxes are imposed on taxpayers to help fund government operations using a *pay-as-you-go* system.
- Form W-2 is the starting point for Form 1040.

LO 10-2: Calculate federal income tax withholding, social security, and Medicare taxes on wages and tips.

- Withholding of taxes is an approximation of the proportionate share of total tax liability the employee will owe to the federal government.
- Form W-4 is completed by the employee to list filing status and claim withholding allowances. This information is used by the employer to calculate withholding.
- Two withholding methods are allowed: the wage bracket method and the percentage method.
- FICA taxes encompass social security taxes and Medicare taxes.
- Social security tax withholding is 6.2% of each employee's wages up to a maximum of $127,200 of wages for 2017. Medicare withholding is 1.45% of all wages.
- The employer must pay an additional amount equal to the amount withheld from employees.
- The employer must withhold a 0.9% additional Medicare tax on wages paid in excess of $200,000. This is an employee-only tax.
- The 0.9% additional Medicare tax is assessed on combined wage and self-employment income in excess of the threshold amounts. A loss on self-employment is excluded from this calculation.

LO 10-3: Describe the rules for reporting and paying payroll taxes, including deposit penalties and Form 941.

- Employers must make payroll tax deposits of amounts withheld from employees' wages.
- Employers typically deposit taxes monthly or semiweekly. A lookback period generally determines the frequency of required deposits.
- Employers must make timely deposits through the Electronic Federal Tax Payment System (EFTPS).
- Payroll taxes not paid on a timely basis are subject to deposit penalties that range from 2% to 15%.
- Form 941 is used to report amounts withheld for income, social security, and Medicare taxes for the quarter. It is due by the end of the month following the end of a quarter.
- With IRS permission, Form 944 can be filed for small business employers, or there can be an election to file quarterly Forms 941.

LO 10-4: Calculate self-employment taxes, unemployment taxes, Form 940, taxes for household employees, and Schedule H.

- Self-employment taxes are based on net earnings of $400 or more generated by a sole proprietor taxpayer. The rate paid is based on both the employee and employer portions.
- 50% of self-employment taxes is a permitted *for* AGI deduction on Form 1040.
- The federal unemployment tax (FUTA) is 6.0% of wages up to $7,000. The maximum credit for state unemployment taxes (SUTA) is 5.4%, reducing the amount due to the IRS to 0.6%.
- Form 940 is filed annually by the employer to report and reconcile FUTA liabilities and payments.
- Household workers are considered employees subject to federal income, social security, Medicare, and FUTA taxes.
- Schedule H reports tax information for household workers. It is filed with Form 1040.

LO 10-5: Determine employer payroll reporting requirements, including Forms W-2 and W-3.	• Employers report wages earned and taxes withheld to employees on Form W-2. • A Form W-2 must be given to each employee no later than January 31 with a copy to the Social Security Administration by January 31 as well. • Form W-3 is a transmittal form that summarizes all employee W-2s prepared by a company and is due no later than January 31.
LO 10-6: Explain supplemental wage payments, backup withholding, Form W-9, estimated tax payments, and Form 1040-ES.	• Supplemental wages are compensation paid in addition to an employee's regular wages. • Withholding on supplemental wages can be calculated using one of two methods: using a flat tax rate of 25% or combining the supplemental wages with regular wages. • Anyone required to file an information return with the IRS must supply the payer a correct taxpayer ID number (TIN) using Form W-9. • Failure of a taxpayer to furnish a TIN to a requester can result in a $50 penalty. A taxpayer making a false statement that results in no backup withholding is subject to a civil penalty of $500. • Failure to provide a correct TIN can result in 28% withholding on certain taxable payments. • Form 1040-ES is used when a taxpayer must make tax payments for estimated taxes due. • Estimated payments are required if unpaid tax liability ≥ $1,000 and withholding and credits do not meet certain "safe harbor" thresholds. • Estimated taxes are due April 15, June 15, September 15, and January 15 or on the next business day if any of these dates falls on a weekend or holiday.

Discussion Questions connect

All applicable discussion questions are available with ***Connect***©

LO 10-2 1. What type of compensation is subject to employer withholding?

LO 10-2 2. Who completes Form W-4, and what is its purpose? What information does it provide to employers?

LO 10-2 3. If a taxpayer makes $30,000 per year, will the annual withholding differ, depending on whether the taxpayer is paid weekly, semimonthly, or monthly? Explain.

LO 10-2 4. If a taxpayer works more than one job, will the withholding from the various jobs necessarily cover his or her tax liability? Explain.

LO 10-2 5. In addition to federal tax withholding, what other taxes are employers required to withhold from an employee's paycheck? How are the calculations made?

LO 10-2 6. Who pays FICA? What are the percentages and limits on the payments?

LO 10-2 7. When are employees required to report tips to their employer? Are tips subject to the same withholding requirements as regular salary?

LO 10-2 8. What are the reporting tip-requirements for large food and beverage establishments?

LO 10-3 9. When must employers make payroll tax deposits?

LO 10-3 10. What is a *lookback* period?

LO 10-3 11. When must monthly and semiweekly schedule depositors make their deposits? What taxes must be deposited?

LO 10-3 12. What are the penalties for not making timely payroll deposits?

LO 10-3 13. If a business fails to make payroll deposits, who is held responsible?

LO 10-3 14. How often must employers report payroll taxes to the IRS? What form must the employer file?

LO 10-3 15. Why are self-employed taxpayers allowed a deduction for self-employment tax in determining adjusted gross income (AGI)?

LO 10-4 16. What is the FUTA tax, and at what percentage is it assessed?

LO 10-4 17. What individuals are subject to the payroll taxes on household employees?

LO 10-4 18. How are household payroll taxes reported? When are they due?

LO 10-5 19. How does an employer report wages to the employee, the federal government, and the Social Security Administration? When is this notification due?

LO 10-5 20. What are the penalties imposed on employers for filing incorrect W-2s?

LO 10-6 21. What are supplemental wage payments?

LO 10-6 22. Explain the two methods for income tax withholding on supplemental wage payments.

LO 10-6 23. Explain the provisions of backup withholding and the conditions under which an employer must comply with these provisions.

____

____

____

LO 10-6 24. What is a Form W-9? Why must this form be filed?

____

____

____

LO 10-6 25. Explain the purpose of Form 1040-ES. Under what conditions are taxpayers required to file 1040-ES? When is Form 1040-ES filed?

____

____

____

Multiple-Choice Questions connect

All applicable multiple-choice questions are available with ***Connect***©

LO 10-2 26. Employees claim withholding allowances on Form W-4. Each withholding allowance claimed lowers their annual withholding base by what amount for calendar year 2017?

a. $3,900.

b. $3,950.

c. $4,000.

d. $4,050.

LO 10-2 27. Ely is single and is paid $1,190 per week and claims one allowance. What is the amount of federal income tax withheld on Ely's gross wages for the week? Use the wage bracket table in the Appendix at the end of the chapter.

a. $184.

b. $186.

c. $203.

d. $206.

LO 10-2 28. Marla is married, is paid $2,565 semimonthly, and claims four withholding allowances. What is the amount of federal income tax withheld on Marla's gross wages for the semimonthly period? Use the percentage method table in the Appendix at the end of the chapter.

a. $190.57.

b. $197.50.

c. $200.51.

d. $207.56.

LO 10-2 29. Erica earned $128,800 during 2017. How much will her employer withhold from her, in total, for FICA taxes?

a. $9,069.60.

b. $9,214.60.

c. $9,741.00.

d. $9,754.00.

LO 10-2 30. Adenike has two jobs and earned $110,000 from her first job and $20,000 from her second job. How much total FICA taxes will Adenike have withheld from her wages from working two jobs?

a. $9,730.80.

b. $9,732.00.

c. $9,771.40.

d. $9,945.00.

LO 10-2 31. Carlos earned a total of $225,000 for 2017. How much in FICA tax will his employer be required to withhold in his name?

a. $10,834.50.

b. $11,148.90.

c. $11,373.90.

d. $12,029.10.

LO 10-2 32. Dewoun has two jobs, and both employers withheld FICA tax. From his first job, he earned $102,100, and from his second job, he earned $28,200. How much can Dewoun claim as an additional payment on his Form 1040 as excess social security paid in 2017?

a. $0.

b. $173.60.

c. $192.20.

d. $204.60.

LO 10-2 33. Carmen earned $75 in tips in September. When must she inform her employer of her tips on Form 4070 for federal income tax and FICA withholding purposes?

a. By September 30.

b. By October 10.

c. By October 31.

d. She is not subject to payroll taxes on tips of less than $80 in any one month.

LO 10-2 34. In a large food or beverage establishment, any tip shortfall from a directly tipped employee is recorded on the employee's W-2 as

a. W-2 box 8—Allocated tips.

b. W-2 box 14—Other.

c. W-2 box 1—Wages, tips, other compensation.

d. W-2 box 7—Social security tips.

LO 10-3 35. An employer will prepare Schedule B of Form 941 under which circumstances?

a. Line 12 on the Form 941 is less than $2,500.

b. The employer is a semimonthly depositor.

c. The employer is a monthly depositor.

d. The employer is a semiweekly depositor.

LO 10-3 36. Lauer Company started its business on July 25, 2017. On August 11 it paid wages for the first time and accumulated a tax liability of $48,000. On Friday, August 18, it incurred a tax liability of $52,000. How is Lauer Company treated as a depositor?

a. Monthly because new companies do not have a lookback period.

b. Semiweekly because its accumulated tax liability is $100,000.

c. Monthly because its accumulated tax liability is not more than $100,000 on any one day.

d. Semiweekly for this pay period only and then monthly for the remainder of the year.

LO 10-3 37. What is the penalty for sending a required tax payment (unless specifically allowed) directly to the IRS?

a. 2%.

b. 5%.

c. 10%.

d. 15%.

LO 10-3 38. A semiweekly schedule depositor's payroll period ends and is paid on Friday, June 24. The depositor (employer) must deposit the federal taxes for this pay period on or before

a. The following Wednesday.

b. The following Friday.

c. June 25.

d. June 29.

LO 10-3 39. To what amount of employer tax accumulation does the one-day deposit rule apply?

a. $75,000.

b. $100,000.

c. More than $100,000.

d. An amount between $75,000 and $99,999.

LO 10-4 40. Employers are required to deposit FUTA taxes when their liability exceeds

a. $100.

b. $500.

c. $1,000.

d. $1,500.

LO 10-4 41. Household employees are subject to FICA withholding if they are paid at least what amount during 2017?

a. $1,500.

b. $1,800.

c. $1,900.

d. $2,000.

LO 10-4 42. Employers pay a maximum federal unemployment tax of 6.0% on how much of an employee's taxable wages for 2017?

a. $1,800.

b. $3,800.

c. $5,800.

d. $7,000.

LO 10-2, 10-4 43. Carlos has two jobs; he is an attorney (not a partner) in a law firm and he has a small legal practice (sole proprietorship) providing real estate legal services. How does he compute his federal income tax for the year?

a. His wages from the law firm are taxed as an employee, as are his wages from the private practice.

b. His wages from the law firm are considered self-employment, as are the earnings from his private practice.

c. His wages from the law firm are taxed as an employee, and his earnings from his private practice are taxed as a self-employed proprietor.

d. His wages from the law firm are taxed as an employee, and his earnings from self-employment are taxed up to the maximum for social security only.

LO 10-4 44. Adrienne is a self-employed attorney. She has net earnings (profit) from her practice of $106,800. Her self-employment taxes for the year are

a. $13,117.76.

b. $13,338.85.

c. $14,204.40.

d. $15,090.36.

LO 10-4 45. Carol works for ABC Company and earned $63,000 for the entire year 2017. How much in FUTA tax is her employer required to withhold in her name? Assume that the employer receives the maximum credit for state unemployment taxes.

a. $0.

b. $42.00.

c. $43.40.

d. $420.00.

LO 10-4 46. On January 2, 2017, Jane employed a part-time household worker in her home. She paid the household worker $350 per month for 2017. What amount of FICA tax is Jane required to record on Schedule H?

a. $237.30.

b. $321.30.

c. $558.60.

d. $642.60.

LO 10-6 47. A taxpayer with 2017 AGI of $160,000 has no income tax withholding and is required to pay estimated taxes. The taxpayer can avoid an underpayment penalty by paying

a. At least 90% of the 2017 tax liability ratably over four quarterly payments.

b. At least 110% of the 2017 tax liability ratably over four quarterly payments.

c. At least 90% of the 2016 tax liability ratably over four quarterly payments.

d. 100% of the 2017 tax liability ratably over four quarterly payments.

LO 10-6 48. Adam received a bonus of $4,400 from his employer. Which one of the following federal income withholding tax amounts is *not* in accordance with IRS rules regarding supplemental wage payments? Adam earns biweekly wages of $3,500, is single, and claims one allowance. Assume his employer uses the percentage method of withholding.

a. $1,237.85 on his bonus if taxes had already been withheld from his regular pay.

b. $1,543.84 if his bonus and wages are paid on different dates within the pay period.

c. $1,750.10 if his bonus is taxed at the supplemental wage percentage and added to his regular wages paid in the same period.

d. $1,887.95 if his bonus and wages are paid at the same time during the pay period.

Problems connect

All applicable problems are available with ***Connect***©

LO 10-2 49. Allison is paid $1,325 per week. What is the amount of federal income tax withheld from Allison's paycheck under the following conditions? Use the percentage method table in the Appendix to this chapter.

a. Allison is single and claims two withholding allowances.

____

b. Allison is married and claims two withholding allowances.

____

c. Allison is single and claims no withholding allowance.

____

LO 10-2 50. Martin is married and claims four exemptions on his W-4. What is his federal income tax withholding under the following conditions? Use the percentage method table in the Appendix to this chapter.

a. Martin is paid semimonthly, and his gross pay is $3,600 per paycheck.

____

b. Martin is paid monthly, and his gross pay is $6,700 per paycheck.

____

c. Martin is paid weekly, and his gross pay is $4,750 per paycheck.

____

LO 10-2 51. Lisa earns $65,000 per year. She is married and claims three allowances. Use the wage bracket tables available online.

a. If she is paid weekly, what is her withholding per paycheck?

____

b. If she is paid monthly, what is her withholding per paycheck?

____

c. If she is paid biweekly, what is her withholding per paycheck?

____

d. If she is paid semimonthly, what is her withholding per paycheck?

____

LO 10-2 52. Henry, who earned $93,840 during 2017, is paid on a monthly basis, is married, and claims four allowances.

a. What is Henry's federal tax withholding for each pay period?

____

b. What is Henry's FICA withholding for each pay period?

____

LO 10-2 53. Roberto's salary is $129,600 in 2017. Roberto is paid on a semimonthly basis, is single, and claims one allowance.

a. What is Roberto's federal tax withholding per pay period?

____

b. What is Roberto's FICA withholding per pay period before he reaches the social security limit?

____

c. For the last pay period in 2017, what is Roberto's FICA withholding?

____

LO 10-3 54. Baker Company is trying to determine how often it needs to deposit payroll taxes for calendar year 2017. The company made the following quarterly payroll tax deposits during the last two years:

Quarter beginning January 1, 2015	$10,000
Quarter beginning April 1, 2015	10,000
Quarter beginning July 1, 2015	11,000
Quarter beginning October 1, 2015	12,000
Quarter beginning January 1, 2016	12,000
Quarter beginning April 1, 2016	12,000
Quarter beginning July 1, 2016	11,000
Quarter beginning October 1, 2016	12,000

a. What is the amount from the lookback period?

____

b. In 2017, how often must Baker Company make payroll deposits?

____

LO 10-4 55. CFG Company has the following employees:

	Wages Paid
Eddie	$12,000
Melanie	6,000
Shelly	22,000

CFG receives the maximum credit for state unemployment taxes. What is the FUTA tax that CFG Company would owe for the year?

LO 10-4 56. Jacob Turner hired Jen Hatcher as a housekeeper starting on January 2 at $750 monthly. Jacob does not withhold any federal taxes. Assume that Jen is not a housekeeper for anyone else. Assume that Jacob paid $2,250 in wages for the fourth quarter of 2017.

a. How much in social security tax should Jacob pay? ______________________

____

b. How much Medicare tax should Jacob pay?

____

c. How much FUTA tax should Jacob pay?

____

LO 10-2, 10-4 57. Lauprechta Inc. Company has the following employees on payroll:

	Semimonthly Payroll	Withholding Allowances	Marital Status
Naila	$5,800	4	Married
Wilfred	$5,000	3	Married
Byron	$3,200	1	Single
Annie	$3,600	2	Single

Complete the table for taxes to be withheld for each pay period.

Employee	Federal Withholding Tax	Social Security Tax	Medicare Tax	Total Taxes Withheld
Naila	________	________	________	________
Wilfred	________	________	________	________
Byron	________	________	________	________
Annie	________	________	________	________

Tax Return Problems connect

All applicable tax return problems are available with ***Connect***©

These problems are intended to be completed manually. Go to the IRS Web site at www.irs.gov to obtain 2017 forms.

Tax Return Problem 1 Use the information from Problem 57. Prepare Form 941 including Schedule B for the second quarter of 2017. Assume that the payroll is consistent every pay period beginning in April through June 30 and that all tax deposits were made on a timely basis as required. Lauprecht Inc.'s Employer Identification Number (EIN) is 36-1238975, and its address is 1825 Elkhart Way, Columbus, GA 31904.

Tax Return Problem 2 Use the information from Problem 57. Prepare Form 940 for 2017. Assume that Lauprecht Inc. has timely paid all amounts due to the state unemployment fund (assume a total amount of $3,471) and that the payroll was consistent throughout the entire year. No FUTA deposits were made during the year.

Tax Return Problem 3 Use the information from Problem 57. Prepare a Form W-2 for Naila Neffa. Her SSN is 412-34-5670, and her address is 988 Main Street, Midland, GA 31820. The EIN for Lauprecht Inc. is 36-1238975, and its address is 1825 Elkhart Way, Columbus, GA 31904.

We have provided selected filled-in source documents that are available in the *Connect Library*

Appendix

PARTIAL WAGE BRACKET METHOD WITHHOLDING

Percentage Method Tables for Income Tax Withholding

(For Wages Paid in 2017)

TABLE 1—WEEKLY Payroll Period

(a) SINGLE person (including head of household)—

If the amount of wages (after subtracting withholding allowances) is: Not over $44 .... The amount of income tax to withhold is: $0

Over—	But not over—		of excess over—
$44	—$224	$0.00 plus 10%	—$44
$224	—$774	$18.00 plus 15%	—$224
$774	—$1,812	$100.50 plus 25%	—$774
$1,812	—$3,730	$360.00 plus 28%	—$1,812
$3,730	—$8,058	$897.04 plus 33%	—$3,730
$8,058	—$8,090	$2,325.28 plus 35%	—$8,058
$8,090	....	$2,336.48 plus 39.6%	—$8,090

(b) MARRIED person—

If the amount of wages (after subtracting withholding allowances) is: Not over $166 .... The amount of income tax to withhold is: $0

Over—	But not over—		of excess over—
$166	—$525	$0.00 plus 10%	—$166
$525	—$1,626	$35.90 plus 15%	—$525
$1,626	—$3,111	$201.05 plus 25%	—$1,626
$3,111	—$4,654	$572.30 plus 28%	—$3,111
$4,654	—$8,180	$1,004.34 plus 33%	—$4,654
$8,180	—$9,218	$2,167.92 plus 35%	—$8,180
$9,218	....	$2,531.22 plus 39.6%	—$9,218

TABLE 2—BIWEEKLY Payroll Period

(a) SINGLE person (including head of household)—

If the amount of wages (after subtracting withholding allowances) is: Not over $88 .... The amount of income tax to withhold is: $0

Over—	But not over—		of excess over—
$88	—$447	$0.00 plus 10%	—$88
$447	—$1,548	$35.90 plus 15%	—$447
$1,548	—$3,623	$201.05 plus 25%	—$1,548
$3,623	—$7,460	$719.80 plus 28%	—$3,623
$7,460	—$16,115	$1,794.16 plus 33%	—$7,460
$16,115	—$16,181	$4,650.31 plus 35%	—$16,115
$16,181	....	$4,673.41 plus 39.6%	—$16,181

(b) MARRIED person—

If the amount of wages (after subtracting withholding allowances) is: Not over $333 .... The amount of income tax to withhold is: $0

Over—	But not over—		of excess over—
$333	—$1,050	$0.00 plus 10%	—$333
$1,050	—$3,252	$71.70 plus 15%	—$1,050
$3,252	—$6,221	$402.00 plus 25%	—$3,252
$6,221	—$9,308	$1,144.25 plus 28%	—$6,221
$9,308	—$16,360	$2,008.61 plus 33%	—$9,308
$16,360	—$18,437	$4,335.77 plus 35%	—$16,360
$18,437	....	$5,062.72 plus 39.6%	—$18,437

TABLE 3—SEMIMONTHLY Payroll Period

(a) SINGLE person (including head of household)—

If the amount of wages (after subtracting withholding allowances) is: Not over $96 .... The amount of income tax to withhold is: $0

Over—	But not over—		of excess over—
$96	—$484	$0.00 plus 10%	—$96
$484	—$1,677	$38.80 plus 15%	—$484
$1,677	—$3,925	$217.75 plus 25%	—$1,677
$3,925	—$8,081	$779.75 plus 28%	—$3,925
$8,081	—$17,458	$1,943.43 plus 33%	—$8,081
$17,458	—$17,529	$5,037.84 plus 35%	—$17,458
$17,529	....	$5,062.69 plus 39.6%	—$17,529

(b) MARRIED person—

If the amount of wages (after subtracting withholding allowances) is: Not over $360 .... The amount of income tax to withhold is: $0

Over—	But not over—		of excess over—
$360	—$1,138	$0.00 plus 10%	—$360
$1,138	—$3,523	$77.80 plus 15%	—$1,138
$3,523	—$6,740	$435.55 plus 25%	—$3,523
$6,740	—$10,083	$1,239.80 plus 28%	—$6,740
$10,083	—$17,723	$2,175.84 plus 33%	—$10,083
$17,723	—$19,973	$4,697.04 plus 35%	—$17,723
$19,973	....	$5,484.54 plus 39.6%	—$19,973

TABLE 4—MONTHLY Payroll Period

(a) SINGLE person (including head of household)—

If the amount of wages (after subtracting withholding allowances) is: Not over $192 .... The amount of income tax to withhold is: $0

Over—	But not over—		of excess over—
$192	—$969	$0.00 plus 10%	—$192
$969	—$3,354	$77.70 plus 15%	—$969
$3,354	—$7,850	$435.45 plus 25%	—$3,354
$7,850	—$16,163	$1,559.45 plus 28%	—$7,850
$16,163	—$34,917	$3,887.09 plus 33%	—$16,163
$34,917	—$35,058	$10,075.91 plus 35%	—$34,917
$35,058	....	$10,125.26 plus 39.6%	—$35,058

(b) MARRIED person—

If the amount of wages (after subtracting withholding allowances) is: Not over $721 .... The amount of income tax to withhold is: $0

Over—	But not over—		of excess over—
$721	—$2,275	$0.00 plus 10%	—$721
$2,275	—$7,046	$155.40 plus 15%	—$2,275
$7,046	—$13,479	$871.05 plus 25%	—$7,046
$13,479	—$20,167	$2,479.30 plus 28%	—$13,479
$20,167	—$35,446	$4,351.94 plus 33%	—$20,167
$35,446	—$39,946	$9,394.01 plus 35%	—$35,446
$39,946	....	$10,969.01 plus 39.6%	—$39,946

Source: U.S. Department of the Treasury, Internal Revenue Service, Form 1040-ES. Washington, DC: 2017.

TABLES

Wage Bracket Method Tables for Income Tax Withholding

SINGLE Persons—**WEEKLY** Payroll Period

(For Wages Paid through December 31, 2017)

And the wages are–		And the number of withholding allowances claimed is—										
At least	But less than	0	1	2	3	4	5	6	7	8	9	10
		The amount of income tax to be withheld is—										
$ 0	$55	$0	$0	$0	$0	$0	$0	$0	$0	$0	$0	$0
55	60	1	0	0	0	0	0	0	0	0	0	0
60	65	2	0	0	0	0	0	0	0	0	0	0
65	70	2	0	0	0	0	0	0	0	0	0	0
70	75	3	0	0	0	0	0	0	0	0	0	0
75	80	3	0	0	0	0	0	0	0	0	0	0
80	85	4	0	0	0	0	0	0	0	0	0	0
85	90	4	0	0	0	0	0	0	0	0	0	0
90	95	5	0	0	0	0	0	0	0	0	0	0
95	100	5	0	0	0	0	0	0	0	0	0	0
100	105	6	0	0	0	0	0	0	0	0	0	0
105	110	6	0	0	0	0	0	0	0	0	0	0
110	115	7	0	0	0	0	0	0	0	0	0	0
115	120	7	0	0	0	0	0	0	0	0	0	0
120	125	8	0	0	0	0	0	0	0	0	0	0
125	130	8	1	0	0	0	0	0	0	0	0	0
130	135	9	1	0	0	0	0	0	0	0	0	0
135	140	9	2	0	0	0	0	0	0	0	0	0
140	145	10	2	0	0	0	0	0	0	0	0	0
145	150	10	3	0	0	0	0	0	0	0	0	0
150	155	11	3	0	0	0	0	0	0	0	0	0
155	160	11	4	0	0	0	0	0	0	0	0	0
160	165	12	4	0	0	0	0	0	0	0	0	0
165	170	12	5	0	0	0	0	0	0	0	0	0
170	175	13	5	0	0	0	0	0	0	0	0	0
175	180	13	6	0	0	0	0	0	0	0	0	0
180	185	14	6	0	0	0	0	0	0	0	0	0
185	190	14	7	0	0	0	0	0	0	0	0	0
190	195	15	7	0	0	0	0	0	0	0	0	0
195	200	15	8	0	0	0	0	0	0	0	0	0
200	210	16	8	1	0	0	0	0	0	0	0	0
210	220	17	9	2	0	0	0	0	0	0	0	0
220	230	18	10	3	0	0	0	0	0	0	0	0
230	240	20	11	4	0	0	0	0	0	0	0	0
240	250	21	12	5	0	0	0	0	0	0	0	0
250	260	23	13	6	0	0	0	0	0	0	0	0
260	270	24	14	7	0	0	0	0	0	0	0	0
270	280	26	15	8	0	0	0	0	0	0	0	0
280	290	27	16	9	1	0	0	0	0	0	0	0
290	300	29	17	10	2	0	0	0	0	0	0	0
300	310	30	18	11	3	0	0	0	0	0	0	0
310	320	32	20	12	4	0	0	0	0	0	0	0
320	330	33	21	13	5	0	0	0	0	0	0	0
330	340	35	23	14	6	0	0	0	0	0	0	0
340	350	36	24	15	7	0	0	0	0	0	0	0
350	360	38	26	16	8	0	0	0	0	0	0	0
360	370	39	27	17	9	1	0	0	0	0	0	0
370	380	41	29	18	10	2	0	0	0	0	0	0
380	390	42	30	19	11	3	0	0	0	0	0	0
390	400	44	32	20	12	4	0	0	0	0	0	0
400	410	45	33	22	13	5	0	0	0	0	0	0
410	420	47	35	23	14	6	0	0	0	0	0	0
420	430	48	36	25	15	7	0	0	0	0	0	0
430	440	50	38	26	16	8	0	0	0	0	0	0
440	450	51	39	28	17	9	1	0	0	0	0	0
450	460	53	41	29	18	10	2	0	0	0	0	0
460	470	54	42	31	19	11	3	0	0	0	0	0
470	480	56	44	32	21	12	4	0	0	0	0	0
480	490	57	45	34	22	13	5	0	0	0	0	0
490	500	59	47	35	24	14	6	0	0	0	0	0
500	510	60	48	37	25	15	7	0	0	0	0	0
510	520	62	50	38	27	16	8	0	0	0	0	0
520	530	63	51	40	28	17	9	1	0	0	0	0
530	540	65	53	41	30	18	10	2	0	0	0	0
540	550	66	54	43	31	19	11	3	0	0	0	0
550	560	68	56	44	33	21	12	4	0	0	0	0
560	570	69	57	46	34	22	13	5	0	0	0	0
570	580	71	59	47	36	24	14	6	0	0	0	0
580	590	72	60	49	37	25	15	7	0	0	0	0
590	600	74	62	50	39	27	16	8	1	0	0	0

Wage Bracket Method Tables for Income Tax Withholding

SINGLE Persons—**WEEKLY** Payroll Period

(For Wages Paid through December 31, 2017)

And the wages are–		And the number of withholding allowances claimed is—										
At least	But less than	0	1	2	3	4	5	6	7	8	9	10
		The amount of income tax to be withheld is—										
$600	$610	$75	$63	$52	$40	$28	$17	$9	$2	$0	$0	$0
610	620	77	65	53	42	30	18	10	3	0	0	0
620	630	78	66	55	43	31	20	11	4	0	0	0
630	640	80	68	56	45	33	21	12	5	0	0	0
640	650	81	69	58	46	34	23	13	6	0	0	0
650	660	83	71	59	48	36	24	14	7	0	0	0
660	670	84	72	61	49	37	26	15	8	0	0	0
670	680	86	74	62	51	39	27	16	9	1	0	0
680	690	87	75	64	52	40	29	17	10	2	0	0
690	700	89	77	65	54	42	30	19	11	3	0	0
700	710	90	78	67	55	43	32	20	12	4	0	0
710	720	92	80	68	57	45	33	22	13	5	0	0
720	730	93	81	70	58	46	35	23	14	6	0	0
730	740	95	83	71	60	48	36	25	15	7	0	0
740	750	96	84	73	61	49	38	26	16	8	0	0
750	760	98	86	74	63	51	39	28	17	9	1	0
760	770	99	87	76	64	52	41	29	18	10	2	0
770	780	101	89	77	66	54	42	31	19	11	3	0
780	790	103	90	79	67	55	44	32	20	12	4	0
790	800	106	92	80	69	57	45	34	22	13	5	0
800	810	108	93	82	70	58	47	35	23	14	6	0
810	820	111	95	83	72	60	48	37	25	15	7	0
820	830	113	96	85	73	61	50	38	26	16	8	0
830	840	116	98	86	75	63	51	40	28	17	9	1
840	850	118	99	88	76	64	53	41	29	18	10	2
850	860	121	101	89	78	66	54	43	31	19	11	3
860	870	123	104	91	79	67	56	44	32	21	12	4
870	880	126	106	92	81	69	57	46	34	22	13	5
880	890	128	109	94	82	70	59	47	35	24	14	6
890	900	131	111	95	84	72	60	49	37	25	15	7
900	910	133	114	97	85	73	62	50	38	27	16	8
910	920	136	116	98	87	75	63	52	40	28	17	9
920	930	138	119	100	88	76	65	53	41	30	18	10
930	940	141	121	102	90	78	66	55	43	31	20	11
940	950	143	124	104	91	79	68	56	44	33	21	12
950	960	146	126	107	93	81	69	58	46	34	23	13
960	970	148	129	109	94	82	71	59	47	36	24	14
970	980	151	131	112	96	84	72	61	49	37	26	15
980	990	153	134	114	97	85	74	62	50	39	27	16
990	1,000	156	136	117	99	87	75	64	52	40	29	17
1,000	1,010	158	139	119	100	88	77	65	53	42	30	18
1,010	1,020	161	141	122	102	90	78	67	55	43	32	20
1,020	1,030	163	144	124	105	91	80	68	56	45	33	21
1,030	1,040	166	146	127	107	93	81	70	58	46	35	23
1,040	1,050	168	149	129	110	94	83	71	59	48	36	24
1,050	1,060	171	151	132	112	96	84	73	61	49	38	26
1,060	1,070	173	154	134	115	97	86	74	62	51	39	27
1,070	1,080	176	156	137	117	99	87	76	64	52	41	29
1,080	1,090	178	159	139	120	100	89	77	65	54	42	30
1,090	1,100	181	161	142	122	103	90	79	67	55	44	32
1,100	1,110	183	164	144	125	105	92	80	68	57	45	33
1,110	1,120	186	166	147	127	108	93	82	70	58	47	35
1,120	1,130	188	169	149	130	110	95	83	71	60	48	36
1,130	1,140	191	171	152	132	113	96	85	73	61	50	38
1,140	1,150	193	174	154	135	115	98	86	74	63	51	39
1,150	1,160	196	176	157	137	118	99	88	76	64	53	41
1,160	1,170	198	179	159	140	120	101	89	77	66	54	42
1,170	1,180	201	181	162	142	123	103	91	79	67	56	44
1,180	1,190	203	184	164	145	125	106	92	80	69	57	45
1,190	1,200	206	186	167	147	128	108	94	82	70	59	47
1,200	1,210	208	189	169	150	130	111	95	83	72	60	48
1,210	1,220	211	191	172	152	133	113	97	85	73	62	50
1,220	1,230	213	194	174	155	135	116	98	86	75	63	51
1,230	1,240	216	196	177	157	138	118	100	88	76	65	53
1,240	1,250	218	199	179	160	140	121	101	89	78	66	54
$1,250 and over		Use Table 1(a) for a **SINGLE person** on page 45. Also see the instructions on page 43.										

Wage Bracket Method Tables for Income Tax Withholding

MARRIED Persons—WEEKLY Payroll Period

(For Wages Paid through December 31, 2017)

And the wages are–		And the number of withholding allowances claimed is—										
At least	But less than	0	1	2	3	4	5	6	7	8	9	10
		The amount of income tax to be withheld is—										
$ 0	$170	$0	$0	$0	$0	$0	$0	$0	$0	$0	$0	$0
170	175	1	0	0	0	0	0	0	0	0	0	0
175	180	1	0	0	0	0	0	0	0	0	0	0
180	185	2	0	0	0	0	0	0	0	0	0	0
185	190	2	0	0	0	0	0	0	0	0	0	0
190	195	3	0	0	0	0	0	0	0	0	0	0
195	200	3	0	0	0	0	0	0	0	0	0	0
200	210	4	0	0	0	0	0	0	0	0	0	0
210	220	5	0	0	0	0	0	0	0	0	0	0
220	230	6	0	0	0	0	0	0	0	0	0	0
230	240	7	0	0	0	0	0	0	0	0	0	0
240	250	8	0	0	0	0	0	0	0	0	0	0
250	260	9	1	0	0	0	0	0	0	0	0	0
260	270	10	2	0	0	0	0	0	0	0	0	0
270	280	11	3	0	0	0	0	0	0	0	0	0
280	290	12	4	0	0	0	0	0	0	0	0	0
290	300	13	5	0	0	0	0	0	0	0	0	0
300	310	14	6	0	0	0	0	0	0	0	0	0
310	320	15	7	0	0	0	0	0	0	0	0	0
320	330	16	8	0	0	0	0	0	0	0	0	0
330	340	17	9	1	0	0	0	0	0	0	0	0
340	350	18	10	2	0	0	0	0	0	0	0	0
350	360	19	11	3	0	0	0	0	0	0	0	0
360	370	20	12	4	0	0	0	0	0	0	0	0
370	380	21	13	5	0	0	0	0	0	0	0	0
380	390	22	14	6	0	0	0	0	0	0	0	0
390	400	23	15	7	0	0	0	0	0	0	0	0
400	410	24	16	8	1	0	0	0	0	0	0	0
410	420	25	17	9	2	0	0	0	0	0	0	0
420	430	26	18	10	3	0	0	0	0	0	0	0
430	440	27	19	11	4	0	0	0	0	0	0	0
440	450	28	20	12	5	0	0	0	0	0	0	0
450	460	29	21	13	6	0	0	0	0	0	0	0
460	470	30	22	14	7	0	0	0	0	0	0	0
470	480	31	23	15	8	0	0	0	0	0	0	0
480	490	32	24	16	9	1	0	0	0	0	0	0
490	500	33	25	17	10	2	0	0	0	0	0	0
500	510	34	26	18	11	3	0	0	0	0	0	0
510	520	35	27	19	12	4	0	0	0	0	0	0
520	530	36	28	20	13	5	0	0	0	0	0	0
530	540	37	29	21	14	6	0	0	0	0	0	0
540	550	39	30	22	15	7	0	0	0	0	0	0
550	560	40	31	23	16	8	0	0	0	0	0	0
560	570	42	32	24	17	9	1	0	0	0	0	0
570	580	43	33	25	18	10	2	0	0	0	0	0
580	590	45	34	26	19	11	3	0	0	0	0	0
590	600	46	35	27	20	12	4	0	0	0	0	0
600	610	48	36	28	21	13	5	0	0	0	0	0
610	620	49	38	29	22	14	6	0	0	0	0	0
620	630	51	39	30	23	15	7	0	0	0	0	0
630	640	52	41	31	24	16	8	0	0	0	0	0
640	650	54	42	32	25	17	9	1	0	0	0	0
650	660	55	44	33	26	18	10	2	0	0	0	0
660	670	57	45	34	27	19	11	3	0	0	0	0
670	680	58	47	35	28	20	12	4	0	0	0	0
680	690	60	48	37	29	21	13	5	0	0	0	0
690	700	61	50	38	30	22	14	6	0	0	0	0
700	710	63	51	40	31	23	15	7	0	0	0	0
710	720	64	53	41	32	24	16	8	0	0	0	0
720	730	66	54	43	33	25	17	9	1	0	0	0
730	740	67	56	44	34	26	18	10	2	0	0	0
740	750	69	57	46	35	27	19	11	3	0	0	0
750	760	70	59	47	36	28	20	12	4	0	0	0
760	770	72	60	49	37	29	21	13	5	0	0	0
770	780	73	62	50	38	30	22	14	6	0	0	0
780	790	75	63	52	40	31	23	15	7	0	0	0
790	800	76	65	53	41	32	24	16	8	1	0	0

Wage Bracket Method Tables for Income Tax Withholding

MARRIED Persons—**WEEKLY** Payroll Period

(For Wages Paid through December 31, 2017)

And the wages are–		And the number of withholding allowances claimed is—										
At least	But less than	0	1	2	3	4	5	6	7	8	9	10
		The amount of income tax to be withheld is—										
$800	$810	$78	$66	$55	$43	$33	$25	$17	$9	$2	$0	$0
810	820	79	68	56	44	34	26	18	10	3	0	0
820	830	81	69	58	46	35	27	19	11	4	0	0
830	840	82	71	59	47	36	28	20	12	5	0	0
840	850	84	72	61	49	37	29	21	13	6	0	0
850	860	85	74	62	50	39	30	22	14	7	0	0
860	870	87	75	64	52	40	31	23	15	8	0	0
870	880	88	77	65	53	42	32	24	16	9	1	0
880	890	90	78	67	55	43	33	25	17	10	2	0
890	900	91	80	68	56	45	34	26	18	11	3	0
900	910	93	81	70	58	46	35	27	19	12	4	0
910	920	94	83	71	59	48	36	28	20	13	5	0
920	930	96	84	73	61	49	37	29	21	14	6	0
930	940	97	86	74	62	51	39	30	22	15	7	0
940	950	99	87	76	64	52	40	31	23	16	8	0
950	960	100	89	77	65	54	42	32	24	17	9	1
960	970	102	90	79	67	55	43	33	25	18	10	2
970	980	103	92	80	68	57	45	34	26	19	11	3
980	990	105	93	82	70	58	46	35	27	20	12	4
990	1,000	106	95	83	71	60	48	36	28	21	13	5
1,000	1,010	108	96	85	73	61	49	38	29	22	14	6
1,010	1,020	109	98	86	74	63	51	39	30	23	15	7
1,020	1,030	111	99	88	76	64	52	41	31	24	16	8
1,030	1,040	112	101	89	77	66	54	42	32	25	17	9
1,040	1,050	114	102	91	79	67	55	44	33	26	18	10
1,050	1,060	115	104	92	80	69	57	45	34	27	19	11
1,060	1,070	117	105	94	82	70	58	47	35	28	20	12
1,070	1,080	118	107	95	83	72	60	48	37	29	21	13
1,080	1,090	120	108	97	85	73	61	50	38	30	22	14
1,090	1,100	121	110	98	86	75	63	51	40	31	23	15
1,100	1,110	123	111	100	88	76	64	53	41	32	24	16
1,110	1,120	124	113	101	89	78	66	54	43	33	25	17
1,120	1,130	126	114	103	91	79	67	56	44	34	26	18
1,130	1,140	127	116	104	92	81	69	57	46	35	27	19
1,140	1,150	129	117	106	94	82	70	59	47	36	28	20
1,150	1,160	130	119	107	95	84	72	60	49	37	29	21
1,160	1,170	132	120	109	97	85	73	62	50	38	30	22
1,170	1,180	133	122	110	98	87	75	63	52	40	31	23
1,180	1,190	135	123	112	100	88	76	65	53	41	32	24
1,190	1,200	136	125	113	101	90	78	66	55	43	33	25
1,200	1,210	138	126	115	103	91	79	68	56	44	34	26
1,210	1,220	139	128	116	104	93	81	69	58	46	35	27
1,220	1,230	141	129	118	106	94	82	71	59	47	36	28
1,230	1,240	142	131	119	107	96	84	72	61	49	37	29
1,240	1,250	144	132	121	109	97	85	74	62	50	39	30
1,250	1,260	145	134	122	110	99	87	75	64	52	40	31
1,260	1,270	147	135	124	112	100	88	77	65	53	42	32
1,270	1,280	148	137	125	113	102	90	78	67	55	43	33
1,280	1,290	150	138	127	115	103	91	80	68	56	45	34
1,290	1,300	151	140	128	116	105	93	81	70	58	46	35
1,300	1,310	153	141	130	118	106	94	83	71	59	48	36
1,310	1,320	154	143	131	119	108	96	84	73	61	49	38
1,320	1,330	156	144	133	121	109	97	86	74	62	51	39
1,330	1,340	157	146	134	122	111	99	87	76	64	52	41
1,340	1,350	159	147	136	124	112	100	89	77	65	54	42
1,350	1,360	160	149	137	125	114	102	90	79	67	55	44
1,360	1,370	162	150	139	127	115	103	92	80	68	57	45
1,370	1,380	163	152	140	128	117	105	93	82	70	58	47
1,380	1,390	165	153	142	130	118	106	95	83	71	60	48
1,390	1,400	166	155	143	131	120	108	96	85	73	61	50
1,400	1,410	168	156	145	133	121	109	98	86	74	63	51
1,410	1,420	169	158	146	134	123	111	99	88	76	64	53
1,420	1,430	171	159	148	136	124	112	101	89	77	66	54
1,430	1,440	172	161	149	137	126	114	102	91	79	67	56
1,440	1,450	174	162	151	139	127	115	104	92	80	69	57
1,450	1,460	175	164	152	140	129	117	105	94	82	70	59
1,460	1,470	177	165	154	142	130	118	107	95	83	72	60
1,470	1,480	178	167	155	143	132	120	108	97	85	73	62
1,480	1,490	180	168	157	145	133	121	110	98	86	75	63
$1,490 and over		Use Table 1(b) for a **MARRIED person** on page 45. Also see the instructions on page 43.										

Wage Bracket Method Tables for Income Tax Withholding

SINGLE Persons—**BIWEEKLY** Payroll Period

(For Wages Paid through December 31, 2017)

And the wages are–		And the number of withholding allowances claimed is—										
At least	But less than	0	1	2	3	4	5	6	7	8	9	10
		The amount of income tax to be withheld is—										
$ 0	$105	$0	$0	$0	$0	$0	$0	$0	$0	$0	$0	$0
105	110	2	0	0	0	0	0	0	0	0	0	0
110	115	2	0	0	0	0	0	0	0	0	0	0
115	120	3	0	0	0	0	0	0	0	0	0	0
120	125	3	0	0	0	0	0	0	0	0	0	0
125	130	4	0	0	0	0	0	0	0	0	0	0
130	135	4	0	0	0	0	0	0	0	0	0	0
135	140	5	0	0	0	0	0	0	0	0	0	0
140	145	5	0	0	0	0	0	0	0	0	0	0
145	150	6	0	0	0	0	0	0	0	0	0	0
150	155	6	0	0	0	0	0	0	0	0	0	0
155	160	7	0	0	0	0	0	0	0	0	0	0
160	165	7	0	0	0	0	0	0	0	0	0	0
165	170	8	0	0	0	0	0	0	0	0	0	0
170	175	8	0	0	0	0	0	0	0	0	0	0
175	180	9	0	0	0	0	0	0	0	0	0	0
180	185	9	0	0	0	0	0	0	0	0	0	0
185	190	10	0	0	0	0	0	0	0	0	0	0
190	195	10	0	0	0	0	0	0	0	0	0	0
195	200	11	0	0	0	0	0	0	0	0	0	0
200	205	11	0	0	0	0	0	0	0	0	0	0
205	210	12	0	0	0	0	0	0	0	0	0	0
210	215	12	0	0	0	0	0	0	0	0	0	0
215	220	13	0	0	0	0	0	0	0	0	0	0
220	225	13	0	0	0	0	0	0	0	0	0	0
225	230	14	0	0	0	0	0	0	0	0	0	0
230	235	14	0	0	0	0	0	0	0	0	0	0
235	240	15	0	0	0	0	0	0	0	0	0	0
240	245	15	0	0	0	0	0	0	0	0	0	0
245	250	16	0	0	0	0	0	0	0	0	0	0
250	260	17	1	0	0	0	0	0	0	0	0	0
260	270	18	2	0	0	0	0	0	0	0	0	0
270	280	19	3	0	0	0	0	0	0	0	0	0
280	290	20	4	0	0	0	0	0	0	0	0	0
290	300	21	5	0	0	0	0	0	0	0	0	0
300	310	22	6	0	0	0	0	0	0	0	0	0
310	320	23	7	0	0	0	0	0	0	0	0	0
320	330	24	8	0	0	0	0	0	0	0	0	0
330	340	25	9	0	0	0	0	0	0	0	0	0
340	350	26	10	0	0	0	0	0	0	0	0	0
350	360	27	11	0	0	0	0	0	0	0	0	0
360	370	28	12	0	0	0	0	0	0	0	0	0
370	380	29	13	0	0	0	0	0	0	0	0	0
380	390	30	14	0	0	0	0	0	0	0	0	0
390	400	31	15	0	0	0	0	0	0	0	0	0
400	410	32	16	1	0	0	0	0	0	0	0	0
410	420	33	17	2	0	0	0	0	0	0	0	0
420	430	34	18	3	0	0	0	0	0	0	0	0
430	440	35	19	4	0	0	0	0	0	0	0	0
440	450	36	20	5	0	0	0	0	0	0	0	0
450	460	37	21	6	0	0	0	0	0	0	0	0
460	470	39	22	7	0	0	0	0	0	0	0	0
470	480	40	23	8	0	0	0	0	0	0	0	0
480	490	42	24	9	0	0	0	0	0	0	0	0
490	500	43	25	10	0	0	0	0	0	0	0	0
500	520	45	27	11	0	0	0	0	0	0	0	0
520	540	48	29	13	0	0	0	0	0	0	0	0
540	560	51	31	15	0	0	0	0	0	0	0	0
560	580	54	33	17	1	0	0	0	0	0	0	0
580	600	57	35	19	3	0	0	0	0	0	0	0
600	620	60	37	21	5	0	0	0	0	0	0	0
620	640	63	40	23	7	0	0	0	0	0	0	0
640	660	66	43	25	9	0	0	0	0	0	0	0
660	680	69	46	27	11	0	0	0	0	0	0	0
680	700	72	49	29	13	0	0	0	0	0	0	0
700	720	75	52	31	15	0	0	0	0	0	0	0
720	740	78	55	33	17	2	0	0	0	0	0	0
740	760	81	58	35	19	4	0	0	0	0	0	0
760	780	84	61	38	21	6	0	0	0	0	0	0
780	800	87	64	41	23	8	0	0	0	0	0	0

Wage Bracket Method Tables for Income Tax Withholding

SINGLE Persons—**BIWEEKLY** Payroll Period

(For Wages Paid through December 31, 2017)

And the wages are–		And the number of withholding allowances claimed is—										
At least	But less than	0	1	2	3	4	5	6	7	8	9	10
		The amount of income tax to be withheld is—										
$800	$820	$90	$67	$44	$25	$10	$0	$0	$0	$0	$0	$0
820	840	93	70	47	27	12	0	0	0	0	0	0
840	860	96	73	50	29	14	0	0	0	0	0	0
860	880	99	76	53	31	16	0	0	0	0	0	0
880	900	102	79	56	33	18	2	0	0	0	0	0
900	920	105	82	59	35	20	4	0	0	0	0	0
920	940	108	85	62	38	22	6	0	0	0	0	0
940	960	111	88	65	41	24	8	0	0	0	0	0
960	980	114	91	68	44	26	10	0	0	0	0	0
980	1,000	117	94	71	47	28	12	0	0	0	0	0
1,000	1,020	120	97	74	50	30	14	0	0	0	0	0
1,020	1,040	123	100	77	53	32	16	1	0	0	0	0
1,040	1,060	126	103	80	56	34	18	3	0	0	0	0
1,060	1,080	129	106	83	59	36	20	5	0	0	0	0
1,080	1,100	132	109	86	62	39	22	7	0	0	0	0
1,100	1,120	135	112	89	65	42	24	9	0	0	0	0
1,120	1,140	138	115	92	68	45	26	11	0	0	0	0
1,140	1,160	141	118	95	71	48	28	13	0	0	0	0
1,160	1,180	144	121	98	74	51	30	15	0	0	0	0
1,180	1,200	147	124	101	77	54	32	17	1	0	0	0
1,200	1,220	150	127	104	80	57	34	19	3	0	0	0
1,220	1,240	153	130	107	83	60	36	21	5	0	0	0
1,240	1,260	156	133	110	86	63	39	23	7	0	0	0
1,260	1,280	159	136	113	89	66	42	25	9	0	0	0
1,280	1,300	162	139	116	92	69	45	27	11	0	0	0
1,300	1,320	165	142	119	95	72	48	29	13	0	0	0
1,320	1,340	168	145	122	98	75	51	31	15	0	0	0
1,340	1,360	171	148	125	101	78	54	33	17	2	0	0
1,360	1,380	174	151	128	104	81	57	35	19	4	0	0
1,380	1,400	177	154	131	107	84	60	37	21	6	0	0
1,400	1,420	180	157	134	110	87	63	40	23	8	0	0
1,420	1,440	183	160	137	113	90	66	43	25	10	0	0
1,440	1,460	186	163	140	116	93	69	46	27	12	0	0
1,460	1,480	189	166	143	119	96	72	49	29	14	0	0
1,480	1,500	192	169	146	122	99	75	52	31	16	0	0
1,500	1,520	195	172	149	125	102	78	55	33	18	2	0
1,520	1,540	198	175	152	128	105	81	58	35	20	4	0
1,540	1,560	201	178	155	131	108	84	61	38	22	6	0
1,560	1,580	206	181	158	134	111	87	64	41	24	8	0
1,580	1,600	211	184	161	137	114	90	67	44	26	10	0
1,600	1,620	216	187	164	140	117	93	70	47	28	12	0
1,620	1,640	221	190	167	143	120	96	73	50	30	14	0
1,640	1,660	226	193	170	146	123	99	76	53	32	16	0
1,660	1,680	231	196	173	149	126	102	79	56	34	18	2
1,680	1,700	236	199	176	152	129	105	82	59	36	20	4
1,700	1,720	241	203	179	155	132	108	85	62	38	22	6
1,720	1,740	246	208	182	158	135	111	88	65	41	24	8
1,740	1,760	251	213	185	161	138	114	91	68	44	26	10
1,760	1,780	256	218	188	164	141	117	94	71	47	28	12
1,780	1,800	261	223	191	167	144	120	97	74	50	30	14
1,800	1,820	266	228	194	170	147	123	100	77	53	32	16
1,820	1,840	271	233	197	173	150	126	103	80	56	34	18
1,840	1,860	276	238	200	176	153	129	106	83	59	36	20
1,860	1,880	281	243	204	179	156	132	109	86	62	39	22
1,880	1,900	286	248	209	182	159	135	112	89	65	42	24
1,900	1,920	291	253	214	185	162	138	115	92	68	45	26
1,920	1,940	296	258	219	188	165	141	118	95	71	48	28
1,940	1,960	301	263	224	191	168	144	121	98	74	51	30
1,960	1,980	306	268	229	194	171	147	124	101	77	54	32
1,980	2,000	311	273	234	197	174	150	127	104	80	57	34
2,000	2,020	316	278	239	200	177	153	130	107	83	60	37
2,020	2,040	321	283	244	205	180	156	133	110	86	63	40
2,040	2,060	326	288	249	210	183	159	136	113	89	66	43
2,060	2,080	331	293	254	215	186	162	139	116	92	69	46
2,080	2,100	336	298	259	220	189	165	142	119	95	72	49

$2,100 and over — Use Table 2(a) for a **SINGLE person** on page 45. Also see the instructions on page 43.

Wage Bracket Method Tables for Income Tax Withholding

MARRIED Persons—**BIWEEKLY** Payroll Period

(For Wages Paid through December 31, 2017)

And the wages are–		And the number of withholding allowances claimed is—										
At least	But less than	0	1	2	3	4	5	6	7	8	9	10
		The amount of income tax to be withheld is—										
$ 0	$340	$0	$0	$0	$0	$0	$0	$0	$0	$0	$0	$0
340	350	1	0	0	0	0	0	0	0	0	0	0
350	360	2	0	0	0	0	0	0	0	0	0	0
360	370	3	0	0	0	0	0	0	0	0	0	0
370	380	4	0	0	0	0	0	0	0	0	0	0
380	390	5	0	0	0	0	0	0	0	0	0	0
390	400	6	0	0	0	0	0	0	0	0	0	0
400	410	7	0	0	0	0	0	0	0	0	0	0
410	420	8	0	0	0	0	0	0	0	0	0	0
420	430	9	0	0	0	0	0	0	0	0	0	0
430	440	10	0	0	0	0	0	0	0	0	0	0
440	450	11	0	0	0	0	0	0	0	0	0	0
450	460	12	0	0	0	0	0	0	0	0	0	0
460	470	13	0	0	0	0	0	0	0	0	0	0
470	480	14	0	0	0	0	0	0	0	0	0	0
480	490	15	0	0	0	0	0	0	0	0	0	0
490	500	16	1	0	0	0	0	0	0	0	0	0
500	520	18	2	0	0	0	0	0	0	0	0	0
520	540	20	4	0	0	0	0	0	0	0	0	0
540	560	22	6	0	0	0	0	0	0	0	0	0
560	580	24	8	0	0	0	0	0	0	0	0	0
580	600	26	10	0	0	0	0	0	0	0	0	0
600	620	28	12	0	0	0	0	0	0	0	0	0
620	640	30	14	0	0	0	0	0	0	0	0	0
640	660	32	16	1	0	0	0	0	0	0	0	0
660	680	34	18	3	0	0	0	0	0	0	0	0
680	700	36	20	5	0	0	0	0	0	0	0	0
700	720	38	22	7	0	0	0	0	0	0	0	0
720	740	40	24	9	0	0	0	0	0	0	0	0
740	760	42	26	11	0	0	0	0	0	0	0	0
760	780	44	28	13	0	0	0	0	0	0	0	0
780	800	46	30	15	0	0	0	0	0	0	0	0
800	820	48	32	17	1	0	0	0	0	0	0	0
820	840	50	34	19	3	0	0	0	0	0	0	0
840	860	52	36	21	5	0	0	0	0	0	0	0
860	880	54	38	23	7	0	0	0	0	0	0	0
880	900	56	40	25	9	0	0	0	0	0	0	0
900	920	58	42	27	11	0	0	0	0	0	0	0
920	940	60	44	29	13	0	0	0	0	0	0	0
940	960	62	46	31	15	0	0	0	0	0	0	0
960	980	64	48	33	17	1	0	0	0	0	0	0
980	1,000	66	50	35	19	3	0	0	0	0	0	0
1,000	1,020	68	52	37	21	5	0	0	0	0	0	0
1,020	1,040	70	54	39	23	7	0	0	0	0	0	0
1,040	1,060	72	56	41	25	9	0	0	0	0	0	0
1,060	1,080	75	58	43	27	11	0	0	0	0	0	0
1,080	1,100	78	60	45	29	13	0	0	0	0	0	0
1,100	1,120	81	62	47	31	15	0	0	0	0	0	0
1,120	1,140	84	64	49	33	17	2	0	0	0	0	0
1,140	1,160	87	66	51	35	19	4	0	0	0	0	0
1,160	1,180	90	68	53	37	21	6	0	0	0	0	0
1,180	1,200	93	70	55	39	23	8	0	0	0	0	0
1,200	1,220	96	72	57	41	25	10	0	0	0	0	0
1,220	1,240	99	75	59	43	27	12	0	0	0	0	0
1,240	1,260	102	78	61	45	29	14	0	0	0	0	0
1,260	1,280	105	81	63	47	31	16	0	0	0	0	0
1,280	1,300	108	84	65	49	33	18	2	0	0	0	0
1,300	1,320	111	87	67	51	35	20	4	0	0	0	0
1,320	1,340	114	90	69	53	37	22	6	0	0	0	0
1,340	1,360	117	93	71	55	39	24	8	0	0	0	0
1,360	1,380	120	96	73	57	41	26	10	0	0	0	0
1,380	1,400	123	99	76	59	43	28	12	0	0	0	0
1,400	1,420	126	102	79	61	45	30	14	0	0	0	0
1,420	1,440	129	105	82	63	47	32	16	1	0	0	0
1,440	1,460	132	108	85	65	49	34	18	3	0	0	0
1,460	1,480	135	111	88	67	51	36	20	5	0	0	0
1,480	1,500	138	114	91	69	53	38	22	7	0	0	0

Wage Bracket Method Tables for Income Tax Withholding

MARRIED Persons—**BIWEEKLY** Payroll Period

(For Wages Paid through December 31, 2017)

And the wages are–		And the number of withholding allowances claimed is—										
At least	But less than	0	1	2	3	4	5	6	7	8	9	10
		The amount of income tax to be withheld is—										
$1,500	$1,520	$141	$117	$94	$71	$55	$40	$24	$9	$0	$0	$0
1,520	1,540	144	120	97	74	57	42	26	11	0	0	0
1,540	1,560	147	123	100	77	59	44	28	13	0	0	0
1,560	1,580	150	126	103	80	61	46	30	15	0	0	0
1,580	1,600	153	129	106	83	63	48	32	17	1	0	0
1,600	1,620	156	132	109	86	65	50	34	19	3	0	0
1,620	1,640	159	135	112	89	67	52	36	21	5	0	0
1,640	1,660	162	138	115	92	69	54	38	23	7	0	0
1,660	1,680	165	141	118	95	71	56	40	25	9	0	0
1,680	1,700	168	144	121	98	74	58	42	27	11	0	0
1,700	1,720	171	147	124	101	77	60	44	29	13	0	0
1,720	1,740	174	150	127	104	80	62	46	31	15	0	0
1,740	1,760	177	153	130	107	83	64	48	33	17	2	0
1,760	1,780	180	156	133	110	86	66	50	35	19	4	0
1,780	1,800	183	159	136	113	89	68	52	37	21	6	0
1,800	1,820	186	162	139	116	92	70	54	39	23	8	0
1,820	1,840	189	165	142	119	95	72	56	41	25	10	0
1,840	1,860	192	168	145	122	98	75	58	43	27	12	0
1,860	1,880	195	171	148	125	101	78	60	45	29	14	0
1,880	1,900	198	174	151	128	104	81	62	47	31	16	0
1,900	1,920	201	177	154	131	107	84	64	49	33	18	2
1,920	1,940	204	180	157	134	110	87	66	51	35	20	4
1,940	1,960	207	183	160	137	113	90	68	53	37	22	6
1,960	1,980	210	186	163	140	116	93	70	55	39	24	8
1,980	2,000	213	189	166	143	119	96	73	57	41	26	10
2,000	2,020	216	192	169	146	122	99	76	59	43	28	12
2,020	2,040	219	195	172	149	125	102	79	61	45	30	14
2,040	2,060	222	198	175	152	128	105	82	63	47	32	16
2,060	2,080	225	201	178	155	131	108	85	65	49	34	18
2,080	2,100	228	204	181	158	134	111	88	67	51	36	20
2,100	2,120	231	207	184	161	137	114	91	69	53	38	22
2,120	2,140	234	210	187	164	140	117	94	71	55	40	24
2,140	2,160	237	213	190	167	143	120	97	73	57	42	26
2,160	2,180	240	216	193	170	146	123	100	76	59	44	28
2,180	2,200	243	219	196	173	149	126	103	79	61	46	30
2,200	2,220	246	222	199	176	152	129	106	82	63	48	32
2,220	2,240	249	225	202	179	155	132	109	85	65	50	34
2,240	2,260	252	228	205	182	158	135	112	88	67	52	36
2,260	2,280	255	231	208	185	161	138	115	91	69	54	38
2,280	2,300	258	234	211	188	164	141	118	94	71	56	40
2,300	2,320	261	237	214	191	167	144	121	97	74	58	42
2,320	2,340	264	240	217	194	170	147	124	100	77	60	44
2,340	2,360	267	243	220	197	173	150	127	103	80	62	46
2,360	2,380	270	246	223	200	176	153	130	106	83	64	48
2,380	2,400	273	249	226	203	179	156	133	109	86	66	50
2,400	2,420	276	252	229	206	182	159	136	112	89	68	52
2,420	2,440	279	255	232	209	185	162	139	115	92	70	54
2,440	2,460	282	258	235	212	188	165	142	118	95	72	56
2,460	2,480	285	261	238	215	191	168	145	121	98	74	58
2,480	2,500	288	264	241	218	194	171	148	124	101	77	60
2,500	2,520	291	267	244	221	197	174	151	127	104	80	62
2,520	2,540	294	270	247	224	200	177	154	130	107	83	64
2,540	2,560	297	273	250	227	203	180	157	133	110	86	66
2,560	2,580	300	276	253	230	206	183	160	136	113	89	68
2,580	2,600	303	279	256	233	209	186	163	139	116	92	70
2,600	2,620	306	282	259	236	212	189	166	142	119	95	72
2,620	2,640	309	285	262	239	215	192	169	145	122	98	75
2,640	2,660	312	288	265	242	218	195	172	148	125	101	78
2,660	2,680	315	291	268	245	221	198	175	151	128	104	81
2,680	2,700	318	294	271	248	224	201	178	154	131	107	84
2,700	2,720	321	297	274	251	227	204	181	157	134	110	87
2,720	2,740	324	300	277	254	230	207	184	160	137	113	90
2,740	2,760	327	303	280	257	233	210	187	163	140	116	93
2,760	2,780	330	306	283	260	236	213	190	166	143	119	96
2,780	2,800	333	309	286	263	239	216	193	169	146	122	99
2,800	2,820	336	312	289	266	242	219	196	172	149	125	102
2,820	2,840	339	315	292	269	245	222	199	175	152	128	105
2,840	2,860	342	318	295	272	248	225	202	178	155	131	108
2,860	2,880	345	321	298	275	251	228	205	181	158	134	111

$2,880 and over — Use Table 2(b) for a **MARRIED person** on page 45. Also see the instructions on page 43.

Chapter Eleven

Retirement and Other Tax-Deferred Plans and Annuities

The rules concerning contributions to and distributions from qualified retirement and other tax-deferred plans and annuities are voluminous and often complex. Entire books are devoted to portions of the subject matter we discuss in this chapter. We begin with an explanation of what a tax-deferred plan is and what it is intended to accomplish. We discuss the rules pertaining to contributions to each type of plan and then close with a presentation of plan distribution rules and annuities.

Learning Objectives

When you have completed this chapter, you should understand the following learning objectives (LO):

- **LO 11-1** Discuss the basic tax and operational structure of tax-deferred plans and annuities.
- **LO 11-2** Explain details about and contributions to employer-sponsored retirement plans.
- **LO 11-3** Describe the tax rules related to contributions to individual-sponsored retirement plans.
- **LO 11-4** Explain details about and contributions to tax-deferred nonretirement plans.
- **LO 11-5** Apply the tax rules for distributions from tax-deferred plans and the tax treatment of those distributions.
- **LO 11-6** Determine the tax treatment of annuity contracts.

TAX-DEFERRED PLANS AND ANNUITIES: THE BASICS

LO 11-1

Assume that you have decided to save $100,000 for retirement. You go to the bank, open a savings account, and start to make monthly deposits. At the end of the year, the bank sends you a Form 1099-INT, and you must pay taxes on the interest you earned on your savings account. To pay the taxes, you withdraw some money from your savings account. Because you now do not have as much money in your savings account, you are not as close to your goal of saving $100,000 for retirement. Saving money for retirement is an important goal. You would think that the government would give you some incentives to help you save. It has.

As mentioned in other chapters, tax law is not designed solely to raise tax revenue. Sometimes Congress uses the tax law to encourage or discourage certain activities. For example, the deductibility of mortgage interest encourages home ownership, tax credits or deductions for higher education expenses help individuals attend college, and tax penalties discourage illegal tax avoidance by taxpayers.

Congress believes that it is important for individuals to save for retirement, so it has enacted laws to encourage such activity. These laws allow taxpayers to establish various types of tax-deferred plans.[1] They permit a taxpayer to set aside money in a special account, invest that money, and defer paying taxes on the interest, dividends, or capital gains earned by the investments until the taxpayer withdraws money after retirement.

It is important to note that Congress has not said that taxpayers will *never* need to pay tax on the investment earnings—only that the day of reckoning (the day to pay the tax) can be put off until later. That is why these accounts are called *tax-deferred* accounts, not *tax-free* accounts.

Now that you have a better understanding of why tax-deferred accounts exist, let's take a brief look at how they work. Operationally, an eligible individual who wants to start a tax-deferred account opens an account with a trustee (such as a bank or brokerage firm). The trustee exists to ensure the tax rules are followed; after all, Congress is going to give taxpayers a tax break to support a specific purpose, so it wants to make sure the funds are used for that purpose.

All tax-deferred plans have an accumulation period and a distribution period. In the *accumulation period,* a donor contributes assets (usually cash) to the plan. Making a contribution to a tax-deferred plan is similar in concept to making a deposit in a savings account. Contributions are often made monthly or annually over as many as 30 or 40 years. The plan trustee invests the contributed assets. Investments may be CDs, stocks, bonds, or similar assets. Investment decisions may be made solely by the trustee, solely by the donor, or jointly. During the accumulation period, no taxes are due on the earnings from the plan's investments.

During the *distribution period,* the trustee distributes (pays) accumulated assets to the plan beneficiary (or for her or his benefit) to be used for the purpose for which the plan was established. A distribution from a retirement plan is conceptually similar to a withdrawal from a savings account. If the plan is a retirement plan, the assets are distributed to the beneficiaries during their retirement. If the plan is an education plan, the assets are distributed to pay education-related bills of the beneficiaries while they are in school. Distributions may be in a lump sum or may be spread out in payments over many years.

Plan contributions and distributions are subject to numerous tax rules. For example, contributions are generally limited in amount and timing. Distributions must be for specific purposes and are subject to rules pertaining to when they can be made and how they are taxed.

In this chapter, we cover the tax rules associated with contributions to and distributions from retirement plans, other tax-deferred or tax-advantaged plans, and annuities.

Retirement plans can be categorized into employer-sponsored plans (including plans for the self-employed) and individual-sponsored plans. *Employer-sponsored plans* encompass qualified pension and profit-sharing plans, 401(k) or 403(b) plans, Keogh plans, SEPs, and SIMPLE plans. An employer creates and administers these plans. In some cases, only the employer contributes to the plan; in other cases, both the employer and the employee make contributions. *Individual-sponsored retirement plans* are Individual Retirement Accounts (IRAs), which include traditional IRAs and Roth IRAs. These plans are created and funded by the individual.

Tax-deferred nonretirement plans are also available for health-related or education expenses. The most common health plans are Health Savings Accounts, discussed in Chapter 4. We cover Coverdell Education Savings Accounts (CESAs) in this chapter.

Sometimes the taxability of distributions or the deductibility of contributions can be a source of confusion. A good rule of thumb to keep in mind when learning about retirement and tax-deferred plans is that if the plan is funded with dollars that have *not* been taxed, the distributions

[1] As you will see, most of these accounts are tax-deferred accounts in which taxability of benefits is postponed to a later date. However, some of these accounts receive different types of tax benefits and are sometimes called *tax-advantaged accounts.* For ease of exposition, we generically refer to all of these accounts as *tax-deferred accounts.*

Buzzwords

Annuity: Series of payments made pursuant to a contract usually between an individual and an insurance company, brokerage firm, or bank. Payments are normally uniformly spaced (monthly, quarterly, or annually).

Beneficiary: Person(s) entitled to receive the benefits from a plan.

Contributions: Amounts deposited into the tax-deferred plan by the donor. Contributions may or may not be tax-deductible, depending on the plan. When making a contribution to the plan, the donor is said to have "funded" the plan.

Distributions: Amounts withdrawn from the tax-deferred plan. Distributions are made to, or for the benefit of, the beneficiary and must be made in accordance with applicable tax rules. Distributions may or may not be taxable, depending on the plan.

Donor: Person(s) or entity(ies) responsible for making contributions to a plan. The donor and the beneficiary can be, and often are, the same individual.

Taxability of plan earnings: Except in unusual circumstances, earnings derived from the investment of plan assets are not taxed in the year earned.

Tax-deferred retirement plan: Account held by a trustee to accumulate and invest assets to be distributed to a beneficiary during retirement.

Tax-deferred plans for other purposes: Account held by a trustee to accumulate and invest assets to pay for a specific purpose such as health care or education.

Trustee: Entity—often a bank, brokerage firm, or insurance company—legally responsible to ensure that a plan's contributions and distributions follow legal and tax rules.

will be fully taxed; if the plan is funded with already taxed dollars, some or all of the distributions will not be taxed. This rule of thumb is not always true, but it is a good place to start.

In this chapter, we also discuss the tax rules pertaining to distributions from an *annuity,* which is a series of payments made pursuant to a contract. The contract is usually between an individual and an insurance company, a financial services company, or an employer. Annuities often arise in conjunction with the payout phase of a retirement plan. The primary tax issue associated with an annuity payment is how much of each payment is taxable.

Payments to a tax-advantaged retirement plan are often tax-deductible and are shown as a *for* AGI deduction on Form 1040, line 32 (for an IRA) or line 28 (for Keogh, SEP, or SIMPLE plans). Form 1040A accommodates only IRA contributions (line 17). Deductible payments made by employers (with respect to pension plans and 401(k) plans) are reported on the employer's tax return. Distributions from retirement plans and annuities are usually taxable, at least in part, and are found on Form 1040, lines 15 and 16, or Form 1040A, lines 11 and 12.

CONCEPT CHECK 11-1— LO 11-1

1. Tax-deferred retirement accounts are essentially tax-free accounts. True or false?
2. The period in which accumulated assets are paid to plan beneficiaries is known as the _______________ period.
3. A Keogh plan is an example of an individual-based retirement plan. True or false?
4. Two examples of employer-based retirement plans are _______________ and _______________.
5. Distributions from pension plans are taxable if the contributions were made using dollars that were not previously taxed. True or false?

EMPLOYER-SPONSORED RETIREMENT PLANS

LO 11-2

Qualified Pension Plans

A *qualified pension plan* provides systematic and definite payments to employees and their beneficiaries after retirement. Individuals receive payments over a period of years, often for life. Most often, the payments are made monthly. The *retirement benefit* amount is determined using factors such as years of employee service and compensation received.[2] The amount of payment must be "definitely determinable" using actuarial assumptions in a manner not subject to employer discretion.[3]

A qualified pension plan must meet strict requirements including (1) not discriminating in favor of highly compensated employees, (2) forming and operating for the exclusive benefit of employees or their beneficiaries, (3) having certain vesting and funding requirements, and (4) having certain minimum participation standards.[4]

A qualified pension plan provides significant tax benefits to both employers and employees. The primary benefits follow:

- The employer gets an immediate deduction for contributions.[5]
- Employer contributions are not compensation to the employee.
- Earnings from investments held by the plan are not taxable when earned.[6]
- Plan assets or earnings are not taxable to employees until the amounts are distributed.[7]

Qualified pension plans may be noncontributory or contributory. In a noncontributory plan, only the employer (not the employee) contributes. In a contributory plan, the employee can choose to contribute beyond employer contributions. The employer can require employee contributions as long as the plan is nondiscriminatory toward highly paid individuals.

A pension plan can also be a qualified profit-sharing plan. Contributions are not required on an annual basis, and it does not matter whether the employer has positive income in a contribution year.[8] Profit-sharing plans must have a definite, predetermined formula for allocating plan contributions to participants and for establishing benefit payments. Note that the required formula applies to the allocation of those contributions once made, not to the amount of the contributions.

Qualified plans may be either a defined contribution plan or a defined benefit plan. *Defined contribution plans* establish the contribution but do not establish the amount of retirement benefits. These plans provide an individual account for each participant and pay benefits based on those accounts.[9] Thus the amount of eventual retirement benefits is unknown. *Defined benefit plans* are those plans that are not defined contribution plans.[10] These defined benefit plans provide a stream of definitely determinable retirement benefits. Defined benefit plans are often deemed to be "less risky" to beneficiaries because, by design, they provide greater certainty as to the amount and timing of future benefits.

TAX YOUR BRAIN

Are qualified pension plans likely to be defined contribution or defined benefit plans? Which are qualified profit-sharing plans likely to be?

ANSWER

Pension plans are more likely to be defined benefit plans, and profit-sharing plans are more likely to be defined contribution plans. By their very nature, defined benefit plans require a more precisely defined stream of inputs (contributions) to enable them to provide a precisely defined stream of outputs (benefits). Contributions to profit-sharing plans are more variable, which makes it less likely there will be a "stream of definitely determinable benefits."

[2] An example is a pension plan that pays each retired employee an annual pension (payable on a monthly basis) equal to 2% of the employee's final salary for each year of service to the company. Thus an employee who worked 30 years for the company would receive an annual pension equal to 60% of his or her final annual salary.

[3] IRC § 401(a)(25).

[4] IRC § 401(a).

[5] IRC § 404.

[6] IRC § 501(a).

[7] IRC § 402.

[8] IRC § 401(a)(27).

[9] IRC § 414(i).

[10] IRC § 414(j).

Normally a bank, insurance company, or financial services company administers a trust that receives the contributions made to pension or profit-sharing plans. One reason for the trust arrangement is that, in the event that the business has financial difficulties or declares bankruptcy, creditors cannot attach the assets set aside for the benefit of the employees. From a practical matter, few companies are in the business of running a pension plan.

To obtain and retain qualified status, a pension or profit-sharing plan must meet complex rules, including the following:

- Be for the exclusive benefit of the employees and their beneficiaries.[11]
- Not discriminate in favor of highly compensated employees—employees who either (a) own more than 5% of the corporation's stock in the current or prior year or (b) received more than $120,000 compensation in the previous year and were in the top 20% of employees based on compensation.[12]
- Have adequate coverage for rank-and-file employees. In general, the plan must benefit at least 70% of those employees who are not highly compensated.[13] A defined benefit plan must also meet certain minimum participation requirements.[14]
- Meet certain minimum vesting standards.[15] *Vesting* occurs when an employee obtains a nonforfeitable right to his or her benefits. Employee contributions must vest immediately. Employer contributions must fully vest after five years of service or must vest 20% in the third year of service and increase 20% per year thereafter until fully vested after seven years of service.

TAX YOUR BRAIN

Why would Congress require vesting rules for employer contributions?

ANSWER

It did so for at least two reasons. First, by design, pension plans provide benefits to participants during retirement. By requiring vesting, Congress ensured that participants will receive payments because the payments cannot go to others or back to the company. Second, qualified plans give employers an immediate tax deduction for contributions. With vesting, Congress has reasonable assurance that the employer deductions are valid in the long run.

Qualified plans must also meet certain limitations on contributions and benefits. Annual per employee additions to a defined contribution plan cannot exceed the lower of $54,000 or 100% of the employee's compensation.[16] Annual additions include employer contributions, employee contributions, and forfeitures (for employees leaving the company before full vesting).

Defined benefit plans have no restrictions on contributions. However, these plans are restricted to annual benefits to a participant equal to the lower of $215,000 or 100% of average compensation of the participant for the highest three years.[17]

For profit-sharing plans, employers can take a maximum annual deduction of 25% of compensation paid.[18]

[11] IRC § 401(a).

[12] IRC § 414(q). The 20% criterion is effective only if the taxpayer elects. The $120,000 amount is subject to annual inflation adjustment.

[13] IRC § 410(b).

[14] IRC § 401 (a)(26).

[15] IRC § 411(a).

[16] IRC § 415(c)(1). The contribution limit is subject to annual inflation adjustment.

[17] IRC § 415(b)(1). The contribution limit is subject to annual inflation adjustment.

[18] IRC § 404(a)(3)(A).

401(k) Plans

An employer can provide a 401(k) plan (named after the IRC section from which it comes) in addition to, or in the place of, a qualified pension or profit-sharing plan. A 401(k) plan is a qualified profit-sharing plan under which an employee can choose to receive a specified portion of her or his wages directly in cash or can elect to have the employer pay the amount on the employee's behalf into a qualified trust for the benefit of the employee on retirement.[19] Trust payments are made with pretax dollars. A 403(b) plan (again named after the IRC section that created it) is equivalent to a 401(k) plan but is for employees of educational and certain tax-exempt organizations.

An employee may elect to defer up to $18,000 under a 401(k) plan.[20] Employees age 50 or over can defer an additional $6,000. Any excess contributions must either be returned to the employee by April 15 of the following year or be included in the employee's gross income.

EXAMPLE 11-1

Fouad earns $80,000 in taxable wages. His employer establishes a 401(k) plan in which he participates. Fouad elects to have 3% of his wages paid into the 401(k) plan. For the year, his employer withholds $2,400 ($80,000 × 3%) from his paychecks on a pretax basis and deposits the amount in trust on Fouad's behalf. As a result, Fouad's taxable wages for the year are $77,600 ($80,000 – $2,400).

A 401(k) plan must meet all of the qualification rules established for pension and profit-sharing plans. In addition, amounts held in the trust cannot be distributed except in the case of termination of the plan or the employee's (a) separation from service, death, or disability, (b) attainment of the age of 59½, or (c) hardship.[21] Hardship distributions are permitted if the employee has an "immediate heavy financial need" that can be met with the distribution and that cannot be relieved by alternative sources such as loans or insurance.[22] Additional nondiscrimination rules apply to 401(k) plans as enumerated in IRC § 401(k)(3).

Keogh Plans

Self-employed individuals are not employees, so they cannot participate in a qualified pension or profit-sharing plan established by an employer. However, they can establish an individual Keogh plan, which is subject to the same contribution and benefit limitations as pension or profit-sharing plans. For defined contribution Keogh plans, self-employed individuals can contribute the lower of $54,000 or 25% of earned income from self-employment.[23] For purposes of the calculation, earned income cannot exceed $270,000.[24] Earned income from self-employment is determined after the deduction for one-half of the self-employment taxes paid and after the amount of the Keogh contribution.

EXAMPLE 11-2

Walter is a self-employed architect. In 2017 his earnings, before the Keogh deduction but after deduction for one-half the self-employment tax, are $60,000. His Keogh deduction for purposes of the 25% calculation is

$$\$60{,}000 - 0.25X = X$$

$$\text{Thus } X = \$48{,}000$$

where X is the amount of self-employment income after the Keogh deduction.

Walter is entitled to contribute the lower of $54,000 or $12,000 (25% of $48,000). Thus his maximum Keogh contribution is $12,000.

[19] IRC § 401(k)(2).

[20] IRC § 402(g)(1). The contribution limit is subject to annual inflation adjustment.

[21] IRC § 401(k)(2).

[22] Reg. § 1.401(k)-1(d)(2).

[23] IRC § 415(c). The contribution limit is subject to annual inflation adjustment.

[24] IRC § 404(l). The earned income limit is subject to annual inflation adjustment.

Defined benefit Keogh plans are subject to the $215,000/100% funding rules given previously for qualified defined benefit plans. Keogh plans must be established by the end of the tax year (once established, the plan continues from year to year). Contributions are required no later than the due date of the return, including extensions.[25]

If a self-employed individual has employees, the Keogh plan must also cover full-time employees under the same nondiscrimination, vesting, and other rules established for qualified plans. Contributions for these employees are deductible by the self-employed individual on Schedule C of his or her tax return.

Simplified Employee Pensions

Qualified pension and profit-sharing plans are complex and can be difficult to establish and administer. Small businesses can establish a *Simplified Employee Pension* (SEP).[26] With a SEP, an employer contributes to IRA accounts of its employees, up to a specified maximum contribution. SEPs must conform to the following rules:

- All employees who have reached the age of 21, who have worked for the employer for at least three of the preceding five years, and who received at least $600 in compensation must be covered.[27]
- Contributions cannot discriminate in favor of highly compensated employees.
- Annual deductible contributions cannot exceed the lower of 25% of the employee's compensation (with a maximum of $270,000) or the $54,000 limitation for defined contribution plans.[28]
- The employer cannot restrict the employee's withdrawals.[29]

Initial SEP adoption must be effective no later than the due date of the employer's return, including extensions. Most small employers adopt a SEP by using Form 5305-SEP. Contributions to the SEP are required no later than the due date of the return of the employer, including extensions.

Self-employed individuals can create and contribute to a SEP. Contribution limits are determined in the same manner as for Keogh plans.

SIMPLE Plans

Employers with 100 or fewer employees who do not have a qualified pension or profit-sharing plan can establish a *SIMPLE retirement plan* for their employees.[30] Under a SIMPLE plan, the employer creates an IRA or a 401(k) account for each employee. Eligible employees are those who earned at least $5,000 during any two preceding years and who are reasonably expected to earn at least $5,000 in the current year. Employees are not required to contribute. SIMPLE plans are not subject to the nondiscrimination rules that apply to other qualified plans. Thus there is no requirement that a certain number or percentage of employees must participate in the SIMPLE plan.

Employees can elect to contribute an employer-specified percentage (or dollar amount if the employer agrees) of their pretax wages with a maximum annual contribution of $12,500.[31] Employees age 50 or older can elect to make additional contributions of up to $2,500 (for a maximum of $15,000 per year).

[25] IRC § 404(a)(6).

[26] IRC § 408(k).

[27] IRC § 408(k)(2). The $600 compensation amount is subject to annual inflation adjustment.

[28] Both dollar amounts are subject to annual inflation adjustment.

[29] IRC § 408(k)(4)(B).

[30] IRC § 408(p).

[31] IRC § 408(p)(2)(A)(ii). The maximum contribution is subject to annual inflation adjustment.

From Shoebox to Software

Contributions to qualified plans, Keogh plans, SEPs, and SIMPLE plans are deductible as a *for* AGI deduction to the extent contributed by the individual. The portion contributed by the employer is not deductible (remember that the employer contribution is not taxable to the employee in the first place).

In tax software, employee contributions to these plans are generally reported on a worksheet. You enter the amount of the deductible contribution in the appropriate box, and that amount carries forward to Form 1040, line 28.

The plan's trustee will report for an individual covered by a SEP or SIMPLE plan the amount of employee contribution in box 8 or 9 of Form 5498 (see Exhibit 11-1).

The trustees of qualified pension plans report employee contributions to employees on a similar form.

Employers either must make a matching contribution of up to 3% (in most instances) of the employee's compensation or must make a nonelective contribution of 2% of compensation for each employee eligible to participate (whether or not the employee actually participates). Contributions to a SIMPLE plan fully and immediately vest to the employee.

EXAMPLE 11-3 Acme Corporation established a SIMPLE plan for its 10 eligible employees, each of whom earned more than $5,000 in the current and prior years. Seven employees elect to contribute 5% of their pretax wages while the other three decline to participate. Acme can choose to make either matching contributions of 3% of wages for the seven employees who elected to participate or a contribution of 2% of wages for all 10 employees.

EXHIBIT 11-1

☐ CORRECTED (if checked)

TRUSTEE'S or ISSUER'S name, street address, city or town, state or province, country, and ZIP or foreign postal code	1 IRA contributions (other than amounts in boxes 2–4, 8–10, 13a, and 14a) $ 2 Rollover contributions $	OMB No. 1545-0747 **2017** Form **5498**		**IRA Contribution Information**
TRUSTEE'S or ISSUER'S federal identification no. / PARTICIPANT'S social security number	3 Roth IRA conversion amount $	4 Recharacterized contributions $		**Copy B**
	5 Fair market value of account $	6 Life insurance cost included in box 1 $		**For Participant**
PARTICIPANT'S name	7 IRA ☐ SEP ☐	SIMPLE ☐ Roth IRA ☐		This information is being furnished to the Internal Revenue Service.
	8 SEP contributions $	9 SIMPLE contributions $		
Street address (including apt. no.)	10 Roth IRA contributions $	11 If checked, required minimum distribution for 2018 ☐		
	12a RMD date	12b RMD amount $		
City or town, state or province, country, and ZIP or foreign postal code	13a Postponed contribution $	13b Year	13c Code	
	14a Repayments $	14b Code		
Account number (see instructions)	15a FMV of certain specified assets $	15b Code(s)		

Form **5498** (keep for your records) www.irs.gov/form5498 Department of the Treasury - Internal Revenue Service

Source: U.S. Department of the Treasury, Internal Revenue Service, Form 5498. Washington, DC: 2017.

Employers establish a SIMPLE plan using Form 5305-S or 5305-SA. The employer retains the form and does not file it with the IRS. Employers must initially adopt the plan between January 1 and October 1. The employer must make contributions no later than the due date of the employer's return, including extensions.

CONCEPT CHECK 11-2—
LO 11-2

1. Qualified pension plans are either defined ____________ plans or defined ____________ plans.
2. Employees must make contributions to qualified pension plans. True or false?
3. The maximum contribution to a 401(k) plan is ____________ for individuals under age 50.
4. A Keogh plan can be used by self-employed individuals. True or false?
5. A SIMPLE plan can be used by employers with 100 or fewer employees who also meet other requirements. True or false?

INDIVIDUAL-SPONSORED RETIREMENT PLANS

LO 11-3

Individual-sponsored retirement plans are Individual Retirement Accounts (IRAs). There are two types: a traditional IRA and a Roth IRA. Although the accounts sound similar, they have significant differences.

Traditional IRA

A traditional IRA is a tax-deferred retirement account for individuals with earned income (employees and self-employed individuals). Qualified individuals can make IRA contributions and take a *for* AGI deduction equal to the lower of \$5,500 or the amount of compensation for the year.[32] Individuals who are age 50 or older as of the end of the tax year can contribute the lower of \$6,500 or the amount of annual compensation. Earnings on invested contributions grow tax-deferred until distribution.

A qualified individual is someone who is not an active participant and whose spouse is not an active participant in an employer-sponsored retirement plan (qualified pension or profit-sharing plan, Keogh, 401(k), SEP, SIMPLE). Even if an individual (or spouse) is an active participant, she or he can make a deductible IRA contribution if her or his AGI is below certain limits. The allowed IRA deduction begins to be phased out for active participants when AGI exceeds certain amounts, depending on the filing status of the taxpayer.[33] For joint filers, the amount is \$99,000, for single or head of household filers the amount is \$62,000, and for married filing separately the amount is zero.[34]

Once AGI reaches the indicated amounts, the taxpayer can use the following formula to determine the disallowed portion of the IRA deduction:

$$\frac{\text{AGI} - \text{Applicable limit}}{\$10{,}000 \text{ or } \$20{,}000} \times \$5{,}500 = \text{Disallowed deduction}$$

The denominator of the fraction is \$10,000 for taxpayers filing as single or head of household and \$20,000 for married filing jointly. For taxpayers over 50 years old, the \$5,500 figure is \$6,500.

[32] IRC § 219(b)(1).

[33] IRC § 219(g)(3)(B).

[34] These amounts increase each year in accordance with an IRC schedule.

From Shoebox to Software

Qualified individuals can make deductible contributions to a traditional IRA. Trustees report contributions on Form 5498 (see Exhibit 11-1).

In your software, you generally enter information concerning IRA contributions on a worksheet or directly on Form 5498. If the requirements to make a deductible contribution are met, the amount in box 1 of Form 5498 is entered as a contribution at the top of the form. It is important to realize that the amount in box 1 is only the amount *contributed*—the trustee makes no determination as to whether the amount is deductible. It is the responsibility of the taxpayer or preparer to report the proper deduction.

Information from the worksheet is carried forward to Form 1040, line 32, or Form 1040A, line 17.

If you open the tax return file for Jose and Maria Ramirez and then open the IRA summary sheet, you will see that the maximum allowable IRA contribution for Jose is zero. This is so because he was covered by a retirement plan at work and he earned in excess of the income limitation.

Contributions to a Roth IRA are in box 10 of Form 5498. You record this amount in the appropriate place on the IRA worksheet or the form.

TAX-DEFERRED NONRETIREMENT PLANS

LO 11-4

The two major types of tax-deferred nonretirement plans are health-related plans and education-related plans. In Chapter 4 we discussed Health Savings Accounts. Here we describe the Coverdell Education Savings Account.

Coverdell Education Savings Account

Taxpayers who meet AGI limitations can contribute to a Coverdell Education Savings Account (CESA) exclusively to pay the qualified elementary, secondary, or higher education expenses of the beneficiary.[43] CESAs are similar to Roth IRAs in that contributions are not deductible, earnings accumulate tax-free, and distributions are not taxable (if used for their intended purpose).

Contributions are limited to $2,000 per year per beneficiary, must be in cash, and must be made before the beneficiary turns 18.[44]

Subject to limitations as to the amount, any person can contribute to a CESA for any person (themselves included). The contributor is not required to report a certain amount of earned income, nor must the contributor be related to the beneficiary. A contributor (or contributors) can establish multiple CESAs for multiple beneficiaries, and an individual can be the beneficiary of multiple CESAs. However, for any given tax year, the aggregate contributions to all CESAs for a specific individual beneficiary cannot exceed $2,000.

EXAMPLE 11-7

Roger and Shelly have one child, Caroline. They established a CESA for Caroline. Shelly's parents can establish a separate CESA for Caroline or can contribute to the CESA already established. The total permitted contributions to all CESAs for which Caroline is the beneficiary cannot exceed $2,000. Thus, if Caroline's parents contribute $1,500 to her CESA in 2017, the grandparents can contribute a maximum of $500 in 2017.

Permitted contributions begin to phase out ratably when the contributor's AGI reaches $190,000 for joint returns or $95,000 for single and head of household returns.[45] When AGI

[43] IRC § 530(b)(1).

[44] IRC § 530(b)(1)(A).

[45] AGI is increased by foreign income excluded from AGI under IRC §§ 911, 931, and 933.

exceeds $220,000 for married taxpayers or $110,000 for single or head of household taxpayers, no CESA contribution is allowed. The formulas to determine the disallowed contribution in the phaseout range are as follows.

Use this formula for joint returns:

$$\frac{\text{AGI} - \text{Applicable limit}}{\$30{,}000} \times \$2{,}000 = \text{Disallowed contribution}$$

Use this formula for single or head of household returns:

$$\frac{\text{AGI} - \text{Applicable limit}}{\$15{,}000} \times \$2{,}000 = \text{Disallowed contribution}$$

EXAMPLE 11-8

Vance and Martha file a joint return showing AGI of $196,300. Their disallowed CESA contribution is $420 ([$196,300 − $190,000] / [$30,000 × $2,000]), so their permitted contribution is $1,580 ($2,000 − $420). If their AGI was more than $220,000, Vance and Martha would not be permitted to make a CESA contribution.

Taxpayers establish the trust using a Form 5305-E or 5305-EA. As with the Roth IRA, the form is not filed with the taxpayer's return but is retained in the tax files. The trustee must be a bank or other entity or person who will administer the account properly.[46]

You can find additional information about CESAs in Chapter 7 of IRS Publication 970—Tax Benefits for Education.

CONCEPT CHECK 11-4—
LO 11-4

1. Contributions to Coverdell Education Savings Accounts (CESAs) are not deductible. True or false?
2. The maximum annual contribution to a CESA is $____________.
3. Contributions to CESA accounts begin to be phased out when AGI reaches $____________ for a single taxpayer.

DISTRIBUTIONS FROM TAX-DEFERRED PENSION PLANS

LO 11-5

General

All pension plans have an accumulation period when contributions are received and invested and a distribution period when assets are paid to owners or beneficiaries. Individuals with pension plan assets normally withdraw those assets during their retirement. The payments received during retirement are *distributions* or *withdrawals*.

Recall that a defined benefit plan provides a retiree certain specified distributions over a specified period or for life. Normally retirees receive fixed distributions (often with inflation adjustments) on a regular basis (such as monthly or quarterly). Many large corporations and unions have defined benefit plans. Retirees do not have an ownership interest in any portion of the plan assets; they are simply entitled to a stream of payments (called an *annuity*).

The second category of pension plans is a defined contribution plan. These plans accumulate assets from contributions and earnings that belong to a specific individual but that are not predetermined as to the value upon retirement. An IRA is an example of a defined contribution plan. While the retiree worked, he or she contributed to the IRA and invested those contributions. The IRA assets belong to the retiree, but there is no guarantee as to either

[46] IRC § 530(b)(1)(B).

their value at retirement or the date the assets will be exhausted once withdrawals commence. Because assets in defined contribution plans belong to the retiree, he or she usually can specify the amount and timing of plan withdrawals.

To reduce the chance of living beyond the point that their pension plan assets are exhausted, beneficiaries of defined contribution plans sometimes choose to buy an annuity contract using some or all of the plan assets. In doing so, the beneficiary is trading a lump sum for a stream of payments. Effectively, the beneficiary becomes a participant in a defined benefit plan to the extent of the annuity.

You can find additional information pertaining to distributions from tax-deferred pension plans in IRS Publication 575—Pension and Annuity Income.

Distributions from Qualified Pension Plans

A distribution from a qualified pension plan (pension and profit-sharing plan, Keogh, 401(k), 403(b), IRA, SEP, SIMPLE) may be fully taxable, nontaxable, or a combination of both. Generally proceeds are tax-free if they are attributable to contributions made with taxed dollars (a nondeductible contribution), and proceeds are taxable if they are attributable to contributions made with untaxed dollars (a deduction was allowed or income was excluded) or if they are attributable to tax-deferred earnings. The annuity provisions govern taxability of distributions from qualified employer retirement plans.[47]

To apply the simplified method of taxing payments from a qualified plan, the taxpayer must first determine the amount that she or he contributed to the plan with previously taxed dollars. The previously taxed investment is divided by the number of anticipated future payments (see the following table). The resulting fraction represents the proportion of each payment that will be tax-free. The remainder of the annuity payment is taxable as ordinary income. If the employee contributed nothing to the plan, the entire payment is taxable.

If the annuity is payable over the life of a single individual, the number of anticipated payments is determined as of the starting date of the payments as follows:

Age of the Individual	Number of Anticipated Monthly Payments
55 or under	360
56–60	310
61–65	260
66–70	210
71 or over	160[48]

If the annuity is payable over the life of more than one individual (the lives of a retiree and his or her spouse), the number of anticipated payments is determined as of the starting date of the payments as follows:

Combined Ages of the Individuals	Number of Anticipated Monthly Payments
110 or under	410
111–120	360
121–130	310
131–140	260
141 or over	210[49]

[47] Specifically, the simplified rules under IRC § 72(d).

[48] IRC § 72(d)(1)(B)(iii).

[49] IRC § 72(d)(1)(B)(iv).

EXAMPLE 11-9

Zeke is entitled to monthly payments of $2,000 over his life from his employer's qualified pension plan. He contributed $97,500 to the plan prior to his retirement at age 64. Zeke would be able to exclude $375 ($97,500 / 260) from each payment as a nontaxable return of his contributions. The remaining $1,625 would be taxable at ordinary income rates.

EXAMPLE 11-10

Instead of taking $2,000 a month over his life, Zeke chose to receive monthly payments of $1,800 a month over his life and that of his 62-year-old wife. The combined ages of Zeke and his wife are 126. Thus Zeke would be permitted to exclude $314.52 ($97,500/310) from each payment with the remaining $1,485.48 being taxable.

The anticipated payment tables assume monthly payments. If payments are received other than monthly, appropriate adjustments are made. For example, the number of anticipated monthly payments for an individual age 55 or under is 360. If the actual payments are made quarterly, the number of anticipated quarterly payments will be 120 (360/12 = 30 years × 4 quarters per year). This would be the number used in the denominator to determine the exclusion amount.

Retirement plans (other than Roth IRAs) must make required distributions.[50] For many plans (especially qualified pension and profit-sharing plans), the plan administrator determines the required distribution rules. Such determination is not a concern to the recipient. However, especially in the case of a traditional IRA, the taxpayer may be required to make the appropriate required minimum distribution calculations.

Generally, distributions from a retirement plan can be taken without penalty once the owner (the person who made the contributions) reaches age 59½. However, it is usually good tax planning to defer withdrawals for as long as practical so that the account balance can continue to grow tax-deferred. Tax deferral cannot continue indefinitely—the tax code mandates certain minimum withdrawals. These minimum withdrawals commence once the plan owner reaches age 70½.

The required minimum distribution (RMD) for a year is equal to the account balance at the end of the prior year divided by the minimum distribution period. The minimum distribution period is determined in accordance with life expectancy tables provided by the IRS in Publication 590. Some of these tables are provided in the appendix to this chapter. Table III is the one used by owners of the retirement plan who either are unmarried or whose spouse is not more than 10 years younger. Table I is used by the beneficiary of a retirement plan after the original owner has died. Table II (not provided but available in Publication 590) is used by owners whose spouse is more than 10 years younger. When referring to the tables, the age used is the age of the taxpayer as of the end of the year for which the distribution is calculated.

EXAMPLE 11-11

Arlene is age 77 and must determine her required minimum distribution for tax year 2017. She would use the balance in her retirement account as of the end of 2016 and would refer to the proper life expectancy table using her age as of the end of 2017.

EXAMPLE 11-12

Mort is unmarried and has been receiving distributions from his retirement plan. He must determine his required minimum distribution for 2017. He is age 76 at the end of 2017. At the end of 2016, his plan had a balance of $110,000. Using Table III, his life expectancy is 22.0 years. Mort must receive at least $5,000 ($110,000/22.0) from his retirement plan in 2017. If Mort were married and the age difference between Mort and his spouse was 10 years or less, the answer to this question would be the same. If the age difference were more than 10 years, Mort would need to use Table II in IRS Publication 590 to determine the appropriate life expectancy.

[50] IRC § 401(a)(9).

If a plan owner reaches age 70½ and he or she has not received any distributions from the plan, there are special rules associated with determining and distributing the very first payment.

Plans can distribute each employee's interest either (1) in a lump sum on the required *beginning date* or (2) in payments starting on the required beginning date, over the life expectancy of the employee or of the employee and a designated beneficiary. The required beginning date is April 1 of the calendar year following the year in which the taxpayer reaches age 70½.[51]

Note that the first distribution is calculated for the tax year in which the taxpayer reaches age 70½. However, that first distribution does not need to be made until April 1 of the tax year after the taxpayer reaches age 70½.

EXAMPLE 11-13

Taxpayer A's 70th birthday was February 1, 2017, so the taxpayer reaches age 70½ on August 1 2017. The distribution calculated for 2017 must be distributed to the taxpayer no later than April 1 2018. Taxpayer B's 70th birthday was November 1, 2017, so the taxpayer is 70½ on May 1, 2018. There is no required distribution for 2017. The distribution calculated for 2018 must be distributed to the taxpayer no later than April 1, 2019.

EXAMPLE 11-14

Mort is unmarried. His 70th birthday was March 1, 2017. Thus he reached age 70½ on September 1, 2017, and his required beginning date is April 1, 2018. At the end of 2016, the balance in his retirement plan was $300,000. He needs to calculate his tax year 2017 required minimum distribution (2017 is the year he turned 70½). At the end of 2017 he will be 70 years old. Using Table III, the life expectancy to use in the calculations is 27.4 years. Thus he must receive at least $10,949 ($300,000/27.4) from his retirement plan no later than April 1, 2018.

EXAMPLE 11-15

Assume Mort's 70th birthday was November 1, 2016. Thus he reached age 70½ on May 1, 2017, and his required beginning date is April 1, 2018. At the end of 2016, the balance in his retirement plan was $550,000. He needs to calculate his tax year 2017 required minimum distribution (2017 is the year he turned 70½). At the end of 2017 he will be 71 years old. Using Table III, the life expectancy to use in the calculations is 26.5 years. Thus he must receive at least $20,755 ($550,000/26.5) from his retirement plan no later than April 1, 2018.

When the owner of a retirement plan dies, special rules apply. These rules depend on whether the beneficiary of the plan (the person who inherits the plan assets) is the spouse or someone else. If the sole beneficiary is the spouse, he or she can elect to be treated as the owner. If so, the beneficiary would account for the retirement plan using the rules just indicated. If the beneficiary is not the spouse (or if the spouse does not make the election to be treated as the owner), the beneficiary generally determines the required minimum distribution for the year of death using his or her age with reference to Table I. For each subsequent year, that factor is reduced by 1. There are special rules for beneficiaries that are not individuals.

EXAMPLE 11-16

Conrad died in 2017 at age 80. His nephew Arnold was the sole beneficiary and was age 67. Using Table I, Arnold would use 19.4 as the appropriate factor in 2017, 18.4 in 2018, and so forth.

Caution: The distribution rules for beneficiaries can be complex. Refer to the Internal Revenue Code and to IRS Publication 590 for additional information.

If required minimum distributions are not made properly, the taxpayer is subject to a nondeductible excise tax equal to 50% of the shortfall.[52] The penalty is reported on Form 5329.

[51] In the case of non-IRA accounts, it is the later of 70½ or the year in which the employee retires.

[52] IRC § 4974(a).

TAX YOUR BRAIN

Why are minimum withdrawal provisions required?

ANSWER

Recall that, for the most part, funds in a pension plan have never been taxed. If there were no minimum distribution standards, the assets could remain in the account and continue to accumulate tax-free indefinitely. In an effort to ensure eventual taxation of contributions and earnings, Congress enacted the minimum withdrawal provisions.

Retirement plan distributions that are includable in income are subject to a 10% additional tax unless the distributions meet *one* of the following exceptions:

- Distributed to an employee or retiree at or after age 59½.
- Made to a beneficiary or estate on or after the death of the employee.
- Paid attributable to a disability.
- Made to an employee over the age of 55 after separation from service (in the case of qualified pension and profit-sharing plans).
- Paid for deductible medical expenses (above the 10% threshold) whether or not the employee itemizes.
- Paid from an IRA to unemployed individuals for health insurance premiums.
- Paid from a CESA for higher education expenses
- Paid from an IRA for "first home" purchases with a $10,000 lifetime maximum.
- Paid from a qualified plan to an alternative payee under provisions of a qualified domestic relations order.
- Distributed to pay an IRS tax levy on the plan.
- Paid as part of a series of substantially equal periodic payments over the life expectancy of the employee (an annuity). In the case of qualified pension and profit-sharing plans, these payments can start only after separation from service.[53]

In the case of SIMPLE plans, distributions not meeting one or more of the preceding exceptions made during the first two years of participation are subject to a 25% additional tax rather than 10%.

The purpose of the additional tax is to discourage withdrawals from retirement plans until the beneficiary retires unless the distribution is for one of the special purposes.

Taxpayers can choose to have the plan administrator withhold taxes on distributions. These withholdings are reported on Form 1099-R, box 4 (see Exhibit 11-3 later in this chapter).

CONCEPT CHECK 11-5— LO 11-5

1. A participant in a defined benefit plan is entitled to only a stream of payments. True or false?
2. Distributions from qualified pension plans may be taxable, nontaxable, or both. True or false?
3. The number of anticipated payments from a pension plan for a single individual, age 68, is ____________.
4. The number of anticipated payments from a pension plan for a married couple aged 59 and 63 is ____________.
5. Distributions are required from a traditional IRA. True or false?

Taxation of Traditional IRA Distributions

Distributions from traditional IRAs are fully taxable if the IRA was entirely funded with deductible contributions. If an IRA was funded partially with deductible contributions and

[53] IRC § 72(t)(1) through (8).

partially with nondeductible contributions, a portion of each distribution is nontaxable. If such is the case, the taxpayer must first determine his or her tax basis in the IRA. The tax basis is equal to the sum of all nondeductible contributions made to the IRA minus the sum of all nontaxable distributions received as of the beginning of the year. Calculation of the tax-free portion is determined as follows:

$$\frac{\text{Tax basis in the IRA (i.e., after-tax contributions)}}{\text{End-of-year asset value} + \text{Distribution for the year}} \times \text{Distribution for the year} = \text{Nontaxable distribution}$$

EXAMPLE 11-17

Michael, age 65, retired in 2017. During the year, he received distributions of $7,000 from his IRA. He made nondeductible contributions of $10,000 to the IRA in prior years and has never received a nontaxable distribution. As of December 31, 2017, the value of his IRA was $100,000. The nontaxable portion of Michael's distribution is $654, calculated as follows:

[$10,000 / ($100,000 + $7,000)] × $7,000 = $654

Michael's taxable distribution is $6,346 ($7,000 – $654), and his tax basis carried forward to tax year 2018 is $9,346 ($10,000 – $654). This $9,346 figure will be used as the numerator of the fraction in 2018.

Distributions from IRAs with nondeductible contributions are reported on Form 8606 Part I (see Exhibit 11-2). The exclusion percentage is on line 10, and the nontaxable distribution is on line 13. The distribution and the taxable amount are carried forward to Form 1040 lines 15a and 15b, respectively.

Taxation of Roth IRA Distributions

Unlike traditional IRAs, no minimum withdrawal from a Roth IRA is required. Roth IRA withdrawals are not taxable when distributed unless they fail to meet a five-year holding period requirement.[54] Specifically, the distribution must be made after the five-tax-year period beginning with the first tax year in which a Roth contribution was made.[55] Roth withdrawals are deemed to come first from contributions and then from earnings. Thus withdrawals within the five-year window are not taxable to the extent that they do not exceed contributions.

EXAMPLE 11-18

Jerry and Roxanne established and funded their Roth IRA in tax year 2013 and have made an annual $2,000 contribution in every year since (even though the 2017 contribution maximum is $5,500, the maximum was smaller in prior years so we will assume equal $2,000 contributions). If other distribution requirements are met, Jerry and Roxanne can make tax-free withdrawals from their Roth beginning in 2018. If they were to make a withdrawal in 2017, they could withdraw up to $10,000 tax-free ($2,000 contribution per year for 2013 through 2017).

The 10% additional tax for retirement plan withdrawals does not apply to Roth distributions because the distributions are not included in income. However, after the five-year holding period, Roth distributions are taxable (and subject to a 10% penalty) to the extent they come from earnings unless they are made (1) on or after the taxpayer's reaching age 59½, (2) as a result of death, (3) on account of disability, or (4) for a first-time home purchase with a maximum cap of $10,000.[56]

[54] IRC § 408A(d)(1).

[55] IRC § 408A(d)(2)(B).

[56] IRC § 408A(d)(2)(A).

EXHIBIT 11-2

Form **8606**

Department of the Treasury
Internal Revenue Service (99)

Nondeductible IRAs

▶ Go to *www.irs.gov/Form8606* for instructions and the latest information.

▶ Attach to Form 1040, Form 1040A, or Form 1040NR.

OMB No. 1545-0074

2017

Attachment Sequence No. **48**

Name. If married, file a separate form for each spouse required to file Form 8606. See instructions.			Your social security number
Fill in Your Address Only If You Are Filing This Form by Itself and Not With Your Tax Return ▶	Home address (number and street, or P.O. box if mail is not delivered to your home)		Apt. no.
	City, town or post office, state, and ZIP code. If you have a foreign address, also complete the spaces below.		
	Foreign country name	Foreign province/state/county	Foreign postal code

Part I **Nondeductible Contributions to Traditional IRAs and Distributions From Traditional, SEP, and SIMPLE IRAs**

Complete this part only if one or more of the following apply.

- You made nondeductible contributions to a traditional IRA for 2017.
- You took distributions from a traditional, SEP, or SIMPLE IRA in 2017 **and** you made nondeductible contributions to a traditional IRA in 2017 or an earlier year. For this purpose, a distribution does not include a rollover, qualified charitable distribution, one-time distribution to fund an HSA, conversion, recharacterization, or return of certain contributions.
- You converted part, but not all, of your traditional, SEP, and SIMPLE IRAs to Roth IRAs in 2017 (excluding any portion you recharacterized) **and** you made nondeductible contributions to a traditional IRA in 2017 or an earlier year.

1	Enter your nondeductible contributions to traditional IRAs for 2017, including those made for 2017 from January 1, 2018, through April 17, 2018 (see instructions)		1
2	Enter your total basis in traditional IRAs (see instructions)		2
3	Add lines 1 and 2		3
	In 2017, did you take a distribution from traditional, SEP, or SIMPLE IRAs, or make a Roth IRA conversion? No ▶ Enter the amount from line 3 on line 14. Do not complete the rest of Part I. Yes ▶ Go to line 4.		
4	Enter those contributions included on line 1 that were made from January 1, 2018, through April 17, 2018		4
5	Subtract line 4 from line 3		5
6	Enter the value of **all** your traditional, SEP, and SIMPLE IRAs as of December 31, 2017, plus any outstanding rollovers (see instructions)	6	
7	Enter your distributions from traditional, SEP, and SIMPLE IRAs in 2017. **Do not** include rollovers, qualified charitable distributions, a one-time distribution to fund an HSA, conversions to a Roth IRA, certain returned contributions, or recharacterizations of traditional IRA contributions (see instructions)	7	
8	Enter the net amount you converted from traditional, SEP, and SIMPLE IRAs to Roth IRAs in 2017. **Do not** include amounts converted that you later recharacterized (see instructions). Also enter this amount on line 16	8	
9	Add lines 6, 7, and 8 — 9		
10	Divide line 5 by line 9. Enter the result as a decimal rounded to at least 3 places. If the result is 1.000 or more, enter "1.000"	10 × .	
11	Multiply line 8 by line 10. This is the nontaxable portion of the amount you converted to Roth IRAs. Also enter this amount on line 17	11	
12	Multiply line 7 by line 10. This is the nontaxable portion of your distributions that you did not convert to a Roth IRA	12	
13	Add lines 11 and 12. This is the nontaxable portion of all your distributions		13
14	Subtract line 13 from line 3. This is **your total basis in traditional IRAs for 2017 and earlier years**		14
15	**Taxable amount.** Subtract line 12 from line 7. If more than zero, also include this amount on Form 1040, line 15b; Form 1040A, line 11b; or Form 1040NR, line 16b		15
	Note: You may be subject to an additional 10% tax on the amount on line 15 if you were under age 59½ at the time of the distribution (see instructions).		

For Privacy Act and Paperwork Reduction Act Notice, see separate instructions. Cat. No. 63966F Form **8606** (2017)

Source: U.S. Department of the Treasury, Internal Revenue Service, Form 8606. Washington, DC: 2017.

Distributions from a Coverdell Education Savings Account

Distributions from a CESA are tax-free to the beneficiary if used for his or her qualified education expenses. Qualified expenses include required tuition, fees, books, supplies, tutoring, equipment, and similar expenses incurred in conjunction with the enrollment or attendance of the beneficiary at an elementary or secondary school or at an accredited postsecondary educational institution.[57] Qualified expenses must be reduced by scholarships or other tax-free income. Expenses for room and board are qualified expenses if either (1) the student is enrolled at least half-time at a qualified postsecondary school or (2) the expense is required in the case of eligible elementary or secondary schools.

If distributions exceed qualified expenses, the excess attributable to contributions is tax-free and the amount attributable to earnings is taxable as ordinary income. The taxable excess is generally subject to a 10% penalty tax. Taxable CESA distributions are reported on Form 1040, line 21, other income.

Expenses used to determine American opportunity/Hope or lifetime learning credits or the tuition and fees deduction cannot be used again as qualified expenses for CESA distributions. In other words, you cannot double-count the expenses.

Funds remaining in a CESA when the beneficiary reaches age 30 must be distributed to the beneficiary within 30 days. If the distribution is not used for qualified education expenses, the amount will be taxable to the extent that it represents earnings. The distribution will also be subject to an additional 10% tax.[58] However, if the CESA is transferred (rolled over) within 60 days to a CESA for a member of the beneficiary's family under age 30, the transfer is tax-free.[59]

Rollovers

Taxpayers can transfer plan assets from one retirement plan to another retirement plan tax- and penalty-free if they follow certain rules.[60] Taxpayers may choose to do so to consolidate numerous pension accounts into one account or to change plan administrators.

Normally transfers are from trustee to trustee. In this case, the taxpayer notifies the current plan trustee to transfer some or all of her or his plan assets to the trustee of another plan. The transfer is made directly from the first trustee to the second trustee, and the taxpayer never has any control over the funds. Such transfers are not subject to tax or withholding.[61]

Alternatively, the taxpayer may choose (subject to plan restrictions) to have some or all of the plan assets distributed to him or her and, within a 60-day period, transfer those assets into another eligible retirement plan. The amount distributed is subject to a 20% mandatory withholding.[62] If the taxpayer fails to properly transfer the funds within the 60-day period, the entire amount distributed (including the amount withheld) is taxable as ordinary income.

Permissible types of tax-free rollovers follow:

- From one IRA to the same or another type except that (a) a transfer to a Roth IRA is taxable and (b) a transfer from a SIMPLE during the first two years of an employee's participation can be made only to another SIMPLE.
- From a qualified plan to an IRA.
- From a qualified plan to another qualified plan.
- From a tax-sheltered annuity to another tax-sheltered annuity or to an IRA.

Taxpayers are permitted to roll over a traditional IRA to a Roth IRA without being subject to the 10% penalty tax. This rollover is also called a *Roth conversion.* If the IRA was funded with tax-deductible contributions, the entire amount must be included in taxable income. If the IRA was funded with tax-deductible and non-tax-deductible contributions, then a pro rata allocation is made.

[57] IRC § 529(e)(3)(A), § 529(e)(5)(A), and § 529(e)(3).

[58] IRC § 530(d)(4)(A).

[59] IRC § 530(d)(5).

[60] Any such transfers must meet the administrative requirements set by the plan administrators.

[61] IRC § 401(a)(31)(A).

[62] IRC 3405(c).

TAX YOUR BRAIN

Amounts transferred from a traditional IRA to a Roth IRA are moving from one IRA to another. Why must the amount transferred be included in income?

ANSWER

Even though both accounts are IRAs, they have different deductibility and taxability rules. Recall that the traditional account is funded with untaxed dollars whereas the Roth is funded with dollars that have already been taxed. In addition, distributions from the traditional IRA will normally be fully taxed whereas Roth distributions will be tax-free. Thus the funds are moving from an account that has never been taxed (traditional) to an account that will not be taxed upon withdrawal (Roth). If the government does not tax the transfer when it occurs, it will never collect tax on the funds.

CONCEPT CHECK 11-6— LO 11-5

1. IRA distributions are taxable if funded with deductible contributions. True or false?
2. Distributions are never required from a Roth IRA. True or false?
3. For an individual age 65, Roth IRA distributions are not taxable if they have been held for at least five years. True or false?
4. Distributions from Coverdell Education Savings Accounts can be used for any purpose once the beneficiary reaches age 30. True or false?

TAX TREATMENT OF ANNUITY CONTRACTS

LO 11-6

Taxpayers may choose to invest in an annuity (either taxable or tax-deferred). An *annuity* is defined as a series of payments made under a contract. The payments can be in a variable or fixed amount and can be for a specified period or for the life of the contract holder. The contract can be with an insurance company, a financial services company, a bank, or an employer. Annuities often arise in conjunction with the payout phase of a retirement plan (the taxability of these plans has previously been discussed).

An annuity contract generally requires the taxpayer to pay a lump sum for the right to receive periodic payments (usually monthly, quarterly, or annually). The portion of these payments attributable to the amount invested is tax-free; the remainder is taxable. The taxable/nontaxable split is calculated based on the proportion that the cost of the contract bears to the expected return from the contract.

The expected return on an annuity that will last for a specified amount of time is easy to determine. If a contract will provide payments of $1,000 per month for five years, the expected return is $60,000 ($1,000 × 12 × 5). The expected return on a contract that will provide payments for the life of the contract owner is determined based on the life expectancy tables provided in IRS Publication 939. We have provided Table V, for single life annuities, in the appendix to this chapter. For dual life annuities, refer to Publication 939. The expected return is equal to the annual payout from the contract multiplied by the appropriate factor.

EXAMPLE 11-19

Bart is 57 years old and purchased a single life annuity contract that will pay him $5,000 per year for life. Bart paid $90,000 for the contract. The expected return on Bart's contract is $134,000 ($5,000 × 26.8).

The exclusion ratio is 0.672 ($90,000/$134,000). Thus each $5,000 annual payment will have a tax-free component of $3,360 (5,000 × 0.672) and a taxable component of $1,640 ($5,000 − $3,360).

From Shoebox to Software Reporting Contributions and Distributions

Contributions to employer-provided qualified pension and profit-sharing plans are not reported on Form 1040 or attachments. Employees will receive certain notification from the plan administrator in accordance with the rules of the plan. Generally the employee contribution information is reported in box 9b of Form 1099-R (see Exhibit 11-3) in the year distributions commence.

Contributions to traditional IRAs, Keogh plans, SEPs, and SIMPLE plans are calculated in accordance with the rules outlined in this chapter and, if deductible, are reported as a *for* AGI deduction on line 32 (for an IRA) or line 28 (for the other plans) of Form 1040.

Nondeductible contributions to a traditional IRA are reported on Form 8606, Part I, line 1 (see Exhibit 11-2). These contributions create a tax basis that determines the taxability of future distributions. It is important for a taxpayer to have good recordkeeping practices because, when calculating the nontaxable portion of IRA distributions, the taxpayer will need to use information that may be up to 30 or 40 years old.

In tax software, IRA contributions and contributions to self-employed pension plans are generally reported on a worksheet.

Distributions from pension plans, IRAs, and similar plans are reported to taxpayers on Form 1099-R. If a taxpayer receives distributions from multiple plans, he or she will receive multiple Forms 1099-R, and the amounts therein must be added together. A Form 1099-R is shown in Exhibit 11-3.

The information in the various boxes of Form 1099-R is important when preparing a tax return. The following is an explanation of the information most commonly provided:

- Box 1 represents the total distribution from the pension plan during the year, including any taxes withheld.
- Box 2a is the taxable amount of the distribution. In box 2b, if the "total distribution" box is checked, the entire distribution is taxable. If the "taxable amount not determined" box is checked, the plan administrator does not have sufficient information to determine the amount of the payment that is taxable. In such case, the taxpayer must calculate the appropriate amount.
- Box 4 is the amount of tax withheld by the plan administrator. It is added to other withholdings and reported on Form 1040, line 64. Generally taxpayers must elect to have amounts withheld from pension payments. In the case of a rollover amount distributed directly to the taxpayer, box 4 will reflect the 20% mandatory withholding.
- Box 7 contains the number or letter code that corresponds to the type of distribution being made. The most common code is "7" for a normal distribution. Other codes are 1 for an early distribution; 3 or 4 as a result of the death or disability, respectively, of the employee; G or H for most rollovers; J for a Roth distribution; and M for a Coverdell Education Savings Account distribution.
- Boxes 10 and 13 provide any state or local tax withholdings. These are used as part of any itemized deductions and in preparation of state and local tax returns.

In tax software, information from Form 1099-R is generally entered directly on the Form 1099-R.

The software transfers the information you enter on the worksheets and the Form 1099-R input form onto the appropriate tax return form. Contributions are not normally reported but are used to determine tax basis. An exception is a nondeductible contribution to a traditional IRA.

Distributions from a pension plan will be reported on Form 1040, lines 16a and 16b. Traditional IRA distributions are initially reported on Form 8606, Part 1 (see Exhibit 11-2), and will be transferred to Form 1040, lines 15a and 15b.

Taxpayers also use Form 8606 to report distributions from a Roth IRA and a nondeductible IRA. Distributions from IRAs with nondeductible contributions are also on Form 8606, Part I. The exclusion percentage is on line 10, and the nontaxable distribution is on line 13. The tax software carries the distribution and the taxable amount to Form 1040, lines 15a and 15b, respectively.

Distributions from a Coverdell Education Savings Account are to be used for qualified education expenses. If distributions exceed expenses, report the excess on Form 1040, line 21, Other income.

EXAMPLE 11-20 Beverly is 60 years old and has purchased a single life annuity for $35,000. The annuity contract will provide Beverly payments of $300 per month for the rest of her life. Beverly's life expectancy from Table V in the appendix is 24.2 years. The expected return from the contract is $87,120 ($300 × 12 × 24.2). The exclusion ratio is 0.4017 ($35,000/$87,120). Thus each $300 payment will have a tax-free component of $120.51 ($300 × 0.4017) and a taxable component of $179.49 ($300.00 – $120.51).

EXHIBIT 11-3

☐ CORRECTED (if checked)

PAYER'S name, street address, city or town, state or province, country, and ZIP or foreign postal code	1 Gross distribution $ 2a Taxable amount $	OMB No. 1545-0119 **2017** Form **1099-R**	**Distributions From Pensions, Annuities, Retirement or Profit-Sharing Plans, IRAs, Insurance Contracts, etc.**
	2b Taxable amount not determined ☐	Total distribution ☐	**Copy B Report this income on your federal tax return. If this form shows federal income tax withheld in box 4, attach this copy to your return.** This information is being furnished to the Internal Revenue Service.
PAYER'S federal identification number / RECIPIENT'S identification number	3 Capital gain (included in box 2a) $	4 Federal income tax withheld $	
RECIPIENT'S name	5 Employee contributions /Designated Roth contributions or insurance premiums $	6 Net unrealized appreciation in employer's securities $	
Street address (including apt. no.)	7 Distribution code(s) / IRA/ SEP/ SIMPLE ☐	8 Other $ %	
City or town, state or province, country, and ZIP or foreign postal code	9a Your percentage of total distribution %	9b Total employee contributions $	
10 Amount allocable to IRR within 5 years $ / 11 1st year of desig. Roth contrib. / FATCA filing requirement ☐	12 State tax withheld $ $	13 State/Payer's state no.	14 State distribution $ $
Account number (see instructions)	15 Local tax withheld $ $	16 Name of locality	17 Local distribution $ $

Form **1099-R** www.irs.gov/form1099r Department of the Treasury - Internal Revenue Service

Source: U.S. Department of the Treasury, Internal Revenue Service, Form 1099-R. Washington, DC: 2017.

After the entire cost of the annuity has been recovered, all additional payments are fully taxable. If an individual dies before recovering the entire cost, the unrecovered cost can be used as an itemized deduction on the individual's final return.

TAX YOUR BRAIN

Under what circumstances will the entire cost of an annuity be recovered?

ANSWER

In the case of an annuity that is payable for a fixed period, the entire cost will be recovered when the last payment is received. For annuities payable over the life of the recipient, the entire cost will be recovered if the annuitant lives exactly as long as the life expectancy used to determine the exclusion ratio. Mathematically, once the recipient reaches the life expectancy originally anticipated, the entire cost will have been recovered.

CONCEPT CHECK 11-7— LO 11-6

1. An annuity is a ____________ of payments under a ____________.
2. Annuity payments are always the same amount each period. True or false?
3. Annuity payments often have a taxable component and a nontaxable component. True or false?

Summary

LO 11-1: Discuss the basic tax and operational structure of tax-deferred plans and annuities.	• Specified retirement plans are encouraged and receive tax advantages. • Important related terminology includes *donor, beneficiary, contributions, distributions, annuity,* and *trustee.* • Tax-deferred does not mean tax-free. • Generally, untaxed contributions are taxed on distribution but taxed contributions are not. • Contributions to retirement plans can provide a tax deduction.
LO 11-2: Explain details about and contributions to employer-sponsored retirement plans.	• Employer-sponsored plans include qualified pension and profit-sharing, 401(k), 403(b), Keogh, SEP, and SIMPLE plans. • Plans provide significant benefits to both employers and employees. • Qualified plans are either defined contribution or defined benefit plans. • All employer-sponsored plans have contribution limits that vary by plan.
LO 11-3: Describe the tax rules related to contributions to individual-sponsored retirement plans.	• Individual-sponsored IRAs include both traditional and Roth. • Contributions are limited to the lower of $5,500 or 100% of compensation. Individuals over 50 can contribute up to $6,500. • Special rules apply to compensation for married taxpayers and for individuals covered by employer-related plans. • Contribution restrictions are based on AGI. • Deductibility of contributions and taxability of distributions for traditional and Roth IRAs differ.
LO 11-4: Explain details about and contributions to tax-deferred nonretirement plans.	• A Coverdell Education Savings Account is a tax-deferred plan used for qualified elementary, secondary, or higher education expenses. • The maximum annual contribution is $2,000, subject to AGI limitations.
LO 11-5: Apply the tax rules for distributions from tax-deferred plans and the tax treatment of those distributions.	• Generally, distributions are taxable if contributions were deductible. • The simplified method is used to determine taxability of qualified plan distributions. • Other retirement plans have required minimum distributions that must begin by April 1 of the year after the taxpayer reaches age 70½. • Distributions are determined using life expectancy tables. • Premature distributions are subject to 10% penalty; some exceptions apply. • Rollovers are generally tax-free, but rollovers to a Roth IRA are subject to tax.
LO 11-6: Determine the tax treatment of annuity contracts.	• Normally, annuity payments are partially taxable and partially tax-free. • The tax-free component is based on the cost of the annuity contract. • The expected return must be determined. The expected return is the amount the annuity recipient expects to receive from the contract. Life expectancy tables may be needed to determine the amount.

Appendix

LIFE EXPECTANCY TABLES

Table I
(Single Life Expectancy)
(For Use by Beneficiaries)

Age	Life Expectancy	Age	Life Expectancy
56	28.7	84	8.1
57	27.9	85	7.6
58	27.0	86	7.1
59	26.1	87	6.7
60	25.2	88	6.3
61	24.4	89	5.9
62	23.5	90	5.5
63	22.7	91	5.2
64	21.8	92	4.9
65	21.0	93	4.6
66	20.2	94	4.3
67	19.4	95	4.1
68	18.6	96	3.8
69	17.8	97	3.6
70	17.0	98	3.4
71	16.3	99	3.1
72	15.5	100	2.9
73	14.8	101	2.7
74	14.1	102	2.5
75	13.4	103	2.3
76	12.7	104	2.1
77	12.1	105	1.9
78	11.4	106	1.7
79	10.8	107	1.5
80	10.2	108	1.4
81	9.7	109	1.2
82	9.1	110	1.1
83	8.6	111 and over	1.0

Generally this table is to be used for IRAs by beneficiaries as a result of the death of the original IRA owner.

Source: Life Expectancy Tables, IRA

Table III
(Uniform Lifetime)

(For Use by:

- **Unmarried Owners,**
- **Married Owners Whose Spouses Are Not More Than 10 Years Younger, and**
- **Married Owners Whose Spouses Are Not the Sole Beneficiaries of Their IRAs)**

Age	Distribution Period	Age	Distribution Period
70	27.4	93	9.6
71	26.5	94	9.1
72	25.6	95	8.6
73	24.7	96	8.1
74	23.8	97	7.6
75	22.9	98	7.1
76	22.0	99	6.7
77	21.2	100	6.3
78	20.3	101	5.9
79	19.5	102	5.5
80	18.7	103	5.2
81	17.9	104	4.9
82	17.1	105	4.5
83	16.3	106	4.2
84	15.5	107	3.9
85	14.8	108	3.7
86	14.1	109	3.4
87	13.4	110	3.1
88	12.7	111	2.9
89	12.0	112	2.6
90	11.4	113	2.4
91	10.8	114	2.1
92	10.2	115 and over	1.9

Generally this table is to be used by the original owner of an IRA.

TABLE V—ORDINARY LIFE ANNUITIES
ONE LIFE—EXPECTED RETURN MULTIPLES

AGE	MULTIPLE	AGE	MULTIPLE	AGE	MULTIPLE
5	76.6	42	40.6	79	10.0
6	75.6	43	39.6	80	9.5
7	74.7	44	38.7	81	8.9
8	73.7	45	37.7	82	8.4
9	72.7	46	36.8	83	7.9
10	71.7	47	35.9	84	7.4
11	70.7	48	34.9	85	6.9
12	69.7	49	34.0	86	6.5
13	68.8	50	33.1	87	6.1
14	67.8	51	32.2	88	5.7
15	66.8	52	31.3	89	5.3
16	65.8	53	30.4	90	5.0
17	64.8	54	29.5	91	4.7
18	63.9	55	28.6	92	4.4
19	62.9	56	27.7	93	4.1
20	61.9	57	26.8	94	3.9
21	60.9	58	25.9	95	3.7
22	59.9	59	25.0	96	3.4
23	59.0	60	24.2	97	3.2
24	58.0	61	23.3	98	3.0
25	57.0	62	22.5	99	2.8
26	56.0	63	21.6	100	2.7
27	55.1	64	20.8	101	2.5
28	54.1	65	20.0	102	2.3
29	53.1	66	19.2	103	2.1
30	52.2	67	18.4	104	1.9
31	51.2	68	17.6	105	1.8
32	50.2	69	16.8	106	1.6
33	49.3	70	16.0	107	1.4
34	48.3	71	15.3	108	1.3
35	47.3	72	14.6	109	1.1
36	46.4	73	13.9	110	1.0
37	45.4	74	13.2	111	.9
38	44.4	75	12.5	112	.8
39	43.5	76	11.9	113	.7
40	42.5	77	11.2	114	.6
41	41.5	78	10.6	115	.5

This table is to be used by taxpayers with payments from an annuity not associated with a qualified pension or profit-sharing plan.

Discussion Questions connect

All applicable discussion questions are available with ***Connect***©

LO 11-1 1. What is the purpose of a retirement plan? Why does the government provide tax benefits to retirement plans?

EA LO 11-1 2. What is the rule of thumb noted in the text pertaining to the taxability of retirement plan distributions?

LO 11-1 3. Pension plans have an *accumulation period* and a *distribution period.* Explain what those terms mean.

LO 11-1 4. What are the two broad categories of retirement plans? Give some examples of each.

LO 11-2 5. What are the differences between a defined benefit pension plan and a defined contribution pension plan?

LO 11-2 6. What are the differences between a contributory and a noncontributory pension plan?

LO 11-2 7. What are the similarities and differences between a pension plan and a profit-sharing plan?

LO 11-2 8. Pension plans are subject to certain vesting requirements. What does the word *vesting* mean? Describe the vesting rules for pension plans.

LO 11-2 9. Briefly discuss the conditions necessary for a taxpayer to be permitted to make tax-deductible contributions to a Keogh plan.

LO 11-2 10. What is the maximum annual contribution that can be made to a Keogh plan, and how is the maximum calculated?

LO 11-2 11. Briefly discuss the conditions necessary for a taxpayer to be permitted to make tax-deductible contributions to a SIMPLE plan.

LO 11-2 12. What is the maximum annual contribution that can be made to a SIMPLE plan, and how is the maximum calculated?

LO 11-2 13. Briefly discuss the conditions necessary for a taxpayer to be permitted to make tax-deductible contributions to a simplified employee pension (SEP).

LO 11-2 14. What is the maximum annual contribution that can be made to a SEP, and how is the maximum calculated?

EA LO 11-3 15. Briefly discuss the conditions necessary for a taxpayer to be permitted to make tax-deductible contributions to a traditional IRA.

EA LO 11-3 16. What is the maximum annual contribution that can be made to a traditional IRA, and how is the maximum calculated?

EA LO 11-3 17. What is the deadline by which contributions must be made to a traditional IRA to obtain a tax deduction in the current year?

EA LO 11-3 18. What is the maximum annual contribution that can be made to a Roth IRA, and how is the maximum calculated?

LO 11-3 19. Anne, a single taxpayer under age 50, has wage income of $74,000 and is not covered under a retirement plan by her employer. She would like to start a retirement plan if possible. What options are available to her?

LO 11-4 20. What is the maximum annual contribution that can be made to a Coverdell Education Savings Account? Can an eligible beneficiary have more than one CESA?

LO 11-4 21. Tax-free distributions from a Coverdell Education Savings Account can be used for what purpose? Be specific.

LO 11-5 22. Stan has $20,000 in a traditional IRA at a bank. He decided to change trustees from a bank to a financial services firm. He requests, and receives, a check from the bank that he intends to take to the financial services firm to open a new account. He puts the check in his drawer and forgets it. Three months later, he remembers the check and takes it to the financial services firm and opens an IRA account. What are the tax implications of Stan's actions?

LO 11-6 23. What is meant by an *expected return* on an annuity contract? How do you calculate the expected return for a single person?

Multiple-Choice Questions connect

All applicable multiple-choice questions are available with ***Connect***©

LO 11-1 24. Which of the following is an individual-sponsored pension plan?

a. Defined benefit plan.

b. Keogh plan.

c. Roth IRA.

d. SIMPLE plan.

LO 11-1 25. Which of the following statements is true?

a. Only employers can establish tax-deferred retirement plans.

b. Generally, plan distributions are taxable if the contributions were made with untaxed dollars.

c. The donor and the beneficiary of a retirement plan are almost never the same.

d. Retirement plan distributions can be made for any purpose and at any time.

LO 11-2 26. A participant in a Keogh plan over the age of 50 may contribute up to what amount in 2017?

a. $6,500.

b. $24,000.

c. The lower of $54,000 or 25% of earned income from self-employment.

d. The greater of $54,000 or 25% of earned income from self-employment.

LO 11-2 27. A qualified pension plan provides significant tax benefits to both employers and employees, including

a. Employer contributions are not treated as compensation to the employee.

b. Earnings from the investments held in the plan are tax-deferred.

c. No tax on plan assets until the amounts are distributed.

d. All of the above.

LO 11-2 28. To obtain and retain qualified status, a pension or profit-sharing plan must not discriminate in favor of highly compensated employees, who include

a. Employees who own more than 5% of the corporation's stock.

b. Employees who received more than $100,000 compensation in the previous year.

c. Employees who were in the top 25% of employees based on compensation.

d. All of the above.

LO 11-2 29. A participant in a 401(k) plan under the age of 50 may contribute up to what amount in 2017?

a. $5,500.

b. $12,500.

c. $18,000.

d. $54,000.

LO 11-2 30. Thomas is a self-employed plumber under the age of 50. His earnings from self-employment, before the Keogh deduction but after deducting half of the self-employment tax, are $80,000. What is his deductible Keogh contribution for 2017?

a. $54,000.

b. $20,000.

c. $18,000.

d. $16,000.

LO 11-2 31. Which of the following is true regarding SEPs?

a. The plan cannot discriminate in favor of highly compensated employees.

b. Deductible contributions cannot exceed the lower of 15% of the employee's compensation or $54,000.

c. Self-employed individuals cannot create and contribute to a SEP.

d. The plan must cover all employees who have reached the age of 18, who have worked for the employer for at least two of the preceding five years, and who received at least $600 in compensation.

LO 11-2 32. Generous Corporation provides a SIMPLE plan for its employees. Under the plan, employees can contribute up to 6% of their salary, and Generous Corporation will match each employee's contribution up to 3% of the employee's salary. Erika is an employee of Generous Corporation and elects to contribute 6% of her $60,000 salary to the SIMPLE plan. What is the total contribution made to her SIMPLE account?

a. $12,500.

b. $5,400.

c. $3,600.

d. $1,800.

EA **LO 11-3** 33. Terri is single and age 32. She reported AGI of $64,000 in tax year 2017. She is an active participant in her employer's pension plan. What is the maximum deductible IRA contribution she can make in 2017?

a. $0.

b. $1,100.

c. $4,400.

d. $5,500.

EA **LO 11-3** 34. Ed and Cathy, both under age 50, file a joint return. Neither is covered under an employer pension plan. Cathy earned compensation of $53,000 in 2017. Ed worked part-time and earned $1,200. What is the maximum deductible IRA contribution they can make in 2017?

a. $0.

b. $5,500.

c. $6,700.

d. $11,000.

EA LO 11-3 35. Jack is single and age 53. He reported AGI of $68,000 in 2017. He is an active participant in his employer's pension plan. What is the maximum deductible IRA contribution he can make in 2017?

a. $2,200.

b. $2,600.

c. $3,900.

d. $6,500.

EA LO 11-3 36. Patrice is single and age 26. She reported AGI of $65,000 in tax year 2017. She is an active participant in her employer's pension plan. What is the maximum deductible Roth IRA contribution she can make in 2017?

a. $0.

b. $2,200.

c. $3,300.

d. $5,500.

EA LO 11-3 37. Vickie is single and age 43. She reported AGI of $124,000 in tax year 2017. She is an active participant in her employer's pension plan. What is the maximum Roth IRA contribution she can make in 2017?

a. $0.

b. $2,300.

c. $3,300.

d. $5,500.

LO 11-4 38. Without regard to AGI limitations, what is the maximum contribution permitted to a Coverdell Education Savings Account in 2017?

a. $500.

b. $2,000.

c. $5,500.

d. The lower of $5,500 or 100% of compensation.

LO 11-4 39. Vanessa and Martin file a joint return for 2017. They have one child, age 12. They have combined AGI of $202,000 in 2017. What is their maximum permitted contribution to a Coverdell Education Savings Account for 2017?

a. $0.

b. $800.

c. $1,200.

d. $2,000.

EA LO 11-5 40. Juan is single and retired on January 1, 2017, at age 62. He is entitled to receive monthly payments of $1,500 over his life from his employer's qualified pension plan. The payments began January 1, 2017. He contributed $71,500 to the plan prior to his retirement. Using the simplified method, how much of the payments will be included in his income for 2017?

a. $1,225.

b. $3,300.

c. $14,700.

d. $18,000.

EA LO 11-5 41. If a qualified pension plan is being distributed using joint life expectancy,

a. The taxpayers cannot choose to refigure their life expectancy.

b. If the beneficiary dies, no adjustment of the denominator used to calculate minimum distributions is required.

c. If the beneficiary dies, the life expectancy of a different beneficiary is substituted for the original beneficiary.

d. None of the above.

EA LO 11-5 42. Mark, who is single, must start making distributions from his pension plan beginning April 1, 2017. At the end of 2016 when Mark was 71 years old, the plan had a balance of $220,000. He will use a single life expectancy. What amount must Mark take as a distribution from the pension plan no later than April 1, 2017?

a. $8,302.

b. $12,941.

c. $13,497.

d. $14,193.

EA LO 11-5 43. Juanita, age 62, retired in 2017. During the year, she received distributions of $9,000 from her IRA. She made nondeductible contributions of $20,000 to the IRA in prior years and has never received a nontaxable distribution. As of December 31, 2017, the value of her IRA was $150,000. Calculate the taxable portion of Juanita's distribution.

a. $1,132.

b. $7,800.

c. $7,868.

d. $9,000.

EA LO 11-5 44. Withdrawals from a Roth IRA are

a. Subject to the required minimum distribution rules.

b. Taxable if made after the five-tax-year period beginning with the first tax year in which a Roth contribution was made.

c. Deemed to come first from contributions and then from earnings.

d. Not taxable to the extent they exceed contributions if the five-year holding period requirement is not met.

LO 11-5 45. Regarding a Coverdell Education Savings Account,

a. Distributions are tax-free to the beneficiary if they are used for his or her qualified education expenses.

b. Qualified education expenses include required tuition, fees, books, supplies, and equipment at an eligible education institution.

c. Qualified expenses must be reduced by scholarships or other tax-free income.

d. All of the above apply.

EA LO 11-6 46. Julio is 62 and single. He purchased a single life annuity contract that will pay him $1,000 a month for life with a minimum payout of 10 years. His expected return on the contract

a. Is $120,000.

b. Is $270,000.

c. Is $282,000.

d. Cannot be determined with the information given.

EA LO 11-6 47. June, age 76, and Augustus, age 78, are married. They purchased a single life annuity contract that will pay $1,500 per month for June's lifetime. The expected return on the contract

a. Is $190,800.

b. Is $214,200.

c. Is $405,000.

d. Cannot be determined with the information given.

EA LO 11-6 48. Sanjay purchased a single life annuity contract for $200,000. The contract will pay $15,000 per year beginning in 2017 for the remainder of his life and has an expected return of $330,000. What amount of taxable income must Sanjay report in 2017?

a. $5,909.

b. $9,091.

c. $15,000.

d. $130,000.

Problems connect

All applicable problems are available with ***Connect***©

LO 11-2, 11-3 49. Will, who is single and age 50, is employed as a full-time tax accountant at a local manufacturing company where he earns $73,000 per year. He participates in a pension plan through his employer. Will also operates a small tax practice in his spare time during tax season and has net Schedule C income of $8,000. He is interested in establishing and contributing to other retirement plans. What options are available to Will?

___

___

___

___

___

LO 11-2 50. Cornell Company is considering the establishment of a pension plan. The proposed plan has the following features:

- Contributions for employees earning less than $100,000 will be based on 3% of salary, while contributions for those earning over $100,000 will be based on 4% of salary.
- To reduce employee turnover, company contributions will vest in 10 years.
- Employees with more than five years of service will be required to contribute 2% to the pension plan.
- Employee contributions will completely vest in one year.

Will the proposed pension plan be deemed a qualified pension plan? Why or why not?

___

___

___

___

___

LO 11-2 51. Determine the maximum contribution that can be made to a Keogh plan in each of the following cases. In all instances, the individual is self-employed, and the self-employment tax reduction has already been taken.

a. Self-employment income of $46,000.

b. Self-employment income of $46,000 and wage income of $30,000.

c. Self-employment income of $125,000.

d. Self-employment income of $290,000.

LO 11-2 52. Ken is a self-employed architect in a small firm with four employees: himself, his office assistant, and two drafters, all of whom have worked for Ken full-time for the last four years. The office assistant earns $30,000 per year and each drafter earns $40,000. Ken's net earnings from self-employment (after deducting all expenses and one-half of self-employment taxes) are $310,000. Ken is considering whether to establish a SEP plan and has a few questions:

a. Is he eligible to establish a SEP plan?

b. Is he required to cover his employees under the plan? Why or why not?

c. If his employees must be covered, what is the maximum amount that can be contributed on their behalf?

d. If the employees are not covered, what is the maximum amount Ken can contribute for himself?

e. If Ken is required to contribute for his employees and chooses to contribute the maximum amount, what is the maximum amount Ken can contribute for himself? (*Hint:* Calculate the employee amounts first.) Ignore any changes in Ken's self-employment tax.

LO 11-2 53. Use the same information as in Problem 52. Answer the questions there, assuming that Ken is considering a SIMPLE plan.

EA LO 11-3 54. Under what circumstances is it advantageous for a taxpayer to make a nondeductible contribution to a traditional IRA rather than a contribution to a Roth IRA?

LO 11-3 55. April, who is under age 50, is considering investing in tax-free state government bonds or making a permitted tax-deductible contribution to a traditional IRA. Assume that the amounts are the same for either alternative and that she can reinvest the interest income from the government bonds indefinitely. What tax and nontax factors should she consider?

LO 11-3 56. Lance is single and has a traditional IRA into which he has made deductible contributions for several years. This year he changed employers and is now an active participant in his employer's pension plan. His AGI is $95,000. He wants to make a nondeductible contribution to his IRA in the current year. What advice would you give Lance?

EA LO 11-3, 11-5 57. What are the differences between a traditional IRA and a Roth IRA regarding the deductibility of contributions, taxability of IRA earnings, and taxability of distributions?

EA LO 11-5 58. Using the simplified method, determine the tax-free amount of the following distributions from a qualified pension plan. Contributions, if any, are made with previously taxed dollars.

a. Person A, age 59, made no contributions to the pension plan and will receive a $500 monthly check for life.

b. Person B, age 66, made contributions of $23,000 to the pension plan and will receive a monthly check of $1,300 for life.

c. Person C, age 64, made contributions of $19,000 to the pension plan and will receive monthly payments of $1,200 over her life and the life of her 67-year-old husband.

d. Person D, age 55, made contributions of $32,000 to the pension plan. He will receive quarterly payments of $5,000 over his life and the life of his 58-year-old wife.

EA LO 11-5 59. Pablo and his wife Bernita are both age 45. Their combined AGI is $90,000. Neither is a participant in an employer-sponsored retirement plan. They have been contributing to a traditional IRA for many years and have built up an IRA balance of $120,000. They are considering rolling the traditional IRA into a Roth IRA.

a. Is the couple eligible to make the conversion? Why or why not?

b. Assume that the couple does not make the conversion but, instead, establishes a separate Roth IRA in the current year and properly contributes $2,000 per year for four years at which point the balance in the Roth is $21,000 (contributions plus investment earnings). At the end of four years, they withdraw $12,000 to pay for an addition to their house. What is the tax effect, if anything, of the withdrawal?

c. Does your answer to (b) change if they instead withdraw only $6,000? Why or why not?

d. What if the $12,000 withdrawal is used to pay qualified education expenses for their daughter who is attending college?

EA LO 11-6 60. Determine the tax-free amount of the monthly payment in each of the following instances. Use the life expectancy tables.

a. Person A is age 57 and purchased an annuity for $82,000. The annuity pays $600 per month for life.

b. Person B is 73 and purchased an annuity for $80,000. The annuity pays $950 per month for life.

c. Person C is 68 and purchased an annuity for $40,000 that pays a monthly payment of $550 for 10 years.

Complex Problems

61. Terrance is age 71 and retired. Beginning in 2017, he must start taking minimum distributions from his IRA account that had a balance of $150,000 as of December 31, 2016. Make these three assumptions: His IRA will earn 8% per year, he will withdraw the minimum distribution on the last day of each calendar year, and only one distribution will be taken in 2017. Calculate the amount of his distribution for years 2017 through 2021 and the ending balance in his IRA account on December 31, 2021.

62. Jennifer is age 50 and is seeking your advice. She has a traditional IRA with a balance of $100,000 and is considering whether to convert it (roll it over) to a Roth IRA. She has sufficient money in CDs to pay any required tax resulting from the rollover. Her current AGI is $70,000. She expects her income will be slightly higher upon retirement at age 65.

What advice would you give Jennifer?

63. Use the information from problem 62. Would your advice change if the fact(s) changed in each of the following independent instances? Why or why not?
    a. Jennifer cannot cash the CDs and would need to pay any additional tax liability from the IRA funds.
    b. She expects her income on retirement to decrease slightly.
    c. Jennifer is age 30.

Chapter Twelve

Special Property Transactions

In Chapter 7, we discussed the sale of capital assets and the associated preferential tax treatment as well as the sale of business property and ordinary income property. The Internal Revenue Code (IRC) has other provisions that allow special tax treatment for certain transactions. In this chapter, we cover many special provisions that permit taxpayers to exclude or defer gains in certain situations, including like-kind exchanges, involuntary conversions, installment sales, and the sale of a personal residence. Not all of the provisions discussed in this chapter are favorable to the taxpayer. For example, losses are not allowed on transactions between related parties.

Learning Objectives

When you have completed this chapter, you should understand the following learning objectives (LO):

LO 12-1 Explain how to defer gains using the like-kind exchange rules.

LO 12-2 Describe how to account for and report involuntary conversions.

LO 12-3 Apply the tax rules to report an installment sale.

LO 12-4 Explain how to exclude a gain on the sale of a personal residence.

LO 12-5 Apply the rules affecting related parties and wash sales.

INTRODUCTION

Numerous provisions in the IRC allow the taxpayer either to defer a gain to future years or to exclude the gain entirely from taxable income. A general rule of tax practice is that if a taxpayer must recognize a gain, it is best to defer the gain for as long as legally possible. Other provisions in the IRC disallow losses in certain circumstances. We discuss many of these provisions in this chapter. The topics discussed in this chapter include these:

- Exchange of property held for productive use or investment (like-kind exchanges).
- Involuntary conversions.
- Installment sales.
- Exclusion of gain from the sale of a principal residence.
- Losses with respect to transactions between related parties.
- Wash sales of stock or securities.

LIKE-KIND EXCHANGES

LO 12-1

Consider the following.

EXAMPLE 12-1

Bert and Alice purchased a house for rental in Emerald Isle, North Carolina, in 1964 for $15,000 (now fully depreciated). The same house and land are now worth $500,000. The house produces $25,000 of rental income a year. However, Bert and Alice's children and grandchildren live in Louisiana, so a beach house in Gulf Shores, Alabama, would be better because it could be used by the children when it is not rented. If Bert and Alice sell the property in North Carolina, a taxable § 1231 gain of $500,000 would result. If a 15% capital gains tax rate were assumed, Bert and Alice would pay tax of $75,000 on that gain, thereby reducing the proceeds available to purchase a new house in Alabama.[1] This is a perfect scenario for a like-kind exchange. Instead of selling their North Carolina house and buying another one in Alabama, if Bert and Alice exchange one house for the other, no tax will be owed.

Taxpayers often balk at the idea of a like-kind exchange because of the perceived difficulty in locating a desirable property for which the seller is willing to participate in an exchange. As discussed here, a properly executed like-kind exchange can take place even though the seller has no desire to exchange properties. A properly executed like-kind exchange in Example 12-1 would save $75,000 in taxes and allow the purchase of a nicer property or properties.

Requirements of Nontaxable Exchanges

Three criteria must be met to qualify for a like-kind exchange:

- An exchange must occur.
- The property transferred and the property received must be held for productive use in a trade or business or for investment.
- The property exchanged must be like-kind.[2]

One important aspect of a like-kind exchange is that it is *not* an elective provision. In other words, when an exchange occurs that meets the above criteria, the taxpayer must defer the gain or loss.

Generally, an *exchange* is loosely defined as receiving property of a like (similar) use in trade for similar property. The sale of old property and the purchase of new property are *not* an exchange. Additionally, the property must be held for productive use or investment to qualify. Thus, if a taxpayer trades a personal-use asset for another personal-use asset, the exchange does not qualify as a like-kind exchange.

Exchanges of the following specific properties do *not* qualify for like-kind treatment:[3]

- Stock in trade or other property held primarily for sale (inventory).
- Stocks, bonds, or notes.[4]

[1] As discussed in Chapter 7, the sale of real property results in a § 1250 gain. Thus any of this gain attributable to depreciation is taxed at a 25% gain (unrecaptured § 1250 gain). In this case, only $15,000 is an unrecaptured § 1250 gain. The excess is taxed as a § 1231 gain that could result in a 15% rate, assuming that Bert and Alice are in a regular tax bracket higher than 15%.

[2] IRC § 1031(a).

[3] IRC § 1031(a)(2).

[4] IRC § 1036 allows a nontaxable exchange treatment for an exchange of stock in the same corporation. For example, a taxpayer could exchange common stock for preferred stock in a nontaxable transaction.

- Other securities or evidence of indebtedness or interest.
- Interests in a partnership.
- Certificates of trust or beneficial interests.

Note that because inventory does not qualify for like-kind treatment, a dealer cannot participate in a like-kind exchange on a trade-in.

EXAMPLE 12-2

Marius, a dealer in farm equipment, allows a trade-in of an old combine (large equipment used to harvest crops) toward the purchase of a new combine. He cannot use the like-kind rules to defer any taxable gain. However, the customer could use the like-kind rules to defer gain, assuming the customer is a farmer, not a dealer in farm equipment.

What Is a "Like-Kind" Asset?

The requirement that the property be like-kind does not require the asset received to be an exact duplicate of the property exchanged. To qualify as "like-kind," the property must be of the same nature or character. The grade or quality of the exchanged assets does not matter.[5]

EXAMPLE 12-3

Johnny exchanges a parcel of farm real property for city real property. Because both properties are real properties held for productive use, the exchange would qualify as a like-kind exchange.[6]

When a taxpayer exchanges business personal property, the property must be of the same depreciation class of property.[7] Thus the exchange of a five-year class asset for a seven-year class asset would *not* qualify for "like-kind" treatment.

Boot Property

When two taxpayers wish to exchange properties, the fair market values (FMVs) of the properties rarely are equal. Thus to make an exchange a viable option, one participant gives extra consideration (usually cash or a note payable) to make the exchange values equitable. This extra consideration is called *boot,* defined as property given or received in a like-kind exchange that is *not* like-kind property. The receipt of boot property often triggers the recognition of gain. The following is the general rule concerning the receipt of boot:

When boot is received, the recognized gain is the *lesser* of

1. The FMV of the boot received; or
2. The realized gain on the exchange.[8]

Gain or loss is determined by comparing the FMV received with the basis of the assets given. The receipt of boot causes the recognition of gain but not loss.[9] Giving boot does not trigger gain recognition.

[5] Reg. § 1.1031-1(b).
[6] Reg. § 1.1031(b).
[7] Rev. Proc. 87-56, 1987-2 CB 674; see Chapters 6 and 7 for a discussion of asset classes.
[8] IRC § 1031(b).
[9] IRC § 1031(c).

EXAMPLE 12-4

Sonja exchanges a machine used in business with Kelly for another machine. The basis of Sonja's old machine is $25,000, its FMV is $33,000, and she gives cash of $7,000. Kelly's basis in her machine is $35,000, and its FMV is $40,000.

	Sonja		Kelly
New machine—FMV	$40,000	Amount received	$40,000*
Basis of old	(25,000)	Basis of old	(35,000)
Cash given	(7,000)	Gain—recognized	$ 5,000
Gain—not recognized	$ 8,000		

* The amount received was the $33,000 FMV of Sonja's machine plus the $7,000 cash (boot).

Kelly recognizes the gain because she received boot in the transaction. The gain recognized is $5,000 because it is the lower of the boot received ($7,000 cash) or the gain realized ($5,000). Sonja defers her gain of $8,000.

Tax Basis of New Property Received

An important calculation in a nontaxable exchange is the basis calculation. The basis calculation is the method by which the taxpayer defers gain. Generally, the basis of the new property is calculated as follows:

Basis Calculation of New Property Received[10]	
	Adjusted basis of the property given up
+	Adjusted basis of the boot given
+	Gain recognized
−	FMV of boot received
−	Loss recognized
=	Adjusted basis of new asset

Alternatively, the taxpayer can calculate the adjusted basis by taking the FMV of the property received (like-kind asset) less the gain postponed (or plus the loss postponed).

TAX YOUR BRAIN

Why is the term *deferred* used instead of *excluded* when referring to the realized gain in a nontaxable exchange?

ANSWER

The gain is deferred because the unrecognized gain reduces the basis in the new asset received. Thus the gain is deferred until the new asset is sold or disposed of. The reduced basis also causes less depreciation allowed on the new asset.

[10] IRC § 1031(d).

EXAMPLE 12-5

Assuming the same facts as in Example 12-4, what is the basis in the new properties for Sonja and Kelly?

	Sonja	Kelly
Adjusted basis of property given	$25,000	$35,000
+ Adjusted basis of boot given	7,000	–0–
+ Gain recognized	–0–	5,000
– FMV of boot received	–0–	7,000
– Loss recognized	–0–	–0–
Basis of new machine	$32,000	$33,000

Or	FMV of Property Received	–	Gain Postponed	+	Loss Postponed	=	Basis
Sonja	$40,000	–	$8,000	+	$–0–	=	$32,000
Kelly	33,000	–	–0–	+	–0–	=	33,000

In practice, the FMV is sometimes difficult to assess with used assets. If the item is large and valuable, it may be prudent to have the exchanged property appraised. For most businesses and most exchanges, the exchange is typically a trade-in of an old asset for a new asset. In this case, the new basis is the sales price of the new asset less any deferred gain (or plus any deferred loss).

The holding period used to determine any short-term or long-term treatment on the sale of the new asset includes the holding period of the old asset exchanged. Thus if a taxpayer exchanges a property held for 20 years for a new property, the new property has a holding period of 20 years plus the holding period of the new property.

Time Period for Finding Exchange Property

The taxpayer does not have an unlimited amount of time to find exchange property. After relinquishing his or her property, the taxpayer has 45 days to identify replacement property. In addition, the taxpayer must receive the replacement property within the earlier of 180 days after the property was given up or the due date for filing a return (including extensions) for the year of the transfer.

EXAMPLE 12-6

Dan transfers property to Joey, and Joey places cash with an escrow agent on December 10, 2017. Dan has until January 24, 2018 (45 days), to identify a replacement property and must receive the replacement property by April 15, 2018. f the tax return were extended, Dan would have 180 days from December 10 to receive the property.

Liabilities Assumed on the Exchange

The assumption or release of a liability adds complexity to a nontaxable exchange. When a taxpayer is released from a liability in an exchange, its release is considered boot received.[11] In other words, the taxpayer who assumes the debt is treated as having paid cash, and the taxpayer released from the debt is treated as having received cash. Because liabilities released are boot, the presence of a liability can trigger gain to the lesser of boot received or gain realized.

[11] IRC § 1031(d).

EXAMPLE 12-7

Jack exchanges land used in his business (FMV $200,000) for Dave's land (FMV $150,000). Jack's basis in the land is $75,000 and is subject to a liability of $50,000, which Dave assumes.

Proceeds	$200,000*
Basis	(75,000)
Realized gain	$125,000†

* The FMV of the land received of $150,000 plus the release of a liability of $50,000.

† The realized gain is $125,000, of which $50,000 is recognized (the lesser of boot received or gain realized). The released liability is boot. The basis in the new land is $75,000 (FMV of land received of $150,000 less the deferred gain of $75,000).

Exchanges between Related Parties

Exchanges between related parties are not like-kind exchanges if either party disposes of the property within two years of the exchange. Any gain realized on the exchange is recognized in the year of the subsequent sale.[12] A *related party* includes the taxpayer's spouse, child, grandchild, parent, brother, or sister; or a related corporation, S corporation, partnership, or trust. Death or involuntary conversions within the two-year period do not trigger the gain.[13]

TAX YOUR BRAIN

Why does the tax law disallow a nontaxable exchange between related parties if the property is sold within two years?

ANSWER

Suppose one brother was in the 35% tax bracket and the other brother was in the 15% tax bracket. The brothers could exchange gain property held by the high-bracket brother at no gain, and the low-bracket brother could sell the property and pay tax at a lower tax rate. Corporations and shareholders owning more than 50% of the stock are also related parties. Without the disallowance, the same type of transaction could occur between the corporation and a related shareholder.

Deferred Exchanges

One problem with a like-kind exchange is finding someone willing to exchange properties. However, with a properly executed like-kind exchange, the exchange can be nontaxable even if a seller of a property is unwilling to exchange properties. As noted, a like-kind exchange does not need to be simultaneous to be tax-free. The Ninth Circuit Court held that the contractual right to receive like-kind property is the same as the ownership rights themselves.[14] The court did not specify a time period, so Congress imposed the 45- and 180-day time requirements discussed earlier.

The most common arrangement for a deferred exchange occurs when the title to the property to be exchanged is placed in an escrow account with a custodian (usually an attorney or CPA). The custodian sells the property and places the cash in an escrow account. The taxpayer then has 45 days to identify like-kind property. When the property has been identified, the custodian purchases the new asset and distributes the title to the taxpayer. The main restriction is

[12] IRC § 1031(f).

[13] IRC § 1031(f)(2).

[14] *Starker v. US* (1979, CA9) 79-2 USTC 9541.

From Shoebox to Software

The reporting requirements for like-kind exchanges are not complex for single asset exchanges. The taxpayer is required to file Form 8824. On Form 8824, the taxpayer reports the FMV of property given up, the basis of the property given, and the gain or loss realized. The taxpayer compares the boot property to the realized gain to determine how much gain, if any, must be recognized.

Exhibit 12-1 illustrates the reporting for the exchange in Example 12-7. Recall that Jack traded land with an FMV of $200,000 and a liability of $50,000 for land with an FMV of $150,000.[15] Because the gain of $50,000 is recognized on the like-kind exchange and the land was used in a business, the land is considered §1231 property. Thus the gain transfers to page 1 of Form 4797.

that the taxpayer cannot, at any time, have actual or constructive receipt of the proceeds from the sale of old property. In other words, the taxpayer cannot touch or be able to use the cash proceeds; otherwise, the nontaxable exchange will be disqualified.[16]

EXAMPLE 12-8

On May 1, 2017, David offers to purchase real property from Zack for $100,000. However, David is unwilling to participate in a like-kind exchange. Thus Zack enters into an exchange agreement with Carri (an attorney) to facilitate an exchange with respect to the real property. The exchange agreement between Zack and Carri provides that Zack will deliver a deed conveying real property to Carri, who, in turn, will deliver a deed conveying the real property to David in exchange for $100,000. The exchange agreement expressly limits Zack's rights to receive, pledge, borrow, or otherwise obtain benefits of the money or other property held by Carri. On May 17, 2017, Zack delivers to Carri a deed conveying the real property to Carri. On the same date, Carri delivers to David a deed conveying real property to him, and David deposits $100,000 in escrow. The escrow agreement provides that the money in escrow be used to purchase replacement property. On June 3, 2017 (within 45 days), Zack identifies replacement real property. On August 9, 2017, Carri uses $80,000 from the escrow to purchase the new real property. On the same date (within 180 days), Carri delivers to Zack a deed conveying new real property to him, and the escrow holder pays Zack $20,000, the balance of the escrow account (considered boot). Zack recognizes gain of the lesser of the realized gain or the boot received ($20,000).

CONCEPT CHECK 12-1— LO 12-1

1. With a correctly executed like-kind exchange, gain is never recognized unless the taxpayer receives boot. True or false?
2. For a transaction to qualify for a like-kind exchange, an exchange of assets must occur and the assets must be held for trade or business use or for investment and be like-kind assets. True or false?
3. A taxpayer has 180 days after relinquishing his or her property to identify a replacement property. True or false?
4. The basis in the replacement property is typically the FMV of the property received less the gain postponed. True or false?

INVOLUNTARY CONVERSIONS

LO 12-2

An *involuntary conversion* occurs when property is destroyed, stolen, condemned, or disposed of under the threat of condemnation and the taxpayer receives other property or payment such as an insurance or condemnation award. If the taxpayer receives other property for the converted property of similar or related use, the taxpayer recognizes no gain.[17]

[15] The dates included on the tax form were not given in the example.

[16] Reg. § 1.1031(k)-1(g). This regulation section gives safe harbor rules to protect against the actual or constructive receipt of the money.

[17] IRC § 1033(a)(1).

EXHIBIT 12-1

Form **8824**

Department of the Treasury
Internal Revenue Service

Like-Kind Exchanges

(and section 1043 conflict-of-interest sales)

▶ Attach to your tax return.

▶ Go to *www.irs.gov/Form8824* for instructions and the latest information.

OMB No. 1545-1190

2017

Attachment Sequence No. **109**

Name(s) shown on tax return	Identifying number
Jack A. Trade	**412-34-5670**

Part I **Information on the Like-Kind Exchange**

Note: *If the property described on line 1 or line 2 is real or personal property located outside the United States, indicate the country.*

1 Description of like-kind property given up:
Land located at 519 Exchange Avenue, Anywhere, USA

2 Description of like-kind property received:
Land located at 321 Exchange Avenue, Anywhere, USA

3 Date like-kind property given up was originally acquired (month, day, year) . . . . . . | 3 | **10/15/2014**

4 Date you actually transferred your property to the other party (month, day, year) . . . . | 4 | **05/01/2017**

5 Date like-kind property you received was identified by written notice to another party (month, day, year). See instructions for 45-day written identification requirement . . . . . . | 5 | **05/01/2017**

6 Date you actually received the like-kind property from other party (month, day, year). See instructions | 6 | **05/01/2017**

7 Was the exchange of the property given up or received made with a related party, either directly or indirectly (such as through an intermediary)? See instructions. If "Yes," complete Part II. If "No," go to Part III . . . . ☐ **Yes** ☑ **No**

Note: *Do not file this form if a related party sold property into the exchange, directly or indirectly (such as through an intermediary); that property became your replacement property; and none of the exceptions in line 11 applies to the exchange. Instead, report the disposition of the property as if the exchange had been a sale. If one of the exceptions on line 11 applies to the exchange, complete Part II.*

Part II **Related Party Exchange Information**

8 Name of related party	Relationship to you	Related party's identifying number

Address (no., street, and apt., room, or suite no., city or town, state, and ZIP code)

9 During this tax year (and before the date that is 2 years after the last transfer of property that was part of the exchange), did the related party sell or dispose of any part of the like-kind property received from you (or an intermediary) in the exchange? . . . . ☐ **Yes** ☐ **No**

10 During this tax year (and before the date that is 2 years after the last transfer of property that was part of the exchange), did you sell or dispose of any part of the like-kind property you received? . . . . ☐ **Yes** ☐ **No**

*If both lines 9 and 10 are "No" and this is the year of the exchange, go to Part III. If both lines 9 and 10 are "No" and this is **not** the year of the exchange, stop here. If either line 9 or line 10 is "Yes," complete Part III and report on this year's tax return the deferred gain or (loss) from line 24 **unless** one of the exceptions on line 11 applies.*

11 If one of the exceptions below applies to the disposition, check the applicable box.

a ☐ The disposition was after the death of either of the related parties.

b ☐ The disposition was an involuntary conversion, and the threat of conversion occurred after the exchange.

c ☐ You can establish to the satisfaction of the IRS that neither the exchange nor the disposition had tax avoidance as one of its principal purposes. If this box is checked, attach an explanation. See instructions.

For Paperwork Reduction Act Notice, see the instructions. Cat. No. 12311A Form **8824** (2017)

Source: U.S. Department of the Treasury, Internal Revenue Service, Form 8824. Washington, DC: 2017.

EXHIBIT 12-1 *(concluded)*

Form 8824 (2017) Page **2**

Name(s) shown on tax return. Do not enter name and social security number if shown on other side. | **Your social security number**

Part III **Realized Gain or (Loss), Recognized Gain, and Basis of Like-Kind Property Received**

Caution: *If you transferred* **and** *received* **(a)** *more than one group of like-kind properties or* **(b)** *cash or other (not like-kind) property, see* **Reporting of multi-asset exchanges** *in the instructions.*

Note: *Complete lines 12 through 14* **only** *if you gave up property that was not like-kind. Otherwise, go to line 15.*

12	Fair market value (FMV) of other property given up	12	
13	Adjusted basis of other property given up	13	
14	Gain or (loss) recognized on other property given up. Subtract line 13 from line 12. Report the gain or (loss) in the same manner as if the exchange had been a sale	14	
	Caution: *If the property given up was used previously or partly as a home, see* **Property used as home** *in the instructions.*		
15	Cash received, FMV of other property received, plus net liabilities assumed by other party, reduced (but not below zero) by any exchange expenses you incurred. See instructions	15	50,000
16	FMV of like-kind property you received	16	150,000
17	Add lines 15 and 16	17	200,000
18	Adjusted basis of like-kind property you gave up, net amounts paid to other party, plus any exchange expenses **not** used on line 15. See instructions	18	75,000
19	**Realized gain or (loss).** Subtract line 18 from line 17	19	125,000
20	Enter the smaller of line 15 or line 19, but not less than zero	20	50,000
21	Ordinary income under recapture rules. Enter here and on Form 4797, line 16. See instructions	21	
22	Subtract line 21 from line 20. If zero or less, enter -0-. If more than zero, enter here and on Schedule D or Form 4797, unless the installment method applies. See instructions	22	50,000
23	**Recognized gain.** Add lines 21 and 22	23	50,000
24	Deferred gain or (loss). Subtract line 23 from line 19. If a related party exchange, see instructions	24	75,000
25	**Basis of like-kind property received.** Subtract line 15 from the sum of lines 18 and 23	25	75,000

Part IV **Deferral of Gain From Section 1043 Conflict-of-Interest Sales**

Note: *This part is to be used* **only** *by officers or employees of the executive branch of the Federal Government or judicial officers of the Federal Government (including certain spouses, minor or dependent children, and trustees as described in section 1043) for reporting nonrecognition of gain under section 1043 on the sale of property to comply with the conflict-of-interest requirements. This part can be used* **only** *if the cost of the replacement property is more than the basis of the divested property.*

26 Enter the number from the upper right corner of your certificate of divestiture. (**Do not** attach a copy of your certificate. Keep the certificate with your records.) ▶ ______ - ______

27 Description of divested property ▶ ____________________

28 Description of replacement property ▶ ____________________

29	Date divested property was sold (month, day, year)	29	MM/DD/YYYY
30	Sales price of divested property. See instructions	30	
31	Basis of divested property	31	
32	**Realized gain.** Subtract line 31 from line 30	32	
33	Cost of replacement property purchased within 60 days after date of sale	33	
34	Subtract line 33 from line 30. If zero or less, enter -0-	34	
35	Ordinary income under recapture rules. Enter here and on Form 4797, line 10. See instructions	35	
36	Subtract line 35 from line 34. If zero or less, enter -0-. If more than zero, enter here and on Schedule D or Form 4797. See instructions	36	
37	**Deferred gain.** Subtract the sum of lines 35 and 36 from line 32	37	
38	**Basis of replacement property.** Subtract line 37 from line 33	38	

Form **8824** (2017)

EXAMPLE 12-9

The state of Alabama condemned 300 acres of Art's land. In payment to Art, the state awarded him 300 acres of similar land. In this case, Art recognizes no gain or loss, and the basis of his new land is the same as his old land.

A far more likely scenario is that the taxpayer receives cash either from the condemning authority or from an insurance policy (in the case of a casualty). In this case, the taxpayer must recognize any gain unless he or she elects the nonrecognition provisions.[18] This election provides that, in general, no gain will be recognized on an involuntary conversion if the taxpayer replaces the converted property with similar property of equal or greater value within a certain time.

EXAMPLE 12-10

A tornado destroyed Kelly's building used in a trade or business. Kelly purchased the building in 1984 for $100,000, and it is now fully depreciated (zero adjusted basis). She received $250,000 in insurance proceeds for the replacement cost. Unless Kelly elects to replace the property with similar-use property costing $250,000 or more, she must recognize the $250,000 gain.

To defer the entire gain, the replacement property must be purchased for an amount equal to or greater than the proceeds from the conversion. The gain is recognized at the lower of the gain realized or the proceeds *not* used for replacement. If, in this example, the replacement building costs only $240,000, Kelly would recognize $10,000 of the $250,000 realized gain.

The involuntary conversion provisions do not apply to losses. Losses are deducted without reference to the involuntary conversion rules and are allowed to the extent allowed by the casualty loss rules for either personal property (see Chapter 5) or business property (see Chapter 6).

Replacement Property

To postpone any gain, the taxpayer must purchase qualifying replacement property with the specific purpose of replacing the converted property. However, qualifying property depends on the type of property held prior to the involuntary conversion. If the property lost is anything other than real property, the replacement property must be "similar or related in service or use."[19] This test is more restrictive than the like-kind test.

EXAMPLE 12-11

A delivery van used in Chris's business was destroyed in an auto accident. The van was fully depreciated. Chris received $8,000 in insurance proceeds. To qualify as replacement property, Chris must replace the van with a vehicle of similar or related use.[20]

If the property destroyed or condemned is real property, the similar use restrictions are lowered. The replacement property for real property must be only like-kind.[21]

[18] IRC § 1033(2)(A).

[19] IRC § 1033(a)(2)(A).

[20] If the property was lost in a presidentially declared disaster zone, any tangible property held for productive use in the business qualifies. In this case, any tangible business property qualifies as replacement property.

[21] IRC § 1033(g)(1).

EXAMPLE 12-12

The city condemned an office building owned by Alice. Her basis in the building was $120,000, and she received $200,000 in condemnation proceeds. If Alice invests $200,000 or more in a residential building instead of an office building, she meets the like-kind test even though the similar use test is not met.

The IRC also allows the taxpayer to purchase stock in a corporation that holds property similar to the converted property. However, the taxpayer must have control of the corporation with similar-use property for the acquisition to qualify as replacement property.[22]

Replacement Period

The time to purchase replacement property is limited. The replacement period ends two years after the close of the first taxable year in which any part of the gain is realized.[23]

The two years to replace involuntarily converted property is the norm for most property. However, for real property held for use in a trade or business or investment that is condemned, the replacement period is three years.[24]

EXAMPLE 12-13

The state condemned Connie's land with a $200,000 basis on October 23, 2017. Connie received proceeds of $310,000 on December 12, 2017. Because the $110,000 gain was realized in 2017, she has until December 31, 2020, to replace the property and defer the gain. If the proceeds were received on January 5, 2018, Connie would have until December 31, 2021, to replace the property (three years from the end of the tax year in which the gain was realized because the property was real property).

Basis and Holding Period of Replacement Property

The basis calculation for the replacement property is similar to like-kind exchanges. The basis is calculated as follows when property is converted directly to similar property:[25]

	Adjusted basis of converted property
+	Increased by money reinvested in excess of proceeds received
−	Decreased by money received not used to replace the property
+	Amount of gain recognized by the taxpayer on the conversion
−	Amount of loss recognized by the taxpayer on the conversion
=	Adjusted basis of replacement property

When the conversion results in money received (which is usually the case through either insurance proceeds or a condemnation award) and replacement property is purchased within the two-year period, the basis of the new property is its cost less the deferred gain.[26]

EXAMPLE 12-14

Assume the same facts as in Example 12-13. However, in June 2017, Connie finds suitable replacement land and acquires it for $325,000. She recognizes none of the $110,000 gain because the property is replaced within the three-year period and the acquisition price is more than $310,000. The basis of the new land is $215,000 ($325,000 purchase price less $110,000 deferred gain).

[22] IRC § 1033(a)(2)(A).

[23] IRC § 1033(a)(2)(B)(i).

[24] IRC § 1033(g)(4).

[25] IRC § 1033(b)(1).

[26] IRC § 1033(b)(2).

From Shoebox to Software

As mentioned previously, there is no form to elect deferral of gain on an involuntary conversion. The taxpayer simply attaches a schedule or statement to the end of the tax return noting the election. If the replacement property is purchased in a subsequent tax year, another statement is attached to the subsequent return detailing the replacement property. Exhibit 12-2 is an example of a sample statement attached to a tax return regarding involuntary conversions.

EXHIBIT 12-2

(for year of involuntary conversion)
Connie Erwin
SSN 123-45-6789
Tax Year 2017

The land parcel at 104 Asphalt Drive, Cary, AZ, was taken by eminent domain by the state of Arizona on October 23, 2017. The proceeds from the state amounted to $310,000. I elect the deferral of gain under IRC §1033.

Proceeds	$310,000
Adjusted basis	(200,000)
Deferred gain	$110,000

(for the tax year when replacement property is acquired)
Connie Erwin
SSN 123-45-6789
Tax Year 2018

A land parcel at 112 Fix Drive, Cary, AZ, was purchased for $325,000 as replacement property for land conveyed to the state of Arizona on October 23, 2017. The gain is deferred under IRC §1033.

State proceeds	$310,000
Adjusted basis	(200,000)
Deferred gain	$110,000
Cost of new land	$325,000
Deferred gain	(110,000)
Basis of new land	$215,000

EXAMPLE 12-15 Assume the same facts as in Example 12-14 ($310,000 in condemnation proceeds). Suppose the purchase price of the new land was only $260,000. In this case, $50,000 of the gain is recognized because $50,000 of the proceeds is not used to replace the converted property. The basis of the new property would be $200,000 ($260,000 purchase price less $60,000 deferred gain).

The holding period for the replacement property includes the holding period of the converted property.[27]

In two instances concerning involuntary conversions, taxpayers must file an amended tax return (Form 1040X):

- The taxpayer does not buy replacement property within the replacement period. In this case, the gain on the sale of the asset and any tax due must be reported in the year of the conversion.
- The replacement property purchased by the taxpayer costs less than the amount realized for the converted property.[28]

The taxpayer reports the gain either on Form 4797 for business property or on Schedule D for personal investment property.

[27] IRC § 1223(1)(A).

[28] Source: IRS Publication 544, 7–10.

CONCEPT CHECK 12-2— LO 12-2

Assume these facts to answer the following questions: A fire destroyed Andrew's building used in his woodworking business. He had purchased the building several years ago for $75,000, and it now has a $50,000 adjusted basis. Andrew received $105,000 in insurance proceeds for the replacement cost.

1. If Andrew does not replace the building, what is his taxable gain?
2. How many years does Andrew have to replace the building to defer any recognized gain?
3. How much gain would Andrew be required to recognize if he replaced the building (within the replacement period) with another building costing $95,000?
4. How much gain would Andrew be required to recognize if he replaced the building with another building costing $115,000?
5. Assuming the same facts as in (4), how much would Andrew's basis be in the new building?

INSTALLMENT SALES
LO 12-3

When an asset is sold, any gain or loss is usually recognized in the year of sale. The IRC allows the taxpayer a method to defer some of the gain to future years.[29] An *installment sale* is a disposition of property for which at least one payment is to be received after the year of the sale.[30]

Typically, payments on installment sales consist of three components:

- Interest income.
- Return of adjusted basis in the property sold.
- Gain on the sale.

Taxpayers report the interest income separately (on Form 1040, Schedule B) from the gain on the sale. The return of basis and the gain portion of each payment are determined based on the gross profit percentage of the asset sold. The gross profit percentage is calculated as follows:

Selling price		$100,000
Installment sale basis		
Adjusted basis of the property	$25,000	
Selling expenses	3,000	
Depreciation recapture	–0–	(28,000)
Gross profit		$ 72,000
Contract price		$100,000
Gross profit percentage (gross profit/contract price)	72%	

Most installment payments have an interest component. However, the interest charges do not affect the gross profit calculation. If the taxpayer in the preceding example were to receive

[29] IRC § 453.

[30] IRC § 453(b)(1).

a $20,000 cash down payment and $20,000 for the next four years, income would be recognized as follows:

	Cash Received*	Income	Return of Basis
Year of sale	$ 20,000 × 72%	$14,400	$ 5,600
1st payment	20,000 × 72%	14,400	5,600
2nd payment	20,000 × 72%	14,400	5,600
3rd payment	20,000 × 72%	14,400	5,600
4th payment	20,000 × 72%	14,400	5,600
	$100,000	$72,000	$28,000

* In this example, the interest component is ignored for simplicity. If a 10% interest rate were assumed, the first installment payment would also have $8,000 of interest ($6,000 for payment 2, $4,000 for payment 3, and $2,000 for payment 4). Thus the first year cash received is actually $28,000 ($20,000 installment plus $8,000 in interest).

The contract price is the selling price or the selling price reduced by any debt assumed by the buyer. In the preceding example, the contract price and the selling price are the same.[31]

EXAMPLE 12-16 Assume the same facts as just given except that the buyer agrees to pay $80,000 in cash over four years and assume a $20,000 liability attached to the asset.

Selling price		$100,000
Installment sale basis		
Adjusted basis of the property	$25,000	
Selling expenses	3,000	
Depreciation recapture	–0–	(28,000)
Gross profit		$ 72,000
Contract price ($100,000 – $20,000)		$ 80,000
Gross profit percentage (gross profit/contract price)	90%	

If the taxpayer in the same example were to receive a $20,000 cash down payment and $15,000 for the next four years, income would be recognized as follows:

	Cash Received*	Income	Return of Basis
Year of sale	$20,000 × 90%	$18,000	$2,000
1st payment	15,000 × 90%	13,500	1,500
2nd payment	15,000 × 90%	13,500	1,500
3rd payment	15,000 × 90%	13,500	1,500
4th payment	15,000 × 90%	13,500	1,500
	$80,000	$72,000	$8,000

*Again, the interest component would be separate from the gross profit calculations, but the additional cash for interest would be received.

[31] Reg § 15A.453-1(b)(5), Ex.2.

Dealers, Inventory, and Depreciation Recapture

An installment sale does not include any dispositions by a taxpayer who is a dealer in the item sold (for example, a car dealership cannot use the installment method to account for the sale of a car).[32] Likewise, a taxpayer cannot use the installment method to report a gain from the sale of stock or securities traded on an established securities market.

Note in the preceding examples that depreciation recapture is added to the basis in the gross profit calculation. We discussed depreciation recapture in Chapter 7. Any depreciation deducted on personal assets used in a trade or business (§ 1245 assets) must be recaptured as ordinary income when the asset is disposed of. If that asset is sold on the installment method, the depreciation recapture is recognized in the year of sale and cannot be deferred.

Other limitations apply to installment sales between related parties. If the related party resells the property before *all* installment payments have been made or within two years of the sale, any payment received by the related party on the second sale is treated as an amount received by the original seller.[33]

Electing Out of the Installment Method

Taxpayers must use the installment method for deferred payments unless they elect not to use the installment method.

TAX YOUR BRAIN

Why might a taxpayer wish to elect out of the installment method and not defer any gain?

ANSWER

A taxpayer may want to report the entire gain in the year of sale if the gain were a capital gain and the taxpayer had a large capital loss that would go unused in the current year.

To elect out of the installment method, the taxpayer simply reports the sale in its entirety on Form 4797 or Schedule D, whichever applies.

CONCEPT CHECK 12-3— LO 12-3

1. Tamaria sold a tract of land for $30,000. The land has a basis of $18,000, and she incurred $2,000 of selling expenses. Tamaria received $5,000 down and will receive five additional annual payments of $5,000 each. What is Tamaria's gross profit percentage on the sale?
   a. 33.3%.
   b. 60.0%.
   c. 66.7%.
   d. 100.0%.

2. Assume the same facts. How much income will Tamaria recognize in year 2 when she receives the first additional payment of $5,000?
   a. $0.
   b. $1,667.
   c. $3,335.
   d. $5,000.

[32] IRC § 453(b)(2).

[33] IRC § 453(e).

From Shoebox to Software

A taxpayer initially reports installment sales on Form 6252 and transfers any recognized gain to Schedule D or Form 4797 as appropriate. Exhibit 12-3 illustrates the tax reporting for Example 12-16. In this example, the taxpayer received $80,000 cash ($20,000 down and the remainder over four years). The buyer also assumed a $20,000 liability.

To record an installment sale in most software programs, open Form 6252 on the Forms menu. Fill in the proceeds, basis, commissions, and the amount of cash received during the tax year. The software calculates the gross profit percentage and the recognized gain. The software then transfers the gain to Schedule D or Form 4797.

SALE OF A PERSONAL RESIDENCE

LO 12-4

The Taxpayer Relief Act of 1997 changed the treatment of the sale of personal residences in favor of taxpayers. Under certain conditions (explained later), a taxpayer can exclude up to $500,000 ($250,000 for a single taxpayer) of gain on the sale of his or her primary residence.[34] Note that this provision is an exclusion, not a deferral of gain.

Even though a taxpayer is allowed tax deductions for more than one home for various other provisions in the IRC,[35] the residence exclusion applies only to the taxpayer's principal residence. To qualify for the exclusion, the taxpayer must meet the ownership test and the use test. During the five-year period ending on the date of the sale, the taxpayer must have satisfied

- The ownership test: owned the home for at least two years.
- The use test: lived in the home as his or her main home for at least two years.[36]

The ownership and use tests do not have to be continuous. The taxpayer need only show that he or she lived in the main home for either 24 full months or 730 days during the five-year period.

EXAMPLE 12-17

David purchased a house on May 1, 2015. He lived in the house from May 1, 2015, until April 15, 2016. He then lived in Germany from April 15, 2016, to April 1, 2017. David moved back into the house from April 1, 2017, until June 5, 2018, when he sold the house. Because David has lived in the house for 24 full months in the five years prior to the sale of the home, he is eligible for the exclusion (11 months the first time and 14 months after he returned from Germany).

Reduced Maximum Exclusion

The exclusion applies to only one sale every two years. The taxpayer is ineligible for the exclusion if, during the two-year period ending on the date of sale of the present home, the taxpayer sold another home at a gain and excluded all or part of that gain.[37] If the second sale is caused by a change in the place of employment, health reasons, or other unforeseen circumstances, the taxpayer is still eligible for some reduced exclusion. In this situation, a portion of the gain can be excluded by dividing the number of days used by 730 days and multiplying by the full exclusion amount.[38]

[34] IRC § 121(a) and (b).

[35] For example, a taxpayer can deduct the mortgage interest on a primary residence and a second vacation home as an itemized deduction.

[36] IRC § 121(a).

[37] IRC § 121(b)(3)(A).

[38] IRC § 121(c)(2)(B).

EXHIBIT 12-3

Form **6252** Department of the Treasury Internal Revenue Service	**Installment Sale Income** ▶ Attach to your tax return. ▶ Use a separate form for each sale or other disposition of property on the installment method. ▶ Go to *www.irs.gov/Form6252* for the latest information.	OMB No. 1545-0228 **2017** Attachment Sequence No. **79**

Name(s) shown on return: **Jack Taxpayer** | Identifying number: **412-34-5670**

1	Description of property ▶ **Land, 303 Anywhere Road**		
2a	Date acquired (mm/dd/yyyy) ▶ **02/05/1997**	**b** Date sold (mm/dd/yyyy) ▶	**10/23/2017**
3	Was the property sold to a related party (see instructions) after May 14, 1980? If "No," skip line 4	☐ Yes	☑ No
4	Was the property you sold to a related party a marketable security? If "Yes," complete Part III. If "No," complete Part III for the year of sale and the 2 years after the year of sale	☐ Yes	☐ No

Part I **Gross Profit and Contract Price.** Complete this part for the year of sale only.

5	Selling price including mortgages and other debts. **Don't** include interest, whether stated or unstated			5	100,000
6	Mortgages, debts, and other liabilities the buyer assumed or took the property subject to (see instructions)	6	20,000		
7	Subtract line 6 from line 5	7	80,000		
8	Cost or other basis of property sold	8	25,000		
9	Depreciation allowed or allowable	9			
10	Adjusted basis. Subtract line 9 from line 8	10	25,000		
11	Commissions and other expenses of sale	11	3,000		
12	Income recapture from Form 4797, Part III (see instructions)	12			
13	Add lines 10, 11, and 12			13	28,000
14	Subtract line 13 from line 5. If zero or less, **don't** complete the rest of this form (see instructions)			14	72,000
15	If the property described on line 1 above was your main home, enter the amount of your excluded gain (see instructions). Otherwise, enter -0-			15	0
16	**Gross profit.** Subtract line 15 from line 14			16	72,000
17	Subtract line 13 from line 6. If zero or less, enter -0-			17	0
18	**Contract price.** Add line 7 and line 17			18	80,000

Part II **Installment Sale Income.** Complete this part for the year of sale **and** any year you receive a payment or have certain debts you must treat as a payment on installment obligations.

19	Gross profit percentage (expressed as a decimal amount). Divide line 16 by line 18. (For years after the year of sale see instructions)			19	0.90
20	If this is the year of sale, enter the amount from line 17. Otherwise, enter -0-			20	0
21	Payments received during year (see instructions). **Don't** include interest, whether stated or unstated			21	20,000
22	Add lines 20 and 21			22	20,000
23	Payments received in prior years (see instructions). **Don't** include interest, whether stated or unstated	23	0		
24	**Installment sale income.** Multiply line 22 by line 19			24	18,000
25	Enter the part of line 24 that is ordinary income under the recapture rules (see instructions)			25	0
26	Subtract line 25 from line 24. Enter here and on Schedule D or Form 4797 (see instructions)			26	18,000

Part III **Related Party Installment Sale Income. Don't** complete if you received the final payment this tax year.

27 Name, address, and taxpayer identifying number of related party

28 Did the related party resell or dispose of the property ("second disposition") during this tax year? ☐ Yes ☐ No

29 **If the answer to question 28 is "Yes," complete lines 30 through 37 below unless one of the following conditions is met. Check the box that applies.**

- a ☐ The second disposition was more than 2 years after the first disposition (other than dispositions of marketable securities). If this box is checked, enter the date of disposition (mm/dd/yyyy) ▶
- b ☐ The first disposition was a sale or exchange of stock to the issuing corporation.
- c ☐ The second disposition was an involuntary conversion and the threat of conversion occurred after the first disposition.
- d ☐ The second disposition occurred after the death of the original seller or buyer.
- e ☐ It can be established to the satisfaction of the IRS that tax avoidance wasn't a principal purpose for either of the dispositions. If this box is checked, attach an explanation (see instructions).

30	Selling price of property sold by related party (see instructions)	30	
31	Enter contract price from line 18 for year of first sale	31	
32	Enter the **smaller** of line 30 or line 31	32	
33	Total payments received by the end of your 2017 tax year (see instructions)	33	
34	Subtract line 33 from line 32. If zero or less, enter -0-	34	
35	Multiply line 34 by the gross profit percentage on line 19 for year of first sale	35	
36	Enter the part of line 35 that is ordinary income under the recapture rules (see instructions)	36	
37	Subtract line 36 from line 35. Enter here and on Schedule D or Form 4797 (see instructions)	37	

For Paperwork Reduction Act Notice, see page 4. Cat. No. 13601R Form **6252** (2017)

Source: U.S. Department of the Treasury, Internal Revenue Service, Form 6252. Washington, DC: 2017.

EXHIBIT 12-4 **Worksheet for the Reduced Maximum Exclusion**

Source: IRS *Publication 523*.

Worksheet 3. **Reduced Maximum Exclusion** *Keep for Your Records*

Caution: *Complete this worksheet only if you qualify for a reduced maximum exclusion (see* Reduced Maximum Exclusion*). Complete column (a).*

			(a) You	(b) Your Spouse
1.	Maximum amount	1.	$250,000	$250,000
2a.	Enter the number of days (or months) that you used the property as a main home during the 5-year period* ending on the date of sale	2a.		
b.	Enter the number of days (or months) that you owned the property during the 5-year period* ending on the date of sale. If you used days on line 2a, you also must use days on this line and on lines 3 and 5. If you used months on line 2a, you also must use months on this line and on lines 3 and 5. (If married filing jointly and one spouse owned the property longer than the other spouse, both spouses are treated as owning the property for the longer period.)	b.		
c.	Enter the smaller of line 2a or 2b	c.		
3.	Have you (or your spouse, if filing jointly) excluded gain from the sale of another home during the 2-year period ending on the date of this sale? ☐ **No.** Skip line 3 and enter the number of days (or months) from line 2c on line 4. ☐ **Yes.** Enter the number of days (or months) between the date of the most recent sale of another home on which you excluded gain and the date of sale of this home	3.		
4.	Enter the smaller of line 2c or 3	4.		
5.	Divide the amount on line 4 by 730 days (or 24 months). Enter the result as a decimal (rounded to at least 3 places). But do not enter an amount greater than 1.000	5.		
6.	Multiply the amount on line 1 by the decimal amount on line 5	6.		
7.	**Reduced maximum exclusion.** Add the amounts in columns (a) and (b) of line 6. Enter it here and on Worksheet 2, line 13	7.		

***If you were a member of the uniformed services or Foreign Service, an employee of the intelligence community, or an employee or volunteer of the Peace Corps during the time you owned the home, see *Members of the uniformed services or Foreign Service, employees of the intelligence community, or employees or volunteers of the Peace Corps* to determine your 5-year period.**

EXAMPLE 12-18

Rob (single) sold his house in Charlotte, North Carolina, at a gain of $130,000 on May 5, 2017. He properly excluded the gain. He left Charlotte to take a job in Richmond, Virginia, where he purchased a new home for $325,000 on June 10, 2017. On October 1, 2017, Rob's employer offered him a transfer to Orlando to manage the firm's Orlando office. Rob took the job and sold his Richmond home for $350,000 (a $25,000 gain) on October 10, 2017. Because the move was employment-related, Rob can exclude his gain up to $41,781. He lived in the home for 122 days from June 10, 2017, to October 10, 2017. Rob calculates his exclusion as follows:

122 days / 730 days × $250,000 exclusion[39]

= $41,781 allowed exclusion

Exhibit 12-4 provides a worksheet to help determine the reduced maximum exclusion.

Another exception to the two-year rule involves an individual who has a disability. The use test is modified if during the five-year period before the sale of the home, a taxpayer

- Became physically or mentally unable to care for himself or herself.
- Owned and lived in the home as the main residence for a total of at least one year.

In this case, the taxpayer is deemed to live in the home during any time he or she lived in a care facility licensed by a state or political subdivision.

[39] The exclusion is $250,000 if the taxpayer is single and $500,000 if the taxpayer is married and files a joint return.

From Shoebox to Software

Because most post-1997 sales of residences produce gains of less than $250,000 for single taxpayers and $500,000 for married taxpayers, the reporting requirements involving the sale of a residence are minimal. If no gain is recognized on the sale of a residence, the taxpayer is not required to report the sale on any form or statement. If, however, the gain is larger than the allowed exclusion, the taxpayer is required to report the gain as a sale of a capital asset on Schedule D. When the gain is partially excluded, the taxpayer should write the amount excluded on Schedule D. Exhibit 12-5 illustrates the presentation on Schedule D of a gain recognized on the sale of a residence when some of the gain is excluded.

Tax software usually performs the exclusion calculation for you. With most software programs, you go to the Schedule D Home Sale worksheet and fill in the house sale information.

Special Problems with Married Individuals

Married individuals can exclude up to $500,000 from the gain on a personal residence. However, what happens when one spouse is eligible for the exclusion and the other is not? In this case, each individual is treated separately.

EXAMPLE 12-19

Susan sold her personal residence on July 10, 2017, at a $190,000 gain. She excluded the gain. On August 15, 2017, she married Gus. He sold his house on December 12, 2017, at a gain of $480,000. Because Susan is not eligible for the exclusion (she sold a residence within two years of a previous sale), only $250,000 of the $480,000 gain is excluded from income.

Other special provisions for married individuals are summarized in Table 12-1.

TABLE 12-1
Provisions for Married Individuals

Source: IRS *Publication 523, 13.*

One spouse sells a home	The other spouse is still allowed an exclusion of gain up to $250,000.
Death of spouse before sale	The surviving spouse is deemed to have owned and lived in the property for any period when the decedent spouse owned and lived in the home. Starting in 2008, a surviving spouse can qualify for up to $500,000 if the sale of the residence occurs not later than two years after one spouse's death.
Home transferred from spouse	The transferee spouse is considered to have owned the residence for any period of time when the transferor spouse owned the residence.
Use of home after divorce	The taxpayer is considered to have used the house during any period when (1) the taxpayer owned it and (2) the spouse or former spouse is allowed to live in it under a divorce or separation agreement.

CONCEPT CHECK 12-4— LO 12-4

1. If married taxpayers live in their personal residence for more than two years, the couple can exclude the gain on the sale of their residence up to $500,000. True or false?
2. A taxpayer cannot exclude any gain on the sale of a residence if he or she has lived there less than two years. True or false?
3. Sharon and Johnny were recently married, and Sharon moved into Johnny's house. She then sold her home and took the exclusion. Because Sharon took the exclusion, Johnny must forfeit his exclusion if he were to sell his home within the next two years. True or false?

EXHIBIT 12-5

Part II **Long-Term Capital Gains and Losses—Assets Held More Than One Year**

See instructions for how to figure the amounts to enter on the lines below. This form may be easier to complete if you round off cents to whole dollars.	(d) Proceeds (sales price)	(e) Cost (or other basis)	(g) Adjustments to gain or loss from Form(s) 8949, Part II, line 2, column (g)	(h) Gain or (loss) Subtract column (e) from column (d) and combine the result with column (g)
8a Totals for all long-term transactions reported on Form 1099-B for which basis was reported to the IRS and for which you have no adjustments (see instructions). However, if you choose to report all these transactions on Form 8949, leave this line blank and go to line 8b .				
8b Totals for all transactions reported on Form(s) 8949 with **Box D** checked				
9 Totals for all transactions reported on Form(s) 8949 with **Box E** checked				
10 Totals for all transactions reported on Form(s) 8949 with **Box F** checked.	470,000	325,000	135,000	10,000

11 Gain from Form 4797, Part I; long-term gain from Forms 2439 and 6252; and long-term gain or (loss) from Forms 4684, 6781, and 8824	**11**	
12 Net long-term gain or (loss) from partnerships, S corporations, estates, and trusts from Schedule(s) K-1	**12**	
13 Capital gain distributions. See the instructions	**13**	
14 Long-term capital loss carryover. Enter the amount, if any, from line 13 of your **Capital Loss Carryover Worksheet** in the instructions	**14**	( )
15 **Net long-term capital gain or (loss).** Combine lines 8a through 14 in column (h). Then go to Part III on the back	**15**	10,000

Form 8949 (2017) Attachment Sequence No. **12A** Page **2**

Name(s) shown on return. Name and SSN or taxpayer identification no. not required if shown on other side	**Social security number or taxpayer identification number**
Rob Johnson	**412-34-5670**

Before you check Box D, E, or F below, see whether you received any Form(s) 1099-B or substitute statement(s) from your broker. A substitute statement will have the same information as Form 1099-B. Either will show whether your basis (usually your cost) was reported to the IRS by your broker and may even tell you which box to check.

Part II **Long-Term.** Transactions involving capital assets you held more than 1 year are long term. For short-term transactions, see page 1.

Note: You may aggregate all long-term transactions reported on Form(s) 1099-B showing basis was reported to the IRS and for which no adjustments or codes are required. Enter the totals directly on Schedule D, line 8a; you aren't required to report these transactions on Form 8949 (see instructions).

You *must* check Box D, E, *or* F below. Check only one box. If more than one box applies for your long-term transactions, complete a separate Form 8949, page 2, for each applicable box. If you have more long-term transactions than will fit on this page for one or more of the boxes, complete as many forms with the same box checked as you need.

☐ **(D)** Long-term transactions reported on Form(s) 1099-B showing basis was reported to the IRS (see **Note** above)
☐ **(E)** Long-term transactions reported on Form(s) 1099-B showing basis **wasn't** reported to the IRS
☑ **(F)** Long-term transactions not reported to you on Form 1099-B

1 (a) Description of property (Example: 100 sh. XYZ Co.)	(b) Date acquired (Mo., day, yr.)	(c) Date sold or disposed of (Mo., day, yr.)	(d) Proceeds (sales price) (see instructions)	(e) Cost or other basis. See the **Note** below and see *Column (e)* in the separate instructions	**Adjustment, if any, to gain or loss.** If you enter an amount in column (g), enter a code in column (f). **See the separate instructions.** (f) Code(s) from instructions	(g) Amount of adjustment	(h) **Gain or (loss).** Subtract column (e) from column (d) and combine the result with column (g)
Sale of Personal Residence	**04/05/03**	**05/05/17**	**470,000**	**325,000**	**H**	**(135,000)**	**10,000**
Adj. above is Sec. 121 exclusion							

Source: U.S. Department of the Treasury, Internal Revenue Service, Form 8949. Washington, DC: 2017.

RELATED-PARTY LOSSES AND WASH SALES

LO 12-5

The related-party rules and wash sale rules limit losses (but not gains) when the taxpayer still has control over the property that caused the loss. In other words, these rules apply when the taxpayer creates a tax loss but does not substantially change the ownership of the property.

Related-Party Losses

A taxpayer cannot deduct any loss from the sale or exchange of property, directly or indirectly, between related parties.[40] The following relationships are considered related parties:

- Members of a family including spouse, ancestors, lineal descendants, and brothers and sisters (whether whole or half blood).[41]
- An individual and a corporation when more than 50% in value of the outstanding stock is owned, directly or indirectly, by or for the individual.
- Two corporations that are members of the same controlled group.
- A grantor and a fiduciary of any trust.
- A fiduciary of a trust and a beneficiary of such trust.
- Any corporation or partnership where there is more than 50% ownership.

Constructive ownership rules also apply.[42] With constructive ownership, a taxpayer is deemed to also own the stock of anyone or any entity he or she controls. A taxpayer constructively owns stock in the following instances:

- Stock owned by a corporation, partnership, estate, or trust shall be considered as being owned proportionately by its shareholders, partners, or beneficiaries.
- An individual is considered to own any stock owned by his or her family.
- An individual owning any stock in a corporation is considered to own the stock owned by or for his or her partner in a partnership.

EXAMPLE 12-20

Following are several examples concerning the constructive ownership rules:

Al owns 75% of Mama Corp.
Alice (Al's wife) owns 25% of Mama Corp.
Dad (Alice's dad) owns 0% of Mama Corp.
Pizza Corp. is owned 80% by Mama Corp.
Pizza Corp. is owned 20% by unrelated parties.

Tables 12-2 and 12-3 illustrate the ownership of the two corporations.

TABLE 12-2
Stock Ownership of Mama Corp.

Person	Actual (percentage)	Constructive (percentage)	Total under Section 267 (percentage)
Al	75%	From Alice 25%	100%
Alice	25	From Al 75	100
Dad	–0–	From Alice 25	25

(continued)

[40] IRC § 267(a)(1).
[41] IRC § 267(c)(4).
[42] Reg. § 1.267(c)-1(b).

TABLE 12-3
Stock Ownership of Pizza Corp.

Person	Actual (percentage)	Constructive (percentage)	Total under Section 267 (percentage)
Al	–0–%	60% & 20%*	80%
Alice	–0–	20 & 60†	80
Dad	–0–	20‡	20
Mama Corp.	80	–0–	80

* Deemed ownership through Mama Corp. 80% × 75% = 60% and through Alice 80% × 25% = 20%.
† Deemed ownership through Mama Corp. 80% × 25% = 20% and through Al 80% × 75% = 60%.
‡ Through Alice 80% × 25% = 20%.

Because Al and Alice control Mama Corp. and Mama Corp. controls Pizza Corp., Al and Alice are deemed to own Pizza Corp. Al and Alice are considered related parties to both Mama and Pizza.

EXAMPLE 12-21

Building Supply Inc. is owned 50% by Jake and 50% by his partner, David. Both Jake and David are related parties to Building Supply because each partner is considered as owning the stock of the other partner. Thus both are considered to own more than 50% of the stock of Building Supply Inc.[43]

Once a relationship is considered a related party, any losses on the sale of property between related parties are disallowed. This rule can be especially harsh because the disallowance of the loss does not affect the basis of the property to the buyer. The basis is the cost of the property. IRC § 267(d) does provide some relief in that if the related buyer subsequently sells the property at a gain, the taxpayer reduces the recognized gain by the previously disallowed related-party loss.[44]

EXAMPLE 12-22

Jake sells land (basis $15,000) to related party Building Supply Inc. for $8,000. The $7,000 loss is disallowed to Jake, and the basis to Building Supply is $8,000. If Building Supply Inc. subsequently sells the land to an unrelated party for $10,000, the $2,000 gain is reduced to $0. The $5,000 leftover loss remains unused and is lost.

Wash Sales of Stock

The purpose of the wash sale rules is to disallow a tax loss when the ownership of a company is not reduced. A *wash sale* occurs when a taxpayer sells stock or securities at a loss, and within a period of 30 days before or 30 days after the sale, the taxpayer acquires substantially identical stock or securities.[45]

EXAMPLE 12-23

On December 15, 2017, Kathy sold 300 shares of Electronics Inc. (a publicly traded company) at a loss of $2,500. On January 5, 2018, Kathy repurchased 300 shares of Electronics. The $2,500 loss is disallowed.

The wash sale rule does not apply to dealers in securities.

[43] Reg. § 1.267(c)–1(4)(b) ex. 2.
[44] IRC § 267(d)(2).
[45] IRC § 1091(a).

EXAMPLE 12-24

Jackie made the following acquisitions of ABC Inc.:

January 15, 2017, 300 shares @ $50/share = $15,000
February 1, 2017, 200 shares @ $30/share = $6,000

To offset other capital gains, Jackie sells all 500 shares of ABC Inc. for $25 per share on December 15, 2017. Because she believes ABC is a good investment, she buys 600 shares of ABC on January 5, 2018, for $28 per share. Because she repurchased identical stock, Jackie cannot deduct the losses on the blocks of stock.

EXAMPLE 12-25

Assume the same facts as Example 12-24, but Jackie repurchased only 300 shares of ABC stock. In this case, a proportionate share of the loss is allowed. Because 300 of the 500 shares were repurchased, Jackie can deduct 40% of the losses.

A disallowed loss under the wash sale rule is not lost forever but only deferred. The taxpayer adds any disallowed loss to the basis of the newly acquired stock. Thus the future disposal of the stock results in a reduced gain or greater loss.[46]

EXAMPLE 12-26

Art purchased 100 shares of XYZ Corp. for $10 per share in 2008. He sold the 100 shares on December 1, 2017, for $6 per share. Within 30 days, he subsequently purchased 100 shares for $8 per share. No loss is recognized. The basis of the new 100 shares is $12 per share. This basis is the $8 per share cost plus the deferred loss of $4 per share.

CONCEPT CHECK 12-5— LO 12-5

1. Leslie sold 500 shares of Bluff Co. stock to her brother for $5,000. Leslie purchased the stock three years ago for $7,000. How much of the loss can Leslie deduct on her tax return in the current year?
2. Would the answer to Question 1 change if Leslie had sold the stock to Leslie Co. instead of to her brother? Explain assuming the following facts:
   a. Leslie owns 25% of the outstanding stock in Leslie Co.
   b. Leslie owns 75% of the outstanding stock in Leslie Co.
3. What is the purpose of the wash sale rules?

Summary

LO 12-1: Explain how to defer gains using the like-kind exchange rules.

- There must be an exchange.
- The property exchanged must be held for business use or for investment.
- The property exchanged must be like-kind.
- Boot property received can cause the recognition of gain.

LO 12-2: Describe how to account for and report involuntary conversions.

- If the taxpayer receives other property for the converted property of similar or related use, the taxpayer recognizes no gain.
- If the taxpayer receives cash for the converted property, the taxpayer must use the proceeds to replace the converted property with similar property of equal or greater value within two years (generally) to defer all of the gain.
- The basis of the property is typically its cost less any deferred gain.

[46] Reg. § 1.1091-2(a).

LO 12-3: Apply the tax rules to report an installment sale.	• The taxpayer calculates a gross profit percentage based on the basis of the property sold divided by the selling price. • As the taxpayer receives cash in installments, the gain is recognized based on the gross profit percentage. • The interest income on any note receivable is a separate calculation.
LO 12-4: Explain how to exclude a gain on the sale of a personal residence.	• A taxpayer can exclude up to $500,000 ($250,000 if single) of gain on the sale of a personal residence. • The residence exclusion applies only to the taxpayer's principal residence. • The taxpayer must live there two of the last five years. • Reduced exclusions are available if a move is the result of employment transfers or health issues.
LO 12-5: Apply the rules affecting related parties and wash sales.	• A taxpayer cannot deduct any loss from the sale or exchange of property between related parties. • Related parties include family members and controlled entities. • The wash sale rules disallow a tax loss when the ownership of a company is not reduced. • A wash sale occurs when a taxpayer sells stock and within a period of 30 days (before or after the sale) the taxpayer acquires substantially the same stock.

Discussion Questions connect

All applicable discussion questions are available with ***Connect***©

LO 12-1 1. Can the exchange of personal-use property qualify as a like-kind exchange? Why or why not?

LO 12-1 2. What types of properties do *not* qualify for like-kind exchange treatment?

LO 12-1 3. Discuss the characteristics of a like-kind asset. Must the asset received in a like-kind exchange be an exact duplicate of the asset given? Explain.

LO 12-1 4. What is *boot*? How does the receipt of boot affect a like-kind exchange?

LO 12-1 5. What is the difference between a *deferred gain* and an *excluded gain*?

LO 12-1 6. How is the basis calculated in a like-kind exchange? How does the receipt of boot affect the basis of the asset received? How does the giving of boot affect the basis of the asset received?

LO 12-1 7. Often, when assets are exchanged, liabilities are assumed in the exchange. How does the assumption of liabilities in a like-kind exchange affect the gain or loss recognized? How does it affect the basis of an asset received in a like-kind exchange?

LO 12-1 8. What are the special provisions for like-kind exchanges between related parties? Why are these special provisions included in the IRC?

LO 12-1 9. Must both parties in a potential like-kind exchange agree to the exchange? If not, how can the transaction be structured to defer any gain?

LO 12-2 10. What is an *involuntary conversion*?

LO 12-2 11. When an involuntary conversion occurs and the taxpayer receives insurance proceeds, what must the taxpayer do to guarantee that no gain is recognized?

LO 12-2 12. When faced with an involuntary conversion, does the taxpayer have an unlimited amount of time to replace the converted property? Explain.

LO 12-2 13. How are the basis and holding period of the replacement property in an involuntary conversion determined? Explain.

LO 12-2 14. What information must be reported to the IRS concerning an involuntary conversion?

LO 12-3 15. How is income reported from an installment sale? What are the components of the payments received in an installment sale, and how is the gross profit percentage calculated?

EA LO 12-4 16. Discuss the rules concerning the sale of a personal residence. Include in your discussion the specifics regarding the *ownership test* and the *use test.*

EA LO 12-4 17. Is a taxpayer allowed to take the § 121 exclusion for a vacation home that was never rented? Explain.

EA LO 12-4 18. If a taxpayer moves within two years after moving into a new home and uses the exclusion on his former home, is any gain taxable on the sale of the new home? Under what conditions can some of the exclusion be used?

EA LO 12-4 19. What happens in the following circumstances if a wife, prior to marriage, uses the exclusion on the sale of a residence and subsequently (after marriage) sells a second residence within two years?

a. The new husband sells a residence.

b. The new husband dies within two years and the wife sells the residence.

EA LO 12-5 20. What is a *related-party loss,* and why is it disallowed?

EA LO 12-5 21. Explain the constructive ownership rules and how they relate to related-party transactions.

EA LO 12-5 22. What is a *wash sale,* and why are losses from wash sales disallowed?

Multiple-Choice Questions connect

All applicable multiple-choice questions are available with ***Connect***©

LO 12-1 23. For an exchange to qualify as a nontaxable exchange, what criteria must be present?

a. There must be an exchange.

b. The property transferred and received must be held for use in a trade or business or for investment.

c. The property exchanged must be like-kind.

d. All of these must be present.

LO 12-1 24. For the asset received in a like-kind exchange, how is the holding period of the new asset determined?

a. According to the date the new asset is received.

b. According to the date the old asset is given away.

c. According to the holding period of the old asset.

d. None of the above apply.

LO 12-1 25. Which of the following exchanges qualifies as like-kind property?

a. Partnership interest for partnership interest.

b. Inventory for equipment.

c. Investment land for an apartment building.

d. Business-use delivery truck for a business-use van.

LO 12-1 26. Eric exchanged equipment used in his land-clearing business with Geoff for upgraded equipment. Eric exchanged the equipment with a $75,000 FMV and $45,000 basis along with $15,000 cash. Geoff's basis in his equipment is $60,000, and the FMV is $90,000. Which of the following statements is correct?

a. Geoff must recognize a gain of $15,000 on the exchange.

b. Geoff must recognize a gain of $5,000 on the exchange.

c. Neither Eric nor Geoff must recognize a gain.

d. Eric must recognize a gain of $15,000 on the exchange.

LO 12-1 27. Ava exchanges a machine used in her business with Gail for another machine. The basis of Ava's old machine is $50,000, the FMV is $66,000, and she gives Gail cash of $14,000. Gail's basis in her machine is $70,000, and the FMV is $80,000. What is Ava's adjusted basis in the new machine she receives?

a. $50,000.

b. $64,000.

c. $66,000.

d. $80,000.

LO 12-1 28. Janel exchanges a building she uses in her rental business for a building owned by Russel that she will use in her rental business. The adjusted basis of Janel's building is $160,000, and the FMV is $250,000. The adjusted basis of Russel's building is $80,000, and the FMV is $250,000. Which of the following statements is correct?

a. Janel's recognized gain is $0, and her basis for the building received is $160,000.

b. Janel's recognized gain is $90,000, and her basis for the building received is $160,000.

c. Janel's recognized gain is $0, and her basis for the building received is $250,000.

d. Janel's recognized gain is $90,000, and her basis for the building received is $250,000.

LO 12-1 29. Jason exchanged office furniture (seven-year life) for other furniture (seven-year life). The old furniture had an adjusted basis of $14,000, and the new furniture had an FMV of $22,000. Jason also paid $5,000 cash in the exchange. What are the recognized gain or loss and the basis of the furniture?

a. $0 and $14,000.

b. $0 and $19,000.

c. $6,000 and $14,000.

d. ($8,000) and $9,000.

LO 12-1 30. Gretel exchanges a warehouse with an adjusted basis of $150,000 and an FMV of $160,000 for a mini-storage building with an FMV of $100,000 and $60,000 cash. What are the recognized gain or loss and the basis of the mini-storage building?

a. $0 gain and $150,000 basis.

b. $10,000 gain and $100,000 basis.

c. $10,000 gain and $150,000 basis.

d. $(10,000) loss and $160,000 basis.

LO 12-2 31. What tax form is completed to elect deferral of gain on an involuntary conversion?

a. No form is required.

b. Form 4797.

c. Form 4562.

d. Form 1040, Schedule D.

LO 12-2 32. In order to build a new road, the city of Oxford annexed 20 acres of Michael's farmland with an FMV of $30,000 and basis of $18,000. In return, Michael received 50 acres of similar land, which was appraised at $45,000. In this involuntary conversion, what gain or loss should Michael recognize, and what is his basis in the new land?

a. $0 gain and $18,000 basis.

b. $0 gain and $27,000 basis.

c. $12,000 gain and $30,000 basis.

d. $27,000 gain and $45,000 basis.

LO 12-2 33. A warehouse with an adjusted basis of $125,000 was destroyed by a tornado on April 15, 2017. On June 15, 2017, the insurance company paid the owner $195,000. The owner reinvested $170,000 in another warehouse. What is the basis of the new warehouse if nonrecognition of gain from an involuntary conversion is elected?

a. $100,000.

b. $125,000.

c. $170,000.

d. $195,000.

LO 12-2 34. A warehouse with an adjusted basis of $250,000 was destroyed by a tornado on April 15, 2017. On June 15, 2017, the insurance company paid the owner $395,000. The owner reinvested $470,000 in a new warehouse. What is the basis of the new warehouse if nonrecognition of gain from an involuntary conversion is elected?

a. $105,000.

b. $250,000.

c. $325,000.

d. $395,000.

LO 12-2 35. Kyla owns a convenience store with an adjusted basis of $215,000 that was destroyed by a flood on August 15, 2017. Kyla received a check for $275,000 from her insurance company on January 10, 2018, compensating her for the damage to her store. What is the latest date on which Kyla can buy replacement property to avoid recognition of any realized gain?

a. August 15, 2019.

b. December 31, 2019.

c. January 10, 2020.

d. December 31, 2021.

LO 12-3 36. On June 15, 2017, Allen sold land held for investment to Stan for $50,000 and an installment note of $250,000 payable in five equal annual installments beginning on June 15, 2018, plus interest at 10%. Allen's basis in the land is $150,000. What amount of gain is recognized in 2017 under the installment method?

a. $0.

b. $25,000.

c. $50,000.

d. $150,000.

LO 12-3 37. On July 1, 2017, Andrea sold land held for investment to Taylor. Andrea's land had a $300,000 basis and was subject to a $150,000 mortgage. Under the contractual agreement, Taylor will pay Andrea $85,000 on the date of the sale, will assume the mortgage, and will give Andrea a note for $375,000 (plus interest at the federal rate) due the following year. What is the contract price in the year of sale?

a. $460,000.

b. $525,000.

c. $610,000.

d. $760,000.

LO 12-3 38. Which of the following statements is correct with regard to installment sales?

a. The contract price is generally the amount of cash the seller will receive.

b. Sales by a taxpayer who is a dealer in the item sold are not eligible for installment sale treatment.

c. The installment method cannot be used to report gain from the sale of stock or securities that are traded on an established securities market.

d. All of the above are correct.

LO 12-3 39. A taxpayer who sells her personal residence in 2017 may exclude some or all of the gain on the sale if the residence was owned and lived in for

a. At least four years before the sale date.

b. Any two years of a five-year period before the sale.

c. Any of the last four years of an eight-year period before the sale.

d. At least one year prior to the sale date.

EA LO 12-4 40. Marcus purchased Vinnie and Marie's personal residence for $225,000 cash and the assumption of their $100,000 mortgage. Vinnie and Marie bought the house six years ago for $275,000 and have used it as a primary residence. What amount of gain should Vinnie and Marie recognize on the sale of their personal residence?

a. $0.

b. $50,000.

c. $100,000.

d. $225,000.

EA LO 12-4 41. Daniel, who is single, purchased a house on May 15, 1994, for $115,000. During the years he owned the house, he installed a swimming pool at a cost of $24,000 and replaced the driveway at a cost of $12,000. On April 28, 2017, Daniel sold the house for $470,000. He paid a realtor commission of $28,000 and legal fees of $1,000 connected with the sale of the house. What is Daniel's recognized gain on the sale of the house?

a. $0.

b. $40,000.

c. $290,000.

d. $319,000.

EA LO 12-5 42. All of the following relationships are considered related parties *except*

a. A corporation and a taxpayer whose spouse owns 80% of the corporation's stock

b. A trust and a taxpayer who is the grantor of the trust.

c. A corporation and a taxpayer who owns 20% of the corporation's stock.

d. A partnership and a taxpayer who is a two-thirds partner.

EA LO 12-5 43. On June 1, 2017, Nigel sells land (basis $55,000) to his son Ted for $40,000, the land's FMV on the date of the sale. On September 21, 2017, Ted sells the land to an unrelated party. Which of the following statements is correct?

a. If Ted sells the land for $35,000, he has a $20,000 recognized loss on the sale.

b. If Ted sells the land for $65,000, he has a $25,000 recognized gain on the sale.

c. If Ted sells the land for $45,000, he has a $5,000 recognized gain on the sale.

d. If Ted sells the land for $57,000, he has a $2,000 recognized gain on the sale.

EA LO 12-5 44. Bryce owns 200 shares of Basic Company stock that he purchased for $8,000 three years ago. On December 28, 2017, Bryce sold 100 shares of the stock for $2,500. On January 3, 2018, Bryce repurchased 50 shares for $1,100. How much of the loss can Bryce deduct in 2017?

a. $0.

b. $750.

c. $4,400.

d. $5,500.

Problems connect

All applicable problems are available with ***Connect***©

LO 12-1 45. Carlton holds undeveloped land for investment. His adjusted basis in the land is $200,000, and the FMV is $325,000. On November 1, 2017, he exchanges this land for land owned by his son, who is 31 years old. The appraised value of his son's land is $320,000 with a basis of $310,000.

a. Calculate Carlton's realized and recognized gain or loss from the exchange with his son and on Carlton's subsequent sale of the land to a real estate agent on July 19, 2018, for $375,000.

b. Calculate Carlton's realized and recognized gain or loss from the exchange with his son if Carlton does not sell the land received from his son, but his son sells the land received from Carlton on July 19, 2018. Calculate Carlton's basis for the land on November 1, 2017, and July 19, 2018.

c. What could Carlton do to avoid any recognition of gain associated with the first exchange prior to his sale of the land?

LO 12-1 46. Elaine exchanges a van that is used exclusively for business purposes for another van that also is to be used exclusively for business. The adjusted basis for the old van is $18,000, and its FMV is $14,500.

a. Calculate Elaine's recognized gain or loss on the exchange.

b. Calculate Elaine's basis for the van she receives.

LO 12-1 47. What is the basis of the new property in each of the following situations? Is any gain recognized in the following transactions?

a. Rental house with an adjusted basis of $100,000 exchanged for a personal-use river cottage with an FMV of $130,000.

b. General Motors common stock with an adjusted basis of $19,000 exchanged for Quaker Oats common stock with an FMV of $14,000.

c. Land and building with an adjusted basis of $25,000 used as a furniture repair shop exchanged for land and a building with an FMV of $52,000 used as a car dealership.

d. An office building with an adjusted basis of $22,000 exchanged for a heavy-duty truck with an FMV of $28,000. Both properties are held for 100% business purposes.

e. A residential rental property held for investment with an adjusted basis of $230,000 exchanged for a warehouse to be held for investment with an FMV of $180,000.

LO 12-1 48. Viktor exchanges stock (adjusted basis $18,000, FMV $25,000) and real estate (adjusted basis $18,000, FMV $44,000) held for investment for other real estate to be held for investment. The real estate acquired in the exchange has an FMV of $67,000.

a. What are Viktor's realized and recognized gain or loss?

b. What is the basis of the acquired real estate?

LO 12-1 49. LaRhonda owns an office building that has an adjusted basis of $45,000. The building is subject to a mortgage of $20,000. She transfers the building to Miguel in exchange for $15,000 cash and a warehouse with an FMV of $50,000. Miguel assumes the mortgage on the building.

a. What are LaRhonda's realized and recognized gain or loss?

b. What is her basis in the newly acquired warehouse?

LO 12-1 50. Kim owns equipment that is used exclusively in her business. The equipment has an adjusted basis of $8,500 (FMV $5,000). Kim transfers the equipment and $2,000 cash to David for a computer (also used for business purposes) that has an FMV of $7,000.

a. What is Kim's recognized gain or loss on the exchange?

b. What is Kim's adjusted basis in the computer?

EA LO 12-4 57. Virginia is an accountant for a global CPA firm. She is being temporarily transferred from the Raleigh, North Carolina, office to Tokyo. She will leave Raleigh on October 7, 2017, and will be out of the country for four years. She sells her personal residence on September 30, 2017, for $250,000 (her adjusted basis is $190,000). Upon her return to the United States in 2021, she purchases a new residence in Los Angeles for $220,000, where she will continue working for the same firm.

a. What are Virginia's realized and recognized gain or loss?

b. What is Virginia's basis in the new residence?

EA LO 12-4 58. On February 1, 2017, a 39-year-old widow buys a new residence for $150,000. Three months later, she sells her old residence for $310,000 (adjusted basis of $120,000). Selling expenses totaled $21,000. She lived in the old house for 15 years.

a. What are the widow's realized and recognized gain or loss?

b. What is her basis in the new residence?

EA LO 12-4 59. Dominique is a manager for a regional bank. He is being relocated several states away to act as a temporary manager while a new branch is interviewing for a permanent manager. He will leave on May 1, 2017, and will be at the new location for less than one year. He sells his personal residence on April 15, 2017, for $123,000 (adjusted basis $95,000). Upon completion of the assignment, he purchases a new residence for $200,000.

a. What are Dominique's realized and recognized gain or loss?

b. What is Dominique's basis in the new residence?

c. Assume that Dominique is transferred out of state and sells his new residence for $230,000 two months later (he is single). What are the realized and recognized gains?

EA LO 12-5 60. Crystal owns 150 shares of Carson Inc. stock that has an adjusted basis of $100,000. On December 18, 2017, she sells the 150 shares for FMV ($88,000). On January 7, 2018, she purchases 200 shares of Carson stock for $127,500.

a. What are Crystal's realized and recognized gain or loss on the sale of the 150 shares sold on December 18, 2017?

b. What is Crystal's adjusted basis for the shares purchased on January 7, 2018?

c. How would your answers in (*a*) and (*b*) change if she purchased only 100 shares for $98,000 in January?

EA LO 12-5 61. On January 1, 2017, Myron sells stock that has a $50,000 FMV on the date of the sale (basis $75,000) to his son Vernon. On October 21, 2017, Vernon sells the stock to an unrelated party. In each of the following, determine the tax consequences of these transactions to Myron and Vernon:

a. Vernon sells the stock for $40,000.

b. Vernon sells the stock for $80,000.

c. Vernon sells the stock for $65,000.

EA LO 12-5 62. Harold owns 130 shares of stock in Becker Corporation. His adjusted basis for the stock is $210,000. On December 15, 2017, he sells the stock for $180,000. He purchases 200 shares of Becker Corporation stock on January 12, 2018, for $195,000.

a. What are Harold's realized and recognized gain or loss on the sale?

b. What is Harold's adjusted basis for the 200 shares purchased on January 12, 2018?

c. How would your answers in (*a*) and (*b*) change if he purchased only 100 shares for $95,000 in January?

EA LO 12-5 63. Lewis owns 200 shares of stock in Modlin Corporation. His adjusted basis for the stock is $180,000. On December 15, 2017, he sells the stock for $170,000. He purchases 200 shares of Modlin Corporation stock on January 8, 2018, for $170,000.

a. What are Lewis's realized and recognized gain or loss on the sale?

___

b. What is Lewis's adjusted basis for the 200 shares purchased on January 8, 2018?

___

c. How would your answers in (*a*) and (*b*) change if he purchased only 100 shares for $105,000 in January?

___

d. What tax treatment is Lewis trying to achieve?

___

Tax Return Problems connect

All applicable tax return problems are available with ***Connect***©

Use your tax software to complete the following problems. If you are manually preparing the tax returns, the problem indicates the forms or schedules you will need.

Tax Return Problem 1

Wendy O'Neil (SSN 412-34-5670), who is single, worked full-time as the director at a local charity. She resides at 1501 Front Street, Highland, AZ 85711. For the year, she had the following reported on her W-2:

Wages	$46,200
Federal withholding	6,930
Social security wages	46,200
Social security withholding	2,864
Medicare withholding	670
State withholding	2,310

Other information follows:

1099-INT New Bank		$300
1099-DIV Freeze, Inc.	Ordinary dividends	400
	Qualified dividends	400

Wendy had the following itemized deductions:

State income tax withholding	$2,310
State income tax paid with the 2016 return	100
Real estate tax	2,600
Mortgage interest	8,060

Wendy inherited a beach house in North Carolina (rental only) on January 2, 2017, from her father. The FMV at the father's death was $850,000. He had purchased the house 20 years earlier for $100,000.

Summer rental income	$45,000
Repairs	2,500
Real estate taxes	6,500
Utilities	2,400
Depreciation	(Calculate)

On December 29, 2017, Wendy properly conducted a like-kind exchange for rental real estate located at 128 Lake Blvd., Hot Town, AZ. She received rental property with an FMV of $950,000 and $20,000 cash in exchange for the North Carolina beach house. The Arizona property did not produce any income until 2018.

Prepare Form 1040 for Wendy for 2017. The taxpayer had qualifying health care coverage at all times during the tax year. You will also need Schedule A, Schedule D, Schedule E, Form 4562, and Form 8824.

Tax Return Problem 2

Dave (SSN 412-34-5670) and Alicia (SSN 412-34-5671) Stanley are married and retired at age 51. The couple's income consists of rental property, stock investments, and royalties from an invention. They sold their large house that they had purchased six years ago for $580,000 on October 18, 2017, for $1 million. They now live in a condo at 101 Magnolia Lane, Suite 15, Highland Park, FL 33853.

The rental property is an apartment complex (building cost $1.5 million and was purchased January 5, 2017) with 30 units that rent for $27,000 per month and are at 90% occupancy.

Rental income	$291,600
Salaries	115,000
Payroll taxes	8,798
Real estate taxes	18,750
Interest	45,000
Repairs and maintenance	29,000
Depreciation	(Calculate)

The following information is also for the year:

1099-INT	Old Bank		$ 22,000
1099-DIV	Dell, Inc.	Ordinary dividends	15,250
		Qualified dividends	15,250
1099-DIV	IBM, Inc.	Ordinary dividends	8,650
		Qualified dividends	8,650
1099-DIV	Pepsi, Inc.	Ordinary dividends	18,785
		Qualified dividends	18,785
1099-MISC	Box 2 royalties		152,300

	Purchased	Sold	Sale Price	Basis	Gain/Loss
Dell (held 9 mo.)	12/01/16	09/01/17	$15,000	$ 9,000	$ 6,000
Pepsi (held 4 mo.)	09/01/17	12/29/17	17,000	25,000	(8,000)
IBM (held 30 mo.)	06/05/15	12/05/17	38,000	20,000	18,000

On January 3, 2018, Dave repurchased the exact number of shares he sold on December 29, 2017. The Stanleys paid $13,000 each quarter (four payments) in federal estimated income taxes.

Prepare Form 1040 for the Stanleys. Taxpayers had qualifying health care coverage at all times during the tax year. You will also need Schedule B, Schedule D, Schedule E, Form 4562, and Form 8960.

We have provided selected filled-in source documents that are available in *Connect.*

Chapter **Thirteen**

At-Risk/Passive Activity Loss Rules and the Individual Alternative Minimum Tax

In this chapter, we provide a detailed examination of the at-risk rules and the passive activity loss rules. At-risk rules and passive activity loss rules work together to limit the deductibility of losses from activities in which the taxpayer does not materially participate in the business or in which an economic loss does not occur. We also discuss the alternative minimum tax (AMT) for individual taxpayers. Congress enacted the AMT to ensure that taxpayers with substantial economic income cannot avoid significant tax liability using exclusions, deductions, and credits permitted in the Internal Revenue Code (IRC).

Learning Objectives

When you have completed this chapter, you should understand the following learning objectives (LO):

LO 13-1 Explain the process of applying the at-risk rules.

LO 13-2 Describe the rules and applications related to passive activities.

LO 13-3 Explain how the passive activity loss rules and at-risk rules work together to limit the deductibility of losses.

LO 13-4 Explain the alternative minimum tax and how it is calculated.

INTRODUCTION

A pervasive problem for the government prior to 1976 was taxpayer use of tax shelters to reduce taxable income. Tax shelters were (and still are) investment schemes that produce substantial tax losses but, at the same time, produce either a neutral or a positive cash flow. In 1976 Congress established the *at-risk rules* to combat such tax shelters. When it was apparent that the at-risk rules alone were not sufficient to quell abusive tax shelters, Congress enacted the *passive activity loss* (PAL) rules in 1986.

To understand the rules developed to combat tax shelters, you need to understand the government's problem in the first place. Example 13-1 is an example of a typical tax shelter.

EXAMPLE 13-1

Abbott, Bart, and Calvin had some extra cash to invest. They also wanted to reduce their taxable income. The three individuals each invested $33,333 into a partnership. The partnership borrowed $900,000 on a 10% interest-only nonrecourse note and purchased an equipment-intensive oil and gas venture for $1,000,000.[1] The venture produced $150,000 per year in royalty income.

	Total	Abbott	Bart	Calvin
Income	$150,000	$ 50,000	$ 50,000	$ 50,000
Interest ($900,000 × 10%)	(90,000)	(30,000)	(30,000)	(30,000)
Cash flow	60,000	20,000	20,000	20,000
Depreciation* ($1 million × 15%)	(150,000)	(50,000)	(50,000)	(50,000)
Tax loss	$ (90,000)	$(30,000)	$(30,000)	$(30,000)

* The depreciation rate would vary depending on the type of asset being depreciated. For simplicity, a conservative 15% rate was used.

Assuming no at-risk rules or PAL rules, Abbott, Bart, and Calvin each would have a $30,000 tax loss from this activity, yet the venture has positive cash flow of $20,000 to each taxpayer plus tax savings related to the $30,000 loss. By the end of the tax year, the partners would have received more cash and tax savings than the amount they invested in the first place. Furthermore, if the losses remained the same for year 2, each partner would have deducted a total of $60,000 in tax losses from a venture in which each initially had only $33,333 to lose (the "at-risk" amount).

Congress established the at-risk rules to limit the deductible losses that the taxpayer could economically lose. In Example 13-1, this amount is only $33,333. Thus, if losses in the second year were also $30,000 per partner, the deductible loss of each partner would be limited to $3,333 (the initial $33,333 at-risk amount minus the $30,000 loss in year 1).

AT-RISK RULES

LO 13-1

The following types of activities are subject to the at-risk rules:

1. Holding, producing, or distributing motion picture films or videotapes.
2. Farming.
3. Leasing any § 1245 property.
4. Exploring for, or exploiting, oil and gas resources as a trade or business or for the production of income.
5. Exploring for, or exploiting, geothermal deposits.[2]

In addition to the activities specifically listed, the IRC also includes a catch-all provision that causes *any* activity "engaged in by the taxpayer in carrying on a trade or business or for the production of income" to be subject to the at-risk rules. The film, farming, leasing, and oil and gas exploration ventures are specifically listed because they were the most common tax-sheltering activities at the time. The at-risk rules often affect investments that have some form of limited liability to the investors (such as limited partnerships).

[1] A *nonrecourse debt* is one for which no one is personally liable. The notions of recourse, nonrecourse, and qualified nonrecourse are discussed in greater detail later in the chapter. Financial institutions rarely lend money for which no security is pledged or no individual is personally liable. The availability of nonrecourse financing is the primary reason that the at-risk rules were ineffective in limiting abusive tax shelters, thus leading to the passage of the PAL rules.

[2] IRC § 465(c).

TAX YOUR BRAIN

Assume that Jack invests $20,000 cash in a plant nursery for a 20% share in the business. The 80% owner is Jill, who contributes $20,000 and personally borrows $60,000 to put in the business. Jack does no work in the business and is not liable for any of the debt. Is either Jack or Jill subject to at-risk limitations?

ANSWER

Both Jack and Jill are subject to the at-risk rules. Jack's initial at-risk amount is $20,000 because that is all he can lose. Jill, on the other hand, would have an initial at-risk amount of $80,000 (her $20,000 cash contribution plus the $60,000 she personally borrowed).

What Is At-Risk?

Generally the initial *at-risk* amount is the money plus the adjusted basis of property contributed to the activity. The at-risk amount also includes certain amounts borrowed in connection with the activity.[3] The taxpayer's at-risk amount increases each tax year by income/gain items and any additional contributions of money or property. Likewise, the at-risk amount decreases each tax year by loss items and distributions of money or property. Table 13-1 summarizes the increases and decreases in the at-risk amount.

Factors that either increase or decrease the at-risk amount are considered prior to determining the amount of allowed loss items.[4]

EXAMPLE 13-2

In 2017, Zeke contributed land with an adjusted basis of $15,000 and a fair market value (FMV) of $30,000 to Land Developers Limited Partnership (LDLP) in return for a 5% limited partnership interest. LDLP issued Zeke the K-1 shown in Exhibit 13-1. What are Zeke's allowed losses and ending at-risk amount? Assume, perhaps unrealistically, that LDLP has no liabilities.

Zeke's initial at-risk amount	$15,000
Interest income	123
Dividend income	600
Capital gain	700
At-risk prior to loss	$16,423
Loss allowed under at-risk rules	(7,000)*
Ending at-risk amount	$ 9,423

*The $7,000 loss is allowed under the at-risk rules. However, as noted earlier, the loss may still be disallowed under the passive activity loss rules. We discuss these rules in a few pages.

TABLE 13-1
At-Risk Calculation

+	Cash contributions
+	Property contributions
+	Share of liabilities
+	Income items (net income, interest, dividends, etc.)
+	Gain items (gain on asset sales, capital gains)
(−)	Cash distributions
(−)	Property distributions
(−)	Release of liabilities
=	Amount at risk
(−)	Loss items (i.e., net losses allowed to the extent at-risk)
=	Ending at-risk amount

[3] IRC § 465(b)(1)(A)&(B).

[4] Proposed Regulation § 1.465-39(a). Proposed Regulations are weak authority until they become permanent. However, in this case, the inclusion of increase/decrease items is common and has been treated similarly in practice for numerous years.

EXHIBIT 13-1

651113

☐ Final K-1 ☐ Amended K-1 OMB No. 1545-0123

Schedule K-1 (Form 1065) **2017**

Department of the Treasury
Internal Revenue Service

For calendar year 2017, or tax year

beginning / / 2017 ending / /

Partner's Share of Income, Deductions, Credits, etc. ► **See back of form and separate instructions.**

Part I Information About the Partnership

A Partnership's employer identification number
52-1234567

B Partnership's name, address, city, state, and ZIP code
Land Developers, LP
P.O. Box 999
Wayne, MS 38765

C IRS Center where partnership filed return
Cincinnati, OH

D ☐ Check if this is a publicly traded partnership (PTP)

Part II Information About the Partner

E Partner's identifying number
412-34-5670

F Partner's name, address, city, state, and ZIP code
Zeke Johnson
123 Ash Street
Wayne, MS 38765

G ☐ General partner or LLC member-manager ☐ Limited partner or other LLC member

H ☒ Domestic partner ☐ Foreign partner

I1 What type of entity is this partner? Individual

I2 If this partner is a retirement plan (IRA/SEP/Keogh/etc.), check here ☐

J Partner's share of profit, loss, and capital (see instructions):

	Beginning	Ending
Profit	%	5 %
Loss	%	5 %
Capital	%	5 %

K Partner's share of liabilities at year end:

Nonrecourse . . . . $
Qualified nonrecourse financing . $
Recourse . . . . $

L Partner's capital account analysis:

Beginning capital account . . . $
Capital contributed during the year $
Current year increase (decrease) . $
Withdrawals & distributions . . $ ( )
Ending capital account . . . . $

☐ Tax basis ☐ GAAP ☐ Section 704(b) book
☐ Other (explain)

M Did the partner contribute property with a built-in gain or loss?
☒ **Yes** ☐ **No**
If "Yes," attach statement (see instructions)

Part III Partner's Share of Current Year Income, Deductions, Credits, and Other Items

1	Ordinary business income (loss) (7,000)	**15**	Credits
2	Net rental real estate income (loss)		
3	Other net rental income (loss)	**16**	Foreign transactions
4	Guaranteed payments		
5	Interest income 123		
6a	Ordinary dividends 600		
6b	Qualified dividends 600		
7	Royalties		
8	Net short-term capital gain (loss)		
9a	Net long-term capital gain (loss) 700	**17**	Alternative minimum tax (AMT) items
9b	Collectibles (28%) gain (loss)		
9c	Unrecaptured section 1250 gain		
10	Net section 1231 gain (loss)	**18**	Tax-exempt income and nondeductible expenses
11	Other income (loss)		
		19	Distributions
12	Section 179 deduction		
13	Other deductions	**20**	Other information
14	Self-employment earnings (loss)		

*See attached statement for additional information.

For IRS Use Only

For Paperwork Reduction Act Notice, see Instructions for Form 1065. www.irs.gov/Form1065 Cat. No. 11394R **Schedule K-1 (Form 1065) 2017**

Source: U.S. Department of the Treasury, Internal Revenue Service, Form 1065- Schedule K-1. Washington, DC: 2017.

EXAMPLE 13-3

Assume that in 2018, Zeke's K-1 from LDLP had only one item: an $11,500 ordinary loss on line 1.

Beginning at-risk (Example 13-2)	$9,423
Increase or decrease items	–0–
At-risk prior to loss	9,423
Loss allowed under at-risk rules	(9,423)
Ending at-risk amount	$ –0–

In this case, a $2,077 loss is disallowed under the at-risk rules ($11,500 K-1 loss minus the permitted $9,423 loss).[5] Zeke cannot deduct the disallowed loss until he has additional amounts at-risk. Zeke will increase his at-risk amount by contributing additional capital, by incurring additional liabilities, or by waiting for LDLP to generate income or gain items.

A taxpayer uses Form 6198 to report an activity that is subject to at-risk limitations. The taxpayer is not required to file Form 6198 if the activity has net income or is not subject to the at-risk limitation. Thus in Example 13-2 (for tax year 2017), Zeke would not file Form 6198 because he was not subject to any at-risk limitations. However, because Zeke's loss was limited in Example 13-3, he would file Form 6198 in 2018 (see Exhibit 13-2).

Other income or gain items from Zeke's LDLP investment, if any, are reported on Form 6198, line 2 or 3. Any losses are allowable to the extent of income and gains from the current year. For example, if LDLP reported an additional $200 of interest income in 2018, $200 of the $11,500 loss would have automatically been deductible regardless of the at-risk amount (current year first). Thus a total of $9,623 could have been deducted, although line 10b on Form 6198 would still show only $9,423.

Liabilities for At-Risk Purposes

Liabilities fall into three categories:

1. Recourse.
2. Nonrecourse.
3. Qualified nonrecourse.[6]

A *recourse liability* is one in which the taxpayer is personally liable for the debt. A taxpayer's at-risk amount increases by his or her share of recourse debt.

EXAMPLE 13-4

Lee invested $10,000 cash in S&W Properties General Partnership and received a 25% interest in the partnership. The partnership borrowed $100,000 in full recourse debt. Assuming that Lee is personally liable for $25,000 (25% × $100,000 debt) if the partnership defaults on the loan, Lee's at-risk amount would be $35,000 ($10,000 cash + $25,000 debt).

Recourse debt is not included in the at-risk amount if the amounts are borrowed from any person (or entity) that has an interest in the activity or someone who is related to any person who has an interest in the activity.[7] In this case, the related-party lender would receive the at-risk increase.

[5] Some tax practitioners prefer to say that the at-risk amount is a negative $2,077. However, tax basis can never go below zero. It is true that tax basis and the at-risk amount may or may not be the same. When liabilities are ignored in the at-risk calculation (which often occurs in practice unless they are needed to deduct a loss), the at-risk amount and the tax basis are identical. In this text, we refer to the situation in Example 13-3 as zero at-risk with a disallowed loss.

[6] IRC § 465(b)(2).

[7] IRC § 465(b)(3)(A)(B)(C).

EXHIBIT 13-2

Form **6198** (Rev. November 2009) Department of the Treasury Internal Revenue Service

At-Risk Limitations

▶ **Attach to your tax return.**
▶ **See separate instructions.**

OMB No. 1545-0712
Attachment Sequence No. **31**

Name(s) shown on return: **Zeke Johnson**
Identifying number: 123-45-6789

Description of activity (see page 2 of the instructions): **Land Developers, L.P.**

Part I **Current Year Profit (Loss) From the Activity, Including Prior Year Nondeductible Amounts.** See page 2 of the instructions.

		Line	Amount
1	Ordinary income (loss) from the activity (see page 2 of the instructions)	1	(11,500)
2	Gain (loss) from the sale or other disposition of assets used in the activity (or of your interest in the activity) that you are reporting on:		
a	Schedule D	2a	
b	Form 4797	2b	
c	Other form or schedule	2c	
3	Other income and gains from the activity, from Schedule K-1 of Form 1065, Form 1065-B, or Form 1120S, that were not included on lines 1 through 2c	3	
4	Other deductions and losses from the activity, including investment interest expense allowed from Form 4952, that were not included on lines 1 through 2c	4	( )
5	Current year profit (loss) from the activity. Combine lines 1 through 4. See page 3 of the instructions before completing the rest of this form	5	(11,500)

Part II **Simplified Computation of Amount At Risk.** See page 3 of the instructions before completing this part.

		Line	Amount
6	Adjusted basis (as defined in section 1011) in the activity (or in your interest in the activity) on the first day of the tax year. **Do not** enter less than zero	6	9,423
7	Increases for the tax year (see page 3 of the instructions)	7	0
8	Add lines 6 and 7	8	9,423
9	Decreases for the tax year (see page 4 of the instructions)	9	0
10a	Subtract line 9 from line 8 ▶ 10a 9,423		
b	If line 10a is **more** than zero, enter that amount here and go to line 20 (or complete Part III). Otherwise, enter -0- and see **Pub. 925** for information on the recapture rules	10b	9,423

Part III **Detailed Computation of Amount At Risk.** If you completed Part III of Form 6198 for the prior year, see page 4 of the instructions.

		Line	Amount
11	Investment in the activity (or in your interest in the activity) at the effective date. **Do not** enter less than zero	11	
12	Increases at effective date	12	
13	Add lines 11 and 12	13	
14	Decreases at effective date	14	
15	Amount at risk (check box that applies):		
a	☐ At effective date. Subtract line 14 from line 13. **Do not** enter less than zero.		
b	☐ From your prior year Form 6198, line 19b. **Do not** enter the amount from line 10b of your prior year form.	15	
16	Increases since (check box that applies):		
a	☐ Effective date **b** ☐ The end of your prior year	16	
17	Add lines 15 and 16	17	
18	Decreases since (check box that applies):		
a	☐ Effective date **b** ☐ The end of your prior year	18	
19a	Subtract line 18 from line 17 ▶ 19a		
b	If line 19a is **more** than zero, enter that amount here and go to line 20. Otherwise, enter -0- and see **Pub. 925** for information on the recapture rules	19b	

Part IV **Deductible Loss**

		Line	Amount
20	**Amount at risk.** Enter the **larger** of line 10b or line 19b	20	9,423
21	**Deductible loss.** Enter the **smaller** of the line 5 loss (treated as a positive number) or line 20. See page 8 of the instructions to find out how to report any deductible loss and any carryover	21	(9,423)

Note: *If the loss is from a passive activity, see the Instructions for* **Form 8582,** *Passive Activity Loss Limitations, or the Instructions for* **Form 8810,** *Corporate Passive Activity Loss and Credit Limitations, to find out if the loss is allowed under the passive activity rules. If only part of the loss is subject to the passive activity loss rules, report only that part on Form 8582 or Form 8810, whichever applies.*

For Paperwork Reduction Act Notice, see page 8 of the instructions. Cat. No. 50012Y Form **6198** (Rev. 11-2009)

Source: U.S. Department of the Treasury, Internal Revenue Service, Form 6198. Washington, DC: 2017.

EXAMPLE 13-5

Assume the same facts as in Example 13-4. However, the partnership borrowed $100,000 from Stan, who is a 50% partner in S&W Properties. In this case, the debt would not count as an at-risk amount for Lee. The result would be the same had the $100,000 been borrowed from Stan Corporation, a corporation 100% owned by Stan.

Nonrecourse debts are loans in which no individual is personally liable for the debt. Because no one is personally liable, a taxpayer's share of nonrecourse liabilities does not increase at-risk amounts.

The final category of debt is *qualified nonrecourse financing,* which applies to the activity of holding real property (real estate). Taxpayers are deemed to be at-risk for their share of such amounts.[8] Qualified nonrecourse financing is any debt that meets all of the following criteria:[9]

1. The taxpayer borrowed it with respect to the activity of holding real property.[10]
2. The taxpayer borrowed it from a qualified person or government.[11]
3. No person is personally liable for repayment.
4. The debt is not convertible debt.

This provision limited the effectiveness of the general at-risk rules in reducing tax shelter abuses for real estate investments. Most financial institutions are unwilling to finance business activities without security. In practice, borrowings for real estate ventures often meet the requirements of qualified nonrecourse financing because the financial institution requires the real estate to secure the loan but may not require the individuals to be personally liable.

EXAMPLE 13-6

Jane, Danielle, and Dora each invested $20,000 in a real estate venture. The partnership borrowed $300,000 from a local bank and purchased an apartment building for $360,000. The bank required that the apartment building secure the loan, but none of the partners was personally liable for repayment of the debt. Assuming that each partner is a one-third partner, each has a beginning at-risk amount of $120,000 (1/3 of $300,000 debt + $20,000 cash investment).

Carryover of Disallowed Losses

Losses disallowed under the at-risk rules are carried over indefinitely. The taxpayer can deduct the suspended losses in later years when the taxpayer's at-risk amount increases by income from the activity, cash or property contributions, or an increased share of recourse debt.

[8] IRC § 465(b)(6).

[9] IRC § 465(b)(6)(B).

[10] IRC § 465(b)(6)(E)(ii) specifically excludes holding of mineral property from the definition of holding real property.

[11] A *qualified person* is any person who is actively and regularly engaged in the business of lending money and who is not a related party to the taxpayer or the person from whom the taxpayer acquired the property. Any financial institution qualifies as a qualified person assuming there is no owner relationship with the taxpayer.

EXAMPLE 13-7

Kim invested $100,000 in an activity in 2001. In 2013, Kim's at-risk amount was $25,000 at the beginning of the year. Kim's shares of losses from the activity were as follows (ignore passive loss rules):

Year	Gain (Loss)
2013	$(30,000)
2014	(20,000)
2015	(10,000)
2016	20,000
2017	20,000

For each year, Kim can deduct the following amounts under the at-risk rules:

	At-Risk	Loss Carryover
Beginning at-risk amount	$ 25,000	
2013 loss allowed	(25,000)	$ 5,000 disallowed
Ending at-risk amount	$ –0–	
2014 loss allowed	–0–	20,000 disallowed
Ending at-risk amount	–0–	$25,000 carryover
2015 loss allowed	–0–	10,000 disallowed
Ending at-risk amount	–0–	$35,000 carryover
2016 increase in at-risk amount	20,000	
2016 loss allowed	(20,000)	20,000 allowed
Ending at-risk amount	$ –0–	$15,000 carryover
2017 increase in at-risk amount	20,000	
2017 loss allowed	(15,000)	15,000 allowed
Ending at-risk amount	$ 5,000	$ –0– carryover

On her 2017 tax return, Kim reports $5,000 of net income ($20,000 income minus the $15,000 loss allowed). The amount would be reported on Schedule E (if this were a partnership or S corporation) or Schedule C (if this activity were a sole proprietorship). All of the carryover losses are gone, and the 2018 tax year starts with an at-risk amount of $5,000.

CONCEPT CHECK 13-1— LO 13-1

1. Which of the following items will increase a taxpayer's at-risk amount?
   a. A cash contribution made by the taxpayer into the activity.
   b. The taxpayer's share of income from the activity.
   c. The taxpayer's share of the activity's liabilities for which the taxpayer is personally liable.
   d. All of the above.
2. Which of the following types of liability do *not* increase the taxpayer's at-risk in an activity?
   a. Nonrecourse debt.
   b. Recourse debt.
   c. Qualified nonrecourse debt.
   d. All of the above increase at-risk.
3. When a loss is disallowed by the at-risk rules, which of the following is true?
   a. The loss is lost forever.
   b. The loss can be used only upon the activity's disposal.
   c. The loss is indefinitely carried forward.
   d. The loss can be used only if the taxpayer makes a contribution to the activity.

PASSIVE ACTIVITY LOSSES

LO 13-2

The goal of the passive activity loss (PAL) rules is to restrict deductibility of tax losses created from activities that are not the taxpayer's primary source of income. The PAL rules supplement the at-risk rules. The loss must first be allowed under the at-risk rules and then must pass through PAL rule filters to ultimately be deductible and reduce taxable income.

Definition of Passive Activity

A *passive activity* is one in which the taxpayer does not materially participate. The IRC defines material participation by the taxpayer as participating in the activity on a regular, continuous, and substantial basis.[12]

Most rental activities and limited partnership interests are, by definition, passive activities. An additional potential passive activity is a trade or business in which the taxpayer does not materially participate. Table 13-2 summarizes passive activities.

TABLE 13-2
Passive Activities

Most rental properties
Any ownership interests as a limited partner
Any trade or business in which the taxpayer does not materially participate

TAX YOUR BRAIN

What constitutes regular, continuous, and substantial participation in an activity?

ANSWER

The IRS issued regulations that list seven tests to determine material participation. It is clear, however, that investor-only participation is not sufficient to be classified as a material participant in an activity.

The regulations provide seven tests to help determine whether a taxpayer materially participates in an activity.[13] A taxpayer materially participates if he or she meets any of the following seven tests.

Test 1: The 500-Hour Test

The individual participates in the activity for more than 500 hours. This test is the general test for most activities. The main premise is that if a taxpayer participates more than 500 hours in an activity, that taxpayer is more than a mere investor. Any work normally completed in the activity counts toward the 500-hour requirement.

Test 2: Sole Participant

The individual's participation in the activity for the taxable year constitutes all of the participation in such activity of all individuals (including individuals who are not owners of interest in the activity) for such year. If no one else works in the activity, the taxpayer must be a material participant. This rule is pertinent to many small sole proprietorships that operate cyclical or seasonal businesses.

EXAMPLE 13-8

Nidar is the sole owner and operator of a small coffee and hot chocolate shop in the mountains. The shop is open only in the winter during high-traffic times such as weekends and holidays. Even though Nidar works fewer than 500 hours in the activity, the work is not a passive activity because he is the only one who participates in the business.

[12] IRC § 469(h).

[13] IRS Reg. § 1.469-5(a).

Test 3: More Than 100 Participation Hours

The individual participates in the activity for more than 100 hours during the tax year, and the individual's participation is not less than any other individual for the year.

EXAMPLE 13-9

Assume the same facts as in Example 13-8, but Nidar hires several part-time employees to help run the coffee and hot chocolate shop. If he works more than 100 hours and none of the other employees works more hours, the activity is not a passive activity.

Test 4: Aggregate Significant Participation

The activity is a significant participation activity (participation more than 100 hours) for the tax year, and the individual's aggregate participation in all significant participation activities during such year exceeds 500 hours. Test 4 is important to taxpayers who own and operate several businesses during the year but participate fewer than 500 hours in any one of them.

EXAMPLE 13-10

Let's assume that Nidar operates his coffee and hot chocolate shop in the mountains for 130 hours in the winter, operates a daiquiri shop at the beach for 200 hours in the summer, and works in a landscaping business of which he is a part owner for 250 hours during the year. All of these businesses are significant participation activities because Nidar worked more than 100 hours in each. Furthermore, in aggregate, his participation in all significant participation activities is more than 500 hours. Thus he is a material participant in all three activities.

Test 5: History of Material Participation

The individual materially participated in the activity for any 5 taxable years during the 10 taxable years immediately preceding the current taxable year.

Test 6: Personal Service Activity

The activity is a personal service activity, and the individual materially participated in it for any three taxable years (whether or not consecutive) preceding the taxable year.

Tests 5 and 6 are extremely important to individuals who cease to work in the activity (because of retirement, disability, or otherwise) but retain an ownership interest.

EXAMPLE 13-11

Tom is part owner in a furniture store with his son but retired from working in the business last year. Assuming that Tom worked more than 500 hours for 5 of the last 10 years, the current profit or loss from the activity is not passive. If Tom and his son operated a personal service activity such as a CPA firm, Tom needs to have been a material participant for only any three taxable years preceding the current year.

Test 7: Facts and Circumstances

Based on all of the facts and circumstances, the individual participates in the activity on a regular, continuous, and substantial basis during the tax year.

Test 7 is a catchall for taxpayers who do not meet one of the first six tests. However, the temporary regulations are silent about the conditions required to meet Test 7. Based on the lack of guidance in the regulations regarding Test 7, it would be prudent to rely on Tests 1 through 6 in determining material participation.

Passive Activity Losses: General Rule

Taxpayers subject to PAL rules include any individual, estate, trust, closely held C corporation, or any personal service corporation.[14] The general rule for passive activities generating

[14] IRC § 469(a)(2). In this text, the focus is exclusively on the individual taxpayer. However, these same PAL rules also apply to the other entity types.

a loss is that a taxpayer can deduct the passive loss to the extent of passive income. The PAL rules are applied on an individual-by-individual basis.

TAX YOUR BRAIN

Can two partners in a passive activity with identical passive losses from the activity be treated differently concerning the deductibility of the losses?

ANSWER

Yes, one of the partners who has passive income from another source can deduct the passive loss while the partner with no other passive activity cannot. Remember that PAL rules are applied on an individual basis, and any losses are allowed only to the extent of passive income.

EXAMPLE 13-12

Suppose Edna has an ownership interest in three passive activities. In the current tax year, the activities had the following income and losses:

Partnership A	$10,000
Partnership B	(8,000)
Partnership C	(6,000)

Edna can deduct passive losses only to the extent of passive income. Here she can deduct $10,000 of the $14,000 in passive losses. This assumes that Edna is at-risk for each of the loss activities. The excess $4,000 loss would be suspended and carried forward to future tax years until Edna has additional passive income (or until the activity is sold).

The IRC separates all income/loss items into three categories:[15]

1. **Active income/loss:** includes wages and profit or loss from a trade or business with material participation.
2. **Portfolio income:** includes interest, dividends, royalties, and capital gains.
3. **Passive income/loss:** includes any income or loss from a trade or business in which the taxpayer did not materially participate. It also includes income or loss from most rental activities whether or not there was material participation.[16]

Net passive losses cannot offset portfolio income or active income. In other words, all passive activities are first appropriately combined. If the result is net passive income, the income is reported. If the result is a net passive loss, the loss is suspended until additional passive income is generated.

Rental Activities

A *rental activity* is any activity in which a taxpayer receives payments principally for the use of tangible property. In general, rental activities are passive activities. One exception concerns real estate professionals. A rental business can qualify for active treatment if more than one-half of the personal services performed in a business during the year are performed in a real property trade or business and the taxpayer performs more than 750 hours of services in the activity.[17]

EXAMPLE 13-13

Richard owns and operates several rental houses and apartment complexes in a college town. This is his only business activity, and he works full-time in the venture. In this case, Richard meets the exception as a real estate professional, and the rental income and losses are not passive activities.

[15] IRC § 469(e).

[16] The sale of an asset (such as a piece of equipment) used in the passive activity would be considered passive. This does not include gains on investment property (that is, capital gains or losses).

[17] IRC § 469(c)(7)(B).

From Shoebox to Software

EXAMPLE 13-14 Assume that Jose Ramirez (from the earlier chapters) received a K-1 (shown in Exhibit 13-3) from College Repairs Limited Partnership.

Upon reviewing the K-1, you know that the partnership is a passive activity because the limited partner box is checked (Question G on Schedule K-1). If the general partner box is checked, you must apply one of the seven material participation tests to determine whether the activity is passive. The interest and dividends ($500 and $200, respectively) are portfolio income, which you report on Schedule B. The $1,200 capital gain transfers to Schedule D. However, the $3,523 loss is a passive loss and is deductible on Schedule E only if Jose had passive income from another passive activity.

In Chapter 8 you entered information from a K-1 on Jose Ramirez's return. However, Jose materially participated in that partnership. In the College Repairs partnership, Jose is a limited partner, and thus the activity is passive.

In your tax software, open the Ramirez file and open a new K-1. Enter the information from the College Repairs LP from Exhibit 13-3. Assume that Jose is at-risk for this activity. After you complete the K-1 information, the tax software transfers the information to Schedule B, Schedule D, and Form 8582. Note that the allowed loss on Form 8582 is zero because Jose had no other passive income. Also note that Schedule E, page 2, shows the College Repairs LP, but zero loss is allowed. Form 8582 is shown in Exhibit 13-4.

In addition to the real estate professional exception to the PAL rules, rental activities are not passive activities in six other cases.[18]

Case 1: Average Rental Period Fewer than Seven Days

The average period for customer use is fewer than seven days. Businesses that rent or lease tangible property for short periods are active (nonpassive) activities. For example, businesses that rent automobiles, tools, or DVDs are not passive activities.

Case 2: Average Rental Period 30 or Fewer Days with Significant Personal Services

The average period of customer use is 30 or fewer days, and the owner provides significant personal services. An example meeting this exception for nonpassive classification would be the rental of a large crane for a construction site. If the average use were more than 7 days but fewer than 30 days and the rental company provided the crane operator, the rental would qualify as an active activity.

Case 3: Extraordinary Personal Services

The owner provides extraordinary personal services in connection with the rental of tangible property. The most common rental property meeting this exception includes hospitals and university dormitories. Dorm rooms and hospital rooms are essentially rented, but the extraordinary services provided (the education or medical care) qualify the business for active treatment.

Case 4: Incidental Rental Activity

The rental activity is incidental to a nonrental activity. This occurs if the property was predominantly used in a trade or business for at least two of the last five tax years. The gross rental income must be less than 2% of the lower of the basis of the property or its FMV. For example, suppose that a farmer leases a portion of his rice farm for duck hunting over the winter. If the rent received is less than 2% of the lower of basis or FMV, the rent is incidental to the farming activity.

[18] Reg. § 1.469-1(e)(3).

EXHIBIT 13-3

651117

☐ Final K-1 ☐ Amended K-1

OMB No. 1545-0123

Schedule K-1 (Form 1065) **2017**

Department of the Treasury
Internal Revenue Service

For calendar year 2017, or tax year

beginning / / 2017 ending / /

Partner's Share of Income, Deductions, Credits, etc. ► **See back of form and separate instructions.**

DRAFT AS OF July 17, 2017 DO NOT FILE

Part I Information About the Partnership

A Partnership's employer identification number
57-7234567

B Partnership's name, address, city, state, and ZIP code
College Repairs, LP
123 University Drive
State University, NC 28765

C IRS Center where partnership filed return
Cincinnati, OH

D ☐ Check if this is a publicly traded partnership (PTP)

Part II Information About the Partner

E Partner's identifying number
412-34-5670

F Partner's name, address, city, state, and ZIP code
Jose Ramirez
1234 West Street
Mytown, GA 30294

G ☐ General partner or LLC member-manager ☐ Limited partner or other LLC member

H ☒ Domestic partner ☐ Foreign partner

I1 What type of entity is this partner? Individual

I2 If this partner is a retirement plan (IRA/SEP/Keogh/etc.), check here ☐

J Partner's share of profit, loss, and capital (see instructions):

	Beginning	Ending
Profit	%	5 %
Loss	%	5 %
Capital	%	5 %

K Partner's share of liabilities at year end:

Nonrecourse . . . . $
Qualified nonrecourse financing . $
Recourse . . . . $

L Partner's capital account analysis:

Beginning capital account . . . $
Capital contributed during the year $
Current year increase (decrease) . $
Withdrawals & distributions . . $ ( )
Ending capital account . . . . $

☐ Tax basis ☐ GAAP ☐ Section 704(b) book
☐ Other (explain)

M Did the partner contribute property with a built-in gain or loss?
☐ **Yes** ☒ **No**
If "Yes," attach statement (see instructions)

Part III Partner's Share of Current Year Income, Deductions, Credits, and Other Items

1	Ordinary business income (loss)	(3,523)
2	Net rental real estate income (loss)	
3	Other net rental income (loss)	
4	Guaranteed payments	
5	Interest income	500
6a	Ordinary dividends	200
6b	Qualified dividends	200
7	Royalties	
8	Net short-term capital gain (loss)	
9a	Net long-term capital gain (loss)	1,200
9b	Collectibles (28%) gain (loss)	
9c	Unrecaptured section 1250 gain	
10	Net section 1231 gain (loss)	
11	Other income (loss)	
12	Section 179 deduction	
13	Other deductions	
14	Self-employment earnings (loss)	
15	Credits	
16	Foreign transactions	
17	Alternative minimum tax (AMT) items	
18	Tax-exempt income and nondeductible expenses	
19	Distributions	
20	Other information	

*See attached statement for additional information.

For IRS Use Only

For Paperwork Reduction Act Notice, see Instructions for Form 1065. www.irs.gov/Form1065 Cat. No. 11394R **Schedule K-1 (Form 1065) 2017**

Source: U.S. Department of the Treasury, Internal Revenue Service, Schedule K-1 Form 1065. Washington, DC: 2017.

EXHIBIT 13-4

Form **8582**

Department of the Treasury
Internal Revenue Service (99)

Passive Activity Loss Limitations

► See separate instructions.
► Attach to Form 1040 or Form 1041.
► Go to *www.irs.gov/Form8582* for instructions and the latest information.

OMB No. 1545-1008
2017
Attachment Sequence No. **88**

Name(s) shown on return	Identifying number
Jose and Maria Ramirez	412-34-5670

Part I **2017 Passive Activity Loss**

Caution: Complete Worksheets 1, 2, and 3 before completing Part I.

Rental Real Estate Activities With Active Participation (For the definition of active participation, see **Special Allowance for Rental Real Estate Activities** in the instructions.)

Line	Description	Line	Amount	Line	Amount
1a	Activities with net income (enter the amount from Worksheet 1, column (a))	1a			
b	Activities with net loss (enter the amount from Worksheet 1, column (b))	1b	( )		
c	Prior years' unallowed losses (enter the amount from Worksheet 1, column (c))	1c	( )		
d	Combine lines 1a, 1b, and 1c			1d	

Commercial Revitalization Deductions From Rental Real Estate Activities

Line	Description	Line	Amount	Line	Amount
2a	Commercial revitalization deductions from Worksheet 2, column (a)	2a	( )		
b	Prior year unallowed commercial revitalization deductions from Worksheet 2, column (b)	2b	( )		
c	Add lines 2a and 2b			2c	( )

All Other Passive Activities

Line	Description	Line	Amount	Line	Amount
3a	Activities with net income (enter the amount from Worksheet 3, column (a))	3a			
b	Activities with net loss (enter the amount from Worksheet 3, column (b))	3b	(3,523)		
c	Prior years' unallowed losses (enter the amount from Worksheet 3, column (c))	3c	( )		
d	Combine lines 3a, 3b, and 3c			3d	(3,523)
4	Combine lines 1d, 2c, and 3d. If this line is zero or more, stop here and include this form with your return; all losses are allowed, including any prior year unallowed losses entered on line 1c, 2b, or 3c. Report the losses on the forms and schedules normally used			4	(3,523)

If line 4 is a loss and:
- Line 1d is a loss, go to Part II.
- Line 2c is a loss (and line 1d is zero or more), skip Part II and go to Part III.
- Line 3d is a loss (and lines 1d and 2c are zero or more), skip Parts II and III and go to line 15.

Caution: If your filing status is married filing separately and you lived with your spouse at any time during the year, **do not** complete Part II or Part III. Instead, go to line 15.

Part II **Special Allowance for Rental Real Estate Activities With Active Participation**

Note: Enter all numbers in Part II as positive amounts. See instructions for an example.

Line	Description	Line	Amount	Line	Amount
5	Enter the **smaller** of the loss on line 1d or the loss on line 4			5	
6	Enter $150,000. If married filing separately, see instructions	6			
7	Enter modified adjusted gross income, but not less than zero (see instructions)	7			
	Note: If line 7 is greater than or equal to line 6, skip lines 8 and 9, enter -0- on line 10. Otherwise, go to line 8.				
8	Subtract line 7 from line 6	8			
9	Multiply line 8 by 50% (0.50). **Do not** enter more than $25,000. If married filing separately, see instructions			9	
10	Enter the **smaller** of line 5 or line 9			10	

If line 2c is a loss, go to Part III. Otherwise, go to line 15.

Part III **Special Allowance for Commercial Revitalization Deductions From Rental Real Estate Activities**

Note: Enter all numbers in Part III as positive amounts. See the example for Part II in the instructions.

Line	Description	Line	Amount
11	Enter $25,000 reduced by the amount, if any, on line 10. If married filing separately, see instructions	11	
12	Enter the loss from line 4	12	
13	Reduce line 12 by the amount on line 10	13	
14	Enter the **smallest** of line 2c (treated as a positive amount), line 11, or line 13	14	

Part IV **Total Losses Allowed**

Line	Description	Line	Amount
15	Add the income, if any, on lines 1a and 3a and enter the total	15	0
16	**Total losses allowed from all passive activities for 2017.** Add lines 10, 14, and 15. See instructions to find out how to report the losses on your tax return	16	0

For Paperwork Reduction Act Notice, see instructions. Cat. No. 63704F Form **8582** (2017)

Source: U.S. Department of the Treasury, Internal Revenue Service, Form 8582. Washington, DC: 2017.

Case 5: Nonexclusive Use by Customers

The taxpayer customarily makes the property available during defined business hours for nonexclusive use by customers. The regulations provide the example of the rental of golf carts on a golf course. The carts are customarily available during business hours for nonexclusive use by customers. This example could also qualify for the exception of average rental for fewer than seven days or the rental being incidental to the trade or business activity.

Case 6: Use in a Partnership, S Corporation, or Joint Venture

The property is provided for use in an activity conducted by a partnership, S corporation, or joint venture in which the taxpayer owns an interest. If a taxpayer owns an interest in one of these (other than a rental activity) and rents property to that entity for use in the trade or business, the rental of that property is not considered a passive activity.

$25,000 Offset for Rental Activities with Active Participation

Thus far in our discussion, passive losses are deducted only to the extent of passive income. One exception to this rule is the "$25,000 loss offset" for real estate rental activities for certain lower-income taxpayers.[19] A taxpayer who qualifies for this exception can offset up to $25,000 in passive losses from a rental activity against active and/or portfolio income. To qualify for the $25,000 offset, a taxpayer must actively participate in the rental activity.

To actively participate, an individual must have at least a 10% ownership interest in a rental activity. A taxpayer who participates in making management decisions or arranges for others to provide services (such as repairs) is treated as actively participating in a rental activity. Approving new tenants, deciding on rental terms, and approving expenditures also count in determining active participation.

Do not confuse *active participation* with *material participation.* Material participation is the test to determine whether an activity is passive. Active participation concerns rental property (which is already considered passive) and is a far less stringent requirement than material participation.

The $25,000 loss offset starts to phase out once a taxpayer's Adjusted Gross Income (AGI) reaches $100,000 (before rental loss). The $25,000 amount is reduced by 50% of the taxpayer's AGI in excess of $100,000 and is eliminated when a taxpayer's AGI reaches $150,000.

EXAMPLE 13-15

Alexandra has AGI (before any rental loss) of $85,000. She also owns a rental condo in Florida in which she actively participates. The condo produced a $12,000 loss in the current year. Alexandra has no passive income but can deduct the entire $12,000 rental loss against other active and portfolio income because her AGI is less than $100,000.

EXAMPLE 13-16

Assume the same facts as in Example 13-15 but, in this case, Alexandra's pre-rental AGI is $140,000. With $140,000 in AGI, her deductible rental loss would be only $5,000. The available offset is reduced by $20,000 ([$140,000 AGI − $100,000 threshold] × 50%). If Alexandra's AGI were at or above $150,000, none of the rental loss could offset active or portfolio income. The nondeductible rental loss is a passive loss and would be suspended until passive income is generated or the activity is disposed of.

[19] The $25,000 amount becomes $12,500 for married taxpayers who file separate returns and do not live together at any time during the tax year.

Disposition of a Passive Activity

When a taxpayer disposes of a passive activity in a taxable transaction (taxable gain or loss is recognized), suspended passive losses from past years are allowed, and any excess passive losses can be used to offset nonpassive income.[20]

EXAMPLE 13-17

Jamal sells his entire interest in a rental property in which he actively participated at a gain of $15,525. The activity has a current year loss of $2,800 and $12,650 in prior year suspended losses. The $15,525 would most likely be reported on Form 4797, Part I, as a § 1231 gain. Jamal deducts the total $15,450 in current and suspended losses ($2,800 + $12,650) on Schedule E. If this were Jamal's only passive activity, Form 8582 would not be required. If Jamal had other passive activities, Form 8582 would be required because the sale resulted in a net gain of $75 ($15,525 gain from sale less $15,450 in total losses). The excess $75 is passive income and offsets other passive losses.

If less than the entire interest in a passive activity is sold, the gains and losses from disposition are treated as part of the net income or loss from that activity. In other words, the gain or loss from a partial disposition of a passive activity is passive. The disposition of less than all of a passive interest does not trigger the allowance of prior year suspended losses.

Additionally, a gift of a passive interest does not trigger the use of suspended PALs because a gift is not a taxable transaction. In the gift situation, the suspended PALs are added to the basis assumed by the donee.[21] A similar rule applies when a passive property transfers at death. Typically the beneficiary receives the property with a basis equal to the FMV at the date of death. To the extent any suspended PALs exceed the increase in basis to the beneficiary, the suspended PALs are deducted on the decedent's final tax return.[22]

CONCEPT CHECK 13-2— LO 13-2

1. Rental properties are almost always considered passive activities. True or false?
2. The general rule concerning the deductibility of passive losses is that they can be deducted only to the extent of passive income. True or false?
3. For low-income taxpayers, passive rental losses can be deducted against other income up to a maximum of $50,000. True or false?
4. Generally, suspended passive losses can be deducted against other income when the activity is sold or disposed of. True or false?

AT-RISK AND PAL RULES IN CONJUNCTION

LO 13-3

In this section, we illustrate how the at-risk rules and the PAL rules work together to limit tax shelter abuses. When an investment in an activity is at-risk, a Form 6198 is filed for each at-risk activity. Form 8582 (see Exhibit 13-4) is used to report PALs. A taxpayer files only one Form 8582 regardless of the number of passive activities with losses. The instructions relating to Form 8582 provide worksheets to determine the correct allocations between allowed and disallowed losses.

TAX YOUR BRAIN

Do the PAL rules come into play for an activity that has a loss but has no amount at-risk?

ANSWER

No, the loss must first be allowed under the at-risk rules, and then the PAL rules are applied. The PAL cannot be deducted unless the taxpayer had some passive income or was eligible for the $25,000 loss offset for rental real estate.

[20] IRC § 469(g).

[21] IRC § 469(j)(6)(A).

[22] IRC § 469(g)(2)(A).

EXAMPLE 13-18

At the beginning of 2015, Marcella's at-risk amount in an activity was $60,000. The income/losses from the activity for 2015, 2016, and 2017 are as follows:

Year	Gain/Loss
2015	$(80,000)
2016	(60,000)
2017	100,000

How are the income and losses treated for each year? Apply both the at-risk rules and PAL rules assuming that this is Marcella's only passive activity:

2015		
	Beginning at-risk	$60,000
	Loss	(60,000) $20,000 disallowed at-risk
	Ending at-risk	$ –0–

Therefore, $60,000 of the loss passes through the at-risk rules. The PAL rules are now applied to the $60,000. Because Marcella has no other passive income and did not dispose of the activity, the $60,000 PAL is suspended and carried forward to 2016:

Carryforwards to 2016	$20,000 disallowed at-risk
	$60,000 suspended PAL*

* These carryforward items should be noted in a prominent place (usually on the first page) in the 2014 working papers. When the 2015 tax return is prepared, a quick review of the prior year working papers will bring the suspended losses to the attention of the preparer.

2016		
	Beginning at-risk	$–0–
	Loss	–0–$60,000 disallowed at-risk
	Ending at-risk	$–0–

Because the $60,000 loss did not make it through the at-risk rules, the PAL rules are not applied. The $60,000 disallowed at-risk loss adds to the carryforward:

Carryforwards to 2017	$20,000 disallowed at-risk from 2015
	$60,000 disallowed at-risk from 2016
	$60,000 suspended PAL from 2015
	$–0– suspended PAL from 2016

2017		
	Beginning at-risk	$ –0–
	Income	100,000
	Prior year disallowed losses	(80,000)
	Ending at-risk	$ 20,000

Because the activity had $100,000 of income, the entire amount of prior year disallowed losses is allowed under the at-risk rules. Now that the entire amount of losses ($140,000) has made it through the at-risk rules, the PAL rules are applied. Because the activity now has passive income of $100,000, Marcella can deduct $100,000 of the suspended PAL from 2015 and 2016. See Exhibit 13-5 (Form 8582) and Exhibit 13-6 (page 2 of Schedule E assumes the activity was a partnership) for the tax form presentation for 2017:

Carryforwards to 2018	$–0– disallowed at-risk from 2015
	$–0– disallowed at-risk from 2016
	$40,000 suspended PALs

EXHIBIT 13-5

Form **8582**

Department of the Treasury
Internal Revenue Service (99)

Passive Activity Loss Limitations

▶ See separate instructions.

▶ Attach to Form 1040 or Form 1041.

▶ Go to *www.irs.gov/Form8582* for instructions and the latest information.

OMB No. 1545-1008

2017

Attachment Sequence No. **88**

Name(s) shown on return	Identifying number
Marcella Doe	**412-34-5670**

Part I **2017 Passive Activity Loss**

Caution: Complete Worksheets 1, 2, and 3 before completing Part I.

	Rental Real Estate Activities With Active Participation (For the definition of active participation, see **Special Allowance for Rental Real Estate Activities** in the instructions.)				
1a	Activities with net income (enter the amount from Worksheet 1, column (a))	1a			
b	Activities with net loss (enter the amount from Worksheet 1, column (b))	1b	( )		
c	Prior years' unallowed losses (enter the amount from Worksheet 1, column (c))	1c	( )		
d	Combine lines 1a, 1b, and 1c			1d	
	Commercial Revitalization Deductions From Rental Real Estate Activities				
2a	Commercial revitalization deductions from Worksheet 2, column (a)	2a	( )		
b	Prior year unallowed commercial revitalization deductions from Worksheet 2, column (b)	2b	( )		
c	Add lines 2a and 2b			2c	( )
	All Other Passive Activities				
3a	Activities with net income (enter the amount from Worksheet 3, column (a))	3a	100,000		
b	Activities with net loss (enter the amount from Worksheet 3, column (b))	3b	( )		
c	Prior years' unallowed losses (enter the amount from Worksheet 3, column (c))	3c	(140,000)		
d	Combine lines 3a, 3b, and 3c			3d	(40,000)
4	Combine lines 1d, 2c, and 3d. If this line is zero or more, stop here and include this form with your return; all losses are allowed, including any prior year unallowed losses entered on line 1c, 2b, or 3c. Report the losses on the forms and schedules normally used			4	(40,000)

If line 4 is a loss and:
- Line 1d is a loss, go to Part II.
- Line 2c is a loss (and line 1d is zero or more), skip Part II and go to Part III.
- Line 3d is a loss (and lines 1d and 2c are zero or more), skip Parts II and III and go to line 15.

Caution: If your filing status is married filing separately and you lived with your spouse at any time during the year, **do not** complete Part II or Part III. Instead, go to line 15.

Part II **Special Allowance for Rental Real Estate Activities With Active Participation**

Note: Enter all numbers in Part II as positive amounts. See instructions for an example.

5	Enter the **smaller** of the loss on line 1d or the loss on line 4			5	
6	Enter $150,000. If married filing separately, see instructions	6			
7	Enter modified adjusted gross income, but not less than zero (see instructions)	7			
	Note: If line 7 is greater than or equal to line 6, skip lines 8 and 9, enter -0- on line 10. Otherwise, go to line 8.				
8	Subtract line 7 from line 6	8			
9	Multiply line 8 by 50% (0.50). **Do not** enter more than $25,000. If married filing separately, see instructions			9	
10	Enter the **smaller** of line 5 or line 9			10	

If line 2c is a loss, go to Part III. Otherwise, go to line 15.

Part III **Special Allowance for Commercial Revitalization Deductions From Rental Real Estate Activities**

Note: Enter all numbers in Part III as positive amounts. See the example for Part II in the instructions.

11	Enter $25,000 reduced by the amount, if any, on line 10. If married filing separately, see instructions	11	
12	Enter the loss from line 4	12	
13	Reduce line 12 by the amount on line 10	13	
14	Enter the **smallest** of line 2c (treated as a positive amount), line 11, or line 13	14	

Part IV **Total Losses Allowed**

15	Add the income, if any, on lines 1a and 3a and enter the total	15	100,000
16	**Total losses allowed from all passive activities for 2017.** Add lines 10, 14, and 15. See instructions to find out how to report the losses on your tax return	16	100,000

For Paperwork Reduction Act Notice, see instructions. Cat. No. 63704F Form **8582** (2017)

Source: U.S. Department of the Treasury, Internal Revenue Service, Form 8582. Washington, DC: 2017.

EXHIBIT 13-6

Schedule E (Form 1040) 2017 — Attachment Sequence No. **13** — Page **2**

Name(s) shown on return. Do not enter name and social security number if shown on other side.
Marcella Doe

Your social security number 412-34-5670

Caution: The IRS compares amounts reported on your tax return with amounts shown on Schedule(s) K-1.

Part II Income or Loss From Partnerships and S Corporations **Note:** If you report a loss from an at-risk activity for which **any** amount is **not** at risk, you **must** check the box in column **(e)** on line 28 and attach **Form 6198.** See instructions.

27 Are you reporting any loss not allowed in a prior year due to the at-risk, excess farm loss, or basis limitations, a prior year unallowed loss from a passive activity (if that loss was not reported on Form 8582), or unreimbursed partnership expenses? If you answered "Yes," see instructions before completing this section . . . ☐ **Yes** ☐ **No**

28	(a) Name	(b) Enter **P** for partnership; **S** for S corporation	(c) Check if foreign partnership	(d) Employer identification number	(e) Check if any amount is not at risk
A	Marcella's Partnership	P	☐	56-1234567	☐
B			☐		☐
C			☐		☐
D			☐		☐

	Passive Income and Loss		Nonpassive Income and Loss		
	(f) Passive loss allowed (attach **Form 8582** if required)	**(g)** Passive income from **Schedule K-1**	**(h)** Nonpassive loss from **Schedule K-1**	**(i)** Section 179 expense deduction from **Form 4562**	**(j)** Nonpassive income from **Schedule K-1**
A	100,000	100,000			
B					
C					
D					
29a Totals		100,000			
b Totals	100,000				

30	Add columns (g) and (j) of line 29a . . .	30	100,000
31	Add columns (f), (h), and (i) of line 29b . . .	31	(100,000)
32	**Total partnership and S corporation income or (loss).** Combine lines 30 and 31. Enter the result here and include in the total on line 41 below . . .	32	0

Part III Income or Loss From Estates and Trusts

33	(a) Name	(b) Employer identification number
A		
B		

	Passive Income and Loss		Nonpassive Income and Loss	
	(c) Passive deduction or loss allowed (attach **Form 8582** if required)	**(d)** Passive income from **Schedule K-1**	**(e)** Deduction or loss from **Schedule K-1**	**(f)** Other income from **Schedule K-1**
A				
B				
34a Totals				
b Totals				

35	Add columns (d) and (f) of line 34a . . .	35	
36	Add columns (c) and (e) of line 34b . . .	36	( )
37	**Total estate and trust income or (loss).** Combine lines 35 and 36. Enter the result here and include in the total on line 41 below . . .	37	

Part IV Income or Loss From Real Estate Mortgage Investment Conduits (REMICs)—Residual Holder

38	(a) Name	(b) Employer identification number	(c) Excess inclusion from **Schedules Q,** line 2c (see instructions)	(d) Taxable income (net loss) from **Schedules Q,** line 1b	(e) Income from **Schedules Q,** line 3b

39	Combine columns (d) and (e) only. Enter the result here and include in the total on line 41 below	39	

Part V Summary

40	Net farm rental income or (loss) from **Form 4835.** Also, complete line 42 below . . .	40	
41	**Total income or (loss).** Combine lines 26, 32, 37, 39, and 40. Enter the result here and on Form 1040, line 17, or Form 1040NR, line 18 ▶	41	0
42	**Reconciliation of farming and fishing income.** Enter your **gross** farming and fishing income reported on Form 4835, line 7; Schedule K-1 (Form 1065), box 14, code B; Schedule K-1 (Form 1120S), box 17, code V; and Schedule K-1 (Form 1041), box 14, code F (see instructions) . .	42	
43	**Reconciliation for real estate professionals.** If you were a real estate professional (see instructions), enter the net income or (loss) you reported anywhere on Form 1040 or Form 1040NR from all rental real estate activities in which you materially participated under the passive activity loss rules . .	43	

Schedule E (Form 1040) 2017

Source: U.S. Department of the Treasury, Internal Revenue Service, Schedule E Form 1040. Washington, DC: 2017

EXAMPLE 13-19

Over the years, Lori purchased interests in four passive partnerships. Partnerships A, B and C conduct a trade or business, and Partnership D is a rental real estate company. Lori's AGI prior to the partnership gains/losses is $80,003. The four partnerships had the following gains and losses in the current year. Lori is sufficiently at-risk in each partnership.

Partnership	Income/Loss	Type
A	$60,000	Trade or business
B	(60,000)	Trade or business
C	(30,000)	Trade or business
D	(10,000)	Rental real estate

In this case, Lori can deduct $70,000 of the $100,000 in losses under the PAL rules: $60,000 is allowed to the extent of passive income (allocated to B and C), and the $10,000 loss from the rental real estate is allowed under the $25,000 offset rule. Lori allocates the suspended PALs to the loss properties as follows:

	$30,000 in suspended PAL		
	70,000 in PAL allowed		
Suspended			
Partnership B	$60,000/$90,000 × $30,000 suspended	=	$20,000 suspended to B
Partnership C	30,000/90,000 × 30,000 suspended	=	10,000 suspended to C
PAL allowed			
Partnership B	60,000/90,000 × 60,000 allowed PAL	=	40,000 allowed to B
Partnership C	30,000/90,000 × 60,000 allowed PAL	=	20,000 allowed to C
Partnership D		=	10,000 allowed to D

Partnership A shows $60,000 of income on Schedule E, and Partnerships B, C, and D show losses of $40,000, $20,000, and $10,000, respectively. See Exhibit 13-7 and Exhibit 13-8 for the correct presentation on Form 8582 and Schedule E, page 2, respectively.

TAX YOUR BRAIN

Why is it important that suspended losses be properly allocated to the various loss properties?

ANSWER

The primary reason is that when a passive activity is disposed of, the suspended losses are allowed. The suspended losses should be deducted in proportion to the activities that created the losses.

CONCEPT CHECK 13-3—
LO 13-3

1. Which rules are applied *first* to a passive activity: the at-risk rules or the passive activity loss rules? Explain.
2. Why must suspended passive losses from several passive activities be allocated among the activities?
3. If a taxpayer has AGI of $105,000 before considering a $23,000 loss from a rental activity, how much can the taxpayer deduct from the rental activity, if any?

ALTERNATIVE MINIMUM TAX (AMT)
LO 13-4

The *alternative minimum tax* (AMT) is a separate tax system that attempts to levy tax on individuals (and corporations) who might otherwise escape taxation by using advanced tax incentives and programs provided in the IRC. The following is an excerpt from the Senate Finance Committee report providing the reasoning for the change in AMT rules:

EXHIBIT 13-7

Form **8582** — Department of the Treasury, Internal Revenue Service (99)

Passive Activity Loss Limitations

▶ See separate instructions.
▶ Attach to Form 1040 or Form 1041.
▶ Go to *www.irs.gov/Form8582* for instructions and the latest information.

OMB No. 1545-1008 — **2017** — Attachment Sequence No. **88**

Name(s) shown on return	Identifying number
Lori Doe	412-34-5670

Part I — 2017 Passive Activity Loss

Caution: Complete Worksheets 1, 2, and 3 before completing Part I.

Rental Real Estate Activities With Active Participation (For the definition of active participation, see **Special Allowance for Rental Real Estate Activities** in the instructions.)

Line	Description	Box	Amount	Line	Amount
1a	Activities with net income (enter the amount from Worksheet 1, column (a))	1a			
b	Activities with net loss (enter the amount from Worksheet 1, column (b))	1b	(10,000)		
c	Prior years' unallowed losses (enter the amount from Worksheet 1, column (c))	1c	( )		
d	Combine lines 1a, 1b, and 1c			1d	(10,000)

Commercial Revitalization Deductions From Rental Real Estate Activities

Line	Description	Box	Amount	Line	Amount
2a	Commercial revitalization deductions from Worksheet 2, column (a)	2a	( )		
b	Prior year unallowed commercial revitalization deductions from Worksheet 2, column (b)	2b	( )		
c	Add lines 2a and 2b			2c	( )

All Other Passive Activities

Line	Description	Box	Amount	Line	Amount
3a	Activities with net income (enter the amount from Worksheet 3, column (a))	3a	60,000		
b	Activities with net loss (enter the amount from Worksheet 3, column (b))	3b	(90,000)		
c	Prior years' unallowed losses (enter the amount from Worksheet 3, column (c))	3c	( )		
d	Combine lines 3a, 3b, and 3c			3d	(30,000)
4	Combine lines 1d, 2c, and 3d. If this line is zero or more, stop here and include this form with your return; all losses are allowed, including any prior year unallowed losses entered on line 1c, 2b, or 3c. Report the losses on the forms and schedules normally used			4	(40,000)

If line 4 is a loss and:
- Line 1d is a loss, go to Part II.
- Line 2c is a loss (and line 1d is zero or more), skip Part II and go to Part III.
- Line 3d is a loss (and lines 1d and 2c are zero or more), skip Parts II and III and go to line 15.

Caution: If your filing status is married filing separately and you lived with your spouse at any time during the year, **do not** complete Part II or Part III. Instead, go to line 15.

Part II — Special Allowance for Rental Real Estate Activities With Active Participation

Note: Enter all numbers in Part II as positive amounts. See instructions for an example.

Line	Description	Box	Amount	Line	Amount
5	Enter the **smaller** of the loss on line 1d or the loss on line 4			5	10,000
6	Enter $150,000. If married filing separately, see instructions	6	150,000		
7	Enter modified adjusted gross income, but not less than zero (see instructions)	7	80,003		
	Note: If line 7 is greater than or equal to line 6, skip lines 8 and 9, enter -0- on line 10. Otherwise, go to line 8.				
8	Subtract line 7 from line 6	8	69,997		
9	Multiply line 8 by 50% (0.50). **Do not** enter more than $25,000. If married filing separately, see instructions			9	25,000
10	Enter the **smaller** of line 5 or line 9			10	10,000

If line 2c is a loss, go to Part III. Otherwise, go to line 15.

Part III — Special Allowance for Commercial Revitalization Deductions From Rental Real Estate Activities

Note: Enter all numbers in Part III as positive amounts. See the example for Part II in the instructions.

Line	Description	Line	Amount
11	Enter $25,000 reduced by the amount, if any, on line 10. If married filing separately, see instructions	11	
12	Enter the loss from line 4	12	
13	Reduce line 12 by the amount on line 10	13	
14	Enter the **smallest** of line 2c (treated as a positive amount), line 11, or line 13	14	

Part IV — Total Losses Allowed

Line	Description	Line	Amount
15	Add the income, if any, on lines 1a and 3a and enter the total	15	60,000
16	**Total losses allowed from all passive activities for 2017.** Add lines 10, 14, and 15. See instructions to find out how to report the losses on your tax return	16	70,000

For Paperwork Reduction Act Notice, see instructions. Cat. No. 63704F Form **8582** (2017)

Source: U.S. Department of the Treasury, Internal Revenue Service, Form 8582. Washington, DC: 2017.

EXHIBIT 13-8

Schedule E (Form 1040) 2017 Attachment Sequence No. **13** Page **2**

Name(s) shown on return. Do not enter name and social security number if shown on other side.	**Your social security number**
Lori Doe	**412-34-5670**

Caution: The IRS compares amounts reported on your tax return with amounts shown on Schedule(s) K-1.

Part II **Income or Loss From Partnerships and S Corporations** **Note:** If you report a loss from an at-risk activity for which **any** amount is **not** at risk, you **must** check the box in column **(e)** on line 28 and attach **Form 6198.** See instructions.

27 Are you reporting any loss not allowed in a prior year due to the at-risk, excess farm loss, or basis limitations, a prior year unallowed loss from a passive activity (if that loss was not reported on Form 8582), or unreimbursed partnership expenses? If you answered "Yes," see instructions before completing this section . . . . ☐ **Yes** ☐ **No**

28	(a) Name	(b) Enter **P** for partnership; **S** for S corporation	(c) Check if foreign partnership	(d) Employer identification number	(e) Check if any amount is not at risk
A	**Partnership A**	**P**	☐	**56-1234567**	☐
B	**Partnership B**	**P**	☐	**57-1234567**	☐
C	**Partnership C**	**P**	☐	**58-1234567**	☐
D	**Partnership D**	**P**	☐	**59-1234567**	☐

	Passive Income and Loss		**Nonpassive Income and Loss**		
	(f) Passive loss allowed (attach **Form 8582** if required)	(g) Passive income from **Schedule K-1**	(h) Nonpassive loss from **Schedule K-1**	(i) Section 179 expense deduction from **Form 4562**	(j) Nonpassive income from **Schedule K-1**
A		**60,000**			
B	**40,000**				
C	**20,000**				
D	**10,000**				
29a Totals		**60,000**			
b Totals	**70,000**				

30	Add columns (g) and (j) of line 29a	30	**60,000**
31	Add columns (f), (h), and (i) of line 29b	31	(**70,000**
32	**Total partnership and S corporation income or (loss).** Combine lines 30 and 31. Enter the result here and include in the total on line 41 below	32	**(10,000)**

Part III **Income or Loss From Estates and Trusts**

33	(a) Name	(b) Employer identification number
A		
B		

	Passive Income and Loss		**Nonpassive Income and Loss**	
	(c) Passive deduction or loss allowed (attach **Form 8582** if required)	(d) Passive income from **Schedule K-1**	(e) Deduction or loss from **Schedule K-1**	(f) Other income from **Schedule K-1**
A				
B				
34a Totals				
b Totals				

35	Add columns (d) and (f) of line 34a	35	
36	Add columns (c) and (e) of line 34b	36	( )
37	**Total estate and trust income or (loss).** Combine lines 35 and 36. Enter the result here and include in the total on line 41 below	37	

Part IV **Income or Loss From Real Estate Mortgage Investment Conduits (REMICs)—Residual Holder**

38	(a) Name	(b) Employer identification number	(c) Excess inclusion from **Schedules Q,** line 2c (see instructions)	(d) Taxable income (net loss) from **Schedules Q,** line 1b	(e) Income from **Schedules Q,** line 3b

39	Combine columns (d) and (e) only. Enter the result here and include in the total on line 41 below	39	

Part V **Summary**

40	Net farm rental income or (loss) from **Form 4835.** Also, complete line 42 below	40	
41	**Total income or (loss).** Combine lines 26, 32, 37, 39, and 40. Enter the result here and on Form 1040, line 17, or Form 1040NR, line 18 ▶	41	**(10,000)**
42	**Reconciliation of farming and fishing income.** Enter your **gross** farming and fishing income reported on Form 4835, line 7; Schedule K-1 (Form 1065), box 14, code B; Schedule K-1 (Form 1120S), box 17, code V; and Schedule K-1 (Form 1041), box 14, code F (see instructions) . .	42	
43	**Reconciliation for real estate professionals.** If you were a real estate professional (see instructions), enter the net income or (loss) you reported anywhere on Form 1040 or Form 1040NR from all rental real estate activities in which you materially participated under the passive activity loss rules . .	43	

Schedule E (Form 1040) 2017

Source: U.S. Department of the Treasury, Internal Revenue Service, Schedule E Form1040. Washington, DC: 2017.

> **Reason for Change:** The committee believes that the minimum tax should serve one overriding objective: to ensure that no taxpayer with substantial economic income can avoid significant tax liability by using exclusions, deductions, and credits. Although these provisions may provide incentives for worthy goals, they become counterproductive when taxpayers are allowed to use them to avoid virtually all tax liability. The ability of high-income individuals and highly profitable corporations to pay little or no tax undermines respect for the entire tax system and, thus, for the incentive provisions themselves. In addition, even aside from public perceptions, the committee believes that it is inherently unfair for high-income individuals and highly profitable corporations to pay little or no tax due to their ability to utilize various tax preferences.[23]

The AMT rules are based on the notion of alternative minimum taxable income (AMTI). To determine AMTI, the taxpayer starts with regular taxable income calculated in accordance with the laws discussed throughout this text. The taxpayer then makes adjustments to regular taxable income to arrive at AMTI, which is used to calculate the minimum tax liability using. The AMT tax rate is 26% on the first $187,800 and then moves to 28%. The AMT for an individual taxpayer is reported on Form 6251.

AMT Formula

The base formula for calculating AMT is this:[24]

Regular taxable income	
+	Personal/dependency exemptions and standard deduction if the taxpayer does not itemize.[a]
+/−	Adjustment items[b]
+	Tax preference items[c]
=	Alternative minimum taxable income (AMTI)
−	AMT exemption amount[d]
=	Alternative minimum tax base
×	Tax rate of either 26% (or 28% less $3,756[e])
=	Tentative minimum tax
−	Regular tax
=	Alternative minimum tax

[a] IRC § 56(b)(1)(E).
[b] IRC § 56.
[c] IRC § 57.
[d] IRC § 55(d)(1).
[e] IRC § 55(b)(1)(A).

It is important to note that a taxpayer does not owe any AMT unless the AMT calculation results in an amount higher than the regular tax. Also note that the AMT tax rate is either 26% or 28%. If the taxpayer's AMTI is $187,800 or less, the AMT rate is 26%. If the AMTI amount is more than $187,800, the AMT rate is 28%. When the rate is 28%, $3,756 is then subtracted from the resulting AMT tax calculation. For taxpayers with net capital gains or qualified dividend income, the tax rates for these items are the same for both AMT and regular tax purposes.

AMT Adjustment Items

Adjustments to regular income to arrive at AMTI can be either positive or negative.[25] The adjustments could reduce AMTI to the point that a taxpayer will not be subject to AMT. However, most adjustments increase AMTI. Table 13-3 lists the primary AMT adjustments.[26]

Only those adjustments affecting numerous taxpayers are covered in detail in this section. For more obscure adjustments, see the instructions for Form 6251 and IRC § 56.

[23] Senate Report No. 99-313 (P.L. 99-514), 1986-3 CB (Part 3), p. 518. The Senate Report accompanied the Tax Reform Act of 1986.

[24] The format on Form 6251 is somewhat different, but the calculation is the same.

[25] A positive adjustment increases AMTI, and a negative adjustment decreases AMTI. Thus a negative adjustment is good for the taxpayer.

[26] IRC § 56.

TABLE 13-3
Adjustments to AMT

Standard deduction and personal/dependency exemptions not allowed.
Depreciation placed in service after 1986 and before 1999.
Depreciation exceeding 150% declining balance for some assets placed in service after 1998.
Adjustments to gains and losses on the sale of assets (different gains are caused by different depreciation methods).
Treatment of incentive stock options.
Passive activities (differences in regular tax passive loss and AMT passive loss allowed).
Beneficiaries of estates and trusts (differences in regular income or loss and amount of AMT income or loss).
Treatment of long-term contracts.
Others.

Standard Deduction, Exemptions, and Itemized Deduction Limits

If the taxpayer does not itemize and takes the standard deduction for regular tax purposes, the standard deduction is added back as a positive adjustment to AMTI. Likewise, the personal exemptions are also added as a positive adjustment.[27]

EXAMPLE 13-20

Roland is married, files a joint return, and has two children. Because he rents his home (pays no mortgage interest) and lives in Florida (has no state income tax), he does not itemize his deductions but takes the standard deduction. Roland would have the following positive adjustments for AMTI:

Standard deduction	$12,600
Personal exemptions (4 × $4,050)	16,200*
	$28,800

* Because only high-income taxpayers are usually subject to AMT, the personal exemption may not be an adjustment if it is phased out.

Limitations on Itemized Deductions

Several itemized deductions are either limited or disallowed in determining AMTI. For example, the AGI floor for medical expenses is 10% of AGI even for taxpayers 65 and over who still get the 7.5% floor (after 2017, the 10% limit also applies to seniors). Any itemized deduction for taxes or miscellaneous itemized deductions are totally disallowed for AMT purposes.[28] The itemized deduction for mortgage interest is also modified for AMTI because only mortgage interest used to build, buy, or substantially improve the taxpayer's home or second home is allowed. Interest expense from a home equity loan to purchase an auto or other asset (qualified housing interest) is disallowed for AMT purposes and causes a positive AMT adjustment. This qualified housing interest is treated as investment interest and is deductible only to the extent of investment income. All other itemized deductions are allowed as AMT deductions. If the taxpayer's total itemized deduction is limited by the 3%/80% phaseout, the amount of the phaseout would be a negative AMT adjustment.

Table 13-4 summarizes the AMT adjustments for itemized deductions.

Depreciation Adjustment for AMT

Nearly every taxpayer who calculates depreciation on his or her tax return will have a depreciation adjustment for AMT purposes. For most assets, depreciation must be recalculated using methods allowable for AMT. The method and life used vary depending on when the asset was placed in service and the type of property (real property or personal property).

Real Property Placed in Service after 1986 and before 1999

Depreciation (for regular tax purposes) on all depreciable real property placed in service after 1986 and before 1999 is calculated using the straight-line method. The only difference is the

[27] IRC § 56(b)(1)(E).
[28] IRC § 56(b)(1)(A).

TABLE 13-4
Summary of AMT Adjustments for Itemized Deductions

Medical	AGI floor of 10% for all taxpayers
Taxes	Not allowed for AMT.
Mortgage interest	Allowed for AMT only if the interest is to build, buy, or substantially improve the taxpayer's residence.
Gifts to charity	Allowed for AMT subject to the same limitations as regular tax.
Casualty and theft losses	Allowed for AMT subject to the same limitations as regular tax.
Miscellaneous itemized deductions	Not allowed for AMT.

EXAMPLE 13-21

Suppose that Jergen had the Schedule A shown in Exhibit 13-9 for his regular tax return. The mortgage interest is all qualified mortgage interest to purchase his personal residence.

For AMT purposes, Jergen has the following adjustments:

Itemized Deduction	Regular Tax	Permitted AMT Deduction	AMT Adjustment
Medical	$53,150	$53,150	$ –0–
Taxes	49,350	–0–	49,350
Mortgage interest	15,400	15,400	–0–
Charitable contributions	12,800	12,800	–0–
Miscellaneous deductions	1,880	–0–	1,880
Total AMT adjustment for itemized deductions			$51,230

Because taxes are not allowed as an AMT deduction, any income from tax refunds included in regular taxable income results in a negative AMT adjustment.[29]

depreciation life of 27.5 years for residential real property and 39 years for nonresidential real property.[30] For AMT purposes, the depreciation life is 40 years for *all* real property (straight-line and mid-month conventions stay the same). Table 13 in Revenue Procedure 87-57 is the appropriate table to use for the depreciation calculation for real property under the AMT rules. Table 13 is reproduced in the Appendix to this chapter (Table 13A-1).

EXAMPLE 13-22

Alex purchased a warehouse for $310,000 in August 1998. The regular depreciation and AMT depreciation for 2015 are calculated as follows:

Regular Tax Depreciation (Table 6A-8—Chapter 6)	AMT Depreciation (Appendix Table 13A-1)	Adjustment
$310,000 × 2.564% = $7,948	$310,000 × 2.5% = $7,750	$198

The depreciation adjustment is only $198 for this asset. This is a small adjustment because the depreciation lives are virtually the same: 39 years for regular taxes compared to 40 years for AMT purposes.

[29] A negative AMT adjustment reduces the AMT income subject to tax. Recall that tax refunds are included in income only if the taxpayer deducted the taxes in a prior year.

[30] For assets placed in service prior to 1986, the difference in depreciation is called *a tax preference item* rather than an *adjustment* and thus is discussed in the preference section. Also, nonresidential real property purchased between December 31, 1986, and May 13, 1993, has a depreciable life of 31.5 years.

EXHIBIT 13-9

SCHEDULE A (Form 1040)
Department of the Treasury
Internal Revenue Service (99)

Itemized Deductions

▶ Go to *www.irs.gov/ScheduleA* for instructions and the latest information.
▶ Attach to Form 1040.

OMB No. 1545-0074
2017
Attachment Sequence No. **07**

Name(s) shown on Form 1040: **Jergen Taxpayer**
Your social security number: **412-34-5670**

Section	Line	Description	Line	Amount	Line	Amount
Medical and Dental Expenses		**Caution:** Do not include expenses reimbursed or paid by others.				
	1	Medical and dental expenses (see instructions)	1	77,750		
	2	Enter amount from Form 1040, line 38 — 2: 246,000				
	3	Multiply line 2 by 10% (0.10)	3	24,600		
	4	Subtract line 3 from line 1. If line 3 is more than line 1, enter -0-			4	53,150
Taxes You Paid	5	State and local **(check only one box):** a ☑ Income taxes, **or** b ☐ General sales taxes	5	40,300		
	6	Real estate taxes (see instructions)	6	7,000		
	7	Personal property taxes	7	1,150		
	8	Other taxes. List type and amount ▶	8			
	9	Add lines 5 through 8			9	49,350
Interest You Paid	10	Home mortgage interest and points reported to you on Form 1098	10	15,400		
Note: Your mortgage interest deduction may be limited (see instructions).	11	Home mortgage interest not reported to you on Form 1098. If paid to the person from whom you bought the home, see instructions and show that person's name, identifying no., and address ▶	11			
	12	Points not reported to you on Form 1098. See instructions for special rules	12			
	13	Reserved	13			
	14	Investment interest. Attach Form 4952 if required. See instructions.	14			
	15	Add lines 10 through 14			15	15,400
Gifts to Charity	16	Gifts by cash or check. If you made any gift of $250 or more, see instructions	16	12,800		
If you made a gift and got a benefit for it, see instructions.	17	Other than by cash or check. If any gift of $250 or more, see instructions. You **must** attach Form 8283 if over $500	17			
	18	Carryover from prior year	18			
	19	Add lines 16 through 18			19	12,800
Casualty and Theft Losses	20	Casualty or theft loss(es). Attach Form 4684. See instructions			20	
Job Expenses and Certain Miscellaneous Deductions	21	Unreimbursed employee expenses—job travel, union dues, job education, etc. Attach Form 2106 or 2106-EZ if required. See instructions. ▶	21	6,000		
	22	Tax preparation fees	22	800		
	23	Other expenses—investment, safe deposit box, etc. List type and amount ▶	23			
	24	Add lines 21 through 23	24	6,800		
	25	Enter amount from Form 1040, line 38 — 25: 246,000				
	26	Multiply line 25 by 2% (0.02)	26	4,920		
	27	Subtract line 26 from line 24. If line 26 is more than line 24, enter -0-			27	1,880
Other Miscellaneous Deductions	28	Other—from list in instructions. List type and amount ▶			28	
Total Itemized Deductions	29	Is Form 1040, line 38, over $156,900? ☐ **No.** Your deduction is not limited. Add the amounts in the far right column for lines 4 through 28. Also, enter this amount on Form 1040, line 40. ☑ **Yes.** Your deduction may be limited. See the Itemized Deductions Worksheet in the instructions to figure the amount to enter.			29	132,580
	30	If you elect to itemize deductions even though they are less than your standard deduction, check here ▶ ☐				

For Paperwork Reduction Act Notice, see the Instructions for Form 1040. Cat. No. 17145C **Schedule A (Form 1040) 2017**

Source: U.S. Department of the Treasury, Internal Revenue Service, SCHEDULE A Form1040. Washington, DC: 2017.

EXAMPLE 13-23

Assume the same facts as in Example 13-22, but the property is an apartment building instead of a warehouse.

Regular Tax Depreciation (Table 6A-6—Chapter 6)	AMT Depreciation (Appendix Table 13A-1)	Adjustment
$310,000 × 3.636% = $11,272	$310,000 × 2.5% = $7,750	$3,522

In Example 13-23, the adjustment of $3,522 is higher because the depreciable lives are 27.5 years for regular tax purposes and 40 years for AMT purposes.

Real Property Placed in Service after 1998

Congress changed the law for real property placed in service after 1998. Because the depreciation difference affected only the depreciation life and the difference was only one year in the case of nonresidential real property, Congress eliminated this adjustment. For real property placed in service after 1998, there is no adjustment for depreciation.

Personal Property Placed in Service after 1986 and before 1999

For personal property, both the depreciation method and the class life are different under AMT rules. Regular MACRS depreciation for personal property is 200% declining balance (DB), and the life is determined under the general depreciation system (GDS). However, only 150% declining balance is allowed for AMT, and the life is determined under the alternative depreciation system (ADS). Both Revenue Procedure 87-56 and IRS Publication 946 present the different depreciation systems and corresponding lives.

The AMT lives are almost always longer (*never* shorter) than the regular tax lives. Longer lives and a less aggressive depreciation method (150% DB versus 200% DB) ensure that a positive AMTI adjustment results for personal property. This adjustment is becoming less important because most of these assets were fully depreciated for regular tax purposes during the 2006 tax year and fully depreciated for AMT in the 2009 tax year.

TAX YOUR BRAIN

Will the AMT depreciation adjustment for these assets be larger or smaller as the years progress?

ANSWER

It will be smaller. Because a higher amount of depreciation is taken in the early years with accelerated methods, the 200% declining balance depreciation will decline more rapidly than the 150% declining balance as the assets get older. Thus the difference between the two numbers will narrow. The adjustment will actually become negative in the last years of depreciation.

Personal Property Placed in Service after 1998

In an attempt to simplify AMT calculations, Congress again changed the treatment of AMT depreciation for personal property. For any personal assets placed in service after 1998, the depreciation lives for AMT purposes are the same as for regular taxes (both will use the GDS life). The method still differs (150% DB for AMT and 200% DB for MACRS) for assets placed in service before then.

EXAMPLE 13-24

Andrew has two depreciable business assets. AMT depreciation is calculated using 150% DB; the MACRS method is 200% DB. Depreciation for tax year 2017 (the eighth year of depreciation) yields the following AMT.[31] The AMT depreciation percentages are found in Table 14 of Rev. Proc. 87-57. This table is partially reproduced in Table 13A-2 in the appendix to this chapter.[32]

Asset	Date Purchased	Cost	MACRS Life/ AMT Life	MACRS Depreciation	AMT Depreciation	Adjustment
Furniture 1	02/12/2010	$ 7,000	7-year	$312	$429	$(117)
Furniture 2	11/15/2010	12,000	7-year	535	736	(201)
					AMT adjustment	$(318)

Basis Calculation: Different Gains and Losses for AMT Purposes

Because of the different depreciation methods for AMT and for regular tax, accumulated depreciation and the adjusted basis of the assets are different. The different basis causes different gains and losses when assets are disposed.

EXAMPLE 13-25

Suppose we purchased furniture on February 10, 2015, for $6,000. On March 2, 2017, we sold the furniture for $4,300. The depreciation expense and gain for regular tax purposes are calculated as follows (seven-year, 200% DB):

Year	Adjusted Basis	Depreciation Expense	Accumulated Depreciation
2015	$6,000	$ 857	$ 857
2016	5,143*	1,469	2,326
2017	3,674	525†	2,851
			$3,149
Regular tax gain			$4,300 − $3,149 = $1,151

* The depreciation tables are structured such that depreciation is always calculated by multiplying the original cost basis by the appropriate percentage.

† One-half year of depreciation is allowed in the year of disposal.

The AMT depreciation, AMT adjusted basis, and AMT gain are calculated as follows (seven-year, 150% DB):

Year	Adjusted Basis	Depreciation Expense	Accumulated Depreciation
2015	$6,000	$ 643	$ 643
2016	5,357	1,148	1,791
2017	4,209	451	2,242
			$3,758
AMT gain			$4,300 − $3,758 = $542

The sale of this asset would result in a negative AMT adjustment of $609 ($1,151 regular tax gain less the $542 AMT gain).

[31] Recall that because the half-year convention is used for most assets, the depreciation calculation goes into the eighth year for seven-year assets.

[32] The regular depreciation percentages are found in the appendix of Chapter 6, Table 6A-1. For MACRS depreciation of personal property, the percentages are also found in Table 1 of Rev. Proc. 87-57.

TAX YOUR BRAIN

Why does the difference in gains result in a negative AMT adjustment that reduces AMT income?

ANSWER

The regular tax gain of $1,151 is already included in taxable income (the starting point for AMT calculations). The AMT gain is $609 less than the regular tax gain. Therefore, AMT income should be reduced to reflect the lower gain.

Incentive Stock Options Adjustment

For regular tax purposes, no income is recognized when an incentive stock option is exercised. This is not the case with AMT. For AMT purposes, the positive adjustment is equal to the FMV of the stock less the amount the taxpayer paid for it (including any amount paid for the option).[33]

EXAMPLE 13-26

Bob works for a large publicly traded company and regularly receives incentive stock options as bonuses. Bob exercises options to purchase 1,000 shares at $12 per share when the market value is $18. Bob's AMT adjustment is calculated as follows:

Market value	1,000 shares × $18 per share	=	$18,000
Cost of stock	1,000 shares × $12 per share	=	12,000
AMT adjustment			$ 6,000

The AMT basis in the stock is increased by the amount of the adjustment. Thus, when the stock is sold, the gain or loss will be different for AMT purposes than for regular tax purposes. In Example 13-26, the stock basis is $12,000 for regular tax purposes and $18,000 for AMT.

Passive Activity Adjustment and K-1 Adjustments

AMTI is also adjusted for differences in passive losses and other adjustments originating from flow-through entities such as partnerships, estates, and trusts. The rule that passive activity losses are allowed only to the extent of passive income pertains to both regular tax and AMT calculations. However, the amount of passive loss and passive income will be different for AMT because all of the adjustments and preferences discussed in this chapter also apply to the passive activities (for example, depreciation must be calculated differently using the AMT rules). These adjustments are reported to the taxpayer via the K-1 received from the flow-through entity.

Treatment of Long-Term Contracts

For AMT purposes, a taxpayer must use the percentage of completion method rather than the completed contract method to report the income from long-term contracts. The adjustment is the difference between the income under the percentage of completion method and income determined for regular tax. In the year in question, if AMT income is smaller, the adjustment is negative. A negative adjustment is likely to occur in the year the contract is completed. This adjustment rarely, if ever, affects individual taxpayers.

Tax Preference Items

Unlike adjustments, tax items result only in additions to AMTI. Tax preference items are typically more specific and affect taxpayers only in certain industries. This is true for individual taxpayers because individuals are unlikely to conduct business in certain industries other than a corporation or other entity form. Tax preference items are more likely to flow through from a K-1 than be directly calculated by the taxpayer. Some preference items can, however, affect

[33] IRC § 56(b)(3).

individual taxpayers. The following is a summary of the pertinent tax preference items that could affect an individual taxpayer. Form 6251 gives a complete list of tax preferences.

Depreciation on Pre-1987 Assets

For all real property placed in service prior to 1987 and depreciated under an accelerated method, depreciation must be recalculated for AMT using the straight-line method over a 19-year life. The excess of regular tax depreciation over the straight-line depreciation is a *tax preference item*. Only a positive amount is reported. If the 19-year straight-line method results in more depreciation no preference item is included. In tax year 2008, straight-line depreciation should be higher because the newest asset in this category was purchased in 1986. This preference item is considerably less important as time passes and pre-1986 assets approach the end of their depreciable lives.

IRC § 1202 Exclusion

One preference item that can cause a substantial increase in AMTI for an individual taxpayer is the preference for the § 1202 exclusion (discussed in Chapter 7), which allows 50% (and possibly as much as 75%) of any gain from the sale of "qualified small business stock" to be excluded from regular tax. However, for AMT purposes, 7% of the amount excluded must be added as a tax preference item for post–May 5, 2003, sales.[34] The 2012 Taxpayer Relief Act made the 7% AMT preference item permanent. This preference will not apply to qualified small business stock purchased between September 1, 2010, and January 1, 2014. Additional dates of purchase apply to this provision; see IRC § 57(a)(7) for more information.

EXAMPLE 13-27

Richard invested in a local corporation with gross assets of $15,000,000. He purchased 500 shares for $25,000 in 2001. On June 6, 2017, Richard sold the stock for $45,000. One-half of the $20,000 gain is excluded from gross income for regular tax purposes under § 1202. For AMT, a tax preference item of $700 ($10,000 exclusion × 7%) is added to AMTI.

Other Preference Items

The following is a list of other preference items that an individual taxpayer may be subject to in certain limited situations. A detailed discussion of these items is beyond the scope of this text. Preference items include these:

- Percentage depletion taken in excess of the basis of the property.
- Excess intangible drilling and development costs.
- Tax-exempt interest on private activity bonds.
- Amortization of pollution control facilities placed in service before 1987.[35]

Exemption Amount

After all of the tax preference items and AMT adjustments have been included, the taxpayer reduces AMTI by an exemption amount. The exemption amount varies depending on the filing status of the taxpayer and level of AMTI. The exemption amounts follow:

Filing Status	AMTI Not More Than	2017 Exemption Amount
Single/head of household	$120,700	$54,300
Married filing jointly/qualifying widow(er)	160,900	84,500
Married filing separately	80,450	42,250

The exemption amount is reduced by 25% of AMTI in excess of the income limit in the "AMTI Not More Than" column.

[34]IRC § 57(a)(7).

[35]IRC § 57(a).

EXAMPLE 13-28

After computing all tax preferences and AMT adjustments, Alex and his wife Brooke have AMTI of $255,000. Because Alex and Brooke file a joint tax return, their initial exemption is $84,500. However, because their AMTI is more than $160,900, the exemption is reduced to $60,975: ($84,500 – 0.25[$255,000 – $160,900]).

COMPREHENSIVE AMT EXAMPLE

This comprehensive AMT example uses components of many of the examples throughout this chapter.

Jergen Trade is married with two children. His Form 1040 shows regular taxable income of $97,220 (AGI $246,000 – Itemized deductions of $132,580 – Exemptions of $16,200). His regular tax liability is $15,784. He also has the following AMT adjustments and preferences:

1. Itemized deductions (Example 13-21):

Itemized Deduction	Regular Tax	AMT Deduction	AMT Adjustment
Medical	$53,150	$53,150	$ –0–
Taxes	49,350	–0–	49,350
Mortgage interest	15,400	15,400	–0–
Charitable contributions	12,800	12,800	–0–
Miscellaneous deductions	1,880	–0–	1,880
Total AMT adjustment for itemized deductions			$51,230

2. Depreciation of an apartment purchased in August 1998 for $310,000 (Example 13-23):

Regular Tax Depreciation	AMT Depreciation	Adjustment
2017 $310,000 × 3.636% = $11,272	$310,000 × 2.5% = $7,750	$3,522

3. Depreciation on personal property (Example 13-24):

Asset	Date Purchased	Cost	MACRS Life/AMT Life	MACRS Depreciation	AMT Depreciation	Adjustment
Furniture 1	02/12/10	$ 7,000	7-year	$312	$429	$(117)
Furniture 2	11/15/10	12,000	7-year	535	736	(201)
					AMT adjustment	$(318)

4. Different basis (gain or loss) on the sale of an asset (see Example 13-25 for the calculations):

Regular tax gain	$4,300 – $3,149 = $1,151
AMT gain	$4,300 – $3,758 = 542

The sale of this asset would result in a $609 negative AMT adjustment ($1,151 tax gain – $542 AMT gain).

5. Incentive stock option adjustment (Example 13-26): Jergen exercises options to purchase 1,000 shares at $12 per share when the market value is $18. His AMT adjustment is calculated as follows:

Market value	1,000 shares × $18 per share	=	$18,000
Cost of stock	1,000 shares × $12 per share	=	12,000
AMT adjustment			$ 6,000

Exhibit 13-10 illustrates a completed Form 6251 and the calculated AMT of $8,092.

EXHIBIT 13-10

Form **6251** — Department of the Treasury, Internal Revenue Service (99)

Alternative Minimum Tax—Individuals

► Go to *www.irs.gov/Form6251* for instructions and the latest information.
► Attach to Form 1040 or Form 1040NR.

OMB No. 1545-0074 — **2017** — Attachment Sequence No. 32

Name(s) shown on Form 1040 or Form 1040NR: **Jergen Trade** — Your social security number: **412-34-5670**

Part I Alternative Minimum Taxable Income (See instructions for how to complete each line.)

		Line	Amount
1	If filing Schedule A (Form 1040), enter the amount from Form 1040, line 41, and go to line 2. Otherwise, enter the amount from Form 1040, line 38, and go to line 7. (If less than zero, enter as a negative amount.)	1	113,420
2	Reserved for future use	2	
3	Taxes from Schedule A (Form 1040), line 9	3	49,350
4	Enter the home mortgage interest adjustment, if any, from line 6 of the worksheet in the instructions for this line	4	
5	Miscellaneous deductions from Schedule A (Form 1040), line 27	5	1,880
6	If Form 1040, line 38, is $156,900 or less, enter -0-. Otherwise, see instructions	6	( )
7	Tax refund from Form 1040, line 10 or line 21	7	( )
8	Investment interest expense (difference between regular tax and AMT)	8	
9	Depletion (difference between regular tax and AMT)	9	
10	Net operating loss deduction from Form 1040, line 21. Enter as a positive amount	10	
11	Alternative tax net operating loss deduction	11	( )
12	Interest from specified private activity bonds exempt from the regular tax	12	
13	Qualified small business stock, see instructions	13	
14	Exercise of incentive stock options (excess of AMT income over regular tax income)	14	6,000
15	Estates and trusts (amount from Schedule K-1 (Form 1041), box 12, code A)	15	
16	Electing large partnerships (amount from Schedule K-1 (Form 1065-B), box 6)	16	
17	Disposition of property (difference between AMT and regular tax gain or loss)	17	(609)
18	Depreciation on assets placed in service after 1986 (difference between regular tax and AMT)	18	3,204
19	Passive activities (difference between AMT and regular tax income or loss)	19	
20	Loss limitations (difference between AMT and regular tax income or loss)	20	
21	Circulation costs (difference between regular tax and AMT)	21	
22	Long-term contracts (difference between AMT and regular tax income)	22	
23	Mining costs (difference between regular tax and AMT)	23	
24	Research and experimental costs (difference between regular tax and AMT)	24	
25	Income from certain installment sales before January 1, 1987	25	(
26	Intangible drilling costs preference	26	
27	Other adjustments, including income-based related adjustments	27	
28	**Alternative minimum taxable income.** Combine lines 1 through 27. (If married filing separately and line 28 is more than $249,450, see instructions.)	28	173,245

Part II Alternative Minimum Tax (AMT)

29 Exemption. (If you were under age 24 at the end of 2017, see instructions.)

IF your filing status is . . .	AND line 28 is not over . . .	THEN enter on line 29 . . .
Single or head of household	$120,700	$54,300
Married filing jointly or qualifying widow(er)	160,900	84,500
Married filing separately	80,450	42,250

If line 28 is **over** the amount shown above for your filing status, see instructions. — **29** 81,414

		Line	Amount
30	Subtract line 29 from line 28. If more than zero, go to line 31. If zero or less, enter -0- here and on lines 31, 33, and 35, and go to line 34	30	91,831
31	• If you are filing Form 2555 or 2555-EZ, see instructions for the amount to enter. • If you reported capital gain distributions directly on Form 1040, line 13; you reported qualified dividends on Form 1040, line 9b; **or** you had a gain on both lines 15 and 16 of Schedule D (Form 1040) (as refigured for the AMT, if necessary), complete Part III on the back and enter the amount from line 64 here. • **All others:** If line 30 is $187,800 or less ($93,900 or less if married filing separately), multiply line 30 by 26% (0.26). Otherwise, multiply line 30 by 28% (0.28) and subtract $3,756 ($1,878 if married filing separately) from the result.	31	23,876
32	Alternative minimum tax foreign tax credit (see instructions)	32	0
33	Tentative minimum tax. Subtract line 32 from line 31	33	23,876
34	Add Form 1040, line 44 (minus any tax from Form 4972), and Form 1040, line 46. Subtract from the result any foreign tax credit from Form 1040, line 48. If you used Schedule J to figure your tax on Form 1040, line 44, refigure that tax without using Schedule J before completing this line (see instructions)	34	15,784
35	**AMT.** Subtract line 34 from line 33. If zero or less, enter -0-. Enter here and on Form 1040, line 45	35	8,092

For Paperwork Reduction Act Notice, see your tax return instructions. Cat. No. 13600G Form **6251** (2017)

Source: U.S. Department of the Treasury, Internal Revenue Service, Form 6251. Washington, DC: 2017.

From Shoebox to Software

Tax software performs most of the AMT calculation automatically. All of the itemized deduction adjustments and the AMT depreciation calculations transfer to Form 6251. For some of the unique adjustments, the taxpayer must enter the adjustments and preferences directly on Form 6251.

Some explanation is necessary concerning certain items on Form 6251 in Exhibit 13-10:

Line 1: This is taxable income ($113,420) before personal and dependency exemptions. Recall that personal exemptions are not allowed for AMT purposes. Instead of adding the personal exemptions as an adjustment, taxable income is taken from line 41 of Form 1040. Line 41 is immediately before the exemptions are deducted.

Line 18: The depreciation adjustment of $3,204 is a combination of the real property depreciation adjustment of $3,522 and the personal property depreciation adjustment of $(318).

Line 28: The AMT exemption is $84,500 for married taxpayers. However, the exemption is reduced by 25% of the amount AMTI is over $160,900. The exemption is calculated as $84,500 – (25%[$173,245 – 160,900]) = $81,414.

Line 31: Because AMTI after the exemption is less than $187,800, the AMT rate is 26%. The resulting tentative tax is $23,876 ($91,831 × 26%).

Lines 34 and 35: The regular tax is $15,784. The difference between the tax calculated under the AMT rules and the regular tax is equal to the AMT of $8,092. If the taxpayer had capital gains and the regular tax was calculated on page 2 of Schedule D, the AMT would be calculated on page 2 of Form 6251 (not shown). The preferential capital gain rates are allowed for AMT purposes.

CONCEPT CHECK 13-4—
LO 13-4

1. Medical expenses are allowed in full (same as the regular tax) for AMT purposes. True or false?
2. No taxes are allowed as a deduction for AMT purposes. True or false?
3. If a taxpayer is married and has eight children, his exemptions for regular tax purposes could be $40,500 (10 exemptions × $4,050). None of this amount would be allowed for AMT purposes. True or false?
4. If a taxpayer's AMTI is $187,300 or less, the AMT tax rate would be 26%. True or false?

Summary

LO 13-1: Explain the process of applying the at-risk rules.

- The initial at-risk amount is the money plus the adjusted basis of property contributed.
- The at-risk amount is increased by income/gain items, additional contributions, and the taxpayer's share of recourse liabilities.
- Loss deductions and distributions are limited to the amount that the taxpayer has at-risk.

LO 13-2: Describe the rules and applications related to passive activities.

- A passive activity is one in which the taxpayer does not materially participate.
- A passive loss is generally deductible only to the extent of passive income.
- Low-income taxpayers could be able to offset up to $25,000 of passive rental loss against other income.
- When a passive activity is sold, suspended passive losses from past years are allowed to offset nonpassive income.

LO 13-3: Explain how the passive activity loss rules and at-risk rules work together to limit the deductibility of losses.	• For a loss to be deductible, it must first be allowed under the at-risk rules before the PAL rules can be applied. • Suspended PALs must be allocated to individual properties.
LO 13-4: Explain the alternative minimum tax and how it is calculated.	• The AMT is a separate tax system to limit taxpayers with substantial income from avoiding paying tax by using exclusions, deductions, and credits. • Itemized deductions for taxes and miscellaneous deductions are disallowed for AMT. • Personal exemptions are not allowed for AMT. • The AMT rate is 26% for AMTI of $187,800 or less, and 28% for AMTI over $187,800.

Appendix

Tables 13A-1 and 13A-2 are reproductions of Tables 13 and 14 in Rev. Proc. 87–57.

DEPRECIATION TABLE 13A-1 **Alternative Depreciation System Straight-Line Applicable Recovery Period: 40 Years**

	Mid-Month Convention											
	Month in the First Recovery Year the Property Is Placed in Service											
Recovery Year	**1**	**2**	**3**	**4**	**5**	**6**	**7**	**8**	**9**	**10**	**11**	**12**
1	2.396	2.188	1.979	1.771	1.563	1.354	1.146	.938	.729	.521	.313	.104
2–40	2.500	2.500	2.500	2.500	2.500	2.500	2.500	2.500	2.500	2.500	2.500	2.500
41	.104	.312	.521	.729	.937	1.146	1.354	1.562	1.771	1.979	2.187	2.396

DEPRECIATION TABLE 13A-2
Alternative Minimum Tax 150% Declining Balance Switching to Straight-Line Recovery Period: 2.5–50 Years

	Half-Year Convention					
	Partial Table of Table 14 Rev. Proc. 87-57					
Recovery Year	**4.0**	**5.0**	**6.0**	**7.0**	**10.0**	**12.0**
1	18.75	15.00	12.50	10.71	7.50	6.25
2	30.47	25.50	21.88	19.13	13.88	11.72
3	20.31	17.85	16.41	15.03	11.79	10.25
4	20.31	16.66	14.06	12.25	10.02	8.97
5	10.16	16.66	14.06	12.25	8.74	7.85
6		8.33	14.06	12.25	8.74	7.33
7			7.03	12.25	8.74	7.33
8				6.13	8.74	7.33
9					8.74	7.33
10					8.74	7.33
11					4.37	7.32
12						7.33
13						3.66

Discussion Questions connect

All applicable discussion questions are available with ***Connect***©

LO 13-1 1. Discuss the *at-risk* concept and how it applies to the deductibility of investment losses.

LO 13-1 2. What amounts are considered at-risk when making the determination of a deductible loss?

LO 13-1 3. What are the differences between recourse, nonrecourse, and qualified nonrecourse liabilities? Which liabilities are considered at-risk?

LO 13-2 4. What is a *passive activity*? What types of activities are automatically considered passive?

LO 13-2 5. Discuss the concept of *material participation*. To be considered a material participant, what tests must the taxpayer satisfy?

LO 13-2 6. When a loss is disallowed under the passive activity loss rules, what happens to that loss in future years?

LO 13-2 7. Discuss the rules concerning the $25,000 loss offset for rental activities. Why are losses of $25,000 allowed for some taxpayers?

LO 13-2 8. What are the differences between material participation, active participation, and significant participation?

LO 13-2 9. When a passive activity is sold or otherwise disposed of, what happens to any suspended losses from that activity?

LO 13-3 10. When must Form 6198 and Form 8582 be filed? Does the taxpayer file more than one Form 6198 or Form 8582?

LO 13-3 11. How do the passive loss rules and the at-risk rules work in conjunction to limit losses?

EA LO 13-4 12. Discuss the AMT formula and how it relates to the regular income tax. Include in your discussion factors that cause AMT to be assessed.

EA LO 13-4 13. What AMT adjustment items are likely to affect all taxpayers who itemize their deductions? Give examples.

EA LO 13-4 14. Are medical expenses treated differently for AMT purposes than for regular tax purposes? If so, explain.

EA LO 13-4 15. Are the depreciation lives the same for AMT purposes as for regular tax purposes? If not, how are the lives determined for AMT?

EA LO 13-4 16. Discuss the tax basis calculation adjustment. Why is the gain or loss on the sale of depreciable assets different for AMT purposes than for regular tax purposes?

Multiple-Choice Questions connect

All applicable multiple-choice questions are available with ***Connect***©

LO 13-1 17. Which of the following increases a taxpayer's at-risk amount?

a. Cash and the adjusted basis of property contributed to the activity.

b. Borrowed amounts used in the activity for which the taxpayer is personally liable.

c. Income from the activity.

d. All of the above.

LO 13-1 18. Which of the following increases a taxpayer's at-risk amount?

a. Cash distributions.

b. Property distributions.

c. Increased share of liabilities.

d. Loss items.

LO 13-1 19. In 2017, Kirsten invested $20,000 for a 10% partnership interest (not a passive activity). The partnership has losses of $150,000 in 2017 and $250,000 in 2018. Kirsten's share of the partnership's losses is $15,000 in 2017 and $25,000 in 2018. How much of the losses from the partnership can Kirsten deduct?

a. $0 in 2017 and $0 in 2018.

b. $15,000 in 2017 and $5,000 in 2018.

c. $15,000 in 2017 and $25,000 in 2018.

d. $20,000 in 2017 and $0 in 2018.

LO 13-1 20. Leonard invests $10,000 cash in an equipment-leasing activity for a 15% share in the business. The 85% owner is Rebecca, who contributes $10,000 and borrows $75,000 to put in the business. Only Rebecca is liable for repayment of the loan. The partnership incurs a loss of $125,000 during the year. What amounts of the loss are deductible currently by Leonard and Rebecca (ignore passive loss rules)?

a. $0 by Leonard and $0 by Rebecca.

b. $10,000 by Leonard and $85,000 by Rebecca.

c. $18,750 by Leonard and $106,250 by Rebecca.

d. $21,250 by Leonard and $73,750 by Rebecca.

LO 13-1 21. Myer owns a 20% interest in a partnership (not involved in real estate) in which his at-risk amount was $50,000 at the beginning of the year. During the year, he receives a $40,000 distribution from the partnership. The partnership produces a $160,000 loss during the year. What is Myer's deductible loss for the year (ignore passive loss rules)?

a. $0.

b. $10,000.

c. $32,000.

d. $50,000.

LO 13-1 22. Alcott invested $20,000 for a 25% interest in a partnership (not a passive activity) on January 1, 2017. The partnership borrowed $100,000 (with full recourse to the partners) on January 15, 2017, to cover short-term cash flow requirements. During the year, the partnership generated a $60,000 loss. By December 31, 2017, the partnership had paid off $20,000 of the loan. What is Alcott's at-risk amount on January 1, 2018?

a. $20,000.

b. $25,000.

c. $40,000.

d. $45,000.

LO 13-1 23. Agnes and Aunt Sue each invested $140,000 cash in the A&S Partnership, and each received a 50% interest in the partnership. To finance her investment in the partnership, Agnes borrowed $60,000 on a full recourse basis from her partner, Aunt Sue. Which of the following is correct?

a. Agnes's at-risk amount in her partnership interest is $80,000.

b. Aunt Sue's at-risk amount in her partnership interest is $140,000.

c. Agnes's at-risk amount in her partnership interest is $140,000.

d. Aunt Sue's at-risk amount in her partnership interest is $80,000.

LO 13-2 24. Which of the following would be considered a passive activity?

a. A limited partnership interest.

b. Most rental real estate activities.

c. A trade or business in which the taxpayer does not materially participate.

d. All of the above.

LO 13-2 25. Sylvester, an accountant, owns a mail-order business in which he participates. He has one employee who works part-time in the business. Which of the following statements is *not* correct?

a. If Sylvester participates for 600 hours and the employee participates for 1,000 hours during the year, Sylvester qualifies as a material participant.

b. If Sylvester participates for 120 hours and the employee participates for 125 hours during the year, Sylvester does not qualify as a material participant.

c. If Sylvester participates for 495 hours and the employee participates for 520 hours during the year, Sylvester qualifies as a material participant.

d. If Sylvester participates for 105 hours and the employee participates for 5 hours during the year, Sylvester probably qualifies as a material participant.

LO 13-2 26. Janel owns five small businesses, each of which has its own manager and employees. Janel spends the following number of hours this year working in the various businesses: Business A, 130 hours; Business B, 160 hours; Business C, 110 hours; Business D, 120 hours; Business E, 100 hours. Which of the following statements is correct?

a. Businesses A, B, C, D, and E are all significant participation activities.

b. Businesses A, B, C, and D are all significant participation activities.

c. Janel is considered a material participant in Businesses A, B, C, and D.

d. Both *b* and *c* are correct.

LO 13-2 27. Samuel is a CPA and earns $150,000 from his practice in the current year. He also has an ownership interest in three passive activities. Assume he is sufficiently at risk in each of the three partnerships. In the current tax year, the activities had the following income and losses:

Partnership A	$40,000
Partnership B	(32,000)
Partnership C	(24,000)

What is Samuel's AGI for the current year?

a. $134,000.

b. $144,000.

c. $150,000.

d. $190,000.

LO 13-2 28. Nathaniel has AGI (before any rental loss) of $65,000. He also owns several rental properties in which he actively participates. The rental properties produced a $30,000 loss in the current year. Nathaniel also has $5,000 of income from a limited partnership interest. How much, if any, of the rental loss can he deduct in the current year?

a. $0.

b. $5,000.

c. $25,000.

d. $30,000.

LO 13-2 29. Basil has $130,000 AGI (before any rental loss). He also owns several rental properties in which he actively participates. The rental properties produced a $30,000 loss in the current year. How much, if any, of the rental loss can Basil deduct in the current year?

a. $0.

b. $10,000.

c. $15,000.

d. $25,000.

LO 13-2 30. Raymond sells his entire interest in a rental property in which he actively participated at a gain of $18,000. The activity has a current year loss of $5,500 and $18,500 in prior year suspended losses. During the year, Raymond has $55,000 in salary. What is Raymond's AGI for the year?

a. $49,000.

b. $55,000.

c. $67,500.

d. $73,000.

EA LO 13-4 31. Jacob is single with no dependents. During 2017 he has $48,000 of taxable income. He also has $28,000 of positive AMT adjustments and $12,000 of tax preferences. Jacob does not itemize his deductions but takes the standard deduction. Calculate his AMTI.

a. $88,000.

b. $92,050.

c. $94,350.

d. $98,400.

EA LO 13-4 32. Which of the following itemized deductions is *not* allowed for AMT?

a. Medical expenses.

b. Taxes.

c. Charitable contributions.

d. Interest on loan to purchase principal residence.

EA LO 13-4 33. Which of the following statements is correct with regard to the medical expense deduction?

a. Medical expenses are not deductible for AMT.

b. The medical expense deduction is decreased for AMT.

c. The medical expense deduction is increased for AMT.

d. The same amount of medical expenses that is deductible for regular tax purposes is deductible for AMT for most taxpayers.

EA LO 13-4 34. Paul reported the following itemized deductions on his 2017 tax return. His AGI for 2017 was $65,000. The mortgage interest is all qualified mortgage interest to purchase his personal residence. For AMT, compute his total adjustment for itemized deductions.

Medical expenses (after the 10.0% of AGI floor)	$ 6,000
State income taxes	3,600
Home mortgage interest	11,500
Charitable contributions	3,200
Miscellaneous itemized deductions (after the 2% of AGI floor)	1,800

a. $1,800.

b. $3,600.

c. $5,400.

d. $20,100.

EA LO 13-4 35. After computing all tax preferences and AMT adjustments, Phillip and his wife Carmin have AMTI of $210,000. If Phillip and Carmin file a joint tax return, what exemption amount can they claim for AMT for 2017?

a. $0.

b. $54,300.

c. $72,225.

d. $84,500.

Problems connect

All applicable problems are available with *Connect*©

LO 13-1 36. In 2017, Andrew contributed equipment with an adjusted basis of $20,000 and an FMV of $18,000 to Construction Limited Partnership (CLP) in return for a 3% limited partnership interest. Andrew's shares of CLP income and losses for the year were as follows:

Interest	$ 500
Dividends	300
Capital gains	900
Ordinary loss	(4,325)

CLP had no liabilities. What are Andrew's initial basis, allowed losses, and ending at-risk amount?

LO 13-1 37. Cindy, Casey, and Kara each invested $30,000 in a real estate venture. The partnership borrowed $200,000 and purchased a warehouse for $290,000. The note was secured by the building; there was no personal recourse against the partners. What is each partner's beginning at-risk amount in the venture?

LO 13-2 38. During the current year, Joshua worked 1,300 hours as a tax consultant and 450 hours as a real estate agent. His one other employee (his wife) worked 300 hours in the real estate business. Joshua earned $50,000 as a tax consultant, and together the couple lost $20,000 in the real estate business. How should Joshua treat the loss on his federal income tax return?

LO 13-2 39. Donald has two investments in activities that are considered nonrental passive activities. He acquired Activity A six years ago, and it was profitable until the current year. He acquired Activity B in the current year. His share of the loss from Activity A in the current year is $15,000, and his share of the loss from Activity B is $4,000. What is the total of Donald's suspended losses from these activities as of the end of the current year?

LO 13-2 40. Darrell acquired an activity eight years ago. The loss from it in the current year was $65,000. The activity involves residential rental real estate in which he is an active participant. Calculate Darrell's AGI after considering that Darrell's AGI was $100,000 before including any potential loss.

LO 13-2 41. Evelyn has rental income of $48,000 and passive income of $18,000. She also has $148,000 of losses from a real estate rental activity in which she actively participates. Evelyn's AGI is $95,000 before considering this activity. How much rental loss can she deduct against other income sources without regard to the at-risk rules?

LO 13-2 42. Christine died owning an interest in a passive activity property. The property had an adjusted basis of $210,000, a fair market value of $224,000, and suspended losses of $21,000. What can be deducted on her final income tax return?

LO 13-2 43. Judy acquired passive Activity A in January 2012 and Activity B in July 2013. Until 2017 Activity A was profitable. Activity A produced a loss of $50,000 in 2017 and a loss of $75,000 in 2018. She has $45,000 passive income from Activity B in 2017 and $35,000 in 2018. After offsetting passive income, how much of the net losses may she deduct?

LO 13-2 44. This year Robert had the following income and losses from four passive activities:

Activity 1	$(20,000)
Activity 2	(10,000)
Activity 3	(5,000)
Activity 4	33,000

Activity 4 had $10,000 of passive losses that are carried over from a prior year. Robert also had wages of $110,000.

a. How much income or loss does Robert have from the four activities?

b. How are the suspended PALs allocated?

c. If Activity 1 were sold at an $18,000 gain, what would be the total income or loss from the four activities?

LO 13-2 45. Lucy has AGI of $120,000 before considering losses from some rental real estate she owns (she actively participates). She had the following losses from her rental property:

Rental property 1	$(22,000)
Rental property 2	(5,000)

a. How much of the losses can Lucy deduct?

b. If Lucy's AGI before the losses was $90,000, how much of the losses can she deduct?

LO 13-2 46. Julia acquired passive Activity A in January 2013 and passive Activity B in July 2015. Until 2016 Activity A was profitable. Activity A produced a loss of $150,000 in 2016 and a loss of $150,000 in 2017. She had passive income from Activity B of $50,000 in 2016 and $35,000 in 2017. How much of the net passive losses may she deduct in 2016 and 2017, respectively? (Ignore at-risk rules.)

LO 13-3 47. Jackson invested $190,000 in a passive activity five years ago. On January 1, 2015, his at-risk amount in the activity was $45,000. His shares of the income and losses in the activity were $52,000 loss in 2015, $20,000 loss in 2016, and $80,000 gain in 2017. How much can Jackson deduct in 2015 and 2016? What is his taxable income from the activity in 2017? Keep in mind the at-risk rules as well as the passive loss rules.

LO 13-3 48. Hunter has a $38,000 loss from an investment in a partnership in which he does not participate. His basis in the interest is $35,000.

a. How much of the loss is disallowed by the at-risk rules?

b. How much of the loss is disallowed by the passive loss rules?

LO 13-3 49. Reva gave her daughter a passive activity last year that had an adjusted basis of $75,000. The activity had suspended losses of $35,000 and a fair market value of $120,000. In the current year, her daughter realized income of $18,000 from the passive activity. What is the tax effect on Reva and her daughter last year and in the current year?

LO 13-4 50. In 2015, Jerry acquired an interest in a partnership in which he is not a material participant. The partnership was profitable until 2016. Jerry's basis in the partnership interest at the beginning of 2016 was $55,000. In 2016, his share of the partnership loss was $40,000. In 2017, his share of the partnership income was $18,000. How much can Jerry deduct in 2016 and 2017?

EA LO 13-4 51. Benny sells an apartment building. His adjusted basis for regular income tax purposes is $450,000, and it is $475,000 for AMT purposes. He receives $700,000 from the sale.

a. Calculate Benny's gain for regular income tax purposes.

b. Calculate Benny's gain for AMT purposes.

c. Calculate any applicable AMT adjustment.

EA LO 13-4 52. Carson had the following itemized deductions in 2017:

State income taxes	$ 1,500
Charitable contributions	9,900
Mortgage interest (personal residence)	12,000
Medical expenses ($8,000 – [10.0% × $75,000])	500
Miscellaneous ($2,200 – [2% × $75,000])	700

a. What are Carson's itemized deductions for AMT purposes?

b. What is the amount of the AMT adjustment?

EA LO 13-4 53. William is not married, nor does he have any dependents. He does not itemize deductions. His taxable income for 2017 was $87,000. His AMT adjustments totaled $125,000. What is William's AMT for 2017? (*Hint:* Don't forget the personal exemption.)

EA LO 13-4 54. Herbie is the owner of two apartment buildings. Following is information related to the two buildings:

	Date Acquired	Total Cost	Cost Allocated to Land
Building A	3/15/97	$300,000	$40,000
Building B	8/31/04	600,000	95,000

Herbie elected the maximum depreciation available for each asset. What is the effect of depreciation on AMTI for 2017?

EA LO 13-4 55. Clay Company uses the completed contract method on a contract that requires 14 months to complete. The contract is for $750,000 and has estimated costs of $425,000. At the end of 2017, $210,000 of the costs had been incurred. The contract is completed on schedule; however, total costs equal $435,000. What is the amount of AMT adjustments for 2017 and 2018?

EA LO 13-4 56. Arnold exercised an incentive stock option in 2014, acquiring 1,500 shares of stock at an option price of $80 per share. The FMV of the stock at the date of exercise was $110 per share. In 2016, the rights became freely transferable and were not subject to a substantial risk of forfeiture. Arnold sells the shares in 2017 for $165 per share. How do these transactions affect his AMTI in 2014, 2016, and 2017?

EA LO 13-4 57. Barbara is single and owns a home in the city, which is her primary residence. She also owns a cottage at the beach, which she treats as a vacation home. In April 2017, she borrowed $50,000 on a home equity loan and used the proceeds to pay off credit card obligations and other debt. She paid the following in 2017:

Mortgage interest (personal residence)	$15,000
Mortgage interest (cottage)	8,000
Interest on the home equity loan	5,000
Interest on credit card	2,500

Calculate any AMT adjustment concerning interest in 2017.

Tax Return Problems connect

All applicable tax return problems are available with ***Connect***©

Use your tax software to complete the following problems. If you are manually preparing the tax returns, the problem indicates the forms or schedules you will need.

Tax Return Problem 1 Kia Lopez (SSN 412-34-5670) resides at 101 Poker Street, Apt. 12A, Hickory, FL 34714. Her W-2 shows the following:

Wages	$56,500
Federal withholding	6,100
Social security wages	56,500
Social security withholding	3,503
Medicare withholding	819
State withholding	–0–

In 2017, Kia contributed cash of $7,000 to Apartment Rentals Limited Partnership (ARLP) in return for a 13% limited partnership interest. She is an active participant. Kia's shares of ARLP income and losses for the year per her K-1 were as follows:

Interest	$ 35
Dividends (qualified)	290
Capital gains (long-term)	700
Rental loss	(8,300)

ARLP had no liabilities. Kia does not itemize and has no other investments or passive activities.

Prepare Form 1040 for Kia Lopez for 2017. The taxpayer had qualifying health care coverage at all times during the tax year. You will need Form 1040, Schedule E (page 2), Form 6198, and Form 8582.

Tax Return Problem 2 Kurt and Ashley Tallo (SSNs 412-34-5670 and 412-34-5671) reside at 1901 Princess Ave., Park City, UT 84060. Kurt does not work outside the home. Ashley's W-2 shows the following:

Wages	$340,000
Federal withholding	76,800
Social security wages	127,200
Social security withholding	7,886
Medicare withholding	5,740
State withholding	23,800

The Tallos also have the following:

Mortgage interest	$12,600
Charitable contributions	10,000

Kurt and Ashley have four passive activities. They received K-1s from four partnerships with the following income or loss on line 1. They are at-risk in each activity, so the passive loss rules are the only obstacle.

Activity 1	$(40,000)
Activity 2	(20,000)
Activity 3	(10,000)
Activity 4	63,000

Prepare Form 1040 for the Tallos for 2017. The taxpayers had qualifying health care coverage at all times during the tax year. You will need Form 1040, Schedule A, Schedule E (page 2), Form 6251, and Form 8582. Do not compute the underpayment penalty, if any.

Tax Return Problem 3

Nathan is married with two children and has AGI of $405,000. He also has the following AMT adjustments and preferences:

a. Itemized deductions:

Itemized Deduction	Regular Tax	AMT Deduction	AMT Adjustment
Medical after floor	$ 5,375		
Taxes	34,354		
Mortgage interest	14,900		
Charitable contributions	18,000		
Miscellaneous deductions after floor	540		

b. Depreciation of a rental property purchased in August 2007 for $210,000.

c. Depreciation on personal property:

Asset	Date Purchased	Cost	MACRS Life/ AMT	MACRS Depreciation	AMT Depreciation	Adjustment
Computer 1	02/12/13	$ 2,900				
Furniture 1	02/12/13	12,000				

d. Incentive stock option: Nathan exercises options to purchase 1,000 shares at $19 per share when the market value is $26.

Prepare Form 6251 for the calculation of AMT. The regular tax is $79,375.[36]

We have provided selected filled-in source documents that are available in *Connect.*

[36] This regular tax number may vary slightly if software is used to complete this problem. This number was calculated using the tax rate schedules published prior to software and tax table publication dates.

Chapter Fourteen

Partnership Taxation

In this chapter, we discuss taxation of partnerships. As noted earlier in this text, the partnership itself does not pay income tax. However, a partnership must annually report each partner's share of its income or loss and other items on a Schedule K-1. This chapter presents the tax consequences of the partnership entity from formation to liquidation. We also examine Form 1065, the annual information tax return filed by partnerships.

Learning Objectives

When you have completed this chapter, you should understand the following learning objectives (LO):

- **LO 14-1** Explain the rules dealing with the formation of a partnership.
- **LO 14-2** Be able to report partnership ordinary income or loss.
- **LO 14-3** Determine separately stated items.
- **LO 14-4** Calculate partner basis.
- **LO 14-5** Apply the rules for partnership distributions.
- **LO 14-6** Correctly report partnership liquidations and dispositions.

INTRODUCTION

Taxpayers are increasingly using the partnership organizational form for tax purposes. The partnership form allows substantial flexibility in terms of contributions and distributions. A partnership is subject to tax only at the partner level. In contrast to a corporation that pays a corporate tax, and then the individual shareholder is subject to tax on the dividends (double taxation), a partnership's income flows through to its partners, and the partnership pays no income tax at the entity level.

A historic disadvantage of a general partnership has been a lack of limited liability; all general partners were individually liable for partnership actions and liabilities. With the increasing availability of limited liability companies (LLCs), limited liability partnerships (LLPs), and limited partnerships (LPs), all of which are taxed as partnerships for federal purposes and which also limit the liability of at least some partners, this disadvantage has been eliminated. The discussions in this chapter encompass each of these organizational forms under the generic term *partnerships.*

FORMATION OF A PARTNERSHIP

LO 14-1

Generally a partner recognizes no gain or loss on the formation of a partnership.[1] The most common way to form a partnership is for two or more partners (individuals or entities) to contribute cash, property, or services in exchange for a partnership interest.

[1] IRC § 721.

Holding Periods

Chapter 7 discussed the importance of holding periods for § 1231 assets and capital assets. A partnership interest is a capital asset to the partner. Likewise, partners are likely to contribute capital assets, § 1231 assets, and ordinary assets (such as inventory) when forming partnerships. As a general rule, the holding period of the partnership interest includes the partner's holding period for the § 1231 assets and capital assets contributed.[4] If ordinary assets are contributed (such as inventory or accounts receivable), the holding period of the partnership interest begins on the date of the transfer.[5]

The same holding period concept holds true for the partnership. The partnership holding period for the individual assets includes the contributing partner's holding period for § 1231 and capital assets.

EXAMPLE 14-6

Casey contributed the following business assets to CWS Partnership on June 5, 2017:

	Basis	FMV	Date Purchased by Casey
Building	$175,000	$300,000	07/01/09
Inventory	50,000	100,000	05/08/14

The building is a § 1231 asset and has a $175,000 basis to CWS. The building has a long-term holding period to the partnership. Because the inventory is an ordinary asset, its basis is $50,000 with a short-term holding period.[6]

Contribution of Services

Nonrecognition of gain does not apply when a partner receives a partnership interest in exchange for services. When forming a partnership, one or more partners frequently invest capital and other partners perform services in exchange for a partnership interest. A partner providing services recognizes income to the extent of the fair market value of his or her partnership interest.[7]

EXAMPLE 14-7

Russell, Kevin, and David form a partnership. Russell and Kevin are wealthy investors; David is an expert construction contractor. Russell contributes a 20-acre parcel of land, and Kevin contributes cash. David agrees to perform all of the work to develop the land into a high-end subdivision.

	Basis	FMV	Partnership Percentage
Russell's land	$200,000	$300,000	30%
Kevin's cash	300,000	300,000	30
David's services	–0–	–0–	40

David must recognize $240,000 of income in the tax year of formation ($600,000 FMV of assets × 40% partnership interest). In essence, Russell and Kevin are paying David for his future services.

[4] IRC § 1223.

[5] If a mixture of capital assets and ordinary assets is contributed to a partnership, the holding period of the partnership interest should be fragmented into interests with different holding periods. This is an issue only when the partnership interest is disposed of within a year of contribution. See *Aliber v. Commissioner* for more information [52 TCM 1316 (1987)].

[6] The inventory maintains its inventory characteristic (ordinary income property) for five years even if the partnership does not hold it out for sale to customers; see IRC § 724(b).

[7] Reg. § 1.721-1(b).

Example 14-7 is a drastic example that shows how an unknowing service partner may be burdened with a high unexpected tax liability without cash available to pay the bill.

Contributed Property with Liabilities

Complexities arise when a partnership assumes a partner's liability. A partner who is released of a liability is treated as receiving money from the partnership, which reduces his or her partnership basis. If other partners assume a portion of the liability, they are treated as making a money contribution that increases their partnership basis.[8]

EXAMPLE 14-8

Angie contributes an office building to a newly formed partnership for a 25% interest. The building has a $300,000 FMV and a $160,000 basis and is subject to a $100,000 mortgage. The partnership assumes the mortgage. Each of the other three partners contributes $200,000 cash. The partners calculate their basis as follows:

	Angie	Cherie	Bess	Kiley
Beginning basis	$160,000	$200,000	$200,000	$200,000
Plus: Share of liability ($100,000 × 25%)	25,000	25,000	25,000	25,000
Less: Release of liability	(100,000)	–0–	–0–	–0–
Partner basis	$ 85,000	$225,000	$225,000	$225,000

An important point to note is that a partner's basis can *never* go below zero. If the release of liability causes the basis to become negative, the contributing partner must recognize a gain.[9]

EXAMPLE 14-9

Assume the same facts as in Example 14-8 except that the basis of the office building is $45,000. Angie's basis would change as follows:

Beginning basis	$ 45,000
Plus: Share of liability	25,000
Less: Liability release	(100,000)
Liability in excess of basis	(30,000)
Gain recognized by Angie	30,000
Partnership basis	$ –0–

The gain recognized causes the negative basis to return to zero.

In summary, the only time a partner recognizes a gain on partnership formation is upon contributing services or when the partnership assumes a partner's liability in excess of basis.

CONCEPT CHECK 14-1— LO 14-1

1. Generally a partner does not recognize a gain on the formation of a partnership. True or false?
2. Typically the basis of the assets contributed to a partnership is the same in the hands of the partnership as it was in the hands of the contributing partner. True or false?
3. If two taxpayers form a partnership and each has a 50% interest in it, each partner's outside basis must be equal. True or false?
4. A partner does not have to recognize a gain on the receipt of a partnership interest in exchange for services. True or false?
5. A partner who assumes an increased portion of the partnership debt is treated as making a cash contribution, and his or her basis in the partnership increases. True or false?

[8] IRC § 752. The term *money contribution* is used in place of *cash contribution* because the partner is not actually contributing cash but is assuming a liability. However, the effect on basis is the same.

[9] IRC § 731.

PARTNERSHIP ORDINARY INCOME OR LOSS
LO 14-2

Partnership income consists of two components: ordinary income or loss and separately stated items. Both flow through to the individual partners. *Ordinary income or loss* consists of all ordinary income and expense items; *separately stated items* are those that could affect individual partners differently at the partner level.

Ordinary Income or Loss

See Exhibit 14-1 for the five main pages of Form 1065, the annual informational tax return that every partnership must file. Each partnership calculates ordinary income or loss and reports the amount on page 1 of Form 1065. The tax rules used to calculate ordinary income are generally similar to those used by a Schedule C business. All ordinary income items are accumulated and reduced by ordinary and necessary expenses to derive net ordinary income or loss, shown on line 22 of Form 1065. Several partnership expense items require some additional discussion: guaranteed payments to partners, depreciation, and health insurance premiums.

Guaranteed Payments

Partners of a partnership are not employees of the partnership; thus they cannot receive a salary. Partners are owners of the partnership and are considered self-employed individuals (or entities) that have merged together to run a business. *Guaranteed payments* are payments made to partners for services rendered. To qualify as a guaranteed payment, the payment must be calculated without regard to partnership income.[10]

EXAMPLE 14-10

Junius is a 20% partner in the DJ Real Estate partnership. He does substantial work for the partnership and receives $1,000 per month for his services. The $1,000 a month is a guaranteed payment and, as such, the partnership deducts it from ordinary income on line 10. He would include the $12,000 guaranteed payment on page 2 of his Form 1040, Schedule E.

EXAMPLE 14-11

Donna is an 80% partner in the DJ Real Estate partnership. She also works for the partnership and receives a monthly payment of 50% of the net income for the month. Because Donna's payment is calculated *with regard to partnership income,* it is *not* considered a guaranteed payment, and the partnership cannot take a deduction for the payment.

Guaranteed payments are the only items that are reported both as a deduction for ordinary income and as a separately stated item (discussed in the next section).

TAX YOUR BRAIN

Refer to Examples 14-10 and 14-11. How can Junius and Donna, partners in the same partnership, be treated differently? Donna is an 80% partner in the business but receives only 50% of the net income.

ANSWER

This is one of the benefits of the partnership form. Due to the flexibility of a partnership agreement, the partners can receive the returns of the business in any way they agree upon. In Examples 14-10 and 14-11, Junius may get a flat fee because he works a fixed number of hours in the office, whereas Donna is the sales agent and makes her money based on the sales she makes. How Donna and Junius share the net income at the end of the year is based on their agreement, but in this example it is likely to be 80% to Donna and 20% to Junius. He, however, is guaranteed $12,000 per year no matter the partnership income or loss.

[10] IRC § 707(c).

EXHIBIT 14-1

Form **1065** Department of the Treasury Internal Revenue Service

U.S. Return of Partnership Income

For calendar year 2017, or tax year beginning ______, 2017, ending ______, 20 ____.

▶ Go to *www.irs.gov/Form1065* for instructions and the latest information.

OMB No. 1545-0123 **2017**

	Type or Print	
A Principal business activity	Name of partnership	D Employer identification number
B Principal product or service	Number, street, and room or suite no. If a P.O. box, see the instructions.	E Date business started
C Business code number	City or town, state or province, country, and ZIP or foreign postal code	F Total assets (see the instructions) $

G Check applicable boxes: (1) ☐ Initial return (2) ☐ Final return (3) ☐ Name change (4) ☐ Address change (5) ☐ Amended return
(6) ☐ Technical termination - also check (1) or (2)

H Check accounting method: (1) ☐ Cash (2) ☐ Accrual (3) ☐ Other (specify) ▶

I Number of Schedules K-1. Attach one for each person who was a partner at any time during the tax year ▶

J Check if Schedules C and M-3 are attached ☐

Caution. *Include **only** trade or business income and expenses on lines 1a through 22 below. See the instructions for more information.*

Income	1a	Gross receipts or sales	1a	
	b	Returns and allowances	1b	
	c	Balance. Subtract line 1b from line 1a		1c
	2	Cost of goods sold (attach Form 1125-A)		2
	3	Gross profit. Subtract line 2 from line 1c		3
	4	Ordinary income (loss) from other partnerships, estates, and trusts (attach statement)		4
	5	Net farm profit (loss) (attach Schedule F (Form 1040))		5
	6	Net gain (loss) from Form 4797, Part II, line 17 (attach Form 4797)		6
	7	Other income (loss) (attach statement)		7
	8	**Total income (loss).** Combine lines 3 through 7		8
Deductions (see the instructions for limitations)	9	Salaries and wages (other than to partners) (less employment credits)		9
	10	Guaranteed payments to partners		10
	11	Repairs and maintenance		11
	12	Bad debts		12
	13	Rent		13
	14	Taxes and licenses		14
	15	Interest		15
	16a	Depreciation (if required, attach Form 4562)	16a	
	b	Less depreciation reported on Form 1125-A and elsewhere on return	16b	16c
	17	Depletion **(Do not deduct oil and gas depletion.)**		17
	18	Retirement plans, etc.		18
	19	Employee benefit programs		19
	20	Other deductions (attach statement)		20
	21	**Total deductions.** Add the amounts shown in the far right column for lines 9 through 20		21
	22	**Ordinary business income (loss).** Subtract line 21 from line 8		22

Sign Here

Under penalties of perjury, I declare that I have examined this return, including accompanying schedules and statements, and to the best of my knowledge and belief, it is true, correct, and complete. Declaration of preparer (other than partner or limited liability company member) is based on all information of which preparer has any knowledge.

▶ Signature of partner or limited liability company member ▶ Date

May the IRS discuss this return with the preparer shown below (see instructions)? ☐ Yes ☐ No

Paid Preparer Use Only

Print/Type preparer's name	Preparer's signature	Date	Check ☐ if self-employed	PTIN
Firm's name ▶			Firm's EIN ▶	
Firm's address ▶			Phone no.	

For Paperwork Reduction Act Notice, see separate instructions. Cat. No. 11390Z Form **1065** (2017)

Source: U.S. Department of the Treasury, Internal Revenue Service, Form 1065. Washington, DC: 2017.

(continued)

EXHIBIT 14-1 *(continued)*

Form 1065 (2017) Page **2**

Schedule B Other Information

		Yes	No
1	What type of entity is filing this return? Check the applicable box: **a** ☐ Domestic general partnership **b** ☐ Domestic limited partnership **c** ☐ Domestic limited liability company **d** ☐ Domestic limited liability partnership **e** ☐ Foreign partnership **f** ☐ Other ▶		
2	At any time during the tax year, was any partner in the partnership a disregarded entity, a partnership (including an entity treated as a partnership), a trust, an S corporation, an estate (other than an estate of a deceased partner), or a nominee or similar person?		
3	At the end of the tax year:		
a	Did any foreign or domestic corporation, partnership (including any entity treated as a partnership), trust, or tax-exempt organization, or any foreign government own, directly or indirectly, an interest of 50% or more in the profit, loss, or capital of the partnership? For rules of constructive ownership, see instructions. If "Yes," attach Schedule B-1, Information on Partners Owning 50% or More of the Partnership		
b	Did any individual or estate own, directly or indirectly, an interest of 50% or more in the profit, loss, or capital of the partnership? For rules of constructive ownership, see instructions. If "Yes," attach Schedule B-1, Information on Partners Owning 50% or More of the Partnership		
4	At the end of the tax year, did the partnership:		
a	Own directly 20% or more, or own, directly or indirectly, 50% or more of the total voting power of all classes of stock entitled to vote of any foreign or domestic corporation? For rules of constructive ownership, see instructions. If "Yes," complete (i) through (iv) below		

(i) Name of Corporation	**(ii)** Employer Identification Number (if any)	**(iii)** Country of Incorporation	**(iv)** Percentage Owned in Voting Stock

		Yes	No
b	Own directly an interest of 20% or more, or own, directly or indirectly, an interest of 50% or more in the profit, loss, or capital in any foreign or domestic partnership (including an entity treated as a partnership) or in the beneficial interest of a trust? For rules of constructive ownership, see instructions. If "Yes," complete (i) through (v) below		

(i) Name of Entity	**(ii)** Employer Identification Number (if any)	**(iii)** Type of Entity	**(iv)** Country of Organization	**(v)** Maximum Percentage Owned in Profit, Loss, or Capital

		Yes	No
5	Did the partnership file Form 8893, Election of Partnership Level Tax Treatment, or an election statement under section 6231(a)(1)(B)(ii) for partnership-level tax treatment, that is in effect for this tax year? See Form 8893 for more details		
6	Does the partnership satisfy **all four** of the following conditions?		
a	The partnership's total receipts for the tax year were less than $250,000.		
b	The partnership's total assets at the end of the tax year were less than $1 million.		
c	Schedules K-1 are filed with the return and furnished to the partners on or before the due date (including extensions) for the partnership return.		
d	The partnership is not filing and is not required to file Schedule M-3 If "Yes," the partnership is not required to complete Schedules L, M-1, and M-2; Item F on page 1 of Form 1065; or Item L on Schedule K-1.		
7	Is this partnership a publicly traded partnership as defined in section 469(k)(2)?		
8	During the tax year, did the partnership have any debt that was cancelled, was forgiven, or had the terms modified so as to reduce the principal amount of the debt?		
9	Has this partnership filed, or is it required to file, Form 8918, Material Advisor Disclosure Statement, to provide information on any reportable transaction?		
10	At any time during calendar year 2017, did the partnership have an interest in or a signature or other authority over a financial account in a foreign country (such as a bank account, securities account, or other financial account)? See the instructions for exceptions and filing requirements for FinCEN Form 114, Report of Foreign Bank and Financial Accounts (FBAR). If "Yes," enter the name of the foreign country. ▶		

Form **1065** (2017)

EXHIBIT 14-1 *(continued)*

Form 1065 (2017) Page **3**

Schedule B Other Information *(continued)*

		Yes	No
11	At any time during the tax year, did the partnership receive a distribution from, or was it the grantor of, or transferor to, a foreign trust? If "Yes," the partnership may have to file Form 3520, Annual Return To Report Transactions With Foreign Trusts and Receipt of Certain Foreign Gifts. See instructions		
12a	Is the partnership making, or had it previously made (and not revoked), a section 754 election? . . . . See instructions for details regarding a section 754 election.		
b	Did the partnership make for this tax year an optional basis adjustment under section 743(b) or 734(b)? If "Yes," attach a statement showing the computation and allocation of the basis adjustment. See instructions		
c	Is the partnership required to adjust the basis of partnership assets under section 743(b) or 734(b) because of a substantial built-in loss (as defined under section 743(d)) or substantial basis reduction (as defined under section 734(d))? If "Yes," attach a statement showing the computation and allocation of the basis adjustment. See instructions		
13	Check this box if, during the current or prior tax year, the partnership distributed any property received in a like-kind exchange or contributed such property to another entity (other than disregarded entities wholly owned by the partnership throughout the tax year) . . . . ▶ ☐		
14	At any time during the tax year, did the partnership distribute to any partner a tenancy-in-common or other undivided interest in partnership property?		
15	If the partnership is required to file Form 8858, Information Return of U.S. Persons With Respect To Foreign Disregarded Entities, enter the number of Forms 8858 attached. See instructions ▶		
16	Does the partnership have any foreign partners? If "Yes," enter the number of Forms 8805, Foreign Partner's Information Statement of Section 1446 Withholding Tax, filed for this partnership. ▶		
17	Enter the number of Forms 8865, Return of U.S. Persons With Respect to Certain Foreign Partnerships, attached to this return. ▶		
18a	Did you make any payments in 2017 that would require you to file Form(s) 1099? See instructions		
b	If "Yes," did you or will you file required Form(s) 1099?		
19	Enter the number of Form(s) 5471, Information Return of U.S. Persons With Respect To Certain Foreign Corporations, attached to this return. ▶		
20	Enter the number of partners that are foreign governments under section 892. ▶		
21	During the partnership's tax year, did the partnership make any payments that would require it to file Form 1042 and 1042-S under chapter 3 (sections 1441 through 1464) or chapter 4 (sections 1471 through 1474)?		
22	Was the partnership a specified domestic entity required to file Form 8938 for the tax year (See the Instructions for Form 8938)?		

Designation of Tax Matters Partner (see instructions)

Enter below the general partner or member-manager designated as the tax matters partner (TMP) for the tax year of this return:

Name of designated TMP ▶ Identifying number of TMP ▶

If the TMP is an entity, name of TMP representative ▶ Phone number of TMP ▶

Address of designated TMP ▶

Form **1065** (2017)

(continued)

EXHIBIT 14-1 *(continued)*

Form 1065 (2017) Page 4

DRAFT AS OF August 16, 2017 DO NOT FILE

Schedule K **Partners' Distributive Share Items**

Section	Line	Description			Line	Total amount
Income (Loss)	1	Ordinary business income (loss) (page 1, line 22)			1	
	2	Net rental real estate income (loss) (attach Form 8825)			2	
	3a	Other gross rental income (loss)	3a			
	b	Expenses from other rental activities (attach statement)	3b			
	c	Other net rental income (loss). Subtract line 3b from line 3a			3c	
	4	Guaranteed payments			4	
	5	Interest income			5	
	6	Dividends: a Ordinary dividends			6a	
		b Qualified dividends	6b			
	7	Royalties			7	
	8	Net short-term capital gain (loss) (attach Schedule D (Form 1065))			8	
	9a	Net long-term capital gain (loss) (attach Schedule D (Form 1065))			9a	
	b	Collectibles (28%) gain (loss)	9b			
	c	Unrecaptured section 1250 gain (attach statement)	9c			
	10	Net section 1231 gain (loss) (attach Form 4797)			10	
	11	Other income (loss) (see instructions) Type ▶			11	
Deductions	12	Section 179 deduction (attach Form 4562)			12	
	13a	Contributions			13a	
	b	Investment interest expense			13b	
	c	Section 59(e)(2) expenditures: (1) Type ▶	(2) Amount ▶		13c(2)	
	d	Other deductions (see instructions) Type ▶			13d	
Self-Employment	14a	Net earnings (loss) from self-employment			14a	
	b	Gross farming or fishing income			14b	
	c	Gross nonfarm income			14c	
Credits	15a	Low-income housing credit (section 42(j)(5))			15a	
	b	Low-income housing credit (other)			15b	
	c	Qualified rehabilitation expenditures (rental real estate) (attach Form 3468, if applicable)			15c	
	d	Other rental real estate credits (see instructions) Type ▶			15d	
	e	Other rental credits (see instructions) Type ▶			15e	
	f	Other credits (see instructions) Type ▶			15f	
Foreign Transactions	16a	Name of country or U.S. possession ▶				
	b	Gross income from all sources			16b	
	c	Gross income sourced at partner level			16c	
		Foreign gross income sourced at partnership level				
	d	Passive category ▶	e General category ▶	f Other ▶	16f	
		Deductions allocated and apportioned at partner level				
	g	Interest expense ▶	h Other ▶		16h	
		Deductions allocated and apportioned at partnership level to foreign source income				
	i	Passive category ▶	j General category ▶	k Other ▶	16k	
	l	Total foreign taxes (check one): ▶ Paid ☐ Accrued ☐			16l	
	m	Reduction in taxes available for credit (attach statement)			16m	
	n	Other foreign tax information (attach statement)				
Alternative Minimum Tax (AMT) Items	17a	Post-1986 depreciation adjustment			17a	
	b	Adjusted gain or loss			17b	
	c	Depletion (other than oil and gas)			17c	
	d	Oil, gas, and geothermal properties—gross income			17d	
	e	Oil, gas, and geothermal properties—deductions			17e	
	f	Other AMT items (attach statement)			17f	
Other Information	18a	Tax-exempt interest income			18a	
	b	Other tax-exempt income			18b	
	c	Nondeductible expenses			18c	
	19a	Distributions of cash and marketable securities			19a	
	b	Distributions of other property			19b	
	20a	Investment income			20a	
	b	Investment expenses			20b	
	c	Other items and amounts (attach statement)				

Form **1065** (2017)

EXHIBIT 14-1 *(concluded)*

Form 1065 (2017) Page **5**

Analysis of Net Income (Loss)

1	Net income (loss). Combine Schedule K, lines 1 through 11. From the result, subtract the sum of Schedule K, lines 12 through 13d, and 16l					1	
2	Analysis by partner type:	(i) Corporate	(ii) Individual (active)	(iii) Individual (passive)	(iv) Partnership	(v) Exempt Organization	(vi) Nominee/Other
a	General partners						
b	Limited partners						

DRAFT AS OF August 16, 2017 DO NOT FILE

Schedule L **Balance Sheets per Books**

	Assets	Beginning of tax year (a)	(b)	End of tax year (c)	(d)
1	Cash				
2a	Trade notes and accounts receivable				
b	Less allowance for bad debts				
3	Inventories				
4	U.S. government obligations				
5	Tax-exempt securities				
6	Other current assets (attach statement)				
7a	Loans to partners (or persons related to partners)				
b	Mortgage and real estate loans				
8	Other investments (attach statement)				
9a	Buildings and other depreciable assets				
b	Less accumulated depreciation				
10a	Depletable assets				
b	Less accumulated depletion				
11	Land (net of any amortization)				
12a	Intangible assets (amortizable only)				
b	Less accumulated amortization				
13	Other assets (attach statement)				
14	Total assets				
	Liabilities and Capital				
15	Accounts payable				
16	Mortgages, notes, bonds payable in less than 1 year				
17	Other current liabilities (attach statement)				
18	All nonrecourse loans				
19a	Loans from partners (or persons related to partners)				
b	Mortgages, notes, bonds payable in 1 year or more				
20	Other liabilities (attach statement)				
21	Partners' capital accounts				
22	Total liabilities and capital				

Schedule M-1 **Reconciliation of Income (Loss) per Books With Income (Loss) per Return**
Note. The partnership may be required to file Schedule M-3 (see instructions).

1	Net income (loss) per books		6	Income recorded on books this year not included on Schedule K, lines 1 through 11 (itemize):	
2	Income included on Schedule K, lines 1, 2, 3c, 5, 6a, 7, 8, 9a, 10, and 11, not recorded on books this year (itemize):		a	Tax-exempt interest $	
3	Guaranteed payments (other than health insurance)		7	Deductions included on Schedule K, lines 1 through 13c, and 16l, not charged against book income this year (itemize):	
4	Expenses recorded on books this year not included on Schedule K, lines 1 through 13d, and 16l (itemize):		a	Depreciation $	
a	Depreciation $		8	Add lines 6 and 7	
b	Travel and entertainment $		9	Income (loss) (Analysis of Net Income (Loss), line 1). Subtract line 8 from line 5	
5	Add lines 1 through 4				

Schedule M-2 **Analysis of Partners' Capital Accounts**

1	Balance at beginning of year		6	Distributions: a Cash	
2	Capital contributed: a Cash			b Property	
	b Property		7	Other decreases (itemize):	
3	Net income (loss) per books				
4	Other increases (itemize):		8	Add lines 6 and 7	
5	Add lines 1 through 4		9	Balance at end of year. Subtract line 8 from line 5	

Form **1065** (2017)

Depreciation

A partnership calculates depreciation following the same rules as a sole proprietorship using Schedule C. Form 4562 must be completed and attached. One major exception concerns the § 179 expense deduction. A partnership can use the § 179 expense deduction, but the deduction cannot reduce the partnership ordinary income. § 179 expense must be reported separately to each partner.

TAX YOUR BRAIN

Why must § 179 expense be reported separately to each partner?

ANSWER

If you recall from Chapter 6, each individual is allowed to deduct a maximum of $510,000 of § 179 expense in tax year 2017. If the partnership deducts the § 179 expense and does not separately state it to partners, an individual could set up numerous partnerships for his or her businesses and, effectively, have an unlimited § 179 expense (up to $510,000 for each partnership).

Partner Health Premiums

Most employees can exclude from income the cost of employer-provided health and accident insurance. For employees of a partnership, this is certainly the case. However, because partners are not employees, partners cannot exclude from income the cost of their health insurance premiums paid by the partnership. The partnership treats the premiums as guaranteed payments to the partner, and the partner can deduct the premiums as a *for* AGI deduction on Form 1040.

CONCEPT CHECK 14-2— LO 14-2

1. A partnership can deduct which of the following in determining partnership ordinary income or loss?
   a. All ordinary and necessary expenses.
   b. Guaranteed payments.
   c. Depreciation.
   d. All of the above.
2. What tax form is a partnership required to file each year?
   a. Form 1120.
   b. Form 1040.
   c. Form 1065.
   d. Form 1120S.
3. A payment made to a partner that is calculated without regard to partnership income is a
   a. Partner salary.
   b. Partner withdrawal.
   c. Loan to a partner.
   d. Guaranteed payment.

SEPARATELY STATED ITEMS
LO 14-3

As noted earlier, a partnership must allocate income and expense items between ordinary items and separately stated items. The general rule regarding income and expense items of a partnership and their classification follows:

> All income and expense items of a partnership that may be treated differently at the partner level must be separately stated.

TABLE 14-1
Common Partnership Ordinary and Separately Stated Items

Ordinary Items (page 1, Form 1065)	Separately Stated Items (Schedule K, page 4, Form 1065)
Gross profit	Net income from rental real estate
Ordinary income from Form 4797	Net income from other rentals
Salary and wages (nonpartners)	Interest income
Guaranteed payments (partners)	Guaranteed payments (partners)
Repairs and maintenance	Dividends
Bad debts	Royalty income
Rent	Capital gains and losses
Taxes and licenses	§ 1231 gains and losses
Interest	Charitable contributions
Depreciation	§ 179 expense
Retirement plans	Tax credits
Employee benefits	AMT adjustments and preferences
Other ordinary and necessary expenses	

Table 14-1 lists the most common ordinary items and separately stated items.

Form 1065, Schedule K (page 4), lists the partners' shares of income, credits, and deductions. Schedule K is the total for all partners, whereas Schedule K-1 (discussed later) provides the individual partner's share of each item.

TAX YOUR BRAIN

Why are items such as rental loss or capital gains separately stated?

ANSWER

Rental losses are passive activities. One partner may have rental income or other passive income to offset the losses whereas another partner may not. Thus the rental loss from the partnership could be treated differently from partner to partner. Likewise, an individual partner receives preferential tax treatment for capital gains. A corporate partner, in the same partnership, receives no preferential treatment and can deduct capital losses only to the extent of capital gains. Again, the different tax treatment at the partner level mandates that these items be separately reported to the partners.

Allocations to Partners (Schedule K-1)

Every year, each partner in a partnership must receive a Schedule K-1 (shown in Exhibit 14-2), which reports the partner's share of ordinary income or loss and each separately stated item. Section J of the K-1 shows the partner's percentage share of profit, loss, and ownership. Notice that the line items on the K-1 correspond directly to the line items on Schedule K of Form 1065. The summation (line 1, for example) of all the K-1s, whether for 2 or 5,000 partners, should equal the total on Schedule K. In the majority of cases, the allocation to the partner is the year-end percentage multiplied by the total amount for each item on Schedule K (page 4 of Form 1065).[11] This calculation differs if changes in ownership occurred during the year or special allocations are made between the partners.

[11] This is not always the case. One of the benefits of the partnership form is flexibility in the allocations. Allocations are based on the partnership agreement, and as long as the agreement has substantial economic effect, the allocations can vary. *Substantial economic effect* basically means that tax minimization is not the only reason for the allocation. Complete coverage of substantial economic effect is beyond the scope of this text.

EXHIBIT 14-2

651117

☐ Final K-1 ☐ Amended K-1 OMB No. 1545-0123

Schedule K-1 (Form 1065) **2017**

Department of the Treasury
Internal Revenue Service

For calendar year 2017, or tax year

beginning / / 2017 ending / /

Partner's Share of Income, Deductions, Credits, etc. ► See back of form and separate instructions.

Part I Information About the Partnership

A Partnership's employer identification number
22-7892345

B Partnership's name, address, city, state, and ZIP code
W&J Woodworking
2155 Playground Ave
Kinston, NC 23849

C IRS Center where partnership filed return
Cincinnati, OH

D ☐ Check if this is a publicly traded partnership (PTP)

Part II Information About the Partner

E Partner's identifying number
412-34-5670

F Partner's name, address, city, state, and ZIP code
Luleng Wu
118 Nail Road
Kinston, NC 23849

G ☒ General partner or LLC member-manager ☐ Limited partner or other LLC member

H ☒ Domestic partner ☐ Foreign partner

I1 What type of entity is this partner? Individual

I2 If this partner is a retirement plan (IRA/SEP/Keogh/etc.), check here ☐

J Partner's share of profit, loss, and capital (see instructions):

	Beginning	Ending
Profit	%	40 %
Loss	%	40 %
Capital	%	40 %

K Partner's share of liabilities at year end:

Nonrecourse	$
Qualified nonrecourse financing	$ 26,300
Recourse	$ 43,000

L Partner's capital account analysis:

Beginning capital account	$ 116,900
Capital contributed during the year	$
Current year increase (decrease)	$ 76,000
Withdrawals & distributions	$ (20,000)
Ending capital account	$ 172,900

☒ Tax basis ☐ GAAP ☐ Section 704(b) book
☐ Other (explain)

M Did the partner contribute property with a built-in gain or loss?
☐ Yes ☒ No
If "Yes," attach statement (see instructions)

Part III Partner's Share of Current Year Income, Deductions, Credits, and Other Items

1	Ordinary business income (loss)		60,540
2	Net rental real estate income (loss)		
3	Other net rental income (loss)		
4	Guaranteed payments		42,000
5	Interest income		
6a	Ordinary dividends		1,110
6b	Qualified dividends		1,110
7	Royalties		
8	Net short-term capital gain (loss)		440
9a	Net long-term capital gain (loss)		600
9b	Collectibles (28%) gain (loss)		
9c	Unrecaptured section 1250 gain		
10	Net section 1231 gain (loss)		105
11	Other income (loss)	A	2,600
12	Section 179 deduction		
13	Other deductions		
14	Self-employment earnings (loss)	A	91,940
15	Credits		
16	Foreign transactions		
17	Alternative minimum tax (AMT) items		
18	Tax-exempt income and nondeductible expenses		
19	Distributions		
20	Other information		

*See attached statement for additional information.

For IRS Use Only

For Paperwork Reduction Act Notice, see Instructions for Form 1065. www.irs.gov/Form1065 Cat. No. 11394R Schedule K-1 (Form 1065) 2017

Source: U.S. Department of the Treasury, Internal Revenue Service, Schedule K-1 (Form 1065). Washington, DC: 2017.

EXAMPLE 14-12

Knox is a partner in Knox, Smith, & Wood partnership. He owned 33.3% from January 1, 2017, to March 31, 2017, when he bought Smith's 33.3% interest. He owned 66.6% for the rest of the year. The partnership had $76,000 of ordinary income and $8,000 in long-term capital gains. Barring any special allocations in a partnership agreement, Knox's share of the income items follows:

Ordinary income	$76,000 × 33.3% × 3/12 =	$ 6,333*
	$76,000 × 66.6% × 9/12 =	38,000
Ordinary income allocated to Knox		$44,333
Capital gain	$8,000 × 33.3% × 3/12 =	$ 667
	$8,000 × 66.6% × 9/12 =	4,000
Capital gain allocated to Knox		$ 4,667

* Use of expanded decimal places reduces rounding errors.

Self-Employment Income

Another important item affecting a partner is self-employment income. As we have mentioned, a partner is not an employee of a partnership and, thus, must consider income from the partnership to be self-employment income. In Chapter 6, we noted that a self-employed individual must pay 15.3% of self-employment tax on the first $127,200 of self-employment income (wages in excess of $118,500 will be subject only to the Medicare rate of 2.9%). Normally, only ordinary income and guaranteed payments are included as self-employment income from the partnership.[12] Table 14-2 illustrates the basic computation of self-employment income using the information on the Schedule K-1 in Exhibit 14-2.

The partnership reports self-employment income to the partner on line 14 of Schedule K-1. The sum of all the partners' self-employment income should equal the total self-employment income on Form 1065, Schedule K, line 14a.

TABLE 14-2
Calculation of Self-Employment Income from a Partnership

1. Ordinary income from Schedule K-1, line 1	$ 60,540
2. Plus: Any guaranteed payments from Schedule K-1, line 4	42,000
3. Less: Any § 1231 gain included in ordinary income	–0–
4. Less: Any § 179 expense from Schedule K-1, line 12	(10,600)
Self-employment income Schedule K-1, line 14	$ 91,940

TAX YOUR BRAIN

Why are items such as dividends, capital gains, and royalty income not included in self-employment income? Likewise, why do charitable contributions not reduce self-employment income?

ANSWER

Only income and expenses from the operations of the partnership are included. Dividends, capital gains, and royalty income are not included as self-employment income because they are investment income. The partnership is just a conduit for the partners' charitable contributions.

CONCEPT CHECK 14-3— LO 14-3

1. Why are items such as rental income/loss, capital gains/losses, and charitable contributions that flow through a partnership treated as separately stated?
2. Why is income from a partnership treated as self-employment income?

[12] Rental of real estate may be included in self-employment income if the property is held for sale to customers in the course of a trade or business as a real estate dealer or if the rental income is for rentals for which service is rendered to the occupants (such as a bed and breakfast).

BASIS OF THE PARTNERSHIP INTEREST
LO 14-4

A partner's basis in his or her partnership interest changes over time. It is extremely important to continue to recalculate basis for various reasons. For example, a partner must use the basis to determine any gain or loss on the sale or disposal of the interest, to determine the basis of property distributed from the partnership, and to determine whether losses from the partnership are deductible (see the at-risk rules in Chapter 13). Table 14-3 summarizes the process to calculate a partner's basis.[13]

Although it is advisable to keep a running total of a partner's basis each year, the basis calculation is mandatory at the following times:

1. In a year the partnership had a loss.
2. At the liquidation or disposition of a partner's interest.
3. In a year a partner receives nonliquidating distributions.

Increases and Decreases in Partnership Basis

Table 14-3 notes that the partner's share of separately stated items increases or decreases his or her basis. Do separately stated income items such as tax-exempt income increase basis? Do separately stated nondeductible loss or deduction items (such as life insurance premiums) decrease basis? The answers are yes. All income/gain or expense/loss items increase or decrease outside basis.

TAX YOUR BRAIN

Why do tax-exempt and nondeductible items increase or decrease basis?

ANSWER

If these items do not increase or decrease a partner's basis (outside basis), they will have a tax effect when the partnership interest is sold or disposed of. For example, if a partner's share of tax-exempt interest is $500, that $500 should never be taxed. If the partner's basis does not increase by $500, the partnership basis will be $500 lower. When the interest is sold, $500 in additional gain will be recognized. Thus the tax-exempt interest income will effectively be taxed. The same concept applies to nondeductible items but in the opposite direction.

There is a specific sequence to the basis adjustments. The order of adjustment follows:

1. Basis is first increased and decreased by all adjustments except for losses.
2. The adjustment is reduced by money distributed (including release of liabilities).
3. The adjustment is reduced by the basis of any property distributed.

TABLE 14-3
Basis of the Partnership Interest

Starting basis = Basis of property contributed + FMV of services rendered (or cost if partnership interest was purchased)*
Plus: Basis of property contributions after formation (cash or property)
Plus: Partner's share of partnership ordinary income
Plus: Partner's share of separately stated income or gain items
Plus: Partner's share in partnership liabilities
Less: Basis of property distributed (cash or property—but not below zero)
Less: Partner's share of partnership ordinary loss (but not below zero)
Less: Partner's share of separately stated loss/expense items
Less: Partner's release of partnership liabilities

* A partnership interest could be inherited or received by gift as well. If the interest is inherited, the beginning partnership basis is the FMV at the date of death of the decedent. The gift basis is typically the donor's basis plus any gift tax paid on the appreciation.

[13] IRC § 705(a).

The basis that remains is used for the determination of any deductible losses from the partnership.

EXAMPLE 14-13

Partner Allison has a basis of $5,000 in a partnership at the beginning of the year. She receives $3,000 in cash distributions, her distributive share of income is $2,500, and she receives a land distribution with a basis of $4,000 (FMV $10,000).

Beginning basis	$5,000
Share of income	2,500
Cash distribution	(3,000)
Land distribution	(4,000)
Year-end basis	$ 500

EXAMPLE 14-14

Use the information on the Schedule K-1 shown in Exhibit 14-2. If Luleng Wu's partnership basis at the beginning of 2017 was $22,000, calculate his basis at the end of 2017.

Beginning basis	$22,000
Share of ordinary income	60,540
Share of dividends	1,110
Share of short-term capital gains	440
Share of long-term capital gains	600
Share of net § 1231 gain	105
Charitable contributions	(2,600)
Section 179 expense	(10,600)
Wu's ending basis	$71,595

Notice in Example 14-14 and Table 14-3 that guaranteed payments are *not* used in the basis calculation. Typically, guaranteed payments do not have an impact on basis. The partner recognizes income from the guaranteed payment but receives a payment for the exact amount. Thus the increase (income recognized) and the decrease (cash distribution) exactly cancel out.[14]

Liabilities

In Example 14-14, you may have noticed that we did not include any liabilities in the basis even though the partner's Schedule K-1 clearly shows the partner's share of liabilities in Section K. In practice, most tax preparers calculate basis but ignore the liability implications. In most cases, liabilities are considered only if the increase in basis is necessary to deduct a loss from the partnership. The primary reason for this common practice is that the liability level of the partnership is consistently changing, and most of the time the calculation is simply not necessary.

EXAMPLE 14-15

Using the same facts as in Example 14-14, we calculate the ending basis including liabilities as follows:

Ending basis	$ 71,595
Qualified nonrecourse	26,300
Other debt	43,000
Total basis including liabilities	$140,895

[14] One instance in which this is not the case occurs when a partner receives a capital interest for services to the partnership. Income is recognized as a guaranteed payment but no cash payment is made. The partner's basis is increased in this instance.

CONCEPT CHECK 14-4— LO 14-4

1. A partner must use basis to determine the gain or loss on a sale of the partnership interest and to determine whether losses are deductible. True or false?
2. A partner's basis is not increased by his or her share of tax-exempt income items. True or false?
3. In the calculation of basis, the order of the basis adjustments is not important. True or false?
4. A partner's basis is never increased by his or her share of recourse liabilities. True or false?

PARTNERSHIP DISTRIBUTIONS LO 14-5

One of the convenient features of a partnership is flexibility concerning distributions. As a general rule, a partner recognizes no gain or loss on a nonliquidating distribution.[15]

EXAMPLE 14-16

Davis, a 50% partner in ABCD partnership, has a basis of $85,000 in his partnership interest. He receives a cash distribution of $84,000 at year-end. Davis recognizes no gain or loss on the distribution but reduces his basis to $1,000.

TAX YOUR BRAIN

Why does the IRS allow the tax-free distribution in Example 14-16?

ANSWER

For Davis to have a predistribution basis of $85,000, he would have made past contributions or have been taxed on income to increase his basis. Therefore, he is receiving either a distribution of previously taxed income or a distribution of his own capital, neither of which is taxed. This is a significant advantage of the partnership form over the corporate form. A distribution from a corporation is usually considered a taxable dividend.

Gain on Current Distributions

The two exceptions to the general rule of no gain or loss on current distributions follow

1. When money or marketable securities are distributed in excess of the partner's basis, a gain is recognized to the extent of the excess.[16]
2. The current distribution triggers a precontribution gain.[17]

Basis can never go below zero. Thus if money or marketable securities (cashlike assets) exceed the partner's basis, the partner recognizes the excess as a capital gain.[18]

EXAMPLE 14-17

Assume the same facts as in Example 14-16. If Davis received a cash distribution of $86,000, he must recognize a $1,000 capital gain. After the distribution and recognized gain, he would have a zero basis in the partnership at year-end.

A precontribution gain occurs when a partner contributes appreciated property to a partnership and, within seven years, the partnership distributes the same property to another partner. In essence, the contributing partner is selling the property to the distributing partner and attempting to eliminate the gain by passing it through the partnership. If the contributed property is distributed to another partner within the seven-year time frame, the contributing partner recognizes the deferred gain.

[15] IRC § 731.

[16] Remember that *money* in this case refers to cash distributions and the release of liabilities.

[17] IRC § 737.

[18] IRC § 741.

EXAMPLE 14-18

Bailey contributes land to a partnership with a basis of $8,000 and an FMV of $12,000 in 2015. In 2017, when the FMV of the land is $14,000, the partnership distributes the land to Jessica, another partner. The distribution triggers a precontribution gain of $4,000 to Bailey. Jessica has no gain or loss on the distribution and would have a basis of $12,000 in the land ($8,000 carryover basis plus the $4,000 gain recognized by Bailey).

Basis of Distributed Property

When property is distributed to a partner from a partnership, neither the partner nor the partnership recognizes any gain. The basis and the holding period of the distributed property carry over to the partner.[19] Hence the partner steps into the shoes of the partnership. The only exception to the carryover basis rule occurs when the basis in the distributed property exceeds the basis in the partnership interest. The basis of the distributed property is limited to the basis of the partnership interest. Recall that the partner recognizes a gain only if the distribution exceeds basis and the distribution consists only of money and marketable securities.[20]

EXAMPLE 14-19

Fonda has a partnership basis of $6,000. She receives, from the partnership, a distribution of equipment with a basis to the partnership of $8,000 and an FMV of $5,000. The basis in the equipment to Fonda after the distribution is limited to her basis in the partnership of $6,000. Fonda recognizes no gain or loss and has a zero basis in her partnership interest after the distribution.

EXAMPLE 14-20

Assume the same facts as in Example 14-19 except that Fonda receives a $2,000 cash distribution and the equipment. In this case, she would first reduce her partnership basis by the $2,000 cash distribution. Fonda still does not recognize any gain but now has a basis of $4,000 in the equipment.

CONCEPT CHECK 14-5— LO 14-5

1. Which of the following is true concerning the recognition of gain on a distribution from a partnership?
   a. Gain is recognized if the partner receives property with a basis higher than his or her partnership interest basis.
   b. Gain is recognized if the partner receives cash in excess of his or her basis.
   c. The partner never recognizes a gain on a partnership distribution.
   d. The partner always recognizes a gain on a partnership distribution.
2. Nelson has a partnership basis of $12,000. He receives, from the partnership, a distribution of furniture with a basis to the partnership of $16,000 and an FMV of $10,000. Nelson's basis in the furniture after the distribution from the partnership is
   a. $10,000.
   b. $12,000.
   c. $16,000.
   d. None of the above.
3. Assume the same facts as in Question 2. However, Nelson receives a cash distribution of $4,000 with the furniture. The basis in the furniture after the distributions is
   a. $8,000.
   b. $10,000.
   c. $12,000.
   d. $16,000.

[19] See IRC § 732(a) for the basis and IRC § 735(b) for the holding period.

[20] This is assuming there is no triggered precontribution gain.

DISPOSAL OR LIQUIDATION OF A PARTNERSHIP INTEREST

LO 14-6

The most common way to dispose of a partnership interest is either through partnership liquidation or by selling the interest.[21]

Liquidation of a Partnership Interest

Liquidation occurs when a partner's entire interest is redeemed by the partnership. Most of the rules concerning nonliquidating distributions (discussed previously) also apply to liquidating distributions. Thus a distribution of money in excess of basis causes a capital gain. If property is received in the liquidating distribution, no gain is recognized, and the basis of the property is adjusted as shown in Example 14-19.

One substantial difference in the liquidation rules and regular distribution rules is that a loss can be recognized on liquidating distributions. A loss occurs when the amounts received in liquidation are less than the partner's outside basis. One major caveat is that the loss can be recognized only after the final payment is received from the partnership and when only money, receivables, and/or inventory is/are distributed.

EXAMPLE 14-21

Cassandra has a $20,000 basis in her partnership interest when she receives liquidating distributions from the partnership. She receives cash of $12,000 and equipment with a basis to the partnership of $6,000. Cassandra recognizes no gain or loss on the liquidating distribution. The equipment will have a basis to her of $8,000 ($20,000 partnership basis minus cash received of $12,000).

EXAMPLE 14-22

Assume the same facts as in Example 14-21 except that Cassandra receives cash of $12,000 and inventory with a basis to the partnership of $6,000. Cassandra recognizes a loss of $2,000 on the liquidation (cash and inventory basis of $18,000 minus the $20,000 partnership basis); the inventory will have a basis to her of $6,000.

If several assets are distributed in liquidation and the partner does not have outside basis to cover the basis in the partnership assets distributed, the outside basis is allocated among the distributed assets as follows:

1. The partnership basis is first reduced by money distributions.
2. Any remaining basis covers the basis in receivables and inventory distributed.
3. Any remaining basis is allocated to the other assets distributed in proportion to each asset's basis.[22]

EXAMPLE 14-23

Kelsey has a basis in her partnership interest of $10,000. She receives the following assets in complete liquidation of the partnership interest:

Cash	$3,000
Inventory (basis)	2,000
Equipment (basis)	2,000
Land (basis)	4,000

[21] Of course, a partnership interest could be disposed of through inheritance or by gift, but these disposals have limited income tax effects to the partner. There may be estate tax issues or gift tax considerations, but these are beyond the scope of this text.

[22] Reg. § 1.732-1(c).

Kelsey has no recognized gain or loss, and her $10,000 outside basis is allocated to the assets as follows:

Cash	$3,000
Inventory	2,000
Equipment ($5,000 × $2,000/$6,000)	1,667
Land ($5,000 × $4,000/$6,000)	3,333

Sale of a Partnership Interest

The sale of a partnership interest is similar to the sale of any capital asset. The partner determines the amount realized from the sale and subtracts the basis of the partnership interest at the date of sale. The gain or loss is a capital item, and, assuming that the partner is an individual, he or she reports the transaction on Schedule D of Form 1040.

EXAMPLE 14-24

Bart purchased a 30% partnership interest for $23,000 in February 2015. His share of partnership income in subsequent years was $12,000 in 2015, $15,000 in 2016, and $8,000 in 2017. He made no additional contributions to, or withdrawals from, the partnership. On December 18, 2017, Bart sold his partnership interest for $74,000. His long-term capital gain is $16,000.

Amount realized		$ 74,000
Basis: Beginning	$ 23,000	
2015 income	+12,000	
2016 income	+15,000	
2017 income	+ 8,000	(58,000)
Long-term capital gain		$ 16,000

The partner may be subject to ordinary income from the sale if the partnership has substantially appreciated inventory or accounts receivable.[23] If the partnership sold or collected these items, ordinary income would result, and the partner would share in that ordinary income. A partner who is allowed capital gain treatment on the sale of the partnership interest would effectively convert the ordinary income to capital gain income and benefit from the preferential capital gain rates. IRC § 751 prevents this conversion.

EXAMPLE 14-25

Assume the same facts as in Example 14-24. However, the partnership has uncollected accounts receivable with an FMV of $20,000 and a basis of $0.[24] Because Bart's share in the receivables is $6,000 (30% interest × $20,000), $6,000 of the $16,000 gain is ordinary, and the remaining $10,000 is capital gain.

CONCEPT CHECK 14-6—
LO 14-6

1. Shelly has a basis in her partnership interest of $30,000. She receives the following assets in complete liquidation of the partnership interest:

Cash	$ 9,000
Inventory (basis)	6,000
Equipment (basis)	8,000
Land (basis)	12,000

a. What is Shelly's recognized gain?

b. What is Shelly's basis in each of the assets distributed?

(continued)

[23] IRC § 751.

[24] Typically a cash basis partnership will have a zero basis in accounts receivable because income is not recognized until the partnership collects the cash.

2. Callie purchased a 60% partnership interest for $55,000 in March 2016. She had income of $18,000 from the partnership in 2016 and $26,000 in 2017. She made no additional contributions to, or withdrawals from, the partnership. On December 30, 2017, Callie sold her partnership interest for $107,000.
   a. What is Callie's basis before the sale?
   b. What is Callie's gain or loss?
   c. Is the gain or loss (if any) capital or ordinary?

Comprehensive Example

Shafer and Jones Consulting, LLC, is a partnership formed on January 1, 2014, to perform business consulting services. The business is located at 1482 Jones Business Complex, Anywhere, NC 27858. Its Employer ID is 92-1234567; it uses the tax/cash basis of accounting, is not subject to partnership audit procedures, has no foreign interests, and is not a tax shelter.

The home address for David A. Shafer (SSN 412-34-5670) is 103 Flower Road, Anywhere, NC 27858. He is a 60% partner. Robert B. Jones (SSN 412-34-5671) lives at 534 Bates Road, Anywhere, NC 27858. He is a 40% partner.

In 2017, David received a distribution of $60,000, and Robert received a $40,000 distribution. Both of these distributions are in addition to the guaranteed payments.

SHAFER AND JONES CONSULTING, LLC
Comparative Balance Sheet
As of December 31, 2016, and December 31, 2017

	12/31/16	12/31/17
Assets		
Cash	$ 29,452	$ 35,452
Investments	153,345	105,480
Office equipment	123,000	143,800
Accumulated depreciation (equipment)	(68,880)	(71,852)
Building	245,600	245,600
Accumulated depreciation (building)	(18,616)	(24,913)
Total assets	$463,901	$433,567
Liabilities and equity		
Notes payable	$233,800	$228,333
Capital accounts		
Capital, Shafer	138,061	123,140
Capital, Jones	92,040	82,094
Total liabilities and equity	$463,901	$433,567

SHAFER AND JONES CONSULTING, LLC
Income Statement
For the Year Ending December 31, 2017

Revenue	
Consulting income	$554,897
Interest income	1,231
Dividend income (qualified)	3,234
Long-term capital losses	(12,435)
Total revenue	$546,927

Expenses	
Salaries and wages (nonpartners)	$153,000
Guaranteed payments	
Shafer	100,000
Jones	96,000
Depreciation (MACRS—includes $5,000 § 179 expense)	31,448
Interest expense	15,983
Taxes and licenses	15,548
Utilities	12,132
Travel	11,458
Meals and entertainment (100%)	11,345
Auto	9,880
Insurance (nonpartner health)	5,000
Accounting and legal	4,800
Repairs	3,200
Charitable contributions	1,500
Payroll penalties	500
Total expenses	$471,794
Net income	$ 75,133

See Table 14-4 for a spreadsheet of partnership ordinary income and separately stated items. Exhibits 14-3 and 14-4 show the presentation of Form 1065 and Schedule K-1s for Shafer and Jones Consulting. Form 4562 (depreciation), Schedule D (capital gains and losses), and a statement listing other deductions (line 20 of Form 1065) are omitted from the example.

TABLE 14-4

SHAFER AND JONES CONSULTING, LLC

Income Statement

For the Year Ending December 31, 2017

	Adjustments	Ordinary	Separately Stated
Consulting income		554,897	
Interest income			1,231
Dividend income (qualified)			3,234
Long-term capital losses			(12,435)
Expenses			
Salaries and wages (nonpartners)		153,000	
Guaranteed payments			
Shafer		100,000	100,000
Jones		96,000	96,000
Depreciation (MACRS—includes $5,000 § 179 expense)		26,448	5,000
Interest expense		15,983	
Taxes and licenses		15,548	
Utilities		12,132	
Travel		11,458	
Meals and entertainment (100%)	(5 673)*	5,672*	
Auto		9,880	
Insurance (nonpartner health)		5,000	
Accounting and legal		4,800	
Repairs		3,200	
Charitable contributions			1,500
Payroll penalties	(500)†		
Net income	$ 75,133	$ 95,776	

* Only 50% of meals and entertainment expenses are allowed.
† Penalties are not deductible.

EXHIBIT 14-3

Form **1065**
Department of the Treasury
Internal Revenue Service

U.S. Return of Partnership Income

For calendar year 2017, or tax year beginning ________, 2017, ending ________, 20____.
▶ Go to *www.irs.gov/Form1065* for instructions and the latest information.

OMB No. 1545-0123
2017

A Principal business activity: Consulting	Name of partnership: Shafer and Jones Consulting, LLC	D Employer identification number: 92-1234567
B Principal product or service: Consulting	Type or Print — Number, street, and room or suite no. If a P.O. box, see the instructions.: 1482 Jones Business Complex	E Date business started: 01/01/14
C Business code number: 541600	City or town, state or province, country, and ZIP or foreign postal code: Anywhere, NC 27858	F Total assets (see the instructions): $ 433,567

G Check applicable boxes: (1) ☐ Initial return (2) ☐ Final return (3) ☐ Name change (4) ☐ Address change (5) ☐ Amended return
(6) ☐ Technical termination - also check (1) or (2)
H Check accounting method: (1) ☑ Cash (2) ☐ Accrual (3) ☐ Other (specify) ▶
I Number of Schedules K-1. Attach one for each person who was a partner at any time during the tax year ▶ Two
J Check if Schedules C and M-3 are attached ☐

Caution. *Include **only** trade or business income and expenses on lines 1a through 22 below. See the instructions for more information.*

Income	1a	Gross receipts or sales	1a	554,897		
	b	Returns and allowances	1b			
	c	Balance. Subtract line 1b from line 1a			1c	554,897
	2	Cost of goods sold (attach Form 1125-A)			2	0
	3	Gross profit. Subtract line 2 from line 1c			3	554,897
	4	Ordinary income (loss) from other partnerships, estates, and trusts (attach statement)			4	
	5	Net farm profit (loss) (attach Schedule F (Form 1040))			5	
	6	Net gain (loss) from Form 4797, Part II, line 17 (attach Form 4797)			6	
	7	Other income (loss) (attach statement)			7	
	8	**Total income (loss).** Combine lines 3 through 7			8	554,897
Deductions (see the instructions for limitations)	9	Salaries and wages (other than to partners) (less employment credits)			9	153,000
	10	Guaranteed payments to partners			10	196,000
	11	Repairs and maintenance			11	3,200
	12	Bad debts			12	
	13	Rent			13	
	14	Taxes and licenses			14	15,548
	15	Interest			15	15,893
	16a	Depreciation (if required, attach Form 4562)	16a	26,448		
	b	Less depreciation reported on Form 1125-A and elsewhere on return	16b		16c	26,448
	17	Depletion **(Do not deduct oil and gas depletion.)**			17	
	18	Retirement plans, etc.			18	
	19	Employee benefit programs			19	
	20	Other deductions (attach statement)			20	48,942
	21	**Total deductions.** Add the amounts shown in the far right column for lines 9 through 20			21	459,121
	22	**Ordinary business income (loss).** Subtract line 21 from line 8			22	95,776

Sign Here

Under penalties of perjury, I declare that I have examined this return, including accompanying schedules and statements, and to the best of my knowledge and belief, it is true, correct, and complete. Declaration of preparer (other than partner or limited liability company member) is based on all information of which preparer has any knowledge.

▶ Signature of partner or limited liability company member ▶ Date

May the IRS discuss this return with the preparer shown below (see instructions)? ☐ Yes ☐ No

Paid Preparer Use Only	Print/Type preparer's name	Preparer's signature	Date	Check ☐ if self-employed	PTIN
	Firm's name ▶			Firm's EIN ▶	
	Firm's address ▶			Phone no.	

For Paperwork Reduction Act Notice, see separate instructions. Cat. No. 11390Z Form **1065** (2017)

Source: U.S. Department of the Treasury, Internal Revenue Service, Form 1065. Washington, DC: 2017.

EXHIBIT 14-3 *(continued)*

Form 1065 (2017) Page **2**

Schedule B Other Information

		Yes	No
1	What type of entity is filing this return? Check the applicable box: **a** ☐ Domestic general partnership **b** ☐ Domestic limited partnership **c** ☑ Domestic limited liability company **d** ☐ Domestic limited liability partnership **e** ☐ Foreign partnership **f** ☐ Other ▶		
2	At any time during the tax year, was any partner in the partnership a disregarded entity, a partnership (including an entity treated as a partnership), a trust, an S corporation, an estate (other than an estate of a deceased partner), or a nominee or similar person?		✓
3	At the end of the tax year:		
a	Did any foreign or domestic corporation, partnership (including any entity treated as a partnership), trust, or tax-exempt organization, or any foreign government own, directly or indirectly, an interest of 50% or more in the profit, loss, or capital of the partnership? For rules of constructive ownership, see instructions. If "Yes," attach Schedule B-1, Information on Partners Owning 50% or More of the Partnership		✓
b	Did any individual or estate own, directly or indirectly, an interest of 50% or more in the profit, loss, or capital of the partnership? For rules of constructive ownership, see instructions. If "Yes," attach Schedule B-1, Information on Partners Owning 50% or More of the Partnership	✓	
4	At the end of the tax year, did the partnership:		
a	Own directly 20% or more, or own, directly or indirectly, 50% or more of the total voting power of all classes of stock entitled to vote of any foreign or domestic corporation? For rules of constructive ownership, see instructions. If "Yes," complete (i) through (iv) below		✓

(i) Name of Corporation	**(ii)** Employer Identification Number (if any)	**(iii)** Country of Incorporation	**(iv)** Percentage Owned in Voting Stock

		Yes	No
b	Own directly an interest of 20% or more, or own, directly or indirectly, an interest of 50% or more in the profit, loss, or capital in any foreign or domestic partnership (including an entity treated as a partnership) or in the beneficial interest of a trust? For rules of constructive ownership, see instructions. If "Yes," complete (i) through (v) below		✓

(i) Name of Entity	**(ii)** Employer Identification Number (if any)	**(iii)** Type of Entity	**(iv)** Country of Organization	**(v)** Maximum Percentage Owned in Profit, Loss, or Capital

		Yes	No
5	Did the partnership file Form 8893, Election of Partnership Level Tax Treatment, or an election statement under section 6231(a)(1)(B)(ii) for partnership-level tax treatment, that is in effect for this tax year? See Form 8893 for more details		✓
6	Does the partnership satisfy **all four** of the following conditions?		
a	The partnership's total receipts for the tax year were less than $250,000.		
b	The partnership's total assets at the end of the tax year were less than $1 million.		
c	Schedules K-1 are filed with the return and furnished to the partners on or before the due date (including extensions) for the partnership return.		
d	The partnership is not filing and is not required to file Schedule M-3		✓
	If "Yes," the partnership is not required to complete Schedules L, M-1, and M-2; Item F on page 1 of Form 1065; or Item L on Schedule K-1.		
7	Is this partnership a publicly traded partnership as defined in section 469(k)(2)?		✓
8	During the tax year, did the partnership have any debt that was cancelled, was forgiven, or had the terms modified so as to reduce the principal amount of the debt?		✓
9	Has this partnership filed, or is it required to file, Form 8918, Material Advisor Disclosure Statement, to provide information on any reportable transaction?		✓
10	At any time during calendar year 2017, did the partnership have an interest in or a signature or other authority over a financial account in a foreign country (such as a bank account, securities account, or other financial account)? See the instructions for exceptions and filing requirements for FinCEN Form 114, Report of Foreign Bank and Financial Accounts (FBAR). If "Yes," enter the name of the foreign country. ▶		✓

Form **1065** (2017)

(continued)

EXHIBIT 14-3 *(continued)*

Form 1065 (2017) Page 3

Schedule B Other Information *(continued)*

		Yes	No
11	At any time during the tax year, did the partnership receive a distribution from, or was it the grantor of, or transferor to, a foreign trust? If "Yes," the partnership may have to file Form 3520, Annual Return To Report Transactions With Foreign Trusts and Receipt of Certain Foreign Gifts. See instructions		✓
12a	Is the partnership making, or had it previously made (and not revoked), a section 754 election? See instructions for details regarding a section 754 election.		✓
b	Did the partnership make for this tax year an optional basis adjustment under section 743(b) or 734(b)? If "Yes," attach a statement showing the computation and allocation of the basis adjustment. See instructions		✓
c	Is the partnership required to adjust the basis of partnership assets under section 743(b) or 734(b) because of a substantial built-in loss (as defined under section 743(d)) or substantial basis reduction (as defined under section 734(d))? If "Yes," attach a statement showing the computation and allocation of the basis adjustment. See instructions		✓
13	Check this box if, during the current or prior tax year, the partnership distributed any property received in a like-kind exchange or contributed such property to another entity (other than disregarded entities wholly owned by the partnership throughout the tax year) ▶ ☐		
14	At any time during the tax year, did the partnership distribute to any partner a tenancy-in-common or other undivided interest in partnership property?		✓
15	If the partnership is required to file Form 8858, Information Return of U.S. Persons With Respect To Foreign Disregarded Entities, enter the number of Forms 8858 attached. See instructions ▶		
16	Does the partnership have any foreign partners? If "Yes," enter the number of Forms 8805, Foreign Partner's Information Statement of Section 1446 Withholding Tax, filed for this partnership. ▶		✓
17	Enter the number of Forms 8865, Return of U.S. Persons With Respect to Certain Foreign Partnerships, attached to this return. ▶		
18a	Did you make any payments in 2017 that would require you to file Form(s) 1099? See instructions	✓	
b	If "Yes," did you or will you file required Form(s) 1099?	✓	
19	Enter the number of Form(s) 5471, Information Return of U.S. Persons With Respect To Certain Foreign Corporations, attached to this return. ▶		
20	Enter the number of partners that are foreign governments under section 892. ▶		
21	During the partnership's tax year, did the partnership make any payments that would require it to file Form 1042 and 1042-S under chapter 3 (sections 1441 through 1464) or chapter 4 (sections 1471 through 1474)?		✓
22	Was the partnership a specified domestic entity required to file Form 8938 for the tax year (See the Instructions for Form 8938)?		✓

Designation of Tax Matters Partner (see instructions)

Enter below the general partner or member-manager designated as the tax matters partner (TMP) for the tax year of this return:

Name of designated TMP ▶	**David A. Shafer**	Identifying number of TMP ▶	**412-34-5670**
If the TMP is an entity, name of TMP representative ▶		Phone number of TMP ▶	**252-555-5555**
Address of designated TMP ▶	**103 Flower Road** **Anywhere, NC 27858**		

Form **1065** (2017)

EXHIBIT 14-3 *(continued)*

Form 1065 (2017) Page **4**

Schedule K **Partners' Distributive Share Items**

Section	Line	Item		Line	Total amount
Income (Loss)	1	Ordinary business income (loss) (page 1, line 22)		1	95,776
	2	Net rental real estate income (loss) (attach Form 8825)		2	
	3a	Other gross rental income (loss)	3a		
	b	Expenses from other rental activities (attach statement)	3b		
	c	Other net rental income (loss). Subtract line 3b from line 3a		3c	
	4	Guaranteed payments		4	196,000
	5	Interest income		5	1,231
	6	Dividends: a Ordinary dividends		6a	3,234
		b Qualified dividends	6b 3,234		
	7	Royalties		7	
	8	Net short-term capital gain (loss) (attach Schedule D (Form 1065))		8	
	9a	Net long-term capital gain (loss) (attach Schedule D (Form 1065))		9a	(12,435)
	b	Collectibles (28%) gain (loss)	9b		
	c	Unrecaptured section 1250 gain (attach statement)	9c		
	10	Net section 1231 gain (loss) (attach Form 4797)		10	
	11	Other income (loss) (see instructions) Type ▶		11	
Deductions	12	Section 179 deduction (attach Form 4562)		12	5,000
	13a	Contributions		13a	1,500
	b	Investment interest expense		13b	
	c	Section 59(e)(2) expenditures: (1) Type ▶ (2) Amount ▶		13c(2)	
	d	Other deductions (see instructions) Type ▶		13d	
Self-Employment	14a	Net earnings (loss) from self-employment		14a	286,776
	b	Gross farming or fishing income		14b	
	c	Gross nonfarm income		14c	
Credits	15a	Low-income housing credit (section 42(j)(5))		15a	
	b	Low-income housing credit (other)		15b	
	c	Qualified rehabilitation expenditures (rental real estate) (attach Form 3468, if applicable)		15c	
	d	Other rental real estate credits (see instructions) Type ▶		15d	
	e	Other rental credits (see instructions) Type ▶		15e	
	f	Other credits (see instructions) Type ▶		15f	
Foreign Transactions	16a	Name of country or U.S. possession ▶			
	b	Gross income from all sources		16b	
	c	Gross income sourced at partner level		16c	
		Foreign gross income sourced at partnership level			
	d	Passive category ▶ e General category ▶ f Other ▶		16f	
		Deductions allocated and apportioned at partner level			
	g	Interest expense ▶ h Other ▶		16h	
		Deductions allocated and apportioned at partnership level to foreign source income			
	i	Passive category ▶ j General category ▶ k Other ▶		16k	
	l	Total foreign taxes (check one): ▶ Paid ☐ Accrued ☐		16l	
	m	Reduction in taxes available for credit (attach statement)		16m	
	n	Other foreign tax information (attach statement)			
Alternative Minimum Tax (AMT) Items	17a	Post-1986 depreciation adjustment		17a	
	b	Adjusted gain or loss		17b	
	c	Depletion (other than oil and gas)		17c	
	d	Oil, gas, and geothermal properties—gross income		17d	
	e	Oil, gas, and geothermal properties—deductions		17e	
	f	Other AMT items (attach statement)		17f	
Other Information	18a	Tax-exempt interest income		18a	
	b	Other tax-exempt income		18b	
	c	Nondeductible expenses		18c	6,173
	19a	Distributions of cash and marketable securities		19a	100,000
	b	Distributions of other property		19b	
	20a	Investment income		20a	
	b	Investment expenses		20b	
	c	Other items and amounts (attach statement)			

DRAFT AS OF August 16, 2017 DO NOT FILE

Form **1065** (2017)

(continued)

EXHIBIT 14-3 *(concluded)*

Form 1065 (2017) Page **5**

Analysis of Net Income (Loss)

1	Net income (loss). Combine Schedule K, lines 1 through 11. From the result, subtract the sum of Schedule K, lines 12 through 13d, and 16l	1	277,306

2	Analysis by partner type:	(i) Corporate	(ii) Individual (active)	(iii) Individual (passive)	(iv) Partnership	(v) Exempt Organization	(vi) Nominee/Other
a	General partners		277,306				
b	Limited partners						

Schedule L — Balance Sheets per Books

	Assets	Beginning of tax year (a)	(b)	End of tax year (c)	(d)
1	Cash		29,452		35,452
2a	Trade notes and accounts receivable . . .				
b	Less allowance for bad debts				
3	Inventories				
4	U.S. government obligations				
5	Tax-exempt securities				
6	Other current assets (attach statement) . .				
7a	Loans to partners (or persons related to partners)				
b	Mortgage and real estate loans				
8	Other investments (attach statement) . . .		153,345		105,480
9a	Buildings and other depreciable assets . .	386,600		389,400	
b	Less accumulated depreciation	87,496	281,104	97,765	292,635
10a	Depletable assets				
b	Less accumulated depletion				
11	Land (net of any amortization)				
12a	Intangible assets (amortizable only) . . .				
b	Less accumulated amortization				
13	Other assets (attach statement)				
14	Total assets		463,901		433,567
	Liabilities and Capital				
15	Accounts payable				
16	Mortgages, notes, bonds payable in less than 1 year		233,800		228,333
17	Other current liabilities (attach statement) .				
18	All nonrecourse loans				
19a	Loans from partners (or persons related to partners)				
b	Mortgages, notes, bonds payable in 1 year or more				
20	Other liabilities (attach statement)				
21	Partners' capital accounts		230,101		205,234
22	Total liabilities and capital		463,901		433,567

Schedule M-1 — Reconciliation of Income (Loss) per Books With Income (Loss) per Return

Note. The partnership may be required to file Schedule M-3 (see instructions).

1	Net income (loss) per books	75,133	6	Income recorded on books this year not included on Schedule K, lines 1 through 11 (itemize):	
2	Income included on Schedule K, lines 1, 2, 3c, 5, 6a, 7, 8, 9a, 10, and 11, not recorded on books this year (itemize):		a	Tax-exempt interest $	
3	Guaranteed payments (other than health insurance)	196,000	7	Deductions included on Schedule K, lines 1 through 13d, and 16l, not charged against book income this year (itemize):	
4	Expenses recorded on books this year not included on Schedule K, lines 1 through 13d, and 16l (itemize):		a	Depreciation $	
a	Depreciation $		8	Add lines 6 and 7	
b	Travel and entertainment $ 6,173	6,173	9	Income (loss) (Analysis of Net Income (Loss), line 1). Subtract line 8 from line 5 .	277,306
5	Add lines 1 through 4	277,306			

Schedule M-2 — Analysis of Partners' Capital Accounts

1	Balance at beginning of year . . .	230,101	6	Distributions: **a** Cash	100,000
2	Capital contributed: **a** Cash . . .			**b** Property	
	b Property . .		7	Other decreases (itemize):	
3	Net income (loss) per books	75,133			
4	Other increases (itemize):		8	Add lines 6 and 7	100,000
5	Add lines 1 through 4	305,234	9	Balance at end of year. Subtract line 8 from line 5	205,234

Form **1065** (2017)

EXHIBIT 14-4

651117

☐ Final K-1 ☐ Amended K-1 OMB No. 1545-0123

Schedule K-1 (Form 1065) **2017**

Department of the Treasury
Internal Revenue Service

For calendar year 2017, or tax year

beginning / / 2017 ending / /

Partner's Share of Income, Deductions, Credits, etc. ► See back of form and separate instructions.

Part I Information About the Partnership

A Partnership's employer identification number
92-1234567

B Partnership's name, address, city, state, and ZIP code
Shafer and Jones Consulting, LLC
1842 Jones Business Center
Anywhere, NC 27858

C IRS Center where partnership filed return
Cincinnati, OH

D ☐ Check if this is a publicly traded partnership (PTP)

Part II Information About the Partner

E Partner's identifying number
412-34-5670

F Partner's name, address, city, state, and ZIP code
David A. Shafer
123 Flower Road
Anywhere, NC 27858

G ☐ General partner or LLC member-manager ☐ Limited partner or other LLC member

H ☒ Domestic partner ☐ Foreign partner

I1 What type of entity is this partner? Individual

I2 If this partner is a retirement plan (IRA/SEP/Keogh/etc.), check here ☐

J Partner's share of profit, loss, and capital (see instructions):

	Beginning	Ending
Profit	%	60 %
Loss	%	60 %
Capital	%	60 %

K Partner's share of liabilities at year end:

Nonrecourse	$
Qualified nonrecourse financing	$
Recourse	$ 137,000

L Partner's capital account analysis:

Beginning capital account	$ 138,061
Capital contributed during the year	$
Current year increase (decrease)	$ 45,080
Withdrawals & distributions	$ (60,000)
Ending capital account	$ 123,140

☒ Tax basis ☐ GAAP ☐ Section 704(b) book
☐ Other (explain)

M Did the partner contribute property with a built-in gain or loss?
☐ **Yes** ☒ **No**
If "Yes," attach statement (see instructions)

Part III Partner's Share of Current Year Income, Deductions, Credits, and Other Items

Line	Item	Amount
1	Ordinary business income (loss)	57,466
2	Net rental real estate income (loss)	
3	Other net rental income (loss)	
4	Guaranteed payments	100,000
5	Interest income	739
6a	Ordinary dividends	1,940
6b	Qualified dividends	1,940
7	Royalties	
8	Net short-term capital gain (loss)	
9a	Net long-term capital gain (loss)	(7,461)
9b	Collectibles (28%) gain (loss)	
9c	Unrecaptured section 1250 gain	
10	Net section 1231 gain (loss)	
11	Other income (loss)	
12	Section 179 deduction	3,000
13	Other deductions	A 900
14	Self-employment earnings (loss)	A 154,466
15	Credits	
16	Foreign transactions	
17	Alternative minimum tax (AMT) items	
18	Tax-exempt income and nondeductible expenses	C 3,704
19	Distributions	A 60,000
20	Other information	

*See attached statement for additional information.

For IRS Use Only

For Paperwork Reduction Act Notice, see Instructions for Form 1065. www.irs.gov/Form1065 Cat. No. 11394R **Schedule K-1 (Form 1065) 2017**

Source: U.S Department of the Treasury, Internal Revenue Service, Schedule K-1 (Form 1065). Washington, DC: 2017.

(continued)

EXHIBIT 14-4 *(concluded)*

651117

☐ Final K-1 ☐ Amended K-1 OMB No. 1545-0123

Schedule K-1 (Form 1065) **2017**

Department of the Treasury
Internal Revenue Service

For calendar year 2017, or tax year

beginning / / 2017 ending / /

Partner's Share of Income, Deductions, Credits, etc. ► See back of form and separate instructions.

Part I Information About the Partnership

A Partnership's employer identification number
92-1234567

B Partnership's name, address, city, state, and ZIP code
Shafer and Jones Consulting, LLC
1842 Jones Business Center
Anywhere, NC 27858

C IRS Center where partnership filed return
Cincinnati, OH

D ☐ Check if this is a publicly traded partnership (PTP)

Part II Information About the Partner

E Partner's identifying number
412-34-5671

F Partner's name, address, city, state, and ZIP code
Robert B. Jones
543 Bates Road
Anywhere, NC 27858

G ☐ General partner or LLC member-manager ☐ Limited partner or other LLC member

H ☒ Domestic partner ☐ Foreign partner

I1 What type of entity is this partner? Individual

I2 If this partner is a retirement plan (IRA/SEP/Keogh/etc.), check here ☐

J Partner's share of profit, loss, and capital (see instructions):

	Beginning	Ending
Profit	%	40 %
Loss	%	40 %
Capital	%	40 %

K Partner's share of liabilities at year end:

Nonrecourse	$
Qualified nonrecourse financing	$
Recourse	$ 91,333

L Partner's capital account analysis:

Beginning capital account	$ 92,040
Capital contributed during the year	$
Current year increase (decrease)	$ 30,053
Withdrawals & distributions	$ (40,000)
Ending capital account	$ 82,094

☒ Tax basis ☐ GAAP ☐ Section 704(b) book
☐ Other (explain)

M Did the partner contribute property with a built-in gain or loss?
☐ Yes ☒ No
If "Yes," attach statement (see instructions)

Part III Partner's Share of Current Year Income, Deductions, Credits, and Other Items

Line	Item	Amount
1	Ordinary business income (loss)	38,310
2	Net rental real estate income (loss)	
3	Other net rental income (loss)	
4	Guaranteed payments	96,000
5	Interest income	492
6a	Ordinary dividends	1,294
6b	Qualified dividends	1,294
7	Royalties	
8	Net short-term capital gain (loss)	
9a	Net long-term capital gain (loss)	(4,974)
9b	Collectibles (28%) gain (loss)	
9c	Unrecaptured section 1250 gain	
10	Net section 1231 gain (loss)	
11	Other income (loss)	
12	Section 179 deduction	2,000
13	Other deductions	A 600
14	Self-employment earnings (loss)	A 132,310
15	Credits	
16	Foreign transactions	
17	Alternative minimum tax (AMT) items	
18	Tax-exempt income and nondeductible expenses	C 2,469
19	Distributions	A 40,000
20	Other information	

*See attached statement for additional information.

For IRS Use Only

Summary

LO 14-1: Explain the rules dealing with the formation of a partnership.	• Generally there is no gain or loss on formation. • Basis determination is very important. • *Outside basis* is the tax basis of the partnership interest to the partner. • *Inside basis* is the partner's share of the basis of partnership assets. • The partnership holding period carries over from the contributing partner. • The FMV of services is income to the contributing partner. • Property contributed with liabilities may trigger a gain to the contributing partner.
LO 14-2: Be able to report partnership ordinary income or loss.	• The partnership files an annual information return, Form 1065. • Partnership income is separated into ordinary income or loss and separately stated items. • Income or loss is reported to partners on Schedule K-1. • Ordinary income is calculated as for a Schedule C business. • Guaranteed payments are an expense to the partnership. • The § 179 depreciation expense deduction must be separately stated. • Partner health insurance premiums are treated as a guaranteed payment.
LO 14-3: Determine separately stated items.	• Separately stated items are income or expense items that may be treated differently at the partner level. • Examples of separately stated items include interest, capital gains, charitable contributions, and self-employment income.
LO 14-4: Calculate partner basis.	• In general, partner basis is equal to the basis of property contributed, plus or minus income or loss, plus or minus separately stated items, plus partner share of liabilities.
LO 14-5: Apply the rules for partnership distributions.	• In general, no gain or loss is recorded on a nonliquidating distribution. • Distributions reduce basis. • Partner basis of property received generally equals the partnership basis.
LO 14-6: Correctly report partnership liquidations and dispositions.	• Generally no gain or loss occurs on partnership liquidation. • Exceptions exist if amount in liquidation is less than basis and the distribution is only cash, receivables, or inventory. • Sale of partnership interest is sale of a capital asset. • If a partnership holds appreciated inventory or accounts receivable, part of the gain may be ordinary.

Discussion Questions connect

All applicable discussion questions are available with ***Connect***©

LO 14-1 1. Discuss the formation of a partnership. Is any gain or loss recognized? Explain.

LO 14-1 2. What entity forms are considered partnerships for federal income tax purposes?

LO 14-1 3. How do taxation for the corporate form and taxation for the partnership form differ?

LO 14-1 4. What is the concept of *basis*? In your discussion, differentiate between outside basis and inside basis.

LO 14-1 5. Elaborate on the term *basis-in, basis-out.* What does that phrase mean in the context of a partnership formation?

LO 14-1 6. How can two partners, each with a 50% interest in a partnership, have different amounts of outside basis at the formation of a partnership? Shouldn't the two partners contribute the same amount to have the same interest?

LO 14-1 7. When a partnership receives an asset from a partner, does the partnership ever recognize a gain? What is the basis of the asset in the hands of the partnership after contribution?

LO 14-1 8. Discuss the concept of *steps into the shoes.* Does this concept pertain to the partnership, the partners, or both?

LO 14-2 9. Why would smaller partnerships (and other businesses for that matter) use only the tax basis of accounting, which does not follow GAAP?

LO 14-2 10. How is depreciation calculated by the partnership when a partner contributes a business asset?

LO 14-2 11. Discuss the concepts of *ordinary income* and *separately stated items* concerning partnerships. When must a partnership item of income or loss be separately stated, and why?

LO 14-2 12. Can a partner have a salary from a partnership? Why? What is a *guaranteed payment*?

LO 14-2 13. Are guaranteed payments treated as ordinary items or as separately stated items?

LO 14-2 14. Is the § 179 expense deduction allowed for partnerships? If so, is § 179 an ordinary income item or a separately stated item? Why?

LO 14-3 15. If a partner owns a 20% interest, does that necessarily mean that he or she will receive 20% of the net income from the partnership? Explain.

LO 14-3 16. Is partnership income considered self-employment income? If so, how is it calculated?

LO 14-3 17. Why must some income and gain items be separately stated in a partnership?

LO 14-4 18. Explain why nontaxable income and nondeductible expenses increase or reduce outside basis.

LO 14-4 19. When is it mandatory that a partner calculate his or her partner interest basis (outside basis)? What items affect the outside basis of a partner?

LO 14-4 20. How does a partner's share of partnership liabilities affect his or her outside basis?

LO 14-5 21. The general rule is that partners do not recognize any gain when they receive a distribution. In what circumstances might a partner recognize a gain on a current distribution?

LO 14-5 22. Define *precontribution gain.* What causes a partner to recognize it?

LO 14-5 23. Describe the rules concerning the basis of property distributed to a partner. How does the concept of *basis-in, basis-out* apply to partnership distributions?

LO 14-6 24. How can a partnership interest be disposed of? Which disposal method is more likely to produce a gain or loss? How is the gain or loss calculated?

LO 14-6 25. How is the outside basis of a partner allocated to assets in a liquidation of the partnership interest? Include in your answer the effects of distributing cash, ordinary assets, § 1231 assets, and capital assets.

Multiple-Choice Questions connect

All applicable multiple-choice questions are available with **Connect**©

LO 14-1 26. Carmin performs services in exchange for a 25% interest in Real Estate Rental Partnership. The services were worth $15,000. The tax implications to Carmin are

a. No taxable income and a partnership interest with a basis of $0.

b. No taxable income and a partnership interest with a basis of $15,000.

c. $15,000 of taxable income and a partnership interest with a basis of $0.

d. $15,000 of taxable income and a partnership interest with a basis of $15,000.

LO 14-1 27. Billy contributes land with an FMV of $7,000 and a basis of $3,000 to ABCD Partnership in return for a 5% partnership interest in the partnership. Billy's basis in the partnership

a. Is $0.

b. Is $3,000.

c. Is $7,000.

d. Cannot be determined.

LO 14-1 28. Billy contributes land with an FMV of $7,000 and a basis of $3,000 to ABCD Partnership in return for a 5% partnership interest in the partnership. ABCD's basis in the land

a. Is $0.

b. Is $3,000.

c. Is $7,000.

d. Cannot be determined.

LO 14-1 29. Jake has a Schedule C with the following assets:

	Basis	FMV
Cash	$ 4,500	$ 4,500
Accounts receivable (A/R)	–0–	10,000
Building	95,000	155,000

Jake contributes these assets to form AJ Partnership and receives a 50% interest. His basis in the partnership interest is

a. $0.

b. $99,500.

c. $159,500.

d. $169,500.

LO 14-1 30. Jake has a Schedule C with the following assets:

	Basis	FMV
Cash	$ 4,500	$ 4,500
Accounts receivable (A/R)	–0–	10,000
Building	95,000	155,000

Jake contributes these assets to form AJ Partnership and receives a 50% interest. AJ's basis in the assets is

a. Cash $4,500; A/R $0; building $155,000.

b. Cash $4,500; A/R $10,000; building $155,000.

c. Cash $4,500; A/R $0; building $95,000.

d. Cash $4,500; A/R $10,000; building $95,000.

LO 14-1 31. Allie contributed the following business assets to ASW Partnership on August 1, 2017:

	Basis	FMV	Date Purchased by Allie
Building	$175,000	$300,000	07/01/04
Inventory	50,000	100,000	05/08/14

What is the holding period for the building and the inventory to ASW Partnership?

a. Building—long-term capital or § 1231 asset.

b. Building—short-term ordinary asset.

c. Inventory—short-term ordinary asset.

d. Both *a* and *c*.

LO 14-1 32. Shelly contributed the following business assets to S&S Partnership on March 3, 2017:

	Basis	FMV	Date Purchased by Shelly
Equipment	$75,000	$ 45,000	07/01/16
Accounts receivable	–0–	100,000	Various

What is the basis in the equipment and the accounts receivable to S&S?

a. Equipment $0; accounts receivable $0.

b. Equipment $75,000; accounts receivable $0.

c. Equipment $45,000; accounts receivable $0.

d. Equipment $45,000; accounts receivable $100,000.

LO 14-2 33. Which of the following is considered when calculating ordinary income to a partnership?

a. Dividend income.

b. § 179 expense.

c. Guaranteed payments to partners.

d. Capital gains and losses.

LO 14-3 34. Styron is a partner in Styron, Lee, & Jane Partnership. Styron owned 25% from January 1, 2017, to June 30, 2017, when he bought Lee's 25% interest. He owned 50% for the rest of the year. The partnership had ordinary income of $88,000 and $12,000 in long-term capital gains. Barring any special allocations in a partnership agreement, Styron's share of ordinary income for the year is

a. $11,000.

b. $33,000.

c. $88,000.

d. $100,000.

LO 14-3 35. All of the following are considered separately stated items to a partnership *except*

a. Charitable contributions.

b. § 179 expense.

c. Depreciation.

d. Capital gains and losses.

LO 14-3 36. Which of the following items from a partnership go into the calculation of a partner's self-employment income?

a. Rental income.

b. Dividend income.

c. Interest income.

d. § 179 expense.

LO 14-3 37. A partner's share of ordinary income or loss and separately stated items is reported to the partner via what form?

a. Form 1065.

b. Form 1040, Schedule SE.

c. Form 1065, Schedule K-1.

d. Form 1065, Schedule D.

LO 14-3 38. Retish is a 10% partner in a partnership. The partnership pays Retish a guaranteed payment of $45,000 per year. If the partnership's ordinary income is $38,000 before considering the guaranteed payment, the partnership will report ordinary income of how much?

a. ($7,000).

b. $ 0.

c. $33,500.

d. $38,000.

LO 14-4 39. The calculation of a partner's basis in his or her partnership interest is mandatory in which of the following situations?

a. In a partnership loss year.

b. At the liquidation or disposition of a partner's interest.

c. When the partner receives nonliquidating distributions.

d. All of the above.

LO 14-4 40. Maggie and Davis are equal partners in a partnership. When forming the partnership, Davis contributed a building with an FMV of $550,000 and a basis of $175,000. During the first year of operations, the partnership earned $170,000 in ordinary income and tax-exempt interest of $2,500. Assuming no special allocations, Davis's basis in the partnership interest at the end of the year is

a. $175,000.

b. $261,250.

c. $345,600.

d. $347,500.

LO 14-4 41. All of the following items usually affect the basis of a partnership interest *except*

a. Cash or property contributed.

b. Guaranteed payments.

c. Partnership income or loss items.

d. A partner's share of recourse liabilities.

LO 14-4 42. Partner Beth has a basis of $10,000 in a partnership at the beginning of the year. She receives $6,000 in cash distributions, her distributive share of income is $5,000, and she receives a land distribution with a basis of $8,000 (FMV $20,000). What is Beth's partnership interest basis at the end of the year?

a. $0.

b. $1,000.

c. $9,000.

d. $10,000.

LO 14-5 43. Molly, a 30% partner in XYZ Partnership, has a basis of $55,000 in her partnership interest. She receives a cash distribution of $54,000 at year-end. The distribution has what tax effect on Molly?

a. No gain or loss is recognized, and she has a $55,000 basis in her partnership interest.

b. No gain or loss is recognized, and she has a $1,000 basis in her partnership interest.

c. She has a recognized gain of $37,500 and a basis of $0 in her partnership interest.

d. She has a recognized gain of $55,000 and a basis of $0 in her partnership interest.

LO 14-5 44. A partner recognizes a gain on a current distribution in which of the following situations?

a. When a partner receives a property distribution with a basis in excess of his or her basis.

b. When money or marketable securities are distributed in excess of the partner's basis.

c. When the current distribution triggers a precontribution gain.

d. Both *b* and *c*.

LO 14-5 45. Katlin contributes land to a partnership with a basis of $44,000 and an FMV of $56,000 in 2015. In 2017, when the FMV of the land is $58,000, the partnership distributes the land to Baily, another partner. Which of the following is true?

a. Katlin recognizes no gain or loss.

b. Baily recognizes a gain of $14,000.

c. Katlin recognizes a gain of $12,000.

d. Baily has a basis of $58,000 in the land.

LO 14-6 46. All of the following statements are correct concerning liquidating distributions of a partnership *except*

a. A loss can never be recognized.

b. A distribution of money in excess of basis causes a gain to be recognized.

c. Basis in a property distribution is allocated essentially the same as in a nonliquidating distribution.

d. Generally no gain or loss is recognized when the liquidating distribution consists only of property.

LO 14-6 47. On November 1, Ashton sells her interest in XYZ Partnership to Wayne for $200,000 cash and a release of liability of $30,000. Ashton's basis at the beginning of the year was $125,000 (including the $30,000 of liability). Ashton's share of income through November 1 was $45,000, and she received a $15,000 cash distribution earlier in the year. What are the tax consequences to Ashton of the sale of her partnership interest?

a. $0 tax effect.

b. $45,000 capital gain.

c. $75,000 capital gain.

d. $105,000 capital gain.

Problems connect

All applicable problems are available with ***Connect***©

LO 14-1 48. Denise contributes the following assets to a partnership in exchange for a 25% partnership interest:

	FMV	Basis
Cash	$20,000	$20,000
Office equipment	12,000	5,000
Auto	20,000	6,000

What is Denise's beginning basis in her partnership interest?

LO 14-1 49. On June 1 of the current year, Patti contributes equipment with a $45,000 basis and a $35,000 FMV in exchange for a partnership interest. She purchased the equipment three years ago.

a. What is Patti's basis in her partnership interest?

b. What is Patti's holding period of her partnership interest?

c. What is the basis of the equipment in the hands of the partnership?

d. What is the holding period of the equipment in the hands of the partnership?

e. How will the partnership depreciate the equipment in the year of contribution?

LO 14-1, 14-4 50. Dennis, Suzy, and Katherine form a partnership. Dennis and Suzy give equipment and a building, respectively. Katherine agrees to perform all of the accounting and office work in exchange for a 10% interest.

	FMV	Basis	Partnership Percentage
Dennis's equipment	$100,000	$10,000	45%
Suzy's building	100,000	45,000	45
Katherine's services	–0–	–0–	10

a. Do any of the partners recognize any gain? If so, how much and why?

b. What is the basis for each partner in his or her partnership interest?

c. What is the basis to the partnership of each asset?

LO 14-1, 14-4 51. Moe, Johnny, and Raymond form a partnership and contribute the following assets:

	FMV	Basis	Partnership Percentage
Moe's inventory	$ 50,000	$10,000	33.3%
Johnny's building	110,000	80,000	33.3
Raymond's cash	50,000	50,000	33.3

Johnny's building has a mortgage of $60,000, which the partnership assumes.

a. Do any of the partners recognize any gain? If so, how much and why?

b. What is the basis for each partner in his partnership interest?

c. What is the basis to the partnership in each asset?

d. How would your answer change with respect to Johnny if the basis in the building were $45,000?

LO 14-2 52. Barry and Kurt are equal partners in the BK Partnership. Barry receives a guaranteed payment of $55,000. In addition to the guaranteed payment, Barry withdraws $10,000 from the partnership. The partnership has $24,000 in ordinary income during the year.

a. How much income must Barry report from BK Partnership?

b. What is the effect of the distribution on Barry's partnership basis?

LO 14-2 53. Kerry is a partner in the Kerry, Davis, Smith & Jones Partnership. Kerry owned 25% from January 1, 2017, to June 30, 2017, when he bought Jones's 25% interest. He owned 50% for the rest of the year. The partnership had ordinary income of $146,000 and $15,000 in long-term capital gains. Barring any special allocations in a partnership agreement, what is Kerry's share of income?

LO 14-2, 14-3 54. Wade has a beginning basis in a partnership of $23,000. His share of income and expense from the partnership consists of the following amounts:

Ordinary income	$43,000
Guaranteed payment	12,000
Long-term capital gain	15,500
§ 1231 gain	4,300
Charitable contributions	2,000
§ 179 expense	18,000
Cash distribution	6,000

a. What is Wade's self-employment income?

b. Calculate Wade's basis at the end of the year.

LO 14-2, 14-3 55. Bryan and Gayle are equal partners in BG Partnership. The partnership reports the following items of income and expense:

Ordinary income from operations	$13,000
Interest income	5,000
Long-term capital gains	23,000
§ 179 expense	55,000
Charitable contributions	3,000

a. Which of these items are considered separately stated items? On what form will these items be reported to the partners?

b. Where will these amounts be reported by the partners?

LO 14-4, 14-5 56. Kim has a basis in her partnership interest of $12,000 when she receives a distribution from the partnership of $6,000 cash and equipment with a basis of $8,000 ($12,000 FMV).

a. How much gain or loss must Kim recognize on the distribution?

b. What is Kim's ending partnership basis?

c. What is Kim's basis in the equipment?

LO 14-4, 14-5 57. Zach contributed land with an FMV of $25,000 and a basis of $14,000 to a partnership on April 5, 2011. On June 6, 2017, the partnership distributed the land to Art, a partner in the same partnership. At distribution, the land had an FMV of $29,000.

a. What is the effect of the distribution to Zach, if any?

b. What is the effect of the distribution to Art?

LO 14-5 58. Roberto has a basis of $6,000 in a partnership at the beginning of the year. He receives $7,000 in cash distributions, his distributive share of income is $3,500, and he receives a land distribution with a basis of $6,000 (FMV $12,000).

a. Is Roberto required to recognize any gain? If so, how much is the gain?

b. What is Roberto's basis in the land?

c. What is Roberto's ending basis in his partnership interest?

Chapter **Fifteen**

Corporate Taxation

One legal form under which a business can operate is the corporate form. From a tax perspective, a corporation can be a C corporation or an S corporation, both designations derived from the applicable Internal Revenue Code (IRC) subsection. In this chapter, we introduce the tax rules associated with both corporate forms.

Learning Objectives

When you complete this chapter, you should understand the following learning objectives (LO):

- **LO 15-1** Describe corporate formation and filing requirements.
- **LO 15-2** Calculate corporate and shareholder basis.
- **LO 15-3** Determine corporate taxable income and tax liability.
- **LO 15-4** Explain the tax rules for transactions with shareholders.
- **LO 15-5** Prepare Schedules L, M-1, and M-3.
- **LO 15-6** Discuss other corporate issues.
- **LO 15-7** Know the rules for tax treatment of Subchapter S corporations.

INTRODUCTION

Businesses can choose to operate using a number of different legal structures, the most common of which are sole proprietorships, partnerships, regular corporations (called *C corporations*), and *Subchapter S corporations.* The *C* and *S* designations come from Subchapter C and Subchapter S of the Internal Revenue Code, where much of the tax law pertaining to these two entities is found.

The tax treatment of each of these structures differs, sometimes markedly so. We discussed sole proprietorships in Chapter 6 and partnerships in Chapter 14. In this chapter, we discuss C corporations and S corporations. In short, C corporations are taxed as a separate legal entity, and S corporations are taxed in a manner similar to a partnership.

CORPORATE FORMATION AND FILING REQUIREMENTS

LO 15-1

Organization

An individual or group of individuals can choose to operate a business as a *corporation,* which is a legal entity. Although rules vary slightly from state to state, the general procedure is as follows. First, the individual(s) or other entities that form the corporation (called the *incorporators*) file articles of incorporation and bylaws with the appropriate agency in the state in which they want to become incorporated. Generally the appropriate state agency is the Secretary of State, the Corporation Commission, or something similar. The state agency then issues to the corporation a charter or comparable document indicating that the corporate entity exists and that it can operate in accordance with its corporate documents.

After incorporation, states require corporations to file an annual report and pay a fee. This report and fee indicate to the state that the corporation remains active. When corporations decide to terminate their activities, many states require the corporation to file a notification.

Large C corporations must use the accrual basis of accounting.[1] Corporations with average annual gross receipts of $5 million or less can use the cash basis. Corporations that maintain inventory for sale to customers must use the accrual method of accounting at least for their sales and cost of goods sold.[2] Corporations must choose their method of accounting when they file their first return. If the corporation wishes to change its method of accounting subsequent to its first year of operation, it must file for permission to make the change.

C corporations can choose an accounting period when they file their first tax return without approval of the IRS. Often newly formed corporations do not give much thought to an appropriate fiscal year-end. Corporations should consider a fiscal year-end that occurs during a time of the year other than their busiest time. For example, the fiscal year of many retailers ends on January 31. Disney's fiscal year-end is September 30, right after its busy summer season.

Filing Requirements

Corporations must file an annual Form 1120 (see Exhibit 15-1).[3] Filing is required even if the corporation did not have taxable income.

Beginning in 2016, the due date for corporate tax returns depends on the fiscal year of the corporation. For corporations operating a fiscal year that ends on June 30, the return is due on September 15, which is the 15th day of the third month after year end. A seven-month extension is permitted from that date (to April 15) for a maximum period of 10.5 months.[4]

For all other corporations, the initial filing date is the 15th day of the fourth month after the fiscal year end. So, for example, a calendar year corporate return is due on April 15 and a corporation with a fiscal year that ends on February 28 is required to file by June 15. A six-month extension is allowed from the original due date (for a total of 10.5 months).

CONCEPT CHECK 15-1— LO 15-1

1. A corporation can use either the cash or accrual method of accounting. True or false?
2. Corporate tax returns are due __________ if no extension is requested.
3. The tax year of a corporation must end on December 31. True or false?

BASIS
LO 15-2

As we noted when discussing partnership taxation in Chapter 14, basis involves two critical issues: (1) the basis of the ownership interest (stock in the case of a corporation) in the hands of the owner and (2) the basis to the corporation of property exchanged for the ownership interest.

When a corporation is formed, individuals purchase or otherwise acquire stock in the entity. The stock acquisition is, in effect, an exchange of cash or property for stock and can be a taxable transaction. If the transferors (that is, the shareholders who are forming the corporation) control 80% or more of the corporation immediately after the exchange, the exchange is generally tax-free.[5]

[1] IRC § 448.

[2] Using the accrual basis for cost of goods sold suggests the corporation will also use that method for inventories. Corporations that use the accrual basis for sales and cost of goods sold and the cash basis for other items are said to be using a hybrid method of accounting.

[3] IRC § 6012(a)(2).

[4] Reg. § 1.6081-3(a)(1).

[5] IRC § 351.

EXHIBIT 15-1

Form **1120**
Department of the Treasury
Internal Revenue Service

U.S. Corporation Income Tax Return

For calendar year 2017 or tax year beginning ________, 2017, ending ________, 20 ___

▶ Go to *www.irs.gov/Form1120* for instructions and the latest information.

OMB No. 1545-0123

2017

A Check if:	**TYPE OR PRINT** Name	**B** Employer identification number
1a Consolidated return (attach Form 851) ☐	Number, street, and room or suite no. If a P.O. box, see instructions.	**C** Date incorporated
b Life/nonlife consolidated return ☐	City or town, state, or province, country, and ZIP or foreign postal code	**D** Total assets (see instructions) $
2 Personal holding co. (attach Sch. PH) ☐		
3 Personal service corp. (see instructions) ☐		
4 Schedule M-3 attached ☐	**E** Check if: (1) ☐ Initial return (2) ☐ Final return (3) ☐ Name change (4) ☐ Address change	

Income	1a	Gross receipts or sales	1a	
	b	Returns and allowances	1b	
	c	Balance. Subtract line 1b from line 1a		1c
	2	Cost of goods sold (attach Form 1125-A)		2
	3	Gross profit. Subtract line 2 from line 1c		3
	4	Dividends (Schedule C, line 19)		4
	5	Interest		5
	6	Gross rents		6
	7	Gross royalties		7
	8	Capital gain net income (attach Schedule D (Form 1120))		8
	9	Net gain or (loss) from Form 4797, Part II, line 17 (attach Form 4797)		9
	10	Other income (see instructions—attach statement)		10
	11	**Total income.** Add lines 3 through 10 ▶		11
Deductions (See instructions for limitations on deductions.)	12	Compensation of officers (see instructions—attach Form 1125-E) ▶		12
	13	Salaries and wages (less employment credits)		13
	14	Repairs and maintenance		14
	15	Bad debts		15
	16	Rents		16
	17	Taxes and licenses		17
	18	Interest		18
	19	Charitable contributions		19
	20	Depreciation from Form 4562 not claimed on Form 1125-A or elsewhere on return (attach Form 4562)		20
	21	Depletion		21
	22	Advertising		22
	23	Pension, profit-sharing, etc., plans		23
	24	Employee benefit programs		24
	25	Domestic production activities deduction (attach Form 8903)		25
	26	Other deductions (attach statement)		26
	27	**Total deductions.** Add lines 12 through 26 ▶		27
	28	Taxable income before net operating loss deduction and special deductions. Subtract line 27 from line 11.		28
	29a	Net operating loss deduction (see instructions)	29a	
	b	Special deductions (Schedule C, line 20)	29b	
	c	Add lines 29a and 29b		29c
Tax, Refundable Credits, and Payments	30	**Taxable income.** Subtract line 29c from line 28. See instructions		30
	31	Total tax (Schedule J, Part I, line 11)		31
	32	Total payments and refundable credits (Schedule J, Part II, line 21)		32
	33	Estimated tax penalty. See instructions. Check if Form 2220 is attached ▶ ☐		33
	34	**Amount owed.** If line 32 is smaller than the total of lines 31 and 33, enter amount owed		34
	35	**Overpayment.** If line 32 is larger than the total of lines 31 and 33, enter amount overpaid		35
	36	Enter amount from line 35 you want: **Credited to 2018 estimated tax** ▶	**Refunded** ▶	36

Sign Here

Under penalties of perjury, I declare that I have examined this return, including accompanying schedules and statements, and to the best of my knowledge and belief, it is true, correct, and complete. Declaration of preparer (other than taxpayer) is based on all information of which preparer has any knowledge.

▶ Signature of officer | Date | ▶ Title

May the IRS discuss this return with the preparer shown below? See instructions. ☐ **Yes** ☐ **No**

Paid Preparer Use Only	Print/Type preparer's name	Preparer's signature	Date	Check ☐ if self-employed	PTIN
	Firm's name ▶			Firm's EIN ▶	
	Firm's address ▶			Phone no.	

For Paperwork Reduction Act Notice, see separate instructions. Cat. No. 11450Q Form **1120** (2017)

Source: U.S Department of the Treasury, Internal Revenue Service, Form 1120. Washington, DC: 2017.

(continued)

EXHIBIT 15-1 *(continued)*

Form 1120 (2017) Page **2**

Schedule C **Dividends and Special Deductions** (see instructions)

		(a) Dividends received	(b) %	(c) Special deductions (a) × (b)
1	Dividends from less-than-20%-owned domestic corporations (other than debt-financed stock)		70	
2	Dividends from 20%-or-more-owned domestic corporations (other than debt-financed stock)		80	
3	Dividends on debt-financed stock of domestic and foreign corporations		see instructions	
4	Dividends on certain preferred stock of less-than-20%-owned public utilities		42	
5	Dividends on certain preferred stock of 20%-or-more-owned public utilities		48	
6	Dividends from less-than-20%-owned foreign corporations and certain FSCs		70	
7	Dividends from 20%-or-more-owned foreign corporations and certain FSCs		80	
8	Dividends from wholly owned foreign subsidiaries		100	
9	**Total.** Add lines 1 through 8. See instructions for limitation			
10	Dividends from domestic corporations received by a small business investment company operating under the Small Business Investment Act of 1958		100	
11	Dividends from affiliated group members		100	
12	Dividends from certain FSCs		100	
13	Dividends from foreign corporations not included on line 3, 6, 7, 8, 11, or 12			
14	Income from controlled foreign corporations under subpart F (attach Form(s) 5471)			
15	Foreign dividend gross-up			
16	IC-DISC and former DISC dividends not included on line 1, 2, or 3			
17	Other dividends			
18	Deduction for dividends paid on certain preferred stock of public utilities			
19	**Total dividends.** Add lines 1 through 17. Enter here and on page 1, line 4 ▶			
20	**Total special deductions.** Add lines 9, 10, 11, 12, and 18. Enter here and on page 1, line 29b ▶			

Form **1120** (2017)

EXHIBIT 15-1 *(continued)*

Form 1120 (2017) Page **3**

Schedule J **Tax Computation and Payment** (see instructions)

Part I–Tax Computation

1	Check if the corporation is a member of a controlled group (attach Schedule O (Form 1120)). See instructions ▶ ☐				
2	Income tax. Check if a qualified personal service corporation. See instructions . . . ▶ ☐			2	
3	Alternative minimum tax (attach Form 4626)			3	
4	Add lines 2 and 3			4	
5a	Foreign tax credit (attach Form 1118)	5a			
b	Credit from Form 8834 (see instructions)	5b			
c	General business credit (attach Form 3800)	5c			
d	Credit for prior year minimum tax (attach Form 8827)	5d			
e	Bond credits from Form 8912	5e			
6	**Total credits.** Add lines 5a through 5e			6	
7	Subtract line 6 from line 4			7	
8	Personal holding company tax (attach Schedule PH (Form 1120))			8	
9a	Recapture of investment credit (attach Form 4255)	9a			
b	Recapture of low-income housing credit (attach Form 8611)	9b			
c	Interest due under the look-back method—completed long-term contracts (attach Form 8697)	9c			
d	Interest due under the look-back method—income forecast method (attach Form 8866)	9d			
e	Alternative tax on qualifying shipping activities (attach Form 8902)	9e			
f	Other (see instructions—attach statement)	9f			
10	**Total.** Add lines 9a through 9f			10	
11	**Total tax.** Add lines 7, 8, and 10. Enter here and on page 1, line 31			11	

Part II–Payments and Refundable Credits

12	2016 overpayment credited to 2017			12	
13	2017 estimated tax payments			13	
14	2017 refund applied for on Form 4466			14	( )
15	Combine lines 12, 13, and 14			15	
16	Tax deposited with Form 7004			16	
17	Withholding (see instructions)			17	
18	**Total payments.** Add lines 15, 16, and 17			18	
19	Refundable credits from:				
a	Form 2439	19a			
b	Form 4136	19b			
c	Form 8827, line 8c	19c			
d	Other (attach statement—see instructions)	19d			
20	**Total credits.** Add lines 19a through 19d			20	
21	**Total payments and credits.** Add lines 18 and 20. Enter here and on page 1, line 32			21	

Schedule K **Other Information** (see instructions)

		Yes	No
1	Check accounting method: a ☐ Cash b ☐ Accrual c ☐ Other (specify) ▶		
2	See the instructions and enter the:		
a	Business activity code no. ▶		
b	Business activity ▶		
c	Product or service ▶		
3	Is the corporation a subsidiary in an affiliated group or a parent-subsidiary controlled group? If "Yes," enter name and EIN of the parent corporation ▶		
4	At the end of the tax year:		
a	Did any foreign or domestic corporation, partnership (including any entity treated as a partnership), trust, or tax-exempt organization own directly 20% or more, or own, directly or indirectly, 50% or more of the total voting power of all classes of the corporation's stock entitled to vote? If "Yes," complete Part I of Schedule G (Form 1120) (attach Schedule G)		
b	Did any individual or estate own directly 20% or more, or own, directly or indirectly, 50% or more of the total voting power of all classes of the corporation's stock entitled to vote? If "Yes," complete Part II of Schedule G (Form 1120) (attach Schedule G)		

Form **1120** (2017)

(continued)

EXHIBIT 15-1 *(continued)*

Form 1120 (2017) Page 4

Schedule K **Other Information** *(continued from page 3)*

		Yes	No
5	At the end of the tax year, did the corporation:		
a	Own directly 20% or more, or own, directly or indirectly, 50% or more of the total voting power of all classes of stock entitled to vote of any foreign or domestic corporation not included on **Form 851,** Affiliations Schedule? For rules of constructive ownership, see instructions. If "Yes," complete (i) through (iv) below.		

(i) Name of Corporation	(ii) Employer Identification Number (if any)	(iii) Country of Incorporation	(iv) Percentage Owned in Voting Stock

		Yes	No
b	Own directly an interest of 20% or more, or own, directly or indirectly, an interest of 50% or more in any foreign or domestic partnership (including an entity treated as a partnership) or in the beneficial interest of a trust? For rules of constructive ownership, see instructions. If "Yes," complete (i) through (iv) below.		

(i) Name of Entity	(ii) Employer Identification Number (if any)	(iii) Country of Organization	(iv) Maximum Percentage Owned in Profit, Loss, or Capital

		Yes	No
6	During this tax year, did the corporation pay dividends (other than stock dividends and distributions in exchange for stock) in excess of the corporation's current and accumulated earnings and profits? See sections 301 and 316 . . . . If "Yes," file **Form 5452,** Corporate Report of Nondividend Distributions. See the instructions for Form 5452. If this is a consolidated return, answer here for the parent corporation and on Form 851 for each subsidiary.		
7	At any time during the tax year, did one foreign person own, directly or indirectly, at least 25% of the total voting power of all classes of the corporation's stock entitled to vote or at least 25% of the total value of all classes of the corporation's stock? . For rules of attribution, see section 318. If "Yes," enter: **(a)** Percentage owned ► ______ and **(b)** Owner's country ► ______ **(c)** The corporation may have to file **Form 5472,** Information Return of a 25% Foreign-Owned U.S. Corporation or a Foreign Corporation Engaged in a U.S. Trade or Business. Enter the number of Forms 5472 attached ► ______		
8	Check this box if the corporation issued publicly offered debt instruments with original issue discount . . . . ► ☐ If checked, the corporation may have to file **Form 8281,** Information Return for Publicly Offered Original Issue Discount Instruments.		
9	Enter the amount of tax-exempt interest received or accrued during the tax year ► $ ______		
10	Enter the number of shareholders at the end of the tax year (if 100 or fewer) ► ______		
11	If the corporation has an NOL for the tax year and is electing to forego the carryback period, check here . . . . ► ☐ If the corporation is filing a consolidated return, the statement required by Regulations section 1.1502-21(b)(3) must be attached or the election will not be valid.		
12	Enter the available NOL carryover from prior tax years (do not reduce it by any deduction reported on page 1, line 29a.) . . . . ► $ ______		
13	Are the corporation's total receipts (page 1, line 1a, plus lines 4 through 10) for the tax year **and** its total assets at the end of the tax year less than $250,000? . . . . If "Yes," the corporation is not required to complete Schedules L, M-1, and M-2. Instead, enter the total amount of cash distributions and the book value of property distributions (other than cash) made during the tax year ► $ ______		
14	Is the corporation required to file Schedule UTP (Form 1120), Uncertain Tax Position Statement? See instructions . . . . . If "Yes," complete and attach Schedule UTP.		
15a	Did the corporation make any payments in 2017 that would require it to file Form(s) 1099?		
b	If "Yes," did or will the corporation file required Forms 1099?		
16	During this tax year, did the corporation have an 80% or more change in ownership, including a change due to redemption of its own stock?		
17	During or subsequent to this tax year, but before the filing of this return, did the corporation dispose of more than 65% (by value) of its assets in a taxable, non-taxable, or tax deferred transaction?		
18	Did the corporation receive assets in a section 351 transfer in which any of the transferred assets had a fair market basis or fair market value of more than $1 million?		
19	During the corporation's tax year, did the corporation make any payments that would require it to file Forms 1042 and 1042-S under chapter 3 (sections 1441 through 1464) or chapter 4 (sections 1471 through 1474) of the Code?		

Form **1120** (2017)

EXHIBIT 15-1 *(concluded)*

Form 1120 (2017) Page **5**

Schedule L Balance Sheets per Books

Assets	Beginning of tax year (a)	(b)	End of tax year (c)	(d)
1 Cash				
2a Trade notes and accounts receivable				
b Less allowance for bad debts	( )		( )	
3 Inventories				
4 U.S. government obligations				
5 Tax-exempt securities (see instructions)				
6 Other current assets (attach statement)				
7 Loans to shareholders				
8 Mortgage and real estate loans				
9 Other investments (attach statement)				
10a Buildings and other depreciable assets				
b Less accumulated depreciation	( )		( )	
11a Depletable assets				
b Less accumulated depletion	( )		( )	
12 Land (net of any amortization)				
13a Intangible assets (amortizable only)				
b Less accumulated amortization	( )		( )	
14 Other assets (attach statement)				
15 Total assets				
Liabilities and Shareholders' Equity				
16 Accounts payable				
17 Mortgages, notes, bonds payable in less than 1 year				
18 Other current liabilities (attach statement)				
19 Loans from shareholders				
20 Mortgages, notes, bonds payable in 1 year or more				
21 Other liabilities (attach statement)				
22 Capital stock: a Preferred stock				
b Common stock				
23 Additional paid-in capital				
24 Retained earnings—Appropriated (attach statement)				
25 Retained earnings—Unappropriated				
26 Adjustments to shareholders' equity (attach statement)				
27 Less cost of treasury stock		( )		( )
28 Total liabilities and shareholders' equity				

Schedule M-1 Reconciliation of Income (Loss) per Books With Income per Return

Note: The corporation may be required to file Schedule M-3. See instructions.

1 Net income (loss) per books		7 Income recorded on books this year not included on this return (itemize): Tax-exempt interest $	
2 Federal income tax per books			
3 Excess of capital losses over capital gains			
4 Income subject to tax not recorded on books this year (itemize):		8 Deductions on this return not charged against book income this year (itemize):	
5 Expenses recorded on books this year not deducted on this return (itemize):		a Depreciation $	
a Depreciation $		b Charitable contributions $	
b Charitable contributions $			
c Travel and entertainment $			
		9 Add lines 7 and 8	
6 Add lines 1 through 5		10 Income (page 1, line 28)—line 6 less line 9	

Schedule M-2 Analysis of Unappropriated Retained Earnings per Books (Line 25, Schedule L)

1 Balance at beginning of year		5 Distributions: a Cash	
2 Net income (loss) per books		b Stock	
3 Other increases (itemize):		c Property	
		6 Other decreases (itemize):	
		7 Add lines 5 and 6	
4 Add lines 1, 2, and 3		8 Balance at end of year (line 4 less line 7)	

Form **1120** (2017)

EXAMPLE 15-1

Marty and Sara decide to form Boone Company. Marty transfers $1,000 cash in exchange for 100 shares of stock, and Sara transfers a bond with a fair market value (FMV) of $1,000 (basis of $800) for 100 shares. They are the only two shareholders of Boone Company. Because they control 80% or more of Boone immediately after the exchange, the transaction is tax-free.

Even when the 80% rule is met, a stockholder could be required to recognize a gain in two cases. The first is when the individual transfers property subject to a liability and the relief of liability is greater than the transferor's basis in the property. The gain is equal to the excess of liability over basis.

EXAMPLE 15-2

Gina transfers an apartment building to GGG Company in exchange for all of the stock in the company. The building has a basis of $100,000, an FMV of $500,000, and debt (assumed by the company) of $300,000. Even though Gina controls more than 80% of the company immediately after the exchange, the transaction is taxable because she has debt relief in excess of basis. She has a gain of $200,000 (relief of debt of $300,000 minus building basis of $100,000).

The second case involves an individual who contributes cash or property and receives, in return, stock plus other cash or property (this extra cash or property is called *boot,* discussed in an earlier chapter). In this case, the taxable gain is the lower of the FMV of the property received or the realized gain (the FMV of property contributed less the tax basis of the property contributed).

EXAMPLE 15-3

Ernie receives all the stock of EBU Company in exchange for contributing a machine with a basis of $15,000 and an FMV of $25,000. Ernie also receives $3,000 cash from the company. The gain on transfer is $10,000 (the difference between the basis and FMV of the machine). The gain Ernie must report is $3,000, the lower of gain or cash received.

To the corporate entity, the basis of the cash or property received is equal to the basis in the hands of the shareholder plus any gain recognized by the shareholder. The basis of the stock in the hands of the shareholder is equal to the basis of the property contributed plus any gain recognized, minus any boot received (boot includes relief of liability). The amounts of inside and outside basis for the stockholders in each of the three previous examples are as follows:

	Reported Gain	Stock Basis to Shareholder (Outside)	Property Basis to Corporation (Inside)
Marty	$ –0–	$ 1,000	$ 1,000
Sara	–0–	800	800
Gina	200,000	–0–	300,000
Ernie	3,000	15,000	18,000

Shareholders do not recognize losses as a result of the formation of a corporation when the 80% test is met.

If an individual provides services in exchange for stock upon the formation of a corporation, the individual will recognize ordinary income equal to the FMV of the services.

Unless a C corporation stockholder increases or decreases his or her proportionate ownership (buys or sells stock), there is generally no adjustment to the outside basis over time.

CONCEPT CHECK 15-2— LO 15-2

1. When forming a corporation, if the transferors control at least 80% of the corporate entity, the formation is generally tax-free. True or false?
2. The basis to the corporation of property received is equal to ______________.
3. Arturo contributed land with an FMV of $100,000 and basis of $40,000 to a newly formed corporation in exchange for 90% of the stock. Arturo's basis in the stock is ______________.

TAXABLE INCOME AND TAX LIABILITY

LO 15-3

Corporate taxable income is generally determined using the same operating rules as a trade or business that we discussed in Chapter 6. The general formula to determine corporate taxable income and tax liability follows. The line numbers pertain to Form 1120 in Exhibit 15-1.

Total gross receipts or sales (line 1c)
− Cost of goods sold (line 2)
Gross profit (line 3)
+ Interest, dividends, capital gains, other income (lines 4–10)
Total income (line 11)
− Ordinary and necessary trade or business expenses (lines 12–27)
Taxable income before special deductions (line 28)
− Net operating loss deduction (line 29a)
− Dividends received deduction (line 29b)
= Taxable income (line 30)
× Applicable tax rates
= Tax liability (line 31)
− Tax payments during the tax year and tax credits (line 32)
= Tax due with return (line 34) or refund (line 35)

In corporate taxation, the notion of Adjusted Gross Income (AGI) does not exist.

As mentioned, determination of corporate taxable income generally follows the trade or business rules discussed in Chapter 6. A few differences pertaining to corporations—capital gains and losses, charitable contributions, the dividends received deduction, and some miscellaneous differences—must be noted.

Capital Gains and Losses (Form 1120, line 8)

As we discussed in Chapter 7, individuals (or other noncorporate taxpayers) include capital gains and losses in income. If capital losses exceed capital gains, individuals recognize a net capital loss of up to $3,000 with any excess being carried forward indefinitely. C corporations are not permitted to report any net capital losses. Thus capital losses can only offset capital gains.[6] In other words, the amount on line 8 must be either positive or zero; it cannot be negative.

[6] IRC § 1211(a).

Corporations are permitted to carry back excess capital losses three preceding years (starting with the earliest year) and then forward five years if any loss remains.[7] Corporations can use the carryback and carryforward amounts only against net capital gains in the years noted.

EXAMPLE 15-4

ABC Company, a C corporation, was formed in 2013 and reported net income in each year of its operation. The company had net capital gains and losses as follows:

2013	$ 7,000 gain
2014	10,000 gain
2015	1,000 gain
2016	5,000 gain
2017	21,000 loss

The 2017 capital loss must be carried back three years starting with the earliest year. Thus ABC Company will first apply the $21,000 loss from 2017 to tax year 2014, then to 2015, and finally to 2016. Because the total capital gains in those years were $16,000, ABC Company has a $5,000 capital loss to carry forward to tax years 2018 to 2022.

TAX YOUR BRAIN

Pirate Company was formed in 2012 and reported capital gains and losses, prior to any carryforwards and carrybacks, as follows:

2012	$ 2,000 loss
2013	7,000 gain
2014	10,000 gain
2015	16,000 loss
2016	5,000 gain
2017	14,000 loss

What is the proper tax treatment of the capital gain carryforwards and carrybacks, and what is the resulting net capital gain or loss for each year indicated?

ANSWER

Work from the oldest date to the present. The 2012 loss is carried forward to 2013 resulting in a $5,000 gain in 2013. In 2014, the $10,000 gain will be reported. In 2015, the $16,000 loss will be carried back first to 2013, eliminating the remaining $5,000 gain, and then to 2014, eliminating the $10,000 gain. A $1,000 loss carryforward then remains from 2015. This carryforward will be applied to 2016 resulting in a $4,000 gain in 2016. Finally, the 2017 loss will be carried back to the remaining 2016 gain, giving Pirate Company a $10,000 loss carryforward to be used starting in 2018 and expiring in 2022.

If a corporation carries back a capital loss, it files an amended return for the prior year(s) and will receive a refund.

The other major difference between individual and corporate taxation of capital gains pertains to tax rates. Individuals pay tax on net capital gains at a rate lower than for ordinary income. For corporations, net capital gains are included in income and are taxed at the marginal corporate rate.

[7] IRC § 1212(a).

Charitable Contributions

Corporations are permitted charitable contributions to qualified charitable organizations. The deduction is limited to 10% of taxable income before any of the following:

- Charitable contributions.
- Dividends received deduction (described next).
- Net operating loss carryback.
- Capital loss carryback.[8]

Any contributions in excess of the permitted amount are carried forward for five years, are added to the charitable contributions in that year, and are subject to the 10% limitation. In future years, current contributions are deducted first.[9]

EXAMPLE 15-5

Szabo Company reported $50,000 of taxable income before charitable contributions. The company had charitable contributions of $8,000. Szabo's charitable contributions are limited to $5,000 ($50,000 × 10%). Thus Szabo's taxable income will be $45,000, and its charitable contributions carryforward is $3,000.

In general, if a corporation contributes ordinary income property, the deduction is limited to the corporation's basis in the property.[10] Ordinary income property is property that, if sold, would produce a gain other than a long-term capital gain. An example is inventory held by a corporation.

Taxpayers use carryforward information to determine any charitable contributions limitation but ignore carryback information. In effect, taxpayers use all information available when the return is filed but do not make changes for information that could become available in the future.

Dividends Received Deduction

C corporations are permitted a tax deduction for a portion of the dividends they receive from other domestic corporations. The dividends received deduction (DRD) is a percentage of the dividend and varies, depending on the percentage ownership in the dividend-paying corporation:[11]

Ownership Percentage	Deduction Percentage
Less than 20%	70%
20% to less than 80%	80%
80% or more	100%

EXAMPLE 15-6

Duck Corporation owns 15% of Rose Company. Duck received a $10,000 dividend from Rose and is entitled to a $7,000 dividends received deduction. The deduction means that $3,000 of the dividend is included in Duck's taxable income. If Duck owned 40% of Rose, the DRD would have been $8,000, and only $2,000 of the dividend would have been taxable to Duck.

The DRD can be limited. If taxable income (before DRD or any capital loss carryback) is between 100% of the dividend and 70% (or 80% as appropriate) of the dividend, the DRD is limited to taxable income multiplied by the appropriate percentage.

[8] IRC § 170(b)(2).

[9] IRC § 170(d)(2).

[10] In IRC § 170(e). There are three limited cases in which the deduction can exceed basis.

[11] IRC § 246(b)(3).

EXAMPLE 15-7

Sylva Silverware owns 30% of Fredonia Flatware. Fredonia paid a $20,000 dividend to Sylva. Sylva's taxable income, before the DRD, was $50,000. Sylva's DRD is $16,000 ($20,000 × 80%).

EXAMPLE 15-8

Use the information from the previous example except that Sylva's taxable income, before the DRD, was $5,000. Sylva's taxable income is not between 80% of the dividend ($16,000) and 100% of the dividend ($20,000). Thus the DRD is not limited.

EXAMPLE 15-9

Use the information from Example 15-7 except that Sylva's taxable income before the DRD was $18,000. In this case, Sylva's taxable income is in the limitation area (between $16,000 and $20,000). Thus Sylva's DRD is limited to 80% of taxable income before the DRD, or $14,400 ($18,000 × 80%).

In Examples 15-7 through 15-9, if Sylva had owned less than 20% of Fredonia, the applicable percentage would have been 70% and the lower dollar limit for purposes of the limitation would have been $14,000 (the $20,000 dividend × 70%).

Other Differences

Except for closely held C corporations, the passive loss rules (refer to Chapter 13) do not apply to corporations.[12] A *closely held C corporation* is one in which more than 50% of the value of its outstanding stock is owned, directly or indirectly, by not more than five individuals.[13]

Corporations normally incur various organizational expenses at the time of legal formation. These costs can include legal fees, incorporation fees, and filing fees. In general, capitalized costs are deductible over their useful life. Because the life of a corporation is theoretically indefinite, organizational expenses are recorded as a nonamortizable asset and are not deductible. However, the IRC permits corporations to elect to deduct organizational expenses in an amount equal to the lower of (1) the amount of organizational expenses or (2) $5,000.[14] If total organizational expenses exceed $50,000, then the $5,000 amount is reduced to zero on a dollar-for-dollar basis. Thus, when organizational expenses exceed $55,000, no immediate deduction is permitted. Any remaining organizational expenses are deductible over a 180-month period beginning with the month the corporation begins business. Expenditures must be incurred before the end of the fiscal year in which the corporation begins business, and the election must be filed with the first tax return. Expenditures associated with issuing or selling stock are not deductible.

Organizational expenses are different from *start-up expenses,* which are incurred prior to the time the corporation begins to produce income. If the enterprise is operating as a business the expenses would be deductible as ordinary and necessary business expenses. However, the business is not yet active and is not earning income; thus the expenses are not deductible and must be capitalized. Corporations can elect to treat the expenses as deferred expenses and deduct them initially and/or over a 180-month period in a manner similar to that described for organizational expenses.[15] The 180-month period begins in the month in which the active trade or business begins. The election must be filed with the tax return for the corporation's first year. The calculations and limitations are determined separately for organizational expenses and for start-up expenses.

[12] IRC § 469(a)(2).

[13] IRC § 542(a)(2).

[14] IRC § 248(a).

[15] IRC § 195(b).

Corporate Tax Rates

Once corporate taxable income is determined, the amount of tax liability can be calculated with reference to a tax rate table. Tax rates for C corporations[16] are as follows:

Corporate Tax Rates

Taxable Income Over	But Not Over	The Tax Is	Of the Amount Over
$ –0–	$ 50,000	15%	$ –0–
50,000	75,000	$ 7,500 + 25%	50,000
75,000	100,000	13,750 + 34%	75,000
100,000	335,000	22,250 + 39%	100,000
335,000	10,000,000	113,900 + 34%	335,000
10,000,000	15,000,000	3,400,000 + 35%	10,000,000
15,000,000	18,333,333	5,150,000 + 38%	15,000,000
18,333,333	—	35% of taxable income	18,333,333

Corporate tax rates follow a progressive tax structure, but the rates "wobble around" as income increases. Technically, the tax rate for incomes between $75,000 and $10,000,000 is 34% and the rate above $10,000,000 is 35%.[17] However, the IRC also recaptures the benefit of reduced rates for those corporate taxpayers with higher incomes. In other words, a corporate taxpayer with $60,000 of taxable income pays tax of 15% on the first $50,000 and 25% on the remaining $10,000. A corporate taxpayer with taxable income of $60,000,000 does not get the benefit of lower rates and pays tax at a 35% flat rate on every dollar of income. The tax rate tables are structured to eliminate the benefit of the lower brackets.

EXAMPLE 15-10

Beaufort Company has taxable income of $1,200,000. Its tax liability is $408,000 (calculated as $113,900 + [($1,200,000 − $335,000) × 34%] = $408,000). You will get the same answer if you multiply taxable income by 34%.

Estimated Payments

A corporation must pay *estimated taxes.* The required annual payment is the lower of (1) 100% of the tax due for the year or (2) 100% of the tax due for the prior year.[18] Estimated payments can be made in four installments on the 15th day of the 4th, 6th, 9th, and 12th months of the corporation's fiscal year. For calendar year corporations, the due dates are April 15, June 15, September 15, and December 15. Estimated payments are reported on Form 1120, line 32.

Large corporations (those with taxable income in excess of $1 million in any of the three preceding years) cannot use the prior year tax safe harbor except for the first quarterly installment payment. These corporations must base the final three quarterly payments on their estimate of current year tax due.

The corporate underpayment penalty is based on the same interest rate schedule used for individuals. The penalty is not deductible in any year.

Net Operating Losses

If a corporation has a net operating loss (NOL), it can carry the loss back two years and forward 20 years.[19] Alternatively, the corporation can affirmatively elect to waive the carryback period and only carry the loss forward.[20] The election is irrevocable for the tax year.

[16] IRC § 11(b).

[17] IRC § 11(b)(1)(C) and IRC § 11(b)(1)(D).

[18] IRC § 6655.

[19] IRC § 172 and IRC § 172(b)(1).

[20] IRC § 172(b)(3).

In general, a net operating loss occurs when the corporate entity has negative taxable income for the year.

TAX YOUR BRAIN

Under what circumstances would a corporation choose to forgo the carryback period for a net operating loss and elect to only carry the loss forward?

ANSWER

If tax rates will be higher in the future and if the corporation expects to earn money in the future, it may make sense to only carry the NOL forward. For example, if tax rates in prior years were 30% and are expected to be 40% in the future, the corporation would receive an additional 10 cents for each dollar of NOL if the loss were only carried forward.

CONCEPT CHECK 15-3—
LO 15-3

1. Corporations follow the same tax rules for capital gains as do individuals. True or false?
2. The tax liability of a corporation with taxable income of $520,000 is ____________.
3. A corporation reported taxable income of $390,000 before charitable contributions. The corporation made charitable contributions of $50,000. Its permitted deduction for charitable contributions in the current tax year is ____________.
4. Organizational expenses are automatically deductible over 180 months. True or false?
5. Corporate net operating losses from 2017 can be carried back ____________ years and forward ____________ years.

TRANSACTIONS WITH SHAREHOLDERS
LO 15-4

Dividends and Distributions

Corporations can pay cash or property (called *distributions*) to their shareholders. To the extent that distributions are from the earnings and profits of the corporation, the distribution is a *dividend.*[21] The corporation cannot deduct the cost of the dividend, and the shareholder reports taxable income in an amount equal to the fair market value of the property received.[22]

Earnings and profits (E&P) are conceptually similar to retained earnings except that they are calculated using tax law, not financial accounting standards.

Distributions paid in excess of earnings and profits are nontaxable to the extent of the stockholder's basis in her or his stock. The excess of a distribution over the stockholder's basis is treated as a capital gain (assuming the stock is a capital asset in the hands of the stockholder).[23]

If a corporation makes a distribution of property (not cash) that has a basis less than the fair market value (that is, appreciated property), the corporation is treated as selling the property at its fair market value. Thus the corporation recognizes a gain on the distribution of appreciated property.

EXAMPLE 15-11

Sasha received a $500 cash distribution from the E&P of Alpha Company. The dividend is fully taxable to Sasha.

[21] IRC § 316.

[22] IRC § 301.

[23] IRC § 301(c)(2) and § 301(c)(3).

EXAMPLE 15-12

Assume that Sasha's distribution was in the form of property with an FMV of $500 and a basis to Alpha Company of $400. Alpha will record a $100 gain. Sasha will report dividend income of $500.

EXAMPLE 15-13

Quad Company has E&P of $5,000. It makes a $6,000 cash distribution to Quincy, its sole shareholder. Assuming that Quincy has a basis in his stock of at least $1,000, he will report dividend income of $5,000 and a nontaxable distribution of $1,000. Quincy will reduce the basis of his stock by $1,000.

EXAMPLE 15-14

Use the information from Example 15-13. Assume that the basis of Quincy's stock is $200. In this case, he would report a dividend of $5,000, a nontaxable return of capital of $200, and a capital gain of $800. Quincy will also reduce the basis of his stock to zero.

The preceding discussion assumed that the distribution was made to shareholders on a pro rata basis. In other words, each shareholder receives a distribution proportionate to his or her ownership. Corporations can also make a non–pro rata distribution by which one or more stockholders receive a distribution that is not in proportion to their ownership percentage. If the distribution is in appreciated property, the corporation again has a deemed sale and gain based on FMV. The shareholder reports dividend income equal to the FMV of the cash or property received.

A shareholder may receive a distribution in full liquidation of her or his ownership interest. For example, a shareholder may sell all of her or his stock back to the corporation for cash or property. In such case, he or she will have a capital gain or loss equal to the difference between the amount of the distribution and his or her basis in the stock.

Liquidation

A *corporate liquidation* occurs when a corporation decides to cease doing business and wind up its business affairs. The corporation pays debts and distributes remaining assets to shareholders. In the case of a complete liquidation, the corporation records all assets and liabilities at fair market value (with associated write-ups or write-downs). The shareholder reports a capital gain or loss equal to the difference between his or her basis in the stock and the FMV of the property received.

EXAMPLE 15-15

Tara received cash of $5,000 and other assets with an FMV of $7,000 as a result of the complete liquidation of Blue Corporation. Tara's basis in the stock of Blue was $10,000. Tara will report a return of capital (nontaxable) of $10,000 and a capital gain of $2,000.

CONCEPT CHECK 15-4— LO 15-4

1. Dividends are always taxable to a shareholder. True or false?
2. If a corporation pays a dividend in property, the stockholder will have a dividend equal to the corporate basis in the property. True or false?
3. A corporation has earnings and profits of $10,000 and makes a cash distribution to its sole shareholder in the amount of $11,000. The amount of taxable dividend to the shareholder is ____________.

SCHEDULES L, M-1, AND M-3

LO 15-5

Corporations must provide a beginning and ending balance sheet on Form 1120, Schedule L, as well as a reconciliation of book income to taxable income on Form 1120, Schedule M-1. See page 5 of Form 1120 in Exhibit 15-1 for both schedules. If a corporation's total receipts and total assets are both less than $250,000, the two schedules are not required.

Preparation of Schedule L is straightforward. It is prepared in accordance with the accounting method the corporation uses to keep its financial accounting records (accrual, cash, or mixed model).

Schedule M-1 can be more complex. It reconciles net income per books (line 1) with net income per the tax return (line 10). In effect, this schedule sets out all book/tax differences for the year regardless of whether they are permanent or temporary differences.

It is important to note that Schedule M-1 reconciles from net income per books (financial accounting net income) to net income per the tax law, *not* the other way around. Let's examine each of the lines individually.

Line 2: Federal income tax is an expense for book purposes but is not deductible for tax purposes. The amount of federal income tax expense must be added back to book income. This number is the federal income tax expense deduction on the income statement—*not* the tax expense on page 1 of the tax return.

Line 3: For book purposes, excess capital losses qualify as an expense. For tax purposes, recall that corporate capital losses are deductible only to the extent of capital gains. Thus any excess of capital losses over capital gains must be added back to book income.

Line 4: Certain income may be taxable but may be properly excluded from book income. Examples include the last month's rent collected at lease signing by a landlord or the installment sale income reported in full on the books in a prior year. These items must be added to book income to arrive at taxable income.

Line 5: Certain expenses can be recorded on the books but are not deductible on the tax return. These items include the difference between accelerated depreciation taken on the books and straight-line depreciation for taxes in the early years of an asset's life; the difference between the book and tax deductions if charitable contributions are limited on the tax return and 50% of travel and entertainment expenses that are not deductible on the tax return.

Line 7: Some income is reported on the books but is not reported on the tax return. Examples include life insurance proceeds that can be excluded for taxes but must be included for book purposes; prepayment of the last month of rent that will be included on the tax return at the beginning of the lease but on the books at the end of the lease; and interest from tax-exempt bonds.

Line 8: Deductions can be taken on the tax return but are not deductible in the financial records. Tax return depreciation in excess of book depreciation is an example. Another is the tax deduction for previously disallowed charitable contributions. These were deducted on the financial statements in a prior year.

EXAMPLE 15-16

Martin Company had book income of $50,000 for the year. It also had the following differences between book income and tax income:

Charitable contributions carryforward used in current year	$2,000
Excess depreciation on tax return	6,000

In addition, the company incurred $10,000 of travel and entertainment expense, only 50% of which is deductible for taxes. Martin Company's taxable income is $47,000 ($50,000 – $2,000 – $6,000 + [$10,000 × 50%]). A completed Schedule M-1 for Martin Company is shown in Exhibit 15-2.

EXHIBIT 15-2

Schedule M-1 **Reconciliation of Income (Loss) per Books With Income per Return**
Note: Schedule M-3 required instead of Schedule M-1 if total assets are $10 million or more—see instructions

1	Net income (loss) per books	50,000	7	Income recorded on books this year not included on this return (itemize): Tax-exempt interest $	
2	Federal income tax per books				
3	Excess of capital losses over capital gains				
4	Income subject to tax not recorded on books this year (itemize):		8	Deductions on this return not charged against book income this year (itemize):	
5	Expenses recorded on books this year not deducted on this return (itemize):		a	Depreciation $ 6,000	
a	Depreciation $		b	Charitable contributions $ 2,000	
b	Charitable contributions $				
c	Travel and entertainment $ 5,000				8,000
		5,000	9	Add lines 7 and 8	8,000
6	Add lines 1 through 5	55,000	10	Income (page 1, line 28)—line 6 less line 9	47,000

Source: U.S. Department of the Treasury, Internal Revenue Service, Form 1120. Washington, DC: 2017.

Corporations with total assets of $10 million or more must complete a separate Schedule M-3. This schedule is, in effect, an extremely detailed reconciliation of book income with taxable income. Thus it is an expanded version of Schedule M-1 for large corporations. You can locate a Schedule M-3 on the IRS Web site (www.irs.gov).

CONCEPT CHECK 15-5— LO 15-5

1. Completion of Schedule L is required of all corporations. True or false?
2. Schedule M-1 reconciles book income to taxable income. True or false?
3. A corporation's depreciation expense is lower on the financial statements than it is on the tax return. Would this difference be a negative or positive item on Schedule M-1?

OTHER CORPORATE ISSUES INCLUDING ALTERNATIVE MINIMUM TAX

LO 15-6

Corporations can be part of a controlled group. The most common of these groups are parent–subsidiary groups or brother–sister groups, which we discuss here, in addition to corporate alternative minimum tax.

Parent–Subsidiary Groups

Parent–subsidiary groups are those for which a common parent corporation owns, directly or indirectly, at least 80% of one or more other corporations. The ownership can be one or more chains of corporations connected through stock ownership with the parent corporation.

EXAMPLE 15-17

Garner Corporation owns 90% of Harnett Company. The two corporations are part of a parent–subsidiary group. The relationship holds as long as Garner owns at least 80% of Harnett.

EXAMPLE 15-18

Garner Corporation also owns 95% of Iona Company. Iona, in turn, owns 85% of Jasper Corporation. The entire Garner/Iona/Jasper chain of corporations is part of a parent–subsidiary group.

Parent–subsidiary corporations can elect to file a consolidated tax return. Form 1122 is attached to the first consolidated return for each of the subsidiaries of the group.[24] An appropriate officer of the subsidiary signs the form, thereby consenting to be included in the group. All members of the parent–subsidiary group must be included. Subsidiaries no longer file

[24] Reg. § 1.1502-75(b).

separate returns. In subsequent years, Form 851, which is an affiliation schedule listing the corporations that are part of the consolidated return, is attached to the consolidated return.

Electing to file as a consolidated entity has certain advantages. For example, a consolidated return allows the entity to offset losses from one corporation against profits of another. In addition, profits from intercompany sales are deferred. There are potential disadvantages as well. The election is binding on future tax years, losses on intercompany sales cannot be immediately recognized, and elections made by the parent are binding on all subsidiaries.

Brother–Sister Groups

A *brother–sister group* may exist if five or fewer persons own two or more corporations. The group exists if both of the following tests are met:

- **Total ownership test:** The shareholder group owns stock representing at least 80% of the voting shares of stock or at least 80% of the total value of all shares.
- **Common ownership test:** The shareholder group has common (identical) ownership of more than 50% of the voting power or more than 50% of the value of all shares.

At first glance, the tests seem to be the same with different percentages, but such is not the case. The 80% test examines ownership of an individual corporation. The 50% test, in effect, is based on the smallest common percentage across all of the corporations evaluated.

EXAMPLE 15-19

Three individuals have ownership interests in four different corporations as follows:

	Corporations				Identical
	A	B	C	D	Ownership
Reed	60%	20%	30%	30%	20%
Smith	30	65	30	40	30
Thomas	10	15	40	20	10
Totals	100%	100%	100%	90%	60%

The Identical Ownership column represents the smallest number reading across the column. In other words, it is the identical ownership across all of the corporations. So, for example, Reed owns at least 20% of each of the corporations.

The total ownership test is met because the three individuals own at least 80% of each of the four corporations (in this example for corporations A, B, and C, they actually own all the stock). The common ownership test is met because the common (identical) ownership is more than 50% (it is 60% in this example). Thus the four corporations are all part of a brother–sister group.

TAX YOUR BRAIN

In Example 15-19, if Reed sold half of her ownership in Corporation B to an unrelated third party, would the corporations remain as a brother–sister group?

ANSWER

No. By reducing her ownership in Corporation B to 10% of the total, Reed now has an identical common ownership across the four corporations of 10%. Thus the sum of the common ownership for all three individuals is exactly 50%. The common ownership test must be more than 50%. Thus the entities are no longer a brother–sister group.

One way to think about the two tests is that the 80% test is a "vertical test" (does the group own at least 80% of a specific individual corporation?) whereas the 50% test is a "horizontal test" (what is the smallest percentage that an individual owns across the various corporations?).

Corporations within a brother–sister group continue to file individual tax returns. However, the IRS realizes that the common control within a brother–sister group can result in income or expense being inappropriately allocated between members of the group. Thus the IRS has the authority to reallocate the income, deductions, and credits of the related corporations "in order to prevent the evasion of taxes or clearly reflect the income" of the individual corporations within the group.[25]

For purposes of determining corporate tax brackets, the accumulated earnings credit, and the minimum tax exemption, a controlled group is determined only with reference to the common ownership test. In all other cases, both tests are used.

Corporate Alternative Minimum Tax

Corporations are subject to a corporate alternative minimum tax (AMT).[26] The tax is calculated in a manner similar to AMT for an individual. In general, the corporation starts with regular taxable income, adds or subtracts adjustments, adds tax preference items, subtracts an exemption amount, and multiplies the resulting AMT base by a 20% AMT rate.

Most tax preference items are similar to those for individuals. An additional corporate preference item is for adjusted current earnings (ACE). The ACE adjustment is 75% of the difference between ACE and unadjusted alternative minimum taxable income. In short, ACE is the economic income of the corporation; it takes into account all of the corporation's inflows and outflows (including nontaxable and nondeductible items). The ACE adjustment can be very complex and is beyond the scope of this text.

The AMT exemption amount is $40,000 for corporations with AMT income of $150,000 or less.[27] The exemption is reduced by 25 cents for each dollar that AMT income exceeds $150,000. Thus the exemption is totally phased out at AMT income levels of $310,000 or more.

Small corporations are not subject to the AMT.[28] A *small corporation* is one that has average annual gross receipts of $7,500,000 or less for each of the preceding three tax years. Newly formed corporations are exempt from the AMT in the first year of existence and continue to be exempt from the AMT for the first three years if average annual gross receipts are less than $5 million.

EXAMPLE 15-20

Manteo Company has taxable income of $200,000 and is not a small corporation. It has a regular tax liability of $61,250. The company has $120,000 of tax preferences. Manteo's AMT is calculated as follows:

Regular taxable income	$200,000
Tax preferences	120,000
AMT income	320,000
Exemption (AMT income exceeds $310,000)	–0–
AMT base	320,000
Times tax rate	× 20%
AMT	64,000
Less: Regular corporate tax	61,250
Corporate AMT due	$ 2,750

CONCEPT CHECK 15-6—
LO 15-6

1. To be considered a parent–subsidiary group, the parent corporation must own, directly or indirectly, at least ________ percent of the subsidiary corporation.
2. A brother–sister group may exist if ________ or fewer persons own two or more corporations.
3. For AMT purposes, the corporate exemption amount is $________.

[25] IRC § 482.

[26] IRC § 55 through § 59.

[27] IRC § 55(d)(2).

[28] IRC § 55(e).

SUBCHAPTER S CORPORATIONS

LO 15-7

General

A Subchapter S corporation is a "regular" corporation that has elected to be taxed under the provisions of Subchapter S of the IRC.[29] In effect, a Subchapter S (Sub S) corporation is a corporation for legal purposes but is taxed in a manner similar to a partnership. Thus the shareholders (not the corporation) are taxed based on their proportionate share of net income and separately stated items.

Sub S corporations file their annual tax returns on Form 1120S (see Exhibit 15-3). Tax returns for S corporations are due on the 15th day of the third month after the end of the fiscal year (March 15 for a calendar year Sub S corporation). A six-month extension is permitted.

Subchapter S Election

A corporation must affirmatively elect to be taxed as a Subchapter S corporation. The corporation must be a qualifying small business corporation that meets *all* of the following characteristics:[30]

- Be a domestic corporation.
- Have 100 or fewer shareholders who are all individuals, estates, and certain trusts.[31]
- Have only one class of stock.
- Have shareholders who are U.S. citizens or resident aliens.

For the election to be valid, it must be made on Form 2553, must be signed by all shareholders, and must be filed on a timely basis.[32] If the corporation wants the election to be valid for the current year, Form 2553 must be filed either in the prior fiscal year or before the 15th day of the third month of the current year. Thus elections filed after the 2.5-month deadline are effective for the following year.

The Sub S election is valid until it is statutorily terminated or voluntarily revoked. The election is statutorily terminated if the corporation fails to meet the qualifications to be a Sub S corporation. For example, once the corporation has more than 100 shareholders, the election will be terminated. For statutorily terminated elections, the termination is effective on the day the terminating event occurs.

The corporation can choose to voluntarily revoke the election. If shareholders owning a majority of the voting stock consent, in writing, to revoke the election, the Sub S status will be terminated.[33] If the revocation is made (and filed) during the first 2.5 months of the tax year, the revocation will be effective as of the beginning of the year. If the revocation is made subsequent to that date, the Sub S status will be terminated as of the beginning of the following year. Shareholders can state a revocation date on or after the date the voluntary revocation is filed, and the revocation will be effective on the selected date.

In most circumstances, if an S corporation loses its status because of statutory or voluntary revocation, the corporation must wait five years before reelecting Sub S status.

Taxable Income and Separately Stated Items

Generally items of income and expense are the same for a C corporation as for an S corporation.

As mentioned, a Sub S corporation is taxed as though it were a partnership. In other words, the shareholders, not the corporation, pay tax on the Subchapter S income. Unlike a partnership, a Sub S corporation can amortize organizational expenses and must recognize gains, but not losses, on distributions of property to shareholders. The dividends received deduction does not apply to a Sub S corporation.

[29] IRC § 1361.

[30] IRC § 1361(b).

[31] Members of a family are treated as one shareholder under IRC § 1361(c)(1). A family is defined as a common ancestor, the lineal descendants of that person, and the spouses or former spouses of the common ancestor or lineal descendants.

[32] IRC § 1362(a).

[33] IRC § 1362(d).

EXHIBIT 15-3

Form **1120S**
Department of the Treasury
Internal Revenue Service

U.S. Income Tax Return for an S Corporation

▶ **Do not file this form unless the corporation has filed or is attaching Form 2553 to elect to be an S corporation.**
▶ **Go to *www.irs.gov/Form1120S* for instructions and the latest information.**

OMB No. 1545-0123
2017

For calendar year 2017 or tax year beginning , 2017, ending , 20

A S election effective date	TYPE OR PRINT — Name	**D** Employer identification number
B Business activity code number (see instructions)	Number, street, and room or suite no. If a P.O. box, see instructions.	**E** Date incorporated
C Check if Sch. M-3 attached ☐	City or town, state or province, country, and ZIP or foreign postal code	**F** Total assets (see instructions) $

G Is the corporation electing to be an S corporation beginning with this tax year? ☐ Yes ☐ No If "Yes," attach Form 2553 if not already filed
H Check if: **(1)** ☐ Final return **(2)** ☐ Name change **(3)** ☐ Address change **(4)** ☐ Amended return **(5)** ☐ S election termination or revocation
I Enter the number of shareholders who were shareholders during any part of the tax year . . . ▶

Caution: Include **only** trade or business income and expenses on lines 1a through 21. See the instructions for more information.

Income	1a	Gross receipts or sales	1a	
	b	Returns and allowances	1b	
	c	Balance. Subtract line 1b from line 1a		1c
	2	Cost of goods sold (attach Form 1125-A)		2
	3	Gross profit. Subtract line 2 from line 1c		3
	4	Net gain (loss) from Form 4797, line 17 (attach Form 4797)		4
	5	Other income (loss) (see instructions—attach statement)		5
	6	**Total income (loss).** Add lines 3 through 5 ▶		6
Deductions (see instructions for limitations)	7	Compensation of officers (see instructions—attach Form 1125-E)		7
	8	Salaries and wages (less employment credits)		8
	9	Repairs and maintenance		9
	10	Bad debts		10
	11	Rents		11
	12	Taxes and licenses		12
	13	Interest		13
	14	Depreciation not claimed on Form 1125-A or elsewhere on return (attach Form 4562)		14
	15	Depletion **(Do not deduct oil and gas depletion.)**		15
	16	Advertising		16
	17	Pension, profit-sharing, etc., plans		17
	18	Employee benefit programs		18
	19	Other deductions (attach statement)		19
	20	**Total deductions.** Add lines 7 through 19 ▶		20
	21	**Ordinary business income (loss).** Subtract line 20 from line 6		21
Tax and Payments	22a	Excess net passive income or LIFO recapture tax (see instructions)	22a	
	b	Tax from Schedule D (Form 1120S)	22b	
	c	Add lines 22a and 22b (see instructions for additional taxes)		22c
	23a	2017 estimated tax payments and 2016 overpayment credited to 2017	23a	
	b	Tax deposited with Form 7004	23b	
	c	Credit for federal tax paid on fuels (attach Form 4136)	23c	
	d	Add lines 23a through 23c		23d
	24	Estimated tax penalty (see instructions). Check if Form 2220 is attached ▶ ☐		24
	25	**Amount owed.** If line 23d is smaller than the total of lines 22c and 24, enter amount owed		25
	26	**Overpayment.** If line 23d is larger than the total of lines 22c and 24, enter amount overpaid		26
	27	Enter amount from line 26 **Credited to 2018 estimated tax** ▶ **Refunded** ▶		27

Sign Here

Under penalties of perjury, I declare that I have examined this return, including accompanying schedules and statements, and to the best of my knowledge and belief, it is true, correct, and complete. Declaration of preparer (other than taxpayer) is based on all information of which preparer has any knowledge.

▶ Signature of officer | Date | ▶ Title

May the IRS discuss this return with the preparer shown below (see instructions)? ☐ Yes ☐ No

Paid Preparer Use Only

Print/Type preparer's name	Preparer's signature	Date	Check ☐ if self-employed	PTIN
Firm's name ▶			Firm's EIN ▶	
Firm's address ▶			Phone no.	

For Paperwork Reduction Act Notice, see separate instructions. Cat. No. 11510H Form **1120S** (2017)

Source: U.S. Department of the Treasury, Internal Revenue Service, Form 1120S. Washington, DC: 2017.

(continued)

EXHIBIT 15-3 *(continued)*

Form 1120S (2017) Page 2

Schedule B **Other Information** (see instructions)

		Yes	No
1	Check accounting method: a ☐ Cash b ☐ Accrual c ☐ Other (specify) ▶		
2	See the instructions and enter the: a Business activity ▶ b Product or service ▶		
3	At any time during the tax year, was any shareholder of the corporation a disregarded entity, a trust, an estate, or a nominee or similar person? If "Yes," attach Schedule B-1, Information on Certain Shareholders of an S Corporation		
4	At the end of the tax year, did the corporation:		
a	Own directly 20% or more, or own, directly or indirectly, 50% or more of the total stock issued and outstanding of any foreign or domestic corporation? For rules of constructive ownership, see instructions. If "Yes," complete (i) through (v) below		

(i) Name of Corporation	(ii) Employer Identification Number (if any)	(iii) Country of Incorporation	(iv) Percentage of Stock Owned	(v) If Percentage in (iv) is 100%, Enter the Date (if any) a Qualified Subchapter S Subsidiary Election Was Made

		Yes	No
b	Own directly an interest of 20% or more, or own, directly or indirectly, an interest of 50% or more in the profit, loss, or capital in any foreign or domestic partnership (including an entity treated as a partnership) or in the beneficial interest of a trust? For rules of constructive ownership, see instructions. If "Yes," complete (i) through (v) below		

(i) Name of Entity	(ii) Employer Identification Number (if any)	(iii) Type of Entity	(iv) Country of Organization	(v) Maximum Percentage Owned in Profit, Loss, or Capital

		Yes	No
5a	At the end of the tax year, did the corporation have any outstanding shares of restricted stock? If "Yes," complete lines (i) and (ii) below. (i) Total shares of restricted stock ▶ (ii) Total shares of non-restricted stock ▶		
b	At the end of the tax year, did the corporation have any outstanding stock options, warrants, or similar instruments? If "Yes," complete lines (i) and (ii) below. (i) Total shares of stock outstanding at the end of the tax year ▶ (ii) Total shares of stock outstanding if all instruments were executed ▶		
6	Has this corporation filed, or is it required to file, **Form 8918,** Material Advisor Disclosure Statement, to provide information on any reportable transaction?		
7	Check this box if the corporation issued publicly offered debt instruments with original issue discount ▶ ☐ If checked, the corporation may have to file **Form 8281,** Information Return for Publicly Offered Original Issue Discount Instruments.		
8	If the corporation: **(a)** was a C corporation before it elected to be an S corporation **or** the corporation acquired an asset with a basis determined by reference to the basis of the asset (or the basis of any other property) in the hands of a C corporation **and (b)** has net unrealized built-in gain in excess of the net recognized built-in gain from prior years, enter the net unrealized built-in gain reduced by net recognized built-in gain from prior years (see instructions) ▶ $		
9	Enter the accumulated earnings and profits of the corporation at the end of the tax year. $		
10	Does the corporation satisfy **both** of the following conditions?		
a	The corporation's total receipts (see instructions) for the tax year were less than $250,000		
b	The corporation's total assets at the end of the tax year were less than $250,000 If "Yes," the corporation is not required to complete Schedules L and M-1.		
11	During the tax year, did the corporation have any non-shareholder debt that was canceled, was forgiven, or had the terms modified so as to reduce the principal amount of the debt? If "Yes," enter the amount of principal reduction $		
12	During the tax year, was a qualified subchapter S subsidiary election terminated or revoked? If "Yes," see instructions		
13a	Did the corporation make any payments in 2017 that would require it to file Form(s) 1099?		
b	If "Yes," did the corporation file or will it file required Forms 1099?		

Form **1120S** (2017)

EXHIBIT 15-3 *(continued)*

Form 1120S (2017) Page **3**

Section	Line	**Schedule K — Shareholders' Pro Rata Share Items**			Total amount
Income (Loss)	1	Ordinary business income (loss) (page 1, line 21)		1	
	2	Net rental real estate income (loss) (attach Form 8825)		2	
	3a	Other gross rental income (loss)	3a		
	b	Expenses from other rental activities (attach statement)	3b		
	c	Other net rental income (loss). Subtract line 3b from line 3a		3c	
	4	Interest income		4	
	5	Dividends: a Ordinary dividends		5a	
		b Qualified dividends	5b		
	6	Royalties		6	
	7	Net short-term capital gain (loss) (attach Schedule D (Form 1120S))		7	
	8a	Net long-term capital gain (loss) (attach Schedule D (Form 1120S))		8a	
	b	Collectibles (28%) gain (loss)	8b		
	c	Unrecaptured section 1250 gain (attach statement)	8c		
	9	Net section 1231 gain (loss) (attach Form 4797)		9	
	10	Other income (loss) (see instructions) Type ▶		10	
Deductions	11	Section 179 deduction (attach Form 4562)		11	
	12a	Charitable contributions		12a	
	b	Investment interest expense		12b	
	c	Section 59(e)(2) expenditures (1) Type ▶ (2) Amount ▶		12c(2)	
	d	Other deductions (see instructions) Type ▶		12d	
Credits	13a	Low-income housing credit (section 42(j)(5))		13a	
	b	Low-income housing credit (other)		13b	
	c	Qualified rehabilitation expenditures (rental real estate) (attach Form 3468, if applicable)		13c	
	d	Other rental real estate credits (see instructions) Type ▶		13d	
	e	Other rental credits (see instructions) Type ▶		13e	
	f	Biofuel producer credit (attach Form 6478)		13f	
	g	Other credits (see instructions) Type ▶		13g	
Foreign Transactions	14a	Name of country or U.S. possession ▶			
	b	Gross income from all sources		14b	
	c	Gross income sourced at shareholder level		14c	
		Foreign gross income sourced at corporate level			
	d	Passive category		14d	
	e	General category		14e	
	f	Other (attach statement)		14f	
		Deductions allocated and apportioned at shareholder level			
	g	Interest expense		14g	
	h	Other		14h	
		Deductions allocated and apportioned at corporate level to foreign source income			
	i	Passive category		14i	
	j	General category		14j	
	k	Other (attach statement)		14k	
		Other information			
	l	Total foreign taxes (check one): ▶ ☐ Paid ☐ Accrued		14l	
	m	Reduction in taxes available for credit (attach statement)		14m	
	n	Other foreign tax information (attach statement)			
Alternative Minimum Tax (AMT) Items	15a	Post-1986 depreciation adjustment		15a	
	b	Adjusted gain or loss		15b	
	c	Depletion (other than oil and gas)		15c	
	d	Oil, gas, and geothermal properties—gross income		15d	
	e	Oil, gas, and geothermal properties—deductions		15e	
	f	Other AMT items (attach statement)		15f	
Items Affecting Shareholder Basis	16a	Tax-exempt interest income		16a	
	b	Other tax-exempt income		16b	
	c	Nondeductible expenses		16c	
	d	Distributions (attach statement if required) (see instructions)		16d	
	e	Repayment of loans from shareholders		16e	

Form **1120S** (2017)

(continued)

EXHIBIT 15-3 *(continued)*

Form 1120S (2017) Page **4**

Schedule K **Shareholders' Pro Rata Share Items** (continued)

			Total amount
Other Information	17a	Investment income	17a
	b	Investment expenses	17b
	c	Dividend distributions paid from accumulated earnings and profits	17c
	d	Other items and amounts (attach statement)	
Recon-ciliation	18	**Income/loss reconciliation.** Combine the amounts on lines 1 through 10 in the far right column. From the result, subtract the sum of the amounts on lines 11 through 12d and 14l	18

Schedule L **Balance Sheets per Books**

	Beginning of tax year		End of tax year	
Assets	(a)	(b)	(c)	(d)
1 Cash				
2a Trade notes and accounts receivable				
b Less allowance for bad debts	( )		( )	
3 Inventories				
4 U.S. government obligations				
5 Tax-exempt securities (see instructions)				
6 Other current assets (attach statement)				
7 Loans to shareholders				
8 Mortgage and real estate loans				
9 Other investments (attach statement)				
10a Buildings and other depreciable assets				
b Less accumulated depreciation	( )		( )	
11a Depletable assets				
b Less accumulated depletion	( )		( )	
12 Land (net of any amortization)				
13a Intangible assets (amortizable only)				
b Less accumulated amortization	( )		( )	
14 Other assets (attach statement)				
15 Total assets				
Liabilities and Shareholders' Equity				
16 Accounts payable				
17 Mortgages, notes, bonds payable in less than 1 year				
18 Other current liabilities (attach statement)				
19 Loans from shareholders				
20 Mortgages, notes, bonds payable in 1 year or more				
21 Other liabilities (attach statement)				
22 Capital stock				
23 Additional paid-in capital				
24 Retained earnings				
25 Adjustments to shareholders' equity (attach statement)				
26 Less cost of treasury stock		( )		( )
27 Total liabilities and shareholders' equity				

Form **1120S** (2017)

EXHIBIT 15-3 *(concluded)*

Form 1120S (2017) Page **5**

Schedule M-1 Reconciliation of Income (Loss) per Books With Income (Loss) per Return

Note: The corporation may be required to file Schedule M-3 (see instructions)

1	Net income (loss) per books		5	Income recorded on books this year not included on Schedule K, lines 1 through 10 (itemize):	
			a	Tax-exempt interest $	
2	Income included on Schedule K, lines 1, 2, 3c, 4, 5a, 6, 7, 8a, 9, and 10, not recorded on books this year (itemize)				
3	Expenses recorded on books this year not included on Schedule K, lines 1 through 12 and 14l (itemize):		6	Deductions included on Schedule K, lines 1 through 12 and 14l, not charged against book income this year (itemize):	
a	Depreciation $		a	Depreciation $	
b	Travel and entertainment $				
			7	Add lines 5 and 6	
4	Add lines 1 through 3		8	Income (loss) (Schedule K, line 18). Line 4 less line 7	

Schedule M-2 Analysis of Accumulated Adjustments Account, Other Adjustments Account, and Shareholders' Undistributed Taxable Income Previously Taxed (see instructions)

		(a) Accumulated adjustments account	(b) Other adjustments account	(c) Shareholders' undistributed taxable income previously taxed
1	Balance at beginning of tax year			
2	Ordinary income from page 1, line 21			
3	Other additions			
4	Loss from page 1, line 21	( )		
5	Other reductions	( )	( )	
6	Combine lines 1 through 5			
7	Distributions other than dividend distributions			
8	Balance at end of tax year. Subtract line 7 from line 6			

Form **1120S** (2017)

In a manner similar to partnership taxation, some items of income, expense, or credit are not included in income but are separately stated and allocated to shareholders on a per share, per day basis.[34] Separately stated items are on Schedule K (see pages 3 and 4 of Form 1120S in Exhibit 15-3). The Subchapter S Schedule K is similar to that for a partnership.

EXAMPLE 15-21

Pitt Company is a Subchapter S corporation with two shareholders, Anne and Zeke, who own 60% and 40% of the corporation, respectively. During the year, Pitt has income of $50,000 that includes $3,000 of dividend income and $1,000 of charitable contributions. Pitt's Sub S taxable income is $48,000. The allocation of the income and separately stated items follows:

	Anne (60%)	Zeke (40%)	Total
Taxable income	$28,800	$19,200	$48,000
Dividend income	1,800	1,200	3,000
Charitable contributions	600	400	1,000

Corporate and Shareholder Basis and Distributions

Upon formation, the basis rules for S corporations are the same as those for C corporations (noted previously). Significant differences, however, pertain to income and separately stated items and distributions. In effect, Sub S shareholders are taxed on their proportionate share of income and separately stated items but are not taxed when they receive a distribution. This treatment is similar to that for partners of a partnership.

[34] You might find it instructive to review the rules associated with separately stated items of a partnership in Chapter 14.

A Sub S shareholder who receives a K-1 from the corporation reports each item on her or his tax return in a manner similar to that done for a partnership (see Chapter 14). Each K-1 item increases or decreases the basis of the shareholder's stock. If the Sub S corporation reports a loss, the shareholder can take the loss only to the extent of her or his adjusted basis in the corporation's stock.

A shareholder's basis in the stock is increased or decreased by the following items:

Increases:
- Net income
- Separately stated income items (dividends, interest, capital gains tax exempt income, etc.)
- Capital contributions
- Loans from the shareholder to the corporation

Decreases:
- Net losses
- Separately stated expense items (charitable contributions, capital losses, etc.)
- Distributions from the corporation at fair market value

Decreases cannot reduce the shareholder's basis in stock below zero. Any excess first goes to reduce the basis of any loans from the shareholder to the corporation, and if any remains, it is suspended. When the corporation later recognizes items that increase basis (such as net income), the increases are allocated as follows: (1) increase the basis of shareholder loans, if any, to their original basis, (2) eliminate suspended losses, and (3) increase the basis of the stock for the remainder.

EXAMPLE 15-22

Thangam owns stock in a Subchapter S corporation. At the end of 2016, the tax basis of her stock was $2,000. She had previously made a $1,500 loan to the company. For year 2016, her share of the loss of the company was $4,500. To account for this loss, she would reduce the tax basis of her stock to $0, then would reduce the tax basis of her loan to $0, and would have a remaining $1,000 suspended loss ($4,500 – $2,000 – $1,500 = $1,000). In 2017, her share of corporate net income was $3,000. She would first increase the tax basis in the loan to its original $1,500. Then she would eliminate the $1,000 suspended loss. Finally, she would increase the tax basis of her stock by the remaining $500.

An S corporation differs from a partnership in that the shareholder does not increase his or her stock basis by his or her share of debt in the corporation.

EXAMPLE 15-23

Laurel owns stock in a Subchapter S corporation. At the end of 2016, her tax basis in the stock was $100. In 2017, her share of corporate net income was $150, and her share of a corporate charitable contribution was $300. At the end of 2017, a simple mathematical calculation would indicate that her stock basis is a negative $50 ($100 + $150 – $300 = [$50]). However, basis cannot be negative. Her basis is set to zero and the $50 shortfall is suspended to future years. If, in 2018, Laurel's share of corporate net income was $400, she would increase her stock basis by $400 and decrease her stock basis by the suspended $50, resulting in a December 2018 stock basis of $350.

Schedule M-1

Schedule M-1 for Form 1120S is also a reconciliation between income for books and income for taxes. The substantive difference between an S corporation Schedule M-1 and a C corporation Schedule M-1 is that an S corporation has no line for federal income tax because the Subchapter S corporation does not pay federal income tax; the shareholders pay it.

CONCEPT CHECK 15-7— LO 15-7

1. Corporations with fewer than 100 shareholders are automatically considered Subchapter S corporations. True or false?
2. A Subchapter S corporation is taxed in a manner similar to a partnership. True or false?
3. Subchapter S corporations file a Form ________.
4. Alyssa is a shareholder in a Subchapter S corporation and has a basis of $1,000 in her stock. The corporation gives her a $200 cash dividend. Is this dividend taxable to Alyssa?
5. Similar to a partnership, shareholders of a Subchapter S corporation increase the basis of their stock by their share of corporate debts. True or false?

Summary

LO 15-1: Describe corporate formation and filing requirements.

Corporations
- Are legal entities formed under the laws of a state.
- Can use cash basis of accounting if sales < = $5 million or have no inventory.
- Can choose fiscal year-end in first year.
- File Form 1120.

LO 15-2: Calculate corporate and shareholder basis.

- No gain on formation of corporation if transferors control 80% or more.
- Relief of liability in excess of basis triggers gain equal to the excess.
- Boot received triggers gain.
- Basis to corporation is shareholder basis plus gain recognized by shareholder.
- Basis to shareholder is carryover basis plus gain recognized, minus boot received.

LO 15-3: Determine corporate taxable income and tax liability.

- Taxable income generally follows rules associated with trade or business (Chapter 6).
- Net capital losses are not permitted. Carry back three years and then forward five.
- Charitable contributions are limited to 10% of taxable income before considering charitable contributions. Excess is carried forward five years.
- A deduction is permitted equal to 70%, 80%, or 100% of dividends received from other domestic corporations. DRD may be limited.
- Organizational expenditures and start-up expenses can be deducted over 180 months or more upon election.
- Taxable income is subject to tax rates up to 35%.
- Estimated payments are required.
- Net operating losses can be carried back 2 years and forward 20. Can choose to only carry forward if an affirmative election is made.

LO 15-4: Explain the tax rules for transactions with shareholders.

- Distributions from earnings and profits are dividends and are taxable to shareholder; not deductible by corporation.
- Distributions in excess of E&P are nontaxable to extent of stock basis and a capital gain in excess of basis.
- Distribution of property with FMV in excess of basis creates gain to corporation.
- Distribution in full liquidation of shareholder interest creates gain or loss equal to distribution compared to basis.

LO 15-5: Prepare Schedules L, M-1, and M-3.	• Schedule L is a beginning and ending balance sheet in accordance with financial accounting method. • Schedule M-1 is a reconciliation from book income to taxable income. • M-1 sets forth all book/tax differences, whether permanent or temporary. • M-3, a comprehensive book/tax reconciliation, is for large corporations.
LO 15-6: Discuss other corporate issues.	• Parent–subsidiary groups are those in which a common parent owns, directly or indirectly, at least 80% of one or more other corporations. • Can elect to file consolidated tax return. • Brother–sister group may exist if five or fewer persons own two or more corporations. • Must disclose to IRS. • Most corporations are subject to AMT. • Corporate AMT concepts are similar to AMT for individuals.
LO 15-7: Know the rules for tax treatment of Subchapter S corporations.	Subchapter S corporations • Are "regular" corporations that elect to be taxed in a manner similar to a partnership. • File 1120S. • Must meet four tests to elect Sub S status. • Report taxable income and separately stated items similar to a partnership. • Do not pay tax; shareholders do. • Calculate shareholder basis similar to partnership except corporate debt does not affect basis. • Can have distributions, which are not taxable to shareholders.

Discussion Questions

All applicable discussion questions are available with ***Connect***©

LO 15-1 1. Explain the circumstances in which a corporation can use the accrual basis or the cash basis of accounting.

____

____

____

LO 15-1 2. When must a corporate tax return be filed? Can a corporation receive an extension of time to file a return, and if so, what is the length of the extension?

____

____

____

LO 15-1 3. Without regard to any extensions of time to file, when is the income tax return due for a corporation with a May 31 year-end? An August 31 year-end? A February 28 year-end?

____

____

____

LO 15-2 4. Explain the 80% rule as it pertains to the formation of a corporation.

LO 15-2 5. In what instances could a gain be recorded associated with the issuance of stock upon formation of a corporation? Assume that the 80% test is met.

LO 15-2 6. An individual contributes property with a fair market value in excess of basis to a corporation in exchange for stock. What is the basis of the stock in the hands of the shareholder, and what is the basis of the property contributed in the hands of the corporation?

LO 15-3 7. What is the *dividends received deduction*? What is its purpose?

LO 15-3 8. Explain the rules associated with capital loss carrybacks and carryforwards.

LO 15-3 9. Explain the rules pertaining to the deductibility of charitable contributions for a C corporation.

LO 15-3 10. Explain the difference between *organizational expenses* and *start-up expenditures*. In what circumstances are they deductible?

LO 15-3 11. Why does the marginal tax rate vary up and down for taxable incomes over $100,000?

LO 15-3 12. On what dates are estimated payments due for a calendar year corporation? What are the dates for a corporation with a fiscal year ending August 31?

LO 15-3 13. Explain the rules associated with the carryback and carryforward of net operating losses.

LO 15-4 14. A corporation may make a distribution to its shareholders. Depending on the circumstances, in the hands of the shareholder, the distribution can be classified as a dividend, a tax-free distribution, or a capital gain. Explain the circumstances in which each classification can occur.

LO 15-4 15. In what circumstances does a corporation record a gain related to a distribution to a shareholder?

LO 15-5 16. What is Schedule M-1, and what is its purpose?

LO 15-5 17. What is Schedule L, and what is its purpose?

LO 15-6 18. For purposes of the corporate alternative minimum tax, explain the application of the AMT exemption amount and its phaseout.

LO 15-6 19. Under what circumstances can a parent–subsidiary group file a consolidated income tax return?

LO 15-6 20. Why might a parent–subsidiary group choose to file, or not to file, a consolidated income tax return?

LO 15-6 21. What are the two tests used to determine whether a group of corporations is a brother–sister group?

LO 15-7 22. What criteria must a corporation meet to appropriately elect Subchapter S status?

LO 15-7 23. A calendar year corporation properly files a Subchapter S election on January 10, 2017. On what date is the election effective? What if the election were filed on June 1, 2017?

LO 15-7 24. The Subchapter S status of a calendar year corporation is statutorily terminated on August 12, 2017. The Subchapter S status is deemed to be terminated on what date? What is the answer if the status were voluntarily revoked on that date?

Multiple-Choice Questions

All applicable multiple-choice questions are available with ***Connect***©

LO 15-1 25. Which of the following statements is correct?

a. A calendar year corporation must file its tax return no later than March 15 unless it requests an extension.

b. A corporation is a legal entity that is taxed on its taxable income.

c. Corporations choose their tax year in their first year of operation and can elect to change it in their third year of operation.

d. Large corporations without inventory can choose to use either the cash or accrual method of accounting.

LO 15-1 26. A corporation has a fiscal year-end of June. If the corporation does not receive an automatic extension of time to file its return, the return will be due on the 15th of

a. August.

b. September.

c. October.

d. November.

LO 15-2 27. Two individuals form a corporation and own all of its stock. One individual contributes cash, and the other contributes property encumbered by a mortgage. The new corporation assumes the mortgage. Which of the following statements is true with respect to the individual who contributes the property?

a. Because the 80% test is met, no gain or loss will be recognized.

b. Gain is recognized to the extent of relief of liability.

c. Gain is recognized to the extent of relief of liability in excess of the basis of property contributed.

d. Gain is recognized to the extent that the fair market value of the stock exceeds the basis of the property contributed.

LO 15-2 28. Tameka and Janelle form a corporation in which each will own 50% of the stock. Tameka contributes $50,000 in cash. Janelle contributes property with a basis of $30,000 and an FMV of $60,000. She receives $10,000 of inventory from the corporation. Which of the following statements is true?

a. Janelle will report a gain of $10,000.

b. Janelle will report a gain of $30,000.

c. Tameka will report a gain of $10,000.

d. Neither Tameka nor Janelle will report a gain or loss as a result of these transactions.

LO 15-2 29. Svetlana forms a corporation in which she is the sole shareholder. She contributes a vehicle with a basis of $15,000 and an FMV of $8,000 in exchange for stock. She also contributes cash of $2,000. Svetlana will recognize

a. A $5,000 loss.

b. A $7,000 loss.

c. A $10,000 loss.

d. Neither a gain nor loss.

LO 15-2 30. Annabelle forms a corporation in which she is the sole shareholder. She transfers $20,000 cash plus land with a $100,000 adjusted basis and a $160,000 FMV in exchange for all the stock of the corporation. The corporation assumes the $140,000 mortgage on the land. What is her basis in the stock, and what is the gain she must report (if any)?

a. No gain; stock basis is $120,000.

b. Gain of $20,000; stock basis is $120,000.

c. No gain; stock basis is $100,000.

d. Gain of $20,000; stock basis is zero.

LO 15-3 31. Mountain Company owns 10% of Valley Company. Both are domestic corporations. Valley pays a $60,000 dividend to Mountain. What amount of dividend income will be included in the taxable income of Mountain Company?

a. $6,000.

b. $12,000.

c. $18,000.

d. $60,000.

LO 15-3 32. For Subchapter C corporations, which of the following statements is true?

a. Capital losses can be carried back three years and then carried forward five years.

b. Corporations can elect to forgo the carryback period for capital losses and only carry the losses forward.

c. Capital losses can be carried back 2 years and then carried forward 20 years.

d. Capital losses are permitted up to $3,000 per year.

LO 15-1, 15-3 33. Which of the following statements is false?

a. A corporation with average sales in excess of $5,000,000 must use the accrual method of accounting.

b. The charitable contributions of a corporation may be limited.

c. A corporation may be entitled to a deduction for dividends received from other domestic corporations.

d. Passive loss rules apply to all corporations.

LO 15-3 34. A calendar year corporate taxpayer must make its final estimated tax payment on the 15th of which month?

a. November.

b. December.

c. January.

d. February.

LO 15-4 35. Which, if any, of the following statements concerning the shareholders of a Subchapter C corporation is correct?

a. Shareholders are taxed on their proportionate share of earnings and profits as they are earned.

b. Shareholders are taxed on distributions from corporate earnings and profits.

c. Shareholders are never taxed on earnings and profits or distributions from the corporation.

d. None of these statements is correct.

LO 15-4 36. Parker Company has earnings and profits of $8,000. It distributes capital gain property with a basis of $2,000 and FMV of $9,000 to Gertrude Parker, its sole shareholder. Gertrude has a basis of $10,000 in her stock. Which of the following statements is true with respect to this transaction?

a. Gertrude will report dividend income of $2,000 and a capital gain of $7,000.

b. Gertrude will report dividend income of $8,000.

c. Gertrude will report dividend income of $8,000 and a nontaxable distribution of $1,000.

d. Gertrude will report dividend income of $9,000.

LO 15-5 37. Which of the following is a negative adjustment on Schedule M-1?

a. Federal income tax.

b. Charitable contributions in excess of the 10% limit.

c. Depreciation for books in excess of depreciation for taxes.

d. Tax-exempt interest income.

LO 15-5 38. Which of the following is a positive adjustment on Schedule M-1?

a. Excess of capital losses over capital gains.

b. Excess of capital gains over capital losses.

c. Charitable contribution carryover to the current year.

d. Depreciation for taxes in excess of depreciation for books.

LO 15-6 39. Banana Company is widely held. It owns 85% of Strawberry Corporation. Two individuals hold the remaining 15%. Which of the following statements is true?

a. Banana and Strawberry must file a consolidated tax return.

b. Banana and Strawberry can elect to file a consolidated tax return.

c. Banana and Strawberry can file a consolidated tax return if the other owners of Strawberry agree.

d. Banana and Strawberry are brother–sister corporations.

LO 15-6 40. What missing dollar amounts are correct in the following sentence? The AMT exemption is $________ for corporations with AMT income of $________ or less.

a. $40,000; $150,000.

b. $40,000; $310,000.

c. $150,000; $310,000.

d. This question cannot be answered with the information given.

LO 15-7 41. Which of the following items increase basis for a stockholder of a Subchapter S corporation?

a. Capital contributions.

b. Charitable contributions.

c. Net losses.

d. Distributions from the corporation.

LO 15-7 42. Which of the following statements is incorrect?

a. An S corporation can own stock of a C corporation.

b. A C corporation can own stock of an S corporation.

c. An S corporation can be a partner in a partnership.

d. An estate can own stock of an S corporation.

LO 15-7 43. Which, if any, of the following statements concerning the shareholders of a Subchapter S corporation is correct?

a. Shareholders are taxed on their proportionate share of earnings that are distributed.

b. Shareholders are taxed on the distributions from the corporation.

c. Shareholders are taxed on their proportionate share of earnings whether or not distributed.

d. None of these statements is correct.

LO 15-4, 15-7 44. Chen received a $10,000 dividend from a Subchapter C corporation. He also owns a 50% interest in a Subchapter S corporation that reported $100,000 of taxable income. He received a distribution of $20,000 from the Subchapter S corporation. How much income will Chen report as a result of these events?

a. $30,000.

b. $40,000.

c. $60,000.

d. $80,000.

Problems connect

All applicable problems are available with ***Connect***©

LO 15-2 45. When a corporation is formed, in certain cases the transferor may report a gain. What are the instances in which a gain would be reported? In these cases, what is the basis of the stock held by the transferor?

____

____

____

____

____

____

LO 15-2 46. An individual contributes property with an FMV in excess of basis to a corporation in exchange for stock. The property is subject to a mortgage. In each of the following instances, determine the basis of the stock in the hands of the shareholder and the basis of the property contributed in the hands of the corporation. Assume that the 80% rule is met.

a. The property is subject to a mortgage that is less than basis, and the corporation assumes the mortgage.

b. The property is subject to a mortgage that is more than basis, and the corporation assumes the mortgage.

LO 15-2 47. Determine the basis of stock in the hands of the shareholder in each of the following instances. Assume that the 80% rule is met in all cases.

a. Contribution of property with a basis of $1,000 and an FMV of $1,400.

b. Contribution of property with a basis of $3,000 and an FMV of $3,800. The stockholder also received $500 cash from the corporation as part of the stock transaction.

c. Contribution of property with a basis of $8,200 and an FMV of $12,500. The stockholder also received property with an FMV of $1,700 from the corporation as part of the stock transaction.

d. Contribution of a building with an FMV of $200,000, a mortgage (assumed by the corporation) of $100,000, and a basis of $125,000.

e. Contribution of a building with an FMV of $1,700,000, a mortgage (assumed by the corporation) of $1,000,000, and a basis of $635,000.

LO 15-2 48. Using the information from Problem 47, determine the basis of the property contributed in the hands of the corporation in each instance. Assume that the 80% rule is met in all cases.

LO 15-3 49. Explain the operation of the dividends received deduction.

LO 15-3 50. Determine the amount of the dividends received deduction in each of the following instances. In all cases, the net income figure includes the full dividend.

a. Dividend of $10,000 from a 45% owned corporation; taxable income before DRD of $50,000.

b. Dividend of $19,000 from a 15% owned corporation; taxable income before DRD of $75,000.

c. Dividend of $22,000 from a 60% owned corporation; taxable income before DRD of $11,000.

d. Dividend of $8,000 from a 10% owned corporation; taxable income before DRD of $7,000.

LO 15-3 51. For each of the following cases, determine the amount of capital gain or loss to report in each year (after taking into account any applicable carrybacks) and the capital loss carryforward to 2017 if any. Assume that 2011 is the first year of operation for each corporation.

	Capital Gain or Loss for Year Indicated					
Corporation	**2011**	**2012**	**2013**	**2014**	**2015**	**2016**
A	$ 4,000	$7,000	$(10,000)	$ 5,000	$ 3,000	(1,000)
B	5,000	3,000	3,000	4,000	(20,000)	2,000
C	5,000	9,000	(3,000)	2,000	(20,000)	8,000
D	(50,000)	7,000	3,000	11,000	10,000	2,000

LO 15-3 52. Determine the deductible charitable contribution in each of the following instances:

a. Charitable contribution of $4,000 and taxable income before charitable contribution of $50,000.

b. Charitable contribution of $8,000 and taxable income before charitable contribution of $50,000.

c. Charitable contribution of $4,800 and taxable income before charitable contribution of $50,000. Taxable income includes a net operating loss carryforward of $5,000.

d. Charitable contribution of $4,800 and taxable income before charitable contribution of $40,000. Taxable income includes a capital loss carryback of $5,000.

LO 15-3 53. Determine the amount of tax liability for the corporation in each of the following cases:

a. Taxable income of $45,200.

b. Taxable income of $450,200.

c. Taxable income of $4,500,200.

d. Taxable income of $14,500,200.

e. Taxable income of $45,000,200.

LO 15-3 54. Determine taxable income in each of the following instances. Assume that the corporation is a C corporation and that book income is before any income tax expense.

a. Book income of $50,000 including capital gains of $2,000, a charitable contribution of $1,000, and meals and entertainment expenses of $3,000.

b. Book income of $92,000 including capital losses of $3,000, a charitable contribution of $12,000, and meals and entertainment expenses of $3,000.

c. Book income of $76,000 including municipal bond interest of $2,000, a charitable contribution of $5,000, and dividends of $3,000 from a 10% owned domestic corporation. The corporation also has an $8,000 charitable contribution carryover.

d. Book income of $129,000 including municipal bond interest of $2,000, a charitable contribution of $5,000, and dividends of $7,000 from a 70% owned domestic corporation. The corporation has a capital loss carryover of $6,000 and a capital gain of $2,500 in the current year.

LO 15-3 55. Using the information from Problem 54, calculate the amount of tax liability in each instance.

LO 15-3 56. LMNO Corporation was formed in 2010. It reported net income (loss) over the 2009 through 2016 tax years, before accounting for any net operating losses, as follows:

2010	$ (4,000)
2011	19,000
2012	23,000
2013	(31,000)
2014	11,000
2015	(8,000)
2016	3,000

a. Determine annual taxable income after accounting for any net operating losses for 2010 to 2016 assuming the corporation does not waive the carryback period. Also determine any NOL carryforward to 2017.

b. Determine annual taxable income after accounting for any net operating losses for 2010 to 2016 assuming the corporation waives the carryback period. Also determine any NOL carryforward to 2017.

LO 15-4 57. Determine the amount of taxable dividend, nontaxable distribution, and capital gain for the distributions made in each of the following cases:

a. Corporate E&P of $10,000, shareholder stock basis of $12,000, distribution of $6,000.

b. Corporate E&P of $7,500, shareholder stock basis of $7,000, distribution of $6,500.

c. Corporate E&P of $16,000, shareholder stock basis of $5,000, distribution of $17,000.

d. Corporate E&P of $14,000, shareholder stock basis of $11,000, distribution of $26,000.

LO 15-5 58. Go to the IRS Web site (www.irs.gov) and print page 5 of Form 1120. Complete Schedule M-1 for each of the following cases:

a. Corporate financial statement: net income of $52,000 including tax expense of $15,000, charitable contributions of $3,000, and depreciation expense of $37,000. Depreciation expense for tax purposes is $46,000.

b. Corporate financial statement: net income of $139,000 including tax expense of $68,000, charitable contributions of $28,000, depreciation expense of $103,000, and meals and entertainment expenses of $31,000. Depreciation expense for tax purposes is $145,000.

c. Corporate financial statement: net income of $226,000 including tax expense of $111,000, charitable contributions of $16,000, municipal bond interest of $19,000, meals and entertainment expenses of $41,000, capital gains of $6,000, and depreciation expense of $142,000. Depreciation expense for tax purposes is $131,000, and the corporation has a $7,000 charitable contribution carryforward for the current year.

LO 15-6 59. A corporation has regular taxable income of $370,000 and a regular tax liability of $125,800. It has positive tax preference items totaling $310,000. You have determined that the corporation is subject to alternative minimum tax because it has average annual gross receipts of $9,000,000. Determine the amount of AMT owed by the corporation, if any.

LO 15-7 60. Refer to Problem 54. Determine the amount of taxable income and separately stated items in each case, assuming the corporation is a Subchapter S corporation.

LO 15-7 61. Refer to Problem 58. Determine the amount of taxable income and separately stated items in each case, assuming the corporation is a Subchapter S corporation. Ignore any carryforward items.

Tax Return Problems

All applicable tax return problems are available with ***Connect***®

Tax Return Problem 1 Phil Williams and Liz Johnson are 60% and 40% shareholders, respectively, in WJ Corporation, a Subchapter S corporation. The corporation had the following activity during the year:

Income	$336,123
Interest income	1,259
Dividend income (qualified)	4,586
Long-term capital gains	13,458
Total revenue	$355,426
Expenses	
Salaries and wages (nonofficers)	$ 47,000
Salaries and wages, owners and officers	125,000
Depreciation (MACRS—includes $9,000 § 179 expense)	41,888
Interest expense	5,220
Taxes and licenses	15,548
Meals and entertainment (100%)	15,257
Auto	5,254
Insurance (nonofficer health)	6,000
Accounting and legal	2,800
Repairs	1,200
Charitable contributions	2,500
Payroll penalties	500
Total expenses	$268,167
Net income	$ 87,259

During the year, the corporation made a distribution of $20,000, in total, to its shareholders. Complete page 1, Schedule K, and Schedule M-1 of Form 1120S.

Tax Return Problem 2 Harrell and Smith, Inc., 204 Ambulance Street, Anywhere, CA 92345, is a corporation (EIN 57-1234567) formed on January 1, 2012. Information concerning the corporation and its two shareholders follows. It uses tax/cash basis accounting, did not pay dividends in excess of earnings and profits, has no foreign shareholders, is not publicly traded, and has no NOL carrybacks.

Bruce Harrell (SSN 412-34-5670), 1018 Lexington Downs, Anywhere, CA 92345, is a 60% shareholder. Della Smith (SSN 412-34-5671), 4564 Yates Road, Anywhere, CA 92345, is a 40% shareholder. Bruce received a dividend of $60,000, and Della received a dividend of $40,000. Both of these dividends are in addition to their salaries.

HARRELL AND SMITH, INC.
Comparative Balance Sheet
As of December 31, 2016, and December 31, 2017

	12/31/16	12/31/17
Assets		
Cash	$ 39,955	$ 45,459
Investments	258,456	169,125
Office equipment	225,000	310,759
Accumulated depreciation (equipment)	(156,000)	(165,379)
Building	491,200	491,200
Accumulated depreciation (building)	(37,232)	(49,826)
Total assets	$821,379	$801,338

(continued)

HARRELL AND SMITH, INC. *(concluded)*
Comparative Balance Sheet
As of December 31, 2016, and December 31, 2017

	12/31/16	12/31/17
Liabilities and equity		
Notes payable	$353,600	$335,458
Common stock	10,000	10,000
Retained earnings	457,779	455,880
Total liabilities and equity	$821,379	$801,338

HARRELL AND SMITH, INC.
Income Statement
For the Year Ending December 31, 2017

Revenue	
Consulting income	$866,689
Interest income	4,231
Rental income	9,000
Dividend income (qualified)	8,234
Long-term capital losses	(8,200)
Total revenue	$879,954
Expenses	
Salaries and wages (nonowners)	$253,000
Officers' salaries	
Harrell	225,000
Smith	150,000
Depreciation	21,973
Interest expense	20,127
Taxes and licenses	24,051
Utilities	15,500
Travel	11,850
Meals and entertainment (100%)	12,452
Auto	18,500
Insurance (health)	7,000
Accounting and legal	6,450
Repairs	3,200
Charitable contributions	12,000
Payroll penalties	750
Total expenses	$781,853
Net income	$ 98,101

Prepare Form 1120, pages 1–5, for Harrell and Smith, Inc. Schedule D and Form 4562 can be omitted (the information given is not sufficient to complete these forms).

We have provided selected filled-in source documents that are available in *Connect.*

Appendix A

Amended Tax Returns (Form 1040X)

Over 150 million individual income tax returns are filed each year. The vast majority of those returns are filed correctly. However, on occasion, the information on an already-filed tax return is determined to be incorrect.

There are literally hundreds of reasons why a previously filed return might be incorrect: a math error, a change of filing status, an additional or corrected informational tax form received, the basis or sales price on the sale of a capital asset initially reported incorrectly, a permitted itemized deduction omitted, and so on. There might be one error or multiple errors, and the changes might cause total tax liability to increase or decrease.

If a previously filed tax return is determined to be in error, the taxpayer must file an amended tax return on Form 1040X. On the amended return, the taxpayer provides numerical information concerning the tax return item(s) that is (are) being corrected plus a reconciliation between the original data and the correct data. The form also has a section where the taxpayer must explain the change.

Let us look at an example:

- Exhibit A-1 is the Form 1040 originally filed by Kim Watkins for tax year 2016. She had wage income and interest income, and she took the standard deduction. She originally received a refund of $216. After she had filed her return, she received a corrected Form 1099-INT from State Savings Bank. The corrected Form 1099-INT showed interest income in box 1 that was $250 more than originally reported.
- As a result of receiving this corrected Form 1099-INT, Kim must file an amended tax return. The completed Form 1040X amended tax return is shown in Exhibit A-2.
- Column A of the 1040X amended return provides tax information as it was originally filed. The information in column A comes from the data on the original Form 1040 in Exhibit A-1. Column B is used to indicate the numerical items that have changed. In this case, line 1, Adjusted Gross Income, must increase by $250 to properly report the information from the corrected Form 1099-INT received by Kim. Column C represents the corrected totals. The explanation for the change is provided in Part III on page 2.
- Note that we are preparing an amended return for tax year 2016. Thus the amount of tax on line 6 of Form 1040X is determined using the 2016 tax tables. These tables can be found in the Form 1040 instructions for tax year 2016, available on the IRS Web site at www.irs.gov.
- Because Kim's income increased by $250, she will owe additional tax of $38. That amount is reflected on line 20. When Kim files her amended Form 1040X, she must include a check for $38. Kim is in the 15% tax bracket. The additional tax represents the 15% income tax that is due on the additional $250 of income ($250 × 15% = $37.50, rounded to $38).

Only one item needed to be corrected in our example. If multiple changes are required, the taxpayer should clearly explain each item and provide a detailed summation and reconciliation.

Use the information from our previous example. Assume that Kim received two corrected 1099-INT forms, one from State Savings Bank that increased her interest income by $250 and another from State Bank and Trust that decreased her interest income by $100. In this case, the amount on line 1, column B, of Form 1040X would be $150, the net difference. The explanation in Part III on page 2 needs to clearly explain the change. Here is how Part III, Explanation of Changes, might appear in this case:

Taxpayer received two corrected Forms 1099-INT. One was from State Savings Bank. It showed corrected interest income $250 more than originally reported. The other was from State Bank and Trust. It showed corrected interest income $100 less than originally reported. The amount of Adjusted Gross Income on line 1 is increased by $150, determined as follows:

Change from corrected Form 1099-INT from State Savings Bank	$ 250
Change from corrected Form 1099-INT from State Bank and Trust	(100)
Net change to Adjusted Gross Income	$ 150

It is extremely important to note that the amended return must be prepared using the tax rules in effect for the year of the original return. For example, if we were preparing an amended return for Kim Watkins for tax year 2015, the standard deduction on line 2 of Form 1040X would continue to be $6,300, but the personal exemption on line 4 would be $4,000 because those were the correct amounts for tax year 2015. We would also use the tax tables or tax rate schedules for 2015, not 2016.

Generally Form 1040X must be filed within three years after the date the original return was filed or within two years after the date the taxpayer paid the tax due on the original return, whichever is later.

EXHIBIT A-1

Form **1040** Department of the Treasury—Internal Revenue Service (99)
U.S. Individual Income Tax Return **2016** OMB No. 1545-0074 IRS Use Only—Do not write or staple in this space.

For the year Jan. 1–Dec. 31, 2016, or other tax year beginning , 2016, ending , 20 See separate instructions.

Your first name and initial	Last name	Your social security number
Kim	Watkins	4 1 2 3 4 5 6 7 0
If a joint return, spouse's first name and initial	Last name	Spouse's social security number
Home address (number and street). If you have a P.O. box, see instructions. 123 Main Street	Apt. no.	▲ Make sure the SSN(s) above and on line 6c are correct.
City, town or post office, state, and ZIP code. If you have a foreign address, also complete spaces below (see instructions). Anywhere, TX 77840		**Presidential Election Campaign** Check here if you, or your spouse if filing jointly, want $3 to go to this fund. Checking a box below will not change your tax or refund. ☐ You ☐ Spouse
Foreign country name	Foreign province/state/county	Foreign postal code

Filing Status

Check only one box

1 ☑ Single
2 ☐ Married filing jointly (even if only one had income)
3 ☐ Married filing separately. Enter spouse's SSN above and full name here. ▶
4 ☐ Head of household (with qualifying person). (See instructions.) If the qualifying person is a child but not your dependent, enter this child's name here. ▶
5 ☐ Qualifying widow(er) with dependent child

Exemptions

6a ☑ **Yourself.** If someone can claim you as a dependent, **do not** check box 6a
b ☐ **Spouse**

Boxes checked on 6a and 6b: 1

c **Dependents:** (1) First name Last name	(2) Dependent's social security number	(3) Dependent's relationship to you	(4) ✓ if child under age 17 qualifying for child tax credit (see instructions)
			☐
			☐
			☐
			☐

If more than four dependents, see instructions and check here ▶ ☐

No. of children on 6c who: • lived with you • did not live with you due to divorce or separation (see instructions)
Dependents on 6c not entered above
d Total number of exemptions claimed — Add numbers on lines above ▶ 1

Income

Attach Form(s) W-2 here. Also attach Forms W-2G and 1099-R if tax was withheld.

If you did not get a W-2, see instructions.

7	Wages, salaries, tips, etc. Attach Form(s) W-2	7	45,491
8a	**Taxable** interest. Attach Schedule B if required	8a	1,173
b	**Tax-exempt** interest. **Do not** include on line 8a — 8b		
9a	Ordinary dividends. Attach Schedule B if required	9a	
b	Qualified dividends — 9b		
10	Taxable refunds, credits, or offsets of state and local income taxes	10	
11	Alimony received	11	
12	Business income or (loss). Attach Schedule C or C-EZ	12	
13	Capital gain or (loss). Attach Schedule D if required. If not required, check here ▶ ☐	13	
14	Other gains or (losses). Attach Form 4797	14	
15a	IRA distributions — 15a; b Taxable amount	15b	
16a	Pensions and annuities — 16a; b Taxable amount	16b	
17	Rental real estate, royalties, partnerships, S corporations, trusts, etc. Attach Schedule E	17	
18	Farm income or (loss). Attach Schedule F	18	
19	Unemployment compensation	19	
20a	Social security benefits — 20a; b Taxable amount	20b	
21	Other income. List type and amount	21	
22	Combine the amounts in the far right column for lines 7 through 21. This is your **total income** ▶	22	46,664

Adjusted Gross Income

23	Educator expenses	23	
24	Certain business expenses of reservists, performing artists, and fee-basis government officials. Attach Form 2106 or 2106-EZ	24	
25	Health savings account deduction. Attach Form 8889	25	
26	Moving expenses. Attach Form 3903	26	
27	Deductible part of self-employment tax. Attach Schedule SE	27	
28	Self-employed SEP, SIMPLE, and qualified plans	28	
29	Self-employed health insurance deduction	29	
30	Penalty on early withdrawal of savings	30	
31a	Alimony paid b Recipient's SSN ▶	31a	
32	IRA deduction	32	
33	Student loan interest deduction	33	
34	Tuition and fees. Attach Form 8917	34	
35	Domestic production activities deduction. Attach Form 8903	35	
36	Add lines 23 through 35	36	
37	Subtract line 36 from line 22. This is your **adjusted gross income** ▶	37	46,664

For Disclosure, Privacy Act, and Paperwork Reduction Act Notice, see separate instructions. Cat. No. 11320B Form **1040** (2016)

Source: U.S. Department of the Treasury, Internal Revenue Service, Form 1040. Washington, DC 2016.

(continued)

EXHIBIT A-1 *(concluded)*

Form 1040 (2016) Page 2

Section	Line	Description	Line	Amount
	38	Amount from line 37 (adjusted gross income)	38	46,664
Tax and Credits	39a	Check if: ☐ **You** were born before January 2, 1952, ☐ Blind. ☐ **Spouse** was born before January 2, 1952, ☐ Blind. **Total boxes checked** ▶ 39a		
	b	If your spouse itemizes on a separate return or you were a dual-status alien, check here ▶ 39b☐		
Standard Deduction for— • People who check any box on line 39a or 39b **or** who can be claimed as a dependent, see instructions. • All others: Single or Married filing separately, $6,300; Married filing jointly or Qualifying widow(er), $12,600; Head of household, $9,300	40	**Itemized deductions** (from Schedule A) **or** your **standard deduction** (see left margin)	40	6,300
	41	Subtract line 40 from line 38	41	40,364
	42	**Exemptions.** If line 38 is $155,650 or less, multiply $4,050 by the number on line 6d. Otherwise, see instructions	42	4,050
	43	**Taxable income.** Subtract line 42 from line 41. If line 42 is more than line 41, enter -0-	43	36,314
	44	**Tax** (see instructions). Check if any from: a ☐ Form(s) 8814 b ☐ Form 4972 c ☐	44	4,985
	45	**Alternative minimum tax** (see instructions). Attach Form 6251	45	
	46	Excess advance premium tax credit repayment. Attach Form 8962	46	
	47	Add lines 44, 45, and 46 ▶	47	4,985
	48	Foreign tax credit. Attach Form 1116 if required — 48		
	49	Credit for child and dependent care expenses. Attach Form 2441 — 49		
	50	Education credits from Form 8863, line 19 — 50		
	51	Retirement savings contributions credit. Attach Form 8880 — 51		
	52	Child tax credit. Attach Schedule 8812, if required — 52		
	53	Residential energy credits. Attach Form 5695 — 53		
	54	Other credits from Form: a ☐ 3800 b ☐ 8801 c ☐ — 54		
	55	Add lines 48 through 54. These are your **total credits**	55	0
	56	Subtract line 55 from line 47. If line 55 is more than line 47, enter -0- ▶	56	4,985
Other Taxes	57	Self-employment tax. Attach Schedule SE	57	
	58	Unreported social security and Medicare tax from Form: a ☐ 4137 b ☐ 8919	58	
	59	Additional tax on IRAs, other qualified retirement plans, etc. Attach Form 5329 if required	59	
	60a	Household employment taxes from Schedule H	60a	
	b	First-time homebuyer credit repayment. Attach Form 5405 if required	60b	
	61	Health care: individual responsibility (see instructions) Full-year coverage ☑	61	
	62	Taxes from: a ☐ Form 8959 b ☐ Form 8960 c ☐ Instructions; enter code(s)	62	
	63	Add lines 56 through 62. This is your **total tax** ▶	63	4,985
Payments	64	Federal income tax withheld from Forms W-2 and 1099 — 64: 5,201		
	65	2016 estimated tax payments and amount applied from 2015 return — 65		
If you have a qualifying child, attach Schedule EIC.	66a	**Earned income credit (EIC)** — 66a		
	b	Nontaxable combat pay election — 66b		
	67	Additional child tax credit. Attach Schedule 8812 — 67		
	68	American opportunity credit from Form 8863, line 8 — 68		
	69	Net premium tax credit. Attach Form 8962 — 69		
	70	Amount paid with request for extension to file — 70		
	71	Excess social security and tier 1 RRTA tax withheld — 71		
	72	Credit for federal tax on fuels. Attach Form 4136 — 72		
	73	Credits from Form: a ☐ 2439 b ▇ Reserved c ☐ 8885 d ☐ — 73		
	74	Add lines 64, 65, 66a, and 67 through 73. These are your **total payments** ▶	74	5,201
Refund	75	If line 74 is more than line 63, subtract line 63 from line 74. This is the amount you **overpaid**	75	216
	76a	Amount of line 75 you want **refunded to you.** If Form 8888 is attached, check here ▶ ☐	76a	216
Direct deposit? See instructions.	▶ b	Routing number ▶ c Type: ☐ Checking ☐ Savings		
	▶ d	Account number		
	77	Amount of line 75 you want **applied to your 2017 estimated tax** ▶ 77		
Amount You Owe	78	**Amount you owe.** Subtract line 74 from line 63. For details on how to pay, see instructions ▶	78	
	79	Estimated tax penalty (see instructions) — 79		

Third Party Designee Do you want to allow another person to discuss this return with the IRS (see instructions)? ☐ **Yes.** Complete below. ☐ **No**

Designee's name ▶ Phone no. ▶ Personal identification number (PIN) ▶

Sign Here Under penalties of perjury, I declare that I have examined this return and accompanying schedules and statements, and to the best of my knowledge and belief, they are true, correct, and accurately list all amounts and sources of income I received during the tax year. Declaration of preparer (other than taxpayer) is based on all information of which preparer has any knowledge.

Joint return? See instructions. Keep a copy for your records.

Your signature	Date	Your occupation	Daytime phone number
Spouse's signature. If a joint return, **both** must sign.	Date	Spouse's occupation	If the IRS sent you an Identity Protection PIN, enter it here (see inst.)

Paid Preparer Use Only

Print/Type preparer's name	Preparer's signature	Date	Check ☐ if self-employed	PTIN
Firm's name ▶			Firm's EIN ▶	
Firm's address ▶			Phone no.	

www.irs.gov/form1040 Form **1040** (2016)

EXHIBIT A-2

Form **1040X** (Rev. January 2017)

Department of the Treasury—Internal Revenue Service

Amended U.S. Individual Income Tax Return

▶ Information about Form 1040X and its separate instructions is at *www.irs.gov/form1040x*.

OMB No. 1545-0074

This return is for calendar year ☑ 2016 ☐ 2015 ☐ 2014 ☐ 2013
Other year. Enter one: calendar year **or** fiscal year (month and year ended):

Your first name and initial	Last name	Your social security number
Kim	Watkins	412 34 5670
If a joint return, spouse's first name and initial	Last name	Spouse's social security number

Current home address (number and street). If you have a P.O. box, see instructions.	Apt. no.	Your phone number
123 Main Street		

City, town or post office, state, and ZIP code. If you have a foreign address, also complete spaces below (see instructions).

Anywhere, TX 77840

Foreign country name	Foreign province/state/county	Foreign postal code

Amended return filing status. You **must** check one box even if you are not changing your filing status. **Caution:** In general, you can't change your filing status from joint to separate returns after the due date.

☑ Single ☐ Married filing jointly ☐ Married filing separately ☐ Head of household (If the qualifying person is a child but not your dependent, see instructions.) ☐ Qualifying widow(er)

Full-year coverage. If all members of your household have full-year minimal essential health care coverage, check "Yes." Otherwise, check "No." (See instructions.) ☑ Yes ☐ No

Use Part III on the back to explain any changes		A. Original amount or as previously adjusted (see instructions)	B. Net change—amount of increase or (decrease)—explain in Part III	C. Correct amount
Income and Deductions				
1 Adjusted gross income. If net operating loss (NOL) carryback is included, check here ▶ ☐	1	46,664	250	46,914
2 Itemized deductions or standard deduction	2	6,300		6,300
3 Subtract line 2 from line 1	3	40,364	250	40,614
4 Exemptions. **If changing, complete Part I on page 2 and enter the amount from line 29**	4	4,050		4,050
5 Taxable income. Subtract line 4 from line 3	5	36,314	250	36,564
Tax Liability				
6 Tax. Enter method(s) used to figure tax (see instructions): Tax Tables	6	4,985	38	5,023
7 Credits. If general business credit carryback is included, check here ▶ ☐	7			
8 Subtract line 7 from line 6. If the result is zero or less, enter -0-	8	4,985	38	5,023
9 Health care: individual responsibility (see instructions)	9			
10 Other taxes	10			
11 Total tax. Add lines 8, 9, and 10	11	4,985		5,023
Payments				
12 Federal income tax withheld and excess social security and tier 1 RRTA tax withheld (**If changing**, see instructions.)	12	5,201		5,201
13 Estimated tax payments, including amount applied from prior year's return	13			
14 Earned income credit (EIC)	14			
15 Refundable credits from: ☐ Schedule 8812 Form(s) ☐ 2439 ☐ 4136 ☐ 8863 ☐ 8885 ☐ 8962 or ☐ other (specify):	15			
16 Total amount paid with request for extension of time to file, tax paid with original return, and additional tax paid after return was filed	16			0
17 Total payments. Add lines 12 through 15, column C, and line 16	17			5,201
Refund or Amount You Owe				
18 Overpayment, if any, as shown on original return or as previously adjusted by the IRS	18			216
19 Subtract line 18 from line 17 (If less than zero, see instructions.)	19			4,985
20 **Amount you owe.** If line 11, column C, is more than line 19, enter the difference	20			38
21 If line 11, column C, is less than line 19, enter the difference. This is the amount **overpaid** on this return	21			
22 Amount of line 21 you want **refunded to you**	22			
23 Amount of line 21 you want **applied to your (enter year):** estimated tax	23			

Complete and sign this form on Page 2.

For Paperwork Reduction Act Notice, see instructions. Cat. No. 11360L Form **1040X** (Rev. 1-2017)

Source: U.S. Department of the Treasury, Internal Revenue Service, Form 1040X. Washington, DC: 2017.

(continued)

EXHIBIT A-2 *(concluded)*

Form 1040X (Rev. 1-2017) Page **2**

Part I Exemptions

Complete this part **only** if you are increasing or decreasing the number of exemptions (personal and dependents) claimed on line 6d of the return you are amending.

See *Form 1040 or Form 1040A instructions* and *Form 1040X instructions.*		A. Original number of exemptions or amount reported or as previously adjusted	B. Net change	C. Correct number or amount
24 Yourself and spouse. **Caution:** If someone can claim you as a dependent, you can't claim an exemption for yourself	**24**			
25 Your dependent children who lived with you	**25**			
26 Your dependent children who didn't live with you due to divorce or separation	**26**			
27 Other dependents	**27**			
28 Total number of exemptions. Add lines 24 through 27	**28**			
29 Multiply the number of exemptions claimed on line 28 by the exemption amount shown in the instructions for line 29 for the year you are amending. Enter the result here and on line 4 on page 1 of this form . .	**29**			

30 List **ALL** dependents (children and others) claimed on this amended return. If more than 4 dependents, see instructions.

(a) First name	Last name	**(b)** Dependent's social security number	**(c)** Dependent's relationship to you	**(d)** Check box if qualifying child for child tax credit (see instructions)
				☐
				☐
				☐
				☐

Part II Presidential Election Campaign Fund

Checking below won't increase your tax or reduce your refund.

☐ Check here if you didn't previously want $3 to go to the fund, but now do.

☐ Check here if this is a joint return and your spouse did not previously want $3 to go to the fund, but now does.

Part III Explanation of changes. In the space provided below, tell us why you are filing Form 1040X.

▶ Attach any supporting documents and new or changed forms and schedules.

Taxpayer received a corrected Form 1099-INT from State Savings Bank. The interest income shown in box 1 of the corrected Form 1099-INT was $250 greater than originally reported to the taxpayer. This $250 increase is reported on page 1 above, in box B.

Remember to keep a copy of this form for your records.

Under penalties of perjury, I declare that I have filed an original return and that I have examined this amended return, including accompanying schedules and statements, and to the best of my knowledge and belief, this amended return is true, correct, and complete. Declaration of preparer (other than taxpayer) is based on all information about which the preparer has any knowledge.

Sign Here

▶ Your signature | Date | ▶ Spouse's signature. If a joint return, **both** must sign. | Date

Paid Preparer Use Only

▶ Preparer's signature | Date | Firm's name (or yours if self-employed)

Print/type preparer's name | Firm's address and ZIP code

PTIN | ☐ Check if self-employed | Phone number | EIN

For forms and publications, visit IRS.gov. Form **1040X** (Rev. 1-2017)

Appendix B

Comprehensive Problems

In this Appendix, we provide a series of comprehensive tax return problems. In the text, the scope of the tax return problems is generally limited to the subject matter of the chapter. The comprehensive problems in this Appendix require integration of tax materials across multiple chapters. Each problem does have a primary focus area—Schedule A, C, D, or E. We provide two problems for Schedules A, C, and D. In each case, the first problem is a bit easier than the second.

The problems can be completed using the TaxACT software provided with this text or can be completed using the tax forms found on the IRS Web site (www.irs.gov).

COMPREHENSIVE PROBLEM 1

With Emphasis on Schedule A

James and Esther Johnson live at 45678 S.W. 112th Street, Homestead, FL 33033. James, who is 67 years old (date of birth 12/14/1950), is retired receiving social security benefits, and Esther, who is 66 years old (date of birth 6/11/1951), is also retired but working on a part-time basis. Their social security numbers are 412-34-5670 and 412-34-5671, respectively. The Johnsons had qualifying health care coverage at all times during the tax year.

Annual social security income for Jim is $18,000 (SSA-1099, box 5) and for Esther is $10,800 (SSA-1099, box 5).

Interest received by them from Central Bank is $2,545 (1099-INT, box 1). No income tax withholding was made.

Esther is working part-time as an interior decorator as an employee of Decorating House, a corporation. Her Form W-2 shows the following information:

Wages = $15,000.00
Federal W/H = $ 1,500.00
Social security wages = $15,000.00
Social security W/H = $ 930.00
Medicare wages = $15,000.00
Medicare W/H = $ 217.50

Their itemized deductions are as follows:

1. Mortgage interest on their main home, $8,100.
2. Real estate taxes, $5,600.
3. Personal property taxes, $185.

4. Doctors' expenses unreimbursed by insurance, $5,400.
5. Medical insurance premiums for the year, $2,400.
6. Prescribed medicine, $1,995.
7. Vitamins, $300.
8. Total cash contributions to their church, $675. The contributions were made over the course of the year and no individual contribution was greater than $250.
9. Tax preparation fees for their 2016 return, $325, paid in 2017.
10. Lottery tickets bought by Esther during the year, $750. Winnings received, $940 (W-2G, box 1). Income tax withholding on winnings, $35 (W-2G, box 4).

Because the Johnsons live in Florida, where there is no state income tax, they will deduct the estimation of the general sales tax related to the area in which they live. The most efficient way to do this is by using the Sales Tax Calculator on the IRS Web site at http://apps.irs.gov/app/stdc/. A key point to remember in using the calculator is that "income" for this calculation also includes the nontaxable portion of social security benefits. For more information on using the IRS Sales Tax Calculator, refer to page 5–12 in the text.

Required

Prepare their individual income tax return using the appropriate forms. They do not want to contribute to the presidential election campaign and do not want anyone to be a third-party designee. For any missing information, make reasonable assumptions.

COMPREHENSIVE PROBLEM 2

With Emphasis on Schedule A

Jamie and Cecilia Reyes are husband and wife and file a joint return. They live at 5677 Apple Cove Road, Boise, ID 83722. Jamie's social security number is 412-34-5670 (date of birth 6/15/1968) and Cecilia's is 412-34-5671 (date of birth 4/12/1970). They provide more than half of the support of their daughter, Carmen (age 23), social security number 412-34-5672 (date of birth 9/1/1994), who is a full-time veterinarian school student. Carmen received a $3,200 scholarship covering her room and board at college. She was not required to perform any services to receive the scholarship. Jamie and Cecilia furnish all of the support of Maria (Jamie's grandmother), social security number 412-34-5673 (date of birth 11/6/1947), who is age 70 and lives in a nursing home. They also have a son, Gustavo (age 4), social security number 412-34-5674 (date of birth 3/14/2013). The Reyes and all of their dependents had qualifying health care coverage at all times during the tax year.

Jamie's W-2 contained the following information:

Federal Wages (box 1) =	$145,625.00
Federal W/H (box 2) =	$ 16,812.50
Social Security wages (box 3) =	$127,200.00
Social Security W/H (box 4) =	$ 7,886.00
Medicare Wages (box 5) =	$145,625.00
Medicare W/H (box 6) =	$ 2,111.56
State Wages (box 16) =	$145,625.00
State W/H (box 17) =	$ 5,435.00

Other receipts for the couple were as follows:

Dividends (all qualified dividends)	$2,500
Interest income:	
Union Bank	$ 220
State of Idaho—interest on tax refund	22
City of Boise school bonds	1,250
Interest from U.S. savings bonds (not used for educational purposes)	410
2016 federal income tax refund received in 2017	2,007
2016 state income tax refund received in 2017	218
Idaho lottery winnings	1,100
Casino slot machine winnings	2,250
Gambling losses at casino	6,500

Other information that the Reyeses provided for the 2017 tax year:

Mortgage interest on personal residence	$11,081
Loan interest on fully equipped motor home	3,010
Doctor's fee for a face-lift for Mrs. Reyes	8,800
Dentist's fee for a new dental bridge for Mr. Reyes	3,500
Vitamins for the entire family	110
Real estate property taxes paid	$ 5,025
DMV fees on motor home (tax portion)	1,044
DMV fees on family autos (tax portion)	436
Doctors' bills for grandmother	2,960
Nursing home for grandmother	9,200
Wheelchair for grandmother	1,030
Property taxes on boat	134
Interest on personal credit card	550
Interest on loan to buy public school district bonds	270
Cash contributions to church (all the contributions were in cash and none more than $250 at any one time)	4,100
Cash contribution to man at bottom of freeway off-ramp	25
Contribution of furniture to Goodwill—cost basis	4,000
Contribution of same furniture to listed above Goodwill—fair market value	410
Tax return preparation fee for 2016 taxes	625

Required

Prepare a Form 1040, Schedule A, and Schedule B for the completion of the Reyes's tax return. They do not want to contribute to the presidential election campaign and do not want anyone to be a third-party designee. For any missing information, make reasonable assumptions.

COMPREHENSIVE PROBLEM 3

With Emphasis on Schedule C

Christian Everland (SS# 412-34-5670) is single and resides at 3554 Arrival Road, Apt. 6E, Buckhead, GA 30625.

Last year Christian started his own landscaping business. He now has two employees and had the following business results in 2017:

Revenue	$63,500
Expenses	
Wages	$12,500
Payroll taxes	956
Fuel	3,500
Repairs	2,345
Assets	
Truck, used 100% for business. Original cost of $22,000. Purchased on 03/01/17.	
Mower #1. Original cost of $4,500. Purchased new on 01/05/17.	
Mower #2. Leased for $200 per month for all of 2017.	
Other business equipment. Original cost of $4,000. Purchased new on 01/05/17.	

Christian has no other income, does not itemize, and has no dependents. He paid four quarterly federal tax estimates of $1,000 each.

Required

Prepare Christian's 2017 Form 1040 and supplemental schedules. Schedule C, Form 4562, and Schedule SE are required. He wants to contribute to the presidential election campaign and does not want anyone to be a third-party designee. Christian had qualifying health care coverage at all times during the tax year. For any missing information, make reasonable assumptions.

COMPREHENSIVE PROBLEM 4

With Emphasis on Schedule C

Shelly Beaman (social security number 412-34-5670) is single and resides at 540 Front Street, Ashland, NC 27898.

Shelly's W-2 wages	$55,800
Federal withholding	10,044
Social security wages	55,800
Social security withholding	3,460
Medicare withholding	809
State withholding	3,348
1099-INT New Bank	532
1099-DIV XYZ, Inc.	
Ordinary dividends	258
Qualified dividends	258

Shelly had the following itemized deductions:

State income tax withholding (from W-2)	$ 3,348
State income tax paid with 2016 return	600
Real estate tax	4,200
Mortgage interest	11,800
Charitable contributions	2,500

Shelly also started her own home design consulting business in March 2017. The results of her business operations for 2017 follow:

Gross receipts from clients		$154,000
Vehicle mileage	21,000 business miles (2,100 per month) 32,000 total miles during the year 2010 Chevy Suburban Placed in service 03/01/17	
Postage		(750)
Office supplies		(1,500)
State license fees		(155)
Supplies		(5,300)
Professional fees		(2,500)
Design software		(1,000)
Professional education programs (registration)		(550)
Travel to education program		
Airplane		(350)
Lodging $119/night × 3 nights		
Meals per diem 3 days		
Business Assets	**Date Purchased**	**Cost**
Laptop	6/08/17	$ 2,500
Computer	3/05/17	5,700
Printer	3/01/17	1,800
Copier	6/02/17	1,700
Furniture	4/01/17	5,000
Building	3/01/17	175,000
Phone		(600)
Internet service		(450)
Rent		(8,300)
Insurance		(1,700)

Shelly made a $29,000 estimated tax payment on September 15, 2017.

Required

Prepare Shelly's Form 1040 for 2017 including all of the supplementary schedules. Schedule A, Schedule B, Schedule C, Form 4562, and Schedule SE are required. Section 179 is elected on all eligible assets in 2017. She wants to contribute to the presidential election campaign and does not want anyone to be a third-party designee. Shelly had qualifying health care coverage at all times during the tax year. We have provided filled-in source documents that are available in *Connect*. For any missing information, make reasonable assumptions.

COMPREHENSIVE PROBLEM 5

With Emphasis on Schedule D

Matthew Flaws is a single taxpayer and lives at 5670 Sierra Drive, Honolulu, HI 96822. He has income from a job as a marketing representative, interest income, dividend income, and stock investments. Some of his investments are in a mutual fund. His social security number is 412-34-5670.

Social security numbers for the Watanabe family:

Chris	412-34-5670
Stefani	412-34-5671
Justin	412-34-5672
Jordan	412-34-5673

They paid $4,500 to Friendly Hills Child Care center for after-school care for both Justin and Jordan, allocated equally. The address is 2 River Dr, Riverside, CA and their ID number is 22-1234567.

Stefani's W-2 from the Riverside school district showed the following:

Wages = $56,925.04
Federal W/H = $ 9,085.90
Social security wages = $56,925.04
Social security W/H = $ 3,529.35
Medicare wages = $56,925.04
Medicare W/H = $ $825.41
California W/H = $ 2,105.75

Chris's accounting business is located in downtown Riverside. His business had the following income and expense information for the year:

Gross revenues	$165,000
Expenses:	
Advertising	$ 2,100
Insurance	1,200
Legal fees	10,500
Office supplies	800
Rent	24,000
Travel	6,945
Meals and entertainment	2,400
Utilities	2,800
Wages	34,000
Dues	650

Additionally, Chris and Stefani paid the following expenses during the year:

Medical and dental expenses	$ 4,500
Property tax (home on Victoria Lane)	3,750
State income taxes with the 2016 return	3,900
Donations to the church (cash)	3,500
Mortgage interest (home on Victoria Lane)	14,900
Stefani paid $950 in classroom expenses for her class	

Chris and Stefani also earned $975 of interest income from California Bank during the year.

Lastly, Chris and Stefani own a three-bedroom cabin in Big Bear Lake (they bought it in January of 2005 for $300,000). The address is 3105 Stonehedge Road, Big Bear Lake, CA 92315. They did not use the property for personal use at any time during the year. The revenue and expenses for the Big Bear Lake rental property are as follows:

Rental income	$18,000
Expenses:	
Insurance	$ 1,200
Property taxes	2,500
Auto (standard mileage)	267
Management fees	1,600
Repairs and maintenance	1,100
Mortgage interest	9,000
Depreciation	Calculate
Utilities	450

The Watanabes also made $15,000 and $9,000 in federal and California estimated income tax payments on 12/31/17, respectively, during the year.

Required

Prepare the Watanabes' federal tax return for 2017. Use Form 1040, Schedule A, Schedule C, Schedule E, Schedule SE, and any additional schedules or forms they may need. The Watanabes had qualifying health care coverage at all times during the tax year. They do not want to contribute to the presidential election campaign, and they do not want anyone to be a third-party designee. For any missing information, make reasonable assumptions.

Appendix C

Concept Check Answers

CHAPTER 1

Concept Check 1-1

1. Progressive, proportional, regressive.
2. Proportional.
3. Progressive.

Concept Check 1-2

1. True.
2. 25%. For a married couple, the marginal rate is 25% for taxable income between $75,900 and $153,100.
3. False. The average tax rate is the percentage that a taxpayer pays in tax given a certain amount of taxable income. The marginal tax rate represents the proportion of tax that he or she pays on the next dollar of taxable income.
4. False. All tax returns conform to the basic formula.

Concept Check 1-3

1. False. Only taxpayers with a simple tax structure who meet six criteria can file Form 1040EZ.
2. False. To file Form 1040EZ, a taxpayer must be under age 65.
3. True. With the fact pattern provided, Erma meets the six criteria and can file Form 1040EZ.

Concept Check 1-4

1. Wages, unemployment compensation, and interest. The category wages includes salary and tips.
2. Form 1099-G.
3. Single, married filing jointly.

Concept Check 1-5

1. True. Taxpayers must use the tax tables if their income is under $100,000. If taxpayers are eligible to use Form 1040EZ, they must have income under $100,000 (otherwise they would not be eligible to use the form).
2. $14,796.
3. $14,793.
4. False. The payment is the greater of 2.5% or a flat dollar amount based on the number of family members.

Concept Check 1-6

1. False. Taxpayers pay an estimate of their tax liability during the year with income tax withholdings or quarterly estimated tax payments.
2. Required to pay, $392.
3. False. An Earned Income Credit is subtracted from the tax liability.

Concept Check 1-7

1. Ways and Means.
2. The Internal Revenue Code.
3. True. For any action to become law, both houses of Congress and the president must agree.

Concept Check 1-8

1. False. Statutory tax authority (the law) takes precedence over all other types of tax authority.
2. False. Revenue Procedures are issued by the IRS for use by all taxpayers.
3. IRS Treasury Regulations. See Table 1-6.

Concept Check 1-9

1. False. Tax cases can be appealed to the U.S. Supreme Court.
2. False. The taxpayer can file a suit with the Tax Court, the district court, or the Court of Federal Claims.
3. Tax. The advantage of using the Tax Court is that the taxpayer does not need to pay the IRS's proposed assessment prior to trial.

CHAPTER 2

Concept Check 2-1

1. False. A taxpayer should use the simplest form that is appropriate for his or her situation. This approach will save the taxpayer and the IRS time and money.
2. True. Adjusted Gross Income (AGI) is an important concept because several deductions and credits depend upon the AGI amount. Some examples are the medical deduction and the Earned Income Credit.

Concept Check 2-2

1. True. Yes, couples in the process of obtaining a divorce (where the divorce is not yet final) can file a joint return.
2. True. The social security number and full name of the spouse must be shown on the return.
3. False. The surviving spouse must also meet another rule that states the household needs to be the principal place of abode for the entire year (except for temporary absences) of both the taxpayer and a child, stepchild, or adopted child who can be claimed as a dependent by the taxpayer.

Concept Check 2-3

4. True. The amount of the personal exemption is $4,050 for 2017. On a joint return, the taxpayer is entitled to two personal exemptions: one exemption for himself or herself and another one for his or her spouse, for a total of $8,100.

Concept Check 2-4

1. In addition to the dependent taxpayer test, joint return test, and citizen or resident test, a qualifying child must meet the following five tests: relationship test, age test, residency test, support test, and special test for qualifying child of more than one taxpayer.
2. The child must be under 19 years of age, or under 24 years of age and a full-time student. For years after 2008, the child must be younger than the person claiming the dependency.

Concept Check 2-5

1. False. A taxpayer must meet all of the four tests in order to be a qualifying relative.
2. False. A qualifying relative cannot earn an amount equal to or greater than the exemption amount, which is $4,050.

Concept Check 2-6

1. The amount of the standard deduction is
   a. Taxpayer is single, 42 years of age, and blind = 7,900 ($6,350 + $1,550).
   b. Taxpayer is head of household, 37 years of age, and not blind = $9,350.
   c. Taxpayers are married filing jointly, the husband is 67 and the wife is 61 years of age, and neither is blind = $13,950 ($12,700 + $1,250).

Concept Check 2-7

1. Tax for the single taxpayer is $4,728 and for the married taxpayers is $9,226.
2. The limitation for FICA (social security) for the year 2017 is $127,200.

Concept Check 2-8

1. The failure to file a tax return penalty does not apply because the taxpayer filed an extension before his or her return was due. However, the failure to pay does apply. The amount is $30 ([$3,000 × 0.5%] 2 months).
2. True. The IRS can assess criminal penalties in addition to civil penalties. The former are applicable to tax evasion, willful failure to collect or pay tax, and willful failure to file a return.

CHAPTER 3

Concept Check 3-1

1. In general, an individual must recognize income on his or her tax return if a transaction meets all of the following three conditions: There must be an economic benefit; there must actually be a transaction that has reached a conclusion; and the income must not be tax-exempt income.
2. True. Certain income is statutorily excluded from taxation and will not be included in gross income even though the other two conditions are met. An example is tax-exempt interest.

Concept Check 3-2

1. True. According to Reg. § 1.61-1(a), income may be realized in any form, whether in money, property, or services.
2. True. Receipt of property or services serves to trigger income recognition. Furthermore, taxpayers recognize income even if they receive it indirectly.

Concept Check 3-3

1. False. Interest is taxable if received from state or local bonds issued for private activities, such as convention centers, industrial parks, or stadiums.
2. False. Schedule B is required if an individual receives *over* $1,500 of interest for the tax year.

Concept Check 3-4

1. True. Qualified dividends (1) are made from the earnings and profits of the payer corporation and (2) are from domestic corporations or qualified foreign corporations.
2. False. Corporations normally pay dividends in the form of cash, but they may pay them in property or anything of economic value. The basis of the property received as a dividend in the hands of the shareholder is the property's fair market value at the date of distribution.

Concept Check 3-5

1. The amount is $27,750 (22,000 + 4,500 + 1,250).

Concept Check 3-6

1. Items such as jury duty and gambling winnings are listed under line 21 of the Form 1040.

Concept Check 3-7

1. False. It is not taxable. This is an example of a *de minimis* benefit whose value is so small that keeping track of which employees received the benefit is administratively impractical.
2. True. It is not taxable. The individual must be a degree-seeking student at an educational institution and must use the proceeds for qualified tuition and related expenses (tuition, fees, books, supplies, and equipment). If the scholarship or fellowship payment exceeds permitted expenses, the excess is taxable income.

Concept Check 3-8

1. True. The law limits the ability of taxpayers to create debt instruments with interest rates that materially vary from market rates on the date the instrument is created. Imputing interest will reallocate payments such that more of the payment will be interest and less principal.
2. True. If someone purchases a debt instrument (such as a bond) from an issuer for an amount less than par, the transaction creates original issue discount (OID). The initial OID is equal to the difference between the acquisition price and the maturity value.

CHAPTER 4

Concept Check 4-1

1. At least half-time at an eligible educational institution.
2. Tuition and fees
3. $135,000.

Concept Check 4-2

1. Self-employed.
2. Nontaxable.
3. Form 8889 and Form 1040.

Concept Check 4-3

1. False. Under current IRS regulations, moving expenses can be deducted only as a *for AGI,* or *above-the-line,* deduction.
2. False. In order to deduct moving expenses, taxpayers must meet both tests in addition to the employment test.
3. True. To the extent that the employer reimburses the employee for moving costs, those costs cannot be deducted. However, if the total moving expenses exceed the reimbursement, those expenses in excess of the reimbursement can be deducted.

Concept Check 4-4

1. Net earnings.
2. For 2017, the employee's portion is calculated at 7.65%.
3. $200,000.

Concept Check 4-5

1. False. For self-employed individuals, the deduction is 100% of the costs.
2. False. The limitation on this deduction is that taxpayers cannot deduct the cost of premiums that exceeds *net* earnings from self-employment.
3. True. If the taxpayer is entitled to participate in any subsidized health plan maintained by any employer of the taxpayer or of the taxpayer's spouse, a deduction is not allowed.

Concept Check 4-6

1. As an *above-the-line* deduction.
2. Form 1099-INT.

Concept Check 4-7

1. False. Alimony payments can be made only in cash. If the payment consists of property, it is a property settlement.
2. False. As long as the couple is legally separated and there is a written agreement requiring payments, it will be classified as alimony.
3. True. If alimony payments decrease sharply in the second or third year of payment, this is a signal that the nature of the payments might be a property settlement, not alimony.

Concept Check 4-8

1. 900 hours.
2. $500.
3. Home schooling and non-athletic supplies for health or PE classes.

CHAPTER 5

Concept Check 5-1

1. 10.0% of AGI.
2. Actually paid. Payment by credit card meets this standard.
3. Insurance reimbursement.
4. Age.

Concept Check 5-2

1. True. In addition, the two other criteria are that it must be on personal property and the property must be assessed, at a minimum, on an annual basis.
2. False. When property is sold during the year, both the buyer and the seller receive a deduction for a portion of the real estate tax paid according to the number of days each owner held the property.
3. False. The tax benefit rule states that if you receive a refund of that expense that was previously deducted on the tax return, you are required to include that refund in income when it is received.
4. True. But generally most taxpayers receive a greater benefit by taking the credit.

Concept Check 5-3

1. Acquire, construct, or substantially improve.
2. $1,000,000.
3. Net investment.
4. 1%.

Concept Check 5-4

1. False. Charitable contributions can be taken only as an itemized deduction.
2. False. The overall limitation on the deductibility of charitable contributions is 50% of AGI. The 30% limit relates to the contribution of appreciated capital gain property
3. True. If noncash gifts are worth over $500, the taxpayer must file Form 8283.

Concept Check 5-5

1. Sudden, unexpected, or unusual nature.
2. Form 4684 and then carried to Form 1040.
3. Two; $100.
4. 10%.

Concept Check 5-6

1. False. The threshold is 2% of AGI.
2. True. The amount calculated there goes to line 21 of the Schedule A.
3. False. The law does allow a deduction for uniforms required for employment as long as they would not usually be worn away from work. The accountant's blue suit would not fall into this category. However, a police officer's uniform would qualify for the deduction.

Concept Check 5-7

1. Limit.
2. 3%; 80%.

CHAPTER 6

Concept Check 6-1

1. False. Schedule C is used only for an activity in which the individual is self-employed, not an employee.
2. False. Any income received by the self-employed taxpayer is taxable and should be included on Schedule C. Not all individuals or organizations are required to send a 1099-MISC to the self-employed individual.
3. True. If inventory is a material item, it must be accounted for using the accrual method of accounting. The cash method can be used for all other items.

Concept Check 6-2

1. Ordinary, necessary, and reasonable.
2. Illegal bribes, kickbacks, and other such payments; payments for certain lobbying and political expenses; payments for fines and penalties.

Concept Check 6-3

1. $1,300. When an asset is transferred from personal use to business use, the depreciable basis is the lesser of cost or FMV at transfer.
2. $17,600. The adjusted basis at the end of year 1 is the cost less the accumulated depreciation ($22,000 – $4,400).

Concept Check 6-4

1. B. Autos are 5-year property under the MACRS rules.
2. C. An apartment complex is considered residential real property and thus has a 27.5-year life under the MACRS rules.
3. D. A warehouse is considered nonresidential real property and thus has a 39-year life under the MACRS rules.

Concept Check 6-5

1. False. A taxpayer must use the half-year convention for personal property unless more than 40% of the basis is purchased in the last quarter of the year; then mid-quarter is required. The taxpayer must use the mid-month convention for real property.
2. True. If more than 40% of the basis of personal property is purchased in the fourth quarter, the taxpayer must use the mid-quarter convention.
3. True. The only time the half-year convention is not used is when more than 40% of the personal property is purchased in the fourth quarter.
4. False. Because an apartment complex is residential real property, the mid-month convention is required.
5. True. Once the convention is established, it never changes for an asset. Thus if one half-year of depreciation is taken in the year of purchase, then one half-year of depreciation should be taken in the year of disposal. The same is true for mid-quarter and mid-month assets.

Concept Check 6-6

1. $1,715. Equipment is a 7-year asset ($12,000 × 14.29%).
2. $1,049. 2018 would be the third year of depreciation, and the table percentage is 17.49% for year 3. But only one-half of a year of depreciation would be allowed ($12,000 × 17.49% × ½).
3. $9,501. An apartment complex is 27.5-year, mid-month property purchased in March. The appropriate percentage is the third column of Table 6A-6 ($330,000 × 2.879).

Concept Check 6-7

1. $12,000 in § 179 expense and $0 additional MACRS depreciation.
2. $510,000 in § 179 expense (up to the limit of $510,000 for 2017) and $3,573 in 7-year MACRS depreciation ($25,000 remaining basis × 14.29%).

Concept Check 6-8

1. C. $25,000 in § 179 expense and $2,800 in MACRS depreciation ([$39,000 – $25,000] × 20%) is allowed. The total is $27,800.
2. C. $25,000 × 80% business use = $20,000 in § 179 expense and $2,224 in regular depreciation ([$39,000 × 80%] – $20,000 § 179) × 20% (5-year MACRS percentage). The total is $22,240.

Concept Check 6-9

1. False. The standard mileage rate incorporates depreciation into the mileage rate. A taxpayer uses either the standard mileage rate or the actual costs of operations including depreciation.
2. False. Transportation costs are deductible for all business travel except for commuting.
3. True. Once overnight rest is required with business travel, the taxpayer can then deduct meals and lodging.
4. True. Subject to the 50% limitation, a taxpayer can use the standard per diems of $51/day. The per diems are higher in high-cost areas.
5. True. Subject to the 50% limitation, a taxpayer can deduct entertainment costs for clients assuming they are ordinary, necessary, and reasonable.

Concept Check 6-10

1. D. The external painting is an indirect cost and is deductible based on the business use ratio ($3,000 × 20%). The office painting is a direct expense and is 100% deductible.
2. B. The home office expenses are deductible only to the extent of Schedule C income. Clients do not have to be seen at the home office, and § 179 is never allowed on real property. The home office can be depreciated over 27.5 years as residential real estate.
3. C. A business casualty loss when a property is partially destroyed is calculated using the lesser of the decrease in FMV or the adjusted basis of the property.

Concept Check 6-11

1. True. Typically, if an activity has shown a profit for three of five consecutive years, the activity is not considered a hobby. The burden of proving the activity is a hobby shifts to the IRS.
2. True. The expenses from a hobby can be used only to offset income from the hobby. Thus no net loss can occur.
3. True. Expenses such as real estate taxes and mortgage interest must be the first expenses deducted from hobby income. Otherwise these expenses could be deducted elsewhere (Schedule A) once all of the hobby income was offset.
4. False. If the educational costs help qualify the taxpayer for a new trade or business, the educational costs are not deductible.

Concept Check 6-12

1. \$6,076. \$43,000 × 92.35% × 15.3%.
2. \$1,152. \$43,000 × 92.35% × 2.9%. Kia has already paid through her employer the maximum amount of wages subject to social security. Kia still must pay Medicare because there is no limit.
3. \$5,306. \$43,000 × 92.35% × 2.9% = \$1,152 for Medicare. Because Kia has not reached the social security limit, an additional \$4,924 of social security must be paid (\$127,200 – \$85,000 = \$42,200 limit left; \$43,000 SE × 92.35% × 12.4%).

CHAPTER 7

Concept Check 7-1

1. False. The gain or loss is the difference between the amount realized from the sale and the asset's adjusted basis.
2. False. Form 4797 is used to record the gain or loss from an asset used in a trade or business.
3. True.

Concept Check 7-2

1. False. Inventory sold by a company appears on the income statement as the cost of goods sold and then on Schedule C for a sole proprietorship.
2. C. Property used in a trade or business.
3. False. Assets considered short-term are held for less than one year and are considered to be ordinary income assets.
4. True.
5. True.

Concept Check 7-3

1. False. When an ordinary asset is sold, the gain or loss is termed an "ordinary gain or loss."
2. The distinction is important because of the preferential tax rate treatment on capital gains versus ordinary gains.
3. True.

Concept Check 7-4

1. B. The tax treatment of a capital asset varies only if there is a gain. Losses are included for the netting process.
2. True.
3. False. Inherited property is always long-term property regardless of how long the asset belonged to the decedent or beneficiary.
4. False. The surtax is charged when MAGI is over the threshold amounts.
5. Collectible gains 28%

Collectible gains	28%
§ 1202 gains	28%
Unrecaptured § 1250 gains	25%
Taxpayer's regular rate ≥ 25% and < 39.6%	15%
Taxpayer's regular rate < 25%	0%
Taxpayer's regular rate is > 35%	20%

Concept Check 7-5

1. False. Losses are ordinary and fully deductible.
2. True.
3. Depreciation recapture rules transform some or all of a § 1231 gain into an ordinary gain.
4. § 1245 property is personal trade or business property subject to depreciation. § 1250 property includes depreciable real property used in a trade or business that has never been considered § 1245 property.
5. Unrecaptured gain is taxed at a 25% rate for all straight-line depreciation taken on the property. Recaptured gain is taxed at ordinary rates to the extent the depreciation taken exceeds straight-line depreciation.

Concept Check 7-6

1. First in, first out—The first shares purchased are the first shares sold. This results in the largest gain when the value of the mutual fund units appreciates.

   Specific identification—The taxpayer specifies exactly which units are for sale from the fund.

   Average basis—The taxpayer takes the total cost basis and divides by the total number of units to get an average cost per unit (single category).

2. True.
3. False. The basis for property given as a gift depends on whether the FMV was higher or lower than the basis at the date of the gift.
4. False. The tax treatment of a gain on the sale of inherited property is always considered to be held long term regardless of the holding period of the deceased.

CHAPTER 8

Concept Check 8-1

1. True. Income and expenses associated with rental property are reported on Schedule E unless the taxpayer is a real estate professional and the rental activity is considered a trade or business.
2. False. All ordinary and necessary expenses related to a rental property are deductible in the current year, but capital improvements must be depreciated and deducted over the useful life of the asset category.
3. True. Rental property is depreciated over 27.5 years for residential and 39 years for nonresidential using the straight-line method.
4. False. The income and expenses associated with a rental property that is considered to be the taxpayer's trade or business are reported on Schedule C.
5. False. Expenses paid by the tenant or services provided in lieu of rent payments are components of rental income and must be reported at the fair market value.

Concept Check 8-2

1. B. Primarily personal; rented less than 15 days.
2. A. Primarily rental; rented 15 days or more or personal use was less than 10% of rental days (i.e., less than 18 days).
3. A. Primarily rental; rented 15 days or more and personal use was no more than 14 days. Only 9 days of the 16 days are considered personal days because Darren worked for 7 days repairing the property.
4. C. Personal/rental; rented 15 days or more and personal use was more than 14 days.

Concept Check 8-3

1. Personal/rental. The property was rented for 75 days and used for personal use for 30 days. Rental property used for personal use more than 14 days (or 10% of days rented) and rented for 15 days or more is categorized as personal/rental.
2.

$6,000 × 75/105 =	$4,286
1,000 × 75/105 =	714
1,400 × 75/105 =	1,000
800 × 75/105 =	571
2,000 × 75/105 =	1,429
Allocated expenses	$8,000

3.

$6,000 × 75/365 =	$1,233
1,000 × 75/365 =	205
1,400 × 75/105 =	1,000
800 × 75/105 =	571
2,000 × 75/105 =	1,429
Allocated expenses	$4,438

4.

Rental income	$15,000
Allocated expenses	8,000
Net income	$ 7,000

Concept Check 8-4

1. Schedule C. Royalty received as a result of a trade or business should be reported on Schedule C.
2. Schedule E. Royalty produced by an investment should be reported on Schedule E.
3. Schedule C. Readings based on books written are not royalties but payment for services performed and should be reported on Schedule C.
4. Schedule E. Royalties are payments received for the right to use intangible property. The payments are for the use of Jane's textbook.

Concept Check 8-5

1. True. Flow-through entities supply each owner with a K-1 indicating his or her share of income, expenses, or losses.
2. False. Ordinary income from an S corporation is not considered self-employment income.
3. True. Partners, shareholders, or owners of flow-through entities must report their K-1 information on their individual tax returns on a Form E.
4. True. A taxpayer is allowed up to $25,000 of rental losses against other nonpassive income subject to limitations and phaseouts.

CHAPTER 9

Concept Check 9-1

1. $600
   $4,500 is more than maximum allowed, so use $3,000 × 20% = $600.

2. $4,500

   $500 × 9 months = $4,500; although expenses of $6,000 do not exceed the maximum allowed, the amount used cannot be greater than $4,500 because Katie is a student.

3. $570

   $2,900 – $1,000 = $1,900 × 30% = $570

Concept Check 9-2

1. $150

Base amount	$7,500
Less social security	1,000
Less 1/2 of AGI over $10,000	5,500
Allowable base amount	1,000
Applicable %	× 15%
Credit	$ 150

Concept Check 9-3

1. $ 580

   $2,900 × 20% = $580

2. $1,113

   100% of first $2,000 and 25% of second $900 is the credit allowed of $2,225. However, the credit is phased out due to AGI.

   $2,225 × ($90,000 – $85,000/$10,000) = $1,113

3. $0

   Her AGI is greater than the maximum phaseout amount.

4. $740

   ($1,600 + $2,100) × 20% = $740

Concept Check 9-4

1. $2,240

   ($8,000/$63,000) × $17,640 = $2,240 (less than foreign tax paid of $2,500)

Concept Check 9-5

1. $1,900

   $1,000 per child × 2 = $2,000; however, limitations apply due to AGI.

   ($112,000 – $110,000)/$1000 = 2; therefore,

   $2,000 – (2 × $50) = $1,900

Concept Check 9-6

1. $150

   $1,500 × 10% = $150

2. $1,000

   $2,000 × 50% = $1,000 ($2,200 over the maximum allowed)

Concept Check 9-7

1. $ 0 in 2016.

   $13,570 in 2017.

   $10,500 + $3,950 = $14,450; however, the maximum allowed is $13,570.

2. $13,075

   $16,000 is more than the maximum of $13,570, so use $13,570. The credit must be phased out because of AGI as follows:

   $13,570 × ([$243,540 – $205,000]/$40,000) × $13,570 = $13,075

Concept Check 9-8

1. $3,400
2. $2,110

   $3,400 (maximum credit) – ([$32,000 – $23,930] × 15.98%) = $2,110

3a. $5,616

3b. $4,816 refund

   $5,616 credit – $800 tax liability = $4,816 refund; EIC is a refundable credit.

Concept Check 9-9

1. No. The premium tax credit is only available to taxpayers with household income between 100% and 400% of the federal poverty level for the taxpayer's family size.
2. .0966

CHAPTER 10

Concept Check 10-1

1. True.
2. True.

Concept Check 10-2

1. False. They are also levied on noncash compensation as well as cash compensation other than through wages and salary.
2. False. Form W-4 is completed by the employee so the employer knows how much to withhold in federal income tax from the employee's compensation.
3. $52 if you use the wage bracket table, $51.03 if you use the percentage method.
4. $7,886.40 (limit $127,300) in social security and $1,892.25 in Medicare taxes (no limit).
5. False. Only tips in excess of $20 per month are subject to tax withholding.

Concept Check 10-3

1. False. New employers start as monthly schedule depositors. If in any one day tax liability equals $100,000, they become semiweekly schedule depositors.
2. False. The lookback period runs from the quarters starting July 1 of the current year through June 30 of the next year.
3. True.
4. False. A penalty is assessed only on the amount of tax that was not deposited on time.
5. True.

Concept Check 10-4

1. True.
2. A.
3. Individuals who employ household workers and do not withhold any taxes during the year. The schedule is attached to the taxpayer's Form 1040.
4. They paid any one household employee wages of $2,000 or more in 2017, federal income taxes were withheld from employee wages, and household wages of at least $1,000 were paid to all household workers combined in any calendar quarter in 2016 or 2017.

Concept Check 10-5

1. True.
2. Copy A is sent to the Social Security Administration along with Form W-3, which is the transmittal form. They are due January 31, 2018.
3. An employer who must correct an employee's W-2 must file Forms W-2C and W-3C as soon as possible.
4. The penalties for incorrectly preparing W-2s range from $50 per return to $260 per return with a maximum depending on the size of the business. Also a penalty of $530 per return (with no maximum) for intentional disregard for filing requirements.

Concept Check 10-6

1. Method 1: Withhold at a flat rate of 25%. If taxes are withheld from regular wages, add the two amounts together, calculate the tax as if they are one payment, and subtract the amount of withholding already taken out of the employee's wages. Method 2: If taxes are not already withheld from regular wages, add the two amounts together, and calculate the tax as if they are one payment.
2. True.
3. Form W-9 is used for U.S. persons (including resident aliens) to document their taxpayer identification number (TIN). This form must be on file by the payer.
4. $50 for each failure unless the failure is due to reasonable cause, not to willful neglect. If the taxpayer makes false statements with no reasonable basis that result in backup withholding, a penalty of $500 is assessed. There can also be criminal penalties including fines and imprisonment.
5. False. There is no way of knowing whether the taxpayer will overpay and have a refund. The estimated payments contribute by having taxpayers pay additional taxes to limit the amount of possible underpayment.

CHAPTER 11

Concept Check 11-1

1. False. Tax is only delayed (deferred), not forgiven.
2. Distribution.
3. False. It is an example of an employer-sponsored plan.
4. Employer-sponsored plans include qualified pension and profit-sharing plans, 401(k) or 403(b) plans, Keogh plans, SEPs, and SIMPLE plans. Choose any two.
5. True.

Concept Check 11-2

1. Defined benefit, defined contribution.
2. False. Some plans require employee contributions and some do not.
3. $18,000.
4. True. In fact, they can be used only by self-employed individuals.
5. True.

Concept Check 11-3

1. Traditional IRA and Roth IRA.
2. $6,500.
3. False. As long as neither individual is an active participant in an employer plan, a deductible contribution is permitted regardless of the amount of AGI.
4. True.

Concept Check 11-4

1. True.
2. $2,000.
3. $95,000. The phaseout is complete when AGI reaches $110,000.

Concept Check 11-5

1. True.
2. True.
3. 210.
4. 310.
5. True.

Concept Check 11-6

1. True.
2. True.
3. True.
4. False. Coverdell distributions must be used for higher education expenses (subject to certain restrictions). If not, the distributions are taxable.

Concept Check 11-7

1. An annuity is a series of payments under a contract.
2. False.
3. True.

CHAPTER 12

Concept Check 12-1

1. True. A gain is never recognized with a nontaxable like-kind exchange unless the taxpayer receives boot. Then gain is recognized to the lesser of the realized gain or the FMV of the boot received.
2. True. Those are the three conditions necessary to execute a nontaxable like-kind exchange.
3. False. The taxpayer has 45 days to identify the replacement property and 180 days to actually receive the replacement property.
4. True. The basis in the replacement property is the adjusted basis of the property given up, plus the basis of boot given, plus gain recognized, less the FMV of boot received. This sum is typically the FMV of the property received less the postponed gain.

Concept Check 12-2

1. \$55,000. If the building is not replaced, the insurance proceeds are treated as sale proceeds and the gain is recognized in full.
2. Three years. The typical replacement period is two years. However, for real property held for use in a trade or business, the replacement period increases to three years.
3. \$10,000 gain recognized. The realized gain of \$55,000 is recognized to the lesser of the proceeds not used for replacement or the realized gain. In this case, the amount not used is the lesser of the two (\$10,000).
4. \$0 gain recognized. All of the proceeds were used to replace the property.
5. \$60,000 is the adjusted basis. The basis is calculated as the cost of the new asset less the deferred gain (\$115,000 – \$55,000 deferred gain).

Concept Check 12-3

1. A. The gross profit percentage is calculated by dividing the gross profit by the gross sales prices (\$10,000/\$30,000 = 33.3%).
2. B. The income recognized is \$1,667 (the amount received in year two of \$5,000 × 33.3% gross profit percentage).

Concept Check 12-4

1. True. The maximum gain exclusion is \$500,000 for married taxpayers who file a joint return.
2. False. If the move is caused by an employment change or for health reasons, a taxpayer is eligible for some reduced exclusion. The exclusion is calculated by taking a ratio of the number of days used as a personal residence and dividing it by 730 days.
3. False. Johnny would still be allowed to exclude his gain but only to the maximum exclusion of \$250,000.

Concept Check 12-5

1. \$0. Because Leslie sold the stock to her brother, the related-party rules disallow any loss deduction on the sale by Leslie.
2. A. Leslie could deduct \$2,000 in capital losses. In order for a corporation (or other entity) to be considered a related party, Leslie would have to have control of the corporation (greater than 50% ownership).

   B. \$0. Because Leslie now has control of the corporation, she is considered a related party and the loss would be disallowed.
3. The purpose of the wash sale rules is to disallow a tax loss where the ownership of a company is not reduced. Thus if a taxpayer buys similar stock within 30 days of a stock sale (before or after), any loss on the sale is disallowed.

CHAPTER 13

Concept Check 13-1

1. D. All of the above increase the at-risk of a taxpayer. See Table 13-1 for all of the increases and decreases of at-risk.

2. A. Nonrecourse debt does not increase the taxpayer's at-risk. Nonrecourse debt is debt that the taxpayer is not personally liable for.
3. C. The loss is indefinitely carried forward and can be deducted once the taxpayer gets additional at-risk.

Concept Check 13-2

1. True. The only way a rental property is not a passive activity is when the taxpayer is a real estate professional. A rental business can qualify for nonpassive treatment if more than one-half of the personal services performed in a business during the year is performed in a real property trade or business and the taxpayer performs more than 750 hours of services in the activity.
2. True. Passive losses are allowed only to the extent of passive income. One exception is the $25,000 offset for rental properties.
3. False. The $25,000 offset is limited to $25,000 and is phased out after a taxpayer's AGI reaches $100,000.
4. True. Any suspended passive losses are allowed when the activity is sold.

Concept Check 13-3

1. In order for a loss to be deducted, it must first be allowed under the at-risk rules. Once the loss is allowed under the at-risk rules, the passive loss rules are applied.
2. The main reason is that passive losses are allowed when an activity is sold or disposed of. Thus if a taxpayer were considering the sale of a passive activity, he or she could lump all suspended passive losses on one activity and sell it. All of the losses would then be allowed. The allocation to all loss activities stops this potential abuse.
3. The taxpayer is eligible for the $25,000 offset for rental losses. However, the $25,000 limit is phased out once the taxpayer's AGI reaches $100,000 ([$105,000 − $100,000] × $^1/_2$ = $2,500). Thus only $22,500 of the rental loss would be allowed.

Concept Check 13-4

1. True. The AGI floor for medical expenses is 10% for AMT purposes and regular tax for most taxpayers. Some taxpayers over 65 still get the 7.5% floor until after the 2017 tax year.
2. True. No taxes are allowed as a deduction for AMT. Any taxes deducted on the regular return are added back as a positive adjustment for AMT.
3. True. Personal exemptions are added as a positive adjustment for AMT purposes.
4. True. If AMTI is greater than $187,800, the AMT rate is 28%.

CHAPTER 14

Concept Check 14-1

1. True. The only time gain is recognized by a contributing partner is when the partner receives an interest for services or when he or she is released of a liability in excess of basis.
2. True. The basis of the assets typically carries over from the partner to the partnership.
3. False. The basis is dependent on the basis of the assets the individual partners contributed to the partnership. One partner could have a $0 basis while the other partner might have $100,000, yet both share 50% in the profit and loss of the partnership.
4. False. Gain must be recognized to the extent of the FMV of the partnership interest received for services.
5. True. An increase or decrease in partnership liabilities is treated as a cash contribution or cash distribution and thus increases or decreases partnership basis.

Concept Check 14-2

1. D. All of the above can be deducted from partnership income to determine the net income or loss from the partnership.
2. C. Any form of partnership files a Form 1065 informational return each year.
3. D. A guaranteed payment is a payment, usually for services, that is determined without regard to partnership income and is deductible by the partnership.

Concept Check 14-3

1. All income and expense items of a partnership that may be treated differently at the partner level must be "separately stated." Rental income/loss, capital gains/losses, and charitable contributions all can be treated differently at the partner level. For example, an individual partner can take up to $3,000 of capital losses against ordinary income while a corporate partner in the same partnership cannot.
2. A partner is not an employee of the partnership. Thus income received by the partner from the partnership has no social security or Medicare withheld by the partnership.

Concept Check 14-4

1. True. These are two of the uses of basis. Basis is also used to determine the basis (or whether a gain is recognized) of property distributed.

2. False. If the basis is not increased by tax-exempt income, then the exempt income will eventually be taxed when the partnership interest is sold. The lower basis will cause a higher gain upon sale.
3. False. The basis is first reduced by all adjustments except for losses, then money distributed, and then the basis of any property distributed. After those items, any basis remaining is used to determine the deductibility of losses.
4. False. The basis is always increased by the partner's share of recourse debt.

Concept Check 14-5

1. B. If a cash distribution or a release of liabilities exceeds basis, the partner will have a gain on a distribution from the partnership.
2. B. $12,000—the furniture would be reduced to the basis left in the partnership.
3. A. $8,000—the basis in the partnership is first reduced by the cash distribution. That leaves $8,000 for the furniture.

Concept Check 14-6

1. A. Shelly's recognized gain would be $0. She did not receive cash in excess of her basis.

   B. Shelly's basis in the assets would be as follows:

Cash	$9,000
Inventory	$6,000
Equipment ($15,000 × $8,000/$20,000)	$6,000
Land ($15,000 × $12,000/$20,000)	$9,000

2. A. $99,000 ($55,000 beginning basis + $18,000 + $26,000)

   B. $8,000 ($107,000 sales price – $99,000 *basis*)

   C. Because the partnership interest is a capital asset and there was no mention of inventory or receivables in the partnership, the gain would be a long-term capital gain.

CHAPTER 15

Concept Check 15-1

1. False. Some corporations are prohibited from using the cash basis. Corporations with average annual revenues over $5 million must use the accrual basis. Corporations with inventory must use the accrual basis at least for sales and cost of goods sold.
2. The 15th day of the fourth month after the fiscal year end.
3. False. In the first year of operation, a corporation establishes its tax year. Although many corporations choose December 31, that date is not required.

Concept Check 15-2

1. True. Although an exchange of cash or property can be taxable, if the 80% rule is met, the formation activities are generally tax-free.
2. The basis in the hands of the shareholder plus any gain recognized by the shareholder.
3. $40,000. His basis in the stock is his carryover basis in the land.

Concept Check 15-3

1. False. Corporations cannot report a net capital loss whereas individuals can take up to $3,000 in capital losses in any tax year.
2. $176,800. Tax liability is equal to $113,900 plus 34% of the amount of taxable income over $335,000.
3. $39,000. A corporation can take a charitable contribution in an amount not to exceed 10% of taxable income before charitable contribution.
4. False. Although organizational expenses are deductible over 180 months or more, the corporation must make an affirmative election in its first tax return in order to do so.
5. 2, 20.

Concept Check 15-4

1. True. By definition, a dividend is a distribution from the earnings and profits of a corporation. Dividends are taxable to the shareholder. If a distribution is in excess of the earnings and profits of the corporation, it is not a dividend. It may or may not be taxable depending on the stockholder's basis in his or her stock.
2. False. Property dividends are taxed on the fair value of the property received by the stockholder.
3. $10,000. The amount of the dividend cannot exceed the earnings and profits of the corporation.

Concept Check 15-5

1. False. Corporations with total receipts and total assets under $250,000 are not required to complete Schedule L.
2. True.
3. Negative. Schedule M-1 reconciles from book income to tax income. There is more depreciation on the tax return than on the books. That means book income needs to be reduced to arrive at taxable income.

Concept Check 15-6

1. 80%.
2. Five.
3. $40,000.

Concept Check 15-7

1. False. Not only must a corporation meet tests in addition to the 100 shareholder limit, the corporation must also affirmatively elect Subchapter S status.
2. True. While there are some differences, the tax treatments of a partnership and a Subchapter S corporation are similar.
3. 1120S.
4. Not taxable. Subchapter S dividends are not taxable to a shareholder.
5. False. Corporate debt does not affect shareholders' basis in their stock.

Appendix D

2017 Tax Table

Example. Mr. and Mrs. Reynolds are filing a joint return. Their taxable income on Form 1040A, line 27, is $25,300. First, they find the $25,300-25,350 taxable income line. Next, they find the column for married filing jointly and read down the column. The amount shown where the taxable income line and filing status column meet is $2,866. This is the tax amount they should enter on Form 1040A, line 28.

Sample Table

At Least	But Less Than	Single	Married filing jointly*	Married filing separately	Head of a household
		Your tax is—			
25,200	25,250	3,318	2,851	3,318	3,116
25,250	25,300	3,325	2,859	3,325	3,124
25,300	25,350	3,333	(2,866)	3,333	3,131
25,350	25,400	3,340	2,874	3,340	3,139

If line 27 (taxable income) is— At least	But less than	And you are— Single	Married filing jointly*	Married filing separately	Head of a household
		Your tax is—			
0	5	0	0	0	0
5	15	1	1	1	1
15	25	2	2	2	2
25	50	4	4	4	4
50	75	6	6	6	6
75	100	9	9	9	9
100	125	11	11	11	11
125	150	14	14	14	14
150	175	16	16	16	16
175	200	19	19	19	19
200	225	21	21	21	21
225	250	24	24	24	24
250	275	26	26	26	26
275	300	29	29	29	29
300	325	31	31	31	31
325	350	34	34	34	34
350	375	36	36	36	36
375	400	39	39	39	39
400	425	41	41	41	41
425	450	44	44	44	44
450	475	46	46	46	46
475	500	49	49	49	49
500	525	51	51	51	51
525	550	54	54	54	54
550	575	56	56	56	56
575	600	59	59	59	59
600	625	61	61	61	61
625	650	64	64	64	64
650	675	66	66	66	66
675	700	69	69	69	69
700	725	71	71	71	71
725	750	74	74	74	74
750	775	76	76	76	76
775	800	79	79	79	79
800	825	81	81	81	81
825	850	84	84	84	84
850	875	86	86	86	86
875	900	89	89	89	89
900	925	91	91	91	91
925	950	94	94	94	94
950	975	96	96	96	96
975	1,000	99	99	99	99

If line 27 (taxable income) is— At least	But less than	And you are— Single	Married filing jointly*	Married filing separately	Head of a household
		Your tax is—			
1,000					
1,000	1,025	101	101	101	101
1,025	1,050	104	104	104	104
1,050	1,075	106	106	106	106
1,075	1,100	109	109	109	109
1,100	1,125	111	111	111	111
1,125	1,150	114	114	114	114
1,150	1,175	116	116	116	116
1,175	1,200	119	119	119	119
1,200	1,225	121	121	121	121
1,225	1,250	124	124	124	124
1,250	1,275	126	126	126	126
1,275	1,300	129	129	129	129
1,300	1,325	131	131	131	131
1,325	1,350	134	134	134	134
1,350	1,375	136	136	136	136
1,375	1,400	139	139	139	139
1,400	1,425	141	141	141	141
1,425	1,450	144	144	144	144
1,450	1,475	146	146	146	146
1,475	1,500	149	149	149	149
1,500	1,525	151	151	151	151
1,525	1,550	154	154	154	154
1,550	1,575	156	156	156	156
1,575	1,600	159	159	159	159
1,600	1,625	161	161	161	161
1,625	1,650	164	164	164	164
1,650	1,675	166	166	166	166
1,675	1,700	169	169	169	169
1,700	1,725	171	171	171	171
1,725	1,750	174	174	174	174
1,750	1,775	176	176	176	176
1,775	1,800	179	179	179	179
1,800	1,825	181	181	181	181
1,825	1,850	184	184	184	184
1,850	1,875	186	186	186	186
1,875	1,900	189	189	189	189
1,900	1,925	191	191	191	191
1,925	1,950	194	194	194	194
1,950	1,975	196	196	196	196
1,975	2,000	199	199	199	199

If line 27 (taxable income) is— At least	But less than	And you are— Single	Married filing jointly*	Married filing separately	Head of a household
		Your tax is—			
2,000					
2,000	2,025	201	201	201	201
2,025	2,050	204	204	204	204
2,050	2,075	206	206	206	206
2,075	2,100	209	209	209	209
2,100	2,125	211	211	211	211
2,125	2,150	214	214	214	214
2,150	2,175	216	216	216	216
2,175	2,200	219	219	219	219
2,200	2,225	221	221	221	221
2,225	2,250	224	224	224	224
2,250	2,275	226	226	226	226
2,275	2,300	229	229	229	229
2,300	2,325	231	231	231	231
2,325	2,350	234	234	234	234
2,350	2,375	236	236	236	236
2,375	2,400	239	239	239	239
2,400	2,425	241	241	241	241
2,425	2,450	244	244	244	244
2,450	2,475	246	246	246	246
2,475	2,500	249	249	249	249
2,500	2,525	251	251	251	251
2,525	2,550	254	254	254	254
2,550	2,575	256	256	256	256
2,575	2,600	259	259	259	259
2,600	2,625	261	261	261	261
2,625	2,650	264	264	264	264
2,650	2,675	266	266	266	266
2,675	2,700	269	269	269	269
2,700	2,725	271	271	271	271
2,725	2,750	274	274	274	274
2,750	2,775	276	276	276	276
2,775	2,800	279	279	279	279
2,800	2,825	281	281	281	281
2,825	2,850	284	284	284	284
2,850	2,875	286	286	286	286
2,875	2,900	289	289	289	289
2,900	2,925	291	291	291	291
2,925	2,950	294	294	294	294
2,950	2,975	296	296	296	296
2,975	3,000	299	299	299	299

(Continued)

* This column must also be used by a qualifying widow(er).

Source: U.S. Department of the Treasury, Internal Revenue Service, Form 1040A, 2017 Tax Table. Washington, DC: 2017.

2017 Tax Table — *Continued*

If line 27 (taxable income) is— At least	But less than	And you are— Single	Married filing jointly *	Married filing sepa-rately	Head of a house-hold
		Your tax is—			
3,000					
3,000	3,050	303	303	303	303
3,050	3,100	308	308	308	308
3,100	3,150	313	313	313	313
3,150	3,200	318	318	318	318
3,200	3,250	323	323	323	323
3,250	3,300	328	328	328	328
3,300	3,350	333	333	333	333
3,350	3,400	338	338	338	338
3,400	3,450	343	343	343	343
3,450	3,500	348	348	348	348
3,500	3,550	353	353	353	353
3,550	3,600	358	358	358	358
3,600	3,650	363	363	363	363
3,650	3,700	368	368	368	368
3,700	3,750	373	373	373	373
3,750	3,800	378	378	378	378
3,800	3,850	383	383	383	383
3,850	3,900	388	388	388	388
3,900	3,950	393	393	393	393
3,950	4,000	398	398	398	398
4,000					
4,000	4,050	403	403	403	403
4,050	4,100	408	408	408	408
4,100	4,150	413	413	413	413
4,150	4,200	418	418	418	418
4,200	4,250	423	423	423	423
4,250	4,300	428	428	428	428
4,300	4,350	433	433	433	433
4,350	4,400	438	438	438	438
4,400	4,450	443	443	443	443
4,450	4,500	448	448	448	448
4,500	4,550	453	453	453	453
4,550	4,600	458	458	458	458
4,600	4,650	463	463	463	463
4,650	4,700	468	468	468	468
4,700	4,750	473	473	473	473
4,750	4,800	478	478	478	478
4,800	4,850	483	483	483	483
4,850	4,900	488	488	488	488
4,900	4,950	493	493	493	493
4,950	5,000	498	498	498	498
5,000					
5,000	5,050	503	503	503	503
5,050	5,100	508	508	508	508
5,100	5,150	513	513	513	513
5,150	5,200	518	518	518	518
5,200	5,250	523	523	523	523
5,250	5,300	528	528	528	528
5,300	5,350	533	533	533	533
5,350	5,400	538	538	538	538
5,400	5,450	543	543	543	543
5,450	5,500	548	548	548	548
5,500	5,550	553	553	553	553
5,550	5,600	558	558	558	558
5,600	5,650	563	563	563	563
5,650	5,700	568	568	568	568
5,700	5,750	573	573	573	573
5,750	5,800	578	578	578	578
5,800	5,850	583	583	583	583
5,850	5,900	588	588	588	588
5,900	5,950	593	593	593	593
5,950	6,000	598	598	598	598

If line 27 (taxable income) is— At least	But less than	And you are— Single	Married filing jointly *	Married filing sepa-rately	Head of a house-hold
		Your tax is—			
6,000					
6,000	6,050	603	603	603	603
6,050	6,100	608	608	608	608
6,100	6,150	613	613	613	613
6,150	6,200	618	618	618	618
6,200	6,250	623	623	623	623
6,250	6,300	628	628	628	628
6,300	6,350	633	633	633	633
6,350	6,400	638	638	638	638
6,400	6,450	643	643	643	643
6,450	6,500	648	648	648	648
6,500	6,550	653	653	653	653
6,550	6,600	658	658	658	658
6,600	6,650	663	663	663	663
6,650	6,700	668	668	668	668
6,700	6,750	673	673	673	673
6,750	6,800	678	678	678	678
6,800	6,850	683	683	683	683
6,850	6,900	688	688	688	688
6,900	6,950	693	693	693	693
6,950	7,000	698	698	698	698
7,000					
7,000	7,050	703	703	703	703
7,050	7,100	708	708	708	708
7,100	7,150	713	713	713	713
7,150	7,200	718	718	718	718
7,200	7,250	723	723	723	723
7,250	7,300	728	728	728	728
7,300	7,350	733	733	733	733
7,350	7,400	738	738	738	738
7,400	7,450	743	743	743	743
7,450	7,500	748	748	748	748
7,500	7,550	753	753	753	753
7,550	7,600	758	758	758	758
7,600	7,650	763	763	763	763
7,650	7,700	768	768	768	768
7,700	7,750	773	773	773	773
7,750	7,800	778	778	778	778
7,800	7,850	783	783	783	783
7,850	7,900	788	788	788	788
7,900	7,950	793	793	793	793
7,950	8,000	798	798	798	798
8,000					
8,000	8,050	803	803	803	803
8,050	8,100	808	808	808	808
8,100	8,150	813	813	813	813
8,150	8,200	818	818	818	818
8,200	8,250	823	823	823	823
8,250	8,300	828	828	828	828
8,300	8,350	833	833	833	833
8,350	8,400	838	838	838	838
8,400	8,450	843	843	843	843
8,450	8,500	848	848	848	848
8,500	8,550	853	853	853	853
8,550	8,600	858	858	858	858
8,600	8,650	863	863	863	863
8,650	8,700	868	868	868	868
8,700	8,750	873	873	873	873
8,750	8,800	878	878	878	878
8,800	8,850	883	883	883	883
8,850	8,900	888	888	888	888
8,900	8,950	893	893	893	893
8,950	9,000	898	898	898	898

If line 27 (taxable income) is— At least	But less than	And you are— Single	Married filing jointly *	Married filing sepa-rately	Head of a house-hold
		Your tax is—			
9,000					
9,000	9,050	903	903	903	903
9,050	9,100	908	908	908	908
9,100	9,150	913	913	913	913
9,150	9,200	918	918	918	918
9,200	9,250	923	923	923	923
9,250	9,300	928	928	928	928
9,300	9,350	933	933	933	933
9,350	9,400	940	938	940	938
9,400	9,450	948	943	948	943
9,450	9,500	955	948	955	948
9,500	9,550	963	953	963	953
9,550	9,600	970	958	970	958
9,600	9,650	978	963	978	963
9,650	9,700	985	968	985	968
9,700	9,750	993	973	993	973
9,750	9,800	1,000	978	1,000	978
9,800	9,850	1,008	983	1,008	983
9,850	9,900	1,015	988	1,015	988
9,900	9,950	1,023	993	1,023	993
9,950	10,000	1,030	998	1,030	998
10,000					
10,000	10,050	1,038	1,003	1,038	1,003
10,050	10,100	1,045	1,008	1,045	1,008
10,100	10,150	1,053	1,013	1,053	1,013
10,150	10,200	1,060	1,018	1,060	1,018
10,200	10,250	1,068	1,023	1,068	1,023
10,250	10,300	1,075	1,028	1,075	1,028
10,300	10,350	1,083	1,033	1,083	1,033
10,350	10,400	1,090	1,038	1,090	1,038
10,400	10,450	1,098	1,043	1,098	1,043
10,450	10,500	1,105	1,048	1,105	1,048
10,500	10,550	1,113	1,053	1,113	1,053
10,550	10,600	1,120	1,058	1,120	1,058
10,600	10,650	1,128	1,063	1,128	1,063
10,650	10,700	1,135	1,068	1,135	1,068
10,700	10,750	1,143	1,073	1,143	1,073
10,750	10,800	1,150	1,078	1,150	1,078
10,800	10,850	1,158	1,083	1,158	1,083
10,850	10,900	1,165	1,088	1,165	1,088
10,900	10,950	1,173	1,093	1,173	1,093
10,950	11,000	1,180	1,098	1,180	1,098
11,000					
11,000	11,050	1,188	1,103	1,188	1,103
11,050	11,100	1,195	1,108	1,195	1,108
11,100	11,150	1,203	1,113	1,203	1,113
11,150	11,200	1,210	1,118	1,210	1,118
11,200	11,250	1,218	1,123	1,218	1,123
11,250	11,300	1,225	1,128	1,225	1,128
11,300	11,350	1,233	1,133	1,233	1,133
11,350	11,400	1,240	1,138	1,240	1,138
11,400	11,450	1,248	1,143	1,248	1,143
11,450	11,500	1,255	1,148	1,255	1,148
11,500	11,550	1,263	1,153	1,263	1,153
11,550	11,600	1,270	1,158	1,270	1,158
11,600	11,650	1,278	1,163	1,278	1,163
11,650	11,700	1,285	1,168	1,285	1,168
11,700	11,750	1,293	1,173	1,293	1,173
11,750	11,800	1,300	1,178	1,300	1,178
11,800	11,850	1,308	1,183	1,308	1,183
11,850	11,900	1,315	1,188	1,315	1,188
11,900	11,950	1,323	1,193	1,323	1,193
11,950	12,000	1,330	1,198	1,330	1,198

(Continued)

* This column must also be used by a qualifying widow(er).

2017 Tax Table — *Continued*

If line 27 (taxable income) is—		And you are—			
At least	But less than	Single	Married filing jointly *	Married filing separately	Head of a household
		Your tax is—			
12,000					
12,000	12,050	1,338	1,203	1,338	1,203
12,050	12,100	1,345	1,208	1,345	1,208
12,100	12,150	1,353	1,213	1,353	1,213
12,150	12,200	1,360	1,218	1,360	1,218
12,200	12,250	1,368	1,223	1,368	1,223
12,250	12,300	1,375	1,228	1,375	1,228
12,300	12,350	1,383	1,233	1,383	1,233
12,350	12,400	1,390	1,238	1,390	1,238
12,400	12,450	1,398	1,243	1,398	1,243
12,450	12,500	1,405	1,248	1,405	1,248
12,500	12,550	1,413	1,253	1,413	1,253
12,550	12,600	1,420	1,258	1,420	1,258
12,600	12,650	1,428	1,263	1,428	1,263
12,650	12,700	1,435	1,268	1,435	1,268
12,700	12,750	1,443	1,273	1,443	1,273
12,750	12,800	1,450	1,278	1,450	1,278
12,800	12,850	1,458	1,283	1,458	1,283
12,850	12,900	1,465	1,288	1,465	1,288
12,900	12,950	1,473	1,293	1,473	1,293
12,950	13,000	1,480	1,298	1,480	1,298
13,000					
13,000	13,050	1,488	1,303	1,488	1,303
13,050	13,100	1,495	1,308	1,495	1,308
13,100	13,150	1,503	1,313	1,503	1,313
13,150	13,200	1,510	1,318	1,510	1,318
13,200	13,250	1,518	1,323	1,518	1,323
13,250	13,300	1,525	1,328	1,525	1,328
13,300	13,350	1,533	1,333	1,533	1,333
13,350	13,400	1,540	1,338	1,540	1,339
13,400	13,450	1,548	1,343	1,548	1,346
13,450	13,500	1,555	1,348	1,555	1,354
13,500	13,550	1,563	1,353	1,563	1,361
13,550	13,600	1,570	1,358	1,570	1,369
13,600	13,650	1,578	1,363	1,578	1,376
13,650	13,700	1,585	1,368	1,585	1,384
13,700	13,750	1,593	1,373	1,593	1,391
13,750	13,800	1,600	1,378	1,600	1,399
13,800	13,850	1,608	1,383	1,608	1,406
13,850	13,900	1,615	1,388	1,615	1,414
13,900	13,950	1,623	1,393	1,623	1,421
13,950	14,000	1,630	1,398	1,630	1,429
14,000					
14,000	14,050	1,638	1,403	1,638	1,436
14,050	14,100	1,645	1,408	1,645	1,444
14,100	14,150	1,653	1,413	1,653	1,451
14,150	14,200	1,660	1,418	1,660	1,459
14,200	14,250	1,668	1,423	1,668	1,466
14,250	14,300	1,675	1,428	1,675	1,474
14,300	14,350	1,683	1,433	1,683	1,481
14,350	14,400	1,690	1,438	1,690	1,489
14,400	14,450	1,698	1,443	1,698	1,496
14,450	14,500	1,705	1,448	1,705	1,504
14,500	14,550	1,713	1,453	1,713	1,511
14,550	14,600	1,720	1,458	1,720	1,519
14,600	14,650	1,728	1,463	1,728	1,526
14,650	14,700	1,735	1,468	1,735	1,534
14,700	14,750	1,743	1,473	1,743	1,541
14,750	14,800	1,750	1,478	1,750	1,549
14,800	14,850	1,758	1,483	1,758	1,556
14,850	14,900	1,765	1,488	1,765	1,564
14,900	14,950	1,773	1,493	1,773	1,571
14,950	15,000	1,780	1,498	1,780	1,579
15,000					
15,000	15,050	1,788	1,503	1,788	1,586
15,050	15,100	1,795	1,508	1,795	1,594
15,100	15,150	1,803	1,513	1,803	1,601
15,150	15,200	1,810	1,518	1,810	1,609
15,200	15,250	1,818	1,523	1,818	1,616
15,250	15,300	1,825	1,528	1,825	1,624
15,300	15,350	1,833	1,533	1,833	1,631
15,350	15,400	1,840	1,538	1,840	1,639
15,400	15,450	1,848	1,543	1,848	1,646
15,450	15,500	1,855	1,548	1,855	1,654
15,500	15,550	1,863	1,553	1,863	1,661
15,550	15,600	1,870	1,558	1,870	1,669
15,600	15,650	1,878	1,563	1,878	1,676
15,650	15,700	1,885	1,568	1,885	1,684
15,700	15,750	1,893	1,573	1,893	1,691
15,750	15,800	1,900	1,578	1,900	1,699
15,800	15,850	1,908	1,583	1,908	1,706
15,850	15,900	1,915	1,588	1,915	1,714
15,900	15,950	1,923	1,593	1,923	1,721
15,950	16,000	1,930	1,598	1,930	1,729
16,000					
16,000	16,050	1,938	1,603	1,938	1,736
16,050	16,100	1,945	1,608	1,945	1,744
16,100	16,150	1,953	1,613	1,953	1,751
16,150	16,200	1,960	1,618	1,960	1,759
16,200	16,250	1,968	1,623	1,968	1,766
16,250	16,300	1,975	1,628	1,975	1,774
16,300	16,350	1,983	1,633	1,983	1,781
16,350	16,400	1,990	1,638	1,990	1,789
16,400	16,450	1,998	1,643	1,998	1,796
16,450	16,500	2,005	1,648	2,005	1,804
16,500	16,550	2,013	1,653	2,013	1,811
16,550	16,600	2,020	1,658	2,020	1,819
16,600	16,650	2,028	1,663	2,028	1,826
16,650	16,700	2,035	1,668	2,035	1,834
16,700	16,750	2,043	1,673	2,043	1,841
16,750	16,800	2,050	1,678	2,050	1,849
16,800	16,850	2,058	1,683	2,058	1,856
16,850	16,900	2,065	1,688	2,065	1,864
16,900	16,950	2,073	1,693	2,073	1,871
16,950	17,000	2,080	1,698	2,080	1,879
17,000					
17,000	17,050	2,088	1,703	2,088	1,886
17,050	17,100	2,095	1,708	2,095	1,894
17,100	17,150	2,103	1,713	2,103	1,901
17,150	17,200	2,110	1,718	2,110	1,909
17,200	17,250	2,118	1,723	2,118	1,916
17,250	17,300	2,125	1,728	2,125	1,924
17,300	17,350	2,133	1,733	2,133	1,931
17,350	17,400	2,140	1,738	2,140	1,939
17,400	17,450	2,148	1,743	2,148	1,946
17,450	17,500	2,155	1,748	2,155	1,954
17,500	17,550	2,163	1,753	2,163	1,961
17,550	17,600	2,170	1,758	2,170	1,969
17,600	17,650	2,178	1,763	2,178	1,976
17,650	17,700	2,185	1,768	2,185	1,984
17,700	17,750	2,193	1,773	2,193	1,991
17,750	17,800	2,200	1,778	2,200	1,999
17,800	17,850	2,208	1,783	2,208	2,006
17,850	17,900	2,215	1,788	2,215	2,014
17,900	17,950	2,223	1,793	2,223	2,021
17,950	18,000	2,230	1,798	2,230	2,029
18,000					
18,000	18,050	2,238	1,803	2,238	2,036
18,050	18,100	2,245	1,808	2,245	2,044
18,100	18,150	2,253	1,813	2,253	2,051
18,150	18,200	2,260	1,818	2,260	2,059
18,200	18,250	2,268	1,823	2,268	2,066
18,250	18,300	2,275	1,828	2,275	2,074
18,300	18,350	2,283	1,833	2,283	2,081
18,350	18,400	2,290	1,838	2,290	2,089
18,400	18,450	2,298	1,843	2,298	2,096
18,450	18,500	2,305	1,848	2,305	2,104
18,500	18,550	2,313	1,853	2,313	2,111
18,550	18,600	2,320	1,858	2,320	2,119
18,600	18,650	2,328	1,863	2,328	2,126
18,650	18,700	2,335	1,869	2,335	2,134
18,700	18,750	2,343	1,876	2,343	2,141
18,750	18,800	2,350	1,884	2,350	2,149
18,800	18,850	2,358	1,891	2,358	2,156
18,850	18,900	2,365	1,899	2,365	2,164
18,900	18,950	2,373	1,906	2,373	2,171
18,950	19,000	2,380	1,914	2,380	2,179
19,000					
19,000	19,050	2,388	1,921	2,388	2,186
19,050	19,100	2,395	1,929	2,395	2,194
19,100	19,150	2,403	1,936	2,403	2,201
19,150	19,200	2,410	1,944	2,410	2,209
19,200	19,250	2,418	1,951	2,418	2,216
19,250	19,300	2,425	1,959	2,425	2,224
19,300	19,350	2,433	1,966	2,433	2,231
19,350	19,400	2,440	1,974	2,440	2,239
19,400	19,450	2,448	1,981	2,448	2,246
19,450	19,500	2,455	1,989	2,455	2,254
19,500	19,550	2,463	1,996	2,463	2,261
19,550	19,600	2,470	2,004	2,470	2,269
19,600	19,650	2,478	2,011	2,478	2,276
19,650	19,700	2,485	2,019	2,485	2,284
19,700	19,750	2,493	2,026	2,493	2,291
19,750	19,800	2,500	2,034	2,500	2,299
19,800	19,850	2,508	2,041	2,508	2,306
19,850	19,900	2,515	2,049	2,515	2,314
19,900	19,950	2,523	2,056	2,523	2,321
19,950	20,000	2,530	2,064	2,530	2,329
20,000					
20,000	20,050	2,538	2,071	2,538	2,336
20,050	20,100	2,545	2,079	2,545	2,344
20,100	20,150	2,553	2,086	2,553	2,351
20,150	20,200	2,560	2,094	2,560	2,359
20,200	20,250	2,568	2,101	2,568	2,366
20,250	20,300	2,575	2,109	2,575	2,374
20,300	20,350	2,583	2,116	2,583	2,381
20,350	20,400	2,590	2,124	2,590	2,389
20,400	20,450	2,598	2,131	2,598	2,396
20,450	20,500	2,605	2,139	2,605	2,404
20,500	20,550	2,613	2,146	2,613	2,411
20,550	20,600	2,620	2,154	2,620	2,419
20,600	20,650	2,628	2,161	2,628	2,426
20,650	20,700	2,635	2,169	2,635	2,434
20,700	20,750	2,643	2,176	2,643	2,441
20,750	20,800	2,650	2,184	2,650	2,449
20,800	20,850	2,658	2,191	2,658	2,456
20,850	20,900	2,665	2,199	2,665	2,464
20,900	20,950	2,673	2,206	2,673	2,471
20,950	21,000	2,680	2,214	2,680	2,479

(Continued)

* This column must also be used by a qualifying widow(er).

2017 Tax Table — *Continued*

If line 27 (taxable income) is—		And you are—			
At least	But less than	Single	Married filing jointly *	Married filing sepa-rately	Head of a house-hold
		Your tax is—			
21,000					
21,000	21,050	2,688	2,221	2,688	2,486
21,050	21,100	2,695	2,229	2,695	2,494
21,100	21,150	2,703	2,236	2,703	2,501
21,150	21,200	2,710	2,244	2,710	2,509
21,200	21,250	2,718	2,251	2,718	2,516
21,250	21,300	2,725	2,259	2,725	2,524
21,300	21,350	2,733	2,266	2,733	2,531
21,350	21,400	2,740	2,274	2,740	2,539
21,400	21,450	2,748	2,281	2,748	2,546
21,450	21,500	2,755	2,289	2,755	2,554
21,500	21,550	2,763	2,296	2,763	2,561
21,550	21,600	2,770	2,304	2,770	2,569
21,600	21,650	2,778	2,311	2,778	2,576
21,650	21,700	2,785	2,319	2,785	2,584
21,700	21,750	2,793	2,326	2,793	2,591
21,750	21,800	2,800	2,334	2,800	2,599
21,800	21,850	2,808	2,341	2,808	2,606
21,850	21,900	2,815	2,349	2,815	2,614
21,900	21,950	2,823	2,356	2,823	2,621
21,950	22,000	2,830	2,364	2,830	2,629
22,000					
22,000	22,050	2,838	2,371	2,838	2,636
22,050	22,100	2,845	2,379	2,845	2,644
22,100	22,150	2,853	2,386	2,853	2,651
22,150	22,200	2,860	2,394	2,860	2,659
22,200	22,250	2,868	2,401	2,868	2,666
22,250	22,300	2,875	2,409	2,875	2,674
22,300	22,350	2,883	2,416	2,883	2,681
22,350	22,400	2,890	2,424	2,890	2,689
22,400	22,450	2,898	2,431	2,898	2,696
22,450	22,500	2,905	2,439	2,905	2,704
22,500	22,550	2,913	2,446	2,913	2,711
22,550	22,600	2,920	2,454	2,920	2,719
22,600	22,650	2,928	2,461	2,928	2,726
22,650	22,700	2,935	2,469	2,935	2,734
22,700	22,750	2,943	2,476	2,943	2,741
22,750	22,800	2,950	2,484	2,950	2,749
22,800	22,850	2,958	2,491	2,958	2,756
22,850	22,900	2,965	2,499	2,965	2,764
22,900	22,950	2,973	2,506	2,973	2,771
22,950	23,000	2,980	2,514	2,980	2,779
23,000					
23,000	23,050	2,988	2,521	2,988	2,786
23,050	23,100	2,995	2,529	2,995	2,794
23,100	23,150	3,003	2,536	3,003	2,801
23,150	23,200	3,010	2,544	3,010	2,809
23,200	23,250	3,018	2,551	3,018	2,816
23,250	23,300	3,025	2,559	3,025	2,824
23,300	23,350	3,033	2,566	3,033	2,831
23,350	23,400	3,040	2,574	3,040	2,839
23,400	23,450	3,048	2,581	3,048	2,846
23,450	23,500	3,055	2,589	3,055	2,854
23,500	23,550	3,063	2,596	3,063	2,861
23,550	23,600	3,070	2,604	3,070	2,869
23,600	23,650	3,078	2,611	3,078	2,876
23,650	23,700	3,085	2,619	3,085	2,884
23,700	23,750	3,093	2,626	3,093	2,891
23,750	23,800	3,100	2,634	3,100	2,899
23,800	23,850	3,108	2,641	3,108	2,906
23,850	23,900	3,115	2,649	3,115	2,914
23,900	23,950	3,123	2,656	3,123	2,921
23,950	24,000	3,130	2,664	3,130	2,929
24,000					
24,000	24,050	3,138	2,671	3,138	2,936
24,050	24,100	3,145	2,679	3,145	2,944
24,100	24,150	3,153	2,686	3,153	2,951
24,150	24,200	3,160	2,694	3,160	2,959
24,200	24,250	3,168	2,701	3,168	2,966
24,250	24,300	3,175	2,709	3,175	2,974
24,300	24,350	3,183	2,716	3,183	2,981
24,350	24,400	3,190	2,724	3,190	2,989
24,400	24,450	3,198	2,731	3,198	2,996
24,450	24,500	3,205	2,739	3,205	3,004
24,500	24,550	3,213	2,746	3,213	3,011
24,550	24,600	3,220	2,754	3,220	3,019
24,600	24,650	3,228	2,761	3,228	3,026
24,650	24,700	3,235	2,769	3,235	3,034
24,700	24,750	3,243	2,776	3,243	3,041
24,750	24,800	3,250	2,784	3,250	3,049
24,800	24,850	3,258	2,791	3,258	3,056
24,850	24,900	3,265	2,799	3,265	3,064
24,900	24,950	3,273	2,806	3,273	3,071
24,950	25,000	3,280	2,814	3,280	3,079
25,000					
25,000	25,050	3,288	2,821	3,288	3,086
25,050	25,100	3,295	2,829	3,295	3,094
25,100	25,150	3,303	2,836	3,303	3,101
25,150	25,200	3,310	2,844	3,310	3,109
25,200	25,250	3,318	2,851	3,318	3,116
25,250	25,300	3,325	2,859	3,325	3,124
25,300	25,350	3,333	2,866	3,333	3,131
25,350	25,400	3,340	2,874	3,340	3,139
25,400	25,450	3,348	2,881	3,348	3,146
25,450	25,500	3,355	2,889	3,355	3,154
25,500	25,550	3,363	2,896	3,363	3,161
25,550	25,600	3,370	2,904	3,370	3,169
25,600	25,650	3,378	2,911	3,378	3,176
25,650	25,700	3,385	2,919	3,385	3,184
25,700	25,750	3,393	2,926	3,393	3,191
25,750	25,800	3,400	2,934	3,400	3,199
25,800	25,850	3,408	2,941	3,408	3,206
25,850	25,900	3,415	2,949	3,415	3,214
25,900	25,950	3,423	2,956	3,423	3,221
25,950	26,000	3,430	2,964	3,430	3,229
26,000					
26,000	26,050	3,438	2,971	3,438	3,236
26,050	26,100	3,445	2,979	3,445	3,244
26,100	26,150	3,453	2,986	3,453	3,251
26,150	26,200	3,460	2,994	3,460	3,259
26,200	26,250	3,468	3,001	3,468	3,266
26,250	26,300	3,475	3,009	3,475	3,274
26,300	26,350	3,483	3,016	3,483	3,281
26,350	26,400	3,490	3,024	3,490	3,289
26,400	26,450	3,498	3,031	3,498	3,296
26,450	26,500	3,505	3,039	3,505	3,304
26,500	26,550	3,513	3,046	3,513	3,311
26,550	26,600	3,520	3,054	3,520	3,319
26,600	26,650	3,528	3,061	3,528	3,326
26,650	26,700	3,535	3,069	3,535	3,334
26,700	26,750	3,543	3,076	3,543	3,341
26,750	26,800	3,550	3,084	3,550	3,349
26,800	26,850	3,558	3,091	3,558	3,356
26,850	26,900	3,565	3,099	3,565	3,364
26,900	26,950	3,573	3,106	3,573	3,371
26,950	27,000	3,580	3,114	3,580	3,379
27,000					
27,000	27,050	3,588	3,121	3,588	3,386
27,050	27,100	3,595	3,129	3,595	3,394
27,100	27,150	3,603	3,136	3,603	3,401
27,150	27,200	3,610	3,144	3,610	3,409
27,200	27,250	3,618	3,151	3,618	3,416
27,250	27,300	3,625	3,159	3,625	3,424
27,300	27,350	3,633	3,166	3,633	3,431
27,350	27,400	3,640	3,174	3,640	3,439
27,400	27,450	3,648	3,181	3,648	3,446
27,450	27,500	3,655	3,189	3,655	3,454
27,500	27,550	3,663	3,196	3,663	3,461
27,550	27,600	3,670	3,204	3,670	3,469
27,600	27,650	3,678	3,211	3,678	3,476
27,650	27,700	3,685	3,219	3,685	3,484
27,700	27,750	3,693	3,226	3,693	3,491
27,750	27,800	3,700	3,234	3,700	3,499
27,800	27,850	3,708	3,241	3,708	3,506
27,850	27,900	3,715	3,249	3,715	3,514
27,900	27,950	3,723	3,256	3,723	3,521
27,950	28,000	3,730	3,264	3,730	3,529
28,000					
28,000	28,050	3,738	3,271	3,738	3,536
28,050	28,100	3,745	3,279	3,745	3,544
28,100	28,150	3,753	3,286	3,753	3,551
28,150	28,200	3,760	3,294	3,760	3,559
28,200	28,250	3,768	3,301	3,768	3,566
28,250	28,300	3,775	3,309	3,775	3,574
28,300	28,350	3,783	3,316	3,783	3,581
28,350	28,400	3,790	3,324	3,790	3,589
28,400	28,450	3,798	3,331	3,798	3,596
28,450	28,500	3,805	3,339	3,805	3,604
28,500	28,550	3,813	3,346	3,813	3,611
28,550	28,600	3,820	3,354	3,820	3,619
28,600	28,650	3,828	3,361	3,828	3,626
28,650	28,700	3,835	3,369	3,835	3,634
28,700	28,750	3,843	3,376	3,843	3,641
28,750	28,800	3,850	3,384	3,850	3,649
28,800	28,850	3,858	3,391	3,858	3,656
28,850	28,900	3,865	3,399	3,865	3,664
28,900	28,950	3,873	3,406	3,873	3,671
28,950	29,000	3,880	3,414	3,880	3,679
29,000					
29,000	29,050	3,888	3,421	3,888	3,686
29,050	29,100	3,895	3,429	3,895	3,694
29,100	29,150	3,903	3,436	3,903	3,701
29,150	29,200	3,910	3,444	3,910	3,709
29,200	29,250	3,918	3,451	3,918	3,716
29,250	29,300	3,925	3,459	3,925	3,724
29,300	29,350	3,933	3,466	3,933	3,731
29,350	29,400	3,940	3,474	3,940	3,739
29,400	29,450	3,948	3,481	3,948	3,746
29,450	29,500	3,955	3,489	3,955	3,754
29,500	29,550	3,963	3,496	3,963	3,761
29,550	29,600	3,970	3,504	3,970	3,769
29,600	29,650	3,978	3,511	3,978	3,776
29,650	29,700	3,985	3,519	3,985	3,784
29,700	29,750	3,993	3,526	3,993	3,791
29,750	29,800	4,000	3,534	4,000	3,799
29,800	29,850	4,008	3,541	4,008	3,806
29,850	29,900	4,015	3,549	4,015	3,814
29,900	29,950	4,023	3,556	4,023	3,821
29,950	30,000	4,030	3,564	4,030	3,829

(Continued)

* This column must also be used by a qualifying widow(er).

2017 Tax Table — *Continued*

If line 27 (taxable income) is—		And you are—			
At least	But less than	Single	Married filing jointly *	Married filing sepa-rately	Head of a house-hold
		Your tax is—			
30,000					
30,000	30,050	4,038	3,571	4,038	3,836
30,050	30,100	4,045	3,579	4,045	3,844
30,100	30,150	4,053	3,586	4,053	3,851
30,150	30,200	4,060	3,594	4,060	3,859
30,200	30,250	4,068	3,601	4,068	3,866
30,250	30,300	4,075	3,609	4,075	3,874
30,300	30,350	4,083	3,616	4,083	3,881
30,350	30,400	4,090	3,624	4,090	3,889
30,400	30,450	4,098	3,631	4,098	3,896
30,450	30,500	4,105	3,639	4,105	3,904
30,500	30,550	4,113	3,646	4,113	3,911
30,550	30,600	4,120	3,654	4,120	3,919
30,600	30,650	4,128	3,661	4,128	3,926
30,650	30,700	4,135	3,669	4,135	3,934
30,700	30,750	4,143	3,676	4,143	3,941
30,750	30,800	4,150	3,684	4,150	3,949
30,800	30,850	4,158	3,691	4,158	3,956
30,850	30,900	4,165	3,699	4,165	3,964
30,900	30,950	4,173	3,706	4,173	3,971
30,950	31,000	4,180	3,714	4,180	3,979
31,000					
31,000	31,050	4,188	3,721	4,188	3,986
31,050	31,100	4,195	3,729	4,195	3,994
31,100	31,150	4,203	3,736	4,203	4,001
31,150	31,200	4,210	3,744	4,210	4,009
31,200	31,250	4,218	3,751	4,218	4,016
31,250	31,300	4,225	3,759	4,225	4,024
31,300	31,350	4,233	3,766	4,233	4,031
31,350	31,400	4,240	3,774	4,240	4,039
31,400	31,450	4,248	3,781	4,248	4,046
31,450	31,500	4,255	3,789	4,255	4,054
31,500	31,550	4,263	3,796	4,263	4,061
31,550	31,600	4,270	3,804	4,270	4,069
31,600	31,650	4,278	3,811	4,278	4,076
31,650	31,700	4,285	3,819	4,285	4,084
31,700	31,750	4,293	3,826	4,293	4,091
31,750	31,800	4,300	3,834	4,300	4,099
31,800	31,850	4,308	3,841	4,308	4,106
31,850	31,900	4,315	3,849	4,315	4,114
31,900	31,950	4,323	3,856	4,323	4,121
31,950	32,000	4,330	3,864	4,330	4,129
32,000					
32,000	32,050	4,338	3,871	4,338	4,136
32,050	32,100	4,345	3,879	4,345	4,144
32,100	32,150	4,353	3,886	4,353	4,151
32,150	32,200	4,360	3,894	4,360	4,159
32,200	32,250	4,368	3,901	4,368	4,166
32,250	32,300	4,375	3,909	4,375	4,174
32,300	32,350	4,383	3,916	4,383	4,181
32,350	32,400	4,390	3,924	4,390	4,189
32,400	32,450	4,398	3,931	4,398	4,196
32,450	32,500	4,405	3,939	4,405	4,204
32,500	32,550	4,413	3,946	4,413	4,211
32,550	32,600	4,420	3,954	4,420	4,219
32,600	32,650	4,428	3,961	4,428	4,226
32,650	32,700	4,435	3,969	4,435	4,234
32,700	32,750	4,443	3,976	4,443	4,241
32,750	32,800	4,450	3,984	4,450	4,249
32,800	32,850	4,458	3,991	4,458	4,256
32,850	32,900	4,465	3,999	4,465	4,264
32,900	32,950	4,473	4,006	4,473	4,271
32,950	33,000	4,480	4,014	4,480	4,279

If line 27 (taxable income) is—		And you are—			
At least	But less than	Single	Married filing jointly *	Married filing sepa-rately	Head of a house-hold
		Your tax is—			
33,000					
33,000	33,050	4,488	4,021	4,488	4,286
33,050	33,100	4,495	4,029	4,495	4,294
33,100	33,150	4,503	4,036	4,503	4,301
33,150	33,200	4,510	4,044	4,510	4,309
33,200	33,250	4,518	4,051	4,518	4,316
33,250	33,300	4,525	4,059	4,525	4,324
33,300	33,350	4,533	4,066	4,533	4,331
33,350	33,400	4,540	4,074	4,540	4,339
33,400	33,450	4,548	4,081	4,548	4,346
33,450	33,500	4,555	4,089	4,555	4,354
33,500	33,550	4,563	4,096	4,563	4,361
33,550	33,600	4,570	4,104	4,570	4,369
33,600	33,650	4,578	4,111	4,578	4,376
33,650	33,700	4,585	4,119	4,585	4,384
33,700	33,750	4,593	4,126	4,593	4,391
33,750	33,800	4,600	4,134	4,600	4,399
33,800	33,850	4,608	4,141	4,608	4,406
33,850	33,900	4,615	4,149	4,615	4,414
33,900	33,950	4,623	4,156	4,623	4,421
33,950	34,000	4,630	4,164	4,630	4,429
34,000					
34,000	34,050	4,638	4,171	4,638	4,436
34,050	34,100	4,645	4,179	4,645	4,444
34,100	34,150	4,653	4,186	4,653	4,451
34,150	34,200	4,660	4,194	4,660	4,459
34,200	34,250	4,668	4,201	4,668	4,466
34,250	34,300	4,675	4,209	4,675	4,474
34,300	34,350	4,683	4,216	4,683	4,481
34,350	34,400	4,690	4,224	4,690	4,489
34,400	34,450	4,698	4,231	4,698	4,496
34,450	34,500	4,705	4,239	4,705	4,504
34,500	34,550	4,713	4,246	4,713	4,511
34,550	34,600	4,720	4,254	4,720	4,519
34,600	34,650	4,728	4,261	4,728	4,526
34,650	34,700	4,735	4,269	4,735	4,534
34,700	34,750	4,743	4,276	4,743	4,541
34,750	34,800	4,750	4,284	4,750	4,549
34,800	34,850	4,758	4,291	4,758	4,556
34,850	34,900	4,765	4,299	4,765	4,564
34,900	34,950	4,773	4,306	4,773	4,571
34,950	35,000	4,780	4,314	4,780	4,579
35,000					
35,000	35,050	4,788	4,321	4,788	4,586
35,050	35,100	4,795	4,329	4,795	4,594
35,100	35,150	4,803	4,336	4,803	4,601
35,150	35,200	4,810	4,344	4,810	4,609
35,200	35,250	4,818	4,351	4,818	4,616
35,250	35,300	4,825	4,359	4,825	4,624
35,300	35,350	4,833	4,366	4,833	4,631
35,350	35,400	4,840	4,374	4,840	4,639
35,400	35,450	4,848	4,381	4,848	4,646
35,450	35,500	4,855	4,389	4,855	4,654
35,500	35,550	4,863	4,396	4,863	4,661
35,550	35,600	4,870	4,404	4,870	4,669
35,600	35,650	4,878	4,411	4,878	4,676
35,650	35,700	4,885	4,419	4,885	4,684
35,700	35,750	4,893	4,426	4,893	4,691
35,750	35,800	4,900	4,434	4,900	4,699
35,800	35,850	4,908	4,441	4,908	4,706
35,850	35,900	4,915	4,449	4,915	4,714
35,900	35,950	4,923	4,456	4,923	4,721
35,950	36,000	4,930	4,464	4,930	4,729

If line 27 (taxable income) is—		And you are—			
At least	But less than	Single	Married filing jointly *	Married filing sepa-rately	Head of a house-hold
		Your tax is—			
36,000					
36,000	36,050	4,938	4,471	4,938	4,736
36,050	36,100	4,945	4,479	4,945	4,744
36,100	36,150	4,953	4,486	4,953	4,751
36,150	36,200	4,960	4,494	4,960	4,759
36,200	36,250	4,968	4,501	4,968	4,766
36,250	36,300	4,975	4,509	4,975	4,774
36,300	36,350	4,983	4,516	4,983	4,781
36,350	36,400	4,990	4,524	4,990	4,789
36,400	36,450	4,998	4,531	4,998	4,796
36,450	36,500	5,005	4,539	5,005	4,804
36,500	36,550	5,013	4,546	5,013	4,811
36,550	36,600	5,020	4,554	5,020	4,819
36,600	36,650	5,028	4,561	5,028	4,826
36,650	36,700	5,035	4,569	5,035	4,834
36,700	36,750	5,043	4,576	5,043	4,841
36,750	36,800	5,050	4,584	5,050	4,849
36,800	36,850	5,058	4,591	5,058	4,856
36,850	36,900	5,065	4,599	5,065	4,864
36,900	36,950	5,073	4,606	5,073	4,871
36,950	37,000	5,080	4,614	5,080	4,879
37,000					
37,000	37,050	5,088	4,621	5,088	4,886
37,050	37,100	5,095	4,629	5,095	4,894
37,100	37,150	5,103	4,636	5,103	4,901
37,150	37,200	5,110	4,644	5,110	4,909
37,200	37,250	5,118	4,651	5,118	4,916
37,250	37,300	5,125	4,659	5,125	4,924
37,300	37,350	5,133	4,666	5,133	4,931
37,350	37,400	5,140	4,674	5,140	4,939
37,400	37,450	5,148	4,681	5,148	4,946
37,450	37,500	5,155	4,689	5,155	4,954
37,500	37,550	5,163	4,696	5,163	4,961
37,550	37,600	5,170	4,704	5,170	4,969
37,600	37,650	5,178	4,711	5,178	4,976
37,650	37,700	5,185	4,719	5,185	4,984
37,700	37,750	5,193	4,726	5,193	4,991
37,750	37,800	5,200	4,734	5,200	4,999
37,800	37,850	5,208	4,741	5,208	5,006
37,850	37,900	5,215	4,749	5,215	5,014
37,900	37,950	5,223	4,756	5,223	5,021
37,950	38,000	5,233	4,764	5,233	5,029
38,000					
38,000	38,050	5,245	4,771	5,245	5,036
38,050	38,100	5,258	4,779	5,258	5,044
38,100	38,150	5,270	4,786	5,270	5,051
38,150	38,200	5,283	4,794	5,283	5,059
38,200	38,250	5,295	4,801	5,295	5,066
38,250	38,300	5,308	4,809	5,308	5,074
38,300	38,350	5,320	4,816	5,320	5,081
38,350	38,400	5,333	4,824	5,333	5,089
38,400	38,450	5,345	4,831	5,345	5,096
38,450	38,500	5,358	4,839	5,358	5,104
38,500	38,550	5,370	4,846	5,370	5,111
38,550	38,600	5,383	4,854	5,383	5,119
38,600	38,650	5,395	4,861	5,395	5,126
38,650	38,700	5,408	4,869	5,408	5,134
38,700	38,750	5,420	4,876	5,420	5,141
38,750	38,800	5,433	4,884	5,433	5,149
38,800	38,850	5,445	4,891	5,445	5,156
38,850	38,900	5,458	4,899	5,458	5,164
38,900	38,950	5,470	4,906	5,470	5,171
38,950	39,000	5,483	4,914	5,483	5,179

(Continued)

* This column must also be used by a qualifying widow(er).

2017 Tax Table — *Continued*

If line 27 (taxable income) is— At least	But less than	And you are— Single	Married filing jointly *	Married filing sepa-rately	Head of a house-hold
		Your tax is—			
39,000					
39,000	39,050	5,495	4,921	5,495	5,186
39,050	39,100	5,508	4,929	5,508	5,194
39,100	39,150	5,520	4,936	5,520	5,201
39,150	39,200	5,533	4,944	5,533	5,209
39,200	39,250	5,545	4,951	5,545	5,216
39,250	39,300	5,558	4,959	5,558	5,224
39,300	39,350	5,570	4,966	5,570	5,231
39,350	39,400	5,583	4,974	5,583	5,239
39,400	39,450	5,595	4,981	5,595	5,246
39,450	39,500	5,608	4,989	5,608	5,254
39,500	39,550	5,620	4,996	5,620	5,261
39,550	39,600	5,633	5,004	5,633	5,269
39,600	39,650	5,645	5,011	5,645	5,276
39,650	39,700	5,658	5,019	5,658	5,284
39,700	39,750	5,670	5,026	5,670	5,291
39,750	39,800	5,683	5,034	5,683	5,299
39,800	39,850	5,695	5,041	5,695	5,306
39,850	39,900	5,708	5,049	5,708	5,314
39,900	39,950	5,720	5,056	5,720	5,321
39,950	40,000	5,733	5,064	5,733	5,329
40,000					
40,000	40,050	5,745	5,071	5,745	5,336
40,050	40,100	5,758	5,079	5,758	5,344
40,100	40,150	5,770	5,086	5,770	5,351
40,150	40,200	5,783	5,094	5,783	5,359
40,200	40,250	5,795	5,101	5,795	5,366
40,250	40,300	5,808	5,109	5,808	5,374
40,300	40,350	5,820	5,116	5,820	5,381
40,350	40,400	5,833	5,124	5,833	5,389
40,400	40,450	5,845	5,131	5,845	5,396
40,450	40,500	5,858	5,139	5,858	5,404
40,500	40,550	5,870	5,146	5,870	5,411
40,550	40,600	5,883	5,154	5,883	5,419
40,600	40,650	5,895	5,161	5,895	5,426
40,650	40,700	5,908	5,169	5,908	5,434
40,700	40,750	5,920	5,176	5,920	5,441
40,750	40,800	5,933	5,184	5,933	5,449
40,800	40,850	5,945	5,191	5,945	5,456
40,850	40,900	5,958	5,199	5,958	5,464
40,900	40,950	5,970	5,206	5,970	5,471
40,950	41,000	5,983	5,214	5,983	5,479
41,000					
41,000	41,050	5,995	5,221	5,995	5,486
41,050	41,100	6,008	5,229	6,008	5,494
41,100	41,150	6,020	5,236	6,020	5,501
41,150	41,200	6,033	5,244	6,033	5,509
41,200	41,250	6,045	5,251	6,045	5,516
41,250	41,300	6,058	5,259	6,058	5,524
41,300	41,350	6,070	5,266	6,070	5,531
41,350	41,400	6,083	5,274	6,083	5,539
41,400	41,450	6,095	5,281	6,095	5,546
41,450	41,500	6,108	5,289	6,108	5,554
41,500	41,550	6,120	5,296	6,120	5,561
41,550	41,600	6,133	5,304	6,133	5,569
41,600	41,650	6,145	5,311	6,145	5,576
41,650	41,700	6,158	5,319	6,158	5,584
41,700	41,750	6,170	5,326	6,170	5,591
41,750	41,800	6,183	5,334	6,183	5,599
41,800	41,850	6,195	5,341	6,195	5,606
41,850	41,900	6,208	5,349	6,208	5,614
41,900	41,950	6,220	5,356	6,220	5,621
41,950	42,000	6,233	5,364	6,233	5,629
42,000					
42,000	42,050	6,245	5,371	6,245	5,636
42,050	42,100	6,258	5,379	6,258	5,644
42,100	42,150	6,270	5,386	6,270	5,651
42,150	42,200	6,283	5,394	6,283	5,659
42,200	42,250	6,295	5,401	6,295	5,666
42,250	42,300	6,308	5,409	6,308	5,674
42,300	42,350	6,320	5,416	6,320	5,681
42,350	42,400	6,333	5,424	6,333	5,689
42,400	42,450	6,345	5,431	6,345	5,696
42,450	42,500	6,358	5,439	6,358	5,704
42,500	42,550	6,370	5,446	6,370	5,711
42,550	42,600	6,383	5,454	6,383	5,719
42,600	42,650	6,395	5,461	6,395	5,726
42,650	42,700	6,408	5,469	6,408	5,734
42,700	42,750	6,420	5,476	6,420	5,741
42,750	42,800	6,433	5,484	6,433	5,749
42,800	42,850	6,445	5,491	6,445	5,756
42,850	42,900	6,458	5,499	6,458	5,764
42,900	42,950	6,470	5,506	6,470	5,771
42,950	43,000	6,483	5,514	6,483	5,779
43,000					
43,000	43,050	6,495	5,521	6,495	5,786
43,050	43,100	6,508	5,529	6,508	5,794
43,100	43,150	6,520	5,536	6,520	5,801
43,150	43,200	6,533	5,544	6,533	5,809
43,200	43,250	6,545	5,551	6,545	5,816
43,250	43,300	6,558	5,559	6,558	5,824
43,300	43,350	6,570	5,566	6,570	5,831
43,350	43,400	6,583	5,574	6,583	5,839
43,400	43,450	6,595	5,581	6,595	5,846
43,450	43,500	6,608	5,589	6,608	5,854
43,500	43,550	6,620	5,596	6,620	5,861
43,550	43,600	6,633	5,604	6,633	5,869
43,600	43,650	6,645	5,611	6,645	5,876
43,650	43,700	6,658	5,619	6,658	5,884
43,700	43,750	6,670	5,626	6,670	5,891
43,750	43,800	6,683	5,634	6,683	5,899
43,800	43,850	6,695	5,641	6,695	5,906
43,850	43,900	6,708	5,649	6,708	5,914
43,900	43,950	6,720	5,656	6,720	5,921
43,950	44,000	6,733	5,664	6,733	5,929
44,000					
44,000	44,050	6,745	5,671	6,745	5,936
44,050	44,100	6,758	5,679	6,758	5,944
44,100	44,150	6,770	5,686	6,770	5,951
44,150	44,200	6,783	5,694	6,783	5,959
44,200	44,250	6,795	5,701	6,795	5,966
44,250	44,300	6,808	5,709	6,808	5,974
44,300	44,350	6,820	5,716	6,820	5,981
44,350	44,400	6,833	5,724	6,833	5,989
44,400	44,450	6,845	5,731	6,845	5,996
44,450	44,500	6,858	5,739	6,858	6,004
44,500	44,550	6,870	5,746	6,870	6,011
44,550	44,600	6,883	5,754	6,883	6,019
44,600	44,650	6,895	5,761	6,895	6,026
44,650	44,700	6,908	5,769	6,908	6,034
44,700	44,750	6,920	5,776	6,920	6,041
44,750	44,800	6,933	5,784	6,933	6,049
44,800	44,850	6,945	5,791	6,945	6,056
44,850	44,900	6,958	5,799	6,958	6,064
44,900	44,950	6,970	5,806	6,970	6,071
44,950	45,000	6,983	5,814	6,983	6,079
45,000					
45,000	45,050	6,995	5,821	6,995	6,086
45,050	45,100	7,008	5,829	7,008	6,094
45,100	45,150	7,020	5,836	7,020	6,101
45,150	45,200	7,033	5,844	7,033	6,109
45,200	45,250	7,045	5,851	7,045	6,116
45,250	45,300	7,058	5,859	7,058	6,124
45,300	45,350	7,070	5,866	7,070	6,131
45,350	45,400	7,083	5,874	7,083	6,139
45,400	45,450	7,095	5,881	7,095	6,146
45,450	45,500	7,108	5,889	7,108	6,154
45,500	45,550	7,120	5,896	7,120	6,161
45,550	45,600	7,133	5,904	7,133	6,169
45,600	45,650	7,145	5,911	7,145	6,176
45,650	45,700	7,158	5,919	7,158	6,184
45,700	45,750	7,170	5,926	7,170	6,191
45,750	45,800	7,183	5,934	7,183	6,199
45,800	45,850	7,195	5,941	7,195	6,206
45,850	45,900	7,208	5,949	7,208	6,214
45,900	45,950	7,220	5,956	7,220	6,221
45,950	46,000	7,233	5,964	7,233	6,229
46,000					
46,000	46,050	7,245	5,971	7,245	6,236
46,050	46,100	7,258	5,979	7,258	6,244
46,100	46,150	7,270	5,986	7,270	6,251
46,150	46,200	7,283	5,994	7,283	6,259
46,200	46,250	7,295	6,001	7,295	6,266
46,250	46,300	7,308	6,009	7,308	6,274
46,300	46,350	7,320	6,016	7,320	6,281
46,350	46,400	7,333	6,024	7,333	6,289
46,400	46,450	7,345	6,031	7,345	6,296
46,450	46,500	7,358	6,039	7,358	6,304
46,500	46,550	7,370	6,046	7,370	6,311
46,550	46,600	7,383	6,054	7,383	6,319
46,600	46,650	7,395	6,061	7,395	6,326
46,650	46,700	7,408	6,069	7,408	6,334
46,700	46,750	7,420	6,076	7,420	6,341
46,750	46,800	7,433	6,084	7,433	6,349
46,800	46,850	7,445	6,091	7,445	6,356
46,850	46,900	7,458	6,099	7,458	6,364
46,900	46,950	7,470	6,106	7,470	6,371
46,950	47,000	7,483	6,114	7,483	6,379
47,000					
47,000	47,050	7,495	6,121	7,495	6,38
47,050	47,100	7,508	6,129	7,508	6,39
47,100	47,150	7,520	6,136	7,520	6,40
47,150	47,200	7,533	6,144	7,533	6,40
47,200	47,250	7,545	6,151	7,545	6,41
47,250	47,300	7,558	6,159	7,558	6,42
47,300	47,350	7,570	6,166	7,570	6,43
47,350	47,400	7,583	6,174	7,583	6,43
47,400	47,450	7,595	6,181	7,595	6,44
47,450	47,500	7,608	6,189	7,608	6,45
47,500	47,550	7,620	6,196	7,620	6,46
47,550	47,600	7,633	6,204	7,633	6,46
47,600	47,650	7,645	6,211	7,645	6,47
47,650	47,700	7,658	6,219	7,658	6,48
47,700	47,750	7,670	6,226	7,670	6,49
47,750	47,800	7,683	6,234	7,683	6,49
47,800	47,850	7,695	6,241	7,695	6,50
47,850	47,900	7,708	6,249	7,708	6,51
47,900	47,950	7,720	6,256	7,720	6,52
47,950	48,000	7,733	6,264	7,733	6,52

* This column must also be used by a qualifying widow(er).

(Continued)

2017 Tax Table — *Continued*

If line 27 (taxable income) is—		And you are—			
At least	But less than	Single	Married filing jointly *	Married filing separately	Head of a household
		Your tax is—			
48,000					
48,000	48,050	7,745	6,271	7,745	6,536
48,050	48,100	7,758	6,279	7,758	6,544
48,100	48,150	7,770	6,286	7,770	6,551
48,150	48,200	7,783	6,294	7,783	6,559
48,200	48,250	7,795	6,301	7,795	6,566
48,250	48,300	7,808	6,309	7,808	6,574
48,300	48,350	7,820	6,316	7,820	6,581
48,350	48,400	7,833	6,324	7,833	6,589
48,400	48,450	7,845	6,331	7,845	6,596
48,450	48,500	7,858	6,339	7,858	6,604
48,500	48,550	7,870	6,346	7,870	6,611
48,550	48,600	7,883	6,354	7,883	6,619
48,600	48,650	7,895	6,361	7,895	6,626
48,650	48,700	7,908	6,369	7,908	6,634
48,700	48,750	7,920	6,376	7,920	6,641
48,750	48,800	7,933	6,384	7,933	6,649
48,800	48,850	7,945	6,391	7,945	6,656
48,850	48,900	7,958	6,399	7,958	6,664
48,900	48,950	7,970	6,406	7,970	6,671
48,950	49,000	7,983	6,414	7,983	6,679
49,000					
49,000	49,050	7,995	6,421	7,995	6,686
49,050	49,100	8,008	6,429	8,008	6,694
49,100	49,150	8,020	6,436	8,020	6,701
49,150	49,200	8,033	6,444	8,033	6,709
49,200	49,250	8,045	6,451	8,045	6,716
49,250	49,300	8,058	6,459	8,058	6,724
49,300	49,350	8,070	6,466	8,070	6,731
49,350	49,400	8,083	6,474	8,083	6,739
49,400	49,450	8,095	6,481	8,095	6,746
49,450	49,500	8,108	6,489	8,108	6,754
49,500	49,550	8,120	6,496	8,120	6,761
49,550	49,600	8,133	6,504	8,133	6,769
49,600	49,650	8,145	6,511	8,145	6,776
49,650	49,700	8,158	6,519	8,158	6,784
49,700	49,750	8,170	6,526	8,170	6,791
49,750	49,800	8,183	6,534	8,183	6,799
49,800	49,850	8,195	6,541	8,195	6,806
49,850	49,900	8,208	6,549	8,208	6,814
49,900	49,950	8,220	6,556	8,220	6,821
49,950	50,000	8,233	6,564	8,233	6,829
50,000					
50,000	50,050	8,245	6,571	8,245	6,836
50,050	50,100	8,258	6,579	8,258	6,844
50,100	50,150	8,270	6,586	8,270	6,851
50,150	50,200	8,283	6,594	8,283	6,859
50,200	50,250	8,295	6,601	8,295	6,866
50,250	50,300	8,308	6,609	8,308	6,874
50,300	50,350	8,320	6,616	8,320	6,881
50,350	50,400	8,333	6,624	8,333	6,889
50,400	50,450	8,345	6,631	8,345	6,896
50,450	50,500	8,358	6,639	8,358	6,904
50,500	50,550	8,370	6,646	8,370	6,911
50,550	50,600	8,383	6,654	8,383	6,919
50,600	50,650	8,395	6,661	8,395	6,926
50,650	50,700	8,408	6,669	8,408	6,934
50,700	50,750	8,420	6,676	8,420	6,941
50,750	50,800	8,433	6,684	8,433	6,949
50,800	50,850	8,445	6,691	8,445	6,959
50,850	50,900	8,458	6,699	8,458	6,971
50,900	50,950	8,470	6,706	8,470	6,984
50,950	51,000	8,483	6,714	8,483	6,996
51,000					
51,000	51,050	8,495	6,721	8,495	7,009
51,050	51,100	8,508	6,729	8,508	7,021
51,100	51,150	8,520	6,736	8,520	7,034
51,150	51,200	8,533	6,744	8,533	7,046
51,200	51,250	8,545	6,751	8,545	7,059
51,250	51,300	8,558	6,759	8,558	7,071
51,300	51,350	8,570	6,766	8,570	7,084
51,350	51,400	8,583	6,774	8,583	7,096
51,400	51,450	8,595	6,781	8,595	7,109
51,450	51,500	8,608	6,789	8,608	7,121
51,500	51,550	8,620	6,796	8,620	7,134
51,550	51,600	8,633	6,804	8,633	7,146
51,600	51,650	8,645	6,811	8,645	7,159
51,650	51,700	8,658	6,819	8,658	7,171
51,700	51,750	8,670	6,826	8,670	7,184
51,750	51,800	8,683	6,834	8,683	7,196
51,800	51,850	8,695	6,841	8,695	7,209
51,850	51,900	8,708	6,849	8,708	7,221
51,900	51,950	8,720	6,856	8,720	7,234
51,950	52,000	8,733	6,864	8,733	7,246
52,000					
52,000	52,050	8,745	6,871	8,745	7,259
52,050	52,100	8,758	6,879	8,758	7,271
52,100	52,150	8,770	6,886	8,770	7,284
52,150	52,200	8,783	6,894	8,783	7,296
52,200	52,250	8,795	6,901	8,795	7,309
52,250	52,300	8,808	6,909	8,808	7,321
52,300	52,350	8,820	6,916	8,820	7,334
52,350	52,400	8,833	6,924	8,833	7,346
52,400	52,450	8,845	6,931	8,845	7,359
52,450	52,500	8,858	6,939	8,858	7,371
52,500	52,550	8,870	6,946	8,870	7,384
52,550	52,600	8,883	6,954	8,883	7,396
52,600	52,650	8,895	6,961	8,895	7,409
52,650	52,700	8,908	6,969	8,908	7,421
52,700	52,750	8,920	6,976	8,920	7,434
52,750	52,800	8,933	6,984	8,933	7,446
52,800	52,850	8,945	6,991	8,945	7,459
52,850	52,900	8,958	6,999	8,958	7,471
52,900	52,950	8,970	7,006	8,970	7,484
52,950	53,000	8,983	7,014	8,983	7,496
53,000					
53,000	53,050	8,995	7,021	8,995	7,509
53,050	53,100	9,008	7,029	9,008	7,521
53,100	53,150	9,020	7,036	9,020	7,534
53,150	53,200	9,033	7,044	9,033	7,546
53,200	53,250	9,045	7,051	9,045	7,559
53,250	53,300	9,058	7,059	9,058	7,571
53,300	53,350	9,070	7,066	9,070	7,584
53,350	53,400	9,083	7,074	9,083	7,596
53,400	53,450	9,095	7,081	9,095	7,609
53,450	53,500	9,108	7,089	9,108	7,621
53,500	53,550	9,120	7,096	9,120	7,634
53,550	53,600	9,133	7,104	9,133	7,646
53,600	53,650	9,145	7,111	9,145	7,659
53,650	53,700	9,158	7,119	9,158	7,671
53,700	53,750	9,170	7,126	9,170	7,684
53,750	53,800	9,183	7,134	9,183	7,696
53,800	53,850	9,195	7,141	9,195	7,709
53,850	53,900	9,208	7,149	9,208	7,721
53,900	53,950	9,220	7,156	9,220	7,734
53,950	54,000	9,233	7,164	9,233	7,746
54,000					
54,000	54,050	9,245	7,171	9,245	7,759
54,050	54,100	9,258	7,179	9,258	7,771
54,100	54,150	9,270	7,186	9,270	7,784
54,150	54,200	9,283	7,194	9,283	7,796
54,200	54,250	9,295	7,201	9,295	7,809
54,250	54,300	9,308	7,209	9,308	7,821
54,300	54,350	9,320	7,216	9,320	7,834
54,350	54,400	9,333	7,224	9,333	7,846
54,400	54,450	9,345	7,231	9,345	7,859
54,450	54,500	9,358	7,239	9,358	7,871
54,500	54,550	9,370	7,246	9,370	7,884
54,550	54,600	9,383	7,254	9,383	7,896
54,600	54,650	9,395	7,261	9,395	7,909
54,650	54,700	9,408	7,269	9,408	7,921
54,700	54,750	9,420	7,276	9,420	7,934
54,750	54,800	9,433	7,284	9,433	7,946
54,800	54,850	9,445	7,291	9,445	7,959
54,850	54,900	9,458	7,299	9,458	7,971
54,900	54,950	9,470	7,306	9,470	7,984
54,950	55,000	9,483	7,314	9,483	7,996
55,000					
55,000	55,050	9,495	7,321	9,495	8,009
55,050	55,100	9,508	7,329	9,508	8,021
55,100	55,150	9,520	7,336	9,520	8,034
55,150	55,200	9,533	7,344	9,533	8,046
55,200	55,250	9,545	7,351	9,545	8,059
55,250	55,300	9,558	7,359	9,558	8,071
55,300	55,350	9,570	7,366	9,570	8,084
55,350	55,400	9,583	7,374	9,583	8,096
55,400	55,450	9,595	7,381	9,595	8,109
55,450	55,500	9,608	7,389	9,608	8,121
55,500	55,550	9,620	7,396	9,620	8,134
55,550	55,600	9,633	7,404	9,633	8,146
55,600	55,650	9,645	7,411	9,645	8,159
55,650	55,700	9,658	7,419	9,658	8,171
55,700	55,750	9,670	7,426	9,670	8,184
55,750	55,800	9,683	7,434	9,683	8,196
55,800	55,850	9,695	7,441	9,695	8,209
55,850	55,900	9,708	7,449	9,708	8,221
55,900	55,950	9,720	7,456	9,720	8,234
55,950	56,000	9,733	7,464	9,733	8,246
56,000					
56,000	56,050	9,745	7,471	9,745	8,259
56,050	56,100	9,758	7,479	9,758	8,271
56,100	56,150	9,770	7,486	9,770	8,284
56,150	56,200	9,783	7,494	9,783	8,296
56,200	56,250	9,795	7,501	9,795	8,309
56,250	56,300	9,808	7,509	9,808	8,321
56,300	56,350	9,820	7,516	9,820	8,334
56,350	56,400	9,833	7,524	9,833	8,346
56,400	56,450	9,845	7,531	9,845	8,359
56,450	56,500	9,858	7,539	9,858	8,371
56,500	56,550	9,870	7,546	9,870	8,384
56,550	56,600	9,883	7,554	9,883	8,396
56,600	56,650	9,895	7,561	9,895	8,409
56,650	56,700	9,908	7,569	9,908	8,421
56,700	56,750	9,920	7,576	9,920	8,434
56,750	56,800	9,933	7,584	9,933	8,446
56,800	56,850	9,945	7,591	9,945	8,459
56,850	56,900	9,958	7,599	9,958	8,471
56,900	56,950	9,970	7,606	9,970	8,484
56,950	57,000	9,983	7,614	9,983	8,496

(Continued)

* This column must also be used by a qualifying widow(er).

2017 Tax Table — *Continued*

If line 27 (taxable income) is— At least	But less than	And you are— Single	Married filing jointly *	Married filing sepa-rately	Head of a house-hold
		Your tax is—			
57,000					
57,000	57,050	9,995	7,621	9,995	8,509
57,050	57,100	10,008	7,629	10,008	8,521
57,100	57,150	10,020	7,636	10,020	8,534
57,150	57,200	10,033	7,644	10,033	8,546
57,200	57,250	10,045	7,651	10,045	8,559
57,250	57,300	10,058	7,659	10,058	8,571
57,300	57,350	10,070	7,666	10,070	8,584
57,350	57,400	10,083	7,674	10,083	8,596
57,400	57,450	10,095	7,681	10,095	8,609
57,450	57,500	10,108	7,689	10,108	8,621
57,500	57,550	10,120	7,696	10,120	8,634
57,550	57,600	10,133	7,704	10,133	8,646
57,600	57,650	10,145	7,711	10,145	8,659
57,650	57,700	10,158	7,719	10,158	8,671
57,700	57,750	10,170	7,726	10,170	8,684
57,750	57,800	10,183	7,734	10,183	8,696
57,800	57,850	10,195	7,741	10,195	8,709
57,850	57,900	10,208	7,749	10,208	8,721
57,900	57,950	10,220	7,756	10,220	8,734
57,950	58,000	10,233	7,764	10,233	8,746
58,000					
58,000	58,050	10,245	7,771	10,245	8,759
58,050	58,100	10,258	7,779	10,258	8,771
58,100	58,150	10,270	7,786	10,270	8,784
58,150	58,200	10,283	7,794	10,283	8,796
58,200	58,250	10,295	7,801	10,295	8,809
58,250	58,300	10,308	7,809	10,308	8,821
58,300	58,350	10,320	7,816	10,320	8,834
58,350	58,400	10,333	7,824	10,333	8,846
58,400	58,450	10,345	7,831	10,345	8,859
58,450	58,500	10,358	7,839	10,358	8,871
58,500	58,550	10,370	7,846	10,370	8,884
58,550	58,600	10,383	7,854	10,383	8,896
58,600	58,650	10,395	7,861	10,395	8,909
58,650	58,700	10,408	7,869	10,408	8,921
58,700	58,750	10,420	7,876	10,420	8,934
58,750	58,800	10,433	7,884	10,433	8,946
58,800	58,850	10,445	7,891	10,445	8,959
58,850	58,900	10,458	7,899	10,458	8,971
58,900	58,950	10,470	7,906	10,470	8,984
58,950	59,000	10,483	7,914	10,483	8,996
59,000					
59,000	59,050	10,495	7,921	10,495	9,009
59,050	59,100	10,508	7,929	10,508	9,021
59,100	59,150	10,520	7,936	10,520	9,034
59,150	59,200	10,533	7,944	10,533	9,046
59,200	59,250	10,545	7,951	10,545	9,059
59,250	59,300	10,558	7,959	10,558	9,071
59,300	59,350	10,570	7,966	10,570	9,084
59,350	59,400	10,583	7,974	10,583	9,096
59,400	59,450	10,595	7,981	10,595	9,109
59,450	59,500	10,608	7,989	10,608	9,121
59,500	59,550	10,620	7,996	10,620	9,134
59,550	59,600	10,633	8,004	10,633	9,146
59,600	59,650	10,645	8,011	10,645	9,159
59,650	59,700	10,658	8,019	10,658	9,171
59,700	59,750	10,670	8,026	10,670	9,184
59,750	59,800	10,683	8,034	10,683	9,196
59,800	59,850	10,695	8,041	10,695	9,209
59,850	59,900	10,708	8,049	10,708	9,221
59,900	59,950	10,720	8,056	10,720	9,234
59,950	60,000	10,733	8,064	10,733	9,246

If line 27 (taxable income) is— At least	But less than	And you are— Single	Married filing jointly *	Married filing sepa-rately	Head of a house-hold
		Your tax is—			
60,000					
60,000	60,050	10,745	8,071	10,745	9,259
60,050	60,100	10,758	8,079	10,758	9,271
60,100	60,150	10,770	8,086	10,770	9,284
60,150	60,200	10,783	8,094	10,783	9,296
60,200	60,250	10,795	8,101	10,795	9,309
60,250	60,300	10,808	8,109	10,808	9,321
60,300	60,350	10,820	8,116	10,820	9,334
60,350	60,400	10,833	8,124	10,833	9,346
60,400	60,450	10,845	8,131	10,845	9,359
60,450	60,500	10,858	8,139	10,858	9,371
60,500	60,550	10,870	8,146	10,870	9,384
60,550	60,600	10,883	8,154	10,883	9,396
60,600	60,650	10,895	8,161	10,895	9,409
60,650	60,700	10,908	8,169	10,908	9,421
60,700	60,750	10,920	8,176	10,920	9,434
60,750	60,800	10,933	8,184	10,933	9,446
60,800	60,850	10,945	8,191	10,945	9,459
60,850	60,900	10,958	8,199	10,958	9,471
60,900	60,950	10,970	8,206	10,970	9,484
60,950	61,000	10,983	8,214	10,983	9,496
61,000					
61,000	61,050	10,995	8,221	10,995	9,509
61,050	61,100	11,008	8,229	11,008	9,521
61,100	61,150	11,020	8,236	11,020	9,534
61,150	61,200	11,033	8,244	11,033	9,546
61,200	61,250	11,045	8,251	11,045	9,559
61,250	61,300	11,058	8,259	11,058	9,571
61,300	61,350	11,070	8,266	11,070	9,584
61,350	61,400	11,083	8,274	11,083	9,596
61,400	61,450	11,095	8,281	11,095	9,609
61,450	61,500	11,108	8,289	11,108	9,621
61,500	61,550	11,120	8,296	11,120	9,634
61,550	61,600	11,133	8,304	11,133	9,646
61,600	61,650	11,145	8,311	11,145	9,659
61,650	61,700	11,158	8,319	11,158	9,671
61,700	61,750	11,170	8,326	11,170	9,684
61,750	61,800	11,183	8,334	11,183	9,696
61,800	61,850	11,195	8,341	11,195	9,709
61,850	61,900	11,208	8,349	11,208	9,721
61,900	61,950	11,220	8,356	11,220	9,734
61,950	62,000	11,233	8,364	11,233	9,746
62,000					
62,000	62,050	11,245	8,371	11,245	9,759
62,050	62,100	11,258	8,379	11,258	9,771
62,100	62,150	11,270	8,386	11,270	9,784
62,150	62,200	11,283	8,394	11,283	9,796
62,200	62,250	11,295	8,401	11,295	9,809
62,250	62,300	11,308	8,409	11,308	9,821
62,300	62,350	11,320	8,416	11,320	9,834
62,350	62,400	11,333	8,424	11,333	9,846
62,400	62,450	11,345	8,431	11,345	9,859
62,450	62,500	11,358	8,439	11,358	9,871
62,500	62,550	11,370	8,446	11,370	9,884
62,550	62,600	11,383	8,454	11,383	9,896
62,600	62,650	11,395	8,461	11,395	9,909
62,650	62,700	11,408	8,469	11,408	9,921
62,700	62,750	11,420	8,476	11,420	9,934
62,750	62,800	11,433	8,484	11,433	9,946
62,800	62,850	11,445	8,491	11,445	9,959
62,850	62,900	11,458	8,499	11,458	9,971
62,900	62,950	11,470	8,506	11,470	9,984
62,950	63,000	11,483	8,514	11,483	9,996

If line 27 (taxable income) is— At least	But less than	And you are— Single	Married filing jointly *	Married filing sepa-rately	Head of a house-hold
		Your tax is—			
63,000					
63,000	63,050	11,495	8,521	11,495	10,009
63,050	63,100	11,508	8,529	11,508	10,021
63,100	63,150	11,520	8,536	11,520	10,034
63,150	63,200	11,533	8,544	11,533	10,046
63,200	63,250	11,545	8,551	11,545	10,059
63,250	63,300	11,558	8,559	11,558	10,071
63,300	63,350	11,570	8,566	11,570	10,084
63,350	63,400	11,583	8,574	11,583	10,096
63,400	63,450	11,595	8,581	11,595	10,109
63,450	63,500	11,608	8,589	11,608	10,121
63,500	63,550	11,620	8,596	11,620	10,134
63,550	63,600	11,633	8,604	11,633	10,146
63,600	63,650	11,645	8,611	11,645	10,159
63,650	63,700	11,658	8,619	11,658	10,171
63,700	63,750	11,670	8,626	11,670	10,184
63,750	63,800	11,683	8,634	11,683	10,196
63,800	63,850	11,695	8,641	11,695	10,209
63,850	63,900	11,708	8,649	11,708	10,221
63,900	63,950	11,720	8,656	11,720	10,234
63,950	64,000	11,733	8,664	11,733	10,246
64,000					
64,000	64,050	11,745	8,671	11,745	10,25[illegible]
64,050	64,100	11,758	8,679	11,758	10,27[illegible]
64,100	64,150	11,770	8,686	11,770	10,28[illegible]
64,150	64,200	11,783	8,694	11,783	10,29[illegible]
64,200	64,250	11,795	8,701	11,795	10,30[illegible]
64,250	64,300	11,808	8,709	11,808	10,32[illegible]
64,300	64,350	11,820	8,716	11,820	10,33[illegible]
64,350	64,400	11,833	8,724	11,833	10,34[illegible]
64,400	64,450	11,845	8,731	11,845	10,35[illegible]
64,450	64,500	11,858	8,739	11,858	10,37[illegible]
64,500	64,550	11,870	8,746	11,870	10,38[illegible]
64,550	64,600	11,883	8,754	11,883	10,39[illegible]
64,600	64,650	11,895	8,761	11,895	10,40[illegible]
64,650	64,700	11,908	8,769	11,908	10,42[illegible]
64,700	64,750	11,920	8,776	11,920	10,43[illegible]
64,750	64,800	11,933	8,784	11,933	10,44[illegible]
64,800	64,850	11,945	8,791	11,945	10,45[illegible]
64,850	64,900	11,958	8,799	11,958	10,47[illegible]
64,900	64,950	11,970	8,806	11,970	10,48[illegible]
64,950	65,000	11,983	8,814	11,983	10,49[illegible]
65,000					
65,000	65,050	11,995	8,821	11,995	10,509
65,050	65,100	12,008	8,829	12,008	10,521
65,100	65,150	12,020	8,836	12,020	10,534
65,150	65,200	12,033	8,844	12,033	10,546
65,200	65,250	12,045	8,851	12,045	10,559
65,250	65,300	12,058	8,859	12,058	10,571
65,300	65,350	12,070	8,866	12,070	10,584
65,350	65,400	12,083	8,874	12,083	10,596
65,400	65,450	12,095	8,881	12,095	10,609
65,450	65,500	12,108	8,889	12,108	10,621
65,500	65,550	12,120	8,896	12,120	10,634
65,550	65,600	12,133	8,904	12,133	10,646
65,600	65,650	12,145	8,911	12,145	10,659
65,650	65,700	12,158	8,919	12,158	10,671
65,700	65,750	12,170	8,926	12,170	10,684
65,750	65,800	12,183	8,934	12,183	10,696
65,800	65,850	12,195	8,941	12,195	10,709
65,850	65,900	12,208	8,949	12,208	10,721
65,900	65,950	12,220	8,956	12,220	10,734
65,950	66,000	12,233	8,964	12,233	10,746

(Continued)

* This column must also be used by a qualifying widow(er).

2017 Tax Table — *Continued*

If line 27 (taxable income) is—		And you are—			
At least	But less than	Single	Married filing jointly *	Married filing separately	Head of a household
		Your tax is—			
66,000					
66,000	66,050	12,245	8,971	12,245	10,759
66,050	66,100	12,258	8,979	12,258	10,771
66,100	66,150	12,270	8,986	12,270	10,784
66,150	66,200	12,283	8,994	12,283	10,796
66,200	66,250	12,295	9,001	12,295	10,809
66,250	66,300	12,308	9,009	12,308	10,821
66,300	66,350	12,320	9,016	12,320	10,834
66,350	66,400	12,333	9,024	12,333	10,846
66,400	66,450	12,345	9,031	12,345	10,859
66,450	66,500	12,358	9,039	12,358	10,871
66,500	66,550	12,370	9,046	12,370	10,884
66,550	66,600	12,383	9,054	12,383	10,896
66,600	66,650	12,395	9,061	12,395	10,909
66,650	66,700	12,408	9,069	12,408	10,921
66,700	66,750	12,420	9,076	12,420	10,934
66,750	66,800	12,433	9,084	12,433	10,946
66,800	66,850	12,445	9,091	12,445	10,959
66,850	66,900	12,458	9,099	12,458	10,971
66,900	66,950	12,470	9,106	12,470	10,984
66,950	67,000	12,483	9,114	12,483	10,996
67,000					
67,000	67,050	12,495	9,121	12,495	11,009
67,050	67,100	12,508	9,129	12,508	11,021
67,100	67,150	12,520	9,136	12,520	11,034
67,150	67,200	12,533	9,144	12,533	11,046
67,200	67,250	12,545	9,151	12,545	11,059
67,250	67,300	12,558	9,159	12,558	11,071
67,300	67,350	12,570	9,166	12,570	11,084
67,350	67,400	12,583	9,174	12,583	11,096
67,400	67,450	12,595	9,181	12,595	11,109
67,450	67,500	12,608	9,189	12,608	11,121
67,500	67,550	12,620	9,196	12,620	11,134
67,550	67,600	12,633	9,204	12,633	11,146
67,600	67,650	12,645	9,211	12,645	11,159
67,650	67,700	12,658	9,219	12,658	11,171
67,700	67,750	12,670	9,226	12,670	11,184
67,750	67,800	12,683	9,234	12,683	11,196
67,800	67,850	12,695	9,241	12,695	11,209
67,850	67,900	12,708	9,249	12,708	11,221
67,900	67,950	12,720	9,256	12,720	11,234
67,950	68,000	12,733	9,264	12,733	11,246
68,000					
68,000	68,050	12,745	9,271	12,745	11,259
68,050	68,100	12,758	9,279	12,758	11,271
68,100	68,150	12,770	9,286	12,770	11,284
68,150	68,200	12,783	9,294	12,783	11,296
68,200	68,250	12,795	9,301	12,795	11,309
68,250	68,300	12,808	9,309	12,808	11,321
68,300	68,350	12,820	9,316	12,820	11,334
68,350	68,400	12,833	9,324	12,833	11,346
68,400	68,450	12,845	9,331	12,845	11,359
68,450	68,500	12,858	9,339	12,858	11,371
68,500	68,550	12,870	9,346	12,870	11,384
68,550	68,600	12,883	9,354	12,883	11,396
68,600	68,650	12,895	9,361	12,895	11,409
68,650	68,700	12,908	9,369	12,908	11,421
68,700	68,750	12,920	9,376	12,920	11,434
68,750	68,800	12,933	9,384	12,933	11,446
68,800	68,850	12,945	9,391	12,945	11,459
68,850	68,900	12,958	9,399	12,958	11,471
68,900	68,950	12,970	9,406	12,970	11,484
68,950	69,000	12,983	9,414	12,983	11,496
69,000					
69,000	69,050	12,995	9,421	12,995	11,509
69,050	69,100	13,008	9,429	13,008	11,521
69,100	69,150	13,020	9,436	13,020	11,534
69,150	69,200	13,033	9,444	13,033	11,546
69,200	69,250	13,045	9,451	13,045	11,559
69,250	69,300	13,058	9,459	13,058	11,571
69,300	69,350	13,070	9,466	13,070	11,584
69,350	69,400	13,083	9,474	13,083	11,596
69,400	69,450	13,095	9,481	13,095	11,609
69,450	69,500	13,108	9,489	13,108	11,621
69,500	69,550	13,120	9,496	13,120	11,634
69,550	69,600	13,133	9,504	13,133	11,646
69,600	69,650	13,145	9,511	13,145	11,659
69,650	69,700	13,158	9,519	13,158	11,671
69,700	69,750	13,170	9,526	13,170	11,684
69,750	69,800	13,183	9,534	13,183	11,696
69,800	69,850	13,195	9,541	13,195	11,709
69,850	69,900	13,208	9,549	13,208	11,721
69,900	69,950	13,220	9,556	13,220	11,734
69,950	70,000	13,233	9,564	13,233	11,746
70,000					
70,000	70,050	13,245	9,571	13,245	11,759
70,050	70,100	13,258	9,579	13,258	11,771
70,100	70,150	13,270	9,586	13,270	11,784
70,150	70,200	13,283	9,594	13,283	11,796
70,200	70,250	13,295	9,601	13,295	11,809
70,250	70,300	13,308	9,609	13,308	11,821
70,300	70,350	13,320	9,616	13,320	11,834
70,350	70,400	13,333	9,624	13,333	11,846
70,400	70,450	13,345	9,631	13,345	11,859
70,450	70,500	13,358	9,639	13,358	11,871
70,500	70,550	13,370	9,646	13,370	11,884
70,550	70,600	13,383	9,654	13,383	11,896
70,600	70,650	13,395	9,661	13,395	11,909
70,650	70,700	13,408	9,669	13,408	11,921
70,700	70,750	13,420	9,676	13,420	11,934
70,750	70,800	13,433	9,684	13,433	11,946
70,800	70,850	13,445	9,691	13,445	11,959
70,850	70,900	13,458	9,699	13,458	11,971
70,900	70,950	13,470	9,706	13,470	11,984
70,950	71,000	13,483	9,714	13,483	11,996
71,000					
71,000	71,050	13,495	9,721	13,495	12,009
71,050	71,100	13,508	9,729	13,508	12,021
71,100	71,150	13,520	9,736	13,520	12,034
71,150	71,200	13,533	9,744	13,533	12,046
71,200	71,250	13,545	9,751	13,545	12,059
71,250	71,300	13,558	9,759	13,558	12,071
71,300	71,350	13,570	9,766	13,570	12,084
71,350	71,400	13,583	9,774	13,583	12,096
71,400	71,450	13,595	9,781	13,595	12,109
71,450	71,500	13,608	9,789	13,608	12,121
71,500	71,550	13,620	9,796	13,620	12,134
71,550	71,600	13,633	9,804	13,633	12,146
71,600	71,650	13,645	9,811	13,645	12,159
71,650	71,700	13,658	9,819	13,658	12,171
71,700	71,750	13,670	9,826	13,670	12,184
71,750	71,800	13,683	9,834	13,683	12,196
71,800	71,850	13,695	9,841	13,695	12,209
71,850	71,900	13,708	9,849	13,708	12,221
71,900	71,950	13,720	9,856	13,720	12,234
71,950	72,000	13,733	9,864	13,733	12,246
72,000					
72,000	72,050	13,745	9,871	13,745	12,259
72,050	72,100	13,758	9,879	13,758	12,271
72,100	72,150	13,770	9,886	13,770	12,284
72,150	72,200	13,783	9,894	13,783	12,296
72,200	72,250	13,795	9,901	13,795	12,309
72,250	72,300	13,808	9,909	13,808	12,321
72,300	72,350	13,820	9,916	13,820	12,334
72,350	72,400	13,833	9,924	13,833	12,346
72,400	72,450	13,845	9,931	13,845	12,359
72,450	72,500	13,858	9,939	13,858	12,371
72,500	72,550	13,870	9,946	13,870	12,384
72,550	72,600	13,883	9,954	13,883	12,396
72,600	72,650	13,895	9,961	13,895	12,409
72,650	72,700	13,908	9,969	13,908	12,421
72,700	72,750	13,920	9,976	13,920	12,434
72,750	72,800	13,933	9,984	13,933	12,446
72,800	72,850	13,945	9,991	13,945	12,459
72,850	72,900	13,958	9,999	13,958	12,471
72,900	72,950	13,970	10,006	13,970	12,484
72,950	73,000	13,983	10,014	13,983	12,496
73,000					
73,000	73,050	13,995	10,021	13,995	12,509
73,050	73,100	14,008	10,029	14,008	12,521
73,100	73,150	14,020	10,036	14,020	12,534
73,150	73,200	14,033	10,044	14,033	12,546
73,200	73,250	14,045	10,051	14,045	12,559
73,250	73,300	14,058	10,059	14,058	12,571
73,300	73,350	14,070	10,066	14,070	12,584
73,350	73,400	14,083	10,074	14,083	12,596
73,400	73,450	14,095	10,081	14,095	12,609
73,450	73,500	14,108	10,089	14,108	12,621
73,500	73,550	14,120	10,096	14,120	12,634
73,550	73,600	14,133	10,104	14,133	12,646
73,600	73,650	14,145	10,111	14,145	12,659
73,650	73,700	14,158	10,119	14,158	12,671
73,700	73,750	14,170	10,126	14,170	12,684
73,750	73,800	14,183	10,134	14,183	12,696
73,800	73,850	14,195	10,141	14,195	12,709
73,850	73,900	14,208	10,149	14,208	12,721
73,900	73,950	14,220	10,156	14,220	12,734
73,950	74,000	14,233	10,164	14,233	12,746
74,000					
74,000	74,050	14,245	10,171	14,245	12,759
74,050	74,100	14,258	10,179	14,258	12,771
74,100	74,150	14,270	10,186	14,270	12,784
74,150	74,200	14,283	10,194	14,283	12,796
74,200	74,250	14,295	10,201	14,295	12,809
74,250	74,300	14,308	10,209	14,308	12,821
74,300	74,350	14,320	10,216	14,320	12,834
74,350	74,400	14,333	10,224	14,333	12,846
74,400	74,450	14,345	10,231	14,345	12,859
74,450	74,500	14,358	10,239	14,358	12,871
74,500	74,550	14,370	10,246	14,370	12,884
74,550	74,600	14,383	10,254	14,383	12,896
74,600	74,650	14,395	10,261	14,395	12,909
74,650	74,700	14,408	10,269	14,408	12,921
74,700	74,750	14,420	10,276	14,420	12,934
74,750	74,800	14,433	10,284	14,433	12,946
74,800	74,850	14,445	10,291	14,445	12,959
74,850	74,900	14,458	10,299	14,458	12,971
74,900	74,950	14,470	10,306	14,470	12,984
74,950	75,000	14,483	10,314	14,483	12,996

(Continued)

* This column must also be used by a qualifying widow(er).

2017 Tax Table — *Continued*

If line 27 (taxable income) is—		And you are—			
At least	But less than	Single	Married filing jointly *	Married filing sepa-rately	Head of a house-hold
		Your tax is—			
75,000					
75,000	75,050	14,495	10,321	14,495	13,009
75,050	75,100	14,508	10,329	14,508	13,021
75,100	75,150	14,520	10,336	14,520	13,034
75,150	75,200	14,533	10,344	14,533	13,046
75,200	75,250	14,545	10,351	14,545	13,059
75,250	75,300	14,558	10,359	14,558	13,071
75,300	75,350	14,570	10,366	14,570	13,084
75,350	75,400	14,583	10,374	14,583	13,096
75,400	75,450	14,595	10,381	14,595	13,109
75,450	75,500	14,608	10,389	14,608	13,121
75,500	75,550	14,620	10,396	14,620	13,134
75,550	75,600	14,633	10,404	14,633	13,146
75,600	75,650	14,645	10,411	14,645	13,159
75,650	75,700	14,658	10,419	14,658	13,171
75,700	75,750	14,670	10,426	14,670	13,184
75,750	75,800	14,683	10,434	14,683	13,196
75,800	75,850	14,695	10,441	14,695	13,209
75,850	75,900	14,708	10,449	14,708	13,221
75,900	75,950	14,720	10,459	14,720	13,234
75,950	76,000	14,733	10,471	14,733	13,246
76,000					
76,000	76,050	14,745	10,484	14,745	13,259
76,050	76,100	14,758	10,496	14,758	13,271
76,100	76,150	14,770	10,509	14,770	13,284
76,150	76,200	14,783	10,521	14,783	13,296
76,200	76,250	14,795	10,534	14,795	13,309
76,250	76,300	14,808	10,546	14,808	13,321
76,300	76,350	14,820	10,559	14,820	13,334
76,350	76,400	14,833	10,571	14,833	13,346
76,400	76,450	14,845	10,584	14,845	13,359
76,450	76,500	14,858	10,596	14,858	13,371
76,500	76,550	14,870	10,609	14,870	13,384
76,550	76,600	14,883	10,621	14,883	13,396
76,600	76,650	14,895	10,634	14,897	13,409
76,650	76,700	14,908	10,646	14,911	13,421
76,700	76,750	14,920	10,659	14,925	13,434
76,750	76,800	14,933	10,671	14,939	13,446
76,800	76,850	14,945	10,684	14,953	13,459
76,850	76,900	14,958	10,696	14,967	13,471
76,900	76,950	14,970	10,709	14,981	13,484
76,950	77,000	14,983	10,721	14,995	13,496
77,000					
77,000	77,050	14,995	10,734	15,009	13,509
77,050	77,100	15,008	10,746	15,023	13,521
77,100	77,150	15,020	10,759	15,037	13,534
77,150	77,200	15,033	10,771	15,051	13,546
77,200	77,250	15,045	10,784	15,065	13,559
77,250	77,300	15,058	10,796	15,079	13,571
77,300	77,350	15,070	10,809	15,093	13,584
77,350	77,400	15,083	10,821	15,107	13,596
77,400	77,450	15,095	10,834	15,121	13,609
77,450	77,500	15,108	10,846	15,135	13,621
77,500	77,550	15,120	10,859	15,149	13,634
77,550	77,600	15,133	10,871	15,163	13,646
77,600	77,650	15,145	10,884	15,177	13,659
77,650	77,700	15,158	10,896	15,191	13,671
77,700	77,750	15,170	10,909	15,205	13,684
77,750	77,800	15,183	10,921	15,219	13,696
77,800	77,850	15,195	10,934	15,233	13,709
77,850	77,900	15,208	10,946	15,247	13,721
77,900	77,950	15,220	10,959	15,261	13,734
77,950	78,000	15,233	10,971	15,275	13,746

If line 27 (taxable income) is—		And you are—			
At least	But less than	Single	Married filing jointly *	Married filing sepa-rately	Head of a house-hold
		Your tax is—			
78,000					
78,000	78,050	15,245	10,984	15,289	13,759
78,050	78,100	15,258	10,996	15,303	13,771
78,100	78,150	15,270	11,009	15,317	13,784
78,150	78,200	15,283	11,021	15,331	13,796
78,200	78,250	15,295	11,034	15,345	13,809
78,250	78,300	15,308	11,046	15,359	13,821
78,300	78,350	15,320	11,059	15,373	13,834
78,350	78,400	15,333	11,071	15,387	13,846
78,400	78,450	15,345	11,084	15,401	13,859
78,450	78,500	15,358	11,096	15,415	13,871
78,500	78,550	15,370	11,109	15,429	13,884
78,550	78,600	15,383	11,121	15,443	13,896
78,600	78,650	15,395	11,134	15,457	13,909
78,650	78,700	15,408	11,146	15,471	13,921
78,700	78,750	15,420	11,159	15,485	13,934
78,750	78,800	15,433	11,171	15,499	13,946
78,800	78,850	15,445	11,184	15,513	13,959
78,850	78,900	15,458	11,196	15,527	13,971
78,900	78,950	15,470	11,209	15,541	13,984
78,950	79,000	15,483	11,221	15,555	13,996
79,000					
79,000	79,050	15,495	11,234	15,569	14,009
79,050	79,100	15,508	11,246	15,583	14,021
79,100	79,150	15,520	11,259	15,597	14,034
79,150	79,200	15,533	11,271	15,611	14,046
79,200	79,250	15,545	11,284	15,625	14,059
79,250	79,300	15,558	11,296	15,639	14,071
79,300	79,350	15,570	11,309	15,653	14,084
79,350	79,400	15,583	11,321	15,667	14,096
79,400	79,450	15,595	11,334	15,681	14,109
79,450	79,500	15,608	11,346	15,695	14,121
79,500	79,550	15,620	11,359	15,709	14,134
79,550	79,600	15,633	11,371	15,723	14,146
79,600	79,650	15,645	11,384	15,737	14,159
79,650	79,700	15,658	11,396	15,751	14,171
79,700	79,750	15,670	11,409	15,765	14,184
79,750	79,800	15,683	11,421	15,779	14,196
79,800	79,850	15,695	11,434	15,793	14,209
79,850	79,900	15,708	11,446	15,807	14,221
79,900	79,950	15,720	11,459	15,821	14,234
79,950	80,000	15,733	11,471	15,835	14,246
80,000					
80,000	80,050	15,745	11,484	15,849	14,259
80,050	80,100	15,758	11,496	15,863	14,271
80,100	80,150	15,770	11,509	15,877	14,284
80,150	80,200	15,783	11,521	15,891	14,296
80,200	80,250	15,795	11,534	15,905	14,309
80,250	80,300	15,808	11,546	15,919	14,321
80,300	80,350	15,820	11,559	15,933	14,334
80,350	80,400	15,833	11,571	15,947	14,346
80,400	80,450	15,845	11,584	15,961	14,359
80,450	80,500	15,858	11,596	15,975	14,371
80,500	80,550	15,870	11,609	15,989	14,384
80,550	80,600	15,883	11,621	16,003	14,396
80,600	80,650	15,895	11,634	16,017	14,409
80,650	80,700	15,908	11,646	16,031	14,421
80,700	80,750	15,920	11,659	16,045	14,434
80,750	80,800	15,933	11,671	16,059	14,446
80,800	80,850	15,945	11,684	16,073	14,459
80,850	80,900	15,958	11,696	16,087	14,471
80,900	80,950	15,970	11,709	16,101	14,484
80,950	81,000	15,983	11,721	16,115	14,496

If line 27 (taxable income) is—		And you are—			
At least	But less than	Single	Married filing jointly *	Married filing sepa-rately	Head of a house-hold
		Your tax is—			
81,000					
81,000	81,050	15,995	11,734	16,129	14,509
81,050	81,100	16,008	11,746	16,143	14,521
81,100	81,150	16,020	11,759	16,157	14,534
81,150	81,200	16,033	11,771	16,171	14,546
81,200	81,250	16,045	11,784	16,185	14,559
81,250	81,300	16,058	11,796	16,199	14,571
81,300	81,350	16,070	11,809	16,213	14,584
81,350	81,400	16,083	11,821	16,227	14,596
81,400	81,450	16,095	11,834	16,241	14,609
81,450	81,500	16,108	11,846	16,255	14,621
81,500	81,550	16,120	11,859	16,269	14,634
81,550	81,600	16,133	11,871	16,283	14,646
81,600	81,650	16,145	11,884	16,297	14,659
81,650	81,700	16,158	11,896	16,311	14,671
81,700	81,750	16,170	11,909	16,325	14,684
81,750	81,800	16,183	11,921	16,339	14,696
81,800	81,850	16,195	11,934	16,353	14,709
81,850	81,900	16,208	11,946	16,367	14,721
81,900	81,950	16,220	11,959	16,381	14,734
81,950	82,000	16,233	11,971	16,395	14,746
82,000					
82,000	82,050	16,245	11,984	16,409	14,759
82,050	82,100	16,258	11,996	16,423	14,771
82,100	82,150	16,270	12,009	16,437	14,784
82,150	82,200	16,283	12,021	16,451	14,796
82,200	82,250	16,295	12,034	16,465	14,809
82,250	82,300	16,308	12,046	16,479	14,821
82,300	82,350	16,320	12,059	16,493	14,834
82,350	82,400	16,333	12,071	16,507	14,846
82,400	82,450	16,345	12,084	16,521	14,859
82,450	82,500	16,358	12,096	16,535	14,871
82,500	82,550	16,370	12,109	16,549	14,884
82,550	82,600	16,383	12,121	16,563	14,896
82,600	82,650	16,395	12,134	16,577	14,909
82,650	82,700	16,408	12,146	16,591	14,921
82,700	82,750	16,420	12,159	16,605	14,934
82,750	82,800	16,433	12,171	16,619	14,946
82,800	82,850	16,445	12,184	16,633	14,959
82,850	82,900	16,458	12,196	16,647	14,971
82,900	82,950	16,470	12,209	16,661	14,984
82,950	83,000	16,483	12,221	16,675	14,996
83,000					
83,000	83,050	16,495	12,234	16,689	15,009
83,050	83,100	16,508	12,246	16,703	15,021
83,100	83,150	16,520	12,259	16,717	15,034
83,150	83,200	16,533	12,271	16,731	15,046
83,200	83,250	16,545	12,284	16,745	15,059
83,250	83,300	16,558	12,296	16,759	15,071
83,300	83,350	16,570	12,309	16,773	15,084
83,350	83,400	16,583	12,321	16,787	15,096
83,400	83,450	16,595	12,334	16,801	15,109
83,450	83,500	16,608	12,346	16,815	15,121
83,500	83,550	16,620	12,359	16,829	15,134
83,550	83,600	16,633	12,371	16,843	15,146
83,600	83,650	16,645	12,384	16,857	15,159
83,650	83,700	16,658	12,396	16,871	15,171
83,700	83,750	16,670	12,409	16,885	15,184
83,750	83,800	16,683	12,421	16,899	15,196
83,800	83,850	16,695	12,434	16,913	15,209
83,850	83,900	16,708	12,446	16,927	15,221
83,900	83,950	16,720	12,459	16,941	15,234
83,950	84,000	16,733	12,471	16,955	15,246

(Continued)

* This column must also be used by a qualifying widow(er).

2017 Tax Table — *Continued*

If line 27 (taxable income) is—		And you are—			
At least	But less than	Single	Married filing jointly *	Married filing sepa-rately	Head of a house-hold
		Your tax is—			
84,000					
84,000	84,050	16,745	12,484	16,969	15,259
84,050	84,100	16,758	12,496	16,983	15,271
84,100	84,150	16,770	12,509	16,997	15,284
84,150	84,200	16,783	12,521	17,011	15,296
84,200	84,250	16,795	12,534	17,025	15,309
84,250	84,300	16,808	12,546	17,039	15,321
84,300	84,350	16,820	12,559	17,053	15,334
84,350	84,400	16,833	12,571	17,067	15,346
84,400	84,450	16,845	12,584	17,081	15,359
84,450	84,500	16,858	12,596	17,095	15,371
84,500	84,550	16,870	12,609	17,109	15,384
84,550	84,600	16,883	12,621	17,123	15,396
84,600	84,650	16,895	12,634	17,137	15,409
84,650	84,700	16,908	12,646	17,151	15,421
84,700	84,750	16,920	12,659	17,165	15,434
84,750	84,800	16,933	12,671	17,179	15,446
84,800	84,850	16,945	12,684	17,193	15,459
84,850	84,900	16,958	12,696	17,207	15,471
84,900	84,950	16,970	12,709	17,221	15,484
84,950	85,000	16,983	12,721	17,235	15,496
85,000					
85,000	85,050	16,995	12,734	17,249	15,509
85,050	85,100	17,008	12,746	17,263	15,521
85,100	85,150	17,020	12,759	17,277	15,534
85,150	85,200	17,033	12,771	17,291	15,546
85,200	85,250	17,045	12,784	17,305	15,559
85,250	85,300	17,058	12,796	17,319	15,571
85,300	85,350	17,070	12,809	17,333	15,584
85,350	85,400	17,083	12,821	17,347	15,596
85,400	85,450	17,095	12,834	17,361	15,609
85,450	85,500	17,108	12,846	17,375	15,621
85,500	85,550	17,120	12,859	17,389	15,634
85,550	85,600	17,133	12,871	17,403	15,646
85,600	85,650	17,145	12,884	17,417	15,659
85,650	85,700	17,158	12,896	17,431	15,671
85,700	85,750	17,170	12,909	17,445	15,684
85,750	85,800	17,183	12,921	17,459	15,696
85,800	85,850	17,195	12,934	17,473	15,709
85,850	85,900	17,208	12,946	17,487	15,721
85,900	85,950	17,220	12,959	17,501	15,734
85,950	86,000	17,233	12,971	17,515	15,746
86,000					
86,000	86,050	17,245	12,984	17,529	15,759
86,050	86,100	17,258	12,996	17,543	15,771
86,100	86,150	17,270	13,009	17,557	15,784
86,150	86,200	17,283	13,021	17,571	15,796
86,200	86,250	17,295	13,034	17,585	15,809
86,250	86,300	17,308	13,046	17,599	15,821
86,300	86,350	17,320	13,059	17,613	15,834
86,350	86,400	17,333	13,071	17,627	15,846
86,400	86,450	17,345	13,084	17,641	15,859
86,450	86,500	17,358	13,096	17,655	15,871
86,500	86,550	17,370	13,109	17,669	15,884
86,550	86,600	17,383	13,121	17,683	15,896
86,600	86,650	17,395	13,134	17,697	15,909
86,650	86,700	17,408	13,146	17,711	15,921
86,700	86,750	17,420	13,159	17,725	15,934
86,750	86,800	17,433	13,171	17,739	15,946
86,800	86,850	17,445	13,184	17,753	15,959
86,850	86,900	17,458	13,196	17,767	15,971
86,900	86,950	17,470	13,209	17,781	15,984
86,950	87,000	17,483	13,221	17,795	15,996
87,000					
87,000	87,050	17,495	13,234	17,809	16,009
87,050	87,100	17,508	13,246	17,823	16,021
87,100	87,150	17,520	13,259	17,837	16,034
87,150	87,200	17,533	13,271	17,851	16,046
87,200	87,250	17,545	13,284	17,865	16,059
87,250	87,300	17,558	13,296	17,879	16,071
87,300	87,350	17,570	13,309	17,893	16,084
87,350	87,400	17,583	13,321	17,907	16,096
87,400	87,450	17,595	13,334	17,921	16,109
87,450	87,500	17,608	13,346	17,935	16,121
87,500	87,550	17,620	13,359	17,949	16,134
87,550	87,600	17,633	13,371	17,963	16,146
87,600	87,650	17,645	13,384	17,977	16,159
87,650	87,700	17,658	13,396	17,991	16,171
87,700	87,750	17,670	13,409	18,005	16,184
87,750	87,800	17,683	13,421	18,019	16,196
87,800	87,850	17,695	13,434	18,033	16,209
87,850	87,900	17,708	13,446	18,047	16,221
87,900	87,950	17,720	13,459	18,061	16,234
87,950	88,000	17,733	13,471	18,075	16,246
88,000					
88,000	88,050	17,745	13,484	18,089	16,259
88,050	88,100	17,758	13,496	18,103	16,271
88,100	88,150	17,770	13,509	18,117	16,284
88,150	88,200	17,783	13,521	18,131	16,296
88,200	88,250	17,795	13,534	18,145	16,309
88,250	88,300	17,808	13,546	18,159	16,321
88,300	88,350	17,820	13,559	18,173	16,334
88,350	88,400	17,833	13,571	18,187	16,346
88,400	88,450	17,845	13,584	18,201	16,359
88,450	88,500	17,858	13,596	18,215	16,371
88,500	88,550	17,870	13,609	18,229	16,384
88,550	88,600	17,883	13,621	18,243	16,396
88,600	88,650	17,895	13,634	18,257	16,409
88,650	88,700	17,908	13,646	18,271	16,421
88,700	88,750	17,920	13,659	18,285	16,434
88,750	88,800	17,933	13,671	18,299	16,446
88,800	88,850	17,945	13,684	18,313	16,459
88,850	88,900	17,958	13,696	18,327	16,471
88,900	88,950	17,970	13,709	18,341	16,484
88,950	89,000	17,983	13,721	18,355	16,496
89,000					
89,000	89,050	17,995	13,734	18,369	16,509
89,050	89,100	18,008	13,746	18,383	16,521
89,100	89,150	18,020	13,759	18,397	16,534
89,150	89,200	18,033	13,771	18,411	16,546
89,200	89,250	18,045	13,784	18,425	16,559
89,250	89,300	18,058	13,796	18,439	16,571
89,300	89,350	18,070	13,809	18,453	16,584
89,350	89,400	18,083	13,821	18,467	16,596
89,400	89,450	18,095	13,834	18,481	16,609
89,450	89,500	18,108	13,846	18,495	16,621
89,500	89,550	18,120	13,859	18,509	16,634
89,550	89,600	18,133	13,871	18,523	16,646
89,600	89,650	18,145	13,884	18,537	16,659
89,650	89,700	18,158	13,896	18,551	16,671
89,700	89,750	18,170	13,909	18,565	16,684
89,750	89,800	18,183	13,921	18,579	16,696
89,800	89,850	18,195	13,934	18,593	16,709
89,850	89,900	18,208	13,946	18,607	16,721
89,900	89,950	18,220	13,959	18,621	16,734
89,950	90,000	18,233	13,971	18,635	16,746
90,000					
90,000	90,050	18,245	13,984	18,649	16,759
90,050	90,100	18,258	13,996	18,663	16,771
90,100	90,150	18,270	14,009	18,677	16,784
90,150	90,200	18,283	14,021	18,691	16,796
90,200	90,250	18,295	14,034	18,705	16,809
90,250	90,300	18,308	14,046	18,719	16,821
90,300	90,350	18,320	14,059	18,733	16,834
90,350	90,400	18,333	14,071	18,747	16,846
90,400	90,450	18,345	14,084	18,761	16,859
90,450	90,500	18,358	14,096	18,775	16,871
90,500	90,550	18,370	14,109	18,789	16,884
90,550	90,600	18,383	14,121	18,803	16,896
90,600	90,650	18,395	14,134	18,817	16,909
90,650	90,700	18,408	14,146	18,831	16,921
90,700	90,750	18,420	14,159	18,845	16,934
90,750	90,800	18,433	14,171	18,859	16,946
90,800	90,850	18,445	14,184	18,873	16,959
90,850	90,900	18,458	14,196	18,887	16,971
90,900	90,950	18,470	14,209	18,901	16,984
90,950	91,000	18,483	14,221	18,915	16,996
91,000					
91,000	91,050	18,495	14,234	18,929	17,009
91,050	91,100	18,508	14,246	18,943	17,021
91,100	91,150	18,520	14,259	18,957	17,034
91,150	91,200	18,533	14,271	18,971	17,046
91,200	91,250	18,545	14,284	18,985	17,059
91,250	91,300	18,558	14,296	18,999	17,071
91,300	91,350	18,570	14,309	19,013	17,084
91,350	91,400	18,583	14,321	19,027	17,096
91,400	91,450	18,595	14,334	19,041	17,109
91,450	91,500	18,608	14,346	19,055	17,121
91,500	91,550	18,620	14,359	19,069	17,134
91,550	91,600	18,633	14,371	19,083	17,146
91,600	91,650	18,645	14,384	19,097	17,159
91,650	91,700	18,658	14,396	19,111	17,171
91,700	91,750	18,670	14,409	19,125	17,184
91,750	91,800	18,683	14,421	19,139	17,196
91,800	91,850	18,695	14,434	19,153	17,209
91,850	91,900	18,708	14,446	19,167	17,221
91,900	91,950	18,721	14,459	19,181	17,234
91,950	92,000	18,735	14,471	19,195	17,246
92,000					
92,000	92,050	18,749	14,484	19,209	17,259
92,050	92,100	18,763	14,496	19,223	17,271
92,100	92,150	18,777	14,509	19,237	17,284
92,150	92,200	18,791	14,521	19,251	17,296
92,200	92,250	18,805	14,534	19,265	17,309
92,250	92,300	18,819	14,546	19,279	17,321
92,300	92,350	18,833	14,559	19,293	17,334
92,350	92,400	18,847	14,571	19,307	17,346
92,400	92,450	18,861	14,584	19,321	17,359
92,450	92,500	18,875	14,596	19,335	17,371
92,500	92,550	18,889	14,609	19,349	17,384
92,550	92,600	18,903	14,621	19,363	17,396
92,600	92,650	18,917	14,634	19,377	17,409
92,650	92,700	18,931	14,646	19,391	17,421
92,700	92,750	18,945	14,659	19,405	17,434
92,750	92,800	18,959	14,671	19,419	17,446
92,800	92,850	18,973	14,684	19,433	17,459
92,850	92,900	18,987	14,696	19,447	17,471
92,900	92,950	19,001	14,709	19,461	17,484
92,950	93,000	19,015	14,721	19,475	17,496

(Continued)

* This column must also be used by a qualifying widow(er).

2017 Tax Table — *Continued*

If line 27 (taxable income) is—		And you are—			
At least	But less than	Single	Married filing jointly *	Married filing separately	Head of a household
		Your tax is—			
93,000					
93,000	93,050	19,029	14,734	19,489	17,509
93,050	93,100	19,043	14,746	19,503	17,521
93,100	93,150	19,057	14,759	19,517	17,534
93,150	93,200	19,071	14,771	19,531	17,546
93,200	93,250	19,085	14,784	19,545	17,559
93,250	93,300	19,099	14,796	19,559	17,571
93,300	93,350	19,113	14,809	19,573	17,584
93,350	93,400	19,127	14,821	19,587	17,596
93,400	93,450	19,141	14,834	19,601	17,609
93,450	93,500	19,155	14,846	19,615	17,621
93,500	93,550	19,169	14,859	19,629	17,634
93,550	93,600	19,183	14,871	19,643	17,646
93,600	93,650	19,197	14,884	19,657	17,659
93,650	93,700	19,211	14,896	19,671	17,671
93,700	93,750	19,225	14,909	19,685	17,684
93,750	93,800	19,239	14,921	19,699	17,696
93,800	93,850	19,253	14,934	19,713	17,709
93,850	93,900	19,267	14,946	19,727	17,721
93,900	93,950	19,281	14,959	19,741	17,734
93,950	94,000	19,295	14,971	19,755	17,746
94,000					
94,000	94,050	19,309	14,984	19,769	17,759
94,050	94,100	19,323	14,996	19,783	17,771
94,100	94,150	19,337	15,009	19,797	17,784
94,150	94,200	19,351	15,021	19,811	17,796
94,200	94,250	19,365	15,034	19,825	17,809
94,250	94,300	19,379	15,046	19,839	17,821
94,300	94,350	19,393	15,059	19,853	17,834
94,350	94,400	19,407	15,071	19,867	17,846
94,400	94,450	19,421	15,084	19,881	17,859
94,450	94,500	19,435	15,096	19,895	17,871
94,500	94,550	19,449	15,109	19,909	17,884
94,550	94,600	19,463	15,121	19,923	17,896
94,600	94,650	19,477	15,134	19,937	17,909
94,650	94,700	19,491	15,146	19,951	17,921
94,700	94,750	19,505	15,159	19,965	17,934
94,750	94,800	19,519	15,171	19,979	17,946
94,800	94,850	19,533	15,184	19,993	17,959
94,850	94,900	19,547	15,196	20,007	17,971
94,900	94,950	19,561	15,209	20,021	17,984
94,950	95,000	19,575	15,221	20,035	17,996
95,000					
95,000	95,050	19,589	15,234	20,049	18,009
95,050	95,100	19,603	15,246	20,063	18,021
95,100	95,150	19,617	15,259	20,077	18,034
95,150	95,200	19,631	15,271	20,091	18,046
95,200	95,250	19,645	15,284	20,105	18,059
95,250	95,300	19,659	15,296	20,119	18,071
95,300	95,350	19,673	15,309	20,133	18,084
95,350	95,400	19,687	15,321	20,147	18,096
95,400	95,450	19,701	15,334	20,161	18,109
95,450	95,500	19,715	15,346	20,175	18,121
95,500	95,550	19,729	15,359	20,189	18,134
95,550	95,600	19,743	15,371	20,203	18,146
95,600	95,650	19,757	15,384	20,217	18,159
95,650	95,700	19,771	15,396	20,231	18,171
95,700	95,750	19,785	15,409	20,245	18,184
95,750	95,800	19,799	15,421	20,259	18,196
95,800	95,850	19,813	15,434	20,273	18,209
95,850	95,900	19,827	15,446	20,287	18,221
95,900	95,950	19,841	15,459	20,301	18,234
95,950	96,000	19,855	15,471	20,315	18,246
96,000					
96,000	96,050	19,869	15,484	20,329	18,259
96,050	96,100	19,883	15,496	20,343	18,271
96,100	96,150	19,897	15,509	20,357	18,284
96,150	96,200	19,911	15,521	20,371	18,296
96,200	96,250	19,925	15,534	20,385	18,309
96,250	96,300	19,939	15,546	20,399	18,321
96,300	96,350	19,953	15,559	20,413	18,334
96,350	96,400	19,967	15,571	20,427	18,346
96,400	96,450	19,981	15,584	20,441	18,359
96,450	96,500	19,995	15,596	20,455	18,371
96,500	96,550	20,009	15,609	20,469	18,384
96,550	96,600	20,023	15,621	20,483	18,396
96,600	96,650	20,037	15,634	20,497	18,409
96,650	96,700	20,051	15,646	20,511	18,421
96,700	96,750	20,065	15,659	20,525	18,434
96,750	96,800	20,079	15,671	20,539	18,446
96,800	96,850	20,093	15,684	20,553	18,459
96,850	96,900	20,107	15,696	20,567	18,471
96,900	96,950	20,121	15,709	20,581	18,484
96,950	97,000	20,135	15,721	20,595	18,496
97,000					
97,000	97,050	20,149	15,734	20,609	18,509
97,050	97,100	20,163	15,746	20,623	18,521
97,100	97,150	20,177	15,759	20,637	18,534
97,150	97,200	20,191	15,771	20,651	18,546
97,200	97,250	20,205	15,784	20,665	18,559
97,250	97,300	20,219	15,796	20,679	18,571
97,300	97,350	20,233	15,809	20,693	18,584
97,350	97,400	20,247	15,821	20,707	18,596
97,400	97,450	20,261	15,834	20,721	18,609
97,450	97,500	20,275	15,846	20,735	18,621
97,500	97,550	20,289	15,859	20,749	18,634
97,550	97,600	20,303	15,871	20,763	18,646
97,600	97,650	20,317	15,884	20,777	18,659
97,650	97,700	20,331	15,896	20,791	18,671
97,700	97,750	20,345	15,909	20,805	18,684
97,750	97,800	20,359	15,921	20,819	18,696
97,800	97,850	20,373	15,934	20,833	18,709
97,850	97,900	20,387	15,946	20,847	18,721
97,900	97,950	20,401	15,959	20,861	18,734
97,950	98,000	20,415	15,971	20,875	18,746
98,000					
98,000	98,050	20,429	15,984	20,889	18,759
98,050	98,100	20,443	15,996	20,903	18,771
98,100	98,150	20,457	16,009	20,917	18,784
98,150	98,200	20,471	16,021	20,931	18,796
98,200	98,250	20,485	16,034	20,945	18,809
98,250	98,300	20,499	16,046	20,959	18,821
98,300	98,350	20,513	16,059	20,973	18,834
98,350	98,400	20,527	16,071	20,987	18,846
98,400	98,450	20,541	16,084	21,001	18,859
98,450	98,500	20,555	16,096	21,015	18,871
98,500	98,550	20,569	16,109	21,029	18,884
98,550	98,600	20,583	16,121	21,043	18,896
98,600	98,650	20,597	16,134	21,057	18,909
98,650	98,700	20,611	16,146	21,071	18,921
98,700	98,750	20,625	16,159	21,085	18,934
98,750	98,800	20,639	16,171	21,099	18,946
98,800	98,850	20,653	16,184	21,113	18,959
98,850	98,900	20,667	16,196	21,127	18,971
98,900	98,950	20,681	16,209	21,141	18,984
98,950	99,000	20,695	16,221	21,155	18,996
99,000					
99,000	99,050	20,709	16,234	21,169	19,009
99,050	99,100	20,723	16,246	21,183	19,021
99,100	99,150	20,737	16,259	21,197	19,034
99,150	99,200	20,751	16,271	21,211	19,046
99,200	99,250	20,765	16,284	21,225	19,059
99,250	99,300	20,779	16,296	21,239	19,071
99,300	99,350	20,793	16,309	21,253	19,084
99,350	99,400	20,807	16,321	21,267	19,096
99,400	99,450	20,821	16,334	21,281	19,109
99,450	99,500	20,835	16,346	21,295	19,121
99,500	99,550	20,849	16,359	21,309	19,134
99,550	99,600	20,863	16,371	21,323	19,146
99,600	99,650	20,877	16,384	21,337	19,159
99,650	99,700	20,891	16,396	21,351	19,171
99,700	99,750	20,905	16,409	21,365	19,184
99,750	99,800	20,919	16,421	21,379	19,196
99,800	99,850	20,933	16,434	21,393	19,209
99,850	99,900	20,947	16,446	21,407	19,221
99,900	99,950	20,961	16,459	21,421	19,234
99,950	100,000	20,975	16,471	21,435	19,246

$100,000 or over
use Form 1040

* This column must also be used by a qualifying widow(er).

Appendix E

IRS Tax Forms

Included in this Appendix are copies of select IRS tax forms that are used throughout *Fundamentals of Taxation*. All of these forms are also available for download from the IRS Web site: www.irs.gov.

Form **1040** Department of the Treasury—Internal Revenue Service (99)
U.S. Individual Income Tax Return **2017** OMB No. 1545-0074 IRS Use Only—Do not write or staple in this space.

For the year Jan. 1–Dec. 31, 2017, or other tax year beginning , 2017, ending , 20 — See separate instructions.

Your first name and initial	Last name	Your social security number
If a joint return, spouse's first name and initial	Last name	Spouse's social security number
Home address (number and street). If you have a P.O. box, see instructions.	Apt. no.	▲ Make sure the SSN(s) above and on line 6c are correct.
City, town or post office, state, and ZIP code. If you have a foreign address, also complete spaces below (see instructions).		**Presidential Election Campaign** Check here if you, or your spouse if filing jointly, want $3 to go to this fund. Checking a box below will not change your tax or refund. ☐ You ☐ Spouse
Foreign country name	Foreign province/state/county	Foreign postal code

Filing Status

Check only one box.

1 ☐ Single
2 ☐ Married filing jointly (even if only one had income)
3 ☐ Married filing separately. Enter spouse's SSN above and full name here. ▶
4 ☐ Head of household (with qualifying person). (See instructions.) If the qualifying person is a child but not your dependent, enter this child's name here. ▶
5 ☐ Qualifying widow(er) (see instructions)

Exemptions

6a ☐ **Yourself.** If someone can claim you as a dependent, **do not** check box 6a . . . . .
b ☐ **Spouse** . . . . .

Boxes checked on 6a and 6b

c **Dependents:**

(1) First name Last name	(2) Dependent's social security number	(3) Dependent's relationship to you	(4) ✓ if child under age 17 qualifying for child tax credit (see instructions)
			☐
			☐
			☐
			☐

If more than four dependents, see instructions and check here ▶ ☐

No. of children on 6c who:
• lived with you
• did not live with you due to divorce or separation (see instructions)
Dependents on 6c not entered above

d Total number of exemptions claimed . . . . . **Add numbers on lines above ▶**

Income

Attach Form(s) W-2 here. Also attach Forms W-2G and 1099-R if tax was withheld.

If you did not get a W-2, see instructions.

Line	Description	Box	Line
7	Wages, salaries, tips, etc. Attach Form(s) W-2		7
8a	**Taxable** interest. Attach Schedule B if required		8a
b	**Tax-exempt** interest. **Do not** include on line 8a	8b	
9a	Ordinary dividends. Attach Schedule B if required		9a
b	Qualified dividends	9b	
10	Taxable refunds, credits, or offsets of state and local income taxes		10
11	Alimony received		11
12	Business income or (loss). Attach Schedule C or C-EZ		12
13	Capital gain or (loss). Attach Schedule D if required. If not required, check here ▶ ☐		13
14	Other gains or (losses). Attach Form 4797		14
15a	IRA distributions	15a	b Taxable amount 15b
16a	Pensions and annuities	16a	b Taxable amount 16b
17	Rental real estate, royalties, partnerships, S corporations, trusts, etc. Attach Schedule E		17
18	Farm income or (loss). Attach Schedule F		18
19	Unemployment compensation		19
20a	Social security benefits	20a	b Taxable amount 20b
21	Other income. List type and amount		21
22	Combine the amounts in the far right column for lines 7 through 21. This is your **total income** ▶		22

Adjusted Gross Income

Line	Description	Box	Line
23	Educator expenses	23	
24	Certain business expenses of reservists, performing artists, and fee-basis government officials. Attach Form 2106 or 2106-EZ	24	
25	Health savings account deduction. Attach Form 8889	25	
26	Moving expenses. Attach Form 3903	26	
27	Deductible part of self-employment tax. Attach Schedule SE	27	
28	Self-employed SEP, SIMPLE, and qualified plans	28	
29	Self-employed health insurance deduction	29	
30	Penalty on early withdrawal of savings	30	
31a	Alimony paid b Recipient's SSN ▶	31a	
32	IRA deduction	32	
33	Student loan interest deduction	33	
34	Reserved for future use	34	
35	Domestic production activities deduction. Attach Form 8903	35	
36	Add lines 23 through 35		36
37	Subtract line 36 from line 22. This is your **adjusted gross income** ▶		37

For Disclosure, Privacy Act, and Paperwork Reduction Act Notice, see separate instructions. Cat. No. 11320B Form **1040** (2017)

Source: U.S. Department of the Treasury, Internal Revenue Service, Form 1040. Washington, DC: 2017.

Form 1040 (2017) Page **2**

DRAFT AS OF August 15 DO NOT FILE

Tax and Credits

38	Amount from line 37 (adjusted gross income)		38
39a	Check if: ☐ **You** were born before January 2, 1953, ☐ Blind. ☐ **Spouse** was born before January 2, 1953, ☐ Blind. **Total boxes checked ▶ 39a**		
b	If your spouse itemizes on a separate return or you were a dual-status alien, check here ▶ 39b ☐		
40	**Itemized deductions** (from Schedule A) **or** your **standard deduction** (see left margin)		40
41	Subtract line 40 from line 38		41
42	**Exemptions.** If line 38 is $156,900 or less, multiply $4,050 by the number on line 6d. Otherwise, see instructions		42
43	**Taxable income.** Subtract line 42 from line 41. If line 42 is more than line 41, enter -0-		43
44	**Tax** (see instructions). Check if any from: **a** ☐ Form(s) 8814 **b** ☐ Form 4972 **c** ☐		44
45	**Alternative minimum tax** (see instructions). Attach Form 6251		45
46	Excess advance premium tax credit repayment. Attach Form 8962		46
47	Add lines 44, 45, and 46 ▶		47
48	Foreign tax credit. Attach Form 1116 if required	48	
49	Credit for child and dependent care expenses. Attach Form 2441	49	
50	Education credits from Form 8863, line 19	50	
51	Retirement savings contributions credit. Attach Form 8880	51	
52	Child tax credit. Attach Schedule 8812, if required	52	
53	Residential energy credit. Attach Form 5695	53	
54	Other credits from Form: **a** ☐ 3800 **b** ☐ 8801 **c** ☐	54	
55	Add lines 48 through 54. These are your **total credits**		55
56	Subtract line 55 from line 47. If line 55 is more than line 47, enter -0- ▶		56

Standard Deduction for—
• People who check any box on line 39a or 39b **or** who can be claimed as a dependent, see instructions.
• All others:
Single or Married filing separately, $6,350
Married filing jointly or Qualifying widow(er), $12,700
Head of household, $9,350

Other Taxes

57	Self-employment tax. Attach Schedule SE	57
58	Unreported social security and Medicare tax from Form: **a** ☐ 4137 **b** ☐ 8919	58
59	Additional tax on IRAs, other qualified retirement plans, etc. Attach Form 5329 if required	59
60a	Household employment taxes from Schedule H	60a
b	First-time homebuyer credit repayment. Attach Form 5405 if required	60b
61	Health care: individual responsibility (see instructions) Full-year coverage ☐	61
62	Taxes from: **a** ☐ Form 8959 **b** ☐ Form 8960 **c** ☐ Instructions; enter code(s)	62
63	Add lines 56 through 62. This is your **total tax** ▶	63

Payments

If you have a qualifying child, attach Schedule EIC.

64	Federal income tax withheld from Forms W-2 and 1099	64	
65	2017 estimated tax payments and amount applied from 2016 return	65	
66a	**Earned income credit (EIC)**	66a	
b	Nontaxable combat pay election 66b		
67	Additional child tax credit. Attach Schedule 8812	67	
68	American opportunity credit from Form 8863, line 8	68	
69	Net premium tax credit. Attach Form 8962	69	
70	Amount paid with request for extension to file	70	
71	Excess social security and tier 1 RRTA tax withheld	71	
72	Credit for federal tax on fuels. Attach Form 4136	72	
73	Credits from Form: **a** ☐ 2439 **b** ☐ Reserved **c** ☐ 8885 **d** ☐	73	
74	Add lines 64, 65, 66a, and 67 through 73. These are your **total payments** ▶		74

Refund

75	If line 74 is more than line 63, subtract line 63 from line 74. This is the amount you **overpaid**		75
76a	Amount of line 75 you want **refunded to you.** If Form 8888 is attached, check here ▶ ☐		76a
▶ b	Routing number ▶ **c** Type: ☐ Checking ☐ Savings		
▶ d	Account number		
77	Amount of line 75 you want **applied to your 2018 estimated tax** ▶	77	

Direct deposit? See instructions.

Amount You Owe

78	**Amount you owe.** Subtract line 74 from line 63. For details on how to pay, see instructions ▶		78
79	Estimated tax penalty (see instructions)	79	

Third Party Designee

Do you want to allow another person to discuss this return with the IRS (see instructions)? ☐ **Yes.** Complete below. ☐ **No**

Designee's name ▶ Phone no. ▶ Personal identification number (PIN) ▶

Sign Here

Joint return? See instructions. Keep a copy for your records.

Under penalties of perjury, I declare that I have examined this return and accompanying schedules and statements, and to the best of my knowledge and belief, they are true, correct, and accurately list all amounts and sources of income I received during the tax year. Declaration of preparer (other than taxpayer) is based on all information of which preparer has any knowledge.

Your signature	Date	Your occupation	Daytime phone number
Spouse's signature. If a joint return, **both** must sign.	Date	Spouse's occupation	If the IRS sent you an Identity Protection PIN, enter it here (see inst.)

Paid Preparer Use Only

Print/Type preparer's name	Preparer's signature	Date	Check ☐ if self-employed	PTIN
Firm's name ▶			Firm's EIN ▶	
Firm's address ▶			Phone no.	

Go to *www.irs.gov/Form1040* for instructions and the latest information. Form **1040** (2017)

Form **1040A** Department of the Treasury—Internal Revenue Service
U.S. Individual Income Tax Return (99) **2017** IRS Use Only—Do not write or staple in this space.

Your first name and initial	Last name	OMB No. 1545-0074 **Your social security number**
If a joint return, spouse's first name and initial	Last name	**Spouse's social security number**
Home address (number and street). If you have a P.O. box, see instructions.	Apt. no.	▲ Make sure the SSN(s) above and on line 6c are correct.
City, town or post office, state, and ZIP code. If you have a foreign address, also complete spaces below (see instructions).		**Presidential Election Campaign** Check here if you, or your spouse if filing jointly, want $3 to go to this fund. Checking a box below will not change your tax or refund. ☐ You ☐ Spouse
Foreign country name	Foreign province/state/county	Foreign postal code

Filing status
Check only one box.

1 ☐ Single
2 ☐ Married filing jointly (even if only one had income)
3 ☐ Married filing separately. Enter spouse's SSN above and full name here. ▶
4 ☐ Head of household (with qualifying person). (See instructions.) If the qualifying person is a child but not your dependent, enter this child's name here. ▶
5 ☐ Qualifying widow(er) (see instructions)

Exemptions

6a ☐ **Yourself.** If someone can claim you as a dependent, **do not** check box 6a.
b ☐ **Spouse**

Boxes checked on 6a and 6b

c **Dependents:**

If more than six dependents, see instructions.

(1) First name	Last name	(2) Dependent's social security number	(3) Dependent's relationship to you	(4) ✓ if child under age 17 qualifying for child tax credit (see instructions)
				☐
				☐
				☐
				☐
				☐
				☐

No. of children on 6c who:
• lived with you
• did not live with you due to divorce or separation (see instructions)
Dependents on 6c not entered above

d Total number of exemptions claimed. Add numbers on lines above ▶

Income

Attach Form(s) W-2 here. Also attach Form(s) 1099-R if tax was withheld.

If you did not get a W-2, see instructions.

7	Wages, salaries, tips, etc. Attach Form(s) W-2.		7
8a	**Taxable** interest. Attach Schedule B if required.		8a
b	**Tax-exempt** interest. **Do not** include on line 8a.	8b	
9a	Ordinary dividends. Attach Schedule B if required.		9a
b	Qualified dividends (see instructions).	9b	
10	Capital gain distributions (see instructions).		10
11a	IRA distributions.	11a	**11b** Taxable amount (see instructions). 11b
12a	Pensions and annuities.	12a	**12b** Taxable amount (see instructions). 12b
13	Unemployment compensation and Alaska Permanent Fund dividends.		13
14a	Social security benefits.	14a	**14b** Taxable amount (see instructions). 14b
15	Add lines 7 through 14b (far right column). This is your **total income.** ▶		15

Adjusted gross income

16	Educator expenses (see instructions).	16	
17	IRA deduction (see instructions).	17	
18	Student loan interest deduction (see instructions).	18	
19	Reserved for future use.	19	
20	Add lines 16 through 19. These are your **total adjustments.**		20
21	Subtract line 20 from line 15. This is your **adjusted gross income.** ▶		21

For Disclosure, Privacy Act, and Paperwork Reduction Act Notice, see separate instructions. Cat. No. 11327A Form **1040A** (2017)

Source: U.S. Department of the Treasury, Internal Revenue Service, Form 1040A. Washington, DC: 2017.

Form 1040A (2017) Page **2**

Tax, credits, and payments

22	Enter the amount from line 21 (adjusted gross income).		22
23a	Check if: ☐ **You** were born before January 2, 1953, ☐ Blind; ☐ **Spouse** was born before January 2, 1953, ☐ Blind. **Total boxes checked** ▶ 23a ☐		
b	If you are married filing separately and your spouse itemizes deductions, check here ▶ 23b ☐		
24	Enter your **standard deduction**.		24
25	Subtract line 24 from line 22. If line 24 is more than line 22, enter -0-.		25
26	**Exemptions.** Multiply $4,050 by the number on line 6d.		26
27	Subtract line 26 from line 25. If line 26 is more than line 25, enter -0-. This is your **taxable income.** ▶		27
28	**Tax,** including any alternative minimum tax (see instructions).	28	
29	Excess advance premium tax credit repayment. Attach Form 8962.	29	
30	Add lines 28 and 29.		30
31	Credit for child and dependent care expenses. Attach Form 2441.	31	
32	Credit for the elderly or the disabled. Attach Schedule R.	32	
33	Education credits from Form 8863, line 19.	33	
34	Retirement savings contributions credit. Attach Form 8880.	34	
35	Child tax credit. Attach Schedule 8812, if required.	35	
36	Add lines 31 through 35. These are your **total credits.**		36
37	Subtract line 36 from line 30. If line 36 is more than line 30, enter -0-.		37
38	Health care: individual responsibility (see instructions). Full-year coverage ☐		38
39	Add line 37 and line 38. This is your **total tax.**		39
40	Federal income tax withheld from Forms W-2 and 1099.	40	
41	2017 estimated tax payments and amount applied from 2016 return.	41	
42a	**Earned income credit (EIC).**	42a	
b	Nontaxable combat pay election. 42b		
43	Additional child tax credit. Attach Schedule 8812.	43	
44	American opportunity credit from Form 8863, line 8.	44	
45	Net premium tax credit. Attach Form 8962.	45	
46	Add lines 40, 41, 42a, 43, 44, and 45. These are your **total payments.** ▶		46

Standard Deduction for—
- People who check any box on line 23a or 23b **or** who can be claimed as a dependent, see instructions.
- All others:

Single or Married filing separately, $6,350

Married filing jointly or Qualifying widow(er), $12,700

Head of household, $9,350

If you have a qualifying child, attach Schedule EIC.

Refund

47	If line 46 is more than line 39, subtract line 39 from line 46. This is the amount you **overpaid.**	47
48a	Amount of line 47 you want **refunded to you.** If Form 8888 is attached, check here ▶ ☐	48a
▶ b	Routing number ☐☐☐☐☐☐☐☐☐ ▶ c Type: ☐ Checking ☐ Savings	
▶ d	Account number ☐☐☐☐☐☐☐☐☐☐☐☐☐☐☐☐☐	
49	Amount of line 47 you want **applied to your 2018 estimated tax.** 49	

Direct deposit? See instructions and fill in 48b, 48c, and 48d or Form 8888.

Amount you owe

50	**Amount you owe.** Subtract line 46 from line 39. For details on how to pay, see instructions. ▶	50
51	Estimated tax penalty (see instructions). 51	

Third party designee

Do you want to allow another person to discuss this return with the IRS (see instructions)? ☐ **Yes.** Complete the following. ☐ **No**

Designee's name ▶ Phone no. ▶ Personal identification number (PIN) ▶

Sign here

Joint return? See instructions. Keep a copy for your records.

Under penalties of perjury, I declare that I have examined this return and accompanying schedules and statements, and to the best of my knowledge and belief, they are true, correct, and accurately list all amounts and sources of income I received during the tax year. Declaration of preparer (other than the taxpayer) is based on all information of which the preparer has any knowledge.

Your signature	Date	Your occupation	Daytime phone number
Spouse's signature. If a joint return, **both** must sign.	Date	Spouse's occupation	If the IRS sent you an Identity Protection PIN, enter it here (see inst.)

Paid preparer use only

Print/Type preparer's name	Preparer's signature	Date	Check ▶ ☐ if self-employed	PTIN
Firm's name ▶			Firm's EIN ▶	
Firm's address ▶			Phone no.	

Go to *www.irs.gov/Form1040A* for instructions and the latest information. Form **1040A** (2017)

Form **1040EZ**

Department of the Treasury—Internal Revenue Service

Income Tax Return for Single and Joint Filers With No Dependents (99) **2017**

OMB No. 1545-0074

Your first name and initial	Last name	Your social security number
If a joint return, spouse's first name and initial	Last name	Spouse's social security number
Home address (number and street). If you have a P.O. box, see instructions.	Apt. no.	▲ Make sure the SSN(s) above are correct.
City, town or post office, state, and ZIP code. If you have a foreign address, also complete spaces below (see instructions).		**Presidential Election Campaign** Check here if you, or your spouse if filing jointly, want $3 to go to this fund. Checking a box below will not change your tax or refund. ☐ You ☐ Spouse
Foreign country name	Foreign province/state/county	Foreign postal code

Income

Attach Form(s) W-2 here.

Enclose, but do not attach, any payment.

1 Wages, salaries, and tips. This should be shown in box 1 of your Form(s) W-2. Attach your Form(s) W-2. **1**

2 Taxable interest. If the total is over $1,500, you cannot use Form 1040EZ. **2**

3 Unemployment compensation and Alaska Permanent Fund dividends (see instructions). **3**

4 Add lines 1, 2, and 3. This is your **adjusted gross income.** **4**

5 If someone can claim you (or your spouse if a joint return) as a dependent, check the applicable box(es) below and enter the amount from the worksheet on back.
☐ **You** ☐ **Spouse**
If no one can claim you (or your spouse if a joint return), enter $10,400 if **single;** $20,800 if **married filing jointly.** See back for explanation. **5**

6 Subtract line 5 from line 4. If line 5 is larger than line 4, enter -0-. This is your **taxable income.** ▶ **6**

Payments, Credits, and Tax

7 Federal income tax withheld from Form(s) W-2 and 1099. **7**

8a **Earned income credit (EIC)** (see instructions) **8a**

b Nontaxable combat pay election. 8b

9 Add lines 7 and 8a. These are your **total payments and credits.** ▶ **9**

10 **Tax.** Use the amount on **line 6 above** to find your tax in the tax table in the instructions. Then, enter the tax from the table on this line. **10**

11 Health care: individual responsibility (see instructions) Full-year coverage ☐ **11**

12 Add lines 10 and 11. This is your **total tax.** **12**

Refund

Have it directly deposited! See instructions and fill in 13b, 13c, and 13d, or Form 8888.

13a If line 9 is larger than line 12, subtract line 12 from line 9. This is your **refund.** If Form 8888 is attached, check here ▶ ☐ **13a**

▶ b Routing number ▶ c Type: ☐ Checking ☐ Savings

▶ d Account number

Amount You Owe

14 If line 12 is larger than line 9, subtract line 9 from line 12. This is the **amount you owe.** For details on how to pay, see instructions. ▶ **14**

Third Party Designee

Do you want to allow another person to discuss this return with the IRS (see instructions)? ☐ **Yes.** Complete below. ☐ **No**

Designee's name ▶ Phone no. ▶ Personal identification number (PIN) ▶

Sign Here

Joint return? See instructions.

Keep a copy for your records.

Under penalties of perjury, I declare that I have examined this return and, to the best of my knowledge and belief, it is true, correct, and accurately lists all amounts and sources of income I received during the tax year. Declaration of preparer (other than the taxpayer) is based on all information of which the preparer has any knowledge.

Your signature	Date	Your occupation	Daytime phone number
Spouse's signature. If a joint return, **both** must sign.	Date	Spouse's occupation	If the IRS sent you an Identity Protection PIN, enter it here (see inst.)

Paid Preparer Use Only

Print/Type preparer's name	Preparer's signature	Date	Check ☐ if self-employed	PTIN
Firm's name ▶		Firm's EIN ▶		
Firm's address ▶		Phone no.		

For Disclosure, Privacy Act, and Paperwork Reduction Act Notice, see separate instructions. Cat. No. 11329W Form **1040EZ** (2017)

Source: U.S. Department of the Treasury, Internal Revenue Service, Form 1040EZ. Washington, DC: 2017.

Form **2106**

Department of the Treasury
Internal Revenue Service (99)

Employee Business Expenses

▶ Attach to Form 1040 or Form 1040NR.

▶ Go to *www.irs.gov/Form2106* for instructions and the latest information.

OMB No. 1545-0074

2017

Attachment Sequence No. **129**

Your name	Occupation in which you incurred expenses	Social security number

Part I **Employee Business Expenses and Reimbursements**

Step 1 Enter Your Expenses		**Column A** Other Than Meals and Entertainment	**Column B** Meals and Entertainment
1 Vehicle expense from line 22 or line 29. (Rural mail carriers: See instructions.)	1		
2 Parking fees, tolls, and transportation, including train, bus, etc., that **didn't** involve overnight travel or commuting to and from work	2		
3 Travel expense while away from home overnight, including lodging, airplane, car rental, etc. **Don't** include meals and entertainment.	3		
4 Business expenses not included on lines 1 through 3. **Don't** include meals and entertainment	4		
5 Meals and entertainment expenses (see instructions)	5		
6 **Total expenses.** In Column A, add lines 1 through 4 and enter the result. In Column B, enter the amount from line 5	6		

Note: If you weren't reimbursed for any expenses in Step 1, skip line 7 and enter the amount from line 6 on line 8.

Step 2 Enter Reimbursements Received From Your Employer for Expenses Listed in Step 1

7 Enter reimbursements received from your employer that **weren't** reported to you in box 1 of Form W-2. Include any reimbursements reported under code "L" in box 12 of your Form W-2 (see instructions).	7		

Step 3 Figure Expenses To Deduct on Schedule A (Form 1040 or Form 1040NR)

8 Subtract line 7 from line 6. If zero or less, enter -0-. However, if line 7 is greater than line 6 in Column A, report the excess as income on Form 1040, line 7 (or on Form 1040NR, line 8)	8		
Note: If **both columns** of line 8 are zero, you can't deduct employee business expenses. Stop here and attach Form 2106 to your return.			
9 In Column A, enter the amount from line 8. In Column B, multiply line 8 by 50% (0.50). (Employees subject to Department of Transportation (DOT) hours of service limits: Multiply meal expenses incurred while away from home on business by 80% (0.80) instead of 50%. For details, see instructions.)	9		
10 Add the amounts on line 9 of both columns and enter the total here. **Also, enter the total on Schedule A (Form 1040), line 21** (or on **Schedule A (Form 1040NR), line 7**). (Armed Forces reservists, qualified performing artists, fee-basis state or local government officials, and individuals with disabilities: See the instructions for special rules on where to enter the total.) ▶	10		

For Paperwork Reduction Act Notice, see your tax return instructions. Cat. No. 11700N Form **2106** (2017)

Source: U.S. Department of the Treasury, Internal Revenue Service, Form 2106. Washington, DC: 2017.

(continued)

(concluded)

Form 2106 (2017) Page 2

Part II Vehicle Expenses

Section A—General Information (You must complete this section if you are claiming vehicle expenses.)		**(a)** Vehicle 1	**(b)** Vehicle 2
11 Enter the date the vehicle was placed in service	11	/ /	/ /
12 Total miles the vehicle was driven during 2017	12	miles	miles
13 Business miles included on line 12	13	miles	miles
14 Percent of business use. Divide line 13 by line 12	14	%	%
15 Average daily roundtrip commuting distance	15	miles	miles
16 Commuting miles included on line 12	16	miles	miles
17 Other miles. Add lines 13 and 16 and subtract the total from line 12	17	miles	miles

18 Was your vehicle available for personal use during off-duty hours?	☐ Yes	☐ No
19 Do you (or your spouse) have another vehicle available for personal use?	☐ Yes	☐ No
20 Do you have evidence to support your deduction?	☐ Yes	☐ No
21 If "Yes," is the evidence written?	☐ Yes	☐ No

Section B—Standard Mileage Rate (See the instructions for Part II to find out whether to complete this section or Section C.)

22 Multiply line 13 by 53.5¢ (0.535). Enter the result here and on line 1	22	

Section C—Actual Expenses		**(a)** Vehicle 1	**(b)** Vehicle 2
23 Gasoline, oil, repairs, vehicle insurance, etc.	23		
24a Vehicle rentals	24a		
b Inclusion amount (see instructions)	24b		
c Subtract line 24b from line 24a	24c		
25 Value of employer-provided vehicle (applies only if 100% of annual lease value was included on Form W-2—see instructions)	25		
26 Add lines 23, 24c, and 25.	26		
27 Multiply line 26 by the percentage on line 14	27		
28 Depreciation (see instructions)	28		
29 Add lines 27 and 28. Enter total here and on line 1	29		

Section D—Depreciation of Vehicles (Use this section only if you owned the vehicle and are completing Section C for the vehicle.)

		(a) Vehicle 1	**(b)** Vehicle 2
30 Enter cost or other basis (see instructions)	30		
31 Enter section 179 deduction and special allowance (see instructions)	31		
32 Multiply line 30 by line 14 (see instructions if you claimed the section 179 deduction or special allowance)	32		
33 Enter depreciation method and percentage (see instructions)	33		
34 Multiply line 32 by the percentage on line 33 (see instructions)	34		
35 Add lines 31 and 34	35		
36 Enter the applicable limit explained in the line 36 instructions	36		
37 Multiply line 36 by the percentage on line 14	37		
38 Enter the **smaller** of line 35 or line 37. If you skipped lines 36 and 37, enter the amount from line 35. Also enter this amount on line 28 above	38		

Form **2106** (2017)

Form **4562**

Department of the Treasury
Internal Revenue Service (99)

Depreciation and Amortization

(Including Information on Listed Property)

► **Attach to your tax return.**

► **Go to *www.irs.gov/Form4562* for instructions and the latest information.**

OMB No. 1545-0172

2017

Attachment Sequence No. **179**

Name(s) shown on return	Business or activity to which this form relates	**Identifying number**

Part I Election To Expense Certain Property Under Section 179
Note: If you have any listed property, complete Part V before you complete Part I.

1	Maximum amount (see instructions)	1	
2	Total cost of section 179 property placed in service (see instructions)	2	
3	Threshold cost of section 179 property before reduction in limitation (see instructions)	3	
4	Reduction in limitation. Subtract line 3 from line 2. If zero or less, enter -0-	4	
5	Dollar limitation for tax year. Subtract line 4 from line 1. If zero or less, enter -0-. If married filing separately, see instructions	5	

6	(a) Description of property	(b) Cost (business use only)	(c) Elected cost

7	Listed property. Enter the amount from line 29	7	
8	Total elected cost of section 179 property. Add amounts in column (c), lines 6 and 7	8	
9	Tentative deduction. Enter the **smaller** of line 5 or line 8	9	
10	Carryover of disallowed deduction from line 13 of your 2016 Form 4562	10	
11	Business income limitation. Enter the smaller of business income (not less than zero) or line 5 (see instructions)	11	
12	Section 179 expense deduction. Add lines 9 and 10, but don't enter more than line 11	12	
13	Carryover of disallowed deduction to 2018. Add lines 9 and 10, less line 12 ►	13	

Note: Don't use Part II or Part III below for listed property. Instead, use Part V.

Part II Special Depreciation Allowance and Other Depreciation (Don't include listed property.**)** (See instructions.)

14	Special depreciation allowance for qualified property (other than listed property) placed in service during the tax year (see instructions)	14	
15	Property subject to section 168(f)(1) election	15	
16	Other depreciation (including ACRS)	16	

Part III MACRS Depreciation (Don't include listed property.**)** (See instructions.)

Section A

17	MACRS deductions for assets placed in service in tax years beginning before 2017	17	
18	If you are electing to group any assets placed in service during the tax year into one or more general asset accounts, check here ► ☐		

Section B—Assets Placed in Service During 2017 Tax Year Using the General Depreciation System

(a) Classification of property	(b) Month and year placed in service	(c) Basis for depreciation (business/investment use only—see instructions)	(d) Recovery period	(e) Convention	(f) Method	(g) Depreciation deduction
19a 3-year property						
b 5-year property						
c 7-year property						
d 10-year property						
e 15-year property						
f 20-year property						
g 25-year property			25 yrs.		S/L	
h Residential rental property			27.5 yrs.	MM	S/L	
			27.5 yrs.	MM	S/L	
i Nonresidential real property			39 yrs.	MM	S/L	
				MM	S/L	

Section C—Assets Placed in Service During 2017 Tax Year Using the Alternative Depreciation System

20a Class life					S/L	
b 12-year			12 yrs.		S/L	
c 40-year			40 yrs.	MM	S/L	

Part IV Summary (See instructions.)

21	Listed property. Enter amount from line 28	21	
22	**Total.** Add amounts from line 12, lines 14 through 17, lines 19 and 20 in column (g), and line 21. Enter here and on the appropriate lines of your return. Partnerships and S corporations—see instructions	22	
23	For assets shown above and placed in service during the current year, enter the portion of the basis attributable to section 263A costs	23	

For Paperwork Reduction Act Notice, see separate instructions. Cat. No. 12906N Form **4562** (2017)

Source: U.S. Department of the Treasury, Internal Revenue Service, Form 4562. Washington, DC: 2017.

(continued)

(concluded)

Form 4562 (2017) Page **2**

Part V **Listed Property** (Include automobiles, certain other vehicles, certain aircraft, certain computers, and property used for entertainment, recreation, or amusement.)

Note: For any vehicle for which you are using the standard mileage rate or deducting lease expense, complete **only** 24a, 24b, columns (a) through (c) of Section A, all of Section B, and Section C if applicable.

Section A—Depreciation and Other Information (Caution: See the instructions for limits for passenger automobiles.**)**

24a Do you have evidence to support the business/investment use claimed? ☐ **Yes** ☐ **No** **24b** If "Yes," is the evidence written? ☐ **Yes** ☐ **No**

(a) Type of property (list vehicles first)	**(b)** Date placed in service	**(c)** Business/investment use percentage	**(d)** Cost or other basis	**(e)** Basis for depreciation (business/investment use only)	**(f)** Recovery period	**(g)** Method/Convention	**(h)** Depreciation deduction	**(i)** Elected section 179 cost
25 Special depreciation allowance for qualified listed property placed in service during the tax year and used more than 50% in a qualified business use (see instructions) .							**25**	
26 Property used more than 50% in a qualified business use:								
		%						
		%						
		%						
27 Property used 50% or less in a qualified business use:								
		%				S/L –		
		%				S/L –		
		%				S/L –		
28 Add amounts in column (h), lines 25 through 27. Enter here and on line 21, page 1 .							**28**	
29 Add amounts in column (i), line 26. Enter here and on line 7, page 1								**29**

Section B—Information on Use of Vehicles

Complete this section for vehicles used by a sole proprietor, partner, or other "more than 5% owner," or related person. If you provided vehicles to your employees, first answer the questions in Section C to see if you meet an exception to completing this section for those vehicles.

	(a) Vehicle 1		**(b)** Vehicle 2		**(c)** Vehicle 3		**(d)** Vehicle 4		**(e)** Vehicle 5		**(f)** Vehicle 6	
30 Total business/investment miles driven during the year (**don't** include commuting miles) .												
31 Total commuting miles driven during the year												
32 Total other personal (noncommuting) miles driven												
33 Total miles driven during the year. Add lines 30 through 32												
	Yes	**No**	**Yes**	**No**	**Yes**	**No**	**Yes**	**No**	**Yes**	**No**	**Yes**	**No**
34 Was the vehicle available for personal use during off-duty hours?												
35 Was the vehicle used primarily by a more than 5% owner or related person? . .												
36 Is another vehicle available for personal use?												

Section C—Questions for Employers Who Provide Vehicles for Use by Their Employees

Answer these questions to determine if you meet an exception to completing Section B for vehicles used by employees who **aren't** more than 5% owners or related persons (see instructions).

	Yes	**No**
37 Do you maintain a written policy statement that prohibits all personal use of vehicles, including commuting, by your employees?		
38 Do you maintain a written policy statement that prohibits personal use of vehicles, except commuting, by your employees? See the instructions for vehicles used by corporate officers, directors, or 1% or more owners . .		
39 Do you treat all use of vehicles by employees as personal use?		
40 Do you provide more than five vehicles to your employees, obtain information from your employees about the use of the vehicles, and retain the information received?		
41 Do you meet the requirements concerning qualified automobile demonstration use? (See instructions.) . . .		

Note: If your answer to 37, 38, 39, 40, or 41 is "Yes," don't complete Section B for the covered vehicles.

Part VI **Amortization**

(a) Description of costs	**(b)** Date amortization begins	**(c)** Amortizable amount	**(d)** Code section	**(e)** Amortization period or percentage	**(f)** Amortization for this year
42 Amortization of costs that begins during your 2017 tax year (see instructions):					
43 Amortization of costs that began before your 2017 tax year				**43**	
44 **Total.** Add amounts in column (f). See the instructions for where to report				**44**	

Form **4562** (2017)

Form **4797**

Department of the Treasury
Internal Revenue Service

Sales of Business Property

(Also Involuntary Conversions and Recapture Amounts Under Sections 179 and 280F(b)(2))

► Attach to your tax return.

► Go to *www.irs.gov/Form4797* for instructions and the latest information.

OMB No. 1545-0184

2017

Attachment Sequence No. **27**

Name(s) shown on return | **Identifying number**

1 Enter the gross proceeds from sales or exchanges reported to you for 2017 on Form(s) 1099-B or 1099-S (or substitute statement) that you are including on line 2, 10, or 20. See instructions **1**

Part I Sales or Exchanges of Property Used in a Trade or Business and Involuntary Conversions From Other Than Casualty or Theft—Most Property Held More Than 1 Year (see instructions)

2	**(a)** Description of property	**(b)** Date acquired (mo., day, yr.)	**(c)** Date sold (mo., day, yr.)	**(d)** Gross sales price	**(e)** Depreciation allowed or allowable since acquisition	**(f)** Cost or other basis, plus improvements and expense of sale	**(g) Gain or (loss)** Subtract (f) from the sum of (d) and (e)

3 Gain, if any, from Form 4684, line 39 . . . . **3**

4 Section 1231 gain from installment sales from Form 6252, line 26 or 37 . . . . . . **4**

5 Section 1231 gain or (loss) from like-kind exchanges from Form 8824 . . . . . . **5**

6 Gain, if any, from line 32, from other than casualty or theft **6**

7 Combine lines 2 through 6. Enter the gain or (loss) here and on the appropriate line as follows: **7**

Partnerships (except electing large partnerships) and S corporations. Report the gain or (loss) following the instructions for Form 1065, Schedule K, line 10, or Form 1120S, Schedule K, line 9. Skip lines 8, 9, 11, and 12 below.

Individuals, partners, S corporation shareholders, and all others. If line 7 is zero or a loss, enter the amount from line 7 on line 11 below and skip lines 8 and 9. If line 7 is a gain and you didn't have any prior year section 1231 losses, or they were recaptured in an earlier year, enter the gain from line 7 as a long-term capital gain on the Schedule D filed with your return and skip lines 8, 9, 11, and 12 below.

8 Nonrecaptured net section 1231 losses from prior years. See instructions **8**

9 Subtract line 8 from line 7. If zero or less, enter -0-. If line 9 is zero, enter the gain from line 7 on line 12 below. If line 9 is more than zero, enter the amount from line 8 on line 12 below and enter the gain from line 9 as a long-term capital gain on the Schedule D filed with your return. See instructions **9**

Part II Ordinary Gains and Losses (see instructions)

10 Ordinary gains and losses not included on lines 11 through 16 (include property held 1 year or less):

11 Loss, if any, from line 7 . . . . **11** ( )

12 Gain, if any, from line 7 or amount from line 8, if applicable **12**

13 Gain, if any, from line 31 . . . . **13**

14 Net gain or (loss) from Form 4684, lines 31 and 38a **14**

15 Ordinary gain from installment sales from Form 6252, line 25 or 36 . . . . . . **15**

16 Ordinary gain or (loss) from like-kind exchanges from Form 8824. . . . . . **16**

17 Combine lines 10 through 16 . . . . **17**

18 For all except individual returns, enter the amount from line 17 on the appropriate line of your return and skip lines a and b below. For individual returns, complete lines a and b below:

a If the loss on line 11 includes a loss from Form 4684, line 35, column (b)(ii), enter that part of the loss here. Enter the part of the loss from income-producing property on Schedule A (Form 1040), line 28, and the part of the loss from property used as an employee on Schedule A (Form 1040), line 23. Identify as from "Form 4797, line 18a." See instructions . . **18a**

b Redetermine the gain or (loss) on line 17 excluding the loss, if any, on line 18a. Enter here and on Form 1040, line 14 **18b**

For Paperwork Reduction Act Notice, see separate instructions. Cat. No. 13086I Form **4797** (2017)

Source: U.S. Department of the Treasury, Internal Revenue Service, Form 4797. Washington, DC: 2017.

(continued)

(concluded)

Form 4797 (2017) Page **2**

Part III Gain From Disposition of Property Under Sections 1245, 1250, 1252, 1254, and 1255 (see instructions)

19 (a) Description of section 1245, 1250, 1252, 1254, or 1255 property:	(b) Date acquired (mo., day, yr.)	(c) Date sold (mo., day, yr.)
A		
B		
C		
D		

These columns relate to the properties on lines 19A through 19D. ▶		Property A	Property B	Property C	Property D
20 Gross sales price (**Note:** *See line 1 before completing.*)	20				
21 Cost or other basis plus expense of sale	21				
22 Depreciation (or depletion) allowed or allowable	22				
23 Adjusted basis. Subtract line 22 from line 21	23				
24 Total gain. Subtract line 23 from line 20	24				
25 **If section 1245 property:**					
a Depreciation allowed or allowable from line 22	25a				
b Enter the **smaller** of line 24 or 25a	25b				
26 **If section 1250 property:** If straight line depreciation was used, enter -0- on line 26g, except for a corporation subject to section 291.					
a Additional depreciation after 1975. See instructions	26a				
b Applicable percentage multiplied by the **smaller** of line 24 or line 26a. See instructions	26b				
c Subtract line 26a from line 24. If residential rental property **or** line 24 isn't more than line 26a, skip lines 26d and 26e	26c				
d Additional depreciation after 1969 and before 1976	26d				
e Enter the **smaller** of line 26c or 26d	26e				
f Section 291 amount (corporations only)	26f				
g Add lines 26b, 26e, and 26f	26g				
27 **If section 1252 property:** Skip this section if you didn't dispose of farmland or if this form is being completed for a partnership (other than an electing large partnership).					
a Soil, water, and land clearing expenses	27a				
b Line 27a multiplied by applicable percentage. See instructions	27b				
c Enter the **smaller** of line 24 or 27b	27c				
28 **If section 1254 property:**					
a Intangible drilling and development costs, expenditures for development of mines and other natural deposits, mining exploration costs, and depletion. See instructions	28a				
b Enter the **smaller** of line 24 or 28a	28b				
29 **If section 1255 property:**					
a Applicable percentage of payments excluded from income under section 126. See instructions	29a				
b Enter the **smaller** of line 24 or 29a. See instructions	29b				

Summary of Part III Gains. Complete property columns A through D through line 29b before going to line 30.

30 Total gains for all properties. Add property columns A through D, line 24	30	
31 Add property columns A through D, lines 25b, 26g, 27c, 28b, and 29b. Enter here and on line 13	31	
32 Subtract line 31 from line 30. Enter the portion from casualty or theft on Form 4684, line 33. Enter the portion from other than casualty or theft on Form 4797, line 6	32	

Part IV Recapture Amounts Under Sections 179 and 280F(b)(2) When Business Use Drops to 50% or Less (see instructions)

		(a) Section 179	(b) Section 280F(b)(2)
33 Section 179 expense deduction or depreciation allowable in prior years	33		
34 Recomputed depreciation. See instructions	34		
35 Recapture amount. Subtract line 34 from line 33. See the instructions for where to report	35		

Form **4797** (2017)

SCHEDULE A (Form 1040)

Department of the Treasury Internal Revenue Service (99)

Itemized Deductions

▶ Go to *www.irs.gov/ScheduleA* for instructions and the latest information.

▶ Attach to Form 1040.

OMB No. 1545-0074

2017

Attachment Sequence No. **07**

Name(s) shown on Form 1040 | **Your social security number**

Medical and Dental Expenses		**Caution:** Do not include expenses reimbursed or paid by others.				
	1	Medical and dental expenses (see instructions)	1			
	2	Enter amount from Form 1040, line 38 [2]				
	3	Multiply line 2 by 10% (0.10)	3			
	4	Subtract line 3 from line 1. If line 3 is more than line 1, enter -0-			4	
Taxes You Paid	5	State and local **(check only one box):**				
		a ☐ Income taxes, **or** / b ☐ General sales taxes }	5			
	6	Real estate taxes (see instructions)	6			
	7	Personal property taxes	7			
	8	Other taxes. List type and amount ▶	8			
	9	Add lines 5 through 8			9	
Interest You Paid	10	Home mortgage interest and points reported to you on Form 1098	10			
Note: Your mortgage interest deduction may be limited (see instructions).	11	Home mortgage interest not reported to you on Form 1098. If paid to the person from whom you bought the home, see instructions and show that person's name, identifying no., and address ▶	11			
	12	Points not reported to you on Form 1098. See instructions for special rules	12			
	13	Reserved	13			
	14	Investment interest. Attach Form 4952 if required. See instructions.	14			
	15	Add lines 10 through 14			15	
Gifts to Charity	16	Gifts by cash or check. If you made any gift of $250 or more, see instructions	16			
If you made a gift and got a benefit for it, see instructions.	17	Other than by cash or check. If any gift of $250 or more, see instructions. You **must** attach Form 8283 if over $500 . . .	17			
	18	Carryover from prior year	18			
	19	Add lines 16 through 18			19	
Casualty and Theft Losses	20	Casualty or theft loss(es). Attach Form 4684. See instructions			20	
Job Expenses and Certain Miscellaneous Deductions	21	Unreimbursed employee expenses—job travel, union dues, job education, etc. Attach Form 2106 or 2106-EZ if required. See instructions. ▶	21			
	22	Tax preparation fees	22			
	23	Other expenses—investment, safe deposit box, etc. List type and amount ▶	23			
	24	Add lines 21 through 23	24			
	25	Enter amount from Form 1040, line 38 [25]				
	26	Multiply line 25 by 2% (0.02)	26			
	27	Subtract line 26 from line 24. If line 26 is more than line 24, enter -0-			27	
Other Miscellaneous Deductions	28	Other—from list in instructions. List type and amount ▶			28	
Total Itemized Deductions	29	Is Form 1040, line 38, over $156,900? ☐ **No.** Your deduction is not limited. Add the amounts in the far right column for lines 4 through 28. Also, enter this amount on Form 1040, line 40. ☐ **Yes.** Your deduction may be limited. See the Itemized Deductions Worksheet in the instructions to figure the amount to enter. } . .			29	
	30	If you elect to itemize deductions even though they are less than your standard deduction, check here . . . . ▶ ☐				

For Paperwork Reduction Act Notice, see the Instructions for Form 1040. Cat. No. 17145C **Schedule A (Form 1040) 2017**

Source: U.S. Department of the Treasury, Internal Revenue Service, SCHEDULE A (Form 1040). Washington, DC: 2017.

SCHEDULE B
(Form 1040A or 1040)

Department of the Treasury
Internal Revenue Service (99)

Interest and Ordinary Dividends

► Attach to Form 1040A or 1040.
► Go to *www.irs.gov/ScheduleB* for instructions and the latest information.

OMB No. 1545-0074
2017
Attachment Sequence No. 08

Name(s) shown on return | Your social security number

Part I Interest

(See instructions and the instructions for Form 1040A, or Form 1040, line 8a.)

Note: If you received a Form 1099-INT, Form 1099-OID, or substitute statement from a brokerage firm, list the firm's name as the payer and enter the total interest shown on that form.

			Amount
1	List name of payer. If any interest is from a seller-financed mortgage and the buyer used the property as a personal residence, see the instructions and list this interest first. Also, show that buyer's social security number and address ►	1	
2	Add the amounts on line 1	2	
3	Excludable interest on series EE and I U.S. savings bonds issued after 1989. Attach Form 8815	3	
4	Subtract line 3 from line 2. Enter the result here and on Form 1040A, or Form 1040, line 8a . . . . ►	4	

Note: If line 4 is over $1,500, you must complete Part III.

Part II Ordinary Dividends

(See instructions and the instructions for Form 1040A, or Form 1040, line 9a.)

Note: If you received a Form 1099-DIV or substitute statement from a brokerage firm, list the firm's name as the payer and enter the ordinary dividends shown on that form.

			Amount
5	List name of payer ►	5	
6	Add the amounts on line 5. Enter the total here and on Form 1040A, or Form 1040, line 9a . . . . ►	6	

Note: If line 6 is over $1,500, you must complete Part III.

Part III Foreign Accounts and Trusts

(See instructions.)

You must complete this part if you **(a)** had over $1,500 of taxable interest or ordinary dividends; **(b)** had a foreign account; or **(c)** received a distribution from, or were a grantor of, or a transferor to, a foreign trust.

		Yes	No
7a	At any time during 2017, did you have a financial interest in or signature authority over a financial account (such as a bank account, securities account, or brokerage account) located in a foreign country? See instructions		
	If "Yes," are you required to file FinCEN Form 114, Report of Foreign Bank and Financial Accounts (FBAR), to report that financial interest or signature authority? See FinCEN Form 114 and its instructions for filing requirements and exceptions to those requirements		
b	If you are required to file FinCEN Form 114, enter the name of the foreign country where the financial account is located ►		
8	During 2017, did you receive a distribution from, or were you the grantor of, or transferor to, a foreign trust? If "Yes," you may have to file Form 3520. See instructions		

For Paperwork Reduction Act Notice, see your tax return instructions. Cat. No. 17146N **Schedule B (Form 1040A or 1040) 2017**

Source: U.S. Department of the Treasury, Internal Revenue Service, SCHEDULE B (Form 1040A or 1040). Washington, DC: 2017.

SCHEDULE C (Form 1040)

Department of the Treasury Internal Revenue Service (99)

Profit or Loss From Business

(Sole Proprietorship)

▶ Go to *www.irs.gov/ScheduleC* for instructions and the latest information.

▶ Attach to Form 1040, 1040NR, or 1041; partnerships generally must file Form 1065.

OMB No. 1545-0074

2017

Attachment Sequence No. **09**

Name of proprietor | **Social security number (SSN)**

A Principal business or profession, including product or service (see instructions) | **B Enter code from instructions** ▶

C Business name. If no separate business name, leave blank. | **D Employer ID number (EIN)** (see instr.)

E Business address (including suite or room no.) ▶

City, town or post office, state, and ZIP code

F Accounting method: **(1)** ☐ Cash **(2)** ☐ Accrual **(3)** ☐ Other (specify) ▶

G Did you "materially participate" in the operation of this business during 2017? If "No," see instructions for limit on losses ☐ **Yes** ☐ **No**

H If you started or acquired this business during 2017, check here ▶ ☐

I Did you make any payments in 2017 that would require you to file Form(s) 1099? (see instructions) ☐ **Yes** ☐ **No**

J If "Yes," did you or will you file required Forms 1099? ☐ **Yes** ☐ **No**

Part I Income

1	Gross receipts or sales. See instructions for line 1 and check the box if this income was reported to you on Form W-2 and the "Statutory employee" box on that form was checked ▶ ☐	1	
2	Returns and allowances	2	
3	Subtract line 2 from line 1	3	
4	Cost of goods sold (from line 42)	4	
5	**Gross profit.** Subtract line 4 from line 3	5	
6	Other income, including federal and state gasoline or fuel tax credit or refund (see instructions)	6	
7	**Gross income.** Add lines 5 and 6 ▶	7	

Part II Expenses. Enter expenses for business use of your home **only** on line 30.

8	Advertising	8		18	Office expense (see instructions)	18	
9	Car and truck expenses (see instructions)	9		19	Pension and profit-sharing plans	19	
10	Commissions and fees	10		20	Rent or lease (see instructions):		
11	Contract labor (see instructions)	11		a	Vehicles, machinery, and equipment	20a	
12	Depletion	12		b	Other business property	20b	
13	Depreciation and section 179 expense deduction (not included in Part III) (see instructions)	13		21	Repairs and maintenance	21	
				22	Supplies (not included in Part III)	22	
				23	Taxes and licenses	23	
				24	Travel, meals, and entertainment:		
14	Employee benefit programs (other than on line 19)	14		a	Travel	24a	
15	Insurance (other than health)	15		b	Deductible meals and entertainment (see instructions)	24b	
16	Interest:			25	Utilities	25	
a	Mortgage (paid to banks, etc.)	16a		26	Wages (less employment credits)	26	
b	Other	16b		27a	Other expenses (from line 48)	27a	
17	Legal and professional services	17		b	**Reserved for future use**	27b	

28	**Total expenses** before expenses for business use of home. Add lines 8 through 27a ▶	28	
29	Tentative profit or (loss). Subtract line 28 from line 7	29	
30	Expenses for business use of your home. Do not report these expenses elsewhere. Attach Form 8829 unless using the simplified method (see instructions). **Simplified method filers only:** enter the total square footage of: (a) your home: ______ and (b) the part of your home used for business: ______ . Use the Simplified Method Worksheet in the instructions to figure the amount to enter on line 30	30	
31	**Net profit or (loss).** Subtract line 30 from line 29. • If a profit, enter on both **Form 1040, line 12** (or **Form 1040NR, line 13**) and on **Schedule SE, line 2.** (If you checked the box on line 1, see instructions). Estates and trusts, enter on **Form 1041, line 3.** • If a loss, you **must** go to line 32.	31	
32	If you have a loss, check the box that describes your investment in this activity (see instructions). • If you checked 32a, enter the loss on both **Form 1040, line 12,** (or **Form 1040NR, line 13**) and on **Schedule SE, line 2.** (If you checked the box on line 1, see the line 31 instructions). Estates and trusts, enter on **Form 1041, line 3.** • If you checked 32b, you **must** attach **Form 6198.** Your loss may be limited.	32a ☐ All investment is at risk. 32b ☐ Some investment is not at risk.	

For Paperwork Reduction Act Notice, see the separate instructions. Cat. No. 11334P **Schedule C (Form 1040) 2017**

Source: U.S. Department of the Treasury, Internal Revenue Service, SCHEDULE C (Form 1040). Washington, DC: 2017.

(continued)

(concluded)

Schedule C (Form 1040) 2017 Page 2

Part III **Cost of Goods Sold** (see instructions)

33 Method(s) used to value closing inventory: **a** ☐ Cost **b** ☐ Lower of cost or market **c** ☐ Other (attach explanation)

34 Was there any change in determining quantities, costs, or valuations between opening and closing inventory? If "Yes," attach explanation . . . ☐ **Yes** ☐ **No**

35	Inventory at beginning of year. If different from last year's closing inventory, attach explanation	**35**	
36	Purchases less cost of items withdrawn for personal use	**36**	
37	Cost of labor. Do not include any amounts paid to yourself	**37**	
38	Materials and supplies	**38**	
39	Other costs	**39**	
40	Add lines 35 through 39	**40**	
41	Inventory at end of year	**41**	
42	**Cost of goods sold.** Subtract line 41 from line 40. Enter the result here and on line 4	**42**	

Part IV **Information on Your Vehicle.** Complete this part **only** if you are claiming car or truck expenses on line 9 and are not required to file Form 4562 for this business. See the instructions for line 13 to find out if you must file Form 4562.

43 When did you place your vehicle in service for business purposes? (month, day, year) ▶ ___/___/___

44 Of the total number of miles you drove your vehicle during 2017, enter the number of miles you used your vehicle for:

a Business ________ **b** Commuting (see instructions) ________ **c** Other ________

45 Was your vehicle available for personal use during off-duty hours? ☐ **Yes** ☐ **No**

46 Do you (or your spouse) have another vehicle available for personal use? ☐ **Yes** ☐ **No**

47a Do you have evidence to support your deduction? ☐ **Yes** ☐ **No**

b If "Yes," is the evidence written? ☐ **Yes** ☐ **No**

Part V **Other Expenses.** List below business expenses not included on lines 8–26 or line 30.

48 **Total other expenses.** Enter here and on line 27a	**48**

Schedule C (Form 1040) 2017

SCHEDULE D (Form 1040)

Department of the Treasury Internal Revenue Service (99)

Capital Gains and Losses

► Attach to Form 1040 or Form 1040NR.
► Go to *www.irs.gov/ScheduleD* for instructions and the latest information.
► Use Form 8949 to list your transactions for lines 1b, 2, 3, 8b, 9, and 10.

OMB No. 1545-0074

2017

Attachment Sequence No. 12

Name(s) shown on return | **Your social security number**

Part I Short-Term Capital Gains and Losses—Assets Held One Year or Less

See instructions for how to figure the amounts to enter on the lines below. This form may be easier to complete if you round off cents to whole dollars.	(d) Proceeds (sales price)	(e) Cost (or other basis)	(g) Adjustments to gain or loss from Form(s) 8949, Part I, line 2, column (g)	(h) Gain or (loss) Subtract column (e) from column (d) and combine the result with column (g)
1a Totals for all short-term transactions reported on Form 1099-B for which basis was reported to the IRS and for which you have no adjustments (see instructions). However, if you choose to report all these transactions on Form 8949, leave this line blank and go to line 1b .				
1b Totals for all transactions reported on Form(s) 8949 with **Box A** checked				
2 Totals for all transactions reported on Form(s) 8949 with **Box B** checked				
3 Totals for all transactions reported on Form(s) 8949 with **Box C** checked				

4 Short-term gain from Form 6252 and short-term gain or (loss) from Forms 4684, 6781, and 8824 .	4	
5 Net short-term gain or (loss) from partnerships, S corporations, estates, and trusts from Schedule(s) K-1	5	
6 Short-term capital loss carryover. Enter the amount, if any, from line 8 of your **Capital Loss Carryover Worksheet** in the instructions	6	( )
7 **Net short-term capital gain or (loss).** Combine lines 1a through 6 in column (h). If you have any long-term capital gains or losses, go to Part II below. Otherwise, go to Part III on the back	7	

Part II Long-Term Capital Gains and Losses—Assets Held More Than One Year

See instructions for how to figure the amounts to enter on the lines below. This form may be easier to complete if you round off cents to whole dollars.	(d) Proceeds (sales price)	(e) Cost (or other basis)	(g) Adjustments to gain or loss from Form(s) 8949, Part II, line 2, column (g)	(h) Gain or (loss) Subtract column (e) from column (d) and combine the result with column (g)
8a Totals for all long-term transactions reported on Form 1099-B for which basis was reported to the IRS and for which you have no adjustments (see instructions). However, if you choose to report all these transactions on Form 8949, leave this line blank and go to line 8b .				
8b Totals for all transactions reported on Form(s) 8949 with **Box D** checked				
9 Totals for all transactions reported on Form(s) 8949 with **Box E** checked				
10 Totals for all transactions reported on Form(s) 8949 with **Box F** checked.				

11 Gain from Form 4797, Part I; long-term gain from Forms 2439 and 6252; and long-term gain or (loss) from Forms 4684, 6781, and 8824	11	
12 Net long-term gain or (loss) from partnerships, S corporations, estates, and trusts from Schedule(s) K-1	12	
13 Capital gain distributions. See the instructions	13	
14 Long-term capital loss carryover. Enter the amount, if any, from line 13 of your **Capital Loss Carryover Worksheet** in the instructions	14	( )
15 **Net long-term capital gain or (loss).** Combine lines 8a through 14 in column (h). Then go to Part III on the back	15	

For Paperwork Reduction Act Notice, see your tax return instructions. Cat. No. 11338H **Schedule D (Form 1040) 2017**

Source: U.S. Department of the Treasury, Internal Revenue Service, SCHEDULE D (Form 1040). Washington, DC: 2017.

(continued)

(concluded)

Schedule D (Form 1040) 2017 Page **2**

Part III **Summary**

16	Combine lines 7 and 15 and enter the result	**16**	
	• If line 16 is a **gain,** enter the amount from line 16 on Form 1040, line 13, or Form 1040NR, line 14. Then go to line 17 below. • If line 16 is a **loss,** skip lines 17 through 20 below. Then go to line 21. Also be sure to complete line 22. • If line 16 is **zero,** skip lines 17 through 21 below and enter -0- on Form 1040, line 13, or Form 1040NR, line 14. Then go to line 22.		
17	Are lines 15 and 16 **both** gains? ☐ **Yes.** Go to line 18. ☐ **No.** Skip lines 18 through 21, and go to line 22.		
18	If you are required to complete the **28% Rate Gain Worksheet** (see instructions), enter the amount, if any, from line 7 of that worksheet . . . . ▶	**18**	
19	If you are required to complete the **Unrecaptured Section 1250 Gain Worksheet** (see instructions), enter the amount, if any, from line 18 of that worksheet . . . . ▶	**19**	
20	Are lines 18 and 19 **both** zero or blank? ☐ **Yes.** Complete the **Qualified Dividends and Capital Gain Tax Worksheet** in the instructions for Form 1040, line 44 (or in the instructions for Form 1040NR, line 42). **Don't** complete lines 21 and 22 below. ☐ **No.** Complete the **Schedule D Tax Worksheet** in the instructions. **Don't** complete lines 21 and 22 below.		
21	If line 16 is a loss, enter here and on Form 1040, line 13, or Form 1040NR, line 14, the **smaller** of: • The loss on line 16 or • ($3,000), or if married filing separately, ($1,500) } . . . . **Note:** When figuring which amount is smaller, treat both amounts as positive numbers.	**21**	( )
22	Do you have qualified dividends on Form 1040, line 9b, or Form 1040NR, line 10b? ☐ **Yes.** Complete the **Qualified Dividends and Capital Gain Tax Worksheet** in the instructions for Form 1040, line 44 (or in the instructions for Form 1040NR, line 42). ☐ **No.** Complete the rest of Form 1040 or Form 1040NR.		

Schedule D (Form 1040) 2017

Form **8949**

Department of the Treasury
Internal Revenue Service

Sales and Other Dispositions of Capital Assets

▶ Go to *www.irs.gov/Form8949* for instructions and the latest information.

▶ File with your Schedule D to list your transactions for lines 1b, 2, 3, 8b, 9, and 10 of Schedule D.

OMB No. 1545-0074

2017

Attachment Sequence No. **12A**

Name(s) shown on return	**Social security number or taxpayer identification number**

Before you check Box A, B, or C below, see whether you received any Form(s) 1099-B or substitute statement(s) from your broker. A substitute statement will have the same information as Form 1099-B. Either will show whether your basis (usually your cost) was reported to the IRS by your broker and may even tell you which box to check.

Part I **Short-Term.** Transactions involving capital assets you held 1 year or less are short term. For long-term transactions, see page 2.

Note: You may aggregate all short-term transactions reported on Form(s) 1099-B showing basis was reported to the IRS and for which no adjustments or codes are required. Enter the totals directly on Schedule D, line 1a; you aren't required to report these transactions on Form 8949 (see instructions).

You *must* check Box A, B, *or* C below. Check only one box. If more than one box applies for your short-term transactions, complete a separate Form 8949, page 1, for each applicable box. If you have more short-term transactions than will fit on this page for one or more of the boxes, complete as many forms with the same box checked as you need.

☐ **(A)** Short-term transactions reported on Form(s) 1099-B showing basis was reported to the IRS (see **Note** above)

☐ **(B)** Short-term transactions reported on Form(s) 1099-B showing basis **wasn't** reported to the IRS

☐ **(C)** Short-term transactions not reported to you on Form 1099-B

1 (a) Description of property (Example: 100 sh. XYZ Co.)	(b) Date acquired (Mo., day, yr.)	(c) Date sold or disposed of (Mo., day, yr.)	(d) Proceeds (sales price) (see instructions)	(e) Cost or other basis. See the **Note** below and see *Column (e)* in the separate instructions	**Adjustment, if any, to gain or loss.** If you enter an amount in column (g), enter a code in column (f). **See the separate instructions.** (f) Code(s) from instructions	(g) Amount of adjustment	(h) **Gain or (loss).** Subtract column (e) from column (d) and combine the result with column (g)
2 Totals. Add the amounts in columns (d), (e), (g), and (h) (subtract negative amounts). Enter each total here and include on your Schedule D, **line 1b** (if **Box A** above is checked), **line 2** (if **Box B** above is checked), or **line 3** (if **Box C** above is checked) ▶							

Note: If you checked Box A above but the basis reported to the IRS was incorrect, enter in column (e) the basis as reported to the IRS, and enter an adjustment in column (g) to correct the basis. See *Column (g)* in the separate instructions for how to figure the amount of the adjustment.

For Paperwork Reduction Act Notice, see your tax return instructions. Cat. No. 37768Z Form **8949** (2017)

Source: U.S. Department of the Treasury, Internal Revenue Service, Form 8949. Washington, DC: 2017.

(continued)

(concluded)

Form 8949 (2017) Attachment Sequence No. **12A** Page **2**

Name(s) shown on return. Name and SSN or taxpayer identification no. not required if shown on other side	**Social security number or taxpayer identification number**

Before you check Box D, E, or F below, see whether you received any Form(s) 1099-B or substitute statement(s) from your broker. A substitute statement will have the same information as Form 1099-B. Either will show whether your basis (usually your cost) was reported to the IRS by your broker and may even tell you which box to check.

Part II **Long-Term.** Transactions involving capital assets you held more than 1 year are long term. For short-term transactions, see page 1.

Note: You may aggregate all long-term transactions reported on Form(s) 1099-B showing basis was reported to the IRS and for which no adjustments or codes are required. Enter the totals directly on Schedule D, line 8a; you aren't required to report these transactions on Form 8949 (see instructions).

You *must* check Box D, E, *or* F below. Check only one box. If more than one box applies for your long-term transactions, complete a separate Form 8949, page 2, for each applicable box. If you have more long-term transactions than will fit on this page for one or more of the boxes, complete as many forms with the same box checked as you need.

☐ **(D)** Long-term transactions reported on Form(s) 1099-B showing basis was reported to the IRS (see **Note** above)
☐ **(E)** Long-term transactions reported on Form(s) 1099-B showing basis **wasn't** reported to the IRS
☐ **(F)** Long-term transactions not reported to you on Form 1099-B

1 (a) Description of property (Example: 100 sh. XYZ Co.)	(b) Date acquired (Mo., day, yr.)	(c) Date sold or disposed of (Mo., day, yr.)	(d) Proceeds (sales price) (see instructions)	(e) Cost or other basis. See the **Note** below and see *Column (e)* in the separate instructions	Adjustment, if any, to gain or loss. If you enter an amount in column (g), enter a code in column (f). **See the separate instructions.** (f) Code(s) from instructions	(g) Amount of adjustment	(h) **Gain or (loss).** Subtract column (e) from column (d) and combine the result with column (g)
2 Totals. Add the amounts in columns (d), (e), (g), and (h) (subtract negative amounts). Enter each total here and include on your Schedule D, **line 8b** (if **Box D** above is checked), **line 9** (if **Box E** above is checked), or **line 10** (if **Box F** above is checked) ▶							

Note: If you checked Box D above but the basis reported to the IRS was incorrect, enter in column (e) the basis as reported to the IRS, and enter an adjustment in column (g) to correct the basis. See *Column (g)* in the separate instructions for how to figure the amount of the adjustment.

Form **8949** (2017)

SCHEDULE E (Form 1040)

Department of the Treasury Internal Revenue Service (99)

Supplemental Income and Loss

(From rental real estate, royalties, partnerships, S corporations, estates, trusts, REMICs, etc.)

▶ Attach to Form 1040, 1040NR, or Form 1041.

▶ Go to *www.irs.gov/ScheduleE* for instructions and the latest information.

OMB No. 1545-0074

2017

Attachment Sequence No. **13**

Name(s) shown on return | **Your social security number**

Part I **Income or Loss From Rental Real Estate and Royalties** **Note:** If you are in the business of renting personal property, use **Schedule C** or **C-EZ** (see instructions). If you are an individual, report farm rental income or loss from **Form 4835** on page 2, line 40.

A Did you make any payments in 2017 that would require you to file Form(s) 1099? (see instructions) . . . . ☐ **Yes** ☐ **No**

B If "Yes," did you or will you file required Forms 1099? . . . . ☐ **Yes** ☐ **No**

1a	Physical address of each property (street, city, state, ZIP code)
A	
B	
C	

1b	Type of Property (from list below)	2 For each rental real estate property listed above, report the number of fair rental and personal use days. Check the **QJV** box only if you meet the requirements to file as a qualified joint venture. See instructions.		Fair Rental Days	Personal Use Days	QJV
A			A			☐
B			B			☐
C			C			☐

Type of Property:

1 Single Family Residence
2 Multi-Family Residence
3 Vacation/Short-Term Rental
4 Commercial
5 Land
6 Royalties
7 Self-Rental
8 Other (describe)

	Income:	**Properties:**	A	B	C
3	Rents received	3			
4	Royalties received	4			
	Expenses:				
5	Advertising	5			
6	Auto and travel (see instructions)	6			
7	Cleaning and maintenance	7			
8	Commissions	8			
9	Insurance	9			
10	Legal and other professional fees	10			
11	Management fees	11			
12	Mortgage interest paid to banks, etc. (see instructions)	12			
13	Other interest	13			
14	Repairs	14			
15	Supplies	15			
16	Taxes	16			
17	Utilities	17			
18	Depreciation expense or depletion	18			
19	Other (list) ▶	19			
20	Total expenses. Add lines 5 through 19	20			
21	Subtract line 20 from line 3 (rents) and/or 4 (royalties). If result is a (loss), see instructions to find out if you must file **Form 6198**	21			
22	Deductible rental real estate loss after limitation, if any, on **Form 8582** (see instructions)	22	( )	( )	( )

23a	Total of all amounts reported on line 3 for all rental properties	23a	
b	Total of all amounts reported on line 4 for all royalty properties	23b	
c	Total of all amounts reported on line 12 for all properties	23c	
d	Total of all amounts reported on line 18 for all properties	23d	
e	Total of all amounts reported on line 20 for all properties	23e	
24	**Income.** Add positive amounts shown on line 21. **Do not** include any losses	24	
25	**Losses.** Add royalty losses from line 21 and rental real estate losses from line 22. Enter total losses here	25	( )
26	**Total rental real estate and royalty income or (loss).** Combine lines 24 and 25. Enter the result here. If Parts II, III, IV, and line 40 on page 2 do not apply to you, also enter this amount on Form 1040, line 17, or Form 1040NR, line 18. Otherwise, include this amount in the total on line 41 on page 2	26	

For Paperwork Reduction Act Notice, see the separate instructions. Cat. No. 11344L **Schedule E (Form 1040) 2017**

Source: U.S. Department of the Treasury, Internal Revenue Service, SCHEDULE E (Form 1040). Washington, DC: 2017.

(continued)

(concluded)

Schedule E (Form 1040) 2017 Attachment Sequence No. 13 Page 2

Name(s) shown on return. Do not enter name and social security number if shown on other side.	Your social security number

Caution: The IRS compares amounts reported on your tax return with amounts shown on Schedule(s) K-1.

Part II Income or Loss From Partnerships and S Corporations **Note:** If you report a loss from an at-risk activity for which **any** amount is **not** at risk, you **must** check the box in column **(e)** on line 28 and attach **Form 6198.** See instructions.

27 Are you reporting any loss not allowed in a prior year due to the at-risk, excess farm loss, or basis limitations, a prior year unallowed loss from a passive activity (if that loss was not reported on Form 8582), or unreimbursed partnership expenses? If you answered "Yes," see instructions before completing this section . . . ☐ **Yes** ☐ **No**

28	**(a)** Name	**(b)** Enter **P** for partnership; **S** for S corporation	**(c)** Check if foreign partnership	**(d)** Employer identification number	**(e)** Check if any amount is not at risk
A			☐		☐
B			☐		☐
C			☐		☐
D			☐		☐

	Passive Income and Loss		Nonpassive Income and Loss		
	(f) Passive loss allowed (attach **Form 8582** if required)	**(g)** Passive income from **Schedule K-1**	**(h)** Nonpassive loss from **Schedule K-1**	**(i)** Section 179 expense deduction from **Form 4562**	**(j)** Nonpassive income from **Schedule K-1**
A					
B					
C					
D					
29a Totals					
b Totals					

30	Add columns (g) and (j) of line 29a . . .	30	
31	Add columns (f), (h), and (i) of line 29b . . .	31	( )
32	**Total partnership and S corporation income or (loss).** Combine lines 30 and 31. Enter the result here and include in the total on line 41 below . . .	32	

Part III Income or Loss From Estates and Trusts

33	**(a)** Name	**(b)** Employer identification number
A		
B		

	Passive Income and Loss		Nonpassive Income and Loss	
	(c) Passive deduction or loss allowed (attach **Form 8582** if required)	**(d)** Passive income from **Schedule K-1**	**(e)** Deduction or loss from **Schedule K-1**	**(f)** Other income from **Schedule K-1**
A				
B				
34a Totals				
b Totals				

35	Add columns (d) and (f) of line 34a . . .	35	
36	Add columns (c) and (e) of line 34b . . .	36	( )
37	**Total estate and trust income or (loss).** Combine lines 35 and 36. Enter the result here and include in the total on line 41 below . . .	37	

Part IV Income or Loss From Real Estate Mortgage Investment Conduits (REMICs)—Residual Holder

38	**(a)** Name	**(b)** Employer identification number	**(c)** Excess inclusion from **Schedules Q,** line 2c (see instructions)	**(d)** Taxable income (net loss) from **Schedules Q,** line 1b	**(e)** Income from **Schedules Q,** line 3b

39	Combine columns (d) and (e) only. Enter the result here and include in the total on line 41 below	39	

Part V Summary

40	Net farm rental income or (loss) from **Form 4835.** Also, complete line 42 below . . .	40	
41	**Total income or (loss).** Combine lines 26, 32, 37, 39, and 40. Enter the result here and on Form 1040, line 17, or Form 1040NR, line 18 ▶	41	
42	**Reconciliation of farming and fishing income.** Enter your **gross** farming and fishing income reported on Form 4835, line 7; Schedule K-1 (Form 1065), box 14, code B; Schedule K-1 (Form 1120S), box 17, code V; and Schedule K-1 (Form 1041), box 14, code F (see instructions) . .	42	
43	**Reconciliation for real estate professionals.** If you were a real estate professional (see instructions), enter the net income or (loss) you reported anywhere on Form 1040 or Form 1040NR from all rental real estate activities in which you materially participated under the passive activity loss rules . .	43	

Schedule E (Form 1040) 2017

SCHEDULE EIC (Form 1040A or 1040) Department of the Treasury Internal Revenue Service (99)	**Earned Income Credit** Qualifying Child Information ▶ Complete and attach to Form 1040A or 1040 only if you have a qualifying child. ▶ Go to *www.irs.gov/ScheduleEIC* for the latest information.	1040A 1040 EIC	OMB No. 1545-0074 **2017** Attachment Sequence No. **43**
Name(s) shown on return			**Your social security number**

Before you begin:
- See the instructions for Form 1040A, lines 42a and 42b, or Form 1040, lines 66a and 66b, to make sure that **(a)** you can take the EIC, and **(b)** you have a qualifying child.
- Be sure the child's name on line 1 and social security number (SSN) on line 2 agree with the child's social security card. Otherwise, at the time we process your return, we may reduce or disallow your EIC. If the name or SSN on the child's social security card is not correct, call the Social Security Administration at 1-800-772-1213.

CAUTION
- *You can't claim the EIC for a child who didn't live with you for more than half of the year.*
- *If you take the EIC even though you are not eligible, you may not be allowed to take the credit for up to 10 years. See the instructions for details.*
- *It will take us longer to process your return and issue your refund if you do not fill in all lines that apply for each qualifying child.*

Qualifying Child Information	Child 1	Child 2	Child 3
1 Child's name If you have more than three qualifying children, you have to list only three to get the maximum credit.	First name / Last name	First name / Last name	First name / Last name
2 Child's SSN The child must have an SSN as defined in the instructions for Form 1040A, lines 42a and 42b, or Form 1040, lines 66a and 66b, unless the child was born and died in 2017. If your child was born and died in 2017 and did not have an SSN, enter "Died" on this line and attach a copy of the child's birth certificate, death certificate, or hospital medical records showing a live birth.			
3 Child's year of birth	Year ___ ___ ___ ___ *If born after 1998* ***and*** *the child is younger than you (or your spouse, if filing jointly), skip lines 4a and 4b; go to line 5.*	Year ___ ___ ___ ___ *If born after 1998* ***and*** *the child is younger than you (or your spouse, if filing jointly), skip lines 4a and 4b; go to line 5.*	Year ___ ___ ___ ___ *If born after 1998* ***and*** *the child is younger than you (or your spouse, if filing jointly), skip lines 4a and 4b; go to line 5.*
4 a Was the child under age 24 at the end of 2017, a student, and younger than you (or your spouse, if filing jointly)?	☐ **Yes.** *Go to line 5.* ☐ **No.** *Go to line 4b.*	☐ **Yes.** *Go to line 5.* ☐ **No.** *Go to line 4b.*	☐ **Yes.** *Go to line 5.* ☐ **No.** *Go to line 4b.*
b Was the child permanently and totally disabled during any part of 2017?	☐ **Yes.** *Go to line 5.* ☐ **No.** The child is not a qualifying child.	☐ **Yes.** *Go to line 5.* ☐ **No.** The child is not a qualifying child.	☐ **Yes.** *Go to line 5.* ☐ **No.** The child is not a qualifying child.
5 Child's relationship to you (For example, son, daughter, grandchild, niece, nephew, eligible foster child, etc.)			
6 Number of months child lived with you in the United States during 2017 • If the child lived with you for more than half of 2017 but less than 7 months, enter "7." • If the child was born or died in 2017 and your home was the child's home for more than half the time he or she was alive during 2017, enter "12."	______ months *Do not enter more than 12 months.*	______ months *Do not enter more than 12 months.*	______ months *Do not enter more than 12 months.*

For Paperwork Reduction Act Notice, see your tax return instructions. Cat. No. 13339M **Schedule EIC (Form 1040A or 1040) 2017**

Source: U.S. Department of the Treasury, Internal Revenue Service, SCHEDULE EIC (Form 1040A or 1040). Washington, DC: 2017.

SCHEDULE SE (Form 1040)

Department of the Treasury
Internal Revenue Service (99)

Self-Employment Tax

▶ Go to *www.irs.gov/ScheduleSE* for instructions and the latest information.
▶ Attach to Form 1040 or Form 1040NR.

OMB No. 1545-0074

2017

Attachment Sequence No. **17**

Name of person with **self-employment** income (as shown on Form 1040 or Form 1040NR)	Social security number of person with **self-employment** income ▶	

Before you begin: To determine if you must file Schedule SE, see the instructions.

May I Use Short Schedule SE or Must I Use Long Schedule SE?

Note: Use this flowchart **only if** you must file Schedule SE. If unsure, see *Who Must File Schedule SE* in the instructions.

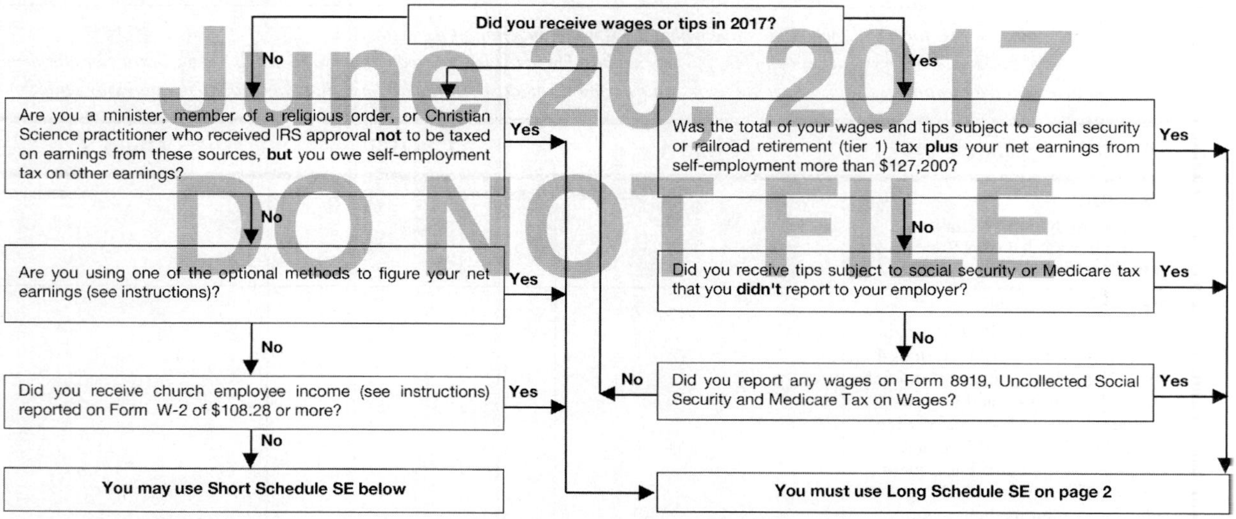

Section A—Short Schedule SE. Caution: Read above to see if you can use Short Schedule SE.

1a	Net farm profit or (loss) from Schedule F, line 34, and farm partnerships, Schedule K-1 (Form 1065), box 14, code A	**1a**	
b	If you received social security retirement or disability benefits, enter the amount of Conservation Reserve Program payments included on Schedule F, line 4b, or listed on Schedule K-1 (Form 1065), box 20, code Z	**1b**	( )
2	Net profit or (loss) from Schedule C, line 31; Schedule C-EZ, line 3; Schedule K-1 (Form 1065), box 14, code A (other than farming); and Schedule K-1 (Form 1065-B), box 9, code J1. Ministers and members of religious orders, see instructions for types of income to report on this line. See instructions for other income to report	**2**	
3	Combine lines 1a, 1b, and 2	**3**	
4	Multiply line 3 by 92.35% (0.9235). If less than $400, you don't owe self-employment tax; **don't** file this schedule unless you have an amount on line 1b . . . . ▶	**4**	
	Note: If line 4 is less than $400 due to Conservation Reserve Program payments on line 1b, see instructions.		
5	**Self-employment tax.** If the amount on line 4 is: • $127,200 or less, multiply line 4 by 15.3% (0.153). Enter the result here and on **Form 1040, line 57,** or **Form 1040NR, line 55** • More than $127,200, multiply line 4 by 2.9% (0.029). Then, add $15,772.80 to the result. Enter the total here and on **Form 1040, line 57,** or **Form 1040NR, line 55**	**5**	
6	**Deduction for one-half of self-employment tax.** Multiply line 5 by 50% (0.50). Enter the result here and on **Form 1040, line 27,** or **Form 1040NR, line 27** **6**		

For Paperwork Reduction Act Notice, see your tax return instructions. Cat. No. 11358Z **Schedule SE (Form 1040) 2017**

Source: U.S. Department of the Treasury, Internal Revenue Service, SCHEDULE SE (Form 1040). Washington, DC: 2017.

Schedule SE (Form 1040) 2017 — Attachment Sequence No. **17** — Page **2**

Name of person with **self-employment** income (as shown on Form 1040 or Form 1040NR) | Social security number of person with **self-employment** income ▶

Section B—Long Schedule SE

Part I Self-Employment Tax

Note: If your only income subject to self-employment tax is **church employee income,** see instructions. Also see instructions for the definition of church employee income.

A If you are a minister, member of a religious order, or Christian Science practitioner **and** you filed Form 4361, but you had $400 or more of **other** net earnings from self-employment, check here and continue with Part I ▶ ☐

DRAFT AS OF June 29, 2017 DO NOT FILE

Line	Description			Box	Amount	
1a	Net farm profit or (loss) from Schedule F, line 34, and farm partnerships, Schedule K-1 (Form 1065), box 14, code A. **Note:** Skip lines 1a and 1b if you use the farm optional method (see instructions)			1a		
b	If you received social security retirement or disability benefits, enter the amount of Conservation Reserve Program payments included on Schedule F, line 4b, or listed on Schedule K-1 (Form 1065), box 20, code Z			1b	(	)
2	Net profit or (loss) from Schedule C, line 31; Schedule C-EZ, line 3; Schedule K-1 (Form 1065), box 14, code A (other than farming); and Schedule K-1 (Form 1065-B), box 9, code J1. Ministers and members of religious orders, see instructions for types of income to report on this line. See instructions for other income to report. **Note:** Skip this line if you use the nonfarm optional method (see instructions)			2		
3	Combine lines 1a, 1b, and 2			3		
4a	If line 3 is more than zero, multiply line 3 by 92.35% (0.9235). Otherwise, enter amount from line 3 **Note:** If line 4a is less than $400 due to Conservation Reserve Program payments on line 1b, see instructions.			4a		
b	If you elect one or both of the optional methods, enter the total of lines 15 and 17 here			4b		
c	Combine lines 4a and 4b. If less than $400, **stop;** you don't owe self-employment tax. **Exception:** If less than $400 and you had **church employee income,** enter -0- and continue ▶			4c		
5a	Enter your **church employee income** from Form W-2. See instructions for definition of church employee income	5a				
b	Multiply line 5a by 92.35% (0.9235). If less than $100, enter -0-			5b		
6	Add lines 4c and 5b			6		
7	Maximum amount of combined wages and self-employment earnings subject to social security tax or the 6.2% portion of the 7.65% railroad retirement (tier 1) tax for 2017			7	127,200	00
8a	Total social security wages and tips (total of boxes 3 and 7 on Form(s) W-2) and railroad retirement (tier 1) compensation. If $127,200 or more, skip lines 8b through 10, and go to line 11	8a				
b	Unreported tips subject to social security tax (from Form 4137, line 10)	8b				
c	Wages subject to social security tax (from Form 8919, line 10)	8c				
d	Add lines 8a, 8b, and 8c			8d		
9	Subtract line 8d from line 7. If zero or less, enter -0- here and on line 10 and go to line 11 ▶			9		
10	Multiply the **smaller** of line 6 or line 9 by 12.4% (0.124)			10		
11	Multiply line 6 by 2.9% (0.029)			11		
12	**Self-employment tax.** Add lines 10 and 11. Enter here and on **Form 1040, line 57,** or **Form 1040NR, line 55**			12		
13	**Deduction for one-half of self-employment tax.** Multiply line 12 by 50% (0.50). Enter the result here and on **Form 1040, line 27,** or **Form 1040NR, line 27**	13				

Part II Optional Methods To Figure Net Earnings (see instructions)

Farm Optional Method. You may use this method **only** if **(a)** your gross farm income[1] wasn't more than $7,800, **or (b)** your net farm profits[2] were less than $5,630.

Line	Description	Box	Amount	
14	Maximum income for optional methods	14	5,200	00
15	Enter the **smaller** of: two-thirds (2/3) of gross farm income[1] (not less than zero) **or** $5,200. Also include this amount on line 4b above	15		

Nonfarm Optional Method. You may use this method **only** if **(a)** your net nonfarm profits[3] were less than $5,630 and also less than 72.189% of your gross nonfarm income,[4] **and (b)** you had net earnings from self-employment of at least $400 in 2 of the prior 3 years. **Caution:** You may use this method no more than five times.

Line	Description	Box	Amount	
16	Subtract line 15 from line 14	16		
17	Enter the **smaller** of: two-thirds (2/3) of gross nonfarm income[4] (not less than zero) **or** the amount on line 16. Also include this amount on line 4b above	17		

[1] From Sch. F, line 9, and Sch. K-1 (Form 1065), box 14, code B.

[2] From Sch. F, line 34, and Sch. K-1 (Form 1065), box 14, code A—minus the amount you would have entered on line 1b had you not used the optional method.

[3] From Sch. C, line 31; Sch. C-EZ, line 3; Sch. K-1 (Form 1065), box 14, code A; and Sch. K-1 (Form 1065-B), box 9, code J1.

[4] From Sch. C, line 7; Sch. C-EZ, line 1; Sch. K-1 (Form 1065), box 14, code C; and Sch. K-1 (Form 1065-B), box 9, code J2.

Schedule SE (Form 1040) 2017

Appendix F

2017 Federal Income Tax Information

2017 Federal Tax Rate Schedules

Schedule X-Single

If taxable income is over:	But not over:	The tax is:
$0	$9,325	10% of taxable income
$9,325	$37,950	$932.50 plus 15% of the excess over $9,325
$37,950	$91,900	$5,226.25 plus 25% of the excess over $37,950
$91,900	$191,650	$18,713.75 plus 28% of the excess over $91,900
$191,650	$416,700	$46,643.75 plus 33% of the excess over $191,650
$416,700	$418,400	$120,910.25 plus 35% of the excess over $416,700
$418,400	—	$121.505.25 plus 39.6% of the excess over $418,400

Schedule Y-1-Married Filing Jointly or Qualifying Widow(er)

If taxable income is over:	But not over:	The tax is:
$0	$18,650	10% of taxable income
$18,650	$75,900	$1,865.00 plus 15% of the excess over $18,650
$75,900	$153,100	$10.452.50 plus 25% of the excess over $75,900
$153,100	$233,350	$29,752.50 plus 28% of the excess over $153,100
$233,350	$416,700	$52,222.50 plus 33% of the excess over $233,350
$416,700	$470,700	$112,728.00 plus 35% of the excess over $416,700
$470,700	—	$131,628.00 plus 39.6% of the excess over $470,700

Schedule Y-2-Married Filing Separately

If taxable income is over:	But not over:	The tax is:
$0	$9,325	10% of taxable income
$9,325	$37,950	$932.50 plus 15% of the excess over $9,325
$37,950	$76,550	$5,226.25 plus 25% of the excess over $37,950
$76,550	$116,675	$14,876.25 plus 28% of the excess over $76,550
$116,675	$208,350	$26,111.25 plus 33% of the excess over $116,675
$208,350	$235,350	$56,364.00 plus 35% of the excess over $208,350
$235,350	—	$65,814.00 plus 39.6% of the excess over $235,350

Schedule Z-Head of Household

If taxable income is over:	But not over:	The tax is:
$0	$13,350	10% of taxable income
$13,350	$50,800	$1,335.00 plus 15% of the excess over $13,350
$50,800	$131,200	$6,952.50 plus 25% of the excess over $50,800
$131,200	$212,500	$27,052.50 plus 28% of the excess over $131,200
$212,500	$416,700	$49,816.50 plus 33% of the excess over $212,500
$416,700	$444,550	$117,202.50 plus 35% of the excess over $416,700
$444,550	—	$126,950.00 plus 39.6% of the excess over $444,550

Qualified Dividends & Capital Gains Tax Rates	
Dividends in 10% or 15% tax brackets	0%
Dividends in higher tax brackets	15%
Dividends in 39.6% tax bracket	20%
Long-term capital gains (held greater than 1 year)	
10% or 15% tax brackets	0%
Higher tax brackets	15%
Capital gains in 39.6% tax bracket	20%
Short-term capital gains (held 1 year or less)	Ordinary Tax Rates

Standard Deduction

Filing Status	Basic Standard Deduction
Single	$6,350
Married filing jointly	$12,700
Married filing separately	$6,350
Head of household	$9,350
Qualifying widow(er)	$12,700
Additional over 65 or blind	
Married, qual. widow(er)	$1,250
Single/Head of household	$1,550

Personal/Dependent Exemption
$4,050/per individual

Standard Mileage Rates

Business miles	$0.535
Charity miles	$0.14
Medical miles	$0.17
Moving miles	$0.17

Social Security, Medicare, & Self-Employment Taxes

Employee	Rate	Income Limit
• Social Security	6.2%	$127,200
• Medicare	1.45%	Unlimited
• Total	7.65%	

Self-employed	Rate	Income Limit
• Social Security	12.4%	$127,200
• Medicare	2.9%	Unlimited
• Total	15.3%	

An additional Medicare tax of 0.9% is assessed on wages and self-employment income in excess of $250,000 (married filing jointly), $125,000 (married filing separately), or $200,000 (all others).

Child Tax Credit

Amount per child under 17	$1,000
Credit reduction—$50 per $1,000 over AGI threshold	
Married filing jointly	$110,000
Single, head of household	$75,000
Married filing separately	$55,000

Coverdell Educational Savings Accounts

Contributions limit—$2,000 per year per beneficiary, must be in cash, and must be made before the beneficiary turns 18.

Phase-out Thresholds

Married filing jointly—AGI	$190,000–$220,000
Single—AGI	$95,000–$110,000

Traditional IRA Contribution Deduction

IRA contributions—Lower of $5,500 or the amount of compensation

Individuals who are age 50 or older—Lower of $6,500 or compensation.

Phase-outs if the individual is a participant in another retirement plan:

Married	$99,000–$119,000	Phase-out range
	Greater than $119,000—no deduction	
Single	$62,000–$72,000	Phase-out range
	Greater than $72,000—no deduction	

Roth IRA Contribution

Roth contribution	$5,500 or compensation
50 or older	$6,500 or compensation

All Roth contributions are not tax deductible

Joint Returns—$186,000 – $196,000 phase-out range

Single or head of household—$118,000 – $133,000 phase-out range

Photo Opener Credits

Chapter 1: ©Purestock/Superstock
Chapter 2: ©Blend Images–Mike Kemp/Brand X/Getty Images
Chapter 3: ©Blend Images–JGI/Jamie Grill/Getty Images
Chapter 4: ©NakoPhotography/Shutterstock
Chapter 5: ©Blend Images/Image Source
Chapter 6: ©ewg3D/E+/Getty Images
Chapter 7: ©Caiaimage/Glow Images
Chapter 8: ©iStockphoto/Getty Images
Chapter 9: ©kristian sekulic/Getty Images
Chapter 10: ©Hill Street Studios/Blend Images LLC
Chapter 11: ©Caia Image/Glow Images
Chapter 12: ©Maskot/Image Source
Chapter 13: ©Robert Nicholas/age fotostock
Chapter 14: ©John Fedele/Blend Images LLC
Chapter 15: ©Chris Ryan/age fotostock

Index

A

D

G

J

K

L

M

N

O

Q

R

T

U